W9-AZE-061

TEACHER'S EDITION

PRENTICE HALL

ECONOMICS

Principles in Action

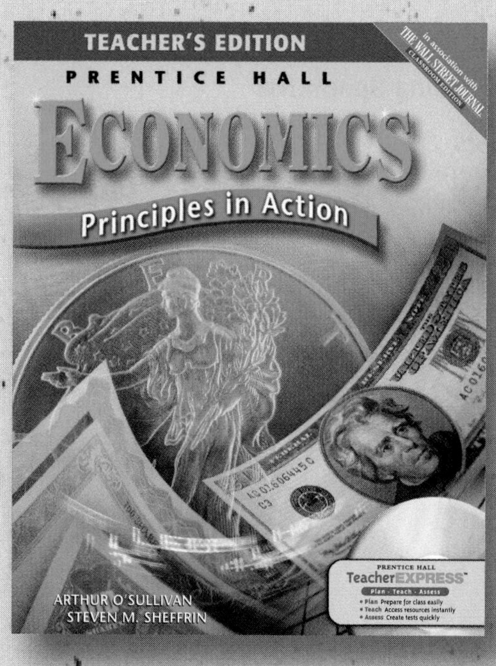

THE WALL STREET JOURNAL.
CLASSROOM EDITION

See pages T16 –T17 for more information on *The Wall Street Journal Classroom Edition* and the resources this partnership offers!

Prentice Hall's exclusive partnership with *The Wall Street Journal Classroom Edition* brings timely articles and information into your classroom to illustrate key economic principles in action.

Boston, Massachusetts
Upper Saddle River, New Jersey

3 4 5 6 7 8 9 10 09 08
ISBN 0-13-133484-0

TEACHER'S EDITION

PRENTICE HALL

ECONOMICS

Principles in Action

PROGRAM REVIEWERS

Teacher Reviewers

Linda Tate Hudson
Central High School Magnet Career Academy
Louisville, Kentucky

Bonnie Meszaros
Center for Economic Education and Entrepreneurship
University of Delaware
Newark, Delaware

Denny L. Schillings
Homewood-Flossmoor High School
Flossmoor, Illinois

John T. Wende
James Bowie High School
Austin, Texas

Internet Reviewer

Vincent M. Seeley
Greenville Central School District
Greenville, New York

Content Area Reading Specialist

Dr. Lois E. Huffman
North Carolina State University
Raleigh, North Carolina

Block Scheduling Consultants

Sharon Dragon
Nimitz High School
Houston, Texas

Dr. Barbara Stern
Assistant Professor
James Madison University
Harrisonburg, Virginia

PROGRAM ADVISORS

Michal Howden
Social Studies Consultant
Zionsville, Indiana

Joe Wieczorek
Social Studies Consultant
Baltimore, Maryland

Professional DEVELOPMENT

Contents

Raising the achievement level of all students is the number one challenge facing teachers today. To assist in meeting this challenge, we've enlisted a team of respected authors and consultants who specialize in economics education and differentiated instruction. In the following pages, you'll find the key elements woven throughout this program that assure teaching and learning success.

Standards-Based Instruction

Daily Pacing Guide T4

Block Scheduling Support T8

National Content Standards in Economics T12

NCEE Twenty Key Concepts T15

The Importance of Making Economic Decisions T16

Math in Economics T18

Differentiated Instruction

Research on Differentiated Instruction by Don Deshler T20

Effective Classroom Implementation T21

Strategies for Specific Student Populations T22

Assessment

Informing Instruction with Assessment T26

Ongoing Assessment T27

Daily Pacing GUIDE

Yearly and semester pacing guides help you plan your course

The following pacing guides show how the units and chapters of *Economics: Principles in Action* can be adapted to fit your specific course focus and time constraints. The yearly guide is representative of a course based on 36 weeks or 180 days. The semester guide is representative of a course with 50-minute periods that lasts for 18 weeks or 90 days.

		One-Year Course (# of DAYS)	One-Semester Course (# of DAYS)
UNIT 1 Introduction to Economics			
Chapter 1	What Is Economics?		
Section 1	Scarcity and the Factors of Production	2	.5
Section 2	Opportunity Cost	1.5	.5
Section 3	Production Possibilities Curves	1.5	1
	Chapter 1 Assessment	1	1
	Total Days for Chapter	**6**	**3**
Chapter 2	Economic Systems		
Section 1	Answering the Three Economic Questions	2	.5
Section 2	The Free Market	2	.5
Section 3	Centrally Planned Economies	3	.5
Section 4	Modern Economies	2	.5
	Chapter 2 Assessment	1	1
	Total Days for Chapter	**10**	**3**
Chapter 3	American Free Enterprise		
Section 1	Benefits of Free Enterprise	1.5	.5
Section 2	Promoting Growth and Stability	2	.5
Section 3	Providing Public Goods	1.5	.5
Section 4	Providing a Safety Net	2	.5
	Chapter 3 Assessment	1	1
	Total Days for Chapter	**8**	**3**
	Unit 1 Assessment	1	1
	Total Days for Unit	25	10
UNIT 2 How Markets Work			
Chapter 4	Demand		
Section 1	Understanding Demand	3	1
Section 2	Shifts of the Demand Curve	3	1
Section 3	Elasticity of Demand	3	1
	Chapter 4 Assessment	1	1
	Total Days for Chapter	**10**	**4**
Chapter 5	Supply		
Section 1	Understanding Supply	3	1
Section 2	Costs of Production	3	1
Section 3	Changes in Supply	3	1
	Chapter 5 Assessment	1	1
	Total Days for Chapter	**10**	**4**

		One-Year Course (# of DAYS)	One-Semester Course (# of DAYS)
Chapter 6	Prices		
Section 1	Combining Supply and Demand	3	1
Section 2	Changes in Market Equilibrium	3	1
Section 3	The Role of Prices	3	1
	Chapter 6 Assessment	1	1
	Total Days for Chapter	**10**	**4**
Chapter 7	Market Structures		
Section 1	Perfect Competition	2	.5
Section 2	Monopoly	2	.5
Section 3	Monopolistic Competition and Oligopoly	2	.5
Section 4	Regulation and Deregulation	2	.5
	Chapter 7 Assessment	1	1
	Total Days for Chapter	**9**	**3**
	Unit 2 Assessment	1	1
	Total Days for Unit	40	16

UNIT 3 Business and Labor

		One-Year Course (# of DAYS)	One-Semester Course (# of DAYS)
Chapter 8	Business Organizations		
Section 1	Sole Proprietorships	2	1
Section 2	Partnerships	2	1
Section 3	Corporations, Mergers, and Multinationals	3	1
Section 4	Other Organizations	2	1
	Chapter 8 Assessment	1	1
	Total Days for Chapter	**10**	**5**
Chapter 9	Labor		
Section 1	Labor Market Trends	2.5	1
Section 2	Labor and Wages	3	1
Section 3	Organized Labor	2.5	1
	Chapter 9 Assessment	1	1
	Total Days for Chapter	**9**	**4**
	Unit 3 Assessment	1	1
	Total Days for Unit	20	10

Daily Pacing GUIDE

		One-Year Course (# of DAYS)	One-Semester Course (# of DAYS)
UNIT 4 Money, Banking, and Finance			
Chapter 10	Money and Banking		
Section 1	Money	2	1
Section 2	The History of American Banking	1.5	1
Section 3	Banking Today	1.5	1
	Chapter 10 Assessment	1	1
	Total Days for Chapter	**6**	**4**
Chapter 11	Financial Markets		
Section 1	Saving and Investing	3	1
Section 2	Bonds and Other Financial Assets	3	1
Section 3	The Stock Market	6	1
	Chapter 11 Assessment	1	1
	Total Days for Chapter	**13**	**4**
	Unit 4 Assessment	1	1
	Total Days for Unit	20	9
UNIT 5 Measuring Economic Performance			
Chapter 12	Gross Domestic Product and Growth		
Section 1	Gross Domestic Product	2	2
Section 2	Business Cycles	2	2
Section 3	Economic Growth	2	2
	Chapter 12 Assessment	1	1
	Total Days for Chapter	**7**	**7**
Chapter 13	Economic Challenges		
Section 1	Unemployment	2	2
Section 2	Inflation	2	2
Section 3	Poverty	2	2
	Chapter 13 Assessment	1	1
	Total Days for Chapter	**7**	**7**
	Unit 5 Assessment	1	1
	Total Days for Unit	15	15

		One-Year Course (# of DAYS)	One-Semester Course (# of DAYS)
UNIT 6 Government and the Economy			
Chapter 14	Taxes and Government Spending		
Section 1	What Are Taxes?	2	1
Section 2	Federal Taxes	14	2
Section 3	Federal Spending	3	2
Section 4	State and Local Taxes and Spending	9	1
	Chapter 14 Assessment	1	1
	Total Days for Chapter	**29**	**7**
Chapter 15	Fiscal Policy		
Section 1	Understanding Fiscal Policy	2	2
Section 2	Fiscal Policy Options	2	2
Section 3	Budget Deficits and the National Debt	2	2
	Chapter 15 Assessment	1	1
	Total Days for Chapter	**7**	**7**
Chapter 16	The Federal Reserve and Monetary Policy		
Section 1	The Federal Reserve System	1.5	1
Section 2	Federal Reserve Functions	2	1
Section 3	Monetary Policy Tools	2	2
Section 4	Monetary Policy and Macroeconomic Stabilization	1.5	2
	Chapter 16 Assessment	1	1
	Total Days for Chapter	**8**	**7**
	Unit 6 Assessment	1	1
	Total Days for Unit	45	22
UNIT 7 The Global Economy			
Chapter 17	International Trade		
Section 1	Why Nations Trade	2	1
Section 2	Trade Barriers and Agreements	2	1
Section 3	Measuring Trade	2	1
	Chapter 17 Assessment	1	1
	Total Days for Chapter	**7**	**4**
Chapter 18	Economic Development and Transition		
Section 1	Levels of Development	1.5	.5
Section 2	Issues in Development	1.5	.5
Section 3	Financing Development	1.5	.5
Section 4	Transitions to Free Enterprise	1.5	.5
	Chapter 18 Assessment	1	1
	Total Days for Chapter	**7**	**3**
	Unit 7 Assessment	1	1
	Total Days for Unit	15	8

Block Scheduling SUPPORT

Block scheduling support throughout the program

Economics: Principles in Action provides a comprehensive array of resources to meet your block scheduling needs. Flexibility is the key to your success in extended class periods. The variety of materials available with this program provide numerous strategies for you to expand coverage of every topic or to cover essential content in limited time.

This pacing chart is for a nine-week teaching block. Each class day is 90 minutes long. Three days of the 45-day block are set aside for review and for final exams.

		Day Section (# of DAYS)
UNIT ONE Introduction to Economics		
Chapter 1	What Is Economics?	
Day 1	Section 1: Scarcity and the Factors of Production	1
Day 2	Section 2: Opportunity Cost	.5
	Section 3: Production Possibilities Curves	.5
Day 3	Chapter 1 Assessment	1
	Total Days for Chapter 1	**3**
Chapter 2	Economic Systems	
Day 4	Section 1: Answering the Three Economic Questions	.5
	Section 2: The Free Market	.5
Day 5	Section 3: Centrally Planned Economies	.5
	Section 4: Modern Economies	.5
Chapter 3	American Free Enterprise	
Day 6	Section 1: Benefits of Free Enterprise	.5
	Section 2: Promoting Growth and Stability	.5
Day 7	Section 3: Providing Public Goods	.5
	Section 4: Providing a Safety Net	.5
Day 8	Chapter 2 and Chapter 3 Assessment	1
	Total Days for Chapters 2 and 3	**5**
UNIT TWO How Markets Work		
Chapter 4	Demand	
Day 9	Section 1: Understanding Demand	.75
Day 10	Section 2: Shifts of the Demand Curve	.75
Day 11	Section 3: Elasticity of Demand	.75
Day 12	Chapter 4 Assessment	.75
	Total Days for Chapter 4	**3**
Chapter 5	Supply	
Day 13	Section 1: Understanding Supply	.5
	Section 2: Costs of Production	.5
Day 14	Section 3: Changes in Supply	1
Day 15	Chapter 5 Assessment	1
	Total Days for Chapter 5	**3**

		Day Section (# of DAYS)
Chapter 6	**Prices**	
Day 16	Section 1: Combining Supply and Demand	.5
	Section 2: Changes in Market Equilibrium	.5
Day 17	Section 3: The Role of Prices	1
Day 18	Chapter 6 Assessment	1
	Total Days for Chapter 6	**3**
Chapter 7	**Market Structures**	
Day 19	Section 1: Perfect Competition	.5
	Section 2: Monopoly	.5
Day 20	Section 3: Monopolistic Competition and Oligopoly	.5
	Section 4: Regulation and Deregulation	.5
Day 21	Chapter 7 Assessment	1
	Total Days for Chapter 7	**3**

UNIT THREE Business and Labor

Chapter 8	**Business Organizations**	
Day 22	Section 1: Sole Proprietorships	.5
	Section 2: Partnerships	.5
Day 23	Section 3: Corporations, Mergers, and Multinationals	.5
	Section 4: Other Organizations	.5
Day 24	Chapter 8 Assessment	1
	Total Days for Chapter 8	**3**
Chapter 9	**Labor**	
Day 25	Section 1: Labor Market Trends	1
	Section 2: Labor and Wages	.5
Day 26	Section 3: Organized Labor	.5
Day 27	Chapter 9 Assessment	1
	Total Days for Chapter 9	**3**

UNIT FOUR Money, Banking, and Finance

Chapter 10	**Money and Banking**	
Day 28	Section 1: Money	.5
	Section 2: The History of American Banking	.5
Day 29	Section 3: Banking Today	.5
Chapter 11	**Financial Markets**	
Day 29	Section 1: Saving and Investing	.5
Day 30	Section 2: Bonds and Other Financial Assets	.5
	Section 3: The Stock Market	.5
Day 31	Chapter 10 and Chapter 11 Assessment	1
	Total Days for Chapters 10 and 11	**4**

Block Scheduling SUPPORT

		Day Section (# of DAYS)
UNIT FIVE Measuring Economic Performance		
Chapter 12	**Gross Domestic Product and Growth**	
Day 32	Section 1: Gross Domestic Product	.33
	Section 2: Business Cycles	.33
	Section 3: Economic Growth	.33
Chapter 13	**Economic Challenges**	
Day 33	Section 1: Unemployment	.33
	Section 2: Inflation	.33
	Section 3: Poverty	.33
Day 34	Chapter 12 and Chapter 13 Assessment	1
	Total Days for Chapters 12 and 13	**3**
UNIT SIX Government and the Economy		
Chapter 14	**Taxes and Government Spending**	
Day 35	Section 1: What Are Taxes?	.5
	Section 2: Federal Taxes	.5
Day 36	Section 3: Federal Spending	.5
	Section 4: State and Local Taxes and Spending	.5
Chapter 15	**Fiscal Policy**	
Day 37	Section 1: Understanding Fiscal Policy	.5
	Section 2: Fiscal Policy Options	.5
Day 38	Section 3: Budget Deficits and the National Debt	1
Day 39	Chapter 14 and Chapter 15 Assessment	1
	Total Days for Chapters 14 and 15	**5**
Chapter 16	**The Federal Reserve and Monetary Policy**	
Day 40	Section 1: The Federal Reserve System	.33
	Section 2: Federal Reserve Functions	.33
	Section 3: Monetary Policy Tools	.33
Day 41	Section 4: Monetary Policy and Macroeconomic Stabilization	.5
Day 41	Chapter 16 Assessment	.5
	Total Days for Chapter 16	**2**

		Day Section (# of DAYS)
UNIT SEVEN	**The Global Economy**	
Chapter 17	International Trade	
Day 42	Section 1: Why Nations Trade	.33
	Section 2: Trade Barriers and Agreements	.33
	Section 3: Measuring Trade	.33
Chapter 18	Economic Development and Transition	
Day 43	Section 1: Levels of Development	.25
	Section 2: Issues in Development	.25
	Section 3: Financing Development	.25
	Section 4: Transitions to Free Enterprise	.25
	Total Days for Chapters 17 and 18	**2**
Day 44	Final Exams/Preparation	1
Day 45	Final Exams	1

NCEE STANDARDS

Economics: Principles in Action uses the *Voluntary National Content Standards in Economics* to ensure solid coverage of the fundamentals. The standards were developed by the National Council on Economic Education (NCEE) in partnership with the National Association of Economic Educators and the Foundation for Teaching Economics.

The chart on the following pages lists the standards for grades 4–12 and shows which chapters in *Economics: Principles in Action* focus on each standard.

	CONTENT STANDARD	CHAPTER
1	Productive resources are limited. Therefore, people cannot have all the goods and services they want; as a result, they must choose some things and give up others.	Chapter 1
2	Effective decision making requires comparing the additional costs of alternatives with the additional benefits. Most choices involve doing a little more or a little less of something; few choices are all-or-nothing decisions.	Chapter 1
3	Different methods can be used to allocate goods and services. People, acting individually or collectively through government, must choose which methods to use to allocate different kinds of goods and services.	Chapter 2
4	People respond predictably to positive and negative incentives.	Chapters 2, 4, and 5
5	Voluntary exchange occurs only when all participating parties expect to gain. This is true for trade among individuals or organizations within a nation, and among individuals or organizations in different nations.	Chapter 17
6	When individuals, regions, and nations specialize in what they can produce at the lowest cost and then trade with others, both production and consumption increase.	Chapter 17

CONTENT STANDARD		CHAPTER
7	Markets exist when buyers and sellers interact. This interaction determines market prices and thereby allocates scarce goods and services.	Chapters 4 and 17
8	Prices send signals and provide incentives to buyers and sellers. When supply or demand changes, market prices adjust, affecting incentives.	Chapters 5 and 6
9	Competition among sellers lowers costs and prices, and encourages producers to produce more of what consumers are willing and able to buy. Competition among buyers increases prices and allocates goods and services to those people who are willing and able to pay the most for them.	Chapter 7
10	Institutions evolve in market economies to help individuals and groups accomplish their goals. Banks, labor unions, corporations, legal systems, and not-for-profit organizations are examples of important institutions. A different kind of institution, clearly defined and well enforced property rights, is essential to a market economy.	Chapters 8, 10, and 11
11	Money makes it easier to trade, borrow, save, invest, and compare the value of goods and services.	Chapter 10
12	Interest rates, adjusted for inflation, rise and fall to balance the amount saved with the amount borrowed, thus affecting the allocation of scarce resources between present and future uses.	Chapters 11 and 16
13	Income for most people is determined by the market value of the productive resources they sell. What workers earn depends, primarily, on the market value of what they produce and how productive they are.	Chapter 9
14	Entrepreneurs are people who take the risks of organizing productive resources to make goods and services. Profit is an important incentive that leads entrepreneurs to accept the risks of business failure.	Chapter 8

NCEE STANDARDS

	CONTENT STANDARD	CHAPTER
15	**Investment in factories, machinery, new technology, and the health, education,and training of people can raise future standards of living.**	Chapters 3, 12, and 18
16	**There is an economic role for government to play in a market economy whenever the benefits of a government policy outweigh its costs. Governments often provide for national defense, address environmental concerns, define and protect property rights, and attempt to make markets more competitive. Most government policies also redistribute income.**	Chapters 3 and 14
17	**Costs of government policies sometimes exceed benefits. This may occur because of incentives facing voters, government officials, and government employees, because of actions by special interest groups that can impose costs on the general public, or because social goals other than economic efficiency are being pursued.**	Chapter 15
18	**A nation's overall levels of income, employment, and prices are determined by the interaction of spending and production decisions made by all households, firms, government agencies, and others in the economy.**	Chapter 12
19	**Unemployment imposes costs on individuals and nations. Unexpected inflation imposes costs on many people and benefits some others because it arbitrarily redistributes purchasing power. Inflation can reduce the rate of growth of national living standards, because individuals and organizations use resources to protect themselves against the uncertainty of future prices.**	Chapter 13
20	**Federal government budgetary policy and the Federal Reserve System's monetary policy influence the overall levels of employment, output, and prices.**	Chapters 13, 15, and 16

Economics: Principles in Action makes complex concepts easy to understand.

To assist understanding, the list of key concepts below correlates to the twenty National Content Standards in Economics shown on pages T10–T12. Clear and simple graphics are used throughout the student text to highlight concept explanations.

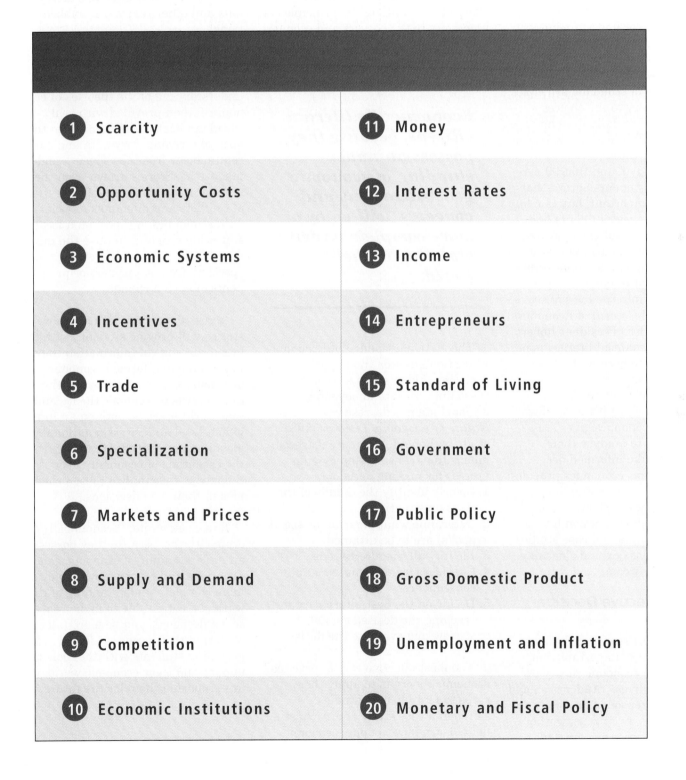

1 Scarcity	11 Money
2 Opportunity Costs	12 Interest Rates
3 Economic Systems	13 Income
4 Incentives	14 Entrepreneurs
5 Trade	15 Standard of Living
6 Specialization	16 Government
7 Markets and Prices	17 Public Policy
8 Supply and Demand	18 Gross Domestic Product
9 Competition	19 Unemployment and Inflation
10 Economic Institutions	20 Monetary and Fiscal Policy

The Importance of Making Economic Decisions

British economist Alfred Marshall said, "Economics is a study of mankind in the ordinary business of life." How should teachers relate these principles to the real world? A key method to enhance student understanding of economic principles is to relate theory to the choices students face in their daily lives and the choices they will face as workers, consumers, and investors.

A recent study found that 90 percent of college students agreed that good credit is important, but as many as one-third of these students had either missed a credit card payment or paid a bill late. Learning how credit card issuers evaluate applications and credit histories can extend the lesson directly into the lives of students. National Council of Economics Education (NCEE) President Robert Duvall said, "Financial literacy is not something you're born with. It's learned behavior. And you're either going to learn it from teachers or you're going to learn it the hard way." The study of economics gives students the tools to analyze their options and make informed decisions.

As a discipline, economics provides a set of rules for understanding daily events and choices. Showing students how to relate common life events to the topics and case studies they learn in class extends learning beyond the classroom.

Teaching Effective Decision-Making

In order to make reasoned decisions as consumers, it is important that students relate economic theory to their everyday lives. Students should learn to make reasoned decisions on economic issues as citizens, workers, consumers, business owners and managers, and members of civic groups. Economics teachers are charged with linking the principles of economics to the careers and economic decisions made by individuals in a free market economy.

Economically literate citizens, because they possess an understanding of economic generalizations and concepts, will enjoy a more complete understanding of their world.

The National Council of Economics Education stresses the importance of decision-making skills in economic reasoning. To extend beyond the national standards, research in *The Nature of Economic Literacy* (1987), a study by Ronald A. Banaszak, recommends the following step-by-step process for making decisions:

1. Clearly identify the details of the decision situation.
2. Determine what personal or social goal(s) are to be attained.
3. Identify all the alternatives.
4. Consider each alternative and its consequences.
5. Decide on the best alternative for reaching the desired goal(s).
6. Review and evaluate the decision.

The most effective way to practice economic theory is to apply these steps to real-life case studies. Through a case study approach, students learn how to apply economic theory by analyzing financial information, current events, research journals and other real world publications.

Applying Decision Making

In addition, students reinforce their understanding of the theories of economics when provided with real world applications of theories in the form of contemporary data and current articles from newspapers and magazines. Stories drawn from the news provide a dramatic illustration of conflicts and dilemmas associated with economics. A report on a local or statewide proposal to raise the minimum wage will include relevant perspectives from supporters or proponents of such a change.

Access to current data and news stories will provide students with the broadest range of information they need to make informed economic decisions. When introduced to the links between economic theory and real-world practice, both on an individual level and across a national or global economy, students will learn the essentials of economic theory and the means to actualize those principles in their own decisions.

Banaszak wrote, "Economically literate citizens, because they possess an understanding of economic generalizations and concepts, will enjoy a more complete understanding of their world, be better able to make reasoned decisions, and be more fully in control of their economic future." By providing students with the tools to understand their economic world, we are preparing them for the future.

Effective Classroom Implementation

Economics: Principles in Action brings economic theory to life by directly linking the principles of microeconomics and macroeconomics to the world that students will explore when they complete their education—a world they already encounter daily when they make choices about their schooling, hobbies, and work.

The program has integrated resources for effective decision-making throughout, examples of which are included below.

Real-World Applications

Through an exclusive relationship with *The Wall Street Journal Classroom Edition, Economics: Principles in Action* provides up-to-date news and opinion features from the pages of *The Wall Street Journal Classroom Edition* to foster economic literacy. These features help students apply decision making to real life events.

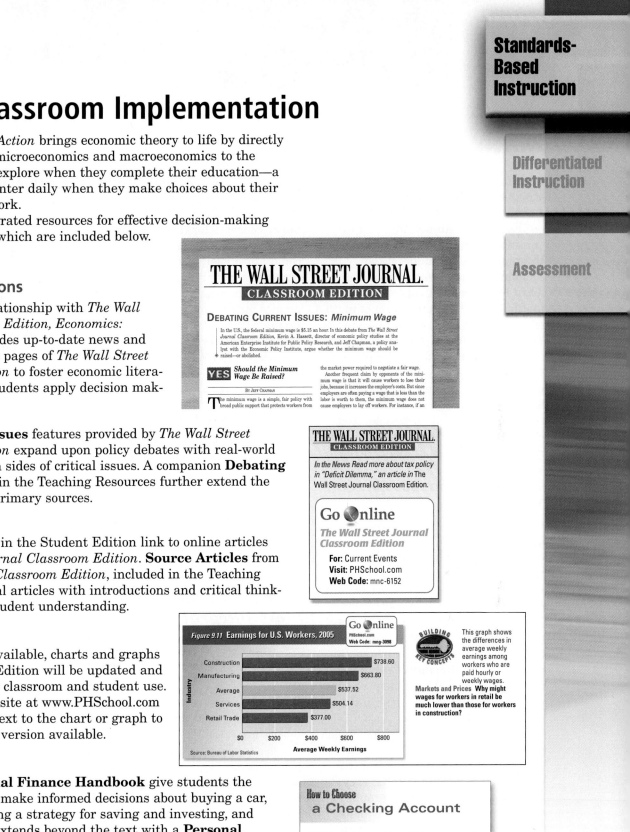

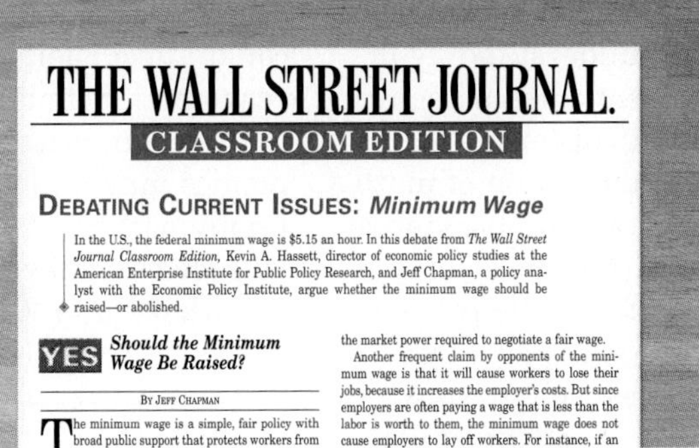

THE WALL STREET JOURNAL.
CLASSROOM EDITION

DEBATING CURRENT ISSUES: *Minimum Wage*

In the U.S., the federal minimum wage is $5.15 an hour. In this debate from *The Wall Street Journal Classroom Edition*, Kevin A. Hassett, director of economic policy studies at the American Enterprise Institute for Public Policy Research, and Jeff Chapman, a policy analyst with the Economic Policy Institute, argue whether the minimum wage should be raised—or abolished.

YES *Should the Minimum Wage Be Raised?*

BY JEFF CHAPMAN

The minimum wage is a simple, fair policy with broad public support that protects workers from the market power required to negotiate a fair wage.

Another frequent claim by opponents of the minimum wage is that it will cause workers to lose their jobs, because it increases the employer's costs. But since employers are often paying a wage that is less than the labor is worth to them, the minimum wage does not cause employers to lay off workers. For instance, if an

Debating Current Issues features provided by *The Wall Street Journal Classroom Edition* expand upon policy debates with real-world examples presenting both sides of critical issues. A companion **Debating Current Issues** booklet in the Teaching Resources further extend the debates with additional primary sources.

THE WALL STREET JOURNAL.
CLASSROOM EDITION

In the News Read more about tax policy in "Deficit Dilemma," an article in The Wall Street Journal Classroom Edition.

Go Online
The Wall Street Journal Classroom Edition
For: Current Events
Visit: PHSchool.com
Web Code: mnc-6152

In the News features in the Student Edition link to online articles from *The Wall Street Journal Classroom Edition*. **Source Articles** from *The Wall Street Journal Classroom Edition*, included in the Teaching Resources, offer additional articles with introductions and critical thinking questions to assess student understanding.

As new data become available, charts and graphs provided in the Student Edition will be updated and posted to the Internet for classroom and student use. Visit Prentice Hall's web site at www.PHSchool.com and enter the web code next to the chart or graph to view the most up-to-date version available.

This graph shows the differences in average weekly earnings among workers who are paid hourly or weekly wages.

Markets and Prices Why might wages for workers in retail be much lower than those for workers in construction?

Lessons in the **Personal Finance Handbook** give students the information they need to make informed decisions about buying a car, applying for a job, choosing a strategy for saving and investing, and paying for college. This extends beyond the text with a **Personal Finance Activities** booklet offering activities for wise money management, including sample financial forms and documents for hands-on practice.

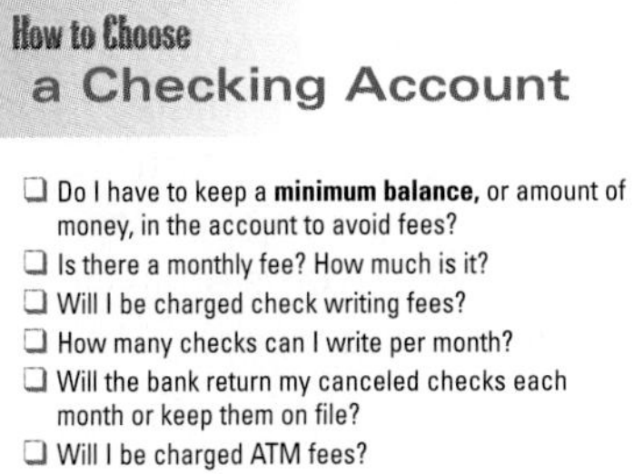

How to Choose a Checking Account

- ❑ Do I have to keep a **minimum balance,** or amount of money, in the account to avoid fees?
- ❑ Is there a monthly fee? How much is it?
- ❑ Will I be charged check writing fees?
- ❑ How many checks can I write per month?
- ❑ Will the bank return my canceled checks each month or keep them on file?
- ❑ Will I be charged ATM fees?
- ❑ What other fees are associated with this account?

REAL-WORLD APPLICATIONS

Math in Economics

Within the fields of social science, economics has the strongest connections to the discipline of mathematics. Educators can use this link to enhance learning in both disciplines. In order to ensure understanding of economic principles, students should learn measurement concepts and methods and the application of mathematical tools such as graphs, statistics, and equations. The study of economics also presents excellent opportunities to practice skills acquired in mathematics courses—increasing math proficiency by applying skills that students need for test success. Emphasizing the mathematics in economics can help all students achieve.

Explaining Economic Concepts Through Math

One state's framework for teaching economics says that in order to master the economic method, "students must use graphs and understand, at the appropriate level, the mathematical equations they represent." Economics draws heavily on mathematics to explain central principles and illustrate key relationships. In economics, mathematical relationships do not merely augment understanding—they are integral to student comprehension.

To illustrate this point, imagine an economics course that did not draw upon the basics of math. Could students read a demand curve if they did not know how to interpret graphs? Could they find elasticity, calculate the unemployment rate, or explain inflation without the language of percentages and algebra? Even a subject as basic as the minimum wage requires an understanding of arithmetic, means, and medians to fully communicate the implications of economic concepts for the workforce.

In fact, students' grasp of math could affect their ability to master economics. Scholars have suggested that the quantitative nature of economics may indicate that a student's familiarity and facility with math will affect achievement in economics (Kourlisky and Wittrock 1987).

Economics draws heavily on mathematics to explain central principles and illustrate key relationships. In economics, mathematical relationships do not merely augment understanding—they are integral to student comprehension.

Research indicates that students with a strong background in mathematics are more likely than others to succeed in their introductory college-level economics classes. Therefore, a strong economics program needs to integrate mathematics into its explanation of economic principles. It should also provide extensive practice with math skills to improve student understanding.

Achieving Math Proficiency

Focusing on math in economics can also assist with building math proficiency. This is important because federal requirements recognize numeracy as being critical to student success. No Child Left Behind requires all U.S. students to demonstrate proficiency in mathematics in order to graduate from high school. To develop this proficiency, students need to apply math to real-life situations. *How People Learn: Brain, Mind, Experience, and School,* a National Research Council publication, makes the connection between math proficiency and how students put math into practice. It argues that "to enable students to become numerate, teachers must encourage them to see and use mathematics in everything they do. Numeracy is driven by the issues that are important to people in their lives and work." Economics is an arena in which these real-life issues can be explored through mathematics. Economics word problems use skills that reinforce lessons learned in math classrooms.

In conclusion, a strong emphasis on math in an economics course can greatly benefit students. This focus both can help illustrate economic theories through math examples and provide practice that strengthens proficiency in math skills. Ideally, students will complete such a course with a thorough understanding of economics and the confidence in the mathematical skills needed to put their education to work.

Effective Classroom Implementation

Economics: Principles in Action was written with the mathematical architecture of economics in mind. Economics principles are explained first on a theoretical level and then illustrated by example. Where it will serve to benefit students, additional math review is provided to make all examples clear and adaptable to new data.

Math Instruction

Important economic concepts are taught using graphs and equations. Instructions walk students through the calculations, step by step, to enhance understanding.

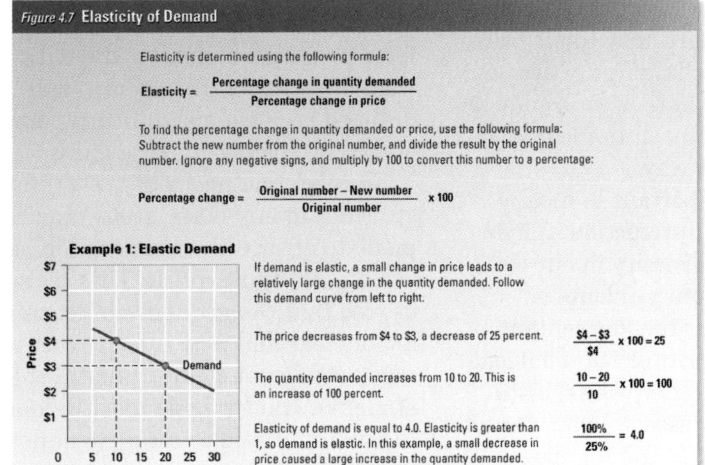

Figure 4.7 **Elasticity of Demand**

Elasticity is determined using the following formula:

$$\text{Elasticity} = \frac{\text{Percentage change in quantity demanded}}{\text{Percentage change in price}}$$

To find the percentage change in quantity demanded or price, use the following formula: Subtract the new number from the original number, and divide the result by the original number. Ignore any negative signs, and multiply by 100 to convert this number to a percentage:

$$\text{Percentage change} = \frac{\text{Original number} - \text{New number}}{\text{Original number}} \times 100$$

Example 1: Elastic Demand

If demand is elastic, a small change in price leads to a relatively large change in the quantity demanded. Follow this demand curve from left to right.

The price decreases from $4 to $3, a decrease of 25 percent. $\frac{\$4 - \$3}{\$4} \times 100 = 25$

The quantity demanded increases from 10 to 20. This is an increase of 100 percent. $\frac{10 - 20}{10} \times 100 = 100$

Elasticity of demand is equal to 4.0. Elasticity is greater than 1, so demand is elastic. In this example, a small decrease in price caused a large increase in the quantity demanded. $\frac{100\%}{25\%} = 4.0$

Caption questions assess understanding and encourage students to apply their skills with new data.

Figure 13.1 **Calculating the Unemployment Rate**

To calculate the unemployment rate, use the following formula:

Number of people unemployed **divided by** number of people in the civilian labor force **multiplied by** 100

For example,
if the number of people unemployed = 7.7 million and the number of people in the civilian labor force = 148.2 million

then,
$7.7 \div 148.2 = .052$
$.052 \times 100 = 5.2$

Therefore,
the unemployment rate is 5.2%.

BUILDING KEY CONCEPTS To calculate the unemployment rate, follow the steps above. **Unemployment In 1982, the civilian labor force was 110.2 million, and 10.68 million were unemployed. What was the unemployment rate?**

Testing Proficiency

Math Practice questions in the section assessment and chapter assessments provide mathematical applications of section and chapter content.

7. ***Math Practice*** Suppose that a very small economy produces only televisions and computers. Determine nominal GDP and real GDP in Year 4, using the following information: *In Year 1, the base year, 10 computers sold at $2,000 each, and 15 televisions sold at $500 each. In Year 4, 17 computers sold at $2,200 each and 20 televisions sold at $550 each.*

In the Teaching Resources, the **Math Practice** booklet provides a variety of math skill application activities, including drawing and interpreting graphs, calculating interest rates, maximizing profit, and choosing between job offers.

Research on Differentiated Instruction

Why do we need differentiated instruction?

The wide range of academic diversity in schools today presents both a challenge and an opportunity to all teachers. Because the challenge of accommodating all students is so urgent, we need to plan and teach to include all learners in a new way.

Why is it so important to modify our planning and instruction in light of the increased diversity in our classes? First, each of our students is expected to master the key content that is tied to district or state outcome examinations. In other words, if students are in our classes, we are expected to teach to enable them to be successful on these high-stakes exams.

Second, when adolescents encounter failure in meeting rigorous curriculum demands, they often lose hope in their ability to be successful—they may mentally disengage from school, seek out "success" by acting out inappropriately, or even drop out of school. Thus, when we work with struggling learners, the costs for not successfully meeting their needs can be significant.

Meeting the needs of highly capable students is equally challenging. They must be "stretched" to learn new materials and engage in higher order thinking about the curriculum. In short, the most successful teachers are those who understand the complexity of the academic diversity in their classes and design their lessons and learning experiences in light of this reality.

What the research tells us

The literature on differentiated instruction tells us three important things: active instruction is that which increases the achievement levels of four major subgroups (special needs, low-, average-, and high-achieving) of students equally. If one subgroup benefits significantly more than others from a teacher's attempt to differentiate instruction for the entire class, eventually the attempt will be dropped because a significant portion of the class is not making gains.

To reach the needs of low-achieving students in any class, steps must be made to ensure that instruction is systematic and explicit. That is, to the degree that the sequence of learning is not clear and new information to be mastered is not clearly taught, the students who struggle most in learning will continue to struggle and will fall further behind their classmates.

Finally, the long-term effects of any instructional practice will be enhanced if a majority of teachers use and reinforce that practice. For example, if Teacher A teaches her class to use a particular learning strategy to master new vocabulary, students will better learn and apply that strategy if it is used and reinforced by all teachers. Effective differentiated instruction is in part dependent on teachers having an opportunity to coordinate the use of similar materials and reinforce critical learning strategies.

How do we provide inclusive instruction?

One of the most important roles that teachers play in effectively providing differentiated instruction is to see themselves as a "mediator" in the learning process. That is, the chances of students learning complex content is greatly enhanced if teachers understand (a) the specific difficulties of learners in their class, (b) why the curriculum content they are teaching is difficult (Is it abstract, dense, etc.?), and (c) the unique features of the curriculum materials and the particular challenges they present in learning. In light of these three factors, the most effective teachers are those who help "mediate" (or manipulate or transform) the content in such a way as to make it understandable and memorable to all their students.

What is the result of differentiated instruction?

While improving student outcomes is a major goal of differentiated instruction, it is important to remember that when teachers are successful in reaching a large majority of students in their classes, an environment of cooperation, learning, and respect emerges. Teachers intent on successfully differentiating their instruction communicate a message that the "work" of this community is learning for everyone. Everyday practices and routines are based on cooperation in accomplishing this work, and the interests and learning needs of everyone in the community are taken seriously.

Don Deshler

Don Deshler, Ph.D., is the Chair of Prentice Hall's Differentiated Instruction Board. He assembled a distinguished panel of national experts to serve on the board, offering extensive experience in special needs, English language learners, less proficient readers, and gifted and talented students. This team informs Prentice Hall's approach to differentiated instruction and offers guidance on the development of new materials based on this approach. He is the Director of the Center for Research on Learning at the University of Kansas.

Effective Classroom Implementation

The mission of *Economics: Principles in Action* is to provide standards-based instruction in ways that allow all learners to participate and to achieve. Because not all students learn in the same manner nor have the same abilities, our program provides options so that all learners work toward the essential understandings and skills, but use different content, processes, and products to get there (Tomlinson, 2001). Our effective support help you close the achievement gap.

Teaching Support Helps You Modify Instruction

The Teacher's Edition provides continuous professional development throughout the program, starting with strategies for specific populations at the beginning of this textbook. The Differentiated Instruction boxes throughout each chapter offers specific suggestions for modifying instruction to accommodate all learners. The direct instruction creates opportunities to build a community of learners, who can learn from and about one another. Together, these tools will help you provide all learners with meaningful access to the curriculum.

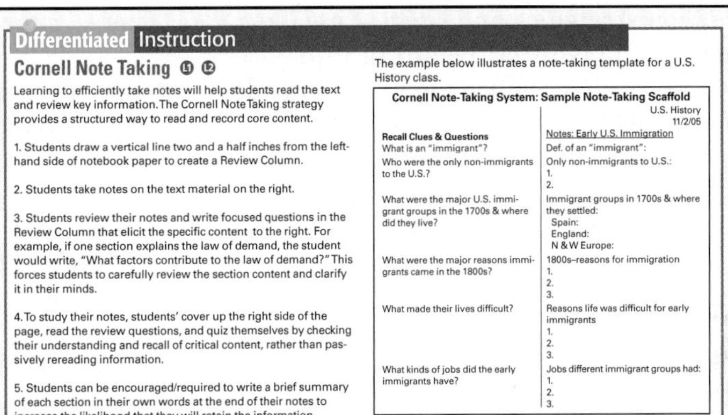

Differentiated Instruction

Cornell Note Taking L1 L2

Learning to efficiently take notes will help students read the text and review key information. The Cornell Note Taking strategy provides a structured way to read and record core content.

1. Students draw a vertical line two and a half inches from the left-hand side of notebook paper to create a Review Column.

2. Students take notes on the text material on the right.

3. Students review their notes and write focused questions in the Review Column that elicit the specific content to the right. For example, if one section explains the law of demand, the student would write, "What factors contribute to the law of demand?" This forces students to carefully review the section content and clarify it in their minds.

4. To study their notes, students' cover up the right side of the page, read the review questions, and quiz themselves by checking their understanding and recall of critical content, rather than passively rereading information.

5. Students can be encouraged/required to write a brief summary of each section in their own words at the end of their notes to increase the likelihood that they will retain the information.

The example below illustrates a note-taking template for a U.S. History class.

Cornell Note-Taking System: Sample Note-Taking Scaffold

U.S. History
11/2/05

Recall Clues & Questions	Notes: Early U.S. Immigration
What is an "immigrant"?	Def. of an "immigrant":
Who were the only non-immigrants to the U.S.?	Only non-immigrants to U.S.: 1. 2.
What were the major U.S. immigrant groups in the 1700s & where did they live?	Immigrant groups in 1700s & where they settled: Spain: England: N & W Europe:
What were the major reasons immigrants came in the 1800s?	1800s–reasons for immigration 1. 2. 3.
What made their lives difficult?	Reasons life was difficult for early immigrants 1. 2. 3.
What kinds of jobs did the early immigrants have?	Jobs different immigrant groups had: 1. 2. 3.

Differentiated Instruction L4

Encourage students to use either a graphing calculator or a spreadsheet program to create a demand schedule and its corresponding demand curve. Ask one or two students to explain how they used this technology to create their schedules and curves. GT

Differentiated Instruction L3

Have students use the following data to prepare a market demand schedule: At a price of 80 cents per pound, the demand for apples is 14,000 pounds. At 60 cents per pound, the demand is 20,000 pounds. At 40 cents per pound, the demand is 26,000 pounds. At 20 cents per pound, the demand is 32,000 pounds.

Then have students graph the demand curve for the given data. Ask them to explain why the demand curve slopes downward and to the right.

Varied Resources Address Different Populations

Economics: Principles in Action is designed to help students of all abilities master core content. **The Guide to the Essentials** offer graphical and text summaries of section content, available in English and Spanish, for students who need extra assistance with reading. The program also delivers content through a wide variety of formats—including text, transparencies, audio, video, and interactive text—appealing to all of your students.

Leveled Review and Assessments Gives You More Options

The **Guided Reading and Review Workbook**, available in English and Spanish, provides a framework for reviewing main ideas and key terms as students read each section. The **ExamView® Test Bank CD-ROM** offers leveled tests, and makes it easy to adapt tests based on individual needs.

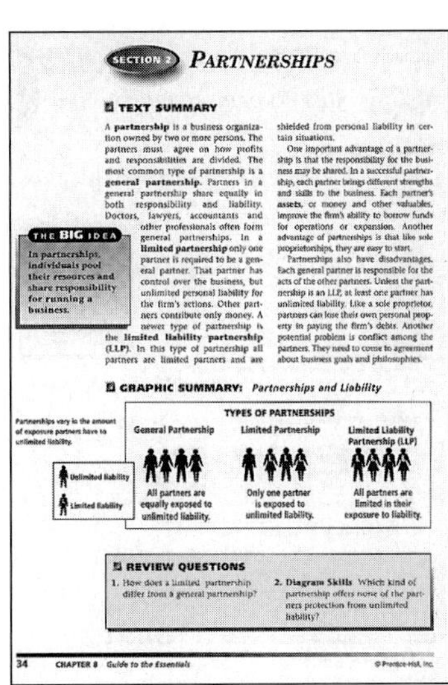

SECTION 2 *PARTNERSHIPS*

TEXT SUMMARY

A **partnership** is a business organization owned by two or more persons. The partners must agree on how profits and responsibilities are divided. The most common type of partnership is a **general partnership**. Partners in a general partnership share equally in both responsibility and liability. Doctors, lawyers, accountants and other professionals often form general partnerships. In a **limited partnership** only one partner is required to be a general partner. That partner has control over the business, but unlimited personal liability for the firm's actions. Other partners contribute only money. A newer type of partnership is the **limited liability partnership (LLP)**. In this type of partnership all partners are limited partners and are shielded from personal liability in certain situations.

One important advantage of a partnership is that the responsibility for the business may be shared. In a successful partnership, each partner brings different strengths and skills to the business. Each partner's **assets**, or money and other valuables, improve the firm's ability to borrow funds for operations or expansion. Another advantage of partnerships is that like sole proprietorships, they are easy to start.

Partnerships also have disadvantages. Each general partner is responsible for the acts of the other partners. Unless the partnership is an LLP, at least one partner has unlimited liability. Like a sole proprietor, partners can lose their own personal property in paying the firm's debts. Another potential problem is conflict among the partners. They need to come to agreement about business goals and philosophies.

THE BIG IDEA

In partnerships, individuals pool their resources and share responsibility for running a business.

GRAPHIC SUMMARY: *Partnerships and Liability*

REVIEW QUESTIONS

1. How does a limited partnership differ from a general partnership?

2. **Diagram Skills** Which kind of partnership offers none of the partners protection from unlimited liability?

34 CHAPTER 8 *Guide to the Essentials* © Prentice-Hall, Inc.

Strategies for Specific Student Populations

Differentiated instruction can be fostered through modifying instruction to address individual needs. To increase student achievement, teachers can use strategies for specific student populations to offer specialized support. Lesson plans in this Teacher's Edition provide differentiated instruction strategies and suggest ancillary support such as the **Guided Reading and Review** workbooks. The following pages provide general guidelines for modifying instruction for students with special needs, less proficient students, English language learners, gifted and talented students and advanced learners.

Special Needs

Students with special education needs are a highly heterogeneous group of learners, presenting unique cognitive, behavioral, social, and physical needs. To help create a classroom culture that supports the participation and achievement of students with such needs, set clear expectations and provide reasonable choices for all students. Lessons should be planned with individual adaptations and modifications. Offer instructional activities that foster the development of relationships among students and between students and teachers.

Preteach

Preteaching helps prepare students for learning.

- Preteach critical social studies terms and high-use academic words using the Vocabulary Builders in the chapter introduction.

- Provide preferred seating in the front of the class, face-to-face talk for students who read lips, interpreters, or space for a guide dog as necessary.

Teach

Using a variety of approaches enhances lessons.

- Provide an overview of key ideas and concepts presented in the text using outlines, maps, or study guides.

- Present all ideas orally and visually, and when possible, incorporate tactile and kinesthetic experiences as well.

- Require students to demonstrate that they are listening and following along (e.g., taking notes, running a finger along the text).

- Incorporate active reading strategies (e.g., choral reading, paired reading) to assist in maintaining attention.

- Provide adaptive materials as appropriate (e.g., enlarged print, Braille edition, captions for the video program).

- Incorporate the same comprehension and learning strategies over time to allow for mastery.

Assess

Students need to know what is expected.

- Assess students' understanding by asking them to write questions about what they have learned, identify what they find unclear of confusing, or complete short quick writes of the key points.

- When having students work in groups or pairs, set up procedures that maintain each student's accountability (e.g., students each having to write, draw, or state a response).

- Make sure that you have adequately scaffolded tasks for special needs students and equipped them with writing instruction and practice that builds the prerequisite skills.

- When appropriate, have students self-manage and chart their academic performance, homework and assignment completion, and behavior.

- Provide outlines of what is to be done, with suggested dates and timelines for project completion.

English Language Learners

Students who are learning English are the fastest-growing segment of the school-age population. These students require frontloading, or preteaching, in order to grasp challenging literacy tasks, such as those encountered in a social studies textbook. Since English Language Learners may be approaching an assignment with impoverished background knowledge and weak English vocabulary, concentrate on activities that build strong conceptual and linguistic foundations, guide them through the text's organization, and model appropriate comprehension strategies. The following practices will support ELL students in making strides in their second-language literacy.

Preteach

English Language Learners require extra preparation.

- Introduce essential words in meaningful contexts, through simple sentences drawing on familiar issues, scenarios, and vocabulary. Ask students to write the definitions in their own words and then present the words when they occur within the reading.
- Utilize realia and visuals (e.g., photographs, objects, color transparencies) to make the concepts less abstract.
- Lead a quick text prereading, or "text tour," focusing student attention on illustrations, title and subtopics, boldfaced words.

Teach

Many of these techniques will benefit all learners.

- Get students physically involved with the page, using sticky notes or small pieces of cardboard to focus and guide their reading.
- Have students engage in repeated readings of the same brief passage to build word recognition, fluency, and reading rate.
- Praise students' efforts to experiment with new language in class, both in writing and in speaking.

Assess

Students will demonstrate learning in different ways.

- Ask students to demonstrate their understanding by drawing upon different language skills: formal and informal writing assignments, posters, small group tasks, and oral presentations.
- Make sure students understand assessment criteria in advance. Distribute rubrics provided in the **Economics Assessment Rubrics.** Whenever possible, provide models of student work to emulate, along with a non-model that fails to meet the specified assessment criteria.

Differentiated INSTRUCTION

Less Proficient Readers

Less proficient readers are individuals who begin the year one or more years below grade level yet do not qualify for special education services. They may or may not be English Language Learners. They may be under-prepared for the academic challenges due to difficulties with attention and memory, learning strategies, or vocabulary and reading fluency. It is especially important to engage these students in challenging lessons while incorporating support or instructional scaffolding to increase their likelihood of success.

Preteach

Preteaching helps build students' confidence.

- For *Difficulties With Attention and Memory*: Gain attention by requesting a simple physic (e.g. "Everyone, eyes on me please"). Then keep the lesson pace brisk—a "perky not pokey" pace is helpful.

- For *Difficulties With Learning Strategies*: Clarify the rationale for learning a new strategy in terms the students value. Directly teach any requisite skills needed to perform the strategy.

- For *Difficulties With Vocabulary and Fluency*: Directly teach meanings of critical vocabulary required for full understanding of the lesson.

Teach

Lessons have to address specific, different needs.

- For *Difficulties With Attention and Memory*: Emphasize connections between new and known information. Engage students in collaborative "read/reflect/discuss/note" cycle, filling out a graphic organizer.

- For *Difficulties With Learning Strategies*: Explicitly model the use of the strategy, including a significant focus on thinking aloud during the execution of each step in the strategy. Discuss where else in or out of school students could use the strategy.

- For *Difficulties With Vocabulary and Fluency*: Intentionally revisit newly acquired vocabulary during discussion.

Assess

Assessment must accommodate special needs.

- For *Difficulties With Attention and Memory*: Ask students to reorganize, prioritize, and otherwise reflect on the key aspects of the lesson. Have them explain their graphic organizers to a partner. Monitor, and reteach as necessary.

- For *Difficulties With Learning Strategies*: Include explicity use of strategies taught as part of the quiz, report, project, and other formal assessments.

- For *Difficulties With Vocabulary and Fluency*: Randomly call on students to provide examples of the vocabulary word under examination.

Gifted and Talented Students and Advanced Learners

Gifted and Talented Students and Advanced Learners need modified instruction to achieve their highest potential. They tend to understand complex concepts quickly, learn more rapidly and in greater depth, and may have interests that are different from their peers. Teachers can modify pacing and offer enrichment to allow for exploring topics in-depth, manipulating ideas in novel ways, and making connections to other disciplines.

Preteach

These students may have extensive background.

- Before beginning a new unit, have students write, verbalize, or draw what they know about the topic and present this information to peers.
- Ask students to brainstorm what they'd like to learn, and then work with them to create a plan for advanced study based on their interests.

Teach

Activate students' ability to think creatively and see connections.

- Help students adjust the pace of their learning, speeding through concepts they master quickly or slowing down to study content in depth. The Teacher's Edition provides ideas for ways to extend content in the Extend part of the lesson plan.
- Challenge students to tackle more complex topics and offer frequent opportunities to focus on abstract ideas.
- Provide opportunities for in-depth research on student-directed topics. Have students explore topics on the Internet and under your direction.
- Encourage students to make connections between content they are learning and other disciplines such as language arts, science, and math. For example, students might want to read about the impact of technology on the economic concept they are studying.

Assess

Assessment can take many forms.

- Have students be responsible for part of the assessment of their learning. Allow them to plan, design, and monitor the project or assignment.
- Encourage students to apply standards-based understandings to new situations. Challenge them to take information and use it in novel ways.

Informing Instruction with Assessment

Assessment is a never-ending cycle. With the spotlight now on improving student performance and providing universal access, it is essential to use assessment to target goals, identify strategies to achieve results, monitor progress, and assess results to inform lesson planning.

Using Adequate Yearly Progress Monitoring Assessments

The key to success is using a variety of assessment tools coupled with data analysis and decision making. The Progress Monitoring Assessments in this program provides four types of assessments.

Types of Assessment	AYP Monitoring Assessments
Screening assessments are brief procedures used to identify at-risk students who are not ready to work at grade-level.	Screening assessments are brief procedures used to identify at-risk students who are not ready to work at grade-level.
Diagnostic assessments provide a more in-depth analysis of strengths and weaknesses that can help teachers make instructional decisions and plan intervention strategies.	Diagnostic assessments provide a more in-depth analysis of strengths and weaknesses that can help teachers make instructional decisions and plan intervention strategies.
Progress-monitoring assessments (sometimes referred to as benchmark tests) provide an ongoing, longitudinal record of student achievement detailing individual student progress toward meeting end-of-year and end of-of-schooling, grade level, district, or state standards.	Progress-monitoring assessments (sometimes referred to as benchmark tests) provide an ongoing, longitudinal record of student achievement detailing individual student progress toward meeting end-of-year and end of-of-schooling, grade level, district, or state standards.
Summative assessments judge students' achievement at the end of a course of study. Large-scale assessments, such as state tests and standardized tests, can be used to determine whether individual students have met the expected standards and whether a school system has made adequate progress in improving its performance.	Summative assessments judge students' achievement at the end of a course of study. Large-scale assessments, such as state tests and standardized tests, can be used to determine whether individual students have met the expected standards and whether a school system has made adequate progress in improving its performance.

Standards-Based Instruction

Differentiated Instruction

Assessment

Ongoing Assessment

Ongoing assessment is a critical part of the assessment process. Used in conjunction with AYP monitoring tools—screeners, diagnostics, benchmark and summative assessments—it can help teachers monitor student progress and adjust instruction on a day-to-day basis.

Periodic Testing

Teachers should use periodic quizzes and tests to measure how students are progressing in what they can do and what they understand, as defined by the standards. Administered between benchmark tests, tests that assess students' analysis skill acquisition and content understanding also inform teacher planning. Assessments include multiple-choice, short answer, and written essays. This program offers printed tests in these formats in the Teaching Resources.

Portfolios

Portfolios are a form of assessment that contain samples of a student's work collected over time. They enable both the teacher and the student to evaluate progress. Portfolios provide students with the opportunity to examine and reflect upon what they have produced so that they can improve their work.

Many Differentiated Instruction activities in the Teacher's Edition were designed for inclusion in a student portfolio. Internet activities linked to section assessments can offer evidence of student understanding.

Assessing Writing

Social studies teachers help build students' writing skills throughout the year and monitor progress through written assessments.

Educators should evaluate student writing based on its alignment with grade-level requirements.

Using Rubrics

Rubrics are a critical component in a successful assessment system. They provide a structure that helps teachers to make expectations clear and provides an equitable way to assess student performance in written or performance-based assessments. Rubrics also allow students to assess their own work.

This program offers analytical rubrics in the Teaching Resources. **Economics Assessment Rubrics** includes reproducible rubrics for students and instruction for rubric use for teachers.

Sample Contents of a Portfolio
Written work • short paragraphs • compositions • short stories • journals
Audio and video cassettes of oral presentations
Quizzes and tests
Individual student projects
Art work
Technology projects and Web research
Storyboards
Evidence of student reflection on his or her own writing

Encouraging Self-Assessment

Students need to evaluate their own progress and accept responsibility for their learning. Students should use the following checks on understanding of skills and concepts before moving on to the next topic:

Caption Questions enhance critical thinking skills and maximize the effectiveness of art, graphics, maps, and narrative.

Standards Monitoring Online lets students assess their understanding of content and get instant remediation.

Using Assessment Technology

Technology can ease the assessment process for teachers. Products with this program generate tests, calculate test results, and analyze assessment data.

Test Generators

Teachers can use test generator software to develop quizzes, tests, and final exams to match their instruction. This program's ExamView® Test Bank CD-ROM allows teachers to easily create customized tests from banks of thousands of questions. The test bank questions, based on textbook content, exactly align with the History-Social Science Standards, and provide specific text page numbers for content to foster remediation. Questions can be sorted by difficulty levels to provide leveled quizzes and tests for universal access.

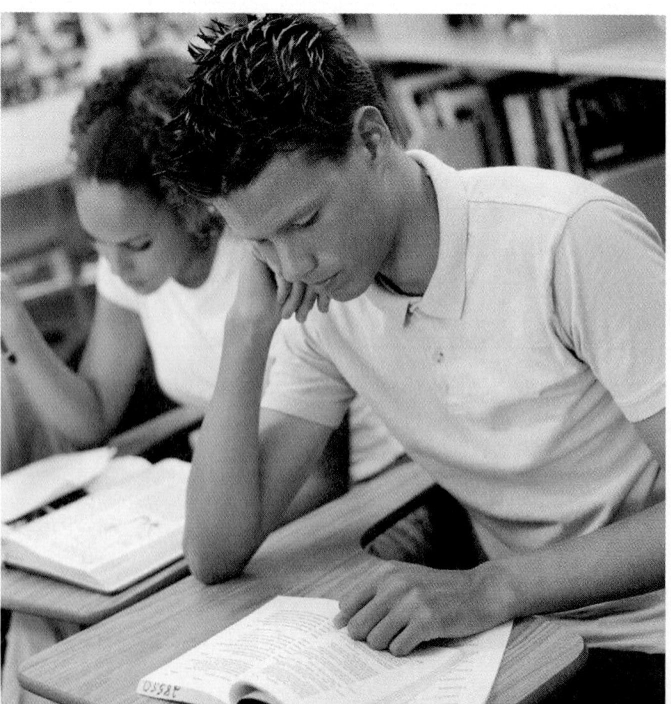

Data Processing Systems

Technology can provide detailed testing results quickly. It also can assist with data gathering and analysis, informing decision making. Teachers can use the testing software for this program with the eInstruction Classroom Performance System—a handheld, instant student response system that allows teachers to evaluate student understanding and track standards mastery. It also works with the EZScanner Scoring System, which grades tests in seconds and generates reports that track performance on standards-based assessments.

References:

T16 Banaszak, Ronald A. *The Nature of Economic Literacy:* ERIC Digest No. 41. ERIC Clearinghouse for Social Studies, 1987.

T16 Borja, Rhea R. *Financial Literacy Challenges Seen.* Education Week: Vol. 24, Issue 37, Page 8; 2005

T18 Bransford, John D, Ann L. Brown, and Rodney R. Cockling. *How People Learn: Brain, Mind, Experience, and School.* National Research Council. Washington, DC. 1999.

T18 Cohn, Elchanan, Sharon Cohn, Donald C. Balch, and James Bradley, Jr. *Do Graphs Promote Learning in Priciples of Economics.* Journal of Economic Education. 2001

T18 Kennedy, Dan, Ph.D, Randall I. Charles, Ph.D, and Art Johnson, Ed.D. *Approaches to Important Content.* http://www.phschool.com/Research/math/

T18 Kourilsky, M., and M. C. Wittrock. 1987. Verbal and graphical strategies in the teaching of economics. *Teaching and Teacher Education* 3 (1): 1-12.

T18 No Child Left Behind http://www.ed.gov/nclb/landing.jhtml?src=pb

Chapter 6 **Prices** 124
1 Combining Supply and Demand 125
2 Changes in Market Equilibrium 133
3 The Role of Prices 139
Case Study: *Government and the Market for Milk* 145
Chapter 6 Assessment 146

Chapter 7 **Market Structures** 150
1 Perfect Competition 151
2 Monopoly 156
3 Monopolistic Competition and Oligopoly 166
4 Regulation and Deregulation 172
Case Study: *Regulating Cable Television* 177
Chapter 7 Assessment 178

THE WALL STREET JOURNAL. CLASSROOM EDITION **Debating Current Issues:**
Oil and Energy Dependence 180

Unit 3 Business and Labor 182

Chapter 8 **Business Organizations** 184
1 Sole Proprietorships 185
2 Partnerships 190
3 Corporations, Mergers, and Multinationals 195
4 Other Organizations 201
Case Study: *Business and Ethics* 205
Chapter 8 Assessment 206

Chapter 9 **Labor** 210
1 Labor Market Trends 211
2 Labor and Wages 219
3 Organized Labor 228
Case Study: *The Paterson Silk Strike of 1913* 235
Chapter 9 Assessment 236

THE WALL STREET JOURNAL. CLASSROOM EDITION **Debating Current Issues:**
Minimum Wage 238

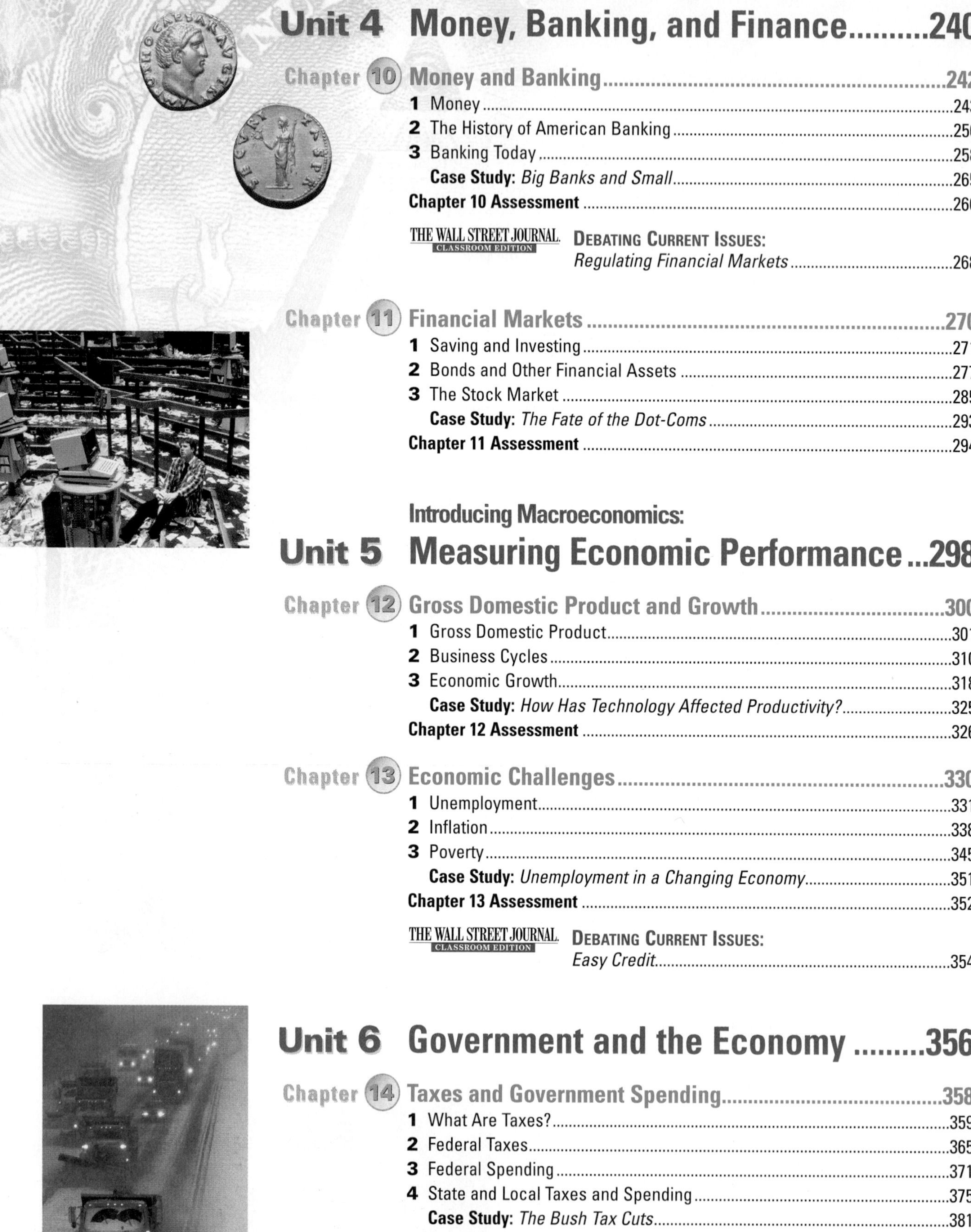

Unit 4 Money, Banking, and Finance..........240

Chapter 10 Money and Banking..........242
1 Money..........243
2 The History of American Banking..........250
3 Banking Today..........258
Case Study: *Big Banks and Small*..........265
Chapter 10 Assessment..........266

THE WALL STREET JOURNAL. CLASSROOM EDITION **Debating Current Issues:** *Regulating Financial Markets*..........268

Chapter 11 Financial Markets..........270
1 Saving and Investing..........271
2 Bonds and Other Financial Assets..........277
3 The Stock Market..........285
Case Study: *The Fate of the Dot-Coms*..........293
Chapter 11 Assessment..........294

Introducing Macroeconomics:

Unit 5 Measuring Economic Performance...298

Chapter 12 Gross Domestic Product and Growth..........300
1 Gross Domestic Product..........301
2 Business Cycles..........310
3 Economic Growth..........318
Case Study: *How Has Technology Affected Productivity?*..........325
Chapter 12 Assessment..........326

Chapter 13 Economic Challenges..........330
1 Unemployment..........331
2 Inflation..........338
3 Poverty..........345
Case Study: *Unemployment in a Changing Economy*..........351
Chapter 13 Assessment..........352

THE WALL STREET JOURNAL. CLASSROOM EDITION **Debating Current Issues:** *Easy Credit*..........354

Unit 6 Government and the Economy 356

Chapter 14 Taxes and Government Spending..........358
1 What Are Taxes?..........359
2 Federal Taxes..........365
3 Federal Spending..........371
4 State and Local Taxes and Spending..........375
Case Study: *The Bush Tax Cuts*..........381
Chapter 14 Assessment..........382

Chapter 15 Fiscal Policy ... 386

1 Understanding Fiscal Policy ... 387
2 Fiscal Policy Options ... 395
3 Budget Deficits and the National Debt ... 403
Case Study: *Will Social Security Survive?* ... 409
Chapter 15 Assessment ... 410

THE WALL STREET JOURNAL. CLASSROOM EDITION **Debating Current Issues:** *Internet Taxation* ... 412

Chapter 16 The Federal Reserve and Monetary Policy ... 414

1 The Federal Reserve System ... 415
2 Federal Reserve Functions ... 420
3 Monetary Policy Tools ... 425
4 Monetary Policy and Macroeconomic Stabilization ... 430
Case Study: *Banking, Monetary Policy, and the Great Depression* ... 435
Chapter 16 Assessment ... 436

Unit 7 The Global Economy ... 438

Chapter 17 International Trade ... 440

1 Why Nations Trade ... 441
2 Trade Barriers and Agreements ... 449
3 Measuring Trade ... 458
Case Study: *NAFTA: Is Free Trade a Good Idea?* ... 465
Chapter 17 Assessment ... 466

Chapter 18 Economic Development and Transition ... 470

1 Levels of Development ... 471
2 Issues in Development ... 478
3 Financing Development ... 485
4 Transitions to Free Enterprise ... 489
Case Study: *The World Bank and Economic Assistance* ... 495
Chapter 18 Assessment ... 496

THE WALL STREET JOURNAL. CLASSROOM EDITION **Debating Current Issues:** *Tariffs and Trade* ... 498

Reference Section

Table of Contents ... 501
Personal Finance Handbook ... 502
Economic Atlas and Databank ... 532
Glossary ... 548
Spanish Glossary ... 559
Index ... 573
Acknowledgments ... 591

Currency rates

Rates for trades of $1 million minimum; includes most credit card transactions.

Country	Currency	Rate in US $	Units for $1
Australia	Dollar	.6539	1.5293
Brazil	Real	.3331	3.0020
Canada	Dollar	.7106	1.4073
Czech Republic	Koruna	.0343	29.19
Denmark	Krone	.1478	6.7639
European Union	Euro	1.0930	.9149
Great Britain	Pound	1.5773	.6340
Hong Kong	Dollar	.1282	7.7983
Hungary	Forint	.0043	233.10
India	Rupee	.0218	45.840
Japan	Yen	.008495	117.71
Mexico	Peso	.091996	10.8700
New Zealand	Dollar	.5845	1.7109
Norway	Krone	.1328	7.5300
Poland	Zloty	.2551	3.92
Singapore	Dollar	.5753	1.7382
South Africa	Rand	.1333	7.5000
South Korea	Won	.000853	1172.80
Sweden	Krona	.1186	8.4300
Switzerland	Franc	.7080	1.4125
Taiwan	Dollar	.0292	34.23

Metals

Special Features

Skills for LIFE

Step-by-step lessons to learn and practice important skills

Interpreting Line Graphs .12
Building Flowcharts .45
Analyzing Primary Sources .61
Analyzing Tables .84
Environmental Policy .107
Determining Cause and Effect .132
Analyzing Political Cartoons .155
Using the Internet for Research .194
Analyzing Statistics .218
Understanding Public Opinion Polls .249
Predicting Consequences .284
Cost-Benefit Analysis .309
Analyzing Bar Graphs .337
Evaluating Historical Debates .364
Comparing Circle Graphs .394
Recognizing Bias in Writing .419
Creating a Multimedia Presentation .448
Using the Writing Process .484

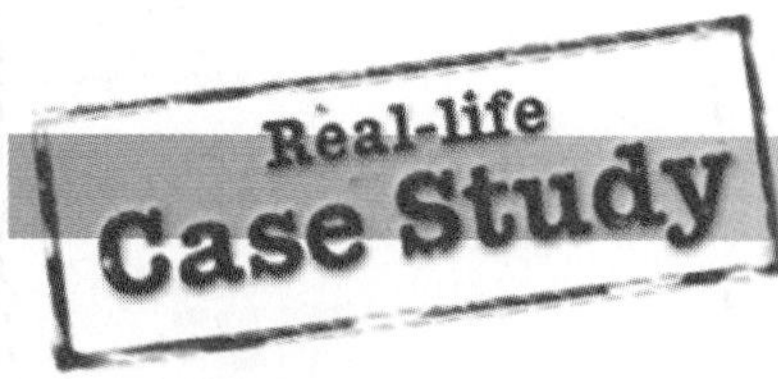

Case Studies show how economic concepts apply to everyday life

Safety at Any Cost? .19
Russia in Crisis .39
Government and the Interstate Highway System .71
What Makes a Person an Entrepreneur? .97
Are Baseball Players Paid Too Much? .121
Government and the Market for Milk .145
Regulating Cable Television .177
Business and Ethics .205
The Paterson Silk Strike of 1913 .235
Big Banks and Small .265
The Fate of the Dot-Coms .293
How Has Technology Affected Productivity? .325
Unemployment in a Changing Economy .351
The Bush Tax Cuts .381
Will Social Security Survive? .409
Banking, Monetary Policy, and the Great Depression .435
NAFTA: Is Free Trade a Good Idea? .465
The World Bank and Economic Assistance .495

Economic Profiles

Biographies of influential and successful economists and entrepreneurs

Economists

Gary Becker .7
Adam Smith .33
Alice Rivlin .56
Karl Marx .227
Henry J. Aaron .370
John Maynard Keynes .402
Alan Greenspan .424
Carla Anderson Hills .457
W. Arthur Lewis .477

Entrepreneurs

Christy Haubegger .89
Robert L. Johnson .115
Michael Dell .138
Bill Gates .165
Jerry Yang .189
Amadeo P. Giannini .257
Warren Buffett .276
Andrew Carnegie .317
Oprah Winfrey .344

THE WALL STREET JOURNAL.
CLASSROOM EDITION

In the News

News items from *The Wall Street Journal Classroom Edition* illustrate economic principles in action

Humans Need Not Apply 5
A New Scholarship Strategy 16
Laying Down the Law 37
Expanding First Amendment 53
Low-Income, Low Tech 69
The Surging Hispanic Economy 87
Blockbuster Stresses Buying Over Renting 102
Ups and Downs 135
Bottom of the Food Chain 170
Wal-Mart Pays at the Pump 175
Best Foot Forward 188
Partnership Prenuptials 192
Worse for the Wear 222
New Colors for the Greenback 252
The Lowdown on Loans 260
How Much Risk Can You Tolerate? 275
How to Get Started in Online Trading 286
The Last Straw? 314
And a Silver Lining 324
Rethinking Layoffs 336
A Grim Undertaking 347
Hard Habit to Break 362
Rethinking the Digital Divide 373
Deficit Dilemma 401
Alan Who? 426
Retirees Forced to Pinch Pennies 433
The Shrinking of the "Big Three" 456
Power Plant 463
Spreading the Wealth 481
Baby Bust 494

Debating Current Issues

Excerpts from *Wall Street Journal Classroom Edition* articles provide background for classroom debates on important economic issues

Health-Care Costs 74
Oil and Energy Dependence 180
Minimum Wage 238
Regulating Financial Markets 268
Easy Credit 354
Internet Taxation 412
Tariffs and Trade 498

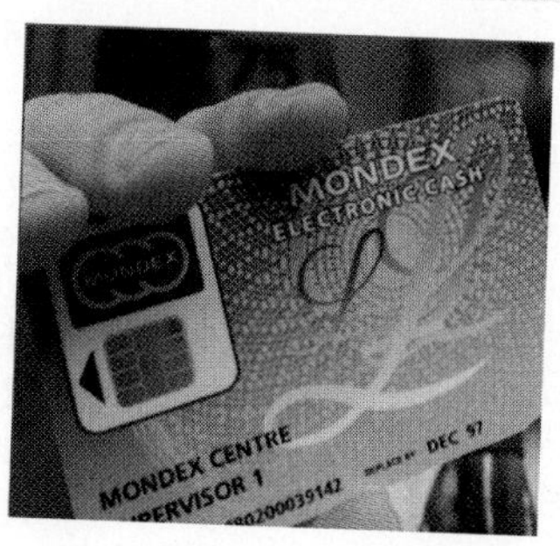

Economics Simulation

Hands-on experiments to help you understand key economic concepts

Designing an Economic System 48
Market Equilibrium 148
Be an Entrepreneur! 208
Making Investment Decisions 296
Increasing Productivity 328
Voluntary Contributions 384
Protectionist Policies 468

Global Connections

Explore economic principles at work in today's changing global economy

Global Trade-Offs 9
Sweden's Mixed Economy 41
New Business in Russia 54
Elasticity in the Kitchen 91
Common Agricultural Policy 118
Rationing and Prices 143
Informed Buyers 152
Nonprofits on a Global Scale 203
Wages Worldwide 225
The Ruble 246
International Bonds 282
Global Economic Decline 314
A Shorter Workweek 335
Value-Added Tax 368
Experimenting in Japan 392
Global Monetary Policy 429
Frankenstein Food? 452
Global Development and the Environment 475

Graphs, Charts, and Tables

More than 250 graphs, charts, and tables to help you visualize key economic concepts

Chapter 1

1.1 The Factors of Production 5
1.2 Karen's Decision-Making Grid 10
1.3 Decision Making at the Margin 11
Hours of Practice vs. Points Scored 12
1.4 Production Possibilities Curve Step 1 14
1.5 Production Possibilities Curve Step 2 15
1.6 Production Possibilities Curve Step 3 16
1.7 The Law of Increasing Costs 17
1.8 Personal Computers per 1,000 People 18
The Costs of Auto Safety 19
Income and Education, 2003 21

Chapter 2

2.1 Combining Factor Resources 24
2.2 Economic Goals 25
2.3 Circular Flow Model of a Market Economy 30
2.4 Circular Flow Model of a Mixed Economy 42
2.5 Continuum of Mixed Economies 43

Chapter 3

3.1 Features of American Free Enterprise 52
3.2 Major Federal Regulatory Agencies 55
3.3 Gross Domestic Product, 1990–2004 58
Unemployment, 1926–1933 61
3.4 The Creation of a Public Good 64
3.5 Positive and Negative Externalities 65
3.6 A Century of Federal Programs to Help Those in Need 68
Uninsured Americans, 2003 75

Chapter 4

4.1 Law of Demand 79
4.2 Building the Law of Demand 80
4.3 Demand Schedules 81
4.4 Ashley's Demand Curve 82

4.5 Market Demand Curve 83
Demand for Selected Goods 84
4.6 Graphing Changes in Demand 86
4.7 Elasticity of Demand 92
4.8 Revenue Table 95
4.9 Elasticity and Revenue 96
Demand Schedule for Selected Services 99

Chapter 5

5.1 Law of Supply 101
5.2 Supply Schedule 103
5.3 Market Supply Schedule 104
5.4 Supply Curves 105
5.5 Elastic Supply 105
5.6 Marginal Product of Labor 109
5.7 Increasing, Diminishing, and Negative Marginal Returns 109
5.8 Fixed and Variable Cost 110
5.9 Production Costs 111
5.10 Marginal Cost Curve 112
5.11 Output and a Change in Price 113
5.12 Shifts in the Supply Curve 117

Chapter 6

6.1 Finding Equilibrium 126
6.2 Excess Demand and Excess Supply 127
6.3 Rent Control 129
6.4 Effects of Minimum Wage 131
6.5 Falling Prices and the Supply Curve 134
6.6 A Change In Supply 135
6.7 A Change In Demand 136

Chapter 7

7.1 Perfect Competition 153
7.2 Market Equilibrium in Perfect Competition 154
7.3 Effect of Economies of Scale 157
7.4 Monopoly 158
7.5 Monopoly Decisions in the National Football League 160
7.6 Demand Schedule for BreatheDeep 161
7.7 Setting a Price in a Monopoly 162
7.8 Monopolistic Competition 167
7.9 Oligopoly 169
7.10 Comparison of Market Structures 170
7.11 Key Events in Federal Antitrust Policy 174
Cable TV Subscribers, 1970–2000 177
United States Oil Imports 181

Chapter 8

8.1 The Entrepreneurial Spirit 186
8.2 Characteristics of Proprietorships 186
8.3 Characteristics of Partnerships 191
8.4 Characteristics of Corporations 196
8.5 Horizontal Merger and Vertical Merger 198
8.6 A Conglomerate 199
Statement of Principles and Code of Conduct ..205

Chapter 9

9.1 Composition of the U.S. Labor Force 212
9.2 Changes in Employment, by Industry 213
9.3 Education and Income, 2003 214
9.4 Women in the U.S. Labor Force, 1960–2010 215
9.5 Earnings of U.S. Workers, 2005 217
Unemployment Rates for American Workers ...218
9.6 Effects of Competition 220
9.7 Labor Supply and Demand 221
9.8 Equilibrium Wage 221
9.9 Comparison: Wages for Doctors, Construction Workers 222
9.10 Comparison: Wages for High-Risk, Low-Risk Jobs 223
9.11 Median Earnings for Full-time Workers, by Gender and Ethnicity, 2003 224
9.12 Key Events in the U.S. Labor Movement 229
9.13 U.S. Economic Changes That Have Affected Unions 232
9.14 Union Membership, 1930–2003 233
Education and Employment 237
Value of the Federal Minimum Wage, 1980–2002 239

Chapter 10

10.1 The Three Functions of Money 244
10.2 Roman Empire, About Second Century A.D. ...245
10.3 Sources of Money's Value 247
Health Care Poll 249
10.4 Developments in American Banking 254
10.5 Major Components of the Money Supply 259
10.6 The Fractional Reserve System 260
10.7 Compound Interest 261
10.8 How Banks Make a Profit 262
Major Bank Mergers Since 1990 265
ATM User Fees Poll 267
SEC Enforcement Actions 269

Chapter 11

11.1 Financial Intermediaries 273
11.2 Types of Risk 274
11.3 Discounts from Par 278
11.4 Bond Ratings 279
11.5 Average Bond Yields, 1992–2003 280
11.6 Treasury Bonds, Notes, and Bills 280

Graphs, Charts, and Tables (continued)

11.7 Reading a Newspaper Stock Report 287
11.8 The Dow, 1896–2005 289
Stock Market Data, 1928–1932 295

Chapter 12

12.1 How GDP is Calculated 302
12.2 Circular Flow of Output and Income 303
12.3 Nominal and Real GDP 304
12.4 Measurements of the Macroeconomy 306
12.5 Aggregate Supply and Demand 307
12.6 Equilibrium Aggregate Supply and Demand 308
12.7 Tracking a Business Cycle 311
12.8 Declining Business Investment 312
12.9 Negative External Shock 313
12.10 U.S. Real GDP, 1929–1945 315
12.11 Real GDP per Capita, 1970–2004 318
12.12 Economic Health of Selected Countries 319
12.13 Effects of Capital Deepening 320
12.14 How Saving Leads to Capital Deepening 321
12.15 Financing the Transcontinental Railroad 322
U.S. Computer Purchases, 1997–2000 325
Transportation Choices 327

Chapter 13

13.1 Calculating the Unemployment Rate 334
13.2 Unemployment Rate, 1968–2004 335
Income and Housing Costs in U.S. Cities 337
13.3 Effect of Inflation on Auto Prices 338
13.4 CPI Market Basket Items 339
13.5 Calculating the Inflation Rate 340
13.6 Inflation Rate, 1970–2004 341
13.7 The Wage-Price Spiral 342
13.8 Poverty Rate, 1964–2002 345
13.9 Poverty Rates by Group, 2003 346
13.10 Income Distribution 348
Poverty by Region 353
Consumer Credit 355

Chapter 14

14.1 Three Types of Tax Structures 360
14.2 Progressive Income Tax 361
14.3 Elasticities of Demand and Tax Effects 363
14.4 Federal Revenue, 2004 365
14.5 Federal Income Tax Rates, 2005 367
14.6 Federal Spending, 2004 371
14.7 State Revenue and Spending, 2002 376
14.8 Local Revenue and Spending, 2002 379

Chapter 15

15.1 Creating the Federal Budget 388
15.2 Effects of Expansionary Fiscal Policy 389
15.3 Flowchart of Effects of Expansionary Fiscal Policy 390
15.4 Effects of Contractionary Fiscal Policy 391
Federal Spending, 1995 and 2004 394
15.5 Keynesian Economics 396
15.6 Annual Change in GDP, 1928–2004 398
15.7 Laffer Curve 399
15.8 Top Marginal Income Tax Rate, 1925–2005 400
15.9 Budget Surpluses and Deficits, 1940–2004 404
15.10 National Debt as a Percentage of GDP 406
15.11 Effects of the Budget Deficit 407
Projected Population, 2000–2050 409
Federal Spending, 1980 and 2004 411
E-commerce, 2003 413

Chapter 16

16.1 Structure of the Federal Reserve System 416
16.2 Federal Reserve Districts 417
16.3 The Path of a Check 421
16.4 Demand for Money 423
16.5 Money Creation 426
16.6 Reserve Requirements 427
16.7 Federal Funds Rate 428
16.8 Open Market Operations 428
16.9 Effects of Monetary Policy 431
16.10 Business Cycles and Stabilization Policy 432
16.11 Fiscal and Monetary Policy Tools 434

Chapter 17

17.1 Resource Distribution 442
17.2 Productivity per Hour 443
17.3 Opportunity Costs for Kate and Carl 444
17.4 Benefits From Specialization and Trade for Carl and Kate 445
17.5 Major Imports and Exports of the United States, 2004 446
17.6 Average Tariff Rates, 1900–2005 450
17.7 Major Trade Organization Members 455
17.8 Foreign Exchange Rates 459
17.9 Effects of a Strong or Weak Dollar on Exports 460
17.10 Exchange Rates of the Dollar and Pound 461
17.11 U.S. Balance of Trade, 1976–2004 463
17.12 Leading Exporters and Importers, 2003 464
Major Provisions of NAFTA 465

Chapter 18

18.1 Per Capita GDP of Selected Nations, 2003 472
18.2 Comparing Australia and India 473
18.3 Levels of Development 476

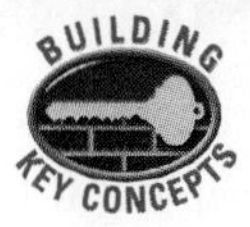

18.4 Population Growth Rates of Selected Nations, 2004 .479
18.5 Age Structures .479
18.6 Education and Literacy .482
Comparison of Three Economies .484
18.7 U.S. Foreign Aid, 2005 .487
18.8 Communist and Noncommunist Nations .490
Per Capita Earnings in Selected Countries .495
Global Economic Organizations .497
U.S. Trade Deficit, 1994–2004 .499

Personal Finance Handbook

Spending and Saving Plan .503
How to Choose a Checking Account .504
Journey of a Personal Check .505
Types of Accounts .506
How to Choose a Savings Account .507
Comparing Investment Options .509
Banking Services .510
How to Choose a Bank .511
Four Steps to Establishing Credit .513
Comparing APR .515
Comparing Terms on an Installment Loan .515
How to Choose a Credit Card .515
College Costs .517
Three Types of Financial Aid .517
Financial Aid Information Sources .518
How to Choose a Car .521
How to Choose an Apartment .523
W-4 Form .529
1040EZ Form .530

Economic Atlas and Databank

Natural Resources

United States Economic Activity and Resources .532
GDP of Agriculture, Forestry, Fishing, Timber-Related Manufacturing, and Mining .534
United States Energy Production, by Source, 2004 .534
U. S. Oil Imports, 1973–2004 .534
Number of Farms .535
Size of Farms .535
Major Agricultural Exports and Imports, 2003 .535

Americans at Work

Characteristics of the United States Work Force, 2005 .536
Real Value of the Minimum Wage .536
Median Weekly Earnings, by Occupation and Sex, 2004 .536
Average Real Hourly Wages, by Education Level, 2003 .537
Earnings Gap .537
Fastest-Growing Occupations .537

Economic Indicators

Real Gross Domestic Product .538
CPI Market Basket, 2005 .538
Consumer Price Index .538
Retail Sales, by Type of Business, 2004 .539
Housing Starts .539
Producer Price Index .539
Consumer Confidence Index .539

The American Consumer

Personal Income and Outlays .540
Personal Savings as a Percentage of Disposable Income .540
Housing Prices .540
Selected Personal Consumption Expenditures, 2004 .541
Per Capita Energy Consumption .541
Consumer Credit Debt .541

The United States Government

Federal Deficit/Surplus .542
Income Taxes per Capita .542
Key Interest Rates .542
Federal Debt .542
Government Receipts, by Source, 2004 .543
Government Spending, by Category, 2004 .543

Trade

U.S. Exports and Imports, by Major Trading Partners, 2003 .544
Major Exports and Imports, 2003 .544
United States Trading Partners .545

The United States and the World

Per Capita Gross Domestic Product .546
Taxes as Percent of GDP .546
National Budgets .547
Health Expenditures as Percent of GDP .547

Studying *Economics: Principles in Action*

Economics is the study of the choices and decisions people make about how to use the world's resources. Understanding economics will help you make informed decisions for yourself and assess the decisions made by others. A number of features in this book are designed to help you understand key economic principles and to show you those principles *in action* in the real world.

Content Standards in Economics

To help guide you in your study of economics, this book incorporates the Voluntary National Content Standards in Economics developed by the National Council on Economic Education. The standards are built around the twenty key concepts listed below.

Building Key Concepts

Each of the graphs, charts, and tables in this textbook includes a question based on one of these twenty key concepts.

Scarcity
Opportunity Cost
Economic Systems
Incentives
Trade
Specialization
Markets and Prices
Supply and Demand
Competition
Economic Institutions
Money
Interest Rates
Income
Entrepreneurs
Standard of Living
Government
Public Policy
Gross Domestic Product
Unemployment and Inflation
Monetary and Fiscal Policy

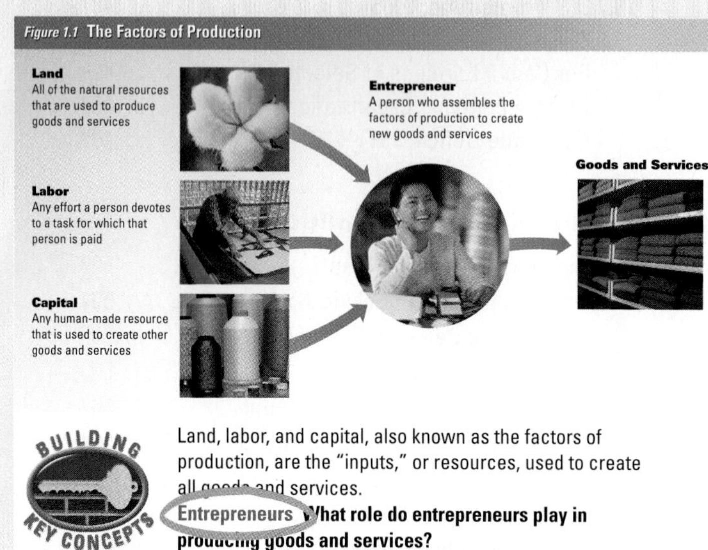

Figure 1.1 The Factors of Production
Land
All of the natural resources that are used to produce goods and services
Labor
Any effort a person devotes to a task for which that person is paid
Capital
Any human-made resource that is used to create other goods and services
Entrepreneur
A person who assembles the factors of production to create new goods and services
Goods and Services
BUILDING KEY CONCEPTS
Land, labor, and capital, also known as the factors of production, are the "inputs," or resources, used to create all goods and services.
Entrepreneurs What role do entrepreneurs play in producing goods and services?

Learning Key Terms

Your study of economics will involve learning the vocabulary economists use. In this book, key terms are listed in each section opener and are clearly defined in the text and in the margins to help you understand the content of each chapter.

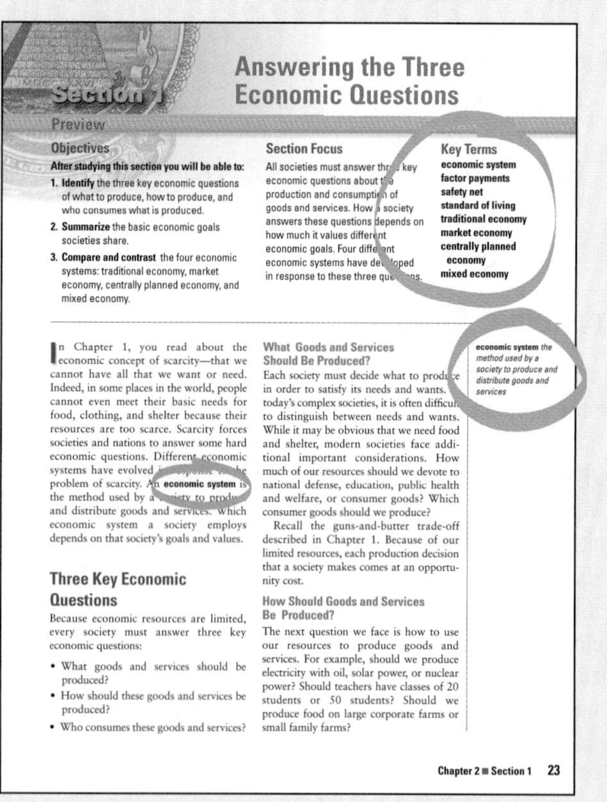

Section 1
Answering the Three Economic Questions
Preview
Objectives
After studying this section you will be able to:
1. Identify the three key economic questions of what to produce, how to produce, and who consumes what is produced.
2. Summarize the basic economic goals societies share.
3. Compare and contrast the four economic systems: traditional economy, market economy, centrally planned economy, and mixed economy.
Section Focus
Key Terms
economic system
factor payments
safety net
standard of living
traditional economy
market economy
centrally planned economy
mixed economy
economic system the method used by a society to produce and distribute goods and services
Three Key Economic Questions
What Goods and Services Should Be Produced?
How Should Goods and Services Be Produced?
Chapter 2 ■ Section 1 23

THE WALL STREET JOURNAL.
CLASSROOM EDITION

In the News Read more about stock trading in "How to Get Started in Online Trading," an article in The Wall Street Journal Classroom Edition.

The Wall Street Journal Classroom Edition

For: Current Events
Visit: PHSchool.com
Web Code: mnc-4113

In the News

Excerpts from ***Wall Street Journal Classroom Edition*** articles appear throughout the book to help you see the connections between economic principles and everyday life.

Debating Current Issues

Debating Current Issues features in every unit provide thought-provoking excerpts from ***Wall Street Journal Classroom Edition*** articles on some of the most controversial economic topics of our day.

THE WALL STREET JOURNAL.
CLASSROOM EDITION

Debating Current Issues: *Oil and Energy Dependence*

The U.S. relies on some of the world's most volatile countries to supply a raw material that is critical to its economy and lifestyle. Despite an increasingly energy-efficient economy, the U.S. remains hooked on imported oil.

In this debate from *The Wall Street Journal Classroom Edition,* Erich Pica, a senior policy analyst with the environmental group Friends of the Earth, and John Felmy and Edward Porter of the American Petroleum Institute present two approaches to reducing oil imports and promoting energy independence in the U.S.

YES ***Should oil prices be raised to promote energy independence?***

By Erich Pica

The price of oil should be increased as part of a price increase on all fossil fuels. Our nation has a problem, and it is not simply a dependence on foreign oil. It is our dependence on oil. The U.S. consumes 25% of the world's oil supply, and has only 3% of its resources. Unless we fundamentally shift our oil consumption patterns, we will remain dependent on foreign oil.

Friends of the Earth, a nonprofit environmental organization, believes that the best way to help solve our dependency problems is with a carbon tax, or a fee on all fossil fuels, including oil. Such a tax would be an efficient way to encourage businesses and individuals to conserve fuel and develop nonfossil-fuel energy sources. And a carbon tax would also fix many of the economic distortions currently not factored into the price of oil.

For example, current oil prices do not reflect the impact of air pollution from our passenger vehicles, which contributes to unhealthy levels of smog that harm human health. And they don't reflect the environmental impact of oil drilling, which damages public lands and coastal areas. Nor do they reflect the growing military and foreign-policy costs of defending oil interests in the Middle East and other turbulent regions.

Using the true cost of oil would raise prices, but it would provide the incentive for consumers to reduce consumption and turn to innovative, clean sources of energy. Ultimately, using less oil is the only way to reduce our dependence on foreign supplies.

A carbon tax is a potential silver bullet that could solve our dependence on oil. Yet, unfortunately, it remains a taboo topic for political leaders. Elected officials and their allies in the oil industry are creating false choices between dependence on foreign oil and reducing the cost of domestic production, knowing that as long as we consume at current rates, our dependency will remain.

Massive oil rigs extract petroleum from beneath the ocean floor. Does the market price of gasoline reflect all the costs of its use?

180

Real-life Case Studies

Case Studies in every chapter provide dramatic examples of economic principles in action in the real world.

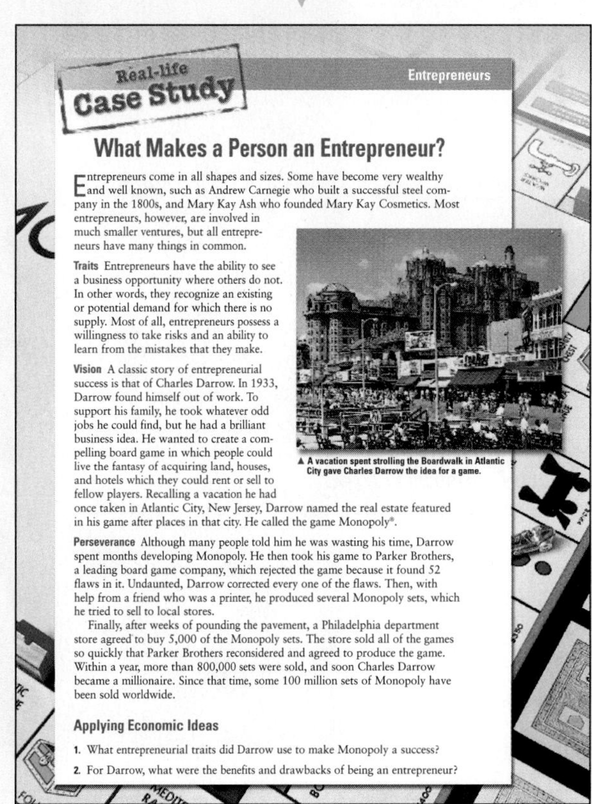

Real-life Case Study

Entrepreneurs

What Makes a Person an Entrepreneur?

Entrepreneurs come in all shapes and sizes. Some have become very wealthy and well known, such as Andrew Carnegie who built a successful steel company in the 1800s, and Mary Kay Ash who founded Mary Kay Cosmetics. Most entrepreneurs, however, are involved in much smaller ventures, but all entrepreneurs have many things in common.

Traits Entrepreneurs have the ability to see a business opportunity where others do not. In other words, they recognize an existing or potential demand for which there is no supply. Most of all, entrepreneurs possess a willingness to take risks and an ability to learn from the mistakes that they make.

Vision A classic story of entrepreneurial success is that of Charles Darrow. In 1933, Darrow found himself out of work. To support his family, he took whatever odd jobs he could find, but he had a brilliant business idea. He wanted to create a compelling board game in which people could live the fantasy of acquiring land, houses, and hotels which they could rent or sell to fellow players. Recalling a vacation he had once taken in Atlantic City, New Jersey, Darrow named the real estate featured in his game after places in that city. He called the game Monopoly®.

▲ A vacation spent strolling the Boardwalk in Atlantic City gave Charles Darrow the idea for a game.

Perseverance Although many people told him he was wasting his time, Darrow spent months developing Monopoly. He then took his game to Parker Brothers, a leading board game company, which rejected the game because it found 52 flaws in it. Undaunted, Darrow corrected every one of the flaws. Then, with help from a friend who was a printer, he produced several Monopoly sets, which he tried to sell to local stores.

Finally, after weeks of pounding the pavement, a Philadelphia department store agreed to buy 5,000 of the Monopoly sets. The store sold all of the games so quickly that Parker Brothers reconsidered and agreed to produce the game. Within a year, more than 800,000 sets were sold, and soon Charles Darrow became a millionaire. Since that time, some 100 million sets of Monopoly have been sold worldwide.

Applying Economic Ideas

1. What entrepreneurial traits did Darrow use to make Monopoly a success?
2. For Darrow, what were the benefits and drawbacks of being an entrepreneur?

Go Online

Use Go Online Web Codes for instant access to Internet activities, data updates, and articles from ***The Wall Street Journal Classroom Edition***.

For: Internet Activity
Visit: PHSchool.com
Web Code: gz-6462

UNIT 1

Introduction to Economics

Introducing the Unit

Unit Summary

Unit 1 provides an introduction to the basic ideas of economics. In Chapter 1 students learn about scarcity, the factors of production, decision making, and opportunity cost. The discussion of scarcity and decision making continues in Chapter 2 with a look at how societies have developed different economic systems to make choices about resource allocation. Chapter 3 examines one of those systems, the American system of free enterprise.

Focus Activity

Introduce Unit 1 to students by asking them to complete the Focus Activity. Students can work alone or in small groups to develop their lists of words related to economics. Once the lists are complete and students have compared them, ask volunteers to suggest subcategories by writing them on the chalkboard. You might have some students create a bulletin board of photos or drawings illustrating these terms. Additional terms can be added to the display as the course continues.

UNIT 1 Introduction to Economics

National Council on Economic Education

The following Voluntary National Content Standards in Economics are addressed in this unit:

★ Standard 1 ★ Standard 3 ★ Standard 15
★ Standard 2 ★ Standard 4 ★ Standard 16

See the Chapter Openers on pp. 2, 22, and 50 for a complete description of the standards addressed in each chapter.

Chapters in This Unit

1. *What Is Economics?*
2. *Economic Systems*
3. *American Free Enterprise*

You have to make a decision . . .

Your favorite band is giving a concert in town, and you really want to go! The tickets are expensive though, and there are so many things you could do with that money. You could buy a concert ticket or . . .

- Use the money to see five movies
- Use the money to buy the band's new CD plus a pair of jeans
- Save the money for your vacation

The choice you will make is rooted in economics. At its core, economics is the study of how people choose to use their limited resources. In this unit you'll read more about the tools that economics offers to help you make decisions as a consumer, seller, worker, and citizen.

Focus Activity

When you hear the word *economics,* what are the first ten words that you think of? Compare your list with those of your classmates. Do the words on your lists fall into any obvious categories?

Bibliography

Print

The Entrepreneur and the Economy. Dallas: The Federal Reserve Bank of Dallas, 1998.

Virtual Economics: An Interactive Center for Economics Education. CD-ROM. Gilliard, June V., and Phillip Saunders. *A Framework for Teaching Basic Economic Concepts.* EconomicsAmerica, National Council on Economic Education, 1997.

Multimedia

Enterprise Series. "Chef's Special." Color video, 28 minutes. Follows the creation of a restaurant from the idea stage through its opening. The Corporation, distributed by Simon and Schuster Communications.

Economics U$A Series. "Resources and Scarcity." Color video, 30 minutes. The segment focuses on resources, scarcity, and choices. Educational Film Center (Annandale, VA): Annenberg/CPB Collection.

Technology Center

Economics Video Library
Includes high-interest, chapter-specific segments produced by CNBC for THE WALL STREET JOURNAL. CLASSROOM EDITION

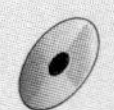

Simulations and Data Graphing CD-ROM
Provides interactive federal budget and stock market simulations and a data graphing tool designed to support instruction in economics.

PRENTICE HALL
TeacherEXPRESS™
Plan · Teach · Assess

Teacher Express CD-ROM offers powerful lesson planning, resource management, testing, and an interactive Teacher's Edition.

Prentice Hall Presentation Pro CD-ROM
Allows you to create custom lectures for every chapter.

Social Studies Skills Tutor CD-ROM
Provides interactive practice in geographic literacy, critical thinking and reading, visual analysis, and communications.

Exam*View*® Test Bank CD-ROM
Allows you to create, edit, and print out chapter level tests.

Transparency Resource Package
Illustrates key economic concepts and provides useful forms and templates for enhancing classroom discussions.

Section Reading Support Transparency System
Delivers the main idea of each section in the student text through graphic organizers.

Offers student-appropriate online activities and links as well as resources for the teacher. Be sure to check out this month's **eTeach** online discussion with a Master Economics Teacher.

Chapter Resource Manager

Chapter 1 What Is Economics?

For more pacing suggestions, see the Economics Pacing Guide in the Program Overview of the Teaching Resources.

Section Objectives	Print and Technology Resources	
1 Scarcity and the Factors of Production *(pp. 3–6)* **Objectives** 1. **Explain** why scarcity and choice are basic problems of economics. 2. **Identify** land, labor, and capital as the three factors of production, and identify the two types of capital. 3. **Explain** the role of entrepreneurs. 4. **Explain** why economists say all resources are scarce.	• **Lesson Planner** Section 1 Lesson Plan, p. 14 • **Learning Styles Lesson Plans folder** Section 1 Lesson Plan, p. 7 • **Lesson Plans folder** Section 1 Lesson Plan, p. 7 • **Economics Assessment Rubrics folder** Writing Assignment, pp. 6–7 • **Unit 1 folder** Guided Reading and Review, p. 2 Careers in Economics, Economist, p. 11 Section 1 Quiz, p. 3	• **Source Articles folder** High-Tech Homework, pp. 3–5 • **Presentation Pro CD-ROM** Section 1 • **Transparency Resource Package** Economics Organizers, G5: Web Graphic Organizer Economics Concepts, 1A: Scarcity and the Factors of Production • **Section Reading Support Transparency System**
2 Opportunity Cost *(pp. 8–11)* **Objectives** 1. Describe why every decision involves trade-offs. 2. Explain the concept of opportunity cost. 3. Explain how people make decisions by thinking at the margin.	• **Lesson Planner** Section 2 Lesson Plan, p. 15 • **Learning Styles Lesson Plans folder** Section 2 Lesson Plan, p. 8 • **Lesson Plans folder** Section 2 Lesson Plan, p. 8 • **Unit 1 folder** Guided Reading and Review, p. 4 Economic Skills, p. 8 Economic Cartoon, p. 12 Section 2 Quiz, p. 5 • **Math Practice folder** Drawing and Interpreting Graphs, p. 2	• **Presentation Pro CD-ROM** Section 2 • **Simulations and Data Graphing CD-ROM** Data Graphing Tool • **Transparency Resource Package** Economics Organizers, G7: Tree Map Graphic Organizer Economics Concepts, 1B: Decision Making at the Margin • **Section Reading Support Transparency System** • **Social Studies Skills Tutor CD-ROM**
3 Production Possibilities Curves *(pp. 13–18)* **Objectives** 1. Interpret a production possibilities curve. 2. Demonstrate how production possibilities graphs show efficiency, growth, and cost. 3. Understand that a country's production possibilities depend on its available resources and technology.	• **Lesson Planner** Section 3 Lesson Plan, p. 16 • **Lesson Plans folder** Section 3 Lesson Plan, p. 9 • **Economics Assessment Rubrics folder** Graphing Data, pp. 8–9 • **Unit 1 folder** Guided Reading and Review, p. 6 Vocabulary Practice, p. 9 Economic Detective, p. 10 Section 3 Quiz, p. 7 • **Case Studies in Free Enterprise folder** Herbert Stein, pp. 2–3 • **Source Articles folder** High-Tech Homework, pp. 3–5	• **Presentation Pro CD-ROM** Section 3 • **Simulations and Data Graphing CD-ROM** Data Graphing Tools • **Transparency Resource Package** Economics Organizers, G5: Web Graphic Organizer Economics Concepts, 1C: Production Possibilities Graph Economics Concepts, 1D: Production Possibilities Graph Overlay • **Section Reading Support Transparency System**

Differentiated Instruction

Creating a Word Bank L2

Research suggests that students will best learn new vocabulary words through frequent encounters. For this reason, the text continues to use high-use words after they are introduced.

You can also encourage frequent encounters by asking students to create a word bank. This can help them process, reflect, and integrate new terms into their vocabulary. To begin, have students make a list of key terms and high-use words from this chapter. Then have students take the list home and see how many examples of these words they can find in current periodicals. Have students bring in their examples and ensure they are accurate. Then have students tape or paste the example on their list next to the word and place these sheets in their notebooks. They may use this as a study guide later.

Responding to Chapter Questions L1 L2

To teach students how to productively answer chapter questions, provide them with the following steps. These will also deepen their understanding of "study reading."

1. Read the chapter question silently and ask yourself—based on the question—what type of information will I be looking for?
   - Why? = For what reasons? What are the reasons?
   - How? = What was the process? What was the sequence?
   - What? = Definition (What is ________?)
   - What + signal word
     - What are the benefits of __________?
     - What was the reaction to __________?

2. Skim the headings to find the section that addresses the question.

3. Re-read the section looking for the answer.

4. Record the answer in your own words, if possible turning the question into part of the answer.

Visit the Social Studies area of the Prentice Hall Web site. There you can find additional links to enrich chapter content for *Economics: Principles in Action* as well as a self-test for students. Be sure to check out this month's **eTeach** online discussion with a Master Economics Teacher.

Web Code: mnf-1011

Running Out of Time?

- Use the **Presentation Pro CD-ROM** to create an outline for this chapter.
- Use the Chapter Summary in the **Chapter 1 Assessment,** p. 20.
- Use the Section Summaries for Chapter 1, from **Guide to the Essentials of Economics (English and Spanish).**

THE WALL STREET JOURNAL. CLASSROOM EDITION

Prentice Hall brings into the classroom the authoritative content of *The Wall Street Journal Classroom Edition.* See the Source Articles, Debating Current Issues, and You and Your Money folders in the **Teaching Resources**. Also, see Economics Video Library, "Groovin' Business."

Assessment Resources

Chapter Assessment

Teaching Resources Unit 1, Chapter 1
- Section Quizzes, pp. 3, 5, 7

Exam *View*® Test Bank CD-ROM Chapter 1

Economics Assessment Rubrics

Chapter 1 Self-Test, **Web Code:** mna-1011

Reading and Skills Evaluation

Progress Monitoring Assessments
- Screening Test
- Diagnostic Test of Social Studies Skills

Standardized Test Preparation

Test Prep Workbook

Test-Taking Strategies With Transparencies

Differentiated Instruction Key

L1	Special Needs	LPR	Less Proficient Readers
L2	Basic to Average	AR	Advanced Readers
L3	All Students	SN	Special Needs Students
L4	Average to Advanced	GT	Gifted and Talented
		ELL	English Language Learner

Chapter 1

What Is Economics?

Introducing the Chapter

In this chapter, students will learn the basic concepts of scarcity, making choices, and the trade-offs that these choices involve. They will also learn what production possibilities graphs show about efficiency, growth, and costs in an economy.

For additional links for *Economics: Principles in Action* provided by Prentice Hall and *The Wall Street Journal Classroom Edition,* visit the Social Studies area. Be sure to check out this month's **eTeach** online discussion with a Master Teacher.

Beyond the Lecture

You may cover the concepts in Chapter 1 in an activity-based style by using the following materials:

- **Technology Resources** appropriate for use with this chapter are noted on pp. 5, 6, 10, 11, 12, 15, 16, 17, 18, and 21.
- **Presentation Pro CD-ROM** with animated graphs gives you an alternative method for organizing and delivering chapter content.
- **Activities** designed to meet the needs of students of mixed abilities and learning styles are noted throughout the chapter in the side columns.
- **Learning Styles Lesson Plans** provide alternate lessons for diverse learning styles. See pp. 7–8 of the Learning Styles Lesson Plans folder located in the Teaching Resources.

Economics Journal

Instruct students to write their responses to the question in their Economics Journals. Students may include completed journal entries in an Economics Portfolio.

Chapter 1 What Is Economics?

Which CD to buy? How many hours to study? Which movie to see? If you're like most people, you constantly face decisions because you don't have enough time and money to do everything. At its most basic level, economics is the study of how people make choices when they face a limited supply of resources. In this chapter you will begin your study of economics by investigating two basic economic ideas: scarcity and trade-offs.

Economics Journal

Quickly jot down three decisions you made within the last 24 hours. For each decision, list two choices you decided against when you made the decision.

Go Online PHSchool.com

For: Current Data
Visit: PHSchool.com
Web Code: mng-1011

NCEE
National Council on Economic Education

The following Voluntary National Content Standards in Economics are addressed in this chapter:

★ **Standard 1** Students will understand that: Productive resources are limited. Therefore, people cannot have all the goods and services they want; as a result, they must choose some things and give up others.

★ **Standard 2** Students will understand that: Effective decision making requires comparing the additional costs of alternatives with the additional benefits. Most choices involve doing a little more or a little less of something; few choices are all-or-nothing decisions.

For more information about the standards, contact the National Council on Economic Education

1140 Avenue of the Americas
New York, NY 10036
1-800-338-1192

Section 1

Scarcity and the Factors of Production

Preview

Objectives

After studying this section you will be able to:

1. **Explain** why scarcity and choice are basic problems of economics.
2. **Identify** land, labor, and capital as the three factors of production, and identify the two types of capital.
3. **Explain** the role of entrepreneurs.
4. **Explain** why economists say all resources are scarce.

Section Focus

People, businesses, and governments must choose among limited or scarce resources. Economics describes how people seek to satisfy their needs and wants by choosing among many alternatives.

Key Terms

- need
- want
- economics
- goods
- services
- scarcity
- shortage
- factors of production
- land
- labor
- capital
- physical capital
- human capital
- entrepreneur

As you begin your study of economics, consider three scenes: In the first scene, members of a household work together to do the laundry, purchase groceries, make meals, earn money, decide how to spend their money, and decide who gets to hold the TV remote.

In the second scene, the leaders of a large corporation sit at a table for their monthly meeting. They discuss whether to add a new product to their product line and advertising options on television and the Internet.

In the third scene, senators in the United States Congress gather to debate the important issues of the day: How can we ensure that people are well fed and have access to health care? What limits should the government place on businesses and international trade? Who gets to control the Internet? Economists look at the decisions made in each of these scenes and study those decisions in greater detail.

Scarcity and Choice

The study of economics begins with the idea that people cannot have everything they **need** and **want.** A need is something like air, food, or shelter that is necessary for survival. A want is an item that we desire but that is not essential to survival. Because people cannot have everything they need or want, they must consider their options and decide which choice will fill their needs best.

To look at the world economically, we can focus on the decisions that people make. You, for example, have to decide what to do with your time—go to a movie or study for a test. Businesses have to decide how many people to employ and how much to produce. A city government may have to decide whether to spend its budget to build a school or a park.

Economics is the study of how people seek to satisfy their needs and wants by making choices. Because people act individually, in groups (such as businesses), and through governments, economists study each of these groups. But why must people make such choices? The reason is scarcity.

Scarcity

Living in a relatively wealthy country, many Americans may find it hard to understand the idea of scarcity. Store shelves brim with goods. **Goods** are physical objects such as shoes and shirts. We have access to countless services. **Services** are actions or activities that one person performs for another. Haircuts, dental checkups, and tutoring are

need *something like air, food, or shelter that is necessary for survival*

want *an item that we desire but that is not essential to survival*

economics *the study of how people seek to satisfy their needs and wants by making choices*

goods *physical objects such as clothes or shoes*

services *actions or activities that one person performs for another*

Building Key Concepts: Graphing the Main Idea

Entrepreneurs To build understanding of the concept of the **entrepreneur,** have students use a web graphic organizer like the one at the right to record details about how entrepreneurs bring together the factors of production. Tell students that a web shows a main idea and its supporting details. Tell students to place the label "Entrepreneur" in the central oval and to place various factors of production in the other ovals.

Section Reading Support Transparencies A template and the answers for this graphic organizer can be found in Chapter 1, Section 1 of the Section Reading Support Transparency System.

Section 1

Scarcity and the Factors of Production

Objectives You may wish to call students' attention to the objectives in the Section Preview. The objectives are reflected in the main headings of the section.

Bellringer Ask students what comes to mind when they hear the word *scarce.* Have students brainstorm a list of items that they think might be scarce. Explain that in this section they will learn that economists see examples of scarcity everywhere.

Vocabulary Builder Have students write definitions in their own words for each key term listed in the Section Preview. Students should check their definitions by locating the words and definitions in the section margins.

Lesson Plan

Teaching the Main Concepts 

1. Focus All resources are scarce, so people make choices to satisfy their wants and needs. Ask students what resources are scarce in their everyday lives.

2. Instruct Discuss with students what they already know about the subject of economics. Suggest that they may be familiar with economic ideas, even if they do not know them as such. Introduce the concepts of scarcity and shortage, and describe the factors of production. Then discuss the role of entrepreneurs in an economy.

3. Close/Reteach Have students create a poster that illustrates the three factors of production. Under each category, have students write a brief description of the factor.

Guided Reading and Review Unit 1 folder, p. 2 asks students to identify the main ideas of the section and to define or identify key terms.

Differentiated Instruction 

You may wish to have students add the following to their portfolios. During the colonial era, farmers, artisans, and some small business owners dominated the economy of the United States. Have students research the early economic history of your community. What choices and decisions did entrepreneurs and others in the area make about land, labor, and capital in the early years of settlement? Ask students to compare the uses of land, labor, and capital then to today's uses. Then have them write two advertisements: one for a business in the early years and one for a business today.

Economics Assessment Rubric
Economics Assessment Rubrics folder, pp. 6–7 provides sample evaluation materials for a writing assignment.

Differentiated Instruction 

Have students copy the section headings and write a sentence summarizing key information under each. ELL

Meeting NCEE Standards

Use the following benchmark activity from the **Voluntary National Content Standards in Economics** to evaluate student understanding of **Standard 1.**

Explain how a high school senior's decision to work 20 hours per week during the school year could reduce her lifetime income. Also, explain how an increase in the legal minimum wage aimed at improving the financial condition of some low-income families could reduce the income of some minimum wage earners.

scarcity *limited quantities of resources to meet unlimited wants*

shortage *a situation in which a good or service is unavailable*

factors of production *land, labor, and capital; the three groups of resources that are used to make all goods and services*

land *natural resources that are used to make goods and services*

labor *the effort that people devote to a task for which they are paid*

capital *any human-made resource that is used to create other goods and services*

physical capital *all human-made goods that are used to produce other goods and services; tools and buildings*

all services. Indeed, we see ads everywhere urging us to purchase goods and services. Yet scarcity exists in all places, at all times.

Defining Scarcity

All of the goods and services we produce are scarce. **Scarcity** implies limited quantities of resources to meet unlimited wants. While one person might be able to buy hundreds of basketballs or pencils or pianos, no one can have an endless supply of everything. Sooner or later, a limit is always reached. At its core, economics is about solving the problem of scarcity.

Scarcity Versus Shortages

Scarcity is not the same as a **shortage**. A shortage occurs when producers will not or cannot offer goods or services at the current prices. Shortages can be temporary or long-term. During the holiday season, a customer may see an empty shelf on Tuesday, but return on Friday to find that same shelf filled to overflowing. Wars and droughts can also create shortages that last for many years.

Scarcity, in contrast, always exists because our needs and wants are always greater than our resource supply. Goods and services are scarce because they are all made from resources that are scarce.

▲ While people's needs and wants are unlimited, the resources available to meet those wants are limited, or scarce. Which scarce resources were used to produce the fruits and vegetables shown here?

Land

Economists call the resources that are used to make all goods and services the **factors of production,** or factor resources. The factors of production are land, labor, and capital.

Economists use the term **land** to refer to all natural resources used to produce goods and services. Natural resources are materials found in nature. They include fertile land for farming and products that are in or on the land, such as coal, water, and forests.

Labor

Another factor of production is **labor.** Labor is the effort that a person devotes to a task for which that person is paid. Labor includes the medical aid provided by a doctor and the tightening of a clamp by an assembly line worker. It is an artist's creation of a painting or the repair of a television.

Capital

Capital is any human-made resource that is used to produce other goods and services. The two categories of capital are physical capital and human capital.

Physical Capital

Human-made objects used to create other goods and services are called **physical capital.** (The term *capital goods* is a synonym for *physical capital.*) Physical capital includes buildings and tools. A shoe factory building and all of the sewing machines and other specialized machinery for making shoes make up part of the shoe company's physical capital.

Physical capital is an important factor of production because it can save people and companies a great deal of time and money. A building is physical capital because it helps workers do their work by providing protection and space. Similarly, tools such as tractors, conveyor belts, and pencils are physical capital because they, too, help workers produce a good or a service.

When we create or buy physical capital to accomplish a job, we usually become more productive. Suppose that your family of 6

Econ 101: Key Concepts Made Easy

Scarcity One of the key concepts in this section is **scarcity.** Students often confuse scarcity with a shortage. Remind students that shortages can be either temporary or long-term. Scarcity, in contrast, always exists because a society's needs and wants are always greater than the supply of resources.

Ask students whether they think that time can be considered a resource. If they think that it is, ask them to consider whether time is a scarce resource. Have students create a chart that shows how, in a typical weekday, they allocate the 24 hours available to them.

Answer to . . .

Photo Caption Fertile land, water, physical labor, and machinery are among the scarce resources used to produce these fruits and vegetables.

Figure 1.1 The Factors of Production

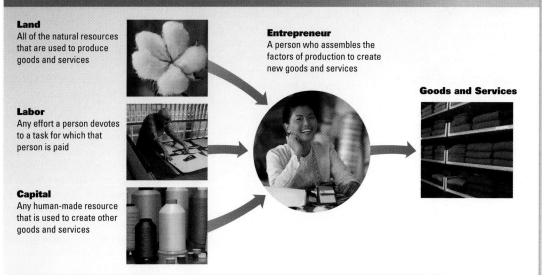

Land
All of the natural resources that are used to produce goods and services
Labor
Any effort a person devotes to a task for which that person is paid
Capital
Any human-made resource that is used to create other goods and services
Entrepreneur
A person who assembles the factors of production to create new goods and services
Goods and Services

BUILDING KEY CONCEPTS

Land, labor, and capital, also known as the factors of production, are the "inputs," or resources, used to create all goods and services.
Entrepreneurs What role do entrepreneurs play in producing goods and services?

people washes dishes by hand every day after every meal—breakfast, lunch, and dinner—for a total of 21 meals per week. It takes 30 minutes per meal for two family members working together to scrape, stack, wash, rinse, dry, and put away the dishes. That's 21 hours per week that could have been spent on other more productive activities.

Now, suppose that your family decides to buy a dishwasher that costs $400. Using the dishwasher, it will take 15 minutes for a single family member to clean up after each meal. At this rate, it will take the entire family only $5\frac{1}{4}$ hours per week to handle this chore. The benefits that your family reaps from the free time will cover the cost of the new dishwasher, which provides the typical benefits of physical capital:

1. *Extra time* Your family no longer has to spend 21 hours per week doing the dishes. Instead, the family gains $15\frac{3}{4}$ hours each week to use for other activities.
2. *More knowledge* By learning how to wash the dishes by machine, family members learn more about using household appliances in general. They can apply that knowledge to the use of other labor-saving devices, such as washing machines, dryers, and microwaves.
3. *More productivity* Because family members now have extra time and extra knowledge, they can use their resources and labor to do additional chores or other activities that are beneficial to the family.

Human Capital

In addition to producing physical capital, people can invest in themselves. **Human capital** is the knowledge and skills a worker gains through education and experience.

An economy requires both physical and human capital to produce goods and services. Doctors use stethoscopes and their schooling in order to provide their services. Assembly-line workers use equipment as well as skills acquired through training and practice to produce goods.

human capital *the skills and knowledge gained by a worker through education and experience*

THE WALL STREET JOURNAL. CLASSROOM EDITION

In the News Read more about capital in "Humans Need Not Apply," an article in The Wall Street Journal Classroom Edition.

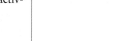

Go Online
The Wall Street Journal Classroom Edition
For: Current Events
Visit: PHSchool.com
Web Code: mnc-1011

Block Scheduling Strategies

Consider these suggestions to take advantage of extended class time:

- Have students work in small groups to complete the first activity on p. 4. You may wish to arrange for a member of a local historical society to talk to the class about the early history of your community.
- Show the Economics Video Library segment "Groovin' Business," about the founding of an Internet retail music business. After viewing the segment, discuss the fact that this business was started with very little land, labor, or capital. Lead a discussion on the unique aspects of Internet businesses; then have students identify other businesses that require little land, labor, or capital.
- Have pairs of students work through the Case Study on Herbert Stein, p. 2 and complete the Free Enterprise Activity in the Case Studies in Free Enterprise folder, pp. 2–3. Ask students to present their reports orally.

Background

Economics in History

Andrew Carnegie, founder of Carnegie Steel, was an entrepreneur who was instrumental in turning American steel manufacturing into a powerful industry. In the years between 1860 and 1900, steel became a key factor of economic development in the United States. It was used in railroad tracks, bridges, and skyscrapers. Using his business sense, Carnegie wisely invested in the expansion of Carnegie Steel by utilizing new manufacturing technologies, such as the Bessemer process and the open-hearth process. By 1900 Carnegie Steel was producing four million tons of steel—a quarter of the total United States production for that year. In 1901 Carnegie sold his company to John Pierpont (J. P.) Morgan, who had just formed the United States Steel Corporation. Carnegie then retired and devoted himself to philanthropy.

Transparency Resource Package
Economics Concepts, 1A: Scarcity and Factors of Production

Learning Styles Activity
Learning Styles Lesson Plans folder, p. 7 asks student groups to create diagrams about the factors of production.

Go Online PHSchool.com Typing in the Web Code when prompted will bring students directly to the article.

THE WALL STREET JOURNAL. CLASSROOM EDITION

For an additional article from *The Wall Street Journal Classroom Edition*, see the Source Articles folder in the **Teaching Resources,** pp. 3–5.

Answer to . . .

Building Key Concepts Entrepreneurs assemble and manipulate the three factors of production and coordinate their use, thus stimulating the production of goods and services.

Guide to the Essentials
Chapter 1, Section 1, p. 2 provides support for students who need additional review of the section content. Spanish support is available in the Spanish edition of the guide on p. 2.

Quiz Unit 1 folder, p. 3 includes questions to check students' understanding of Section 1 content.

Presentation Pro CD-ROM
Quiz provides multiple-choice questions to check students' understanding of Section 1 content.

Answers to . . .

Section 1 Assessment

1. Goods are physical objects (chairs, bananas). Services are actions or activities performed by one person for another (mowing a lawn, teaching).
2. Economics seeks to solve the scarcity problem, which exists because resources are limited whereas needs and wants are unlimited.
3. Scarcity always exists because goods and services are produced from limited resources. Shortages can be temporary or long-term and occur only when producers will not or cannot offer goods or services at current prices.
4. Land includes any natural resources used to produce goods and services, such as fertile soil or coal. Labor is the effort that one person exerts for another and for which the first person is paid. Capital is any human-made resource used to produce goods and services.
5. Physical capital provides extra time, increased knowledge, and/or greater productivity.
6. Entrepreneurs decide how to combine factors of production to create new goods and services.
7. Materials used to make the car are in limited supply. Only so many workers are available to assemble cars. The land that the factory is on is part of a fixed amount of land on Earth.
8. (a) capital (physical) (b) labor (c) land (d) land (e) labor (f) capital (human)
9. You would need a place for your business (land) as well as office help and tutors (labor). You would need economics textbooks and teaching materials (physical capital) as well as the experience of trained economics teachers (human capital).
10. Agree: Capital allows you to have more time, gain knowledge, and be more productive, thus creating more goods or services. This is like interest earned in a savings account. Disagree: Capital is unlike interest because it is not earned; it is an outside factor that allows growth.

FAST FACT

*After fishing in sub-zero temperatures in Labrador during 1912, a man named Clarence Birdseye was astounded that his frozen fish was tasty when he thawed and cooked it weeks later. This **entrepreneur** soon patented a "quick-freeze machine" and started his own seafood company. The result? An entire frozen foods industry was born.*

Entrepreneurs

If land, labor, and capital are the essential ingredients for creating all goods and services, who pulls these resources together? The answer is entrepreneurs. **Entrepreneurs** are ambitious leaders who decide how to combine land, labor, and capital resources to create new goods and services. They are the individuals who take risks to develop original ideas, start businesses, create new industries, and fuel economic growth.

You need not be Bill Gates of Microsoft or Henry Ford to be considered an entrepreneur. An individual who opens a corner food store and transforms it into a 10-store supermarket chain is an entrepreneur.

entrepreneur
ambitious leader who combines land, labor, and capital to create and market new goods and services

Scarce Resources

Economists say that all goods and services are scarce because the land, labor, and capital used to create them are scarce. Consider French fries. A typical portion of French fries started as a potato in a field in Idaho. Seven and one-half gallons of water irrigated the half-foot plot where the potato grew. Nurtured with fertilizers and protected by pesticides, the potato was harvested, processed, frozen, and then transported to Seattle. In Seattle, it was fried in corn oil from Nebraska, sprinkled with salt from Louisiana, and eaten in a restaurant.

All of the economic resources, or factors of production, that were used to create the French fries are scarce. First, the quantity of the land and water available for growing potatoes is limited. Second, the labor available to grow the crop and to process and transport the potatoes is limited by the size, time, age, and energy of a population. Finally, because land and labor are limited, the amount of physical capital available to create the French fries, such as farm equipment, is also limited.

While we have been talking about French fries, we could easily have been talking about a pair of blue jeans or a new space shuttle. No matter what good or service we were to look at, we would discover that the supplies of land, labor, and capital used to produce it are scarce, and that each resource has many alternative uses.

Section 1 Assessment

Progress Monitoring *Online*
For: Self-quiz with vocabulary practice
Web Code: mna-1015

Key Terms and Main Ideas

1. What is the difference between a **good** and a **service?**
2. Why is the idea of **scarcity** a starting point for thinking economically?
3. How is **scarcity** different from **shortages?**
4. Describe the three **factors of production.**
5. What special advantages does **physical capital** offer?
6. What role do **entrepreneurs** play in the economy?

Applying Economic Concepts

7. ***Critical Thinking*** Why might an economist look at hundreds of cars moving along an assembly line and say, "There is an example of scarcity"?
8. ***Decision Making*** Which factor of production is represented by each of the following? **(a)** an office building **(b)** an assembly line worker **(c)** a tree used to make paper **(d)** unused soil **(e)** an artist **(f)** a student
9. ***Try This*** Leaving class today, you decide to start an economics tutoring business. Your first step is to get the two categories of capital. Next you need to obtain the other factors of production. Specifically, what do you need in terms of land, labor, and capital?
10. ***Critical Thinking*** Do you agree or disagree with the following statement? *Creating capital is like depositing money in a savings account. You save now in order to have more in the future.*

For: Research Activity
Visit: PHSchool.com
Web Code: mnd-1011

Progress Monitoring *Online*
For additional assessment, have students access Progress Monitoring Online at **Web Code:** mna-1015

Go Online PHSchool.com Typing in the Web Code when prompted will bring students directly to detailed instructions for this activity.

Economist

Entrepreneur

ECONOMIC
Profile

Gary Becker (b. 1930)

Nobel Prize-winning economist Gary Becker looks at daily life and sees economics at work in all we do. Becker even sees marriage as an economic decision that many people make based on opportunity costs. To understand how Becker arrived at this intriguing conclusion, you have to look at how he came to see the world.

Economics and Social Issues

Like many high school seniors, Becker knew what he was good at—mathematics—but wanted some practical way to apply it. Leaving his small Pennsylvania hometown, Becker went to Princeton University and decided to pursue economics. But he lost interest in the subject because it didn't "deal with important social problems."

Becker briefly considered a degree in sociology, but found the subject "too difficult." Later, as a graduate student at the University of Chicago, he realized that economics could indeed help answer social questions. His first book, based on his studies at Chicago, was an economic analysis of racial discrimination.

"It started me down the path of applying economics to social issues," states Becker, "a path that I have continued to follow." In 1992, that path led to the Nobel Prize in economics, which Becker received for using economic analysis to study a wide range of human behavior. "Economy is the art of making the most of life," he says.

Economics and Personal Decisions

Becker maintains that economics guides even life's most personal decisions. He sees the process of dating as part of a "marriage market." Most people do not marry the first prospect they meet, he notes. The opportunity cost of such a marriage would be high because better prospects are likely to exist. Instead, people try to search for better prospects.

Considering Costs and Benefits

An extended search for a mate, however, consumes time, effort, and other resources. It involves expenditures on personal appearance, in social situations, for education, and for other things that help attract a mate. A person decides to marry, Becker says, when the cost of searching exceeds the possible benefits of finding a better mate.

People measure the benefits of a potential spouse by criteria such as job, appearance, education, and family, Becker says, and they try to judge other traits by these factors. For example, the probability that a person is honest and good-natured may be judged by looking at the person's family. Intelligence is gauged by the person's education. Becker maintains that this process causes people to marry on the basis of imperfect information. Not until later do they truly learn about their partner's personality and compatibility, qualities that take longer to assess.

JUST MARRIED

CHECK FOR UNDERSTANDING

1. **Source Reading** Interpret the following passage from an article by Becker that appeared in *BusinessWeek:* "Human capital is as much a part of the wealth of nations as are factories, housing, machinery, and other physical capital."
2. **Critical Thinking** How does what you've read in this introductory chapter on economics support or conflict with Becker's idea that "economy is the art of making the most of life"?
3. **Decision Making** Do you agree or disagree with Becker's idea that economics guides even life's most personal decisions? Support your position with two or three examples of your own.

Beyond the Classroom: Workplace Skills

Mathematics Tell students that the ability to comprehend numerical data and to solve problems in logical and mathematical ways is important in the workplace. Explain that many jobs require people to make and follow budgets. Jobs may also require such skills as counting money or projecting the time required to complete a job. Ask students to interview three adults about ways that they use mathematics in their jobs. Have students give short oral presentations telling what they discovered.

ECONOMIC Profile
Gary Becker

Background

Winning the Nobel Prize might seem to guarantee instant acceptance of an economist's theories, but that was not the case for Gary Becker. Educated at Princeton University and the University of Chicago and winner of the 1992 Nobel Prize in economics, Becker has excellent credentials. Even so, in the early 1990s some economists viewed Becker's central ideas with distrust.

Becker's premise—that rational economic choices based on self-interest govern most aspects of human behavior, not just decisions about purchasing and investment—has since gained widespread acceptance. He has applied economic theory both to family issues, such as marriage and divorce, and to social issues, including addiction, discrimination, and criminal behavior.

Careers in Economics Activity Unit 1 folder, p. 11 gives students a closer look at the career path of an economist.

Databank, pp. 532–547 contains charts and graphs that can be used to illustrate the work of economists as well as to extend and reinforce skills.

Answers to . . .

1. Becker is describing the value of human resources and the role that people's abilities play in economic systems.
2. Students should relate chapter concepts such as opportunity cost and trade-offs to life decisions.
3. Students who agree might point to such examples as choices in clothing styles and relative amounts of time spent with friends or on schoolwork. Students who disagree might say that these decisions are based on feelings and beliefs, not economics.

Section 2

Opportunity Cost

Objectives You may wish to call students' attention to the objectives in the Section Preview. The objectives are reflected in the main headings of the section.

Bellringer Identify five appealing vacation destinations. Tell students that they can choose just one. Ask volunteers to explain their choices and to describe what they gave up by choosing that vacation over others. Explain that in this section they will learn about trade-offs.

Vocabulary Builder Have students create a brief matching quiz for the key terms listed in the Section Preview. Students should exchange quizzes, answer the questions, and check each other's work by referring to the definitions in the text.

Lesson Plan

Teaching the Main Concepts L3

1. Focus Every decision involves trade-offs—the alternatives we give up by making a choice. Ask students to provide examples of trade-offs.

2. Instruct After discussing trade-offs, examine the concept of opportunity cost and the role of the decision-making grid in making choices. Make the students understand the concept of thinking at the margin by eliciting additional examples of this concept.

3. Close/Reteach Remind students that they consider costs and benefits at the margin in everyday decisions. Have students construct decision-making grids using examples from their own lives (such as the decision to join a club or a sports team).

Answer to . . .

Photo Caption A car would provide convenient transportation and could broaden job opportunities, but the money used for the car could not be saved or used to buy other things.

Section 2 Opportunity Cost

Preview

Objectives

After studying this section you will be able to:

1. **Describe** why every decision involves trade-offs.
2. **Explain** the concept of opportunity cost.
3. **Explain** how people make decisions by thinking at the margin.

Section Focus

All human decisions involve trade-offs. The next best alternative to any choice is called an opportunity cost. Decision-making grids can make it easier to identify the trade-offs and opportunity cost of a decision.

Key Terms

trade-off
guns or butter
opportunity cost
thinking at the margin

trade-off *an alternative that we sacrifice when we make a decision*

guns or butter *a phrase that refers to the trade-offs that nations face when choosing whether to produce more or less military or consumer goods*

Several years ago, a few hotels in Washington, D.C., offered a special service to their guests. A popular art exhibit was in town, but the only way to get tickets was to wait in line for several hours. Many of the hotel's guests were unable or unwilling to do this. Instead, the hotels hired people to stand in line to purchase the $5 tickets. The hotels then sold the tickets to guests for $50 apiece. These guests spent money rather than time in order to get their exhibit tickets. Similarly, when we decide on one alternative, we gain one thing but lose something else.

Trade-Offs

Economists point out that all individuals, businesses, and large groups of people—even governments—make decisions that involve **trade-offs.** Trade-offs are all the alternatives that we give up whenever we choose one course of action over another.

What are some of the trade-offs of buying a car? ▼

Individuals and Trade-Offs

Every decision we make involves trade-offs. For example, if you choose to spend more time at work, you give up watching a movie or going to a baseball game. Choosing to play soccer might prevent you from working on the yearbook or having a part-time job.

Businesses and Trade-Offs

The decisions that businesspeople make about how to use land, labor, and capital resources also create trade-offs. Farmers who plant broccoli cannot use the same land at the same time to grow cauliflower. A manufacturer who decides to use all her equipment to build chairs eliminates the possibility of building tables or desks at that same time.

Society and Trade-Offs

Countries also make decisions that involve trade-offs. Economists simplify their explanations of the trade-offs countries face by using the example of **guns or butter.** In short, a country that decides to produce more military goods ("guns") has fewer resources to devote to consumer goods ("butter") and vice versa. (Remember, resources are limited!) The steel used to make a tank is no longer available for building the dairy equipment needed to make butter.

Graphing the Main Idea

Opportunity Cost To build understanding of the concept of **opportunity costs,** have students use a tree map graphic organizer like the one at the right to explain the types of trade-offs discussed in the text. Tell students that a tree map shows the main topic, main ideas or divisions, and supporting details.

Section Reading Support Transparencies A template and the answers for this graphic organizer can be found in Chapter 1, Section 2 of the Section Reading Support Transparency System.

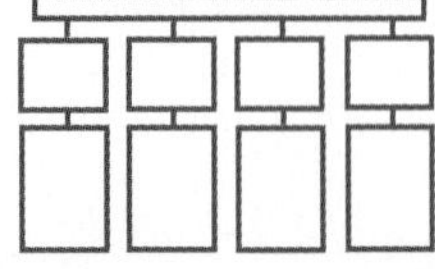

YOU HAVE TWO CHOICES FOR DINNER—
"TAKE IT" OR "LEAVE IT"!

◀ **Because decisions are not always as clear-cut as the one in this cartoon, economists encourage us to consider the trade-offs and opportunity cost of a decision before we make it.**

Defining Opportunity Cost

Whenever individuals, businesses, or governments decide on a course of action, they face many trade-offs. One alternative, though, is usually more desirable than all the others. The most desirable alternative given up as the result of a decision is called the **opportunity cost.**

If a family buys a computer, family members cannot use the same money to pay for their second choice, going on a trip. The trip, then, is the opportunity cost of buying the computer. The farmer who chose to grow broccoli instead of cauliflower experienced the opportunity cost of planting cauliflower. If a government decides to produce more "guns," then having less "butter" is the opportunity cost.

Similarly, every ordinary decision that we make every day involves an opportunity cost. For each of the following choices, which alternative would you choose?

- Sleep late or wake up early for a ski trip?
- Sleep late or wake up early to eat your breakfast?
- Sleep late or wake up early to study for a test?

Most likely, you did not choose "sleep late" for all three decisions. Your decision depended on the specific opportunity cost—whatever you were willing to sacrifice.

Using a Decision-Making Grid

At times, a decision's opportunity cost may be unclear or complicated. Using a decision-making grid like the one in Figure 1.2 can help you determine whether you are willing to accept the opportunity cost of a choice you are about to make. In this particular grid, Karen is trying to decide whether to sleep late or get up early to study for a test. Karen likes to sleep. Getting up early is tough. However, getting up early to study would probably improve her test score.

Karen knows that she is choosing between her two top alternatives: sleeping late and waking up early to study. Because of scarcity, she cannot do both. The time can only be occupied in one way.

To help her decide, Karen lists the benefits of each alternative on the grid. Waking up early to study will probably result in a better grade. Also, she will receive teacher and parental approval and experience the personal satisfaction that comes with doing well on a test. However, she knows she would enjoy sleeping later and that the extra sleep would give her more energy during the day.

opportunity cost *the most desirable alternative given up as the result of a decision*

Global Connections

Global Trade-Offs The same decision made in two different countries can have vastly different opportunity costs. Malaysia bought two warships in 1992, paying a price equal to the cost of providing safe drinking water for the 5 million Malaysians lacking it. In other words, the opportunity cost of the warships was safe drinking water for 5 million people. The opportunity cost of building warships in wealthier countries is not nearly so high. However, there are still costs to consider. In the United States, the number of people employed by the military decreased dramatically following the end of the cold war. In response, the Pentagon developed a new program, "Troops to Teachers," to help former soldiers get jobs teaching in schools. The switch from army duty to teaching reminds us that the opportunity cost of a soldier may be a teacher and vice versa. **Why does the opportunity cost of a decision vary from one situation to another?**

Econ 101: Key Concepts Made Easy

Opportunity Cost Two of the key concepts in this section are **opportunity cost** and **thinking at the margin.** Have students read the paragraph that explains thinking at the margin in terms of an actual margin on a piece of paper. Tell them to think about that example and to consider what the opportunity cost would be of using more and more of the margin in a published book.

At first, students may have a difficult time seeing the opportunity cost of using more of the margin. They may feel that using up as much of the page as possible would be a savings. Lead them to see, however, that a page that is too full of type is difficult to read and may be unattractive. Point out that publishers must (literally) think at the margin to make their books both attractive and economical.

Guided Reading and Review
Unit 1 folder, p. 4 asks students to identify the main ideas of the section and to define or identify key terms.

Learning Styles Activity
Learning Styles Lesson Plans folder, p. 8 asks student groups to consider individual, business, and societal decisions that involve trade-offs.

Differentiated Instruction 

Ask students to write definitions in their own words of the term *opportunity cost.* Ask them to provide examples from their own lives. LPR

Differentiated Instruction 

(Reteaching) Have students work in small groups to discuss stories they have read in which people make decisions and consider opportunity cost. (Students may also use television shows as examples.) Ask a representative from each group to describe one example to the class.

Economic Cartoon
Unit 1 folder, p. 12 gives students practice in interpreting cartoons about section content.

Differentiated Instruction 

Divide students into five groups, each representing one of these products: military aircraft, bridges, school buildings, water purification plants, and hospitals. Have each person in the group make a three-inch square card with the name of their product on one side. Place all the cards, face down, on a table. Have one student from each group draw three cards from the table and then show their group what they drew. Tell the groups that they each represent an underdeveloped country that may trade off two cards for anything left on the table. After they have done so, have each group tell why they chose the cards they did. Explain that this is a simulation of opportunity costs that such nations face. SN

Answer to . . .

Global Connections Opportunity costs vary because every situation has a different set of trade-offs.

Background

Thinking at the Margin and Blackberry Picking

Alfred Marshall was an English economist who lived from 1842 to 1924. In his book *Principles of Economics* (1890), he explains thinking at the margin with the example of a boy picking blackberries to eat. At first the pleasure the boy gains from eating the blackberries more than repays him for the work he has to do in picking. At some point, however, he begins to feel full. After that the opportunity cost (not being able to rest or play with his friends) of adding one more unit (picking another blackberry) becomes too high. He then makes a decision "at the margin" to stop picking.

Transparency Resource Package Economics Concepts, 1B: Decision Making at the Margin

Meeting NCEE Standards

Use the following benchmark activity from the **Voluntary National Content Standards in Economics** to evaluate student understanding of **Standard 2.**

Decide how many workers to hire for a profit-maximizing car wash by comparing the cost of hiring each additional worker to the additional revenues derived from hiring each additional worker.

Differentiated Instruction L4

Ask students to write a paragraph evaluating a public policy decision (such as one involving environmental protection or hiring more police for a city) and summarize the information in terms of opportunity cost and thinking at the margin. GT

Answer to . . .

Building Key Concepts Karen will forgo a better grade, approval from her teacher and parents, and personal satisfaction.

Figure 1.2 **Karen's Decision-Making Grid**

	Alternatives	
	Sleep late	**Wake up early to study**
Benefits	• Enjoy more sleep • Have more energy during the day	• Better grade on test • Teacher and parental approval • Personal satisfaction
Decision	Sleep late	Wake up early to study for test
Opportunity cost	Extra study time	Extra sleep time
Benefits forgone	• Better grade on test • Teacher and parental approval • Personal satisfaction	• Enjoy more sleep • Have more energy during the day

Using a decision-making grid can help us see what we gain and lose when we have to choose between alternatives.
Opportunity Cost What benefits will Karen forgo if she chooses to sleep later?

thinking at the margin *deciding whether to do or use one additional unit of some resource*

Making the Decision

Karen is a practical person. After considering the opportunity cost, she decides that waking up early to study offers the most desirable benefits. She is willing to accept the opportunity cost: extra sleep time. She knows that she is giving up the benefits of sleeping late, namely the pleasure of more sleep and the extra energy it provides.

Karen might have made a different decision when choosing between sleeping and breakfast or sleeping and getting up early to study on a Saturday. With each new situation, the opportunity costs and benefits change.

We always face an opportunity cost, though. When we select one alternative, we have to sacrifice at least one alternative and forgo its benefits. By recognizing what we are sacrificing, we can decide whether the decision is worth it. An economist might say, "Choosing is refusing."

Thinking at the Margin

When economists look at decisions, they point out one more characteristic in addition to opportunity cost. Many decisions involve adding one unit or subtracting one unit, such as one minute or one dollar. From an economist's point of view, when you decide how much more or less to do, you are **thinking at the margin.**

To understand what it means to think at the margin, you might picture a piece of paper with a line drawn down the left side. That line separates the space used for writing from extra space on the paper. You could use some of that extra space or you could leave it blank. Similarly, thinking at the margin means you are thinking about using one additional unit.

Making a Decision at the Margin

When deciding whether or not to study, Karen used the "all or nothing" approach as shown in Figure 1.2. She was either going to wake up early to study or sleep late and not study at all that morning.

In reality, Karen could have decided from among several options rather than just two. She could have decided to get up one, two, or three hours earlier to study or to sleep instead. She could have made her decision by looking specifically at how many extra hours to study that morning. Making a decision about each extra hour would mean that she was thinking at the margin.

Block Scheduling Strategies

Consider these suggestions to take advantage of extended class time:

- Extend the Bellringer activity on p. 8 by having small groups of students research two of the vacation spots you listed. Have each group prepare a report on the trade-offs and opportunity costs of their selections.
- Have students work in pairs or groups of three to complete the activity on this page. Then ask a community leader to speak to the class about the factors that planners must consider when making decisions.
- After students have completed the Economic Cartoon activity in the Unit 1 folder, p. 12, have them create their own economic cartoons on a key concept from this section. Display the cartoons on a bulletin board.

To make a decision at the margin, Karen should look at the opportunity cost of each extra hour of studying and compare it to the benefit. In Figure 1.3, we can see that one hour of studying means an opportunity cost of an hour of sleep and a benefit of probably passing the test with a C. Two hours of studying "cost" two hours of sleep and perhaps getting a B. Three hours of studying mean sacrificing three hours of sleep and probably getting only a slightly higher grade of B+.

What should Karen decide? At three hours, the cost is no longer worth the benefit to Karen because her grade will improve only slightly. Thus, Karen decides to awaken two hours earlier.

Figure 1.3 Decision Making at the Margin

Options	Benefit	Opportunity cost
1st hour of extra study time	Grade of C on test	One hour of sleep
2nd hour of extra study time	Grade of B on test	2 hours of sleep
3rd hour of extra study time	Grade of B+ on test	3 hours of sleep

This person has to decide how many extra hours to study. By comparing the opportunity cost to the benefit of each extra hour, she can decide how much is the right amount. **Opportunity Cost** **At what point is this person paying an added cost with little extra benefit?**

Cost and Benefit at the Margin

Comparing opportunity costs and benefits at the margin enabled Karen to decide how many hours to study. Such a comparison could help someone decide how much money to spend on a car, how many hours to work, and how much time to spend watching television. Employers think at the margin when they decide how many extra workers to hire. Legislators think at the margin when deciding if a government program should include more of a particular benefit. This decision-making process is sometimes called cost/benefit analysis.

Deciding by thinking at the margin is just like making any other decision. Decision makers just have to compare the opportunity costs and the benefits—what they will sacrifice and what they will gain. Once the opportunity cost outweighs the benefits, no more units should be added.

Section 2 Assessment

Progress Monitoring *Online*
For: Self-quiz with vocabulary practice
Web Code: mna-1016

Key Terms and Main Ideas

1. Present three examples that illustrate how all decisions involve **trade-offs.**
2. Why must the **opportunity cost** of a decision always be something desirable?
3. How do economists use the phrase **"guns or butter"?**
4. What does it mean to **"think at the margin"?**

Applying Economic Concepts

5. ***Problem Solving*** Suppose that you can save $50 by buying your car in a different city. If the trip requires only $10 in gasoline, is the trip worthwhile? Why or why not?
6. ***Decision Making*** Determine an opportunity cost for each of the following. **(a)** eating pizza **(b)** going to see a movie on a Tuesday **(c)** going to see a movie on a Saturday **(d)** watching television
7. ***Try This*** Create a decision-making grid like the one in Figure 1.2 to defend a decision you will make today.
8. ***Critical Thinking*** Decide whether to work 2, 4, or 6 hours at an after-school job by comparing the opportunity cost and benefit of each alternative.
9. ***Decision Making*** Which factors would an employer consider if he or she were trying to decide whether to hire an additional worker?

For: Decision-making Activity
Visit: PHSchool.com
Web Code: mnd-1012

Guide to the Essentials
Chapter 1, Section 2, p. 3 provides support for students who need additional review of the section content. Spanish support is available in the Spanish edition of the guide on p. 3.

Quiz Unit 1 folder, p. 5 includes questions to check students' understanding of Section 2 content.

Presentation Pro CD-ROM
Quiz provides multiple-choice questions to check students' understanding of Section 2 content.

Answers to . . .
Section 2 Assessment

1. Students should provide three examples like the following: What shall I do after school: do homework (improve grades), go to the park with friends (have fun), or clean my room (make parents happy)?
2. An opportunity cost must be desirable because there would be no meaningful decision to be made between a desirable option and an undesirable one.
3. "Guns or butter" refers to whether a country chooses to produce more military goods ("guns") or more consumer goods ("butter").
4. "Thinking at the margin" means making a decision about how much more or less to do. It allows people to evaluate options based on available resources.
5. Some students may say yes—the amount saved buying the car in another city is more than the cost of the gasoline to get there (net savings of $40). Some students may say no—time and money will be spent in returning to the dealer for service.
6. Sample answers: (a) enjoying the health benefits of a salad (b) getting a good grade on a test the next day (c) going to an amusement park with friends (d) having fun outdoors
7. Grids will vary, but students should follow the correct format and show logical alternatives for each action.
8. Student comparisons will vary but should show an understanding of the fact that working more hours means earning more money, but less time will be available for other activities.
9. Employers would consider the cost (wages) of hiring an additional worker compared to the benefits gained (more work performed) from having another person in the workforce.

Progress Monitoring *Online*
For additional assessment, have students access Progress Monitoring Online at **Web Code:** mna-1016

Go Online PHSchool.com Typing in the Web Code when prompted will bring students directly to detailed instructions for this activity.

Answer to . . .
Building Key Concepts At the point of adding a third hour of study, the person gains only a higher B.

Skills for LIFE

Interpreting Line Graphs

1. Focus Students will use line graphs to analyze and draw inferences from data.

2. Instruct Ask volunteers to give oral accounts of the information shown on the graph. Compare and contrast the oral accounts with the more concise visual presentation on the graph. Then have students work through the three steps outlined in the skill.

3. Close/Reteach For additional practice, see the Economic Skills Activity below.

Economic Skills Activity
Unit 1 folder, p. 8, "Interpreting Line Graphs," asks students to interpret several graphs in making a choice among several films.

Math Practice Activity
Math Practice folder, p. 2, "Drawing and Interpreting Graphs," gives students a new application skill.

Simulations and Data Graphing CD-ROM offers data graphing tools so that students can practice creating and interpreting line graphs.

Social Studies Skills Tutor CD-ROM offers interactive practice in critical thinking and reading, visual analysis, and communication.

Databank, pp. 532–547 contains charts and graphs to extend and reinforce the skills lesson.

Answers

1. (a) hours of practice per week (b) average points per game (c) between points per game and hours of practice
2. (a) 25 (b) 2 hours (c) about 16
3. The more time you spend practicing, the more points you will score.

Additional Practice

Possible answers: Player C is a naturally better player; Player D plays a more defensive role on the team. There is no absolute correlation between practicing and points scored. Line graphs cannot give us all of the information we may need.

Skills for LIFE

Interpreting Line Graphs

Line graphs easily and clearly present a large quantity of statistical data. Economists use line graphs to illustrate patterns or trends over time and to explain the relationship between two or more variables. A variable is a factor with a value that can change. Use the following steps to read and interpret the line graph below.

1. Identify the type of information presented on the graph. Before you can begin to interpret the information on a graph, you must identify specifically what is being shown. The graph title and the axes' labels indicate the meanings of the points and lines on the graph. Answer the following questions. (a) What do the numbers on the horizontal axis (across) represent? (b) What do the numbers on the vertical axis (up and down) represent? (c) What relationship does the line graph describe?

2. Read the data shown on the graph. Study the graph's axes carefully. Before studying the overall patterns, look carefully at specific points on the graph. Answer the following questions. (a) What is the maximum number of points per game that can be shown on the graph? (b) How many hours a week did Player B practice? (c) How many points per game did Player E average?

3. Study the data shown on the graph to look for relationships or draw conclusions about a topic. Use the graph below to draw conclusions about the relationship between time spent practicing and the number of points scored per game. What could you conclude from the information on the line graph about the relationship between practice and points per game?

Skills: Hours of Practice vs. Points Scored

Average Poins per Game (0, 5, 10, 15, 20, 25); Hours of Practice per Week (0, 2, 4, 6, 8, 10, 12, 14, 16); Player A, Player B, Player C, Player D, Player E, Player F

Additional Practice

Note that the points on the graph do not form a perfectly straight line. For example, Player D did not score as many points per game as Player C, although Player D practiced more hours each week. Why might this be so? What does this information say about the conclusions we can draw from line graphs?

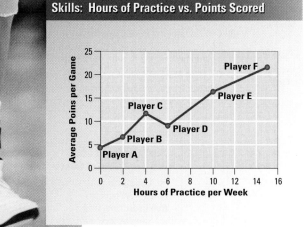

Interdisciplinary Connections: Math

Linking Tables to Graphs Remind students that tables provide another way to organize data. Sometimes, however, a graph shows data patterns more clearly. When creating a graph, students should first identify the least and greatest values for each set of data. They should select a scale that includes these values and that can be divided into equal parts.

Have students work through the following problem: Many people borrow money in order to purchase a car. The term of the loan might be anywhere from 2 to 6 years. The table shows the monthly payments on a loan of $10,000 at 9 percent interest.

a. What can you tell about the relationship between the length of the loan and the monthly payments?
b. Graph the data.
c. Is it easier to see the relationship on a graph or in a table? Explain your answer.

Length of loan (yr.)	2	3	4	5	6
Monthly payment ($)	456.85	318.00	248.85	207.58	180.26

Section 3 Production Possibilities Curves

Preview

Objectives

After studying this section you will be able to:

1. **Interpret** a production possibilities curve.
2. **Demonstrate** how production possibilities curves show efficiency, growth, and cost.
3. **Understand** that a country's production possibilities depend on its available resources and technology.

Section Focus

Decisions about which goods and services to produce affect each of us every day. Production possibilities graphs can help us examine the opportunity cost of these decisions.

Key Terms

production possibilities curve
production possibilities frontier
efficiency
underutilization
cost
law of increasing costs

As the United States entered World War II in 1941, it faced an urgent task: create the weapons and equipment needed to win the war or face defeat. Government agencies took the lead in switching the output of America's factories, farms, and mines from the production of consumer products to the production of military products.

Whether at war or not, nations must choose what to produce. In 2002, farmers in the United States grew about 2 million tons of watermelons. Could they have produced more? If they had, what would have been the opportunity cost?

Production Possibilities

Economists often use graphs to analyze the choices and trade-offs that people make. Why? Because graphs help us see how one value relates to another value. A **production possibilities curve**, or graph, shows alternative ways to use an economy's productive resources. The axes of the graph can show categories of goods and services, such as farm goods and factory goods or capital goods and consumer goods. The axes can also display any pair of specific goods or services, such as hats on one axis and shoes on the other.

production possibilities curve *a graph that shows alternative ways to use an economy's resources*

◀ **During World War II, consumer goods were in short supply as the nation shifted resources to increase production of planes, ships, artillery, and ammunition. Ration coupons (far left) were used to ensure that civilians got a fair share of consumer goods.**

Building Key Concepts: Graphing the Main Idea

Opportunity Costs To build understanding of the concept of **opportunity costs** and trade-offs, have students use a web graphic organizer like the one at the right to explain what a production possibilities graph can show. Tell students that a web shows a main idea and its supporting details.

Section Reading Support Transparencies A template and the answers for this graphic organizer can be found in Chapter 1, Section 3 of the Section Reading Support Transparency System.

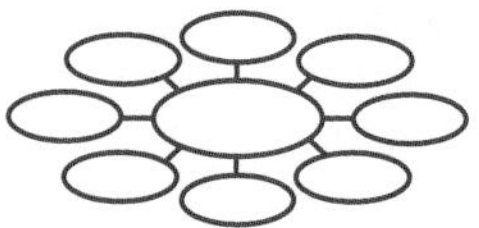

Section 3 Production Possibilities Curves

Objectives You may wish to call students' attention to the objectives in the Section Preview. The objectives are reflected in the main headings of the section.

Bellringer Ask volunteers to explain why graphs sometimes show information more clearly than text or tables. Explain that in this section they will learn about an important category of graphs in economics: production possibilities curves.

Vocabulary Builder Have students work in pairs to find the definition for each key term listed in the Section Preview. One member of each pair should then explain the term's meaning to the other. Students should switch roles for each term.

Lesson Plan

Teaching the Main Concepts 

1. Focus Explain that this section continues the discussion of opportunity cost and trade-offs by describing tools that economists use to analyze these concepts.

2. Instruct Work closely with the text visuals to help students understand the key concepts. Demonstrate how graphs can show efficiency, growth, and cost. Discuss both the historical and the business examples. Be sure that students understand that graphs are an excellent way of showing how one element of an economy affects others.

3. Close/Reteach Remind students that graphic tools are used to assess the global economy as well as the economies of countries. Have students examine the tables and graphs in an almanac. Ask them to describe what some of the visuals show.

Guided Reading and Review Unit 1 folder, p. 6 asks students to identify the main ideas of the section and to define or identify key terms.

Background

Interdisciplinary

Visual images are a powerful way to convince groups of people that a course of action is desirable. During both World War I and World War II, the United States government used poster art to gain support for the war and for the economic policies that the leaders felt would win the war. Posters urging people to buy Liberty Bonds during World War I exhorted them to "Beat Back the Hun." Persuasive posters during World War II showed strong and confident women working in factories. Other posters, designed to help people economize and save scarce resources for the troops, used slogans such as "Food is Ammunition—Don't Waste It" to get their points across.

Differentiated Instruction L4

Have students research the changes in production that occurred in the United States during World War II (for example, changing from producing automobiles to making military vehicles). Ask them to share their research with the class. Hold a discussion in class about what industries might change, and how they would change, during a war today. GT

Answer to . . .

Cartoon Caption Economists use graphs to show complicated data and the relationships between data in a format that is easy to grasp. They also use graphs to illustrate trends.

Building Key Concepts The opportunity cost is the ability to produce watermelons.

"We feel he's either going to be an artist or an economist."

▲ **Why do economists use graphs?**

production possibilities frontier *the line on a production possibilities graph that shows the maximum possible output*

Drawing a Production Possibilities Curve

To draw a production possibilities curve, an economist begins by deciding which goods or services to examine; for example, farm goods and factory goods. In this example shoes and watermelons become the values shown on the two axes of the graph. If the vertical axis in Graphs A and B in Figure 1.4 represents shoes, Graph A indicates that this fictional country, Capeland, could produce 15 million pairs of shoes if it used all of its resources to produce only shoes.

The horizontal axis represents watermelons. Graph B indicates that Capeland could produce 21 million tons of watermelons if that's the only product it chose to produce. So Capeland can produce a maximum of:

15 million pairs of shoes
OR
21 million tons of watermelons

A third, more likely, alternative appears in Figure 1.5. The citizens of Capeland could also produce both shoes and watermelons, and this range of choices appears in the table and graph in that figure. It shows six different ways that Capelanders could use their resources to produce watermelons and shoes. Using the made-up data from the table, we can plot points on the graph and then connect them to draw the line shown in Figure 1.5. This line that we can draw, called the **production possibilities frontier,** shows combinations of the production of both shoes and watermelons. Any spot on

Figure 1.4 Production Possibilities Curve *Step 1*

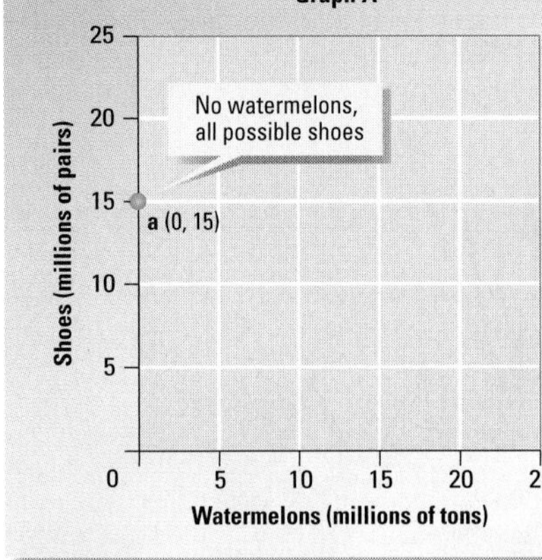

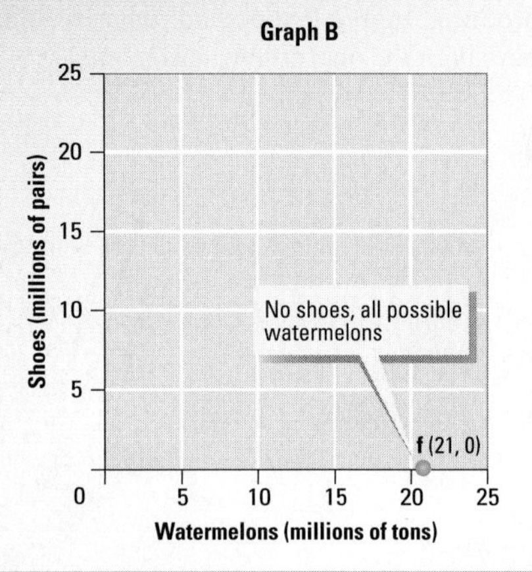

You can begin to build a production possibilities curve by plotting two of the production choices on a grid. Graph A reflects a decision to produce 15 million pairs of shoes. Graph B reflects a decision to produce 21 million tons of watermelons.

Opportunity Cost **What is the opportunity cost of the decision shown in Graph A?**

Econ 101: Key Concepts Made Easy

Scarcity One of the key concepts in this section is that **production possibilities curves** are a useful way for economic planners to make the most productive use of scarce resources. A production possibilities frontier illustrates scarcity. It shows the limits for an economy at a particular point in time, given the existing resources and level of technology. If resources are gained or technology improves, however, a new frontier is created and the graph "shifts to the right."

Ask students to imagine a very simple production possibilities graph illustrating some aspect of their lives. Then ask them to think of a way to add resources or improve technology to "shift" this graph "to the right." Have students share their examples with the class.

Differentiated Instruction

Providing Appropriate Resource Materials (L2)

In order to maximize English language learner success in your social studies class, make sure that your classroom is provisioned with materials that can assist students struggling with English as a second language. These materials can help students better decipher text and assigned readings, write more coherently, and feel confident in their understanding of the content being taught. Materials that a teacher of English language learners should try to obtain include:

1. **English dictionary** for looking up unfamiliar terms.

2. **Two-way translation dictionaries** for looking up words in their native language to obtain the equivalent word in English and for looking up unfamiliar words in English to find a definition in their native language.

3. **Thesaurus** to help students expand their English vocabulary. If a student essay repeatedly uses a basic vocabulary word such as "good", encourage students to use the thesaurus to incorporate a wider variety of words into their writing.

4. **Grammar book** to assist students in their writing.

5. **A set of encyclopedias** that provide brief and clear background information on a variety of topics. Often full-length books found in a school's library are daunting to an English language learner beginning their historical research. Encyclopedias, particularly those aimed at K-12 students, allow students to research information without becoming overwhelmed by lengthy and difficult passages in English.

Visit the Social Studies area of the Prentice Hall Web site. There you can find additional links to enrich chapter content for *Economics: Principles in Action* as well as a self-test for students. Be sure to check out this month's **eTeach** online discussion with a Master Economics Teacher.

Web Code: mnf-1021

Running Out of Time?

- Use the **Presentation Pro CD-ROM** to create an outline for this chapter.
- Use the Chapter Summary in the **Chapter 2 Assessment,** p. 46.
- Use the Section Summaries for Chapter 2, from **Guide to the Essentials of Economics (English and Spanish).**

THE WALL STREET JOURNAL. CLASSROOM EDITION

Prentice Hall brings into the classroom the authoritative content of *The Wall Street Journal Classroom Edition.* See the Source Articles, Debating Current Issues, and the You and Your Money folders in the **Teaching Resources.** Also, see Economics Video Library, "Internet Impact."

Assessment Resources

Chapter Assessment

Teaching Resources Unit 1, Chapter 2
- Section Quizzes, pp. 14, 16, 18, 20

Exam *View*® Test Bank CD-ROM Chapter 2

Economics Assessment Rubrics

Chapter 2 Self-Test, **Web Code:** mna-1021

Reading and Skills Evaluation

Progress Monitoring Assessments
- Screening Test
- Diagnostic Test of Social Studies Skills

Standardized Test Preparation

Test Prep Workbook

Test-Taking Strategies With Transparencies

Differentiated Instruction Key

L1	Special Needs	LPR	Less Proficient Readers
L2	Basic to Average	AR	Advanced Readers
L3	All Students	SN	Special Needs Students
L4	Average to Advanced	GT	Gifted and Talented
		ELL	English Language Learner

Chapter 2

Economic Systems

Introducing the Chapter

In this chapter, students will be introduced to the economic issues and goals shared by all societies and the four principal economic systems: traditional, market, centrally planned, and mixed. Students will learn the advantages and disadvantages of each system and how they are similar and different.

Go Online PHSchool.com

For additional links for *Economics: Principles in Action* provided by Prentice Hall and *The Wall Street Journal Classroom Edition,* visit the Social Studies area. Be sure to check out this month's **eTeach** online discussion with a Master Teacher.

Beyond the Lecture

You may cover the concepts in Chapter 2 in an activity-based style by using the following materials:

- **Technology Resources** appropriate for use with this chapter are noted on pp. 24, 25, 26, 27, 30, 32, 35, 38, 42, 44, and 47.
- **Presentation Pro CD-ROM** with animated graphs gives you an alternative method for organizing and delivering chapter content.
- **Activities** designed to meet the needs of students of mixed abilities and learning styles are noted throughout the chapter in the side columns.
- **Learning Styles Lesson Plans** provide alternate lessons for diverse learning styles. See pp. 9–10 of the Learning Styles Lesson Plans folder located in the Teaching Resources.

Economics Journal

Instruct students to write their responses to the question in their Economics Journals. Students may include completed journal entries in an Economics Portfolio.

Chapter 2 Economic Systems

A system is a way of doing something. The trains, tracks, platforms, routes, and schedules of a subway system move people around a city. Our education system teaches us reading, writing, and arithmetic. Economic systems enable societies to produce and distribute goods and services.

Economics Journal

Make a list of all the different systems you used yesterday. How would your day have been different without these systems?

Go Online PHSchool.com

For: Current Data
Visit: PHSchool.com
Web Code: mng-1021

NCEE National Council on Economic Education

The following Voluntary National Content Standards in Economics are addressed in this chapter:

★ **Standard 3** Students will understand that: Different methods can be used to allocate goods and services. People, acting individually or collectively through government, must choose which methods to use to allocate different kinds of goods and services.

★ **Standard 4** Students will understand that: People respond predictably to positive and negative incentives.

For more information about the standards, contact the National Council on Economic Education

1140 Avenue of the Americas
New York, NY 10036
1-800-338-1192

Answering the Three Economic Questions

Preview

Objectives

After studying this section you will be able to:

1. **Identify** the three key economic questions of what to produce, how to produce, and who consumes what is produced.
2. **Analyze** the societal values that determine how a country answers the three economic questions.
3. **Explain** the characteristics of traditional, command, and market economies and describe the societal values that influence them.

Section Focus

All societies must answer three key economic questions about the production and consumption of goods and services. How a society answers these questions depends on how much it values different economic goals. Four different economic systems have developed in response to these three questions.

Key Terms

economic system
factor payments
patriotism
safety net
standard of living
traditional economy
market economy
centrally planned economy
command economy
mixed economy

In Chapter 1, you read about the economic concept of scarcity—that we cannot have all that we want or need. Indeed, in some places in the world, people cannot even meet their basic needs for food, clothing, and shelter because their resources are too scarce. Scarcity forces societies and nations to answer some hard economic questions. Different economic systems have evolved in response to the problem of scarcity. An **economic system** is the method used by a society to produce and distribute goods and services. Which economic system a society employs depends on that society's goals and values.

economic system *the method used by a society to produce and distribute goods and services*

Three Key Economic Questions

Because economic resources are limited, every society must answer three key economic questions:

- What goods and services should be produced?
- How should these goods and services be produced?
- Who consumes these goods and services?

What Goods and Services Should Be Produced?

Each society must decide what to produce in order to satisfy its needs and wants. In today's complex societies, it is often difficult to distinguish between needs and wants. While it may be obvious that we need food and shelter, modern societies face additional important considerations. How much of our resources should we devote to national defense, education, public health and welfare, or consumer goods? Which consumer goods should we produce?

Recall the guns-and-butter trade-off described in Chapter 1. Because of our limited resources, each production decision that a society makes comes at an opportunity cost.

How Should Goods and Services Be Produced?

The next question we face is how to use our resources to produce goods and services. For example, should we produce electricity with oil, solar power, or nuclear power? Should teachers have classes of 20 students or 50 students? Should we produce food on large corporate farms or on small family farms?

Graphing the Main Idea

Economic Systems To build understanding of the concept of **economic systems,** have students use a tree map graphic organizer like the one at the right. Students should place the label "Economic Systems" in the top box, the labels "Traditional," "Market," "Centrally Planned," and "Mixed" in the next row of boxes, and details about each type of economy in the row below.

Section Reading Support Transparencies A template and the answers for this graphic organizer can be found in Chapter 2, Section 1 of the Section Reading Support Transparency System.

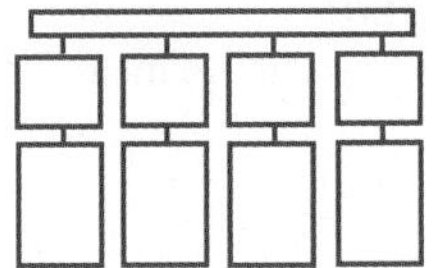

Section 1

Answering the Three Economic Questions

Objectives You may wish to call students' attention to the objectives in the Section Preview. The objectives are reflected in the main headings of the section.

Bellringer Display the following terms: *producer, product, market,* and *consumer.* Ask students to define each term and give related examples for each term. Explain that in this section they will learn how these four forces interact in different economic systems.

Vocabulary Builder Have students write the key terms for Section 1 in their Economics Journals. As they encounter each term in the text and learn its meaning, have them add the definition, a brief example, and a simple illustration.

Lesson Plan

Teaching the Main Concepts (L3)

1. Focus Tell students that each of them plays a vital role in the nation's economy. Ask them what roles they think they play.

2. Instruct Discuss with students what they know about different economies. Explain that all human societies must answer the three key economic questions. Describe the various economic systems. Lead students to understand that although they are learning about distinct economic systems, most countries operate under a mix of systems.

3. Close/Reteach Have each student research the economy of a different country. Then have the class compile a chart showing which type of economy each country uses to illustrate that most economies today are mixed economies.

Guided Reading and Review Unit 1 folder, p. 13 asks students to identify the main ideas of the section and to define or identify key terms.

Differentiated Instruction L4

Remind students that toward the end of the twentieth century, salaries soared for the top executives of major corporations, with some executives earning more in a year than many of their employees would earn in a lifetime. Ask, "Why do you think factor payments vary so widely? Should standards be adopted, and if so, who should determine them?" GT

Transparency Resource Package Economics Concepts, 2A: Three Key Economic Questions

Differentiated Instruction L1

Have students cut out photos of sale items from newspapers or magazines. The items should range widely in price from houses and cars to food items. Divide the photos and place them on two tables. Then randomly give each person in half the class an "income" note ranging from $100,000 down to $50. Allow these students one-at-a-time to come to the table and "purchase" as much as they can, (estimating values) Then invite the other students to come to the table one-at-a-time and distribute the items as equally as possible, after removing three or four of the most expensive for the teacher. Explain the difference between a free market and command system. SN

Today, capital–not labor–dominates the answer to how wheat is produced.

Opportunity Cost **Identify the opportunity costs of each method of farming.**

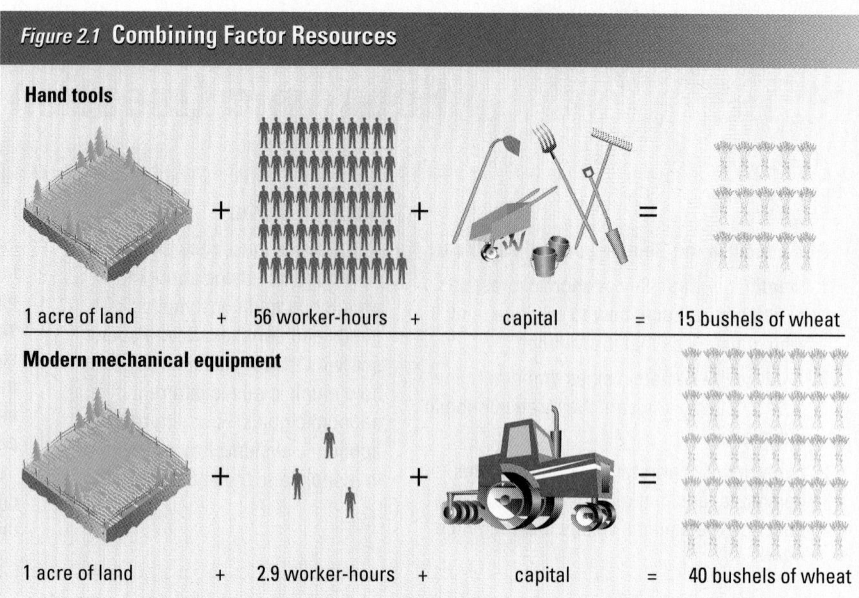

factor payments *the income people receive for supplying factors of production, such as land, labor, or capital*

Although there are countless ways to create all of the things we want and need, all require land, labor, and capital. These factors of production can be combined in different ways. For example, examine the chart above (Figure 2.1). Before the introduction of modern farming equipment, a typical combination of resources for producing 15 bushels of wheat was 56 hours of labor, 1 acre of land, and simple hand tools. With today's mechanical farming equipment, farming is much more efficient. Forty bushels of wheat can be harvested from one acre of land with just 2.9 worker-hours of labor.

Who Consumes Goods and Services?

In recent years, the top 25 goods manufacturers in the United States have launched an average of 13 new products each day. Retail stores, which 50 years ago typically carried about 3,000 items, now offer about 30,000 different products. American farms produce 315 million metric tons of wheat, rice, and corn and maintain about 180 million head of livestock. Despite this staggering output, quantities are not unlimited.

How does this abundance get divided up? Who gets to drive a new luxury car and who can only afford a subway pass? Who attends a concert and who stays home? Who eats a well-balanced diet and who eats nothing but hot dogs for every meal? Who gets access to a good education? Societies must decide how to distribute the available goods and services.

The answer to the question of distribution is determined by how societies choose to distribute income. **Factor payments** are the income people receive for supplying factors of production—land, labor, capital, or entrepreneurship. Landowners receive rent, workers receive wages, and those who lend money to build factories or buy machinery receive payments called interest. Entrepreneurs earn profits if their enterprises succeed.

How much should we pay the owners of the factors of production? How do we decide how much a particular piece of land is worth, how much teachers should earn versus how much doctors should earn, or what the interest rate should be?

The question of who gets to consume which goods and services lies at the very

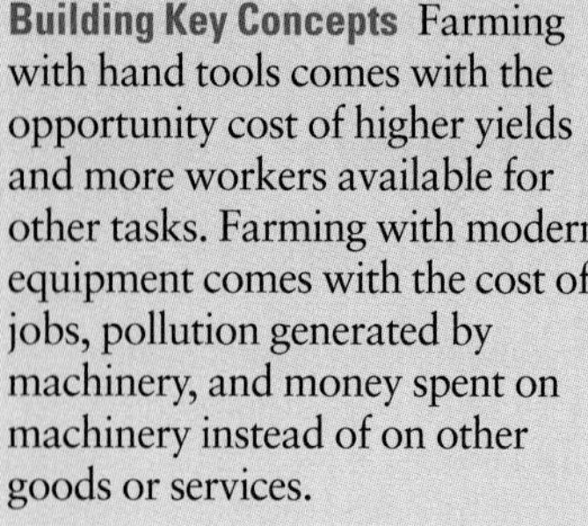

Answer to . . .

Building Key Concepts Farming with hand tools comes with the opportunity cost of higher yields and more workers available for other tasks. Farming with modern equipment comes with the cost of jobs, pollution generated by machinery, and money spent on machinery instead of on other goods or services.

Econ 101: Key Concepts Made Easy

Government One of the key concepts in this section is the notion of a **safety net,** a set of government programs to protect people in unfavorable economic conditions. Students may think that this applies only to those who are poor or unemployed. Stress that the various safety nets provided by the government are meant to help all citizens—poor, middle-class, or wealthy—in times of crisis. Ask students to create a list of safety net programs offered by the government. Tell them to be sure to include programs that operate during both good times and bad, such as Social Security.

heart of the differences between economic systems today. Each society answers the question of distribution based on its unique combination of social values and goals.

Economic Goals and Societal Values

Different societies answer the three economic questions based on the importance they attach to various economic goals. Figure 2.2 lists some general economic goals that most economic systems try to address. Bear in mind that societies pursue each of these goals, to some degree, at the expense of the others.

Economic Efficiency

Because resources are always scarce—that is, they always involve an opportunity cost—most societies try to maximize what they can get for the resources they have to work with. If a society can accurately assess what to produce, it increases its economic efficiency. A manufacturer would be wasting resources producing record albums if people prefer to buy CDs. Knowing the best way to produce a product cuts waste, too. Of course, in the end, products need to reach consumers. An economy that can't deliver goods isn't efficient.

Economic Freedom

Most of us value the opportunity to make our own choices. How do you feel about laws that keep you from earning an income? What about laws that forbid you to make certain purchases or possess certain items? The economic systems of different nations allow different degrees of economic freedoms. In general, however, people all over the world face limitations on economic freedom.

In the United States, the economic freedoms that we as Americans enjoy are an important reason for our patriotism. **Patriotism** is the love of one's country—the passion that inspires a person to serve his or her country, either in defending it from invasion or protecting its rights and maintaining its laws and institutions. The freedoms that allow any American who so chooses to become an entrepreneur, for example, are continuing sources of pride and patriotism.

Economic Security and Predictability

Most people don't like uncertainty. We want to know that we can get milk and bread every time we go to the grocery store, or that the gas pumps will be full when we

patriotism *the love of one's country; the passion that inspires a person to serve his or her country*

This family (left) will need to rebuild their home after a devastating hurricane. Government **Which economic goal could help them recover from the storm?**

Figure 2.2 Economic Goals

Economic efficiency	Making the most of resources
Economic freedom	Freedom from government intervention in the production and distribution of goods and services
Economic security and predictability	Assurance that goods and services will be available, payments will be made on time, and a safety net will protect individuals in times of economic disaster
Economic equity	Fair distribution of wealth
Economic growth and innovation	Innovation leads to economic growth, and economic growth leads to a higher standard of living.
Other goals	Societies pursue additional goals, such as environmental protection.

Block Scheduling Strategies

Consider these suggestions to take advantage of extended class time:

- Extend the Vocabulary Builder on p. 23 by having students write each of their definitions or examples of the key terms on a different piece of paper. Have students form teams for a quiz show; let them take turns identifying which key term each definition or example represents.
- Extend the Focus portion of the Lesson Plan on p. 23 by asking students to create a chart showing all the roles they play in the economy as producers and consumers. Ask students to use specific examples from their everyday lives.
- Have pairs of students work through the case study on Berry Gordy and complete the Free Enterprise Activity in the Case Studies in Free Enterprise folder, pp. 4–5. Ask small groups to present brief marketing plans based on their research.

Background

Consumer Preferences

Statistics on the sales of recorded music in recent years reflect consumers' increasing preference for compact discs (CDs) over cassettes. For example, 46.5 percent of all recorded music sold in 1992 was in the form of CDs, followed by cassettes at 43.6 percent. Five years later, in 1997, CDs made up 70.2 percent of all recorded music sold, whereas cassettes made up only 18.2 percent. By 2002 the sale of CDs had risen to 90.5 percent. Cassette sales, on the other hand, had dropped to a mere 2.4 percent.

Transparency Resource Package Economics Concepts, 2B: Economic Goals

Differentiated Instruction 

Ask students to create posters that explain the three key economic questions and the basic economic goals presented in Section 1. Posters should include both words and illustrations to clarify concept.

Differentiated Instruction 

Ask students to write a sentence that summarizes the content under each subhead in Section 1. *(For "Economic Efficiency" students might write: "Societies strive for efficiency; they try to maximize what they can get for the resources they have.")* LPR

Answer to . . .

Building Key Concepts The goals of efficiency and economic security and predictability would help most.

Background

Economics in History

The Fair Labor Standards Act of 1938 stipulated that certain workers had to be paid a minimum hourly wage, which was initially set at $0.25 an hour. Since then, the numbers and types of workers covered by this law have expanded, and the hourly minimum wage has steadily increased. However, in the late 1960s and early 1970s, the purchasing power of the minimum wage began to decrease due to inflation. For example, in February 1968 the minimum wage was raised to $1.60 an hour. In 1996 dollars, the purchasing power of that $1.60 was $7.21. By January 1980 the minimum wage had risen to $3.10 an hour, but its purchasing power was down to $5.90. In April 1990 the minimum wage was $3.50, or $0.40 an hour higher, but its purchasing power had slid to $4.56.

Differentiated Instruction L3

Ask students to identify the four economic systems presented in Section 1. Then have each student write an essay detailing the similarities and differences between any two of the systems.

Transparency Resource Package Economics Concepts, 2C: Comparing Economic Systems

Economic Cartoon Unit 1 folder, p. 25 gives students practice in interpreting cartoons about section content.

safety net *government programs that protect people experiencing unfavorable economic conditions*

standard of living *level of economic prosperity*

traditional economy *economic system that relies on habit, custom, or ritual to decide questions of production and consumption of goods and services*

go to gas up our cars. We want to feel confident that we will get our paychecks every payday. Ideally, economic systems reassure people that goods and services will be available when they need them and that they can count on receiving expected payments on time.

We also want the security of knowing that help is available if we are elderly, poor, unemployed, or facing some other potential economic disadvantage. Most people feel that the government should provide some kind of **safety net,** or set of government programs that protect people experiencing unfavorable economic conditions. These include injuries, layoffs, natural disasters, or severe shortages. Most countries also believe in providing some sort of base income for retired persons to ensure that older people can support themselves after retirement.

Economic Equity

Each society must decide the best way to divide its economic pie. What constitutes a fair share? Should everyone get the same, or should one's consumption depend on how much one produces? How much should society provide for those who are unable or unwilling to produce?

Many people believe in equal pay for equal work, but society does not value all jobs equally. Most lawyers earn more than most nurses. Most computer programmers earn more than most truck drivers. Not everyone is able to work. How should we provide for the ill and infirm?

Economic Growth and Innovation

A nation's economy must grow for a nation to improve its **standard of living,** or level of economic prosperity. This is especially true if a country's population is growing. The economy also must grow to provide new jobs and income for people.

Innovation plays a huge role in economic growth. Think of the changes brought about by the shift from nomadism to agriculture, from the agricultural age to the industrial age, from the industrial age to the information age. Innovations in technology increase the efficiency of production and usher in new goods and services. In your lifetime, you are witnessing innovations in computer and networking technology that are changing the ways people work, shop, conduct business, locate information, and communicate.

Additional Goals

A society may value goals in addition to those described above. Environmental protection, full employment, universal medical care, and other important concerns may be among a nation's chief economic goals.

All nations must prioritize their economic goals, or arrange them in order of importance. No matter how a nation prioritizes its goals, one fact remains: achieving any economic goal comes only with some kind of economic trade-off.

▼ **The traditional economy of Guatemala's Quiché Maya includes regular market days.**

Economies and Values

Four different economic systems have developed to address the three key economic questions. Each system reflects a different prioritization of economic goals. It also reflects the values of the societies in which these systems are present.

Traditional Economies

A **traditional economy** relies on habit, custom, or ritual to decide what to

Preparing for Standardized Tests

Have students read the section titled "Economic Growth and Innovation" and then answer the question below.

According to the text, which of the following is a benefit of economic growth?

(A) The standard of living improves.

B Nomadism declines.

C Economic equity is increased.

D The economy becomes more predictable.

produce, how to produce it, and to whom to distribute it. There is little room for innovation or change. The traditional economic system revolves around the family. Work tends to be divided along gender lines. Boys tend to take up the occupations of their fathers, while girls follow in the footsteps of their mothers.

Traditional economies are usually communities that tend to stay relatively small and close. Often these societies work to support entire groups, rather than just themselves or their immediate families. Agricultural and hunting practices usually lie at the very heart of the people's lives, laws, and religious beliefs.

Societies with traditional economies have few mechanisms in place to deal effectively with the effects of environmental disaster, such as a flood or drought. They also tend to remain stagnant, resisting change at both the individual and community level. They may be slow to adopt new technology or radical new ideas. They may not have access to goods you see every day at the grocery store. In most cases, these communities lack modern conveniences and have a low standard of living.

Market Economies

In a **market economy,** economic decisions are made by individuals and are based on exchange, or trade. The choices made by individuals determine what gets made and how, as well as who consumes the goods and services produced. Market economies are also called free markets, or capitalism. You will read about the free market in detail in Section 2.

Command Economies

In a **centrally planned economy,** the central government alone decides how to answer all three key economic questions. Centrally planned economies are sometimes called **command economies,** because a central authority is in command of the economy. Section 3 discusses the theories behind centrally planned economies.

Mixed Economies

Most modern economies are **mixed economies**—market-based economic systems in which government plays a limited role. Section 4 describes the reasons for mixed economies and the various ways government is involved in such economies.

market economy *economic system in which decisions on production and consumption of goods and services are based on voluntary exchange in markets*

centrally planned economy *economic system in which the central government makes all decisions on the production and consumption of goods and services*

command economy *economic system in which a central authority is in command of the economy; a centrally planned economy*

mixed economy *market-based economic system with limited government involvement*

Section 1 Assessment

Progress Monitoring *Online*
For: Self-quiz with vocabulary practice
Web Code: mna-1025

Key Terms and Main Ideas

1. What is an **economic system?**
2. How do a **traditional economy,** a **market economy,** a **command economy,** and a **mixed economy** differ?
3. Why aren't all people paid the same amount in **factor payments** for the resources they provide? Provide your own example of two unequal factor payments.
4. Why do governments provide **safety nets** for their citizens?
5. Give at least one example of a traditional, a command, and a market economic system.

Applying Economic Concepts

6. *Using the Databank* Examine the graph "Government Spending, by Category" on page 543. Based on the information in the graph, identify what you think are some economic goals of the United States.
7. *Critical Thinking* Create a chart in which you list the societal values of each of the four economic systems described in the section.
8. *Try This* You and your friends decide to earn money by washing cars. How are the three economic questions answered in this market?

For: Research Activity
Visit: PHSchool.com
Web Code: mnd-1021

GTE Guide to the Essentials
Chapter 2, Section 1, p. 6 provides support for students who need additional review of the section content. Spanish support is available in the Spanish edition of the guide on p. 6.

Quiz Unit 1 folder, p. 14 includes questions to check students' understanding of Section 1 content.

Presentation Pro CD-ROM
Quiz provides multiple-choice questions to check students' understanding of Section 1 content.

Answers to . . .

Section 1 Assessment

1. An economic system is the way in which a society decides to produce and distribute goods and services.
2. The differences between the economic systems arise from the ways that each system answers production and distribution questions.
3. Factor payments differ because societies place different values on different resources and products. A possible example is doctors' wages compared to sanitation workers' wages.
4. Governments provide safety nets to fulfill the goal of economic security and predictability.
5. Answers may include: the Amish (traditional), Cuba (command), and the United States (market).
6. Students may suggest military security and a high standard of living for citizens.
7. traditional economy—values custom rather than innovation; market economy—values individual freedom, growth, efficiency; centrally planned economy—values economic equity, security; mixed economy—values economic freedom, limited government involvement
8. service to be produced—car washing; how it is produced—by my friends and me; consumers—people who want to have their cars washed

Progress Monitoring *Online*
For additional assessment, have students access Progress Monitoring Online at **Web Code:** mna-1025

Go Online PHSchool.com Typing in the Web Code when prompted will bring students directly to detailed instructions for this activity.

Section 2

The Free Market

Objectives You may wish to call students' attention to the objectives in the Section Preview. The objectives are reflected in the main headings of the section.

Bellringer Ask students what comes to mind when they hear the term *self-interest*. Explain that in this section they will learn how self-interest motivates the marketplace.

Vocabulary Builder Ask students to define each key term in their own words and then check their definitions against what they read in Section 2. Then have them explain how each term is related to the free market.

Lesson Plan

Teaching the Main Concepts (L3)

1. Focus Tell students that from the moment they came into the world, their wants and needs were a part of the free market—even when they were being fulfilled by a parent. Have students suggest ways that newborn babies affect the free market.

2. Instruct Discuss with students the nature of markets and their importance to economic systems. Explain that in a free market economy, producers and consumers interact freely, each in his or her own self-interest, to regulate aspects of the market. Be sure that students understand that freedom and self-interest combine to create a marketplace that satisfies most economic goals.

3. Close/Reteach Remind students that although a pure free market offers many benefits, it fails to achieve some economic goals. Have small groups create charts listing the advantages and disadvantages of allowing self-interest and competition to guide the market.

Guided Reading and Review
Unit 1 folder, p. 15 asks students to identify the main ideas of the section and to define or identify key terms.

Section 2 The Free Market

Preview

Objectives

After studying this section you will be able to:

1. **Explain** why markets exist.
2. **Analyze** a circular flow model of a free market economy.
3. **Understand** the self-regulating nature of the marketplace.
4. **Identify** the advantages of a free market economy.

Section Focus

Markets exist so that people can exchange what they have for what they want. A free market is a self-regulating economic system directed by individuals acting in their own self-interest.

Key Terms

market
specialization
household
firm
factor market
profit
product market
self-interest
incentive
competition
invisible hand
consumer sovereignty

market *an arrangement that allows buyers and sellers to exchange things*

What do a farmers' market, a sporting goods store, the New York Stock Exchange, and the sign you posted on your community bulletin board advertising baby-sitting services have in common? All are examples of markets. A **market** is an arrangement that allows buyers and sellers to exchange things.

Why Markets Exist

Markets exist because no one is self-sufficient. In other words, none of us produces all we require to satisfy our needs and wants. You probably didn't grow the plants to make the fibers to weave the cloth to make the shirt you're wearing. Instead, you purchased your shirt at a store, which is an example of a market. Markets allow us to exchange the things we have for the things we want.

Specialization

Instead of being self-sufficient, each of us produces just one or a few products. A nurse specializes in caring for the sick. A

▶ **This Thai spice stand, Brazilian stock exchange, and Indian barber shop (left to right) are all examples of markets.**

Graphing the Main Idea

Economic Systems To build understanding of the concept of **economic systems,** have students use a web graphic organizer like the one at the right to describe circular flow. Tell students that a web shows a main idea and its supporting details. Explain that students should place the label "Circular Flow" in the central oval. In the surrounding ovals they should record how various parts of the system interact with each other.

Section Reading Support Transparencies A template and the answers for this graphic organizer can be found in Chapter 2, Section 2 of the Section Reading Support Transparency System.

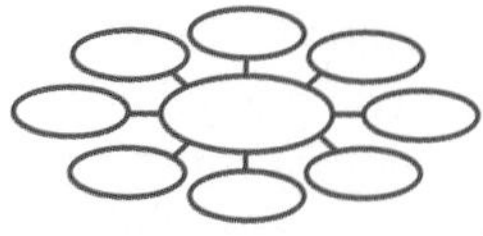

marine mechanic specializes in repairing machinery aboard sea craft. A baker specializes in making breads, cakes, and cookies. **Specialization** is the concentration of the productive efforts of individuals and firms on a limited number of activities.

Specialization leads to efficient use of resources, including capital, land, and labor. It is easier to learn one task or a few tasks very well than to learn them all.

Buying and Selling

Because each of us specializes in producing just a few products, we need markets to sell what we have and to buy what we want. The typical person earns an income (specializing at a particular job) and uses this income to buy the products that he or she wants to consume. If each person were self-sufficient, producing everything he or she wanted to consume, there would be no need for markets.

Free Market Economy

Economic systems that are based on voluntary exchanges in markets are called free market economies. In a free market economy, individuals and businesses use markets to exchange money and products.

In a free market system, individuals and privately owned businesses own the factors of production, make what they want, and buy what they want. In other words, individuals answer the three key economic questions of what to produce, how to produce it, and who consumes that which is produced. As you might guess, a free market economy functions best in an environment of decentralized decision-making such as enjoyed in the United States.

We can represent a free market economy in a special kind of drawing called a circular flow diagram, or model. A circular flow diagram shows at a glance how individuals and businesses exchange money, resources, and products in the marketplace. Figure 2.3 shows a circular flow diagram of a free market economy. The inner ring of the diagram represents the flow of resources and products. The outer ring represents the flow of money.

Households and Firms

The players in the free market economy are households and firms. A **household** is a person or group of people living in the same residence. Households own the factors of production—land, labor, and capital. Households are also the consumers of goods and services.

A business, or **firm,** is an organization that uses resources to produce a product, which it then sells. Firms transform "inputs," or factors of production, into "outputs," or products.

Factor Market

As you can see from the lower half of the circular flow diagram in Figure 2.3, firms purchase factors of production from households. This arena of exchange is called the **factor market.** Firms purchase or rent land (natural resources). They hire workers, paying them wages or salaries for their labor. They also borrow money from households to purchase capital, paying households interest or profits in return. **Profit** is the financial gain made in a transaction.

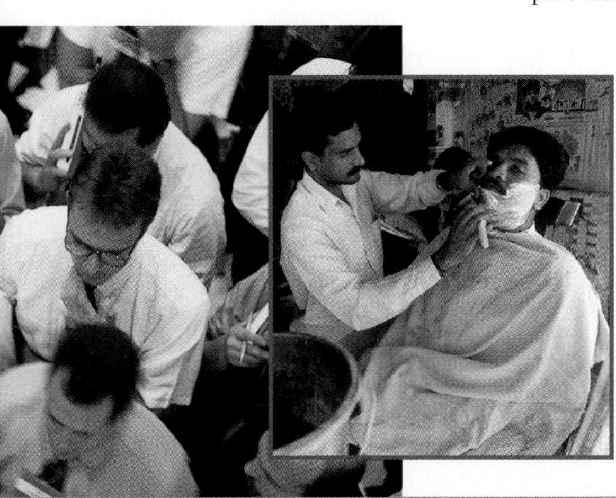

Product Market

Take a close look at the top half of the circular flow diagram in

specialization *the concentration of the productive efforts of individuals and firms on a limited number of activities*

household *a person or group of people living in the same residence*

firm *an organization that uses resources to produce a product, which it then sells*

factor market *market in which firms purchase the factors of production from households*

profit *the financial gain made in a transaction*

Background

Economics in History

From the earliest days of trading between societies, markets were located where the transportation was, usually near seaports and rivers. The importance of transportation to markets can be illustrated by the rise and fall of one of Europe's most active market centers—Brugge, Belgium. This city is sometimes referred to by its French name, Bruges.

Although not located on the coast, Brugge was connected to the North Sea by a canal called the Zwyn. By the 1300s Brugge was not only an international trading center but a financial center as well.

In the 1400s competition from the harbor at Antwerp began to diminish Brugge's importance, but the city was hurt most by the continual accumulation of silt in the Zwyn. Eventually the Zwyn completely silted over, and Brugge lost its connection to the sea. By the end of the 1500s, Brugge had ceased to be a center for trade in Europe. Today its economy is dependent mainly on tourism.

Differentiated Instruction 

(Reteaching) Ask students to write a paragraph that explains why markets exist, giving real-life examples of the reasons provided. *(An example of the reason "people are not self-sufficient" would be "I cannot grow all of my own food.")*

Differentiated Instruction 

To help students understand a circular flow diagram, designate a desk on one side of the room as a "household" and a desk on the other side of the room as a "firm." Have volunteers, holding labels that say "Goods and Services" and "Land, Labor, and Capital," act out the principles of circular flow. Ask students to relate this kinesthetic activity to the self-regulating nature of the marketplace.

Econ 101: Key Concepts Made Easy

Economic Systems One of the key concepts in this section is the **invisible hand,** an idea that students may find confusing. Explain that the "invisible hand" is the interaction between self-interest and competition that acts as a force to set the price of goods and services.

Ask students to think about the introduction of an innovative electronic product, such as a high-definition television. Explain that initially the price is high because the product is new and may have little or no competition. When and if consumers decide that they want this new technology, producers begin competing to manufacture the most appealing version. This competition causes the price to moderate, because price is part of a product's appeal. The price will continue to drop until it reaches a level that offers producers an acceptable profit and consumers an affordable product.

Differentiated Instruction L3

You may wish to have students add the following to their portfolios. Ask students what they plan to do after graduation. Will they get jobs, go to college, travel, start their own businesses? Tell students to write a paragraph about how their choices are motivated by self-interest. Then ask them to think about the specifics of their choices. Which college? Where will they travel? What kind of job or business? Ask them to write a second paragraph explaining how these choices are also motivated by self-interest. Finally, ask them to write a third paragraph explaining how their self-interest might be affected by competition.

Economics Assessment Rubric
Economics Assessment Rubrics folder, pp. 6–7 provides sample evaluation materials for a writing assignment.

Transparency Resource Package
Economics Concepts, 2D: Circular Flow Diagram of a Market Economy

Differentiated Instruction L2

English language learners may benefit from completing the Student Portfolio activity on this page orally. ELL

BUILDING KEY CONCEPTS

A circular flow model shows the interactions between households and businesses in the free market.

Economic Systems
What is exchanged in the factor market? In the product market?

Figure 2.3 **Circular Flow Model of a Market Economy**

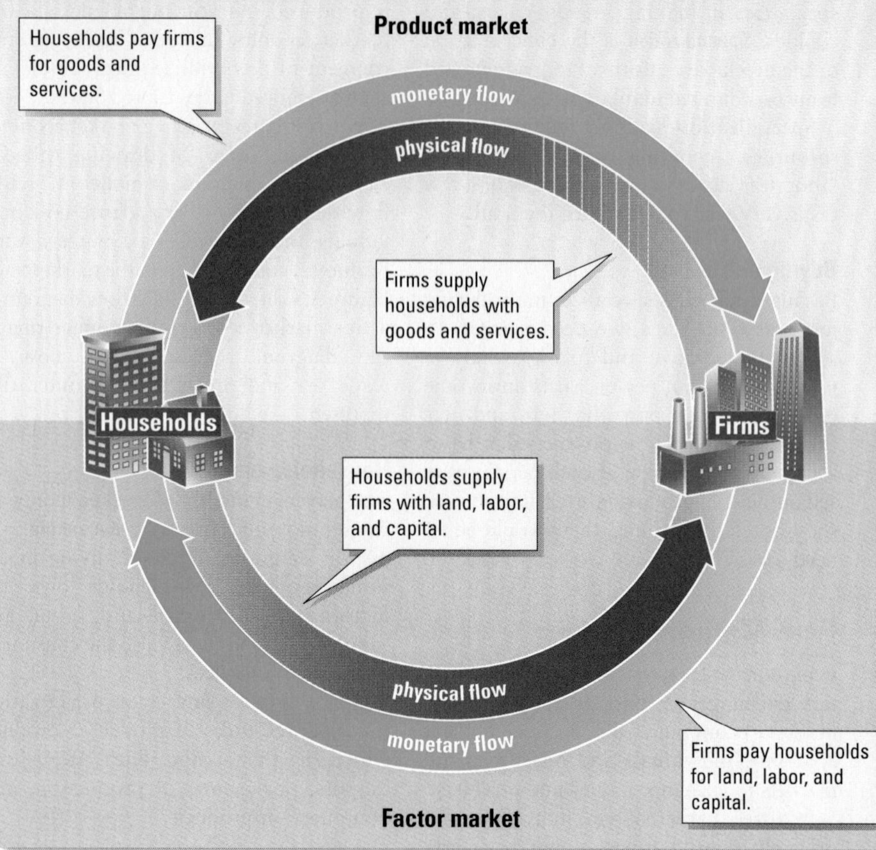
Product market
Households pay firms for goods and services.
monetary flow
physical flow
Firms supply households with goods and services.
Households
Firms
Households supply firms with land, labor, and capital.
physical flow
monetary flow
Firms pay households for land, labor, and capital.
Factor market

product market
the market in which households purchase the goods and services that firms produce

Figure 2.3. You can see that the goods and services that firms produce are purchased by households in the **product market.**

If you follow the rings of the diagram, you will see that households purchase the products made by firms with the money they received from firms in the factor market. The flow between the factor market and the product market is truly circular.

The Self-Regulating Nature of the Marketplace

How is it that firms and households cooperate to give each other what they want—factor resources, in the case of firms, and products, in the case of households? As anyone knows who has tried out for the track team, a part in a play, or has applied for a job or to a college, we live in a competitive society. According to Adam Smith, it is, in fact, competition and our own self-interest that keep the marketplace functioning.

Self-Interest

Adam Smith was a Scottish social philosopher who, in 1776, published a book titled *The Wealth of Nations,* in which he described how the market functions. Smith observed that an economy is made up of countless individual transactions. In each transaction, the buyer and seller consider

Block Scheduling Strategies

Consider these suggestions to take advantage of extended class time:

- Show the Economics Video Library segment "Internet Impact," about the Internet as a perfect free market situation. Then hold a discussion of how the Internet benefits both consumers and businesses. Ask students also to examine possible negative effects of the Internet on these groups.
- Expand the Meeting NCEE Standards activity on p. 31 into a group activity. Organize the class into four groups, one representing each individual noted. Have each group brainstorm a list of incentives for that individual. Then ask students to choose five incentives and to show how they would benefit the economy of the United States as a whole. Allow time for the groups to present their incentives and benefits to the class.

Answer to . . .

Building Key Concepts Firms purchase factors of production from households in the factor market, and households purchase goods and services from firms in the product market.

only their **self-interest**, or their own personal gain. Self-interest, in other words, is the motivating force in the free market.

"Son, your mother and I have decided to let the free market take care of you."

▲ **How could the free market take care of this young man?**

Competition

Consumers (households), in pursuit of their self-interest, have the incentive to look for lower prices. An **incentive** is the hope of reward or the fear of punishment that encourages a person to behave in a certain way. Adam Smith observed that people respond predictably to both positive and negative incentives. As for consumers, we can predict that they will respond to the positive incentive of lower prices, because spending less money on a good lowers the opportunity cost of the purchase.

Firms, meanwhile, seek to make greater profits by increasing sales. Let's take, for example, a shirt manufacturer. The manufacturer finds that striped shirts are far outselling polka-dotted shirts. The manufacturer has the incentive—from more potential sales and profits—to produce more striped shirts. Other manufacturers, observing consumers' desire for striped shirts, also have the incentive to sell them. With all these manufacturers in the market, consumers have all the striped shirts they want.

Manufacturers also have a second incentive—to make the most profit in selling striped shirts. What keeps manufacturers' pursuit of profit from causing prices to skyrocket? If one begins charging $30.00 for a striped shirt, another can sell striped shirts for $25.00. If the first manufacturer wants to sell any more striped shirts, he or she had better drop the selling price. Consumers, pursuing their self-interest, will buy the lower-priced shirt. Economists call this struggle among producers for the dollars of consumers **competition.** While self-interest is the motivating force behind the free market, competition is the regulating force.

Incentives come in two forms. Profit is a *monetary* incentive, or an incentive that rewards in the form of money. *Nonmonetary* incentives reward consumers and business in other ways, such as gifts, services, and other goods.

self-interest *one's own personal gain*

incentive *an expectation that encourages people to behave in a certain way*

competition *the struggle among producers for the dollars of consumers*

The Invisible Hand

Self-interest and competition work together to regulate the marketplace. Self-interest spurs consumers to purchase certain goods

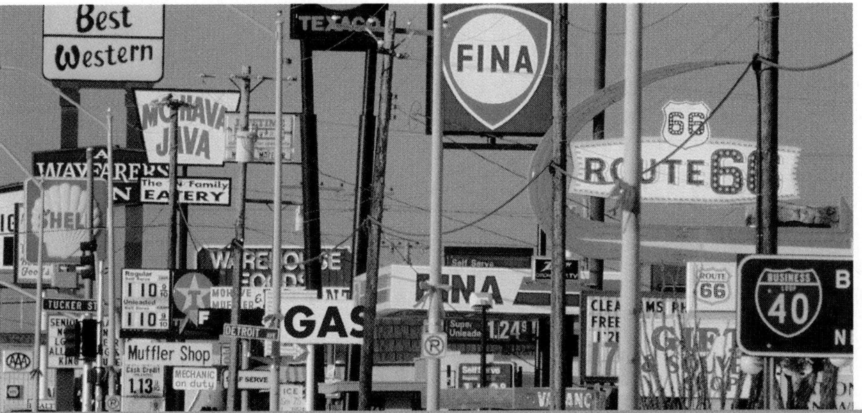

◀ **Competing businesses scream for the attention of consumers.**

Meeting NCEE Standards

Use the following benchmark activity from the **Voluntary National Content Standards in Economics** to evaluate student understanding of **Standard 4.**

Compare and contrast the incentives an individual might face in serving as an elected official, the owner of a small business, the president of a large company, and the director of a local United Way office.

Differentiated Instruction  L2

Ask students to write and illustrate a simplified version of the "striped shirts versus polka-dotted shirts" scenario on this page to demonstrate their understanding of competition. Guide this activity by engaging students in a prewriting discussion of what to do. LPR

Learning Styles Activity

Learning Styles Lesson Plans folder, p. 9 asks students to present panel discussions demonstrating the strengths and shortcomings of the free market in the United States.

Differentiated Instruction  L3

(Reteaching) After students have read the section, ask pairs of students to create an advertisement for the free market, highlighting its advantages. Encourage them to think creatively.

Preparing for Standardized Tests

Have students read the section titled "Competition" and then answer the question below.

Which of the following is an accurate definition of *competition?*

A the hope of reward that encourages a person to behave in a certain way
(B) the struggle among producers for the dollars of consumers
C the financial gain made in a transaction
D an organization that uses resources to produce a product

Answer to . . .

Cartoon Caption He could sell his labor in the factor market and use the income he earns to make purchases in the product market.

GTE Guide to the Essentials
Chapter 2, Section 2, p. 7 provides support for students who need additional review of the section content. Spanish support is available in the Spanish edition of the guide on p. 7.

Quiz Unit 1 folder, p. 16 includes questions to check students' understanding of Section 2 content.

Presentation Pro CD-ROM
Quiz provides multiple-choice questions to check students' understanding of Section 2 content.

Answers to . . .

Section 2 Assessment

1. Specialization allows each of us to focus on individual tasks and not worry about all of our basic needs at once, thus making us more efficient.
2. Factor markets provide goods and services that are necessary to produce more goods and services, whereas product markets provide finished goods to consumers.
3. Profit is the financial gain made in a transaction.
4. Households provide the factors of production in factor markets and the buying power in product markets; firms are the buyers of factors of production and the suppliers of goods and services.
5. Competition benefits consumers by causing firms to sell higher-quality goods at lower prices.
6. Smith meant that the combination of consumers' self-interest and competition among firms would naturally lead to an economy in which consumers can buy products they want at reasonable prices.
7. Consumer sovereignty has to do with the power that consumers have to choose what they will buy, so that they exert control over what is produced by creating the incentive for firms to produce high-quality goods and services.
8. Economic equity is difficult to achieve in a free market economy because not every person functions in the market with the same skills and abilities, and therefore differences in compensation arise.
9. Students should complete the activity and present data on the results. Students should find that they can make more fold-its when they specialize.

FAST FACT

***Self-interest** and the **free market** will provide social services—if there's a **profit** to be gained. One large temporary employee agency recruits and trains workers from the ranks of the urban poor. Bypassing the social-welfare agencies that are charged with getting people off public assistance, it finds work for individuals and employees for businesses, and makes a **profit** for itself.*

and services and firms to produce them. Competition causes more production and moderates firms' quests for higher prices. The overall result is that consumers get the products they want at prices that closely reflect the cost of producing them. All of this happens without any central plan or direction. Adam Smith called this phenomenon "the **invisible hand** of the marketplace."

Advantages of the Free Market

Competition and the pursuit of self-interest serve the public interest. The free market, on its own, meets many economic goals.

invisible hand *term economists use to describe the self-regulating nature of the marketplace*

consumer sovereignty *the power of consumers to decide what gets produced*

1. *Economic efficiency* Because it is self-regulating, a free market economy responds efficiently to rapidly changing conditions. Producers make only what consumers want, when they want it, and generally at prices they are willing to pay.
2. *Economic freedom* Free market economies have the highest degree of economic freedom of any system. This includes the freedom of workers to work where they want, of firms to produce what they want, and of individuals to consume what they want.
3. *Economic growth* Because competition encourages innovation, free markets encourage growth. Entrepreneurs are always seeking profitable opportunities, contributing new ideas and innovations.
4. *Additional goals* Free markets offer a wider variety of goods and services than any other system, because producers have incentives to meet consumers' desires. Consumers, in essence, decide what gets produced. This is called **consumer sovereignty.**

Despite its advantages, no pure market economy exists on any meaningful scale. The same features that make free markets attractive also represent the weaknesses of the free market. The goals of economic equity and economic security are difficult to achieve in a pure market system. In Section 4, you will read about how the free market system has been modified by various nations in order to better meet the entire array of economic goals.

Section 2 Assessment

Progress Monitoring *Online*
For: Self-quiz with vocabulary practice
Web Code: mna-1026

Key Terms and Main Ideas

1. How does **specialization** make us more efficient?
2. What is the difference between the **factor market** and the **product market?**
3. What is **profit?**
4. What are the roles of **households** and **firms** in a market economy?
5. How does **competition** among firms benefit consumers?
6. Explain what Adam Smith meant by "the **invisible hand** of the marketplace."
7. What is the connection between **incentives** and **consumer sovereignty** in a free market economy?

Applying Economic Concepts

8. ***Critical Thinking*** Why is economic equity difficult to achieve in a free market economy?
9. ***Try This*** You will need a stack of paper and two staplers. You and a friend create "fold-its" by folding each sheet of paper in thirds and stapling both ends. How many fold-its can you make in two minutes? Next, try specializing: one of you folds while the other staples. Now how many fold-its can you make in two minutes?
10. ***Critical Thinking*** Provide at least three real-world examples to illustrate the circular flow model of a market economy.

For: Current Events Activity
Visit: PHSchool.com
Web Code: mnd-1022

10. Answers should reflect an understanding that a change in one part of the economy will lead to a change elsewhere in the economy. For example, a frost in Florida will result in losses for orange juice manufacturers and higher prices for consumers.

Progress Monitoring *Online*
For additional assessment, have students access Progress Monitoring Online at **Web Code:** mna-1026

Go Online PHSchool.com Typing in the Web Code when prompted will bring students directly to detailed instructions for this activity.

ECONOMIC

Profile

Economist

Entrepreneur

Adam Smith (1723–1790)

One of the first people to offer an explanation of how a market economy works was the Scottish philosopher Adam Smith. Beginning in his early twenties, Smith enjoyed a long career teaching at universities in Scotland. Although more than a little absent-minded, Smith was adored by his students and respected by his fellow professors. More importantly, his ideas won him fame and influence across Britain.

The Wealth of Nations

Today, we most remember Adam Smith for the theories expressed in his book *The Wealth of Nations*. Published in 1776, *The Wealth of Nations* still stands as an authoritative description of how a market system can flourish.

In the book, Smith identifies land, labor, and capital as the factors of production that generate a nation's wealth. When the production of goods is divided into many steps, and workers specialize in only one step, productivity increases. Higher productivity increases the overall wealth of the nation.

Laissez Faire

Adam Smith also called for restricting the role of government in the economy. Smith insisted that government must leave individuals as free as possible to pursue their own interests if a market economy is to run smoothly. This policy is known as *laissez faire,* which means "let them do (as they please)." In Smith's view, individuals left alone to try to better themselves will produce a multiplication of riches: more jobs and more goods and services.

The Invisible Hand and Self-Interest

Adam Smith also noticed that businesses could provide the goods and services that consumers needed without the help of a central plan telling them what to do. How do they do it? Smith gave credit to an invisible hand.

In Smith's view, the invisible hand guides a nation's resources to their most productive use. One of the invisible hand's tools is self-interest. Individuals, each pursuing what is best for him or her, make decisions that ultimately benefit the nation.

For example, consumers can satisfy their self-interest by buying goods. Business people satisfy their self-interest by making the goods consumers want and selling them for a profit. As sales increase, businesses can raise prices. At this point the invisible hand takes over. Another person sees the profits and starts a competing business, charging a slightly lower price. Other businesses must follow if they want to keep their customers, and balance is restored to the market.

CHECK FOR UNDERSTANDING

1. Source Reading Rewrite the following passage from *The Wealth of Nations* in your own words: "It is not from the benevolence [kindness] of the butcher, the brewer, or the baker that we expect our dinner, but from their regard to their own interest."

2. Critical Thinking What are the forces that together comprise the invisible hand?

3. Learn More Conduct further research and describe the similarities between two 1776 publications: *The Wealth of Nations* and the Declaration of Independence.

ECONOMIC Profile
Adam Smith

Background

As a young man, Adam Smith won a scholarship to Oxford. The open system of the university allowed Oxford students to study and read what they pleased as long as the books that they chose were not deemed subversive. According to one anecdote, which may or may not be true, Smith was almost disciplined for reading David Hume's *A Treatise of Human Nature,* a philosophy book that Hume's contemporaries considered an atheistic heresy.

After leaving Oxford, Smith went home to Scotland and became a professor of logic, and then of moral philosophy, at the University of Glasgow. Later in his life he became a tutor and traveled to France, where he met and was influenced by Voltaire and François Quesnay, a doctor who developed early theories to explain how economic systems worked.

Careers in Economics Activity Unit 1 folder, p. 24 gives students a closer look at the career path of a financial reporter.

Databank, pp. 532–547 contains charts and graphs that can be used to illustrate the work of economists as well as to extend and reinforce skills.

Beyond the Classroom: Workplace Skills

Writing Tell students that the ability to write persuasively is important in many jobs. Explain that in the workplace, people often have to write formal proposals, letters, or memorandums to persuade others to take certain actions. Ask students to suggest why a company might prefer to read a written proposal for a new project rather than have a discussion about it. Elicit responses such as the following: *Companies might prefer written proposals because they can be copied and distributed to a large number of people.*

Answers to . . .

1. Smith is referring to the idea that the market will provide for people's needs with goods that individuals can sell at a fair price in their own best interests.
2. self-interest and competition
3. Answers will vary, but students should point out the centrality of economic and political freedom in both works.

Section 3

Centrally Planned Economies

Objectives You may wish to call students' attention to the objectives in the Section Preview. The objectives are reflected in the main headings.

Bellringer Ask students to imagine they are workers with guaranteed jobs in a centrally planned economy. They are told what and how much to produce and when to produce it. How deeply committed would they be to efficiency, quality, and innovation? Explain that in this section they will learn about the advantages and disadvantages of central planning.

Vocabulary Builder Ask students to read the definitions of the key terms in the margins of Section 3. Have students use each term in a sentence that makes its meaning clear.

Lesson Plan

Teaching the Main Concepts L3

1. Focus Explain that the breakup of the Soviet Union in 1991 was partly due to the collapse of its centrally planned economy. Ask students to speculate why centrally planned economies might be more vulnerable to sudden turmoil.

2. Instruct Discuss with students the features of a centrally planned economy. When discussing the Soviet Union, ask students to explain the reasons for shortages and shoddy construction. Lead them to see that central economic planning has serious flaws.

3. Close/Reteach Remind students that the collapse of the Soviet Union was partly due to the disadvantages of a centrally planned economy. Have students work in pairs to create tables comparing the advantages and disadvantages of a centrally planned economy and a free market economy.

Guided Reading and Review Unit 1 folder, p. 17 asks students to identify the main ideas of the section and to define or identify key terms.

Section 3 Centrally Planned Economies

Preview

Objectives

After studying this section you will be able to:

1. **Describe** how a centrally planned economy is organized.
2. **Analyze** the centrally planned economy of the former Soviet Union.
3. **Identify** the problems of a centrally planned economy.

Section Focus

In a centrally planned, or command, economy, the central government controls the economy. Central planning has limitations and disadvantages not found in market economies.

Key Terms

socialism
communism
authoritarian
collective
heavy industry

Centrally planned economies operate in direct contrast to free market systems. Centrally planned economies oppose private property, free market pricing, competition, and consumer choice.

How Is a Centrally Planned Economy Organized?

In a centrally planned economy, the central government, rather than individual producers and consumers in markets, answers the key economic questions of production and consumption. A central bureaucracy makes all the decisions about what items to produce, how to produce them, and who gets them. After collecting information, bureaucrats tell each firm what and how much to produce. It is up to the bureaucrats to ensure that each firm has enough raw materials and workers to meet its production goals.

Government Control of Factor Resources and Production

In a centrally planned economy, the government owns both land and capital. In a sense it owns labor, too, by controlling

▶ **Government posters in Cuba (left) and Cambodia (right) try to inspire worker productivity in these centrally planned economies.**

Building Key Concepts: Graphing the Main Idea

Economic Systems To build understanding of the concept of **economic systems,** have students fill in a multi-flow chart graphic organizer like the one at the right to record the advantages and disadvantages of a centrally planned economy. Have them place the label "Centrally Planned Economy" in the center. The advantages are located in the upper boxes, and the disadvantages in the lower boxes.

Section Reading Support Transparencies A template and the answers for this graphic organizer can be found in Chapter 2, Section 3 of the Section Reading Support Transparency System.

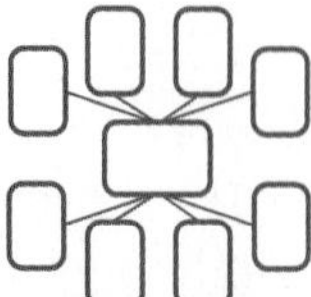

where individuals work and what wages they are paid. The government decides what to produce, how much to produce, and how much to charge. Each year, it directs workers to produce a certain number of trucks, so many yards of cotton fabric, a certain amount of glass, and so on. Farmers are told what to plant, how to plant, and where to send their crops. The free market forces of self-interest and competition are absent from the system.

For example, let's follow the decision-making process for the production of military uniforms and a consumer product—sweaters.

1. The top planners decide that more military uniforms than sweaters will be made. They send this decision to the materials committee.
2. Knowing how much cotton is available, the materials committee decides how many sweaters and how many military uniforms will be made. They send their decision to the cotton makers, the button makers, and the elastic makers.
3. The cotton, the buttons, and the elastic arrive at sweater factories and uniform factories where they are manufactured into sweaters and uniforms.

As you can see, decisions on what to produce and how much to produce are not determined by consumers. Chances are that many citizens living under this economy would still need new sweaters. This lack of consumer voice in production and distribution shows that under centrally planned economies, consumers do not have consumer sovereignty.

▲ **How would you describe production in this Romanian factory?**

Socialism and Communism

The words most often associated with centrally planned economies are *socialism* and *communism.* They are often used interchangeably, but we need to make a distinction between the two terms.

Socialism is a social and political philosophy based on the belief that democratic means should be used to distribute wealth evenly throughout a society. Real equality, socialists argue, can only exist when political equality is coupled with economic equality. Economic equality is possible only if the public controls the centers of economic power. Although socialist nations may be democracies, socialism requires a high degree of central planning to achieve economic equality.

In socialist countries the government often owns major industries, such as utilities. Socialism, as you will see in Section 4, exists to varying degrees in different nations throughout the world.

Communism is a political system that arose out of the philosophy of socialism. **Communism** is characterized by a centrally planned economy with all economic and political power resting in the hands of the central government.

Unlike socialists, however, communists believed that a socialist society can only come about after a violent revolution. While socialist economies can still allow for democracy, communist governments are **authoritarian.** Authoritarian governments exact strict obedience from their citizens and do not allow individuals freedom of judgment and action. Throughout history, communist nations have been dominated by a single political

socialism *a social and political philosophy based on the belief that democratic means should be used to evenly distribute wealth throughout a society*

communism *a political system characterized by a centrally planned economy with all economic and political power resting in the hands of the central government*

authoritarian *requiring strict obedience to an authority, such as a dictator*

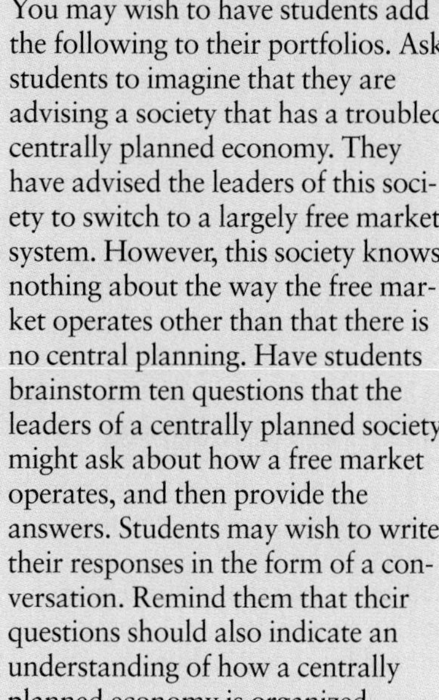

Differentiated Instruction L3

You may wish to have students add the following to their portfolios. Ask students to imagine that they are advising a society that has a troubled centrally planned economy. They have advised the leaders of this society to switch to a largely free market system. However, this society knows nothing about the way the free market operates other than that there is no central planning. Have students brainstorm ten questions that the leaders of a centrally planned society might ask about how a free market operates, and then provide the answers. Students may wish to write their responses in the form of a conversation. Remind them that their questions should also indicate an understanding of how a centrally planned economy is organized.

Economics Assessment Rubric
Economics Assessment Rubrics folder, pp. 6–7 provides sample evaluation materials for a writing assignment.

Transparency Resource Package
Economics Concepts, 2E: Centrally Planned Economies

Econ 101: Key Concepts Made Easy

Economic Systems One of the key concepts in this section is **socialism.** Students may wonder why a socialist state controls the most important factors of production if socialists believe that economic equality is possible only when the *people* control the centers of economic power. Explain to students that in a socialist democracy, the people elect their leaders. Therefore, the elected government manages the most important factors of production *in the name of the people.* If the government mismanages the people's resources, the people can—and usually do—elect a new government. (This is not true when a government is authoritarian, however.) Thus, in effect, the people do control the centers of economic power.
Ask students to relate this situation to the interaction between the performance of the economy of the United States and the approval ratings of government leaders, as well as their chances for reelection.

Answer to . . .

Photo Caption Students may describe assembly line production or give their impressions of the working conditions in the factory.

Differentiated Instruction L4

Remind students that after the breakup of the Soviet Union, most of the other formerly Communist republics abandoned their centrally planned economies and began a transition to largely free market economies. Ask students to think about the differences between these two economic systems and to speculate about the major challenges that accompany such a transition. GT

Differentiated Instruction L2

To help students better understand the Soviet economy, have them find images of the Soviet Union from the 1940s through the 1990s. These images should depict the Soviet standard of living, agriculture, heavy industry, medicine, science and technology, and so on. Have students assemble the images on posterboard or scan them into a software presentation program. Finally, ask students to share their images as part of a presentation on life in a centrally planned economy. LPR

Background

Comparing Economic Performance

The depths to which the Russian economy had sunk by 1996 can be illustrated by several statistics. The 1996 per capita Gross National Product (GNP) in the Russian Federation was only $2,410. The real growth rate of the GNP per capita from 1990 to 1996 in the Russian Federation was -9.2 percent. China, whose 1996 GNP per capita was only $750, showed a real growth rate of 11 percent. In comparison, the United States had a 1996 GNP per capita of $28,870 and a real growth rate of 1.2 percent.

Answer to . . .

Photo Caption labor-intensive and lacking advanced technology

▶ **Karl Marx (left) and Friedrich Engels (center) introduced their socialist philosophy in *The Communist Manifesto* in 1848. The term *communist* was adopted by the Bolsheviks who, led by Vladimir Lenin (right), took control of Russia in 1917.**

collective *large farm leased from the state to groups of peasant farmers*

party or dictator. The former Soviet Union was a communist nation that provides us with a good case study of how a centrally planned economy works—and doesn't work.

The Former Soviet Union

The Soviet Union arose out of a pair of revolutions in Russia in 1917. In March, imperial rule in Russia came to an end when Czar Nicholas II was forced from the throne. A provisional republican government was set up, but by November it, too, was toppled. It was taken over by the Bolsheviks, revolutionary socialists led by Vladimir Lenin. Once in power, they renamed themselves communists. Under the control of the Communist party, central planning was introduced during the 1920s and continued to operate until the breakup of the Soviet Union in 1991.

Soviet planners were most concerned with building national power and prestige in the international community. As a result, they allocated the best land, labor, and capital to the armed forces, space program, and production of capital goods such as farm equipment and factories. The committees that ran the system were responsible for deciding the quantity, production process, and distribution of 24 million different goods and services.

Soviet Agriculture

In the Soviet Union, the central government created large state-owned farms and collectives for most of the country's agricultural production. On state-run farms, the state provided farmers with all equipment, seed, and fertilizer. Farmers worked for daily wages set by economic planners.

Collectives were large farms leased from the state to groups of peasant farmers. Farmers managed operation of the collectives, though they still were required to produce what the government instructed them to. Farmers either received a share of what they produced or income from its sale.

Agricultural workers were guaranteed employment and income, and the govern-

▶ **How would you describe the farming techniques shown in this photo of a Soviet collective?**

Block Scheduling Strategies

Consider these suggestions to take advantage of extended class time:

- Extend the activity on p. 35 by having students work in small groups to brainstorm questions and answers. A designated reporter from each group can then present each group's work to the class.
- Have students complete the activity on p. 37 as a class. Students may role-play Soviet consumers waiting in long lines, living in tiny apartments, and so on. A consumer profile will emerge from the emotions the students experience.
- Form five groups within the class. Ask each group to determine the origins of two of the following terms: *socialism, communism, authoritarian, collective, soviet, quota, incentive, democracy, industry, consumer.* Then have each group make a short oral presentation to the class on their terms and their significance in the section.

ment established quotas and distribution. Under such a system, individuals had few incentives to produce more or better crops. While Russia had been a major exporter of wheat until 1913, before long the Soviet Union could not keep its own people fed. Soviet agriculture bore much of the opportunity cost of Soviet central planning decisions.

Soviet Industry

Soviet factories also were state-owned. Planners favored the defense industry, the space program, and **heavy industry.** (Heavy industry requires a large capital investment to produce items used in other industries. Chemical, steel, and heavy machinery manufacturing are heavy industries.) The makers of consumer goods and services paid the opportunity cost of this concentration of resources. They were stuck with leftover, lower-quality resources with which to create their products.

Like agriculture, industry was characterized by a lack of incentives. Jobs were guaranteed, and wages were set by the government. Once a production quota was met, there was no reason to produce more goods. Workers had little incentive to work harder or to innovate. In fact, it was illegal for workers to exhibit entrepreneurial behavior and start their own businesses.

▲ **Shifting from communism to a free market economy has been a difficult transition. Consumers often waited hours in long lines only to discover nearly empty store shelves.**

Soviet Consumers

Consumers, too, experienced the opportunity cost of central planners' decisions. A popular joke in the Soviet Union went, "We pretend to work, and they pretend to pay us." A worker's wages were not worth much because consumer goods were scarce and usually of poor quality. Manufacturers had the incentive to focus on quantity, not quality. For example, a manufacturer assigned to produce a certain number of suits could loosely stitch the buttons and mismatch coats and trousers. Still, the state store had to accept delivery of the suits. Consumers would be left with no alternatives.

Consumers often had difficulty getting goods, too. They wasted countless hours waiting in line to purchase goods and services. Luxuries such as meat were made affordable by government price setting, but they were rarely available. Housing shortages forced people to live in crowded and poorly constructed apartments. Because of the long waiting list for apartments, it was not unusual to find a family living in just two rooms.

heavy industry *industry that requires a large capital investment and that produces items used in other industries*

THE WALL STREET JOURNAL.
CLASSROOM EDITION

In the News Read more about the former Soviet Union in "Laying Down the Law," an article in The Wall Street Journal Classroom Edition.

The Wall Street Journal Classroom Edition

For: Current Events
Visit: PHSchool.com
Web Code: mnc-1023

Background

Biography

Although Soviet leader Mikhail Gorbachev was born into a peasant farmer family, he attended college and earned a degree in law. Gorbachev then began working for the Communist Party and rose quickly to a position of prominence. In 1982 the Soviet leader Yuri Andropov named Gorbachev to direct the nation's economy. Gorbachev became the leader of the Soviet Union in 1985.

Soon after he assumed his new position, Gorbachev told the Soviet people that their centrally planned economy was in trouble and must be modernized to make it more productive. His new economic and political reform policy was *perestroika,* which means "restructuring." Unfortunately for Gorbachev, his reforms faced great opposition, and the economy grew worse. Inflation soared; goods were in short supply. Economic chaos led to political unrest, and the Soviet Union began to break apart. On December 25, 1991, Gorbachev resigned as president, and the Soviet Union officially ceased to exist.

Differentiated Instruction 

Ask students to create a personality profile of the Soviet consumer described in this section. Students should consider the goods and services that were or were not available, the quality of these goods and services, the political atmosphere in the country, the standard of living, and so on. Then ask students to link their profile to problems that result from a centrally planned economy. GT

Go Online PHSchool.com Typing in the Web Code when prompted will bring students directly to the article.

Preparing for Standardized Tests

Have students read the section titled "Soviet Industry" and then answer the question below.

Which of the following is not a reason why Soviet workers lacked incentives?

A Jobs were guaranteed.

B Wages were set by the government.

(C) There were no production quotas.

D Entrepreneurial behavior was illegal.

GTE **Guide to the Essentials**
Chapter 2, Section 3, p. 8 provides support for students who need additional review of the section content. Spanish support is available in the Spanish edition of the guide on p. 8.

Quiz Unit 1 folder, p. 18 includes questions to check students' understanding of Section 3 content.

Presentation Pro CD-ROM
Quiz provides multiple-choice questions to check students' understanding of Section 3 content.

Answers to . . .

Section 3 Assessment

1. In socialist countries the government often owns major industries. Socialism has been achieved peacefully through democracy. In Communist nations all economic and political power rests in the hands of the central government. Communist governments are authoritarian.
2. Authoritarian governments are strongly centralized and demand strict obedience from their citizens. They do not allow individuals freedom of judgment and action.
3. The government paid farmers a set wage and told them what to produce, thus providing very little incentive to produce more or to produce goods more efficiently.
4. The emphasis on heavy industry in the Soviet Union cost the nation adequate consumer goods and services.
5. Centrally planned economies eliminate competition, giving businesses no incentive to produce consumer goods of high quality. Also, the large bureaucracy needed in this type of economy is not flexible enough to respond to consumer demands.
6. a, d

▲ **Statues of Lenin were toppled after the collapse of communism in the Soviet Union in 1991.**

Problems of Centrally Planned Economies

Central planning can be used to jumpstart selected industries and guarantee jobs and income. The other side of the coin, however, is poor quality, serious shortages of nonpriority goods and services, and diminishing production.

In theory, centrally planned economies can work effectively toward explicitly stated goals. For example, in 1928, Soviet leader Joseph Stalin instituted the first of several five-year plans to boost production. While a disaster in terms of agriculture, Stalin had some success in increasing output in heavy industries.

Perhaps the greatest disadvantage of centrally planned economies is that their performance almost always falls far short of the ideals upon which the system is built. In addition, such systems generally cannot meet consumers' needs or wants. Since the government owns all production factors, workers lack any incentive to work hard. These systems also do not reward innovation, actively discouraging any kind of change. The large, expensive bureaucracy necessary to make the thousands of production and distribution decisions to run the economy lacks the flexibility to adjust to consumer demands. Decisions become overly complicated. Finally, command economies sacrifice individual freedoms in order to pursue societal goals.

Many areas of the world, especially less developed countries, have experimented with centrally planned economies, but most of these experiments have failed. Instead, most of these nations have moved toward mixed economies over the past twenty years. In the next section, you will read about today's mixed economies.

Section 3 Assessment

Progress Monitoring *Online*
For: Self-quiz with vocabulary practice
Web Code: mna-1027

Key Terms and Main Ideas

1. How do **socialism** and **communism** differ?
2. What characterizes an **authoritarian** government?
3. Why did Soviet **collectives** offer little incentive to farmers?
4. In the Soviet Union, what was the opportunity cost of the emphasis on **heavy industry?**

Applying Economic Concepts

5. ***Critical Thinking*** Why do centrally planned economies have difficulty meeting consumer needs?
6. ***Decision Making*** Which of the following economic goals are difficult to achieve in a centrally planned economy? **(a)** economic efficiency **(b)** economic security and predictability **(c)** economic equity **(d)** economic growth and innovation

For: Current Events Activity
Visit: PHSchool.com
Web Code: mnd-1023

Progress Monitoring *Online*
For additional assessment, have students access Progress Monitoring Online at **Web Code:** mna-1027

Go Online PHSchool.com Typing in the Web Code when prompted will bring students directly to detailed instructions for this activity.

Economic Systems

Russia in Crisis

In 1991, when the Communist system in Russia collapsed, many Russians rejoiced at the prospect of living under a freer political and economic system. Many specifically looked forward to living in a Western-style free market economy.

During the next decade, Russians experienced an economic crisis. Although economists had predicted that switching to a free enterprise system would be difficult, few predicted how traumatic it would be.

▲ Many Western businesses saw the collapse of Communism as a business opportunity.

Corruption The confusion caused by the sudden upheaval of both the political and economic systems opened the door for crime and corruption on an enormous scale. Some businessmen and politicians took advantage of the nation's inexperience with a market economy and abused their power by robbing the nation's assets.

Financial Problems Russia's gross domestic product fell sharply until 1997. The nation had to devalue its currency and postpone payments on loans owed to Western nations. Hardest hit of all have been Russia's citizens, many of whom survive on incomes of less than $40 a month. Retirees were squeezed when prices increased much faster than the value of their government pensions.

Success in Sight Despite these problems, Russia's economy has improved considerably since 1998. As the devaluation of the ruble made foreign imports more expensive, consumers bought more locally-made goods. A new president, Vladimir Putin, brought political and financial stability to the government.

Growth has been uneven. The streets of the capital, Moscow, shine with fine restaurants and fashionable stores while the rest of country lags behind. Much of the nation's good fortune is due to exports of oil and natural gas, leaving Russia vulnerable to price changes on international markets.

Russia has not yet succeeded in building a stable, modern free market economy. Officials actively discourage start-ups by imposing unpredictable regulations and occasionally demanding bribes. Insolvent businesses can still stay afloat because of the elaborate system of bartering among suppliers. This discourages Russian businesses from becoming more efficient.

It is now obvious that Russia's problems in making the transition were seriously underestimated. As this painful process continues, Russians look forward to the day when a prosperous free market economy becomes a reality.

Applying Economic Ideas

1. What problems has Russia experienced in switching from a state-controlled to a free market economy?
2. Why might Western nations be willing to make loans to troubled Russia?

Real-life Case Study: Economic Systems

1. Focus Making the transition from a command economy to a free market economy can be a long and difficult process if the change is not managed efficiently.

2. Instruct Point out some of the specific problems Russia has encountered as it struggles to establish a free market economy. Then ask students to speculate, based on what they know about centrally planned and free market economies, what Russian leaders could have done to make their economic transition less traumatic and less corrupt.

3. Close/Reteach Have students research economic conditions in Russia today.

Case Studies Activity
Case Studies in Free Enterprise folder, pp. 4–5, "Berry Gordy," helps students apply economic principles in an additional case study.

Economic Detective Activity
Unit 1 folder, p. 23, "Economic Recovery in Sunnhilla," provides an additional application of chapter concepts.

Preparing for Standardized Tests

Have students read the case study and then answer the question below.

Which of the following is one reason why Poland's transition to a market economy was more successful than Russia's?

(A) encouragement of start-up companies
B Poland's larger size and larger labor force
C government subsidization of insolvent firms
D requiring government licensing and regulation

Answers to . . .

1. Answers may include crime, corruption, financial difficulties, and food shortages.
2. Students may mention concern over what could happen if a nation armed with thousands of nuclear weapons were thrown into chaos or the desire for an economically sound Russia, capable of buying Western goods and producing necessary goods.

Section 4

Modern Economies

Objectives You may wish to call students' attention to the objectives in the Section Preview. The objectives are reflected in the main headings of the section.

Bellringer Ask students how they would feel if they had to pay a monthly book-rental fee at their community library or buy a ticket to use most highways. Explain that in this section they will learn that mixed economies offer many advantages not found in a pure free market economy.

Vocabulary Builder Ask students to write definitions for those key terms which they already understand. Have them check their definitions against those in the margins of this section and make corrections as necessary. Then have them copy the definitions of any terms they did not know and use the terms in sentences.

Lesson Plan

Teaching the Main Concepts L3

1. Focus Remind students that no one economic system can adequately satisfy everyone's wants and needs. That is why most modern economies are a mix of economic systems.

2. Instruct Discuss with students the concept of laissez faire and how it works in modern economies. Be sure that students understand government participation by examining the circular flow diagram in this section. Finally, discuss the advantages and drawbacks of the economies of North Korea, China, Hong Kong, Sweden, and the United States.

3. Close/Reteach Remind students that government intervention is a feature of all economies to some degree. Have students create charts comparing the levels of government intervention in North Korea, China, Hong Kong, Sweden, and the United States.

Guided Reading and Review
Unit 1 folder, p. 19 asks students to identify the main ideas of the section and to define or identify key terms.

Section 4 Modern Economies

Preview

Objectives

After studying this section you will be able to:

1. **Explain** the rise of mixed economic systems.
2. **Interpret** a circular flow model of a mixed economy.
3. **Compare** the mixed economies of various nations along a continuum between centrally planned and free market systems.
4. **Understand** the role of free enterprise in the economy of the United States.

Section Focus

It is doubtful that any nation can exist successfully under a pure centrally planned economy or a pure market economy. Most modern economies mix features of both systems. The economy of the United States is based on the principles of the free market.

Key Terms

laissez faire
private property
free enterprise
continuum
transition
privatize

You cannot find today any economic system that relies exclusively on central planning or the individual initiative of the free market. Instead, most economies are a mixture of economic systems. Most contemporary mixed economies blend the market with government intervention, or involvement, in the marketplace.

The Rise of Mixed Economies

No single economic system has all the answers. Centrally planned economies are cumbersome, do not adequately meet consumer needs, and limit freedom. Traditional economies have little potential for growth or change. Even market economies, with all their advantages, have certain drawbacks.

The Limits of Laissez Faire

Adam Smith and other early free market philosophers believed that, left to its own devices, the free market system would provide the greatest benefit for consumers and raise the standard of living. They

▶ **Most public parks rely on government dollars for support.**

Graphing the Main Idea

BUILDING KEY CONCEPTS

Economic Systems To build understanding of **economic systems** and the differences among them, have students use a double web graphic organizer like the one at the right to show the differences between the economy of North Korea and that of the United States. Tell students that a double web can be used to compare and contrast information about two groups.

Section Reading Support Transparencies A template and the answers for this graphic organizer can be found in Chapter 2, Section 4 of the Section Reading Support Transparency System.

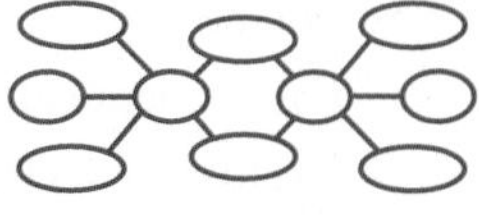

preached **laissez faire,** the doctrine that government generally should not intervene in the marketplace. (See the Profile of Adam Smith on page 33.) Even Smith acknowledged, however, the need for a certain limited degree of government intervention in the economy.

As market economies have evolved since Smith's time, government intervention has become greater because some needs and wants of modern society are difficult to answer in the marketplace. How well, for example, could the marketplace provide for national defense or for roads and highway systems?

Some needs that markets could meet fall to governments so that all members of society can participate. Education is one example. Other needs that could fall into this category are health care and mass transit.

Governments create laws protecting property rights and enforcing contracts. There would be little incentive to develop new products without property rights or patent laws (laws that give the inventor of a new product the exclusive right to sell it for a certain period of time). Without laws insisting on competition, many people fear that some firms would dominate others in their industry and be able to charge consumers any price.

You will recall from your study of American history that the 5th and 14th amendments to the Constitution declare that no person may be deprived of "Life, liberty, or property, without due process of law." The 5th Amendment also says that "just compensation" must be paid to owners when private property is taken for public use. **Private property** is property that is owned by individuals or companies, not by the government or the people as a whole. The Framers of the Constitution ensured that the United States government would protect this fundamental right.

Balancing Control and Freedom

A society must assess its values and prioritize its economic goals. Some goals are better met by the open market and others are better met by government action. In addition, societies must evaluate the opportunity cost of pursuing each goal.

Each nation decides what it is willing to give up to meet its goals. What are you willing to give up? Are you willing to pay taxes to fund the army? To give money to people without jobs? To give all people an education? To subsidize farms? Should the government establish job-safety guidelines or a minimum wage?

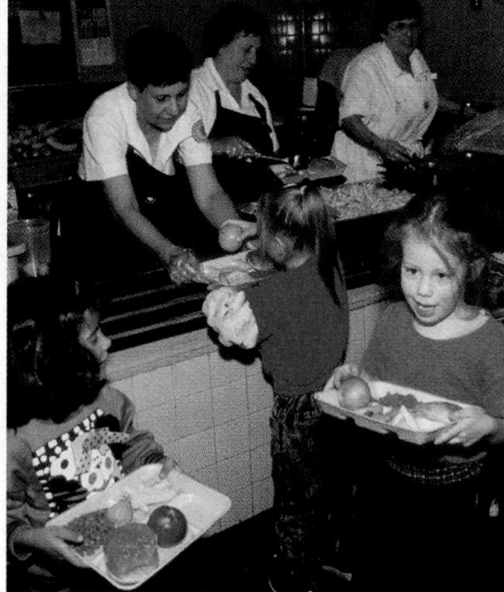

◀ **These kindergarten students in this school lunch program are enjoying a benefit of government intervention.**

laissez faire *the doctrine that states that government generally should not intervene in the marketplace*

private property *property owned by individuals or companies, not by the government or the people as a whole*

Global Connections

Sweden's Mixed Economy Sweden's mixed economy has mixed benefits for the Swedish people. The Swedish government redistributes more than half of Sweden's wealth through social benefit programs. When a child is born, his or her parents are entitled to a combined 450 days of parental leave, with three quarters of their base salary paid by the government. Swedish patients rarely pay more than 1,800 Swedish kronor (about $230) per year for prescriptions. If you were a teen in Sweden, your new braces would be free. Employers are required to give employees a minimum of 30 days vacation. The trade-off for these benefits is the second-highest tax burden of any industrialized country. Swedes pay around 56 percent of their gross domestic product in taxes, compared to only 32 percent in the United States. **How would you describe the level of government involvement in Sweden's economy?**

Econ 101: Key Concepts Made Easy

Government One of the key concepts in this section is the **transferring** of money by the government. The government transfers money not to penalize the rich or to make everyone financial equals but rather to provide financial assistance to those who need it most. Offer students this example: a late-night explosion at an auto parts factory destroys the building. In that instant the factory's workers have lost their income. The workers then apply for unemployment compensation, a government program that collects money from employers to fund unemployment insurance and redistributes the funds to those who have lost their jobs. The workers will receive income from the government until they find new jobs or until their unemployment compensation expires.
Ask students to think of other examples of the government transferring money. Have them share their examples with the class.

Background

Economics in History

When Franklin D. Roosevelt became president in 1933, the nation was in the grip of the Great Depression. The prosperity of the Roaring Twenties had crashed along with the stock market, and people were looking for economic salvation. Roosevelt's policies illustrate one method for balancing economic control and economic freedom.

Roosevelt saw government action as the best way to accomplish his goal of improving America's ravaged economy. Toward that end Roosevelt, his advisors, and members of Congress developed a plan for government intervention in the economic crisis. The plan was called the New Deal. During a period that came to be known as the Hundred Days, Roosevelt proposed and Congress passed sweeping legislation to help the nation weather the economic storm. This legislation included the following:

- **Emergency Banking Act**—enabled financially sound banks to reopen
- **Glass-Steagall Banking Act**—created the Federal Deposit Insurance Corporation (FDIC) to insure bank deposits
- **Civilian Conservation Corps** and **Public Works Administration**—put people to work, at government expense, in conservation projects and the building of courthouses, dams, bridges, and other public structures.

The "Second Hundred Days" saw the passage of the Social Security Act and the National Labor Relations Act as well as the creation of the Works Progress Administration.

The New Deal did not end the Great Depression, but most economists agree that it did much to relieve economic suffering and preserve the basics of the free enterprise system.

Answer to . . .

Global Connections Most students are likely to describe the level of government involvement as high, especially in comparison to the United States.

Differentiated Instruction L3

You may wish to have students add the following to their portfolios. Have students use an almanac to investigate four of the world's economies. Ask them to create a chart that shows economic data for two countries in which government intervention dominates the mixed economy and two countries in which the market system dominates the mixed economy. Then have students write a brief report summarizing the data. Students should create an economic model using a circular flowchart to illustrate their findings and should include it with their report.

Transparency Resource Package
Economics Concepts, 2F: Circular Flow Diagram of a Mixed Economy

Differentiated Instruction L2

Ask students to create a poster that arranges the economies profiled in the "Comparing Mixed Economies" section from the most centrally planned to the most purely free market. Students may want to illustrate their work with pictures of economic activities in each country. LPR

Learning Styles Activity
Learning Styles Lesson Plans folder, p. 10 asks students to prepare written reports assessing the degree to which government and free enterprise dominate the mixed economies of selected countries.

This circular flow model shows how government typically interacts with households and businesses in the marketplace.
Economic Systems **Explain how government actions affect the circular flow model in a mixed economy.**

Figure 2.4 **Circular Flow Model of a Mixed Economy**

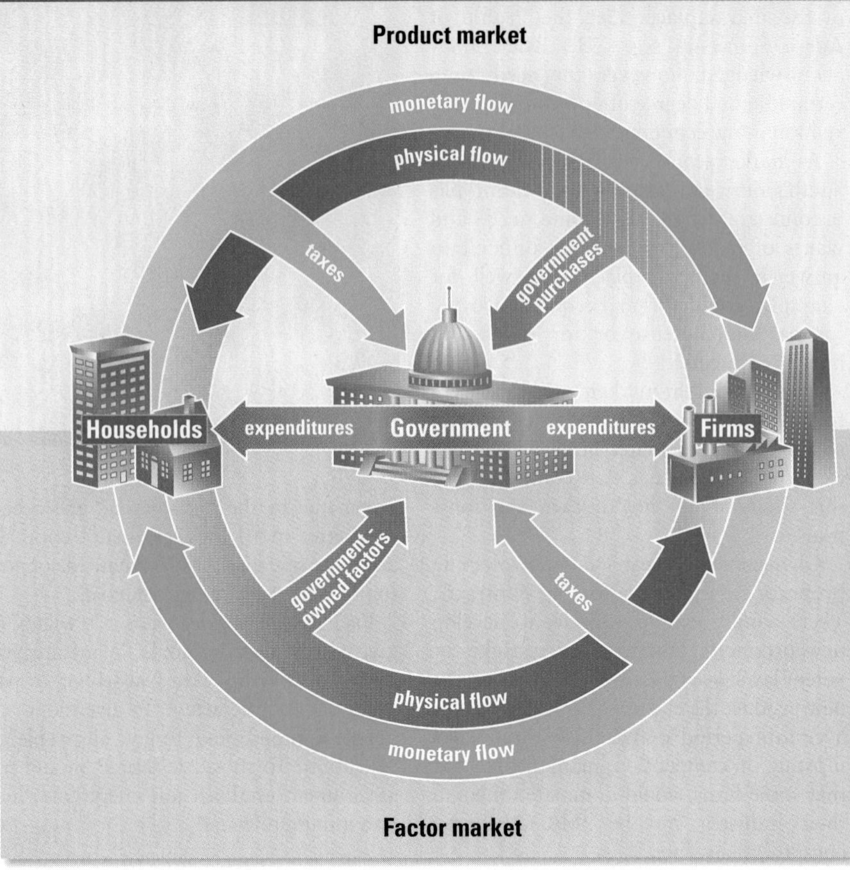

A Circular Flow Model of a Mixed Economy

To illustrate the structure of most modern economies accurately, we need to add government to our picture of the circular flow of economic activity. Figure 2.4 illustrates the government's role in the marketplace in a mixed economy. The government can enter the circular flow of economic activity in many ways.

Government in the Factor Market

Just like businesses, the government purchases land, labor, and capital from households in the factor market. For example, the United States government pays 2.8 million employees $9.7 billion a year for their labor.

Government in the Product Market

Governments purchase goods and services in the product market. They need buildings and office supplies, telephones, computers, and fax machines, for example.

Governments also provide certain goods and services through the factor resources that they combine. The federal, state, and local governments in the United States, for example, provide 4 million miles of roads.

Block Scheduling Strategies

Consider these suggestions to take advantage of extended class time:

- Extend the Bellringer activity on p. 40 by having students work as a group to compile a list of goods and services that the government, rather than the free market, provides. Then discuss how students' lives would be different if these goods and services were left up to the free market to provide.
- Present the Background note on p. 41. Then have students find and read a short story, an excerpt from a book, or a contemporary news article that discusses the Depression and Roosevelt's economic decisions. Ask students to give short oral presentations that focus on how control and freedom were balanced during this era.
- Have students bring the results of the first activity described on this page to class. Have students compare data and draw conclusions about which type of mixed economy seems to produce the best results.

Answer to . . .

Building Key Concepts Students should mention taxes, government purchases, and various other government expenditures.

Transferring Money

As you can see from the outer ring of Figure 2.4, governments collect taxes from both households and businesses. Governments then transfer the money they collect to businesses and individuals for a variety of reasons ranging from worker disability to the survival of an industry. The greatest expenditure of the United States government is Social Security.

Comparing Mixed Economies

The foundation of the United States economy is the free market. An economic system characterized by private or corporate ownership of capital goods is called **free enterprise.** In a free enterprise system investments are determined in a free market by private decision rather than by state control. Figure 2.5 below shows a continuum of mixed economies. A **continuum** is a range with no clear divisions. On one end of the scale is the centrally planned economy. On the opposite end is the free market economy.

Mixed Economies Where Government Intervention Dominates

Reflecting an economy almost totally dominated by the government, North Korea occupies one end of the scale. Government owns all the property and all economic output. State-owned industries produce 95 percent of North Korea's goods. Almost all imports are banned, and production of goods and services by foreign companies is forbidden.

In China, where the economy is dominated by government, one quarter of all enterprises are at least partly owned by individuals. China, like many nations that have relied heavily on central planning in the past, is in **transition,** a period of change in which an economy moves away from central planning toward a market-based system. To make the transition, state firms must be **privatized,** or sold to individuals, and then allowed to compete with one another in the marketplace. As you will read in Chapter 18, economic transition is a difficult, and often painful, process.

Mixed Economies Where the Market System Dominates

At the other end of the scale, with one of the world's freest markets, is Hong Kong. Hong Kong, once administered by Great Britain, is now a special administrative region of China. It continues, at the beginning of the twenty-

FAST FACT

In competition with foreign fast-food restaurant chains, Chinese entrepreneur Shen Qing started his own restaurant chain—the Baked Pig Face restaurants. The seasoned pigs' heads, served in a modern setting, are wildly popular. Mr. Shen benefits by receiving profits, and consumers benefit by being able to choose a traditional Chinese dish over Western-style fast food.

free enterprise *an economic system characterized by private or corporate ownership of capital goods; investments that are determined by private decision rather than by state control; and determined in a free market*

continuum *a range with no clear divisions*

transition *period of change in which an economy moves away from a centrally planned economy toward a market-based system*

privatize *to sell state-run firms to individuals*

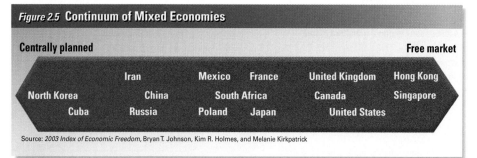

Figure 2.5 Continuum of Mixed Economies

Centrally planned → Free market

North Korea, Cuba, Iran, China, Russia, Mexico, South Africa, Poland, France, Japan, United Kingdom, Canada, United States, Hong Kong, Singapore

Source: *2003 Index of Economic Freedom,* Bryan T. Johnson, Kim R. Holmes, and Melanie Kirkpatrick

BUILDING KEY CONCEPTS

The degree of government intervention in the marketplace varies among nations.
Economic Systems How would you explain China's position on this continuum? Why is Hong Kong, technically part of China, so far to the right on this diagram?

Differentiated Instruction L3

(Reteaching) Organize the class into two groups. One group will play the part of a group of economic planners from North Korea. The other group will play economic planners from Hong Kong. Each group of planners must address the following situation:

North Korea and Hong Kong each have 10 idle factories that must be brought up to full production within a year. The planners must answer the questions below and explain how they arrived at their answers.

- What will we produce?
- To whom will we sell our products?
- How will we find workers for the factories?
- How much will we charge for our products?

When both groups have formulated their plans, a volunteer from each should present the plans to the class. Be sure to remind students that their plans must reflect the economic system of the country they represent.

Differentiated Instruction L3

After students have read this section, ask them to create a web graphic organizer that shows the significance of free enterprise in the economy of the United States.

Economic Detective Activity

Unit 1 folder, p. 23, "Economic Recovery in Sunnhilla," provides an integrated application of chapter concepts.

Economic Video Library

Video segment "Internet Impact" discusses the impact of the Internet on modern business.

Preparing for Standardized Tests

Have students read the section titled "Comparing Mixed Economies" and then answer the question below.

Which of the following is true of North Korea's economy?

A Private enterprise produces 95 percent of its goods.
B North Korea imports many foreign goods.
C "Black markets" do not exist.
(D) Its economy is almost completely state controlled.

Answer to...

Building Key Concepts China is in a transition, moving away from central planning toward a market-based system. Hong Kong is a special administrative district of China that uses a largely free economic system.

GTE Guide to the Essentials
Chapter 2, Section 4, p. 9 provides support for students who need additional review of the section content. Spanish support is available in the Spanish edition of the guide on p. 9.

Quiz Unit 1 folder, p. 20 includes questions to check students' understanding of Section 4 content.

Presentation Pro CD-ROM
Quiz provides multiple-choice questions to check students' understanding of Section 4 content.

Answers to . . .

Section 4 Assessment

1. Laissez faire is the doctrine that states that government should not intervene in the marketplace.
2. Some centrally planned nations are switching to free enterprise systems in order to keep pace with the evolving global economy.
3. Privatization is usually a slow process in centrally planned economies because, typically, few enterprises or businesses exist when privatization begins.
4. Answers should focus on the freedoms inherent in the U.S. free enterprise system. And on the fact that individuals, not government, make economic decisions.
5. Citizens would probably gain more economic freedom and consumer choices.
6. Students should locate articles from reliable sources and be able to place them appropriately on the bulletin board.

▶ What type of economic system do you see reflected in this busy mall?

first century, largely under the free economic system it enjoyed under British rule.

In Hong Kong, the private sector rules. The government protects private property and rarely interferes in the free market, aside from establishing wage and price controls on rent and some public services. It is highly receptive to foreign investment and imposes virtually no barriers on foreign trade. Banks in Hong Kong operate independently of the government, and foreign-owned banks have nearly all the same rights as domestic ones.

The United States Economy

The United States has a free enterprise economy. Still, the government intervenes to keep order, provide vital services, and to promote the general welfare. Some people argue for more government services, while others say that the government already intervenes too much in the economy. Nevertheless, the United States enjoys a high level of economic freedom.

United States law protects private property. The marketplace operates with a low level of government regulation. Foreign investment is encouraged. So, too, is free trade, although the United States does protect some domestic industries and does retaliate against trade restrictions imposed by other nations. The banking industry operates under relatively few restrictions, and foreign-owned banks have few additional restrictions. In the next chapter, you will read in detail about the government and the free enterprise economy of the United States.

Section 4 Assessment

Progress Monitoring *Online*
For: Self-quiz with vocabulary practice
Web Code: mna-1028

Key Terms and Main Ideas

1. What is **laissez faire?**
2. Why have some nations begun a **transition** to **free enterprise?**
3. Why are nations with centrally planned economies sometimes slow to succeed when they **privatize** industry?
4. Compare the U.S. free enterprise system with other economic systems you have read about in this chapter.

Applying Economic Concepts

5. ***Critical Thinking*** What benefits might citizens of a centrally planned economy derive from a move toward a market-based system?
6. ***Try This*** Survey newspapers and magazines to find articles describing life in different economic systems. Construct a bulletin board of the continuum of economies in Fig. 2.5. Place each article on the appropriate location on the continuum.

For: Research Activity
Visit: PHSchool.com
Web Code: mnd-1024

Progress Monitoring *Online*
For additional assessment, have students access Progress Monitoring Online at **Web Code:** mna-1028

Go Online PHSchool.com Typing in the Web Code when prompted will bring students directly to detailed instructions for this activity.

Answer to . . .

Photo Caption the free enterprise system

Skills for LIFE

Building Flowcharts

A flowchart is a visual guide to a process that breaks the process down into individual steps. Arrows often indicate the order and relationships among the steps. In economics, flowcharts help people visualize the ways goods are produced, how money flows through the economy, and how decisions can affect many people. Use the following steps to analyze the flowchart below.

1. **Identify the steps of the process.** Read the labels in the boxes to familiarize yourself with the process of writing an article. (a) What does Laura do after she interviews people for the article? (b) What are the two choices for step one of the process?

2. **Analyze the relationships among steps.** A flowchart shows a series of actions and decisions. (a) According to this particular chart, who can make a decision that directly affects the flow? (b) Why does the path split into two new paths after Laura submits the article to her editor?

3. **Predict possible future developments.** New arrows and steps can be added anywhere along the flowchart, not just at the ends. Picture how different decisions and actions might change the look of Laura's flowchart. (a) Where else might the flowchart split into two new paths? (b) Give an example of a new step that could be added to start a new path.

Laura hears about a story that would make a good article.

Laura's editor assigns her a story to research for an article.

Laura interviews several students.

Laura writes an article and submits it to her editor.

Laura's editor decides not to print the article in the next issue.

Laura's editor revises the article and includes it in the next issue.

Laura's article appears in the newspaper that week.

Additional Practice

Construct a flowchart to show the steps that you could take to offer a new product for sale in your small food store.

Skills for LIFE

Building Flowcharts

1. Focus Students will build flowcharts to illustrate the steps in a process.

2. Instruct Ask students to analyze the sequence of the flowchart and explain why it shows multiple boxes leading to a single box as well as a single box branching out to multiple boxes. Also ask why one box is a dead end. Then have students work through the three steps outlined in the skills feature.

3. Close/Reteach To provide additional practice, see the Economic Skills Activity below.

Economic Skills Activity
Unit 1 folder, p. 21, "Building Flowcharts," asks students to use a flow chart to solve a problem.

Social Studies Skills Tutor CD-ROM offers interactive practice in critical thinking and reading, visual analysis, and communication.

Answers

1. (a) Laura writes an article and submits it to her editor. (b) Laura could hear about a story that might make a good article, or Laura's editor could assign her a story to research for an article.
2. (a) Laura's editor (b) It splits because Laura's editor could decide to print the article or not to print it in the next issue.
3. (a) Based on the results of her interviews, Laura might give up on the article or write it as assigned. (b) After Laura's editor hears that the interviews were unsuccessful, the editor could send Laura out to do research on a different article.

Additional Practice

Students should create a flowchart that shows all of the steps of offering a new product for sale. Steps might include doing market research, producing the product, advertising the product, and offering it for sale at various prices depending on demand.

Interdisciplinary Connections: Science

Visualizing Scientific Processes The study of a science is often the study of processes, sequences of steps or events that lead to some result. For example, astronomers study the process that leads to the birth of a star. Geneticists study the events that transform a normal cell into a malignant one. These processes can be presented visually through the use of flowcharts.

Have students work through the following problem: Medical science has so far found no cure for the common cold. Still, we all know the symptoms that signal a mild or severe cold, the remedies we can employ, and the results of doing nothing. Drawing from your own experience, create a flowchart that describes the events of a cold, from the first sniffle to the last cough.

Chapter 2 Assessment

Key Terms

1. mixed economy
2. self-interest
3. laissez faire
4. centrally planned economy
5. competition
6. market economy

Using Graphic Organizers

7. Students should fill spaces with advantages for each type of economy. Examples for free market economies include economic freedom and efficiency. Examples for mixed economies include equity and economic security. A shared advantage is the incentive for private producers to provide reasonably priced goods that people want.

Reviewing Main Ideas

8. Students should identify a local business and describe its possible factor and product markets. These could include rent, wages, land, products sold, and services offered.
9. An assembly line provides a unique task for each member on the line to do in order to complete a whole product. This is similar to specialization in markets, where each person produces a particular type of good as part of the activity of the entire economy.
10. Pure free markets do not exist in the world because there are many factors that need to be addressed, such as national defense and education, which free markets have difficulty handling on their own. Also, governments need to intervene by creating and enforcing laws about commerce.
11. In a free market economy, the government is not part of the circular flow diagram. In a mixed economy, the government intervenes through such aspects as taxes, government-owned factors, and government expenditures to firms and households.

Critical Thinking

12. Students should make a list of the three economic questions and how these are answered in their own homes. They should then make a judgment based on this information as to what style of economic system their household is most like. For example, some students might say that their households are like centrally planned economies because parents make the major economic decisions and own the means of production.
13. Students should present three ways their lives would change under a pure free market or a centrally planned system. For example, under a pure free market system there would be no public education. Under a pure centrally planned economy they could not start their own business.
14. Students should state advantages and disadvantages of each system that highlight the value placed on economic freedom in free markets and economic equity in centrally planned economies.

Chapter 2 Assessment

Chapter Summary

A summary of the major ideas in Chapter 2 appears below. See also the **Guide to the Essentials of Economics,** which provides additional review and test practice of key concepts in Chapter 2.

Section 1 Answering the Three Economic Questions (pp. 23–27)

The three basic economic questions societies ask are (1) What goods and services should be produced? (2) How should these goods and services be produced? and (3) Who consumes these goods and services? An **economic system** is the way a society decides to answer these three economic questions. There are four general types of economic systems: **traditional economies, market economies, centrally planned** (or **command**) **economies,** and **mixed economies.**

Section 2 The Free Market (pp. 28–32)

A free market is a self-regulating economic system powered by individuals acting in their own **self-interest.** In a free market economy, the factors of production are privately owned, and individuals decide how to answer the three economic questions.

Section 3 Centrally Planned Economies (pp. 34–38)

In a **centrally planned economy** the central government controls the factors of production and answers the three basic economic questions for all of society. Two systems often mentioned when centrally planned economies are discussed are **socialism** and **communism.**

Section 4 Modern Economies (pp. 40–44)

Most of the economic systems in the world today are mixed economies. These systems use a combination of government involvement and free markets. Throughout the world there are different levels of government intervention in mixed economies.

Key Terms

Match the following terms with the definitions listed below. You will not use all of the terms.

competition | **socialism** | **mixed economy** | **self-interest** | **command economy** | **laissez faire** | **privatize** | **consumer sovereignty** | **market economy**

1. System that combines the free market with some government intervention
2. One's own personal gain
3. The doctrine that states that government generally should not intervene in the marketplace
4. System in which the central government makes all decisions on the production and consumption of goods and services
5. The struggle among producers for the dollars of consumers
6. System in which decisions on production and consumption of goods and services are based entirely on exchange, or trade

Using Graphic Organizers

7. On a separate sheet of paper, copy the web map below showing the advantages and values of a mixed economy. Complete the web map with examples from your knowledge or experience.

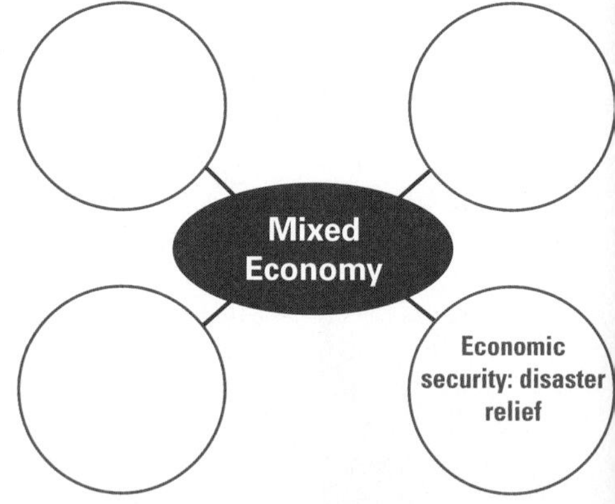

Reviewing Main Ideas

8. Think of a business in your local area. Describe its operation in terms of factor markets and product markets.
9. Explain how a factory assembly line is an example of specialization.
10. Why are there no pure free market economies in the world?
11. Compare the circular flow diagrams of a free market and a mixed economy. Describe how they differ, and why.

Critical Thinking

12. **Synthesizing Information** Suppose that your household is its own society. How are the three key economic questions answered?
13. **Predicting Consequences** Think of three ways your life would change if the United States began using a pure free market system or a pure centrally planned system instead of the free enterprise system.
14. **Analyzing Information** Review the advantages and disadvantages of both free market economies and centrally planned economies. Assess the way each system values economic freedom and economic equity.

Problem-Solving Activity

15. Suppose that you are opening a new music store in your town. What resources would you need from the factor market? What would you offer in the product market? How would the government affect your business?

Skills for Life

Building Flowcharts Review the steps on page 45; then answer the following questions using the flowchart below.

16. What does Megan do to try to make extra money this weekend?
17. Why does the flowchart split into two paths after Megan sets up her stand?
18. What step does Megan take if the neighbors like her cookies?
19. If the neighbors do not like cookies, where could a step or steps be added so Megan could succeed next time?
20. Organize a flowchart for yourself depicting a goal that you did not achieve. (a) Take a close look at the steps you took. (b) What errors did you make? (c) Decide which steps you can change so you can succeed in the future.

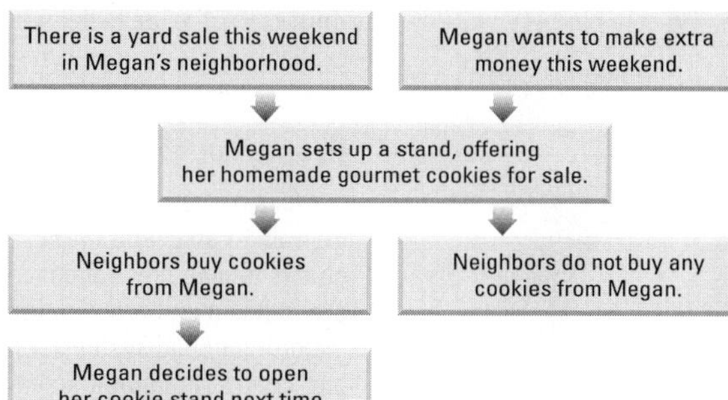
There is a yard sale this weekend in Megan's neighborhood.
Megan wants to make extra money this weekend.
Megan sets up a stand, offering her homemade gourmet cookies for sale.
Neighbors buy cookies from Megan.
Neighbors do not buy any cookies from Megan.
Megan decides to open her cookie stand next time a neighbor has a yard sale.

Economics Journal

Organizing Ideas Review your personal list of systems. Rewrite your list in two columns. In one column, list the systems that are more influenced by central planning. In the other column, list the ones that are more influenced by the free market. Add to each list other systems you use on a regular basis.

Progress Monitoring *Online*

For: Chapter 2 Self-Test **Visit:** PHSchool.com
Web Code: mna-1021

As a final review, take the Economics Chapter 2 Self-Test and receive immediate feedback on your answers. The test consists of 20 multiple-choice questions designed to test your understanding of the chapter content.

Problem-Solving Activity

15. Resources from the factor market would include rented space and hired workers. Offerings in the product market might include compact discs, musical instruments, and music lessons. Examples of how the government would affect the music store would include having to pay taxes and comply with local regulations.

Skills for Life

16. Megan decides to sell gourmet cookies at the neighborhood yard sale.
17. The neighbors will either buy or not buy Megan's cookies.
18. Megan opens her stand again the next time a neighbor has a garage sale.
19. Students should hypothesize additional options for Megan, such as asking the neighbors what snacks they would like.
20. Students should prepare a flow chart of a failed opportunity and use the models and steps provided to synthesize their responses.

Go Online
PHSchool.com

Additional support materials and activities for Chapter 2 of *Economics: Principles in Action* can be found in the Social Studies area of **PHSchool.com.**

Economics Journal

Students should organize their lists by level of government intervention. The highway system, for example, has a relatively high level of government intervention; the Internet is more influenced by the free market.

Review and Assessment

Vocabulary Practice Unit 1 folder, p. 22 uses a fill-in-the-blanks exercise to reinforce understanding of key terms.

GTE **Guide to the Essentials** Chapter 2 Test, p. 10

Test Bank CD-ROM, Chapter 2 Test

Go Online PHSchool.com Students may use the Chapter 2 Self-Test on **PHSchool.com** to prepare for the Chapter Test.

Economics **Simulation**

Objectives Upon completion of this simulation, students should be able to:

- demonstrate knowledge of economic systems by designing an economic system for an imaginary island society;
- explain the advantages and disadvantages of different economic systems.

Bellringer Ask students to divide a piece of paper into two columns: "Free Market Economy" and "Centrally Planned Economy." Have them list as many features of each type of economy as they can think of in five minutes. Then have students compare their lists.

1. Focus Build on the Bellringer activity by reviewing any differences between free market and centrally planned economies that were not mentioned. Explain to students that in this simulation they will use their knowledge of economic systems to develop an economic system for an imaginary island country.

2. Instruct Have students prepare for and conduct the simulation, using the procedures noted in the text.

3. Close/Reteach After students have presented their conclusions, discuss answers to the first three analysis questions as a class. Assign the Making Comparisons question as a follow-up.

Economic Simulation
Economic Simulations folder, pp. 3–8, "Trade-Offs and Decision Making: Should Cooper's Point Be Developed?" provides an additional simulation on a unit topic.

Economics Simulation Designing an Economic System

Most people live and work within an established economic system. Sometimes government economic policy decisions bring gradual shifts or changes to an established system. For example, in the United States during the Great Depression, many new federal programs—notably Social Security—changed the role of government in the American economy. Occasionally, a revolution overthrows an established economic system and puts in place a new one, as you read in Chapter 2.

What if you could design an economic system from scratch? Suppose that you are part of a group of people who have inherited an uninhabited island. As the first settlers on this island, one of your tasks will be to establish an economic system.

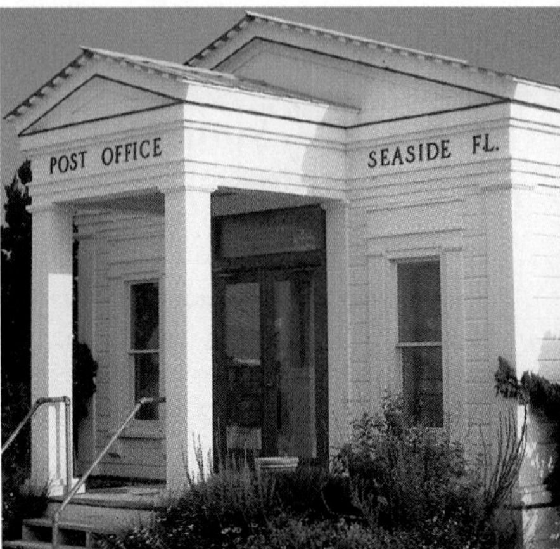

▲ **Will services such as postal delivery be provided by the government or by private companies?**

Materials
Notebook paper
Box or paper bag

Preparing the Simulation

In this simulation, your group will play the role of an island's first settlers. Your goal is to plan an economic system. Each group has members who represent the major economic systems—free market and centrally planned economies. As the founders of a new community, you may choose either of those systems or you may take elements from different systems and create a new one.

Step 1: The teacher or several student volunteers should prepare one slip of paper for each student in the class, as follows:

One half labeled **"Free Market Economy (Capitalist, Democratic)"**

One half labeled **"Centrally Planned Economy (Socialist, Authoritarian)"**

Step 2: Place the slips in a box or paper bag. Form groups of six to eight people, representing Island A, Island B, Island C, and so on. When the groups are set, each member should draw one of the labeled slips of paper, which will determine the economic system that member argues for in the discussion.

Be aware that the groups will probably not be evenly balanced between both economies. (If any group has representatives of only one system, redo the drawing.)

Step 3: Review the basics of the economic system that you represent. You will be advocating this system, so play your role as if this is the system you grew up in and are most familiar with.

Conducting the Simulation

This simulation will consist of four phases. Each group will identify and discuss its options, reach an agreement, and present its plan to the class.

Presentation of Options: Within your group, determine the options for your island economy. Delegates for each of the economic systems represented in the group should present the benefits of their systems in a persuasive manner.

Discussion: After the benefits of both systems have been explained, each group should debate the benefits and drawbacks of each economic system. You may want to make a decision-making grid to see the trade-offs.

Negotiation: Then your group should decide whether you wish to accept one of the systems as a whole or create a new system using elements of both systems.

You should answer these questions:
a) Who decides how resources will be allocated?
b) Who owns the factors of production?
c) Who determines what goods and services will be produced?
d) Who determines prices?
e) How is income distributed?
f) Must all members contribute equally?
g) What social benefits does the system supply?
h) What is the role of government in the economy?
Create a chart like the one on this page to summarize the structure of your island's economy.

Class Presentation: Each group should choose a speaker to present the system to the class. After each presentation, class members may ask questions about the system, so the spokesperson should be ready to defend the group's decisions.

Summary of Island Economic System

Feature of Economic System	How Defined in Island Economy
Role of Government	
Ownership of Land and Capital	
Decision Makers for Production and Pricing	
Income Distribution	
Social Benefits	

Simulation Analysis

After listening to each group's speaker present the group's conclusions, answer the following questions:

1. Did the systems your class created closely resemble the systems of any specific countries? If so, which ones?
2. How much did the roles of group members influence the economic decisions you made?
3. What was the most problematic issue for each group?
4. **Making Comparisons** How does living in a free market economy affect your view of another economic system?

Background

Economics in History

The economic systems of primitive societies were very different from either free market or centrally planned economies. In primitive societies kinship ties regulated the economy. If a member of a tribe killed an animal, for example, the meat would be distributed according to fixed, traditional kinship rules. Property rights did not exist but developed later. Instead groups practiced their own elaborate gift-giving customs, in which gifts were exchanged and remained in constant circulation. This practice symbolized the mutual aid and cooperation that were essential to early societies.

Differentiated Instruction 

Ask groups of three to four students to research the economic systems of one European country. (Assign each group a different country.) Have them prepare short oral reports that describe the country's economy and discuss whether it is based on a free market or a centrally planned system.

Answers to . . .

1. Students should indicate any resemblance between the systems they created and systems of specific countries such as the United States or China.
2. Students are likely to answer that the roles had a strong influence, since individuals argued for a particular system.
3. Answers will depend on interactions within particular groups but are likely to stem from the fact that various economic backgrounds were represented in each group.
4. Students should recognize that they are likely to be biased toward a free market economy and thus may be unwilling to accept even beneficial aspects of other economic systems.

Interdisciplinary Connections: History

Feudalism Before capitalism evolved, the economic system of western Europe was based on feudalism. In feudal societies, which were primarily agricultural, complex systems of allegiances tied serfs, the people who worked the land, to lords, the people who owned the land. Lords in turn owed allegiance to nobles, who owed allegiance to a more powerful ruler. In return for their labor and allegiance, those lower in the hierarchy received military and some social protection from those above. Over time, as cities grew and craftspersons gained more power, the feudal system began to dissolve.

Making the Connection Ask students to research feudalism and the Commercial Revolution. Have them investigate the factors that led to the death of feudalism and the rise of commerce. Then have students prepare a report on the subject.

Chapter 3 American Free Enterprise

For more pacing suggestions, see the Economics Pacing Guide in the Program Overview of the Teaching Resources.

Section Objectives	Print and Technology Resources	
1 Benefits of Free Enterprise *(pp. 51–55)* **Objectives** 1. Describe the tradition of free enterprise in the United States and the constitutional protections that underlie it. 2. Explain the basic principles of the U.S. free enterprise system. 3. Identify the role of the consumer in the U.S. free enterprise system. 4. Describe the role of the government in the U.S. free enterprise system.	• **Lesson Planner** Section 1 Lesson Plan, p. 21 • **Lesson Plans folder** Section 1 Lesson Plan, p. 14 • **Economics Assessment Rubrics folder** Writing Assignment, pp. 6–7 • **Unit 1 folder** Guided Reading and Review, p. 26 Careers in Economics, Budget Analyst, p. 37 Section 1 Quiz, p. 27 • **Source Articles folder** Road Warriors, pp. 9–11	• **Presentation Pro CD-ROM** Section 1 • **Transparency Resource Package** Economics Organizers, G5: Web Graphic Organizer Economics Concepts, 3A: Features of American Free Enterprise • **Section Reading Support Transparency System**
2 Promoting Growth and Stability *(pp. 57–60)* **Objectives** 1. Explain how the government tracks and seeks to influence business cycles. 2. Analyze how the government promotes economic strength. 3. Analyze the effect of technology on productivity.	• **Lesson Planner** Section 2 Lesson Plan, p. 22 • **Lesson Plans folder** Section 2 Lesson Plan, p. 11 • **Lesson Plans folder** Section 2 Lesson Plan, p. 15 • **Economics Assessment Rubrics folder** Graphing Data, pp. 8–9 • **Unit 1 folder** Guided Reading and Review, p. 28 Vocabulary Practice, p. 35 Section 2 Quiz, p. 29	• **Case Studies in Free Enterprise folder** Mary Kay Ash, pp. 6–7 • **Math Practice folder** Determining Economic Growth, p. 3 • **Presentation Pro CD-ROM** Section 2 • **Transparency Resource Package** Economics Organizers, G6: Double Web Graphic Organizer Economics Concepts, 3B: Technological Progress in the U.S. • **Section Reading Support Transparency System** • **Social Studies Skills Tutor CD-ROM**
3 Providing Public Goods *(pp. 62–66)* **Objectives** 1. Identify examples of public goods. 2. Analyze market failures. 3. Evaluate how the government allocates some resources by managing externalities.	• **Lesson Planner** Section 3 Lesson Plan, p. 23 • **Lesson Plans folder** Section 3 Lesson Plan, p. 16 • **Economics Assessment Rubrics folder** Position Paper, pp. 22–23 • **Unit 1 folder** Guided Reading and Review, p. 30 Section 3 Quiz, p. 31 Economic Detective, p. 36 • **Presentation Pro CD-ROM** Section 3	• **Transparency Resource Package** Economics Organizers, G7: Tree Map Graphic Organizer Economics Concepts, 3C: Externalities • **Section Reading Support Transparency System**
4 Providing a Safety Net *(pp. 67–70)* **Objectives** 1. Summarize the U.S. political debate on ways to fight poverty. 2. Describe the main programs through which the government redistributes income.	• **Lesson Planner** Section 4 Lesson Plan, p. 24 • **Learning Styles Lesson Plans folder** Section 4 Lesson Plan, p. 12 • **Lesson Plans folder** Section 4 Lesson Plan, p. 17 • **Economics Assessment Rubrics folder** Graphing Data, pp. 8–9 • **Unit 1 folder** Guided Reading and Review, p. 32 Economic Skills, p. 34 Economic Cartoon, p. 38 Section 4 Quiz, p. 33	• **Presentation Pro CD-ROM** Section 4 • **Simulations and Data Graphing CD-ROM** Data Graphing Tools • **Transparency Resource Package** Economics Organizers, G6: Double Web Graphic Organizer Economics Concepts, 3D: Major Redistribution Programs • **Section Reading Support Transparency System**

Differentiated Instruction

Primary Source Jigsaw L2

One way to help students decipher primary sources is to use the jigsaw strategy. Each group will become an "expert" on an assigned material and then teach that material to their peers. For example, if the class is analyzing three primary sources, place the students into groups of three and assign each group one of the sources. After these groups have cooperatively analyzed their source, they are reassigned in a second group that has a representative for each of the three sources. Numerically, this group assigned appears as follows:

1. The first group: 111, 111, 111

2. The second group: 123, 123, 123

In their new groups, ask students to explain and teach their primary source material to the others. Students at a variety of learning abilities can benefit from cooperative learning. The key is to use heterogeneous groups that include high- and low-achieving students.

Deciphering Idioms L2

Some vocabulary and idiomatic expressions are potentially problematic for English Language Learners and Less Proficient Readers. The meanings of statements such as "providing a safety net" and "free rider problem" are not obvious to all students. To help students understand the meaning of these phrases, model these steps for the phrase "providing a safety net."

1. Use context clues to decipher meaning. Look at visuals to help determine meaning.

2. Cite specific examples.—*To clarify this, compare it with sayings high school students will likely hear (e.g., You should have a back-up plan.)*

3. Discuss the appeal of this phrase.—*Would the phrase "a safety system" be just as powerful? The word "net" signifies something that saves and protects.*

4. Ask students to find examples of this phrase in the text.

Go Online PHSchool.com

Visit the Social Studies area of the Prentice Hall Web site. There you can find additional links to enrich chapter content for *Economics: Principles in Action* as well as a self-test for students. Be sure to check out this month's **eTeach** online discussion with a Master Economics Teacher.

Web Code: mnf-1031

Running Out of Time?

- Use the **Presentation Pro CD-ROM** to create an outline for this chapter.
- Use the Chapter Summary in the **Chapter 3 Assessment**, p. 72.
- Use the Section Summaries for Chapter 3, from **Guide to the Essentials of Economics (English and Spanish)**.

THE WALL STREET JOURNAL. CLASSROOM EDITION

Prentice Hall brings into the classroom the authoritative content of *The Wall Street Journal Classroom Edition.* See the Source Articles, Debating Current Issues, and You and Your Money folders in the **Teaching Resources**. Also, see Economics Video Library, "Forced Out."

Assessment Resources

Chapter Assessment

Teaching Resources Unit 1, Chapter 3
- Section Quizzes, pp. 27, 29, 31. 33

Exam *View*® Test Bank CD-ROM Chapter 3

Economics Assessment Rubrics

Chapter 3 Self-Test, **Web Code:** mna-1031

Reading and Skills Evaluation

Progress Monitoring Assessments
- Screening Test
- Diagnostic Test of Social Studies Skills

Standardized Test Preparation

Test Prep Workbook

Test-Taking Strategies With Transparencies

Differentiated Instruction Key

L1 Special Needs	LPR Less Proficient Readers
L2 Basic to Average	AR Advanced Readers
L3 All Students	SN Special Needs Students
L4 Average to Advanced	GT Gifted and Talented
	ELL English Language Learner

Chapter 3

American Free Enterprise

Introducing the Chapter

In this chapter, students will learn the specifics of the American free enterprise system, including how the public sector and the private sector interact to maintain a stable, efficient, and growing economy.

For additional links for *Economics: Principles in Action* provided by Prentice Hall and *The Wall Street Journal Classroom Edition,* visit the Social Studies area. Be sure to check out this month's **eTeach** online discussion with a Master Teacher.

Beyond the Lecture

You may cover the concepts in Chapter 3 in an activity-based style by using the following materials:

- **Technology Resources** appropriate for use with this chapter are noted on pp. 53, 55, 60, 65, 66, 68, 70, and 73.
- **Presentation Pro CD-ROM** with animated graphs gives you an alternative method for organizing and delivering chapter content.
- **Activities** designed to meet the needs of students of mixed abilities and learning styles are noted throughout the chapter in the side columns.
- **Learning Styles Lesson Plans** provide alternate lessons for diverse learning styles. See pp. 11–12 of the Learning Styles Lesson Plans folder located in the Teaching Resources.

Economics Journal

Instruct students to write their responses to the question in their Economics Journals. Students may include completed journal entries in an Economics Portfolio.

Chapter 3 American Free Enterprise

In the United States, economic opportunity is abundantly evident, from corporate headquarters in gleaming cities like Miami, shown here, to neighborhood mom-and-pop businesses, to drive-through franchises in suburban strip malls. This chapter examines the benefits of American free enterprise and the factors that make it so prosperous, adaptive, and enduring.

Economics Journal

In what ways do the benefits of free enterprise affect your daily life? List as many examples as you can. Consider neighborhood businesses, jobs you have held, and other ways in which you benefit from our nation's prosperity.

Go Online PHSchool.com

For: Current Data
Visit: PHSchool.com
Web Code: mng-1031

National Council on Economic Education

The following Voluntary National Content Standards in Economics are addressed in this chapter:

★ **Standard 15** Students will understand that: Investment in factories, machinery, new technology, and the health, education, and training of people can raise future standards of living.

★ **Standard 16** Students will understand that: There is an economic role for government to play in a market economy whenever the benefits of a government policy outweigh its costs. Governments often provide for national defense, address environmental concerns, define and protect property rights, and attempt to make markets more competitive. Most government policies also redistribute income.

For more information about the standards, contact the National Council on Economic Education
1140 Avenue of the Americas
New York, NY 10036
1-800-338-1192

Section 4 Providing a Safety Net

Preview

Objectives

After studying this section you will be able to:

1. **Summarize** the U.S. political debate on ways to fight poverty.
2. **Describe** the main programs through which the government redistributes income.

Section Focus

Sometimes the United States government has to step in to create programs to aid poor, disabled, and elderly people.

Key Terms

poverty threshold
welfare
cash transfers
in-kind benefits

Prosperity is a hazy memory in East St. Louis. Tumble-down buildings and weed-covered lots scar the urban landscape. Poverty and unemployment are constant companions in this Illinois city of 40,000 or so residents.

The city hugs the banks of the Mississippi River across from its prosperous big brother, St. Louis, Missouri, a city of more than 330,000 people. At one time, both cities profited from their locations on the busy river. But in the 1970s the firms of East St. Louis packed up and fled, having found better business opportunities elsewhere. With few businesses to tax and a jobless population, the city edged toward bankruptcy, unable to provide even the most basic services, like garbage collection and police and fire protection. At the end of the twentieth century, while much of the United States enjoyed economic growth, East St. Louis struggled merely to exist.

The Poverty Problem

While the free market has proven better at generating wealth than has any other economic system, that wealth is spread unevenly throughout society. This leaves some people below the **poverty threshold,** an income level below that which is needed to support families or households. The poverty threshold is a relative figure determined by the federal government and adjusted periodically. In 2004, the poverty threshold for a single parent under age 65, with one child, was $12,490. For a four-person family with two children, it was $18,850. In East St. Louis, 42 percent of families with children live below the poverty line. The median household income is about $25,000 a year.

poverty threshold *an income level below that which is needed to support families or households*

The Government's Role

The opportunities that the free market offers can lift the working poor into the middle class. Yet, in poor areas from East St. Louis to rural Appalachia to south-central Los

▲ **Members of the East St. Louis Action Research Project, founded in 1990, help rehabilitate an economically depressed neighborhood.**

Graphing the Main Idea

Standard of Living To help students understand the major types of redistribution programs designed to raise people's **standard of living** (cash transfers and in-kind benefits), have them use a double web graphic organizer like the one at the right. Tell students that a double web can be used to compare or contrast information about two groups.

Section Reading Support Transparencies A template and the answers for this graphic organizer can be found in Chapter 3, Section 4 of the Section Reading Support Transparency System.

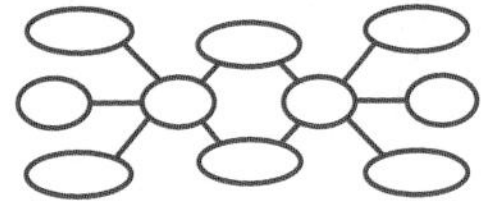

Section 4

Providing a Safety Net

Objectives You may wish to call students' attention to the objectives in the Section Preview. The objectives are reflected in the main headings of the section.

Bellringer Ask students to volunteer personal definitions of *poverty* as part of a class discussion. Explain that in Section 4 they will learn how the government works to raise the standard of living.

Vocabulary Builder Have students look up the meaning of each key term in Section 4. Ask each student to create a crossword puzzle with the terms and to share it with a classmate.

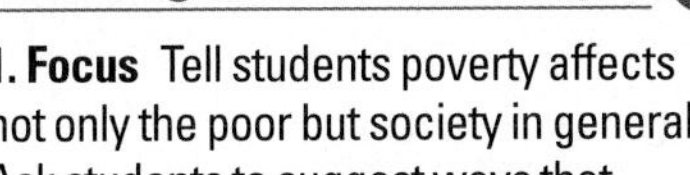

Lesson Plan

Teaching the Main Concepts (L3)

1. Focus Tell students poverty affects not only the poor but society in general. Ask students to suggest ways that poverty touches the lives of everyone.

2. Instruct Be sure students understand that poverty can strike anyone—the young, the old, the disabled. Because poverty affects the marketplace, the government recognizes the need to attack poverty and raise the standard of living throughout society. Describe the types of redistribution programs and how each is designed to provide assistance.

3. Close/Reteach Although the free enterprise system does not guarantee everyone the same degree of wealth, it does allow for government intervention to give people the opportunities they need to maintain a minimum standard of living. Ask students to provide examples of successes and failures of government redistribution programs.

Guided Reading and Review
Unit 1 folder, p. 32 asks students to identify the main ideas of the section and to define or identify key terms.

Differentiated Instruction 

Have students examine statistics on poverty in the United States in an almanac or the *Statistical Abstract of the United States*. Ask them to choose a set of statistics that will allow them to create a graph that illustrates an aspect of poverty. Encourage students to add color and illustrations as appropriate. Then ask students to write a paragraph to accompany their graph. This paragraph should relate the information in their graph to the larger political debate on ways to fight poverty and should demonstrate understanding of that debate.

Economics Assessment Rubric Economics Assessment Rubrics folder, pp. 8–9 provides sample evaluation materials for a data graphing assignment.

Simulations and Data Graphing CD-ROM offers data graphing tools so students can practice creating and interpreting line graphs.

Economic Cartoon Unit 1 folder, p. 38 gives students practice in interpreting cartoons about section content.

welfare *government aid to the poor*

Angeles, economic opportunities are limited because of factors such as a lack of local jobs and few educational opportunities.

As a society, we recognize some responsibilities to the very young, the very old, the sick, the poor, and the disabled. For these people, the government tries to provide a safety net. Various federal, state, and local government programs help to raise people's standard of living, their level of economic well-being as measured by the ability to purchase the goods and services they need and want.

Yet, in a society that prefers limited government activity in the economy, poverty poses tough questions: What can the government do to combat poverty? What should it do? Is government regulation the best way to help the poor?

BUILDING KEY CONCEPTS

Throughout the 1900s, federal spending on social programs grew to include more and more people in need.

Opportunity Costs

What are some of the trade-offs involved in spending on social programs?

The Welfare System

Since the 1930s, the main government effort to ease poverty has been to collect taxes from individuals and redistribute some of those funds in the form of welfare. **Welfare** is a general term that refers to government aid for the poor. It includes many types of redistribution programs.

The nation's welfare system began under President Franklin Delano Roosevelt, following the Great Depression. Welfare spending increased considerably in the 1960s under President Lyndon B. Johnson's "War on Poverty."

Welfare payments soared in the 1970s and 1980s. In the 1990s, critics of welfare voiced increasing concern about people becoming dependent on welfare and being unable or unwilling to get off it. Some also pointed out that income redistribution discourages productivity, thus actually aggravating poverty. In 1996, Congress made sweeping changes in the welfare system.

Redistribution Programs

Income data are gathered by the U.S. Bureau of the Census, an agency within the Labor Department. The Census Bureau conducts monthly surveys of households to track key economic data. Using the data, the Census Bureau estimates how many people are living in poverty.

Chapter 13 will treat the causes of poverty in detail. In the meantime, here is an overview of the major types of redistribution programs through which the federal government helps the poor and the elderly.

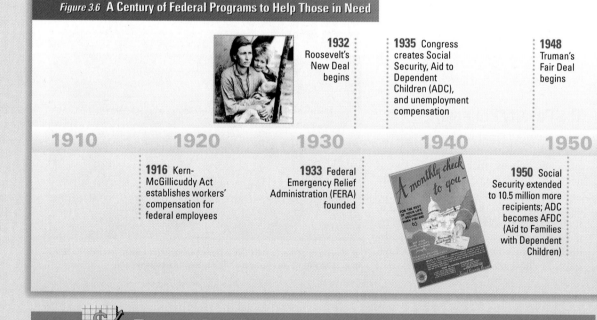

Figure 3.6 **A Century of Federal Programs to Help Those in Need**

1910 | 1920 | 1930 | 1940 | 1950

1916 Kern-McGillicuddy Act establishes workers' compensation for federal employees

1932 Roosevelt's New Deal begins

1933 Federal Emergency Relief Administration (FERA) founded

1935 Congress creates Social Security, Aid to Dependent Children (ADC), and unemployment compensation

1948 Truman's Fair Deal begins

1950 Social Security extended to 10.5 million more recipients; ADC becomes AFDC (Aid to Families with Dependent Children)

Econ 101: Key Concepts Made Easy

Government The key concept **redistribution programs** may confuse or trouble some students. Such programs are often viewed as "government giveaways" by taxpayers who believe that the recipients of such aid are undeserving and that taxpayers should not have to support other people, here or abroad.

To help students understand that such programs can be in the public interest, ask what the social and economic impact would be if each of the following redistribution programs was canceled: workers' compensation, Social Security, and federal school lunch programs. Then have students consider alternate solutions for addressing these issues.

Answer to . . .

Building Key Concepts Students might suggest lower taxes, a freer marketplace, and funds available for reinvestment in the economy to create more jobs and raise the standard of living.

Cash Transfers

State and federal governments provide **cash transfers,** direct payments of money to poor, disabled, and retired people. The following programs distribute direct cash transfers:

1. *Temporary Assistance for Needy Families* (TANF) This program grew out of the 1990s debate about how to ease poverty while decreasing government payments to the poor. TANF replaced the earlier welfare program, Aid to Families with Dependent Children (AFDC). Critics of AFDC said that it made people dependent on welfare and did not encourage them to take responsibility for their lives.

   Launched in 1996 as part of comprehensive welfare reform, TANF discontinues direct federal welfare payments to recipients. Instead, federal money goes to the states, which design and run their own welfare programs. States must adhere to federal rules that create work incentives and establish a lifetime limit for benefits. The program aims to move people from welfare dependence to the work force.
2. *Social Security* The Social Security program was created in 1935, during the Great Depression, when many of the elderly lost their life savings and had no new income. Social Security provides cash transfers of retirement income to the elderly and living expenses to disabled Americans. The program collects payroll taxes from current workers and then redistributes that money to current recipients.
3. *Unemployment insurance* Another cash transfer is the unemployment insurance program, which is funded jointly by federal and state governments. Unemployment compensation checks provide money to eligible workers who have lost their jobs. Workers must show that they have made efforts to get work during each week that they receive benefits.
4. *Workers' compensation* This program provides a cash transfer of state funds to workers injured on the job. Most employers must pay workers' compensation insurance to cover any future claims their employees might make. This insurance has become more and more expensive as medical expenses and the number of reported on-the-job injuries have increased.

THE WALL STREET JOURNAL.
CLASSROOM EDITION

In the News Read more about income redistribution in "Low-Income, Low Tech," an article in The Wall Street Journal Classroom Edition.

The Wall Street Journal Classroom Edition

For: Current Events
Visit: PHSchool.com
Web Code: mnc-1034

cash transfers *direct payments of money to eligible poor people*

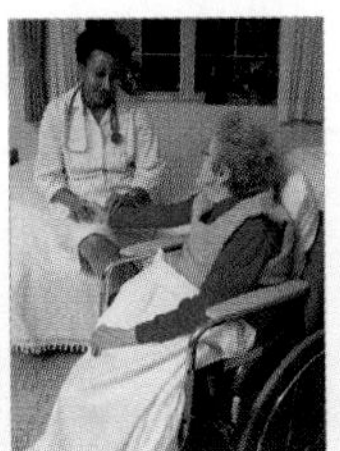

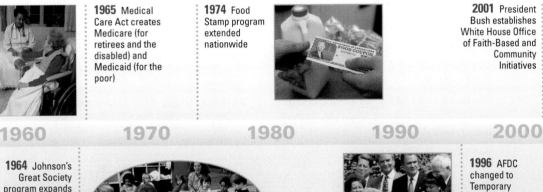

1965 Medical Care Act creates Medicare (for retirees and the disabled) and Medicaid (for the poor)

1974 Food Stamp program extended nationwide

2001 President Bush establishes White House Office of Faith-Based and Community Initiatives

1960 1970 1980 1990 2000

1964 Johnson's Great Society program expands welfare with new programs such as Head Start preschool education

1996 AFDC changed to Temporary Assistance for Needy Families (TANF)

Block Scheduling Strategies

Consider these suggestions to take advantage of extended class time:

- To extend the activity on p. 68, have students use the Simulations and Data Graphing CD-ROM to create graphs. Then have students give oral presentations about the data.
- Have students complete the Economic Cartoon Activity on p. 38 of the Unit 1 folder. Then ask students to search news magazines and newspapers for additional cartoons on the subject of welfare or welfare reform. Have small groups choose two cartoons and prepare a presentation that compares or contrasts their points of view.
- Engage students in a discussion of welfare. First discuss the Florida plan (Background note, this page) in terms of its fairness. Then ask students to brainstorm ideas that could make welfare more equitable, more efficient, and more productive.

Go Online PHSchool.com Typing in the Web Code when prompted will bring students directly to the article.

Background

Reforming Welfare

As a result of a program of welfare reform launched in 1996, states began to set up and administer their own welfare programs. Florida instituted a program called Work and Gain Economic Self-Sufficiency (WAGES). This program gives temporary assistance to poor families with children and provides parents with employment opportunities and support services. WAGES is a "work-first" program. When people apply for assistance, they are immediately referred for employment. Unless exempted, each participant must participate in work activities to the full extent of the federal guidelines. Cash assistance is limited, and after collecting the maximum assistance, a recipient must work, train for work, provide community service, or provide child care for others. A single parent must work at least 30 hours a week, and two-parent families must work a combined minimum of 35 hours.

Learning Styles Activity

Learning Styles Lesson Plans folder, p. 12 asks student groups to put themselves in the place of social groups in need of assistance and to create posters that will help them act as advocates for their groups.

Differentiated Instruction 

Ask students to turn each main head and subhead in Section 4 into a question. Then have students demonstrate their understanding of the text by answering each question. LPR

Transparency Resource Package Economics Concepts, 3D: Major Redistribution Programs

GTE Guide to the Essentials Chapter 3, Section 4, p. 14 provides support for students who need additional review of the section content. Spanish support is available in the Spanish edition of the guide on p. 14.

Quiz Unit 1 folder, p. 33 includes questions to check students' understanding of Section 4 content.

Presentation Pro CD-ROM Quiz provides multiple-choice questions to check students' understanding of Section 4 content.

Answers to . . .

Section 4 Assessment

1. Welfare attempts to raise poor people's standard of living by collecting tax money from individuals and businesses and redistributing it to people with little or no income.
2. Poverty exists because a free market economy generates wealth but does not spread it evenly throughout society. The system rewards the most productive members of society. As a result, people with fewer opportunities to be productive may suffer.
3. Cash transfers provide people with direct payments of money. In-kind benefits provide goods and services free or at reduced cost.
4. The Social Security Administration taxes a portion of citizens' income while they are working and redistributes it to the nation's elderly and the disabled.
5. (a) $8,980 ÷ 52 weeks per year = $172.69 ÷ 40 hrs per week = $4.31 per hour. (b) $12,120 ÷ 52 weeks per year = $233.08 ÷ 40 hrs per week = $5.82 per hour.
6. Student responses should demonstrate an understanding of the statement and of government welfare programs. Students might suggest that TANF or government educational programs reflect this statement.

In-Kind Benefits

The government also provides poor people with **in-kind benefits,** goods and services provided for free or at greatly reduced prices. The most common in-kind benefits include food giveaways, food stamps, subsidized housing, and legal aid.

in-kind benefits *goods and services provided for free or at greatly reduced prices*

Medical Benefits

Another social service that the U.S. government provides is health insurance for the elderly, the disabled, and the poor. Medicare covers Americans over age 65 as well as the disabled. Medicaid covers some poor people who are unemployed or not covered by their employer's insurance plans. Administered under the Social Security program, Medicare and Medicaid are enormously expensive programs. We will examine them further in Chapter 14.

Education

Federal, state, and local governments all provide educational opportunities to the poor. The federal government funds programs from preschool to college. State and local programs aid students with learning disabilities.

Education programs add to the nation's human capital and labor productivity. As you saw in Chapter 1, improved education and technology can make an entire economy more productive by shifting the production possibilities frontier outward.

Faith-Based Initiatives

In 2001, President George W. Bush announced an initiative to rely on nongovernmental support for people in need. His administration "will look first to faith-based organizations, charities, and community groups that have shown the ability to save and change lives."

The President believes that religious organizations have frequently been among the most successful groups delivering social services. These groups not only spend money to solve problems, but also provide a special compassion. He therefore proposed as a next step in welfare reform that faith-based organizations be allowed to compete for federal funds. In 2003, both houses of Congress passed bills enacting some of President Bush's proposals.

Mr. Bush established an Office of Faith-Based and Community Initiatives to help faith-based groups work more effectively with the federal government. He also encouraged the states to create state offices of faith-based action.

Section 4 Assessment

Progress Monitoring *Online*
For: Self-quiz with vocabulary practice
Web Code: mna-1038

Key Terms and Main Ideas

1. How does **welfare** attempt to raise poor people's standard of living?
2. Why does poverty exist in a free market economy?
3. What is the difference between **cash transfers** and **in-kind benefits?**
4. How is Social Security an example of income redistribution?

Applying Economic Concepts

5. ***Math Practice*** Assume that the poverty threshold is $8,980 for an individual and $12,120 for a two-person household. Based on a 40-hour work week, how much would you need to earn per hour in order to be above the poverty threshold for **(a)** an individual and **(b)** a two-person household?
6. ***Critical Thinking*** An old adage states, "Give a person a fish, feed him for a day; teach a person how to fish, feed him for a lifetime." Do any of the government programs in this section reflect this saying? Explain your answer.

For: Decision-making Activity
Visit: PHSchool.com
Web Code: mnd-1034

Progress Monitoring *Online*
For additional assessment, have students access Progress Monitoring Online at **Web Code:** mna-1038

Go Online PHSchool.com Typing in the Web Code when prompted will bring students directly to detailed instructions for this activity.

Government

Government and the Interstate Highway System

The United States did not always have a good network of roads. In the 19th century, when horse-drawn vehicles were dominant, almost all roads were unpaved. Many became rutted and uneven, making travel difficult, slow, and uncomfortable. The push to build a network of smoother roads began in the 1880s—through the efforts of a bicycle club.

▲ President Dwight Eisenhower signed the Federal Aid-Highway Act on June 29, 1956.

Early Efforts In 1886, a bicycling craze was sweeping the nation. Many American cyclists belonged to the League of American Wheelmen, an organization that wanted smoother roads for cycling. This club was the first to convince Congress to consider building a national highway system. As motor vehicles later became more common, automobile manufacturers, road builders, and gasoline companies took up the crusade for better roads.

State Highways By the early 1900s, Congress began to provide funding to the states to build highways. Each state, however, focused on building highways within its own borders with its own numbering and sign systems—and the highways did not always connect at state borders.

Federal Highways In 1921, the Federal Highway Act got the U.S. government directly involved in highway construction by setting up a system of major highways that connected from state to state, so that drivers could travel between states without ever having to leave a high-speed highway. The government then created a simple system of numbering and marking these interstate highways, to make navigating the system easy. In the 1950s, the Cold War raised concerns about the military's ability to defend the country with existing roads. In 1956, the Federal Aid-Highway Act authorized the construction of 41,000 miles of highways to tie the nation together, creating the interstate highway system we know today.

Today, America's interstate highway system is one of the most important features of the country's infrastructure. It allows people and goods to travel quickly from one part of the country to another, reducing transportation costs and speeding up commerce.

Applying Economic Ideas

1. Why was it inefficient to leave highway construction to individual states?
2. Why do you think it took Congress so long to authorize funds for highway construction?

Real-life Case Study: Government

1. Focus The interstate highway system in the United States is an excellent example of government resources being allocated for the public good.

2. Instruct Explain to students that the interstate highway system, which many Americans take for granted, plays a critical role in the transportation of goods and services. The other means of transportation are by rail, ship, and air. Ask students to think of other examples of government resources that Americans may take for granted.

3. Close/Reteach Have students list specific ways in which the interstate highway system benefits them.

Case Studies Activity
Case Studies in Free Enterprise folder, pp. 6–7, "Mary Kay Ash," lets students apply economic principles to an additional case study.

Economic Detective Activity
Unit 1 folder, p. 36, "Blockster, U.S.A.," provides an additional application of chapter concepts.

Preparing for Standardized Tests

Have students read the case study and then answer the question below.

Which of the following was not a result of the federal highway acts of 1921 and 1956?

A Highways in neighboring states were connected.
B A single highway numbering system was instituted.
(C) The League of American Wheelmen was created.
D Transportation costs declined as commerce accelerated.

Answers to . . .

1. Individual state highway numbering systems varied, and these highways did not always connect between states.
2. Students may say that Congress believed it was the states' job to construct the roads and that it would be an overextension of congressional power to do it on the federal level.

Chapter 3 Assessment

Key Terms

1. externality
2. open opportunity
3. free contract
4. free rider
5. in-kind payment
6. gross domestic product
7. macroeconomics

Using Graphic Organizers

8. Students' answers should include examples of government programs and interventions that meet public policy goals. Examples include: welfare (to fight poverty); environmental protection laws (to promote positive externalities); laboratory tests on foods and medicines (to protect public health).

Reviewing Main Ideas

9. (a) The government supports free enterprise with contract law, private property rights, copyrights, and patents. It protects public interest by monitoring the effects of externalities and creating public policy. (b) Answers will vary, but should include an understanding of government involvement in free enterprise such as: patents, copyrights, health warnings, environmental protections.
10. Students answers should illustrate a clear understanding of the basic principles of free enterprise: profit motive, open opportunity, private property rights and economic rights.
11. The U.S. government tracks and influences business cycles to prevent wild swings in economic behavior.
12. (a) cash transfer: direct funds are provided for those who have lost their jobs (b) cash transfer: direct payment is made to those who qualify for benefits (c) in-kind payment; food stamps provide coupons for buying food

Critical Thinking

13. Student answers should show clear understanding of how a federal agency limits negative externalities. For example, the EPA sets pollution standards to limit environmental damage and health problems.
14. Students paragraphs will vary, but should illustrate an understanding of the constitutional rights provided to businesses as well as the rights and freedoms inherent to the free enterprise system.
15. The production possibilities frontier would be moved out toward the right (overall production possibility would increase), which would probably increase the nation's GDP.

Chapter 3 Assessment

Chapter Summary

A summary of major ideas in Chapter 3 appears below. See also the **Guide to the Essentials of Economics**, which provides additional review and test practice of key concepts in Chapter 3.

Section 1 Benefits of Free Enterprise (pp. 51–55)

The benefits of the American free enterprise system are the result of the basic principles of **profit motive, voluntary exchange, private property rights,** and **competition.** These benefits include individual freedom for consumers and producers and a wide variety of goods. To protect economic freedoms, the government intervenes in matters of **public interest**. Federal agencies monitor and regulate certain types of businesses. **Public disclosure laws** provide critical information to consumers.

Section 2 Promoting Growth and Stability (pp. 57–60)

Macroeconomics concerns the behavior of whole economies, while **microeconomics** concerns the behavior of smaller economic units, such as households. When necessary, the government takes action to influence macroeconomic **business cycles.** It aids the growth of the economy, as measured by **GDP.** It encourages the creation of new **technologies** by giving patents and copyrights to entrepreneurs.

Section 3 Providing Public Goods (pp. 62–66)

The government provides **public goods,** such as roads, when it would be impractical for individuals to pay for them. Providing public goods produces positive and negative **externalities.**

Section 4 Providing a Safety Net (pp. 67–70)

The government uses tax money to raise the standard of living of people in **poverty.** The nation's welfare system includes programs that distribute various benefits, including **cash transfers, in-kind payments,** and medical benefits.

Key Terms

Choose the italicized word in parentheses that best completes each sentence.

1. Acid rain is an example of a(n) *(externality/free rider)*.
2. The tradition of *(private property/open opportunity)* allows everyone to compete in the free market.
3. The right of *(free contract/voluntary exhange)* allows people to decide what agreements they want to enter into.
4. Someone who benefits from a good without paying for it is an example of a *(free rider/public good)*.
5. Food stamps are an example of a/an *(cash transfer/in-kind payment)*.
6. We can use figures on *(gross domestic product/public goods)* to measure economic growth.
7. Study of the behavior of the entire U.S. economy is an example of *(macroeconomics/microeconomics)*.

Using Graphic Organizers

8. On a separate sheet of paper, copy the tree map below to help you organize information about the American free enterprise system. Complete the tree map by writing descriptions and examples for each of the headings shown. You may add branches to the tree.

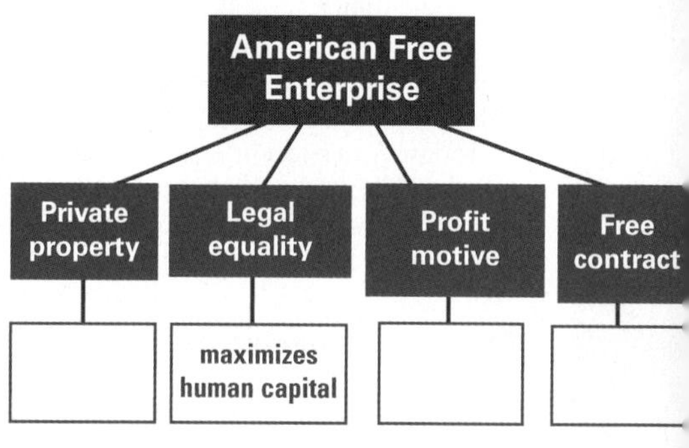

Reviewing Main Ideas

9. **(a)** How does the government support free enterprise and protect public interest? **(b)** Describe and evaluate the government rules and regulations described in this chapter.
10. Explain the basic principles of free enterprise in your own words.
11. Why does the U.S. government track and influence business cycles?
12. Explain why each of the following is either a cash transfer or an in-kind payment. **(a)** unemployment insurance **(b)** Social Security **(c)** food stamps

Critical Thinking

13. **Drawing Inferences** Choose one of the federal agencies mentioned in Section 1, and explain how it acts to limit negative externalities.
14. **Synthesizing Information** Based on your reading of the chapter, write a paragraph in which you describe and analyze the economic rights of businesses.
15. **Predicting Consequences** How might the invention of a new, powerful fuel source for cars and trucks affect the country's production possibilities frontier? How might the new fuel affect GDP?

Problem-Solving Activity

16. Suppose that there is a three-person city. The three residents are considering having a fireworks display. Gabriela is willing to contribute $100 toward the display, while Jerome is willing to pay $80, and Katelyn is willing to pay $60. The fireworks display costs $120. (a) Will any single citizen alone be willing to pay for the fireworks? (b) What recommendation can you make to this city that will benefit all three citizens?

Economics Journal

Brainstorming Reread your Economics Journal entry for Chapter 3. Of the benefits of free enterprise that you listed, which are most important to you and your family?

Skills for Life

Analyzing Primary Sources Review the steps shown on page 61; then read the primary source below and answer the following questions.

17. What course of action is President Johnson suggesting in this speech?
18. In your own words, state three economic reasons Johnson uses to support his argument.
19. For what type of assignment might you use this primary source quotation? Explain.

> The war on poverty is not a struggle simply to support people, to make them dependent on the generosity of others. It is a struggle to give people a chance. . . . We do this, first of all, because it is right that we should. . . . We do it also because helping some will increase the prosperity of all. Our fight against poverty will be an investment in the most valuable of our resources—the skills and strength of our people. And in the future, as in the past, this investment will return its cost many fold to our entire economy.
>
> If we can raise the annual earnings of 10 million among the poor by only $1,000 we will have added $14 billion a year to our national output. In addition we can make important reductions in public assistance payments which now cost us $4 billion a year, and in the large costs of fighting crime and delinquency, disease and hunger. . . .
>
> This is only part of the story. Our history has proved that each time we broaden the base of abundance, giving more people the chance to produce and consume, we create new industry, higher production, increased earnings and better income for all.
>
> —President Lyndon B. Johnson, *Public Papers of the Presidents of the United States,* 1965

Progress Monitoring *Online*

For: Chapter 3 Self-Test **Visit:** PHSchool.com
Web Code: mna-1031

As a final review, take the Economics Chapter 3 Self-Test and receive immediate feedback on your answers. The test consists of 20 multiple-choice questions designed to test your understanding of the chapter content.

Problem-Solving Activity

16. (a) no (b) Students might suggest that each individual be charged $40 for the display, since each one will have an equal opportunity to make use of it. Other students might suggest graduating the "tax" according to the amount each person was willing to pay ($50, $40, $30).

Skills for Life

17. The President is suggesting the investment of funds to fight poverty.
18. Students might mention that Johnson states that it will raise everyone's standard of living, it is a good investment, and it will pay for itself many times over in the future.
19. Students might suggest a paper on changing views of public policy over time or a biographical sketch of Lyndon Johnson.

Additional support materials and activities for Chapter 3 of *Economics: Principles in Action* can be found in the Social Studies area of **PHSchool.com.**

Review and Assessment

Vocabulary Practice Unit 1 folder, p. 35 uses a crossword puzzle to reinforce understanding of key terms.

GTE **Guide to the Essentials** Chapter 3 Test, p. 15

Test Bank CD-ROM Chapter 3 Test

Go Online PHSchool.com Students may use the Chapter 3 Self-Test on **PHSchool.com** to prepare for the Chapter Test.

Economics Journal

Students answers will vary, but may include: the ability to choose what and when to buy (voluntary exchange), the ability to purchase items by cash and credit (free contract); the ability to start a business at any time and in any field (open opportunity).

THE WALL STREET JOURNAL.
CLASSROOM EDITION

DEBATE: HEALTH-CARE COSTS

1. Focus Have students find the meaning of each of these words before they begin to read: *bias, capitation, competence, diminished, dispensed, ethical, incentive,* and *rendered.*

Explain to students that they will be conducting a debate on whether doctors should consider costs when treating their patients. Inform them that they will be responsible for arguing one side of the issue. Remind students that a well-prepared debater supports a position with valid evidence, logical arguments, and responsible appeals to emotion.

2. Instruct The authors have both researched the delicate balance between cost and care in the treatment of patients. Have students conduct further research on health-care costs from credible sources before conducting the debate.

Remind students that they should use the following debate format:
The affirmative side will:
- State the problem to be solved. Why is this problem significant?
- Explain who or what is harmed if this problem is not resolved. Use factual evidence to quantify the harm.
- Propose a plan of action. Explain why it is better than the current system.
- Provide factual evidence to show how the plan will solve the problem.

The opposing side will:
- Refute the arguments of the affirmative side, using factual evidence to quantify and support its position.
- If necessary, support the status quo's ability to solve the problem.

3. Close/Reteach When the debate is concluded, encourage students to discuss their opinions on the issue. Ask them whether they were persuaded by the other side's arguments. Conclude by having students write their own statements supporting or opposing using cost as a factor in patient treatments.

THE WALL STREET JOURNAL.
CLASSROOM EDITION

DEBATING CURRENT ISSUES: *Health-Care Costs*

As health-care costs have skyrocketed in recent years, both patients and caregivers have had to ask a difficult question: Should cost be a deciding factor in medical treatment? In this debate from *The Wall Street Journal Classroom Edition,* Abbie Leibowitz, an executive at Health Advocate and former chief medical officer at Aetna, and Dr. David Rogers, a physician in private practice, discuss the role of costs in the health-care system.

YES *Should doctors consider cost when treating a patient?*

BY ABBIE LEIBOWITZ

It is absolutely reasonable and ethical for physicians to consider the costs of care when evaluating treatment options.

The principle of "first do no harm" that all doctors are taught has broader implications than just its application to the patient. Do no harm in your treatment of the patient for the patient's sake, do no harm in treating your patient from a public-health perspective, and do no harm to the system of health care we all depend upon.

As a percentage of our gross domestic product, the U.S. has the most expensive health-care system in the world. Medical-insurance premiums in the private sector have been increasing far faster than the pace of general inflation. They are projected to double between 2003 and 2012 to $3.1 trillion or 17.7% of the nation's GDP. Such increases are unsustainable and are a prescription for an economic and public-health disaster.

As costs increase, payors—whether the government or employers—shift more financial responsibility to the individual in the form of diminished benefits or increasing co-payments and deductibles. The increasing burden of paying for otherwise uncompensated care is like a hidden tax on those who pay for medical services. Providers simply build these costs into the rates they charge those who pay.

Is it good care to so burden a patient with expenses that could have been avoided? Is it good care to prescribe an expensive brand-name product when there is an equally effective generic equivalent that costs less than half as much? If because they cannot afford the cost of care or medicine, patients do not get their prescriptions filled, have we helped them? We have no choice but to exert a conscious control over medical costs.

Resources are not limitless. When given the choice of equally effective diagnostic tests, treatment approaches, or medication options, physicians must consider which is likely to cost less. Our patients' needs are our first priority, but the health-care system we all depend upon is also our "patient."

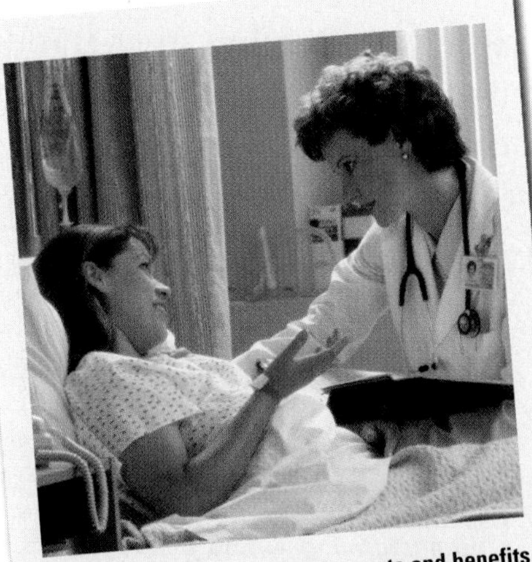

Doctors must consider both the costs and benefits of treatments when choosing the best treatment for a sick patient.

Debate Activity
Debating Current Issues folder, p. 5 asks students to find facts to support either side of the health-care debate.

Economic Assessment Rubric
Economics Assessment Rubrics folder, pp. 14–15 provides sample evaluation materials for participation in debates.

Background

About the Authors

Abbie Leibowitz is an executive at Health Advocate, a company that helps patients cope with health-insurance troubles. Ms. Leibowitz argues that balancing cost and care is the only way to stabilize the health care system. On the other side of the issue is David Rogers, a physician in private practice who says doctors should have one primary concern: their patients' health.

NO Should doctors consider cost when treating a patient?

By David E. Rogers, M.D.

As stated in the American Medical Association's Declaration of Professional Responsibility, one of the duties of all physicians is to "Treat the sick and injured with competence and compassion and without prejudice." "Without prejudice" means to avoid any bias that could possibly interfere with or reduce the quality of care the patient receives. In my opinion, this would include considering costs when making treatment decisions.

Of course, a physician should not provide any unnecessary care just because the cost is covered. On the other hand, limiting or withholding care or choosing potentially inferior options just to reduce cost would be unethical. For physicians, the quality of the patient's medical care should always be the first and foremost consideration. I have always felt that "managed care" created cost-related, ethical dilemmas for physicians trying to act in a patient's best interest.

One economic model that brings physicians into direct conflict with cost considerations is the capitation system that is the basis of managed care. This is a system where a uniform or set fee is paid to the physician per patient (per capita) and in return the physician agrees to provide all the health care needed for those covered patients. The payment is not reduced if few services are necessary, so the physician makes more money when fewer services are rendered. However, the payment is no greater than if many services are provided. Physicians in this situation may actually be forced to operate at a loss. From a business standpoint, the incentive is to take care of only well patients and provide as little service as possible. Fortunately, most "capitation" agreements have disappeared because physicians refuse to compromise their patients' care in such a way.

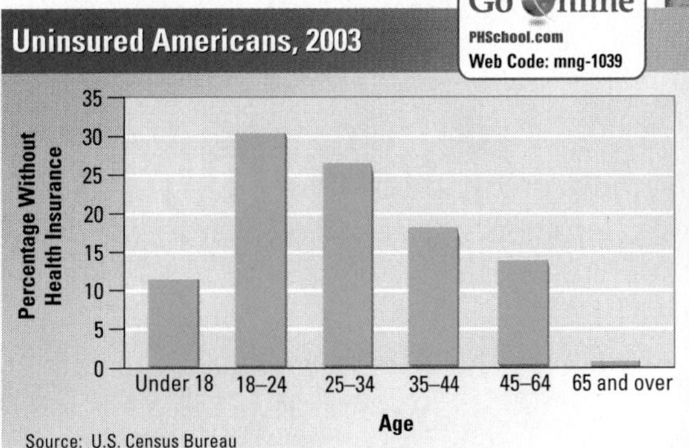

Increasing health-care costs have led to higher prices for health insurance. As a result, more and more younger Americans do not have health insurance.

One example of where cost has played a role in medical decision-making can be found at your local pharmacy. Often, doctors will prescribe a brand-name drug and the patient will find that the generic version of the drug has been substituted. That's because many insurers require that if a generic version of a drug is available, that is what should be dispensed.

In most situations, generic drugs are just as effective as their brand-name counterparts. But there are many instances where the patient does not get the same desired effect.

We all like to say we are worried about costs—until we are the one who is sick or injured. When that happens, all we care about is getting well, regardless of the cost.

DEBATING THE ISSUE

1. Why does David Rogers disagree with "managed care"?
2. What data does Abbie Leibowitz cite to show that the health-care system is facing a crisis?
3. **Drawing Conclusions** The two authors disagree about whether a doctor's obligations extend beyond the patient to the overall public-health system. With which author do you agree? Why?
4. **Reading Graphs** Which age group's members are most likely to lack health insurance?

For: You Decide Poll
Visit: PHSchool.com
Web Code: mnp-1031

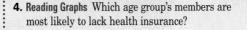

Interdisciplinary Connections: History

Health-Insurance Funding In 1965, the U.S. Congress created the Medicare program. This program pays for hospital care and physician services for people over the age of 65 as well as covering some specific disabilities and diseases. Wage earners pay for this health-insurance system by taxes withheld from their paychecks. The federal and state governments fund Medicaid, another health-insurance system for low-income families. In 2002, Medicare had 41 million enrollees and spent more than $230 billion. In 2000, 9.4 percent of people under 65 years of age were covered by Medicaid, an increase from the 8.8 percent covered in 1998, according to the National Center for Health Statistics.

Making the Connection Have students discuss the role of state and federal governments in paying health-insurance costs. When it comes to allocating tax revenue to fund government programs, what priority should these health-insurance programs receive? Why? What other alternatives could the government adopt to provide health coverage and keep costs down?

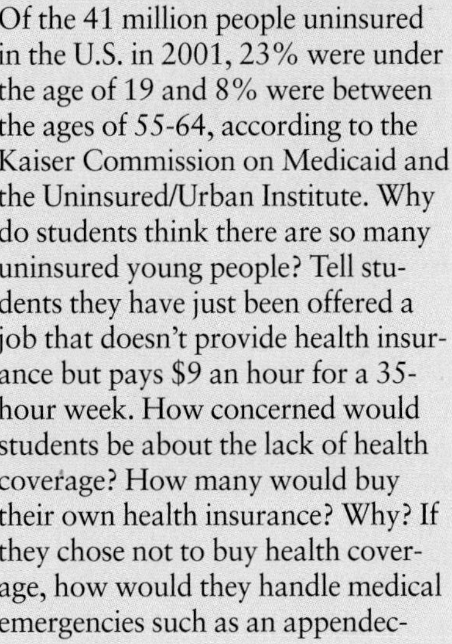

Differentiated Instruction L2

Of the 41 million people uninsured in the U.S. in 2001, 23% were under the age of 19 and 8% were between the ages of 55-64, according to the Kaiser Commission on Medicaid and the Uninsured/Urban Institute. Why do students think there are so many uninsured young people? Tell students they have just been offered a job that doesn't provide health insurance but pays $9 an hour for a 35-hour week. How concerned would students be about the lack of health coverage? How many would buy their own health insurance? Why? If they chose not to buy health coverage, how would they handle medical emergencies such as an appendectomy? LPR

Go Online PHSchool.com Students can find additional links related to the debate by visiting the *Economics: Principles in Action* site at **PHSchool.com.**

Answers to . . .

1. Dr. Rogers objects to the capitation system.
2. There is a growing population of nearly 45 million uninsured Americans who don't buy health insurance because they can't afford their share of the cost, or they work for employers who don't offer this benefit. Over the past three years, medical insurance premiums in the private sector have increased faster than inflation. They are projected to reach 17.7% of the nation's GDP or $3.1 trillion by 2012.
3. Answers will vary but should refer to details from the debate sources.
4. Age 18–24

UNIT 2

How Markets Work

Introducing the Unit

Unit Summary

Unit 2 discusses the factors that affect the way markets perform. In Chapter 4 students learn about demand—consumer desire for a product—and how it is affected by other economic factors. Chapter 5 covers supply, which along with demand is one of the basic building blocks of the marketplace. Both of these factors affect prices, the subject of Chapter 6. Chapter 7 covers the four types of market structures and how the government intervenes to protect competition—a key element of free enterprise—in the marketplace.

Focus Activity

Introduce Unit 2 to students by asking them to complete the Focus Activity. Give students 5 to 10 minutes to brainstorm their lists of goods that either are in limited supply or are in great demand. Then allow students to make generalizations about the items on their lists. Finally, hold a class discussion in which students compare lists and develop hypotheses about causal links between supply, demand, and price.

UNIT 2

How Markets Work

National Council on Economic Education

The following Voluntary National Content Standards in Economics are addressed in this unit:

★ Standard 4 ★ Standard 8
★ Standard 7 ★ Standard 9

See the Chapter Openers on pp. 78, 100, 124, and 150 for a complete description of the standards addressed in each chapter.

Chapters in This Unit

4. *Demand*
5. *Supply*
6. *Prices*
7. *Market Structures*

Today is the Super Bowl . . .

Your favorite team is playing, the stadium is right across town, and you really want to go!

- How many other people are trying to get tickets?
- How many tickets are available?
- What determines the price of the tickets?
- From whom are you going to buy your ticket? Is there more than one ticket outlet?

Answers to all of these questions are based on the laws of supply and demand—two of the most important tools of economic analysis. In this unit you will study supply and demand to see how the prices of goods and services are affected by all sorts of changes in the economy, including higher incomes, technological innovation, and changes in consumer preferences.

Focus Activity

Brainstorm a list of goods that have either a limited supply or are in great demand. What generalizations can you make about the prices of these items? Compare your list with those of your classmates.

Bibliography

Print

Virtual Economics: An Interactive Center for Economics Education. CD-ROM. Santoni, Gary. *Economic Activity and Markets.* EconomicsAmerica, National Council on Economic Education, 1997.

Multimedia

The People of Market Street Series. Board of Governors of the Federal Reserve System, distributed by Corelco, 32 Oak Terrace, St. Louis, MO 63119-3615.

"Demand." Color video, 21 minutes. Explains the law of demand, illustrating that many other factors besides price affect demand.

"Supply." Color video, 20 minutes. Shows how amounts of goods produced and supplied respond to market price as well as the other factors that guide a potential producer.

Technology Center

Economics Video Library

Includes high-interest, chapter-specific segments produced by CNBC for

THE WALL STREET JOURNAL.
CLASSROOM EDITION

Simulations and Data Graphing CD-ROM

Provides interactive federal budget and stock market simulations and a data graphing tool designed to support instruction in economics.

PRENTICE HALL
TeacherEXPRESS™
Plan · Teach · Assess

Teacher Express CD-ROM offers powerful lesson planning, resource management, testing, and an interactive Teacher's Edition.

Prentice Hall Presentation Pro CD-ROM

Allows you to create custom lectures for every chapter.

Social Studies Skills Tutor CD-ROM

Provides interactive practice in geographic literacy, critical thinking and reading, visual analysis, and communications.

Exam*View*® Test Bank CD-ROM

Allows you to create, edit, and print out chapter level tests.

Transparency Resource Package

Illustrates key economic concepts and provides useful forms and templates for enhancing classroom discussions.

Section Reading Support Transparency System

Delivers the main idea of each section in the student text through graphic organizers.

Offers student-appropriate online activities and links as well as resources for the teacher. Be sure to check out this month's **eTeach** online discussion with a Master Economics Teacher.

Chapter 4 Demand

For more pacing suggestions, see the Economics Pacing Guide in the Program Overview of the Teaching Resources.

Section Objectives	Print and Technology Resources
1 Understanding Demand *(pp. 79–83)* **Objectives** 1. Explain the law of demand. 2. Understand how the substitution effect and the income effect influence decisions. 3. Create a demand schedule for an individual and a market. 4. Interpret a demand graph using demand schedules.	• **Lesson Planner** Section 1 Lesson Plan, p. 25 • **Learning Styles Lesson Plans folder** Section 1 Lesson Plan, p. 13 • **Lesson Plans folder** Section 1 Lesson Plan, p. 18 • **Economics Assessment Rubrics folder** Graphing Data, pp. 8–9 • **Unit 2 folder** Guided Reading and Review, p. 2 Economic Skills, p. 8 Section 1 Quiz, p. 3 • **Presentation Pro CD-ROM** Section 1 • **Transparency Resource Package** Economics Organizers, G5: Web Graphic Organizer Economics Concepts, 4A: Individual Demand Curve Economics Concepts, 4B: Market Demand Curve • **Section Reading Support Transparency System** • **Social Studies Skills Tutor CD-ROM**
2 Shifts of the Demand Curve *(pp. 85–88)* **Objectives** 1. Understand the difference between a change in quantity demanded and a shift in the demand curve. 2. Identify the determinants that create changes in demand and that can cause a shift in the demand curve. 3. Explain how the change in the price of one good can affect demand for a related good.	• **Lesson Planner** Section 2 Lesson Plan, p. 26 • **Learning Styles Lesson Plans folder** Section 2 Lesson Plan, p. 14 • **Lesson Plans folder** Section 2 Lesson Plan, p. 19 • **Unit 2 folder** Guided Reading and Review, p. 4 Careers in Economics, Buyer, p. 11 Economic Cartoon, p. 12 Section 2 Quiz, p. 5 • **Source Articles folder** Walking on Clamshells, pp. 12–14 • **Presentation Pro CD-ROM** Section 2 • **Transparency Resource Package** Economics Organizers, G9: Multi-Flow Chart Graphic Organizer Economics Concepts, 4C: Change Along a Demand Curve Economics Concepts, 4D: Change in Demand • **Section Reading Support Transparency System**
3 Elasticity of Demand *(pp. 90–96)* **Objectives** 1. Explain how to calculate elasticity of demand. 2. Identify factors that affect elasticity. 3. Explain how firms use elasticity and revenue to make decisions.	• **Lesson Planner** Section 3 Lesson Plan, p. 27 • **Lesson Plans folder** Section 3 Lesson plan, p. 20 • **Economics Assessment Rubrics folder** Position Paper, pp. 22–23 • **Unit 2 folder** Guided Reading and Review, p. 6 Vocabulary Practice, p. 9 Economic Detective, p. 10 Section 3 Quiz, p. 7 • **Case Studies in Free Enterprise folder** Howard Schultz, pp. 8–9 • **Math Practice folder** Determining Elasticity of Demand, p. 4 • **Presentation Pro CD-ROM** Section 3 • **Transparency Resource Package** Economics Organizers, G7: Tree Map Graphic Organizer Economics Concepts, 4E: Elasticity of Demand • **Section Reading Support Transparency System**

Differentiated Instruction

Cornell Note Taking L1 L2

Learning to efficiently take notes will help students read the text and review key information. The Cornell NoteTaking strategy provides a structured way to read and record core content.

1. Students draw a vertical line two and a half inches from the left-hand side of notebook paper to create a Review Column.

2. Students take notes on the text material on the right.

3. Students review their notes and write focused questions in the Review Column that elicit the specific content to the right. For example, if one section explains the law of demand, the student would write, "What factors contribute to the law of demand?" This forces students to carefully review the section content and clarify it in their minds.

4. To study their notes, students' cover up the right side of the page, read the review questions, and quiz themselves by checking their understanding and recall of critical content, rather than passively rereading information.

5. Students can be encouraged/required to write a brief summary of each section in their own words at the end of their notes to increase the likelihood that they will retain the information.

The example below illustrates a note-taking template for a U.S. History class.

Cornell Note-Taking System: Sample Note-Taking Scaffold

	U.S. History 11/2/05
Recall Clues & Questions	Notes: Early U.S. Immigration
What is an "immigrant"?	Def. of an "immigrant":
Who were the only non-immigrants to the U.S.?	Only non-immigrants to U.S.: 1. 2.
What were the major U.S. immigrant groups in the 1700s & where did they live?	Immigrant groups in 1700s & where they settled: Spain: England: N & W Europe:
What were the major reasons immigrants came in the 1800s?	1800s–reasons for immigration 1. 2. 3.
What made their lives difficult?	Reasons life was difficult for early immigrants 1. 2. 3.
What kinds of jobs did the early immigrants have?	Jobs different immigrant groups had: 1. 2. 3.

Go Online PHSchool.com

Visit the Social Studies area of the Prentice Hall Web site. There you can find additional links to enrich chapter content for *Economics: Principles in Action* as well as a self-test for students. Be sure to check out this month's **eTeach** online discussion with a Master Economics Teacher.

Web Code: mnf-2041

Running Out of Time?

- Use the **Presentation Pro CD-ROM** to create an outline for this chapter.
- Use the Chapter Summary in the **Chapter 4 Assessment,** p. 98.
- Use the Section Summaries for Chapter 4, from **Guide to the Essentials of Economics (English and Spanish).**

THE WALL STREET JOURNAL. CLASSROOM EDITION

Prentice Hall brings into the classroom the authoritative content of *The Wall Street Journal Classroom Edition.* See the Source Articles, Debating Current Issues, and You and Your Money folders in the **Teaching Resources**. Also, see Economics Video Library, "Home Sweet Home."

Assessment Resources

Chapter Assessment

Teaching Resources Unit 2, Chapter 4

- Section Quizzes, pp. 3, 5, 7

Exam *View*® Test Bank CD-ROM Chapter 4

Economics Assessment Rubrics

Chapter 4 Self-Test, **Web Code:** mna-2041

Reading and Skills Evaluation

Progress Monitoring Assessments

- Screening Test
- Diagnostic Test of Social Studies Skills

Standardized Test Preparation

Test Prep Workbook

Test-Taking Strategies With Transparencies

Differentiated Instruction Key

L1 Special Needs	LPR Less Proficient Readers
L2 Basic to Average	AR Advanced Readers
L3 All Students	SN Special Needs Students
L4 Average to Advanced	GT Gifted and Talented
	ELL English Language Learner

Chapter 4

Demand

Introducing the Chapter

In this chapter, students are introduced to the concept of demand. The chapter moves from general definitions of demand to an exploration of demand curves and their shifts, and finally, to a discussion of the elasticity of demand.

Go Online
PHSchool.com

For additional links for *Economics: Principles in Action* provided by Prentice Hall and *The Wall Street Journal Classroom Edition,* visit the Social Studies area. Be sure to check out this month's **eTeach** online discussion with a Master Teacher.

Beyond the Lecture

You may cover the concepts in Chapter 4 in an activity-based style by using the following materials:

- **Technology Resources** appropriate for use with this chapter are noted on pp. 82, 83, 86, 87, 88, 91, 96, and 99.
- **Presentation Pro CD-ROM** with animated graphs gives you an alternative method for organizing and delivering chapter content.
- **Activities** designed to meet the needs of students of mixed abilities and learning styles are noted throughout the chapter in the side columns.
- **Learning Styles Lesson Plans** provide alternate lessons for diverse learning styles. See pp. 13–14 of the Learning Styles Lesson Plans folder located in the Teaching Resources.

Economics Journal

Instruct students to write their responses to the question in their Economics Journals. Students may include completed journal entries in an Economics Portfolio.

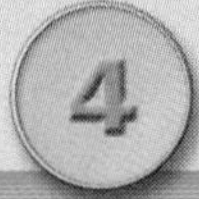

Chapter 4 Demand

Andrea couldn't wait to get the new CD on the shelves of the music store she managed. She sold more than 50 copies at $18.99 each on the first day. Six months later, Andrea moved the CDs to shelves in the middle of the store and cut the price to $14.99. Three years later, a new manager moved the four remaining CDs to the bargain bin. Customers could take one home for only $5.99.

Each of Andrea's decisions was shaped by the needs and wishes of her customers. Economists use the term *demand* to describe the ability and desire of consumers to buy a good. Paired with supply, demand forms one of the building blocks of the marketplace.

Economics Journal

Quickly list the last five goods or services you purchased and how much you spent on each. What led you to buy each one?

Go Online
PHSchool.com

For: Current Data
Visit: PHSchool.com
Web Code: mng-2041

NCEE
National Council on Economic Education

The following Voluntary National Content Standards in Economics are addressed in this chapter:

★ **Standard 4** Students will understand that: People respond predictably to positive and negative incentives.

★ **Standard 7** Students will understand that: Markets exist when buyers and sellers interact. This interaction determines market prices and thereby allocates scarce goods and services.

For more information about the standards, contact the National Council on Economic Education

1140 Avenue of the Americas
New York, NY 10036
1-800-338-1192

Section 1 Understanding Demand

Preview

Objectives

After studying this section you will be able to:

1. **Explain** the law of demand.
2. **Understand** how the substitution effect and the income effect influence decisions.
3. **Create** a demand schedule for an individual and a market.
4. **Interpret** a demand graph using demand schedules.

Section Focus

According to the law of demand, people buy less of a good when its price rises. Demand schedules and demand curves illustrate how people and markets react to different prices.

Key Terms

demand
law of demand
substitution effect
income effect
demand schedule
market demand schedule
demand curve

In Chapter 2, you read about *economic systems,* which are different ways of answering the three economic questions of *what to produce, how much to produce,* and *who gets what.* In the United States, most goods are allocated through a market system. In a market system, the interaction of buyers and sellers determines the prices of most goods as well as what quantity of a good will be produced. Buyers demand goods, sellers supply those goods, and the interactions between the two groups lead to an agreement on the price and the quantity traded.

Demand is the desire to own something and the ability to pay for it. We will look at the demand side of markets in this chapter. In the next chapter we will look at the actions of sellers, which economists call the supply side. In Chapter 6, we will look at supply and demand together and study how they interact to establish the prices that we pay for most goods.

The Law of Demand

Anyone who has ever spent money will easily understand the **law of demand**. The law of demand says that when a good's price is lower, consumers will buy more of it. When the price is higher, consumers will buy less of it. All of us act out this law of demand in our everyday purchasing decisions. Whether your income is \$10 or \$10 million, the price of a good will strongly influence your decision to buy.

Ask yourself this question: Would you buy a slice of pizza for lunch if it cost \$1? Many of us would, and some of us might

demand *the desire to own something and the ability to pay for it*

law of demand *consumers buy more of a good when its price decreases and less when its price increases*

Figure 4.1 **Law of Demand**

PRICE
As prices go down . . .
DEMAND
quantity demanded goes up.

PRICE
As prices go up . . .
DEMAND
quantity demanded goes down.

If the price of pizza rises, people will buy fewer slices.
Incentives What does the law of demand say about lower prices?

Understanding Demand

Objectives You may wish to call students' attention to the objectives in the Section Preview. The objectives are reflected in the main headings of the section.

Bellringer Ask students what is most important when they consider buying something. (Many will say *price.*) Explain that in this section they will learn how price affects the demand for goods and services.

Vocabulary Builder Have students read Section 1 to discover the meanings of the key terms. Ask students to use each key term in a sentence that displays their understanding of the term without simply repeating its definition.

Lesson Plan

Teaching the Main Concepts 

1. Focus Demand for goods is usually directly linked to price. Ask students to suggest ways of increasing demand for certain goods.

2. Instruct Explain the law of demand. Discuss with students how consumer spending habits are affected by the substitution effect and the income effect. Help students understand that demand schedules and curves offer snapshots of consumer demand.

3. Close/Reteach Remind students that as prices rise, demand generally falls. Ask students to illustrate this principle using examples from their own lives.

Graphing the Main Idea

Incentives To build understanding of the concept of **incentives,** have students use a web graphic organizer like the one below to show the details of the law of demand. Remind students that a web shows a main idea and its supporting details.

Section Reading Support Transparencies A template and the answers for this graphic organizer can be found in Chapter 4, Section 1 of the Section Reading Support Transparency System.

Answer to . . .

Building Key Concepts Lower prices increase quantity demanded.

Guided Reading and Review
Unit 2 folder, p. 2 asks students to identify the main ideas of the section and to define or identify key terms.

Meeting NCEE Standards

Use the following benchmark activity from the **Voluntary National Content Standards in Economics** to evaluate student understanding of **Standard 4.**

Analyze the impact (on consumers, producers, workers, savers, and investors) of an increase in the minimum wage, a new tax policy, or a change in interest rates.

Differentiated Instruction 

Ask students to explain each of the key terms in their own words, either orally or in writing. Ask students to think of an example that illustrates each key term. ELL

Differentiated Instruction 

(Reteaching) Organize the class into groups of three or four students. Ask each group to brainstorm a scenario that illustrates the role of the substitution effect and the income effect on demand. Have groups share their scenarios and answer any questions from the class.

FAST FACT

Do you know your rights as an online shopper? The Federal Trade Commission (FTC) requires firms that sell products online to (1) ship the merchandise within 30 days of receiving your order, (2) notify you if the shipment cannot be made on time, and (3) cancel your order and return your payment unless you agree to a delay.

even buy more than one slice. But would you buy the same slice of pizza if it cost $2? Fewer of us would buy it at that price. Even real pizza lovers might reduce their consumption from 3 or 4 slices to just 1 or 2. How many of us would buy a slice for $10? Probably very few. As the price of pizza gets higher and higher, fewer of us are willing to buy it. That is the law of demand in action.

substitution effect *when consumers react to an increase in a good's price by consuming less of that good and more of other goods*

income effect *the change in consumption resulting from a change in real income*

The law of demand is the result of not one pattern of behavior, but of two separate patterns that overlap. These two behavior patterns are the **substitution effect** and the **income effect**. The substitution effect and income effect describe two different ways that a consumer can change his or her spending patterns. Together, they explain why an increase in price decreases the quantity purchased. Figure 4.2 describes how the substitution effect and the income effect can change a consumer's buying habits.

Figure 4.2 **Building the Law of Demand**

	Price of A increases		Price of A decreases	
	Consumption of A	Consumption of other goods	Consumption of A	Consumption of other goods
Income effect	↓	↓	↑	↑
Substitution effect	↓	↑	↑	↓
Combined effect	↓	↕	↑	↕

Both the substitution effect and the income effect lead consumers to buy less of good A when it becomes more expensive. However, the income effect leads consumers to spend less on other goods so they can afford good A, while the substitution effect encourages consumers to replace expensive good A with other, less expensive substitutes.
Incentives **Explain in your own words how an increase in the price of A affects consumption of other goods.**

The Substitution Effect

When the price of pizza rises, pizza becomes more expensive compared to other foods, such as tacos and salads. So, as the price of a slice of pizza rises, consumers have an incentive to buy one of those alternatives as a substitute for pizza. This causes a drop in the amount of pizza demanded. For example, instead of eating pizza for lunch on Mondays and Fridays, a student could eat pizza on Mondays and a bagel on Fridays. This change in spending is known as the substitution effect. The substitution effect takes place when a consumer reacts to a rise in the price of one good by consuming less of that good and more of a substitute good.

The substitution effect can also apply to a drop in prices. If the price of pizza drops, pizza becomes cheaper compared to other alternatives. Consumers will now substitute pizza for tacos, salads, and other lunch choices, causing the quantity of pizza demanded to rise.

The Income Effect

Rising prices have another effect that we have all felt. They make us feel poorer. When the price of movie tickets, shoes, or pizza increases, your limited budget just won't buy as much as it used to. It feels as if you have less money. You can no longer afford to buy the same combination of goods, and you must cut back your purchases of some goods. If you buy fewer slices of pizza without increasing your purchases of other foods, that is the income effect.

One important fact to remember is that economists measure consumption in the amount of a good that is bought, not the amount of money spent to buy it. Although you are spending more on pizza, you are consuming fewer slices, so your consumption has gone down. If the price rises from $1 a slice to $2 a slice, you may decide to pay extra and order your usual lunch, but you certainly would not choose to buy more slices than before. Although people spend more of their money on pizza, when

Answer to . . .

Building Key Concepts Students should explain the concepts in their own words. They should describe how the increased price of good A may decrease the quantity purchased of good B (income effect) or may cause consumers to buy more of good B (substitution effect).

Econ 101: Key Concepts Made Easy

Markets and Prices If students are having difficulty distinguishing between a **demand schedule** and a **market demand schedule,** ask them to consider themselves as individuals in relation to the class as a whole. A demand schedule shows what quantity of a good an individual student will purchase at different prices.

A market demand schedule shows what quantity of a good the entire class will purchase at different prices. Ask students to discuss why the demand schedule for a particular student might be very different from the market demand schedule for the entire class.

◀ Photographers at a school newspaper might buy a new camera every two years. If the price of a camera has fallen by $100 since the last purchase, students could spend the savings on other goods to make the newspaper better. This is the income effect in action.

the price goes up, the quantity demanded goes down. In this sense, the income effect leads to the law of demand.

Remember, too, that the income effect also operates when the price is lowered. If the price of pizza falls, all of a sudden you feel wealthier. If as a result you buy more pizza, that's the income effect.

A Demand Schedule

The law of demand explains how the price of any item affects the quantity demanded of that item. Before we look at the relationship between price and quantity demanded for a specific good, we need to look more closely at how economists use the word *demand*.

Understanding Demand

To have demand for a good, you must be willing and able to buy it at the specified price. This means that you want the good, and you can afford to buy it. You may desperately want a new car, a laptop computer, or a trip to Alaska, but if you can't truly afford any of these goods, then you do not demand them. You might demand compact discs, though, if at the current price you have enough money and want to buy some.

A **demand schedule** is a table that lists the quantity of a good that a person will purchase at each price in a market. For example, the table on the left in Figure 4.3 illustrates individual "demand for pizza." The schedule shows specific quantities that a student named Ashley is willing and able to purchase at specific prices. For example, at a price of $2.00, Ashley's "quantity demanded" of pizza is two slices per day.

Market Demand Schedules

If you owned a store, knowing the demand schedule of one customer might not be very helpful. You would want to know how

demand schedule *a table that lists the quantity of a good a person will buy at each different price*

Figure 4.3 **Demand Schedules**

Individual Demand Schedule		Market Demand Schedule	
Price of a slice of pizza	Quantity demanded per day	Price of a slice of pizza	Quantity demanded per day
$.50	5	$.50	300
$1.00	4	$1.00	250
$1.50	3	$1.50	200
$2.00	2	$2.00	150
$2.50	1	$2.50	100
$3.00	0	$3.00	50

BUILDING KEY CONCEPTS

Demand schedules show that demand for a good falls as the price rises.

Supply and Demand How does the market demand for pizza change when the price falls from $2.50 to $1.00 a slice? Be specific.

Block Scheduling Strategies

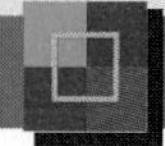

Consider these suggestions to take advantage of extended class time:

- Organize the class into groups of six to eight students. Tell groups that each is to prepare and perform a skit that illustrates the law of demand. Give them time to create and practice their skits, then have each group perform its skit for the class.
- Take a class survey to produce a market demand schedule for a popular product. Then ask volunteers to translate the demand schedule into a demand curve.
- Have students work in small groups to complete the Economic Cartoon activity in the Unit 2 folder, p. 12. Then ask them to suggest examples of other products that have not lasted long on the market because of low demand. Tell students to create their own cartoons for the products they have identified.

Background

Common Misconceptions

This is a tale of two T-shirts. Both are white, and both are made of 100 percent Egyptian cotton. Each has a single pocket, and both are extra-large. One shirt costs $10.95. The other costs $49.95. Why?

The value of any good is influenced by many factors, including demand. When the demand for a product rises, manufacturers can charge more for it. Of course, the law of demand says that when prices rise, people buy less of a product. So how can T-shirts costing $50 be in such demand when nearly identical T-shirts costing $11 are sitting neglected on the next display table? The answer is still related to demand. The description of the two T-shirts omitted an important detail: The more expensive T-shirt has a small nautical flag on the pocket. That flag is the logo of one of the country's hottest designers. Even though the labor and materials that went into manufacturing the two T-shirts are virtually the same, the value of one is nearly 400 percent greater than that of the other. That is a lot to pay for a logo, but if the market demands it, someone will produce it, and consumers will pay for it.

Differentiated Instruction L3

Have each student create an individual demand schedule. Tell students first to think of a good (such as a snack item) and to create a series of price levels. Each student should then go to a classmate, ask how much of the good he or she would buy at each price, and create an individual demand schedule based on the data collected.

Answer to . . .

Building Key Concepts Demanded increases by 150 slices a day.

Differentiated Instruction L4

Encourage students to use either a graphing calculator or a spreadsheet program to create a demand schedule and its corresponding demand curve. Ask one or two students to explain how they used this technology to create their schedules and curves. GT

Differentiated Instruction L3

Have students use the following data to prepare a market demand schedule: At a price of 80 cents per pound, the demand for apples is 14,000 pounds. At 60 cents per pound, the demand is 20,000 pounds. At 40 cents per pound, the demand is 26,000 pounds. At 20 cents per pound, the demand is 32,000 pounds.

Then have students graph the demand curve for the given data. Ask them to explain why the demand curve slopes downward and to the right.

Economics Assessment Rubric
Economics Assessment Rubrics folder, pp. 8–9 provides sample evaluation materials for graphing data.

Learning Styles Activity
Learning Styles Lesson Plans folder, p. 13 asks student groups to create a demand schedule, a market demand schedule, and a market demand curve for a frequently used product.

Transparency Resource Package
Economics Concepts, 4A: Individual Demand Curve

▲ **A sale can encourage consumers to buy more.**

customers as a whole would react to price changes. When you add up the demand schedules of every buyer in the market, you can create a market demand schedule. A **market demand schedule** shows the quantities demanded at each price by all consumers in the market. A market demand schedule for pizza would allow a restaurant owner to predict the total sales of pizza at several different prices.

market demand schedule *a table that lists the quantity of a good all consumers in a market will buy at each different price*

demand curve *a graphic representation of a demand schedule*

The owner of a pizzeria could create a market demand schedule for pizza slices by surveying his or her customers and then adding up the quantities demanded by all individual consumers at each price. The resulting market demand schedule will look like Ashley's demand schedule, but the quantities will be larger, as shown in Figure 4.3.

Note that the market demand schedule on the right in Figure 4.3 contains the same prices as Ashley's individual demand schedule, since those are the possible prices that may be charged by the pizzeria. The schedule also exhibits the law of demand. At higher prices the quantity demanded is lower. The only difference between the two demand schedules is that the market schedule lists larger quantities demanded. This is the case, since now we are talking about the purchase decisions of *all* potential consumers in the market.

Ashley's demand curve shows the number of slices of pizza she is willing and able to buy at each price.

Supply and Demand
How many slices of pizza does she demand when the price is $1.50?

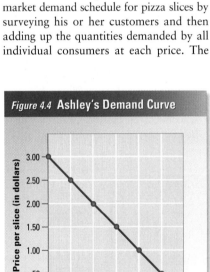

Figure 4.4 **Ashley's Demand Curve**

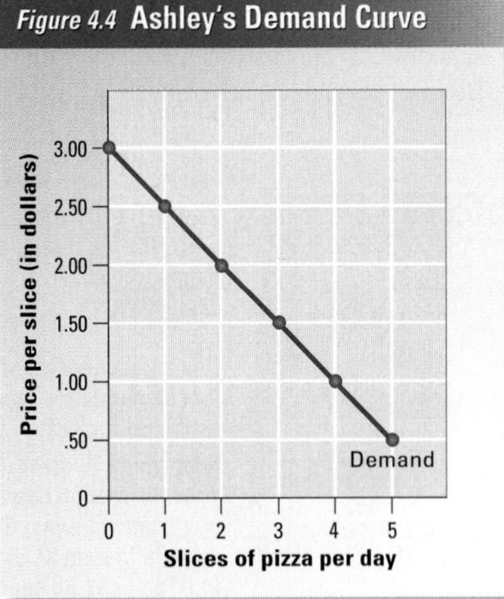

The Demand Graph

What if you took the numbers in Ashley's demand schedule in Figure 4.3 and plotted them on a graph? The result would be a **demand curve.** A demand curve is a graphic representation of a demand schedule.

How do economists create a demand curve? When they transfer numbers from a demand schedule to a graph, they always label the vertical axis with the lowest possible prices at the bottom and the highest at the top. Likewise, they always label the quantities demanded on the horizontal axis with the lowest possible quantity at the left and the highest possible quantity at the right. As Figure 4.4 shows, each pair of price and quantity-demanded numbers on the schedule is plotted as a point on the graph. Connecting the points creates a demand curve.

Reading a Demand Curve

Note two facts about the graph shown in Figure 4.4. First, the graph shows only the relationship between the price of this good and the quantity that Ashley will purchase. It assumes that all other factors that would affect Ashley's demand for pizza—like the price of other goods, her income, and the quality of the pizza—are held constant.

Second, the demand curve on the graph slopes downward to the right. If you follow the curve with your finger from the top left

Preparing for Standardized Tests

Have students read the section titled "The Demand Curve" and then answer the question below.

Which of the following is plotted on the vertical axis of a demand curve?

A demand schedule
(B) price
C quantity
D market demand schedule

Answer to . . .

Building Key Concepts Ashley's demand is 3 slices.

to the bottom right, you will notice that as price decreases, the quantity demanded increases. This is just another way of stating the law of demand, which states that higher prices will always lead to lower quantities demanded. All demand schedules and curves reflect the law of demand.

The demand curve in Figure 4.4 shows Ashley's demand for slices of pizza. A market demand curve shows the quantities demanded by all consumers at the same prices. Thus, in Figure 4.5, the prices listed on the vertical axis are identical to those in Ashley's demand curve. The quantities listed on the horizontal axis are much larger, corresponding to those in the market demand schedule in Figure 4.3.

Figure 4.5 **Market Demand Curve**

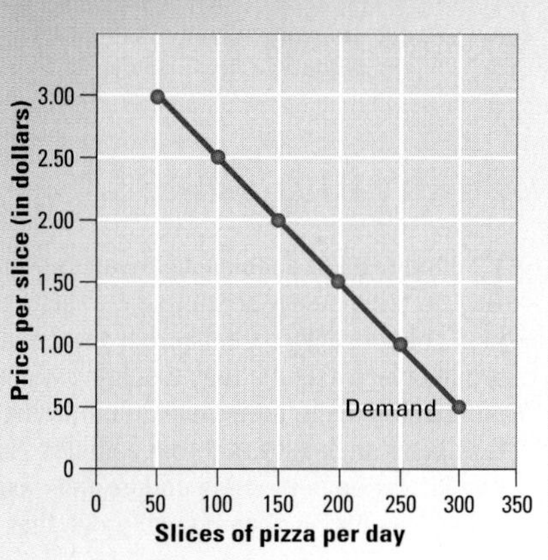

BUILDING KEY CONCEPTS

The market demand curve illustrates demand for pizza in an entire market.

Supply and Demand
How is the market demand curve similar to Ashley's demand curve?

Limits of a Demand Curve

The market demand curve can be used to predict how people will change their buying habits when the price of a good rises or falls. For example, if the price of pizza is $1.50 a slice, the pizzeria will sell 200 slices a day.

This market demand curve is only accurate for one very specific set of market conditions. If a nearby factory were to close, so that fewer people were in the area at lunchtime, the pizzeria would sell less pizza even if the price stayed the same. In the next section, you will read about how demand curves can shift because of changes in factors other than price.

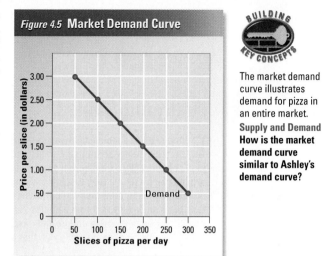

Section 1 Assessment

Progress Monitoring *Online*
For: Self-quiz with vocabulary practice
Web Code: mna-2045

Key Terms and Main Ideas

1. Define and give an example of the **income effect.**
2. What are three characteristics of a **demand curve?**

Applying Economic Concepts

3. ***Critical Thinking*** Explain why the law of demand can apply only in a free market economy.
4. ***Try This*** Create an individual demand schedule like the one in Figure 4.3 for your demand for CDs. Fill in six different prices for CDs. Assume that you have a part-time job that pays $80 a week. How many CDs would you buy at each of the six different prices? Compare your demand schedule to those of your classmates.
5. ***Critical Thinking*** Some economists believe that there are goods that do not obey the law of demand, because the demand for them would actually drop if their price fell. One example is a top-of-the-line luxury car. Why do you think prospective buyers might feel differently about these goods?
6. ***Math Practice*** Use the market demand schedule below to draw a demand curve for miniature golf.

Cost to Play a Game	Games Played per Month
$1.50	350
$2.00	250
$3.00	140
$4.00	80

For: Current Events Activity
Visit: PHSchool.com
Web Code: mnd-2041

Progress Monitoring *Online*
For additional assessment, have students access Progress Monitoring Online at **Web Code:** mna-2045

Go Online PHSchool.com Typing in the Web Code when prompted will bring students directly to detailed instructions for this activity.

Transparency Resource Package Economics Concepts, 4B: Market Demand Curve

GTE Guide to the Essentials Chapter 4, Section 1, p. 16 provides support for students who need additional review of the section content. Spanish support is available in the Spanish edition of the guide on p. 16.

Quiz Unit 2 folder, p. 3 includes questions to check students' understanding of Section 1 content.

Presentation Pro CD-ROM Quiz provides multiple-choice questions to check students' understanding of Section 1 content.

Answers to . . .
Section 1 Assessment

1. The income effect occurs when a consumer responds to a price increase by spending more on that good. If you always buy a particular brand of fruit juice and the price goes up, you may still buy it, but you may also cut down on your consumption because your money does not go as far.
2. The curve shows the relationship between the price of the good and the quantity a person will purchase; the curve assumes that other factors remain constant; the curve slopes downward to the right.
3. In a free market economy, prices fluctuate according to the market. According to the law of demand, consumer's purchasing decisions are based on these free-market price fluctuations.
4. Each student should complete an individual demand schedule. These will vary, but should reflect realistic data.
5. Students may answer that consumers consider these items luxuries and might suspect that such an item was inferior if it were not expensive. Other responses might mention the status value of being able to afford a very expensive item; this value would decline if the item were cheaper.
6. Student graphs should reflect the data provided. The curve should slope downward and to the right.

Answer to . . .

Building Key Concepts The two curves slope down and to the right in a similar manner.

Skills for LIFE

Analyzing Tables

1. Focus Students will learn how to evaluate economic activity patterns using tables.

2. Instruct Explain to students that a table is a way of organizing information so that relationships between facts and figures are easily seen. Be sure that students understand that an effective table can present information visually that otherwise would have to be explained at great length as part of the text. Advise students not to skip tables when reading; in today's print and electronic texts, graphics are an important source of information. Have students work through the three steps outlined in the skills feature.

3. Close/Reteach To provide additional practice, see the Economic Skills Activity below.

Economic Skills Activity
Unit 2 folder, p. 8, "Analyzing Tables," asks students to read a table and analyze the effect of a price increase on pizza sales.

Social Studies Skills Tutor CD-ROM offers interactive practice in critical thinking and reading, visual analysis, and communication.

Answers

1. (a) Demand for Selected Goods (b) the demand by students for certain goods at a cost of $5.00
2. (a) 13 (b) 37 (c) a movie ticket
3. (a) movie ticket (b) asthma medicine; it is probably a necessity for people with this condition
(c) Demand decreased. (d) Possible responses: Parents were willing to pay higher prices for most of the items, probably as they had larger incomes. Parents placed a higher demand on restaurant meals, students usually have food prepared for them or eat at fast-food chains.

Additional Practice

Student charts should reflect the expected levels of demand for these items. Students should be able to tell why they suggested various levels of demand at various prices.

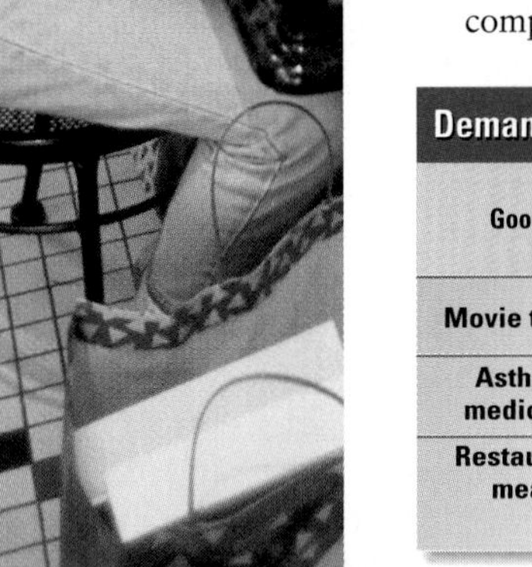

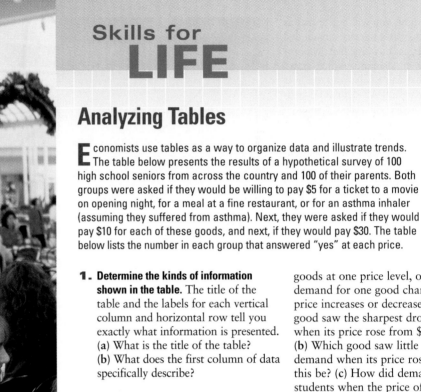

Skills for LIFE

Analyzing Tables

Economists use tables as a way to organize data and illustrate trends. The table below presents the results of a hypothetical survey of 100 high school seniors from across the country and 100 of their parents. Both groups were asked if they would be willing to pay $5 for a ticket to a movie on opening night, for a meal at a fine restaurant, or for an asthma inhaler (assuming they suffered from asthma). Next, they were asked if they would pay $10 for each of these goods, and next, if they would pay $30. The table below lists the number in each group that answered "yes" at each price.

1. **Determine the kinds of information shown in the table.** The title of the table and the labels for each vertical column and horizontal row tell you exactly what information is presented. (a) What is the title of the table? (b) What does the first column of data specifically describe?

2. **Read the information in the table.** Note that each dollar value has two sets of data, one for students, and the other for parents. Answer the following questions. (a) How many students were willing to pay $30 for the meal? (b) How many parents? (c) Which item were nearly all members of both groups unwilling to buy for $30?

3. **Study the table to find relationships among the data and draw conclusions.** You can use the data in this table to compare the demand for different goods at one price level, or to see how demand for one good changes as the price increases or decreases. (a) Which good saw the sharpest drop in demand when its price rose from $5 to $30? (b) Which good saw little change in demand when its price rose? Why might this be? (c) How did demand change for students when the price of a meal went up? (d) Name two conclusions you can draw about the differences between the patterns of demand of the students and their parents.

Additional Practice

Draw a new chart reflecting the data that you might expect to gather if you repeated this survey with different goods, such as a weekly bus pass, a concert ticket, and a best-selling novel.

Demand for Selected Goods

Goods	$5		$10		$30	
	Students	Parents	Students	Parents	Students	Parents
Movie ticket	70	67	11	35	1	0
Asthma medicine	91	94	86	88	79	85
Restaurant meal	94	96	62	80	13	37

Interdisciplinary Connections: Science

Analyzing Scientific Tables Communicating information clearly is a critical skill for scientists. Scientists let others know about their work through forums such as professional journals, conference presentations, and university Web sites, often using tables to organize and summarize their findings.

Have students work through the following activity: Let students look through popular science magazines, such as *Discover* and *Scientific American,* for examples of tables that present information clearly. Tell students to photocopy at least two tables and write a brief analysis of each, providing such information as the name of the table, its purpose, the kinds of information presented in the vertical columns and the horizontal rows, and the relationships among them.

Section 2 Shifts of the Demand Curve

Preview

Objectives

After studying this section you will be able to:

1. **Understand** the difference between a change in quantity demanded and a shift in the demand curve.
2. **Identify** the determinants that create changes in demand and that can cause a shift in the demand curve.
3. **Explain** how the change in the price of one good can affect demand for a related good.

Section Focus

Several factors can change the demand for a good at any price. A change in demand causes the entire demand curve to shift to the left or right.

Key Terms

ceteris paribus
normal good
inferior good
complements
substitutes

The market demand schedule for pizza in Figure 4.3 would appear to give the pizzeria owner all the information she needs to set the prices for her menu. All she has to do is look at the list, pick the price and quantity combination that will earn her the highest profit, and start baking.

Other factors, however, might have an effect. What would happen if the day after she printed a menu, the government announced that tomato sauce had a natural chemical that strengthened the immune system? Demand for pizza at all prices would climb.

When we counted the number of pizza slices that would sell as the price went up or down, we assumed that nothing besides the price of pizza would change. Economists refer to this assumption as ***ceteris paribus,*** the Latin phrase for "all other things held constant." The demand schedule took only changes in price into account. It did not take the news reports into account, or any one of thousands of other factors that change from day to day. In this section, you will learn how economists consider the impact of these other changes on the demand for goods like pizza.

Changes in Demand

A demand curve is accurate only as long as there are no changes other than price that could affect the consumer's decision. In other words, a demand curve is accurate only as long as the *ceteris paribus* assumption is true. When the price changes, we move along the curve to a different quantity demanded. For example, in the graph of Ashley's demand for slices of pizza, an increase in the price from $1.00 per slice to $1.50 will make Ashley's quantity demanded fall from four slices to three slices per day. This movement along the demand curve is referred to as a

ceteris paribus *a Latin phrase that means "all other things held constant"*

▼ A sudden winter storm can increase the demand for snow shovels.

Section 2

Shifts of the Demand Curve

Objectives You may wish to call students' attention to the objectives in the Section Preview. The objectives are reflected in the main headings of the section.

Bellringer Ask students what might happen to sales of a particular type of car if its producer announced that its new engine emitted no pollution, was more powerful than previous engines, and would cost the same. Explain that in this section they will discover how factors other than price can influence demand.

Vocabulary Builder Have students read through the section to find definitions of the key terms. Then ask them to think of a real-life example for each term. (Example of a normal good: *casual clothing*)

Lesson Plan

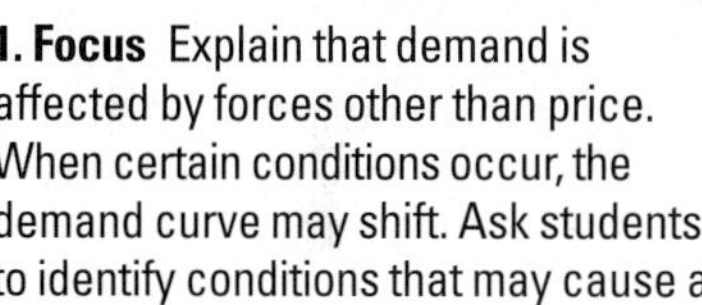

Teaching the Main Concepts L3

1. Focus Explain that demand is affected by forces other than price. When certain conditions occur, the demand curve may shift. Ask students to identify conditions that may cause a shift in demand.

2. Instruct Begin by explaining the difference between an increase or decrease in the quantity demanded and an actual change in demand. Discuss with students the factors that can cause demand to shift. Finally, discuss how complements and substitutes can alter demand.

3. Close/Reteach Remind students that a shift in the demand curve occurs when forces other than price cause consumers to buy more or less of a good at every price than they did before. Ask students to recall real-life examples of products for which demand skyrocketed or plummeted and to explain why demand changed.

Graphing the Main Idea

Markets and Prices To build understanding of the concept of **markets and prices,** have students complete several multi-flow chart graphic organizers like the one below to show the effects of different forces on demand. Tell students that a multi-flow chart shows causes and effects. For example, students might list causes in the outer boxes and the effect in the center box.

Section Reading Support Transparencies A template and the answers for this graphic organizer can be found in Chapter 4, Section 2 of the Section Reading Support Transparency System.

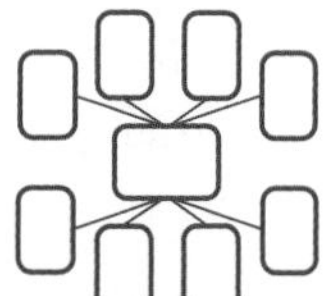

Guided Reading and Review
Unit 2 folder, p. 4 asks students to identify the main ideas of the section and to define or identify key terms.

Meeting NCEE Standards

Use the following benchmark activity from the **Voluntary National Content Standards in Economics** to evaluate student understanding of **Standard 7.**

Explain what happens (and why) to the price of tickets to sporting events purchased from scalpers when many more people want to attend those events than the number of seats in the stadium or arena. Also, explain what will happen to the price of a rare misprinted stamp if the postal service prints another 100,000 stamps in the same way.

Transparency Resource Package
Economics Concepts, 4C: Change Along a Demand Curve

Differentiated Instruction L3

Ask students to think of a single product and speculate on how demand for that product might change due to income fluctuations, population trends, consumer expectations and tastes, and advertising. Tell students that to learn about fluctuations in demand, they will write an essay entitled "A Month in the Life of [product name]." Encourage students to be creative in imagining changing scenarios for their product as the forces that affect it change.

Learning Styles Activity
Learning Styles Lesson Plans folder, p. 14 asks student groups to analyze changes in demand and shifts in a demand curve.

Economic Cartoon
Unit 2 folder, p. 12 gives students practice in interpreting cartoons about section content.

Answer to . . .

Building Key Concepts The effect on demand of an increase in price would be shown by the demand curve; the curve itself would not shift.

Figure 4.6 **Graphing Changes in Demand**

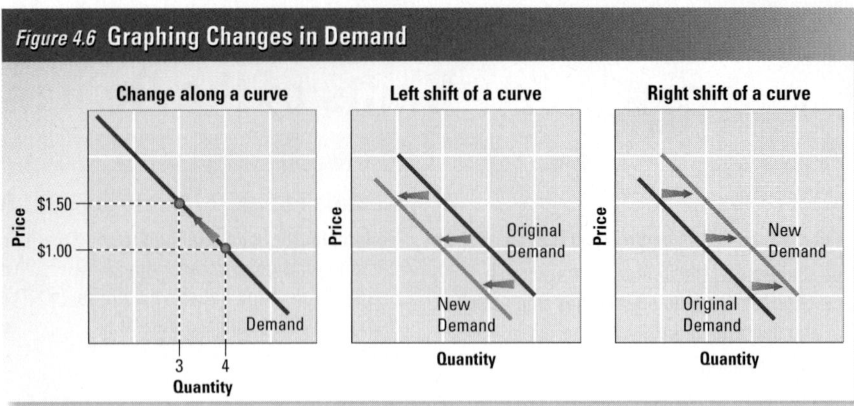

A change in quantity demanded caused by a change in price is shown as a movement *along* a demand curve. The curve does not shift. When factors other than price cause demand to fall, the demand curve shifts to the left. An increase in demand appears as a shift to the right. **Supply and Demand If the price of a book rose by $1.00, how would you represent the change on one of these graphs?**

normal good *a good that consumers demand more of when their incomes increase*

decrease in the quantity demanded. By the same reasoning, a decrease in the price of pizza would lead to an *increase* in the quantity demanded.

When we drop the *ceteris paribus* rule and allow other factors to change, we no longer move along the demand curve. Instead, the entire demand curve shifts. A shift in the demand curve means that at every price, consumers buy a different quantity than before. This shift of the entire curve is what economists refer to as a *change in demand.*

Suppose, for example, that Ashley's town is hit by a heat wave, and Ashley no longer feels as hungry for pizza. She will demand fewer slices at every price. The middle graph in Figure 4.6 shows her original demand curve and her new demand curve, adjusted for hot weather.

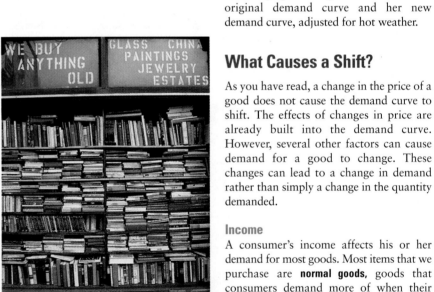

▶ **Used paperback books are often inferior goods. When consumers can afford new, clean books, they will buy fewer old paperbacks.**

What Causes a Shift?

As you have read, a change in the price of a good does not cause the demand curve to shift. The effects of changes in price are already built into the demand curve. However, several other factors can cause demand for a good to change. These changes can lead to a change in demand rather than simply a change in the quantity demanded.

Income

A consumer's income affects his or her demand for most goods. Most items that we purchase are **normal goods,** goods that consumers demand more of when their incomes increase. In other words, an increase

Econ 101: Key Concepts Made Easy

Supply and Demand To help students comprehend the difference between **normal goods** and **inferior goods,** first explain that the terms have meanings specific to economics that differ from their everyday usage. Ask them to relate the economic meanings to their own lives. Display the following:

normal = What I Want

inferior = What I Can Afford

Ask students to make a list of normal and inferior goods that affect their lives and to describe how the list might change if their incomes were to rise.

in Ashley's income from $50 per week to $75 per week will cause her to buy more of a normal good at every price level. If we were to draw a new demand schedule for Ashley, it would show a greater demand for slices of pizza at every price. Plotting the new schedule on a graph would produce a curve to the right of Ashley's original curve. For each of the prices on the vertical axis, the quantity demanded would be greater. This shift to the right of the curve is called an *increase in demand.* A fall in income would cause the demand curve to shift left. This shift is called a *decrease in demand.*

There are also other goods called **inferior goods.** They are called inferior goods because an increase in income causes demand for these goods to fall. Inferior goods are goods that you would buy in smaller quantities, or not at all, if your income were to rise and you could afford something better. Possible examples of inferior goods include macaroni and cheese, generic cereals, and used cars.

Consumer Expectations

Our expectations about the future can affect our demand for certain goods today. Suppose that you have had your eye on a new bicycle for several months. One day you walk in the store to look at the bike, and the salesperson mentions that the store will be raising the price in one week. Now that you expect a higher price in the near future, you are more likely to buy the bike today. In other words, the expectation of a higher price in the future has caused your immediate demand to increase.

If, on the other hand, the salesperson were to tell you that the bike will be on sale next week, your immediate demand for the bicycle would fall to zero. You would rather wait until next week to buy the bike at a lower price.

The current demand for a good is positively related to its expected future price. If you expect the price to rise, your current demand will rise, which means you will buy the good sooner. If you expect the price to drop, your current demand will fall and you will wait for the lower price.

Population

Changes in the size of the population will also affect the demand for most products. For example, a growing population needs to be housed and fed. Therefore, a rise in population will increase demand for houses, food, and many other goods and services.

Population trends can have a particularly strong effect on certain goods. For example, when American soldiers returned from World War II in the mid- to late 1940s, record numbers of them married and started families. This trend led to the "baby boom," a jump in the birthrate from the mid-1940s through 1964. Initially, the baby boom led to higher demand for baby clothes, baby food, and books on baby care. In the 1950s and 1960s, towns had to build thousands of new schools. Later, universities opened new classrooms, dormitories, and even whole new campuses to make room for the flood of new students. The baby boomers have now begun to retire. Over the next few decades the market will face rising demand for the goods and services that are desired by senior citizens, including medical care, recreational vehicles, and homes in the Sunbelt.

Consumer Tastes and Advertising

Who can explain why bell-bottom blue jeans were everywhere one year and rarely seen the next? Is it the result of clever advertising campaigns, social trends, the influence of television shows, or some combination of these factors? Although economists cannot always isolate the reasons why some fads begin, advertising and publicity often play an important role.

Changes in tastes and preferences cannot be explained by changes in income or population or worries about future price increases. Advertising is considered a factor

THE WALL STREET JOURNAL. CLASSROOM EDITION

In the News Read more about changes in demand in "The Surging Hispanic Economy," an article in The Wall Street Journal Classroom Edition.

The Wall Street Journal Classroom Edition

For: Current Events
Visit: PHSchool.com
Web Code: mnc-2042

inferior good *a good that consumers demand less of when their incomes increase*

▲ **When New York City announced that the price of a subway token would rise 25 cents, commuters rushed to buy tokens at the old price. To prevent this, the city introduced a new token (bottom) to replace the older token commuters had bought. Expectations of higher prices had affected demand.**

Background

The Beef Battle

In 1996 some British cattle were found to be infected with bovine spongiform encephalopathy (BSE). Medical research showed a link between BSE and a fatal human brain-wasting disease, Creutzfeldt-Jakob disease (CJD). Panic spread through Europe. Imports of British beef were banned by the European Union, and Great Britain considered slaughtering hundreds of thousands of cattle.

On April 16, 1996, Chicago talk show host Oprah Winfrey aired a program about BSE and its potentially fatal effects on people who ate contaminated beef. The program was aired after news sources had reported that at least 10 Britons had died from CJD after eating beef from contaminated cattle. Winfrey ended her show by declaring that she would never eat another hamburger.

Later, a group of Texas cattlemen filed a suit against Winfrey. They claimed her remarks had affected the demand for beef, driving cattle prices down to 10-year lows. The cattlemen estimated that they had lost more than $10 million in revenue, and they blamed Winfrey's show.

After a 6-week trial, Winfrey won the case. The jury concluded that Winfrey, her producers, and a guest on the show had not hurt the cattle companies.

Go Online PHSchool.com Typing in the Web Code when prompted will bring students directly to the article.

Block Scheduling Strategies

Consider these suggestions to take advantage of extended class time:

- Share the Background note on this page with students. Then hold a debate on the issue of whether Oprah Winfrey's statement caused the demand curve for Texas beef to shift.
- Organize the class into groups of three. Have each group work through the Case Studies in Free Enterprise activity on Howard Schulz. Then ask groups to find additional data on Starbucks. Have each group create a graph or chart of its data and present it to the class.
- Have students view the Economics Video Library segment "Home Sweet Home," about the rising prices of houses caused by the income effect. Have students research local trends in housing prices over the last decade. Then have them write several paragraphs about what factors might have influenced these trends.

Differentiated Instruction L3

(Reteaching) Ask students to think of three examples of goods (such as the skis and ski boots discussed in the section) that are complements.

Transparency Resource Package Economics Concepts, 4D: Change in Demand

GTE **Guide to the Essentials**
Chapter 4, Section 2, p. 17 provides support for students who need additional review of the section content. Spanish support is available in the Spanish edition of the guide on p. 17.

Quiz Unit 2 folder, p. 5 includes questions to check students' understanding of Section 2 content.

Presentation Pro CD-ROM
Quiz provides multiple-choice questions to check students' understanding of Section 2 content.

Answers to . . .

Section 2 Assessment

1. Examples will vary but should include goods students would buy less of, or not at all, if their incomes increased, such as macaroni and cheese or generic brands of breakfast cereal.
2. Examples may include in-line skates and safety gear, or peanut butter and jelly.
3. Examples may include in-line skates and roller skates, or a car and a motorcycle.
4. *Ceteris paribus* allows the demand curve to exist as a constant without variables other than price affecting it.
5. Demand probably fell, since prices rose steadily. The law of demand says that higher prices decrease demand.
6. A shift along a demand curve always reflects only a change in price, while a shift of a demand curve indicates that an outside factor has changed the entire relationship between prices and quantities demanded.
7. (a) change in quantity demanded (b) change in demand (c) change in quantity demanded
8. The curve should reflect the data given. (a) Any point along the normal demand curve will show an increase in quantity demanded. (b) Any point to the right of the curve will show an increase in demand. (c) Any point to the left of the curve will show a decrease in demand.

▲ **Ski boots and skis are two goods that are complements.**

that shifts demand curves because it plays an important role in many trends. Companies spend money on advertising because they hope that it will increase the demand for the goods they sell. Considering the growing sums of money spent on advertising in the United States each year, companies must feel that this investment is paying off.

Prices of Related Goods

complements *two goods that are bought and used together*

substitutes *goods used in place of one another*

The demand curve for one good can be affected by a change in the demand for another good. There are two types of related goods that interact this way: complements and substitutes.

- ***Complements*** are two goods that are bought and used together.
- ***Substitutes*** are goods used in place of one another.

When we consider the demand for skis, ski boots are considered a complement. An increase in the price of ski boots will cause people to buy fewer boots. Because skis are useless without boots, the demand for skis will fall at all prices—after all, why buy new skis if you can't afford the ski boots you need to ski safely?

Now consider the effect on the demand for skis when the price of snowboards rises. Snowboards are a substitute for skis, because consumers will often buy one or the other, but not both. A rise in the price of snowboards will cause people to buy fewer snowboards, and therefore people will buy *more* pairs of new skis at every price. Likewise, a fall in the price of snowboards will lead consumers to buy fewer skis at all price levels.

Section 2 Assessment

Progress Monitoring *Online*
For: Self-quiz with vocabulary practice
Web Code: mna-2046

Key Terms and Main Ideas

1. What is an example of something you consider an **inferior good**?
2. What is one good that can be considered a **complement** for another?
3. What are two goods that can be considered **substitutes?**
4. How does the ***ceteris paribus*** assumption affect a demand curve?

Applying Economic Concepts

5. ***Using the Databank*** According to the law of demand and the chart of median house prices on page 540, how do you think demand for houses changed between 1998 and 2004? Explain.
6. ***Critical Thinking*** What is the difference between a shift along a demand curve and a shift of a demand curve?
7. ***Decision Making*** Decide whether each of these events would cause a change in *demand* or only a change in the *quantity demanded* of the good in parentheses, and explain why. **(a)** A computer manufacturer lowers its prices. (computers) **(b)** A volleyball maker convinces high schools to fund varsity volleyball teams. (volleyballs) **(c)** A freeze ruins the orange crop, and orange juice prices rise. (apple juice)
8. ***Math Practice*** Use the following demand schedule to draw a demand curve. Then find and label a combination of output and price that could result from: **(a)** an increase in the quantity demanded, **(b)** an increase in demand, and **(c)** a decrease in demand.

Price	Quantity Demanded
$1.00	250
$2.00	200
$3.00	150
$4.00	100
$5.00	50

For: Current Events Activity
Visit: PHSchool.com
Web Code: mnd-2042

Progress Monitoring *Online*
For additional assessment, have students access Progress Monitoring Online at **Web Code:** mna-2046

Go Online PHSchool.com Typing in the Web Code when prompted will bring students directly to detailed instructions for this activity.

ECONOMIC *Profile*

Economist

Entrepreneur

Christy Haubegger (b. 1968)

It took a tragedy to awaken the nation to the economic power of Hispanic Americans. In March 1995, the Tejano singer Selena was murdered. The outpouring of grief in the Latino community was tremendous. American businesses took notice. If Latinos were buying millions of records by a Latina singer, entrepreneur Christy Haubegger reasoned that there were other products, such as magazines, that could be marketed specifically to their community.

The Birth of an Entrepreneur

At the time of Selena's death, Christy Haubegger, a recent Stanford University Law School graduate, was already planning the nation's first magazine for Hispanic American women. The adopted Mexican American daughter of Anglo parents, Christy grew up in a Houston, Texas, neighborhood with few Hispanic residents. "Other Hispanic kids were frustrated by the lack of popular images in the media," she recalls, "but at least when they went home they found people who looked like they did."

As Haubegger went on to college and law school, she and her Latina classmates continued to have trouble finding role models. None of the women's magazines that they read reflected their cultural, professional, or beauty concerns. "I felt [a Hispanic publication] was the one women's magazine that I'd want to read," Haubegger says. "I kept thinking 'Somebody should do it,' and finally I realized that that somebody was going to have to be me."

Haubegger approached Edward Lewis, founder in the 1970s of *Essence Magazine*, the first magazine for African American women. Impressed by her ideas, Lewis invested several million dollars. In 1996, the first issue of *Latina* hit the newsstands.

Hispanic Women and Demand

Latina is marketed to Hispanic American women between the ages of 18 and 45. The articles, which are in English with Spanish summaries, focus on people and topics of specific interest to Latinas. "It's 100 percent Latina, cover to cover," Haubegger says proudly of her magazine.

Although many of the ads are in Spanish, Haubegger has had little trouble convincing mainstream companies like Revlon, Honda, and The Gap to advertise in her magazine. With the Hispanic American population growing at four times the national average, companies have taken notice. "I show them the numbers that say we buy 15 percent of the country music and 10 percent of the lipstick," Haubegger says, "and suddenly they're interested."

CHECK FOR UNDERSTANDING

1. Source Reading Explain why the death of Selena led to a growth in the number of consumer products targeted specifically at the Latino community.

2. Critical Thinking How is the growth rate of the Hispanic American population likely to affect the way products are marketed in the future?

3. Decision Making If you were going to create a publication to sell to a segment of the population in your community, what factors would you consider in deciding which group to target?

ECONOMIC *Profile*
Christy Haubegger

Background

When Christy Haubegger begain publishing the magazine *Latina* in 1996, she joined a growing publishing industry aimed at Hispanic Americans. In 1995 *Latina Style* and *Sí* hit the newsstands.

What accounts for the explosion of Latino-oriented media? Demand is the answer. As Haubegger said in a 1995 *New York Times* article, "I was a lawyer and found there was no magazine for me. I want to read about raising my son bilingually. I want to update my mother's enchilada recipe with less fat."

These media products are aimed at middle-class households with incomes of $30,000 to $120,000. That includes nearly half of the Latino households in the United States. That is why, in 1995 alone, advertisers spend nearly $190 million on Latino print media. The success of *Latina* and its sister publications was summed up by Brooke White, a spokeswoman for Nordstrom department stores: "The Hispanic market has a lot of spending power." This is important because in a free market economy, spending power, coupled with demand, equals product.

Careers in Economics Activity
Unit 2 folder, p. 11 gives students a closer look at the career path of a buyer.

Beyond the Classroom: Career Connections

The graph on page 537 lists the Fastest-Growing Occupations. Have students think about how, if they were to start up a new business, they might take advantage of these potential growth occupations. Have them pick one of these occupational areas and think about how they might begin a business. What could the business add to what is usually offered the consumer in this area? Have the students describe the employees who might be likely to work in the occupation selected. How could they, as entrepreneurs and bosses, make their employees more productive, better workers?

Answers to . . .

1. It revealed the size of the demand for Latino-oriented products.
2. The growth rate will result in more products targeted at Latinos. Producers will move into a market where demand is growing.
3. Students' criteria will vary, but should reflect understanding of potential demand for the product. They should consider factors such as market size, future growth, and income.

Section 3 Elasticity of Demand

Preview

Objectives

After studying this section you will be able to:

1. **Explain** how to calculate elasticity of demand.
2. **Identify** factors that affect elasticity.
3. **Explain** how firms use elasticity and revenue to make decisions.

Section Focus

Elasticity of demand describes how consumers will react to a change in the price of a good. Their reaction depends on the original price of the good and the way that good is used by consumers.

Key Terms

elasticity of demand
inelastic
elastic
unitary elastic
total revenue

elasticity of demand *a measure of how consumers react to a change in price*

inelastic *describes demand that is not very sensitive to a change in price*

elastic *describes demand that is very sensitive to a change in price*

Are there some goods that you would always find money to buy, even if the price were to rise drastically? Are there other goods that you would cut back on, or even stop buying altogether, if the price were to rise just slightly?

Economists describe the way that consumers respond to price changes as **elasticity of demand.** Elasticity of demand dictates how drastically buyers will cut back or increase their demand for a good when the price rises or falls, respectively. Your demand for a good that you will keep buying despite a price increase is **inelastic,** or relatively unresponsive to price changes. In the second example, in which you buy much less of a good after a small price increase, your demand is **elastic.** A consumer with highly elastic demand for a good is very responsive to price changes.

"After taxes, operating expenses and profits to stockholders, I'm lucky if I see a nickel of it!"

▲ **Misspelling "lemonade" might not be this entrepreneur's only mistake. How many people will buy lemonade if the price rises to $25.00 a glass?**

Calculating Elasticity

To compute elasticity of demand, take the percentage change in the demand of a good, and divide this number by the percentage change in the price of the good. You can find the equation for elasticity in Figure 4.7 on page 92. The law of demand implies that the result will always be negative. This is because an increase in the price of a good will always decrease the quantity demanded, and a decrease in the price of a good will always increase the quantity demanded. For the sake of simplicity, economists drop the negative sign.

Price Range

The elasticity of demand for a good varies at every price level. Demand for a good can be highly elastic at one price and inelastic at a different price. For example, demand

Section 3 Elasticity of Demand

Objectives You may wish to call students' attention to the objectives in the Section Preview. The objectives are reflected in the main headings of the section.

Bellringer Ask students to list five products they could not do without. Then ask them how their lists might change if the price of each product doubled, tripled, or even quadrupled. Explain that in this section they will learn how economists characterize goods and services that people can and cannot do without.

Vocabulary Builder Have students read the section to learn the meaning of each key term. Then have them add the terms and either their definitions or illustrations of their meanings to their Economics Journals.

Lesson Plan

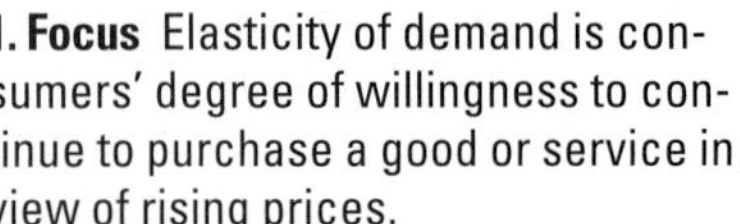

Teaching the Main Concepts L3

1. Focus Elasticity of demand is consumers' degree of willingness to continue to purchase a good or service in view of rising prices.

2. Instruct Begin by explaining *elasticity of demand.* Discuss the differences between inelastic and elastic demand, and show students how elasticity is calculated. Then explain to students how elasticity of demand affects revenue and helps businesses plan for the future.

3. Close/Reteach Point out that the demand for certain goods and services is highly sensitive to price fluctuations, whereas the demand for other goods and services remains relatively unaffected. Ask students how they think producers predict elasticity of demand for a new product.

Answer to . . .

Cartoon Caption Most students will say that no one would buy lemonade at such a price.

Graphing the Main Idea

Markets and Prices To build understanding of the concept of **markets and prices,** have students use a tree map graphic organizer like the one below to explain the factors that determine elasticity. Tell students that a tree map shows a main topic, main ideas or divisions, and supporting details.

Section Reading Support Transparencies A template and the answers for this graphic organizer can be found in Chapter 4, Section 3 of the Section Reading Support Transparency System.

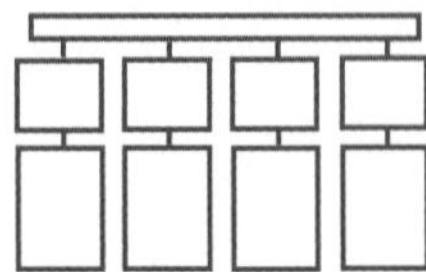

for a glossy magazine will be inelastic when the price rises 50 percent from 20 cents to 30 cents. The price is still very low, and people will buy almost as many copies as they did before. However, when the price increases 50 percent from $4.00 to $6.00, demand will be much more elastic. Many readers will refuse to pay $2.00 more for the magazine. Yet in percentage terms, the change in the magazine's price is exactly the same as when the price rose from 20 cents to 30 cents.

Values of Elasticity

We have been using the terms *inelastic* and *elastic* to describe consumers' responses to price changes. These terms have precise mathematical definitions. If the elasticity of demand for a good at a certain price is *less* than 1, we describe demand as inelastic. If the elasticity is *greater* than one, demand is elastic. If elasticity is exactly equal to 1, we describe demand as **unitary elastic.**

When elasticity of demand is unitary, the percentage change in quantity demanded is exactly equal to the percentage change in the price. Suppose the elasticity of demand for a magazine at $2 is unitary. When the price of the magazine rises by 50 percent to $3, the newsstand will sell exactly half as many copies as before.

Think back to Ashley's demand schedule for pizza in Section 1. Ashley's demand schedule shows that if the price per slice were to rise from $1.00 to $1.50, her quantity demanded would fall from 4 slices to 3 slices per day. The change in price from $1.00 to $1.50 is a 50 percent increase. The change in quantity demanded from 4 to 3 slices is a 25 percent decrease. Dividing the 25 percent decrease in quantity demanded by the 50 percent increase in price gives us an elasticity of demand of 0.5.

Since Ashley's elasticity of demand at prices of $1.00 to $1.50 is less than 1, we say that Ashley's demand for pizza is inelastic. In other words, a price increase has a relatively small effect on the number of slices of pizza she buys.

Suppose that we survey another customer and find that, when the price of pizza rises by 40 percent, this person's quantity demanded falls by 60 percent. The change in the quantity demanded of 60 percent is divided by the change in price of 40 percent, equaling an elasticity of demand of 1.5 (60 percent/40 percent = 1.5). Since this result is greater than 1, this customer's demand is elastic. In other words, this customer is very sensitive to changes in the price of pizza.

Factors Affecting Elasticity

Why is the demand for some goods so much less elastic than for other goods? Rephrase the question and ask yourself, "What is essential to me? What goods must I have, even if the price rises greatly?" The goods you list might have some traits that set them apart from other goods and make your demand for those goods less elastic. Several different factors can affect a person's elasticity of demand for a specific good.

Availability of Substitutes

If there are few substitutes for a good, then even when its price rises greatly, you might still buy it. You feel you have no good alternatives. For example, if your favorite musical group plans to give a concert, and you want to attend, there really is no substitute for a ticket. You could go to a concert to hear some other band, but that would not be as good. You've got to have

unitary elastic *describes demand whose elasticity is exactly equal to 1*

Global Connections

Elasticity in the Kitchen Cooking varies from country to country, and so does **elasticity of demand** for certain foods. If the price of a gallon of milk or a pound of ground beef doubled in the United States, consumers might demand intervention by the government. Do you think this would happen if the price rise affected onions and potatoes? These two vegetables are essential to Indian cooking, and when floods ruined crops in India, their prices more than doubled. In November 1998, angry citizens voted the ruling party out of office in several states in part because of the high price of onions.

Econ 101: Key Concepts Made Easy

Supply and Demand If students are having trouble understanding **elasticity of demand,** show them several pieces of elastic. Then ask them to think about the material that gives its name to the concept. When something is elastic, it can be stretched out and then returned to its original shape. In a similar way, elastic demand rises and falls—as easily as elastic can be stretched out and snapped back. Material that is not elastic does not stretch; it remains the same. Show students a piece of tightly woven cloth to illustrate inelasticity. Inelastic demand remains the same, despite price fluctuations.

Guided Reading and Review
Unit 2 folder, p. 6 asks students to identify the main ideas of the section and to define or identify key terms.

Differentiated Instruction 

To help students transfer information from one medium to another (written to visual), have them create illustrations that demonstrate the principles of elastic and inelastic demand. The illustrations can be drawings, photographs, or photocopies from magazines—anything that clarifies the concepts visually. Suggest that students with access to appropriate computer software enhance the clarity of their presentations with its use.

Differentiated Instruction 

Have students write down the main heads and subheads for Section 3. Then ask them to write a sentence or two that summarizes the content under each head. LPR

Differentiated Instruction 

Draw a grid on the chalkboard with three columns and five lines. Label the first column "Product" and list the names of several products: salt, steak, sports car, Picasso painting, chocolate bar. Label the second column "Demand Elasticity." Label the last column "Reason." Invite students, one at a time to come up and fill in "elastic" or "inelastic" for any product and write a reason for their choice. Discuss the answers. SN

Math Practice Activity
Math Practice folder, p. 4, "Determining Elasticity of Demand," gives students an opportunity to calculate elasticity of demand from data about price and quantity demanded.

Transparency Resource Package
Economics Concepts, 4E: Elasticity of Demand

Differentiated Instruction 

Ask students to interview classmates to create a demand schedule for one of the following goods: popcorn at a movie theater, shoelaces, milk, or running shoes. Tell them to draw a demand curve that displays that schedule. Finally, ask them to write a paragraph that explains the elasticity of demand for that good as shown by the demand schedule and demand curve.

Differentiated Instruction 

English language learners may benefit from working with a peer tutor in class to learn how to calculate elasticity and to interpret the graphs on this page. Pair proficient students with English language learners, either one-on-one or as part of a larger group. Encourage students to share what they learn. ELL

Differentiated Instruction 

Have students examine the concept of elasticity of demand by researching airline ticket prices. Suggest that they choose a destination and then check fares for the next day, a month from now, and three months from now. Ask them to write a short report that examines differences in the elasticity of demand in those three situations and the factors involved. GT

Figure 4.7 Elasticity of Demand

Elasticity is determined using the following formula:

$$\text{Elasticity} = \frac{\text{Percentage change in quantity demanded}}{\text{Percentage change in price}}$$

To find the percentage change in quantity demanded or price, use the following formula: Subtract the new number from the original number, and divide the result by the original number. Ignore any negative signs, and multiply by 100 to convert this number to a percentage:

$$\text{Percentage change} = \frac{\text{Original number} - \text{New number}}{\text{Original number}} \times 100$$

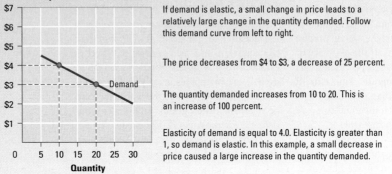

Example 1: Elastic Demand

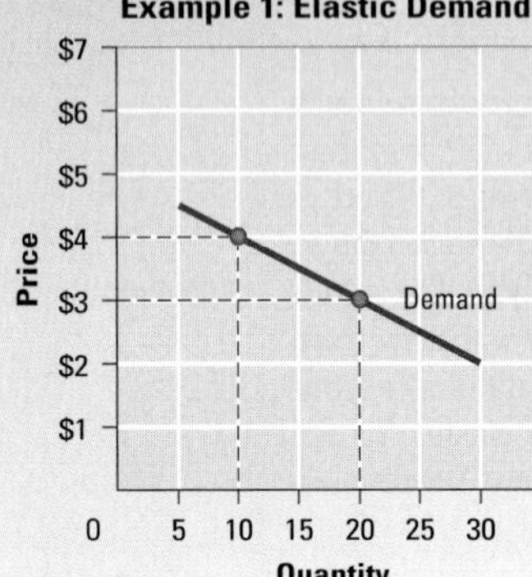

If demand is elastic, a small change in price leads to a relatively large change in the quantity demanded. Follow this demand curve from left to right.

The price decreases from \$4 to \$3, a decrease of 25 percent. $\frac{\$4 - \$3}{\$4} \times 100 = 25$

The quantity demanded increases from 10 to 20. This is an increase of 100 percent. $\frac{10 - 20}{10} \times 100 = 100$

Elasticity of demand is equal to 4.0. Elasticity is greater than 1, so demand is elastic. In this example, a small decrease in price caused a large increase in the quantity demanded. $\frac{100\%}{25\%} = 4.0$

Example 2: Inelastic Demand

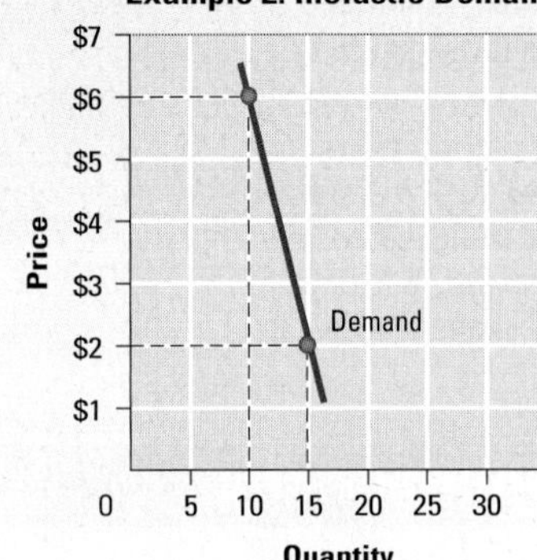

If demand is inelastic, consumers are not very responsive to changes in price. A decrease in price will lead to only a small change in quantity demanded, or perhaps no change at all. Follow this demand curve from left to right as the price decreases sharply from \$6 to \$2.

The price decreases from \$6 to \$2, a decrease of about 67 percent. $\frac{\$6 - \$2}{\$6} \times 100 \approx 67$

The quantity demanded increases from 10 to 15, an increase of 50 percent. $\frac{10 - 15}{10} \times 100 = 50$

Elasticity of demand is about 0.75. The elasticity is less than 1, so demand for this good is inelastic. The increase in quantity demanded is small compared to the decrease in price. $\frac{50\%}{67\%} \approx 0.75$

Unitary elastic demand is a special case. When demand is unitary elastic, an increase (or decrease) in price will be met by an equal percentage decrease (or increase) in quantity demanded. Elasticity of demand is exactly 1.

Elasticity of demand describes how strongly consumers will react to a change in price.
Supply and Demand If a good's elasticity of demand is 0.2, how will consumers react to an increase in price?

Block Scheduling Strategies

Consider these suggestions to take advantage of extended class time:

- Extend the first activity on p. 91 by asking groups of three or four students to combine their individual projects with narration, role-playing, audio accompaniment, or other techniques to create a group presentation on elasticity of demand. Give each group time in class to share its product.
- Extend the second activity on p. 94 by leading a class discussion. Ask students to research the ethical issues of organ transplants. Then, in class, have students answer the question: "When, if ever, do medical ethics take precedence over the normal operation of the free market?"

Answer to . . .

Building Key Concepts There will be little change in quantity demanded.

tickets for this concert, and nothing else will do. Under these circumstances, a moderate change in price is not going to change your mind. Your demand is inelastic.

Similarly, demand for life-saving medicine is usually inelastic. For many prescription drugs, the only possible substitute is to try an unproven treatment. For this reason, people with an illness will continue to buy as much needed medicine as they can afford, even when the price goes up.

If the lack of substitutes can make demand inelastic, a wide choice of substitute goods can make demand elastic. The demand for a particular brand of apple juice is probably elastic because people can choose from dozens of good substitutes if the price of their preferred brand rises.

Relative Importance

A second factor in determining a good's elasticity of demand is how much of your budget you spend on the good. If you already spend a large share of your income on a good, a price increase will force you to make some tough choices. Unless you want to cut back drastically on the other goods in your budget, you must reduce consumption of that good by a significant amount to keep your budget under control. The higher the jump in price, the more you will have to adjust your purchases.

If you currently spend half of your budget on clothes, then even a modest increase in the cost of clothing will probably cause a large reduction in the quantity you purchase. In other words, your demand will be elastic.

However, if the price of shoelaces doubled, would you cut back on your shoelace purchases? Probably not. You may not even notice the difference. Even if you spend twice as much on shoelaces, they will still account for only a tiny part of your overall budget. Your demand for shoelaces is inelastic.

Necessities Versus Luxuries

The third factor in determining a good's elasticity varies a great deal from person to person, but it is nonetheless important. Whether a person considers a good to be a necessity or a luxury has a great impact on the good's elasticity of demand for that person. A necessity is a good people will always buy, even when the price increases. Parents often regard milk as a necessity. They will buy it at any reasonable price. If the price of a gallon of milk rises from $2.49 to $4.49, they will still buy as much milk as their children need to stay healthy. Their demand for milk is inelastic.

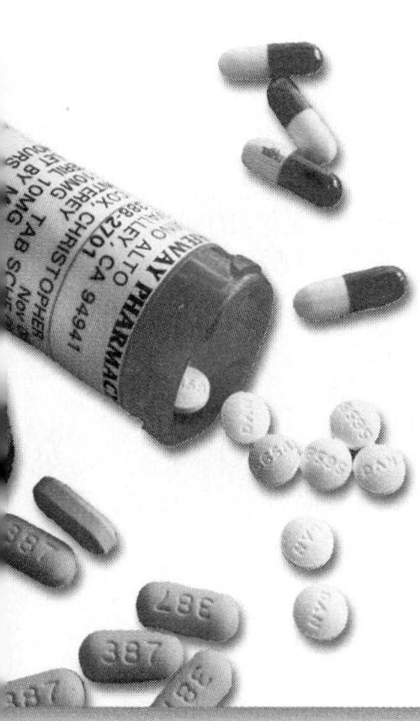

▲ **Demand for some prescription drugs is relatively inelastic because the patient has few alternatives. Demand for any one of these drinks would be much more elastic because a consumer can easily find a less expensive choice.**

Background

Economics in History

Can yesterday's luxury good ever become today's necessity? The answer is yes, and its elasticity of demand can change from very elastic to very inelastic. Here's an interesting example.

Today the telephone is everywhere. Most people cannot imagine life without at least one. However, this was not always the case.

In 1920 only 35 percent of all households in the United States had a telephone. That figure jumped to nearly 41 percent by 1930. During the next decade, however, the Great Depression ravaged the nation's economy, and for some families the telephone was a luxury that they could no longer afford. By 1940 the percentage of households with a telephone actually dropped to about 37 percent as families searched for ways to spend less money.

After winning World War II, the nation's military personnel came home, fueling a demand for phone service. Approximately 60 percent of United States households had become telephone users by 1950. The numbers continued to rise until, by 1997, the figure had reached about 94 percent. What had once been both a novelty and a luxury had clearly become a necessity.

Differentiated Instruction 

(Reteaching) Display the following list of goods: *frozen orange juice, Italian sports car, insulin, cellular phone,* and *house* or *apartment.* Then write the following personal profile: Name—Alice; Age—55; Yearly Income—$50,000; Occupation—Sales Manager, Medical Instruments Corporation; Other factors—has insulin-dependent diabetes.

Ask each student to predict Alice's elasticity of demand for each of the five goods. Ask students to speculate on how Alice's elasticity of demand is affected by substitute goods, the relative importance of goods, necessities versus luxuries, and change over time.

Preparing for Standardized Tests

Have students read the section titled "Factors Affecting Elasticity" and then answer the question below.

Which of the following is not a factor that affects elasticity?

A availability of substitutes

B relative importance of a good

C necessities versus luxuries

(D) total revenue

Differentiated Instruction L3

(Enrichment) As energy prices skyrocketed in the 1970s, the United States government tried various ways to reduce the demand for fossil fuels, such as promoting alternate energy sources and encouraging energy-saving practices. Ask students to investigate this period in history and report on the efforts undertaken by the government and how successful they were in reducing demand. Tell them to consider what they have learned about the elasticity of demand for energy in their reports.

Differentiated Instruction L4

You may wish to have students add the following to their portfolios. Explain to students that demand is not always just an economic principle. It can become an ethical issue as well. As a result of advances in medical science, physicians are having great success in performing organ transplants. Ask students if a person who has severe heart disease has an elastic or inelastic demand for a heart transplant. If that demand is inelastic—meaning that price is no object—should available organs be sold to the highest bidder? How should medical science address this highly personal and often time-sensitive issue of demand? Ask students to write a position paper detailing their thoughts on the ethics of demand in relation to organ transplants. GT

Economics Assessment Rubric
Economics Assessment Rubrics folder, pp. 22–23 provides sample evaluation materials for a position paper.

▲ **Many people consider lobster a luxury and can easily cut it out of their budget.**

The same parents may regard steak as a luxury. When the price of steak increases by a little bit, say 20 percent, parents may cut their monthly purchases of steak by more than 20 percent, or skip steak altogether. Steak is a luxury, and consumers can easily reduce the quantity they consume. Because it is easy to reduce the quantity of luxuries demanded, demand is elastic.

Change over Time

When a price changes, consumers often need time to change their shopping habits. Consumers do not always react quickly to a price increase because it takes time to find substitutes. Because they cannot respond quickly to price changes, their demand is inelastic in the short term. Demand sometimes becomes more elastic over time, however, because people can eventually find substitutes that allow large adjustments to what they buy.

Consider the example of gasoline. When a person purchases a vehicle, he or she might choose a large vehicle that requires a greater volume of gasoline per mile to run. This same person might work at a job many miles away from home and shop at a supermarket that is far from both work and home. These factors determine how much gasoline this person demands, and none can be changed easily.

In the early 1970s, several oil-rich countries cut their oil exports to the United States, and gasoline prices rose quickly. In the short run, there was very little that people could do to reduce their consumption of gasoline. They still needed to drive to school and work. At first, drivers were more likely to pay more for the same amount of gasoline than they were to buy fuel-efficient cars or move closer to their schools and workplaces.

However, because gas prices stayed high for a considerable period of time, some people eventually switched to more fuel-efficient cars. Others formed car pools, walked or rode bicycles, and used public transportation. In the long run, people reduced their consumption of gasoline by finding substitutes. Demand for gasoline, inelastic in the short term, is more elastic in the long term.

As another example, consider what happened to gasoline prices from the early 1980s through the early 2000s. Adjusting for inflation, the price of a gallon of gas fell

▲ **When gas prices rose in the 1970s, auto manufacturers advertised how little fuel their cars used. In recent years when gas prices were low, new advertising emphasized strength and size, even though those cars used more gasoline.**

Interdisciplinary Connections: Literature

Literary Demand Students may not realize it, but literature is quite responsive to demand. Even Charles Dickens, today considered a classic author, created plots and characters in response to his readers' likes and dislikes. Today the current best-sellers, whether they are historical romances, detective thrillers, or government spy capers, are sure to spawn plenty of imitations.

Making the Connection Ask students whether the demand for books is elastic or inelastic and why. Then ask if they can think of any book or type of book that people would buy even at a very high price. *(Students may suggest volumes of great personal value, such as religious texts, or reference books such as dictionaries or encyclopedias. Some students will suggest that the availability of on-line information makes the demand for books more elastic.)*

Differentiated Instruction

Debate L4

Debates challenge students by asking them to use higher level thinking to consider, defend, and refute two opposing arguments. In order to do this effectively, they need to be well-versed in the topic being considered. Debates can be structured in a variety of ways. Here is one model that can be particularly effective:

1. Present an opinion-based question to students that can be logically answered several different ways.

2. Students form two groups, one representing each side.

3. Have students brainstorm justifications for their positions. Make sure that a "scribe" is appointed to write down group members' ideas.

4. Provide time for students to research their position.

5. Instruct students on each side to prepare a two-minute opening statement that makes a compelling case for their position.

6. Begin the debate. A student from each side should read their opening statement, followed by questions from the opposing side. Any member of the group can respond to questions.

7. Conclude the debate by giving each team several minutes to create a brief closing statement to be read to the class.

Poster Assessments L2

Less Proficient Readers often have trouble discerning main points when they read a selection of text. To help them find the key ideas, provide assignments that assist them in finding key information. Additionally, assignments that have an artistic or verbal component often heighten student interest and confidence.

Suggest that students create informative posters. They should use the text to find key points and present this information in an engaging manner. Provide students with a specific number of bullet points that they are required to put on their poster. Each bullet point should list an important main idea about their assigned topic. Students should add an illustration to accompany each bullet point. These poster assessments can be shared with classmates to review key information or displayed around the classroom for students to view.

Visit the Social Studies area of the Prentice Hall Web site. There you can find additional links to enrich chapter content for *Economics: Principles in Action* as well as a self-test for students. Be sure to check out this month's **eTeach** online discussion with a Master Economics Teacher.
Web Code: mnf-2051

Running Out of Time?

- Use the **Presentation Pro CD-ROM** to create an outline for this chapter.
- Use the Chapter Summary in the **Chapter 5 Assessment,** p. 122.
- Use the Section Summaries for Chapter 5, from **Guide to the Essentials of Economics (English and Spanish).**

THE WALL STREET JOURNAL.
CLASSROOM EDITION

Prentice Hall brings into the classroom the authoritative content of *The Wall Street Journal Classroom Edition.* See the Source Articles, Debating Current Issues, and You and Your Money folders in the **Teaching Resources**. Also, see Economics Video Library, "Plummeting Prices."

Assessment Resources

Chapter Assessment

Teaching Resources Unit 2, Chapter 5
- Section Quizzes, pp. 14, 16, 18, 20

Exam *View*® Test Bank CD-ROM Chapter 5
Economics Assessment Rubrics
Chapter 5 Self-Test, **Web Code:** mna-2051

Reading and Skills Evaluation

Progress Monitoring Assessments
- Screening Test
- Diagnostic Test of Social Studies Skills

Standardized Test Preparation

Test Prep Workbook
Test-Taking Strategies With Transparencies

Differentiated Instruction Key

L1 Special Needs	LPR Less Proficient Readers
L2 Basic to Average	AR Advanced Readers
L3 All Students	SN Special Needs Students
L4 Average to Advanced	GT Gifted and Talented
	ELL English Language Learner

Introducing the Chapter

In this chapter, students are introduced to the concepts of supply, costs of production, and factors that cause supply to shift. Students will also see how supply schedules and curves parallel those for demand.

Go Online PHSchool.com

For additional links for *Economics: Principles in Action* provided by Prentice Hall and *The Wall Street Journal Classroom Edition,* visit the Social Studies area. Be sure to check out this month's **eTeach** online discussion with a Master Teacher.

Beyond the Lecture

You may cover the concepts in Chapter 5 in an activity-based style by using the following materials:

- **Technology Resources** appropriate for use with this chapter are noted on pp. 103, 104, 106, 110, 111, 112, 114, 119, 120, and 123.
- **Presentation Pro CD-ROM** with animated graphs gives you an alternative method for organizing and delivering chapter content.
- **Activities** designed to meet the needs of students of mixed abilities and learning styles are noted throughout the chapter in the side columns.
- **Learning Styles Lesson Plans** provide alternate lessons for diverse learning styles. See pp. 15–16 of the Learning Styles Lesson Plans folder located in the Teaching Resources.

Economics Journal

Instruct students to write their responses to the assignment in their Economics Journals. Students may include completed journal entries in an Economics Portfolio.

Chapter 5 Supply

A family buys a half-gallon of orange juice at the supermarket. An author hires a graduate student to translate a book. A store sells a bicycle to a woman over the Internet.

Each of these exchanges involves a buyer and a seller. In this chapter you'll read about the "supply side" of the marketplace, where sellers decide how much to produce or supply. After reading the chapter, you'll better understand the factors that influence sellers' decisions on how much orange juice to produce, how many hours a week to work as a translator, or how many bicycles to export.

Economics Journal

Write down a list of three goods: one that is usually available and "on sale," another that is popular but difficult to find, and a third that falls somewhere in between. What prices do stores charge for these goods?

Go Online PHSchool.com

For: Current Data
Visit: PHSchool.com
Web Code: mng-2051

NCEE
National Council on Economic Education

The following Voluntary National Content Standards in Economics are addressed in this chapter:

★ **Standard 4** Students will understand that: People respond predictably to positive and negative incentives.

★ **Standard 8** Students will understand that: Prices send signals and provide incentives to buyers and sellers. When supply or demand changes, market prices adjust, affecting incentives.

For more information about the standards, contact the National Council on Economic Education

1140 Avenue of the Americas
New York, NY 10036
1-800-338-1192

Section 1 Understanding Supply

Preview

Objectives

After studying this section you will be able to:

1. **Explain** the law of supply.
2. **Interpret** a supply graph using a supply schedule.
3. **Explain** the relationship between elasticity of supply and time.

Section Focus

The law of supply predicts that producers will offer more of a good as its price goes up. How strongly producers react to a change in price depends on their ability to raise or lower output.

Key Terms

supply
law of supply
quantity supplied
supply schedule
variable
market supply schedule
supply curve
market supply curve
elasticity of supply

If you were running a business, what would you do if you discovered that customers were suddenly willing to pay twice as much for your product? If you were like most entrepreneurs, you would try to produce more in order to take advantage of the higher prices. Even if you used the higher prices as a way to work fewer hours while earning the same income, you could be sure that someone else would jump into the market and start selling the same good.

The Law of Supply

Supply is the amount of goods available. How do producers decide how much to supply? According to the **law of supply,** the higher the price, the larger the quantity produced. Economists use the term **quantity supplied** to describe how much of a good is offered for sale at a specific price.

The law of supply develops from the choices of both current and new producers of a good. As the price of a good rises, existing firms will produce more in order to earn additional revenue. At the same time, new firms will have an incentive to enter the market to earn a profit for themselves. If the price of a good falls, some firms will produce less, and others might drop out of the market. These two movements—individual firms changing their level of production and firms entering or exiting the market—combine to create the law of supply.

Higher Production

If a firm is already earning a profit by selling a good, then an increase in the price—*ceteris paribus*—will increase the

supply *the amount of goods available*

law of supply *tendency of suppliers to offer more of a good at a higher price*

quantity supplied *the amount a supplier is willing and able to supply at a certain price*

Figure 5.1 Law of Supply

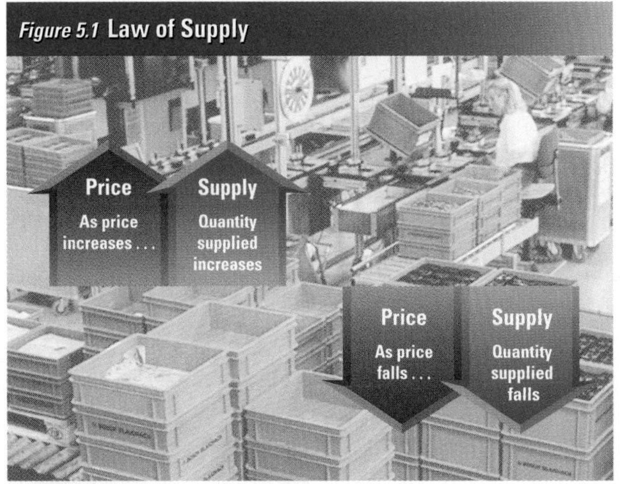

The law of supply predicts that higher prices lead to more production.
Incentives **How is the law of supply different from the law of demand?**

Graphing the Main Idea

Supply and Demand To build understanding of the concept of **supply and demand,** have students complete a tree map graphic organizer like the one shown below. Tell them to write the title of the section in the top box and the main headings of the section in the next row of boxes. In the boxes beneath each heading, they should record main ideas and supporting details.

Section Reading Support Transparencies A template and the answers for this graphic organizer can be found in Chapter 5, Section 1 of the Section Reading Support Transparency System.

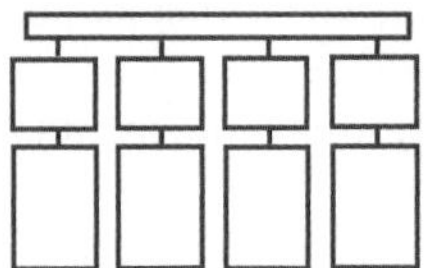

Section 1 Understanding Supply

Objectives You may wish to call students' attention to the objectives in the Section Preview. The objectives are reflected in the main headings of the section.

Bellringer Tell students to imagine that they own a factory that produces sunglasses and that the price of sunglasses begins to rise rapidly. Ask students whether they think that they would produce more pairs of sunglasses, fewer pairs, or the same number as before. Tell them that in this section they will learn what the law of supply says about this situation.

Vocabulary Builder Ask students to use each key term in a sentence that demonstrates understanding of the term. Then have students replace each key term with a blank, trade papers with a classmate, and fill in each other's blanks with the correct terms.

Lesson Plan

Teaching the Main Concepts 

1. Focus The law of supply helps producers decide how much of a good to offer for sale. Ask students to suggest factors that affect this decision.

2. Instruct Begin by discussing the law of supply and how it differs from the law of demand. Explain that supply schedules and curves function just like demand schedules and curves, except that the issue is rising prices and increased supply. Finally, discuss elasticity of supply.

3. Close/Reteach Remind students that as prices rise, producers are willing to supply more of a good or service. Ask them to share examples of this.

Answer to . . .

Photo Caption The law of supply describes how price affects producers. The law of demand describes how price affects consumers.

Guided Reading and Review
Unit 2 folder, p. 13 asks students to identify the main ideas of the section and to define or identify key terms.

Background

Market District to Market Phenomenon

Not many years ago, West Randolph Street in Chicago was home to the Market District, a collection of meat wholesalers. Although chefs and restaurant owners would descend on the Market District every morning to select the day's meat, by three in the afternoon, the proprietors in the district had closed up shop. For the rest of the day, West Randolph was taken over by vagrants, gangs, and other undesirables.

That all changed in 1991, when a restaurant group called KDK opened Vivo, an upscale Italian eatery. Porsches and Mercedes soon replaced refrigerated trucks and the Market District became a laboratory for the law of supply.

KDK realized that Vivo was the start of a new trend, so they decided to increase the supply of such establishments. Another restaurant, Marché, debuted in 1994, followed by Red Light. The crowds grew. It didn't hurt that the area had been spruced up in preparation for the 1996 Democratic National Convention and that the location gave easy suburban access.

Within a few years, a total of eight pricey restaurants were firmly established in the district. Today wholesale businesses stand side by side with trendy restaurants and art galleries, proving that when there is money to be made, producers are happy to supply more of what consumers are willing to pay for.

Go Online PHSchool.com Typing in the Web Code when prompted will bring students directly to the article.

THE WALL STREET JOURNAL.
CLASSROOM EDITION

In the News Read more about supply in *"Blockbuster Stresses Buying Over Renting,"* an article in The Wall Street Journal Classroom Edition.

The Wall Street Journal Classroom Edition
For: Current Events
Visit: PHSchool.com
Web Code: mnc-2051

firm's profits. The promise of higher revenues for each sale also encourages the firm to produce more. Consider the pizzeria you read about in Chapter 4. The pizzeria is probably making a reasonable profit by selling a certain number of slices a day at the market price. If the pizzeria weren't making a profit, the owner would soon try to raise the price or switch from pizzas to something more profitable.

If the price of pizza rises, but the firm's cost of making pizza stays the same, then the pizzeria will earn a higher profit on each slice of pizza. A sensible entrepreneur would try to produce and sell more pizza to take advantage of the higher prices.

Similarly, if the price of pizza goes down, the pizzeria will earn less profit per slice or even lose money. The owner will choose to sell less pizza and produce something else, such as calzones or sandwiches, that will yield more profit.

In both cases, the search for profit drives the supplier's decision. When the price goes up, the supplier recognizes the chance to make more money and works harder to produce more pizza. When the price falls, the same entrepreneur is discouraged from producing as much as before.

Market Entry

Profits appeal both to producers already in the market and people who may decide to join the market. As you have seen, when the price of pizza rises, a pizzeria stands out as a good opportunity to make money. If you were considering opening a restaurant of your own, a pizzeria would look like a safe bet. In this way, rising prices draw new firms into a market and add to the quantity supplied of the good.

Consider the market for music. In the late 1970s, disco music became popular among young people. The music industry quickly recognized the popularity of disco, and more and more groups began releasing disco recordings. Even some groups that once performed soul music and rhythm and blues chose to record disco albums. New entrants crowded the market to take advantage of the potential for profit. Disco, however, proved to be a short-lived fad. By the early 1980s, disco music was gone from the radio, and stores couldn't sell the albums on their shelves.

► **The music industry illustrates how profit drives suppliers' decisions. As different musical styles become popular, new groups make recordings to profit from the current fad.**

Econ 101: Key Concepts Made Easy

Supply and Demand Help students to understand the **law of supply** by pointing out that producers will naturally supply more of a good, if they can, in order to earn more revenue. Suppose that a lemonade stand owner sees that the price of lemonade is rising. The owner will naturally produce and offer more lemonade to make more revenue. In addition, several other lemonade stands may open in the neighborhood.

Ask students to recall the features of free enterprise, listed in a chart on p. 52. Ask students to explain how economic freedom, self-interest, and the profit motive are involved in the law of supply. *(Americans have the freedom to start new businesses; they make decisions about production based on self-interest; they may produce more at higher prices to make a greater profit.)*

This pattern of sharp increases and decreases in supply occurs again and again in the music industry. In the early 1990s, "grunge" music emerged from Seattle to become widely popular among high school and college students across the country. How did the market react? Record labels soon hired many grunge groups. Music stores devoted more and more space to this style of music. Within a few years, however, grunge lost its appeal, and many groups disbanded or moved on to new styles. Other styles of music, such as salsa, achieved new popularity.

In each of the examples above, many musicians joined the market for a particular style of music to profit from a trend. Their actions reflected the law of supply, which says that the output or quantity supplied of a good increases as the price of the good increases.

The Supply Schedule

Similar to a demand schedule, a **supply schedule** shows the relationship between price and quantity supplied for a specific good. The pizzeria discussed earlier might have a supply schedule that looks like the one in Figure 5.2. This table compares two **variables,** or factors that can change. These variables are the price of a slice and the number of slices supplied by a pizzeria. We could collect this information by asking the pizzeria owner how many slices she is willing and able to make at different prices, or we could look at records to see how the quantity supplied has varied as the price has changed. We will almost certainly find that at higher prices, the pizzeria owner is willing to make more pizza. At a lower price she prefers to make less pizza and to devote her limited resources to other, more profitable, items.

Like a demand schedule, a supply schedule lists supply for a very specific set of conditions. The schedule shows how the price of pizza, and only the price of pizza, affects the pizzeria's output. All of the other factors that could change the restaurant's output decisions, such as the costs of tomato sauce, labor, and rent, are assumed to remain constant.

Figure 5.2 **Supply Schedule**

Price per slice of pizza	Slices supplied per day
$ .50	100
$1.00	150
$1.50	200
$2.00	250
$2.50	300
$3.00	350

This supply schedule lists how many slices of pizza one pizzeria will offer at different prices. **Incentives What does this chart tell you about the pizzeria owner's decisions?**

A Change in the Quantity Supplied

Economists use the word *supply* to refer to the relationship between price and quantity supplied, as shown in the supply schedule. The pizzeria's supply of pizza includes all possible combinations of price and output. According to this supply schedule, the pizzeria's supply is 100 slices at $ .50 a slice, 150 slices at $1.00 a slice, 200 slices at $1.50 a slice, and so on. The number of slices that the pizzeria offers at a specific price is called the quantity supplied at that price. At $2.50 per slice, the pizzeria's quantity supplied is 300 slices per day.

A rise or fall in the price of pizza will cause the quantity supplied to change, but not the supply schedule. In other words, a change in a good's price moves the seller from one row to another in the same supply schedule, but does not change the supply schedule itself. When a factor other than the price of pizza affects output, we have to build a whole new supply schedule for the new market conditions.

Market Supply Schedule

All of the supply schedules of individual firms in a market can be added up to create a **market supply schedule.** A market supply schedule shows the relationship between prices and the total quantity supplied by all

supply schedule *a chart that lists how much of a good a supplier will offer at different prices*

variable *a factor that can change*

market supply schedule *a chart that lists how much of a good all suppliers will offer at different prices*

Transparency Resource Package Economics Concepts, 5A: Supply

Differentiated Instruction L3

(Enrichment) Have each student write a paragraph that explains the law of supply as it applies to a current music or clothing trend. If possible, have them track rising prices and increases in supply by providing market statistics.

Economic Cartoon
Unit 2 folder, p. 23 gives students practice in interpreting cartoons about section content.

Differentiated Instruction L2

Ask students to write a few sentences explaining the law of supply in their own words. Then ask them to create a drawing or collage that illustrates the law of supply in terms of an example given in the text. They might, for example, show pictures of movies that have popularized disco and of artists who later entered the market. LPR

Block Scheduling Strategies

Consider these suggestions to take advantage of extended class time:

- Extend the Bellringer activity on p. 101 by having small groups present skits based on that scenario. Allow time for groups to create their skits and then to perform them.
- Extend the activity on p. 104 by having students use the Simulations and Data Graphing CD-ROM to create their graphs. Work with the class to create a bulletin board display showing the individual and market supply schedules and supply curves.
- Invite a local business owner to talk about how he or she decides how much of a product to produce and responds to fluctuations in the prices of products. After the presentation, have students write a summary and specify whether the business owner's supply is elastic or inelastic.

Answer to . . .

Building Key Concepts The owner chose to increase supply as the price increased.

Differentiated Instruction L3

(Reteaching) Tell students to imagine that they are ice cream parlor owners. Ask individual students to create a supply schedule for ice cream cones similar to the one on p. 103. Then have them turn this supply schedule into a supply curve like the one on p. 105. Work with the class to create a market supply schedule. Ask volunteers to turn this schedule into a curve.

Transparency Resource Package Economics Concepts, 5B: Individual Supply Curve Economics Concepts, 5C: Market Supply Curve

Differentiated Instruction L1

Have students build a supply curve and supply schedule for a product of their choice. Explain that the schedule should increase prices at a regular rate, perhaps ten percent, and the quantity supplied should also increase by a regular amount or percentage. Prices should increase on the vertical axis from bottom to top. Quantity supplied should increase on the horizontal axis, left to right. SN

Figure 5.3 **Market Supply Schedule**

Price per slice of pizza	Slices supplied per day
$ .50	1,000
$1.00	1,500
$1.50	2,000
$2.00	2,500
$2.50	3,000
$3.00	3,500

A market supply schedule represents all suppliers in a market. **Supply and Demand How does this market supply schedule compare to the individual supply schedule?**

supply curve *a graph of the quantity supplied of a good at different prices*

market supply curve *a graph of the quantity supplied of a good by all suppliers at different prices*

elasticity of supply *a measure of the way quantity supplied reacts to a change in price*

firms in a particular market. The information in a market supply schedule becomes important when we want to determine the total supply of pizza at a certain price in a large area, like a city.

The market supply schedule for pizza resembles the supply schedule at a single pizzeria, but the quantities are much larger. Figure 5.3 shows the supply of pizza for a hypothetical city.

This market supply schedule lists the same prices as those in the supply schedule for the single pizzeria, since all restaurants will charge prices within the same range. The quantities supplied are much larger because there are many pizzerias in the community. Like the individual supply schedule, this market supply schedule reflects the law of supply. Pizzerias supply more pizza at higher prices.

The Supply Graph

When the data points in the supply schedule are graphed, they create a **supply curve.** A supply curve is very similar to a demand curve, except that the horizontal axis now measures the quantity of the good supplied, not the quantity demanded. Figure 5.4 shows a supply curve for one pizzeria and a **market supply curve** for all the pizzerias in the city. The data used to draw the two curves are from the supply schedules in Figures 5.2 and 5.3. The prices shown along the vertical axes are the same in both graphs. However, the quantities of pizza supplied at each price are much larger in the market supply curve.

The key feature of the supply curve is that it always rises from left to right. As your finger traces the curve from left to right, it moves toward higher and higher output levels (on the horizontal axis) and higher and higher prices (on the vertical axis). This illustrates the law of supply, which says that a higher price leads to higher output.

Supply and Elasticity

In Chapter 4, you learned that elasticity of demand measures how consumers will react to a change in price. **Elasticity of supply** is based on the same concept. Elasticity of supply is a measure of the way suppliers respond to a change in price.

Elasticity of supply tells how firms will respond to changes in the price of a good. The labels *elastic, inelastic,* and *unitary elastic* represent the same values of elasticity of supply as those of elasticity of demand. When elasticity is greater than one, supply is very sensitive to changes in price and is considered elastic. If supply is not very responsive to changes in price, and elasticity is less than one, supply is considered inelastic. When a percentage change in price is perfectly matched by an equal percentage change in quantity supplied, elasticity is exactly one, and supply is unitary elastic.

Elasticity of Supply and Time

What determines whether the supply of a good will be elastic or inelastic? The key factor is time. In the short run, a firm cannot easily change its output level, so supply is inelastic. In the long run, firms are more flexible, so supply is more elastic.

Elasticity of Supply in the Short Run

An orange grove is one example of a business that has difficulty adjusting to a change in price in the short term. Orange trees take several years to mature and grow

Preparing for Standardized Tests

Have students read the section titled "Market Supply Schedule" and then answer the question below.

A market supply schedule shows the relationship between:

A demand and the total quantity supplied by one company in a market.
(B) prices and the total quantity supplied by all firms in a market.
C prices and the total quantity supplied by one company in a market.
D demand and the total quantity supplied by all firms in a market.

Answer to . . .

Building Key Concepts Students should note that the relationship between price and supply is similar in both but that the quantities supplied are greater in the market supply curve.

Figure 5.4 Supply Curves

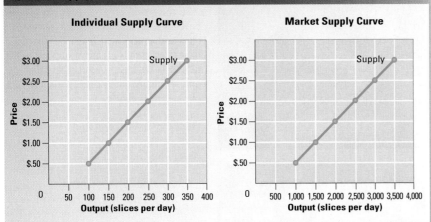

Individual Supply Curve

Price: $3.00, $2.50, $2.00, $1.50, $1.00, $.50
Supply
0, 50, 100, 150, 200, 250, 300, 350, 400
Output (slices per day)

Market Supply Curve

Price: $3.00, $2.50, $2.00, $1.50, $1.00, $.50
Supply
0, 500, 1,000, 1,500, 2,000, 2,500, 3,000, 3,500, 4,000
Output (slices per day)

BUILDING KEY CONCEPTS

Supply curves always rise from left to right, as predicted by the law of supply. As price increases, so does the quantity supplied.

Supply and Demand How many slices will one pizzeria produce at $2.00 a slice?

fruit. If the price of oranges goes up, an orange grower can buy and plant more trees, but he will have to wait several years for his investment to pay off. In the short term, the grower could take smaller steps to increase output. For example, he could use a more effective pesticide. While this step might increase his output somewhat, it would probably not increase the number of oranges by very much. Economists would say that his supply is inelastic, because he cannot easily change his output. The same factors that prevent the owner of the orange grove from expanding his supply will also prevent new growers from entering the market and supplying oranges in the short term.

In the short run, supply is inelastic whether the price increases or decreases. If the price of a crate of oranges falls, the grove owner has few ways to cut his supply. He invested years ago in land and trees, and his grove will provide oranges no matter what the price is. Even if the price drops drastically, the grove owner will probably pick and sell nearly as many oranges as before. The grove owner's competitors have also invested heavily in land and trees and won't drop out of the market if they can survive. In this case, supply is inelastic whether prices rise or fall.

While orange groves illustrate a business in which supply is inelastic, other businesses benefit from more elastic supply. For example, a business that provides a service, such as a haircut, is highly elastic. Unlike oranges, the supply of haircuts is easily expanded or reduced. If the price rises, barber shops and salons can hire workers quickly.

Figure 5.5 Elastic Supply

SUPPLY
Price
Supply
When supply is elastic, a small increase in price has a big effect on supply.

BUILDING KEY CONCEPTS

When supply is elastic, it reacts strongly to changes in price. **Supply and Demand If supply is inelastic, how will supply react to a small increase in price?**

Differentiated Instruction L3

Organize students into groups of three or four. Ask each group to analyze the following situations and explain how elasticity of supply would affect producer decisions in each case.

- The price of apples increases. *(Supply is relatively inelastic; an apple grower could not increase the supply greatly in the short term.)*
- The price of an oil change increases. *(Supply is relatively elastic; a repair shop could hire more workers and increase the supply.)*
- The price of dry cleaning services increases. *(Supply is relatively elastic; a dry cleaner could hire more workers and increase the supply.)*
- The price of tickets to a football game increases. *(Supply is relatively inelastic; stadium owners cannot increase the supply of seats greatly in the short term.)*

Differentiated Instruction L2

Have students create two multi-flow chart graphic organizers that depict the factors that affect elasticity of supply. The center of one organizer should be labeled "Inelastic Supply," and the center of the other should be labeled "Elastic Supply." Have students fill in the factors that lead to each condition. LPR

Econ 101: Key Concepts Made Easy

Supply and Demand Students may have difficulty understanding what is meant by **inelastic supply.** After all, if the price of a good goes up, surely someone will find a way to produce more of it, right? Ask students to think about the paintings of Vincent Van Gogh. During the 1980s and 1990s, art collectors paid enormous sums of money for Van Gogh's work. Nevertheless, no matter how high the prices went, the supply remained constant. After all, a dead artist cannot paint! Van Gogh's artwork is an extreme example of inelastic supply. Ask students to think of other examples of inelastic supply (for example, homes in a highly developed area or cut-your-own Christmas trees).

Answer to . . .

Building Key Concepts 250 slices
Building Key Concepts Supply will not increase.

GTE Guide to the Essentials
Chapter 5, Section 1, p. 20 provides support for students who need additional review of the section content. Spanish support is available in the Spanish edition of the guide on p. 20.

Quiz Unit 2 folder, p. 14 includes questions to check students' understanding of Section 1 content.

Presentation Pro CD-ROM
Quiz provides multiple-choice questions to check students' understanding of Section 1 content.

Answers to . . .

Section 1 Assessment

1. Student responses should adequately summarize the law of supply, which states that producers will offer more of a good as its price increases.
2. A price change will cause a change in the quantity supplied, whereas an outside factor, such as inclement weather, causes a change in supply.
3. A good with a large elasticity of supply will be very responsive to changes in price. Supply will rise swiftly in response to a price increase.
4. Oil production in Texas will increase because the law of supply dictates that as prices increase, suppliers will produce more.
5. (a) inelastic: the number of hotel rooms can be increased, but not quickly or easily (b) elastic: taxi drivers could work more or fewer hours, or taxi companies could put more taxis into use (c) elastic: more or fewer photographs could be produced if the price changed
6. If the market price rises, an entrepreneur might be able to produce less and still make the same amount of money as before.

▶ While the supply of oranges is inelastic, the supply of goods made from oranges is elastic. For example, producers can choose whether to produce more or less orange juice from the oranges.

In addition, new barber shops and salons will open, and existing businesses might stay open later in the evening. This means that a small increase in price will cause a large increase in quantity supplied, even in the short term.

If the price of a haircut drops, some barbers will close their shops earlier in the day, and others will leave the market for jobs elsewhere. Quantity supplied will fall quickly. Because haircut suppliers can quickly change their operations, the supply of haircuts is elastic.

Elasticity in the Long Run

Like demand, supply can become more elastic over time. Consider the example of the orange grower who could not increase his output much when the price of oranges rose. Over time, he could plant more trees to increase his supply of oranges. These changes will become more effective over time as trees grow and bear fruit. After several years, he will be able to sell many more oranges at the high market price.

If the price drops and stays low for several years, orange growers who survived the first two or three years of losses might decide to give up and grow something else. Given five years to respond instead of six weeks, the supply of oranges will be far more elastic. Just like demand, supply becomes more elastic if the supplier has a long time to respond to a price change.

Section 1 Assessment

Progress Monitoring *Online*
For: Self-quiz with vocabulary practice
Web Code: mna-2055

Key Terms and Main Ideas

1. Explain the **law of supply** in your own words.
2. What is the difference between supply and **quantity supplied?**
3. How does the quantity supplied of a good with a large **elasticity of supply** react to a price change?

Applying Economic Concepts

4. ***Problem Solving*** If the price of oil rises around the world, what will happen to oil production in Texas? Explain your answer.
5. ***Decision Making*** Explain whether you think the supply of the following goods is elastic or inelastic, and why. **(a)** hotel rooms **(b)** taxi rides **(c)** photographs
6. ***Critical Thinking*** When the price of a good rises, total supply in the market will rise, but some entrepreneurs might actually choose to work less. Why might they make this choice?

Go Online PHSchool.com
For: Research Activity
Visit: PHSchool.com
Web Code: mnd-2051

Progress Monitoring *Online*
For additional assessment, have students access Progress Monitoring Online at **Web Code:** mna-2055

Go Online PHSchool.com Typing in the Web Code when prompted will bring students directly to detailed instructions for this activity.

Skills for
LIFE

Environmental Policy

Environmental policy deals with the way humans interact with the natural world. Environmental policy should help set guidelines for how people can best use natural resources without having a long-term negative effect on the world around us. This sample environmental policy report discusses a situation where the actions of people have had an effect on the landscape.

1. Identify the people and places in the report. Environmental policy deals with both the natural world and the way people use it. In this policy report, the author has described a particular kind of natural landscape and also a particular kind of human activity. (a) What is the natural landscape discussed in the report? (b) What are the human actions discussed in the report?

For decades, we have worked to manage fire danger in the national forests and parklands by putting out all fires as soon as possible. Fire suppression was believed to be in the best interests of the forest, and served to protect the houses built in or near forests. More than thirty-four million people live in areas at a high risk of fire, and for many years we thought that fire suppression was the best way to protect those people.

Experts on forest and forests fires now say that fire suppression may not be the best thing for the forests, or for the people living near the forests. The normal life cycle for a forest probably involves regular small fires and the occasional large fire. Under those conditions, the underbrush plants between the large trees will be cleared out on a regular basis. If we suppress fires in the forest areas, then the underbrush becomes too tall and crowded, which eventually puts the whole forest area at a higher risk for the type of large and difficult to control fires that swept through Southern California in 2004. We are recommending that the forestry service adopt a new policy of not suppressing smaller fires.

2. Describe the impact of human action on the environment. When there are different courses of action open to people, it's not always easy to choose between them. (a) The report describes two different ways people can act in this situation. What are they? (b) List the advantages and disadvantages of each course of action.

3. Identify the different needs of different groups. Most environmental policy statements have to deal with the different needs of all of the groups involved in the decision. (a) Do you think the needs of people who live closer to the fire risk areas are different than the needs of people who don't live as close? (b) Does this report discuss any ways that people who live near fire risk areas can act to protect themselves from the regular small fires?

Additional Practice

Find a natural landscape near your home that has been affected by human use, and write a sample environmental policy report. Do you think that the human use of that area should continue the way it has been going so far? Do you think that people should change their use of that area? Why or why not?

Skills for LIFE

Environmental Policy

1. Focus Students will learn to evaluate environmental policy decisions.

2. Instruct Explain to students that some environmental concerns are not easily resolved. In every decision, there may be trade-offs. While some people benefit, others may not. The object is to make decisions that serve the best interests of the whole community.

3. Close/Reteach To provide additional practice, see the Economic Skills Activity below.

Economic Skills Activity
Unit 2 folder, p. 19

Social Studies Skills Tutor CD-ROM offers interactive practice in critical thinking and reading, visual analysis, and communication.

Answers

1. (a) national forests and parklands; (b) fire suppression, building houses in or near the forests
2. (a) clear out underbrush to suppress small fires; allow the underbrush to grow and control the small fires (b) Suppressing the small fires protects houses in or near the forests but results in large uncontrollable fires; allowing the underbrush to grow results in small fires that affect some homes but prevents fires from getting out of control.
3. (a) yes (b) (no)

Interdisciplinary Connections: Government

Endangered Species and Environmental Policy Many environmental policy reports must take into account the provisions of the Endangered Species Act. Passed in 1973, this law protects plants and animals from extinction by limiting human behavior that threatens their habitats. The presence of endangered species at a spot designated for economic development has caused conflicts between the federal government and private property owners.

Have students work through the following activity: Ask students to research a recent court case where the federal government or an environmental group cited the Endangered Species Act to stop an economic development project. How did the project threaten the endangered species? What were the financial trade-offs involved in protecting the habitat? How did the courts rule on the dilemma?

Additional Practice

Students' reports should address all concerns discussed in the activity.

Section 2

Costs of Production

Objectives You may wish to call students' attention to the objectives in the Section Preview. The objectives are reflected in the main headings of the section.

Bellringer Ask students to think about fast-food restaurants. Ask: "How do the owners of these restaurants know how much food to produce each day? What would happen to the owner's profits if the restaurant produced too much or too little food?" Then explain that in this section students will learn how producers of goods and services determine ideal levels of output.

Vocabulary Builder Have students read the section to discover the meaning of each key term. Then ask them to write definitions of the terms in their own words.

Lesson Plan

Teaching the Main Concepts L3

1. Focus Explain that marginal costs and returns are the key factors in any company's decision about how much of a good or service to produce.
2. Instruct Begin by discussing the effects of labor on output, stressing the causes of increasing and diminishing marginal returns. Next, introduce the concepts of fixed and variable costs, explaining how they combine to determine total cost and how total cost is used to determine marginal cost. Then, discuss how profit is calculated and how it leads to the determination of ideal output. Finally, explain how a firm decides to shut down an unprofitable business.
3. Close/Reteach Remind students that ideal output is determined by maximizing the use of labor and capital and calculating the production level at which marginal revenue equals marginal cost. Have students define marginal revenue and marginal costs and explain how they are calculated.

Section 2 Costs of Production

Preview

Objectives

After studying this section you will be able to:

1. **Explain** how firms decide how much labor to hire to produce a certain level of output.
2. **Analyze** the production costs of a firm.
3. **Understand** how a firm chooses to set output.
4. **Explain** how a firm decides to shut down an unprofitable business.

Section Focus

Entrepreneurs consider marginal benefits and costs when deciding how much output to produce. Ordinarily, firms earn their highest profits when the cost of making one more unit is the same as the market price of the good.

Key Terms

marginal product of labor
increasing marginal returns
diminishing marginal returns
fixed cost
variable cost
total cost
marginal cost
marginal revenue
operating cost

marginal product of labor *the change in output from hiring one additional unit of labor*

In Section 1, we identified how producers respond to a change in price. The law of supply states that producers will offer more goods as the price goes up and fewer as the price falls. In this section, we will explain how a supplier decides *how much* to produce.

Consider a firm that produces beanbags. The firm's factory has one sewing machine and one pair of scissors. The firm's inputs are workers and materials, including cloth, thread, and beans. Assume that each beanbag requires the same amount of materials. As the number of workers increases, what happens to the quantity of beanbags produced?

The supply of beanbag chairs in the market depends on several factors, including the cost of labor and capital. ▼

Labor and Output

One of the basic questions any business owner has to answer is how many workers to hire. To answer this question, owners have to consider how the number of workers they hire will affect their total production. For example, at the beanbag factory, one worker can produce four beanbags per hour. Two workers can make a total of ten bags per hour, and three can make a total of seventeen beanbags an hour. As new workers join the company, total output increases. After the seventh worker is hired, production peaks at 32 beanbags per hour. When the firm hires the eighth worker, however, total output drops to 31 bags per hour.

Figure 5.6 shows the relationship between labor, measured by the number of workers in the factory, and the number of beanbags produced.

Marginal Product of Labor

The third column of Figure 5.6 shows the **marginal product of labor,** or the change in output from hiring one more worker. This is called the marginal product because it measures the change in output at the margin, where the last worker has been hired or fired.

Graphing the Main Idea

Incentives To build understanding of the concept of **incentives** and the costs of production, have students complete a tree map graphic organizer like the one shown below. Tell them to put the title of the section in the top box and the main headings of the section in the next row of boxes. In the boxes beneath each heading, they should record main ideas and supporting details.

Section Reading Support Transparencies A template and the answers for this graphic organizer can be found in Chapter 5, Section 2 of the Section Reading Support Transparency System.

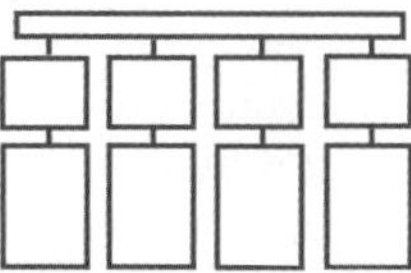

The first worker to be hired produces four bags an hour, so her marginal product is four bags. The second worker raises total output from four bags an hour to ten, so her marginal product of labor is six. Looking at this column, we see that the marginal product of labor increases for the first three workers, rising from four to seven.

Increasing Marginal Returns

The marginal product of labor increases for the first three workers because there are three tasks involved in making a beanbag. Workers cut and sew cloth into the correct shape, stuff it with beans, and sew the bag closed. In our example, a single worker performing all these tasks would only produce four bags per hour. Adding a second worker would allow each worker to specialize in one or two tasks. If each worker focuses on only one part of the process, she will waste less time switching between tasks and will become more skillful at her assigned tasks. In other words, specialization increases output per worker, so the second worker adds more to output than the first. The firm enjoys **increasing marginal returns.**

In our example, there are benefits from specialization for the first three workers. The firm enjoys a rising marginal product of labor for the first three workers.

Diminishing Marginal Returns

When the fourth through the seventh workers are hired, the marginal product of labor is still positive. Each new worker still adds to total output. However, the marginal product of labor shrinks as each worker joins the company. The fourth worker increases output by six bags, while the seventh increases output by only one bag. Why?

After the beanbag firm hires its first three workers, one for each task, the benefits of specialization end. At that point, adding more workers increases total output, but at a decreasing rate. This situation is known as **diminishing marginal returns.** A firm with diminishing marginal returns of labor will produce less and less output from each additional unit of labor added to the mix.

The firm suffers from diminishing marginal returns from labor because its workers must work with a limited amount of capital. Remember that capital is any human-made resource that is used to produce other goods. In this example, capital is represented by the factory's single sewing machine and pair of scissors. When there are three workers, but only one needs to use the sewing machine, this worker will never have to wait to get to

Figure 5.6 **Marginal Product of Labor**

Labor (number of workers)	Output (beanbags per hour)	Marginal product of labor
0	0	—
1	4	4
2	10	6
3	17	7
4	23	6
5	28	5
6	31	3
7	32	1
8	31	-1

The marginal product of labor is the increase in output added by the last unit of labor.
Specialization
Why does the marginal product of labor decrease with more than four workers in this example?

increasing marginal returns *a level of production in which the marginal product of labor increases as the number of workers increases*

diminishing marginal returns *a level of production in which the marginal product of labor decreases as the number of workers increases*

Figure 5.7 **Increasing, Diminishing, and Negative Marginal Returns**

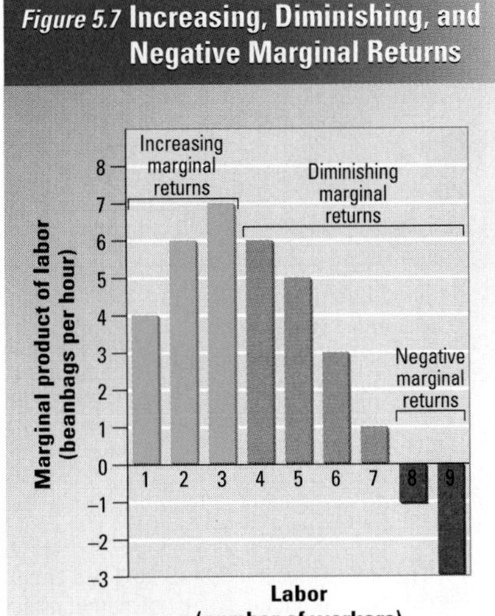

Labor has increasing and then diminishing marginal returns.
Opportunity Cost
What is the marginal product of labor when the factory currently employs five workers?

Guided Reading and Review
Unit 2 folder, p. 15 asks students to identify the main ideas of the section and to define or identify key terms.

Differentiated Instruction 

To help students transfer information from one medium to another (statistical to written), ask students to use the graphics on this page to explain how firms decide how much labor to hire. Tell them to write one or more paragraphs and to refer to both of the figures on this page.

Differentiated Instruction 

Pair each student with a peer tutor who is a native English speaker. Encourage these student pairs to sit together in class so that comprehension difficulties can be addressed quickly. Suggest that each pair meet for a few minutes every day to discuss any key terms or concepts that need clarification. ELL

Econ 101: Key Concepts Made Easy

Opportunity Cost Some students may have difficulty grasping the concept of something that is **marginal.** Explain that in economic terms, *marginal* simply means "additional." Display the following list, and encourage students to copy it into their Economics Journals:

marginal product of labor = output change from hiring one **additional** worker

marginal cost = the **additional** cost of producing one **additional** unit

marginal revenue = the **additional** revenue from producing one **additional** unit

Answer to . . .

Building Key Concepts It decreases because the workers are working with a limited amount of capital.
Building Key Concepts Five beanbags per hour.

Background

Corporate Downsizing

Workers used to assume that if they were doing a good job for a growing, profitable company, their jobs were secure. During the 1990s, however, hundreds of thousands of such workers discovered just how insecure their jobs really were when they unexpectedly found themselves victims of a corporate trend—downsizing. When a company downsizes, it lays off a percentage of its workers.

Why would growing, profitable companies put loyal employees through such pain? Blame it on diminishing marginal returns. In today's highly competitive marketplace the companies that thrive are lean, tightly focused, and extremely cost-conscious. During the early 1990s, such diverse companies as IBM, General Motors, Boeing, and Eastman Kodak looked at their corporate structures and saw inefficient organizations that would lose their competitive edge if they didn't shape up. As a result, employees had to go: 85,000 at IBM; 74,000 at General Motors; 30,000 at Boeing; and 14,000 at Eastman Kodak—all between 1991 and 1994. According to some economists, those jobs are lost forever.

That's why it is important for companies to pay close attention to hiring levels and what they will gain from their investment. Careful planning today can prevent unnecessary pain tomorrow.

Transparency Resource Package Economics Concepts, 5D: Increasing, Diminishing, and Negative Marginal Returns

FAST FACT

*To understand the **diminishing marginal returns** of capital, consider an Internet service provider that mailed millions of free copies of its software on compact discs. The first discs sent out got customers interested in the product and provided a good return on investment. After consumers received several additional discs, however, the discs no longer caught their attention and more often than not ended up in the trash.*

work. When there are more than three workers, the factory will assign more than one to work at the sewing machine. While one is working, the other will have to wait. She may be able to help cut fabric or stuff bags in the meantime, but every bag must be sewn up at some point, so she cannot greatly increase the speed of the production process.

The problem gets worse as more workers are hired and the amount of capital remains constant. Wasted time waiting for the sewing machine or scissors means that additional workers will add less and less to total output at the factory.

Negative Marginal Returns

As the table in Figure 5.6 shows, adding the eighth worker at the beanbag factory can actually decrease output by one bag. At this stage, workers get in each other's way and disrupt the production process, so overall output decreases. Of course, few companies ever hire so many workers that their marginal product of labor becomes negative.

Production Costs

Paying workers and purchasing capital are all costs of producing goods. Economists

Figure 5.8 **Fixed and Variable Cost**

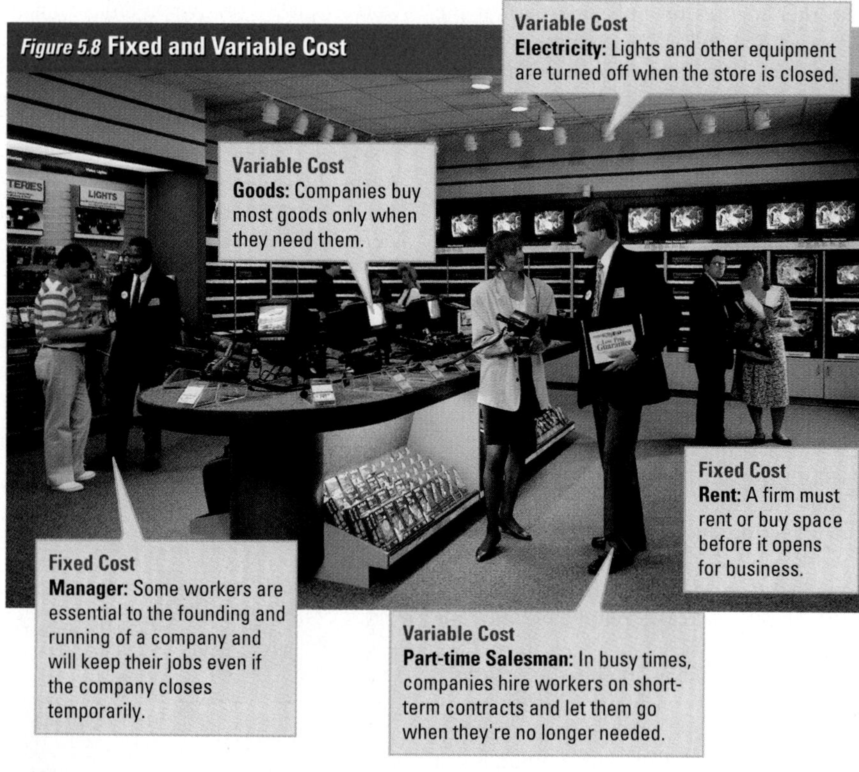

Variable Cost
Electricity: Lights and other equipment are turned off when the store is closed.
Variable Cost
Goods: Companies buy most goods only when they need them.
TERIES
LIGHTS
Fixed Cost
Rent: A firm must rent or buy space before it opens for business.
Fixed Cost
Manager: Some workers are essential to the founding and running of a company and will keep their jobs even if the company closes temporarily.
Variable Cost
Part-time Salesman: In busy times, companies hire workers on short-term contracts and let them go when they're no longer needed.

Firms must separate fixed costs from variable costs to determine whether or not to produce at a given market price.
Entrepreneurs Why are some employees considered variable costs?

Block Scheduling Strategies

Consider these suggestions to take advantage of extended class time:

- Show the Economics Video Library segment "Plummeting Prices," about the lowering of prices for personal computers. After they view the segment, have students create graphs that illustrate the trends over the last two decades.
- Have students use the Internet to learn more about fixed and variable costs. Links with activities can be found within *Economics: Principles in Action* in the Social Studies area of the Prentice Hall Web site. **www.phschool.com**

Answer to . . .

Photo Caption Part-time workers are variable costs because they can be asked to work more or fewer hours.

Figure 5.9 **Production Costs**

Beanbags (per hour)	Fixed cost	Variable cost	Total cost (fixed cost + variable cost)	Marginal cost	Marginal revenue (market price)	Total revenue	Profit (total revenue – total cost)
0	$36	$0	$36	—	$24	$0	$–36
1	36	8	44	$8	24	24	–20
2	36	12	48	4	24	48	0
3	36	15	51	3	24	72	21
4	36	20	56	5	24	96	40
5	36	27	63	7	24	120	57
6	36	36	72	9	24	144	72
7	36	48	84	12	24	168	84
8	36	63	99	15	24	192	93
9	36	82	118	19	24	216	98
10	36	106	142	24	24	240	98
11	36	136	172	30	24	264	92
12	36	173	209	37	24	288	79

Firms consider a variety of costs when deciding how much to produce.
Markets and Prices
Why is the marginal revenue always equal to $24?

divide a producer's costs into two categories: fixed costs and variable costs.

Fixed Costs

A **fixed cost** is a cost that does not change, no matter how much of a good is produced. Most fixed costs involve the production facility, the cost of building and equipping a factory, office, store, or restaurant. Examples of fixed costs include rent, machinery repairs, property taxes on a factory, and the salaries of workers who keep the business running even when production temporarily stops.

Variable Costs

Variable costs are costs that rise or fall depending on the quantity produced. They include the costs of raw materials and some labor. For example, to produce more beanbags, the firm must purchase more beans and hire more workers to stuff the beanbags. If the company wants to produce less and cut costs, it can stop buying beans or have some workers work fewer hours a week. The cost of labor is a variable cost because it changes with the number of workers, which changes with the quantity produced. Electricity and heating bills are also variable costs, because the company can cut off heat and electricity for the factory and its machines when they are not in use.

Total Cost

Figure 5.9 shows some cost data for the firm that produces beanbags. The firm has a factory that is fully equipped to produce beanbags. How does the cost of producing beanbags change as the output increases?

In our example, the fixed costs are the costs of the factory building and all the machinery and equipment inside. As shown in the second column in Figure 5.9, the fixed costs are $36.00 per hour.

Variable costs include the cost of beans, fabric, and most of the workers hired to produce the beanbags. As shown in the third column, variable costs rise with the number of beanbags produced. Fixed costs and variable costs are added together to find **total cost.** Total cost is shown in the fourth column.

Marginal Cost

If we know the total cost at several levels of output, we can determine the **marginal cost** of production at each level. Marginal cost is the additional cost of producing one more unit.

As shown in Figure 5.9, even if the firm is not producing a single beanbag, it still

fixed cost *a cost that does not change, no matter how much of a good is produced*

variable cost *a cost that rises or falls depending on how much is produced*

total cost *fixed costs plus variable costs*

marginal cost *the cost of producing one more unit of a good*

Differentiated Instruction L3

(Enrichment) Remind students about the human cost of downsizing. (You may wish to read them the Background note on p. 110.) Ask them to consider what financial or ethical obligations, if any, employers have to employees who get caught in the corporate numbers game and lose their jobs. Have students write an essay that either (a) makes a convincing argument that companies do not have this obligation, or (b) describes steps that employers could take to help downsized workers get their lives and careers back on track.

Differentiated Instruction 

In order to reinforce understanding of how firms make decisions, have students imagine that they have just started their own businesses to produce greeting cards. How will they decide how many employees to hire? What are their fixed and variable costs? Ask students to write a brief proposal that addresses both of these questions.

Transparency Resource Package
Economics Concepts, 5E: Fixed Versus Variable Costs

Meeting NCEE Standards

Use the following benchmark activity from the **Voluntary National Content Standards in Economics** to evaluate student understanding of **Standard 4.**

Analyze the impact (on consumers, producers, workers, savers, and investors) of an increase in the minimum wage, a new tax policy, or a change in interest rates.

Preparing for Standardized Tests

Have students read the sections titled "Fixed Costs" and "Variable Costs" and then answer the question below.

All of the following are examples of variable costs except

A rent.
B electricity.
C labor.
D heat.

Answer to . . .

Building Key Concepts The marginal revenue equals the market price.

Differentiated Instruction 

You may wish to have students add the following to their portfolios. To help students create a product on a contemporary economic topic using critical methods of inquiry, ask them to assume that they are business consultants who have been asked to analyze the production costs of a firm. The problem is that total costs have begun to exceed total revenues. Facts about the company follow. Ask students to write a proposal that suggests ways for the company to cut costs and increase revenues.

Company: MGQQ Solutions
Product: Customized computer programs for small businesses
Location: Beverly Hills, California; in newly constructed office complex
Employees: 10—owner, receptionist, file clerk, secretary, 4 programmers, 2 accountants
Clients: 5 regular, 2 occasional GT

Economics Assessment Rubric
Economics Assessment Rubrics folder, pp. 6–7 provides sample evaluation materials for a writing assignment.

Differentiated Instruction 

Ask students to use the graphics on pp. 112 and 113 to explain how firms make output decisions. You might also display Transparency 5F and have students use it to demonstrate understanding of these concepts.

Transparency Resource Package
Economics Concepts, 5F: Setting Output

marginal revenue *the additional income from selling one more unit of a good; sometimes equal to price*

must pay $36.00 an hour for fixed costs. If the firm decides to produce just one beanbag an hour, its total cost rises $8.00 from $36.00 to $44.00 an hour. The marginal cost of the first beanbag is $8.00.

For the first three beanbags, the marginal cost falls as output increases. The marginal cost of the second beanbag is $4.00, and the marginal cost of the third beanbag is $3.00. Each additional beanbag is cheaper to make because of increasing marginal returns resulting from specialization.

With the fourth beanbag, the marginal cost starts to rise. The marginal cost of the fifth per hour is $7.00, the sixth costs $9.00, and the seventh, $12.00. The rising marginal cost reflects diminishing returns to labor. The benefits of specialization are exhausted at three beanbags per hour, and diminishing returns set in as more and more workers share a fixed production facility.

Setting Output

Behind all of the decisions about how many workers to hire is the firm's basic goal: to maximize profits. Profit is defined as total revenue minus total cost. As you read in Chapter 4, a firm's total revenue is the money the firm gets by selling its product. Total revenue is equal to the price of each good multiplied by the number of goods sold. Figure 5.9 shows total revenue when the price of a beanbag is $24.00. To find the level of output with the highest profit, we look for the biggest gap between total revenue and total cost. The gap is biggest and profit is highest when the firm makes 9 or 10 beanbags per hour. At this rate, the firm can expect to make a profit of $98.00 an hour.

Marginal Revenue and Marginal Cost

Another way to find the best level of output is to find the output level where **marginal revenue** is equal to marginal cost. Marginal revenue is the additional income from selling one more unit of a good. If the firm has no control over the market price, marginal revenue equals the market price. Each beanbag sold at $24.00 increases the firm's total revenue by $24.00, so marginal revenue is $24.00. According to the table, price equals marginal cost with 10 beanbags, so that's the quantity that maximizes profit at $98 an hour.

To understand how an output of 10 beanbags maximizes the firm's profits, suppose that the firm picked a different level of output. If the firm made only 4 beanbags per hour, is it making as much money as it can?

From Figure 5.9, we know that the marginal cost of the fifth beanbag is $7.00. The market price for a beanbag is $24.00, so the marginal revenue from that beanbag is $24.00. The $17.00 difference between the marginal revenue and marginal cost represents pure profit for the company from making and selling the fifth beanbag. The company should increase its production to five beanbags an hour to capture that profit on the fifth beanbag.

If we do the same calculations for a sixth beanbag, we find that the company can capture a profit of $15.00 by producing the sixth beanbag per hour. The price of the seventh beanbag is $12.00 higher than its marginal cost, so that beanbag earns an

Figure 5.10 Marginal Cost Curve

Marginal cost (in dollars)
40
30
20
10
0
Marginal cost
0 1 2 3 4 5 6 7 8 9 10 11 12
Output (beanbags per hour)

For most firms, the marginal cost of production falls as output rises from zero, but eventually begins to rise.

Markets and Prices How many beanbags an hour should this firm make to produce at the lowest possible marginal cost?

Interdisciplinary Connections: Dramatic Arts

Production Costs When the Drama Club gets ready to stage a new play, it must deal with many of the same production costs as a business. On opening night the actors, director, costume designers, musicians, lighting crew, and set builders will present their product to consumers and hope to make a profit.

Making the Connection Ask students to list the fixed and variable costs for the production of a musical. Then ask how the Drama Club can decide what to charge for each ticket so that they will make a profit.

Answer to . . .

Building Key Concepts Three beanbags per hour.

additional $12.00 in profit for the company. The profit is available any time the company receives more for the last beanbag than it cost to produce. Any rational entrepreneur would take this opportunity to increase profit.

Now suppose that the firm is producing so many beanbags an hour that marginal cost is *higher* than price. If the firm produces eleven beanbags an hour, it receives $24.00 for that eleventh beanbag, but the $30.00 cost of that beanbag wipes out the profit. The firm actually loses $6.00 on the sale of the eleventh beanbag. Because marginal cost is increasing, and price is constant in this example, the losses would get worse at higher levels of output. The company would be better off producing less and keeping costs down.

The ideal level of output is where marginal revenue (price) is equal to marginal cost. Any other quantity of output would generate less profit.

Figure 5.11 Output and a Change in Price

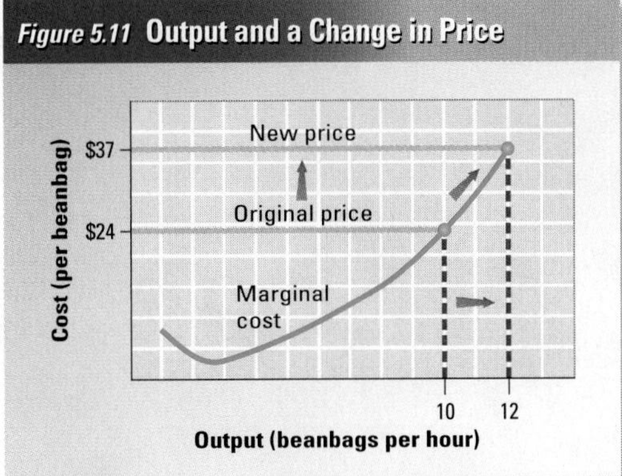

The most profitable level of output is where price (or marginal revenue) is equal to marginal cost.
Markets and Prices What would happen to output if the market price fell to $20?

Responding to Price Changes

What would happen if the price of a beanbag rose from $24.00 to $37.00? Thinking at the margin, we would predict that the firm would increase production to twelve beanbags per hour. That's the quantity at which the marginal cost is equal to the new, higher price. At the original price of $24.00, the firm would not produce more than ten beanbags, according to Figure 5.11. When the price rises to $37.00, marginal revenue soars above marginal cost at that output level. Raising production to twelve beanbags an hour would allow the firm to capture profits on the eleventh and twelfth beanbags.

This example shows the law of supply in action. An increase in price from $24.00 to $37.00 causes the firm to increase the quantity supplied from ten to twelve beanbags an hour.

The Shutdown Decision

Consider the problems faced by a factory that is losing money. The factory is producing at a level of output at which marginal revenue is equal to marginal cost. As you have read, this is the most profitable level of output. However, the market price is so low that the factory's total revenue is still less than its total cost, and the firm is losing money. Should this factory continue to produce goods and lose money, or should its owners shut the factory down?

This may seem like a silly question. In fact, there are times when keeping a money-losing factory open is the best choice. The firm should keep the factory open if the total revenue from the goods and services the factory produces is greater than the cost of keeping it open.

For example, if the price of beanbags drops to $7, and the factory produces at the profit-maximizing level of five beanbags per hour, the total revenue of the business is $35 per hour. Weigh this against the factory's **operating cost**, or the cost of operating the facility. The operating cost includes the variable costs the owners must pay to keep the factory running, but not the fixed costs, which the owners must pay whether the factory is open or closed.

According to Figure 5.9, if the factory produces five beanbags, the variable cost is $27 per hour. Therefore, the benefit of operating the facility (total revenue of $35)

operating cost *the cost of operating a facility, such as a store or factory*

Background

Profits and More Profits

In the world of business, the term *profit* has a straightforward definition: "The excess of total revenue over total cost." Economists, however, classify profits in varying ways.

Let's say that Mr. Denson discovers a new technique for manufacturing snowboards that enables him to produce them for much less than the market price. His excess total revenues are known as *entrepreneurial profits.*

Suppose that there is a sudden huge increase in the number of people who want to take up snowboarding. Mr. Denson's excess total revenues are called *windfall profits.*

Mr. Denson knows that increased interest in snowboarding will mean increased competition, and that could hurt his profits. Therefore, he gets together with his biggest competitor, and the two agree to restrict their output so that demand will outstrip supply; thus, prices and profits will remain high. Now Mr. Denson's excess total revenues have a new name: *monopoly profits.*

Differentiated Instruction 

(Reteaching) Ask students to explain what goes into a firm's decision to shut down an unprofitable business.

Learning Styles Activity
Learning Styles Lesson Plans folder, p. 15 asks students to build a production costs table and use it to determine the most profitable level of output for a hypothetical sweatshirt producer.

✓ Preparing for Standardized Tests

Have students read the section titled "Setting Output" and then answer the question below.

Which of the following best describes the ideal level of output?

A Marginal revenue is more than marginal cost.
B Marginal revenue is more than total cost.
(C) Marginal revenue is equal to marginal cost.
D Marginal revenue is less than total cost.

Answer to . . .
Building Key Concepts Output of beanbags would decrease.

GTE Guide to the Essentials
Chapter 5, Section 2, p. 21 provides support for students who need additional review of the section content. Spanish support is available in the Spanish edition of the guide on p. 21.

Quiz Unit 2 folder, p. 16 includes questions to check students' understanding of Section 2 content.

Presentation Pro CD-ROM
Quiz provides multiple-choice questions to check students' understanding of Section 2 content.

Answers to . . .

Section 2 Assessment

1. The marginal product of labor increases up to a point and then decreases as still more workers are hired.
2. Diminishing marginal returns will probably have a negative effect on labor: As the firm experiences less new output per worker, fewer new workers will be hired, and some may be let go.
3. Examples of fixed costs may include the building rent or mortgage or the property taxes. Variable costs include the prices of the wheat, yeast, and milk used to produce baked goods.
4. Marginal cost is calculated by finding out how much additional cost results from each additional unit produced. For example, in the duffel bag example, the marginal cost of the first duffel bag was $8.00 because total cost rose from $36.00 to $44.00 with the production of one bag.
5. The smaller factory will experience diminishing returns first because it most likely has half as much capital for workers to use to produce goods.
6. Student answers should include reasonable explanations for their decisions. (a) variable (b) variable (c) variable (d) fixed (e) variable
7. (a) $32 (b) $28 (c) 2

▲ **When a factory begins losing money, the owner must consider its operating cost and revenue when deciding what to do.**

is greater than the variable cost ($27), so it makes sense to keep the facility running.

Consider the effects of the other choice. If the firm were to shut down the factory, it would still have to pay all of its fixed costs. The factory's total revenue would be zero because it would be producing nothing for sale. Therefore, the firm would lose an amount of money equal to its fixed costs.

For this beanbag factory, the fixed costs equal $36 per hour, so the factory would lose $36 for each hour it is closed. If the factory were to keep producing five beanbags per hour, its total cost would be $63 ($36 in fixed costs plus $27 in variable costs) per hour, but it would lose only $28 ($63 in total cost minus $35 in revenue) for each hour it is open. The factory would lose less money while producing because the total revenue ($35) would exceed the variable costs ($27), leaving $8 to cover some of the fixed costs. Although the factory would lose money in either situation, it would lose less money by continuing to produce and sell beanbags.

How long will a business continue to operate a factory at a loss before it decides to replace the facility? The firm will build a new factory and stay in the market only if the market price of beanbags is high enough to cover all the costs of production, including the cost of building a new factory.

Section 2 Assessment

Progress Monitoring *Online*
For: Self-quiz with vocabulary practice
Web Code: mna-2056

Key Terms and Main Ideas

1. How does the **marginal product of labor** change as more workers are hired?
2. What is the impact of **diminishing marginal returns** on labor?
3. Give an example of a **fixed cost** and a **variable cost** of a bakery.
4. How does a firm calculate **marginal cost?**

Applying Economic Concepts

5. ***Critical Thinking*** A firm has two factories, one twice as large as the second. As the number of workers at each factory increases, which factory will experience diminishing returns first?
6. ***Decision Making*** Explain whether each of these expenses of a textile mill is a fixed cost or a variable cost, and why. **(a)** repairs to a leaking roof **(b)** cotton **(c)** food for the mill's cafeteria **(d)** night security guard **(e)** electricity
7. ***Math Practice*** Use the table below to answer the following questions. **(a)** What is the total cost when output is 2? **(b)** What is the marginal cost of the third unit? **(c)** How much should this firm produce if the market price is $24?

Output	Fixed Cost	Variable Cost
1	$5	$10
2	$5	$27
3	$5	$55
4	$5	$91
5	$5	$145

For: Simulation Activity
Visit: PHSchool.com
Web Code: mnd-2052

Progress Monitoring *Online*
For additional assessment, have students access Progress Monitoring Online at **Web Code:** mna-2056

Go Online PHSchool.com Typing in the Web Code when prompted will bring students directly to detailed instructions for this activity.

ECONOMIC

Profile

Economist

Entrepreneur

Robert L. Johnson (b. 1946)

In 1979, while working as chief lobbyist for the National Cable Television Association, Robert Johnson was asked by a businessman to support a proposed cable channel for older Americans. Existing channels targeted young white viewers, leaving older Americans underserved. Johnson immediately realized that this statement applied to African Americans as well. In that moment, the idea for Black Entertainment Television—BET—was born.

Launching BET

Searching for investors, Johnson approached Tele-Communications Incorporated (TCI), a large cable operator that was hoping to expand. He pointed out that a cable company supplying quality programming with appeal to the African American community would have an advantage over its competitors in cities with large black populations. TCI bought a 20 percent stake in his venture.

In January 1980, Johnson launched BET—the first black-owned and -operated television network. Its first broadcasts were limited to two hours each Friday night on another cable network's channel. However, he soon added a gospel show, coverage of college sports, and a music program featuring black recording artists. By 1982, using music videos that record companies provided for free, BET had increased its airtime to six hours a day.

In 1984, Johnson sold another share in BET to Home Box Office (HBO), a division of Time Warner. This provided the money he needed to expand his programming. Johnson now had access to the country's two largest cable providers, Time Warner and TCI, as well as to HBO's satellite, so he could broadcast 24 hours a day. By 1989, BET was reaching 23 million homes. Fifteen years later, that figure had grown to nearly 75 million households, including more than 90 percent of African American households with cable.

Creating a Brand

"When I see BET, I don't see a cable network," Johnson says. "I see a black media conglomerate." In the 1990s, Johnson used the network's commercial airtime and its strong reputation among African Americans to create a BET "umbrella brand."

Besides adding four more cable channels, Johnson launched BET Arabesque Films to produce movies for theaters and for his cable network. Arabesque Books, a line of African American romance novels that Johnson purchased in 1998, provided the material for the first movies. "I want to grow my brand to be like Disney," Johnson said of his goals.

Viacom bought BET for $2.3 billion in 2000, making Johnson a billionaire. In 2002, Johnson broke new ground by launching the first majority African-American-owned team in major pro sports—the NBA's Charlotte Bobcats.

CHECK FOR UNDERSTANDING

1. **Source Reading** Describe how Johnson's BET affected the supply of television entertainment available to cable viewers.
2. **Critical Thinking** Using clues in the text above, explain the meaning of the term *umbrella brand.*
3. **Learn More** Use the Internet and other sources to research and report on the variety of products and services that BET currently has or is planning for the future.

Beyond the Classroom: Career Connections

Venture Capitalist Entrepreneurs like Robert Johnson don't lack ideas. However, they often lack the funds to turn those ideas into reality. That's where venture capitalists enter the picture. Venture capitalists seek out entrepreneurs whose business plans are solid and have profit potential. Then the venture capitalists put up money to finance the venture in return for a share of future profits. If the business succeeds, the venture capitalists have a new source of revenue that can continue for many years. Have students research venture capitalist firms, finding out how they operate and what talents a venture capitalist needs to succeed.

ECONOMIC *Profile*
Robert Johnson

Background

At the time Robert Johnson sold BET to Viacom, no African-American had ever owned a controlling interest in a team in the professional baseball, football, hockey, or basketball leagues. Johnson's opportunity came when the struggling Charlotte Hornets basketball team moved to New Orleans in 2003. Local business leaders convinced the NBA's Board of Governors that their town deserved a new basketball franchise to replace the Hornets. In the past, the Hornets had led all other NBA teams in attendance. It was believed that a new team based in a new stadium could revive the popularity of professional basketball in Charlotte.

The NBA's Board of Governors chose Johnson over retired Celtics player Larry Bird to lead the new Charlotte Bobcats in July 2003. Johnson had demonstrated his commitment to Charlotte basketball through two unsuccessful attempts to buy the Hornets in the past. His dedication to the game and his wealth helped him to prevail. Johnson's friend Michael Jordan said, "I think Bob's going to do well. He has the first things that you need in owning a basketball team... which is loving the game.... He's going to do a great job."

Careers in Economics Activity Unit 2 folder, p. 22 gives students a closer look at the career path of a store manager.

Answers to . . .

1. Johnson increased the supply of television programming.
2. Students should deduce that an umbrella brand is a single brand name, such as BET or Disney, that labels a wide variety of products.
3. Students should list products and services that BET offers or has plans to develop; answers should be based on current information available on the Internet.

Section 3

Changes in Supply

Objectives You may wish to call students' attention to the objectives in the Section Preview. The objectives are reflected in the main headings of the section.

Bellringer Ask students to speculate on how an artist might react if the cost of oil paints were to skyrocket. Lead students to understand that the artist would probably have to reduce his or her output of paintings. Explain that in this section they will learn how output at all prices can, like demand, shift because of a variety of factors.

Vocabulary Builder Have students read the section to learn the meaning of each key term. Then ask them to find a photo that illustrates each term or to draw an illustration of their own. Have students write the term and definition on the back of each illustration.

Lesson Plan

Teaching the Main Concepts L3

1. Focus As with demand, the entire supply curve can shift to the right or left because of factors other than price. Ask students to speculate on what these factors might be.
2. Instruct Begin by explaining how rising or falling costs of production can cause supply to increase or decrease. Then discuss how the government can affect supply through subsidies, taxes, and regulation. Finally, explain how expectations of future prices and the number of firms in the market can also affect supply.
3. Close/Reteach Remind students that a variety of factors can cause supply to increase or decrease at all price levels. Ask students to suggest factors that might cause either an increase or a decrease in the supply of sugar.

Guided Reading and Review
Unit 2 folder, p. 17 asks students to identify the main ideas of the section and to define or identify key terms.

Section 3 Changes in Supply

Preview

Objectives

After studying this section you will be able to:

1. **Identify** how determinants such as input costs create changes in supply.
2. **Identify** three ways that the government can influence the supply of a good.
3. **Understand** supply and demand in the global economy.
4. **Analyze** the effects of other factors that affect supply.

Section Focus

Changes in the costs of inputs can raise or lower the supply of a good at all prices. The number of firms in a market and the price and supply of other goods can also have an effect on the supply of a good.

Key Terms

subsidy
excise tax
regulation

Just as several factors can affect demand at all price levels, a separate set of factors can affect supply. In this section, you will read about these factors that can affect supply, and the factors that shift an entire supply curve to the left or right.

▲ **New technology has lowered the costs of production in many markets.**

Input Costs

Any change in the cost of an input used to produce a good—such as raw materials, machinery, or labor—will affect supply. A rise in the cost of an input will cause a fall in supply at all price levels because the good has become more expensive to produce. On the other hand, a fall in the cost of an input will cause an increase in supply at all price levels.

Effect of Rising Costs

Think of the effects of input costs on the relationship between marginal revenue (price) and marginal cost. A supplier sets output at the most profitable level, where price is equal to marginal cost. Marginal cost includes the cost of the inputs that go into production, so a rise in the cost of labor or raw materials will translate directly into a higher marginal cost. If the cost of inputs increases enough, the marginal cost may become higher than the price, and the firm may not be as profitable as it could be.

If a firm has no control over the price, the only solution is to cut production and lower marginal cost until marginal cost equals the lower price. Supply falls at each price, and the supply curve shifts to the left, as illustrated in Figure 5.12.

Graphing the Main Idea

Supply and Demand To enhance students' understanding of the concept of **supply and demand,** have them complete a web graphic organizer like the one below to show the factors that can cause changes in supply. Remind students that a web shows a main idea with its supporting details.

Section Reading Support Transparencies A template and the answers for this graphic organizer can be found in Chapter 5, Section 3 of the Section Reading Support Transparency System.

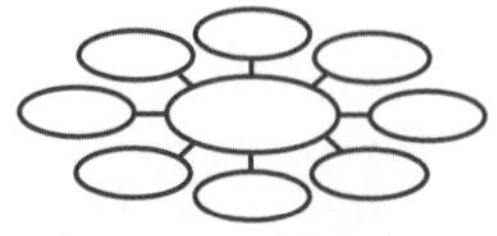

Figure 5.12 **Shifts in the Supply Curve**

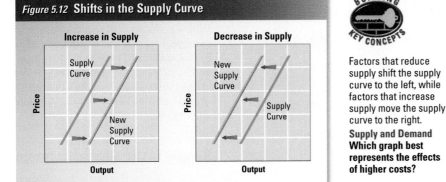

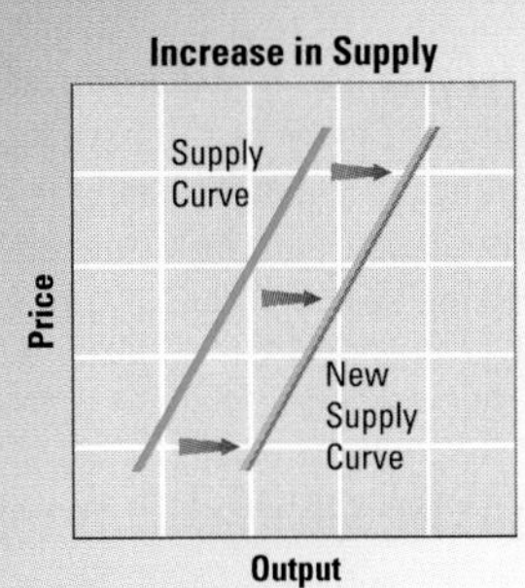

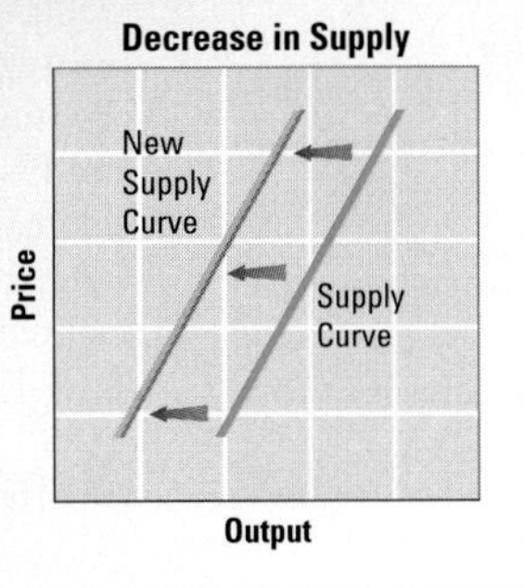

Factors that reduce supply shift the supply curve to the left, while factors that increase supply move the supply curve to the right.

Supply and Demand Which graph best represents the effects of higher costs?

Technology

Input costs can drop as well. Advances in technology, for example, can lower production costs in many industries. Sophisticated robots have replaced many workers on assembly lines and allowed manufacturers to spend less on salaries. Computers have simplified tasks and cut costs in fields as diverse as journalism and architecture. E-mail that can be sent and received in an instant can replace slowly delivered letters and expensive long-distance phone calls.

Technology lowers costs and increases supply at all price levels. This effect is seen in a rightward shift in the supply curve in Figure 5.12.

Government's Influence on Supply

The government has the power to affect the supplies of many goods. By raising or lowering the cost of producing goods, the government can encourage or discourage an entrepreneur or an industry within the country or abroad.

Subsidies

One method used by governments to affect supply is to give subsidies to the producers of a good, particularly food. A **subsidy** is a government payment that supports a business or market. The government often pays a producer a set subsidy for each unit of a good produced.

Governments have several reasons for subsidizing producers. European countries faced food shortages during and after World War II. Although imported food is cheaper, European governments protect farms so that some will be available to grow food in case imports are ever cut off. The government of France also subsidizes small farms because French citizens want to protect the lifestyle and character of the French countryside.

Governments in developing countries often subsidize manufacturers to protect young, growing industries from strong foreign competition. In the past, countries such as Indonesia and Malaysia have subsidized a national car company as a source of pride, even though imported cars were less expensive to build. In Western Europe, banks and national airlines were allowed to suffer huge losses with the assurance that the government would cover their debts. In many countries, governments have stopped providing industrial subsidies in the interest of free trade and fair competition.

In the United States, the federal government subsidizes producers in many industries. Farm subsidies are particularly controversial, however, especially when farmers are paid to take land out of cultivation to keep prices high. In these cases, more efficient farmers are penalized, and farmers use more herbicides and pesticides

subsidy *a government payment that supports a business or market*

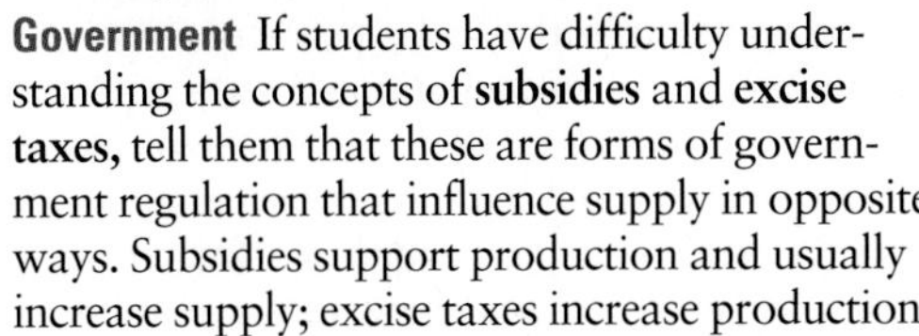

Econ 101: Key Concepts Made Easy

Government If students have difficulty understanding the concepts of **subsidies** and **excise taxes,** tell them that these are forms of government regulation that influence supply in opposite ways. Subsidies support production and usually increase supply; excise taxes increase production costs and therefore decrease the supply of a good. Ask students what other methods they think governments might use to affect supply of a good or service.

Differentiated Instruction 

Time: 90 minutes

Activity: Present a scenario in which the supply of tomatoes is affected by various input costs, such as higher wages for farm workers, or higher or lower fertilizer costs.

Grouping: Groups of four to six students.

Purpose: Have students study the section on input costs in the textbook. Then have them work together to create and present a scenario that displays how changes in input costs could affect the supply of tomatoes.

Roles: Farmworker, grocery clerk, fertilizer salesperson, production technology sales representative, tomato grower.

Outcome: Students will understand how one factor or a combination of factors can affect the supply of a product.

Meeting NCEE Standards

Use the following benchmark activity from the **Voluntary National Content Standards in Economics** to evaluate student understanding of **Standard 8.**

Predict the changes in supply and market price for domestic cars when the cost of labor increases, more robotics are used to produce cars, the prices of domestic utility vehicles rise, or the number of imported cars increases.

Differentiated Instruction 

Have students create a cause-and-effect chart for each of the major concepts in this section: the effects on supply of changes in input costs, government intervention, and so on. Point out that their charts can be a useful study aid. LPR

Answer to . . .

Building Key Concepts the graph in which the curve shifts to the left (Decrease in Supply)

Background

Excise Taxes

Excise taxes have a long history and existed as far back as ancient Rome. An excise tax is actually a type of sales tax that is levied on the manufacture, purchase, sale, or consumption of a specific product. Excise taxes have often been the subject of controversy. Supporters of excise taxes point out that they can be used to place the burden of taxation on luxuries or nonessential goods. Also, some supporters point out that the taxes can be set up so that the burden of the tax falls on the people who will benefit from it—for example, when taxes on gasoline are used to build and maintain roads. Others argue against excise taxes, saying that their reduction of supply is unfair. Also, because excise taxes are often the same for expensive and cheaper brands of the same good, people with lower incomes are more strongly affected by such taxes because a larger percentage of their income goes toward paying the tax.

Differentiated Instruction 

(Reteaching) Ask students to write short essays in which they imagine a fictitious company that produces a popular product. Ask students to describe three examples of government intervention that might influence the supply of their product. Essays should describe the methods of government intervention used and the effects of each method.

Differentiated Instruction 

Ask students to explain, in a captioned cause-and-effect diagram, how a company's supply can be affected each time interest rates increase or decrease. GT

Global Connections

Common Agricultural Policy The European Union, a group of fifteen countries in Europe, protects its farms through its Common Agricultural Policy (CAP). Under CAP, the European Union **subsidizes** farms to keep them running and to encourage farmers to produce more food. Although this may have made sense in difficult times after World War II, farms have since modernized, and subsidies have led to a tremendous amount of unneeded food. In 1994, the CAP cost Europe $40 billion while producing a "wine lake" and "butter mountain" that no one would buy. Since then, Europe has tried to cut subsidies and introduce voluntary limits on production.

excise tax *a tax on the production or sale of a good*

regulation *government intervention in a market that affects the production of a good*

on lands they do cultivate to compensate for production lost on the acres the government pays them not to plant.

Taxes

A government can reduce the supply of some goods by placing an **excise tax** on them. An excise tax is a tax on the production or sale of a good. An excise tax increases production costs by adding an extra cost for each unit sold.

Excise taxes are sometimes used to discourage the sale of goods that the government thinks are harmful to the public good, like cigarettes, alcohol, and high-pollutant gasoline. Excise taxes are built into the prices of these and other goods, so consumers may not realize that they are paying them. Like any increase in cost, an excise tax causes the supply of a good to decrease at all price levels. The supply curve shifts to the left.

Regulation

Subsidies and excise taxes represent ways that government directly affects supply by changing revenue or production costs. Government can also raise or lower supply through indirect means. Government regulation often has the effect of raising costs. **Regulation** is government intervention in a market that affects the price, quantity, or quality of a good.

For many years, pollution from automobiles harmed the environment. Starting in 1970, the federal government required car manufacturers to install technology to reduce pollution from auto exhaust. For example, new cars had to use lead-free fuel because scientists linked health problems to lead in gasoline. Regulations such as these increased the cost of manufacturing cars and reduced the supply. The supply curve shifted to the left.

Supply in the Global Economy

As you read in earlier chapters, a large and rising share of goods and services is produced in one country and imported by another to be sold to consumers. The supplies of imported goods are affected by changes in other countries. Here are some examples of possible changes in the supply of products imported by the U.S.

- The U.S. imports carpets from India. An increase in the wages of Indian workers would decrease the supply of carpets to the U.S. market, shifting the supply curve to the left.
- The U.S. imports telephones from Japan. A new technology that decreases the cost of producing telephones would increase the supply of telephones to the U.S. market, shifting the supply curve to the right.
- The U.S. imports oil from Russia. A new oil discovery in Russia would increase the supply of oil to the U.S. market and shift the supply curve to the right.

Import restrictions also affect the supply curves of restricted goods. The total supply of a product equals the sum of imports and domestically produced products. An import ban on sugar would eliminate foreign sugar suppliers from the market, shifting the market supply curve to the left. At any price, a smaller quantity of sugar would be supplied. If the government restricted imports by establishing an import quota, the supply curve would shift to the left, but the shift would be smaller than it would be for an absolute ban on sugar imports.

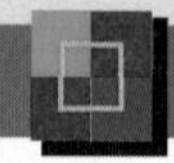

Block Scheduling Strategies

Consider these suggestions to take advantage of extended class time:

- Have pairs of students work through the case study on Steven Spielberg and complete the Free Enterprise Activity in the Case Studies in Free Enterprise folder, pp. 10–11. Ask students to prepare a report on a popular movie released in the last year, analyzing the extent of its effects on the U.S. economy.
- Explain to students that government regulation initiated by the Occupational Health and Safety Administration (OSHA) is a form of government intervention that some business owners believe adds to their costs and thus affects their output. Facilitate a class debate on the question: "Should businesses be allowed to set their own safety standards?"

Other Influences on Supply

While government can have an important influence on the supply of goods, there are also other important factors that influence supply.

Future Expectations of Prices

If you were a soybean farmer, and you expected the price of soybeans to double next month, what would you do with the crop that you just harvested? Would you sell it right now, or hold on to it until soybean prices rise? Most farmers would store their soybeans until the price rose, cutting back supply in the short term.

If a seller expects the price of a good to rise in the future, the seller will store the goods now in order to sell more in the future. On the other hand, if the price of the good is expected to drop in the near future, sellers will earn more money by placing goods on the market immediately before the price falls. Expectations of higher prices will reduce supply now and increase supply later, and expectations of lower prices will have the opposite effect.

Inflation is a condition of rising prices. During periods of inflation, the value of cash in a person's pocket decreases from day to day as prices rise. Not too long ago, one dollar could buy a movie ticket or a small meal, but inflation over many years has reduced the value of the dollar. However, a good will continue to hold its value, provided that it can be stored for a long period of time. When faced with inflation, suppliers prefer to hold on to goods that will maintain their value rather than sell them for cash that loses its value rapidly. As a result, inflation can affect supply by encouraging suppliers to hold on to goods as long as possible. In the short term, supply can fall dramatically.

During the Civil War, the South faced terrible inflation. The prices of most goods rose very quickly. There were shortages of food, and shopkeepers knew that prices on basic food items like flour, butter, and salt would rise each month. A few decided to hoard their food and wait for higher prices. They succeeded too well; the supply of food fell so much that prices rose out of the reach of many families. Riots broke out in Virginia and elsewhere when hungry people decided they weren't going to wait for the food to be released from the warehouses, and the shopkeepers lost their goods and their profits.

▲ As prices for fossil fuels have risen, electric companies have looked to alternative sources of supply, such as wind.

Number of Suppliers

One additional factor to consider when looking at changes in supply is the number of suppliers in the market. If more suppliers enter a market to produce a certain good, the market supply of the good will rise, and the supply curve will shift to the right. On the other hand, if suppliers stop producing the good and leave the market, the supply will decline. There is a positive relationship between the number of suppliers in a market and the market supply of the good.

Where Do Firms Produce?

So far we have ignored the issue of where firms locate their production facilities. For many firms, the key factor is the cost of transportation—the cost of transporting

Transparency Resource Package
Economics Concepts, 5G: Changes in Supply

Differentiated Instruction L3

Ask students to predict how the following conditions will affect the supply of private luxury airplanes. Have them show their predictions in the form of a simple graphic organizer.

- The cost of premium leather rises sharply.
- The government subsidizes the manufacture of small jet engines.
- Congress passes a law that greatly increases the number of safety devices required on private aircraft.
- The number of private airplane manufacturers in the United States doubles.
- Computer simulation programs enable manufacturers to design and test aircraft before parts are built.
- The U.S. government imposes an import ban on private luxury airplanes.

Differentiated Instruction L2

Form groups of three or four. Each English language learner in the class should be in a different group. Ask the groups to study the illustrations in this section and to write new, longer captions for each illustration that explain the main ideas of the section. ELL

Learning Styles Activity
Learning Styles Lesson Plans folder, p. 16 asks student groups to write letters to the editor supporting or opposing government subsidies, excise taxes, or regulations.

Economic Detective Activity
Unit 2 folder, p. 21, "Elmo Entrepreneur," provides an integrated application of chapter concepts.

Preparing for Standardized Tests

Have students read the section titled "Future Expectations of Prices" and then answer the question below.

How would the supply of apples probably be affected if the price of apples was expected to drop in the near future?

A The supply would not be affected.
B The supply would decrease just before the price drop as suppliers held on to goods.
C The supply would increase only if inflation was occurring.
(D) The supply would increase just before the price drop as suppliers placed goods on the market.

GTE **Guide to the Essentials**
Chapter 5, Section 3, p. 22 provides support for students who need additional review of the section content. Spanish support is available in the Spanish edition of the guide on p. 22.

Quiz Unit 2 folder, p. 18 includes questions to check students' understanding of Section 3 content.

Presentation Pro CD-ROM
Quiz provides multiple-choice questions to check students' understanding of Section 3 content.

Answers to . . .

Section 3 Assessment

1. A subsidy lowers marginal cost and thus increases supply.
2. Governments may use excise taxes to discourage sales of products that are thought to be harmful to the public.
3. Government regulation may make a good more costly to produce, thereby decreasing supply.
4. The government could provide a subsidy to mining companies to encourage an increase in production.
5. (a) decrease (b) decrease (c) increase
6. Lowering marginal revenue decreases the incentive to produce. This is also the effect of raising the marginal cost. Both result in less profit for the producer.

▲ **High levels of inflation, like the 70 percent annual price increases affecting Turkey, can cause suppliers to hoard their goods to sell later at a higher price.**

inputs to a production facility and the cost of transporting the finished product to consumers. A firm will locate close to input suppliers when inputs, such as raw materials, are expensive to transport. A firm will locate close to its consumers when output is more costly to transport.

For an example of a firm that locates close to its input suppliers, consider a firm that cooks tomatoes into tomato sauce. Suppose that a firm uses seven tons of tomatoes to produce one ton of sauce. The firm locates its plant close to the tomato fields—and far from its consumers—because it is much cheaper to ship one ton of sauce to consumers than to ship seven tons of tomatoes to the plant. Tomato sauce producers cluster in places like California's Central Valley where weather and soil conditions are favorable for the growing of tomatoes.

For an example of a firm that locates close to its consumers, consider a firm that bottles soft drinks. The firm combines concentrated syrup with local water, so the firm's output (canned drinks) weighs more than its transportable input (syrup). As a result, the firm locates close to its consumers—and far from its syrup supplier—because the firm saves more on transporting soft drinks than it pays to transport its syrup. In general, if a firm's output is bulky or perishable, the firm will locate close to its consumers.

Other firms locate close to inputs that cannot be transported at all. Some firms are pulled toward concentrations of specialized workers such as artists, engineers, and programmers. Other firms are pulled toward locations with low energy costs. Many firms locate in cities because of the rich variety of workers and business services available in urban areas.

Section 3 Assessment

Progress Monitoring *Online*
For: Self-quiz with vocabulary practice
Web Code: mna-2057

Key Terms and Main Ideas

1. How does a **subsidy** affect supply?
2. Why does the government impose **excise taxes?**
3. How can **regulation** affect a producer's output decisions?

Applying Economic Concepts

4. ***Using the Databank*** Turn to the graph on page 534 that lists the production of the American agriculture, timber, and mining industries. If the government wanted the mining industry to produce $120 billion next year, what step could it take?
5. ***Decision Making*** Decide whether each of these events would cause an increase or decrease in the supply of American-made backpacks. **(a)** The government raises the minimum wage of backpack workers to $40 an hour. **(b)** A new regulation requires firms to make backpacks out of expensive clear plastic. **(c)** An engineer invents a machine that can sew ten backpacks a minute, speeding up production.
6. ***Critical Thinking*** Explain why a change that lowers the marginal revenue (price) changes the quantity produced in the same direction as a change that raises the marginal cost of production.

For: Art History Activity
Visit: PHSchool.com
Web Code: mnd-2053

Progress Monitoring *Online*
For additional assessment, have students access Progress Monitoring Online at **Web Code:** mna-2057

Go Online PHSchool.com Typing in the Web Code when prompted will bring students directly to detailed instructions for this activity.

Supply and Demand

Are Baseball Players Paid Too Much?

Major league baseball provides us with a prime example of the ways in which supply and demand affect wages. Millions of people are willing to buy tickets to watch major leaguers in person. Even more watch the games on television. Most team owners make enormous amounts of money from the sale of tickets and television rights, as well as licensing fees.

Supply and Demand The salaries of top baseball players are determined by supply and demand. The public creates a high demand for watching professional sports, but the supply of truly talented athletes is relatively small. This drives their salaries up. On the other hand, most people could be trained to work as store clerks or fast-food restaurant employees, so wages for those positions tend to be low.

▲ Baseball commissioner Bud Selig has presided over a 232-day players' strike that resulted in the cancellation of the World Series for the first time since 1904.

Free Agency Up until the 1970s, players received relatively low salaries. This was because most were required to play only for the team that first signed them to a contract, or to the team that they had been traded to. In the mid-1970s, players went to court seeking the right to become "free agents." Free agency would allow them, after playing for a team for a certain number of years, to sell their services to any other team willing to pay them the salaries they asked for. Although team owners strongly opposed free agency, the players won their case.

A Price to Pay This victory has led to bidding wars which have resulted in the astronomical salaries that top stars now receive. Yet, while these players have benefited greatly from free agency, both fans and major league baseball itself have had to pay a price. The intense loyalty that fans once demonstrated toward their favorite teams has diminished as players switch from one team to another in search of higher salaries. Owners have sharply increased ticket prices to afford the huge increases in players' salaries.

Now, only teams that operate in the largest television markets or have the wealthiest owners can afford to pay the best players. Some fans believe that only the richest teams can make it to the World Series, while the less-wealthy teams are left behind. The result of this development has been a growing cynicism on the part of many fans who feel—rightly or wrongly—that baseball championships are now purchased rather than won.

Applying Economic Ideas

1. What arguments might players make for free agency?
2. How do the laws of supply and demand affect baseball players' salaries?

Real-life Case Study: Supply and Demand

1. Focus Free agency has significantly increased the earning potential of major league baseball players; at the same time, however, such high salaries have led to increases in ticket prices and the perception that the best teams will always be those with the most money.

2. Instruct Ask students whether they believe that current salaries for athletes are justified on the basis of supply and demand, and why. Then ask students to argue whether salaries should be based instead on the importance of the job to society.

3. Close/Reteach Ask students to think of other examples of jobs for which salaries are driven up on the basis of supply and demand.

Case Studies Activity
Case Studies in Free Enterprise folder, p. 10–11, "Steven Spielberg," helps students apply economic principles in an additional case study.

Economic Detective Activity
Unit 2 folder, p. 21, "Elmo Entrepreneur," provides an additional application of chapter concepts.

Interdisciplinary Connections: Music

Supply and Demand The interaction of supply and demand transcends prices and salaries. These economic forces can exert their influence in many aspects of daily life that may not appear to have anything to do with economics.

Making the Connection Present students with the following scenario. Three students have applied for scholarships to a prestigious music school. One is a top-notch guitarist. Another is a first-rate viola player. The third is a master of the flugelhorn. Two of the students receive partial scholarships. One receives a full scholarship. Who probably received which music scholarship, and why? *(Students should provide answers that demonstrate an understanding of factors that affect supply and demand.)*

Answers to . . .

1. Players might have pointed out that the free enterprise system allows for free agency or that they deserve a chance to earn high salaries because of the time and energy they devote to playing baseball.
2. Since there are few top baseball players (small supply), the demand for them is high and therefore drives up their salaries (price).

Chapter 5 Assessment

Key Terms
1. fixed cost
2. marginal revenue
3. excise tax
4. elasticity of supply
5. subsidy
6. law of supply
7. marginal cost

Using Graphic Organizers
8. Examples of fixed costs include rent, machinery upkeep, and property taxes. Examples of variable costs include the costs of raw materials and some labor.

Reviewing Main Ideas
9. The marginal product of labor increases up to a certain point; once a certain point is reached, however, total output still increases, but at a decreasing rate.
10. Fixed costs and variable costs combine to create total cost. Fixed costs, or overhead, are costs that are the same no matter how much is produced. Variable costs rise or fall depending on the quantity produced.
11. Factors that may change supply include changes in input costs; future expectations; technological changes; and government subsidies, taxes, and regulations.
12. Diminishing marginal returns occur when output declines with each additional unit of labor. They generally result when the supply of capital does not increase with the work force, such as when there are not enough sewing machines or scissors for the added workers to use.
13. Global economic events such as increases in wages, technological innovation, or trade restrictions will affect the supply of goods to the United States.

Chapter 5 Assessment

Chapter Summary

A summary of major ideas in Chapter 5 appears below. See also the **Guide to the Essentials of Economics**, which provides additional review and test practice of key concepts in Chapter 5.

Section 1 Understanding Supply (pp. 101–106)

The **law of supply** states that when the price of a good rises, the **quantity supplied** of that good also rises because existing firms produce more and new firms join the market. Economists list the quantity supplied of a good at each price in a **supply schedule** and graph this data on a **supply curve** that rises from left to right. Supply can be elastic or inelastic depending upon how easily a producer can change the level of output.

Section 2 Costs of Production (pp. 108–114)

As an entrepreneur invests more in labor while keeping capital constant, the **marginal product of labor** first increases, then falls. A firm adds its **fixed costs** and **variable costs** to determine its **total cost** at each level of output. The most profitable level of output is where the **marginal cost** of producing the last unit is the same as the **marginal revenue** the firm receives when that unit is sold.

Section 3 Changes in Supply (pp. 116–120)

Several factors can raise or lower the supply of a good at all prices. When inputs such as capital and labor become more expensive, supply falls and the supply curve shifts to the left. New technology can lower the cost of production and increase supply, shifting the supply curve to the right. Government encourages suppliers with **subsidies** and reduces supply with **excise taxes.** Other factors that affect supply are the number of suppliers in the market and competition from suppliers in other countries.

Key Terms

Match the following definitions with the terms listed below. You will not use all of the terms.

marginal costs	**supply schedule**
marginal revenue	**regulation**
elasticity of supply	**excise tax**
law of supply	**variable costs**
subsidy	**fixed cost**

1. An expense that costs the same whether or not a firm is producing a good or service
2. The income that the supplier receives from selling one more unit
3. A tax on the sale or manufacture of a good
4. A measure of how suppliers will respond to a change in price
5. A government payment to support a business or market
6. The tendency of suppliers to offer more of a good at a higher price
7. The additional cost of producing one more unit of output

Using Graphic Organizers

8. On a separate sheet of paper, copy the multiflow map below. Organize information on how firms determine their total costs by completing the multiflow map with examples of fixed and variable costs.

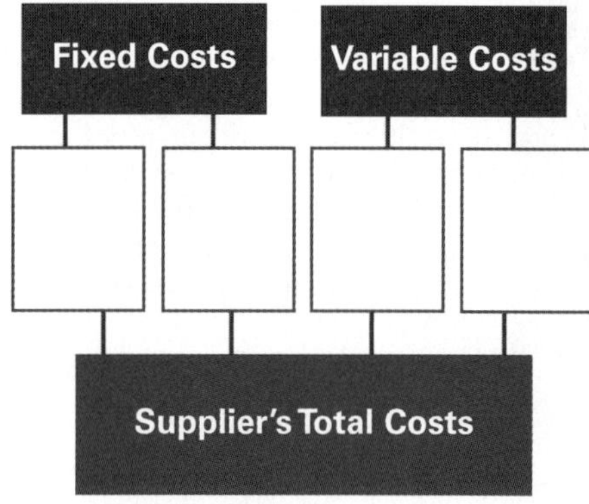

Critical Thinking
14. The supply curve will move to the left.
15. Students should point out that she should not shut down the store. The total revenue ($7,000) is greater than the cost of keeping the shop open ($6,000).
16. A sample scenario for increasing marginal returns might involve a toy factory that makes molded plastic toys that also require assembly. The factory owns one plastic-molding machine. As more workers are hired, workers specialize, and output per worker increases. Diminishing marginal returns will occur as even more workers are hired, but there is still only one molding machine. Time will be wasted as workers wait for parts to be made and output per worker decreases.

Reviewing Main Ideas

9. How does the marginal product of labor change as more people are hired?
10. What categories of costs combine to create a firm's total cost?
11. Name and describe three factors that can cause a change in supply.
12. What circumstances cause a firm to experience diminishing marginal returns?
13. How can the global economy affect the supply of a good in the United States?

Critical Thinking

14. **Recognizing Cause and Effect** Assume that a $1 per pound tax has been placed on fish. What effect will this have on the supply curve for fish?
15. **Analyzing Information** A local coffee shop has the following expenses: $5,000 a month for rent; $3,000 a month for a full-time manager; $4,000 a month for part-time workers; and $2,000 a month for coffee beans, milk, and cups. In July, the owner can expect to earn $7,000 in revenue. If she chooses to close down the store, she will not have to pay for part-time workers or supplies. Explain whether she should close the shop for the month of July, and why or why not.
16. **Making Comparisons** Compare the two terms *increasing marginal returns* and *diminishing marginal returns*. Describe two scenarios, one to explain and demonstrate each term.

Problem-Solving Activity

17. Suppose that you plan to open a T-shirt factory. Create a list of fixed costs and variable costs that you would encounter. How would each of these costs affect the number of T-shirts you make?

Economics Journal

Recognizing Cause and Effect For each item on your list, explain if you think supply is elastic or inelastic, and why. Brainstorm five specific events that could increase the supply of each item.

Skills for Life

Environmental Policy Review the steps shown on page 107, and then complete the following activity based on your own experiences.

18. (a) What natural landscapes are identified in the report? (b) Identify three locations in the report that are defined by human settlement.
19. What are the human needs for the land described in this report?
20. What environmental considerations are balanced against these human needs?
21. (a) How does the report propose to meet both the environmental and human needs of the region? (b) List two possible benefits and two possible negative results from this solution.

> The announcement that the Navy would close the Naval Weapons Station in Concord, California, brings new opportunities to this city of about 120,000. The base includes 5,170 acres inland next to the city and 7,630 acres of islands, tidal lands, and port facilities on the water. The San Francisco metropolitan area faces an affordable housing crisis that can be helped by building new homes on the former base.
>
> The tidal portion of the base is home to many species of birds, fish, and shellfish. Industrial development in the port threatened their habitat in the past. We expect wildlife to flourish on the islands if they become free of human interference.
>
> The inland portion of the base provides a less fragile environment that is better suited to development. The city proposes to build multi-family housing and schools on sections of this parcel of land. By setting aside 30% of the land for parks and open spaces, we believe that the city can meet both the environmental demands of the inland ecosystem with the housing needs of the San Francisco area.

Progress Monitoring *Online*

For: Chapter 5 Self-Test **Visit:** PHSchool.com
Web Code: mna-2051

As a final review, take the Economics Chapter 5 Self-Test and receive immediate feedback on your answers. The test consists of 20 multiple-choice questions designed to test your understanding of the chapter content.

Problem-Solving Activity

17. Student responses may include such fixed costs as rent and administrative salaries and such variable costs as electricity, gas, fabric, and production labor. The fixed costs remain the same as long as the factory is open and must be covered in any case. Producing more shirts makes all the variable costs rise, and the decision about how many shirts to produce would be based on estimates of marginal revenue and marginal cost.

Skills for Life

18. (a) inland acreage, islands, and tidal lands (b) the naval base, San Francisco, and Concord
19. new housing for 33,000 Concord residents
20. Birds, fish, and shellfish living near the tidal portion of the base; the inland ecosystem
21. (a) The city proposes to build only on the inland area and to set aside 30% of the land for parks and open spaces. (b) Benefits include affordable housing and open recreation areas. Possible negative results could be shrinking and disturbing wildlife habitats and straining the ecosystem.

Additional support materials and activities for Chapter 5 of *Economics: Principles in Action* can be found in the Social Studies area of **PHSchool.com**

Economics Journal

Students' responses will vary. Answers should demonstrate an understanding of elastic and inelastic supply and the factors that affect supply.

Review and Assessment

Vocabulary Practice Unit 2 folder, p. 20 uses a crossword puzzle to reinforce understanding of key terms.

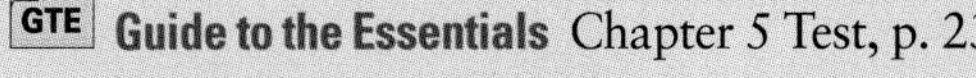

GTE **Guide to the Essentials** Chapter 5 Test, p. 23

Test Bank CD-ROM Chapter 5 Test

Go Online PHSchool.com Students may use the Chapter 5 Self-Test on **PHSchool.com** to prepare for the Chapter Test.

Chapter Resource Manager

Chapter 6 Prices

For more pacing suggestions, see the Economics Pacing Guide in the Program Overview of the Teaching Resources.

Section Objectives	Print and Technology Resources
1 Combining Supply and Demand *(pp. 125–131)* **Objectives** 1. Explain how supply and demand create balance in the marketplace. 2. Compare a market in equilibrium with a market in disequilibrium. 3. Identify how the government sometimes intervenes in markets to control prices. 4. Analyze the effects of price ceilings and price floors.	• **Lesson Planner** Section 1 Lesson Plan, p. 31 • **Learning Styles Lesson Plans folder** Section 1 Lesson Plan, p. 17 • **Lesson Plans folder** Section 1 Lesson Plan, p. 24 • **Economics Assessment Rubrics folder** Writing Assignment, pp. 6–7 • **Unit 2 folder** Guided Reading and Review, p. 24 Economic Skills, p. 30 Section 1 Quiz, p. 25 • **Presentation Pro CD-ROM** Section 1 • **Transparency Resource Package** Economics Organizers, G7: Tree Map Graphic Organizer Economics Concepts, 6A: Supply and Demand Economics Concepts, 6B: Equilibrium Economics Concepts, 6C: Excess Demand Economics Concepts, 6D: Excess Supply Economics Concepts, 6E: Rent Control Economics Concepts, 6F: Price Floors Economics Concepts, 6G: Price Floors Overlay • **Section Reading Support Transparency System** • **Social Studies Skills Tutor CD-ROM**
2 Changes in Market Equilibrium *(pp. 133–137)* **Objectives** 1. Identify the determinants that create changes in price. 2. Explain how a market reacts to a fall in supply by moving to a new equilibrium. 3. Explain how a market reacts to shifts in demand by moving to a new equilibrium.	• **Lesson Planner** Section 2 Lesson Plan, p. 32 • **Lesson Plans folder** Section 2 Lesson Plan, p. 25 • **Unit 2 folder** Guided Reading and Review, p. 26 Careers in Economics, Financial Advisor, p. 33 Economic Cartoon, p. 34 Section 2 Quiz, p. 27 • **Source Articles folder** Hot Ticket, Higher Price, pp. 18–20 • **Presentation Pro CD-ROM** Section 2 • **Section Reading Support Transparency System** • **Transparency Resource Package** Economics Organizers, G9: Multi-Flow Chart Graphic Organizer Economics Concepts, 6H: Shifts in Supply Economics Concepts, 6I: Shifts in Supply Overlay Economics Concepts, 6J: Fall in Supply Economics Concepts, 6K: Shifts in Demand Economics Concepts, 6L: Shifts in Demand Overlay Economics Concepts, 6M: Fall in Demand
3 The Role of Prices *(pp. 139–144)* **Objectives** 1. Analyze the role of prices in a free market. 2. List the advantages of a price-based system. 3. Explain how a price-based system leads to a wider choice of goods and efficient allocation of resources. 4. Describe the relationship between prices and the profit incentive.	• **Lesson Planner** Section 3 Lesson Plan, p. 33 • **Learning Styles Lesson Plans folder** Section 3 Lesson Plan, p. 18 • **Lesson Plans folder** Section 3 Lesson Plan, p. 26 • **Economics Assessment Rubrics folder** Writing Assignment, pp. 6–7 • **Unit 2 folder** Guided Reading and Review, p. 28 Vocabulary Practice, p. 31 Economic Detective, p. 32 Section 3 Quiz, p. 29 • **Case Studies in Free Enterprise folder** William Mow, pp. 12–13 • **Math Practice folder** Comparing Prices, p. 5 • **Presentation Pro CD-ROM** Section 3 • **Transparency Resource Package** Economics Organizers, G6: Double Web Graphic Organizer Economics Concepts, 6N: The Advantages of Prices • **Section Reading Support Transparency System**

Differentiated Instruction

Finding High-Interest Ideas L1 L2

Students will be more willing and more interested in engaging in discussion if they are discussing a topic of high interest. As students read the chapter, ask them to write down one idea that could be used to conduct an interesting discussion. Ideas could relate to something they do not understand, something that seems interesting, or something that relates to something else they know, but should provoke interest and more ideas.

Model the process by giving students both rich and poor ideas for a discussion.

Rich idea: How do buyers and sellers achieve equilibrium in the real world?

Poor idea: How does rent control work?

Visit the Social Studies area of the Prentice Hall Web site. There you can find additional links to enrich chapter content for *Economics: Principles in Action* as well as a self-test for students. Be sure to check out this month's **eTeach** online discussion with a Master Economics Teacher.

Web Code: mnf-2061

Running Out of Time?

- Use the **Presentation Pro CD-ROM** to create an outline for this chapter.
- Use the Chapter Summary in the **Chapter 6 Assessment,** p. 146.
- Use the Section Summaries for Chapter 6, from **Guide to the Essentials of Economics (English and Spanish).**

THE WALL STREET JOURNAL. CLASSROOM EDITION

Prentice Hall brings into the classroom the authoritative content of *The Wall Street Journal Classroom Edition.* See the Source Articles, Debating Current Issues, and You and Your Money folders in the **Teaching Resources.** Also, see Economics Video Library, "Money Pit."

Assessment Resources

Chapter Assessment

Teaching Resources Unit 2, Chapter 6

- Section Quizzes, pp. 25, 27, 29

Exam*View*® Test Bank CD-ROM Chapter 6

Economics Assessment Rubrics

Chapter 6 Self-Test, **Web Code:** mna-2061

Reading and Skills Evaluation

Progress Monitoring Assessments

- Screening Test
- Diagnostic Test of Social Studies Skills

Cumulative Testing and Remediation

Progress Monitoring Assessments

- Benchmark Test #1

Standardized Test Preparation

Test Prep Workbook

Test-Taking Strategies With Transparencies

Differentiated Instruction Key

L1 Special Needs	LPR Less Proficient Readers
L2 Basic to Average	AR Advanced Readers
L3 All Students	SN Special Needs Students
L4 Average to Advanced	GT Gifted and Talented
	ELL English Language Learner

Chapter 6

Prices

Introducing the Chapter

In this chapter, students will learn how supply, demand, and prices work together in the marketplace to create a balance. Students will understand that a price-based system is both more flexible and more efficient than a centrally planned system.

For additional links for *Economics: Principles in Action* provided by Prentice Hall and *The Wall Street Journal Classroom Edition,* visit the Social Studies area. Be sure to check out this month's **eTeach** online discussion with a Master Teacher.

Beyond the Lecture

You may cover the concepts in Chapter 6 in an activity-based style by using the following materials:

- **Technology Resources** appropriate for use with this chapter are noted on pp. 126, 127, 128, 130, 131, 134, 135, 136, 137, 142, 144, and 147.
- **Presentation Pro CD-ROM** with animated graphs gives you an alternative method for organizing and delivering chapter content.
- **Activities** designed to meet the needs of students of mixed abilities and learning styles are noted throughout the chapter in the side columns.
- **Learning Styles Lesson Plans** provide alternate lessons for diverse learning styles. See pp. 17–18 of the Learning Styles Lesson Plans folder located in the Teaching Resources.

Economics Journal

Instruct students to write their responses in their Economics Journals. Students may include completed journal entries in an Economics Portfolio.

Chapter 6 Prices

Anyone who has ever haggled over the price of a used car, a stereo, or even an old lamp at a garage sale knows about the opposing interests of buyers and sellers. Buyers always want to pay the lowest possible price, while sellers hope to sell at the highest possible price. With buyers and sellers at odds, how can a market system satisfy both groups?

In a free market system, supply and demand work together. The result is a price that both sides can agree on.

Economics Journal

Write down how much you feel you should be paid for an hour of doing each of the following tasks: washing dishes, sweeping floors, baby-sitting a neighbor's child, and bagging groceries at the supermarket.

Go Online PHSchool.com

For: Current Data
Visit: PHSchool.com
Web Code: mng-2061

National Council on Economic Education

The following Voluntary National Content Standard in Economics is addressed in this chapter:

★ **Standard 8** Students will understand that: Prices send signals and provide incentives to buyers and sellers. When supply or demand changes, market prices adjust, affecting incentives.

For more information about the standards, contact the National Council on Economic Education

1140 Avenue of the Americas
New York, NY 10036
1-800-338-1192

Section 1 Combining Supply and Demand

Preview

Objectives

After studying this section you will be able to:

1. **Explain** how supply and demand create balance in the marketplace.
2. **Compare** a market in equilibrium with a market in disequilibrium.
3. **Identify** how the government sometimes intervenes in markets to control prices.
4. **Analyze** the effects of price ceilings and price floors.

Section Focus

In an uncontrolled market, the price of a good and quantity sold will settle at a point where the quantity supplied equals the quantity demanded. The government can set a maximum or minimum price, but that can lead to an imbalance between supply and demand.

Key Terms

equilibrium
disequilibrium
excess demand
excess supply
price ceiling
price floor
rent control
minimum wage

The market system makes certain that consumers can buy the products they want, that sellers make enough profit to stay in business, and that sellers respond to changing needs and tastes of consumers. Other economic systems have been tried—most notably, central planning—and have been judged by most observers to be less successful than the market system.

In this section we will combine our tools for studying demand and supply to learn how markets operate and how markets can turn competing interests into a positive outcome for both sides. In the process we will discover that free markets usually produce some of their best outcomes when they are left alone, without government intervention.

Balancing the Market

Just as buyers and sellers come together in a market, the study of demand and supply will come together in this section. We begin by looking at the supply and demand schedules. As you will recall, a demand schedule shows how much consumers are willing to buy at various prices. A supply schedule shows how much sellers are willing to sell at various prices. Comparing these schedules should allow us to find common ground for the two sides of the market.

The combined supply and demand schedule in Figure 6.1 combines the market demand and supply schedules for pizza slices that you saw in Chapters 4 and 5. For each price, this schedule lists both the number of slices that consumers are willing to buy and the number of slices that pizzerias are willing to supply.

Defining Equilibrium

The point where demand and supply come together at the same number of slices is called the **equilibrium.** Equilibrium is the point of balance between price and quantity. At equilibrium, the market for a good is stable.

equilibrium *the point at which quantity demanded and quantity supplied are equal*

▼ In the market equilibrium, prices adjust to make the quantity supplied equal to the quantity demanded.

Graphing the Main Idea

Supply and Demand To build understanding of the concept of **supply and demand,** have students use a tree map graphic organizer like the one below. Remind students that a tree map shows an outline for a main topic, main ideas, and supporting details. They should put the title of the section in the top box, the main section headings in the next row of boxes, and main ideas and supporting details in the boxes below that.

Section Reading Support Transparencies A template and the answers for this graphic organizer can be found in Chapter 6, Section 1 of the Section Reading Support Transparency System.

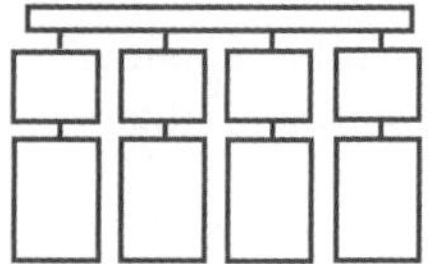

Section 1 Combining Supply and Demand

Objectives You may wish to call students' attention to the objectives in the Section Preview. The objectives are reflected in the main headings of the section.

Bellringer Ask students whether they have ever been on an amusement park ride that affected their sense of balance. Ask them how they felt when they regained their balance. Explain that in this section they will learn that a marketplace that is out of balance naturally wants to return to a balanced state.

Vocabulary Builder Have students pick out the six terms that form pairs in the list of key terms. Then have them illustrate the difference between the terms in each pair with a cartoon or simple drawing.

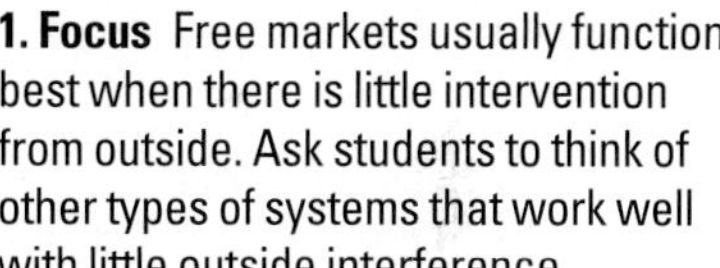

Lesson Plan

Teaching the Main Concepts (L3)

1. Focus Free markets usually function best when there is little intervention from outside. Ask students to think of other types of systems that work well with little outside interference.

2. Instruct Be sure that students understand the concept of *equilibrium.* Work through the text examples to show how the conditions of excess demand and excess supply tend to resolve themselves in the free market. Then explain the effects and varying viewpoints on price ceilings and price floors.

3. Close/Reteach Remind students that the competing interests in the free market tend to keep it in a state of equilibrium. Ask students how this situation differs from a centrally planned system.

Guided Reading and Review
Unit 2 folder, p. 24 asks students to identify the main ideas of the section and to define or identify key terms.

Differentiated Instruction 

Have students study the table and graph on this page. Then ask volunteers to use the table and the graph to demonstrate how supply and demand create balance in the marketplace. They should use data from these visuals along with narrative they create to explain this phenomenon.

Transparency Resource Package
Economics Concepts, 6A: Supply and Demand
Economics Concepts, 6B: Equilibrium

Differentiated Instruction 

Time: 90 minutes

Activity: Create and perform a skit.

Grouping: Groups of four to six students

Purpose: To script and present a skit that compares a market in equilibrium with a market in disequilibrium. Students should work with products different from those used as examples in the text.

Roles: Producers, consumers, narrator

Outcome: Students will understand the difference between market equilibrium and market disequilibrium and will understand the factors that contribute to each. GT

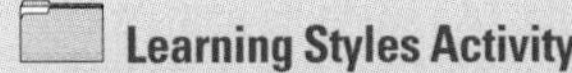

Learning Styles Lesson Plans folder, p. 17 asks students to use a supply and demand schedule to identify market equilibrium and to construct graphs illustrating equilibrium and disequilibrium.

Figure 6.1 Finding Equilibrium

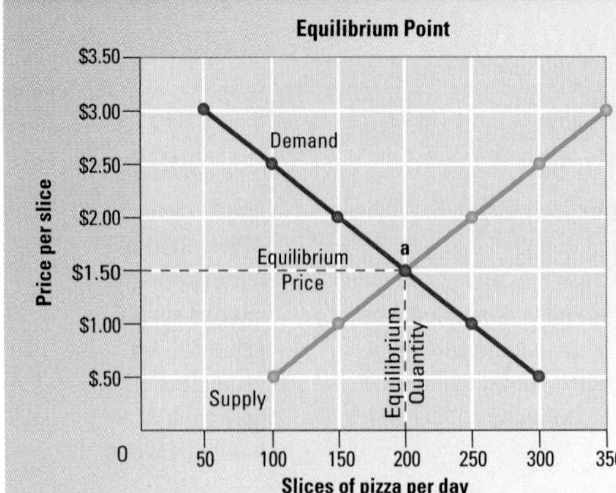

Combined Supply and Demand Schedule

Price of a slice of pizza	Quantity demanded	Quantity supplied	Result
$ .50	300	100	Shortage from excess demand
$1.00	250	150	
$1.50	200	200	Equilibrium
$2.00	150	250	Surplus from excess supply
$2.50	100	300	
$3.00	50	350	

Market equilibrium will be found at the price at which the quantity demanded is equal to the quantity supplied. **Markets and Prices** **How many slices are sold at $2.50 a slice? How many slices are sold at equilibrium?**

To find the equilibrium price and equilibrium quantity, simply look for the price at which the quantity supplied equals the quantity demanded. Do you see that in Figure 6.1 this occurs at a price of $1.50 per slice? At that price, and only at that price, the quantity demanded and the quantity supplied are equal, at 200 slices per day. This is the market equilibrium.

In the market for pizza, as in any market, quantities supplied and demanded will be equal at only one price and one quantity. At this equilibrium price, buyers will purchase exactly as much of the product as firms are willing to sell. Buyers who are willing to purchase the goods at the equilibrium price will find ample supplies on store shelves. Firms that are willing to sell at the equilibrium price will find enough buyers for their goods.

disequilibrium *describes any price or quantity not at equilibrium; when quantity supplied is not equal to quantity demanded in a market*

excess demand *when quantity demanded is more than quantity supplied*

Graphing Equilibrium

We can also illustrate equilibrium with a supply and demand graph. In Figure 6.1, we have plotted on the same graph the market supply curve and the market demand curve for slices of pizza. The equilibrium price and quantity can be found where quantity supplied equals quantity demanded, or the point where the supply curve crosses the demand curve. On the graph, this is point a.

Disequilibrium

If the market price or quantity supplied is anywhere but at the equilibrium, the market is in a state that economists call **disequilibrium.** Disequilibrium occurs when quantity supplied is not equal to quantity demanded in a market. In the above example, disequilibrium will occur with any price other than $1.50 per slice or any quantity other than 200 slices. Disequilibrium can produce one of two outcomes, excess demand or excess supply.

Excess Demand

The problem of **excess demand** occurs when quantity demanded is more than quantity supplied. When the actual price in a market is below the equilibrium price, you have excess demand, because a low price encourages buyers and discourages sellers.

For example, in Figure 6.1, a price of $1.00 per slice of pizza will lead to a quantity demanded of 250 slices per day and a quantity supplied of only 150 slices

Econ 101: Key Concepts Made Easy

Markets and Prices Two of the key concepts in this section are market **equilibrium** and **disequilibrium.** Ask students to think of a seesaw. When one end is up and the other down, the seesaw is in disequilibrium. When people adjust to each other and balance their weights, the seesaw is in equilibrium. Ask students to speculate about why the market tends toward equilibrium. What would occur, for example, if demand increased but prices did not also rise? *(Supply would probably run out because people would buy more of the same group of goods.)* What if supply increased but prices stayed the same? *(There would be a growing surplus because people would not increase consumption.)*

Answer to . . .

Building Key Concepts 100; 200

per day. At this price, there is excess demand of 100 slices per day.

When customers want to buy 100 more slices of pizza than restaurants are prepared to sell, these customers will have to wait in long lines for their pizza, and some will have to do without. In Figure 6.2, below, we have illustrated the excess demand at $1.00 per slice by drawing a dotted line across the graph at that price. As you can see, at $1.00 a slice, the quantity demanded is 250 slices, and the quantity supplied is 150 slices.

If you were running the pizzeria, and you noticed long lines of customers waiting to buy your pizza at $1.00 per slice, what would you do? Assuming that you like to earn profits, you would probably raise the price. As you increased the price of pizza, you would be willing to work harder and bake more, because you would know you could earn more money for each slice you sell.

Of course, as the price rises, customers will buy less pizza, since it is becoming relatively more expensive. When the price reaches $1.50 per slice, you will find that you are earning more profits and can keep up with demand, but the lines are much shorter. Some days you may throw out a few leftover slices, and other days you have to throw an extra pizza or two in the oven to keep up with customers, but on the whole, you are meeting the needs of your customers. In other words, the market is now at equilibrium.

As long as there is excess demand, and the quantity demanded exceeds the quantity supplied, suppliers will keep raising the price. When the price has risen enough to close the gap, suppliers will have found the

FAST FACT

Excess supply was a major problem for the tourism industry in the last months of 1999. Hotels, restaurants, and cruise lines assumed that people would be willing to pay a very high price to celebrate the start of the year 2000, and doubled or tripled their usual rates for special "millennium" travel packages. Unfortunately, many people decided not to travel around January 1, 2000, and many who did travel refused to pay thousands of dollars for dinner or one night in a hotel. High prices and the large number of choices led to a problem of excess supply.

Figure 6.2 Excess Demand and Excess Supply

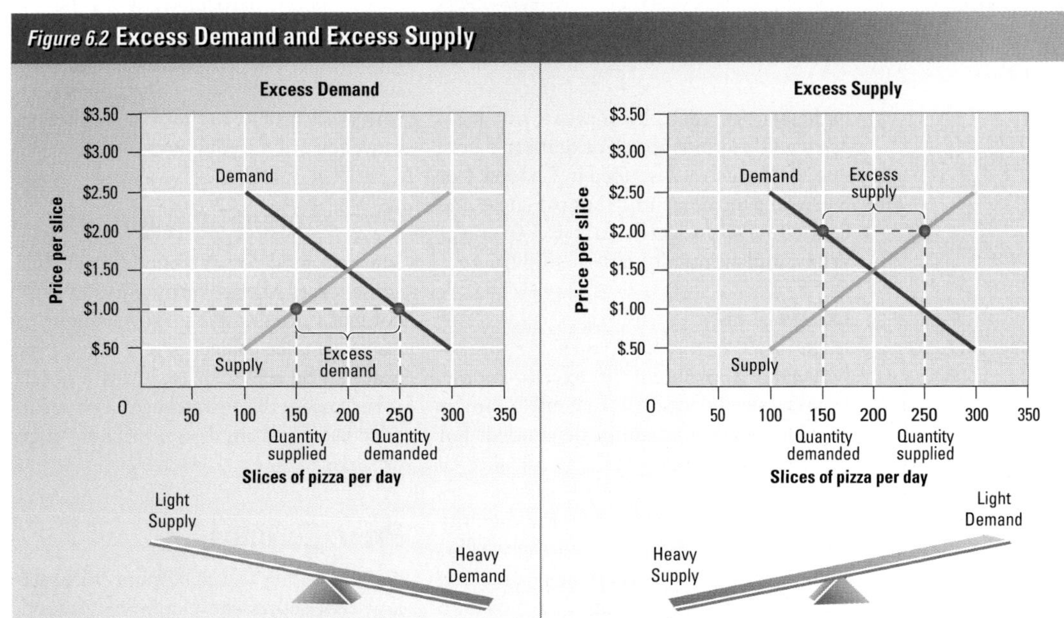

Excess demand and excess supply both lead to a market with fewer sales than at equilibrium.
Supply and Demand **Why are sales lower at $1.00 a slice than at $2.00 a slice?**

Block Scheduling Strategies

Consider these suggestions to take advantage of extended class time:

■ Extend the first activity on this page. Have students use Internet resources to locate articles on global shifts in supply and demand. Then have them summarize these shifts, using the links provided in the *Economics: Principles in Action* segment in the Social Studies area at the following Web site: **www.phschool.com**

■ Show the Economics Video Library segment "Money Pit," about the high value placed on upscale housing, the increase in home renovation, and the increase in the economic resources devoted to renovation. After viewing the segment, ask students to make a list of local businesses and industries that would be affected by increased home renovation. Have them write a short report that speculates on the local impact of an increase in renovation.

Transparency Resource Package
Economics Concepts, 6C: Excess Demand

Differentiated Instruction  L2

Have English language learners work with groups of two to three native English-speaking students to develop a set of five questions and answers about section content. Ask groups to exchange their questions and check each other's answers. ELL

Differentiated Instruction  L3

(Reteaching) Have students examine the graphs at the bottom of this page. Each illustrates an example provided in the text. Form groups of three to four students, and assign each group either the situation of excess demand or that of excess supply. Ask them to create a realistic scenario illustrating their situations (using a different product) and then create an economic model to analyze the economic data by drawing a supply and demand graph that shows supply, demand, and the area of disequilibrium.

Differentiated Instruction  L2

Have students analyze the following global examples of supply and demand in light of what they have learned about equilibrium and disequilibrium in this section.

There is an oversupply of wheat in the United States. The United States begins exporting wheat to Russia. There is an increase in per capita income in Russia, increasing the demand for wheat from the United States. What will happen to the price of wheat in the United States? *(It will rise.)*

The United States imports oil from Russia. Russia discovers a new oil field, increasing its supply of oil. What will happen to the price that the United States pays for Russian oil? *(It will decrease.)* LPR

Answer to . . .

Building Key Concepts There is excess demand that cannot be supplied at $1 per slice.

Differentiated Instruction L3

Ask students to write a short paragraph that explains the point of view of this economic issue: why the government sometimes intervenes in a market to control prices and what methods the government uses to intervene in markets. Ask students whether they think that these interventions serve the public good.

Differentiated Instruction L2

Ask students to rewrite the following incorrect statements as correct statements.

- Equilibrium is the point at which quantity demanded *exceeds* quantity supplied. *(equals)*
- Markets tend toward *disequilibrium*. *(equilibrium)*
- Rent control is an example of government intervention called a *price floor*. *(price ceiling)* LPR

Transparency Resource Package
Economics Concepts, 6D: Excess Supply

Answer to . . .

Photo Caption Amounts stated will vary, but students should explain their answers based on supply and demand.

▼ **How much would you be willing to pay to live in one of these apartments?**

highest price that the market will bear. They will continue to sell at that price until one of the factors described in Chapter 4 or 5 changes the demand or supply curve and creates new pressures to raise or lower prices, and eventually, a new equilibrium.

Excess Supply

If the price is too high, then the market will face a problem of excess supply. **Excess supply** occurs when quantity supplied exceeds quantity demanded. For example, at a price of $2.00 per slice of pizza, the quantity supplied of 250 slices per day is much greater than the quantity demanded of 150 slices per day. This means that pizzeria owners will be making 100 more slices of pizza each day than they can sell at that price. The relatively high price encourages pizzeria owners to work hard and bake lots of pizza, but it discourages customers from buying pizza, since it is relatively more expensive than other menu items. Some customers will buy one slice instead of two, while others will eat elsewhere. The problem is shown graphically in Figure 6.2. At the end of the day, it is likely that 100 slices will have to be thrown out.

excess supply *when quantity supplied is more than quantity demanded*

price ceiling *a maximum price that can be legally charged for a good or service*

price floor *a minimum price for a good or service*

After a short time, pizzeria owners will get tired of throwing out unsold pizza at closing time and will cut their prices. As the price falls, the quantity demanded will rise, and more customers will buy more pizza. At the same time, pizzeria owners will prepare fewer pizzas. As the price of pizza falls, the quantity demanded rises and the quantity supplied falls. This process will continue until the price reaches $1.50 per slice. At that price, the amount of pizza that pizzeria owners are willing to sell is exactly equal to the amount that their customers are willing to buy.

Whenever the market is in disequilibrium and prices are flexible, market forces will push the market toward the equilibrium. Sellers do not like to waste their resources on excess supply, particularly when the goods cannot be stored for long, like pizza. And when there is excess demand, profit-seeking sellers realize that they can raise prices to earn more profits. In this way, market prices move toward the equilibrium level.

Government Intervention

Markets tend toward equilibrium, but in some cases the government steps in to control prices. The government can impose a **price ceiling,** or a maximum price that can be legally charged for a good. In other cases, the government can create a **price floor,** or a minimum price for a good or service.

Price Ceilings

A price ceiling is a maximum price, set by law, that sellers can charge for a good or service. The government places price ceilings on some goods that are considered "essential" and might become too expensive for some consumers. For example, some local governments, notably New York City, have

Econ 101: Key Concepts Made Easy

Markets and Prices Remind students of Adam Smith's concept of the **invisible hand,** which was discussed in the Economic Profile in Chapter 2. This idea states that individuals, acting in self-interest, tend to make decisions that result in market equilibrium. If, for example, a producer raises prices too high, people tend to stop buying from that producer. The firm has to lower prices to sell its goods and make a profit. Ask students to give examples from this section of the work of the invisible hand.

experimented with ceilings on apartment rents, called **rent control.** Rent control was introduced to prevent inflation during a housing crisis in the early 1940s and continued after World War II. More recently, other cities imposed rent control, often motivated by a desire to help poor households by cutting their housing costs and permitting them to live in neighborhoods they could otherwise not afford. As we'll see, rent control reduces the quantity and quality of housing, so it helps some households but harms others, including many poor households. If the ceiling is established below the equilibrium price, the result will look like graph A in Figure 6.3 below.

In this market, the supply and demand curves for two-bedroom apartments meet at the equilibrium shown at point c in graph B. At this point, rents are $900 a month. Consumers will demand 30,000 apartments and suppliers will offer 30,000 apartments for rent.

Suppose that the city government passes a law that limits the rent on two-bedroom apartments to $600 per month. At that price, the quantity of apartments demanded is 40,000 (point b), and the quantity supplied is 20,000 (point a). At such a low price, apartments seem inexpensive, and many people will try to rent apartments instead of living with their families or investing in their own houses.

However, some landlords will have difficulty earning profits or breaking even at these low rents. Fewer new apartment buildings will be built, and older ones might be converted into offices, stores, or condominiums.

As you can see in graph A of Figure 6.3, the result is excess demand of 20,000 apartments. The price ceiling increases the quantity demanded but decreases the quantity supplied. Since rents are not allowed to rise, this excess demand will last as long as the price ceiling holds.

The Cost of Price Ceilings

When the price cannot rise to the equilibrium level, the market must determine which 20,000 of the 40,000 households will get an apartment, and which 20,000 will do without. Although governments usually pass rent control laws to help renters with the greatest need, few of these renters benefit from rent control. Methods besides prices, including long waiting lists, discrimination by landlords, and even bribery, are used to allocate the scarce supply of apartments among the many people who want them. Luck becomes an important factor, and sometimes the only way to get a rent-controlled apartment is to inherit it from a parent or grandparent.

New York City revised its laws in the 1990s to exclude the wealthiest renters

rent control *a price ceiling placed on rent*

Differentiated Instruction L4

You may wish to have students add the following to their portfolios. Have them read through the information on price ceilings and rent control. Then ask them to write an editorial explaining whether they think that price ceilings in the form of rent control really help the poor. GT

Economics Assessment Rubric

Economics Assessment Rubrics folder, pp. 6–7 provides sample evaluation materials for a writing assignment.

Figure 6.3 **The Effects of Rent Control**

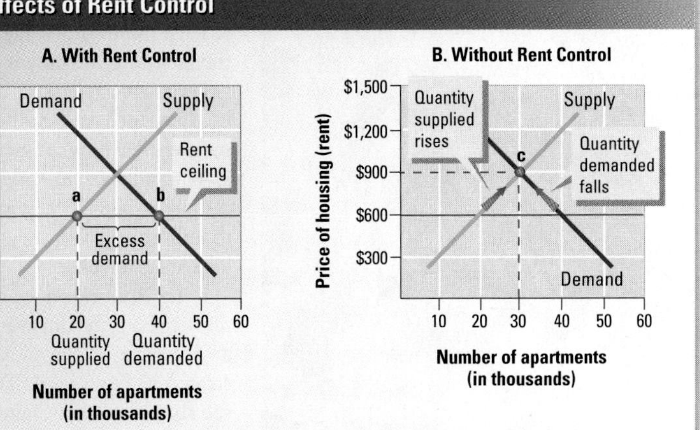

Rent control helps some people, but it also creates a housing market with fewer, less-desirable homes.
Supply and Demand
At what price does the market for apartments reach equilibrium without rent control?

Preparing for Standardized Tests

Have students read the section titled "The Cost of Price Ceilings" and then answer the question below.

Which of the following has not been cited as a cost of rent control?

A bribery being used to allocate scarce apartments
B poor maintenance in rent-controlled apartment buildings
(C) a surplus of apartments
D rent-controlled apartments in the hands of wealthy individuals

Answer to . . .

Building Key Concepts $900

Background

The Minimum Wage

The minimum wage, an example of a price floor, has risen steadily since it was instituted in 1938 at $0.25 an hour: It tripled in 12 years, quadrupled in 18 years, and rose in six decades to more than 20 times the original rate. However, when the actual purchasing power of this wage is figured using constant dollars, the progress is much more gradual. Its purchasing power rose and fell until about 1950, when it began a gradual increase. It reached a peak in 1968—in that year it bought nearly 2.5 times as much as in 1938—but it has been declining fairly steadily since that time. Today its purchasing power is less than twice what it was in 1938.

Transparency Resource Package
Economics Concepts, 6E: Rent Control
Economics Concepts, 6F: Price Floors
Economics Concepts, 6G: Price Floors Overlay

Differentiated Instruction L1

Prepare a number of "landlord" cards equal to the number of students in class. Print $1000, $800, or $600 on one side and "landlord" on the other. Prepare corresponding "renter" cards with $1000, $800, or $600 on one side and "renter" on the other. Divide all the "landlord" cards equally among three students and give a "renter" card to each of the rest. Tell the renters to find an apartment they can afford, exchanging their cards for a landlord's card. Everyone should find an apartment. Three apartments will be unrented. Collect the cards. Announce, "Rent controls are in effect. No landlord may charge more than $800." Distribute the cards as before, except the $1000 landlord cards. Tell the renters to find an apartment at any price at or below the amount listed on their card. Discuss reasons for the "shortage" of rental property. SN

minimum wage *a minimum price that an employer can pay a worker for an hour of labor.*

from rent control protection after newspapers discovered that some very wealthy people rented spacious apartments at prices much less than market value.

Additionally, since the rent controls limit landlords' profits, landlords may try to increase their income by cutting costs. Why should a landlord give a building a fresh coat of paint and a new garden if he or she can't earn the money back through higher rent? Besides, if there's a waiting list to get an apartment, the landlord has no incentive to work hard and attract renters. As a result, many rent-controlled apartment buildings become run-down, and renters may have to wait months to have routine problems fixed.

Ending Rent Control

If rents were allowed to rise to the market equilibrium level, which is $900 per month, the quantity of apartments in the market would actually rise to 30,000 apartments. The market would be in equilibrium, and people who could afford $900 a month would have an easier time finding vacant apartments. Instead of spending time and money searching for apartments, and then having to accept an apartment in a poorly maintained building, many renters would be able to find a wider selection of apartments. Landlords would also have a greater incentive to properly maintain their buildings and invest in new construction.

On the other hand, people lucky enough to live in a rent-controlled apartment may no longer be able to afford to stay there once rent control is ended and the landlord can legally raise the rent. As soon as the neighborhood improves, these renters may be priced out of their own apartments, to be replaced by people willing to pay the equilibrium price. Remember that ending rent control increases the number of apartments on the market by 10,000.

Certainly, the end of rent control benefits some people and hurts others. Economists agree that the benefits of ending rent control exceed the costs, and suggest that there are better ways to help poor households find affordable housing.

▼ The minimum wage has a strong impact on teens in the work force.

Price Floors

A price floor is a minimum price, set by the government, that must be paid for a good or service. Price floors are often imposed when government wants sellers to receive some minimum reward for their efforts.

The Minimum Wage

One well-known price floor is the **minimum wage,** which sets a minimum price that an employer can pay a worker for an hour of labor. The federal government sets a base level for the minimum wage, and states can set their own minimum wages even higher. A full-time worker being paid the federal minimum wage will earn less than the federal government says is necessary to support a couple with one child. However, it does provide some lower limit for workers' earnings. The important question, as you will read in *Debating Current Issues* on pages 238–239, is whether the benefits to minimum wage workers outweigh the loss of some jobs.

If the minimum wage is set above the market equilibrium wage rate, the result is a decrease in employment, as demonstrated in Figure 6.4. This figure illustrates the supply curve of labor, which shows the number of worker-hours offered at various

Interdisciplinary Connections: Math

Fluctuations in the Minimum Wage The Background note on this page discusses the changes in the minimum wage since 1938. Although the minimum wage has continued to rise, its purchasing power has not risen in the same way.

Making the Connection Use the following information to construct a line graph. Then use the graph to verify the information in the Background note on this page.

Year	Minimum Wage	Purchasing Power*	Year	Minimum Wage	Purchasing Power*
1938	$0.25	$3.27	1975	$2.10	$7.21
1940	$0.30	$3.96	1980	$3.10	$6.94
1950	$0.75	$5.74	1985	$3.35	$5.75
1955	$0.75	$5.17	1990	$3.80	$5.37
1960	$1.00	$6.24	1995	$4.25	$5.15
1967	$1.40	$7.74	2000	$5.15	$5.52
1970	$1.60	$7.61	2003	$5.15	$5.15

*in constant 2003 dollars

wage rates, and a demand curve for labor, which shows the number of workers employers will hire at various wages.

If the market equilibrium wage for low-skilled labor is \$4.50 per hour, and the minimum wage is set at \$5.15, the result is an excess supply of labor. There are now 4 million more people looking for work than employers are willing to hire. (Remember that in this example, the worker is the supplier because he or she supplies labor that is bought by an employer.) Firms will employ 2 million fewer workers than they would at the equilibrium wage rate because the price floor on labor keeps the wage rate artificially high. If the minimum wage is below the equilibrium rate, it will have no effect because employers would have to pay at least the equilibrium rate anyway to find workers in a free market.

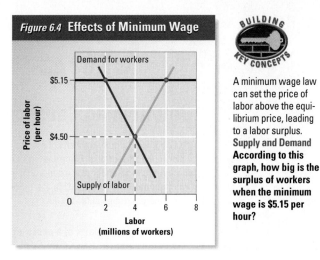

Figure 6.4 Effects of Minimum Wage

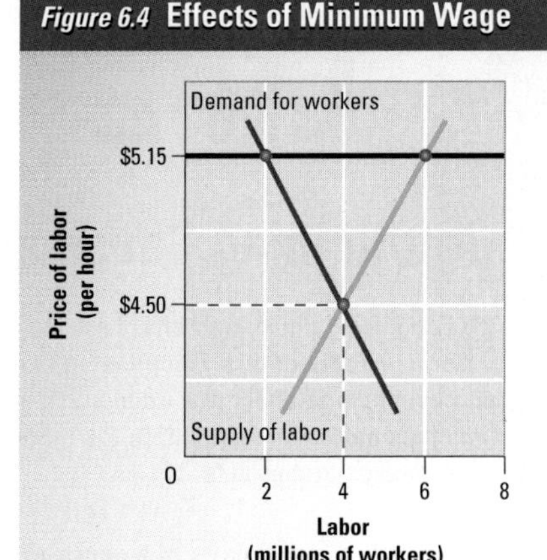

A minimum wage law can set the price of labor above the equilibrium price, leading to a labor surplus.

Supply and Demand According to this graph, how big is the surplus of workers when the minimum wage is \$5.15 per hour?

Price Supports in Agriculture

Price floors are used for many farm products around the world. Until 1996, the United States set minimum prices for several commodities, although these price floors were not legal limits. Instead, whenever the price fell below the price floor, the government created demand by buying excess crops.

Congress abolished these programs in 1996 because they conflicted with free enterprise. Today, the federal government responds to low commodity prices by providing emergency financial aid to farmers.

Section 1 Assessment

Progress Monitoring *Online*
For: Self-quiz with vocabulary practice
Web Code: mna-2065

Key Terms and Main Ideas

1. What is unique about an **equilibrium** price?
2. What situation can lead to **excess demand?**
3. How is a **price floor** different from a **price ceiling?**
4. How does **rent control** work?

Applying Economic Concepts

5. ***Using the Databank*** Turn to the graph of median weekly earnings on page 536 in the Databank. Suppose that the federal government has raised the minimum wage to \$600 per week. **(a)** Which category of jobs would be least affected by the change? **(b)** Which two categories would be most affected by the new minimum wage? **(c)** What are the likely consequences for workers in these two fields?
6. ***Critical Thinking*** What are the benefits and drawbacks of a price ceiling?
7. ***Math Practice*** The graph below shows supply and demand curves in the notebook market. Use what you have learned in this section to identify the following elements of the graph: price floor, supply curve, equilibrium point, disequilibrium point, demand curve, price ceiling.

For: Current Events Activity
Visit: PHSchool.com
Web Code: mnd-2061

GTE Guide to the Essentials
Chapter 6, Section 1, p. 24 provides support for students who need additional review of the section content. Spanish support is available in the Spanish edition of the guide on p. 24.

Quiz Unit 2 folder, p. 25 includes questions to check students' understanding of Section 1 content.

Presentation Pro CD-ROM
Quiz provides multiple-choice questions to check students' understanding of Section 1 content.

Answers to . . .

Section 1 Assessment

1. The equilibrium price is unique because it is the point where the price and amount supplied are equal to the price and amount demanded.
2. Excess demand occurs when the quantity demanded is more than the quantity supplied. This can occur when the actual price in a market is lower than the equilibrium price.
3. A price floor is a government-set minimum price for certain goods or services (such as minimum wage). A price ceiling is a government-set maximum price that can be charged for a good or service (as in rent control).
4. Rent control is a price ceiling placed on rent that is often motivated by a desire to help poor households by cutting their housing costs.
5. (a) managerial and professional (b) farming, forestry, and fishing; service (c) Wages will probably increase; some workers may lose their jobs as companies cut back to save money.
6. Price ceilings benefit lower-income people by keeping prices from rising beyond their means. Drawbacks include possible shortages, such as waiting lists for apartments.
7. Price ceiling (E), supply curve (C), equilibrium point (a), disequilibrium point (b), demand curve (F), price floor (D)

Progress Monitoring *Online*
For additional assessment, have students access Progress Monitoring Online at **Web Code:** mna-2065

Go Online PHSchool.com Typing in the Web Code when prompted will bring students directly to detailed instructions for this activity.

Answer to . . .
Building Key Concepts The surplus is 4,000,000 workers.

Skills for LIFE

Determining Cause and Effect

1. Focus Students will analyze information by identifying cause-and-effect relationships and draw conclusions on what are causes and effects.

2. Instruct Present students with several simple cause-effect statements, such as *Because traffic was stopped on the bridge, I was late to work.* Ask volunteers to suggest examples as well. Then have students work through the three steps outlined in the skills feature.

3. Close/Reteach To provide additional practice, see the Economic Skills Activity below.

Economic Skills Activity
Unit 2 folder, p. 30, "Recognizing Cause and Effect," asks students to identify causes and effects.

Social Studies Skills Tutor CD-ROM offers interactive practice in critical thinking and reading, visual analysis, and communication.

Answers

1. (a) A, C, E, F (b) A: floods > poor coffee crop; C: poor harvest > rise in prices > stores stop selling expensive brands; E: poor crop > coffee shops raise prices despite declining quality; heat wave > servers lost jobs and chain did not open new stores; F: coffee is expensive > consumers switch to tea and soft drinks > importers buy more tea > growers plant more tea > South American farmers struggle to rebuild, but farmers in Southeast Asia prosper (c) A: because; C: due to, as a result; E: led to, when; F: when, while
2. (a) poor harvest, heat wave (b) rise in prices, loss of jobs, stores not opening
3. Diagrams should accurately link causes to effects.

Additional Practice

Students may answer that a new tax will result in higher costs for importers. Importers will pass on costs to coffee shops, and as a result customers will pay more for coffee. Consequently, customers will decrease coffee consumption, and as a result growers will make less money.

Skills for LIFE

Determining Cause and Effect

Recognizing cause and effect means examining how one event or action brings about others. Because an economy is a complex web of choices and events, one challenge economists face is finding and defining the relationships between events. Use the following steps to learn how to determine causes and effects.

1. Identify the two parts of a cause-effect relationship. A cause is an event or an action that brings about an effect. Words such as *because, due to,* and *on account of* signal causes. Words such as *so, thus, therefore,* and *as a result* signal effects. Read statements A through F at the left and answer the following: (a) Which statements are cause-effect statements? (b) Identify the cause and the effect in each cause-effect statement. (c) Which word or words signal the cause-effect relationship?

STATEMENTS LIST

A. Because of floods in South America, last year's coffee crop was poor.
B. Coffee is grown in Brazil, Colombia, and several countries in West Africa.
C. Because of the poor harvest, there was not enough good coffee available for American distributors to buy. As a result, prices went up, and many stores chose to stop selling the most expensive blends.
D. Many Americans drink coffee in the morning to wake up, while others drink coffee in the afternoon or after dinner.
E. The poor state of this year's crop led coffee shops to raise prices even as the quality of their coffee declined. When a heat wave hit the Northeast in July and August, sales dropped by 30 percent, many servers lost their jobs, and a major chain decided to delay opening new stores in Philadelphia and Washington, D.C.
F. When high quality coffee became expensive and difficult to find, many consumers switched to tea and soft drinks instead. Importers bought more tea in Southeast Asia to meet the new demand, and tea plantations planted more crops for the following year. While farmers in South America struggled to rebuild, farmers in India and Indonesia made more money and were able to invest in new machinery.

2. Remember that an event can have more than one cause and more than one effect. Read statement E at the left and answer the following questions. (a) What are the causes presented in the statement? (b) What are the effects of those causes?

3. An event can be both a cause and an effect. Causes and effects can form a chain of events. Read statement F at the left and use arrows to draw a diagram of the causes and effects that show the chain of related events.

Additional Practice

Based on what you have learned in this chapter, construct a chain of events to show the impact of a new tax on the coffee market.

Interdisciplinary Connections: Philosophy

Understanding Cause and Effect Through Logic Logic is a branch of philosophy that is concerned with correct reasoning. The basic form of reasoning, called an argument, consists of a set of premises (assertions) followed by a conclusion. If the premises support the conclusion adequately, the argument is correct, or valid.

Have students work through the following activity: Tell students that there are two basic types of arguments or reasoning—deductive and inductive. Ask groups of two or three students to find out about each of these types of reasoning and to provide an explanation and examples in verbal or graphic form.

Section 2 Changes in Market Equilibrium

Preview

Objectives

After studying this section you will be able to:

1. **Identify** the determinants that create changes in price.
2. **Explain** how a market reacts to a fall in supply by moving to a new equilibrium.
3. **Explain** how a market reacts to shifts in demand by moving to a new equilibrium.

Section Focus

When a supply or demand curve shifts, a new equilibrium occurs. The market price and quantity sold move toward the new equilibrium.

Key Terms

surplus
shortage
search costs

Economists say that a market will tend toward equilibrium, which means that the price and quantity will gradually move toward their equilibrium levels. Why does this happen? Remember that excess demand will lead firms to raise prices. Higher prices induce the quantity supplied to rise and the quantity demanded to fall until the two values are equal.

On the other hand, excess supply will force firms to cut prices. Falling prices will cause quantity demanded to rise and quantity supplied to fall until, once again, they are equal. Through these relationships, the market price and quantity sold of a good will move toward their equilibrium values.

Remember from Chapters 4 and 5 that all of the changes in demand and supply described above are changes along a demand or supply curve. Assuming that a market starts at equilibrium, there are two factors that can push it into disequilibrium: a shift in the entire demand curve and a shift in the entire supply curve.

Changes in Price

In Chapter 5, you read about the different factors that shift a supply curve to the left or to the right. These factors include advances in technology, new government taxes and subsidies, and changes in the prices of the raw materials and labor used to produce the good.

Since market equilibrium occurs at the intersection of a demand curve and a supply curve, a shift of the entire supply curve will change the equilibrium price and quantity. A shift in the supply curve to the left or the right creates a new equilibrium. Since markets tend toward equilibrium, a change in supply will set market forces into motion that lead the market to this new equilibrium price and quantity sold.

◀ **A functioning market will carefully balance supply and demand.**

Graphing the Main Idea

Supply and Demand To help students understand **supply and demand,** have students use two multi-flow chart graphic organizers like the one below. Tell students that a multi-flow chart shows causes and effects. Have them construct a multi-flow chart titled "Shifts in Supply" and one titled "Shifts in Demand."

Section Reading Support Transparencies A template and the answers for this graphic organizer can be found in Chapter 6, Section 2 of the Section Reading Support Transparency System.

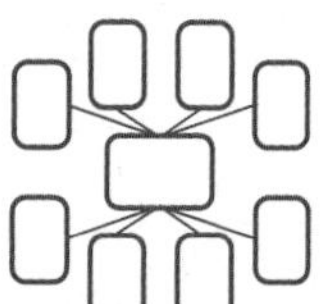

Section 2 Changes in Market Equilibrium

Objectives You may wish to call students' attention to the objectives in the Section Preview. The objectives are reflected in the main headings of the section.

Bellringer Ask students to provide examples of items that have undergone price changes in the past six months. Explain that in this section they will learn how and why prices change.

Vocabulary Builder Ask students to read the definitions of the key terms in the margins of this section. Have them use each term in a sentence that helps explain its meaning.

Lesson Plan

Teaching the Main Concepts 

1. Focus Ask a volunteer to define *equilibrium* and *disequilibrium.* Tell students that in this section they will learn how the market reacts to changes in supply or demand by moving to a new equilibrium.

2. Instruct Explain to students that this section discusses how prices change in the marketplace. First, work through the section on shifts in supply, helping students to see that excess supply leads to lower prices, whereas a shortage leads to higher prices. Conversely, increased demand leads to higher prices, and a decrease in demand leads to lower prices. Be sure that students understand how the factors work together and influence one another.

3. Close/Reteach Ask students to provide current examples of changes in demand or supply of items. Encourage them to examine the causes and effects of these shifts in the marketplace.

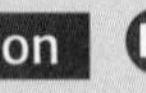

Guided Reading and Review
Unit 2 folder, p. 26 asks students to identify the main ideas of the section and to define or identify key terms.

Transparency Resource Package
Economics Concepts, 6H: Shifts in Supply
Economics Concepts, 6I: Shifts in Supply Overlay

Differentiated Instruction L3

Have groups of four to six students plan and present brief skits that demonstrate the basic movement toward equilibrium in the marketplace. They should present situations in which demand and supply interact, resulting in a price change. Encourage the groups to be creative in their presentations, but also limit them to a presentation time of five minutes or less. Stress that their brief skit should dramatize the market tendency toward equilibrium.

As CD players become cheaper to produce, the supply increases at all but the lowest prices.
Supply and Demand Why do the 1985 and 1990 supply curves begin so high up on the graph?

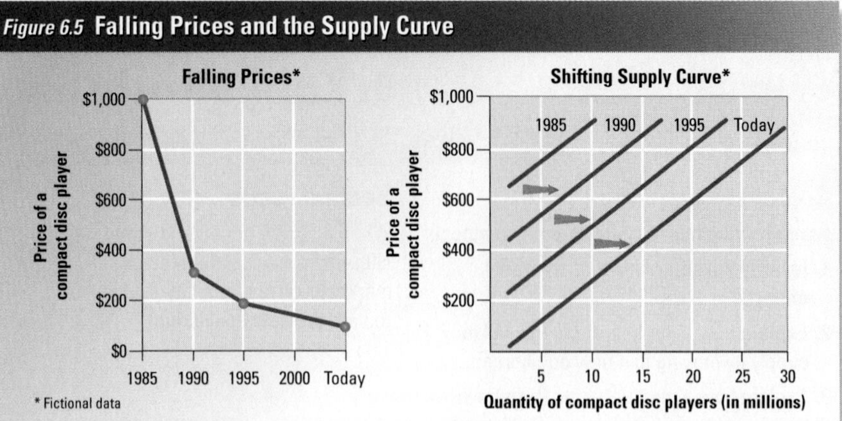

Understanding a Shift in Supply

When compact disc players were first introduced in the early 1980s, a basic, single-disc machine cost around $1,000. The early compact disc players were much more expensive and less sophisticated than the compact disc players people use today. Gradually, as firms developed better technology for producing compact disc players, their prices fell. In 1990, a consumer could purchase a fancy single-disc player for $300; just five years later, in 1995, a similar player could be purchased for about $200. Today, consumers can buy a compact disc player for less than $100.

Not only have the prices of compact disc players fallen, but the machines on sale today have many more features and options than the original $1,000 machine. Technology has lowered the cost of manufacturing compact disc players and has also reduced the costs of some of the inputs, like computer chips. These advances in production have allowed manufacturers to produce compact disc players at lower costs. Producers have passed on these lower costs to consumers in the form of lower market prices.

We can use the tools developed in Chapter 5 to graph the effect of these changes on the CD market's supply curve. Figure 6.5 shows how the supply curve shifted outward, or to the right, as manufacturers offered more and more CD players at lower prices. In the early 1980s, no compact disc players were offered for $300. They were simply too expensive to develop and manufacture. Today, manufacturers can offer millions of CD players at this price.

surplus *situation in which quantity supplied is greater than quantity demanded; also known as excess supply*

Finding a New Equilibrium

Picture the point in time when compact disc players were evolving from an expensive luxury good to a mid-priced good. A new generation of computer chips has just reduced the cost of production. These lower costs have shifted the supply curve to the right where at each price, producers are willing to supply a larger quantity.

This shift, shown in Figure 6.6 using fictional quantities, has thrown the market into disequilibrium. At the old equilibrium price, suppliers are now willing to offer 4,000,000 compact disc players, up from 2,000,000.

In Figure 6.6, the increase in quantity supplied at the old equilibrium price is shown as the change from point a to point b. However, the quantity demanded at this price has not changed, and consumers will only buy 2,000,000 compact disc players. At this market price, unsold compact disc players will begin to pile up in the warehouse. When quantity supplied exceeds quantity demanded at a given price, economists call this a **surplus.** The surplus compact disc players are

Econ 101: Key Concepts Made Easy

Supply and Demand The key concepts in this section are how the market reacts to a change in **supply** and how the market reacts to a change in **demand.** Help students to see that the market naturally moves toward equilibrium but that the market's reactions to these two forces are opposites: a rise in supply causes lower prices, whereas a rise in demand causes higher prices. A drop in supply causes higher prices, but a drop in demand causes lower prices.

It may help students to look back at the Skills for Life feature on p. 132 and to think of changes in supply or demand as a series of cause-effect statements. Ask students to draw a diagram with cause-effect arrows to illustrate one of the text examples.

Answer to . . .

Building Key Concepts Prices were high because producers were still trying to make up for the costs of developing the new technology.

excess supply, so something will have to change to bring the market to equilibrium.

As you read in Section 1, suppliers will respond to excess supply by reducing prices. As the price falls from $600 to $400, more consumers decide to buy compact disc players, and the quantity demanded rises. The combined movement of falling prices and increasing quantity demanded can be seen in Figure 6.6 as a change from point a to point c. Notice that this change is a movement along the demand curve, not a shift of the entire demand curve.

Eventually, the price falls to a point where quantity supplied and quantity demanded are equal, and excess supply is no longer a problem. This new equilibrium point, shown at point c in Figure 6.6, marks a lower equilibrium price and a higher equilibrium quantity sold than before the supply curve shifted. This is how equilibrium changes when supply increases, and the entire supply curve shifts to the right.

Changing Equilibrium

As the price of compact disc players fell due to better technology, more and more people bought them. The equilibrium in this market, then, started moving gradually downward and to the right. This is where the quantities demanded and supplied are higher, and the prices are lower.

The supply curve for compact disc players has been moving to the right ever since the first $1,000 compact disc players were sold. The curve continues to shift today as new technology continues to drive down the production cost and market price of the most basic machines.

Equilibrium is usually not an unchanging, single point on a graph. The equilibrium in the compact disc player market has always been in motion. The market equilibrium follows the intersection of the demand curve and the supply curve as that point moves downward along the demand curve.

Equilibrium is a "moving target" that changes as market conditions change.

Figure 6.6 A Change in Supply

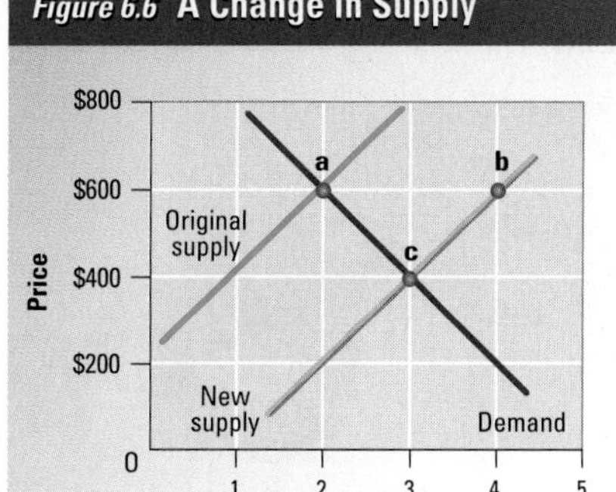

When supply increases, prices fall, and quantity demanded increases to reach a new equilibrium.

Supply and Demand How would you compare the point of the new equilibrium to the old equilibrium?

Manufacturers and retail sellers of compact disc players are constantly searching for a new equilibrium as technology and methods of production change. Consumers recognize this "searching" by the frequent price changes, sales, and rebates on compact disc players. Each of these tactics is designed to keep the machines moving out of stores as fast as new machines come in.

A Fall in Supply

Just as new technology or lower costs can shift the supply curve to the right, so other factors that reduce supply can shift the supply curve to the left. Consider the market for cars. If the price of steel rises, automobile manufacturers will produce fewer cars at all price levels, and the supply curve will shift to the left. If auto workers strike for higher wages, and the company must pay more for labor to build the same number of cars, supply will decrease. If the government imposes a new tax on car manufacturers, supply will decrease. In all of these cases, the supply curve will move to the left, because the quantity supplied is lower at all price levels.

THE WALL STREET JOURNAL. CLASSROOM EDITION

In the News Read more about supply in "Ups and Downs," an article in The Wall Street Journal Classroom Edition.

Go Online
The Wall Street Journal Classroom Edition
For: Current Events
Visit: PHSchool.com
Web Code: mnc-2062

Differentiated Instruction L4

Ask students to identify several high-tech products that are currently on the market that they would like to own but think are too expensive to purchase at this time. Have students choose one of these products. Then have each student create a cause-effect chart highlighting factors that are likely to change the supply, demand, and price, thus leading to a new equilibrium. Encourage volunteers to explain their charts to the class. GT

Transparency Resource Package
Economics Concepts, 6J: Fall in Supply

Go Online PHSchool.com Typing in the Web Code when prompted will bring students directly to the article.

THE WALL STREET JOURNAL. CLASSROOM EDITION

For an additional article from *The Wall Street Journal Classroom Edition,* see the Source Articles folder in the **Teaching Resources,** pp. 18–20.

Economic Cartoon
Unit 2 folder, p. 34 gives students practice in interpreting cartoons about section content.

Block Scheduling Strategies

Consider these suggestions to take advantage of extended class time:

- Extend the Close/Reteach section of the Lesson Plan to have students gather articles on shifts in demand or supply of various items that directly affect them. Ask students to focus on one or two examples and to write a short essay that discusses factors that led to the shift as well as the economic results of the shift and the move toward market equilibrium.
- Extend the Meeting NCEE Standards activity on p. 136 by asking groups of four to six students to create similar scenarios that exhibit changes in supply and demand. Groups should provide solutions to other groups' scenarios.
- Have pairs complete the Economic Cartoon activity in the Unit 2 Folder, p. 34. Then have pairs create their own cartoons that show one of the changes in market equilibrium discussed in this section.

Answer to . . .

Building Key Concepts Price is lower and output is higher.

Meeting NCEE Standards

Use the following benchmark activity from the **Voluntary National Content Standards in Economics** to evaluate student understanding of **Standard 8.**

Predict the change in demand for a particular brand of jeans when an extensive ad campaign for the brand targets teenagers, their allowances double, the price of corduroy pants skyrockets, or jeans become a popular item among adults.

Transparency Resource Package
Economics Concepts, 6K: Shifts in Demand
Economics Concepts, 6L: Shifts in Demand Overlay
Economics Concepts, 6M: Fall in Demand

Background Note

Supply and Demand

For an example of a change in demand caused by a change in a related market, consider the interactions between the markets for airline and rail travel. The September 11, 2001, attacks on the World Trade Center and the Pentagon changed our expectations about the safety of airline travel, increasing its perceived cost. As a result, the demand for alternative travel modes increased. For example, the demand for rail travel in the corridor from Washington to New York to Boston, which accounts for over half of Amtrak's passenger revenue, increased by about 25%. In other words, the demand curve for rail travel shifted to the right, with more passengers at every price level.

▲ **Almost every fall, a trendy toy emerges as one that every child "must have." Demand for these toys increases.**

shortage *situation in which quantity demanded is greater than quantity supplied; also known as excess demand*

search costs *the financial and opportunity costs consumers pay when searching for a good or service*

When the supply curve shifts to the left, the equilibrium price and quantity sold will change as well. This process is the exact opposite of the change that results from an increase in supply. As the supply curve shifts to the left, suppliers raise their prices and the quantity demanded falls. The new equilibrium point will be at a spot along the demand curve above and to the left of the original equilibrium point. The market price is higher than before, and the quantity sold is lower.

Figure 6.7 A Change in Demand

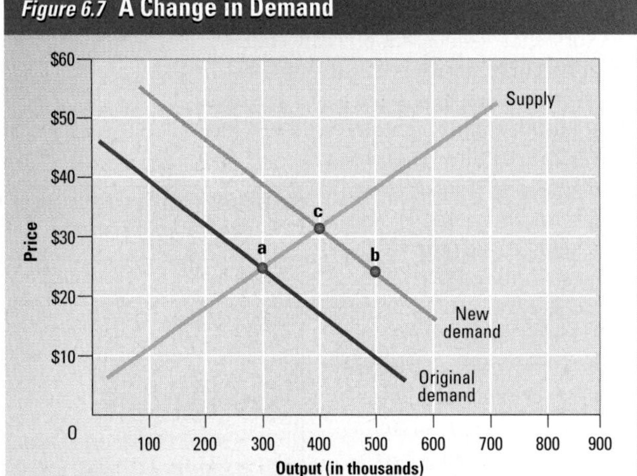

When demand shifts, price and quantity supplied change to create a new equilibrium.
Prices and Markets What happens to prices when the demand curve shifts to the right?

Shifts in Demand

Almost every year, around November, a new doll or toy emerges as a nationwide fad. People across the country race to stores at opening time and stand in long lines to buy that year's version of Tickle Me Elmo or Pokémon.

As you read in Chapter 4, these fads reflect the impact of consumer tastes and advertising on consumer behavior. Fads like these, in which demand rises quickly, are real-life examples of a rapid, rightward shift in a market demand curve. Figure 6.7 shows how a rapid, unexpected increase in market demand will affect the equilibrium in a market for a hypothetical, trendy toy.

The Problem of Excess Demand

In Figure 6.7, the fad causes a sudden increase in market demand, and the demand curve shifts to the right. This shift leads to excess demand at the original price of $24 (point b). Before the fad began, quantity demanded and quantity supplied were equal at 300,000 dolls, shown at point a. On the graph, excess demand appears as a gap between the quantity supplied of 300,000 dolls and the new quantity demanded of 500,000 at $24, shown at point b. This is an increase of 200,000 in the quantity demanded. Economists would also describe this as a **shortage** of 200,000 dolls.

In the stores that carry the dolls, excess demand appears as bare shelves and long lines. Excess demand also appears in the form of **search costs**—the financial and opportunity costs consumers pay in searching for a good or service. Driving to different stores and calling different towns to find an available doll are both examples of search costs.

In the meantime, the available dolls must be rationed, or distributed, in some other manner. In this case, long lines, limits on the quantities each customer may buy, and

Preparing for Standardized Tests

Have students read the section titled "The Problem of Excess Demand" and answer the question below.

According to the text, which of the following are forms of search costs?

A long lines at stores
B limits on the quantities purchased
(C) driving to a different town to find a product
D increasing the cost of a good that is in high demand

Answer to . . .
Building Key Concepts Prices rise.

"first come, first serve" policies are used to distribute the dolls among customers.

Return to Equilibrium

As time passes, firms will react to the signs of excess demand and raise their prices. In fact, customers may actually push prices up on their own if there is "bidding" in the market, as there is for real estate, antiques, fine art, and hard-to-find items.

If a parent cannot find the doll he wants at the store, he might offer the store keeper an extra $5 to guarantee him a doll from the next shipment. Through these methods, the market price will rise until the quantity supplied equals the quantity demanded at 300,000 dolls. All of these dolls are sold at the new equilibrium price of $30, shown at point c in Figure 6.7.

When demand increases, both the equilibrium price and the equilibrium quantity also increase. The demand curve has shifted, and the equilibrium point has moved, setting in motion market forces that push the price and quantity toward their new equilibrium values.

A Fall in Demand

When a fad passes its peak, demand can fall as quickly as it rose. Excess demand turns into excess supply for the once-popular toy as parents look for a new, more trendy gift for their children. Overflowing store shelves and silent cash registers, the symptoms of excess supply, replace long lines and bidding wars.

When demand falls, the demand curve shifts to the left. Suppliers respond by cutting prices on their inventory. Price and quantity sold slide down along the supply curve to a new equilibrium point at point a in Figure 6.7. The end of the fad restores the original price and quantity supplied.

Section 2 Assessment

Progress Monitoring *Online*
For: Self-quiz with vocabulary practice
Web Code: mna-2066

Key Terms and Main Ideas

1. What conditions lead to a **surplus?**
2. What is an example of a **search cost?**

Applying Economic Concepts

3. ***Decision Making*** Explain how the equilibrium price and quantity sold of eggs will change in the following cases. Remember that they need not move in the same direction. **(a)** An outbreak of food poisoning is traced to eggs. **(b)** Scientists breed a new chicken that lays twice as many eggs each week. **(c)** A popular talk show host convinces her viewers to eat an egg a day.
4. ***Critical Thinking*** What will happen to suppliers in a market if there is a surplus of the good they sell, but no supplier can afford to lower prices?
5. ***Math Practice*** The graph at the right shows the effects of a demand shift on a particular market. **(a)** Has demand increased or decreased? Explain. **(b)** What are the original equilibrium price and quantity sold? **(c)** What are the new equilibrium price and quantity sold? **(d)** A new tax raises the cost of production. How does the supply curve react? **(e)** Give a market price and quantity sold that might be a new equilibrium point after this cost increase.

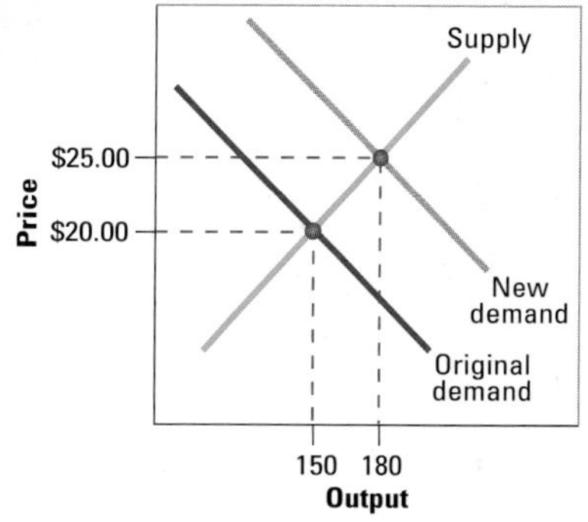

For: Research Activity
Visit: PHSchool.com
Web Code: mnd-2062

Progress Monitoring *Online*
For additional assessment, have students access Progress Monitoring Online at **Web Code:** mna-2066

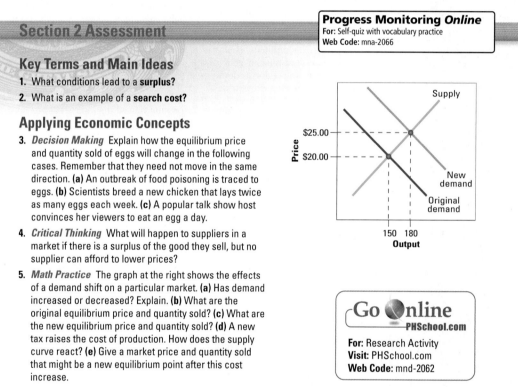

Go Online PHSchool.com Typing in the Web Code when prompted will bring students directly to detailed instructions for this activity.

GTE Guide to the Essentials
Chapter 6, Section 2, p. 25 provides support for students who need additional review of the section content. Spanish support is available in the Spanish edition of the guide on p. 25.

Quiz Unit 2 folder, p. 27 includes questions to check students' understanding of Section 2 content.

Presentation Pro CD-ROM
Quiz provides multiple-choice questions to check students' understanding of Section 2 content.

Answers to . . .

Section 2 Assessment

1. Surpluses are caused by shifts in the supply curve, which cause quantity supplied to exceed quantity demanded. Surpluses can also occur if consumers demand far less of a good than they did previously.
2. An example of a search cost is the time and gas money spent looking for a hard-to-find item.
3. (a) Quantity sold decreases; equilibrium price decreases. (b) Quantity sold may increase; equilibrium price decreases. (c) Quantity sold increases; equilibrium price increases.
4. Suppliers will be left at the mercy of the product's elasticity of demand. If demand is inelastic, they should be able to sell the product at the price they have been asking and will need to adjust production to make sure that they do not produce more of it until the surplus is gone. If demand is elastic, they may be stuck with the surplus unless some other market factor increases sales.
5. (a) Increased; the curve has shifted to the right. (b) Original equilibrium price is $20; original quantity sold is 150. (c) New equilibrium price is $25; new quantity sold is 180. (d) The supply curve will shift to the left. (e) Possible answer—Equilibrium price: $22; quantity sold: 162.

ECONOMIC *Profile*
Michael Dell

Background

The same kind of forward thinking that made Michael Dell a successful entrepreneur continues to fuel his success today. Dell sees the trend toward high-speed Internet access as a boost to personal computer sales. Consumers, he believes, will want faster and better access, and Dell wants his company to be there to provide the computers and other devices to make it possible.

At the same time, faster access will make Dell's on-line marketing efforts even more effective. Dell hopes to expand his Web site to include on-line conferences and broadcast programming on how to get the most out of a Dell PC. It will come as no surprise that at the same time Dell will use his Web site to sell more computers more effectively.

Careers in Economic Activity Unit 2 folder, p. 33 gives students a closer look at the career path of a financial advisor.

Answers to . . .

1. Dell uses a direct-marketing approach that allows his company to custom-build each product. This practice avoids large inventories and eliminates price markups by retailers. For this reason Dell can undersell competitors while providing a product that meets customers' exact needs.
2. Prices would probably go up because Dell's overhead would rise due to increased costs for facilities, employees, and the inventory needed to maintain a retail chain.
3. Answers will vary depending on the sources used by students for research but should point to Dell's reaction to imitations by competitors of Dell's direct approach.

Economist

Entrepreneur

ECONOMIC *Profile*

In 1984, Michael Dell took $1,000 and an idea, and began to build a computer business. Defying the odds against the success of a new business, Dell built what is now the largest direct-sale computer manufacturer in the world. In the process, he made millionaires out of investors who had faith in a young person and his ideas.

"I often wonder what new development will come along and totally change the face of our industry," says computer magnate Michael Dell. This visionary Texan has not only adapted well to change, he has revolutionized the way products are marketed and sold. Dell has been called the Henry Ford of the computer industry.

As a teenager in the early 1980s, Dell saw a future in personal computers (PCs). During his freshman year at the University of Texas, he sold PCs from his dorm room. Business was so good that the next year he quit school and, with $1,000 in capital, started a company. Fifteen years later, Dell Computer Corporation was a $19.9 billion business, with more than $18 million a day in sales on its Internet site alone.

Direct From Dell

When Dell started his company in 1984, PC manufacturers were all selling standard models through retail stores. Dell's vision was to sell his computers directly to consumers. This approach allowed him to customize each computer to the customer's needs. It also enabled Dell to sell PCs for less than his competitors did because there were no retailers marking up his prices to make a profit for their stores.

Dell's direct-marketing model had cost advantages as well. By custom-building each computer, he did not have to maintain warehouses full of unsold goods. The company took each order by phone or fax and shipped the finished computer within two weeks. The low inventory costs were also reflected in Dell's pricing. Not only did Dell's customers receive exactly what they needed, they got it at a lower price than that of his competitors' standard PCs.

Dell in Cyberspace

As the Internet grew in the early 1990s, Dell saw new opportunities. Most people at the time viewed the Internet as a source of information. "Commerce . . . was pretty much restricted to ordering T-shirts," Dell says. "But it . . . struck me that if you could order a T-shirt online, you could order anything—including a computer." In 1996, Dell became one of the first manufacturers to offer products via the Internet. The Dell Web site allows visitors to create a computer system, calculate its price, place an order, pay, and even arrange financing online.

The success of this "Dell direct" approach to the sale of computers has shaped how other business sectors, such as banking and the auto industry, market and sell their products.

CHECK FOR UNDERSTANDING

1. **Source Reading** Summarize the factors that allowed Dell Computer Corporation to sell personal computers at lower prices than its competitors could.
2. **Critical Thinking** What would be likely to happen to its prices if Dell Computer Corporation opened stores across the country? Explain why.
3. **Learn More** How has Dell Computer Corporation strived to maintain its success against competitors who have imitated the Dell direct sales approach?

Beyond the Classroom: Career Connections

Computer Programmer All computers depend on a set of extremely detailed instructions, called "software" or "programs," to perform any task from simple calculations to word processing to flight simulation. Computer programmers write, test, and maintain these instructions, working in special computer languages such as FORTRAN, Prolog, or Visual Basic. Programmers are employed in almost every industry, but the largest concentration of programmers is found in the computer and data processing services industries. Ask students what traits or talents they think that computer programmers would need to have to be successful.

Section 3 The Role of Prices

Preview

Objectives

After studying this section you will be able to:

1. **Analyze** the role of prices in a free market.
2. **List** the advantages of a price-based system.
3. **Explain** how a price-based system leads to a wider choice of goods and more efficient allocation of resources.
4. **Describe** the relationship between prices and the profit incentive.

Section Focus

Goods and services can be divided up among buyers and sellers by a central plan or a price-based market system. Prices allow an efficient, flexible exchange of goods.

Key Terms

supply shock
rationing
black market
spillover costs

In Section 1, you read how supply and demand interact to determine the equilibrium price and quantity sold in a market. You also read about how those prices change over time. Prices are a key element of equilibrium. Price changes can move markets toward equilibrium and solve problems of excess supply and excess demand. In this section we will discuss the importance of prices and the role they play.

In a free market, prices are a tool for distributing goods and resources throughout the economy. Prices are nearly always the most efficient way to allocate, or distribute, resources. The alternative method for distributing goods and resources, namely a centrally planned economy, is not nearly as efficient as a market system based on prices.

Prices in the Free Market

Prices serve a vital role in a free market economy. Prices help move land, labor, and capital into the hands of producers, and finished goods into the hands of buyers. The following example shows the benefits of a system based on free market prices.

Kevin decides to buy a sweater for his sister for her birthday next month. He goes to a nearby shopping center and compares the prices of several different sweaters. Kevin finds that a department store offers cotton cable-knit sweaters for $30 to $50 and soft cashmere sweaters for $110. He visits other stores and finds that he can spend as little as $20 for an acrylic sweater or as much as $350 for a designer cashmere sweater. Kevin considers his sister's tastes and his own income and buys his sister one of the less expensive cotton sweaters.

Later, Kevin uses his computer to browse catalogs of mail-order stores. He's surprised to find a sweater very similar to the one he bought, but it's on sale for $5 less, shipping

▼ **Sweaters sell for different prices, depending on quality, style, and type of yarn.**

Graphing the Main Idea

Markets and Prices To build understanding of the concepts of **markets and prices,** have students use a double web graphic organizer like the one below to record the characteristics of a price-based system as compared to a centrally planned economy. Remind students that a double web graphic organizer can be used to compare and contrast information about two subjects.

Section Reading Support Transparencies A template and the answers for this graphic organizer can be found in Chapter 6, Section 3 of the Section Reading Support Transparency System.

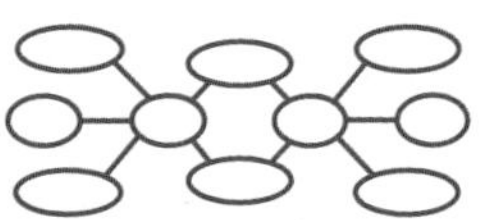

Section 3

The Role of Prices

Objectives You may wish to call students' attention to the objectives in the Section Preview. The objectives are reflected in the main headings of the section.

Bellringer Ask whether any students have been involved in purchases that involved barter, such as an exchange between friends or a market situation in another country. Ask volunteers to talk about their experiences. Point out that in this section they will examine the role of preset prices.

Vocabulary Builder Have students read the section to learn the meaning of each key term. Then have them add the terms and their definitions to their Economics Journals.

Lesson Plan

Teaching the Main Concepts 

1. Focus Remind students that although they may not always like the prices they see in stores, prices play an important role in the economy. Ask them to explain how they react to dramatic price changes.
2. Instruct Examine the advantages of prices as an incentive and as signals to both producers and consumers. Then discuss the flexibility of prices that allows for changing conditions and provides the wide variety of goods and services enjoyed by nations with free enterprise systems. Help students to analyze the efficiency of price-based systems and their self-correcting aspects.
3. Close/Reteach Display the terms *Price-Based Market System* and *Centrally Planned Economy.* Ask volunteers to list advantages under the "Price-Based" heading and corresponding disadvantages or problems under the "Centrally Planned" heading.

Guided Reading and Review
Unit 2 folder, p. 28 asks students to identify the main ideas of the section and to define or identify key terms.

Differentiated Instruction 

(Reteaching) Have students make a list of the roles that prices play in a price-based system. They will find many points in the section material, but they also may come up with some additional roles on their own. Encourage students to share their lists and to create a class master list.

Math Practice Activity
Math Practice folder, p. 5, "Comparing Prices," allows students to compare the price of products of different sizes to determine which is the best value.

Learning Styles Activity
Learning Styles Lesson Plans folder, p. 18 asks students to make determinations about the effect of prices on consumer choices.

included. Kevin decides to buy the sweater on-line with his credit card and return the sweater he bought at the mall.

Kevin's story, familiar to anyone who has shopped for a gift, demonstrates the importance of prices to the free market system. The simple process of buying a gift for a friend or relative would be much more complicated and inefficient without the price system.

The Advantages of Prices

Prices provide a language for buyers and sellers. Could you conceive of a marketplace without prices? Without prices as a standard measure of value, a seller would have to barter for goods by bidding shoes or apples to purchase a sweater. A sweater might be worth two pairs of shoes to one customer, but another customer might be willing to trade three pairs of shoes for the same sweater. The supplier would have no consistent and accurate way to measure demand for a product.

Price as an Incentive

Buyers and sellers alike look at prices to find information on a good's demand and supply. The law of supply and the law of demand describe how people and firms respond to a change in prices. In these cases, prices are a signal that tell a consumer or producer how to adjust. Prices communicate to both buyers and sellers whether goods are in short supply or readily available.

In the example of the popular doll discussed in Section 2, the increased demand for the doll told suppliers that people wanted more dolls, and soon! However, the signal that producers respond to is not simply the demand, but the high price consumers are willing to pay for the doll, well above the usual retail price. This higher price tells firms that people want more dolls, but also that the firms can earn more profit by producing more dolls, because they are in demand. Therefore, rising prices in a market will cause existing firms to produce more goods and will attract new firms to enter a market.

Prices as Signals

Think of prices as a traffic light. A relatively high price is a green light that tells producers that a specific good is in demand and that they should use their resources to produce more. New suppliers will also join the market. A low price, however, is a red light to producers that a good is being overproduced. In this case, low prices tell a supplier that he or she might earn higher profits by using existing resources to produce a different product.

For consumers, a low price is a green light to buy more of a good. A low price indicates that the good carries a low opportunity cost for the consumer, and offers a good buying opportunity. By the same token, a high price is a red light to stop and think carefully before buying.

Flexibility

Another important aspect of prices is that they are flexible. When a supply shift or a demand shift changes the equilibrium in a market, price and quantity supplied need to change to solve problems of too much or too little demand. In many markets, prices are much more flexible than output levels.

▼ **Drought, floods, or frost can kill crops and cause a supply shock.**

ECONOMY
U.S. Cuts Crop Forecasts Amid Drought

ECONOMY
North Carolina Hurricane Damages Rise
Losses Are Expected to Hit At Least $6 Billion Total; New Storm Is Awaited

Floyd Fallout

Harvest's Prospects Wilt in Heat Wave, Drought in East

Down on the Farm

Econ 101: Key Concepts Made Easy

Economic Systems Help students understand the role of prices as promoting both **flexibility** and **efficiency.** Students who have lived in the United States all their lives may not realize how wide a variety of goods is available in our free enterprise system, compared to a centrally planned economy, and how efficiently the free market works.

Ask a speaker who has lived in a country with a centrally planned economy to speak to the class about inefficiencies and other problems. Encourage students both to ask questions and to make comparisons.

Prices can be easily increased to solve a problem of excess demand, and they can be just as easily decreased to eliminate a problem of excess supply.

For example, a **supply shock** is a sudden shortage of a good, such as gasoline or wheat. A supply shock creates a problem of excess demand because suppliers can no longer meet the needs of consumers. The immediate problem is how to divide up the available supply among consumers.

What are the options? Increasing supply can be a time-consuming and difficult process. For example, wheat takes time to plant, grow, and harvest. **Rationing,** or dividing up goods and services using criteria other than price, is expensive and can take a long time to organize. Rationing is the basis of central planning, which you read about in Chapter 2.

Raising prices is the quickest way to resolve excess demand. A quick rise in prices will reduce quantity demanded to the same level as quantity supplied and avoid the problem of distribution. The people who have enough money and value the good most highly will pay the most for the good. These consumers will be the only consumers still in the market at the higher price, and the market will settle at a new equilibrium.

Price System Is "Free"

Unlike central planning, a distribution system based on prices costs nothing to administer. Central planning requires central planners who collect information on production and decide how resources are to be distributed. In the former Soviet Union, the government employed thousands of bureaucrats in an enormous agency called GOSPLAN to organize the economy. During World War II, the United States government set up the Office of Price Administration to prevent inflation and coordinate rationing of important goods.

On the other hand, free market pricing distributes goods through millions of decisions made daily by consumers and suppliers. Kevin, from the beginning of the section, looks at the prices of sweaters and decides which one to buy for his sister and which supplier to buy it from. A farmer reads the reports from the commodity exchanges and decides whether to grow corn instead of soybeans next year. Everyone is familiar with how prices work and knows how to use them. In short, prices help goods flow through the economy without a central plan.

A Wide Choice of Goods

One of the benefits of a market-based economy is the diversity of goods and services consumers can buy. Price gives suppliers a way to allow consumers to choose among similar products. Kevin could buy his sister an acrylic sweater for $20, a cotton sweater for $40, or a cashmere sweater for much more. Based on his income and his sister's tastes, Kevin decided on a cotton sweater at the lower end of the price range. The prices provided an easy way for Kevin to narrow his choices to a certain price range. Prices also allow producers to target the audience they want with the products that will sell best to that audience.

In a command economy, however, one organization decides what goods are produced and how much stores will charge for these goods. To limit their costs,

supply shock *a sudden shortage of a good*

rationing *a system of allocating scarce goods and services using criteria other than price*

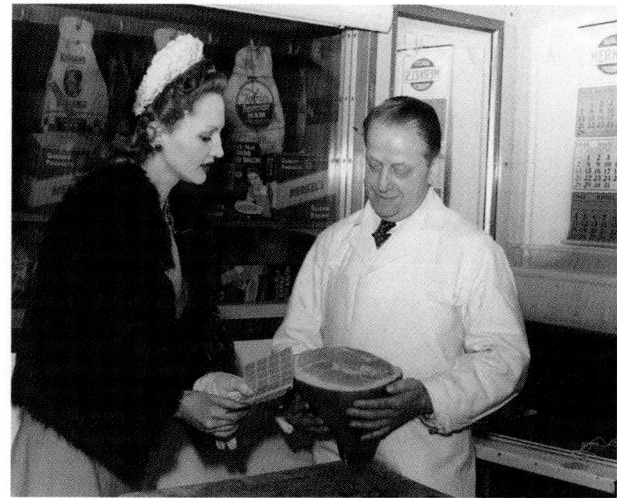

▼ During the World War II era, civilians could only buy a certain amount of meat and other goods each month. People needed both cash and ration points to buy.

Differentiated Instruction L3

Have students write a persuasive letter in support of a price-based market system. Suggest that they focus on the advantages of this system in terms of flexibility and a wider variety of goods. Encourage students to include as many real-life examples as they can.

Differentiated Instruction 

You may wish to have students add the following to their portfolios. Ask them to research the progress of China's transition from central planning to a free market economy. (Their history textbooks may have information on this subject, but they will need to check some news sources or almanacs for the most recent information.) Ask them to write a two- to three-page article on what they have learned. GT

Economics Assessment Rubric

Economics Assessment Rubrics folder, pp. 6–7 provides sample evaluation materials for a writing assignment.

Block Scheduling Strategies

Consider these suggestions to take advantage of extended class time:

- Extend the first activity on this page by organizing groups of four to six students to create persuasive "commercials" for a price-based market system. Encourage students to use drama, humor, and effective visual presentation to get their points across to their audience. Have all groups present their commercials in class.
- Have students conduct interviews with people who have experienced rationing situations, from water rationing during a drought to rationing of food and other goods during wartime. Ask students to create questions that examine the reasons for and the effects of rationing. Be sure that students distinguish between short-term rationing for a specific purpose and rationing as an economic policy.

Differentiated Instruction L3

Have students write ten statements that demonstrate the cause-effect relationship between a price-based system and the efficient use of resources. Some of these sentences may be paraphrases of section material. Others should be examples from students' own experience or from outside reading or observation. (Possible cause-effect statement: *Predictions of hot weather would lead to greater demand for air conditioners, which would lead to higher prices, which would lead to a greater supply of air conditioners to meet this demand.*)

Differentiated Instruction L4

Have students analyze the complexities of rationing. Ask them to think of a specific situation in which rationing has occurred or might occur. Their analyses should evaluate the potential costs of rationing, the difficulties involved in controlling people's behavior, and the possibility of fraud when people try to bypass the rationing system. To help students transfer information from one medium to another (written to oral), ask them to present their analyses in front of the class. If available, have the student use the Powerpoint or similar computer program in their presentation. GT

Transparency Resource Package
Economics Concepts, 6N: The Advantages of Prices

▲ **North Korea's Communist government has built identical apartment blocks for its citizens, who do not get to choose where to live.**

black market *a market in which goods are sold illegally*

central planners restrict production to a few varieties of each product. As a result, consumers in the former Communist states of Eastern Europe and the Soviet Union had far fewer choices of goods than consumers in Western Europe and the United States. You may ask why Communist governments used a command economic system. The answer is, in part, that they hoped to distribute wealth evenly throughout their society. As a result, the government of the Soviet Union built whole neighborhoods of identical apartment blocks and supermarkets with names such as "Supermarket No. 3."

Rationing and Shortages

Although goods in the Soviet Union were inexpensive, consumers could not always find them. When they did, they often had to wait hours for eggs or soap, years for apartments or telephones. The United States experienced similar problems, although far less severe, when the government instituted temporary price controls during World War II.

Although rationing in the United States was only a short-term hardship, like rationing in the Soviet Union it was expensive and left many consumers unhappy. The needs of the U.S. armed forces for food, metal, and rubber during World War II created tremendous shortages at home, and the government controlled the distribution of food and consumer goods. Choices were limited, and consumers felt, rightly or wrongly, that some people fared better than others. However, rationing was chosen because a price-based system might have put food and housing out of the reach of some Americans, and the government wanted to guarantee every civilian a minimum standard of living in wartime.

The Black Market

Despite the ration system, the federal government was unable to control the supply of all goods passing through the economy. A butcher could sell a steak without asking for ration points, or a landlord might be willing to rent an apartment at the rate fixed by the government only if the renter threw in a cash "bonus" or an extra two months' rent as a "deposit."

When people conduct business without regard for government controls on price or quantity, they are said to do business on the **black market**. Black markets allow consumers to pay more so they can buy a good when rationing makes it otherwise unavailable. Although black markets are a nearly inevitable consequence of rationing, such trade is illegal and strongly discouraged by governments.

Efficient Resource Allocation

All of the advantages of a free market allow prices to allocate resources efficiently. Efficient resource allocation means that economic resources—land, labor, and capital—will be used for their most valuable purposes. A market system, with its freely changing prices, ensures that resources go to the uses that consumers value most highly. A price-based system also ensures that resource use will adjust to the changing demands of consumers.

Preparing for Standardized Tests

Have students read the section titled "Efficient Resource Allocation" and then answer the question below.

According to the text, what is one reason resources are allocated efficiently in a market system?

A Land, labor, and capital are often used in a wasteful way.
B Central control manages resource allocation.
C Resources are sold to the lowest bidder.
(D) Changing prices ensure that resources are used in ways most highly valued by consumers.

These changes take place without any central control, because the people who own resources—landowners, workers who sell their labor, and people who provide capital to firms—seek the largest possible returns. How do people earn the largest returns? By selling their resources to the highest bidder. The highest bidder will be that firm that produces goods that are in the highest demand. Therefore, the resources will flow to the uses that are most highly valued by consumers. This flow is the most efficient way to use our society's scarce resources.

Global Connections

Rationing and Prices Cuba has two different systems for distributing goods. Some goods are rationed, while many others are sold in stores at different prices. The difference between the two systems is that the price-based system uses not Cuba's currency, the peso, but the United States dollar. Many Cubans earn dollars by working in tourism or as gifts from family members outside the country. Cubans with dollars can buy a variety of food and clothing at stores and restaurants that only accept dollars. Cubans who are paid in pesos must get their food through the state's rationing system. Prices are very low, but food is rationed, and the government provides each person with a limited amount of grain, coffee, salt, and other basic foods.

Prices and the Profit Incentive

Suppose that scientists predicted extremely hot weather for the coming summer. In most parts of the country, consumers would buy up air conditioners and fans, to prepare for the heat. Power companies would buy reserves of oil and natural gas to supply these appliances with enough power. Since demand would exceed supply, consumers would bid up the price of fans, and power plants would bid up the price of fuel. Suppliers would recognize the possibility for profit in the higher prices charged for these goods, and they would produce more fans and air conditioners. Oil and natural gas fields would hire workers to pump more fuel for power plants. Eventually, more fans, air conditioners, and fuel would move into the market. The potential heat wave would have created a need for certain goods, and the rise in prices would have given producers an incentive to meet this need.

As we previously noted, efficient resource allocation occurs naturally in a market system as long as the system works reasonably well. Landowners tend to use their scarce property in the most profitable manner. Workers usually move toward high-paying jobs, and capital will be invested in the firms that pay the highest returns.

The Wealth of Nations

Adam Smith made this point in his famous book *The Wealth of Nations,* published in 1776. Smith explained that it was not because of charity that the baker and the butcher provided people with their food. Rather, they provide people with bread and meat because prices are such that they

▼ The People's Republic of China is moving away from a command economy and rationing to a more market-based economy.

Econ 101: Key Concepts Made Easy

Economic Systems Some students might have difficulty understanding why **free enterprise** works so effectively and **central planning** does not. This section provides many examples to show why this is true. However, students may be interested in considering the possibility that free enterprise, with its frank understanding of what motivates people best (their self-interest), is a much more practical system. Central planning, onthe other hand, assumes that individuals will continue to work for the good of the group, whether or not the individual prospers. Hold a class discussion on what assumptions lie behind the two systems and how these assumptions work to each system's advantage or disadvantage.

Differentiated Instruction 

Organize groups of two to three students. Within groups have each member illustrate one concept from the section, such as rationing, the black market, or spillover costs. Then have individuals explain their concepts to the other group members. LPR

Differentiated Instruction 

Ask students to study the photos in this section and read the captions. Then have them use the photos to write sentences that explain the section's main ideas. ELL

Economic Detective Activity
Unit 2 folder, p. 32, "Hy Feshn Neckties," provides an additional application of chapter concepts.

GTE Guide to the Essentials
Chapter 6, Section 3, p. 26 provides support for students who need additional review of the section content. Spanish support is available in the Spanish edition of the guide on p. 26.

Quiz Unit 2 folder, p. 29 includes questions to check students' understanding of Section 3 content.

Presentation Pro CD-ROM
Quiz provides multiple-choice questions to check students' understanding of Section 3 content.

Answers to . . .

Section 3 Assessment

1. Supply shock will cause the market to move into a brief disequilibrium and will usually cause an increase in the price of the good thus decreasing the quantity demanded.
2. Rationing distributes scarce goods and services according to criteria other than price, so it is the exact opposite of a price-based economy.
3. (1) Price-based systems allow for flexibility in the marketplace between consumers and suppliers. (2) Price-based systems allow for a larger selection of goods and services. (3) Command economies are very inefficient at delivering consumer goods to the marketplace despite their lower prices.
4. Students' examples should demonstrate understanding of chapter concepts.
5. (a) Answers will vary depending on student participation in the activity. (b) Students may say that they are worth more or are in greater demand. (c) Students should suggest that bids would be lower.
6. Adam Smith would probably be against any form of rationing because it goes against his theory of the "invisible hand" guiding the market, and it involves aspects of central planning.

▲ The price of water affects how efficiently it is used. When water is provided to farmers at a higher price, they have an incentive to irrigate more efficiently.

will profit from doing so. In other words, businesses prosper by finding out what people want, and then providing it. This has proved to be a more efficient system than any other that has been tried in the modern era.

Market Problems

spillover costs *costs of production that affect people who have no control over how much of a good is produced*

There are some exceptions to the general idea that markets lead to an efficient allocation of resources. The first problem, imperfect competition, can affect prices, and higher prices can affect consumer decisions. If only a few firms are selling a product, there might not be enough competition among sellers to lower the market price down to the cost of production. When only one producer sells a good, this producer will usually charge a higher price than we would see in a market with several competitive businesses. In the following chapter, you will read more about how markets behave under conditions of imperfect competition.

A second problem can involve **spillover costs,** also known as externalities, that include costs of production, such as air and water pollution, that "spill over" onto people who have no control over how much of a good is produced. Since producers do not have to pay spillover costs, their total costs seem artificially low, and they will produce more than the equilibrium quantity of the good. The extra costs will be paid by consumers.

Imperfect information is a third problem that can prevent a market from operating smoothly. If buyers and sellers do not have enough information to make informed choices about a product, they may not make the choice that is best for them.

Section 3 Assessment

Progress Monitoring *Online*
For: Self-quiz with vocabulary practice
Web Code: mna-2067

Key Terms and Main Ideas

1. How does a **supply shock** affect equilibrium price and quantity?
2. How is **rationing** different from a price-based market system?

Applying Economic Concepts

3. ***Decision Making*** List three reasons why a price-based system works more efficiently than central planning.
4. ***Critical Thinking*** Give two examples of situations in which prices gave you an incentive to purchase or not purchase a good or service.
5. ***Try This*** Distribute $50 in play money to each student in your class. Then, ask students to bid for items from the following basket of goods and services: 10 pairs of movie tickets, 20 fine restaurant dinners, 40 bagels, 5 pairs of running shoes, and 30 hours of dog walking. **(a)** What prices were bid for these goods? **(b)** Why do you think some goods received higher bids than others? **(c)** What do you think would happen to the bids if the number of items for sale doubled?
6. ***Critical Thinking*** What do you think Adam Smith would think of rationing? Explain.

For: Critical Thinking Activity
Visit: PHSchool.com
Web Code: mnd-2063

Progress Monitoring *Online*
For additional assessment, have students access Progress Monitoring Online at **Web Code:** mna-2067

Go Online PHSchool.com Typing in the Web Code when prompted will bring students directly to detailed instructions for this activity.

Reviewing Main Ideas

9. What factors can lead to disequilibrium? Describe these factors in your own words.
10. What role does the government play in determining some prices?
11. What problem can a price floor cause?
12. How do prices act as a "language" in the free market?
13. Turn to Figure 6.1 on page 126. Explain how to interpret the supply and demand graph (left), using the supply and demand schedule (right).

Critical Thinking

14. **Recognizing Cause and Effect** Why have some cities and towns passed rent control laws? How do these laws affect price equilibrium? What happens when these laws are repealed?
15. **Drawing Inferences** How do computers lower search costs for producers and consumers? What effect does this have on price equilibrium?
16. **Synthesizing Information** How do prices in the free market lead to efficient resource allocation? Describe an example from your experience.

Problem-Solving Activity

17. Suppose that a recent snowstorm has caused a supply shock in the market for sugar in the United States. How would you attempt to solve the problems that follow the storm? What actions are available to both consumers and producers?

Skills for Life

Determining Cause and Effect Review the steps shown on page 132; then answer the following questions using the statements below.

18. Which of the statements describe cause-effect relationships?
19. Identify three phrases used to identify the cause of a cause-effect relationship in these statements.
20. Identify three terms used to identify the effect of a cause-effect relationship in these statements.
21. Which statement includes more than one cause-effect relationship?
22. Read statement (f). Create a flowchart describing the cause-effect relationships shown.

STATEMENTS

a) Oranges are grown mainly in the South and West, especially Florida and California.

b) The price of oranges in the United States rose this year because of a small harvest.

c) Some people enjoy orange juice with breakfast, while others like to drink it after exercise.

d) Due to the early frost in much of the South, this year's orange crop was poor.

e) Overall orange juice production was down this year, and several national brands lost money. However, the American dairy industry saw an increase in milk sales. Americans did not drink as much orange juice as they had in recent years.

f) This year's disastrous orange crop caused many brands to raise their prices. Because of the high prices, many consumers switched to other juices. Several national brands reduced orange juice production and researched new products that would meet this alternative demand.

Economics Journal

Essay Writing Compare your list of minimum wages for chores with the lists of other students. How do they compare? Use your classroom data to create four supply curves, one for each task. How might the minimum wage affect the supply of labor for these chores? Draw a line representing the current minimum wage in your city or state as a price floor.

Progress Monitoring *Online*

For: Chapter 6 Self-Test **Visit:** PHSchool.com
Web Code: mna-2061

As a final review, take the Economics Chapter 6 Self-Test and receive immediate feedback on your answers. The test consists of 20 multiple-choice questions designed to test your understanding of the chapter content.

Problem-Solving Activity

17. Solutions to solve the problem caused by the storm will vary, but students should explain their reasonings. Students might suggest voluntary consumer limitation of sugar consumption, rationing, or price hikes by producers.

Skills for Life

18. b, d, f
19. b: because of, d: due to, f: caused to raise, because of
20. b: price rose, d: crop was poor, f: raise prices, switched to other juices
21. f
22. Students should create flowcharts that accurately reflect the particular cause-effect relationships listed in the statements.

Additional support materials and activities for Chapter 6 of *Economics: Principles in Action* can be found in the Social Studies area of **PHSchool.com.**

Economics Journal

Students' responses will vary. Students should prepare accurate supply curves and equilibrium wages based on the data gathered.

Review and Assessment

Vocabulary Practice Unit 2 folder, p. 31 uses a fill-in-the-blanks word puzzle to reinforce understanding of key terms.

GTE **Guide to the Essentials** Chapter 6 Test, p. 27

Test Bank CD-ROM Chapter 6 Test

Go Online PHSchool.com Students may use the Chapter 6 Self-Test on **PHSchool.com** to prepare for the Chapter Test.

Economics **Simulation**

Objectives Upon completion of this simulation, students should be able to:
- explain how a free market reaches a state of equilibrium;
- describe the effect of supply and demand on prices.

Bellringer Display the word *equilibrium.* Ask students for definitions of the term and for examples from everyday life or from other fields, such as science. Lead students to understand that *equilibrium* simply means "balance."

1. Focus Give students this example to start them thinking about equilibrium: There are 10 red wagons for sale and 10 children who want them. Point out that in this situation demand is equal to supply. Ask students what they think would happen to the price if, suddenly, 50 children wanted red wagons but there were still only 10 wagons. *(The price will rise and demand will decrease until an equilibrium point is reached.)*

2. Instruct Have students prepare for and conduct the simulation, using the procedures noted in the text.

3. Close/Reteach Have students complete the transaction chart. After they have presented their conclusions, discuss answers to the first three analysis questions as a class. Assign the Predicting Consequences question as a follow-up.

Economic Simulation
Economic Simulations folder, pp. 9–14, "Monopolies: Is the Law Being Broken?" provides an additional simulation on a unit topic.

Economics Simulation Market Equilibrium

The supply of a good (or service) and the demand for it interact in the market. If the quantity supplied or demanded goes up or down, the price of that good or service will also be affected. Similarly, changes in supply or demand influence the quantity produced. At a certain point, the quantity that people want is equal to the quantity available, and the price stabilizes. This situation is called *market equilibrium.*

Materials
20 slips of paper (one color)
20 slips of paper (contrasting color)
2 small boxes
notebook paper

Preparing the Simulation

How does the market reach a state of equilibrium? In this simulation, you and your peers will act as apple producers and consumers. You will meet in the market to agree on an exchange of apples at a certain price. You'll see how both producers and consumers change their requirements in order to reach an agreement.

Step 1: Your class will be divided into two equal groups, Producers and Consumers.

Step 2: The Consumers group will prepare 20 slips of colored paper that represent the prices a Consumer is willing to pay for a bushel of apples. Consumers will number the first 10 slips from $4 to $40 by fours ($4, $8, and so on), and repeat for the second 10 slips. Meanwhile, the Producers group will prepare 20 slips of paper in a contrasting color that represent the cost of producing a bushel of apples. Producers will number the first 10 slips from $5 to $50 by fives ($5, $10, and so on), and repeat for the second 10 slips.

Step 3: Put the Consumer slips into a box. Each person in the Consumer group should draw a slip. If you are a Consumer, the amount on the slip is the maximum price you are willing to pay for a bushel of apples.

Step 4: Put the Producer slips into a box. Each person in the Producer group should draw a slip from the box. If you are a Producer, the amount on the slip is your cost of producing a bushel of apples.

▲ **The profit from the sale of these apples is the difference between the sale price and the cost to produce the apples.**

Conducting the Simulation

There will be three trading periods. Your goal is to make the best deal you can—to buy below your maximum price if you are a Consumer, and to sell for more than your cost if you are a Producer.

If you are a Consumer, your score will be the difference between the price you are willing to pay for apples and the price you actually pay. For example, if the price on your slip is $50, and you buy apples for $30, your score is $20. If you are an apple Producer, your score is your profit—the difference

Trading Period 1

Producers and Consumers will meet in a trading area and try to make deals. Each person can buy or sell one bushel of apples in each period. When you reach an agreement, report the price and your own score to the teacher. The trading period will end when no more pairs of Producers and Consumers can make a deal.

Trading Period 2

Negotiate as in Trading Period 1. You have another chance to save money (Consumers) or increase your profits (Producers). Again, report your deals to your teacher.

Trading Period 3

Before this trading period begins, one third of the Producers will move into the Consumer group. (The costs on their slips of paper now become the maximum prices they are willing to pay.) Then make trades as in the first two periods. This trading period will end when no more pairs of Producers and Consumers can make a deal. Take note of any price differences produced by an increase in the number of Consumers and a decrease in the number of Producers. Record your transaction with your teacher.

between your cost of producing the apples and the price at which you can sell them.

You do not have to buy or sell apples in any trading period. If you do not, however, your score for that round will be $0. Your teacher will keep a record of all the transactions made. You should also keep a record of your own scores. The final score is the sum of all your savings (Consumers) or profits (Producers).

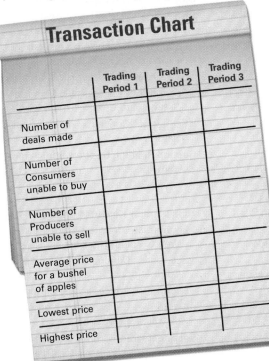

Transaction Chart

	Trading Period 1	Trading Period 2	Trading Period 3
Number of deals made			
Number of Consumers unable to buy			
Number of Producers unable to sell			
Average price for a bushel of apples			
Lowest price			
Highest price			

Simulation Analysis

On a sheet of notebook paper, create a transaction chart like the one on this page. As a class, complete the transaction chart using information that you reported to your teacher. Then discuss the following questions as a group.

1. In Trading Periods 1 and 2, when was it a good idea for a Consumer not to buy apples?
2. When might a Producer choose not to sell his or her apples?
3. What was the effect of increasing the total number of Consumers in Trading Period 3? What would happen to the apple market if the number of Producers increased instead?
4. **Predicting Consequences** What would happen in this market if all the Producers got together and agreed on one price for apples?

Meeting NCEE Standards

Use the following benchmark activity from the **Voluntary National Content Standards in Economics** to evaluate student understanding of Standard 7.

Explain why there is often a late-season surplus of tickets available for the home contests of a baseball team that loses most of its games.

Background

Global Connections

The Tulip Mania, or Tulip Craze, is a historical example of the free market forces of supply and demand—as well as of their perils. Tulips were introduced into Europe from Turkey in the mid-1500s. Over time the demand for these flowers began to exceed the supply, and prices started to rise. Prices for particularly rare bulbs became astronomical. In the early 1600s just one bulb was accepted as a dowry for a bride, and once an entire brewery was given in exchange for an especially rare bulb. In Holland the mania reached its peak in the 1630s. Homes and even estates were mortgaged to buy bulbs, which were resold at constantly rising prices.

Eventually the market for tulips crashed, and prices fell almost overnight. Many people were left bankrupt and debt-ridden, having spent all their savings and borrowed large sums to trade in tulips.

Answers to . . .

1. It was a good idea not to buy apples when the costs to the Producers were higher than the maximum price.
2. A Producer might choose not to sell if the maximum price of apples available to Consumers was lower than the cost.
3. Increasing the number of consumers increased the asking price, thus giving the Producers greater profits. Increasing the number of Producers would have lowered the asking price, thus reducing Producers' profits.
4. Consumers would most likely have to pay higher prices or not buy apples.

Interdisciplinary Connections: Science

Equilibrium in the Lab In physics equilibrium is said to be achieved when all the forces acting on an object cancel each other out, resulting in the object remaining stationary.

Making the Connection Have students research the concept of equilibrium in science (chemistry as well as physics) and then brainstorm comparisons to market equilibrium. Students may, for example, chart the forces involved in the market for a certain good (primarily demand, supply, and price) and show how a market at equilibrium can be thrown off by an increase or a decrease in any factor. Finally, ask students to give their opinions on the differences between equilibrium in science and in economics. Ask whether students think that people's economic choices are as predictable as the effects of natural forces on an object.

Chapter 7 Market Structures

For more pacing suggestions, see the Economics Pacing Guide in the Program Overview of the Teaching Resources.

Section Objectives	Print and Technology Resources	
1 Perfect Competition *(pp. 151–154)* **Objectives** 1. Describe the four conditions that are in place in a perfectly competitive market. 2. List two common barriers that prevent firms from entering a market. 3. Describe prices and output in a perfectly competitive market.	• **Lesson Planner** Section 1 Lesson Plan, p. 34 • **Lesson Plans folder** Section 1 Lesson Plan, p. 27 • **Unit 2 folder** Guided Reading and Review, p. 35 Economic Skills, p. 43 Section 1 Quiz, p. 36 • **Presentation Pro CD-ROM** Section 1	• **Transparency Resource Package** Economics Organizers, G7: Tree Map Graphic Organizer Economics Concepts, 7A: Perfect Competition Economics Concepts, 7B: Barriers to Entry • **Section Reading Support Transparency System** • **Social Studies Skills Tutor CD-ROM**
2 Monopoly *(pp. 156–164)* **Objectives** 1. Describe characteristics and give examples of monopoly. 2. Describe how monopolies are formed, including government monopolies. 3. Explain how a firm with a monopoly sets output and price, and why companies practice price discrimination.	• **Lesson Planner** Section 2 Lesson Plan, p. 35 • **Lesson Plans folder** Section 2 Lesson Plan, p. 28 • **Economics Assessment Rubrics folder** Position Paper, pp. 22–23 • **Unit 2 folder** Guided Reading and Review, p. 37 Careers in Economics, Regional Sales Manager, p. 46 Economic Cartoon, p. 47 Section 2 Quiz, p. 38 • **Math Practice folder** Maximizing Profit, p. 6	• **Presentation Pro CD-ROM** Section 2 • **Simulations and Data Graphing CD-ROM** Data Graphing Tools • **Transparency Resource Package** Economics Organizers, G5: Web Graphic Organizer Economics Concepts, 7C: Monopoly Economics Concepts, 7D: Monopoly Setting Output Economics Concepts, 7E: Monopoly Setting Price • **Section Reading Support Transparency System**
3 Monopolistic Competition and Oligopoly *(pp. 166–171)* **Objectives** 1. Describe characteristics and give examples of monopolistic competition. 2. Explain how firms compete without lowering prices. 3. Understand how firms in a monopolistically competitive market set output. 4. Describe characteristics and give examples of oligopoly.	• **Lesson Planner** Section 3 Lesson Plan, p. 36 • **Learning Styles Lesson Plans folder** Section 3 Lesson Plan, p. 19 • **Lesson Plans folder** Section 3 Lesson Plan, p. 29 • **Unit 2 folder** Guided Reading and Review, p. 39 Section 3 Quiz, p. 40 • **Source Articles folder** A Healthy Marketplace, pp. 21–23 • **Presentation Pro CD-ROM** Section 3	• **Transparency Resource Package** Economics Organizers, G6: Double Web Graphic Organizer Economics Concepts, 7F: Monopolistic Competition Economics Concepts, 7G: Oligopoly Economics Concepts, 7H: Comparison of Market Structures • **Section Reading Support Transparency System**
4 Regulation and Deregulation *(pp. 172–176)* **Objectives** 1. Understand how firms use market power. 2. List three market practices that the government regulates or bans to protect competition. 3. Define deregulation, and list its effects on several industries.	• **Lesson Planner** Section 4 Lesson Plan, p. 37 • **Learning Styles Lesson Plans folder** Section 4 Lesson Plan, p. 20 • **Lesson Plans folder** Section 4 Lesson Plan, p. 30 • **Economics Assessment Rubrics folder** Participating in Debates, pp. 14–15 • **Unit 2 folder** Guided Reading and Review, p. 41 Vocabulary Practice, p. 44 Economic Detective, p. 45 Section 3 Quiz, p. 42	• **Case Studies in Free Enterprise folder** Joan Robinson, pp. 14–15 • **Source Articles folder** Playing Oligopoly, pp. 21–23 • **Presentation Pro CD-ROM** Section 4 • **Transparency Resource Package** Economics Organizers, G5: Web Graphic Organizer Economics Concepts, 7I: Government Regulatory Agencies • **Section Reading Support Transparency System**

Differentiated Instruction

Utilizing Images L1 L2

It cannot be stressed enough how important images can be in a social studies classroom. Photographs, political cartoons, paintings, and artifacts can help students comprehend concepts addressed in the text. For example, a political cartoon can visually represent two candidates' stances on an issue and a painting can reveal the context of an era through its depiction of clothing.

Visuals can also help students compare and contrast concepts. For example, an image of shelves full of tomatoes or oranges to illustrate perfect competition, contrasted with a supermarket aisle full of breakfast cereals or soft drinks, can show the different range of choices offered in different market structures. Overall, visuals can make an individual, event, or time period "come alive" by giving students concrete examples of what they are studying. As you come across each visual, ask students to describe what they are seeing and ask them to make connections to the text.

Creating a Dialogue L2

In addition to learning social studies content, English Language Learners face the more daunting challenge of developing proficiency in English. To encourage students to use both written and spoken English and apply core content, have them create a dialogue. Follow these steps:

1. Divide students into groups and assign each group a scenario.

2. List key terms and high-use words on the board that must be included in the dialogue.

3. Require that every student in the group have a speaking role.

4. Have students submit a written copy of the script as part of the assessment on this activity.

5. Ask each group to perform their dialogues for the class to enhance the English language listening skills of students in the audience.

Visit the Social Studies area of the Prentice Hall Web site. There you can find additional links to enrich chapter content for *Economics: Principles in Action* as well as a self-test for students. Be sure to check out this month's **eTeach** online discussion with a Master Economics Teacher.

Web Code: mnf-2071

Running Out of Time?

- Use the **Presentation Pro CD-ROM** to create an outline for this chapter.
- Use the Chapter Summary in the **Chapter 7 Assessment,** p. 178.
- Use the Section Summaries for Chapter 7, from **Guide to the Essentials of Economics (English and Spanish).**

THE WALL STREET JOURNAL. CLASSROOM EDITION

Prentice Hall brings into the classroom the authoritative content of *The Wall Street Journal Classroom Edition.* See the Source Articles, Debating Current Issues, and You and Your Money folders in the **Teaching Resources.** Also, see Economics Video Library, "Down on the Farm."

Assessment Resources

Chapter Assessment

Teaching Resources Unit 2, Chapter 7
- Section Quizzes, pp. 36, 38, 40, 42

Exam *View*® Test Bank CD-ROM Chapter 7
Economics Assessment Rubrics
Chapter 7 Self-Test, **Web Code:** mna-2071

Reading and Skills Evaluation

Progress Monitoring Assessments
- Screening Test
- Diagnostic Test of Social Studies Skills

Standardized Test Preparation

Test Prep Workbook
Test-Taking Strategies With Transparencies

Differentiated Instruction Key

L1 Special Needs	LPR Less Proficient Readers
L2 Basic to Average	AR Advanced Readers
L3 All Students	SN Special Needs Students
L4 Average to Advanced	GT Gifted and Talented
	ELL English Language Learner

Chapter 7

Market Structures

Introducing the Chapter

In this chapter students will learn the characteristics of the four types of market structures: perfect competition, monopoly, monopolistic competition, and oligopoly. They will also learn how the government intervenes in the market to protect competition.

Go Online
PHSchool.com

For additional links for *Economics: Principles in Action* provided by Prentice Hall and *The Wall Street Journal Classroom Edition,* visit the Social Studies area. Be sure to check out this month's **eTeach** online discussion with a Master Teacher.

Beyond the Lecture

You may cover the concepts in Chapter 7 in an activity-based style by using the following materials:

- **Technology Resources** appropriate for use with this chapter are noted on pp. 152, 153, 154, 157, 161, 162, 164, 167, 170, 171, 173, 176, and 179.
- **Presentation Pro CD-ROM** with animated graphs gives you an alternative method for organizing and delivering chapter content.
- **Activities** designed to meet the needs of students of mixed abilities and learning styles are noted throughout the chapter in the side columns.
- **Learning Styles Lesson Plans** provide alternate lessons for diverse learning styles. See pp. 19–20 of the Learning Styles Lesson Plans folder located in the Teaching

Economics Journal

Instruct students to write their responses to the question in their Economics Journals. Students may include completed journal entries in an Economics Portfolio.

Chapter 7 Market Structures

If a single firm produced all computer software, life might be easier because all software would be compatible. So why has the government tried to prevent one company from dominating the software market? When there are only one or two firms in a market, consumers have fewer choices, and prices are likely to be higher.

In this chapter you will read about four different types of markets, or market structures. The four structures differ mainly in the number of firms that compete within them.

Economics Journal

Write down the names of three major companies: one with very little competition, one with one or two important competitors, and one with many competitors. Which situation do you think describes most markets?

Go Online
PHSchool.com

For: Current Data
Visit: PHSchool.com
Web Code: mng-2071

National Council on Economic Education

The following Voluntary National Content Standards in Economics are addressed in this chapter:

★ **Standard 9** Students will understand that: Competition among sellers lowers costs and prices, and encourages producers to produce more of what consumers are willing and able to buy. Competition among buyers increases prices and allocates goods and services to those people who are willing and able to pay the most for them.

For more information about the standards, contact the National Council on Economic Education

1140 Avenue of the Americas
New York, NY 10036
1-800-338-1192

Section 1 Perfect Competition

Preview

Objectives

After studying this section you will be able to:

1. **Describe** the four conditions that are in place in a perfectly competitive market.
2. **List** two common barriers that prevent firms from entering a market.
3. **Describe** prices and output in a perfectly competitive market.

Section Focus

Perfect competition exists when a market has many buyers and sellers of the same good. Few markets are perfectly competitive because barriers keep companies from entering or leaving the market easily.

Key Terms

perfect competition
commodity
barrier to entry
imperfect competition
start-up costs

The simplest market structure is known as **perfect competition.** It is also called pure competition. A perfectly competitive market is one with a large number of firms all producing essentially the same product. Pure competition assumes that the market is in equilibrium and that all firms sell the same product for the same price. However, each firm produces so little of the product compared to the total supply that no single firm can hope to influence prices. The only decision such producers can make is how much to produce, given their production costs and the market price.

perfect competition *a market structure in which a large number of firms all produce the same product*

Four Conditions for Perfect Competition

While very few industries meet all of the conditions for perfect competition, some come close. Examples include the markets for many farm products and the stocks traded on the New York Stock Exchange. Both of these examples fulfill four strict requirements for a perfectly competitive market:

1. Many buyers and sellers participate in the market.
2. Sellers offer identical products.
3. Buyers and sellers are well informed about products.
4. Sellers are able to enter and exit the market freely.

Many Buyers and Sellers

Perfectly competitive markets require many participants on both the buying and the selling sides. No individual can be powerful enough to buy or sell enough goods to influence the total market quantity or the market price. Everyone in the market must accept the market price as given.

As we saw in Chapter 6, supply and demand interact to determine both price and output. If a market has many independent buyers and sellers, it is not very likely that large enough groups of either buyers or sellers will work together to bargain for better prices. Instead, the market determines price without any influence from individual suppliers or consumers.

▼ **The market for tomatoes comes close to perfect competition because a large number of firms sell tomatoes, and one tomato is very much like another.**

Graphing the Main Idea

Competition To build understanding of the concept of **competition,** have students use a tree map graphic organizer like the one below to record details about the factors needed to meet the conditions for perfect competition. Remind students that a tree map shows a main topic, main ideas, and supporting details.

Section Reading Support Transparencies A template and the answers for this graphic organizer can be found in Chapter 7, Section 1 of the Section Reading Support Transparency System.

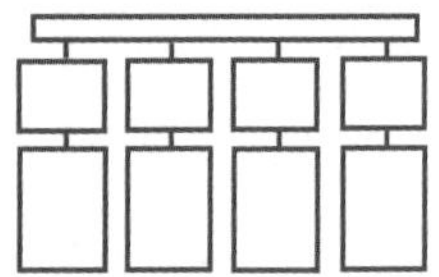

Section 1

Perfect Competition

Objectives You may wish to call students' attention to the objectives in the Section Preview. The objectives are reflected in the main headings of the section.

Bellringer Display the word *competition.* Ask students to describe how they face competition in their daily lives. Then ask them how competition applies to economics. Explain that in this section they will learn about competition in business and about the four conditions that must be met for perfect competition to exist in the market.

Vocabulary Builder Have students create index flash cards for the five key terms. Remind them to put a term on one side of each card and the term's definition on the other.

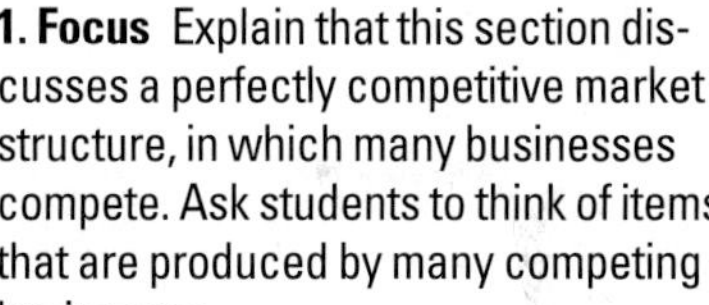

Lesson Plan

Teaching the Main Concepts (L3)

1. Focus Explain that this section discusses a perfectly competitive market structure, in which many businesses compete. Ask students to think of items that are produced by many competing businesses.

2. Instruct Stress to students that barriers to entry do not exist in a perfectly competitive market. Have students identify barriers to entry that are not described in the section. Remind students that a perfectly competitive market fulfills the four requirements listed in the text.

3. Close/Reteach Have students choose a product that they use regularly. Then ask them to try to determine how close the industry that manufactures their product comes to a perfectly competitive market. Have students create charts that display their findings.

Guided Reading and Review Unit 2 folder, p. 35 asks students to identify the main ideas of the section and to define or identify key terms.

Differentiated Instruction 

Display a basic outline of the section, using the section headings. Explain to students that using headings is a helpful outlining strategy for many informational texts. Organize students into three groups, and have each group read a different part of the section. Ask members of each group to fill in their part of the outline. Then have students copy the entire outline on a piece of paper. ELL

Differentiated Instruction 

Have students create a poster about perfect competition. Instruct them first to choose a market that comes close to perfect competition. The poster should list and illustrate the four conditions for perfect competition with drawings, cartoons, or pictures from newspapers or magazines. Display the posters in the classroom.

Transparency Resource Package
Economics Concepts, 7A: Perfect Competition

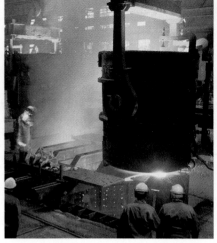

▶ **A pushcart business is easy and inexpensive to begin, while a steel mill requires a large building and costly machinery.**

commodity *a product that is the same no matter who produces it, such as petroleum, notebook paper, or milk*

Identical Products

In a perfectly competitive market, there are no differences between the products sold by different suppliers. This is the second condition for perfect competition. If a rancher needs to buy corn to feed his cattle, he will not care which farmer grew the corn, as long as every farm is willing to deliver the corn he needs for the same price. If an investor buys a share of a company's stock, she will not care which particular share she is buying.

A product that is considered the same regardless of who makes or sells it is called a **commodity.** Examples of commodities include low-grade gasoline, notebook paper, and milk. Identical products are key to perfect competition for one reason: the buyer will not pay extra for one particular company's goods. The buyer will always choose the supplier with the lowest price.

Informed Buyers and Sellers

The third condition for a perfectly competitive market is that buyers and sellers know enough about the market to find the best deal they can get. Under conditions of perfect competition, the market provides the buyer with full information about the features of the product and its price. For the market to work effectively, both buyers and sellers have clear incentives to gather as much information as possible.

In most markets, a buyer's willingness to find information about prices and availability represents a trade-off. The time spent gathering information must be worth the amount of money that will be saved. For example, most buyers would not search the Internet or visit a dozen convenience stores to save five cents on a pack of chewing gum.

Free Market Entry and Exit

The final condition of perfectly competitive markets is that firms must be able to enter them when they can make money and leave them when they can't earn enough to stay in business. For example, when the first pioneering companies began earning a lot of money selling frozen dinners, several competitors jumped into the market with

Global Connection

Informed Buyers The French government ensures that travelers will have complete information about the market for hotel rooms and restaurant meals. While hotels in the United States usually advertise only special discounts, every hotel in France must post in its lobby a list of rates for single and double rooms, with and without a sink, shower, or full bathroom. Restaurants must go further and post a long list of prices for dozens of items, leaving spaces blank if some common items are not on the menu.

Econ 101: Key Concepts Made Easy

Competition A key concept in this section is **perfect competition.** A perfectly competitive market has a very large number of firms, each producing identical products, and each accepting the market price as given. Help students understand that an example of a perfectly competitive market is the market created by stocks traded on the New York Stock Exchange. There are a large number of participants. Each acts as a tiny part of the market. No one participant is powerful enough to influence the total market quantity or the price of goods.

their own products. Later, the firms withdrew from the market those dinners that consumers didn't buy.

Studies show that markets with more firms, and thus more competition, have lower prices. When one firm can keep others out of the market, it can sell its product at a higher price.

Barriers to Entry

Factors that make it difficult for new firms to enter a market are called **barriers to entry.** Barriers to entry can lead to **imperfect competition.** Common barriers to entry include start-up costs and technology.

Start-Up Costs

Entrepreneurs need to invest money in a new firm long before they can start earning income. Before a new sandwich shop can open, the owner needs to rent a store, buy a refrigerator, freezer, and oven, and print menus. The expenses that a new business must pay before the first product reaches the customer are called **start-up costs.**

When the start-up costs in a market are high, entrepreneurs are less likely to enter that market. As a result, markets that involve high start-up costs are less likely to be perfectly competitive markets. For example, the costs of starting up a sandwich shop are much lower than those involved in starting up a lumber mill or a giant supermarket. So, an entrepreneur with a small income is much more likely to try her luck with a sandwich shop.

Use of the Internet reduced start-up costs in many markets, including books and music. However, many entrepreneurs discovered that a Web page did not attract and hold customers as easily as a shop window. The high costs of advertising, shipping, and discounting goods pushed many out of business. With a few exceptions, the Internet-based companies that have succeeded paid substantial start-up costs.

Technology

When a school group needs to raise money, its members could sell goods like flowers, cookies, or candy. Some technically skilled students could offer to fix cars or bicycles. Very few student groups would be able to create and sell a new word-processing program.

Some markets require a high degree of technological know-how. A carpenter, pharmacist, or electrician can spend years in training before he or she has learned all the important skills. As a result, new entrepreneurs cannot easily enter these markets without a lot of preparation and study. Barriers of technology and know-how can keep a market from becoming perfectly competitive.

Price and Output

One of the primary characteristics of perfectly competitive markets is that they are efficient. Competition within these markets keeps both prices and production costs low. Firms must use all inputs—land,

barrier to entry *any factor that makes it difficult for a new firm to enter a market*

imperfect competition *a market structure that does not meet the conditions of perfect competition*

start-up costs *the expenses a firm must pay before it can begin to produce and sell goods*

Figure 7.1 **Perfect Competition**

Number of firms: Many

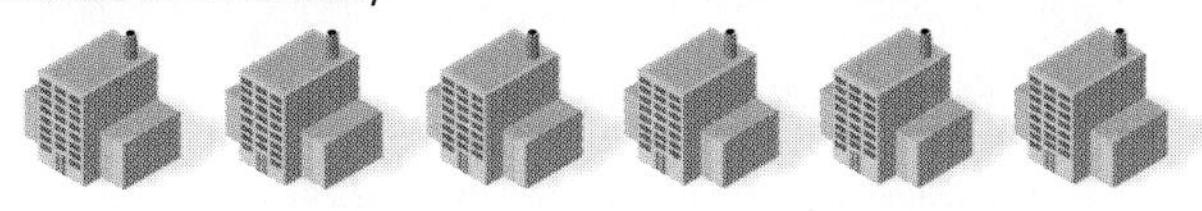

Variety of goods: None

Barriers to entry: None

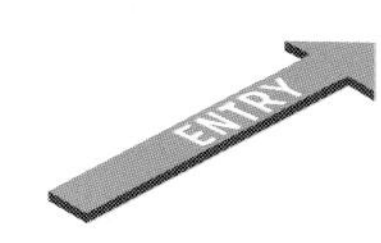

Control over prices: None

A perfectly competitive market must include a large number of suppliers selling the same good. **Competition What prevents any one firm from raising its prices?**

Differentiated Instruction L3

To help students understand the difficulties of starting a high-tech business, have them write a paragraph in which they explain what barriers to entry might exist in starting a computer repair service. Encourage students to include specific reasons in their explanations.

Meeting NCEE Standards

Use the following benchmark activity from the **Voluntary National Content Standards in Economics** to evaluate student understanding of **Standard 9.**

Explain why, in the last 10 years, there have been no U.S. companies emerging to manufacture locomotives, but many emerging to manufacture silk-screen T-shirts and sports clothing. Also, predict what happened to prices of resold tickets to sporting events after Arizona required all ticket scalpers to operate only in a small roped-off area near the stadium or arena in the two hours before an event.

Transparency Resource Package
Economics Concepts, 7B: Barriers to Entry

Differentiated Instruction L3

(Reteaching) Have students write one or two paragraphs explaining the following statement: *One of the primary characteristics of perfectly competitive markets is that they are efficient in terms of both price and output.*

Block Scheduling Strategies

Consider these suggestions to take advantage of extended class time:

- Extend the Bellringer activity on p. 151 by holding an informal debate on whether competition has positive or negative effects on the economy. Allow students to choose a position, and have teams face each other. Each student may make a statement without being interrupted, and students may switch to the other side as points are made.
- Show the Economics Video Library segment "Down on the Farm," about the struggles of small farmers. After viewing the segment, hold a discussion on the way perfect competition affects family farms.
- Invite an entrepreneur to speak about barriers to entry in his or her business. Then ask students to write on how barriers to entry could be minimized.

Answer to . . .

Building Key Concepts If one firm raised its prices, people would stop buying its products, since other identical products would be cheaper. The company would eventually go out of business.

GTE Guide to the Essentials
Chapter 7, Section 1, p. 28 provides support for students who need additional review of the section content. Spanish support is available in the Spanish edition of the guide on p. 28.

Quiz Unit 2 folder, p. 36 includes questions to check students' understanding of Section 1 content.

Presentation Pro CD-ROM
Quiz provides multiple-choice questions to check students' understanding of Section 1 content.

Answers to . . .

Section 1 Assessment

1. Characteristics include: many buyers and sellers participate in the market (farmers market); sellers offer identical products (oranges, shoes); informed buyers and sellers (car dealerships, computers); and ability for sellers to enter or exit the market freely (restaurants, consultant services).
2. High start-up costs discourage new ventures by creating the potential for large losses. Many people are unwilling to take the risk of starting a new business.
3. Student responses will vary, but examples may include start-up costs such as office space and word processing equipment.
4. Perfectly competitive markets require identical products, and commodities are defined as identical products.
5. b, f, g
6. Examples of expenses are store rental, inventory costs, employee salaries, and advertising. Final student estimates should be sound and based on tangible information that they have gathered from various sources.
7. Answers will vary but should demonstrate ability to identify barriers to entry based on knowledge gained from this section. Possible answers may include patent regulations or restriction of the number of firms in the market by an industrial association.

Answer to . . .

Building Key Concepts Students may mention the presence of many buyers and sellers, identical products, informed buyers/sellers, and a market that can be entered and exited freely.

In a perfectly competitive market, price and output reach their equilibrium levels.

Competition What factors allow a perfectly competitive market to reach equilibrium?

Figure 7.2 Market Equilibrium in Perfect Competition

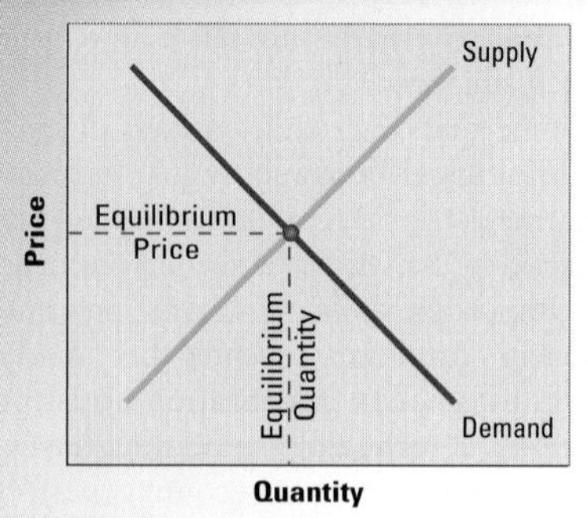

labor, organizational skills, machinery and equipment—to their best advantage. As a result, the prices that consumers pay and the revenue that suppliers receive accurately reflect how much the market values the resources that have gone into the product. In a perfectly competitive market, prices correctly represent the opportunity costs of each product.

Prices in a perfectly competitive market are the lowest sustainable prices possible. Because many sellers compete to offer their commodities to buyers, intense competition forces prices down to the point where the prices just cover the most-efficient sellers' costs of doing business. As you read in Chapter 6, this equilibrium is usually the most efficient state a market can achieve.

We saw in Chapter 5 that producers earn their highest profits when they produce enough that their cost to produce one more unit exactly equals the market price of the unit. Since no supplier can influence prices in perfectly competitive markets, producers will make their output decisions based on their most efficient use of available land, labor, capital, and management skills.

In the long run, output will reach the point where each supplying firm just covers all of its costs, including paying the firm's owners enough to make the business worthwhile.

Section 1 Assessment

Progress Monitoring *Online*
For: Self-quiz with vocabulary practice
Web Code: mna-2075

Key Terms and Main Ideas

1. Describe characteristics and give examples of **perfect competition** (pure competition).
2. How do **start-up costs** discourage entrepreneurs from entering a market?
3. What are two examples of **barriers to entry** in the magazine market?
4. Why must perfectly competitive markets always deal in **commodities?**

Applying Economic Concepts

5. ***Decision Making*** Which of these markets come close to perfect competition? **(a)** televisions **(b)** bottled water **(c)** pizza **(d)** school buses **(e)** white socks **(f)** baseballs **(g)** paper clips
6. ***Try This*** Suppose that you and your friends plan to open a new convenience store. Brainstorm a list of ten expenses that would be your start-up costs. Next, use the Sunday newspapers and the Internet to estimate how much each item on your list will cost. How much do you estimate you will spend before the store can open?
7. ***Critical Thinking*** Other than technology and start-up costs, what are two specific examples of barriers that could prevent a company or individual from entering a market?

For: Simulation Activity
Visit: PHSchool.com
Web Code: mnd-2071

Progress Monitoring *Online*
For additional assessment, have students access Progress Monitoring Online at **Web Code:** mna-2075

Go Online PHSchool.com Typing in the Web Code when prompted will bring students directly to detailed instructions for this activity.

Skills for
LIFE

Analyzing Political Cartoons

Political cartoons express the cartoonist's opinion on a recent issue or current event. The artist's purpose is to sway the opinions of the reader. To achieve this goal, cartoonists often use humor and exaggeration. When analyzing a political cartoon, be sure to examine all the images and words to help you fully understand the artist's intent. Use the following steps to analyze the cartoon below.

1. **Identify the symbols in the cartoon.** Symbolism plays a major role in helping political cartoons convey their messages. For example, Uncle Sam is often used as a symbol for the federal government of the United States. (a) What company's symbol is depicted in this cartoon? (b) Who is the old man?

2. **Analyze the meaning of the cartoon.** (a) What industry is being represented in this cartoon? (b) Why would the artist use Alexander Graham Bell? (c) What is Mr. Bell reading? Why is that relevant to this cartoon?

3. **Draw conclusions about the cartoonist's intent.** (a) What point is the artist trying to make about AT&T's telephone rates? (b) Does the artist believe the telephone industry has perfect competition? (c) Are you swayed by the cartoonist's opinion?

Additional Practice

Create your own political cartoon based on a current economic event or issue. Include symbolism, humor, and exaggeration in your cartoon.

Interdisciplinary Connections: History

Learning About the Past Through Cartoons Point out to students that from the earliest years of the nation's history, newspapers and magazines have published political cartoons. Explain to students that reading these cartoons today can help them understand how people who lived during earlier periods of the nation's history felt about the issues of those times.

Have students work through the following activity: Have students look through books of political cartoons or history texts to locate political cartoons from various eras in the nation's history. Have students bring examples to class and explain what issues the cartoons address and what views they reflect. Encourage students to focus on cartoons dealing with economic concepts.

Skills for LIFE

Analyzing Political Cartoons

1. Focus Students will analyze political cartoons to find and explain the main idea of the cartoonist's view on an economic issue.

2. Instruct Work with students to follow the steps for analyzing the political cartoon in the feature. Use cartoons from the editorial pages of your local newspaper or a business magazine to provide more opportunities for students to use these steps.

3. Close/Reteach To provide additional practice, see the Economic Skills Activity below.

Economic Skills Activity
Unit 2 folder, p. 43, "Analyzing Political Cartoons," asks students to analyze an 1889 cartoon about the effectiveness of the first federal antitrust laws.

Social Studies Skills Tutor CD-ROM offers interactive practice in critical thinking and reading, visual analysis, and communication.

Answers

1. (a) AT&T (b) Alexander Graham Bell
2. (a) the telecommunications industry (b) Bell invented the telephone. (c) He is reading a telephone bill. It shows how unreasonable phone service prices can be.
3. (a) AT&T's prices are too high. (b) no (c) Opinions will vary, but students should explain their reasoning.

Additional Practice

Students' political cartoons should demonstrate an understanding of the event depicted as well as effective symbolism, humor, and exaggeration.

Section 2

Monopoly

Objectives You may wish to call students' attention to the objectives in the Section Preview. The objectives are reflected in the main headings of the section.

Bellringer Ask students if they have ever played the game Monopoly®. Ask them to explain the reason for its name. Explain to students that in this section they will learn about the characteristics of monopoly markets.

Vocabulary Builder Have students find the definitions of each key term listed in the Section Preview. Then have students create fill-in-the-blank sentences for each term. Ask students to read their sentences aloud, letting their classmates identify the correct terms.

Lesson Plan

Teaching the Main Concepts L3

1. Focus A major characteristic of a monopoly is that it is made up of a single seller. Ask students to give examples of firms that they think are monopolies and to identify any elements they have in common.

2. Instruct Begin by making sure that students understand what a monopoly is. Then discuss how monopolies are formed, including government monopolies. Be sure that students understand that a monopolist maximizes profits by producing at a level of output at which marginal cost equals marginal revenue.

3. Close/Reteach Ask small groups of students to create scenarios similar to the Leland/BreatheDeep example on p. 159. Suggest that they illustrate their work. Have them present their scenarios to the class along with any graphics they have created.

Guided Reading and Review Unit 2 folder, p. 37 asks students to identify the main ideas of the section and to define or identify key terms.

Section 2 Monopoly

Preview

Objectives

After studying this section you will be able to:

1. **Describe** characteristics and give examples of monopoly.
2. **Describe** how monopolies are formed, including government monopolies.
3. **Explain** how a firm with a monopoly sets output and price, and why companies practice price discrimination.

Section Focus

A firm has a monopoly when it controls an entire market. Because a monopolist controls the price of its product, a monopoly produces less and charges higher prices than would a perfectly competitive firm.

Key Terms

monopoly
economies of scale
natural monopoly
government monopoly
patent
franchise
license
price discrimination
market power

monopoly *a market dominated by a single seller*

You've gone to the emergency room with a high fever and a sharp pain in your leg. The doctor diagnoses a rare infection and writes a prescription for ten pills of a new medication that the government approved just last year. The doctor tells you that without this medication, your recovery will be slow.

At the pharmacy, you find that the medicine costs $97.35, or nearly ten dollars a pill! The pharmacist tells you that only one company has the right to produce the medicine, and it charges a high price because its scientists worked for years to develop the medication. You feel that you have no choice, so you hand over the cash.

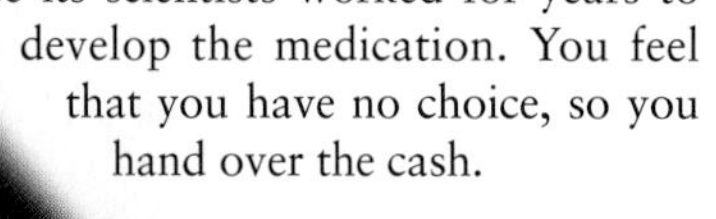

▼ **One company, DeBeers of South Africa, has almost total control over the world's diamond supply.**

The market for prescription medicines is one of many markets in which monopolies can develop. In this section you will read about different types of monopolies and how they form.

Describing Monopoly

A **monopoly** forms when barriers prevent firms from entering a market that has a single supplier. While a perfectly competitive market has many buyers and sellers, monopoly markets have only one seller, but any number of buyers. In fact, barriers to entry are the principal condition that allows monopolies to exist.

While you can probably think of several companies that look and act like monopolies, economists use a strict set of requirements to define a monopoly. If we define the good or service provided by a company broadly enough, we can usually find substitute goods from a different source. For example, you might think that a convenience store on a highway in the middle of the desert has a monopoly. However, you could have carried more water in the car, or, if you had enough money, you might have flown across the desert instead of paying high prices for food and water during the car trip.

Graphing the Main Idea

Competition To build understanding of the concept of **competition,** have students use a web graphic organizer like the one below to explain the various conditions that lead to monopolies. Remind students that a web shows a main idea and its supporting details.

Section Reading Support Transparencies A template and the answers for this graphic organizer can be found in Chapter 7, Section 2 of the Section Reading Support Transparency System.

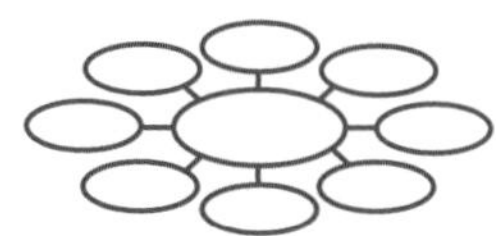

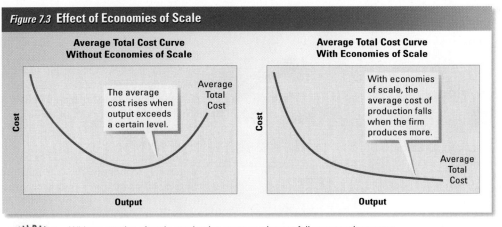

Figure 7.3 **Effect of Economies of Scale**

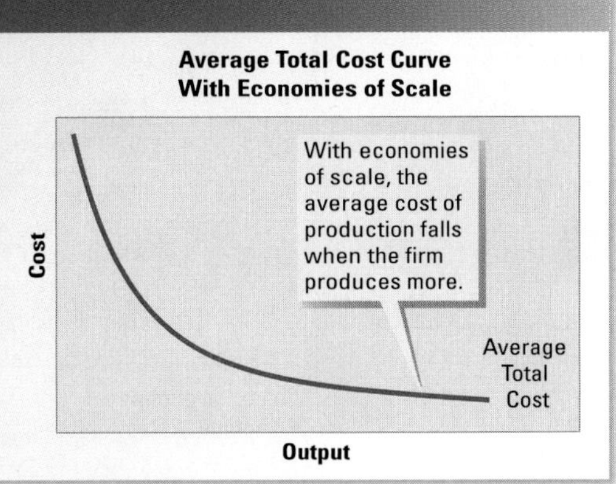

With economies of scale, production costs continue to fall as output increases.
Markets and Prices Describe the cost curve for a firm without economies of scale.

The problem with monopolies is that they can take advantage of their market power and charge high prices. Given the law of demand, this means that the quantity of goods sold is lower than in a market with more than one seller. For this reason, the United States has outlawed some monopolistic practices, as you will read in Section 4.

Forming a Monopoly

All monopolies have one trait in common: a single seller in a market. However, different market conditions can create different types of monopolies.

Economies of Scale

If a firm's start-up costs are high, and its average costs fall for each additional unit it produces, then it enjoys what economists call **economies of scale.** Economies of scale are characteristics that cause a producer's average cost to drop as production rises.

The graph on the left in Figure 7.3 above shows an average total cost curve for a firm without economies of scale. Follow the curve from left to right. As output increases from zero, the average cost of each good drops, and the curve initially slopes downward. This is because large, initial, fixed costs, like the cost of the factory and machinery, can be spread out among more and more goods as production rises. If the factory cost $1,000 to build and each unit of output costs $10 to make, producing one unit will cost $1,010, but producing two units will cost $1,020, or only $510 each. However, if the industry has limited economies of scale, output will eventually rise to a level at which the limited scale economies are exhausted, and the cost of making each unit will rise. The average cost of producing each good increases as output increases, and the curve slopes upward to match the rising cost per unit.

A factory in an industry with economies of scale never reaches this second stage of rising costs per unit. As production increases, the firm becomes more efficient, even at a level of output high enough to supply the entire market. The graph on the right in Figure 7.3 above shows how cost and output are related in economies of scale. Follow the curve from left to right. As output increases, the cost per unit falls, and continues to fall.

A good example is a hydroelectric plant, which generates electricity from a dam on a river. A large dam is expensive to build.

economies of scale *factors that cause a producer's average cost per unit to fall as output rises*

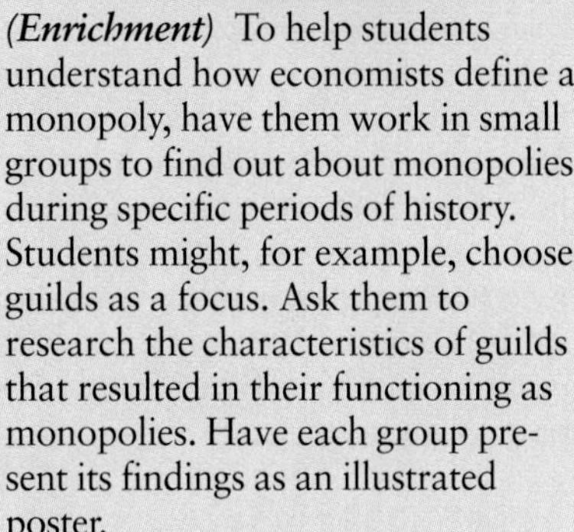

Differentiated Instruction  L3

(Enrichment) To help students understand how economists define a monopoly, have them work in small groups to find out about monopolies during specific periods of history. Students might, for example, choose guilds as a focus. Ask them to research the characteristics of guilds that resulted in their functioning as monopolies. Have each group present its findings as an illustrated poster.

Differentiated Instruction L3

To help students transfer information from one medium to another (data to graph), display the following aluminum production data in table form. (Create two columns: "Quantity Produced" and "Average Cost.") *0.5 million pounds of aluminum produced/$2.80 per pound; 1 million pounds/$2.10 per pound; 1.5 million pounds/$1.80 per pound; 2 million pounds/$1.60 per pound; 2.5 million pounds/$1.53 per pound.* Ask students to plot a graph that shows these data. If available, have students use a computer graphing software in this activity. Display the graphs and discuss what they show about economies of scale.

Transparency Resource Package
Economics Concepts, 7C: Monopoly

Answer to . . .

Building Key Concepts When economies of scale do not exist, increasing production beyond a certain point becomes costly. Other firms may enter the industry and produce additional units profitably.

Econ 101: Key Concepts Made Easy

Markets and Prices One of the key concepts in this section is that output affects **marginal revenue.** Total revenue is the money a firm gets by selling its product—the price multiplied by the quantity sold. A firm's marginal revenue is the change in total revenue that results from selling two different quantities of output.

To help students understand how marginal revenue is determined, refer them to the table on p. 161. Explain to students that to compute the marginal revenue that results from selling 10,000 doses rather than 9,000 doses, they should first find the difference between the total revenues for the two outputs. *($1,000)* Then have them divide that figure by the difference in the quantities *(1,000)*. The marginal revenue at a price of $10 per unit is $1.

Differentiated Instruction L3

This section contains an extended discussion of how one monopoly, public water, is formed. Ask students to consider another monopoly that occurs in their own community. *(Students may suggest public sewers, public electricity, freight railroads, or mass transit.)* Then ask them to write a paragraph explaining why a monopoly occurs in this sector of the marketplace.

Background

Interdisciplinary

Sometimes the government is able to prevent monopolies from occurring through changes in technology. For example, in late 1999, telephone companies such as AT&T were buying large cable networks to gain access to the growing high-speed Internet access, or broadband, market. This tactic could have given those telephone companies a natural monopoly over broadband by forcing consumers to choose the owners of the cable networks as their Internet service providers (ISPs). Although the federal government was wary of forcing cable companies to share their networks, many major cities—such as Portland, Oregon—have declared that the cable companies must share their networks with other ISPs, such as America Online, Inc.

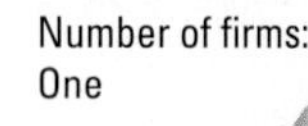

Figure 7.4 **Monopoly**

Number of firms:
One

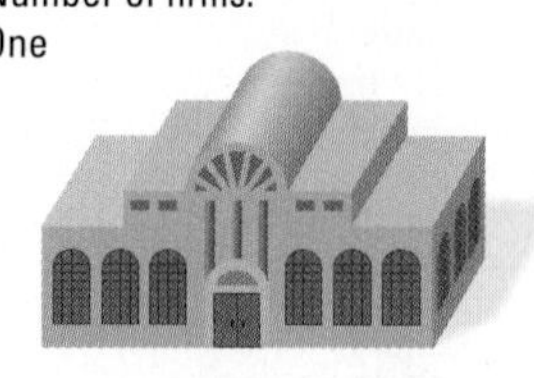

Variety of goods:
None

Barriers to entry:
Complete

Control over prices:
Complete

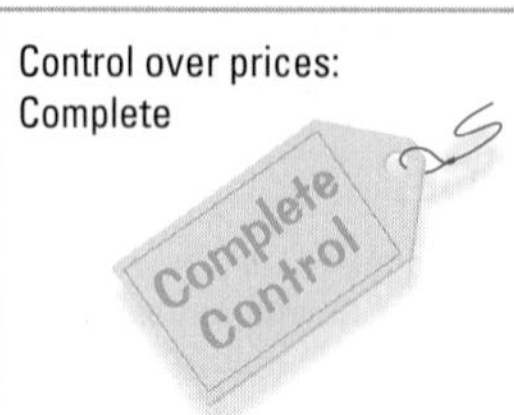

In a monopoly, one company controls the market.
Markets and Prices Why is public water a monopoly?

However, once the dam is built, the plant can produce energy at a very low additional cost simply by letting water flow through the dam. The average cost of the first unit of electricity produced is very high because the cost of the dam is so high. As output increases, the fixed costs of the dam can be spread over more units of electricity, so the average cost drops. In a market with economies of scale, bigger is better. An industry that enjoys economies of scale can easily become a natural monopoly.

natural monopoly *a market that runs most efficiently when one large firm supplies all of the output*

Natural Monopolies

A **natural monopoly** is a market that runs most efficiently when one large firm provides all of the output. If a second firm enters the market, competition will drive down the market price charged to customers and decrease the quantity each firm can sell. One or both of the firms will not be able to cover their costs and will go out of business.

Public water provides a good example of a natural monopoly. In a competitive market, different water companies would dig reservoirs and set up overlapping networks of pipes and pumping stations to deliver water to the same town. Companies would use more land and water than necessary. Each company would have to pay for all of the unneeded pipes and would serve customers no better than a single network.

In cases like this, the government often steps in to allow just one firm in each geographic area to provide these necessary services. The government action ensures that we don't waste resources building additional plants when only one is needed. In return for monopoly status, a firm with a natural monopoly agrees to let government control the prices it can charge and what services it must provide.

Technology and Change

Sometimes the development of a new technology can destroy a natural monopoly. A new innovation can cut fixed costs and make small companies as efficient as one large firm.

▶ **Before cellular phones became popular, telephone service was a natural monopoly because no one wanted to build more than one network of wires.**

Block Scheduling Strategies

Consider these suggestions to take advantage of extended class time:

- Refer students to the map on p. 160. Point out that the cost of an expansion football team has skyrocketed. Have students research the cost of buying an NFL franchise over the last 25 years and graph their findings. Hold a discussion about these costs and the monopolistic management of the league.
- Have students work in pairs to complete the first activity on p. 163. Then have the pairs create similar examples and present them to the class as problems to be solved.
- Organize students into groups of three or four. Assign each group a different industry, and ask group members to gather production and cost data about that industry. Then have groups graph their data.

Answer to . . .

Building Key Concepts Competition in the area of public water would create inefficiency.

▲ A national park can give one company a franchise for, or monopoly over, food service within the park.

When telephone calls were carried by thick copper wires, local telephone service was considered a natural monopoly. No one wanted to build more than one network of wires to connect thousands of homes and businesses. In the 1980s and 1990s, consumers began using cellular phones, which were portable and could carry phone calls via radio waves rather than through wires. Cellular technology reduced the barriers to entry in the local telephone market. Now that cellular phone companies can link to thousands or millions of customers with a few, well-placed towers, they don't need to invest in an expensive infrastructure of cables and telephone poles. Cellular phone companies are becoming as efficient as traditional wire-based phone services.

Government Monopolies

In the case of a natural monopoly, the government allows the monopoly to form and then regulates it. In other cases, however, government actions themselves can create barriers to entry in markets and thereby create monopolies. A **government monopoly** is a monopoly created by the government.

Technological Monopolies

One way that the government can give a company monopoly power is by issuing a **patent.** A patent gives a company exclusive rights to sell a new good or service for a specific period of time. Suppose that Leland Pharmaceuticals developed a new asthma medication called BreatheDeep that helped people with asthma develop stronger lungs. If Leland's researchers could prove to the government that they had invented BreatheDeep, the Food and Drug Administration would grant Leland a patent. This patent would give Leland the exclusive right to sell BreatheDeep for twenty years.

Why would the government want to give a company monopoly power? Patents guarantee that companies can profit from their own research without competition. For this reason, patents encourage firms to research and develop new products that benefit society as a whole, even though the research and development costs may be very high. The market power that comes with the patent allows firms to set prices that maximize their opportunity to make a profit.

Franchises and Licenses

A **franchise** is a contract issued by a local authority that gives a single firm the right to sell its goods within an exclusive market. For example, the National Park Service picks a single firm to sell food and other goods at national parks, such as Yellowstone, Yosemite, and the Everglades. Your school may have contracted with one soft-drink company to install and stock vending machines. The franchise may include a condition that no other soft drinks will be sold in the building. Governments, parks, and schools use franchises to keep small markets under control.

On a larger scale, governments can issue a **license** granting firms the right to operate a business. Examples of scarce resources that require licensing include radio and television broadcast frequencies

government monopoly *a monopoly created by the government*

patent *a license that gives the inventor of a new product the exclusive right to sell it for a certain period of time*

franchise *the right to sell a good or service within an exclusive market*

license *a government-issued right to operate a business*

FAST FACT

Many villages in India and Bangladesh have never had phone service, even though most of the population lives in the countryside. Stretching a cable to every village was too expensive and inefficient, even for a ***natural monopoly.*** *Using a cellular network, Grameen Telecom now plans to bring pay phones to 68,000 villages in Bangladesh and serve 100 million new customers.*

Differentiated Instruction 

(Reteaching) Have students work with partners to read the information under the heading "Government Monopolies." After they have read the material, ask partners to explain to each other the way in which these monopolies are formed. Then have students show their understanding of the material by creating a captioned poster or a graphic that illustrates the ways in which the government extends market power.

Differentiated Instruction L2

Have students divide a piece of paper into two columns. Ask them to describe a natural monopoly in one column. In the other column, have them describe the different kinds of government monopolies. Then have them write a sentence or two summarizing the differences between the two. ELL

Background

Economics in History

The word *franchise* comes from the Old French word *franc,* which meant "free." During the Middle Ages, a franchise was a right or a privilege. The lord who owned a piece of land would grant private individuals certain rights. These might include the right to hold markets or fairs, to operate ferries, or to conduct other commercial activities.

In the United States during the latter part of the 1800s, franchises were granted for the provision of such services as electricity and water. Eventually public utility commissions took over these tasks, and by the 1950s franchises were becoming a popular form of private business organization. Restaurants, convenience stores, printing shops, and dry-cleaning shops are popular types of franchises today.

Preparing for Standardized Tests

Have students read the section titled "Government Monopolies" and then answer the question below.

According to the text, which of the following might the government use to encourage firms to research and develop new products?

A licenses to control specific resources
(B) patents for a specific length of time
C franchises to sell goods
D restrictions on the number of firms

Differentiated Instruction L3

Have students study the map on this page. Ask them to use the information in the map along with their own knowledge to explain how a monopolistic organization, in this case the National Football League, may control output or price in an industry.

Differentiated Instruction L4

You may wish to have students add the following to their portfolios. Have them use the information in the section as well as other resources to find more information about monopolies. Then have them write a position paper on the following question: Are monopolies harmful to consumers? Students' papers should include examples to support their positions. GT

Economics Assessment Rubric
Economics Assessment Rubrics folder, pp. 22–23 provides sample evaluation materials for a position paper.

and land. The Federal Communications Commission issues licenses for individual radio and television stations. Some cities select a single firm to own and manage all of their public parking lots.

Industrial Organizations

In rare cases, the government allows the companies in an industry to restrict the number of firms in a market. For example, the United States government lets Major League Baseball and other sports leagues restrict the number and location of their teams. The government allows team owners of the major professional sports leagues to choose new cities for their teams and does not charge them with violating the laws that prevent competitors from working together.

Major League Baseball has an exemption from these laws, which are known as antitrust laws, because they were originally passed to break up an illegal form of monopoly known as a trust. Other sports leagues do not have an official exemption, but the government treats them as it treats baseball. The restrictions that the leagues impose help keep team play orderly and stable by preventing other cities from starting their own major league teams and crowding the schedule.

The problem with this type of monopoly is that team owners may charge high prices for tickets. In addition, if you're a sports fan in a city without a major league team, you're out of luck.

Output Decisions

If you had severe asthma, which can be fatal, what would BreatheDeep be worth to you? You would probably want the medicine no matter how much it cost. So Leland, the company that invented and patented the drug, could charge a very high price for its new medication. In fact, they

Figure 7.5 Monopoly Decisions in the National Football League

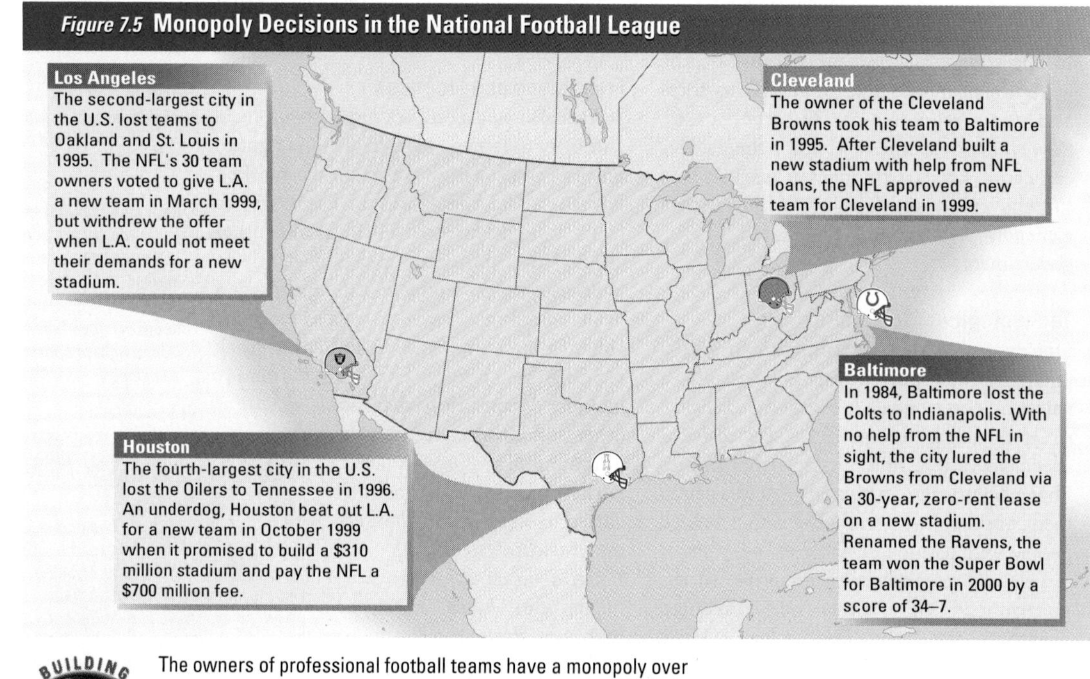

Los Angeles
The second-largest city in the U.S. lost teams to Oakland and St. Louis in 1995. The NFL's 30 team owners voted to give L.A. a new team in March 1999, but withdrew the offer when L.A. could not meet their demands for a new stadium.
Cleveland
The owner of the Cleveland Browns took his team to Baltimore in 1995. After Cleveland built a new stadium with help from NFL loans, the NFL approved a new team for Cleveland in 1999.
Houston
The fourth-largest city in the U.S. lost the Oilers to Tennessee in 1996. An underdog, Houston beat out L.A. for a new team in October 1999 when it promised to build a $310 million stadium and pay the NFL a $700 million fee.
Baltimore
In 1984, Baltimore lost the Colts to Indianapolis. With no help from the NFL in sight, the city lured the Browns from Cleveland via a 30-year, zero-rent lease on a new stadium. Renamed the Ravens, the team won the Super Bowl for Baltimore in 2000 by a score of 34–7.

The owners of professional football teams have a monopoly over membership in the National Football League. Cities have to apply to the NFL for a new team or pay top dollar for an existing team.
Supply and Demand Why do team owners limit the number of teams?

Interdisciplinary Connections: History

Thomas Alva Edison Thomas Alva Edison obtained 1,093 patents from the United States government—the greatest number of patents issued to a single person. In the early 1900s Edison attempted to control the U.S. motion picture industry by pooling his patents with those of other movie inventors. Together they formed the Motion Picture Patents Company, which controlled the production, distribution, and exhibition of motion pictures. However, in 1917 the Supreme Court of the United States ruled that the company was an illegal monopoly, dissolving Edison's control over the industry.

Making the Connection Have students research patents that Edison received for inventions outside the movie industry. Ask them to report how these inventions continue to affect life today.

Answer to...

Building Key Concepts Having fewer teams in the National Football League allows each team to have less competition in its region and, therefore, more fans.

Figure 7.6 Demand Schedule for BreatheDeep

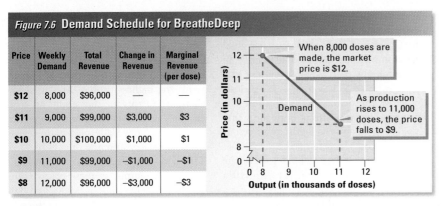

Price	Weekly Demand	Total Revenue	Change in Revenue	Marginal Revenue (per dose)
$12	8,000	$96,000	—	—
$11	9,000	$99,000	$3,000	$3
$10	10,000	$100,000	$1,000	$1
$9	11,000	$99,000	–$1,000	–$1
$8	12,000	$96,000	–$3,000	–$3

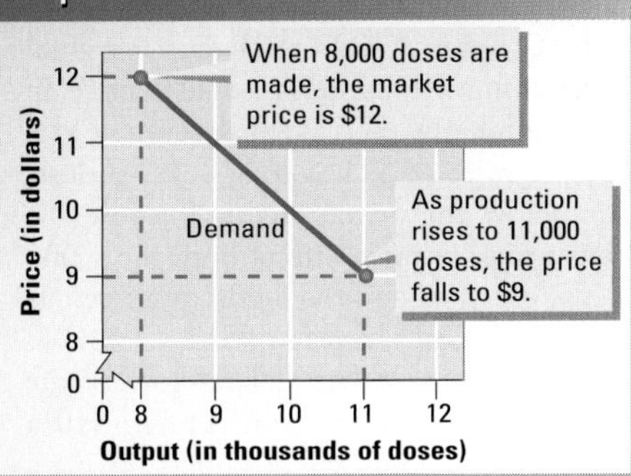

When 8,000 doses are made, the market price is $12.
As production rises to 11,000 doses, the price falls to $9.
Demand
Price (in dollars)
Output (in thousands of doses)

BUILDING KEY CONCEPTS

By increasing output, a monopolist lowers the price of the good. Above a certain level of output, revenue also begins to decrease. **Markets and Prices Why does revenue fall when production increases from 10,000 doses to 11,000 doses?**

could charge enough to earn well above what it cost to research and manufacture the drug. The resulting profits would give the company a reason, or incentive, for inventing the new medication in the first place. But could Leland sell as much medication as it wanted to at whatever price it chose?

Even a monopolist faces a limited choice—it can choose either output or price, but not both. The monopolist looks at the big picture and tries to maximize profits. This usually means that, compared to a perfectly competitive market for the same good, the monopolist produces fewer goods at a higher price.

The Monopolist's Dilemma

The law of demand states that buyers will demand more of a good at lower prices and less at higher prices. Figure 7.6 shows a possible demand curve for BreatheDeep, with prices in dollars on the vertical axis and doses on the horizontal axis. Many people with life-threatening asthma will pay whatever the medicine costs. But some people with milder asthma will choose a cheaper, weaker medicine if the price rises too high.

Trace the demand curve from left to right. At $12 per dose, consumers might demand 8,000 doses of BreatheDeep each week. But at $9 per dose, as many as 11,000 doses will sell. The law of demand means that when the monopolist increases the price, it will sell less, and when it lowers the price, it will sell more. Another way to interpret this graph is that if a monopolist produces more, the price of the good will fall, and if it produces less, the price will rise.

Falling Marginal Revenue

Remember from Chapter 5 that to maximize profits, a seller should set its marginal revenue, or the amount it earns from the last unit sold, equal to its marginal cost, or the extra cost from producing that unit. This same rule applies to a firm with a monopoly. The key difference is that in a perfectly competitive market, marginal revenue is always the same as price, and each firm receives the same price no matter how much it produces. Neither assumption is true in a monopoly.

To understand how this happens, consider the demand schedule for BreatheDeep in Figure 7.6. When BreatheDeep is sold at $12 a dose, consumers buy 8,000 doses, providing $96,000 in revenue. If Leland lowers the price to $11 a dose, 9,000 doses will be bought for a total revenue of $99,000. The

Differentiated Instruction L3

(Reteaching) To help students understand the example of Leland and BreatheDeep, form groups of four to five students. Explain to the members of each group that they are to create a simple illustration—a table or chart—that will display the effects of changing prices as described in "The Monopolist's Dilemma." Have groups work for about 15 minutes on their illustrations. Then have a representative from each group present the graphic to the class. This illustration will prepare them to understand the graph on the next page.

Transparency Resource Package
Economics Concepts, 7D: Monopoly Setting Output
Economics Concepts, 7E: Monopoly Setting Price

Background Note

Monopoly and Patents

The patent system is often tested in times of crisis. As a result of the anthrax poisonings of 2001, the U.S. government decided to stockpile millions of doses of drugs that provide resistance and treatment for anthrax infection. Bayer, the German multinational company that holds the patent for Cipro, agreed to sell 100 million tablets to the government at 95 cents per tablet, half the normal price. The company agreed to sell the second hundred million at 85 cents each, and the third 100 million at 75 cents each.

Answer to...

Building Key Concepts Although more units are being sold, all of the units are sold at a lower price than before production expanded. Therefore, the marginal revenue is a negative number.

Differentiated Instruction 

Ask students to create a captioned version of the graph on this page. Suggest that they redraw the graph on a larger piece of paper and then use material from the textbook to write paragraphs that explain the significance of the axes, curves, and points on the graph.

Simulations and Data Graphing CD-ROM offers data graphing tools so that students can practice creating and interpreting line graphs.

Math Practice Activity
Math Practice folder, p. 6, "Maximizing Profit," gives students additional practice in calculating total revenue and marginal revenue to maximize profits.

sale of 1,000 more doses brought Leland $3,000 in new revenue.

In Chapter 5, you read that marginal revenue in most markets is equal to price. In this monopoly, the marginal revenue at a market price of $11 is roughly $3 a dose, far below the price. This is because the lower market price affects both the 1,000 new doses sold and the 8,000 doses people buy for $11 each instead of $12.

Now suppose that Leland lowers the price of BreatheDeep from $11 to $10 a dose. 10,000 doses will be bought, giving a total revenue of $100,000. This time, the sale of 1,000 more doses brought only $1,000 in additional revenue. $10,000 in revenue from 1,000 new sales barely exceeds the $9,000 fall in revenue from the 9,000 doses which are sold for $10, not $11. The market price is $10 a dose, but the marginal revenue has fallen to a mere $1 for each dose of BreatheDeep sold.

As you've seen, when a firm has some control over price—and can cut the price to sell more—marginal revenue is *less* than price. In contrast, in a perfectly competitive market, the price would not drop at all as output increased, so marginal revenue would remain the same as price. The firm's total revenue would increase at a steady rate with production.

The table in Figure 7.6 lists marginal revenues for several different prices. Note that marginal revenue actually becomes negative when the quantity demanded is greater than 10,000 doses a week.

Setting a Price

Leland will choose a level of output that yields the highest profits. As you read in Chapter 6, this is the point at which marginal revenue is equal to marginal cost.

In Figure 7.6 we have plotted the demand for BreatheDeep at market prices of $8, $9, $10, $11, and $12 a dose. According to Figure 7.6, output at these prices will be 12,000, 11,000, 10,000, 9,000, and 8,000 doses, respectively. These points form the market demand curve for BreatheDeep shown in purple.

Then, based on this data, we plotted Leland's marginal revenue at these levels of output. These points form the marginal revenue curve shown in blue in Figure 7.7. The marginal revenue curve is at the bottom of the graph because a monopolist's marginal revenue is lower than the market price.

Marginal cost equals marginal revenue at point a in Figure 7.7. This is the most profitable level of output. The monopolist produces 9,000 units, the quantity at which marginal revenue and marginal cost are both $3. According to the market demand curve, the market price is $11 when 9,000 units are sold (point b). Therefore, the monopolist will set the price of each dose at $11 or set production at 9,000 units.

Figure 7.7 also shows how price and output would be different if dozens of firms sold BreatheDeep and the market were perfectly competitive. In a perfectly competitive market, marginal revenue is always equal to market price, so the marginal revenue curve would be the same as the purple demand curve. Firms will set output where marginal revenue is equal to marginal cost, shown at point c. As you can see, a perfectly competitive market for BreatheDeep would have more units sold *and* a lower market price than a monopoly.

How much profit does a monopolist earn? The profit per dose is the difference between the market price and the average

A monopolist sets output at a point (a) where marginal revenue is equal to marginal cost.

Markets and Prices
How does this affect output and price compared to a perfectly competitive market?

Figure 7.7 **Setting a Price in a Monopoly**

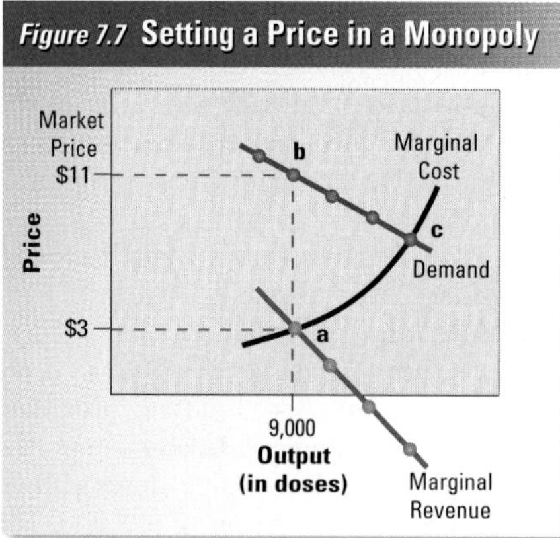

Answer to...

Building Key Concepts A monopolist's marginal revenue is lower than the market price, so output must be set at the point where marginal cost equals marginal revenue. In a perfectly competitive market, marginal revenue remains the same as price. Under monopoly, output will be lower and price higher than they would be under perfect competition.

Preparing for Standardized Tests

Have students study Figure 7.7 and then answer the question below.

Which of the following would be an accurate description of Point a on this graph?

A the point at which marginal revenue exceeds marginal cost
B the point at which demand exceeds supply
(C) the point at which marginal revenue equals marginal cost
D the point at which supply exceeds demand

▲ Price discrimination can take the form of discounts for senior citizens, children, and students.

total cost at that level of production. Suppose the average total cost of 9,000 doses is $5 per dose. Each dose is sold for $11, so the monopolist will earn $6 of profit per dose. Total profit is $54,000, or $6 per dose for 9,000 doses.

Price Discrimination

The previous example assumed that the monopolist must charge the same price to all consumers. But in some cases, the monopolist may be able to divide consumers into two or more groups and charge a different price to each group. This practice is known as **price discrimination.**

Price discrimination is based on the idea that each customer has his or her own maximum price he or she will pay for a good. If a monopolist sets the good's price at the highest maximum price of all the buyers in the market, the monopolist will only sell to the one customer willing to pay that much. If the monopolist sets a low price, the monopolist will gain a lot of customers, but the monopolist will lose the profits it could have made from the customers who bought at the low price but were willing to pay more.

Although price discrimination is a feature of monopoly, it can be practiced by any company with **market power**. Market power is the ability to control prices and total market output. As you will read in the next section, many companies have some market power without having a true monopoly. Market power and price discrimination may be found in any market structure except for perfect competition.

Targeted Discounts

In the monopolist's ideal world, the firm could charge each customer the maximum that he or she is willing to pay, and no less. However, this is impractical, so companies divide consumers into large groups and design pricing policies for each group. One common form of price discrimination identifies some customers who are not willing to pay the regular price and offers those customers a discount. Price discrimination can also mean that a company finds the customers who need the good the most, and charges them more for that good. Here are some examples of price discrimination.

1. *Discounted airline fares* Airlines offer discounts to travelers who buy tickets several weeks in advance or are willing to spend a Saturday night at their destinations. Business travelers would prefer not to stay over on a Saturday night, but these tickets are appealing to vacationers who wouldn't otherwise pay to fly and don't mind the restrictions.
2. *Manufacturers' rebate offers* At times, manufacturers of refrigerators, cars, televisions, and other items will refund a small part of the purchase price to buyers who fill out a form and mail it back. People who take the time to fulfill

price discrimination *division of customers into groups based on how much they will pay for a good*

market power *the ability of a company to change prices and output like a monopolist*

Preparing for Standardized Tests

Have students read the section titled "Targeted Discounts" and then answer the question below.

According to the text, why do companies offer targeted discounts?

A They offer discounts to appeal to all of their customers.

B They offer discounts to allow all people to enjoy luxuries.

C They offer discounts to get people to buy products they don't need.

(D) They offer discounts to entice people who might not normally purchase their goods or services.

Background

Global Connections

Price discrimination on an international scale is known as *dumping.* When this occurs, a firm charges a lower price in a foreign market than it does in its home country. Sometimes the price is even lower than the actual production cost.

Why would a firm engage in dumping? Usually the firm has a monopoly in its own home market but faces competition in a foreign market. The firm is using its market power at home to discriminate against consumers. Sometimes dumping is an attempt to drive rival firms out of business in the foreign market. For this reason dumping is illegal under international trade agreements.

Differentiated Instruction 

Provide students with the following scenarios:

- Students receive discounts on movie theater tickets when they show their student identification.
- Consumers pay much more for fruit early in the harvest season than they do in the middle of the harvest season.

Ask students if these situations are examples of price discrimination. Have them provide reasons for their answers. *(The first is an example of price discrimination; the second is not, because the price reflects the forces of supply and demand in a perfectly competitive market.)* GT

Differentiated Instruction 

(Enrichment) Ask students to compare how supply, demand, and price operate in perfectly competitive markets and in monopolies. Have them create graphs or tables to display their comparisons.

GTE Guide to the Essentials
Chapter 7, Section 2, p. 29 provides support for students who need additional review of the section content. Spanish support is available in the Spanish edition of the guide on p. 29.

Quiz Unit 2 folder, p. 38 includes questions to check students' understanding of Section 2 content.

Presentation Pro CD-ROM
Quiz provides multiple-choice questions to check students' understanding of Section 2 content.

Answers to . . .

Section 2 Assessment

1. A company with market power can control prices and output.
2. Natural monopolies operate at a lower cost to both consumers and producers, so they are generally allowed because they are the most efficient source of that good or service.
3. Students should list three of the following: discounted airline fares, manufacturer's rebate offers, senior citizen or student discounts, and kids fly or stay free promotions.
4. Sample answer: When economies of scale exist, a firm's start-up costs are high, but its average costs fall for each unit it produces, even at a level of output high enough to supply the entire market.
5. Answers will vary but should show an understanding of price discrimination. Students may list any of the types listed in the text on pp. 163–164 or others, such as kids eat free offers in restaurants.
6. As a supporting reason, students may say that this would allow the government to exercise close control of the market for meats in the town. As a reason not to grant the request, students may say that competition among several butcher shops would provide greater choice and higher quality.

the rebate requirements are likely more price-conscious than those who don't, and may be unwilling to pay full price.

3. *Senior citizen or student discounts* Many senior citizens or students have lower incomes than people who work full time. Zoos, theaters, and restaurants often offer discounts to senior citizens and students because they are unlikely to be able to pay full price for what some consider luxuries.
4. *Children fly or stay free promotions* Families with young children spend more of their income on food, clothing, and school expenses. As a result, they have less to spend on vacations. Once again, firms would rather have their business and earn lower profits than earn no profits at all, so they offer discounts for families with children.

Limits of Price Discrimination

For price discrimination to work, a market must meet three conditions. Firms that use price discrimination must have some market power, customers must be divided into distinct groups, and buyers must not be in a position in which they can easily resell the good or service.

1. *Some market power* Price-discriminating firms must have some control over prices. For this reason, price discrimination is rare in highly competitive markets.
2. *Distinct customer groups* The price-discriminating firm must be able to divide customers into distinct groups based on their sensitivity to price. In other words, monopolists must be able to guess the demand curves of different groups, one of which is more elastic, or price-sensitive, than the others.
3. *Difficult resale* If one set of customers could buy the product at the lower price and then resell the product for a profit, the firm could not enforce its price discrimination. Because consumer goods like shoes, groceries, and clothes are easily resold, price discrimination works best in marketing services that are consumed on the spot. Examples include theme park admissions and restaurant meals. Airlines can offer senior discounts because the company can ask for identification and proof of age before letting the customer board.

Although most forms of price discrimination are perfectly legal, sometimes firms use price discrimination to drive other firms out of business. This illegal form of the practice is called predatory pricing, and you will read more about it in Section 4.

Section 2 Assessment

Progress Monitoring *Online*
For: Self-quiz with vocabulary practice
Web Code: mna-2076

Key Terms and Main Ideas

1. What can a firm with **market power** do?
2. Why does government usually approve of **natural monopolies?**
3. What are three different forms of **price discrimination?**
4. Define the term ***economies of scale*** in your own words.

Applying Economic Concepts

5. ***Try This*** Look through a recent newspaper for advertisements and coupons. List five examples of price discrimination.
6. ***Decision Making*** Suppose that you are the mayor of your town, and a local butcher asks you to **franchise** his shop as the only approved butcher shop in town. List a reason for and a reason against granting his request.
7. ***Critical Thinking*** Do you believe that public education is a natural monopoly? Why or why not?

For: Research Activity
Visit: PHSchool.com
Web Code: mnd-2072

7. Student responses should demonstrate an understanding of the concept of natural monopoly. Most students will probably say that public education is a natural monopoly because state boards determine what will be offered. Students who disagree may point to the school choice movement and the way it affects the natural monopoly.

Progress Monitoring *Online*
For additional assessment, have students access Progress Monitoring Online at **Web Code:** mna-2076

Go Online PHSchool.com Typing in the Web Code when prompted will bring students directly to detailed instructions for this activity.

Economist

Entrepreneur

ECONOMIC *Profile*

Bill Gates (b. 1955)

When Bill Gates was 12 years old, the school he attended in Seattle, Washington, bought a computer terminal that was connected to a large computer at a local company. He immediately became hooked on computers and their potential uses. Today, as the Chief Executive Officer and Chairman of Microsoft, the world's largest software company, Gates says his goal is "to have a computer on every desk and in every home, all running Microsoft software."

A Young Entrepreneur

While still a teenager, Gates and some friends developed a computer program to analyze and graph traffic data. In marketing the completed system to city governments, Gates and his friends rang up $20,000 in sales before customers realized they were dealing with students. The company soon folded, but Gates never lost his entrepreneurial spirit.

Growing a Company

In 1975, longtime friend Paul Allen learned that a company in New Mexico was manufacturing a kit to build a small computer. Allen convinced 19-year-old Gates to leave Harvard University and form a company to produce an operating system for this first personal computer, or PC. They named their venture Microsoft.

Five years later, Microsoft landed the contract to develop the operating system for computer giant IBM's new PCs. By 1983, 40 percent of all personal computers were running on Microsoft's operating system.

In the late 1980s, Gates launched Windows, a new, PC-compatible operating system that used graphics and a mouse to perform computer functions. Microsoft's market share for operating systems jumped to 70 percent. Windows also allowed Gates to capture the market for software such as word processing programs, because competitors' products still depended on Microsoft's old, less user-friendly operating system. Those competitors began to complain that Microsoft had a monopoly.

Defending Microsoft

In 1997, the U.S. government claimed that by linking Microsoft's Internet browser to its operating system, Microsoft was unfairly using Windows' huge market share against rival browser companies. Gates angrily denied the charge. "Any operating system without a browser is going to be . . . out of business," he said. "Shall we improve our product or go out of business?"

Some former associates have another view. "He doesn't look for win-win situations with others," one says, "but for ways to make others lose. Success is defined as flattening the competition." Gates rejects such assessments. However, even today, surrounded by the success that being the world's richest person represents, he maintains his competitive edge. Having settled Microsoft's dispute with the federal government, Gates must focus on the changing technological environment ahead.

CHECK FOR UNDERSTANDING

1. **Source Reading** Identify and explain the steps by which Microsoft used its operating systems to gain what critics called a monopoly of the entire computer software industry.
2. **Critical Thinking** Gates claims that his competitive practices improve the industry. His critics claim that they damage it. With which side do you agree, and why?
3. **Decision Making** How important do you think competitiveness is in building a successful company? Why?

Beyond the Classroom: Career Connections

Computer Scientist The wide use of computers has generated a need for highly skilled workers who are trained in designing computers and the software systems that run them. Computer scientists work in both academic institutions and private industry. Their responsibilities range from working with programming language to designing computer games. Have students find out more about the work of computer scientists, such as the academic requirements needed to enter the field, the outlook for the career, and the specific kinds of work that computer scientists perform. Students might also find out the projected salary ranges for people who enter the field.

ECONOMIC *Profile*
Bill Gates

Background

Bill Gates continues to be involved in management decisions and technical development at Microsoft. He has combined his interest in computer technology with his interest in the arts. The Corbis Corporation, which he founded, is developing a comprehensive digital archive of art from private and public collections around the world.

In addition to his computer-related projects, Gates has endowed a philanthropic foundation with more than $17 billion to support health and learning initiatives throughout the world. Part of the endowment has been used to provide computers and Internet access to libraries in low-income communities throughout the United States and Canada.

Careers in Economics Activity
Unit 2 folder, p. 46 gives students a closer look at the career path of a regional sales manager.

Economic Cartoon
Unit 2 folder, p. 47 gives students practice in interpreting cartoons about profile content.

Answers to . . .

1. Microsoft provided the operating system for the PCs made by IBM. This gave the firm a large share of the market for PCs. Next it launched the user-friendly Windows, so Microsoft had an even larger market share. Finally Microsoft captured the market for software such as word processing programs because competitors' products still ran on the old Microsoft operating system.
2. Opinions will vary but should demonstrate reasoned judgment and an understanding of the concepts and issues surrounding the controversy.
3. Some students will say that competitiveness gives a person the drive to succeed. Other students will say that all that is needed to succeed is an excellent product that satisfies a demand.

Section 3

Monopolistic Competition and Oligopoly

Objectives You may wish to call students' attention to the objectives in the Section Preview. The objectives are reflected in the main headings of the section.

Bellringer Display the following terms: *bread, soft drinks, athletic shoes*. Have students list their favorite brands of each of these products. Explain that in this section they will learn that most of these items are produced by firms that are monopolistically competitive.

Vocabulary Builder Have students find the definition of each key term listed in the Section Preview in the margins. Then ask groups of three to four students to act out the terms *price war*, *price fixing*, and *cartel*.

Lesson Plan

Teaching the Main Concepts L3

1. Focus Point out to students that the monopolistic competition market structure is closest to the perfect competition market structure while the oligopoly is closest to the monopolistic market structure.

2. Instruct Discuss with students the characteristics of monopolistic competition and oligopoly. Ask them to think of examples of firms in these types of market structures.

3. Close/Reteach Refer students to the chart on p. 170 that summarizes the characteristics of market structures. Have them create another row that explains how each type of market structure affects consumers.

Guided Reading and Review Unit 2 folder, p. 39 asks students to identify the main ideas of the section and to define or identify key terms.

Section 3 Monopolistic Competition and Oligopoly

Preview

Objectives

After studying this section you will be able to:

1. **Describe** characteristics and give examples of monopolistic competition.
2. **Explain** how firms compete without lowering prices.
3. **Understand** how firms in a monopolistically competitive market set output.
4. **Describe** characteristics and give examples of oligopoly.

Section Focus

Monopolistic competition is similar to perfect competition, except that companies sell slightly different goods. Oligopoly, which is closer to monopoly, describes a market with only a few large producers.

Key Terms

monopolistic competition
differentiation
nonprice competition
oligopoly
price war
collusion
price fixing
cartel

monopolistic competition *a market structure in which many companies sell products that are similar but not identical*

So far, you have studied the two extremes of the range of market structures: perfect competition and monopoly. Very few markets fall into either of these categories. Instead, most fall into two additional categories that economists call monopolistic competition and oligopoly.

Monopolistic Competition

In **monopolistic competition,** many companies compete in an open market to sell products that are similar but not identical. Each firm holds a monopoly over its own particular product. You can think of monopolistic competition as a modified version of perfect competition with minor differences in products.

The differences between perfect competition and monopolistic competition arise because monopolistically competitive firms sell goods that are similar enough to be substituted for one another but are not identical. Monopolistic competition does not involve identical commodities. An example of a monopolistically competitive market is the market for jeans. All jeans can be described as denim pants, but in the shops, buyers can choose from a variety of colors, brand names, styles, and sizes.

Unlike perfect competition, monopolistic competition is a fact of everyday life. You

▶ The market for denim jeans is monopolistically competitive because jeans can vary by size, color, style, and designer.

Graphing the Main Idea

Markets and Prices To build understanding of the concepts of **markets and prices,** have students use a double web graphic organizer like the one below to record details about the elements of monopolistic competition and oligopoly. Remind students that a double web organizer can be used to compare and contrast information about two topics.

Section Reading Support Transparencies A template and the answers for this graphic organizer can be found in Chapter 7, Section 3 of the Section Reading Support Transparency System.

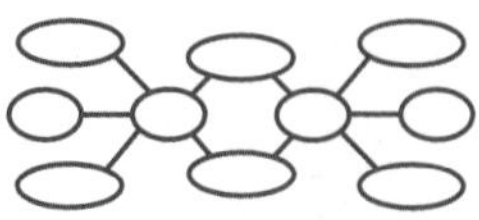

and your friends probably buy from monopolistically competitive firms several times a week. Common examples include bagel shops, ice cream stands, gas stations, and retail stores.

Four Conditions of Monopolistic Competition

Monopolistic competition develops from four conditions. As you read about the types of markets that favor monopolistic competition, note how similar they are to the rules that define perfect competition.

1. *Many firms* As a rule, monopolistically competitive markets are not marked by economies of scale or high start-up costs. Because firms can start selling goods and earning money after a small initial investment, new firms spring up quickly to join the market.
2. *Few artificial barriers to entry* Firms in a monopolistically competitive market do not face the high barriers to entry discussed in Section 1. Patents do not protect anyone from competition, either because they have expired or because each firm sells a product that is distinct enough to fall outside the zone of patent protection. Just like a perfectly competitive market, a monopolistically competitive market includes so many competing firms that producers cannot work together to keep out new competitors.
3. *Slight control over price* Firms in a monopolistically competitive market structure have some freedom to raise or lower their prices because each firm's goods are a little different from everyone else's, and some people are willing to pay more for the difference. However, unlike a monopoly, a monopolistically competitive firm has only limited control over price. This is because consumers will substitute a rival's product if the price rises too high. For example, many customers will choose a can of brand-name cola over a generic cola even if it costs a quarter more per can. If the brand-name cola cost $5 more per can, however, most people would buy the cheaper cola or drink something else.
4. *Differentiated products* Firms have some control over their selling price because they can differentiate, or distinguish, their goods from the other products in the market. The main difference between perfect competition and monopolistic competition is that **differentiation** enables a monopolistically competitive seller to profit from the differences between his or her products and competitors' products.

Figure 7.8 **Monopolistic Competition**

Number of firms: Many

Variety of goods: Some

Barriers to entry: Low

Control over prices: Little

Many firms provide a variety of goods in a monopolistically competitive market.
Competition Why do firms in monopolistic competition have some control over prices?

Nonprice Competition

Firms try not to compete on price alone. The alternative is **nonprice competition,** or competition through ways other than lower prices. Nonprice competition takes several different forms.

1. *Physical characteristics* The simplest way for a firm to distinguish its products is to offer a new size, color, shape,

differentiation *making a product different from other similar products*

nonprice competition *a way to attract customers through style, service, or location, but not a lower price*

Econ 101: Key Concepts Made Easy

Competition Two of the key concepts in this section are **differentiation** and **nonprice competition.** The presence of differentiated products is a defining characteristic of a monopolistically competitive market. Differentiation results in nonprice competition, in which firms try to compete not through price alone but through other factors that set their products apart from the competitors' products.

Ask students to read the section titled "Nonprice Competition." Then have them look at magazine ads and television commercials to find examples of the various forms of nonprice competition. Have students share their examples with the class.

Differentiated Instruction  L2

Work with students to help them change the section's main headings and subheadings into questions. Then organize the class into small groups. Assign each group one of the main headings. Ask group members to work together to answer the questions related to it. Have the groups share their answers. ELL

Differentiated Instruction  L3

(Reteaching) Have students choose a product category (such as pain relievers, shampoos, or cosmetics) that is sold by monopolistically competitive firms. Ask students to create posters that use product pictures and text to explain elements of monopolistic competition (nonprice competition, the relationship between price and output, profit).

Transparency Resource Package Economics Concepts, 7F: Monopolistic Competition

Differentiated Instruction  L1

Explain that monopolistic competition includes many forms of nonprice competition, such as product differentiation, branding, and advertising. Ask students to name products that they would buy, even at a higher price because of one or more of these factors. SN

Answer to . . .

Building Key Concepts The firms have some control because each firm's goods are slightly different from the rest, and some people are willing to pay more for the difference.

Differentiated Instruction L4

Have students find examples of businesses in their community that are in monopolistic competition, such as restaurants, hardware stores, and so on. Ask students to examine local advertising and visit locations to find out what each business does to differentiate its product or service from that of the competition. Have students present their findings in oral reports to the class. GT

Differentiated Instruction L3

Have students choose a product they use that is manufactured by a variety of firms, such as a hair care product. Ask them to identify the reasons why they choose one brand over other available brands. Have students present their reasons in an advertisement for the product. Encourage them to evaluate whether the differences between the product they use and other, similar products are more a matter of perception than of reality.

texture, or taste. Running shoes, pens, cars, and toothpaste are good examples of products that can be easily differentiated by their physical characteristics. A pen is always a writing tool that uses ink, but many people will pay extra for a pen that looks or writes differently. Similarly, you can probably describe a "car" in only a few words, but factories around the world manufacture thousands of car models to fit a range of personalities, jobs, families, and incomes.

2. *Location* Real estate agents say that the three most important factors when buying property are "location, location, location." Some goods can be differentiated by *where* they are sold. Gas stations, movie theaters, and grocery stores succeed or fail based on their locations. A convenience store in the middle of a desert differentiates its product simply by selling it hundreds of miles away from the nearest competitor. Such a location allows the seller to charge a lot more for a quart of water.
3. *Service level* Some sellers can charge higher prices because they offer their customers a high level of service. Conventional restaurants and fast-food restaurants both offer meals to customers. However, conventional restaurants provide servers who bring the food to your table, whereas fast-food restaurants offer a more barebones, do-it-yourself atmosphere. Conventional restaurants and fast-food chains sell many of the same food items, but fast-food chains sell their meals for less. Customers at conventional restaurants pay more for the service and the relaxing atmosphere.
4. *Advertising, image, or status* Some firms use advertising to create apparent differences between their own offerings and other products in the marketplace. These product differences are often more a matter of perception than reality. For example, a designer can apply his or her name to a plain white T-shirt and charge a higher price, even if the quality of fabric and stitching is no different than what generic T-shirts offer. Customers who pay extra for a designer T-shirt do so because the image and status that go with the designer's name are worth the extra money to them.

Price, Output, and Profits

When economists look at price, output, and profits under monopolistic competition, they find the market looks very much as it would under perfect competition.

Prices

Prices under monopolistic competition will be higher than they would be in perfect competition, because firms have some power to raise prices. However, the number of firms and ease of entry prevent companies

▼ **A gas station built in the right location can charge more for gasoline.**

Block Scheduling Strategies

Consider these suggestions to take advantage of extended class time:

- Extend the Vocabulary Builder activity by discussing the presentations. Then form small groups, and have each group write a story that uses at least three key terms. Ask a representative from each group to read the completed story aloud.
- Have students complete the Learning Styles activity on this page. Then ask students to identify the brand of a favorite food. Have them work with partners to set up blind taste tests. Have students compare their final choices with their stated preferences.

from raising prices as high as they would if they were a true monopoly. As you have read, if a monopolistically competitive firm raised prices too high, most customers would ignore any differences and buy the cheaper product. Because customers can choose among many substitute products, monopolistically competitive firms face more elastic demand curves than true monopolists do.

Output

The law of demand says that output and price are negatively related. As one rises, the other falls. Because monopolistically competitive firms sell their products at higher prices than do perfectly competitive firms, but at lower prices than a monopoly, total output under monopolistic competition falls somewhere between that of monopoly and that of perfect competition.

Profit

Like perfectly competitive firms, monopolistically competitive firms earn just enough to cover all of their costs, including salaries for the workers. If a monopolistically competitive firm started to earn profits well above its costs, two market trends would work to take those profits away.

First, fierce competition would encourage rivals to think of new ways to differentiate their products and lure customers back. If one company hires a basketball star to promote its soft drink, a rival might hire a popular singer, while another rival could invest in an advertising blitz on television. The rivalries among firms prevent any one firm from earning excessive profits for long.

Secondly, new firms will enter the market with slightly different products that cost a lot less than the market leaders. If the original good costs too much, consumers will switch to these substitutes. You've seen this happen when a brand-name line of clothing, video games, or stuffed animals becomes popular. Competitors quickly flood the market with cheap imitations for people who can't afford the original or don't know or care about the difference.

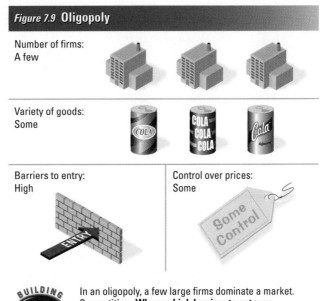

Figure 7.9 Oligopoly

Number of firms:
A few

Variety of goods:
Some

Barriers to entry:
High

Control over prices:
Some

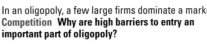

In an oligopoly, a few large firms dominate a market. **Competition Why are high barriers to entry an important part of oligopoly?**

While monopolistically competitive firms can earn profits in the short run, they have to work hard to keep their product distinct to stay ahead of their rivals. Often, they don't succeed.

Production Costs and Variety

Some economists note that firms in monopolistic competition may not be able to produce their goods at the lowest possible average cost. Monopolistically competitive markets have many firms, each producing too little output to minimize costs and use resources efficiently. On the other hand, consumers in these markets enjoy a wide variety of goods to choose from.

Oligopoly

Oligopoly describes a market dominated by a few large, profitable firms. Oligopoly looks like an imperfect form of monopoly. Economists usually call an industry an oligopoly if the four largest firms produce at least 70 to 80 percent of the output.

oligopoly *a market structure in which a few large firms dominate a market*

Differentiated Instruction 

To help students create a product on a contemporary economic issue or topic using critical methods of inquiry, have them choose one of the following industries: domestic automobiles, air travel, soft drinks, breakfast cereals, or household appliances. Ask students to research the industry and explain why it can be considered an oligopoly. Students should specify how characteristics of the industry reflect those of an oligopoly. Ask them to present their findings in an annotated poster.

Differentiated Instruction 

Time: 90 minutes

Activity: Create an infomercial comparing monopolistic competition to monopoly, perfect competition, and oligopoly.

Grouping: Groups of four to six students

Purpose: To create an infomercial that can be used as a teaching tool for other students of economics. Students work together to create script with illustrations and graphics that would provide instruction about and comparisons of the market structures discussed in Chapter 7.

Roles: Illustrator, writer, narrator

Outcome: Students will understand the major characteristics of each of the market structures.

Preparing for Standardized Tests

Have students read the section titled "Price, Output, and Profits" and then answer the question below.

Which of the following best describes prices in a monopolistically competitive market?

A Prices can be raised as high as in a true monopoly.

B Prices are higher when output increases.

C Prices are lower than in a perfectly competitive market.

(D) Prices are higher than in a perfectly competitive market.

Answer to . . .

Building Key Concepts If it were easy for firms to enter the market, more firms would enter, so an oligopoly would not exist.

Background

Economics in History

In 1993 the three major producers of baby formula paid $200 million to retailers and wholesalers of their products. The money was part of a settlement of lawsuits that had been brought against the three firms, claiming that they had conspired to fix prices.

Learning Styles Activity
Learning Styles Lesson Plans folder, p. 19 asks students to compare and contrast characteristics of three market structures—perfect competition, monopolistic competition, and oligopoly—using Venn diagrams.

Transparency Resource Package
Economics Concepts, 7G: Oligopoly
Economics Concepts, 7H: Comparison of Market Structures

Go Online PHSchool.com Typing in the Web Code when prompted will bring students directly to the article.

THE WALL STREET JOURNAL. CLASSROOM EDITION

For an additional article from *The Wall Street Journal Classroom Edition,* see the Source Articles folder in the **Teaching Resources**, pp. 21–23.

Markets can be grouped into four basic structures: perfect competition, monopolistic competition, oligopoly, and monopoly.
Competition
How does a monopolistic competition differ from monopoly?

Figure 7.10 Comparison of Market Structures

	Perfect Competition	Monopolistic Competition	Oligopoly	Monopoly
Number of firms	Many	Many	A few dominate	One
Variety of goods	None	Some	Some	None
Control over prices	None	Little	Some	Complete
Barriers to entry	None	Low	High	Complete
Examples	Wheat, shares of stock	Jeans, books	Cars, movie studios	Public water

Acting on their own or as a team, the biggest firms in an oligopoly may well set prices higher and output lower than in a perfectly competitive market. Examples of oligopolies in the United States include the markets for air travel, breakfast cereals, and household appliances.

Barriers to Entry

An oligopoly can form when significant barriers to entry keep new companies from entering the market to compete with existing firms. Sometimes these barriers are created by a system of government licenses or patents.

In other cases, the economic realities of the market lead to an oligopoly. High start-up costs, such as expensive machinery or a large advertising campaign, can scare firms away from the market. Many small airlines have had trouble competing with larger, better-financed rivals because airplanes are very expensive to buy and maintain. The biggest airlines compound the problem because they often own the most desirable gates at the airport, and already enjoy name recognition and the trust of the consumer. As another example, the two big cola manufacturers have invested so much money in their brand names and sales networks over the last century that few companies think they can successfully challenge their grip on the market.

In the News Read more about oligopoly in "Bottom of the Food Chain," an article in The Wall Street Journal Classroom Edition.

Go Online
The Wall Street Journal Classroom Edition
For: Current Events
Visit: PHSchool.com
Web Code: mnc-2073

Some oligopolies occur because of economies of scale. As you have read, when a firm experiences economies of scale, the average cost of production decreases as output increases. In a monopoly market, only one company can produce enough goods to earn a profit. In an oligopoly, perhaps three or four companies can reach a profitable level of output before the market becomes too crowded and revenue falls below costs.

Cooperation and Collusion

Oligopoly presents a big challenge to government, because oligopolistic firms often *seem* to work together to form a monopoly, even when they are not actually doing so. Many government regulations try to make oligopolistic firms act more like competitive firms. When determined oligopolists work together illegally to set prices and bar competing firms from the market, they can become as damaging to the consumer as a monopoly.

The three practices that concern government the most are price leadership, collusion, and cartels. While these three practices represent ways that firms in an oligopoly can try to control a market, they don't always work. Each tactic includes an incentive for firms to cheat and undo any benefits.

Interdisciplinary Connections: Geography

The Organization of Petroleum Exporting Countries (OPEC) A primary reason for the formation of OPEC was to increase the individual revenues of the member nations, thereby benefiting their economies. The oil reserves in these nations make up about three-fourths of the world's reserves, and oil from these countries makes up about 40 percent of the world's oil trade.

Making the Connection First have students locate the members of OPEC on a world map. Then ask them to research economic development in the OPEC countries. Have them find out to what extent oil revenue has affected those nations' economies and the reasons for these effects. Have students present their findings in oral reports.

Answer to . . .

Building Key Concepts Monopolistic competition consists of many firms, has a variety of goods, little control over prices, and low barriers to entry. A monopoly consists of one firm, no variety in goods, complete control over prices, and complete barriers.

Sometimes the market leader in an oligopoly can start a round of price increases and cuts by making its plans clear to other firms. Price leaders can set prices and output for entire industries as long as other member firms go along with the leader's policy. But disagreements among member firms can spark a **price war,** when competitors cut their prices very low to win business. A price war is harmful to producers but good for consumers.

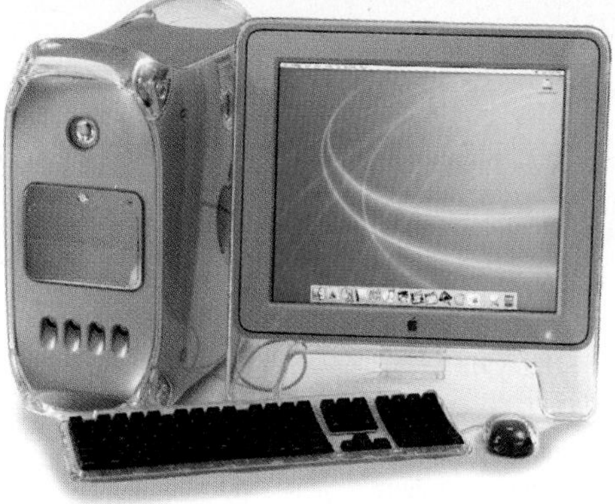

◀ **A computer manufacturer can distinguish its computers with bright colors or a sleek design.**

Collusion refers to an agreement among members of an oligopoly to set prices and production levels. One outcome of collusion is called **price fixing,** an agreement among firms to sell at the same or very similar prices. Collusive agreements set prices and output at the levels that would be chosen by a monopolist. Collusion is illegal in the United States, but the lure of monopolistic profits can tempt businesses to make such agreements despite the illegality and risks.

Collusion is not, however, the only reason for identical pricing in oligopolistic industries. Such pricing may actually result from intense competition, especially if advertising is vigorous and new lines of products are being introduced.

Cartels

Stronger than a collusive agreement, a **cartel** is an agreement by a formal organization of producers to coordinate prices and production. Although other countries and international organizations permit them, cartels are illegal in the United States. Cartels can only survive if every member keeps to its agreed output levels and no more. Otherwise, prices will fall, and firms will lose profits. However, each member has a strong incentive to cheat and produce more than its quota. If every cartel member cheats, too much product reaches the market, and prices fall. Cartels can also collapse if some producers are left out of the group and decide to lower their prices below the cartel's levels. Therefore, cartels usually do not last very long.

price war *a series of competitive price cuts that lowers the market price below the cost of production*

collusion *an agreement among firms to divide the market, set prices, or limit production*

price fixing *an agreement among firms to charge one price for the same good*

cartel *a formal organization of producers that agree to coordinate prices and production*

Section 3 Assessment

Progress Monitoring *Online*
For: Self-quiz with vocabulary practice
Web Code: mna-2077

Key Terms and Main Ideas

1. What are the four conditions of **monopolistic competition?**
2. How do economists determine whether a market is an **oligopoly?**
3. Give three examples of **nonprice competition.**
4. How would **price fixing** and **collusion** help producers?

Applying Economic Concepts

5. ***Using the Databank*** The map on page 545 indicates which countries are members of OPEC, a cartel made up of oil-exporting countries. In the 1970s, OPEC successfully raised oil prices by cutting production. Based on what you have read in this section, explain how this situation illustrates **(a)** how cartels operate **(b)** why cartels can be dangerous.
6. ***Decision Making*** Would you describe the following markets as monopolistic competition or oligopoly? **(a)** refrigerators **(b)** video game systems **(c)** gourmet ice cream **(d)** sunscreen **(e)** cable sports channels
7. ***Critical Thinking*** Which of the four forms of nonprice competition described on pp. 167–168 would you emphasize for the following products? Explain your reasoning. **(a)** a new brand of bottled water **(b)** in-home computer repair **(c)** protein bars

For: Research Activity
Visit: PHSchool.com
Web Code: mnd-2073

Progress Monitoring *Online*
For additional assessment, have students access Progress Monitoring Online at **Web Code:** mna-2077

Go Online PHSchool.com Typing in the Web Code when prompted will bring students directly to detailed instructions for this activity.

GTE Guide to the Essentials
Chapter 7, Section 3, p. 30 provides support for students who need additional review of the section content. Spanish support is available in the Spanish edition of the guide on p. 30.

Quiz Unit 2 folder, p. 40 includes questions to check students' understanding of Section 3 content.

Presentation Pro CD-ROM
Quiz provides multiple-choice questions to check students' understanding of Section 3 content.

Answers to . . .

Section 3 Assessment

1. many firms, few artificial barriers to entry, slight control over price, differentiated products
2. An industry is usually called an oligopoly if the four largest firms produce at least 70 to 80 percent of the market's output.
3. Students may mention any three of the following: physical characteristics; location; service level; advertising, image, or status.
4. Price fixing aids producers by inflating prices unnaturally. Collusion occurs when sellers group together, set higher prices for goods and services, and then earn greater revenues as a result.
5. (a) Cartels set prices and production levels for entire industries as long as other member firms go along with the leader's policy, in effect monopolizing the industry and accruing significant profit from the consumer. (b) Cartels can control the market and significantly raise prices, requiring consumers to pay unnecessarily high prices.
6. (a) monopolistic competition (b) oligopoly (c) monopolistic competition (d) monopolistic competition (e) oligopoly
7. (a) advertising, image, or status (b) service level (c) physical characteristics

Section 4

Regulation and Deregulation

Objectives You may wish to call students' attention to the objectives in the Section Preview. The objectives are reflected in the main headings of the section.

Bellringer Ask students to speculate about how the government regulates aspects of their personal lives. List their responses. Lead a discussion of the reasons for each government regulation. Explain to students that in this section they will learn about ways in which the government intervenes in the market to protect competition.

Vocabulary Builder Have students create a matching quiz for the key terms in the Section Preview. Ask students to exchange quizzes, complete them, and check each other's answers.

Lesson Plan

Teaching the Main Concepts L3

1. Focus The government intervenes in the market when firms try to control the prices and supply of important goods. Ask volunteers to suggest ways in which firms might do this, giving real-life examples if possible.

2. Instruct Point out that unfair business practices in the past have led to government regulation of some aspects of business. Discuss with students the kinds of practices the government regulates or forbids. As students study the information in the section, discuss the reasons for government regulation of various practices and the benefits and drawbacks of such regulation.

3. Close/Reteach Remind students that regulation and deregulation are ways in which the government protects and promotes competition in the market. Have students read the business section of a newspaper and bring in articles about regulation.

Section 4 Regulation and Deregulation

Preview

Objectives

After studying this section you will be able to:

1. **Understand** how firms use market power.
2. **List** three market practices that the government regulates or bans to protect competition.
3. **Define** deregulation, and list its effects on several industries.

Section Focus

The federal government sometimes steps into markets to promote competition and the lower prices it brings. In recent years, the government has also deregulated several markets to promote competition.

Key Terms

predatory pricing
antitrust laws
trust
merger
deregulation

It's 1946. The soldiers have come home from World War II, the cities are booming, and you're a city planner who needs to get people to work each morning. You can build wide roads and parking lots and encourage people to buy cars, you can invest in a fleet of buses, or you can expand the streetcar lines and train tracks that already criss-cross the town center. Ideally, you will choose the most efficient system.

However, you never get to decide. A company called National City Lines (NCL) buys your city's streetcar network and decides to raise fares and shut down several lines. Service gets so bad that commuters stay away, and NCL soon shuts down the system. It's now 1966, and your streetcars are gone. Since the roads are too crowded for more cars, you must buy buses.

▼ After World War II, National City Lines used its mass transit monopoly to shut down streetcar lines.

In the newspaper, you read that National City Lines was secretly funded by companies that make tires, automobiles, and gasoline—the same companies that now offer to sell you 200 new buses.

This really happened in cities like Los Angeles and Baltimore, where National City Lines turned a mass transit oligopoly into a monopoly by buying up its rivals. National City Lines then used its monopoly to close down the streetcar lines. Although some experts argue that the streetcars might have died out anyway, many critics blame National City Lines for the end result. No one can know what might have happened in a competitive market.

If you think what National City Lines did was unfair, the federal government agrees. In this section, you will read about anticompetitive practices and the tools the government uses to stop them.

Market Power

As you have read, monopoly and oligopoly can sometimes be bad for the consumer and the economy as a whole. Markets dominated by a few large firms tend to have higher prices and lower output than markets with many sellers. Before we look at antitrust policies, let's think about how a firm might try to increase its market power.

Graphing the Main Idea

Government To build understanding of the concept of **government,** have students use a web graphic organizer like the one below to explain how the government breaks up and prevents the growth of monopolies. Remind students that a web shows a main idea with its supporting details.

Section Reading Support Transparencies A template and the answers for this graphic organizer can be found in Chapter 7, Section 4 of the Section Reading Support Transparency System.

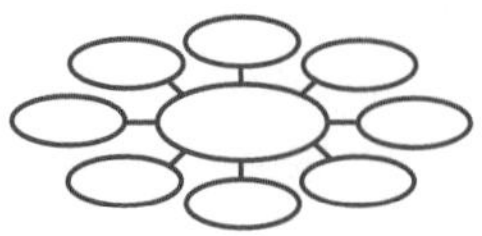

To control prices and output like a monopoly, the leading firms in the market can form a cartel, merge with one another, or set the market price below their costs for the short term to drive competitors out of business. The last practice is known as **predatory pricing.** Economists are skeptical about most claims of predatory pricing because the predator loses money each time it drives an endless series of rivals out of business.

◀ **Public outrage with powerful trusts in the late 1800s led Congress to pass antitrust legislation.**

Government and Competition

The federal government has a number of policies that keep firms from controlling the price and supply of important goods. If a firm controls a large share of a market, the Federal Trade Commission and the Department of Justice's Antitrust Division will watch that firm closely to ensure that it does not unfairly force out its competitors. These government policies are known as **antitrust laws** because a **trust** is a business combination similar to a cartel.

In 1890, Congress passed the Sherman Antitrust Act, which outlawed mergers and monopolies that limit trade between states. This and other laws gave the government the power to regulate industry, to stop firms from forming cartels or monopolies, and to break up existing monopolies. Over the years, Congress passed new laws to outlaw other anticompetitive practices.

Despite the antitrust laws, companies have used many strategies to gain control over their markets. Some firms require a customer who buys one product to buy other products from the same company, whether or not the customer wants them. For example, a tennis shoe manufacturer can demand that a chain buy and resell its brand-name shirts, windbreakers, and watches if it wants to sell its shoes. Another tactic, the one employed by National City Lines, is to buy out competitors.

Regulating Business Practices

The government has the power to regulate all of these practices if they give too much power to a company that already has few competitors. Microsoft sells operating systems, software that tells a computer how to run. In 1997, the Department of Justice accused Microsoft of using a monopoly in operating systems to control the market for a program known as a browser. A browser allows people to access Web sites.

Microsoft insisted that computer manufacturers that sold its operating system also include its browser. The government accused Microsoft of predatory pricing because the company gave away its browser for free, which would ruin the other browser company, Netscape. Microsoft's power in one market gave it a big—and possibly unfair—advantage in related markets.

Microsoft argued that the browser was part of its operating system and could not be sold separately. Microsoft's defenders said that companies *do* compete with Microsoft, and people buy Microsoft software because they like it. In November 1999, a federal judge ruled against Microsoft. Microsoft appealed, and in 2001, President Bush settled the case. According to the settlement, Microsoft could link its browser to its operating system but could not force computer manufacturers to provide only Microsoft software on new computers.

predatory pricing *selling a product below cost to drive competitors out of the market*

antitrust laws *laws that encourage competition in the marketplace*

trust *like a cartel, an illegal grouping of companies that discourages competition*

Guided Reading and Review
Unit 2 folder, p. 41 ask students to identify the main ideas of the section and to define or identify key terms.

Background

Economics in History

John Sherman, younger brother of Civil War general William Tecumseh Sherman, was a United States senator from 1861 to 1877 and from 1881 to 1897. Although the Sherman Antitrust Act of 1890 bears his name, it was a piece of compromise legislation of which he did not fully approve. The act outlaws all combinations that restrain trade between states or with foreign nations and bars attempts to monopolize any part of trade or commerce in the United States. Its language was vague, however, and it provided large corporations with many loopholes. In 1914 the Sherman Antitrust Act was clarified and strengthened by the Clayton Antitrust Act. This act specified many illegal practices that contribute to or result from monopolies.

Differentiated Instruction 

Have students summarize the government's case against Microsoft. Then ask them to research Microsoft's defense. Finally, have students write a position paper in support of one side or the other.
GT

Transparency Resource Package
Economics Concepts, 7I: Government Regulatory Agencies

Econ 101: Key Concepts Made Easy

Markets and Prices One of the key concepts in this section is **predatory pricing.** Explain to students that with predatory pricing, one firm (the predator) sets a price so low that the firm actually loses money. However, the price also makes other firms set even lower prices or lose sales. The predator hopes to drive those other firms out of business. Then the predatory firm can raise prices again and recover its losses—as well as increase its share of the market.

Ask students why a large firm or one with vast resources would be more likely to act as a predator. Then have them explain why the government outlaws this practice.

Differentiated Instruction 

Ask students to list the key terms and then use them in one or several paragraphs in which they summarize the reasons why the government steps in to protect competition in the market. LPR

Differentiated Instruction 

Explain to students that breaking up monopolies and blocking mergers are two different ways of preventing large firms from dominating the market. Ask students to think about how these two tactics approach the problem from different sides. When students have considered this question, hold a class discussion so that they can share their conclusions.

Economic Detective Activity

Unit 2 folder, p. 45, "The Business of Buck Bidness," provides an integrated application of chapter concepts.

Background Note

Airline Policy

The September 11 attacks precipitated a new twist on government policies toward the airlines. After the attack, the demand for air travel decreased, and airlines announced that they were losing money fast enough that they were threatened with bankruptcy. The national government responded by providing $5 billion in cash and $10 billion in loan guarantees. One motivation for the aid package was to cover the airlines' losses resulting from closing the airports for four days after the attacks—an action ordered by the national government. The costs of the four-day closure was about $1.2 billion, a small fraction of the bailout package. The question is, Why did the airline industry receive a bailout package when other industries did not?

Figure 7.11 Key Events in Federal Antitrust Policy

1900 — 1915 — 1925 — 1940

1901 Theodore Roosevelt becomes President and begins enforcing the 1890 Sherman Antitrust Act, which outlaws mergers and monopolies that restrain trade between states

1911 Supreme Court breaks up John D. Rockefeller's Standard Oil Trust

1914 Clayton Antitrust Act outlaws practices that limit competition or lead to monopoly

1936 Robinson-Patman Act defines and outlaws several forms of price discrimination

▲ **Over the past century, the federal government has acted often to promote competition in American industry.**

Breaking Up Monopolies

The government used antitrust legislation to break up existing monopolies such as the American Tobacco Company and John D. Rockefeller's Standard Oil Trust in 1911. In 1982, the government broke American Telephone and Telegraph (AT&T) into seven regional phone companies, including BellSouth, USWest, and PacificBell. Because the government treated local telephone service as a natural monopoly, AT&T legally controlled all the cables and networks that linked telephones in homes and businesses. The government stepped in only when AT&T used its legal monopoly in local phone service to take control of other markets for long-distance phone calls and communications equipment. Today, there are many firms in the market for long-distance service and the market is more competitive. Although thousands of workers lost their jobs, consumers benefit from lower prices and better technology.

Blocking Mergers

In addition to breaking up monopolistic companies, the government has the power to prevent the rise of monopolies. The government does this by blocking company **mergers** that might reduce competition and lead to higher prices. A merger occurs when a company joins with another company or companies to form a single firm. Government regulators also follow the effects of past mergers to check that they did not lead to unfair market control. You read in Section 1 that prices often fall when the number of firms in a market increases. The reverse is also true. Prices often rise when the number of firms in an industry falls.

merger *combination of two or more companies into a single firm*

The government tries to predict the effects of a merger on prices and service when it decides whether or not to approve a merger. Recently, the Department of Justice has looked at data collected by scanners at supermarket check-out lines to see how prices vary when two competitors join forces. In 1997, the Justice Department examined the proposed merger of two companies that sell office supplies. Their studies showed that one company charged less in cities where the other company also had stores. Using this data, the Federal Trade Commission (FTC) convinced the courts that the merger would hurt competition and force customers to pay higher prices. In the end, the Department of Justice did not allow the two companies to merge.

Block Scheduling Strategies

Consider these suggestions to take advantage of extended class time:

- Refer students to the cartoon on p. 173. Ask them to find additional examples of cartoons that express opinions about business practices today or in the past. Then have students draw their own cartoons on this subject. Display the cartoons and discuss them in class.
- Refer students to the time line on pp. 174–175. Review the legislation that has been enacted to promote competition. Then ask students to research the regulatory agencies that the government has created to promote competition and restrict unfair practices. Have students present their findings in a chart.

1974 Department of Justice sues to end AT&T's monopoly over local phone service

2001 Department of Justice settles its lawsuit with Microsoft

1955 1970 1985 2000

1950 Celler-Kefauver Act allows government to stop mergers that could hurt competition

1982 AT&T agrees to break up its local phone service into several companies

Preserving Incentives

While some mergers hurt the consumer by reducing competition, others can actually leave the consumer better off. In these cases, corporate mergers will lower overall average costs and lead to lower prices, more reliable products or service, and a more efficient industry. The government must act carefully to make the right decision. In 1997, the Justice Department and the FTC released new guidelines for proposed mergers. Now, companies that want to merge have the chance to prove that the merger would lower costs and consumer prices or lead to a better product.

Deregulation

In the late 1970s and 1980s, Congress passed laws to deregulate several industries. **Deregulation** means that the government no longer decides what role each company can play in a market and how much it can charge its customers. Over several years, the government deregulated the airline, trucking, banking, railroad, natural gas, and television broadcasting industries. Depending on the degree of deregulation, the government's action allowed—or forced—firms in these industries to compete more in markets by eliminating many entry barriers and price controls.

While deregulation weakens government control, antitrust laws strengthen it. Yet the government uses both of these tools, deregulation and antitrust laws, for the same purpose: to promote competition.

Many critics say that government efforts to regulate industries have created inefficiencies. In some cases, the economic facts that created the need for regulation in the first place have changed. For example, in Section 1 you read how the invention of cellular phones challenged the natural monopoly of local phone service and opened the market to new companies. The trucking industry was also regulated as a natural monopoly from the early 1900s until 1978. By then, many had decided that the government was regulating industries that were not natural monopolies at all.

Judging Deregulation

Deregulation has met with mixed success. In most cases, many new firms entered the

deregulation *the removal of some government controls over a market*

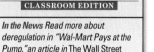

THE WALL STREET JOURNAL.
CLASSROOM EDITION

In the News Read more about deregulation in "Wal-Mart Pays at the Pump," an article in The Wall Street Journal Classroom Edition.

Go Online
The Wall Street Journal Classroom Edition
For: Current Events
Visit: PHSchool.com
Web Code: mnc-2074

Interdisciplinary Connections: History

Theodore Roosevelt In 1901 many Americans were concerned about industrial combinations called trusts. People felt that these trusts were causing continuing price increases. President Theodore Roosevelt responded by reviving the Sherman Antitrust Act, which had been in place since 1890 but had not been enforced.

Making the Connection Have students find out more about Theodore Roosevelt and his antitrust activities against railroad, beef, oil, and other monopolies. Have students research legislation that was passed and court rulings that were handed down during Roosevelt's administration as well as the results of these laws and rulings on monopolistic practices. Hold a class discussion of how these historic events affect today's government regulations.

Differentiated Instruction 

You may wish to have students add the following to their portfolios. Explain that the class will hold a debate on the effects of deregulation. The debate will address the following question: *Has deregulation been successful in promoting competition in the marketplace?*

Form two groups, one representing each side of the debate. Within these large groups have students form smaller groups to gather information. Students should research the effects of deregulation on the airline, banking, and trucking industries and find facts to support their side. Have them present the results of their research in the form of fact sheets or position papers. When students have finished their research, hold the debate, including a follow-up discussion or evaluation. GT

Economics Assessment Rubric
Economics Assessment Rubrics folder, pp. 14–15 provides sample evaluation materials for participation in debates.

Differentiated Instruction 

Display the words *antitrust* and *deregulation.* Explain how the prefixes and roots of these words help to reveal their meanings. Have volunteers explain the meaning of each term. Then supply examples of other words with these prefixes, and ask students to define them. ELL

Learning Styles Activity
Learning Styles Lesson Plans folder, p. 20 asks student groups to illustrate events in a firm's attempts to increase market power as well as to examine possible government action.

Go Online PHSchool.com Typing in the Web Code when prompted will bring students directly to the article.

GTE **Guide to the Essentials**
Chapter 7, Section 4, p. 31 provides support for students who need additional review of the section content. Spanish support is available in the Spanish edition of the guide on p. 31.

Quiz Unit 2 folder, p. 42 includes questions to check students' understanding of Section 4 content.

Presentation Pro CD-ROM
Quiz provides multiple-choice questions to check students' understanding of Section 4 content.

Answers to . . .

Section 4 Assessment

1. Antitrust laws are designed to encourage competition in the marketplace.
2. The government approves mergers only when the combined company will not be able to exert unfair control over markets or prices.
3. Predatory pricing usually leads to one or more firms being forced out of a market, limiting consumer choice and competition and resulting in higher prices.
4. Banking deregulation led to the Savings and Loan Crisis of the 1980s, as banks had more freedom to make riskier investments. Airline deregulation led to some mergers and some firms dropping out of the business but also to lower air fares for consumers.
5. These industries were considered natural monopolies. The government regulated these and other industries to prevent businesses from using market power to control prices and output.
6. Students' answers should demonstrate understanding of both editorials as well as skills in comparing and contrasting arguments.
7. Students should point out that the government intervenes because competition is an important part of the free enterprise system and should be protected. Students may disagree on how consistent the behavior of the government is with the ideas of laissez faire and free markets, but they should support their assertions with facts.

▲ **Many people blamed companies such as Enron for an electricity shortage that affected California in 2000 after deregulation. Other states have deregulated their electricity markets with no difficulties.**

deregulated industries right away. Competition certainly increased in the airline, trucking, and banking industries. Typically, years of wild growth were followed by the disappearance of some firms. This weeding out of weaker players is considered healthy for the economy, but it can be hard on workers in the short term.

In the 1990s, several states deregulated their electricity markets to allow private, competing companies to produce and sell energy to homeowners. In some markets, energy prices fell, but elsewhere, customers paid more. California experienced a massive energy crisis in 2000 that forced the state government to pay extraordinarily high rates for electricity. Many attributed this crisis to companies like Enron that may have used the state deregulation rules to create an electricity shortage.

Airlines: A Complicated Deregulation

Many new airlines started operating after President Carter deregulated the industry in 1978, but some eventually failed or were acquired. Freed from regulatory restriction, many of the large airlines competed aggressively for the busiest routes. For most travelers, the increased competition created lower prices. Another result is that many busy airports now have one dominant airline, and in some cases fares are actually higher than before deregulation.

In the early 2000s, changing conditions transformed the airlines. Over-expansion and sharply rising labor costs squeezed profits. The terrorist hijackings on September 11, 2001, followed by an economic downturn, caused many people to stop flying. Revenues plunged while costs of security and insurance rose. Although the federal government provided some aid, the future of the airline industry is uncertain as several major carriers struggle against bankruptcy.

Section 4 Assessment

Progress Monitoring *Online*
For: Self-quiz with vocabulary practice
Web Code: mna-2078

Key Terms and Main Ideas

1. What is the purpose of **antitrust laws?**
2. Under what conditions will the government approve a **merger?**
3. How does **predatory pricing** hurt competition?
4. How did **deregulation** change the banking and air travel industries?

Applying Economic Concepts

5. *Decision Making* Why did government once regulate the banking, trucking, and airline industries?
6. *Try This* Use the library to find an editorial from 1911 in support of the breakup of Standard Oil, and compare it to a recent editorial that criticizes Microsoft. Which arguments are the same? Which are different?
7. *Critical Thinking* Why does the government believe it has the right to intervene in markets to promote competition? Is this consistent with the idea of laissez faire and free markets?

For: Research Activity
Visit: PHSchool.com
Web Code: mnd-2074

Progress Monitoring *Online*
For additional assessment, have students access Progress Monitoring Online at **Web Code:** mna-2078

Go Online PHSchool.com Typing in the Web Code when prompted will bring students directly to detailed instructions for this activity.

Answer to . . .

Building Key Concepts Government regulation had prevented banks from making some of the risky investments that later led to bank failures.

Government

Regulating Cable Television

Cable television systems offer more than 100 channels featuring continuous news, sports, weather, business reports, and coverage of local activities. This growth in popularity, however, has led to a need for regulation.

The FCC The Federal Communication Commission (FCC) oversees the cable industry. During the 1950s, the FCC maintained a "hands-off" policy. In the 1960s, however, the FCC began to impose regulations. Responding to complaints from over-the-air broadcasters that cable stations were refusing to carry local stations, the FCC ruled that every cable system had to carry the programs of all local stations as well as those of their own.

By the 1970s, the FCC began to impose more regulations. The agency mandated that cable systems provide at least 20 channels in major markets, provide public access channels, and obtain public approval of changes in their rates.

▲ Many cable channels run specialized programming, such as all home improvement shows or all sports.

Deregulation In the 1980s, the FCC ruled that rates for cable services would be deregulated. This led to skyrocketing cable rates and poor service in certain parts of the country. This resulted in a move in the 1990s to regulate the industry once more.

The Cable Television Consumer Protection Act of 1992 allowed competition in the cable industry for the first time. It was hoped that competition would cause cable rates to stabilize or even decrease, while service would improve.

Today, cable television has grown so popular that cable networks now challenge and often surpass the popularity of the original broadcast giants ABC, CBS, and NBC. How much further will cable television grow? No one is sure. What seems certain, however, is that with growth will come further regulation.

Cable TV Subscribers, 1970–2000

Year	Number of Subscribers
1970	4,500,000
1975	9,800,000
1980	16,000,000
1985	32,000,000
1990	50,000,000
1995	58,000,000
2000	70,000,000 (est.)

Source: *Statistical Abstract of the United States*

Applying Economic Ideas

1. Should government regulate the cable television industry? Why or why not?
2. The table at the right shows the number of cable subscribers from 1970 to 2000. What do you think accounts for the increase in subscribers in the 1980s and 1990s?

Preparing for Standardized Tests

Have students read the case study on this page and then answer the question below.

What happened when rates for all cable services were deregulated in the 1980s?

A Cable television ceased to exist.
(B) Cable rates in some areas of the country skyrocketed although service was poor.
C Fewer channels were offered by cable companies.
D Cable rates became lower because of increased competition.

Real-life Case Study: Government

1. Focus In an effort to level the playing field for both cable and over-the-air broadcasters, the government issued regulations to control the way cable television companies conducted their business.

2. Instruct Discuss with students the impact that cable television has had on the average viewer. Ask students why they think cable is such an attractive option for viewers.

3. Close/Reteach Ask students to speculate on the impact of satellite-broadcast television on cable and broadcast television.

Case Studies Activity
Case Studies in Free Enterprise folder, pp. 14–15, "Joan Robinson," helps students apply economic principles in an additional case study.

Economic Detective Activity
Unit 2 folder, p. 45, "The Business of Buck Bidness," provides an integrated application of chapter concepts.

Answers to . . .

1. Some students may say yes, that the cable industry is so large that it needs supervision. Deregulation in the 1970s and 1980s led to skyrocketing prices. Others may say no, that the government should let the marketplace regulate itself. Students should offer support for their opinions.
2. Students may say that the technology began to catch on.

Chapter 7 Assessment

Key Terms

1. Price discrimination
2. perfect competition
3. oligopoly
4. Commodities
5. patent
6. natural monopoly
7. collusion

Using Graphic Organizers

8. Other causes include poor service and inefficiency. Other effects include better service and increased competition.

Reviewing Main Ideas

9. The stock market is a good example of perfect competition because it has many buyers and sellers, identical goods (stocks), informed buyers and sellers, and low barriers to entry.
10. Natural monopolies exist in markets where it would be inefficient for more than one producer to exist. Government monopolies offer franchises or licenses to firms for a specific purpose. They are similar in that both allow a monopoly to exist. Students may also provide examples of each.
11. many firms, few artificial barriers to entry, slight control over price, differentiated products
12. The government intervenes through antitrust legislation and by blocking some mergers. The government sanctions some natural monopolies and government monopolies.

Critical Thinking

13. Monopolies have the ability to set prices and reap all profits, but output is sometimes inefficient. Monopolistically competitive firms share profits within a market, their output levels are more competitive, and their prices are more subject to market conditions (unless they are acting illegally by colluding or fixing price). Similarities between the two structures include the fact that both types of structures involve holding a monopoly and that in both cases the variety of goods is limited—more so in a monopoly.
14. Antitrust policies interfere with the free market, but this interference is designed to ensure that the market remains competitive. Such actions are usually taken in the public interest, but they are still an intrusion into free enterprise.

Chapter 7 Assessment

Chapter Summary

A summary of major ideas in Chapter 7 appears below. See also the **Guide to the Essentials of Economics,** which provides additional review and test practice of key concepts in Chapter 7.

Section 1 Perfect Competition (pp. 151–154)

Perfect competition describes a market with many well-informed buyers and sellers, identical goods, and no **barriers to entry** to stop companies from joining the market. Perfect competition is only found in markets that deal in **commodities,** or goods that are identical no matter who produces or sells them. These markets are efficient at setting output and prices at a level that is beneficial to all.

Section 2 Monopoly (pp. 156–164)

A firm is a monopolist when it is the only seller in a market. A **natural monopoly** is an industry that works best when only one firm serves the entire market. Government can create a monopoly by issuing a **patent, franchise,** or a **license.** A monopolist can set prices or output. Firms use **price discrimination** to divide consumers into groups based on their ability to pay, and then offer a different price to each group.

Section 3 Monopolistic Competition and Oligopoly (pp. 166–171)

Most markets fall somewhere between perfect competition and monopoly. **Monopolistic competition** is similar to perfect competition, except that companies sell slightly different goods and have a little power to set prices. Closer to monopoly, **oligopoly** describes a market dominated by a few large producers. Firms in an oligopoly can practice **collusion** or form a **cartel** to set prices like a monopoly.

Section 4 Regulation and Deregulation (pp. 172–176)

Firms in an oligopoly can merge to try to gain monopoly power. Because monopoly power can lead to inefficient markets, the federal government has passed laws to promote competition and break up monopolies. In the late 1970s and 1980s, government gave up power to regulate several markets. **Deregulation** has led to lower prices in most deregulated markets.

Key Terms

Complete each sentence by choosing the correct answer from the list of terms below. You will not use all of the terms.

perfect competition	**natural monopoly**
oligopoly	**economies of scale**
patent	**price fixing**
commodities	**deregulation**
price discrimination	**collusion**

1. ____ is when a monopolist divides consumers into groups and charges different prices for the same good.
2. A market with many firms producing the same good is in ____.
3. Economists define ____ as a market structure with a few large firms, each of which has some market power.
4. ____ are products that are identical no matter who produces them.
5. A(n) ____ grants the right to sell an invention without competition.
6. A(n) ____ may exist in markets where it is most efficient for only one large firm to provide a product.
7. Economists use the term ____ to describe agreements among firms to set prices and production levels.

8. Using Graphic Organizers

On a separate sheet of paper, copy the multiflow map below. Organize information on government deregulation by completing the map with causes for deregulation on the left and possible effects on the right. You may add more causes or effects.

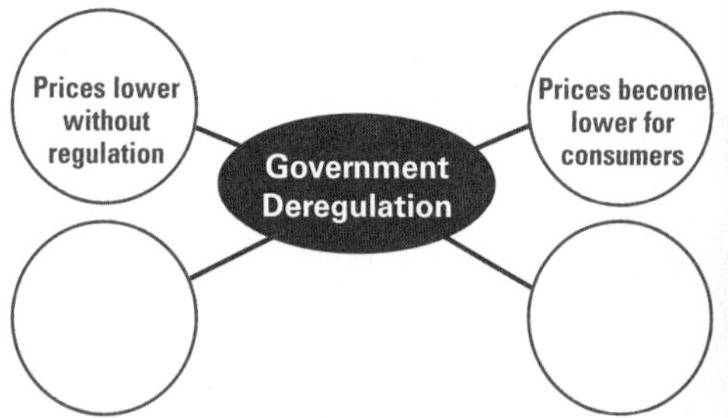

Reviewing Main Ideas

9. How does the buying and selling of stock fit the model for perfect competition?

10. Compare and contrast the characteristics of natural monopolies and monopolies created by government.

11. What four conditions are necessary for a market to be considered monopolistically competitive?

12. How does the United States government intervene in the economy in regard to monopolies and competition?

Critical Thinking

13. Making Comparisons How do prices, output, and profits differ between monopolies and monopolistically competitive firms? Are there similarities?

14. Synthesizing Information What are the trade-offs between free enterprise and government intervention associated with the United States' antitrust policies?

15. Analyzing Information Using the reference to the hydroelectric plant found in Section 2 as an example of economies of scale, think of three examples of industries that benefit from economies of scale.

Problem-Solving Activity

16. Assume that you are the owner of the only music store in town because your town limits the number of shops. The town now wants to repeal that law and allow more music stores to open. Describe what actions you could take as a business owner once the law is repealed.

Skills for Life

Analyzing Political Cartoons Review the steps shown on page 155; then answer the following questions using the cartoon below.

17. Identify the symbols in the cartoon. **(a)** What is symbolized by the oil pump? **(b)** What is symbolized by the man's living room?

18. Analyze the intent of the cartoon. **(a)** Describe the proposed solution to the energy crisis as illustrated in the cartoon. **(b)** Describe this solution as it might be applied to the entire state of California.

19. Draw conclusions about the cartoonist's intent. **(a)** Does the artist believe his solution is a good solution? **(b)** Were you swayed or convinced of the cartoonist's opinion in this case?

solving California's electricity crisis

Economics Journal

Brainstorming Reread your Economics Journal entry for Chapter 7. Write a paragraph for each of the three companies you listed, explaining what market structure each company competes in and how you came to this decision.

Progress Monitoring *Online*

For: Chapter 7 Self-Test **Visit:** PHSchool.com
Web Code: mna-2071

As a final review, take the Economics Chapter 7 Self-Test and receive immediate feedback on your answers. The test consists of 20 multiple-choice questions designed to test your understanding of the chapter content.

15. Students should present three industries that would benefit from economies of scale, such as a nuclear power plant, a printing plant, and a transatlantic shipping firm.

Problem-Solving Activity

16. Student responses will vary but should represent an understanding of the concept of competitive markets and the effects of possible price wars. Answers may include lowering prices, offering extra services, or investing in additional advertising.

Skills for Life

17. (a) oil drilling (b) people's living areas

18. (a) Energy companies should drill for oil in people's homes to produce enough energy to end California's energy crisis. (b) California should relax regulations to allow for the maximum amount of energy production, even if that requires drilling in previously protected areas.

19. (a) no (b) Students' answers will vary but they should explain their reasoning.

Go Online PHSchool.com

Additional support materials and activities for Chapter 7 of *Economics: Principles in Action* can be found in the Social Studies area of **PHSchool.com.**

Review and Assessment

Vocabulary Practice Unit 2 folder, p. 44 uses a crossword puzzle to reinforce understanding of key terms.

GTE **Guide to the Essentials** Chapter 7 Test, p. 32

Test Bank CD-ROM Chapter 7 Test

Go Online PHSchool.com Students may use the Chapter 7 Self-Test on **PHSchool.com** to prepare for the Chapter Test.

Economics Journal

Students' responses should include a paragraph for each of their three examples. Each paragraph should correctly identify the market structure in which the company competes and demonstrate understanding of chapter concepts.

THE WALL STREET JOURNAL.
CLASSROOM EDITION

Debate: Oil and Energy Dependence

1. Focus Have students find the meaning of each of these words before they begin to read: *distortions, fossil fuels, implausible, incentive, inherently, innovative, manipulation, taboo,* and *volatile.*

Explain to students that they will be conducting a debate on whether oil prices should be raised to promote energy conservation and independence. Inform them that they will be responsible for arguing one side of the issue. Remind students that a well-prepared debater supports a position with valid evidence, logical arguments, and responsible appeals to emotion.

2. Instruct The authors have both researched the impact of raising oil prices. Have students conduct further research on this subject from credible sources before conducting the debate.

Remind students that they should use the following debate format:
The affirmative side will:
- State the problem to be solved. Why is this problem significant?
- Explain who or what is harmed if the problem is not resolved. Use factual evidence to quantify the harm.
- Propose a plan of action. Explain why it is better than the current system.
- Provide factual evidence to show how this plan will solve the problem.

The opposing side will:
- Refute the arguments of the affirmative side, using factual evidence to quantify and support its position.
- If necessary, support the status quo's ability to solve the problem.

3. Close/Reteach When the debate is concluded, encourage students to discuss their opinions on the issue. Ask them whether they were persuaded by the other side's arguments. Conclude by having students write their own statements supporting or opposing raising the price of oil to promote energy conservation and independence.

THE WALL STREET JOURNAL.
CLASSROOM EDITION

Debating Current Issues: *Oil and Energy Dependence*

The U.S. relies on some of the world's most volatile countries to supply a raw material that is critical to its economy and lifestyle. Despite an increasingly energy-efficient economy, the U.S. remains hooked on imported oil.

In this debate from *The Wall Street Journal Classroom Edition,* Erich Pica, a senior policy analyst with the environmental group Friends of the Earth, and John Felmy and Edward Porter of the American Petroleum Institute present two approaches to reducing oil imports and promoting energy independence in the U.S.

YES *Should oil prices be raised to promote energy independence?*

By Erich Pica

The price of oil should be increased as part of a price increase on all fossil fuels. Our nation has a problem, and it is not simply a dependence on foreign oil. It is our dependence on oil. The U.S. consumes 25% of the world's oil supply, and has only 3% of its resources. Unless we fundamentally shift our oil consumption patterns, we will remain dependent on foreign oil.

Friends of the Earth, a nonprofit environmental organization, believes that the best way to help solve our dependency problems is with a carbon tax, or a fee on all fossil fuels, including oil. Such a tax would be an efficient way to encourage businesses and individuals to conserve fuel and develop nonfossil-fuel energy sources. And a carbon tax would also fix many of the economic distortions currently not factored into the price of oil.

For example, current oil prices do not reflect the impact of air pollution from our passenger vehicles, which contributes to unhealthy levels of smog that harm human health. And they don't reflect the environmental impact of oil drilling, which damages public lands and coastal areas. Nor do they reflect the growing military and foreign-policy costs of defending oil interests in the Middle East and other turbulent regions.

Using the true cost of oil would raise prices, but it would provide the incentive for consumers to reduce consumption and turn to innovative, clean sources of energy. Ultimately, using less oil is the only way to reduce our dependence on foreign supplies.

A carbon tax is a potential silver bullet that could solve our dependence on oil. Yet, unfortunately, it remains a taboo topic for political leaders. Elected officials and their allies in the oil industry are creating false choices between dependence on foreign oil and reducing the cost of domestic production, knowing that as long as we consume at current rates, our dependency will remain.

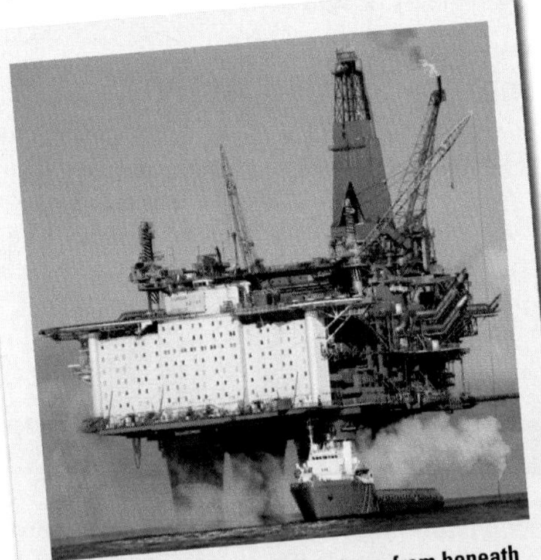

Massive oil rigs extract petroleum from beneath the ocean floor. Does the market price of gasoline reflect all the costs of its use?

Debate Activity Debating Current Issues folder, p. 8 asks students to analyze how the concept of *elasticity of demand* works to set the target price for oil.

Economic Assessment Rubric
Economics Assessment Rubrics folder, pp. 14–15 provides sample evaluation materials for participation in debates.

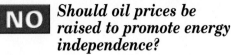

NO Should oil prices be raised to promote energy independence?

By John Felmy and Edward Porter

The notion that we should raise the price of oil is an old idea that resurfaces frequently, especially as the level of U.S. imports increases. But it is an idea based on incorrect assumptions that oil consumption is inherently harmful, its use can be reduced dramatically without cost to the economy, and that by boosting prices we might enjoy a net gain to the environment and reduce dependence on foreign supplies.

These notions are simply implausible. Energy is a productive input into economic activity, and oil is the pre-eminent form used in transportation. If we raise its price, we reduce its use and lose the added value of all economic activity associated with that use. Throughout the last century, there are no examples of sustained growth occurring without increasing energy, and no examples of economic development without increased transportation. Energy, and in particular oil, are essential to sustained economic growth worldwide. And, because of spectacular advances in technology in the production and use of oil, old trade-offs between energy use and the environment often have been reduced or eliminated.

The real problem is not the price of oil or the level of U.S. imports, but the secure supply of energy to a growing world economy in a manner consistent with the highest environmental standards. Although over 180 billion barrels of oil have been produced in the U.S. since 1859, it is estimated that there are over 140 billion barrels left. But the U.S. is not the main player in this market, as oil is now produced by about one hundred countries worldwide. In fact, it is competition among this diverse group of suppliers that is the most effective way to secure both moderate prices and the oil needed to sustain future economic growth.

The policy failures of the past five decades have all shared a common theme—they have sought to defeat the global market by manipulation of price. All past attempts to do so have failed. Given the degree of globalization in the world economy, they are even more likely to fail today. The only effect of raising oil prices in the U.S. today would be to put U.S. firms at a competitive disadvantage in the global market.

What is now needed is responsible development of our domestic resources along with a vigorous commitment to freedom of trade and investment worldwide, not a return to failed policies of the past.

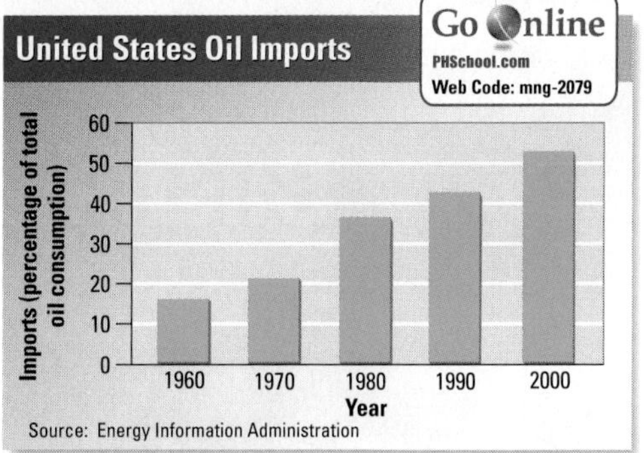

More than half the oil consumed in the U.S. is produced in other countries.

DEBATING THE ISSUE

1. In addition to the price of oil, what does Erich Pica say are the costs of U.S. dependence on oil?
2. According to John Felmy and Edward Porter, why have oil pricing policies failed in the past?
3. **Critical Thinking** Do you agree that raising oil prices would put U.S. firms at a competitive disadvantage in the global market?
4. **Reading Graphs** What share of U.S. oil consumption was imported in 1970? What share was imported in 2000?

For: You Decide Poll
Visit: PHSchool.com
Web Code: mnp-2071

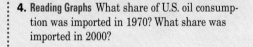

Background

About the Authors

Erich Pica, a senior policy analyst with the environmental group Friends of the Earth, argues that oil prices should be increased through a carbon tax, as a way of reducing consumption and dependence on foreign oil. Arguing against such a tax are John Felmy, chief economist, and Edward Porter, research manager, of the American Petroleum Institute.

Differentiated Instruction 

Oil prices are set by the interaction of buyers and sellers in an exchange where all parties expect to gain. As buyers, what alternatives do students have to shift the demand for oil or to find substitutes for oil? Ask students to explain what they or their family would do differently if the price of oil and gasoline remained high for the next five years. Have them list five changes they could make. What impact would shifts in the demand for oil have on the U.S. economy?

Go Online PHSchool.com Students can find additional links related to the debate by visiting the *Economics: Principles in Action* site at **PHSchool.com.**

Answers to . . .

1. There is the impact of air pollution from our passenger vehicles, which harms human health; the environmental impact of oil drilling, which damages public lands and coastal areas; and the military and foreign-policy costs of defending oil interests in the Middle East and other turbulent regions.
2. These policies have sought to defeat the global market by manipulation of oil price.
3. Answers will vary, but higher oil prices would raise production costs unless a suitable and less expensive energy alternative could be substituted.
4. 21 percent; 52 percent

Interdisciplinary Connections: History

Oil Imports Founded in 1960, the Organization of Petroleum Exporting Countries (OPEC) is an international cartel that is a major supplier of oil. In 1974, an Arab oil embargo caused oil prices to quadruple. As a result of this event, in 1974, the U.S. spearheaded the creation of the International Energy Agency. This agency's purpose was to gather a stockpile of oil to offset any future supply shortage. In 2002, OPEC and the IEA worked together to reach an understanding that would keep oil prices within a range of $20 to $30 a barrel.

Making the Connection Have students research America's current dependence on oil. What is government doing to increase the supply of or reduce the demand for oil? Would students support boosting supplies of oil by drilling in the Alaska National Wildlife Reserve? Why? Should government subsidize or provide incentives for developing alternative energy sources? Why?

UNIT 3 Business and Labor

Introducing the Unit

Unit Summary

Unit 3 describes how the world of work is organized. In Chapter 8 students develop an understanding of the types of business organizations, including sole proprietorships, partnerships, and corporations. In Chapter 9 students learn about labor—the history and development of organized labor as well as factors that determine wages. The chapter also discusses trends in the makeup of the labor force and in wages and benefits.

Focus Activity

Introduce Unit 3 to students by asking them to complete the Focus Activity. Have students work alone to list occupations, and then form groups of three to five students who have at least one occupation in common. Have these groups work together to list specific information about the occupation (for example, educational requirements, working conditions, and companies involved in the field).

3 Business and Labor

National Council on Economic Education

The following Voluntary National Content Standards in Economics are addressed in this unit:

★ Standard 10 ★ Standard 14
★ Standard 13

See the Chapter Openers on pp. 184 and 210 for a complete description of the standards addressed in each chapter.

Chapters in This Unit

8. *Business Organizations*
9. *Labor*

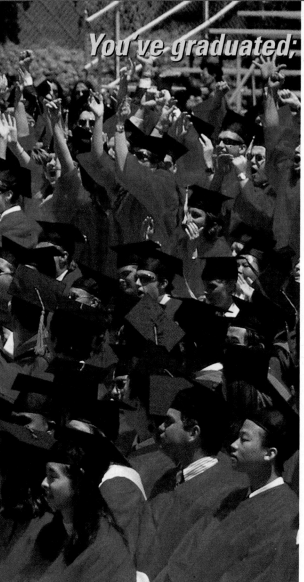

You've graduated; you're off to work . . .

Most Americans spend a large proportion of their lives working. Picture yourself going off to work when you finish your education.

- What type of business do you work for?
- Who are your co-workers?
- Who's your boss? Are you in business for yourself?
- How much do you earn?

Economists categorize businesses according to the way they are organized. Economists also study the composition of the country's labor force and the impact of supply and demand on labor and wages. In this unit you'll read about possible answers you might be giving years from now to the questions above.

Focus Activity

Write down five occupations that you're considering for your future. Categorize each of your choices based on who your employer might be for each job.

Bibliography

Print

Virtual Economics: An Interactive Center for Economics Education. CD-ROM. Federal Reserve Bank of Dallas. *Labor, the Economy, and Monetary Policy.* EconomicsAmerica, National Council on Economic Education, 1997.

Multimedia

From the Social Studies School Service, 10200 Jefferson Blvd., Box 802, Culver City, CA 90232.

"At Work in the New Economy." Color video, 25 minutes. Explores changes in the American workplace. Includes coverage of the impact of advanced technology, the entry of women into the workplace, and the need for job retraining.

"Organizing America: A History of Trade Unions in the U.S." Color and B&W video, 40 minutes. Recounts the history of labor unions in the United States.

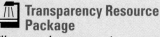

Technology Center

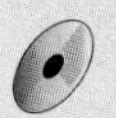

Economics Video Library

Includes high-interest, chapter-specific segments produced by CNBC for

THE WALL STREET JOURNAL. CLASSROOM EDITION

Simulations and Data Graphing CD-ROM

Provides interactive federal budget and stock market simulations and a data graphing tool designed to support instruction in economics.

PRENTICE HALL TeacherEXPRESS™ Plan · Teach · Assess

Teacher Express CD-ROM offers powerful lesson planning, resource management, testing, and an interactive Teacher's Edition.

Prentice Hall Presentation Pro CD-ROM

Allows you to create custom lectures for every chapter.

Social Studies Skills Tutor CD-ROM

Provides interactive practice in geographic literacy, critical thinking and reading, visual analysis, and communications.

ExamView® Test Bank CD-ROM

Allows you to create, edit, and print out chapter level tests.

Transparency Resource Package

Illustrates key economic concepts and provides useful forms and templates for enhancing classroom discussions.

Section Reading Support Transparency System

Delivers the main idea of each section in the student text through graphic organizers.

Offers student-appropriate online activities and links as well as resources for the teacher. Be sure to check out this month's **eTeach** online discussion with a Master Economics Teacher.

Chapter 8 Business Organizations

For more pacing suggestions, see the Economics Pacing Guide in the Program Overview of the Teaching Resources.

Section Objectives	Print and Technology Resources	
1 Sole Proprietorships *(pp. 185–188)* **Objectives** 1. Explain the characteristics of sole proprietorships. 2. Analyze the advantages of a sole proprietorship. 3. Analyze the disadvantages of a sole proprietorship.	• **Lesson Planner** Section 1 Lesson Plan, p. 38 • **Learning Styles Lesson Plans folder** Section 1 Lesson Plan, p. 21 • **Lesson Plans folder** Section 1 Lesson Plan, p. 31 • **Economics Assessment Rubrics folder** Writing Assignment, pp. 6–7 • **Unit 3 folder** Guided Reading and Review, p. 2 Careers in Economics, Business Proprietor, p. 13 Section 1 Quiz, p. 3	• **Presentation Pro CD-ROM** Section 1 • **Transparency Resource Package** Economics Organizers, G10: Venn Diagram Economics Concepts, 8A: Business License Application • **Section Reading Support Transparency System**
2 Partnerships *(pp. 190–193)* **Objectives** 1. Compare and contrast the different types of partnerships. 2. Analyze the advantages of partnerships. 3. Analyze the disadvantages of partnerships.	• **Lesson Planner** Section 2 Lesson Plan, p. 39 • **Lesson Plans folder** Section 2 Lesson Plan, p. 32 • **Unit 3 folder** Guided Reading and Review, p. 4 Economic Skills, p. 10 Section 2 Quiz, p. 5 • **Source Articles folder** Notice What It Takes, pp. 24–26	• **Presentation Pro CD-ROM** Section 2 • **Transparency Resource Package** Economics Organizers, G7: Tree Map Graphic Organizer Economics Concepts, 8B: Partnerships • **Section Reading Support Transparency System** • **Social Studies Skills Tutor CD-ROM**
3 Corporations, Mergers, and Multinationals *(pp. 195–200)* **Objectives** 1. Explain the characteristics of corporations. 2. Analyze the advantages of incorporation. 3. Analyze the disadvantages of incorporation. 4. Compare and contrast corporate combinations. 5. Describe the role of multinational corporations.	• **Lesson Planner** Section 3 Lesson Plan, p. 40 • **Learning Styles Lesson Plans folder** Section 3 Lesson Plan, p. 22 • **Lesson Plans folder** Section 3 Lesson Plan, p. 33 • **Economics Assessment Rubrics folder** Position Paper, pp. 22–23 • **Unit 3 folder** Guided Reading and Review, p. 6 Economic Cartoon, p. 14 Section 3 Quiz, p. 7	• **Presentation Pro CD-ROM** Section 3 • **Transparency Resource Package** Economics Organizers, G7: Tree Map Graphic Organizer Economics Concepts, 8C: Corporate Structures Economics Concepts, 8D: Corporate Mergers Economics Concepts, 8E: Top U.S. and World Employers • **Section Reading Support Transparency System**
4 Other Organizations *(pp. 201–204)* **Objectives** 1. Understand how a business franchise works. 2. Identify the different types of cooperative organizations. 3. Understand the purpose of nonprofit organizations, including professional and business organizations.	• **Lesson Planner** Section 4 Lesson Plan, p. 41 • **Lesson Plans folder** Section 4 Lesson Plan, p. 34 • **Unit 3 folder** Guided Reading and Review, p. 8 Vocabulary Practice, p. 11 Economic Detective, p. 12 Section 4 Quiz, p. 9 • **Case Studies in Free Enterprise folder** Lloyd Ward, pp. 16–17	• **Presentation Pro CD-ROM** Section 4 • **Transparency Resource Package** Economics Organizers, G5: Web Graphic Organizer Economics Concepts, 8F: Business Franchises • **Section Reading Support Transparency System**

Differentiated Instruction

Question-and-Answer Relationships (L2)

For students to craft better answers, they first need to understand what a question is asking. Explain the different types of questions below.

1. **Right There** questions with answers that are found explicitly in one or two sentences in the book.

2. **Think and Search** questions with answers that are found in several different paragraph in the book.

3. **Author and You** questions with answers that are not found directly in the book, but require you to think about what you've read.

4. **On Your Own** questions with answers that are not found directly in the book and which you can answer out of your own knowledge.

Mapping Word Definitions (L2)

To help students learn unfamiliar words, introduce them to the strategy of mapping word definitions. Research shows that this technique helps students develop the ability to investigate word meanings independently and provide elaborated definitions (as opposed to simple one- or two-word definitions). Research also shows that effective vocabulary strategies require students to go beyond simply looking up dictionary definitions or examining the context. Vocabulary learning must be based on the learner's dynamic engagement in constructing understanding.

- Model mapping word definitions by using the following steps for the high-use word *liability*.
- Define the word in their own words—*the loss that may result from a gamble or investment*
- Provide a synonym or example—*risk, chance, venture*
- Use the word in a sentence—*The entrepreneur was liable for her complete $80,000 investment if her shop failed.*
- Provide a non-example—*limited investment*

Visit the Social Studies area of the Prentice Hall Web site. There you can find additional links to enrich chapter content for *Economics: Principles in Action* as well as a self-test for students. Be sure to check out this month's **eTeach** online discussion with a Master Economics Teacher.

Web Code: mnf-3081

Running Out of Time?

- Use the **Presentation Pro CD-ROM** to create an outline for this chapter.
- Use the Chapter Summary in the **Chapter 8 Assessment,** p. 206.
- Use the Section Summaries for Chapter 8, from **Guide to the Essentials of Economics (English and Spanish).**

THE WALL STREET JOURNAL. CLASSROOM EDITION

Prentice Hall brings into the classroom the authoritative content of *The Wall Street Journal Classroom Edition.* See the Source Articles, Debating Current Issues, and You and Your Money folders in the **Teaching Resources.** Also, see Economics Video Library, "Finding Funds."

Assessment Resources

Chapter Assessment

Teaching Resources Unit 3, Chapter 8

- Section Quizzes, pp. 3, 5, 7, 9

Exam *View*® Test Bank CD-ROM Chapter 8

Economics Assessment Rubrics

Chapter 8 Self-Test, **Web Code:** mna-3081

Reading and Skills Evaluation

Progress Monitoring Assessments

- Screening Test
- Diagnostic Test of Social Studies Skills

Standardized Test Preparation

Test Prep Workbook

Test-Taking Strategies With Transparencies

Differentiated Instruction Key

L1 Special Needs
L2 Basic to Average
L3 All Students
L4 Average to Advanced

LPR Less Proficient Readers
AR Advanced Readers
SN Special Needs Students
GT Gifted and Talented
ELL English Language Learner

Chapter 8

Business Organizations

Introducing the Chapter

In this chapter students are introduced to various forms of business organizations, including sole proprietorships, partnerships, corporations, franchises, and cooperatives. The chapter discusses the purpose, structure, and advantages and disadvantages of each type of organization.

For additional links for *Economics: Principles in Action* provided by Prentice Hall and *The Wall Street Journal Classroom Edition,* visit the Social Studies area. Be sure to check out this month's **eTeach** online discussion with a Master Teacher.

Beyond the Lecture

You may cover the concepts in Chapter 8 in an activity-based style by using the following materials:

- **Technology Resources** appropriate for use with this chapter are noted on pp. 186, 188, 191, 193, 196, 199, 200, 202, 204, and 207.
- **Presentation Pro CD-ROM** with animated graphs gives you an alternative method for organizing and delivering chapter content.
- **Activities** designed to meet the needs of students of mixed abilities and learning styles are noted throughout the chapter in the side columns.
- **Learning Styles Lesson Plans** provide alternate lessons for diverse learning styles. See pp. 21–22 of the Learning Styles Lesson Plans folder located in the Teaching Resources.

Economics Journal

Instruct students to write their responses and descriptions in their Economics Journals. Students may include completed journal entries in an Economics Portfolio.

Chapter 8 Business Organizations

Taking care of business can mean working by yourself out of your home or managing a company with thousands of employees and offices across the globe. It can mean being the sole owner of a company or one of thousands. It can also mean working for something other than a for-profit business.

Economics Journal

List the four businesses you and your family visit the most often. Are they local businesses or national chains? Describe each one in a few sentences.

Go Online PHSchool.com

For: Current Data
Visit: PHSchool.com
Web Code: mng-3081

National Council on Economic Education

★ **Standard 10** Students will understand that: Institutions evolve in market economies to help individuals and groups accomplish their goals. Banks, labor unions, corporations, legal systems, and not-for-profit organizations are examples of important institutions. A different kind of institution, clearly defined and well enforced property rights, is essential to a market economy.

★ **Standard 14** Students will understand that: Entrepreneurs are people who take the risks of organizing productive resources to make goods and services. Profit is an important incentive that leads entrepreneurs to accept the risks of business failure.

For more information about the standards, contact the National Council on Economic Education

1140 Avenue of the Americas
New York, NY 10036
1-800-338-1192

Section 1 Sole Proprietorships

Preview

Objectives

After studying this section you will be able to:

1. **Explain** the characteristics of sole proprietorships.
2. **Analyze** the advantages of a sole proprietorship.
3. **Analyze** the disadvantages of a sole proprietorship.

Section Focus

A business is an economic institution that seeks a profit by allocating resources to satisfy customers. Sole proprietorships are the most common form of business in the United States. They are easy to establish and offer owners both the benefits and drawbacks that come with full control of a business.

Key Terms

business organization
sole proprietorship
business license
zoning law
liability
fringe benefit

Entrepreneurs must make many decisions as they start up new businesses. One of the first decisions they face is what form of business organization best serves their interests. A **business organization** is an establishment formed to carry on commercial enterprise. In other words, a business organization is a company, or firm. Sole proprietorships are the most common forms of business organization.

The Role of Sole Proprietorships

A **sole proprietorship** is a business owned and managed by a single individual. That person earns all of the firm's profits and is responsible for all of the firm's debts. This type of firm is by far the most popular in the United States. According to the Internal Revenue Service, about 75 percent of all businesses are sole proprietorships. Most sole proprietorships are small, however. All together they generate only about 6 percent of all United States sales.

Many types of businesses can flourish as sole proprietorships. Look around your town. Chances are good that your local bakery, your barber shop or hair salon, your bike-repair shop, and the corner store are all sole proprietorships.

Advantages of Sole Proprietorships

While you need to do more than just hang out a sign to start your own business, a sole proprietorship is simple to establish. It also offers the owner numerous advantages.

business organization *an establishment formed to carry on commercial enterprise*

sole proprietorship *a business owned and managed by a single individual*

◀ **Personal pride motivates many sole proprietors.**

Graphing the Main Idea

Entrepreneurs To build understanding of **entrepreneurs,** ask students to complete a Venn diagram like the one at the right on the advantages and disadvantages of sole proprietorships. Point out that a Venn diagram can be used to illustrate two sides of an issue. Have students list advantages in one circle; disadvantages in the other circle; and characteristics that can be both in the overlap section.

Section Reading Support Transparencies A template and the answers for this graphic organizer can be found in Chapter 8, Section 1 of the Section Reading Support Transparency System.

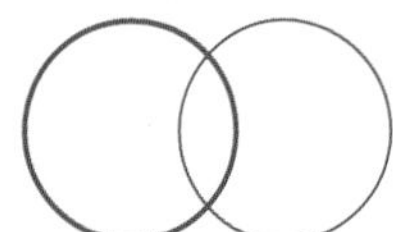

Section 1

Sole Proprietorships

Objectives You may wish to call students' attention to the objectives in the Section Preview. The objectives are reflected in the main headings of the section.

Bellringer Ask students whether they have ever received payment for shoveling snow, baby-sitting, or caring for vacationing families' pets. Explain that any such businesses they operated by themselves were examples of sole proprietorships.

Vocabulary Builder Have students write an extended definition for each key term without including the term itself. Group students into pairs in which one student reads a definition and the other student offers a question that the definition would answer. *(Extended definition: Payments to employees other than salary, such as vacation and retirement pay. Question: What are fringe benefits?)*

Lesson Plan

Teaching the Main Concepts 

1. Focus Explain to students that sole proprietorships are the most common business organization. Ask students to speculate on why people choose to run their own businesses.

2. Instruct Discuss with students the advantages and disadvantages of sole proprietorships, and ask them to weigh one against the other. Ask students whether they think that most Americans feel that the advantages outweigh the disadvantages.

3. Close/Reteach Remind students that the trade-off in a sole proprietorship is absolute control weighed against absolute responsibility. Ask students to create a personality profile of a successful sole proprietor.

Guided Reading and Review Unit 3 folder, p. 2 asks students to identify the main ideas of the section and to define or identify key terms.

Meeting NCEE Standards

Use the following benchmark activity from the **Voluntary National Content Standards in Economics** to evaluate student understanding of **Standard 14.**

Identify an entrepreneur and describe how the entrepreneur's decisions affect job opportunities.

Differentiated Instruction 

Have students interpret the circle graphs on this page to answer the following questions:

1. How much money do the vast majority of proprietorships earn? *(under $25,000)*
2. Which type of proprietorship is most common? *(services)* Which types are least common? *(manufacturing, wholesale trade, finance and insurance)*

Differentiated Instruction 

Ask students to change each of the headings and subheadings in this section into a question. Then ask them to skim the text under the headings to answer their questions before reading the section. LPR

Learning Styles Activity
Learning Styles Lesson Plans folder, p. 21 has student groups analyze the concept of sole proprietorship by creating want ads and role-playing an interview.

Transparency Resource Package
Economics Concepts, 8A: Business License Application

It takes a certain type of personality to start up a business.
Entrepreneurs **Describe some times when you exhibited entrepreneurial spirit.**

Figure 8.1 The Entrepreneurial Spirit

Entrepreneurs . . .

- ★ Seek out responsibility
- ★ Are willing to take risks
- ★ Believe in themselves
- ★ Desire to reach their full potentials
- ★ Have high energy levels
- ★ Are upbeat and optimistic
- ★ Look toward the future rather than the past
- ★ Value achievement over money
- ★ Maintain flexibility as they face new challenges
- ★ Are strongly committed to their goals

Ease of Start-Up

Easy start-up is one of the main advantages of the sole proprietorship. With just a small amount of paperwork and legal expense, just about anyone can start a sole proprietorship.

business license
authorization to start a business issued by the local government

To start a new business, a sole proprietor must meet a small number of government requirements, which can vary from city to city and state to state. Typically, sole proprietors must meet the following minimum requirements:

1. *Authorization* Sole proprietors must obtain a **business license,** which is an authorization from the local government. Certain professionals, such as doctors and day-care providers, may also be required to obtain a special license from the state.
2. *Site permit* If not operating out of the home, a sole proprietor must obtain a certificate of occupancy to use another building for business.
3. *Name* If not using his or her own name as the name of the business, a sole proprietor must register a business name.

This paperwork often takes only a day or two to complete. The most difficult part of starting a new business is coming up with a good idea!

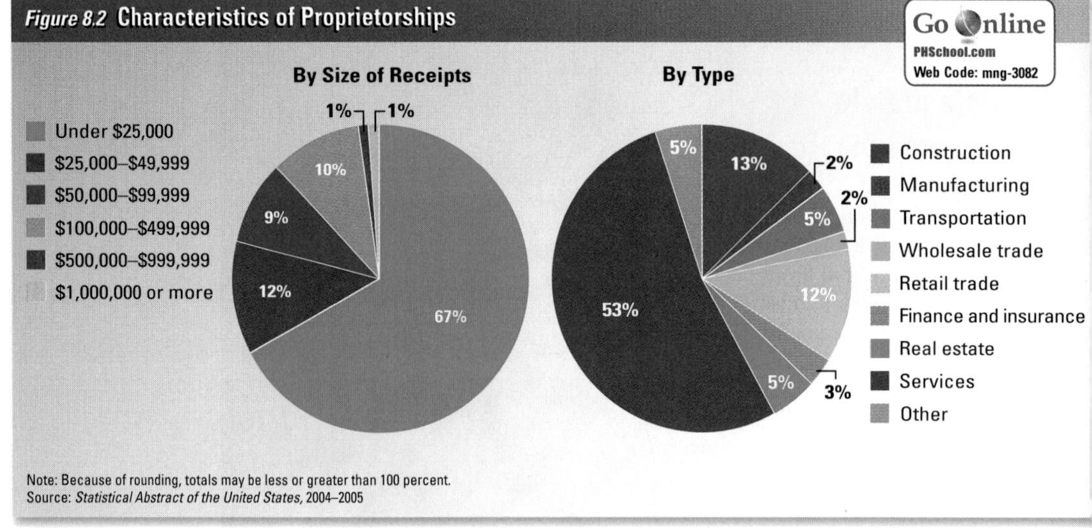

Figure 8.2 Characteristics of Proprietorships

Note: Because of rounding, totals may be less or greater than 100 percent.
Source: *Statistical Abstract of the United States,* 2004–2005

Most sole proprietorships take in relatively small amounts of money, or receipts. Many proprietors run their businesses part-time.
Specialization **What percentage of sole proprietorships is engaged in retail trade? Why might more sole proprietors be engaged in services rather than manufacturing?**

Econ 101: Key Concepts Made Easy

Entrepreneurs One of the key concepts in Section 1 is **liability.** To help students understand this concept, ask them to think of a sole proprietorship as being somewhat like a family. Rent, mortgages, credit cards, and taxes are all examples of the liabilities—financial obligations—of a family. Just as the head of a family is personally responsible for that family's debts, a sole proprietor is personally responsible for the debts of the business.

Answer to . . .

Building Key Concepts Students should describe entrepreneurial ventures they've partaken in.
Building Key Concepts 12 percent, students may suggest that services have lower start-up costs and a lower overall requirement for capital.

Relatively Few Regulations

A proprietorship is the least-regulated form of business organization. Even the smallest business, however, is subject to some regulation, especially industry-specific regulations. For example, a gourmet soft pretzel stand would be subject to health codes, and a furniture refinishing business would be subject to codes regarding dangerous chemicals.

Sole proprietorships may also be subject to local **zoning laws.** Cities and towns often designate separate areas, or zones, for residential use and for business. Zoning laws may prohibit sole proprietors from operating businesses out of their homes.

Otherwise, these small businesses face few legal requirements. Because they require little legal paperwork, sole proprietorships are usually the least expensive form of ownership to establish.

Sole Receiver of Profit

A major advantage of the sole proprietorship is that the owner gets to keep all profits after paying income taxes. Potential profits motivate many people to start their own businesses. If the business succeeds, the owner does not have to share the success with anyone else.

Full Control

Another advantage of sole proprietorship is that sole proprietors can run their businesses as they wish. This means that they can respond quickly to changes in the marketplace. Such a degree of freedom appeals to entrepreneurs. Fast, flexible decision making allows sole proprietorships to take full advantage of sudden opportunities.

Easy to Discontinue

Finally, if sole proprietors decide to stop operations and do something else for a living, they can do so easily. They must, of course, pay all debts and other obligations like taxes, but they do not have to meet any other legal obligations to stop doing business.

▲ **What are the benefits of running a business from home?**

Disadvantages of Sole Proprietorships

As with everything else, there are trade-offs with sole proprietorships. The independence of a sole proprietorship comes with a high degree of responsibility.

Unlimited Personal Liability

The biggest disadvantage of sole proprietorship is unlimited personal liability. **Liability** is the legally bound obligation to pay debts. Sole proprietors are fully and personally responsible for all their business debts. If the business fails, the owner may have to sell personal property to cover any outstanding obligations.

For example, let's say you took out a loan to buy a ride-on lawn mower as part of your landscaping business. Even if you don't make enough money to stay in business, you must still repay the loan for the lawn mower. Business debts can ruin a sole proprietor's personal finances.

Limited Access to Resources

If your landscaping business takes off and grows quickly, you might need to expand

zoning law *law in a city or town that designates separate areas for residency and for business*

liability *the legally bound obligation to pay debts*

Differentiated Instruction L4

You may wish to have students add the following to their portfolios. Ask them to research an American entrepreneur, either a contemporary or a historical figure, who started as a sole proprietor, and write a brief biographical essay detailing that person's accomplishments. Biographical essays should include the following information: the subject's background, business idea or inspiration, funding or lack of it, steps toward the goal, and a description of successes or failures. GT

Economics Assessment Rubric

Economics Assessment Rubrics folder, pp. 6–7 provides sample evaluation materials for a writing assignment.

Differentiated Instruction L3

(Enrichment) Organize the class into four or more groups. Each group will be responsible for one segment of the community (for example, a business district, a residential neighborhood, the area around the school, an industrial district). Have each group use community resources to determine what types of businesses are and are not allowed in each area of the community. Students should also investigate the area's zoning laws and determine why certain businesses are restricted from certain areas. A representative from each group should make a short oral presentation to the class.

Differentiated Instruction L3

Have students make brief (two- to three-minute) presentations on "Why I Would (or Would Not) Want to be a Sole Proprietor." Explain that the presentations should show an understanding of the advantages and disadvantages of sole proprietorship.

Block Scheduling Strategies

Consider these suggestions to take advantage of extended class time:

- Extend the Student Portfolio activity on this page by having an Entrepreneurs' Corner in the school lobby or cafeteria. During class time, encourage students to create posters or handouts illustrating each entrepreneur's activities. Additional class time will be needed to set up the display, or student volunteers may set it up as an after-school project.
- Have the class examine a sole proprietor's business plan. After students have had a chance to read through the plan, ask them to suggest modifications that they think would make the business more successful.

Answer to . . .

Photo Caption Students may note that there would be no need to rent or buy space.

GTE Guide to the Essentials
Chapter 8, Section 1, p. 33 provides support for students who need additional review of the section content. Spanish support is available in the Spanish edition of the guide on p. 33.

Quiz Unit 3 folder, p. 3 includes questions to check students' understanding of Section 1 content.

Presentation Pro CD-ROM
Quiz provides multiple-choice questions to check students' understanding of Section 1 content.

Go Online PHSchool.com Typing in the Web Code when prompted will bring students directly to the article.

Answers to . . .

Section 1 Assessment

1. A business organization is an establishment formed to carry on a commercial enterprise.
2. A sole proprietorship is a business owned and managed by one individual.
3. Business licenses grant permission to undertake and carry out business, while zoning laws influence where businesses may be located.
4. Sole proprietors are responsible for all debts that the business may acquire. They are said to have unlimited personal liability.
5. Most sole proprietorships are small, so they have limited resources to allocate for benefits to both employees and owners.
6. Students may suggest several of the categories of aides, saying that a sole proprietor could hire a staff and manage client contact. Students may also mention desktop publishing specialists, who could run businesses from their homes.
7. Student answers will vary but should show self-understanding and an understanding of entrepreneurship. They may, for example, say that they possess many of the traits and that they would like to own a business because it would be challenging and provide a feeling of accomplishment.

THE WALL STREET JOURNAL.
CLASSROOM EDITION

In the News Read more about entrepreneurship in "Best Foot Forward," an article in The Wall Street Journal Classroom Edition.

The Wall Street Journal Classroom Edition
For: Current Events
Visit: PHSchool.com
Web Code: mnc-3081

your business by buying more equipment. But as a sole proprietor, you may have to expand by paying for the equipment out of your own pocket. This is because banks are sometimes unwilling to offer financing in the early days of a business. Many small business owners use all of their available savings and other personal resources to start up their businesses. This makes it difficult or impossible for them to expand quickly.

Physical capital may not be the only factor resource in short supply. Human capital may be lacking, too. A sole proprietor, no matter how ambitious, may lack some of the skills necessary to run a business successfully. All individuals have strengths and weaknesses. Some aspects of your business may suffer if your skills don't match the needs of the business. For example, you may be great at sales, but not at bookkeeping and accounting. You may love working outdoors landscaping, but hate to call on people to drum up business.

Finally, as a sole proprietor, you may have to turn down work because you simply don't have enough hours in the day or enough workers to keep up with demand. A small business often presents its owner with too many demands, and that can be exhausting both personally and financially.

Lack of Permanence

A sole proprietorship has a limited life. If a sole proprietor dies or closes shop due to retirement, illness, loss of interest in the business, or for any other reason, the business simply ceases to exist.

Sole proprietorships often have trouble finding and keeping good employees. Small businesses generally cannot offer the security and advancement opportunities that many employees look for in a job. In addition, many sole proprietorships are able to offer employees little in the way of fringe benefits. **Fringe benefits** are payments to employees other than wages or salaries, such as paid vacation, retirement pay, and health insurance. Lack of experienced employees can hurt a business. Once again, the flip side of total control is total responsibility: a sole proprietor cannot count on anyone else to maintain the business.

fringe benefit *payment other than wages or salaries*

Section 1 Assessment

Progress Monitoring *Online*
For: Self-quiz with vocabulary practice
Web Code: mna-3085

Key Terms and Main Ideas

1. What is a **business organization?**
2. What is a **sole proprietorship?**
3. What role do **business licenses** and **zoning laws** play in sole proprietorships?
4. What kinds of **liabilities** are sole proprietors subject to?
5. Why do you think many sole proprietorships are able to offer few **fringe benefits** to workers?

Applying Economic Concepts

6. ***Using the Databank*** Examine the graph "Fastest-Growing Occupations" on page 537. Which of these occupations do you think could operate successfully as sole proprietorships? Explain your reasoning.
7. ***Try This*** Refer to Figure 8.1, "The Entrepreneurial Spirit," on page 186. How many of these traits do you have? Would you like to start your own business someday? Why or why not?

For: Simulation Activity
Visit: PHSchool.com
Web Code: mnd-3081

Progress Monitoring *Online*
For additional assessment, have students access Progress Monitoring Online at **Web Code:** mna-3085

Go Online PHSchool.com Typing in the Web Code when prompted will bring students directly to detailed instructions for this activity.

Economist

Entrepreneur

ECONOMIC Profile

Jerry Yang (b. 1968)

When 10-year-old Jerry Yang arrived in California from Taiwan with his brother, mother, and grandmother, the only English word he knew was shoe. *Some 15 years later he had mastered the language well enough to come up with "Yet Another Hierarchical Officious Oracle!" as the name for an on-line directory of Internet addresses that he and his friend David Filo had developed. The initials gave the directory the name Yang really wanted: Yahoo!*

The Birth of Yahoo!

Yang and Filo were graduate students in engineering and shared an office at Stanford University in 1993. At the time, the World Wide Web was in its infancy, and the two office mates began to spend time exploring the new Web. When they could not remember the addresses of interesting Web sites they had visited, they decided to make a reference list. In early 1994, they put their list on-line for friends to use. As the list got longer, Filo and Yang divided it into categories, and the Internet directory Yahoo! was born.

A Hobby Becomes a Business

By the end of 1994, word of a great, free catalog of Web pages had spread well beyond the university. Yang and Filo's site was getting a million visits a day, and Stanford began to rethink letting the university's equipment be tied up in this way. Yahoo! produced no revenue to cover expenses, so Yang and Filo began to consider how they might turn their hobby into a self-sustaining company. With the help of a business student friend, they developed a business plan and began to look for financing.

In April 1995, an investment firm put up $1 million to get Yahoo! Corporation started. America Online (AOL), the world's largest Internet service provider, asked Yahoo! to be its search engine. The prospect of visits from millions of AOL subscribers convinced Filo and Yang to sell advertising space on the Yahoo! site.

The Yahoo! Explosion

In 1996, Yang and Filo offered Yahoo! stock to the public for the first time. The money raised allowed the company to greatly expand its services. Although going public eventually reduced their ownership to 25 percent, the founders still participated in the company. Yang remained involved in business operations and Filo in technical development. Yahoo! survived the dot-com crash on the strength of its brand and advertising revenues. By 2003, Yahoo! had become a $20 billion business. Except for the fact that both were now multimillionaires, little had changed since 1994 for Yang and Filo. Yahoo!'s success "hasn't changed my life at all," reports Yang, "except that I think more about taxes."

CHECK FOR UNDERSTANDING

1. **Source Reading** Explain why Yahoo!'s agreement with AOL assured that Yahoo! would be a success.
2. **Critical Thinking** Why are Yang and Filo much wealthier today than they were when they owned 100 percent of the company?
3. **Learn More** Use the Internet and other sources to learn more about Yahoo!'s legal status as a business organization. Has the company's business organization changed over time?

ECONOMIC Profile Jerry Yang

Background

Although Yahoo! wasn't the first search engine ever created, it has consistently stood out from the crowd because of its user-friendly features and its whimsical quality. In December 2002, more than 200 million unique users visited a Yahoo! Web site. Yahoo! counted more than 100 million registered users.

When asked in an ABC interview what his biggest challenges have been so far, Yang mentioned attracting top people to his organization and continuing to motivate them. As for his success, Yang attributes it partly to Asian values: "Being humble and modest at the right times and being able to endure and persevere are two key values that have been key to successful entrepreneurship."

Careers in Economics Activity
Unit 3 folder, p. 13 gives students a closer look at the career path of a business proprietor.

Beyond the Classroom: Career Connections

Web Designer Explain to students that Web sites like Yahoo! could not exist without the work of Web designers, who create the look and feel of a Web site. They code text in Hypertext Markup Language (HTML) and design the images that give the site its visual appeal. Have students use the links provided in the *Economics: Principles in Action* segment in the Social Studies area of the Prentice Hall Web site (**www.phschool.com**) to examine job listings for Web designers. What is the size of the job market? What types of companies are hiring? What qualifications are needed? What responsibilities are to be expected?

Answers to . . .

1. The agreement ensured that AOL's millions of customers nationwide would be exposed to Yahoo! This would not only make Yahoo! a well-known national name among Internet users but would also allow Yahoo! to sell highly desirable advertising space on its Web site.
2. They gained much wealth from the sale of stock in their company.
3. Students' answers should demonstrate that they have been able to extract information on subjects such as the company's legal status, structure, size, and revenues.

Section 2

Partnerships

Objectives You may wish to call students' attention to the objectives in the Section Preview. The objectives are reflected in the main headings of the section.

Bellringer Ask students to recall times when they worked with a partner to fulfill a school assignment, pursue a hobby, or participate in some volunteer effort. Ask them to identify successful experiences and explain what made them work well.

Vocabulary Builder Have students read Section 2 to discover the meanings of the key terms. Then have them create a fill-in-the-blanks quiz, writing one sentence for each of the seven terms. Finally, have students exchange quizzes and fill in the correct answers.

Lesson Plan

Teaching the Main Concepts L3

1. Focus Explain to students that when two or more people join to start a business, they form a partnership. Depending on the type of partnership, each partner plays a specific role. Ask students how these roles might vary.

2. Instruct Discuss the general idea of a partnership and the specific partnership types. Be sure that students understand how general, limited, and limited liability partnerships are different. Explain to students that partnerships, like proprietorships, have advantages and disadvantages. Discuss examples of each.

3. Close/Reteach Remind students that partnerships require cooperation and a willingness to make the needs of the business a top priority. Ask students to explain how partnerships differ from proprietorships.

Guided Reading and Review
Unit 3 folder, p. 4 asks students to identify the main ideas of the section and to define or identify key terms.

Section 2 Partnerships

Preview

Objectives

After studying this section you will be able to:

1. **Compare and contrast** the different types of partnerships.
2. **Analyze** the advantages of partnerships.
3. **Analyze** the disadvantages of partnerships.

Section Focus

Partnerships let individuals pool their resources and share responsibility for the forming and running of a business.

Key Terms

partnership
general partnership
limited partnership
limited liability partnership (LLP)
articles of partnership
Uniform Partnership Act (UPA)
assets

---

partnership *a business organization owned by two or more persons who agree on a specific division of responsibilities and profits*

general partnership *partnership in which partners share equally in both responsibility and liability*

limited partnership *partnership in which only one partner is required to be a general partner*

limited liability partnership (LLP) *partnership in which all partners are limited partners*

A **partnership** is a business organization owned by two or more persons who agree on a specific division of responsibilities and profits. In the United States, partnerships account for about 7 percent of all businesses. They generate about 5 percent of all sales and about 10 percent of all income.

Types of Partnerships

Partnerships fall into three categories: general partnerships, limited partnerships, and limited liability partnerships. Each divides responsibility and liability differently.

Sometimes three heads are better than one. ▶

General Partnership

The most common type of partnership is the **general partnership.** Partners in a general partnership share equally in both responsibility and liability. Many of the same kinds of businesses that operate as sole proprietorships could operate as general partnerships. Doctors, lawyers, accountants, and other professionals often form partnerships with colleagues. Small retail stores, farms, construction companies, and family businesses often form partnerships as well.

Limited Partnership

In a **limited partnership,** only one partner is required to be a general partner. That is, only one partner has unlimited personal liability for the firm's actions. The remaining partner or partners contribute only money. They do not actively manage the business. Limited partners can lose only the amount of their initial investment. A limited partnership must have at least one general partner, but may have any number of limited partners. The main advantage of being a general partner is in having control of the business. The main drawback, of course, is the extent of liability.

Limited Liability Partnerships

The **limited liability partnership (LLP)** is a newer type of partnership recognized by

Building Key Concepts: Graphing the Main Idea

Entrepreneurs To build understanding of the concept of **entrepreneurs,** have students complete a tree map graphic organizer like the one at the right on partnerships. Remind students that a tree map shows an outline with a main topic, main ideas, and supporting details. Students should place the section title in the top box, a main heading in each of the boxes below, and main ideas and supporting details in the box or boxes below each heading.

Section Reading Support Transparencies A template and the answers for this graphic organizer can be found in Chapter 8, Section 2 of the Section Reading Support Transparency System.

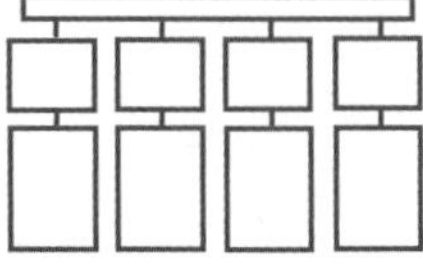

Figure 8.3 **Characteristics of Partnerships**

Go Online
PHSchool.com
Web Code: mng-3083

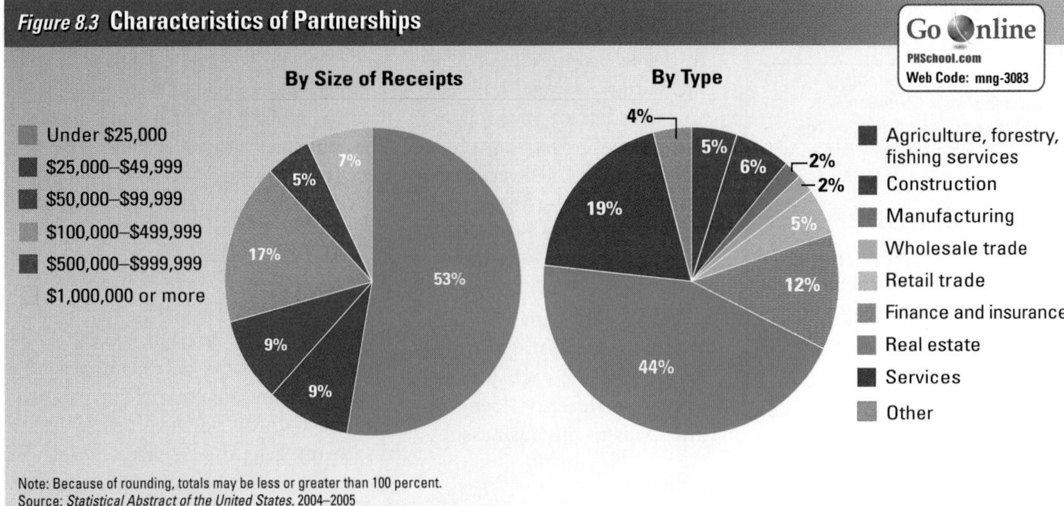

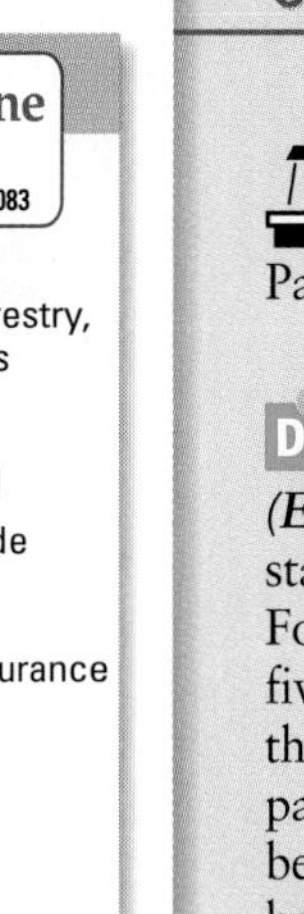

Note: Because of rounding, totals may be less or greater than 100 percent.
Source: *Statistical Abstract of the United States*, 2004–2005

Partnerships can range in size from a pair of house painters to an accounting firm with thousands of partners.
Specialization **Using the information in these graphs, describe partnerships in terms of industry and income.**

many states. In this type of partnership, all partners are limited partners. An LLP functions like a general partnership, except that all partners are limited from personal liability in certain situations, such as another partner's mistakes. Not all types of businesses are allowed to register as limited liability partnerships. Most states allow professionals such as attorneys, physicians, dentists, and accountants to register as LLPs.

Advantages of Partnerships

Partnerships are easy to establish and are subject to few government regulations. They provide entrepreneurs with a number of advantages.

Ease of Start-Up

Like proprietorships, partnerships are easy and inexpensive to establish. The law does not require a written partnership agreement. Most small business experts, however, advise partners to work with an attorney to develop **articles of partnership,** or a partnership agreement. This legal document spells out each partner's rights and responsibilities. It outlines how partners will share profits or losses. Partnership agreements may also address other details, such as the ways new partners can join the firm, duration of the partnership, and tax responsibilities.

If partners do not establish their own articles of partnership, they will fall under the rules of the **Uniform Partnership Act (UPA)**. The Uniform Partnership Act is a uniform state law adopted by most states to establish rules for partnerships. The UPA requires common ownership interests, profit and loss sharing, and shared management responsibilities.

Like sole proprietorships, partnerships are subject to little government regulation. The government does not dictate how partnerships conduct business. Partners can distribute profits as they wish, as long as they abide by the partnership agreement or by the UPA.

articles of partnership *a partnership agreement*

Uniform Partnership Act (UPA) *act ordering common ownership interests, profit and loss sharing, and shared management responsibilities in a partnership*

Transparency Resource Package
Economics Concepts, 8B: Partnerships

Differentiated Instruction L3

(Enrichment) Obtain a copy of a state's Uniform Partnership Act. Form the class into groups of four or five. Assign each group a section of the act that discusses some aspect of partnerships such as how they may be formed or dissolved, relationships between partners, or mergers with other businesses. Have each group determine what its section says about partnerships and present that information to the class. Encourage students to prepare visuals to accompany their presentations.

Differentiated Instruction L2

To help students understand partnerships, display the following words: *who, what, when, where, why,* and *how.* After students have read this section, have them create questions about partnerships, using each of the words *(for example, How does the government regulate partnerships?).* Then have students review the section to answer their own questions. ELL

Differentiated Instruction L3

Have students create charts or other graphics that explain clearly the similarities and differences among the types of partnerships. Encourage students to use creative writing, visual images, and other methods to make their graphic presentations interesting and informative. Display the finished graphics in the classroom.

Econ 101: Key Concepts Made Easy

Entrepreneurs Students may have difficulty understanding the idea of a **limited liability partnership.** Ask them to recall times in school when the entire class was disciplined for the actions of one or two students. Did they think that this was fair? Many people think that it is not fair in business. Explain that limited liability partnerships are formed to prevent all partners from being punished for the reckless or mistaken actions of a few. Ask students to provide some real-life examples that make clear why physician partnerships or attorney partnerships are allowed to register as LLPs.

Answer to . . .

Building Key Concepts Students should point out that over half of all partnerships are involved in services or in the closely related fields of finance, insurance, and real estate and that the majority of partnerships are small (receipts of under $25,000).

Background

Risky Business

People who start new businesses generally do so with good intentions and high hopes. The reality, however, is that starting a new business is a risky proposition. Every year in the United States, new businesses are born, and every year existing businesses fail. A business can fail for a variety of reasons. Perhaps the economy turns unfavorable, competition is unexpectedly fierce, or the individuals who run the business simply lack the necessary skills. Whatever the cause of a business failure, the statistics tell a cautionary tale.

In 1992, for example, nearly 165,000 new businesses made their debuts, adding more than 800,000 jobs to the economy. However, in the same year approximately 97,000 businesses failed. The year 1997 saw nearly 167,000 new businesses provide over 900,000 new jobs. Unfortunately, that same year more than 83,000 American companies failed.

Go Online PHSchool.com Typing in the Web Code when prompted will bring students directly to the article.

THE WALL STREET JOURNAL. CLASSROOM EDITION

For an additional article from *The Wall Street Journal Classroom Edition*, see the Source Articles folder in the **Teaching Resources**, pp. 24–26.

Differentiated Instruction L3

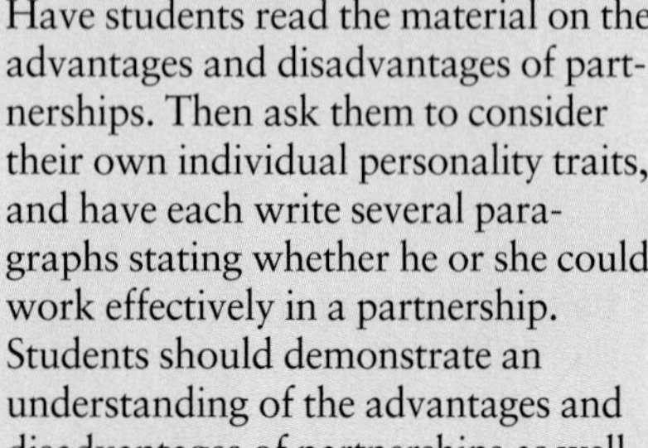

Have students read the material on the advantages and disadvantages of partnerships. Then ask them to consider their own individual personality traits, and have each write several paragraphs stating whether he or she could work effectively in a partnership. Students should demonstrate an understanding of the advantages and disadvantages of partnerships as well as self-awareness.

THE WALL STREET JOURNAL. CLASSROOM EDITION

In the News Read more about partnerships in "Partnership Prenuptials," an article in The Wall Street Journal Classroom Edition.

The Wall Street Journal Classroom Edition

For: Current Events
Visit: PHSchool.com
Web Code: mnc-3082

Shared Decision Making and Specialization

In a sole proprietorship, the individual owner has the sole burden of making all the business decisions. In a partnership, the responsibility for the business may be shared. A sole proprietorship requires the owner to wear many hats, some of which might not fit very well. In a successful partnership, however, each partner brings different strengths and skills to the business.

Larger Pool of Capital

Each partner's **assets**, or money and other valuables, improve the firm's ability to borrow funds for operations or expansion. Partnership agreements may allow firms to add limited partners to raise funds.

Partnerships offer more advantages to employees, enabling them to attract and keep talented employees more easily than proprietorships can. Graduates from top accounting schools, for example, often seek jobs with large and prestigious accounting LLPs, hoping to become partners themselves someday. Similarly, many law school graduates seek out successful partnerships for employment.

assets *money and other valuables belonging to an individual or business*

Taxation

Partnerships, like sole proprietorships, are not subject to any special taxes. Partners pay taxes on their share of the income that the partnership generates. The business itself, however, does not have to pay taxes.

Disadvantages of Partnerships

Partnerships also present some disadvantages. Many of the disadvantages of sole proprietorships are present in partnerships. Limited liability partnerships have fewer disadvantages than partnerships with general partners. All partnerships, however, have the potential for conflict.

Unlimited Liability

Unless the partnership is an LLP, at least one partner has unlimited liability. As in a sole proprietorship, any general partner could lose everything, including personal property, in paying the firm's debts. Limited partners do not face the same threat. They can lose only their investment.

In a partnership, each general partner is bound by the acts of all other general partners. If one partner's actions cause the firm losses, then all of the general partners suffer. If one doctor in a partnership is

Like sole proprietors, ▶ partners must maintain their entrepreneurial spirit to stay in business.

Block Scheduling Strategies

Consider these suggestions to take advantage of extended class time:

- Use the Background note on this page as a point of departure for a student investigation of business start-ups. Have them research business start-ups in the United States since the mid-1900s. Ask students to speculate on which economic or political situations would favor new businesses and which would hinder them.
- Show the Economics Video Library segment "Finding Funds," about ways new business owners find capital and the effects that investors have on the running of a business. Organize the class into groups of three or four, and have them create and perform short skits that depict challenges faced by business owners as they search for capital.

▲ **These partners must find positive ways to deal with conflict if they want to keep their business running smoothly.**

sued for malpractice, all of the doctors in the partnership stand to lose. General partners do not enjoy absolute control over the firm's actions like sole proprietors do. The risk from other people's actions means that people must choose their business partners carefully.

Potential for Conflict

As in any close relationship, partnerships have the potential for conflict. Partnership agreements address technical aspects of the business, such as profit and loss. Many important considerations exist outside these legal guidelines, however. Partners need to ensure that they agree about work habits, goals, management styles, ethics, and general business philosophies. Still, friction between partners often arises and can be difficult to resolve. Many partnerships dissolve because of interpersonal conflicts. Partners must learn to communicate openly and find ways to resolve conflicts.

Section 2 Assessment

Progress Monitoring *Online*
For: Self-quiz with vocabulary practice
Web Code: mna-3086

Key Terms and Main Ideas

1. Explain the characteristics of **partnerships.**
2. How do **general partnerships, limited partnerships,** and **limited liability partnerships** differ?
3. What issues are addressed in **articles of partnership?**
4. What is the purpose of the **Uniform Partnership Act?**

Applying Economic Concepts

5. ***Critical Thinking*** Why might accountants and physicians find limited liability partnerships attractive?
6. ***Critical Thinking*** Do you think the advantages of partnerships outweigh the disadvantages? Why or why not?
7. ***Problem Solving*** You and your general partners are operating under the Uniform Partnership Act, not your own articles of partnership. Now you cannot agree who should be responsible for which duties. How will you resolve your conflict?
8. ***Try This*** With a partner or two, draw up articles of partnership for a fictional business. Decide which type of partnership best suits your business and your personal preferences and skills.

For: Research Activity
Visit: PHSchool.com
Web Code: mnd-3082

Progress Monitoring *Online*
For additional assessment, have students access Progress Monitoring Online at **Web Code:** mna-3086

Go Online PHSchool.com Typing in the Web Code when prompted will bring students directly to detailed instructions for this activity.

GTE Guide to the Essentials
Chapter 8, Section 2, p. 34 provides support for students who need additional review of the section content. Spanish support is available in the Spanish edition of the guide on p. 34.

Quiz Unit 3 folder, p. 5 includes questions to check students' understanding of Section 2 content.

Presentation Pro CD-ROM Quiz provides multiple-choice questions to check students' understanding of Section 2 content.

Answers to . . .

Section 2 Assessment

1. A partnership is a business organization owned by two or more persons who agree on a particular division of responsibilities and profits.
2. A general partnership is a partnership in which partners share equally in both responsibility and liability. A limited partnership is a partnership in which only one partner has unlimited personal liability for the firm's actions; the other partners contribute only money. A limited liability partnership is a partnership in which all partners are limited partners with limited liability.
3. Articles of partnership list each partner's rights and responsibilities, including how partners will share profits and losses. They may also address issues such as the duration of the partnership and tax responsibilities.
4. The Uniform Partnership Act ensures that partnerships are formed according to a common set of rules and standards.
5. Answers will vary, but students may point out that these professionals are more likely than some others to be sued and that individuals need not be held liable for the mistakes of others.
6. Answers will vary depending on students' personalities and opinions. Students who think that the advantages outweigh the disadvantages may point to the opportunity for shared decisions and assets. Other students may disagree because of the potential for conflict.
7. Answers should focus on finding a compromise, such as by creating a new partnership agreement that may use the Uniform Partnership Act as a guideline.
8. Agreements should demonstrate an understanding of differing types of partnerships, the suitability of each for particular businesses, and the students' personalities.

Skills for LIFE

Using the Internet for Research

1. Focus Students will use Internet search engines to conduct research.

2. Instruct Discuss with students the value of search engines for finding information on the Web. Have volunteers describe their experience with search engines and why the choice of search words is so important. Have them follow the steps presented in the feature, giving examples of the types of information available as a result of the technological innovation of the Internet.

3. Close/Reteach To provide additional practice, see the Economic Skills Activity below.

Economic Skills Activity
Unit 3 folder, p. 10, "Using the Internet for Research," asks students to use Internet sources to find out about a corporate merger or acquisition.

Social Studies Skills Tutor CD-ROM offers interactive practice in critical thinking and reading, visual analysis, and communication.

Answers

1. (a) Students may identify chemical or pharmaceutical companies. (b) They may suggest using a news search service or the Web sites of environmental, safety, and government groups.
2. (a) Possible answers: *mission, goal, outlook, standards, philosophy*
(b) Answers will vary but should show an understanding of which term(s) brought inappropriate listings.
3. (a) Possible answers: *ethical, private, unethical* (b) Students may say yes, it provides adequate standards and could be followed. Other students may say no, having read about suspect practices. (c) Students should point to words that seem unethical or in contradiction to the stated mission.

Additional Practice

Have students look up the ethics statement of a company that has recently been in the news because of a controversial decision or action and analyze the statement in light of the recent news.

Skills for
LIFE

Using the Internet for Research

The Internet is a comprehensive network of computers that links businesses, universities, and individuals around the world. The World Wide Web is one part of the Internet. Because the Internet has no central organization, finding a Web page with the information you need can be difficult. Search engines, databases that track thousands of Web pages by subject, can help you focus your search.

In addition to advertising and product information, many corporations use their Internet sites to post corporate ethics statements like the one below. An ethics statement typically describes how the company approaches the law, the community in which it works, and its employees. Use the steps below to locate a corporate ethics statement on the Web.

1. Prepare your search. American companies can face ethical dilemmas over issues like pollution, safety, and working conditions. (a) Identify two companies that you think might face ethical issues. (b) How could you use the Internet to find these companies?

ETHICS STATEMENT OF ALPINE INVESTMENTS, INC.

Alpine Investments, Inc., and each of its employees will:

- Individually and collectively maintain a high level of ethical conduct with clients, coworkers, members of allied professions, and the public.
- Practice a method of financial planning founded on a legal and practical basis, not voluntarily associating with anyone who violates this principle.
- Seek advice in doubtful or difficult cases, and whenever it appears that the services of members of other professions would provide more complete and better quality or degree of advice.
- Not reveal the private information we may observe in any client's affairs, unless required to do so by law.
- Obey all laws and uphold the dignity and honor of the profession and accept the profession's self-imposed rules.
- Oppose, without hesitation, illegal or unethical conduct of fellow members of our profession.

2. Refine your search. Many search engines offer an advanced search option that allows you to refine your search. (a) Which words other than "ethics," "statement," and the company name might help you find the documents you are looking for? (b) Based on your first set of results, what word could you *exclude* from your search to eliminate inappropriate listings?

3. Analyze the document. Answer the following questions using the ethics statement at left. (a) List three significant phrases that the company uses in its ethics statement. (b) Do you find the company's statement convincing? Why or why not? (c) Which words or phrases are not convincing?

Additional Practice

Use the Internet to find an ethics statement for a company that has recently been in the news for a controversial decision or action.

Interdisciplinary Connections: Geography

Searching the Internet Because the Internet is truly a "World Wide Web," it is a rich source of information about countries and cultures. The Internet can bring a vast amount of information about the world and its people directly to your computer screen.

Have students work through the following activity: Ask each student to select a continent and then choose a country on that continent. Students should visit three sites that provide information about nations of the world and rate each site's effectiveness at presenting information. They should answer questions such as: Who created the site? What types of information are presented? How interesting is the site visually? How easy is it to navigate? Would you recommend this site to others? Have students use the links provided in the *Economics: Principles in Action* segment in the Social Studies area at the Prentice Hall Web site. **www.phschool.com**

Section 3 Corporations, Mergers, and Multinationals

Preview

Objectives

After studying this section you will be able to:

1. **Explain** the characteristics of corporations.
2. **Analyze** the advantages of incorporation.
3. **Analyze** the disadvantages of incorporation.
4. **Compare and contrast** corporate combinations.
5. **Describe** the role of multinational corporations.

Section Focus

Corporations are complex business organizations that can be combined to form even larger businesses. Some corporate enterprises span the globe.

Key Terms

corporation
stock
closely held corporation
publicly held corporation
bond
certificate of incorporation
dividend
horizontal merger
vertical merger
conglomerate
multinational corporation (MNC)

Businesses often rely on investment to expand operations. One way for a business to increase investment is to form a corporation. A corporation can grow even larger by combining with other corporations. Some corporations are so large that they do business all over the world.

Corporations

The most complex form of business organization is the corporation. A **corporation** is a legal entity, or being, owned by individual stockholders, each of whom faces limited liability for the firm's debts. Stockholders own **stock**, a certificate of ownership in a corporation. In other words, if you own stock in a corporation, you are a part-owner of that corporation. If a corporation issues 1,000 shares of stock, and you purchase 1 share, you own 1/1000th of the company.

Corporations differ from sole proprietorships, which have no identity beyond that of the owners. A corporation is defined as an "entity" because it has a legal identity separate from those of its owners. Legally, it is regarded much like an individual. A

corporation *a legal entity owned by individual stockholders*

stock *a certificate of ownership in a corporation*

Many corporations make their headquarters in large cities. ▼

Graphing the Main Idea

Economic Institutions To build understanding of the concept of **economic institutions,** have students complete a tree map graphic organizer like the one at the right on corporations, using the main heads of this section in the second row of the map. Remind students that a tree map can help them visualize main ideas and supporting details.

Section Reading Support Transparencies A template and the answers for this graphic organizer can be found in Chapter 8, Section 3 of the Section Reading Support Transparency System.

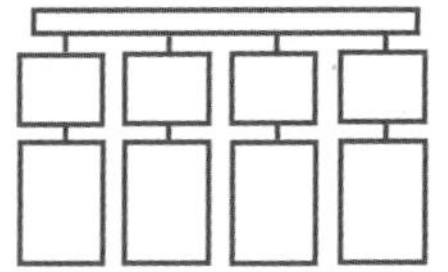

Section 3

Corporations, Mergers, and Multinationals

Objectives You may wish to call students' attention to the objectives in the Section Preview. The objectives are reflected in the main headings of the section.

Bellringer Ask students to recall news stories about companies that bought other companies to create business empires. Explain that this section will introduce the complex world of corporations—how they come to be, how they operate, and why they merge.

Vocabulary Builder Have students read the section to find the meanings of the key terms. Then ask them to create a pictorial or verbal clue that can help in recalling each key term.

Lesson Plan

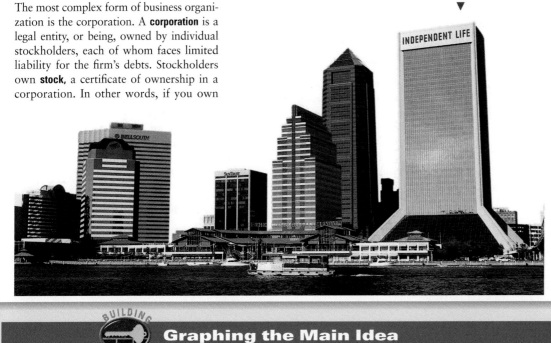

Teaching the Main Concepts 

1. Focus Explain to students that the most complex type of business organizations, corporations, account for about 90 percent of the products sold in the United States and generates about 70 percent of net income. Have students list five products that they have purchased lately and tell whether the products were produced by corporations.

2. Instruct Introduce students to the various types and structures of corporations. Discuss the advantages and disadvantages of incorporation, noting that corporations are the most strictly regulated type of business organization. Finally, explain how and why corporations merge as well as the role of multinational corporations.

3. Close/Reteach Remind students that corporations are complex, closely regulated organizations. Ask them to list some American corporations that also operate in other countries.

 **Guided Reading and Review**
Unit 3 folder, p. 6 asks students to identify the main ideas of the section and to define or identify key terms.

Differentiated Instruction L3
Have students study the circle graphs on this page. Ask students to imagine that they are business reporters for a newspaper and must turn these data into a feature article that offers a snapshot of corporate America. Remind them that their articles should be interesting as well as informative.

Differentiated Instruction L2
Before students read this section, have them write each main head and subhead and then write a sentence or two that predicts what each section of text will say. Then have students read the section and note the accuracy of their predictions. LPR

 **Transparency Resource Package**
Economics Concepts, 8C: Corporate Structures

Differentiated Instruction L1
Have students prepare an organizational chart of the corporation. Stockholders should be at the top, followed by Board of Directors, The Chief Executive Officer or President, Department Managers, and Employees. SN

Figure 8.4 **Characteristics of Corporations**

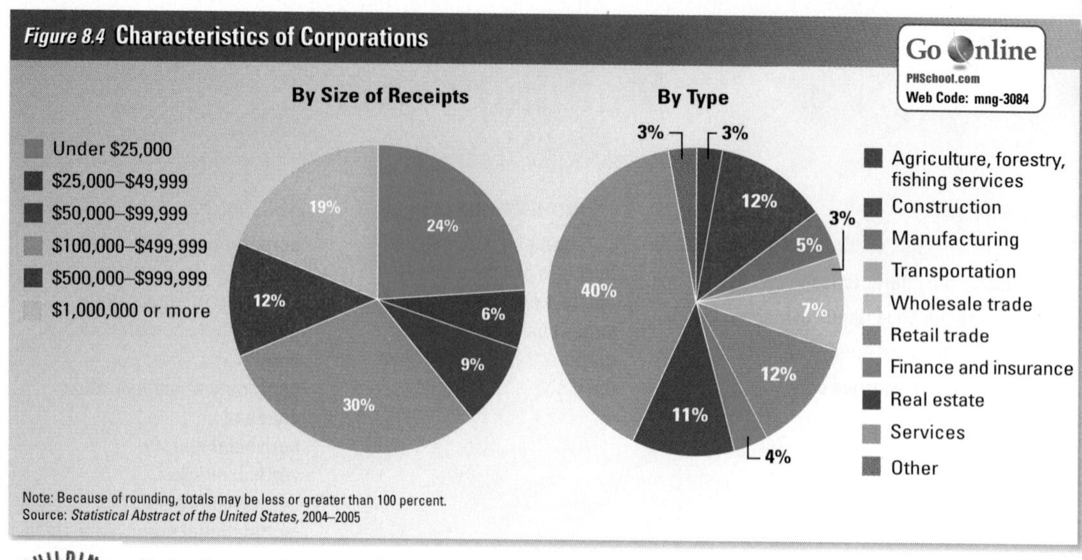

Note: Because of rounding, totals may be less or greater than 100 percent.
Source: *Statistical Abstract of the United States*, 2004–2005

Notice that over 60 percent of corporations are engaged in services, manufacturing, wholesale trade, and retail trade.
Incentives What incentives do businesses in these particular industries have to form corporations?

closely held corporation
corporation that issues stock to only a few people, often family members

publicly held corporation
corporation that sells stock on the open market

corporation pays taxes, may engage in business, make contracts, sue other parties, and get sued by others.

In the United States, corporations account for about 20 percent of all businesses, yet sell about 90 percent of all products sold in the nation. They generate about 70 percent of the net income earned in the nation. Because of the advantages of corporations, most large business firms do incorporate. Supermarkets, high-tech companies, and machinery manufacturers are just some of the types of firms that usually form corporations. Corporations' profits are about ten percent of their income.

Types of Corporations

Some corporations issue stock to only a few people, often family members. These stockholders rarely trade their stock, but pass it on within families. Such corporations are called **closely held corporations.** They are also known as privately held corporations.

A **publicly held corporation,** on the other hand, has many shareholders who can buy or sell stock on the open market. Stocks are bought and sold at financial markets called stock exchanges, such as the New York Stock Exchange. You will read about these financial markets in Chapter 11.

Corporate Structure

While the exact organization varies from firm to firm, all corporations have the same basic structure. Corporation owners—the stockholders—elect a board of directors. The board of directors makes all the major decisions of the corporation. It appoints corporate officers, who run the corporation and oversee production. Corporate officers, in turn, hire managers and employees, who work in various departments like finance, sales, research, marketing, and production.

Advantages of Incorporation

Incorporation, or forming a corporation, offers advantages to both the individual owners, or stockholders, and to the corporation itself. These include

Econ 101: Key Concepts Made Easy

Economic Institutions Some students may have difficulty understanding **double taxation.** Ask students to imagine that they own stock in General Motors (GM). When GM reports its revenue for the year, it must pay income tax on that revenue. Paying the tax reduces the amount of money GM can use to pay dividends to its shareholders. In a sense the shareholders, by receiving a smaller dividend, are helping GM pay its income tax. Then the shareholders have to pay their own income tax on the amount of the dividend they *do* receive—a second tax. Ask students to speculate on why, considering the level of taxation, stocks are such a popular investment.

Answer to . . .
Building Key Concepts Students may suggest that incorporation may increase a firm's ability to gain capital.

- limited liability for owners
- transferable ownership
- ability to attract capital
- long life

Advantages for Stockholders

The primary reason that entrepreneurs choose to incorporate, or form a corporation, is to gain the benefit of limited liability. Individual investors do not carry responsibility for the corporation's actions. They can lose only the amount of money they have invested in the business.

Corporations usually also provide stockholders with more flexibility than other ownership forms. Shares of stock are transferable, which means that stockholders can sell their stocks to others and get money in return.

Advantages for the Corporation

The corporate structure also presents advantages for the firm itself. Corporations have more potential for growth than other business forms. By selling shares on the stock market, corporations can raise money to purchase capital. A corporation can offer as many shares of stock as its corporate charter allows. As long as investors have confidence in the firm's success, companies should be able to sell stock fairly easily.

Corporations can also raise money by borrowing it. They do this by selling bonds. A **bond** is a formal contract to repay borrowed money with interest at fixed intervals.

Because ownership is separate from the running of the firm, corporation owners—that is, stockholders—do not need any special managerial skills. Instead, the corporation can hire various experts—the best financial analysts, the best engineers, and so forth—to create and market the best services or goods possible.

Corporations also have the advantage of long life. Unlike a sole proprietorship, the company does not end with the death of an owner. Because stock is transferable, that is, it can be bought and sold, corporations are able to exist longer than simple proprietorships. Unless it has stated in advance a specific termination date, the corporation can continue doing business indefinitely.

Disadvantages of Incorporation

Corporations are not without their disadvantages. These include

- expense and difficulty of start-up
- double taxation
- potential loss of control by the founders
- more legal requirements and regulations

Difficulty and Expense of Start-Up

Corporate charters can be difficult, expensive, and time consuming to establish. Though most states allow people to form corporations without legal help, few experts would recommend this cheaper shortcut. Applications are complex and confusing.

Firms that wish to incorporate must first file for a state license known as a **certificate of incorporation,** or corporate charter. The application includes crucial information such as

- the corporate name
- statement of purpose
- length of time that the business will run (usually "for perpetuity," or without limit)
- founders' names and addresses
- headquarters' business address
- method of fund-raising
- the rules for the corporation's management

Once state officials review and approve the application, they grant a corporate charter. Then the corporation may organize itself to produce and sell a good or service.

Double Taxation

The law considers corporations legal entities separate from their owners. Corporations, therefore, must pay taxes on their income.

bond *a formal contract to repay borrowed money with interest at fixed intervals*

certificate of incorporation *license to form a corporation issued by state government*

Meeting NCEE Standards

Use the following benchmark activity from the **Voluntary National Content Standards in Economics** to evaluate student understanding of **Standard 10.**

Play the role of a business consultant hired to advise a partnership on the advantages it could enjoy by incorporating; write a letter outlining these benefits for their client.

Differentiated Instruction 

(Reteaching) Read through the Meeting the Standards activity on this page. In addition, have students switch to the role of a business consultant who advises *against* incorporating. Ask them to write a letter that describes the disadvantages of incorporation.

Economic Cartoon

Unit 3 folder, p. 14 gives students practice in interpreting cartoons about section content.

Block Scheduling Strategies

Consider these suggestions to take advantage of extended class time:

- Extend the activities on this page by forming two groups: consultants and partners. Among the consultants, create several subgroups. Have each consultant group choose one student's letter to read to the partner group. After all letters have been read, let the class discuss the merits of each.
- Use the Background note "Keeping the Playing Field Level" on p. 198 as a springboard for a class discussion on government intervention in the economy. Have students research other interventions and then write a newspaper editorial on government intervention or nonintervention. Students should use examples from their research to support their point of view.

Background

Keeping the Playing Field Level

One important role that the government plays in the economy is to scrutinize all proposed mergers so that the marketplace remains competitive—no one player becomes so strongly dominant that other players cannot enter the market. That's exactly what the government did in 1994, when Microsoft announced its intention to buy Intuit, then the maker of the most popular financial software, Quicken.

At that time Quicken held a 70 percent share of the financial software market. Microsoft's financial software was running a distant second. If Microsoft, the dominant producer of computer operating systems, could join with the dominant financial software company, the result would be nearly total control of an emerging software niche.

For that reason the Department of Justice moved in, announcing its opposition to the deal. According to the Justice Department, the proposed transaction could have led to higher software prices and reduced competition and innovation. In mid-1995, faced with the probability of a costly legal battle, Microsoft called off the merger.

Differentiated Instruction 

Have students prepare a written report about one of the following mergers or acquisitions that occurred in the early 2000s: Time Warner and America Online; Compaq and Hewlett-Packard; AT&T Broadband and Comcast. Students should examine reactions to the merger and its effects. GT

Answer to . . .

Building Key Concepts Horizontal mergers combine competing firms. Vertical mergers join firms that are involved in different stages of producing the same good or service.

dividend *the portion of corporate profits paid out to stockholders*

Profit is a form of income. When stockholders receive income from the corporation in the form of **dividends**—the portion of corporate profits paid out to stockholders—the stockholders must pay personal income tax on those dividends. This double taxation keeps many firms from incorporating.

When stockholders sell their shares, they must pay a special tax, called a capital gains tax, if they have made a profit. In 2003, Congress reduced double taxation by lowering the dividend and capital gains tax rates to 15 percent.

Loss of Control

Unlike the owner of a sole proprietorship, the original owners of a corporation often lose control of the company. Managers and boards of directors, not owners, manage corporations. These professional managers do not always act in the owners' best interests. They might be more interested in protecting their own jobs or salaries today than in making difficult decisions that would benefit the firm tomorrow.

More Regulation

Corporations also face more regulations than other kinds of business organizations. Corporations must hold annual meetings for shareholders and keep careful records of all business transactions. Publicly held corporations are required to file quarterly and annual reports to the Securities and Exchange Commission (SEC). The SEC is a federal agency that regulates the stock market.

Corporate Combinations

As a corporation continues to grow, managers and owners may decide it makes

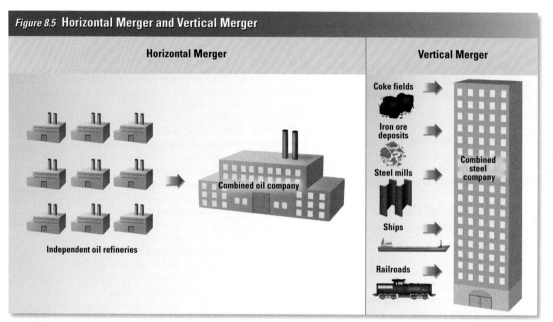

Figure 8.5 **Horizontal Merger and Vertical Merger**

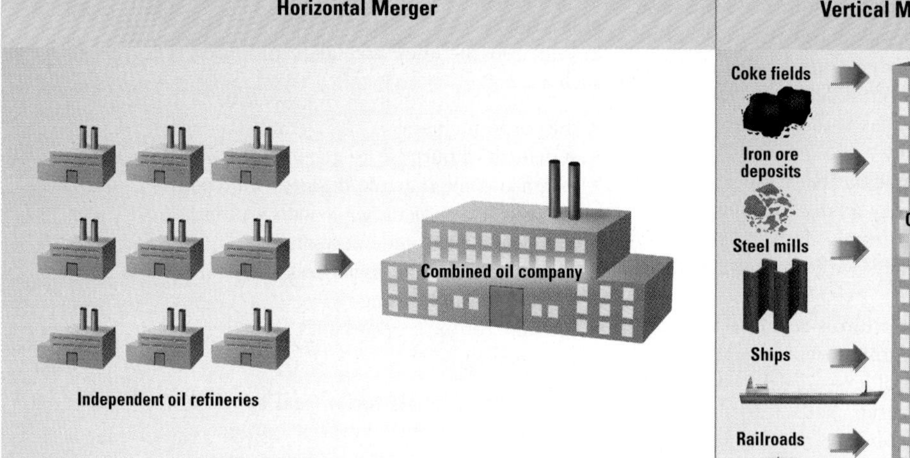

Beginning in the 1880s, John D. Rockefeller's Standard Oil Company combined horizontally (left) with 40 other oil refineries. The power gained by Standard Oil and similar monopolies prompted passage of the Sherman Antitrust Act in 1890. In 1899, Andrew Carnegie established the Carnegie Steel Company. He used the vertical merger (right) to purchase ore mines, furnaces and mills, and even the shipping and railroad lines needed to move his products to market. Within a short time, Carnegie controlled the steel industry. Most vertical mergers, however, do not result in monopolies. **Competition** **Explain the difference between horizontal and vertical mergers.**

Interdisciplinary Connections: Science

Corporate Science The 1990s and 2000s saw significant activity among corporations dedicated to scientific research, especially medical research. Pharmaceutical and bioengineering companies led the way, producing dramatic breakthroughs in the prevention and treatment of disease.

Making the Connection Ask students to research one of the major pharmaceutical or bioengineering corporations and draw up a simple financial profile of the company. What does it produce? How many people does it employ? If it is publicly traded, how has its stock performed over the past five years? What important products has it introduced in the past five years? Have students combine their findings on a bulletin board to facilitate comparison of corporations.

sense to merge, or combine, the firm with another company or companies. The three kinds of mergers are horizontal mergers, vertical mergers, and conglomerates.

Each of these corporate combinations can lead to larger, more efficient firms. Often, larger firms can produce and sell their products at lower prices. However, their size can also give some of these combinations more monopoly power, as discussed in Chapter 7.

Horizontal mergers

Horizontal mergers join two or more firms competing in the same market with the same good or service. For example, in late 1998, two giant automakers, Chrysler Corporation and Daimler-Benz, merged to form DaimlerChrysler.

Two firms might choose to merge if the newly resulting firm would result in economies of scale or would otherwise improve efficiency. At the time of the merger, Chrysler Corporation and Daimler-Benz predicted that their merger would reduce costs and boost revenues as much as $3 billion dollars annually.

As you read in Chapter 7, the federal government watches horizontal mergers carefully. The resulting single firm might gain monopoly power in its market.

Vertical Mergers

Vertical mergers join two or more firms involved in different stages of producing the same good or service. A vertical merger can allow a firm to operate more efficiently. A vertically combined firm can control all phases of production, rather than rely on the goods or services of outside suppliers. Sometimes firms combine vertically out of fear that they may otherwise lose crucial supplies. To ensure production, these firms simply buy their suppliers.

Antitrust regulators become concerned when many firms in the same industry merge vertically if that merger drives supplying firms out of business. Most vertical mergers do not substantially lessen competition, however, so they are usually allowed.

Figure 8.6 **A Conglomerate**

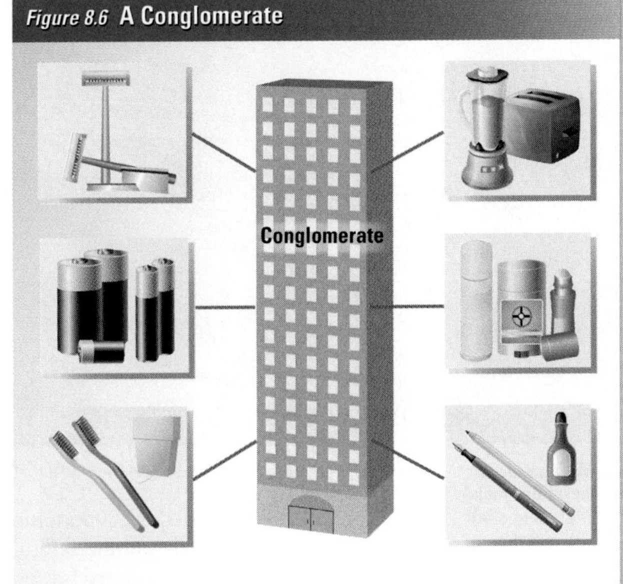

Conglomerates combine diverse businesses.
Competition Why don't conglomerates generally decrease competition?

Conglomerates

Sometimes firms buy other companies that produce totally unrelated goods or services. These combinations, called **conglomerates,** have more than three businesses that make unrelated products. In a conglomerate, no one business earns the majority of the firm's profits. The government usually allows this kind of merger, because it does not result in decreased competition.

Multinational Corporations

The world's largest corporations produce and sell their goods and services throughout the world. They are called **multinational corporations (MNCs)**. MNCs are corporations that operate in more than one country at a time. They usually have headquarters in one country and branches in other countries. Multinationals, which are sometimes called transnational corporations, must obey laws and pay taxes in each country in which they operate. In the

horizontal merger *the combination of two or more firms competing in the same market with the same good or service*

vertical merger *the combination of two or more firms involved in different stages of producing the same good or service*

conglomerate *business combination merging more than three businesses that make unrelated products*

multinational corporation (MNC) *large corporation that produces and sells its goods and services throughout the world*

Differentiated Instruction 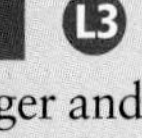

Have students research merger and acquisition activity in the United States over the past 20 years. Ask students to create graphs to display their research.

Differentiated Instruction 

(Reteaching) Have pairs of students create graphic organizers to explain the types of corporate combinations. Each pair should come up with a real-life example of each type of combination.

Transparency Resource Package
Economics Concepts, 8D: Corporate Mergers
Economics Concepts, 8E: Top U.S. and World Employers

Learning Styles Activity
Learning Styles Lesson Plans folder, p. 22 asks students to examine the advantages and disadvantages of corporations going multinational.

Differentiated Instruction 

You may wish to have students add the following to their portfolios. Ask students to read the information about multinationals in this section. Then ask them to use this information and any other knowledge they may have to write a position paper on the positive or negative role of multinationals. Remind students that their papers should explain both sides of the argument, and support a position. GT

Economics Assessment Rubric
Economics Assessment Rubrics folder, pp. 22–23 provides sample evaluation materials for a position paper.

Preparing for Standardized Tests

Have students read the section titled "Horizontal Mergers" and then answer the question below.

Which of the following describes a horizontal merger?

A The Pluto Motor Company merges with the Acme Tire Company.
(B) The Sunshine Rice Cereal Company merges with the New Dawn Oat Cereal Company.
C Megabux Film Studios merges with Good Earth Organic Food Stores.
D Futurama Video Games merges with the Lightning Battery Company.

Answer to . . .

Building Key Concepts The firms combined are in different industries.

GTE Guide to the Essentials
Chapter 8, Section 3, p. 35 provides support for students who need additional review of the section content. Spanish support is available in the Spanish edition of the guide on p. 35.

Quiz Unit 3 folder, p. 7 includes questions to check students' understanding of Section 3 content.

Presentation Pro CD-ROM
Quiz provides multiple-choice questions to check students' understanding of Section 3 content.

Answers to . . .

Section 3 Assessment

1. A corporation has a legal identity beyond that of the owner or partners. It is owned by individual stockholders.
2. A closely held corporation has a limited stock offering, whereas publicly held corporations offer stock on the open market.
3. Information such as the following is required: corporate name, statement of purpose, length of time the business will run, founders' names and addresses, headquarters' business address, method of fund-raising, and rules for management.
4. Stock is a share representing an owned portion of a corporation.
5. Profit is a form of income, and dividends are the portion of corporate profits that is paid to stockholders. Stockholders must then pay income tax on the profit they receive from dividends.
6. A merger is the combination of two or more corporations. Horizontal mergers join two or more firms that had competed in the same market to sell the same good or service. Vertical mergers join two or more firms that are involved in different stages of producing the same good or service. Conglomerates are combinations of more than three businesses that sell unrelated goods or services.
7. Multinational corporations operate in more than one country at a time.
8. Students should have an understanding of the advantages of incorporation (more potential for growth, ease of raising money through bond sales, long life) and the disadvantages (cost and difficulty of start-up, double taxation, potential loss of control by founders, more legal requirements and regulations).
9. Answers will vary, but explanations should show understanding of the benefits and drawbacks of incorporation.
10. As they help to improve the standard of living in other countries, they'll also increase sales there.
11. Students should state their decision and explain their reasoning.

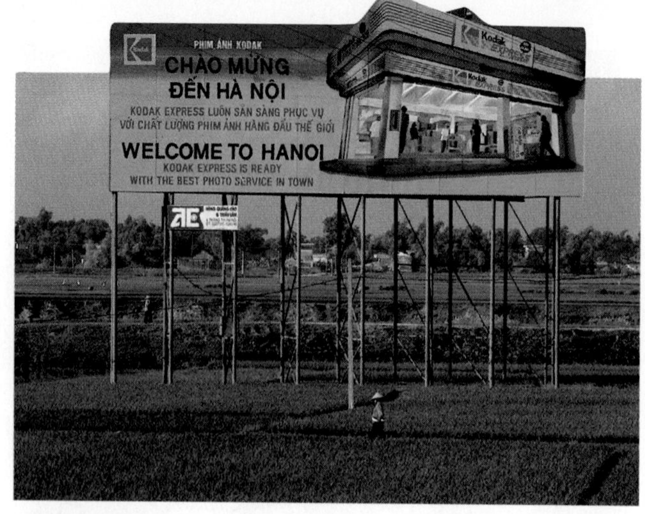

▲ **Multinational corporations make their presence felt throughout the world.**

early 2000s, an estimated 63,000 multinational firms operated about 690,000 foreign branches. They accounted for more than $3 trillion of worldwide assets. Many multinational corporations have operating budgets much bigger than most governments' budgets.

Corporations in the United States and Great Britain operated the world's largest multinationals in the 1970s and early 1980s. The picture today shows many different home countries for these giants, including Japan, South Korea, the Netherlands, and Italy.

Advantages of Multinationals

Multinationals benefit consumers and workers worldwide by providing jobs and products around the world. They also spread new technologies and production methods across the globe. Often the jobs they provide help poorer nations gain better living standards for their people.

Disadvantages of Multinationals

On the downside, many people feel that multinational firms unduly influence the culture and politics in the countries in which they operate. While some people feel that MNCs provide much needed jobs, critics are concerned about the low wages and poor working conditions provided by MNCs in some poorer countries. Whatever the advantages and disadvantages, trends suggest that MNCs will become increasingly visible and important in the world economy in the years ahead.

Section 3 Assessment

Progress Monitoring *Online*
For: Self-quiz with vocabulary practice
Web Code: mna-3087

Key Terms and Main Ideas

1. How does a **corporation** differ from a sole proprietorship or partnership?
2. What is the difference between a **closely held corporation** and a **publicly held corporation?**
3. What information is required in a **certificate of incorporation?**
4. What is **stock?**
5. Why must stockholders pay taxes on **dividends?**
6. What is a merger? How do **horizontal mergers, vertical mergers,** and **conglomerates** differ?
7. Why are some corporations called **multinational corporations?**

Applying Economic Concepts

8. ***Critical Thinking*** Suppose you are deciding whether to incorporate your house-cleaning business. Analyze the consequences of this economic decision.
9. ***Try This*** Identify several sole proprietorships and partnerships in your neighborhood or town. Which of these businesses might benefit from incorporation? Explain your reasoning.
10. ***Critical Thinking*** How might a corporation benefit by being multinational?
11. ***Problem Solving*** You want to incorporate your family business. Will you form a closely held corporation or a publicly held corporation? Explain your reasoning.

For: Current Events Activity
Visit: PHSchool.com
Web Code: mnd-3083

Progress Monitoring *Online*
For additional assessment, have students access Progress Monitoring Online at **Web Code:** mna-3087

Go Online PHSchool.com Typing in the Web Code when prompted will bring students directly to detailed instructions for this activity.

Entrepreneurs

Business and Ethics

When George Abbot Morison retired to the family farm in Peterborough, New Hampshire, in the 1940s, the state had high unemployment and very little industry. Morison decided to do something that would create new jobs and help revitalize the state's industrial base. He had read about Hitchiner Manufacturing Company, Inc., a small company that specialized in producing metal parts. Morison saw a growing need for precision metal parts and realized that Hitchiner's metal casting process had great commercial potential. In 1949, he and his son John H. Morison bought the company, and John became president.

Statement of Principles and Code of Conduct

WE EMBRACE RESPONSIBILITY.
WE ACT IN GOOD FAITH, HONESTLY AND FAIRLY.
WE HONOR THE LAW.
WE NURTURE ACHIEVEMENT.
WE DELIVER QUALITY AND VALUE.
WE RESPECT THE EARTH.
WE ADVANCE TECHNOLOGY.
WE ARE GOOD CITIZENS.
WE GUARD OUR INTEGRITY.

Rights and Responsibilities For the Morisons' investment to pay off, they had to develop the company so that it would make money. To do so, they benefited from their rights to enter into contracts, to use the courts to enforce their contractual rights, and to receive equal protection of law.

Hitchiner also had responsibilities. It had to comply with health and safety laws to reduce the chances of on-the-job injuries. The company had to pay employees at least minimum wage and had to make contributions to the state workers compensation fund. It also had to pay taxes on its profits.

Most importantly, the company strove to maintain "the highest standards of ethical and good-spirited conduct." Key points of its ethics policy appear in the Statement of Principles and Code of Conduct on this page.

Helping Employees Morison realized that the company's success depended on having an educated and trained work force. Hitchiner began sending employees for courses in many disciplines, from basic literacy and mathematics to statistical process control, for apprenticeships in specialized technical fields, and for business-management seminars. In 1953, Hitchiner became one of the first American companies to give its employees an ownership interest in the company.

Continued Success Today, Hitchiner markets its metal castings and licenses its technology and processes worldwide. Its current sales total about $200 million a year.

▼ Hitchiner uses the latest technologies in metal casting.

Applying Economic Ideas

1. **(a)** How were the Morisons able to help themselves and help their community at the same time? **(b)** What were their rights and responsibilities?
2. Analyze Hitchiner's ethics policy. Why was this policy an important part of its business success?

Real-life Case Study: Entrepreneurs

1. Focus Point out that a small business was languishing in a state with high unemployment when an entrepreneurial father and son team stepped in. The Morisons saw the potential for a business that specialized in producing metal parts, they kept up with technology, and they created opportunities for the workforce—from education to ownership—that forged a relationship of mutual respect and productivity.

2. Instruct Discuss the ways an organization like the Hitchiner Company can help shape the lives of its employees beyond providing a useful paycheck. How does such a company gain by such actions?

3. Close/Reteach Ask students to speculate about how the town of Peterborough, N.H., benefits from the changes in the Hitchiner Company.

Case Studies Activity
Case Studies in Free Enterprise folder, pp. 16–17, "Lloyd Ward," helps students apply economic principles in an additional case study.

Economic Detective Activity
Unit 3 folder, p. 12, "Midland Welcomes Your Business!," provides an additional application of chapter concepts.

Answers to . . .

1. (a) Answers may include the following: The business rewarded the Morison family financially, the employees found good jobs with access to training and other benefits, and the town profited from the company's taxes. (b) Morisons' rights included the right to contract, to use courts to enforce contracts, and the right to equal protection. The company was responsible for complying with OSHA, paying minimum wage or more, paying workers' compensation, and paying taxes.
2. Students' responses will vary, but the code reveals a pride in the company and in its human and professional standards. The code sets a tone and a goal for behavior. It sets the expectation that the employees will do and be their best.

Case Studies Activity
Case Studies in Free Enterprise folder, pp. 16–17, "Lloyd Ward," helps students apply economic principles in an additional case study.

Economic Detective Activity
Unit 3 folder, p. 12, "Midland Welcomes Your Business!," provides an additional application of chapter concepts.

Chapter 8 Assessment

Key Terms

1. vertical merger
2. liability
3. corporation
4. sole proprietorship
5. consumer cooperative
6. conglomerate
7. royalties
8. limited partnership

Using Graphic Organizers

9. Flowcharts will vary. One possible arrangement would include *partnership* before the decision to incorporate, with *horizontal merger* and *vertical merger* as choices on the same line as *conglomerate*. Answers should demonstrate an understanding of chapter content.

Reviewing Main Ideas

10. Possible trade-offs include large amount of personal liability measured against full control, limited access to resources measured against ease of start-up, and lack of permanence measured against ease of discontinuing the business.
11. A partnership is easy to start, allows for increased specialization and shared decision making in the business, provides a larger pool of capital, and is not subject to special taxes.
12. Stockholders may benefit financially from their investment in a corporation while not actually having to do any work for it. Also, their liability is limited.
13. Advantages of opening a franchise include management training and support, standardized quality, national advertising programs, financial assistance, and centralized buying power. Disadvantages include some loss of freedom, high franchising fees and royalties, strict operating standards, purchasing restrictions, and a limited product line.
14. Horizontal mergers join two or more firms that compete in the same market with the same good or service. Vertical mergers join two or more firms that are involved in different stages of producing the same good or service. Conglomerates combine more than three businesses that make unrelated products.
15. Multinational corporations operate in more than one country at a time.
16. Lower prices are the main advantage of cooperatives.

Chapter 8 Assessment

Chapter Summary

A summary of major ideas in Chapter 8 appears below. See also the **Guide to the Essentials of Economics**, which provides additional review and test practice of key concepts in Chapter 8.

Section 1 Sole Proprietorships (pp. 185–188)

Sole proprietorships are the most common form of business in the United States. They are easy to establish and offer owners both the benefits and drawbacks that come with full control of the business.

Section 2 Partnerships (pp. 190–193)

Partnerships let individuals pool their resources and share responsibility in the forming and running of a business. Three types of partnerships are the **general partnership**, the **limited partnership**, and the **limited liability partnership**.

Section 3 Corporations, Mergers, and Multinationals (pp. 195–200)

Corporations are complex business organizations that can be owned by a few or a great many individuals. **Mergers** combine corporations in various ways to form even larger businesses. Some corporate enterprises, the **multinationals**, span the globe.

Section 4 Other Organizations (pp. 201–204)

Business franchises are business organizations that give business owners support from a parent company. Other types of organizations serve to aid business owners, consumers, producers, industries, workers, or society at large. Many operate as **nonprofit organizations**.

Key Terms

Match the following definitions with the terms listed below. You will not use all of the terms.

liability	**limited partnership**
corporation	**royalties**
conglomerate	**nonprofit organization**
general partnership	**consumer cooperative**
sole proprietorship	
vertical merger	

1. the combination of two or more firms involved in different stages of producing the same good or service
2. the legally bound obligation to pay debts
3. a legal entity owned by individual stockholders
4. a business owned and managed by a single individual
5. a retail outlet owned and operated by consumers
6. a business combination merging more than three businesses that make unrelated products
7. share of earnings given as payment
8. a form of partnership in which only one partner is required to be a general partner

Using Graphic Organizers

9. On a separate sheet of paper, copy the flowchart below. Use the flowchart to organize information about how a business might grow. Complete the flowchart by writing descriptions and examples for each cell in the chart. You may add cells to the chart.

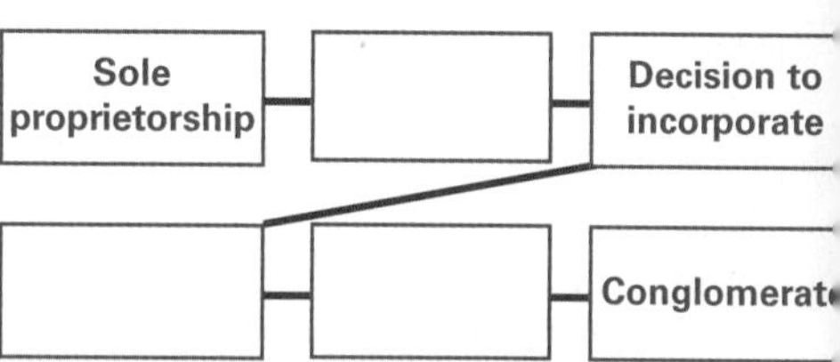

17. Answers may include: sole proprietorship (industry-specific regulations, health codes, zoning laws); partnerships (government regulations, agreements, UPA); corporations (government regulations, annual reports); MNCs (country-specific laws and regulations).

Critical Thinking

18. Answers should demonstrate an understanding of business organizations. Possible answer: what kind of business I want to run; how large I want my business to be; how much liability I am willing to accept.
19. Conglomerates are usually allowed because their mixed nature does not decrease competition. Vertical mergers are usually allowed unless competition would be decreased, as might occur if too many firms in the same industry merge vertically. Horizontal mergers are closely scrutinized to ensure that no firm gains a monopoly.
20. Liability levels for sole proprietorships are greatest: The owner has unlimited personal liability. Partnerships allow for varied levels of liability: Partners may share liability, one partner may assume unlimited liability, or all partners may have limited liability. The

Reviewing Main Ideas

10. List three trade-offs of running a sole proprietorship.
11. What are the advantages of forming a partnership when creating a new business?
12. What benefits do corporations bring to their stockholders?
13. Compare the advantages and disadvantages of opening a business franchise.
14. Describe the difference between vertical mergers, horizontal mergers, and conglomerates.
15. What are multinational corporations?
16. What are the advantages of cooperatives?
17. Identify and evaluate the ordinances and regulations that apply to the various types of businesses described in the chapter.

Critical Thinking

18. **Drawing Conclusions** Suppose you are opening a new business. List three choices that you would need to make to decide what style of business organization to form.
19. **Analyzing Information** How are the three types of corporate combinations usually affected by antitrust policy?
20. **Making Comparisons** Compare the different levels of individual liability among the three main types of business organizations: sole proprietorships, partnerships, and corporations.
21. **Drawing Inferences** How can stockholders influence the actions of the corporation they own?

Problem-Solving Activity

22. Recommend a cooperative for your community. Describe the type of cooperative it would be (consumer, service, or producer) and how your community could benefit from it.

Economics Journal

Identifying Alternatives Revisit your list of local businesses. Pick one and recommend a particular business form for it. Draft a proposal outlining why you think the business or the owner(s) would benefit from your plan.

Skills for Life

Using the Internet for Research Review the steps shown on page 194. Then complete the following activity.

Mergers lead to the formation of new business organizations. Corporate mergers sometimes have far-reaching effects on the companies and employees involved. Use the steps below to prepare a summary of one recent corporate merger and its effects on the employees of the companies involved.

23. **Prepare your search.** Identify one recent merger that has taken place. The Federal Trade Commission (FTC) oversees all mergers to make sure that they do not interfere with competition. Begin by visiting the FTC Web site. **(a)** How can you use the Internet to obtain information about these mergers? **(b)** List three key terms you might use in your search.
24. **Refine your search.** Once you have identified one merger to research, you need to refine your search. **(a)** How can you refine your search? **(b)** Identify two Internet sources that contain specific information about the merger.
25. **Analyze your results.** After you have located specific documents referring to the merger you have selected, you can begin to analyze the information. Print the documents if possible. **(a)** Look at the source of your documents. Could the source be biased? **(b)** What effect has the merger had on employees?

Progress Monitoring *Online*

For: Chapter 8 Self-Test **Visit:** PHSchool.com
Web Code: mna-3081

As a final review, take the Economics Chapter 8 Self-Test and receive immediate feedback on your answers. The test consists of 20 multiple-choice questions designed to test your understanding of the chapter content.

corporation as a separate entity has liability, while individual stockholders have limited liability.

21. Stockholders have influence in electing the board of directors and can also voice discontent as a group.

Problem-Solving Activity

22. Answers should demonstrate an understanding of the nature of cooperatives and of the community. For example, students may suggest a health food store as a consumer cooperative, saying that the community would benefit because these types of foods are not available locally and that the community would experience better health as well as lower prices from the purchasing power of the cooperative.

Skills for Life

23. (a) Students can use the FTC Web site to investigate merger activity. (b) Responses may include *merger, antitrust, competition,* or *corporation.*
24. (a) Students can refine their searches by focusing on effects on the company and its employees or by focusing on a particular time span. (b) Student responses will vary but may include any reputable news source, such as on-line newspapers, magazines, and journals.
25. (a) Students should identify their sources and give reasons why they might be biased or unbiased. (b) Answers should include information on the merger and what it has meant to employees, such as layoffs or increased opportunities.

Additional support materials and activities for Chapter 8 of *Economics: Principles in Action* can be found in the Social Studies area of **PHSchool.com.**

Review and Assessment

Vocabulary Practice Unit 3 folder, p. 11 uses a fill-in-the-blanks word puzzle to reinforce understanding of key terms.

GTE **Guide to the Essentials** Chapter 8 Test, p. 37

Test Bank CD-ROM Chapter 8 Test

Go Online PHSchool.com Students may use the Chapter 8 Self-Test on **PHSchool.com** to prepare for the Chapter Test.

Economics Journal

Students' responses will vary. Proposals should be logical and clear and should outline the benefits of the plan.

Economics Simulation

Objectives Upon completion of this simulation, students should be able to:
- identify the decisions an entrepreneur must make when starting a business;
- apply their knowledge of cost-benefit analysis to make decisions relevant to starting a business.

Bellringer Ask students to think about businesses they could start while they are still in school. Have them list specific businesses or types of businesses that they might begin on a part-time basis.

1. Focus Tell students that in this simulation they will be role-playing entrepreneurs who are writing a business plan for a business they want to start. Ask them to identify factors that an entrepreneur would have to take into account when starting a business. Discuss with students why careful planning is such an important part of starting a business.

2. Instruct Have students prepare for and conduct the simulation, using the procedures noted in the text.

3. Close/Reteach Have students present their business plans. After they have presented their conclusions, discuss answers to the first three analysis questions as a class. Assign the Formulating Questions query as a follow-up.

Economic Simulation
Economic Simulations folder, pp. 15–20, "Organized Labor: Compromise and Negotiation," provides an additional simulation on a unit topic.

Economics Simulation Be an Entrepreneur!

Many people dream of starting their own businesses. Here's your chance to practice doing just that. In this simulation, you and your classmates will form a partnership to run a small business. You plan to sell a line of souvenir baseball caps out of a rented vendor's cart in a nearby shopping mall.

Each partnership group will work independently. First, you will calculate your monthly costs. Then, you will price your product. Next, you will try to project how you would do in the first month of business. At the end of the simulation, all the partnerships will compare results.

▲ Careful planning will improve your business's chances of success.

Materials
Paper
Calculator

Preparing the Simulation

Step 1: Form groups of four to six people. Each group will be a separate business partnership.

Step 2: Choose a name for your company.

Conducting the Simulation

Step 1: Now, get started with your business plan! You and your partners already have $3,000 in start-up capital. Before you spend any of it, you need to figure out what your expenses will be. On a piece of paper, make a monthly expenses chart like the one on the next page. As you figure out each monthly expense, record it on the chart.

Business Loan Should you work within your $3,000 budget, or should you borrow money? You have learned that the best small-business loan that you qualify for charges an interest rate of 10% and requires monthly payments over 5 years:
- $5,000 loan: $106 per month
- $10,000 loan: $212 per month

Vendor License Your community requires you to get a vendor license. This will cost you $60 per year.

Banking Costs You need a business checking account. This will cost $12 per month.

Business Space The monthly rental costs for the vendor's cart depend on size and location:
- Cart in well-traveled, central location: $2,000 per month
- Cart in low-traffic area: $600 per month

Advertising Should you advertise? If you think you'll get enough "walk-in" traffic in the mall, you may not need to. Or, you may want to be more aggressive and use advertising to bring people directly to you:
- Medium-sized ad in the major city newspaper: $400 per week
- Small ad in neighborhood newspaper: $40 per week

Labor Should you and your partners work the cart, or should you hire a salesperson? Your vendor's cart will need to be staffed from 9:30 A.M. to 9:30 P.M. If you hire a salesperson, you will need to pay wages plus another 25 percent for benefits and taxes. Use the following formula:

Number of hours per month × hourly wage × 1.25 = total monthly labor cost

Step 2: Now you need to make decisions about your inventory. How many caps will you order from the manufacturer? Refer to the catalog page at right to determine which kind you'll order. Make an order/pricing form like the one on this page, and record the quantities and costs of the caps you want to buy.

Step 3: Next, you need to set a price for your caps. Keep in mind what the caps cost you and what you think people will pay for them. Add the prices to the order/pricing form and calculate your profit per cap.

Step 4: Finally, you need to determine how many caps you need to sell in order to make a profit after having paid your monthly expenses. Assume, for the moment, that you sell equal numbers of each cap. How many caps do you need to sell each month to break even? How many do you need to sell to make a profit large enough to pay salaries to you and your partners?

Step 5: Present your business plan to the rest of your class.

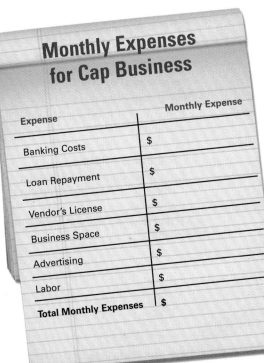

Monthly Expenses for Cap Business

Expense	Monthly Expense
Banking Costs	$
Loan Repayment	$
Vendor's License	$
Business Space	$
Advertising	$
Labor	$
Total Monthly Expenses	$

Good Quality! Cotton caps with plastic snap tabs
Colors: khaki, green, blue, charcoal, red

Item Number	Quantity	Price per cap
Style 101	100	$2.53
Silk Screened	500	$2.37
	1,000	$2.09
Style 102	100	$5.20
Embroidered	500	$4.82
	1,000	$4.60

Best Quality! Cotton twill caps with adjustable leather strap and brass buckle
Colors: black, white, navy blue, pine green

Item Number	Quantity	Price per cap
Style 202	100	$6.05
Embroidered	500	$5.60
	1,000	$5.40

Simulation Analysis

After all the partnerships in your class have presented their business plans, answer the following questions.

1. Which business plan was the most cautious? Which group took the most chances?
2. Where do you get the greatest savings for additional quantities—the least-expensive or most-expensive caps?
3. Suppose that you began the first month with equal numbers of silk-screened and embroidered caps. At the end of the month, you sold out of caps with silk-screened designs but had 20 embroidered caps left. What would this tell you about your market?
4. **Formulating Questions** What other information would you need if you were actually going to set up a small business?

Meeting NCEE Standards

Use the following benchmark activity from the **Voluntary National Content Standards in Economics** to evaluate student understanding of Standard 14.

Explain how entrepreneurial activity is affected by a tax policy that affects income from profits and capital investment.

Background

The Pokémon Craze

Japanese video game creators Satoshi Tajiri and Tsunekaz Ishihara spent six years developing the characters for Pokémon. It was time well spent because it resulted in the video game that took off in Japan, the United States, and Australia in the late 1990s, generating about $700 million in retail sales in the United States in 1999.

The game became popular in Japan in 1996. At first Nintendo executives were not convinced that the game would succeed in the United States. Therefore, they introduced it in September 1998 not as a game but as a television show. Before they knew it, however, the video game had become the lead product. By the end of 1999, trading cards, comic books, notebooks, key chains, and CD soundtracks were selling briskly as well.

Interdisciplinary Connections: Science

Entrepreneurship Scientists can be entrepreneurs, too. Scientists often invent or enhance products or processes that ultimately have significant market value. Engineers such as Henry Bessemer have made discoveries about large-scale processes and products that revolutionized the industrial world. Today discoveries and inventions at a microscopic level may have similar effects.

Making the Connection Have students research recent entrepreneurs who have made their mark in the sciences, and ask them to prepare a short presentation. Since many new patents today come not from individuals but from corporate development teams, you may want to expand this activity beyond individuals and allow students to research small, daring companies that have been pioneers in technology.

Answers to . . .

1. Answers will depend on the business plans that students submit.
2. The greatest savings for additional quantities is with the most-expensive caps.
3. The market has a higher demand for silk-screened caps than for embroidered caps.
4. Students should suggest information that demonstrates an understanding of business start-up, such as marketing data on the demand for caps in their area and information on area competition.

Chapter Resource Manager

Chapter 9 Labor

For more pacing suggestions, see the Economics Pacing Guide in the Program Overview of the Teaching Resources.

Section Objectives	Print and Technology Resources	
1 Labor Market Trends *(pp. 211–217)* **Objectives** 1. Describe how trends in the labor force are tracked. 2. Analyze past and present occupational trends. 3. Summarize how the U.S. labor force is changing. 4. Identify and explain trends in the wages and benefits paid to U.S. workers.	• **Lesson Planner** Section 1 Lesson Plan, p. 42 • **Learning Styles Lesson Plans folder** Section 1 Lesson Plan, p. 23 • **Lesson Plans folder** Section 1 Lesson Plan, p. 35 • **Economics Assessment Rubrics folder** Writing Assignment, pp. 6–7 • **Unit 3 folder** Guided Reading and Review, p. 15 Economic Skills, p. 21 Vocabulary Practice, p. 22 Economic Detective, p. 23 Section 1 Quiz, p. 16 • **Math Practice folder** Real Dollar Value of Minimum Wage, p. 7	• **Presentation Pro CD-ROM** Section 1 • **Transparency Resource Package** Economics Organizers, G7: Tree Map Graphic Organizer Economics Concepts, 9A: Growth in Selected Occupations Economics Concepts, 9B: Earnings and Education Level Economics Concepts, 9C: Characteristics of the U.S. Work Force • **Section Reading Support Transparency System** • **Social Studies Skills Tutor CD-ROM**
2 Labor and Wages *(pp. 219–226)* **Objectives** 1. Analyze the relationship between supply and demand in the labor market. 2. Understand the connection between wages and skill levels. 3. Explain how laws against wage discrimination affect wage levels. 4. Describe other actors affecting wages, such as minimum wage and workplace safety laws.	• **Lesson Planner** Section 2 Lesson Plan, p. 43 • **Lesson Plans folder** Section 2 Lesson Plan, p. 36 • **Economics Assessment Rubrics folder** Writing Assignment, pp. 6–7 • **Unit 3 folder** Guided Reading and Review, p. 17 Careers in Economics, Labor Relations Specialist, p. 24 Section 2 Quiz, p. 18 • **Source Articles folder** Money Isn't Everything, pp. 27–29	• **Presentation Pro CD-ROM** Section 2 • **Transparency Resource Package** Economics Organizers, G5: Web Graphic Organizer Economics Concepts, 9D: Job Migration by State Economics Concepts, 9E: Median Weekly Earnings, by Occupation and Sex • **Section Reading Support Transparency System**
3 Organized Labor *(pp. 228–234)* **Objectives** 1. Describe why historically some American workers have joined labor unions. 2. Trace the history of the labor movement in the United States. 3. Analyze reasons for the decline of the labor movement. 4. Explain how labor and management negotiate contracts.	• **Lesson Planner** Section 3 Lesson Plan, p. 44 • **Learning Styles Lesson Plans folder** Section 3 Lesson Plan, p. 24 • **Lesson Plans folder** Section 3 Lesson Plan, p. 37 • **Economics Assessment Rubrics folder** Writing Assignment, pp. 6–7 • **Unit 3 folder** Guided Reading and Review, p. 19 Economic Cartoon, p. 25 Section 3 Quiz, p. 20	• **Case Studies in Free Enterprise folder** Craig McCaw, pp. 18–19 • **Presentation Pro CD-ROM** Section 3 • **Transparency Resource Package** Economics Organizers, G7: Tree Map Graphic Organizer Economics Concepts, 9F: Rise and Fall of Union Membership Economics Concepts, 9G: Collective Bargaining • **Section Reading Support Transparency System**

Differentiated Instruction

Time Lines (L3)

Too often, high school students have difficulty placing important events or persons in their correct century or context. They may not understand simultaneous developments across an economy. A large time line at the front of the classroom can help students make these connections.

To help students sequence events, create a layered time line. Parallel to the line that marks the years, have students create a line for each trend discussed in this chapter. To begin, divide the class into groups and assign each group one trend in U.S. manufacturing or labor relations. Have them list the important events and sequence them correctly on the time line. Then have students place their respective timelines on a wall, one timeline above the next.

Historical Precedents (L4)

Modern events do not happen in a vacuum; they are usually shaped by many preceding causes and situations. Students should place the labor movement within its greater context in American History. Ask them to draw upon previously learned information to understand the motives and perspectives of involved parties.

To help students develop an understanding of the continuum of history, ask them to formulate a list of causes of the event begin studied. Then have them determine which cause was the most significant in ultimately shaping the outcome of the event being studied. As a class, vote on which cause was the most significant. Ask students, if this cause was removed, might the event have been altered or prevented?

Visit the Social Studies area of the Prentice Hall Web site. There you can find additional links to enrich chapter content for *Economics: Principles in Action* as well as a self-test for students. Be sure to check out this month's **eTeach** online discussion with a Master Economics Teacher.

Web Code: mnf-3091

Running Out of Time?

- Use the **Presentation Pro CD-ROM** to create an outline for this chapter.
- Use the Chapter Summary in the **Chapter 9 Assessment,** p. 236.
- Use the Section Summaries for Chapter 9, from **Guide to the Essentials of Economics (English and Spanish).**

THE WALL STREET JOURNAL. CLASSROOM EDITION

Prentice Hall brings into the classroom the authoritative content of *The Wall Street Journal Classroom Edition.* See the Source Articles, Debating Current Issues, and You and Your Money folders in the **Teaching Resources**. Also, see Economics Video Library, "Pay Equity."

Assessment Resources

Chapter Assessment

Teaching Resources Unit 2, Chapter 9

- Section Quizzes, pp. 16, 18, 20

Exam *View*® Test Bank CD-ROM Chapter 9

Economics Assessment Rubrics

Chapter 9 Self-Test, **Web Code:** mna-3091

Reading and Skills Evaluation

Progress Monitoring Assessments

- Screening Test
- Diagnostic Test of Social Studies Skills

Standardized Test Preparation

Test Prep Workbook

Test-Taking Strategies With Transparencies

Differentiated Instruction Key

L1 Special Needs	LPR Less Proficient Readers
L2 Basic to Average	AR Advanced Readers
L3 All Students	SN Special Needs Students
L4 Average to Advanced	GT Gifted and Talented
	ELL English Language Learner

Chapter 9

Labor

Introducing the Chapter

In this chapter students are introduced to the labor market. They will learn about current and future trends in the labor market, the relationship between labor and wages, and organized labor.

For additional links for *Economics: Principles in Action* provided by Prentice Hall and *The Wall Street Journal Classroom Edition,* visit the Social Studies area. Be sure to check out this month's **eTeach** online discussion with a Master Teacher.

Beyond the Lecture

You may cover the concepts in Chapter 9 in an activity-based style by using the following materials:

- **Technology Resources** appropriate for use with this chapter are noted on pp. 212, 213, 215, 217, 221, 224, 226, 231, 233, 234, and 237.
- **Presentation Pro CD-ROM** with animated graphs gives you an alternative method for organizing and delivering chapter content.
- **Activities** designed to meet the needs of students of mixed abilities and learning styles are noted throughout the chapter in the side columns.
- **Learning Styles Lesson Plans** provide alternate lessons for diverse learning styles. See pp. 23–24 of the Learning Styles Lesson Plans folder located in the Teaching Resources.

Economics Journal

Instruct students to write their interview notes in their Economics Journals. Students may include completed journal entries in an Economics Portfolio.

Chapter 9 Labor

Why do some people earn a lot of money while others work hard and earn little? With a little information, and a little theory, you can begin answering this and other puzzling questions. In the process, you will learn how the government measures the unemployment rate, how workers' wages are determined, and how labor unions influence workers' earnings, job security, and benefits in today's economy.

Economics Journal

Interview a parent, grandparent, or other older adult, and ask that person to describe his or her first job. Ask about hours, pay, working conditions, and co-workers. Take detailed notes of the responses to your questions.

Go Online
PHSchool.com

For: Current Data
Visit: PHSchool.com
Web Code: mng-3091

National Council on Economic Education

The following Voluntary National Content Standard in Economics is addressed in this chapter:

★ **Standard 13** Students will understand that: Income for most people is determined by the market value of the productive resources they sell. What workers earn depends, primarily, on the market value of what they produce and how productive they are.

For more information about the standards, contact the National Council on Economic Education

1140 Avenue of the Americas
New York, NY 10036
1-800-338-1192

Section 1 Labor Market Trends

Preview

Objectives

After studying this section you will be able to:

1. **Describe** how trends in the labor force are tracked.
2. **Analyze** past and present occupational trends.
3. **Summarize** how the U.S. labor force is changing.
4. **Identify and explain** trends in the wages and benefits paid to U.S. workers.

Section Focus

The Bureau of Labor Statistics (BLS) tracks trends in the labor market. These trends include the movement toward a service economy, the hiring of more college graduates, women, and temporary employees, an overall decline in real wages, and rising costs for employee benefits.

Key Terms

labor force
learning effect
screening effect
contingent employment

What are the hottest jobs for the new millennium? If you guessed computer-related occupations, you are right. The number of computer engineers and computer support specialists is expected to nearly double between 2000 and 2010 despite an economic slowdown. (See "Fastest-Growing Occupations" in the Economic Atlas and Databank on page 537 for more information on the ten fastest-growing occupations.)

The labor force is transforming before our eyes. Soaring growth in computer-related jobs is just one of the ways in which the job market is changing.

Tracking the Labor Force

How do we know the direction of changes in the job market? Each month, the Bureau of Labor Statistics (BLS) of the United States Department of Labor surveys households to assemble information on the labor force. Economists define the **labor force** as all nonmilitary people who are employed or unemployed.

labor force *all nonmilitary people who are employed or unemployed*

Employment

Economists consider people to be employed if they are 16 years or older and meet at least one of the following requirements:

- they worked at least one hour for pay within the past week;
- they worked 15 or more hours without pay in a family business, such as a farm;
- they held jobs but did not work due to illnesses, vacations, labor disputes, or bad weather.

Unemployment

People who do not meet these criteria are counted as unemployed if they are either temporarily without work or are not working but have looked for jobs within the last 4 weeks. So to be counted as unemployed, a person either must have work lined up for the future, or must be actively searching for a new job.

The labor force is made up of people with jobs and those who are looking for jobs or are waiting to report to work. Some examples of people outside the labor force are full-time students, parents who stay at home to raise children, and retirees. These people are not considered unemployed, and thus are not counted in employment statistics.

▼ **The labor force includes many small business owners.**

Building Key Concepts: Graphing the Main Idea

Supply and Demand To build understanding of how **supply and demand** have brought about changes in the labor market, have students complete a tree map graphic organizer like the one at the right. Remind students that a tree map shows an outline for a main topic, main ideas, and supporting details. Students should put the section title in the top box, main headings in the next row of boxes, and main ideas and supporting details in the boxes below each heading.

Section Reading Support Transparencies A template and the answers for this graphic organizer can be found in Chapter 9, Section 1 of the Section Reading Support Transparency System.

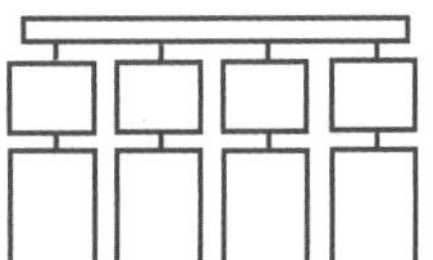

Section 1

Labor Market Trends

Objectives You may wish to call students' attention to the objectives in the Section Preview. The objectives are reflected in the main headings of the section.

Bellringer Ask students to list reasons for the movement of U.S. manufacturing jobs to other countries. Explain that in this section they will learn how the loss of such jobs signals important changes in the U.S. economy and its labor market.

Vocabulary Builder Have students read the section to discover the meaning of the key terms. Ask them to use each term in a sentence that shows its relationship to trends in the labor market.

Lesson Plan

Teaching the Main Concepts (L3)

1. **Focus** The U.S. labor market is taking on new characteristics as the economy moves its emphasis from the manufacture of goods to the provision of services. Ask students to speculate about how these factors change the working environment.
2. **Instruct** Describe the changes that are taking place in the economy, and explain how those changes have affected the labor force. Then discuss the learning effect and the screening effect. Finally, explain how the new economy has affected wages and benefits.
3. **Close/Reteach** As the U.S. economy changed, so did its labor market. Ask students to write a brief essay about how their own personal careers or job choices are likely to differ from the available choices of 30 years ago.

 **Guided Reading and Review**
Unit 3 folder, p. 15 asks students to identify the main ideas of the section and to define or identify key terms.

Differentiated Instruction L4

You may wish to have students add the following to their portfolios. Ask them to write an essay in which they compare and contrast the effects in the United States of the Industrial Revolution of the early nineteenth century and the Electronic/Information Revolution of the late twentieth century. Essays should address technological innovations, the movement of people, how work and the work force changed, and the impact of these factors on the economy. Encourage students to use a data chart to help them organize material during the prewriting stage. GT

Economics Assessment Rubric
Economics Assessment Rubrics folder, pp. 6–7 provides sample evaluation materials for a writing assignment.

Transparency Resource Package
Economics Concepts, 9A: Growth in Selected Occupations

Differentiated Instruction L3

(Reteaching) Ask students to study the labor force tree map on this page and then expand it by adding those characteristics that define *employed* and *unemployed*. Then ask students to create profiles of four members of the labor force—two employed and two unemployed—and explain why each fits his or her category.

FAST FACT

Technological innovations have resulted in new ways to compile and understand economic information. For example, working on the 1880 Census, Herman Hollerith was dismayed by the slowness of the process. So Hollerith designed a mechanical tabulator using punched cards to record information. This developed into a system of punchcard devices with a variety of applications. His Tabulating Machine Co. later became part of International Business Machines (IBM).

"Discouraged workers," people who once sought work but have given up looking for a job, are not counted in employment statistics either.

The Bureau of Labor Statistics

The Bureau of Labor Statistics (BLS) provides answers to two important economic questions: How many people are in the labor force? How many are employed and unemployed at any given time? You can find BLS data in the Census Bureau's *Statistical Abstract of the United States,* available in print or on the Internet.

The BLS provides information about historical trends. For example, the percentage of the U.S. population in the labor force has increased from 59.2 percent in 1950 to 66.6 percent in 2003. In June 2003, the national unemployment rate of 6.4 percent was higher than average by recent standards. The number of employed civilians in the U.S. in 2003 was about 137,738,000.

The BLS also reports the unemployment rate each month. Economists studying the health of the macroeconomy monitor these monthly unemployment figures, which indicate the health of the labor market.

Figure 9.1 Composition of the U.S. Labor Force

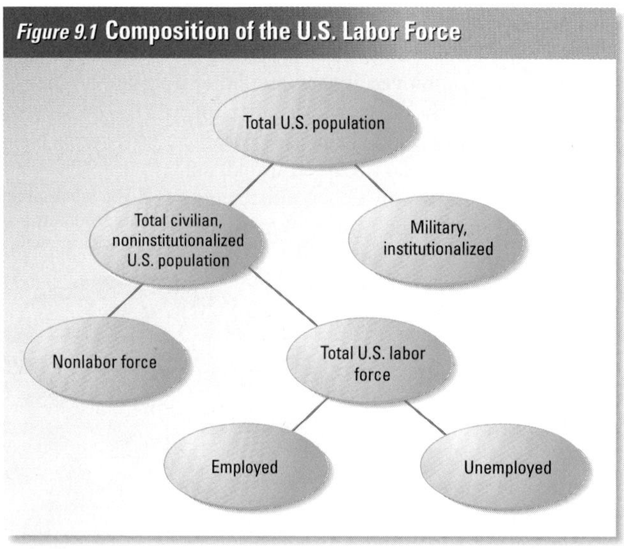

This flowchart shows how the Bureau of Labor Statistics defines who is in the U.S. labor force and who in the labor force is employed and unemployed.
Economic Systems **How does being unemployed differ from not being part of the labor force?**

Occupational Trends

Shifts in the job market reflect major shifts in what our economy produces. To understand these changes, let's look at them in a historical context.

A Changing Economy

At its founding, the United States was a nation of farmers. Most people had few job opportunities beyond the corn, wheat, cotton, and tobacco fields. In the 1800s in the North, however, this agricultural tradition gradually yielded to the Industrial Revolution. The coming of the machine age energized the economy and created new jobs in textile mills, shoe factories, and other new manufacturing enterprises.

By the early decades of the 1900s, heavy manufacturing had become the powerhouse of the U.S. economy. New corporate empires were born, employing thousands of workers: John D. Rockefeller's Standard Oil in 1863; Andrew Carnegie's steelworks in the 1870s; Henry Ford's automobile company in 1903.

The mid-twentieth-century boom in electronics—led by radio and television—produced a new surge of factory jobs. Employment growth centered in the Northeast and Midwest, in companies such as General Electric, Westinghouse, Carrier, and Goodyear.

In the 1970s, the revolution in personal computers opened another new horizon for employment. As computer use continues to rise, computer-related occupations are booming. Many of the new jobs involve the storage, use, and transfer of information. In this "Information Age," even some traditional jobs, from trucking to farming

Answer to . . .

Building Key Concepts To be considered unemployed, an individual must be temporarily out of work or have looked for a job within the last four weeks. An individual who is not part of the labor force is considered neither unemployed nor employed. This category includes full-time students, full-time parents, and retirees.

Econ 101: Key Concepts Made Easy

Income To help students understand the economic justification for **contingent employment,** ask them to conduct research into just-in-time manufacturing, the practice of maintaining just enough inventory for one day's manufacturing output. Just as this practice saves money by keeping a manufacturer's supply highly elastic, hiring contingent employees also saves money because these workers can be hired and discharged as quickly and as often as a company's needs dictate.

to car sales, now require some computer skills. By the late 1900s, over half of American workers reported some use of computers on the job.

Fewer Goods, More Services

The increase in information management jobs is part of an overall shift in the United States from a manufacturing economy to a service economy. Our production of services is increasing faster than our production of goods. Jobs in the service sector include financial services (banking, insurance, investment), online services (Web design, online advertising), health care, and desktop publishing.

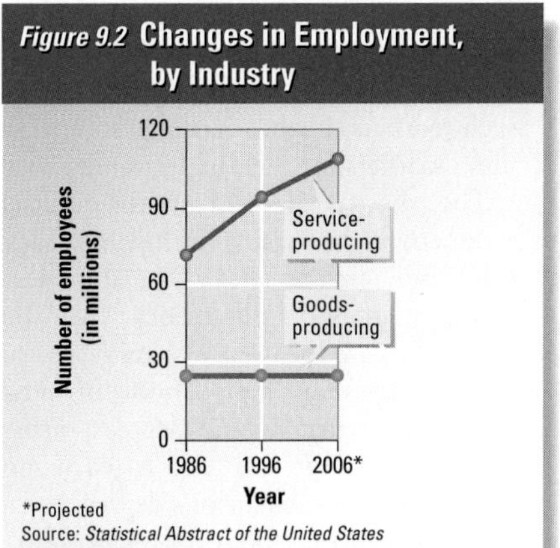

This chart shows the shift from a goods-producing, or manufacturing, economy to a service economy in the United States. **Supply and Demand Describe the changes in the U.S. economy during the period shown.**

Effects of International Competition

As service jobs increase, the United States is losing manufacturing jobs. Many workers have been laid off due to plant closings or moves, too little work, or the elimination of their positions.

In the past, limits on the mobility of capital and labor meant that most goods sold in the United States were made by American workers in American factories. Today, capital and labor are highly mobile. Investment in capital and labor—if not individual workers—crosses international borders easily. American firms can build factories and hire workers in countries where costs are lower. American stores can buy a wide range of goods made in foreign countries to sell in the United States.

As less-skilled manufacturing jobs move overseas, there is less and less demand for the services of unskilled American workers. These employees may receive lower pay or may lose their jobs entirely. This decrease in demand for less-skilled workers pushes these workers to go back to school or to enter job-training programs to gain new skills.

Notice that these shifts in demand for workers are another example of supply and demand in operation. Demand for skilled labor is rising, so wages for skilled workers go up, and the supply of skilled workers increases to meet the demand. Meanwhile, as demand for low-skilled labor drops off, there is a surplus of less-skilled workers who find that they must become more skilled in order to compete in the job market.

The Changing Labor Force

In the 1950s, a typical American worker was a white man who had graduated from high school and had found a secure 40-hour-a-week job where he would hope to stay until retiring at age 65. Not anymore. Today, someone entering the work force can expect to have four or five different jobs during his or her working life and retire at around age 62, or even earlier. The face of the U.S. labor force has changed.

College Graduates

To get jobs, people must have human capital—the education, training, and experience that make them useful in the workplace. More and more, a high-school diploma alone won't prepare a person for financial success. Getting a good education, however, is costly. It requires money, time, and effort. (See "Paying for Education" in

Differentiated Instruction 

(Enrichment) Ask students to suppose that they are reporters who have been given the task of writing a feature article about trends in the manufacturing and service industries in the United States in the last 50 years. Ask them to write an interesting, informative article of one to two pages that provides historical context and summarizes trends.

Differentiated Instruction 

Have students create charts or graphs that summarize trends in the composition of the U.S. labor force in the past fifty years. Charts should focus on college graduates, women, and temporary workers.

Transparency Resource Package Economics Concepts, 9B: Earnings and Education Level

Differentiated Instruction 

Ask students to define the term *trends*. Once they understand this meaning of the word, ask them to describe in their own words one or more trends that have occurred in occupations, the labor force, and wages and benefits in the last 40 years. ELL

Block Scheduling Strategies

Consider these suggestions to take advantage of extended class time:

- Extend the second activity on p. 214 by inviting a female executive to speak to the class about new roles for women in the upper ranks of U.S. businesses. Have students prepare questions.
- To spark an interesting discussion about women in the labor force, show excerpts from one of the following films: *His Girl Friday* (1940, Columbia); *State of the Union* (1948, MGM); *Woman of the Year* (1942, MGM); *Adam's Rib* (1949, MGM). Each features a strong working woman and reveals prevailing attitudes about working women during the 1940s.
- Extend the activity on p. 216 by working with the class to calculate the value of a typical benefits package for an administrative assistant and for a senior executive. Discuss with students how benefits increase the value of employee compensation beyond the wages paid.

Answer to . . .

Building Key Concepts The graph illustrates the number of employees in goods-producing industries remaining constant during the years shown; however, it also indicates the number of employees in the service-producing industries increasing over the period of time indicated on the graph.

Differentiated Instruction 

Organize students into groups of three. Have each group research and prepare an oral report on a prominent female business executive. Encourage each group to select someone who is either running a company or is part of a company's senior management team. Explain to students that they can start by contacting the National Association for Female Executives. Reports should address such issues as the executive's education, career path, current occupation, and management philosophy. Students may even want to write to the subjects of their reports for some specific information or advice.

Differentiated Instruction 

Ask students to call or visit local temporary placement agencies to find out what kinds of jobs temporary workers are hired to do. Have students ask agency personnel to list some reasons why people seek temporary rather than permanent positions. Students should evaluate their findings in a brief essay. GT

learning effect *the theory that education increases productivity and results in higher wages*

screening effect *the theory that the completion of college indicates to employers that a job applicant is intelligent and hard-working*

the Personal Finance Handbook on page 516.) Relatively few people become highly educated; thus, there is a smaller supply of such workers. Higher earnings compensate these workers for their high training costs.

The theory that education increases productivity and results in higher wages is called the **learning effect.** The statistics in Figure 9.3 support this theory. They show that college-educated workers typically earn more than high-school dropouts. People with professional degrees, such as doctors and lawyers, tend to earn more than people with bachelor's degrees.

Another theory about the relationship of education to wages is called the **screening effect**. This theory suggests that the completion of college indicates to employers that a job applicant is intelligent and hard-working. The skills and determination necessary to complete college may also be useful qualities for employees. According to the screening theory, a college degree does not increase productivity, but simply identifies people who may be good employees because of their innate skills.

Women at Work

The changing face of the labor force can be seen right at your local bank. A few decades ago, men greeted customers at the tellers' windows and served as loan officers. Today, most bank tellers and many loan officers are women.

Figure 9.4 shows that in 1960, almost 38 percent of women belonged to the labor force. By 2000, that rate had jumped to over 60 percent.

The increase may be due to several factors. One is that women were encouraged to get a higher education and add to their human capital. By increasing their human capital, they increased their productivity and thus increased their earnings. In addition, as more and more jobs become available in the service sector of the economy, fewer jobs call for physical strength. Instead, jobs require brainpower

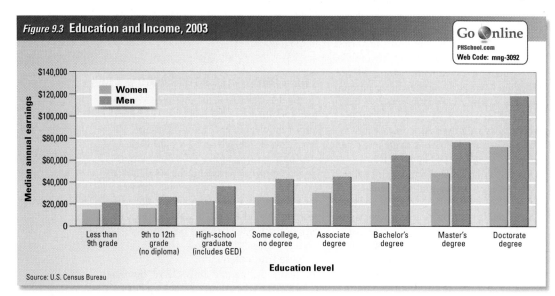

***Figure 9.3* Education and Income, 2003**

Go Online PHSchool.com Web Code: mng-3092

Median annual earnings: $0 – $140,000 (Women, Men)

Education level: Less than 9th grade; 9th to 12th grade (no diploma); High-school graduate (includes GED); Some college, no degree; Associate degree; Bachelor's degree; Master's degree; Doctorate degree

Source: U.S. Census Bureau

As you make your career plans, one factor to consider is the statistic shown here: Education has a big effect on earnings.
Incentives (a) As a man moves up one educational level at a time, when is he likely to see the greatest potential increase in earnings? (b) When is a woman likely to see the greatest potential increase in earnings? (c) What can you conclude about the opportunity costs for men and women of moving up to that higher-paying level?

Preparing for Standardized Tests

Have students read the section titled "Women at Work" and then answer the question below.

Which of the following is not a factor in the rising percentage of women in the labor force?

A higher levels of education
B need for a second income
(C) decreasing levels of human capital
D rise in divorce rates

Answer to . . .

(a) between a master's degree and a doctorate degree (b) between a master's degree and a doctorate (c) There are opportunity costs in terms of both time and money spent on further education, but for many people they are well worth it.

and personal skills, placing men and women on equal footing.

The presence of women in the labor market is expected to continue rising. The BLS projects that the rate of participation of women in the labor force will inch even higher, to more than 61 percent by 2006.

Temporary Workers

In another important trend both in the United States and abroad, more and more businesses are replacing permanent, full-time workers with part-time and temporary workers. Some temporary workers come from "temp" agencies. Others are hired directly by firms as contract workers, people hired for a specified time period or to complete a certain task. These temporary and part-time jobs are known as **contingent employment**.

Contingent employment is becoming more common even in white-collar, professional occupations that have traditionally offered some of the most secure jobs in the economy. For example, some software engineers and attorneys are now hired as contract workers, paid a certain amount of money to complete a certain project, and then released. Such highly skilled workers, when hired directly by employers, are well paid. Some earn as much as permanent workers. On the other hand, workers who get their jobs through temp agencies tend to earn less compared to both permanent employees and directly hired temporary workers.

Why are some companies relying more on temporary employees? Several reasons have been suggested.

1. Flexible work arrangements allow a firm to easily adjust its work force to changing demands for its output. During off-peak seasons or times of reduced demand for their products, companies can easily lay off temporary workers or reduce workers' hours instead of keeping idle employees on the payroll. When business picks up, companies can rehire whatever workers they need.
2. Discharging temporary workers is much easier than discharging regular, permanent employees, since temporary workers do not receive severance pay (money that companies give to employees who are laid off), and temporary workers have fewer legal rights in the workplace.
3. Temporary workers in many industries are paid less and given fewer benefits (if any) than their permanent, full-time counterparts. This advantage has become more important as the cost of medical insurance has risen.
4. Some workers actually prefer these flexible arrangements to traditional, permanent jobs; thus, the market reflects their preferences.

Some people enter and exit the labor force regularly, or prefer the freedom to move from one job to another. However, BLS studies show that a majority of temporary workers would prefer permanent jobs.

Figure 9.4 **Women in the U.S. Labor Force, 1960–2010**

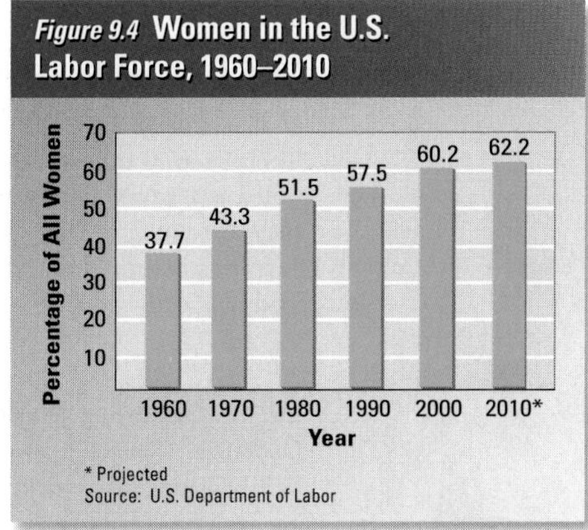

* Projected
Source: U.S. Department of Labor

Participation by women in the labor force has climbed steadily in recent decades.
Income **By what percent will the number of women in the work force have changed between 1960 and 2010?**

contingent employment *a temporary or part-time job*

In the News Read more about the changing labor force in "Temps Can Become Permanent Workers," an article in The Wall Street Journal Classroom Edition.

Go Online
The Wall Street Journal Classroom Edition
For: Current Events
Visit: PHSchool.com
Web Code: mnc-2051

Transparency Resource Package Economics Concepts, 9C: Characteristics of the U.S. Work Force

Economic Detective Activity Unit 3 folder, p. 23, "Ciona Meets the Working World," provides an integrated application of chapter concepts.

Go Online PHSchool.com Typing in the Web Code when prompted will bring students directly to the article.

Differentiated Instruction L1

Choose four pairs of students to prepare and conduct job interviews. Each pair should have an applicant and an employer. Two of these pairs should set up interviews with potential full-time employees. The other two should do interviews with potential temporary hires. Instruct the interviewers to ask appropriate questions regarding the applicants' experience and interests. Instruct the applicants to ask appropriate questions about the job, its benefits, and requirements. SN

Interdisciplinary Connections: Language Arts

Changing Vocabulary Changes in the work force have added new words to the English language. Dissatisfied workers who labored for long hours at the Microsoft "campus" in Redmond, Washington, began calling themselves *microserfs*. Disgruntled members of Generation X who felt locked into generic occupations—where everyone did more or less the same work for very little pay—referred to their positions as *McJobs*. And college grads who had dreamed of corner offices and fat paychecks but instead found themselves sitting in row upon row of square, walled workstations dubbed their environment *cubeland* or *the cube farm*.

Making the Connection Have several students read *Microserfs* (1995) and/or *Generation X: Tales for an Accelerated Culture* (1991), both written by Douglas Coupland.

Answer to . . .
Building Key Concepts 24.5 percent

Differentiated Instruction 

(Enrichment) Ask students to investigate the types of benefits that are offered to employees. Why and how are these benefits significant? Ask them to consider what these benefits cost employers and employees and why some workers receive more benefits than others. Have them find out whether there are any workers who do not get benefits at all. Ask students to share their findings and to relate them to information about the trends in wages and benefits described in the text.

Background

Luring Workers

Perhaps students have heard someone say: "You couldn't *pay* me to take that job." At times the tight labor market of the late 1990s forced employers to do just that—pay people to accept jobs. Called a "signing bonus," this practice was once limited to professional athletics. However, when employers had difficulty hiring skilled workers because the unemployment rate had plunged to a historic low, signing bonuses became an expected benefit—and not just for executives. In the late 1990s these bonuses were sometimes offered to teachers, government employees, and fast-food restaurant managers. When unemployment rose in the early 2000s, signing bonuses became less common.

Math Practice Activity
Math Practice folder, p. 7, "Real Dollar Value of Minimum Wage," gives students an additional application of this skill.

Learning Styles Activity
Learning Styles Lesson Plans folder, p. 23 asks student groups to present a living time line depicting five stages in U.S. labor market trends.

▲ **Employers may offer a wide range of benefits, including medical insurance, life insurance, and retirement savings plans.**

Trends in Wages and Benefits

Labor economists study not only who is in and out of the work force, but how they are doing in terms of earnings and benefits. Today, the picture is mixed.

Earnings Up for Some, Down for Others

While American workers are well paid compared to their counterparts in some other countries, the trend over the last 20 years has been toward slightly lower earnings. The Bureau of Labor Statistics reports that average weekly earnings in the United States increased from $275 in 1980 to $278 in 2003, as measured in inflation-adjusted dollars, or $523 in current dollars.

The slightly higher *average* earnings don't tell the whole story, however. In the past, most employees were paid in wages. Today, added benefits such as health insurance, retirement funds, employee stock options, and year-end bonuses mean that average weekly earnings are much higher than BLS statistics suggest. Many employees today also enjoy the intangible benefits of telecommunicating from their homes and "flex-time," or flexible working hours. Overall, the earnings of college graduates actually increased, while the earnings of workers without college degrees decreased.

Why have average wages not increased more in the last couple of decades? One reason, as you have read, is that greater competition from foreign companies has decreased the demand for low-skilled workers. For example, the last 30 years have brought foreign competition in such industries as steel, textiles, and auto production. Deregulation of many domestic industries, such as trucking, air travel, and telecommunications, may have forced firms to cut employees' wages as competition has intensified.

Cost of Benefits

For many workers, benefits such as pensions and health insurance are a significant share of total compensation. This share rose fairly steadily during the 1900s and early 2000s. Benefits now make up about 28 percent of total compensation in the United States economy today. This adds

▲ **The downsizing trend in the 1990s and 2000s was caused in part by employers wanting to hire temporary workers instead of permanent full-time employees.**

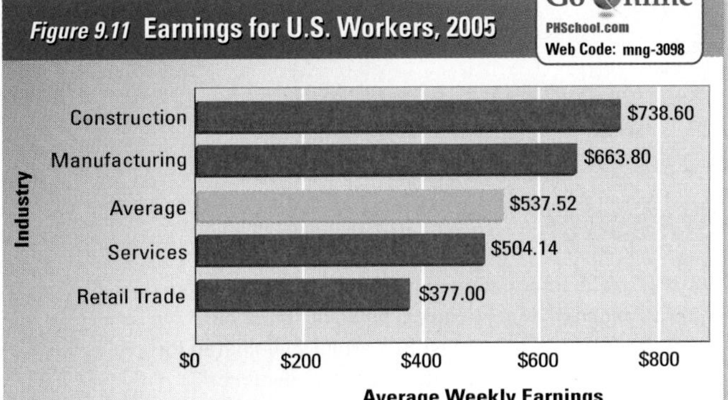

Building Key Concepts This graph shows the differences in average weekly earnings among workers who are paid hourly or weekly wages.

Markets and Prices Why might wages for workers in retail be much lower than those for workers in construction?

up to a large cost for employers—especially since benefits are becoming more expensive.

Company payments into the Social Security system may also be regarded as benefits, since they will be used to pay benefits to retired and disabled workers. Most employees know that Social Security taxes are deducted from their paychecks each month, but may not realize that their employers are also paying a matching amount. Thus, workers and employers share this cost. In addition, Social Security tax rates have risen substantially since the program was created during the 1930s, causing further increases in employers' benefits costs.

Employers are finding that these rising benefits costs increase the cost of doing business and thus cut into their profits. The use of contingent employment is one way some firms are cutting their benefits expenses. Other responses include moving production facilities overseas, where wages are lower and benefits often are nonexistent.

If benefits costs continue to rise, companies will be pressured to respond even further. These responses are likely to be unpopular with workers.

Section 1 Assessment

Progress Monitoring *Online*
For: Self-quiz with vocabulary practice
Web Code: mna-3095

Key Terms and Main Ideas

1. What groups of people does the government consider to be **(a)** in the **labor force; (b)** employed; **(c)** unemployed?
2. What were the major steps in the United States' progression from an agricultural economy to a service economy?
3. How does the **screening effect** differ from the **learning effect?**

Applying Economic Concepts

4. ***Critical Thinking*** Are you part of the labor force? If so, would the government consider you employed during the past week, or unemployed? If not, explain why.
5. ***Problem Solving*** Would you hire permanent workers or contingent workers if you owned **(a)** a pool and garden shop in Minnesota; **(b)** an architectural firm **(c)** a laundromat **(d)** a tax preparation service? Explain your reasoning.
6. ***Decision Making*** You are the manager of a medium-sized publishing company with 90 permanent employees, all of whom receive competitive wages, health insurance, and retirement benefits. The health insurance provider announces a 20 percent increase. Describe at least two possible ways you could respond.

For: Current Events Activity
Visit: PHSchool.com
Web Code: mnd-3091

GTE Guide to the Essentials
Chapter 9, Section 1, p. 38 provides support for students who need additional review of the section content. Spanish support is available in the Spanish edition of the guide on p. 40.

Quiz Unit 3 folder, p. 16 includes questions to check students' understanding of Section 1 content.

Presentation Pro CD-ROM
Quiz provides multiple-choice questions to check students' understanding of Section 1 content.

Answers to . . .

Section 1 Assessment

1. (a) all nonmilitary people who are employed or unemployed; (b) individuals over 16 years of age who have worked at least one hour for pay within the past week, worked 15 or more hours without pay in a family business, or held jobs but did not work due to illnesses, vacations, labor disputes, or bad weather; (c) temporarily without work or are not working but have looked for jobs within the last four weeks.
2. The U. S. progression from an agricultural economy to a service economy began with the shift from agriculture to manufacturing during the Industrial Revolution (1800s), followed by a shift to heavy manufacturing (early 1900s), then the manufacturing of electronics (mid-1900s), and finally to the service economy of the "Information Age."
3. The screening effect is the theory that the completion of college indicates that a job applicant is intelligent and hard-working. The learning effect is the theory that education increases productivity and results in higher wages.
4. Students' answers will vary depending on whether or not they currently hold a job, have held a job, or were never employed. Answers should reflect an understanding of the labor force and the difference between the terms "employed" and "unemployed."
5. (a) contingent workers because the demand for pool and garden supplies is likely to be seasonal in Minnesota (b) permanent workers because architectural projects would be large in scope, and demand would be constant (c) permanent workers because laundromat services are always in demand (d) contingent workers because tax preparation occurs mainly at one time of year
6. Students may suggest passing some or all of the 20 percent increase on to the workers or reducing other benefits to offset the cost increase.

Progress Monitoring *Online*
For additional assessment, have students access Progress Monitoring Online at **Web Code:** mna-3095

Go Online PHSchool.com Typing in the Web Code when prompted will bring students directly to detailed instructions for this activity.

Answer to . . .

Building Key Concepts Students may suggest that construction is harder and more dangerous work.

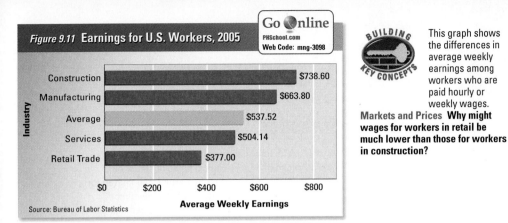

Skills for LIFE

Analyzing Statistics

1. Focus Well-researched and reliable statistics enable economists to analyze past economic performance and predict future economic trends.

2. Instruct Begin by defining *statistics* as the collection and analysis of numerical data. Remind students to analyze the statistical data objectively and critically before drawing inferences and conclusions from it. Note that statistics often can be manipulated to reflect a biased opinion. Have students work through the steps in the skills feature.

3. Close/Reteach To provide additional practice, see the Economic Skills Activity below.

Economic Skills Activity
Unit 3 folder, p. 21, "Analyzing Statistics," asks students to analyze statistics in a college catalog.

Social Studies Skills Tutor CD-ROM offers interactive practice in critical thinking and reading, visual analysis, and communication.

Databank, pp. 534–547 contains a variety of charts and graphs that can be used to extend and reinforce the skills lesson.

Answers

1. (a) Bureau of Labor Statistics (b) The source is the U.S. government and should be considered reliable.
2. (a) Unemployment rates for American workers (by gender and age) in spring 2000 and 2003. (b) Men and women at different age levels and marital statuses.
3. (a) Unemployment increased. (b) no (c) both sexes, ages 16–19 (d) Inexperience and lack of higher education may have made finding jobs difficult. (e) Perhaps that women supporting their families would be actively looking for work, while others might not need or want to work outside their homes.

Additional Practice

Students' answers should reflect the current unemployment statistics and an understanding of how the state of the economy affects unemployment.

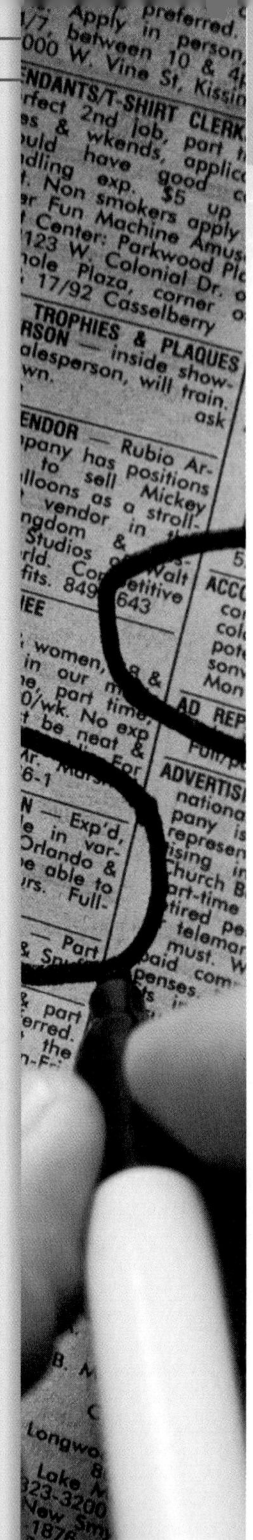

Skills for LIFE

Analyzing Statistics

Statistics provide us with useful information about economic and historical trends. The patterns suggested by statistics, however, must be carefully analyzed, and sources of statistics must be carefully evaluated for reliability. Statistics also need to be verified by other forms of evidence.

During a recent economic boom, unemployment rates dropped as millions of Americans found jobs. Follow the steps below to read and interpret the statistical data found in the table.

1. **Determine the source of the statistics and decide whether the source is reliable.** (a) What is the source of the statistics below? (b) In your opinion, is the source reliable?

2. **Study the statistics to determine what information they provide.** Read the row and column titles carefully, and answer the following questions. (a) What do the data describe? (b) What groups of people are described by the data?

3. **Analyze the data to determine social trends or patterns.** You may be able to use statistical data to draw conclusions about trends or patterns. Answer the following questions: (a) How did the unemployment rate for all workers change between 2000 and 2005? (b) Was the change even across all groups in the work force? (c) Which group suffered from the highest unemployment in 2005? (d) Why do you think this group had the most difficulty finding work? (e) Women who maintain families have a higher rate of unemployment than married women who live with their husbands. Why might this be? (Note: Remember that the unemployment rate only includes people looking for work, not all Americans.)

Additional Practice

Use the Internet to find the most recent government statistics on unemployment, and compare them to the data shown here. What changes do you find? What do these changes indicate about the economy?

Unemployment Rates for U.S. Workers

	Spring 2000	Spring 2005
All workers	4.0%	5.2%
Men, age 20 and up	3.3%	4.4%
Woman, age 20 and up	3.6%	4.6%
Both sexes, 16 to 19 years	12.8%	17.7%
Married women, spouse present	2.7%	3.3%
Woman who maintain families	6.2%	7.7%
Source: Bureau of Labor Statistics		

Interdisciplinary Connections: Math

The World of Statistics Statistics is actually a branch of mathematics with its own mathematical formulas. Nevertheless, statisticians have much in common with scientists and economists. Statistical methods are much like the scientific method. It should be noted that the words used to define an issue are critical to the integrity of the data collected. For instance, if medical researchers want to know the incidence of a certain infection in urban children, they must first define exactly what they mean by *urban children*. Age ranges and a definition of *urban* would make the statistics meaningful.

Have students work through the following activity: Organize students into groups of four. Assign each group a graph from the Databank or from an almanac. Then have groups explain to the class what data are analyzed in their graphs and what characteristics are used to define each group for which data have been provided.

Section 2 Labor and Wages

Objectives

After studying this section you will be able to:

1. **Analyze** the relationship between supply and demand in the labor market.
2. **Understand** the connection between wages and skill levels.
3. **Explain** how laws against wage discrimination affect wage levels.
4. **Describe** other factors affecting wages, such as minimum wage and workplace safety laws.

Section Focus

In a competitive labor market, laws of supply and demand are the main factors responsible for determining wages. Wages are also affected by skill levels and legislation prohibiting wage discrimination. Other factors, such as minimum wage laws, workplace safety laws, and labor unions also affect wages.

derived demand
productivity
equilibrium wage
unskilled labor
semi-skilled labor
skilled labor
professional labor
glass ceiling
labor union
featherbedding

If you are considering what career to pursue, you've probably thought about how much money you can earn in various professions. Most surgeons, for example, earn a lot of money. Social workers generally do not. Why? What determines the size of our paychecks?

It's a matter of supply and demand. Like eggs or airplanes or pet iguanas, labor is a commodity that is bought and sold. Wages are high in professions where supply is low and demand is high. Doctors, for example, are in relatively short supply but in high demand. Relatively large numbers of people become social workers compared to the number of social work jobs available. Hardly anyone needs a widget maker, so widget makers earn very little if anything at all. Thus workers' earnings—the price of labor—depend on conditions in the labor market.

Supply and Demand for Labor

Employment or unemployment in a labor market depends on how closely the demand for workers—the number of available jobs—meets the supply of workers seeking jobs. Let's examine how supply and demand operate in labor markets.

Labor Demand

The demand for labor comes from private firms and government agencies that hire workers to produce goods and services. In most labor markets dozens, or sometimes hundreds, of firms compete with one another to hire workers.

Demand for labor is a **derived demand** because it is derived, or set, by the demand for what a worker produces. For example, the demand for cooks in a market depends on the demand for restaurant meals.

derived demand *demand that is determined by demand for another good or service*

In a competitive labor market, workers are usually paid according to the value of what they produce. For example, competition among restaurants results in a wage for cooks that reflects the cook's productivity. **Productivity** is the value of output, which in this example is the cost of a meal. Suppose that most of the restaurants in your city pay $12 an hour for cooks who generate $20 an hour in revenue for the restaurants. The possibility of profit will attract other restaurant entrepreneurs. Competition will push up the wage for cooks to nearly $20. As a result, cooks will be paid close to the value of their productivity. The flow-

productivity *value of output*

FAST FACT

The top three employers in the United States are Wal-Mart, General Motors, and McDonald's, respectively. Wal-Mart employs about four times as many workers (1.2 million) as General Motors (324,000), its closest competitor in the labor market.

Graphing the Main Idea

Income To build understanding of the concept of **income** and the labor force, have students complete two web graphic organizers like the one at the right. Remind students that a web shows a main idea with its supporting details. In the center of one organizer, they should place the label "Labor Force," and in the center of the other, "How Wages Are Determined." Then have them fill in supporting details for each main idea.

Section Reading Support Transparencies A template and the answers for this graphic organizer can be found in Chapter 9, Section 2 of the Section Reading Support Transparency System.

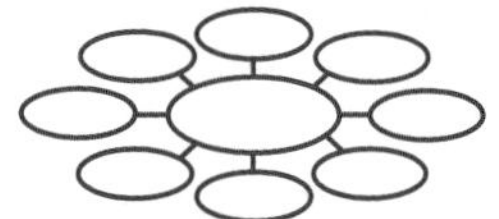

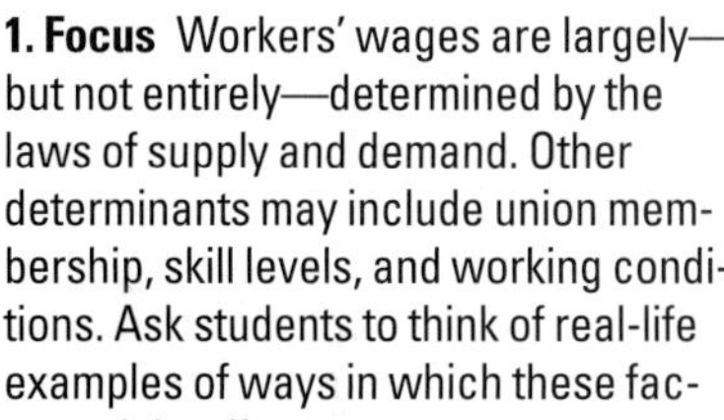

Section 2 Labor and Wages

Objectives You may wish to call students' attention to the objectives in the Section Preview. The objectives are reflected in the main headings of the section.

Bellringer Ask students whether they think it is fair or unfair that there is such a disparity in the wages and salaries individuals receive for the various kinds of work they do. Explain that in this section they will learn the causes and justification for this disparity.

Vocabulary Builder Have students read the section to learn the meaning of each key term. Ask students to write the definition of each term in their Economics Journals and provide an example for each term.

Lesson Plan

Teaching the Main Concepts (L3)

1. Focus Workers' wages are largely—but not entirely—determined by the laws of supply and demand. Other determinants may include union membership, skill levels, and working conditions. Ask students to think of real-life examples of ways in which these factors might affect wages.

2. Instruct Begin by discussing how the forces of supply and demand affect wages. Tell students that factors other than supply and demand also affect wages; then discuss skill levels, working conditions, and the various forms of wage discrimination. Finally, explain the ways in which unions can determine wage scales.

3. Close/Reteach Remind students that the most important determinants of wages are the laws of supply and demand. Ask them to use an almanac to graph data illustrating other factors that can affect wages.

Guided Reading and Review
Unit 3 folder, p. 17 asks students to identify the main ideas of the section and to define or identify key terms.

Meeting NCEE Standards

Use the following benchmark activity from the **Voluntary National Content Standards in Economics** to evaluate student understanding of **Standard 13.**

Explain the impact of an increase in the minimum wage on their ability to secure an after-school job; also explain the impact of the increase on their willingness to work.

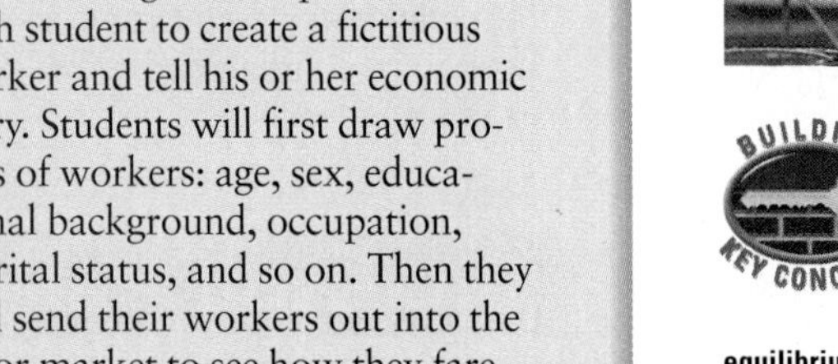

Differentiated Instruction L4

You may wish to have students add the following to their portfolios. Ask each student to create a fictitious worker and tell his or her economic story. Students will first draw profiles of workers: age, sex, educational background, occupation, marital status, and so on. Then they will send their workers out into the labor market to see how they fare. Explain to students that their characters should encounter economic situations such as the following: demand (or lack of demand) for their skills, the effect this has on their wages, response of employers to wages that they feel are too high, and response of workers to wages that are too low. Encourage students to have fun with their narratives as they explore the economic realities of supply and demand in the work force. GT

Figure 9.6 Effects of Competition

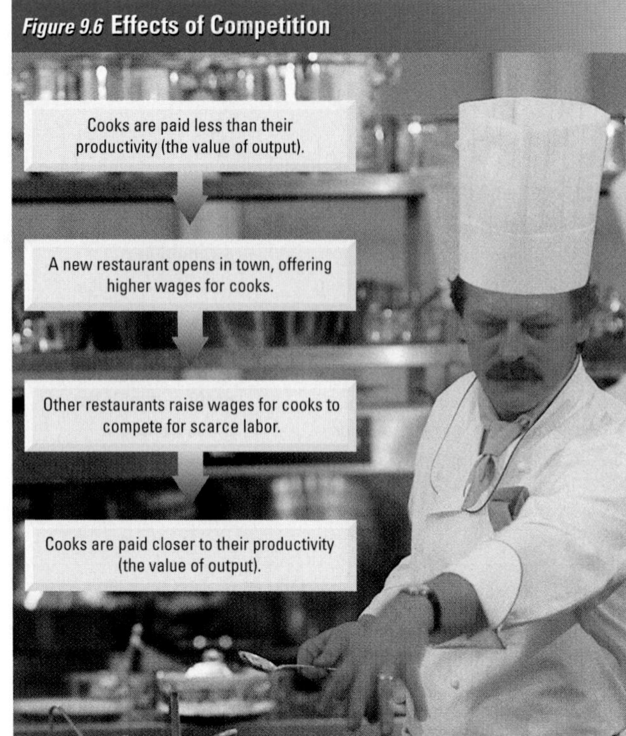
Cooks are paid less than their productivity (the value of output).
A new restaurant opens in town, offering higher wages for cooks.
Other restaurants raise wages for cooks to compete for scarce labor.
Cooks are paid closer to their productivity (the value of output).

BUILDING KEY CONCEPTS

This flowchart shows how competition causes workers to be paid a wage close to their productivity.
Markets and Prices Explain how the outcome of this scenario affects (a) the cooks, (b) the restaurants.

equilibrium wage *the wage rate that produces neither an excess supply of workers nor an excess demand for workers in the labor market*

chart in Figure 9.6 (above) shows the ripple effect that occurs when the new restaurant hires cooks at a higher wage.

Now look at the demand curve for labor, shown in the right-hand graph of Figure 9.7 on page 221. Notice that it is negatively sloped, reflecting the law of demand. The higher the price of labor, the smaller the quantity of labor demanded by firms and government.

Labor Supply

The supply of labor comes from people who provide labor in exchange for wages. As the left-hand graph in Figure 9.7 shows, the supply curve is positively sloped, reflecting the law of supply. In other words, the higher the wage, the larger the quantity of labor supplied.

This is sensible because the higher the wage for a job, the greater the number of people attracted to the job. A higher wage for cooks encourages people who would choose other occupations to acquire the training—that is, the human capital—required to become a cook. For example, if the wage for chefs were high enough, some servers and other staff would be willing to invest the time and money required to complete cooking school.

Equilibrium Wage

We know that at the market equilibrium, the quantity of a good supplied will equal the quantity demanded. Because the equilibrium price makes the quantity that suppliers want to sell equal to the quantity that demanders want to buy, there is no tendency for the price or quantity to change. Economic factors—the supply of labor and the demand for it—combine to determine an equilibrium price. These factors may be different in different parts of the country, or at different times.

The **equilibrium wage** is the wage rate that produces neither an excess supply of workers nor an excess demand for workers in the labor market. On a graph, the equilibrium wage is shown by the intersection of the supply and demand curves. (See Figure 9.8.) At equilibrium, there is no pressure to raise or lower the price.

How do these theories affect how much you should expect to earn working in a pet store or a grocery store next summer? It depends on the supply and demand conditions in your area. If your local pet stores and grocery stores won't hire many additional workers during the summer and a lot of teenagers will be looking for work, the wage will be relatively low. On the other hand, if stores want to hire a lot of teenagers and not many teens want to work, the wage will be higher.

Wages and Skill Levels

Why do lawyers earn more money than carpenters, and carpenters more than cashiers? Wages vary according to workers'

Econ 101: Key Concepts Made Easy

Economic Institutions To help students understand how the **glass ceiling** got its name, ask them to imagine just such a ceiling and its effects. A glass ceiling would be barely visible, but it would act as a barrier nonetheless. Lead students to understand that those below the ceiling can see and appreciate everything happening on the floor above; at the same time, however, they have no access to that level or the activities that take place there, no matter how well qualified they might be. Discuss with students some of the reasons for the existence of the glass ceiling and how it might be circumvented.

Answer to...

Building Key Concepts (a) Although cooks get paid more, they are in less demand. (b) Restaurants are forced to raise prices and lose business.

Figure 9.7 Labor Supply and Demand

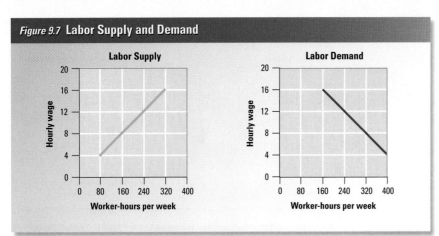

Labor Supply

Hourly wage: 0, 4, 8, 12, 16, 20

Worker-hours per week: 0, 80, 160, 240, 320, 400

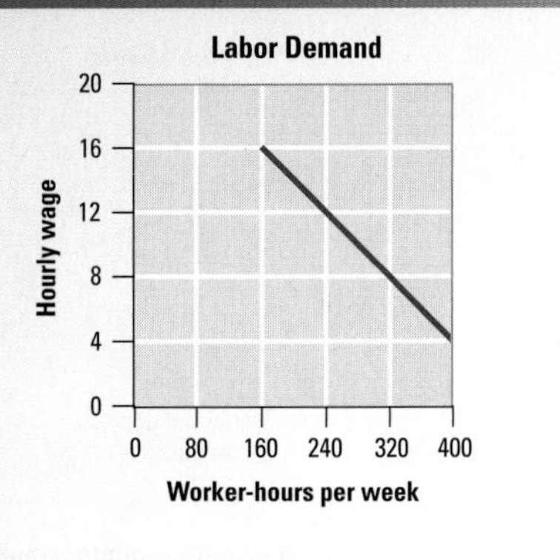

The graph on the right shows how the quantity of labor demanded varies depending on the price of labor. The graph on the left shows how the labor supply varies depending on the wage rate. **Supply and Demand (a) According to the demand curve, if each cook works a 40-hour week, how many cooks will be hired at $12 an hour and at $20 an hour? (b) Why is the supply curve positively sloped?**

skill levels and education, as well as according to supply and demand. Jobs are often categorized into four skill levels:

1. **Unskilled labor** requires no specialized skills, education, or training. Workers in these jobs usually earn an hourly wage. They include dishwashers, messengers, janitors, and many factory and farm workers.
2. **Semi-skilled labor** requires minimal specialized skills and education, such as operation of certain types of equipment. Semi-skilled workers usually earn an hourly wage. They include lifeguards, word processors, short-order cooks, and some construction workers.
3. **Skilled labor** requires specialized abilities and training to do tasks such as operating complicated equipment. Skilled workers need little supervision, yet usually earn an hourly wage rather than a salary. They include auto mechanics, bank tellers, plumbers, firefighters, chefs, and carpenters.
4. **Professional labor** demands advanced skills and education. Professionals are usually white-collar workers who receive a salary. Professionals include managers, teachers, bankers, doctors, actors, professional athletes, and computer programmers.

We can graph the difference in pay scales for workers with various skills. The left-hand graph in Figure 9.9 shows the labor

Figure 9.8 Equilibrium Wage

Hourly wage: 0, 4, 8, 12, 16, 20

Demand curve

Equilibrium

Equilibrium wage

Supply curve

Worker-hours per week: 0, 80, 160, 240, 320, 400

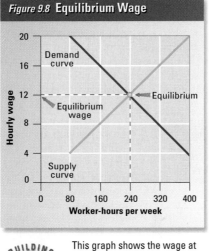

This graph shows the wage at which the quantity demanded equals the quantity supplied. **Supply and Demand Explain why a stable wage means stable restaurant prices.**

unskilled labor *labor that requires no specialized skills, education, or training*

semi-skilled labor *labor that requires minimal specialized skills and education*

skilled labor *labor that requires specialized skills and training*

professional labor *labor that requires advanced skills and education*

Economics Assessment Rubric
Economics Assessment Rubrics folder, pp. 6–7 provides sample evaluation materials for a writing assignment.

Transparency Resource Package
Economics Concepts, 9D: Job Migration by State

Preparing for Standardized Tests

Have students read the section titled "Labor Supply" and then answer the question below.

What is the wage rate called at which there is neither excess supply of or demand for workers?

A occupation wage
B demand wage
C union wage
(D) equilibrium wage

Answer to . . .

Building Key Concepts (a) 6; none (b) At higher wages more workers will be available to do the job.
Building Key Concepts A stable wage keeps labor costs fixed, which means that, if other costs remain stable, restaurant owners will have no reason to raise prices.

Meeting NCEE Standards

Use the following benchmark activity from the **Voluntary National Content Standards in Economics** to evaluate student understanding of **Standard 13.**

Review income data for jobs in manufacturing and service industries over the last 25 years. Explain how changes in the structure of the economy, gross domestic product, technology, government, prices, and discrimination have influenced income for jobs in these two areas.

Go Online PHSchool.com Typing in the Web Code when prompted will bring students directly to the article.

THE WALL STREET JOURNAL. CLASSROOM EDITION

For an additional article from *The Wall Street Journal Classroom Edition,* see the Source Articles folder in the **Teaching Resources,** pp. 27–29.

Figure 9.9 Comparison: Wages for Doctors, Construction Workers

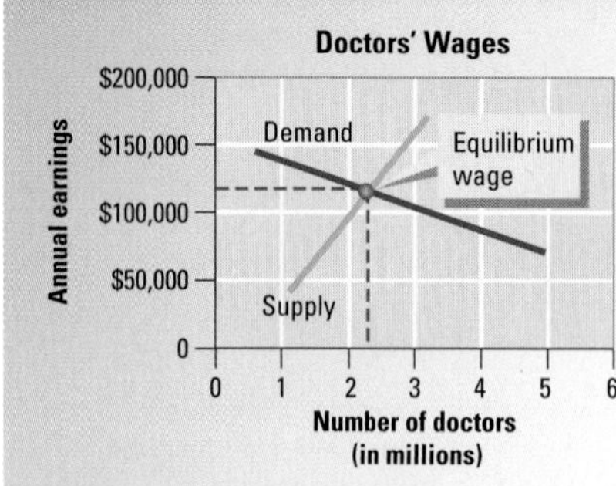

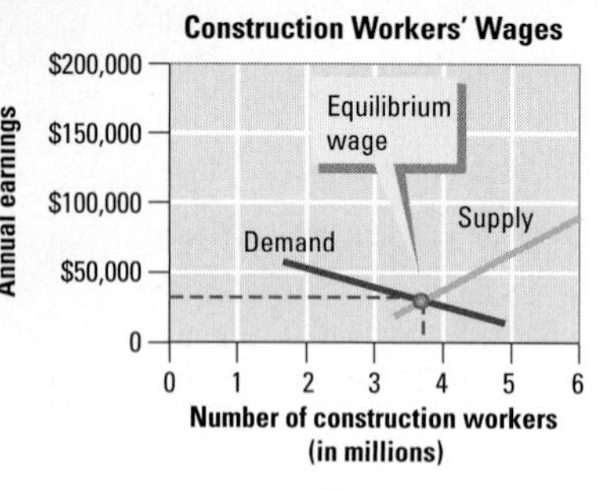

Anyone who pays doctors' bills already knows what the graph on the left shows: Wages for doctors are high. By comparison, construction workers' wages are lower, as shown in the graph on the right. **Supply and Demand Give reasons to explain why the supply of doctors is low and the supply of construction workers is high.**

market for medical doctors. Note that the supply of doctors is relatively low and the demand is relatively high. This produces a high equilibrium wage.

By comparison, the right-hand graph in Figure 9.9 shows that the supply of construction workers is high relative to the demand for them. Hence, the equilibrium wage for construction workers is lower than that for doctors.

Doctors and other highly educated workers, as well as those with much training and experience, enjoy demand for their services that is high relative to the supply, leading to higher earnings. The demand for workers with less education and training tends to be lower relative to the supply, so their earnings are lower.

Another reason that earnings vary is differences in working conditions. Many factors affect the number of workers who are willing to do a certain job: the level of danger, the physical or emotional stress involved, the location, and weather conditions in the area.

Economic studies have shown that jobs with high accident and fatality rates pay relatively high wages. Workers who do dangerous jobs require compensation for the risks they take. Thus, there is a higher equilibrium wage rate for dangerous jobs, as shown in Figure 9.10.

THE WALL STREET JOURNAL. CLASSROOM EDITION

In the News Read more about labor and wages in "Worse for the Wear," an article in The Wall Street Journal Classroom Edition.

Go Online
The Wall Street Journal Classroom Edition
For: Current Events
Visit: PHSchool.com
Web Code: mnc-3092

Wage Discrimination

By seeing labor as something that is bought and sold, we have seen that wages for a particular job should end up at the equilibrium price of labor for that job, depending on the supply and demand for workers in that field. In some situations, however, national or state legislators have decided that there are policy reasons for interfering with the "invisible hand" that sets the wage level. One example is legislation prohibiting wage discrimination.

Wage discrimination occurs when people with the same job, same skills and education, same job performance, and same seniority receive unequal pay. Some companies, for example, have paid lower wages to women and minority employees.

Some employers defended wage discrimination against women by claiming that men needed the money to support families, while women were simply working to earn some extra cash. Job discrimination was also based on the assumption that women

Block Scheduling Strategies

Consider these suggestions to take advantage of extended class time:

- Locate and play a recording of the song "Sixteen Tons." Ask students what it is about. If no one can answer, explain that it deals with the futility of working in a company town. Have students research what a company town is and how it affects workers. Then ask students to write several paragraphs in which they summarize what they have learned and express an opinion about it.
- Show the Economics Video Library segment "Pay Equity," about fighting wage discrimination. After viewing the segment, have students discuss the idea of pay scales as a method of correcting wage discrimination. Ask them to research a pay scale system (for example, for federal employees or the military) and report on how it affects wage discrimination.

Answer to . . .

Building Key Concepts Students may point out that the training and time required to become a doctor keeps the supply low and that much less training is required to work in construction.

would leave their jobs at some point to have children. Discrimination against African Americans and other minority workers reflected racial and ethnic prejudice in society.

Laws Against Wage Discrimination

In the 1960s, the United States Congress passed several anti-discrimination laws that prevent companies from paying lower wages to some employees based on factors like gender or race that are not related to skill or productivity. The Equal Pay Act of 1963 required that male and female employees in the same workplace performing the same job receive the same pay. Title VII of the Civil Rights Act of 1964 prohibited job discrimination on the basis of race, sex, color, religion, or nationality. (Religious institutions and small businesses are exempt from the law.) The Civil Rights Act also created the Equal Employment Opportunity Commission (EEOC) to enforce the law's provisions. The EEOC handles complaints of job discrimination. If necessary, it takes companies to court to force them to comply with the law.

Pay Levels for Women

Despite these protections, the earnings gap that many people see between the wages of men and women is only gradually being closed. Historically, this gap has been the result of social conditions for women.

1. *"Women's work."* Women have historically been denied entrance to certain high-paying occupations, such as doctors, lawyers, and corporate managers. Instead, they have been encouraged to pursue careers in lower-paying fields such as teaching, nursing, and clerical work. With so many women seeking work in these occupations, the labor supply has been generally high. A large supply of labor tends to produce a relatively low equilibrium wage.
2. *Human capital.* Overall, women have had less education, training, and experience in certain occupations than men. This lack of human capital makes women's labor, in economic terms, less productive. As a result, fewer women are eligible for the higher-paying, traditionally male-dominated jobs in fields such as engineering.
3. *Women's career paths.* Even today, some employers assume that female employees are not interested in career advancement. This perception can be a roadblock for women in the workplace. The difficulty many women face in trying to balance child rearing and a career adds to this perception.

Figure 9.10 **Comparison: Wages for High-Risk, Low-Risk Jobs**

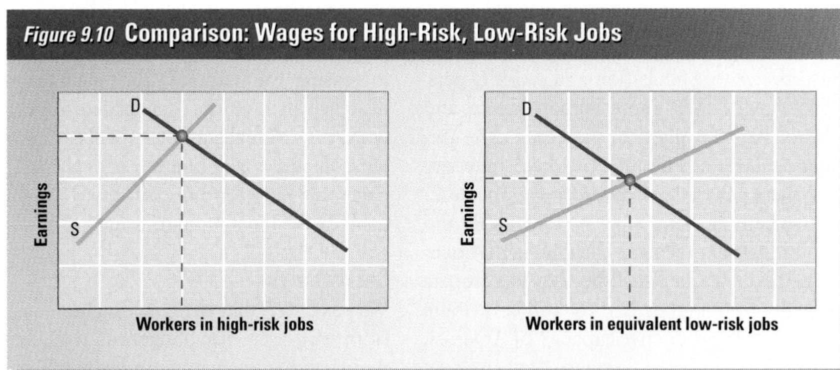

These graphs show how wages compare for similar jobs with different degrees of risk. **Supply and Demand Write one sentence that compares the demand curves on the two graphs and one sentence that compares the two supply curves.**

Background

Stress Sometimes Pays

Job stress usually means a big paycheck, but not always. The following are the ten most stressful jobs, according to the *National Business Employment Weekly Jobs Rated Almanac:* U.S. President, firefighter, senior corporate executive, Indy-class race car driver, taxi driver, surgeon, astronaut, police officer, football player, and air-traffic controller. Except for firefighters, police officers, and taxi drivers, stress seems to pay.

What does this source consider the ten *least* stressful jobs? Here they are: medical records technician, janitor, forklift operator, musical instrument repairer, florist, actuary, appliance repairer, medical secretary, librarian, and bookkeeper. In keeping with their lower levels of stress, these jobs do not carry salaries in the highest ranges.

Differentiated Instruction L3

Have students check one or more almanacs to find out the ten highest-paying and the ten lowest–paying full-time occupations in the United States. Ask students to show the information on a bar graph and then to speculate about the relationships between jobs and salaries.

Preparing for Standardized Tests

Have students read the section titled "Pay Levels for Women" and then answer the question below.

Which of the following describes one reason women's wages are lower than men's?

A Women have been forced to accept menial jobs.

(B) Women have kept the occupations that are considered "women's work" well supplied.

C Women were not included in the Equal Pay Act of 1963.

D Unlike men, women do not have to support families.

Answer to . . .

Building Key Concepts The shapes of the demand curves are similar, but supply and demand meet at a higher point on the curve for high-risk jobs. The supply curve for high-risk jobs is much steeper than the curve for low-risk jobs.

Differentiated Instruction L2

Ask students to list each of the main heads in the section. Then, under each head, students should write a few sentences that summarize the content of that section. LPR

Transparency Resource Package
Economics Concepts, 9E: Median Weekly Earnings, by Occupation and Sex

Despite much progress made toward eliminating wage discrimination, significant wage differences exist between men and women and among workers of various ethnic groups. **Markets and Prices** **According to the graph, which group has the lowest earnings?**

Go Online
PHSchool.com
Web Code: mng-3093

Figure 9.11 **Median Income for Full-time Workers, by Gender and Ethnicity, 2003**

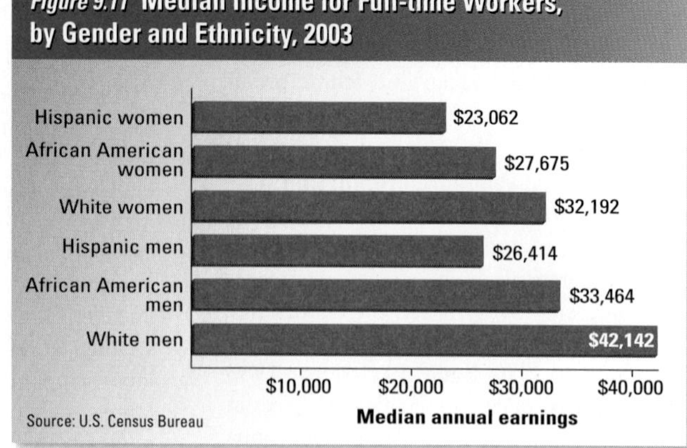

Source: U.S. Census Bureau

glass ceiling *an unofficial, invisible barrier that prevents women and minorities from advancing in businesses dominated by white men*

Much progress has been made in creating job opportunities for women. Yet some qualified women still find that they cannot advance beyond a certain level in the companies they work for. In some companies, men dominate the high managerial positions, and women find it difficult to receive top-level promotions. This unofficial, invisible barrier that sometimes prevents some women and minorities from advancing to the top ranks of business is called a **glass ceiling.**

Pay Levels for Minorities

Minorities tend to earn lower pay than whites do. Income differences between minority workers and white workers are caused partly by productivity differences. On average, whites historically have had access to more education and work experience, giving them more human capital and hence higher wages. In part, non-discrimination laws are designed to help minority workers get more access to job opportunities where they can improve their skills and build their experience. The goal is that over time these workers will be able to compete equally in the labor market and contribute more to the productive capacity of America.

Other Factors Affecting Wages

In addition to laws forbidding discrimination, several other factors can affect wages. These include minimum wage laws, workplace safety laws, employer decisions, and labor unions.

Minimum Wage Laws

In 1938, Congress passed the Fair Labor Standards Act. This law created a minimum wage—the lowest amount employers could lawfully pay for most types of work—and required employers to pay overtime for work beyond 40 hours a week. Many states also have their own minimum wage laws. Because of these laws, employers may be forced to pay more than the equilibrium wage for unskilled labor.

Supporters of the minimum wage argue that it helps the poorest American workers earn enough to support themselves. Opponents point out that artificially increasing the price of labor will cause a decrease in quantity demanded. In other words, individual employees will earn more, but companies will hire fewer of them. (See pages 238–239 for more information on the debate over the minimum wage.)

Safety Laws

We have seen that there is a higher equilibrium wage rate for dangerous jobs. Laws requiring certain minimum levels of workplace safety may also have an effect on wages. If a law or policy increases safety at work, it may also decrease wages because workers are willing to work for lower

Interdisciplinary Connections: Literature

Literary Labor Portrait An extraordinary portrait of the American labor force can be found in Studs Terkel's oral history, *Working: People Talk About What They Do All Day and How They Feel About What They Do.* Terkel interviewed workers, asking them to discuss all aspects of their jobs—what they did, what they enjoyed about their work, what frustrated them, and how they view the condition of the labor force. Terkel's carefully edited conversations reveal insights into working men and women that no mere statistics can provide.

Making the Connection Have students interview several generations of family members, neighbors, or friends who are or have been a part of the American labor force, using the same questions for each interview. Ask students to prepare a written history of how responses to these questions vary with each generation.

Answer to . . .

Building Key Concepts Hispanic women

wages when jobs are safer. It thus would lower the employer's costs. Of course, the employer will usually have to spend money to comply with safety regulations, which may more than offset the employer's savings from any wage reduction.

Employers Respond to Wage Levels

Employers may also take actions to try to affect wage levels. For example, a company might try to cut labor costs by substituting machines for people. In other words, employers can replace human capital with physical capital.

Take furniture, for example. In countries where labor is relatively cheap, furniture may be hand-made by workers. In the United States, where labor is relatively expensive, manufacturers have substituted sophisticated machinery for more expensive human labor. Other examples of substituting physical for human capital include automated teller machines (ATMs) and mechanized assembly lines (such as in automobile manufacturing plants). These technological advances have greatly reduced the number of employees that banks and manufacturing companies hire.

Even if firms cannot use technology to replace labor, they may be able to reduce their labor costs in other ways. Companies may build production plants in other parts of the world where labor is more plentiful, and therefore cheaper. Check the labels on your jeans and shirts to see where they come from!

Similarly, employees who are unhappy with their wages have several choices. In a competitive labor market, they might get higher-paying jobs elsewhere. Other people may change careers entirely, either by choice or out of necessity. Although labor unions are becoming less of a force in the American economy, workers might decide to join a union and press for higher pay.

Unions

An organization of workers that tries to improve working conditions, wages, and benefits for its members is called a **labor union.** Although labor unions today have fewer members than in the past, they are another force that may affect the level of wages for certain jobs. One of the key goals of unions is to get wage increases for their members. As you will see in Section 3, unions allow workers to negotiate wage levels as a group rather than having to deal individually with employers.

Nationally, union members do tend to earn higher wages than nonunion workers in similar jobs. In 2003, the average weekly union wage was $792, compared with $600 a week for nonunion wage earners.

Some evidence suggests that unions depress the wages of nonunion workers. Consider this reasoning:

1. Unions press employers to raise their members' wages.
2. When wages go up, the quantity of labor demanded goes down. Thus, the number of union jobs decreases.
3. As union jobs are cut, more workers are forced to seek nonunion jobs.
4. An increase in the supply of available nonunion workers causes the wage rate for nonunion jobs to fall.

In addition, some unions have engaged in **featherbedding,** negotiating labor contracts that keep unnecessary workers on the company payroll. A notable example of featherbedding occurred in the railroad industry.

In the early days of railroads, a "cabooseman" had to ride at the back of the train to operate a rear brake that stopped the train. Yet even after design

labor union *an organization of workers that tries to improve working conditions, wages, and benefits for its members*

featherbedding *the practice of negotiating labor contracts that keep unnecessary workers on a company's payroll*

Global Connections

Wages Worldwide An average production worker in the United States makes $31,300 a year, according to the U.S. Census Bureau. If you were a worker in a country other than the United States, what would you earn? An average production worker in Germany makes the equivalent of $35,863 a year, while the average worker in Hungary makes $9,916 a year. Wages in Western Europe range from $40,995 in Belgium to $28,198 in France. A worker in Japan makes $27,664, in Turkey $15,825, and in Mexico, just $8,662. These figures are adjusted according to the relative purchasing power in the various countries.

Differentiated Instruction L3

(Reteaching) Ask students to create a chart that illustrates the effects working conditions, discrimination, and unions have on wages. The chart should have two columns, one headed "Wages Go Up" and the other "Wages Go Down." In each column students should include examples to show how the three forces can cause wages to rise or fall.

Differentiated Instruction L2

Have students study the graphs and captions in this section. Then have them use that information to write sentences that explain the main ideas of the section. ELL

Interdisciplinary Connections: Science

Scientific Options If students are looking for incentives to apply themselves in science classes, they might be interested to know that some of the highest-paid people in the United States have degrees in some branch of science. These occupations, all of which averaged $900 or more per week, included engineers, mathematicians and computer scientists, physicians, and pharmacists.

Making the Connection Ask students to write a brief paragraph speculating about why science is such a lucrative career. Make sure that they look into the requirements for degrees in scientific fields.

GTE **Guide to the Essentials**
Chapter 9, Section 2, p. 39 provides support for students who need additional review of the section content. Spanish support is available in the Spanish edition of the guide on p. 39.

Quiz Unit 3 folder, p. 18 includes questions to check students' understanding of Section 2 content.

Presentation Pro CD-ROM Quiz provides multiple-choice questions to check students' understanding of Section 2 content.

Answers to . . .

Section 2 Assessment

1. When demand for labor is high and there is lack of labor supplied to meet this demand, wages and employment opportunities for workers increase; when demand for labor is low and the supply of labor is high, wages and employment opportunities decrease.
2. (a) The equilibrium wage decreases. (b) The equilibrium wage increases.
3. Skilled labor is labor requiring specialized abilities and training, and little supervision. Skilled laborers earn an hourly wage and are generally blue-collar workers (auto mechanics, bank tellers, carpenters). Professional labor demands advanced skills and education. Professionals earn salaries and are white-collar workers (doctors, computer programmers, managers).
4. Minimum wage laws help poor workers earn enough to support themselves; however, by increasing the price of labor, a minimum wage potentially removes employment opportunities from those that need it most. Laws increasing safety at the work place may decrease wages because workers are willing to work for lower wages when jobs are safer.
5. Students' answers will vary, but should include an understanding of the effects of supply and demand on labor as well as the effects of education, training, and skill levels.
6. (a) Medical assistants, network systems and data communications analysts, and physician assistants. (b) No, they are in traditionally nonunion occupations.

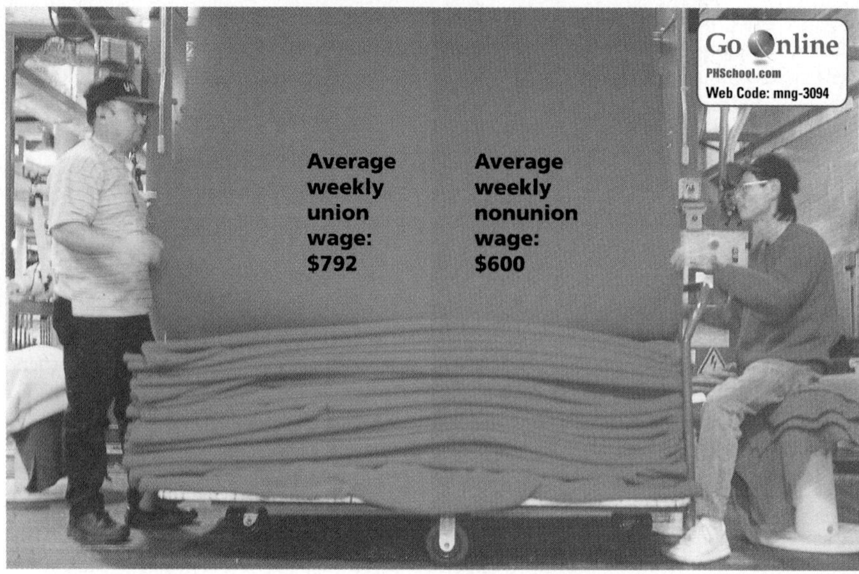

▲ **In 2003, union workers earned higher wages than nonunion workers.**

changes allowed the engineer at the front of the train to operate rear brakes, unions managed to keep caboosemen on the payroll, receiving full wages and benefits for doing nothing.

Unions have been criticized not only for featherbedding, but also because the above-market union wages they negotiate can curtail capital formation. In addition, higher prices for union-made goods can cut sales and consumer purchasing power. The next section will trace the history of unions in the United States and further describe their advantages and disadvantages.

Section 2 Assessment

Progress Monitoring *Online*
For: Self-quiz with vocabulary practice
Web Code: mna-3096

Key Terms and Main Ideas

1. How do the laws of supply and demand affect the labor market?
2. What generally happens to the **equilibrium wage** when **(a)** demand for workers is low and supply is high; **(b)** demand for workers is high and supply is low?
3. How does **skilled labor** differ from **professional labor**? Give an example of each.
4. How do minimum wage and safety laws affect wages?

Applying Economic Concepts

5. ***Critical Thinking*** Choose two occupations, one that pays high wages and one that pays low wages. Explain the reasons for the difference in wages in terms of supply and demand. Are there any additional factors that could also help explain the difference?
6. ***Using the Databank*** Turn to the chart of "Fastest-Growing Occupations" on page 537. **(a)** What types of jobs are being created at the fastest pace? **(b)** Are the fastest-growing occupations in traditionally unionized industries?

For: Research Activity
Visit: PHSchool.com
Web Code: mnd-3092

Progress Monitoring *Online*
For additional assessment, have students access Progress Monitoring Online at **Web Code:** mna-3096

Go Online PHSchool.com Typing in the Web Code when prompted will bring students directly to detailed instructions for this activity.

ECONOMIC

Profile

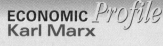

Economist

Entrepreneur

Karl Marx (1818–1883)

While Adam Smith described the orderliness and benefits of a free market economy, Karl Marx focused on its disorders. Marx looked at the factories and slums of nineteenth-century Europe and created a controversial new way to look at economics. Marx's radical ideas eventually led to his exile from his homeland and the eruption of violent revolutions in Russia and China.

Marx the Revolutionary

Karl Marx studied philosophy in his native Germany and earned a doctorate at the age of 23. However, because his radical writings criticized the government, he could find no work as a teacher and was soon forced to flee to Paris. There, in 1848, he and Friedrich Engels published the pamphlet for which Marx is best known: the *Communist Manifesto*.

In the *Communist Manifesto*, Marx argued that history is a struggle between the owners of capital, or "capitalists," and the workers, or "proletariat." He believed that as wealth became concentrated in the hands of the capitalists, the proletariat would become more and more dissatisfied. The result, he predicted, would be revolution and a classless society.

Marx returned to Germany after the publication of his pamphlet, but was soon expelled. In 1849, he settled permanently in London.

Das Kapital

Although Marx is known more for his social and political theories than for his economic ideas, much of his work concerned economics. In 1867, Marx completed the first volume of *Das Kapital*, a three-volume study of the economics of capitalism. Drawing heavily on the writings of Adam Smith and David Ricardo, Marx explored the relationship between labor, profit, and the distribution of wealth. By the time the final volume appeared in 1894, *Das Kapital* had established Marx as one of the most prominent economists of the nineteenth century.

The Theory of Surplus Value

In *Das Kapital*, Marx claimed that human labor is the source of all added value. Marx used the textile industry as an example. The capitalist buys cotton thread and pays workers in his factory to weave it into fabric. The capitalist then sells the fabric for more than the combined value of the thread and the workers' wages. The workers' labor has therefore added value to the capitalist's goods. However, the capitalist does not return this "surplus value" to the workers, but keeps it as profit, thereby "exploiting" the workers. This conclusion was the basis for Marx's radical social and political views.

CHECK FOR UNDERSTANDING

1. **Source Reading** Explain the following passage from *Das Kapital* in your own words: "Capital buys the labour power and pays the wages for it. By means of his work the labourer creates new value which does not belong to him, but to the capitalist."
2. **Critical Thinking** If, as Marx advocated, "surplus value" were returned to the workers, how might this retard economic growth and development?
3. **Problem Solving** Research "profit sharing" and explain how you think Marx would have viewed this method of compensation.

Beyond the Classroom: Workplace Skills

Acquiring and Evaluating Information Explain to students that the ability to acquire and evaluate data is critical in many careers, especially in an economy that is shifting its emphasis from manufacturing goods to providing services. Knowing how to acquire and evaluate data enables workers to assess past activities, spot future trends, and interpret consumer wants and needs—all of which are essential to understanding and delivering the services that people desire. Ask students to discuss how gathering and analyzing data in public-opinion polls can affect the behavior of service providers.

ECONOMIC *Profile*
Karl Marx

Background

Had Karl Marx lived to see his economic theories play out, he would probably have felt both vindicated and disillusioned. Vindication would have come by way of the Russian Revolution (and similar, smaller revolutions), during which the workers really did rise up, replace the ruling class, and put all capital in the hands of the state. Still, Marx probably would have been disillusioned by the events of the last two decades of the twentieth century. During this period his two central beliefs—that capitalism was fatally flawed and that socialism was inevitable—were disproved by the collapse of communism around the world into economic and political disarray while western capitalism thrived.

Careers in Economics Activity
Unit 3 folder, p. 24 gives students a closer look at the career path of a labor relations specialist.

Answers to . . .

1. Marx was saying that workers are paid to transform raw materials into a more valuable product. The added value created is the worth of the new product over the cost of the materials and labor. The value added does not go to those whose work created it, however, but to the business owner as profit.
2. Students should recognize that if workers, instead of capitalists, kept profits, this would likely slow new investment and modernization of equipment and therefore be detrimental to economic growth.
3. Students should learn that profit sharing is a system in which workers receive a portion of a company's earnings after costs. Some students may speculate that Marx would have approved of it as a step in the right direction. Others may argue that he would have rejected it as a half-measure that still left the capitalists in control.

Section 3

Organized Labor

Objectives You may wish to call students' attention to the objectives in the Section Preview. The objectives are reflected in the main headings of the section.

Bellringer Ask students to explain the meaning of Abraham Lincoln's statement, "A house divided against itself cannot stand." Explain that in this section they will learn how two adversaries learned to work together to improve conditions in the United States.

Vocabulary Builder Have students read this section to discover the meaning of each key term. Then tell them to create a photo and headline collage that illustrates the key terms.

Lesson Plan

Teaching the Main Concepts L3

1. Focus Although the rise of the labor movement in the United States was marked by suspicion, distrust, and violence, the laws written in response to the movement have strengthened and lent stability to the labor force. Ask students to describe what they know of the early years of the labor movement.

2. Instruct Begin by discussing the emergence and growth of organized labor in the United States. Next, explain the conditions that have led to a decline in union ranks. Describe how collective bargaining works. Finally, discuss the pros and cons of labor strikes and explain how settlements are reached.

3. Close/Reteach Ask students to summarize how the activities of labor unions have affected the lives of American workers.

Guided Reading and Review Unit 3 folder, p. 19 asks students to identify the main ideas of the section and to define or identify key terms.

Section 3 Organized Labor

Preview

Objectives

After studying this section you will be able to:

1. **Describe** why historically some American workers have joined labor unions.
2. **Trace** the history of the labor movement in the United States.
3. **Analyze** reasons for the decline of the labor movement.
4. **Explain** how labor and management negotiate contracts.

Section Focus

Historically, American workers have tried to gain some control over their working conditions by joining together in labor unions. Labor unions rose to great power and economic influence in the mid-1900s, but have declined since then.

Key Terms

strike
right-to-work law
blue-collar worker
white-collar worker
collective bargaining
mediation
arbitration

Today we think of Labor Day as the traditional end of the summer, a time for picnicking and perhaps shopping for school supplies. You might not know that the holiday has its roots in 1882, when labor leader Peter J. McGuire suggested a day celebrating the American worker. On September 5, 1882, some 10,000 workers took to the streets of New York City in a parade sponsored by a labor group called the Knights of Labor. The Knights later proposed making the first Monday in September a Labor Day holiday. The idea caught on quickly. In 1894, Congress made Labor Day a federal holiday.

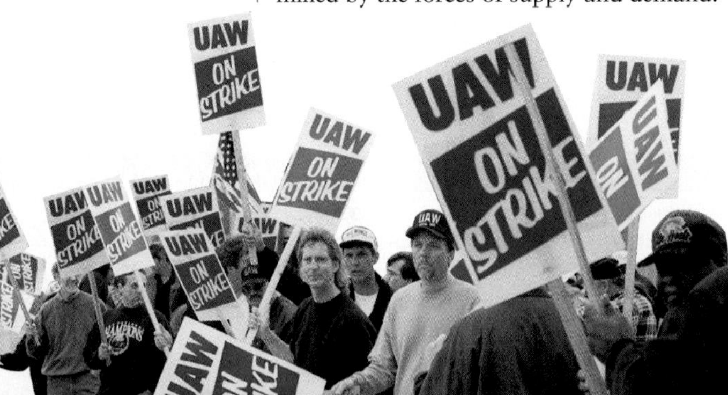

▼ In 1998, United Auto Workers in Flint, Michigan, went on strike against General Motors to force the company to address "unresolved health and safety, subcontracting and production standards issues."

Labor and Labor Unions

As you read in Section 2, wages are determined by the forces of supply and demand. Competition among firms keeps a worker's wages close to his or her level of productivity. In general, workers who command the highest wages are workers with specialized skills and who are in short supply—brain surgeons, for example.

What if, however, an individual employee feels that he or she is being paid too little, working too many hours, or working under unsafe conditions? One option is for the worker to quit his or her current job and find an employer who offers better wages and working conditions. Many economists, in fact, argue that it is a competitive labor market that helps prevent low pay and dangerous working conditions because workers will leave such firms to work elsewhere.

Historically, American workers have also tried to gain some control over their working conditions by joining together to bring their concerns to the attention of company management. Today, only about one out of seven workers in the United States belongs to a labor union. However, this number does not accurately reflect the strong influence that unions have had on the nation's economy in the past. In order to understand the role of labor unions today, we will look at how labor unions rose to power in the United States.

Graphing the Main Idea

Economic Institutions To build understanding of the concept of **economic institutions** and the rise of organized labor in the United States, ask students to complete a tree map graphic organizer like the one at the right. Remind them that a tree map shows an outline for a main topic, main ideas, and supporting details. Suggest that they put the section title across the top of the organizer and main headings in each of the boxes below, followed by main ideas and details.

Section Reading Support Transparencies A template and the answers for this graphic organizer can be found in Chapter 9, Section 3 of the Section Reading Support Transparency System.

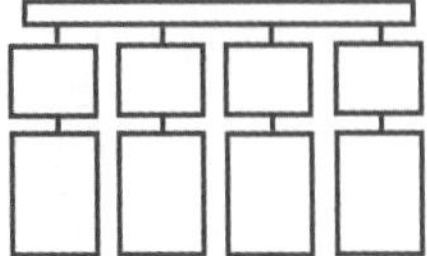

The Labor Movement

The union movement took shape over the course of more than a century. It faced many obstacles along the way, including violence and legal opposition from companies. Figure 9.12 highlights some of the major events in the history of organized labor.

Workers in the 1800s

Labor unions arose largely in response to changes brought by the Industrial Revolution in the early and mid-1800s. Manufacturing brought a new type of occupation to America: the factory job.

By today's standards, it was not an enviable job. In garment factories, iron plants, and gunpowder mills, laborers worked 12 to 16-hour days, 7 days a week, for meager wages. The long workday was not new to those who had worked on farms, but the working conditions were. Men, women, and children as young as age 5 operated clattering machines so dangerous that many people lost their sight, their hearing, even fingers and limbs. Injured workers often lost their jobs.

Today, many firms emphasize that one of their major goals is to attract, hire, and retain the most highly skilled workers. This means treating workers well. In 1855, however, a factory boss bluntly summarized his attitude toward workers:

> "*I regard people just as I regard my machinery. So long as they can do my work for what I choose to pay them, I keep them, getting out of them all I can.*"
>
> —Manager of a textile mill in Fall River, Massachusetts, 1855

Unions Take Hold

As early as the 1790s, whispers of worker discontent grew into organized protests. Skilled workers such as shoemakers and carpenters began to form unions in order to protect their interests. The tool of unions was the **strike,** an organized work stoppage intended to force an employer to address union demands. Initially, the courts regarded unions as illegal. Employers simply fired and replaced workers who caused trouble by trying to organize.

The man who truly started the United States labor movement was Samuel Gompers. The young cigarmaker in New York City rose within union ranks, focusing on three workplace reforms: higher wages, shorter hours, and safer work environments. In 1886, he founded the American Federation of Labor (AFL).

strike *an organized work stoppage intended to force an employer to address union demands*

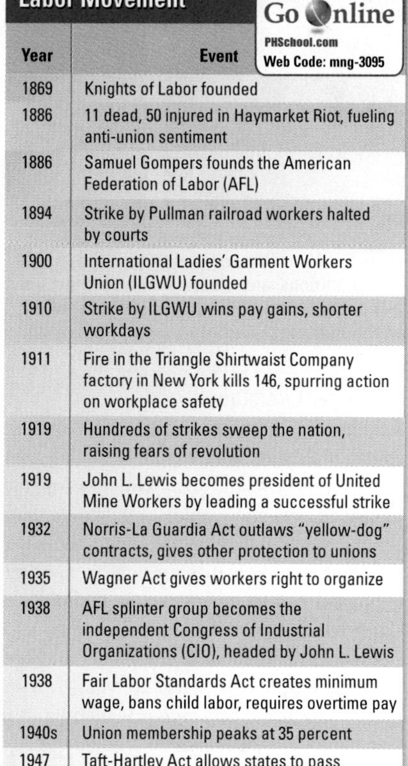

Figure 9.12 **Key Events in the U.S. Labor Movement**

Go Online PHSchool.com Web Code: mng-3095

Year	Event
1869	Knights of Labor founded
1886	11 dead, 50 injured in Haymarket Riot, fueling anti-union sentiment
1886	Samuel Gompers founds the American Federation of Labor (AFL)
1894	Strike by Pullman railroad workers halted by courts
1900	International Ladies' Garment Workers Union (ILGWU) founded
1910	Strike by ILGWU wins pay gains, shorter workdays
1911	Fire in the Triangle Shirtwaist Company factory in New York kills 146, spurring action on workplace safety
1919	Hundreds of strikes sweep the nation, raising fears of revolution
1919	John L. Lewis becomes president of United Mine Workers by leading a successful strike
1932	Norris-La Guardia Act outlaws "yellow-dog" contracts, gives other protection to unions
1935	Wagner Act gives workers right to organize
1938	AFL splinter group becomes the independent Congress of Industrial Organizations (CIO), headed by John L. Lewis
1938	Fair Labor Standards Act creates minimum wage, bans child labor, requires overtime pay
1940s	Union membership peaks at 35 percent
1947	Taft-Hartley Act allows states to pass right-to-work laws
1955	AFL and CIO merge to create AFL-CIO
1960s	Government employees begin to organize
1962	Cesar Chavez begins organizing the first farmworkers' union, which eventually establishes the first labor agreement with growers
1970s	Rise in anti-union measures by employers
2000s	Increase in public-sector unions; decline in overall union membership

The American labor movement had its roots in the 1800s, when the rise of factories led to difficult and dangerous working conditions. **Economic Institutions** **Describe the relationship shown here between labor laws and union membership in the 1900s.**

Differentiated Instruction 

(Reteaching) Ask students to create cause-effect charts that illustrate how unions in the United States got their start, rose to power and prominence, and then declined in prominence. Stress that the charts should show historical causal relationships.

Differentiated Instruction 

Ask students to choose one of the events in the chart on this page and write a brief paragraph explaining the significance of that particular event. Have students share their paragraphs.

Econ 101: Key Concepts Made Easy

Economic Institutions To help students remember the difference between **mediation** and **arbitration,** remind them that the former results in a suggestion, whereas the latter results in a decision. The result of mediation may or may not be a solution, depending on whether or not the two parties decide to accept the mediator's proposal. The result of arbitration offers no such choice: The arbitrator's decision is final. Ask students why both parties of a labor dispute might be wise to accept mediation instead of moving to arbitration.

Answer to . . .

Building Key Concepts As union membership grew, more laws were enacted to protect laborers.

Background

The Workers' Minstrel

Woody Guthrie (1912–1967) was an American folk singer and composer who took a particular interest in working men and women. Many of the more than 1,000 songs he wrote detailed the struggles of workers to make better lives for themselves.

In "Union Maid," Guthrie sang of a proud woman who organized workers and defied the "union-busting" tactics of management, declaring in the song's chorus: "Oh, you can't scare me, I'm sticking to the union." "Union Burying Ground" tells of the deaths of union organizers and members at the hands of management. Guthrie also wrote of the terrible violence that stalked the labor movement in "Ludlow Massacre" and "The 1913 Massacre."

▲ At left, this poster of the United Mine Workers union, founded in 1890, celebrates its efforts to secure fair pay, safe working conditions, and other benefits for mine workers. The photograph at right shows the aftermath of the Triangle Shirtwaist Factory fire of 1911 in which 146 workers died. The tragedy brought national attention to the issues of workplace safety and workers' rights.

Employer Resistance

Attempts to unionize brought swift responses from employers. Viewing strikers as threats to free enterprise and social order, companies identified and fired union organizers. They forced workers to sign so-called yellow-dog contracts, agreements in which workers promised not to join a union. (*Yellow* was slang for "coward.") Companies also used court orders called *injunctions* to order striking employees back to work. Some companies hired their own private militias to harass union organizers.

Congressional Protections

As the nation struggled through the effects of the Great Depression in the 1930s, Congress took up the labor cause, passing a number of pro-union measures. The expansion of workers' rights in the 1930s contributed to a new rise in union strength. Membership peaked in the 1940s at about 35 percent of the nation's non-farm work force.

Unions became a dominant force in many industries. They controlled the day-to-day operations of businesses from shipyards to garbage collection to steel production. Unions amassed billions of dollars in union dues to cover the costs of union activities including organizing, making political donations, and providing aid to striking workers.

Decline of the Labor Movement

As they grew, some unions began to abuse their new power. Some sought to preserve outdated and inefficient production methods in order to protect jobs and benefits. As you read in Section 2, sometimes unions even negotiated to preserve job positions that were really unnecessary—called "featherbedding"—in order to keep more union members employed.

Preparing for Standardized Tests

Have students read the section titled "The Labor Movement" and then answer the question below.

Which of the following was NOT a focus of Samuel Gompers' workplace reforms?

A higher wages
B safer work environments
(C) individual and family health coverage
D shorter hours

Reviewing Main Ideas

9. Who does the government include in its definition of the labor force?
10. What is a labor union?
11. Describe how collective bargaining works.
12. Why is the equilibrium wage high for some workers and low for others?
13. Why is the United States producing fewer goods and more services?
14. How do wage increases affect the demand for and supply of labor?
15. How does discrimination affect wages?
16. How does education affect wages?

Critical Thinking

17. **Predicting Consequences** How might technological changes affect labor demand in the future? Give specific examples.
18. **Drawing Conclusions** Reread the Fast Fact on page 212 describing how the invention of a punch card tabulator sped up data analysis after the 1880 Census. **(a)** What types of information related to labor might the new tabulator have helped to analyze? **(b)** Give other examples of types of economic information available as a result of technological innovations.
19. **Analyzing Information** Describe the reasons why companies are turning to contingent labor. How might this trend affect the work force in the future?

Problem-Solving Activity

20. Suppose you are a business owner competing for employees in a tight labor market. How might you attract employees without raising wages?

Skills for Life

Analyzing Statistics Review the steps shown on page 218; then answer the following questions using the statistics in the table below.

21. What is the source of these statistics?
22. What is being shown by these data?
23. According to the table, who has the lower earnings, a man without a college education or a woman without a college education?
24. Which category of worker shown has the lowest percentage of low-wage employment?
25. Which category of worker shown has the highest percentage of low-wage employment?

Education and Employment

Adult men, ages 25 – 54	No low-wage employment	Low-wage* employment
College or more	90.6%	9.4%
High school or less	70%	30%

Adult women, ages 25 – 54	No low-wage employment	Low-wage* employment
College or more	83.1%	16.9%
High school or less	57.9%	42.1%

*average hourly earnings below $5.70
Source: U.S. Census Bureau

Economics Journal

Essay Writing Review your interview of an older adult. Interview a young adult about his or her job, or compare your own job experience to that of your interview subject. Write an essay describing your impressions of how the workplace has changed over the years.

Progress Monitoring *Online*

For: Chapter 9 Self-Test **Visit:** PHSchool.com
Web Code: mna-2091

As a final review, take the Economics Chapter 9 Self-Test and receive immediate feedback on your answers. The test consists of 20 multiple-choice questions designed to test your understanding of the chapter content.

Problem-Solving Activity

20. Students may suggest offering flexible hours, a pleasant working environment, or a profit-sharing plan.

Skills for Life

21. U.S. Census Bureau
22. The table is showing the statistical relationships between income, gender, and education.
23. woman without a college education
24. adult men with a college education or more
25. adult women with high school education or less

Additional support materials and activities for Chapter 9 of *Economics: Principles in Action* can be found in the Social Studies area of **PHSchool.com.**

Economics Journal

Essays should demonstrate comprehension of interview data as well as a grasp of workplace changes over the years.

Review and Assessment

Vocabulary Practice Unit 3 folder, p. 22 uses a fill-in-the-blanks word puzzle to reinforce understanding of key terms.

GTE **Guide to the Essentials** Chapter 9 Test, p. 41

Test Bank CD-ROM, Chapter 9 Test

Go Online PHSchool.com Students may use the Chapter 9 Self-Test on **PHSchool.com** to prepare for the Chapter Test.

THE WALL STREET JOURNAL.
CLASSROOM EDITION

Debate: Minimum Wage

1. Focus Have students find the meaning of each of these words before they begin to read: *cost of living, exploiting, leeway, living standards, productivity,* and *stagnating.*

Explain to students that they will be conducting a debate on the minimum wage and its impact on the price of labor. Inform them that they will be responsible for arguing one side of the issue. Remind students that a well-prepared debater supports a position with valid evidence, logical arguments, and responsible appeals to emotion.

2. Instruct The authors have both researched the impact of the minimum wage on the cost of labor. Have students conduct further research on the minimum wage from credible sources before conducting the debate.

Remind students that they should use the following debate format:
The affirmative side will:
- State the problem to be solved. Why is this problem significant?
- Explain who or what is harmed if this problem is not resolved. Use factual evidence to quantify the harm.
- Propose a plan of action. Explain why it is better than the current system.
- Provide factual evidence to show how this plan will solve the problem.

The opposing side will:
- Refute the arguments of the affirmative side, using factual evidence to quantify and support its position.
- If necessary, support the status quo's ability to solve the problem.

3. Close/Reteach When the debate is concluded, encourage students to discuss their opinions on the issue. Ask them whether they were persuaded by the other side's arguments. Conclude by having students write their own statements supporting or opposing a legally mandated and enforced minimum wage.

Debate Activity
Debating Current Issues folder, p. 11 asks students to evaluate how higher labor costs can affect the employability of workers. In a market economy who is helped and who is hurt by paying higher wages to workers?

Economic Assessment Rubric
Economics Assessment Rubrics folder, pp. 14–15 provides sample evaluation materials for participation in debates.

THE WALL STREET JOURNAL.
CLASSROOM EDITION

Debating Current Issues: *Minimum Wage*

In the U.S., the federal minimum wage is $5.15 an hour. In this debate from *The Wall Street Journal Classroom Edition,* Kevin A. Hassett, director of economic policy studies at the American Enterprise Institute for Public Policy Research, and Jeff Chapman, a policy analyst with the Economic Policy Institute, argue whether the minimum wage should be raised—or abolished.

YES *Should the Minimum Wage Be Raised?*

By Jeff Chapman

The minimum wage is a simple, fair policy with broad public support that protects workers from exploitation and increases the ability of working families to make ends meet. Despite the effectiveness of the minimum wage, the federal government has failed to raise the minimum wage regularly to account for the rising cost of living.

A strong minimum wage provides income to families who need it the most. More than one-third of families with workers who would benefit from an increase in the minimum wage rely solely on the earnings of those workers. The result of the declining value of the minimum wage has been stagnating or even falling wages.

A class in beginning economics teaches that market forces set wages and prices very efficiently. But low-wage workers don't have the option of not working if employers aren't willing to pay enough to match the market equilibrium. They have to work to survive, while employers have considerable leeway in setting wages, especially for low-wage workers. Thus, without a high enough minimum, employers will often set wages below the actual value of the work and in violation of basic fairness.

Some have claimed that the minimum wage is unfair because it prevents some willing laborers from working for less than the minimum wage. In fact, the minimum wage only prevents low-wage employers from exploiting the fact that many workers do not have the market power required to negotiate a fair wage.

Another frequent claim by opponents of the minimum wage is that it will cause workers to lose their jobs, because it increases the employer's costs. But since employers are often paying a wage that is less than the labor is worth to them, the minimum wage does not cause employers to lay off workers. For instance, if an hour's labor is worth $8 to the employer, but he can get a worker to work for $3, that worker will still be employed if the minimum wage was set at $6.

Years of research has shown that the minimum wage does exactly what it is intended to do. It corrects an imbalance of power and raises the living standards of working families.

According to proponents of a minimum wage hike, people with few job skills would benefit most from an increase.

Background

About the Authors

Kevin A. Hassett, director of economic policy studies at the American Enterprise Institute for Public Policy Research, is opposed to raising the minimum wage and further argues that the law should be abolished. Jeff Chapman, a policy analyst with the Economic Policy Institute in Washington, D.C., researches minimum-wage laws and assists state and local organizations working on living-standards issues.

NO Should the Minimum Wage Be Raised?

By Kevin A. Hassett

The minimum wage is a terrible and counterproductive policy. While it may appear that the minimum wage helps the poor, it does not.

The case against the minimum wage is based on simple economics and mounds of scientific evidence. Suppose that you run a small factory that makes hammers. You employ a large number of minimum-wage workers, and sell your product around the world. If the minimum wage is increased, then your costs increase. In response to this increase, you will have to raise the price that you charge for your product. Since your price for hammers is now higher, other manufacturers in states or countries that have not raised their minimum wages find that their hammers are suddenly cheaper than yours. Their sales go up, and yours go down. With sales down, you are forced to lay off workers.

This scenario describes the cycle that has been observed by economists who study minimum wages. While some minimum-wage workers receive higher pay, others lose their jobs entirely, and the number of people living in poverty likely increases.

The minimum wage denies individuals opportunities they may desire. Think of it this way: If you asked your parents to allow you to take a summer job and they replied that you could, but only if you found a job that paid you at least $15 an hour, you might think that their requirement is unfair. They are not allowing you to decide to work for someone unless you find an employer willing to pay you a salary that they think is fair. Shouldn't you get to make up your own mind about that? The same is true when the government sets high minimum wages. By doing so, government takes away opportunity, especially for disabled individuals and first-time workers.

Some people have expressed concern that employers may set wages unfairly low. But in a competitive marketplace, employers must compete to attract workers. Those who pay wages that are too low will lose workers and business to employers that pay wages based on the productivity of the individuals they hire.

Value of the Minimum Wage, 1980–2004

Year	Nominal Dollars*	1996 Dollars**
1980	3.10	5.90
1982	3.35	5.45
1984	3.35	5.06
1986	3.35	4.80
1988	3.35	4.44
1990	3.80	4.56
1992	4.25	4.75
1994	4.25	4.50
1996	4.75	4.75
1998	5.15	4.96
2000	5.15	4.69
2002	5.15	4.49
2004	5.15	4.28

* Face-value dollars ** Dollars adjusted for inflation

Source: Bureau of Labor Statistics

Go Online PHSchool.com Web Code: mng-3099

Even though the minimum wage has risen, its value has not increased because of inflation.

DEBATING THE ISSUE

1. Why does Jeff Chapman think market forces alone can't set the price for labor effectively?
2. What evidence does Kevin Hassett offer to prove that minimum wage increases affect unemployment? Would you agree that the minimum wage denies workers the opportunity to earn a living?
3. **Critical Thinking** Based on this debate, what role do you think government should have in ensuring that workers earn a "living wage"?
4. **Drawing Conclusions** Explain why you agree or disagree with Hassett: "While it may appear that the minimum wage helps the poor, it does not."
5. **Reading Graphs** Between 1980 and 2004, how much has the minimum wage increased in nominal dollars? What is the percentage increase between 1980 and 2004 in nominal dollars?

For: You Decide Poll
Visit: PHSchool.com
Web Code: mnp-3091

Interdisciplinary Connections: History

Minimum Wage Since the federal minimum wage went into effect in 1938, some changes or amendments have been made which have extended the law's coverage to additional employees. 1961 amendments greatly expanded the FLSA's scope in the retail trade sector and increased the minimum. 1966 amendments extended coverage to public schools, nursing homes, laundries, the entire construction industry, and large farms.

In addition to increasing the minimum wage to $4.75 an hour, the 1996 amendments established a youth sub-minimum wage of $4.25 an hour for newly hired employees under age 20 during their first 90 consecutive calendar days after being hired by their employer.

Making the Connection Have students research additional changes to the minimum wage since its inception. For a complete history of changes in federal minimum wage rates, go to **PHSchool.com**. **Web Code:** mne-3091.

Differentiated Instruction 

Some states have minimum wage laws: Workers receive whichever is higher, the state or the federal rate. Have students research minimum-wage laws in their state. Ask them to find out how their state compares with the federal rate. If the state rate is higher than the federal rate, ask them to give a possible explanation for this situation. How does a minimum-wage law affect the unemployment rate, costs of housing and cost of living? For state information, go to PHSchool.com and use **Web Code:** mne-3092.

Go Online PHSchool.com Students can find additional links related to the debate by visiting the *Economics: Principles in Action* site at **PHSchool.com.**

Answers to . . .

1. Low-wage workers don't have the option of not working if employers aren't willing to pay enough.
2. The 1923 case of *Adkins* v. *Children's Hospital* cites evidence that after the city had increased its minimum wage for nurses, the employer, Children's Hospital, had to reduce the number of nurses it employed; answers will vary.
3. Answers will vary.
4. Students should examine the concepts of equilibrium wage, labor supply, and labor demand in their explanation. Supporters of the minimum wage argue that labor markets aren't competitive and the supply and demand model can't explain the effects of an increase in the minimum wage on employment. Opponents would argue that higher wages set by government result in a decrease in the quantity of workers demanded. With a higher wage, employers may substitute machines or foreign labor, and some small businesses may shut down.
5. The minimum wage has increased by $2.05, which is an increase of 66 percent.

UNIT 4

Money, Banking, and Finance

Introducing the Unit

Unit Summary

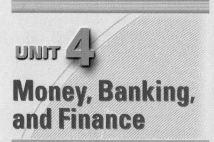

Unit 4 introduces students to the world of money, banking, and finance. In Chapter 10 students learn about the characteristics of money, the historical role of banks, and trends in banking today. In Chapter 11 they examine the world of finance and develop an understanding of savings and investment, including investment options such as stocks and bonds.

Focus Activity

Introduce Unit 4 to students by asking them to complete the Focus Activity. Remind them that a flowchart shows a series of events, and then allow them time to complete their flowcharts. When students have completed their flowcharts, discuss them as a class and then display them on a bulletin board.

UNIT 4

Money, Banking, and Finance

NCEE

National Council on Economic Education

The following Voluntary National Content Standards in Economics are addressed in this unit:

★ Standard 10 ★ Standard 12
★ Standard 11

See the Chapter Openers on pp. 242 and 270 for a complete description of the standards addressed in each chapter.

Chapters in This Unit

10. *Money and Banking*
11. *Financial Markets*

You've just won a million dollars . . .

While most people work to earn wages, you've just been handed a check for a million dollars. Now it's time to go to the bank and collect your winnings.

- Where does the bank get the money to cash your check?
- Should you be investing your money in stock or bonds instead of keeping it in a savings account?
- What happens to the money you've deposited in your savings account? Is it safe?

Money plays a central role not just in economic theory, but also in our lives. For economists, "money" has a special meaning, though. In this unit you'll read about how economists define money, as well as how banks and other institutions help channel money from savers to investors.

Focus Activity

Create a flowchart showing some of the possible paths that a one-dollar bill might take over the course of two days. Include different paths showing how the money may be spent or saved.

Bibliography

Print

Virtual Economics: An Interactive Center for Economics Education. CD-ROM. The Federal Reserve Bank of Boston. *Banking Basics.* EconomicsAmerica, National Council on Economic Education, 1997.

Fundamental Facts About U.S. Money. Atlanta: The Federal Reserve Bank of Atlanta, 1998.

Multimedia

"Demystifying the Stock Market." Multimedia kit with color video, 25 minutes. A detailed but easy-to-understand overview of the stock market. Includes information on the history of stock trading, how the stock market works, and the relationship between the stock market and the U.S. economy. Zenger Media, 10200 Jefferson Blvd., Box 802, Culver City, CA 90232.

Technology Center

Economics Video Library
Includes high-interest, chapter-specific segments produced by CNBC for

THE WALL STREET JOURNAL. CLASSROOM EDITION

Simulations and Data Graphing CD-ROM
Provides interactive federal budget and stock market simulations and a data graphing tool designed to support instruction in economics.

PRENTICE HALL TeacherEXPRESS™ Plan · Teach · Assess

Teacher Express CD-ROM offers powerful lesson planning, resource management, testing, and an interactive Teacher's Edition.

Prentice Hall Presentation Pro CD-ROM
Allows you to create custom lectures for every chapter.

Social Studies Skills Tutor CD-ROM
Provides interactive practice in geographic literacy, critical thinking and reading, visual analysis, and communications.

Exam*View*® Test Bank CD-ROM
Allows you to create, edit, and print out chapter level tests.

Transparency Resource Package
Illustrates key economic concepts and provides useful forms and templates for enhancing classroom discussions.

Section Reading Support Transparency System
Delivers the main idea of each section in the student text through graphic organizers.

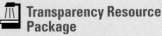

Offers student-appropriate online activities and links as well as resources for the teacher. Be sure to check out this month's **eTeach** online discussion with a Master Economics Teacher.

Chapter 10 Money and Banking

For more pacing suggestions, see the Economics Pacing Guide in the Program Overview of the Teaching Resources.

Section Objectives	Print and Technology Resources	
1 Money *(pp. 243–248)* **Objectives** 1. Describe the three uses of money. 2. Explain the six characteristics of money. 3. Understand the sources of money's value.	• **Lesson Planner** Section 1 Lesson Plan, p. 45 • **Learning Styles Lesson Plans folder** Section 1 Lesson Plan, p. 25 • **Lesson Plans folder** Section 1 Lesson Plan, p. 38 • **Economics Assessment Rubrics folder** Writing Assignment, pp. 6–7 • **Unit 4 folder** Guided Reading and Review, p. 2 Economic Skills, p. 8 Section 1 Quiz, p. 3	• **Presentation Pro CD-ROM** Section 1 • **Transparency Resource Package** Economics Organizers, G5: Web Graphic Organizer Economics Concepts, 10A: The Three Functions of Money • **Section Reading Support Transparency System** • **Social Studies Skills Tutor CD-ROM**
2 The History of American Banking *(pp. 250–256)* **Objectives** 1. Describe the shifts between centralized and decentralized banking before the Civil War. 2. Explain how the banking system was stabilized in the later 1800s. 3. Describe developments in banking during the twentieth century.	• **Lesson Planner** Section 2 Lesson Plan, p. 46 • **Learning Styles Lesson Plans folder** Section 2 Lesson Plan, p. 26 • **Lesson Plans folder** Section 2 Lesson Plan, p. 39 • **Unit 4 folder** Guided Reading and Review, p. 4 Careers in Economics, Banking Customer Service Representative, p. 11 Economic Cartoon, p. 12 Section 2 Quiz, p. 5	• **Source Articles folder** The Power of Compounding, pp. 27–29 • **Presentation Pro CD-ROM** Section 2 • **Transparency Resource Package** Economics Organizers, G8: Flow-Chart Graphic Organizer Economics Concepts, 10B: Metallic Content of U.S. Coins Economics Concepts, 10C: Components of the Money Supply • **Section Reading Support Transparency System**
3 Banking Today *(pp. 258–264)* **Objectives** 1. Explain how the money supply in the United States is measured. 2. Explain the functions of financial institutions. 3. Identify different types of financial institutions. 4. Understand the changes brought about by electronic banking.	• **Lesson Planner** Section 3 Lesson Plan, p. 47 • **Lesson Plans folder** Section 3 Lesson Plan, p. 40 • **Economics Assessment Rubrics folder** Writing Assignment, pp. 6–7 • **Unit 4 folder** Guided Reading and Review, p. 6 Vocabulary Practice, p. 9 Economic Detective, p.10 Section 3 Quiz, p. 7 • **Case Studies in Free Enterprise folder** Dineh Mohajer, pp. 20–21 • **Math Practice folder** Comparing Credit Cards Payments, p. 9 • **Presentation Pro CD-ROM** Section 3	• **Transparency Resource Package** Economics Organizers, G7: Tree Map Graphic Organizer Economics Concepts, 10D: Anti-Counterfeiting Measures Economics Concepts, 10E: Savings Rates Economics Concepts, 10F: Simple and Compound Interest • **Section Reading Support Transparency System**

Differentiated Instruction

Sorting (L2)

A sorting activity is a great way for English Language Learners to show their understanding of a concept without being completely reliant on language skills. It also allows students to practice making choices, differentiating between concepts, and language skills. To reinforce a concept, ask students to work independently. To help students practice their vocabularies, ask students to work in small groups. To begin, follow these guidelines.

1. To help students distinguish between bonds, stocks, and bank accounts, prepare strips of paper that describe different investments. Give each students or groups of students a group of these descriptive phrases and three different containers in which they can place their sorts.

2. Explain and model the activity. Take a stack of descriptions, and as you sort them into their respective containers, explain the rationale behind your decision.

3. To check this assignment, ask students to defend their sorts. You may ask students to explain their decisions in a brief essay, discuss their choices as a class, or instruct students to hand in their sorts for you to look over.

Compare and Contrast (L2)

Point out that comparing and contrasting helps students analyze information. Comparing examines similarities, while contrasting highlights differences. A Venn diagram provides an effective way to compare and contrast information. To make this graphic organizer, draw two overlapping circles. List differences in the outside portions and list similarities in the overlapping oval. Model this skill by reading through the paragraphs under the header *Sources of Money's Value* in Section 1 and compare the ways that different types of money function.

Go Online
PHSchool.com

Visit the Social Studies area of the Prentice Hall Web site. There you can find additional links to enrich chapter content for *Economics: Principles in Action* as well as a self-test for students. Be sure to check out this month's **eTeach** online discussion with a Master Economics Teacher.

Web Code: mnf-4101

Running Out of Time?

- Use the **Presentation Pro CD-ROM** to create an outline for this chapter.
- Use the Chapter Summary in the **Chapter 10 Assessment**, p. 266.
- Use the Section Summaries for Chapter 10, from **Guide to the Essentials of Economics (English and Spanish)**.

THE WALL STREET JOURNAL.
CLASSROOM EDITION

Prentice Hall brings into the classroom the authoritative content of *The Wall Street Journal Classroom Edition.* See the Source Articles, Debating Current Issues, and You and Your Money folders in the **Teaching Resources**. Also, see Economics Video Library, "The Euro, Part 1."

Assessment Resources

Chapter Assessment

Teaching Resources Unit 4, Chapter 10

- Section Quizzes, pp. 3, 5, 7

Exam *View*® Test Bank CD-ROM Chapter 10

Economics Assessment Rubrics

Chapter 10 Self-Test, **Web Code:** mna-4101

Reading and Skills Evaluation

Progress Monitoring Assessments

- Screening Test
- Diagnostic Test of Social Studies Skills

Standardized Test Preparation

Test Prep Workbook

Test-Taking Strategies With Transparencies

Differentiated Instruction Key

L1	Special Needs	LPR	Less Proficient Readers
L2	Basic to Average	AR	Advanced Readers
L3	All Students	SN	Special Needs Students
L4	Average to Advanced	GT	Gifted and Talented
		ELL	English Language Learner

Chapter 10

Money and Banking

Introducing the Chapter

In this chapter students will learn about mediums of exchange and how contemporary U.S. currency evolved. In addition the chapter explains the history and purposes of banking and other financial institutions in the United States and discusses how technology is redefining both the concept of money and the banking system.

Go Online
PHSchool.com

For additional links for *Economics: Principles in Action* provided by Prentice Hall and *The Wall Street Journal Classroom Edition,* visit the Social Studies area. Be sure to check out this month's **eTeach** online discussion with a Master Teacher.

Beyond the Lecture

You may cover the concepts in Chapter 10 in an activity-based style by using the following materials:

- **Technology Resources** appropriate for use with this chapter are noted on pp. 244, 248, 252, 256, 260, 261, 264, and 267.
- **Presentation Pro CD-ROM** with animated graphs gives you an alternative method for organizing and delivering chapter content.
- **Activities** designed to meet the needs of students of mixed abilities and learning styles are noted throughout the chapter in the side columns.
- **Learning Styles Lesson Plans** provide alternate lessons for diverse learning styles. See pp. 25–26 of the Learning Styles Lesson Plans folder located in the Teaching Resources.

Economics Journal

Instruct students to write their responses in their Economics Journals. Students may include completed journal entries in an Economics Portfolio.

Chapter 10 Money and Banking

Picture shopping at an Egyptian market and paying with a packet of salt, or walking into the bank with paper money and walking out with a pouch of gold. Seem unlikely? Actually, these scenarios might well have happened at various times in the past. They illustrate how much money and banking have changed over the centuries to meet society's changing needs.

Economics Journal

Record each time you use cash, checks, credit cards, and ATM cards during an average week. Include any trips you make to a bank or ATM.

Go Online
PHSchool.com

For: Current Data
Visit: PHSchool.com
Web Code: mng-4101

National Council on Economic Education

The following Voluntary National Content Standards in Economics are addressed in this chapter:

★ **Standard 10** Students will understand that: Institutions evolve in market economies to help individuals and groups accomplish their goals. Banks, labor unions, corporations, legal systems, and not-for-profit organizations are examples of important institutions. A different kind of institution, clearly defined and well enforced property rights, is essential to a market economy.

★ **Standard 11** Students will understand that: Money makes it easier to trade, borrow, save, invest, and compare the value of goods and services.

For more information about the standards, contact the National Council on Economic Education

1140 Avenue of the Americas
New York, NY 10036
1-800-338-1192

Section 1 Money

Preview

Objectives

After studying this section you will be able to:

1. **Describe** the three uses of money.
2. **Explain** the six characteristics of money.
3. **Understand** the sources of money's value.

Section Focus

Money serves as a medium of exchange, a unit of account, and a store of value. Although many objects have served as money in the past, the coins and bills we use today meet the needs of modern society.

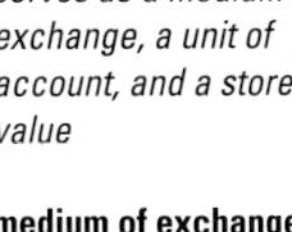

Key Terms

money
medium of exchange
barter
unit of account
store of value
currency
commodity money
representative money
fiat money

Suppose you have just arrived at your neighborhood store after playing basketball on a hot day. You grab a soda and fish around in your jeans pockets for some money. You find a pen, keys, and a chewing gum wrapper, but, unfortunately, no money. Then you reach into your jacket pocket. Finally!—a crumpled dollar bill. You hand the money to the clerk and take a long, cold drink.

Money is a part of our daily lives. Without it, we can't get the things we need and want. That's not the whole story of money, however. In fact, money has functions and characteristics that you might never have thought about.

The Three Uses of Money

If you were asked to define money, you would probably think of the coins and bills in your wallet or the paychecks you receive for your part-time job. Economists define money in terms of its three uses. For an economist, **money** is anything that serves as a medium of exchange, a unit of account, and a store of value.

Money as a Medium of Exchange

A **medium of exchange** is anything that is used to determine value during the exchange of goods and services. Without money, people acquire goods and services through **barter,** or the direct exchange of one set of goods or services for another. Barter is still used in many parts of the world, especially in traditional economies in Asia, Africa, and Latin America. It is also sometimes used informally in the United States. For example, a person might agree to help paint a neighbor's house in exchange for vegetables from the neighbor's garden. In general, however, as an economy becomes more specialized, bartering becomes too difficult and time-consuming to be practical.

To appreciate how much easier money makes exchanges, suppose that money did not exist, and that you wanted to trade your video cassette recorder (VCR) for an audio CD player. You probably would have a great deal of trouble making the exchange. First, you would need to find someone who wanted to both sell the model of CD player you want and buy your particular VCR. Second, this person would need to agree that your VCR is worth the same as his or her CD player. As you might guess, people in barter economies spend a great deal of time and effort exchanging the goods they have for the goods they need and want. That's why barter generally works well only in small, traditional economies.

Now consider how much easier your transaction would be if you used money as

money *anything that serves as a medium of exchange, a unit of account, and a store of value*

medium of exchange *anything that is used to determine value during the exchange of goods and services*

barter *the direct exchange of one set of goods or services for another*

Section 1

Money

Objectives You may wish to call students' attention to the objectives in the Section Preview. The objectives are reflected in the main headings of the section.

Bellringer Ask students to think about a favorite possession. Then ask them what they think the value of that possession is and how they determine its value. Explain that in this section they will learn how a stable currency enables producers and consumers to assign realistic, consistent values to goods and services.

Vocabulary Builder Have students find the key terms in the section and read their definitions. Then have them search magazines for images that depict the meaning of each term. Encourage students to share their findings or to contribute to a class bulletin board.

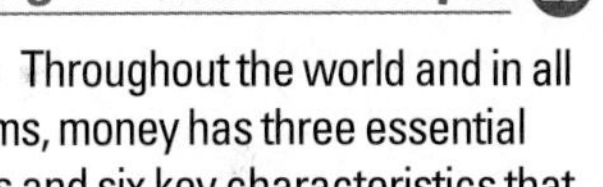

Lesson Plan

Teaching the Main Concepts (L3)

1. Focus Throughout the world and in all of its forms, money has three essential functions and six key characteristics that contribute to its utility as a medium of exchange. Ask students to speculate about these functions and characteristics.

2. Instruct Begin by discussing the three principal functions of money. Then move on to the six characteristics of money, encouraging students to provide examples to illustrate each one. Finally, explain each of the three sources of money's value.

3. Close/Reteach In contemporary society money has become the principal medium of exchange, facilitating the orderly conduct of national and global commerce. Ask students to list ways in which monetary transactions are completed without the exchange of any paper or coins.

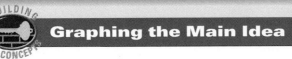

Graphing the Main Idea

Money To build understanding of the concept of **money** and its value, have students use two web graphic organizers like the one shown at the right. Remind students that a web shows a main idea and its supporting details. Suggest that in the center of one organizer, they put the label "Uses of Money" and that in the center of the other, they put the label "Characteristics of Money."

Section Reading Support Transparencies A template and the answers for this graphic organizer can be found in Chapter 10, Section 1 of the Section Reading Support Transparency System.

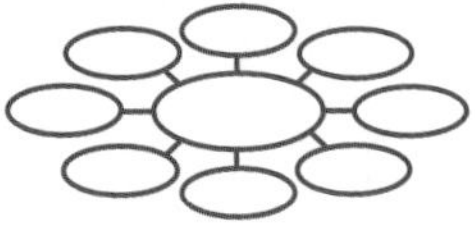

Guided Reading and Review
Unit 4 folder, p. 2 asks students to identify the main ideas of the section and to define or identify key terms.

Transparency Resource Package
Economics Concepts, 10A: The Three Functions of Money

Meeting NCEE Standards

Use the following benchmark activity from the **Voluntary National Content Standards in Economics** to evaluate student understanding of **Standard 11.**

Select examples of money from a collection of pictures that show coins, currency, checks, savings account passbooks, ATM cards, and various types of credit cards and explain whether each is considered money.

Differentiated Instruction L4

You may wish to have students add the following to their portfolios. Ask them to write a brief "day in the life" story about a group of friends and their money. As the group goes through the day, they repeatedly use money as a medium of exchange, a unit of account, and a store of value. The story should contain three examples of each use of money. Encourage students to be creative in detailing the escapades of their characters. GT

Economics Assessment Rubric
Economics Assessment Rubrics folder, pp. 6–7 provides sample evaluation materials for a writing assignment.

Learning Styles Activity
Learning Styles Lesson Plans folder, p. 25 asks student groups to evaluate the six characteristics of money in a cultural perspective.

Answer to . . .

Building Key Concepts The illustrations illustrate money's characteristics of portability, divisibility, acceptability, and durability.

Figure 10.1 The Three Functions of Money

Medium of Exchange	Unit of Account	Store of Value

Money serves as a medium of exchange, a unit of account, and a store of value.
Money How does each illustration represent a characteristic of money?

unit of account *a means for comparing the values of goods and services*

store of value *something that keeps its value if it is stored rather than used*

a medium of exchange. All you would have to do is find someone who is willing to pay you $100 for your VCR. Then you could use that money to buy a CD player from someone else. The person selling you the CD player can use the $100 however he or she wishes. By the same token, the person who buys your VCR can raise that money however he or she wishes. Because money makes exchanges so much easier, people have been using it for thousands of years.

Money as a Unit of Account

In addition to serving as a medium of exchange, money serves as a **unit of account.** In other words, money provides a means for comparing the values of goods and services. For example, suppose you see a jacket on sale for $30. You know this is a good price because you have checked the price of the same or similar jackets in other stores. You can compare the cost of the jacket in this store with the cost in other stores because the price is expressed in the same way in every store in the United States—in terms of dollars and cents. Similarly, you would expect a movie in the theater to cost about $7.00, a video rental about $3.50, and so forth.

Other countries have their own forms of money that serve as units of account. The Japanese quote prices in terms of yen, the Russians in terms of rubles, Mexicans in terms of nuevo pesos, and so forth.

Money as a Store of Value

Money also serves as a **store of value.** This means that money keeps its value if you decide to hold on to—or store—it instead of spending it. For example, when you sell your VCR to purchase a CD player, you might not have a chance to purchase a CD player right away. In the meantime, you can keep the money in your wallet or in a bank. The money will still be valuable and will be recognized as a medium of exchange weeks or months from now when you go to buy the CD player.

Money serves as a good store of value with one important exception. Sometimes economies experience a period of rapid inflation, or a general increase in prices. For example, suppose the United States experiences 10 percent inflation during a particular year. If you sold your VCR at the beginning of that year for $100, the money you received would have 10 percent less value, or buying power, at the

Econ 101: Key Concepts Made Easy

Supply and Demand To help students understand why money must be **scarce** to have any value, ask them to recall what they have learned about supply, demand, and prices. When the quantity supplied of a good or service is low and the quantity demanded is high, the good or service is more valuable than it would be otherwise. The same is true of money. If the supply were unlimited, its perceived value would fall, and eventually consumers would need huge sums of money to pay for even small things, from a haircut to a bag of groceries. By restricting the supply of money, the Federal Reserve keeps its value stable.

end of the year. This is because the price of the CD player would have increased by 10 percent during the year, to $110. The $100 you received at the beginning of the year would no longer be enough to buy the CD player.

In short, when an economy experiences inflation, money does not function as well as a store of value. You will read more about the causes and effects of inflation in Chapter 13.

The Six Characteristics of Money

The coins and paper bills used as money are called **currency.** In the past, societies have also used an astoundingly wide range of other objects as currency. Cattle, salt, dried fish, furs, precious stones, gold, and silver have all served as currency at various times in various places. So have porpoise teeth, rice, wheat, shells, tulip bulbs, and olive oil. These items all worked well in the societies in which they were used. None of them, however, would function very well in our economy today. Each lacks at least one of the six characteristics that economists use to judge how well an item serves as currency. These six characteristics are durability, portability, divisibility, uniformity, limited supply, and acceptability.

Durability

Objects used as money must withstand the physical wear and tear that comes with being used over and over again. If money wears out or is easily destroyed, it cannot be trusted to serve as a store of value.

Unlike wheat or olive oil, coins last for many years. In fact, some collectors have ancient Roman coins that are more than 2,000 years old. While our paper money may not seem very durable, its rag (cloth) content helps $1 bills typically last at least a year in circulation. When paper bills wear out, the United States government can easily replace them.

Portability

People need to be able to take money with them as they go about their daily business. They also must be able to easily transfer money from one person to another when they use money for purchases. Paper money and coins are very portable, or easily carried, because they are small and light.

Divisibility

To be useful, money must be easily divided into smaller denominations, or units of value. When money is divisible, people only have to use as much of it as necessary for any exchange. In the 16th and 17th centuries, people actually used pieces of coins to pay exact amounts for their purchases. Spanish coins called doubloons had lines scored or etched on

currency *coins and paper bills used as money*

▼ **Roman coins**

Figure 10.2 **Roman Empire, About Second Century A.D.**

Coins used throughout the Roman Empire provide a good example of the six characteristics of money. They were durable, portable, divisible into denominations, uniform, in limited supply, and accepted throughout the Empire.
Money What does the fact that Roman coins have been found in places as far from Rome as Britain and Egypt suggest about how well the coins served as currency?

Background

Interdisciplinary

The designs of U.S. paper currency feature many different illustrations. One of the most mysterious is the Great Seal of the United States that appears on the back of the one-dollar bill.

The face of the seal depicts a bald eagle. Above the eagle's head is a burst of light with 13 stars, representing the original 13 colonies. The eagle's right talons hold an olive branch with 13 leaves, representing peace. The left talons clutch 13 arrows, symbolizing war. The eagle's head is turned toward the olive branch to signal the nation's desire for peace. The shield on the eagle's breast includes 13 stripes. The motto *E Pluribus Unum* means "out of many, one."

The back of the seal shows an unfinished pyramid. The pyramid symbolizes strength and endurance. The fact that it is unfinished indicates that the nation is striving for growth and perfection. Above the pyramid is a triangle with an eye in the center, both set in a burst of light. The eye symbolizes divine guidance. Above the eye is another Latin motto, *Annuit Coeptis,* which means "He has favored our undertakings." At the base of the pyramid is engraved the date *1776* in Roman numerals. Below that appears still another Latin motto, *Novus Ordo Seclorum,* which means "a new order of the ages."

Differentiated Instruction

Choose seven students to prepare for and participate in a skit about the characteristics of money. Have six students each bring an article to class that does **not** fulfill a characteristic of useful money. A leaf from a tree is a good example because it is not durable. Each student should approach the seventh student—the "merchant"— and try to buy something with the money. The merchant should explain why it is not acceptable. SN

Block Scheduling Strategies

Consider these suggestions to take advantage of extended class time:

- Extend the Background note on this page by having students research and prepare reports on the symbolism found in coins. Students may present their reports orally or use material from them in a bulletin board display.
- Organize the class into groups of four to six students, and have groups search the Web site of the Bureau of Engraving and Printing for information on measures the government has taken to foil counterfeiters. Then discuss how new technologies continue to challenge the government's attempts to safeguard currency. Have students use the links provided in the *Economics: Principles in Action* segment of the Social Studies area at the following Web site: **www.phschool.com**

Answer to . . .

Building Key Concepts It suggests that they served well, since they were widely used.

Differentiated Instruction 

(Reteaching) Organize the class into groups of four. Display the following list of items: *sugar, emeralds, horses, coins, seashells,* and *government-issued currency.* Ask students in each group to evaluate each item with respect to its usefulness as money. Tell students to consider the six characteristics of money as they make their evaluations: durability, portability, divisibility, uniformity, scarcity, and acceptability. Have each group report its evaluations to the rest of the class.

Differentiated Instruction 

Ask students to research the history of money throughout the world and to construct an illustrated time line showing major milestones in the development of modern currency. If students are familiar with authoring software, encourage them to create an interactive time line that can be stored on a server or posted at an Internet site for others to use and enjoy. GT

them so that they could be easily divided into eight parts. Spanish coins, in fact, came to be called "pieces of eight."

Today, of course, if you use a $20 bill to pay for a $5 lunch, the cashier will not rip your bill into four pieces in order to make change. That's because American currency, like currencies around the world, consists of various denominations—$5 bills, $10 bills, and so on.

Uniformity

Any two units of money must be uniform—that is, the same—in terms of what they will buy. In other words, people must be able to count and measure money accurately.

Suppose everything were priced in terms of dried fish. One small dried fish might buy an apple. One large dried fish might buy a sandwich. This method of pricing is not a very accurate way of establishing the standard value of products because the size of a dried fish can vary. Picture the arguments people would have when trying to agree whether a fish was small or large. A dollar bill, however, always buys $1 worth of goods.

Limited Supply

Suppose a society uses certain pebbles as money. These pebbles have only been found on one beach. One day, however, someone finds an enormous supply of similar pebbles on a different beach. Now anyone can scoop up these pebbles by the handful. Since these pebbles are no longer in limited supply, they are no longer useful as currency.

commodity money *objects that have value in themselves and that are also used as money*

In the United States, the Federal Reserve System controls the supply of money in circulation. By its actions, the Federal Reserve is able to keep just the right amount of money available. You'll read more about how the Federal Reserve monitors and adjusts the money supply in Chapter 16.

Acceptability

Finally, everyone in an economy must be able to exchange the objects that serve as money for goods and services. When you go to the store, why does the person behind the counter accept your money in exchange for a carton of milk or a box of pencils? After all, money is just pieces of metal or paper. Your money is accepted because the owner of the store can spend it elsewhere to buy something he or she needs or wants.

In the United States, we expect that other people in the country will continue to accept paper money and coins in exchange for our purchases. If people suddenly lost confidence in our currency's value, they would no longer be willing to sell goods and services in return for dollars. (See *Global Connections* below to learn more about what happens when people lose confidence in their country's currency.)

Sources of Money's Value

Think about the bills and coins in your pocket. They are durable and portable. They are also easily divisible, uniform, in limited supply, and accepted throughout the country. As convenient and practical as they may be, however, bills and coins have very little value in and of themselves. What, then, makes money valuable? The answer is that there are actually several possible sources of money's value, depending on whether the money is commodity, representative, or fiat money.

Commodity Money

A commodity is an object. **Commodity money** consists of objects that have value in and of

Global Connections

The Ruble Russia's currency is facing trouble as a store of value. In 1998, it was devalued by the official Russian state bank from 6.3 rubles to the dollar to 9.5 rubles to the dollar. This slippage hurt average Russians, as their savings were now worth only two thirds of their previous value. Many Russians turned to buying American dollars with the rubles they had left, fearing another devaluation and having more faith in the stability of the dollar. By 2003, the ruble was valued at 31 to the dollar, or about 3.2 cents.

Preparing for Standardized Tests

Have students read the section titled "The Six Characteristics of Money" and then answer the question below.

The Federal Reserve controls the supply of money that is in circulation. This results in the following characteristic of money:

A acceptability
(B) scarcity
C uniformity
D divisibility

Figure 10.3 Sources of Money's Value

Commodity money

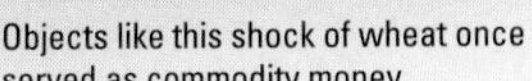

Objects like this shock of wheat once served as commodity money.

Representative money

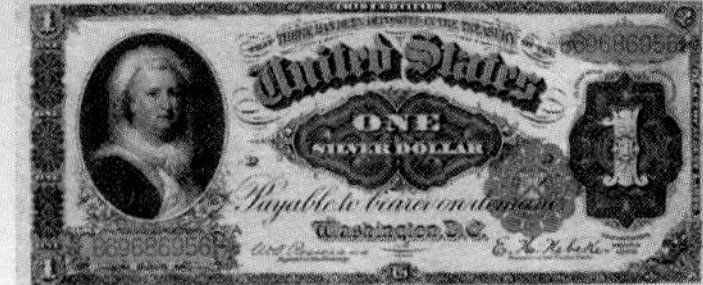

Representative money like this silver certificate could be exchanged for silver.

Fiat money

Today, Federal Reserve notes are fiat money, decreed by the federal government to be an acceptable way to pay debts.

Americans used both commodity and representative money during the colonial period. Representative money was used until 1913, when the first Federal Reserve notes were issued. **Money** **What are the advantages of fiat money over commodity and representative money?**

themselves and that are also used as money. For example, salt, cattle, and precious stones have been used in various societies as commodity money. These objects have other uses as well. If not used as money, salt can preserve food and make it tastier. Cattle can be slaughtered for their meat, and gems can be made into jewelry. Tobacco, corn, and cotton all served as commodity money in the American colonies.

As you can guess, commodity money tends to lack several of the characteristics that make objects good sources of money. For example, it is often not portable, durable, or divisible. That's why commodity money only works in simple economies. As the American colonies developed more complex economic systems, tobacco and other objects were no longer universally accepted as money. The colonies needed a more convenient payment system. They turned to representative money to meet their needs.

Representative Money

Representative money makes use of objects that have value because the holder can exchange them for something else of value. For example, if your brother gives you an IOU, the piece of paper itself is worth nothing. The promise that he will do all of your chores for a month may be worth quite a lot, however. The piece of paper simply represents his promise to you.

Early representative money took the form of paper receipts for gold and silver. Gold or silver money was heavy and thus inconvenient for customers and merchants to carry around. Each time someone made a transaction, the coins would have to be weighed and tested for purity. People therefore started to leave their gold in goldsmiths' safes. Customers would carry paper ownership receipts from the goldsmith to show how much gold they owned. After a while merchants began to accept goldsmiths' receipts instead of the gold itself. In this way, the paper receipts became an early form of paper money.

Colonists in the Massachusetts Bay Colony first used representative money in the late 1600s when the Colony's treasurer issued bills of credit to lenders to help finance King William's War. The bills of credit showed the exact amount that colonists had loaned to the Massachusetts government. Billholders could redeem the

representative money *objects that have value because the holder can exchange them for something else of value*

Background

Common Misconceptions

For centuries diamonds have been accorded almost mythic status throughout the world. In many western cultures today it is the gift of a diamond that symbolizes the promise of undying love, a promise reflected in the advertising slogan, "A diamond is forever."

This symbol of eternal love, however, has its price. Diamonds are among the world's most expensive gems, and many people assume that diamonds are valuable because of their scarcity. It turns out, however, that diamonds are not as scarce as some people would like them to be. In fact, were it not for the vigilance of De Beers Consolidated Mines Ltd., diamonds might last just as long but not be nearly as expensive.

De Beers is the South African diamond mining company that in 1992 controlled approximately 80 percent of the world's diamond sales. De Beers leads a cartel, the Central Selling Organization (CSO), that dictates the terms for diamond selling and pricing around the world. When some nations began to circumvent the CSO and sell directly to dealers during the 1990s, De Beers grew concerned. If the supply of diamonds were uncontrolled, their value would plummet—especially since demand had been falling. For this reason, De Beers began buying up the excess diamonds. In 1992 De Beers spent $350 million on diamond purchases from Angola alone. Diamonds are valuable because De Beers hoards the supply and releases only as many diamonds as the market can sell at a high price.

Interdisciplinary Connections: History

Wampum and Exchange *Wampum* is a Native American word for white and purple beads carved from seashells. Making wampum was time-intensive and required great skill. Wampum beads were about ⅛ inch in diameter and ¼ inch long. Each brittle bead had a tiny hole drilled through the center, and the beads were often strung or sewn onto fabric or animal skins. Thousands of beads might be used to make belts, which were exchanged as pledges. Important events were often recorded in special designs. The early Dutch and English settlers in North America adopted the Native American wampum as their initial currency. This use declined in the middle 1600s, when metal coins became available.

Making the Connection Ask students to evaluate wampum according to the three uses and the six characteristics of money.

Answer to . . .

Building Key Concepts Fiat money is more convenient than commodity or representative money, and the government can stabilize its value by limiting its supply.

GTE Guide to the Essentials
Chapter 10, Section 1, p. 42 provides support for students who need additional review of the section content. Spanish support is available in the Spanish edition of the guide on p. 42.

Quiz Unit 4 folder, p. 3 includes questions to check students' understanding of Section 1 content.

Presentation Pro CD-ROM
Quiz provides multiple-choice questions to check students' understanding of Section 1 content.

Answers to . . .

Section 1 Assessment

1. Money serves as a store of value by retaining worth even though goods are not immediately purchased with it.
2. (a) corn, cattle, precious stones (b) bills of credit, IOUs (c) U.S. currency
3. The face value of U.S. currency is decreed by the federal government.
4. Disadvantages of commodity money vary depending on the commodity but often include lack of portability, durability, or divisibility.
5. Continentals became worthless because people came to believe that they would not be able to redeem them for specie, since the federal treasury held little gold or silver.
6. Students may say that they can shop around for the best bargain, knowing that their money will retain its value.
7. Neither would make good money. Movie tickets lack divisibility, uniformity, scarcity, and acceptability. Popcorn lacks durability, divisibility, uniformity, scarcity, and acceptability.
8. Selling the hockey stick for money is the best solution because the money functions as an accepted medium of exchange. It might be difficult to find someone who wants to exchange a calculator for a hockey stick, but it is relatively simple to sell a hockey stick and to buy a calculator.
9. Student proposals should meet the six characteristics of money. They should choose a durable metal, for example, but not one that is too plentiful.
10. Students' answers should demonstrate understanding of the concept of bartering. For example, students may suggest that they might have trouble settling on a price or that they might not have something of appropriate value to offer in barter.

FAST FACT

Some government agencies estimate that only about one third of all existing pennies are in circulation. The rest sit in jars, fountains, desk drawers, and pockets. Many merchants would prefer to do away with pennies altogether and round up prices to the nearest nickel. While pennies seem insignificant, however, rounding up to the nearest nickel could cost American consumers approximately $600 million per year.

paper for specie, that is, gold and silver coins.

Representative money was not without its problems. During the American Revolution, the Second Continental Congress issued representative money called Continentals to finance the war against England. Unfortunately, few people were able to redeem these early paper currencies for specie because the federal government had no power to collect taxes. Until the Constitution replaced the Articles of Confederation in 1789, the federal government depended on the states' voluntary contributions to fill the treasury. As a result, the federal treasury held very little gold or silver. Continentals became worthless because people came to believe that they would not be able to redeem their bills for gold and silver coins. People even began to use the phrase "not worth a Continental" to refer to something useless.

fiat money *money that has value because the government has ordered that it is an acceptable means to pay debts*

Later, the United States government issued representative money in the form of silver and gold certificates. These certificates were "backed" by gold or silver. In other words, holders of such certificates could redeem them for gold or silver at a local bank. The United States government thus had to keep vast supplies of gold and silver on hand to be able to convert all paper dollars to gold if the demand arose. Some silver certificates circulated until 1971, but for the most part, the government stopped converting paper money into silver or gold in the 1930s.

Fiat Money

If you examine a dollar bill, you will see George Washington's picture on one side, and on the other side the words, "This note is legal tender for all debts, public and private." In essence, these words mean that our money is valuable because our government says it is.

United States money today is fiat money. A fiat is an order or decree. **Fiat money,** also called "legal tender," has value because the government has decreed that it is an acceptable means to pay debts. It remains in limited supply, and therefore valuable, because the Federal Reserve controls its supply. This control of the money supply is essential for a fiat system to work.

Section 1 Assessment

Progress Monitoring *Online*
For: Self-quiz with vocabulary practice
Web Code: mna-4105

Key Terms and Main Ideas

1. How does **money** serve as a **store of value?**
2. Give examples of (a) **commodity money,** (b) **representative money,** and (c) **fiat money.**
3. Why does United States **currency** have value?
4. What are the disadvantages of **commodity money?**
5. Why did Continentals become worthless?

Applying Economic Concepts

6. ***Critical Thinking*** Suppose you are shopping for a new backpack and want to get the best value for your money. Explain how the fact that money functions as a unit of account helps you to make your choice.
7. ***Try This*** Would movie tickets or popcorn make good money? Describe how well these items meet each of the six characteristics of an ideal currency.
8. ***Decision Making*** Suppose you need a graphing calculator. Should you plan to trade your hockey stick for one or should you try to sell your hockey stick and use the money to buy one from a classmate? Explain your reasoning.
9. ***Problem Solving*** What material(s) would you use if you were creating a new United States coin? Why?
10. ***Critical Thinking*** Suppose you live in a society that has a barter economy. What difficulties might you encounter in paying for such services as medical care and education?

For: Internet Activity
Visit: PHSchool.com
Web Code: mnd-4101

Progress Monitoring *Online*
For additional assessment, have students access Progress Monitoring Online at **Web Code:** mna-4105

Go Online PHSchool.com Typing in the Web Code when prompted will bring students directly to detailed instructions for this activity.

Skills for LIFE

Understanding Public Opinion Polls

Public opinion polls measure what people think about a particular subject. Although pollsters take several steps to ensure that their results mirror the population as a whole, there are many pitfalls. For example, the same question phrased in different ways can result in widely different answers, even if all the questions are essentially the same. Because a poll can only measure a small sample of the population, pollsters include a statistical margin of error that indicates the degree to which the poll is accurate for the entire population. Public opinion polls should be read critically to understand exactly what they say. Use the following steps to analyze the hypothetical poll below.

1. **Establish the purpose of the poll.** Read the statements in the poll. (a) What is the subject of the poll. (b) What, specifically, were people asked?

2. **Analyze the response.** Look at the change in the rate of people who agreed with the statements as the statements changed. A politician reading only the responses to the first question might assume that the American people would support an expensive system of free clinics. (a) Which details seemed to provoke a negative reaction? (b) Can we say that a majority of Americans would agree with statement B? Why or why not?

3. **Expand upon the original question.** The lessons learned from one poll can help make the next poll more accurate. If you were a politician trying to obtain accurate and precise information about the public's opinions on health care, how might you rephrase the questions in the poll?

Health Care Poll

"The government today does not spend enough to provide all Americans, including the 40 million Americans without health insurance, with good health care. Keeping this in mind, do you agree or disagree with the following statements?"

	I Agree	I Disagree
A. "Every American should have access to good health care."	64%	36%
B. "The government should guarantee that every American has good health care."	53%	47%
C. "The government should spend more to guarantee that every American has good health care."	42%	58%

Note: Random sample of 1,400 people surveyed by phone; margin of error ± 4 percent

Additional Practice

Use the Internet to find the results of a recent poll. Look at the question or questions asked. How does the pollster try to keep the question as neutral as possible?

Interdisciplinary Connections: Language Arts

Spotting Persuasive Techniques Language can be manipulated in many ways to obscure a person's real meaning or intent. False logic, biased word choice, and other linguistic techniques may be used by public speakers, advertisers, and persuasive writers to convince listeners or readers to support a point of view or buy a product.

Have students work through the following activity: Ask students to read and analyze the introduction to the poll presented on this page. Ask them to explain how reading this introduction could affect the response a person gives to the poll taker. Then have students rewrite the introduction to make it less biased.

Skills for LIFE

Understanding Public Opinion Polls

1. Focus Public opinion polls assess the public's ideas. The questions asked and the results obtained, however, must be carefully analyzed to detect bias or inaccuracy.

2. Instruct Ask students to list the types of situations that typically initiate public opinion polls. Reinforce the importance of analyzing and evaluating questions and responses for the validity of the source for bias, propaganda, point of view, and frame of reference. Point out that poorly worded questions or inadequate analysis of responses can lead to inaccurate results. Then have students work through the three steps presented in the skills feature.

3. Close/Reteach For additional practice, see the Economic Skills Activity below.

Economic Skills Activity
Unit 4 folder, p. 8, "Understanding Public Opinion Polls," asks students to analyze a poll on banking fees and services.

Social Studies Skills Tutor CD-ROM offers interactive practice in critical thinking and reading, visual analysis, and communication.

Answers

1. (a) the American health care system (b) whether or not they agreed or disagreed with several statements about the American health care system
2. (a) mention of guarantee and increased government spending (b) No. The margin of error of the percentage could drop below a majority.
3. Students' answers should demonstrate an understanding of the flaws in the poll questions shown. They may say that they would ask about a specific program or for agreement or disagreement about specific program features.

Additional Practice

Students should be able to locate a poll on the Internet and demonstrate how the pollster kept the questions neutral.

Section 2

The History of American Banking

Objectives You may wish to call students' attention to the objectives in the Section Preview. The objectives are reflected in the main headings of the section.

Bellringer Have students look at the front of a dollar bill. Ask who, if anyone, knows what "Federal Reserve Note" means. Tell students that in this section they will learn about the creation of the Federal Reserve System.

Vocabulary Builder Have students read the section to learn the meaning of each key term. Then ask them to write a question for each of the key terms. Each question should be worded so that the key term is the correct answer.

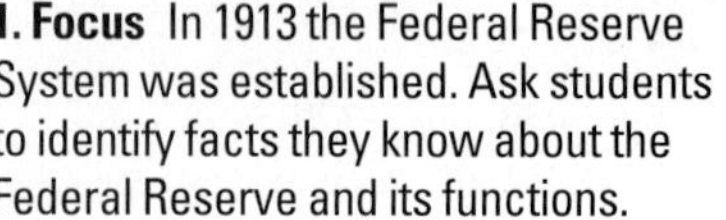

Lesson Plan

Teaching the Main Concepts L3

1. Focus In 1913 the Federal Reserve System was established. Ask students to identify facts they know about the Federal Reserve and its functions.

2. Instruct Begin by discussing the disagreements between the Federalists and Antifederalists over the need for a national bank. Then explain the difficulties that ensued during the period known as the Free Banking Era. Discuss the establishment of the Federal Reserve System and the banking reforms that followed the Great Depression. Finally, explain developments in banking during the twentieth century.

3. Close/Reteach Ask students to identify ways in which the banking system has changed since the birth of our nation.

Answer to . . .

Photo Caption Hamilton favored a national bank; Jefferson opposed it.

Section 2

The History of American Banking

Preview

Objectives

After studying this section you will be able to:

1. **Describe** the shifts between centralized and decentralized banking before the Civil War.
2. **Explain** how the banking system was stabilized in the later 1800s.
3. **Describe** developments in banking during the twentieth century.

Section Focus

The history of banking in the United States is the story of shifts between a centralized, national banking system and independent state and local banks. Out of these shifts has developed the stable banking system in which we place our confidence today.

Key Terms

bank
national bank
bank run
greenback
gold standard
Federal Reserve System
central bank
member bank
Federal Reserve note
Great Depression
Federal Deposit Insurance Corporation (FDIC)

bank *an institution for receiving, keeping, and lending money*

▲ What were the views of Alexander Hamilton (top) and Thomas Jefferson (bottom) on the creation of a national bank?

Chances are there is at least one **bank**—an institution for receiving, keeping, and lending money—near your home. That's because banks have become a fact of everyday life in the United States. This was not always the case, however. American banking as we know it today has developed over the course of the nation's history to meet the needs of a growing and changing population.

American Banking Before the Civil War

During the first part of our nation's history, banks were very informal businesses that merchants managed in addition to their regular trade. For example, a merchant who sold cloth, grain, or other goods might allow customers to deposit money. He would then charge a small fee to keep the money safe. He would also charge a fee if a customer wanted to take out a loan. These informal banks were not completely safe, however. If a merchant went out of business or was untrustworthy, customers could lose all of their savings.

Two Views of Banking

After the American Revolution, the leaders of the new nation agreed that one of their main goals must be to establish a safe, stable banking system. Such a system was important for increasing trade with other countries and ensuring the economic growth of the new United States. The nation's leaders did not, however, agree on how that goal should be accomplished. Their debate on banking during the 1780s and 1790s was part of a larger political debate about the role of government in the young country.

As you may remember from your study of American history, the Federalists believed that the country needed a strong central government to establish economic and social order. The Antifederalists favored leaving most powers in the hands of the states. These two groups viewed the country's banking needs quite differently.

The Federalists, led by Alexander Hamilton, believed that a centralized banking system was necessary for the United States to develop healthy industries and trade. When President Washington appointed Hamilton as Secretary of the Treasury in 1789, Hamilton proposed a

Graphing the Main Idea

Economic Institutions To build understanding of the concept of **economic institutions**, have students complete a flowchart graphic organizer like the one shown at the right. Remind students that a flowchart shows a sequence of events. Tell them to show important events in American banking from the early part of U.S. history through the twentieth century.

Section Reading Support Transparencies A template and the answers for this graphic organizer can be found in Chapter 10, Section 2 of the Section Reading Support Transparency System.

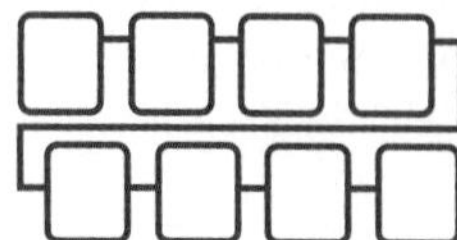

national bank (a bank chartered, or licensed, by the national government) that could issue a single currency for the entire nation, manage the federal government's funds, and monitor other banks throughout the country.

The Antifederalists, however, led by Thomas Jefferson, supported a decentralized banking system. In this system, the states would establish and regulate all banks within their borders.

The First Bank of the United States

At first, the Federalists were successful in creating a strong central bank. In 1791, Congress set up the Bank of the United States, granting it a twenty-year charter, or license to operate. The United States Treasury used the Bank for the following purposes:

- to hold the money that the government collected in taxes
- to help the government carry out its powers to tax, borrow money in the public interest, and regulate interstate and foreign commerce
- to issue representative money in the form of bank notes, which were backed by gold and silver
- to ensure that state-chartered banks held sufficient gold and silver to exchange for bank notes should the demand arise

The Bank succeeded in bringing order and stability to American banking. Many people worried, however, that the Bank would lend only to wealthy people and large businesses. They feared that ordinary people who needed to borrow money to maintain or expand their farms and small businesses would be refused loans. In addition, Jefferson and other Antifederalists pointed out that the Constitution does not explicitly give Congress the power to create a national bank. Therefore, they argued, the creation of a national bank was unconstitutional. When Alexander Hamilton died in a famous duel with Vice President Aaron Burr in 1804, the Bank lost its main backer. The Bank functioned only until 1811, when its charter ran out.

Chaos in American Banking

Once the Bank's charter expired, state banks (banks chartered by state governments) began issuing bank notes that they could not back with specie, or gold and silver coins. The states also chartered many banks without considering whether these banks would be stable and creditworthy.

Without any kind of supervision or regulation, financial confusion resulted. Prices rose rapidly. Neither merchants nor customers had confidence in the value of the paper money in circulation. Different banks issued different currencies, and bankers always faced the temptation to print more money than they had gold and silver to back. Merchants had to keep lists of which notes were redeemable by gold and silver and which were not.

The Second Bank of the United States

To eliminate this financial chaos, Congress chartered the Second Bank of the United States in 1816. Like the first Bank, the Second Bank was limited to a twenty-year charter. The Second Bank slowly managed to rebuild the public's confidence in a national banking system, although many people, including President Andrew Jackson, continued to oppose the idea.

national bank *a bank chartered, or licensed, by the national government*

▲ **In this cartoon, Andrew Jackson drags bank supporter Henry Clay behind him as he attacks the monster national bank. How does the artist suggest that the danger is not real?**

Guided Reading and Review
Unit 4 folder, p. 4 asks students to identify the main ideas of the section and to define or identify key terms.

Differentiated Instruction L3

(Reteaching) Have students construct a captioned time line that details important events in the history of U.S. banking before the Civil War. As students work their way through the first three pages of the section, have them add to their time lines. Ask students to construct their time lines so that they clearly display the shifts between centralized and decentralized banking before the Civil War. For example, they may show moves toward centralized banking above the line and moves toward decentralized banking below, or they may show the two in different colors of ink.

Differentiated Instruction L2

Ask students to copy the three main headings of this section onto a sheet of paper. Then have them write five important facts from each section under each heading. Remind students that the subheadings within each main heading give clues as to the most important concepts. LPR

Econ 101: Key Concepts Made Easy

Money If students have trouble understanding how the **gold standard** was used to secure U.S. currency, ask them to think about how a checking account operates. Checking account holders can issue checks totaling only as much money as they have deposited into their accounts. Merchants and others accept the checks on faith—that is, they trust that the checks are covered by deposits. Similarly, people accepted government currency on faith, believing that the government had enough gold reserves to cover the currency. Because gold had been a valued commodity since ancient times, currency backed by gold inspired trust and confidence.

Answer to . . .

Cartoon Caption The bank is represented by a mythical creature and the action is highly exaggerated.

Differentiated Instruction 

After students have read "The Second Bank of the United States," ask them to explain how Nicholas Biddle challenged the state banks to prove that they had the reserves to back up the currency they issued. ELL

Meeting NCEE Standards

Use the following benchmark activity from the **Voluntary National Content Standards in Economics** to evaluate student understanding of **Standard 10.**

Predict what might happen if there were no legal way to settle boundary disputes or if every state had its own system of weights and measures or currency; explain how liability for product defects affects the behavior of consumers and producers and how it affects the price of a good or service.

Go Online PHSchool.com Typing in the Web Code when prompted will bring students directly to the article.

THE WALL STREET JOURNAL. CLASSROOM EDITION

For an additional article from *The Wall Street Journal Classroom Edition,* see the Source Articles folder in the **Teaching Resources**, pp. 30–32.

Transparency Resource Package
Economics Concepts, 10B: Metallic Content of U.S. Coins

▲ **During the Free Banking Era (1837–1863), state-chartered banks and even individual companies issued their own currency. What were some of the difficulties that arose from this practice?**

bank run *widespread panic in which great numbers of people try to redeem their paper money*

Nicholas Biddle, the Second Bank's president starting in 1823, was responsible for restoring stability. If Biddle thought that a particular state bank was issuing bank notes without enough reserves (that is, gold and silver to back them), he would surprise the bank with a great number of its notes all at once, asking for gold or silver in return. Some state banks, caught without the necessary reserves, went out of business. Others quickly learned to limit how many notes they issued.

Despite the difficulties arising from decentralized banking, many people continued to distrust the federal government's banking power. In addition, although the Supreme Court had ruled a national bank constitutional in 1819, the same groups who had opposed the first Bank also opposed the Second Bank. Finally, President Jackson's extreme distrust of the Second Bank led him to veto the renewal of the Bank in 1832.

THE WALL STREET JOURNAL. CLASSROOM EDITION

In the News Read more about U.S. currency in "New Colors For the Greenback," an article in The Wall Street Journal Classroom Edition.

The Wall Street Journal Classroom Edition

For: Current Events
Visit: PHSchool.com
Web Code: mnc-4102

The Free Banking Era

The fall of the Second Bank once again triggered a period dominated by state-chartered banks. For this reason, the period between 1837 and 1863 is known as the Free Banking, or "Wildcat," Era. Between 1830 and 1837 alone, the number of state-chartered banks nearly tripled. As you might expect, the sheer number of banks and currencies gave rise to a variety of problems.

1. *Bank runs and panics* State-chartered banks often did not keep enough gold and silver to back the paper money that they issued. Customers found it increasingly difficult to exchange their paper money for gold and silver, setting off **bank runs.** These were widespread panics in which great numbers of people tried to redeem their paper money at once. Many banks failed as a result, and public confidence plummeted. An especially severe panic occurred in 1837.
2. *Wildcat banks* Some banks were located on the edges of settled areas. They were called "wildcat banks" because people joked that only wildcats lived in such remote areas. Wildcat banks had a high rate of failure.
3. *Fraud* A few banks engaged in out-and-out fraud, or cheating. They issued bank notes, collected gold and silver money from customers who bought the notes, and then disappeared. Anyone who had bought the notes lost their money.
4. *Many different currencies* State-chartered banks—as well as cities, private banks, railroads, stores, churches, and individuals—were allowed to issue currency. Notes of the same denominations often had different values, so that a dollar issued by the "City of Atlanta" was not necessarily worth the same as a dollar issued by the "City of New York." Many notes were counterfeits, or worthless imitations of real notes.

The Later 1800s

By 1860, an estimated 8,000 different banks were circulating currency. To add to the confusion, the federal government played no role in providing paper currency or regulating reserves of gold or silver. The

Block Scheduling Strategies

Consider these suggestions to take advantage of extended class time:

- Show the Economics Video Library segment "The Euro, Part 1," about the history of Europe's struggle for a unified currency. After viewing the segment ask students to draw comparisons and contrasts between the struggles described in this video and the currency problems that occurred in the young United States.
- Have groups of three to four students research the savings and loan crisis of the late 1980s and early 1990s. Ask each group to prepare a report that addresses such questions as how the crisis began, how it was resolved, and what action has been taken to prevent a similar crisis from recurring. Allow time for students to present their reports to the class.

Answer to . . .

Photo Caption Notes had different value and merchants could not tell whether the bills would be redeemable or valuable.

Civil War, which erupted in 1861, made existing problems worse.

Currency in the North and South

During the Civil War, both the Union and Confederacy needed to raise money to finance their military efforts. In 1861, the United States Treasury issued its first paper currency since the Continental. The official name of the currency was "demand notes," but they were called **"greenbacks"** because they were printed with green ink.

In the South, the Confederacy issued currency backed by cotton, hoping that a Confederate victory would ensure the currency's value. As the Confederate economy suffered under the strain of the war, however, Confederate notes became worthless.

Unifying American Banks

With war raging, the federal government enacted reforms aimed at restoring confidence in paper currency. These reforms resulted in the National Banking Acts of 1863 and 1864. Together, these Acts gave the federal government three important powers:

1. the power to charter banks
2. the power to require banks to hold adequate gold and silver reserves to cover their bank notes
3. the power to issue a single national currency

The new national currency led to the elimination of the many different state currencies in use and helped stabilize the country's money supply.

The Gold Standard

Despite the reforms made during the Civil War, the country was still plagued by money and banking problems. In the 1870s, the nation adopted a **gold standard**—a monetary system in which paper money and coins are equal to the value of a certain amount of gold. The gold standard had two advantages:

1. It set a definite value for the dollar, so that one ounce of gold equaled about $20. Since the value was set, people knew that they could redeem the value of their paper money at any time. Confident in that knowledge, people felt comfortable carrying around the lighter and more convenient paper money.
2. The government could issue currency only if it had gold in the treasury to back the notes. Because of the limited supply of gold, the government was prevented from printing an unlimited number of notes.

The gold standard thus fulfilled an essential requirement of a banking system: a stable currency that inspires the confidence of the public.

Banking in the Early Twentieth Century

Reforms such as the creation of a single national currency and the gold standard helped stabilize American banking. They did not, however, provide for a central decision-making authority. Such an authority could help banks provide funds

greenback *paper currency issued during the Civil War*

gold standard *a monetary system in which paper money and coins are equal to the value of a certain amount of gold*

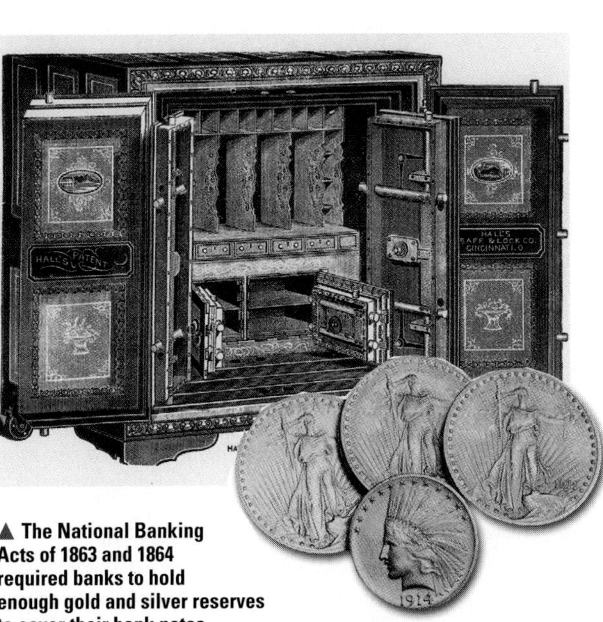

▲ The National Banking Acts of 1863 and 1864 required banks to hold enough gold and silver reserves to cover their bank notes.

Background

Biography

William Jennings Bryan will be remembered for many accomplishments, among them the fiery speech in which he attacked the gold standard at the 1896 Democratic National Convention. In 1890 Bryan was elected to Congress, where he made his mark as an opponent of high tariffs and a proponent of the Free Silver Movement, which advocated coining silver dollars. The silver dollar had been omitted from the list of authorized coins by an act of Congress in 1873.

In Chicago on July 8, 1896, Bryan strode to the podium at the Democratic National Convention and delivered what has become one of the most famous speeches in American politics. In defense of the Free Silver Movement, Bryan challenged the idea that U.S. currency should be backed by gold. He ended his impassioned speech by declaring, "You shall not press down upon the brow of labor this crown of thorns, you shall not crucify mankind upon a cross of gold." The Republicans won the election, however, and enacted the Gold Standard Act in 1900.

Among the supporters of the Free Silver Movement were both silver-mine owners and farmers who hoped that an expanded currency would allow them to obtain higher prices for their crops. The movement died after discoveries of gold in Alaska increased the supply of gold.

Differentiated Instruction  L3

Have students write paragraphs in which they describe the progression from chaos and confusion in banking (before the Civil War) to relative stability (by 1900). Remind them to describe the role of the National Banking Acts of 1863 and 1864 and the shift to the gold standard.

Preparing for Standardized Tests

Have students read the section titled "Unifying American Banks" and then answer the question below.

Which of the following powers was not granted to the government in the National Banking Acts of 1863 and 1864?

A power to charter banks
B power to require banks to hold adequate gold and silver reserves
(C) power to adopt the gold standard
D power to issue a single national currency backed by government bonds

Differentiated Instruction L3

As the year 2000 approached, many dire predictions circulated throughout the United States about the calamities that would befall the nation on January 1, beginning at the stroke of midnight—all due to the fact that many computers and software programs would be unable to recognize the new date. One scenario suggested that people would withdraw so much money from banks prior to the new year that the Federal Reserve would be unable to maintain a stable money supply, a responsibility with which they had been charged by the Federal Reserve Act of 1913.

Ask students to research how the Federal Reserve prepared for the year 2000. Have them write brief reports on what actually occurred.

Differentiated Instruction L3

(Reteaching) Have students review developments in banking during the twentieth century by creating a series of newspaper headlines that might have been seen between 1900 and 1989. Then tell them to choose one of the headlines and write a short newspaper story about the event. Have students examine newspapers of the times on microfilm in order to create headlines and articles with an authentic flavor.

Learning Styles Activity
Learning Styles Lesson Plans folder, p. 26 asks student groups to create a time line of American banking.

Figure 10.4 Developments in American Banking

Date	Development	Example
1780s	The nation has no reliable medium of exchange. Federalists and Antifederalists disagree about a banking system.	▶ 1780s Continental
1791	First Bank of the United States is established.	
1811–1816	Period of instability follows expiration of First Bank's charter.	
1816	Second Bank of the United States reestablishes stability.	
1830s–1860s	President Jackson vetoes recharter of Second Bank in 1832, giving rise to Free Banking Era.	
1861–1863	Civil War makes clear the need for a better monetary and banking system.	◀ 1861–1863 Greenback
1863–1864	National Banking Acts of 1863 and 1864 establish national banking system and uniform national currency.	
1907	Panic of 1907 leads to creation of the Federal Reserve System.	
1913	President Wilson signs the Federal Reserve Act.	
1929	The Great Depression begins.	
1933	President Roosevelt helps restore confidence in the nation's banks by establishing the FDIC.	▶ 1933 FDIC
1940s–1960s	Period of government regulation and long-term stability	
Late 1960s–1970s	New laws make clear the rights and responsibilities of banks and consumers.	
1980s	Period of deregulation; S&Ls face bankruptcies	
2000s	After two decades of mergers, the banking system emerges stable and healthy.	

The history of American banking shows a series of shifts between stability and instability.
Government What does the chart suggest about the role of government in banking during the twentieth century?

Federal Reserve System *the nation's central banking system*

central bank *bank that can lend to other banks in times of need*

member bank *bank that belongs to the Federal Reserve System*

for growth and manage the money supply based on what the economy needed.

Continuing problems in the nation's banking system resulted in the Panic of 1907. Because they lacked adequate reserves, many banks had to stop exchanging gold for paper money. Several long-standing New York banks failed, and many people lost their jobs because businesses did not have access to money for investing in future projects. Clearly, the economy needed a central banking system so that the country could avoid such panics in the future. As a result of the 1907 crisis, the government made plans to reinstate a central bank.

The Federal Reserve System

Passed in late 1913, the Federal Reserve Act established the **Federal Reserve System.** The Federal Reserve System, or Fed, served as the nation's first true **central bank,** or bank that can lend to other banks in time of need. It reorganized the federal banking system as follows:

- *Member banks* The system created up to twelve regional Federal Reserve Banks throughout the country. All banks chartered by the national government were required to become members of the Fed. The Federal Reserve Banks were the central banks for their districts. **Member banks**—banks that belong to the Fed—stored some of their cash reserves at the Federal Reserve Bank in their district.
- *Federal Reserve Board* All of the Federal Reserve Banks were supervised by a Federal Reserve Board appointed by the President of the United States.
- *Short-term loans* Each of the regional Federal Reserve Banks allowed member

Interdisciplinary Connections: History

Wall Street Since before the Civil War, Wall Street has been recognized as the nation's financial center. This narrow, seven-block street in Manhattan was named after an earthen wall built by Dutch settlers in 1653. The wall was intended to act as a barrier against an expected English invasion.

Making the Connection Ask each student to make a list of 5 to 10 terms he or she associates with Wall Street. The terms may be current or historical. *(Students may suggest terms such as* trading, the crash, stock market, commodities, *and so on.)* Combine their lists, and discuss the significance of Wall Street and other financial districts in the history of the United States.

Answer to . . .

Building Key Concepts The government has played an increasingly important role in maintaining bank stability in the twentieth century.

banks to borrow money to meet short-term demands. This helped to prevent bank failures that occurred when large numbers of depositors withdrew funds during a panic.

- *Federal Reserve notes* The system also created the national currency we use today in the United States—**Federal Reserve notes.** This allowed the Federal Reserve to increase and decrease the amount of money in circulation according to business needs.

You will read more about the role of the Federal Reserve and how the system works today in Chapter 16.

Banking and the Great Depression

The Fed helped to restore confidence in the nation's banking system. It was unable, however, to prevent the terrifying **Great Depression**—the severe economic decline that began in 1929 and lasted more than a decade.

During the 1920s, banks loaned large sums of money to many high-risk businesses. Many of these businesses proved unable to pay back their loans. Farmers were also unable to pay back loans due to crop failures and hard times on the nation's farms. In addition, the 1929 stock market crash resulted in widespread bank runs as nervous depositors rushed to withdraw their money. The combination of unpaid loans and bank runs resulted in the failure of thousands of banks across the country.

Banking Reforms

After becoming President in 1933, Franklin D. Roosevelt acted to restore public confidence in the nation's banking system. On March 5, 1933, Roosevelt declared a national "bank holiday" and closed the nation's banks. Within a matter of days, sound banks began to reopen. The "bank holiday" was not a time of festivities, as the name implies, but a desperate last resort to restore trust in the nation's financial system.

Later in 1933, Congress passed the act that established the **Federal Deposit Insurance Corporation (FDIC).** The FDIC insures customer deposits if a bank fails. At first, FDIC insurance covered losses up to $2,500. Today the amount insured has risen to $100,000 per account.

In addition, federal legislation passed during the Great Depression severely restricted individuals' ability to redeem dollars for gold. Eventually, currency became fiat money backed only by the government's decree that establishes its value. In this way, the Federal Reserve could maintain a money supply at adequate levels to support a growing economy.

Banking in the Later Twentieth Century

As a result of the many bank failures of the Great Depression, banks were closely regulated from 1933 through the 1960s. Restrictions included the interest rates banks could pay depositors and the rates that banks could charge consumers for loans. Banks could also lend money only to customers who had a history of paying back loans on time.

By the 1970s, banks were eager for relief from federal regulation. In the late 1970s and 1980s, Congress passed laws to deregulate several industries. Deregulation

Federal Reserve note *the national currency we use today in the United States*

Great Depression *the severe economic decline that began in 1929 and lasted for more than a decade*

Federal Deposit Insurance Corporation (FDIC) *the government agency that insures customer deposits if a bank fails*

▼ Widespread bank runs at the start of the Great Depression led to the failure of thousands of banks nationwide.

Background

Economics in History

When President Franklin Roosevelt took office on March 4, 1933, the bank crisis had reached a critical juncture. Some states had even suspended all banking activities in an effort to stem the panic.

Realizing the gravity of the situation, Roosevelt declared a "bank holiday" on March 5, suspending all banking and halting gold trading. Although there was some question about the legal basis for Roosevelt's declaration, the situation was so desperate that the "bank holiday" took place unopposed. On March 9 Roosevelt submitted the Emergency Banking Bill, which gave the government authorization to reorganize and reopen solvent banks. The banks began reopening on March 13, and deposits actually exceeded withdrawals in the reopened banks.

Interestingly, most of the reopened banks had never been audited to establish their soundness. Roosevelt simply expected the American people to trust his leadership—and they did. As Raymond Moley, a member of Roosevelt's "brain trust," noted: "Capitalism was saved in eight days."

Economic Cartoon
Unit 4 folder, p. 12 gives students practice in interpreting cartoons about section content.

Preparing for Standardized Tests

Have students read the section titled "Banking Reforms After the Great Depression" and then answer the question below.

The purpose of the FDIC, established in 1933, is to

(A) insure customer deposits if a bank fails.
B eliminate the gold standard.
C declare bank holidays.
D create a new national currency known as Federal Reserve Notes.

GTE Guide to the Essentials
Chapter 10, Section 2, p. 43 provides support for students who need additional review of the section content. Spanish support is available in the Spanish edition of the guide on p. 43.

Quiz Unit 4 folder, p. 5 includes questions to check students' understanding of Section 2 content.

Presentation Pro CD-ROM
Quiz provides multiple-choice questions to check students' understanding of Section 2 content.

Answers to . . .

Section 2 Assessment

1. The purpose of the First Bank of the United States was to hold U.S. government tax revenues; to help the government carry out its powers to tax, borrow money, and regulate interstate and foreign commerce; to issue representative money; and to ensure that state-chartered banks held sufficient gold and silver.
2. The National Banking Acts of 1863 and 1864 gave the federal government the power to charter banks, to require banks to hold adequate reserves of specie, and to establish a single national currency.
3. The FDIC insures bank deposits (currently up to $100,000 per depositor) in order to ease the danger of depositors' losing money, as happened after the collapse of the stock market in 1929.
4. Student answers should include highlights of several periods of American banking and illuminate swings between centralization and decentralization. Disputes between the Federalists and the Antifederalists, fragmentation during the Civil War, and the centralization of the National Banking Acts should be among the evidence cited.
5. Many students will probably say yes, that they would seek a unified banking system that would be stable. Some students may say that if they lived in a southern state, they would not want to be ruled by a northern central organization.
6. Students' notes should be based on arguments for and against national banking as found in the section.
7. Students may say that they would be wary of banks and of financial institutions in general.

Answer to . . .

Cartoon Caption The cartoon suggests that few banks were unaffected by the mergers.

▲ **What does the cartoonist suggest about the large number of recent bank mergers?**

is the removal, or relaxation, of government restrictions on business. Unfortunately, this deregulation contributed to a crisis in a class of banks known as Savings and Loans (S&Ls).

The Savings and Loan Crisis

Deregulation was one cause of the S&L crisis. High interest rates, inadequate capital, and fraud were others.

1. *Deregulation* S&Ls had previously been protected by government regulation. S&Ls were unprepared for competition after deregulation.
2. *High interest rates* During the 1970s, S&Ls had made long-term loans at low rates. By the 1980s, interest rates had skyrocketed. This meant that S&Ls had to pay out high interest rates to their depositors. At the same time, however, they were receiving low rates on the money they had loaned out in the 1970s.
3. *Bad loans* Risky loans made in the early 1980s hit the S&L industry especially hard, forcing many out of business, as the graph on page 176 of Chapter 7 shows.
4. *Fraud* A few financially important institutions fraudulently made large loans to businesses that had little chance of succeeding. When these businesses failed, a tremendous drain was put on the reserves of the FSLIC, the federal agency that insured S&Ls.

In 1989, Congress passed the Financial Institutions Reform, Recovery, and Enforcement Act (FIRREA). This Act essentially abolished the independence of the savings and loan industry and transferred insurance responsibilities to the FDIC.

Recent Trends

In 1999, in some of the most sweeping legislation since the Great Depression, Congress repealed the 1933 Glass-Steagall Act. This action paved the way for banks to sell financial assets such as stocks and bonds while establishing new privacy rules for customer data. In addition, the 1990s and 2000s saw a growing trend toward bank mergers. You can read more about these mergers in the Case Study on page 265.

Section 2 Assessment

Progress Monitoring *Online*
For: Self-quiz with vocabulary practice
Web Code: mna-4106

Key Terms and Main Ideas

1. What was the purpose of the first Bank of the United States?
2. What were three results of the National Banking Acts of 1863 and 1864?
3. Explain the purpose of the **Federal Deposit Insurance Corporation (FDIC).**

Applying Economic Concepts

4. ***Critical Thinking*** Use evidence from your reading to explain how the role of financial institutions has changed over time.
5. ***Decision Making*** Picture yourself living in the period following the Civil War. Would you support a central banking system? Why or why not?
6. ***Try This*** Suppose you are a Federalist or Antifederalist. Write notes for one side of a debate on the creation of a national bank. Then organize a classroom debate.
7. ***Critical Thinking*** Suppose you were living during the Great Depression. How might the events of that era have affected your future banking decisions?

For: Research Activity
Visit: PHSchool.com
Web Code: mnd-4102

Progress Monitoring *Online*
For additional assessment, have students access Progress Monitoring Online at **Web Code:** mna-4106

Go Online PHSchool.com Typing in the Web Code when prompted will bring students directly to detailed instructions for this activity.

Economist

Entrepreneur

ECONOMIC *Profile*

Amadeo P. Giannini (1870–1949)

When other banks refused to make loans to working-class people, this son of immigrants established one that would. On the strength of his low-income customer base, Amadeo Peter Giannini built the largest commercial bank in the world and contributed to the United States' economic development.

From Dockworker to Banker

Giannini was born in San Jose, California, to Italian immigrant parents. After his father died, his mother remarried, and the family moved to San Francisco. At age 12, Giannini went to work on the docks, loading and unloading fruits and vegetables for his stepfather's produce market. As a young man, he traveled throughout the state, signing farmers to contracts to supply him with produce. Over time, Giannini gained a reputation as a shrewd but honest businessman. He also developed a respect for people who worked with their hands.

In 1902, Giannini's business success led him to be invited to join the board of directors of a local bank. As a director he learned that the bank would loan only to wealthy San Franciscans. When the other bank directors refused to make loans to low-income workers, he quit the board to start his own bank.

Founding a Community Bank

In 1904, Giannini opened the Bank of Italy in San Francisco's heavily Italian North Beach section. He went door-to-door in the neighborhood, explaining to immigrant workers what the bank could do for them if they were to become customers.

About 18 months later, a devastating earthquake destroyed much of the city, including Giannini's bank. While other banks stayed closed, Giannini put a plank across two barrels in front of his ruined bank and made loans from this "desk." As a result, working-class North Beach was the first section of the city to be rebuilt.

The Bank of America

The earthquake bolstered Giannini's belief that banks should serve the public at large, and he decided to offer his banking services in other communities. In 1909, he opened his first branch in nearby San Jose. By 1918, the Bank of Italy had expanded across California, becoming the first bank in America with a statewide system of branches. In the 1920s, Giannini started a new bank network, which he named the Bank of America. In 1930, he merged the Bank of Italy into this new bank.

Giannini had retired in 1930, but his successor's conservative policies soon brought him out of retirement to retake control. In the 1930s, he made the Bank of America the world's largest commercial bank. At the time of Giannini's death, the Bank of America had roughly 500 branches and $6 billion in deposits.

CHECK FOR UNDERSTANDING

1. Source Reading In your own words, summarize Amadeo Giannini's ideas about a bank's function and role in society.

2. Critical Thinking How does the establishment of new branches benefit both a bank and the public?

3. Learn More Use the Internet and other sources to learn about the Community Reinvestment Act. Write a brief report on what it requires banks to do.

Beyond the Classroom: Career Connections

Loan Officer Lending institutions employ loan officers to work with customers who want to borrow money. Typically, a loan officer will explain the types of loans the institution offers and help the customer complete the loan application. Then, using guidelines established by the institution, the loan officer evaluates the application to determine, for example, whether the applicant has a good credit history and sufficient income to make the monthly payments while meeting other financial obligations. Ask students to suggest reasons why people might obtain loans *(examples: college tuition, home improvements, purchasing an automobile).*

ECONOMIC *Profile*
Amadeo P. Giannini

Background

Amadeo Giannini's success in financing the dreams of immigrants has been duplicated by others, notably a Polish immigrant named Leon Murstein. In 1937 Murstein bought a New York medallion (the license needed to operate a taxi in New York City) for $10. Through the years he used his earnings to buy other medallions, until by the 1970s he had purchased 150.

When Murstein decided to sell his medallions, he ran into the same problem Giannini had discovered many decades before. Banks would not lend money to recent immigrants with no credit history—the very people who wanted to buy Murstein's medallions. Murstein therefore set up his own lending institution, Medallion Financial, and over the next 20 years it made loans totaling $700 million to cab drivers who wanted to be their own bosses. Medallion Financial continues to thrive. In 1998 a New York City taxi medallion sold for $250,000.

Careers in Economics Activity Unit 4 folder, p. 11 gives students a closer look at the career path of a banking customer service representative.

Answers to . . .

1. Giannini believed that a bank's role was to help all members of a community to prosper by supporting development through lending.
2. New branches offer convenient locations to new customers. The community benefits as the bank makes loans accessible. The bank benefits from the income it makes through interest on new loans.
3. Students' reports should demonstrate that they have researched the Community Reinvestment Act, which requires bank branches to make a significant portion of their loans in the geographic areas they serve.

Section 3

Banking Today

Objectives You may wish to call students' attention to the objectives in the Section Preview. The objectives are reflected in the main headings of the section.

Bellringer Ask students to list the kinds of money they have with them today. Students may list only bills and coins, or some may mention credit cards. Explain that in this section they will learn about the many types of money and banking services that exist today.

Vocabulary Builder Ask students to read the section to find the meanings of the key terms. Then ask them to create a matching quiz using the terms and their definitions. Have students exchange quizzes, complete them, and return them for correction.

Lesson Plan

Teaching the Main Concepts L3

1. Focus Banking in the United States has come a long way since the country was founded. Ask students to identify ways in which banking has changed in the last 20 years.

2. Instruct Discuss the money supply, including the classifications M1 and M2. Explain that modern banks provide a variety of services, including checking and savings accounts, loans, credit cards, and so on. When discussing loans, be sure that students understand the difference between simple and compound interest. Finally, discuss the differing types of financial institutions that serve customers today and the impact of technology on the banking industry.

3. Close/Reteach Banking has changed radically in the last half of the twentieth century, and technological innovations continue to promise exciting developments. Ask students to speculate on how banking might change in the twenty-first century.

Section 3 Banking Today

Preview

Objectives

After studying this section you will be able to:

1. **Explain** how the money supply in the United States is measured.
2. **Explain** the functions of financial institutions.
3. **Identify** different types of financial institutions.
4. **Understand** the changes brought about by electronic banking.

Section Focus

Banking has changed greatly in recent decades. Today, many people are likely to use credit or debit cards instead of cash or checks. Banks provide a large array of services, and electronic banking is revolutionizing the way people conduct banking transactions.

Key Terms

money supply
liquidity
demand deposit
money market mutual fund
fractional reserve banking
default
mortgage
credit card
interest
principal
debit card
creditor

money supply *all the money available in the United States economy*

liquidity *the ability to be used as, or directly converted to, cash*

demand deposit *the money in checking accounts*

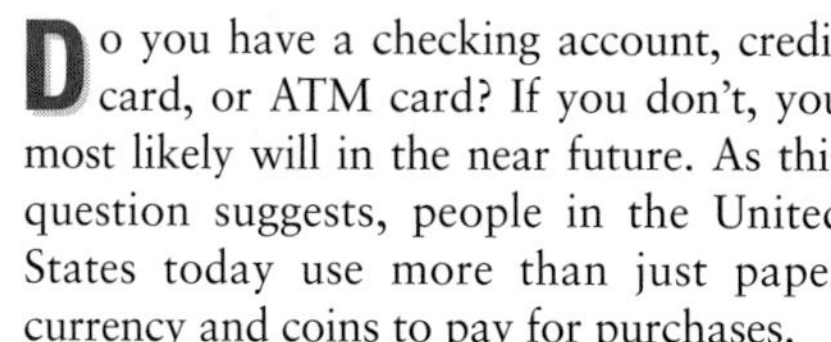

Do you have a checking account, credit card, or ATM card? If you don't, you most likely will in the near future. As this question suggests, people in the United States today use more than just paper currency and coins to pay for purchases.

Measuring the Money Supply

You are familiar with paying for the items you need with currency—the bills and coins in your pocket. Money consists of currency. It also consists of traveler's checks, checking account deposits, and a variety of other components. All of these components make up the United States **money supply**—all the money available in the United States economy. To more easily keep track of these different kinds of money, economists divide the money supply into several categories. The main categories are called M1 and M2.

▲ **Assets that have liquidity include currency, funds in checking accounts, and traveler's checks.**

M1

M1 represents money that people can gain access to easily and immediately to pay for goods and services. In other words, M1 consists of assets that have **liquidity**, or the ability to be used as, or directly converted into, cash.

As you can see from Figure 10.5, about 48 percent of M1 is made up of currency held by the public, that is, all currency held outside of bank vaults. Another large part of M1 is deposits in checking accounts. Funds in checking accounts are also called **demand deposits** because checks can be paid "on demand," that is, at any time. Until the 1980s, checking accounts did not pay interest, and a new category, called *other checkable deposits,* was introduced to describe checking accounts that did pay interest. Today this distinction is not as meaningful as it once was since many checking accounts pay interest if your balance is sufficiently high.

Traveler's checks make up a very small component of M1. Unlike personal checks, traveler's checks can be easily turned into cash.

M2

M2 consists of all the assets in M1 plus several additional assets. These additional M2 funds cannot be used as cash directly, but can be converted to cash fairly easily. M2 assets are also called *near money.*

For example, deposits in savings accounts are included in M2. They are not included in M1 because they cannot be used directly in financial exchanges. You cannot hand a sales clerk your savings account passbook to pay for a new backpack. You can, however, withdraw

Graphing the Main Idea

Economic Institutions To build understanding of today's **economic institutions**, have students complete a tree map graphic organizer like the one shown at the right. Remind students that a tree map shows an outline for a main topic, main ideas, and supporting details. Tell students to place the section title, "Banking Today," in the top box; the main headings in the next row of boxes; and main ideas and supporting details in the boxes below that.

Section Reading Support Transparencies A template and the answers for this graphic organizer can be found in Chapter 10, Section 3 of the Section Reading Support Transparency System.

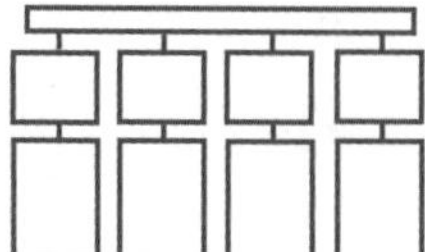

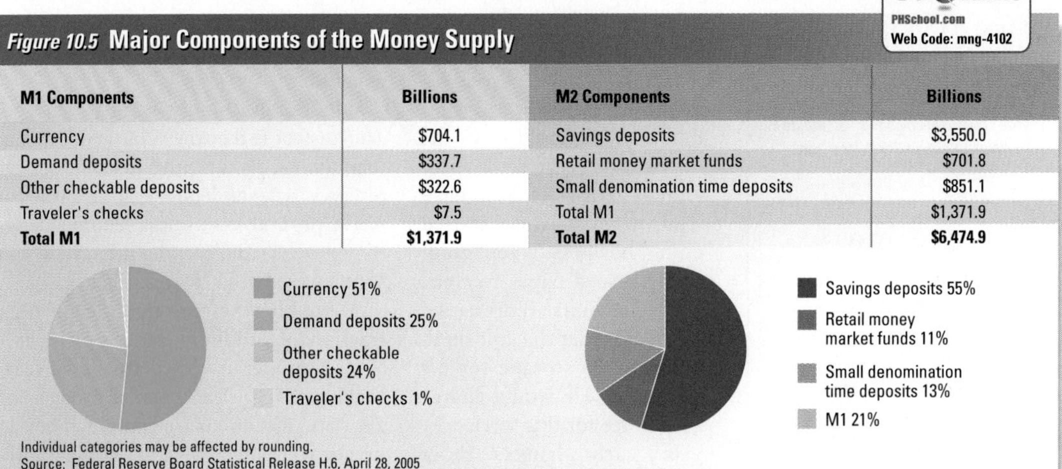

Go Online PHSchool.com Web Code: mng-4102

Figure 10.5 Major Components of the Money Supply

M1 Components	Billions	M2 Components	Billions
Currency	$704.1	Savings deposits	$3,550.0
Demand deposits	$337.7	Retail money market funds	$701.8
Other checkable deposits	$322.6	Small denomination time deposits	$851.1
Traveler's checks	$7.5	Total M1	$1,371.9
Total M1	**$1,371.9**	**Total M2**	**$6,474.9**

Individual categories may be affected by rounding.
Source: Federal Reserve Board Statistical Release H.6, April 28, 2005

The components of M1 can be used as cash or can be easily converted into cash. M2 consists of the assets in M1 plus assets that can be converted to cash fairly easily.
Money What is the largest component of M1? Of M2?

money from your savings account and then use that money to buy a backpack.

Deposits in **money market mutual funds** are also included as part of M2. These are funds that pool money from small savers to purchase short-term government and corporate securities. They earn interest and can be used to cover checks written over a certain minimum amount, such as $250. You will read more about money market mutual funds in Chapter 11.

Functions of Financial Institutions

Banks and other financial institutions are essential to managing the money supply. They also perform many functions and offer a wide range of services to consumers.

Storing Money

Banks provide a safe, convenient place for people to store money. Banks keep cash in fireproof vaults and are insured against the loss of money in the event of a robbery. As you read in Section 2, FDIC insurance protects people from losing their money if the bank is unable to repay funds.

Saving Money

Banks offer a variety of ways for people to save money. Four of the most common ways are the following:

- *Savings accounts*
- *Checking accounts*
- *Money market accounts*
- *Certificates of deposit (CDs)*

Savings accounts and checking accounts are the most common types of bank accounts. They are especially useful for people who need to make frequent withdrawals. Savings accounts and most checking accounts pay a small amount of interest at an annual rate.

Money market accounts and certificates of deposits (CDs) are special kinds of savings accounts that pay a higher rate of interest than do savings and checking accounts. Money market accounts allow you to save and to write a limited number of checks. Interest rates are not fixed, but can move up or down. CDs, on the other hand, offer a guaranteed rate of interest over a certain period of time. Funds placed in a CD, however, cannot be removed until the end of a certain time period, such as one or two years. Customers who remove their

money market mutual fund *a fund that pools money from small savers to purchase short-term government and corporate securities*

Guided Reading and Review
Unit 4 folder, p. 6 asks students to identify the main ideas of the section and to define or identify key terms.

Background

The Two Faces of Money

Money isn't just M1 or M2, paper or coins, checks or credit cards. Some money is good, and some is bad, according to the theories of Sir Thomas Gresham, who was a treasury official in England in the 1500s. He formalized a principle that others had observed before him—that bad money tends to drive out good money. This has become known as Gresham's law.

It works like this: If gold coins are worth more than silver coins, people will hoard the gold coins (good money) and use the silver (bad money). Thus gold coins tend to disappear from, or be driven out of, circulation. The same effect occurred in the United States after 1965, when the government began minting dimes and quarters with more copper and less silver in them. Pre-1965 dimes and quarters quickly disappeared from circulation, driven out by the "bad" new coins.

Differentiated Instruction 

(Reteaching) Ask students to classify each of the following as M1, M2, neither, or both: a savings account, a dollar bill, a personal check, a new car, a traveler's check, a 1-carat diamond, a certificate of deposit (CD), a savings bond, and an Individual Retirement Account (IRA).

Econ 101: Key Concepts Made Easy

Money Help students understand **liquidity** by asking them to think about the difference between a glass of water and an ice cube. Water flows, so you can use it instantly to do many things. You can drink it, shower in it, water plants with it, wash your car with it, and so on. Ice, on the other hand, often is not very helpful in its frozen state. You sometimes have to change its form before it becomes useful. Ask students to make comparisons between liquid assets and water.

Answer to . . .

Building Key Concepts The main component of M1 is currency. The main component of M2 is savings deposits.

Differentiated Instruction 

To help students understand M1 and M2, ask them to find illustrations or examples of each type of money and use these to create an M1/M2 collage. ELL

Differentiated Instruction 

Organize students into groups of three or four. Tell each group to create a fact sheet that lists and briefly describes the various services that banks provide: storing money, saving money, loaning money (including mortgages), issuing credit cards, and so on. Suggest that the fact sheet can be organized around questions *(What if I need to borrow money?)* or descriptive headings *(Storing Money)*. Remind students that they are creating a fact sheet, so the information should be brief and to the point.

Go Online PHSchool.com Typing in the Web Code when prompted will bring students directly to the article.

Transparency Resource Package
Economics Concepts, 10C: Components of the Money Supply
Economics Concepts, 10D: Anti-Counterfeiting Measures
Economics Concepts, 10E: Savings Rates

THE WALL STREET JOURNAL. CLASSROOM EDITION

In the News Read more about loans in "The Lowdown on Loans," an article in The Wall Street Journal Classroom Edition.

The Wall Street Journal Classroom Edition
For: Current Events
Visit: PHSchool.com
Web Code: mnc-4103

money before that time pay a penalty for early withdrawal.

Loans

Banks also perform the important service of providing loans. As you have read, the first banks started doing business when goldsmiths issued paper receipts. These receipts represented gold coins that the goldsmith held in safe storage for his customers. He would charge a small fee for this service.

In early banks, those receipts were fully backed by gold—every customer who held a receipt could be sure that the goldsmith kept the equivalent amount of gold in his safe. Gradually, however, goldsmiths realized that their customers seldom, if ever, asked for all of their gold on one day. Goldsmiths could thus lend out half or even three quarters of their gold at any one time and still have enough gold to handle customer demand.

fractional reserve banking *a banking system that keeps only a fraction of funds on hand and lends out the remainder*

Why did goldsmiths want to lend gold? The answer is that they charged interest on their loans. By keeping just enough gold reserves to cover demand, goldsmiths could run a profitable business lending deposits to borrowers and earning interest. The first banks were based on this practice.

A banking system that keeps only a fraction of funds on hand and lends out the remainder is called **fractional reserve banking.** Like the early banks, today's banks also operate on this principle. They lend money to homeowners for home improvements, to families to pay for college tuition, and to businesses. The more money a bank lends out, and the higher the interest rate it charges borrowers, the more profit a bank is able to make.

By making loans, banks help new businesses get started, and they help established businesses grow. When a business gets a

Figure 10.6 **The Fractional Reserve System**

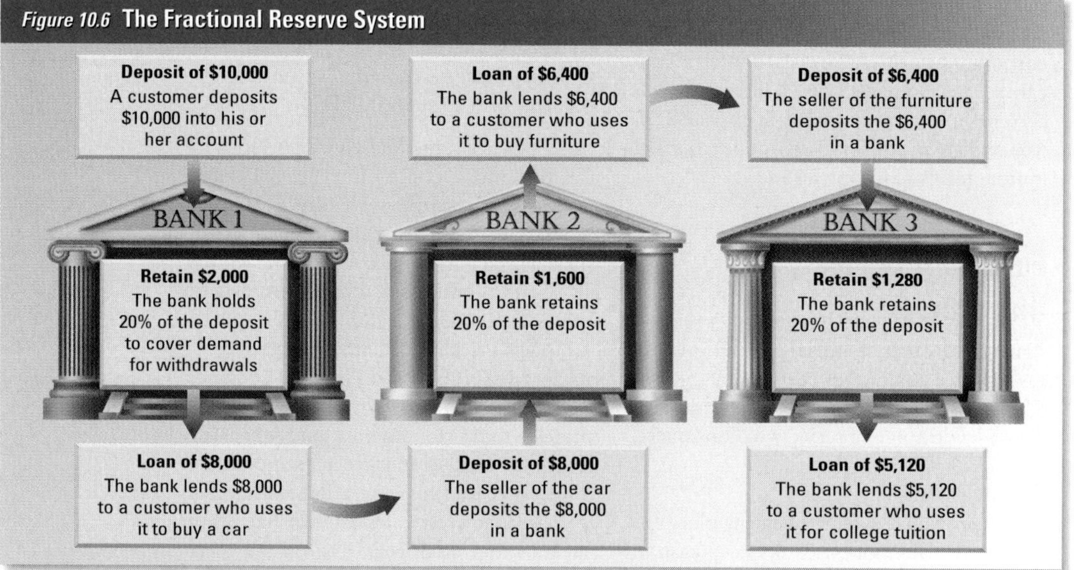
Deposit of $10,000
A customer deposits $10,000 into his or her account
BANK 1
Retain $2,000
The bank holds 20% of the deposit to cover demand for withdrawals
Loan of $8,000
The bank lends $8,000 to a customer who uses it to buy a car
Deposit of $8,000
The seller of the car deposits the $8,000 in a bank
BANK 2
Retain $1,600
The bank retains 20% of the deposit
Loan of $6,400
The bank lends $6,400 to a customer who uses it to buy furniture
Deposit of $6,400
The seller of the furniture deposits the $6,400 in a bank
BANK 3
Retain $1,280
The bank retains 20% of the deposit
Loan of $5,120
The bank lends $5,120 to a customer who uses it for college tuition

In a fractional reserve system, banks keep only a fraction of funds on hand and lend out the rest. The funds lent out fuel the economy and ensure continued growth.
Money **Why does the bank retain a percentage of the money it receives from depositors?**

Block Scheduling Strategies

Consider these suggestions to take advantage of extended class time:

- Conduct an in-class tour of Internet sites created by financial institutions: banks, credit unions, brokerage houses, and so on. Ask students to speculate about the advantages and disadvantages of banking in cyberspace. Use the links provided in the *Economics: Principles in Action* segment in the Social Studies area at the following Web site: **www.phschool.com**
- To reinforce a discussion of credit cards, bring a credit card application to class and work with students to fill it out for a fictitious applicant. Help students to understand what types of information are asked for and why. Discuss with students how credit cards can be used responsibly. Then discuss irresponsible ways in which they are sometimes used.

Answer to...

Building Key Concepts The FED requires certain reserve percentages to cover demand for withdrawals.

loan, that business can create new jobs by hiring new workers or investing in physical capital in order to increase production.

A business that gets a loan may also help other businesses grow. For example, suppose you and a friend want to start a window-washing business. Your business will need supplies like window cleaner and ladders, so the companies that make your supplies will also benefit. They may even hire workers to expand their businesses.

Bankers must, however, consider the security of the loans they make. Suppose borrowers **default**, or fail to pay back their loans? Then the bank loses money. Bankers therefore always face a trade-off between profits and safety. If they make too many bad loans—loans that are not repaid—they may go out of business altogether. (See pages 510–511 of the Personal Finance Handbook to learn more about banks and the services they offer.)

Mortgages

A **mortgage** is a specific type of loan that is used to buy real estate. Suppose the Lee family wants to buy a house for $200,000. They are unlikely to have the cash on hand to be able to pay for the house. Like almost all home-buyers, they will need to take out a mortgage.

The Lees can afford to make a down payment of 20 percent of the price of the house, or $40,000. After investigating the Lees's creditworthiness, their bank agrees to lend them the remaining $160,000 so that they can purchase their new house. Mortgages usually last for 15, 25, or 30 years. According to the terms of their loan, the Lees are responsible for paying back the loan plus whatever interest the bank charges over a period of 25 years.

Credit Cards

If you look at a credit card, somewhere you will see the name of a bank printed on it. Another service that banks provide is issuing **credit cards**—cards entitling their holders to buy goods and services based on the cardholder's promise to pay for these goods and services.

Figure 10.7 Compound Interest

Start of year	Principal amount	Interest earned at 5%	Principal at end of year
–	$100.00	$5.00	$105.00
1	$105.00	$5.25	$110.25
2	$110.25	$5.51	$115.76
3	$115.76	$5.79	$121.55
4	$121.55	$6.08	$127.63
5	$127.63	$6.38	$134.01
6	$134.01	$6.70	$140.71
7	$140.71	$7.04	$147.75
8	$147.75	$7.39	$155.14
9	$155.14	$7.76	$162.90
10	$162.90	$8.14	$171.04
11	$171.04	$8.55	$179.59
12	$179.59	$8.98	$188.57
13	$188.57	$9.43	$198.00
14	$198.00	$9.90	$207.90
15	$207.90	$10.39	$218.29

This chart shows the money earned on a $100 deposit when interest is compounded yearly at 5 percent.

Income How many years does it take for the original deposit to double?

How do credit cards work? Suppose you buy a sleeping bag and tent for $100 on May 3. You do not actually pay for the gear until you receive your credit-card bill and pay it in June. In the meantime, however, the credit-card issuer (the bank) will have paid the sporting goods store. Your payment repays the bank for the "loan" of $100.

Simple and Compound Interest

As you have read, **interest** is the price paid for the use of borrowed money. The amount borrowed is called the **principal**. Simple interest is interest paid only on principal. For example, if you deposit $100 in a savings account at 5 percent simple interest, you will make $5 in a year (assuming that interest is paid annually).

Suppose that you leave the $5 in interest in the bank, so that at the end of the year you have $105 in your account—$100 in principal and $5 in interest. Compound interest is interest paid on both principal and accumulated interest. That means that in the second year, as long as you leave both the principal and the interest in your account, interest will be paid on $105. Figure 10.7 shows how an account paying compound interest grows over time.

default *failure to pay back a loan*

mortgage *a specific type of loan that is used to buy real estate*

credit card *a card entitling its holder to buy goods and services based on the holder's promise to pay for these goods and services*

interest *the price paid for the use of borrowed money*

principal *the amount of money borrowed*

Background

Common Misconceptions

Beth has just returned from the bank with a savings account deposit receipt tucked inside her wallet. What will happen to the money Beth has deposited? Contrary to what some people think, it isn't put into a vault and simply stored until Beth wants it again.

Some of Beth's money is loaned to people who want to buy houses or cars. Because these borrowers pay interest, Beth's money earns revenue for the bank. Some of Beth's money is invested in government securities. These also pay interest. When Kelvyn takes $20 out of a cash machine, some of that money comes from Beth's deposit, too.

But how does Beth profit from her hard-working money? Banks pay interest on savings accounts and sometimes on checking accounts. Interest is the bank's way of thanking Beth for letting it use her money. When Beth is ready to borrow money for college or to finance her new business, someone else's money will be there to help her out.

Transparency Resource Package
Economics Concepts, 10F: Simple and Compound Interest

Math Practice Activity
Math Practice folder, p. 9, "Comparing Credit Cards Payments," allows students to examine the effects of interest rates and time on credit card payments.

Preparing for Standardized Tests

Have students read the section titled "Simple and Compound Interest" and then answer the question below.

Which of the following best describes compound interest?

A interest paid on the principal of borrowed money

B interest paid by mortgage lenders

(C) interest paid on the principal and interest of borrowed money

D interest paid on bank profits

Answer to . . .

Building Key Concepts It takes 14 years for the amount to double.

Differentiated Instruction L4

You may wish to have students add the following to their portfolios. Ask them to create a pamphlet that explains the functions of the financial institutions covered in the section: commercial banks, savings and loan associations, savings banks, and credit unions. Suggest that they provide an overview of each type of institution, its function, and how it differs from the other institutions. Have students share their pamphlets with peers to review important concepts. GT

Economics Assessment Rubric

Economics Assessment Rubrics folder, pp. 6–7 provides sample evaluation materials for a writing assignment.

Differentiated Instruction L3

(Enrichment) Explain to students that some banks are global in nature. Ask students to research the origins and purposes of the World Bank and the International Monetary Fund and to write an expository essay explaining how each functions. Essays should include a real-life example of each institution in action.

After customers deposit money, a bank lends it to businesses and other borrowers and collects interest. The bank uses this income from interest to cover its costs and make a profit.

Income **What are the sources of a bank's income?**

Figure 10.8 How Banks Make a Profit

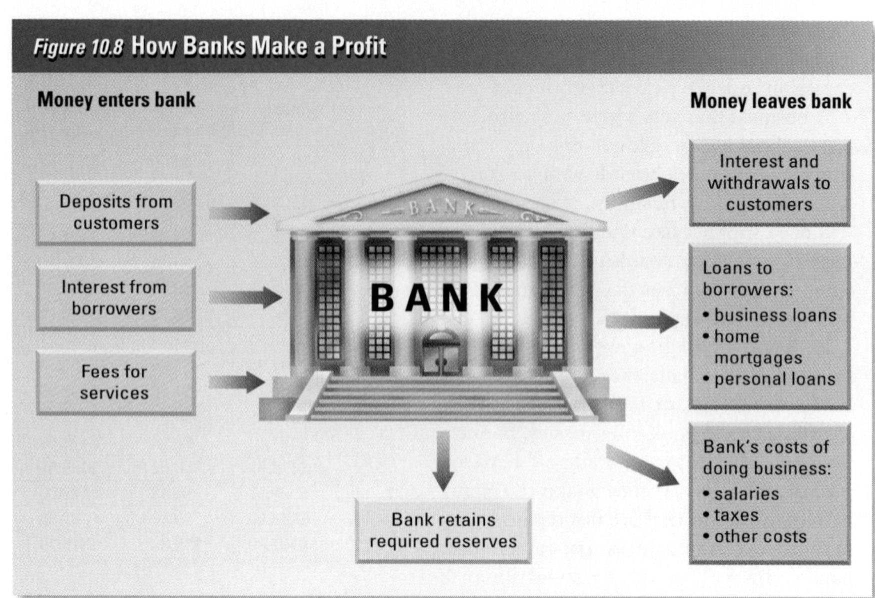

Banks and Profit

The largest source of income for banks is the interest they receive from customers who have taken loans. Banks, of course, also pay out interest on customers' savings and most checking accounts. The amount of interest they pay out, however, is less than the amount of interest they charge on loans. The difference in the amounts is how banks cover their costs and make a profit.

Types of Financial Institutions

Several kinds of financial institutions operate in the United States. These include commercial banks, savings and loan associations, mutual savings banks, and credit unions. During the 1990s, these financial institutions became more similar than dissimilar, although differences still remain.

Commercial Banks

Commercial banks, which traditionally provided services to businesses, offer a wide range of services today. Commercial banks offer checking services, accept deposits, and make loans. Some commercial banks are chartered by states and are regulated by state authorities and by the Federal Deposit Insurance Corporation (FDIC). About one third of all commercial banks are national banks and are part of the Federal Reserve System. Commercial banks provide the most services and play the largest role in the economy of any type of bank.

Savings and Loan Associations

Savings and Loan Associations (S&Ls), which you read about in Section 2, were originally chartered to lend money for building homes during the mid-1800s. Members of Savings and Loan Associations deposited funds into a large general fund and then borrowed enough money to buy their own houses. Savings and Loans are also called *thrifts* because they originally enabled "thrifty" working-class people—that is, people who were careful with their money—to save up and borrow enough to buy their own homes. Over time, Savings and Loan Associations have taken on many of the same functions as commercial banks.

Answer to . . .

Building Key Concepts Sources of income are deposits from customers, interest from borrowers, and fees for services.

Savings Banks

Mutual savings banks (MSBs) originated in the early 1800s to serve people who made smaller deposits and transactions than commercial banks wished to handle. Mutual savings banks were owned by the depositors themselves, who shared in any profits. Later, many MSBs began to sell stock to raise additional capital. These institutions became simply savings banks because depositors no longer owned them.

Although savings banks were traditionally concentrated in the Northeast, they had an important influence on the national economy. In 1972, the Consumer's Savings Bank of Worcester, Massachusetts, introduced a Negotiable Order of Withdrawal (NOW) account, a type of checking account that pays interest. NOW accounts became available nationwide in 1980.

Credit Unions

Credit unions are cooperative lending associations for particular groups, usually employees of a specific firm or government agency. Credit unions are commonly fairly small and specialize in home mortgages and car loans, usually at interest rates favorable to members. Some credit unions also provide checking account services.

Finance Companies

Finance companies make installment loans to consumers. These loans spread the cost of major purchases like computers, cars, refrigerators, and recreational vehicles over a number of months. Because people who borrow from finance companies more frequently fail to repay the loans, finance companies generally charge higher interest rates than banks do.

Electronic Banking

Banks began to use computers in the early 1970s to keep track of transactions. As computers have become more common in the United States, their role in banking has also increased dramatically. In fact, computerized banking may revolutionize banking in much the same way that paper currency changed banking long ago.

Automated Teller Machines

If you use an Automated Teller Machine (ATM), you are already familiar with one of the most common types of electronic banking. ATMs are computers that customers can use to deposit money, withdraw cash, and obtain account information at their convenience. Instead of having to go to the bank during the bank's hours of operation to conduct banking business face-to-face with a teller, you can take care of your finances at an ATM.

ATMs are convenient for both banks and for customers, since they are available 24 hours a day and reduce banks' labor costs. The overwhelming popularity of ATMs suggests that they are likely to be a permanent feature of modern banking.

Debit Cards

Debit cards are used to withdraw money. You may use a debit card to withdraw

debit card *a card used to withdraw money*

◀ **Electronic banking has greatly changed the way customers interact with their banks.**

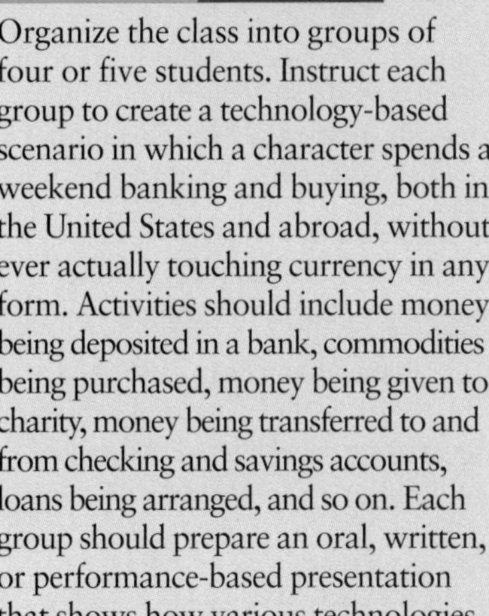

Differentiated Instruction L3

Organize the class into groups of four or five students. Instruct each group to create a technology-based scenario in which a character spends a weekend banking and buying, both in the United States and abroad, without ever actually touching currency in any form. Activities should include money being deposited in a bank, commodities being purchased, money being given to charity, money being transferred to and from checking and savings accounts, loans being arranged, and so on. Each group should prepare an oral, written, or performance-based presentation that shows how various technologies make these transactions possible.

Economic Detective Activity
Unit 4 folder, p. 10, "Tortoise Domain," provides an integrated application of chapter concepts.

Preparing for Standardized Tests

Have students read the section titled "Electronic Banking" and then answer the question below.

Which of the following transactions cannot be completed at an Automated Teller Machine (ATM)?

A deposit money in a savings account
B withdraw money from a checking account
C check the balance of a checking or savings account
(D) withdraw money from a certificate of deposit

GTE **Guide to the Essentials**
Chapter 10, Section 3, p. 44 provides support for students who need additional review of the section content. Spanish support is available in the Spanish edition of the guide on p. 44.

Quiz Unit 4 folder, p. 7 includes questions to check students' understanding of Section 3 content.

Presentation Pro CD-ROM
Quiz provides multiple-choice questions to check students' understanding of Section 3 content.

Answers to . . .

Section 3 Assessment

1. M1 includes all money that is immediately accessible for people to use to pay for goods and services. Examples: cash, money in checking accounts, traveler's checks. M2 includes all of M1 plus all assets that are easily transferred into M1. Examples: savings account deposits and money market mutual funds.
2. A debit card withdraws money directly from a checking or savings account when it is used to make a purchase, whereas when a credit card is used to make a purchase, it functions as a loan that then needs to be paid off.
3. Students should describe any three of the following: storing money safely, lending money, offering mortgages, or issuing credit cards.
4. The more a bank lends out, the more profit a bank makes. However, the bank must not lend out too much of its money, since it needs to keep some in reserve for withdrawals and for safety. Also, banks cannot make loans to everyone who asks but must assess a person's ability to pay back the loan.
5. Students may suggest incentives such as premiums, free checking accounts, or initial low interest rates on loans. Profit plans may include investing deposits, collecting interest on loans, and charging user fees for electronic transfers.
6. Students may mention convenience of branch locations, availability of interest on checking accounts, or convenient electronic options.
7. (a) Personal savings as a percentage of disposable income rose through 1975 and then dropped quickly. (b) During the 1970s consumers often spent money as quickly as possible because of inflation. Other explanations include increases in consumerism and in stock and bond trading.
8. Student's answers will vary, but should include an understanding of loans, savings and checking accounts, mutual funds, ATMs, and credit cards.

FAST FACT

Electronic banking has clear economic benefits. While the cost of processing a paper check is 35 cents, the cost of processing an electronic payment is only 7 cents. The percentage of transactions completed electronically is growing dramatically. Electronic payments account for about 90 percent of the total dollar value of all transactions.

money at an ATM. You may also use a debit card in stores equipped with special machines. When you "swipe" your card through one of these machines, your debit card sends a message to your bank to transfer money from your checking account directly into the store's bank account. For security, debit cards require customers to use personal identification numbers, or PINs, to authorize financial transactions.

Home Banking

More and more people are using the Internet to conduct their financial business. Many banks, credit unions, and other financial institutions allow people to check account balances, transfer money to different accounts, pay their bills, and automatically deposit their paychecks via computer.

Automatic Clearing Houses

creditor *person or institution to whom money is owed*

Automatic Clearing Houses (ACHs), located at Federal Reserve Banks and their branches, allow customers to pay bills without writing checks. An ACH transfers funds automatically from customers' accounts to creditors' accounts. (A **creditor** is a person or institution to whom money is owed.) People usually use ACHs to pay regular monthly bills like mortgage payments, rent, utility bills, and insurance premiums. They save time, postage costs, and any worries about forgetting to make a payment.

Stored Value Cards

Stored value cards, or smart cards, are similar to debit cards. These cards are embedded with either magnetic strips or computer chips with account balance information. Smart cards include cards issued to college students living in dormitories to pay for cafeteria food, computer time, or photocopying. Phone cards, with which customers prepay for a specified amount of long-distance calling, are also smart cards.

Will stored value smart cards someday replace cash altogether? No one can know for sure, but private companies and public facilities have continued to explore new uses for smart card technology.

Section 3 Assessment

Progress Monitoring Online
For: Self-quiz with vocabulary practice
Web Code: mna-4107

Key Terms and Main Ideas

1. What is the difference between M1 and M2? Give an example of each.
2. How does a **debit card** differ from a **credit card?**
3. Describe three services that banks provide.
4. Explain why banks must balance profit and security when making loans.

Applying Economic Concepts

5. ***Try This*** Suppose you are setting up a classroom bank. What incentives will you offer so your classmates will use your bank? How will your bank make a profit?
6. ***You Decide*** Suppose that you are planning to open a checking account so you can deposit checks from your summer job. How will you decide on a bank?
7. ***Using the Databank*** Turn to the graph entitled "Personal Savings as a Percentage of Disposable Income" on page 540. **(a)** Describe the pattern of personal savings shown on the graph. **(b)** What factors could have caused the steady drop in savings since the 1970s?
8. ***Critical Thinking*** Write a paragraph in which you analyze how financial institutions affect households and businesses.

Go Online PHSchool.com
For: Writing Activity
Visit: PHSchool.com
Web Code: mnd-4103

Progress Monitoring *Online*
For additional assessment, have students access Progress Monitoring Online at **Web Code:** mna-4107

Go Online PHSchool.com Typing in the Web Code when prompted will bring students directly to detailed instructions for this activity.

NO Should the government increase its regulation of financial markets?

By Rep. Jeff Flake

It did not take long after the wave of corporate wrongdoing for the populist calls for more government regulation of our financial markets to start.

Some argue that a lack of regulation allowed unscrupulous companies to deceive investors. An unregulated market exists only in theory, but in such an environment, companies could keep important information to themselves and away from investors. Investment has to begin at some point, however, and the first potential investors—if they have any degree of concern for their investment—would only agree to take ownership in the company in exchange for influence over management.

If the initial and subsequent investors do not receive acceptable returns, they will demand more information from the company, a change in management, or they may withdraw their investments. This is the incentive for companies to provide accurate and complete disclosure.

Regulators say that we need to protect investors and the broader marketplace from debacles like the Enron mess. But the economic system that allows for possible risks like Enron has also allowed for the solid lasting profitability and success of thousands of other companies. Restraining the system with more regulation may catch some failures, but it will also hold back many success stories.

Finally, many make the case for more government regulation by arguing that government needs to do more to prevent fraud and manipulation. However, as soon as new regulations are in place, new loopholes will inevitably be created. Frauds and manipulators, who have shown little regard for existing regulations, would not likely respect new regulations.

The long-term impact of increasingly strict rules and regulations can be just as damaging as the fraud and manipulation that occurs in an open system—probably more so. The increase of rules and regulation adds costs and administrative effort. In effect, companies face disincentives to engage in fair and honest exchange. Thus, overregulation is also a destructive activity.

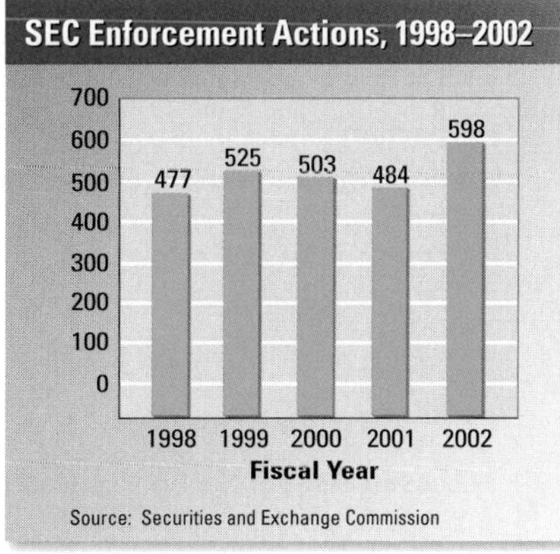

The Securities and Exchange Commission (SEC) begins an "enforcement action" if a public company is believed to have broken SEC rules.

DEBATING THE ISSUE

1. According to Randall Dodd, how do fraud and manipulation of market prices hurt the economy?
2. Why does Rep. Flake believe that a new set of financial regulations prohibiting corporate abuses won't solve current problems?
3. **Testing Conclusions** What evidence is there to support Rep. Flake's belief that new regulations will have unintended consequences?
4. **Reading Graphs** In which year between 1998 and 2002 did the SEC launch the most enforcement actions against companies?

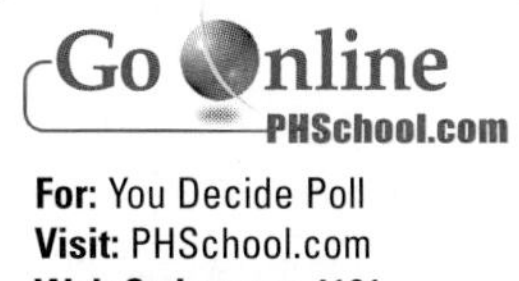

For: You Decide Poll
Visit: PHSchool.com
Web Code: mnp-4101

Differentiated Instruction L3

Sarbanes-Oxley, which addressed Wall Street, corporate, and accounting-industry reform, was set up to improve the quality of corporate financial information, and to make it less likely companies are manipulating their earnings numbers. Ask students to assume the role of stock-market investor. Have them discuss and prepare a report on the benefits and risks of investing in the stock market today. How much confidence would students place in buying shares of companies that are operating under this new legislation? Do they think that investors are receiving accurate earnings information? How risky is it to invest in the stock market today? Why?

Go Online PHSchool.com Students can find additional links related to the debate by visiting the *Economics: Principles in Action* site at **PHSchool.com.**

Interdisciplinary Connections: History

Corporate Scandals The corporate scandals of the early 2000s shook investor confidence in the stock market and resulted in many workers losing their pension or retirement funds. But this was not the first time that investors had become victims of fraudulent-accounting practices and other corporate wrongdoing. Other episodes occurred during the populist and progressive eras at the turn of the last century and at the start of the Great Depression of the 1930s.

Making the Connection In groups, have students research one of the following time periods: 1920, 1930, or 2002. Have groups present an illustrated essay or PowerPoint presentation on this topic: "Periods of United States History Marked by Government Intervention in Private Enterprise." For each time period, groups should discuss the president in office, the business problem, the group(s) affected, and the government action taken.

Answers to . . .

1. They rob investors of a fair return on their money, which discourages investment and harms the entire economy.
2. In the corporate scandals of 2002, it mattered little that laws were already on the books prohibiting many of the actions that led to these scandals.
3. Rep. Flake offers his opinions on regulations. He uses the "corporate inversion" example to illustrate the consequences of unfair federal tax policy.
4. FY02

Chapter Resource Manager

Chapter 11 Financial Markets

For more pacing suggestions, see the Economics Pacing Guide in the Program Overview of the Teaching Resources.

Section Objectives	Print and Technology Resources
1 Saving and Investing *(pp. 271–275)* **Objectives** 1. Understand how investing contributes to the free enterprise system. 2. Explain how the financial system brings together savers and borrowers. 3. Describe how financial intermediaries link savers and borrowers. 4. Identify the trade-offs among risk, liquidity, and return.	• **Lesson Planner** Section 1 Lesson Plan, p. 48 • **Learning Styles Lesson Plans folder** Section 1 Lesson Plan, p. 27 • **Lesson Plans folder** Section 1 Lesson Plan, p. 41 • **Unit 4 folder** Guided Reading and Review, p. 13 Careers in Economics, Stockbroker, p. 22 Section 1 Quiz, p. 14 • **Math Practice folder** Determining Net Worth, p. 10 • **Source Articles folder** Smart Investing, pp. 33–35 • **Presentation Pro CD-ROM** Section 1 • **Transparency Resource Package** Economics Organizers, G5: Web Graphic Organizer Economics Concepts, 11A: Financial Intermediaries Economics Concepts, 11B: Risk and Return • **Section Reading Support Transparency System**
2 Bonds and Other Financial Assets *(pp. 277–283)* **Objectives** 1. Describe the characteristics of bonds as financial assets. 2. Identify different types of bonds. 3. Describe the characteristics of other types of financial assets. 4. Explain four different types of financial asset markets.	• **Lesson Planner** Section 2 Lesson Plan, p. 49 • **Lesson Plans folder** Section 2 Lesson Plan, p. 42 • **Unit 4 folder** Guided Reading and Review, p. 15 Section 2 Quiz, p. 16 • **Case Studies in Free Enterprise folder** Edward L. Bernays, pp. 22–23 • **Presentation Pro CD-ROM** Section 2 • **Transparency Resource Package** Economics Organizers, G7: Tree Map Graphic Organizer Economics Concepts, 11C: Bond Reports • **Section Reading Support Transparency System** • **Social Studies Skills Tutor CD-ROM**
3 The Stock Market *(pp. 285–292)* **Objectives** 1. Understand the benefits and risks of buying stock. 2. Describe how stocks are traded. 3. Identify how stock performance is measured. 4. Explain the causes and effects of the Great Crash of 1929.	• **Lesson Planner** Section 3 Lesson Plan, p. 50 • **Learning Styles Lesson Plans folder** Section 3 Lesson Plan, p. 28 • **Lesson Plans folder** Section 3 Lesson Plan, p. 43 • **Unit 4 folder** Guided Reading and Review, p. 17 Economic Skills, p. 19 Economic Cartoon, p. 23 Vocabulary Practice, p. 20 Economic Detective, p. 21 Section 3 Quiz, p. 18 • **Presentation Pro CD-ROM** Section 3 • **Transparency Resource Package** Economics Organizers, G9: Multi-Flow Chart Graphic Organizer Economics Concepts, 11D: Stock Splits Economics Concepts, 11E: The Dow Jones Industrial Average • **Section Reading Support Transparency System**

Differentiated Instruction

Summarize L3

The ability to summarize effectively can help improve students' abilities to understand and remember the text. Tell students that good summarizes take notes on the text and reread as they write. Poor summarizers read the text once and begin writing.

Model how to create a useful summary of Section 1. First review structural aids, such as headings, key terms, reading checks, visual information, and captions. Point out that many of these show financial investments. Then, predict what you think you will learn about the text: saving and investing. Next, read the selection and go through the main ideas and details. Then reread the section and take notes on key words and key topics, such as *investment* and *return.* Next, organize your ideas and cluster ideas that go together. Finally, write your summary. As you write, cross out any information that does not seem important.

1. Review structural aids, such as headings, key terms, reading checks, visual information, and captions

2. Predict what you think you will learn about the text

3. Read the selection and sort through the main ideas and details. Reread the section and take notes on key words from topic sentences that express the main idea of each paragraph.

4. Organize the ideas in our notes. Cluster ideas that go together.

5. Write your summary. As you write, be sure to cross out any information that does not seem important.

Visit the Social Studies area of the Prentice Hall Web site. There you can find additional links to enrich chapter content for *Economics: Principles in Action* as well as a self-test for students. Be sure to check out this month's **eTeach** online discussion with a Master Economics Teacher.

Web Code: mnf-4111

Running Out of Time?

- Use the **Presentation Pro CD-ROM** to create an outline for this chapter.
- Use the Chapter Summary in the **Chapter 11 Assessment,** p. 294.
- Use the Section Summaries for Chapter 11, from **Guide to the Essentials of Economics (English and Spanish).**

THE WALL STREET JOURNAL. CLASSROOM EDITION

Prentice Hall brings into the classroom the authoritative content of *The Wall Street Journal Classroom Edition.* See the Source Articles, Debating Current Issues, and You and Your Money folders in the **Teaching Resources**. Also, see Economics Video Library, "Getting Started."

Assessment Resources

Chapter Assessment

Teaching Resources Unit 4, Chapter 11
- Section Quizzes, pp. 14, 16, 18

Exam *View*® Test Bank CD-ROM Chapter 11

Economics Assessment Rubrics

Chapter 1 Self-Test, **Web Code:** mna-4111

Reading and Skills Evaluation

Progress Monitoring Assessments
- Screening Test
- Diagnostic Test of Social Studies Skills

Standardized Test Preparation

Test Prep Workbook

Test-Taking Strategies With Transparencies

Differentiated Instruction Key

L1 Special Needs	LPR Less Proficient Readers
L2 Basic to Average	AR Advanced Readers
L3 All Students	SN Special Needs Students
L4 Average to Advanced	GT Gifted and Talented
	ELL English Language Learner

Chapter 11

Financial Markets

Introducing the Chapter

This chapter introduces students to the world of financial markets, including financial institutions and financial assets. The chapter also discusses the operation of the stock market and the forces that led to the Great Crash of 1929.

Go Online PHSchool.com

For additional links for *Economics: Principles in Action* provided by Prentice Hall and *The Wall Street Journal Classroom Edition,* visit the Social Studies area. Be sure to check out this month's **eTeach** online discussion with a Master Teacher.

Beyond the Lecture

You may cover the concepts in Chapter 11 in an activity-based style by using the following materials:

- **Technology Resources** appropriate for use with this chapter are noted on pp. 273, 274, 275, 279, 283, 286, 289, 292, and 295.
- **Presentation Pro CD-ROM** with animated graphs gives you an alternative method for organizing and delivering chapter content.
- **Activities** designed to meet the needs of students of mixed abilities and learning styles are noted throughout the chapter in the side columns.
- **Learning Styles Lesson Plans** provide alternate lessons for diverse learning styles. See pp. 27–28 of the Learning Styles Lesson Plans folder located in the Teaching Resources.

Economics Journal

Instruct students to write their lists and questions in their Economics Journals. Students may include completed journal entries in an Economics Portfolio.

Chapter 11 Financial Markets

What is the Dow? Where is Wall Street? What does a daytrader do? You may have heard these terms but be unsure of exactly what they mean. In this chapter you will learn the meaning of these and other terms from the world of investment. You will also learn how the stock market works and how investors choose from among stocks, bonds, and other standard investments.

Economics Journal

Look through the financial pages of a major newspaper for stock and bond reports. Jot down the kinds of information you find. Then make a list of questions about the information that you don't understand.

Go Online PHSchool.com

For: Current Data
Visit: PHSchool.com
Web Code: mng-4111

National Council on Economic Education

★ **Standard 10** Institutions evolve in market economies to help individuals and groups accomplish their goals. Banks, labor unions, corporations, legal systems, and not-for-profit organizations are examples of important institutions. A different kind of institution, clearly defined and well enforced property rights, is essential to a market economy.

★ **Standard 12** Interest rates, adjusted for inflation, rise and fall to balance the amount saved with the amount borrowed, thus affecting the allocation of scarce resources between present and future uses.

For more information about the standards, contact the National Council on Economic Education

1140 Avenue of the Americas
New York, NY 10036
1-800-338-1192

Section 1 Saving and Investing

Preview

Objectives

After studying this section you will be able to:

1. **Understand** how investing contributes to the free enterprise system.
2. **Explain** how the financial system brings together savers and borrowers.
3. **Describe** how financial intermediaries link savers and borrowers.
4. **Identify** the trade-offs among risk, liquidity, and return.

Section Focus

Investment promotes economic growth and contributes to a nation's wealth. The financial system includes savers and borrowers, as well as the institutions that transfer savers' dollars to borrowers. When borrowers invest these funds, they fuel economic growth.

Key Terms

investment
financial system
financial asset
financial intermediary
mutual fund
diversification
portfolio
prospectus
return

If you go to school today, you give up your time now so that you will be prepared for a career in the future. If a firm builds a new plant, it spends money today for the sake of earning more money in the future. A government may spend money today to build a dam to ensure that people will have a source of hydroelectric power in the future. All of these actions represent investments.

In its most general sense, **investment** is the act of redirecting resources from being consumed today so that they may create benefits in the future. In more narrow, economic terms, investment is the use of assets to earn income or profit.

investment *the act of redirecting resources from being consumed today so that they may create benefits in the future; the use of assets to earn income or profit*

Investing and Free Enterprise

As you have read, one of the chief advantages of the free enterprise system is that it allows people to make a profit. This profit motive leads individuals and businesses to make investments. Investing, in fact, is an essential part of the free enterprise system.

Investment promotes economic growth and contributes to a nation's wealth. When people deposit money in a savings account in a bank, for example, the bank may then lend the funds to businesses. The businesses, in turn, may invest that money in new plants and equipment to increase their production. As these businesses use their investments to expand and grow, they create new and better products and provide new jobs.

◀ **How does this illustration suggest that investment promotes economic growth?**

Section 1 Saving and Investing

Objectives You may wish to call students' attention to the objectives in the Section Preview. The objectives are reflected in the main headings of the section.

Bellringer Ask students to recall when and how they first began saving money. Explain that in this section they will learn some basic principles of saving and investing.

Vocabulary Builder Have students read through the section to learn the meaning of each key term. Then ask them to use the dictionary to investigate each term's origins and meaning.

Lesson Plan

Teaching the Main Concepts 

1. Focus Savers and borrowers are brought together in the financial marketplace by specialized institutions. Ask students what firms fulfill this role.

2. Instruct Begin by discussing the role of investing in our economy. Describe how financial intermediaries bring together savers and borrowers. After explaining risk, diversification, liquidity, and return, discuss the financial trade-offs of saving and investing.

3. Close/Reteach Remind students that saving and investing involve risk and potential gain. Ask them what factors might affect how much risk an investor is willing to take.

Guided Reading and Review Unit 4 folder, p. 13 asks students to identify the main ideas of the section and to define or identify key terms.

Graphing the Main Idea

Economic Institutions To help students understand the roles played by **economic institutions,** ask them to complete a web graphic organizer like the one shown at the right. Remind students that a web shows a main idea and its supporting details. Around the center circle, labeled "Financial Intermediaries," they should fill in types of intermediaries and their roles.

Section Reading Support Transparencies A template and the answers for this graphic organizer can be found in Chapter 11, Section 1 of the Section Reading Support Transparency System.

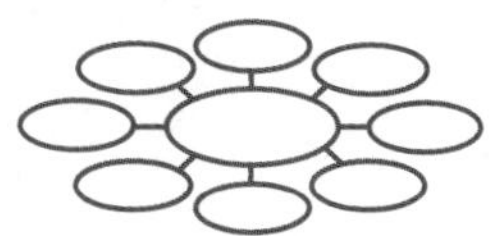

Answer to . . .

Illustration Caption Investment is like sowing seeds, promoting future growth.

Background

Investment Clubs

Americans can invest their money in many ways. One popular way is to organize a group of investors, pool their money, and invest that money according to the wishes of the majority. Such groups have been around for nearly 50 years, according to the National Association of Investment Clubs.

In 1956 the association reported 1,967 clubs. By 1960 that number had risen to 5,608. The strong economy of the 1960s boosted the number of clubs to 13,678 by 1970. During the 1970s, however, the Arab oil embargo sent inflation soaring in the United States. People began to put their limited financial resources into secured investments, such as certificates of deposit. By 1980 the number of investment clubs had dropped to 3,642.

Investor confidence returned in the 1980s, however, and by 1990 the number of investment clubs had grown to 7,085. In 2002 the National Association of Investment Clubs reported 28,235 clubs throughout the United States.

Differentiated Instruction 

(Reteaching) Have students work together in groups of three to create a three-minute advertisement showing how investment contributes to the private enterprise system. Ask them to show through words or actions how investment promotes economic growth and contributes to a nation's wealth.

Meeting NCEE Standards

Use the following benchmark activity from the **Voluntary National Content Standards in Economics** to evaluate student understanding of **Standard 12.**

Explain why people who save money receive interest payments while people who borrow money make interest payments.

Math Practice Activity

Math Practice folder, p. 10, "Determining Net Worth," allows students to calculate their own net worth.

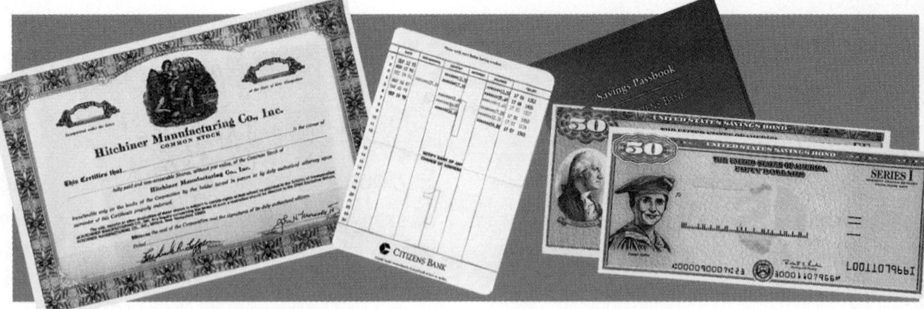

▶ **Documents such as (from left to right) a stock certificate, a savings passbook, and savings bonds are financial assets.**

financial system *the system that allows the transfer of money between savers and borrowers*

financial asset *claim on the property or income of a borrower*

financial intermediary *institution that helps channel funds from savers to borrowers*

mutual fund *fund that pools the savings of many individuals and invests this money in a variety of stocks, bonds, and other financial assets*

The Financial System

In order for investment to take place, an economy must have a financial system. A **financial system** includes savers and borrowers and allows the transfer of money between them to take place.

Financial Assets

When people save, they are, in essence, lending funds to others. As you read in Chapter 10, people can save money in a variety of ways. They may put money in a savings account, purchase a certificate of deposit, or buy a government or corporate bond. In each case, savers obtain a document that confirms their purchase or deposit. These documents may be passbooks, computer printouts, bond certificates, or other records.

Such documents represent claims on the property or income of the borrower. These claims are called **financial assets,** or securities. If the borrower fails to pay back the loan, these documents can serve as proof in court that money was borrowed and that repayment is expected.

For example, suppose you have $100 in a savings account at your local bank. Your passbook (or computer printout) is proof of the money in your account.

The Flow of Savings and Investments

Figure 11.1 shows how the financial system brings together savers and borrowers, fueling investment and economic growth. On one side are savers—households, individuals, and businesses that lend out their savings in return for financial assets. On the other side are borrowers—governments and businesses—who invest the money they borrow to build roads, factories, and homes. Borrowers may also use these funds to develop new products, create new markets, or provide new services.

Financial Intermediaries

Savers and borrowers may be linked directly. As you examine Figure 11.1, you will notice that borrowers and savers may also be linked through a variety of institutions pictured as "in between" the two. These **financial intermediaries** are institutions that help channel funds from savers to borrowers. They include the following:

- *Banks, Savings and Loan Associations, and Credit Unions* As you read in Chapter 10, banks, S&Ls, and credit unions take in deposits from savers, then lend out some of these funds to businesses and individuals.
- *Finance companies* Finance companies make loans to consumers and small businesses. Because finance companies sometimes lend money to people who do not repay their loans, they take on a high degree of risk. Finance companies, therefore, charge borrowers higher fees and interest rates to cover their losses from the loans that are not repaid.
- *Mutual funds* **Mutual funds** pool the savings of many individuals and invest this money in a variety of stocks, bonds, and other financial assets. Mutual funds allow people to invest in a broad range of companies in the stock market. This way,

Econ 101: Key Concepts Made Easy

Economic Institutions Help students understand the function and importance of **financial intermediaries** by asking them to recall what they learned in Chapter 10 about the chaotic banking system in the United States during the 1800s. With no central bank to set the rules, borrowers and investors were on their own, often with disastrous results. In today's highly structured nationwide financial system, intermediaries act as go-betweens, uniting like-minded investors and borrowers and helping to keep the economy growing. Ask students to suggest descriptive analogies for financial intermediaries. (Students may suggest *trip planners, dating services,* or *personal shoppers.*)

investors do not risk their savings by purchasing the stock of only one or two companies that might do poorly.

- *Life insurance companies* The main function of life insurance is to provide financial protection for the family or other beneficiaries of the insured. Working members of a family, for example, may buy life insurance policies so that if they die, money will be paid to survivors to make up for lost income. Insurance companies collect payments called premiums from the people who buy insurance. They lend out part of the premiums they collect to investors.
- *Pension funds* A pension is income that a retiree receives after working a certain number of years or reaching a certain age. In some cases, injuries may qualify a working person for pension benefits. Employers may contribute to the pension fund on behalf of their employees, they may withhold a percentage of workers' salaries to deposit in a pension fund, or they may do both. Employers set up pension funds to collect deposits and distribute payments. Pension fund managers invest these deposits in stocks, bonds, and other financial assets.

Now that you know something about the types of financial intermediaries, you may wonder why savers don't deal directly with investors. The answer is that, in general, dealing with financial intermediaries offers three advantages. Intermediaries share risks, provide information, and provide liquidity to investors.

Sharing Risk

As a saver, you may not want to invest your entire life savings in a single company or enterprise. For example, if you had $500 to invest and your neighbor was opening a new restaurant, would you give her the entire $500? Since it is estimated that more than half of all new businesses fail, you probably would not want to risk all of your money. Instead, you would want to spread the money around to various businesses to reduce the chances of losing your entire investment.

This strategy of spreading out investments to reduce risk is called **diversification.** If you deposited $500 in the bank or bought shares of a mutual fund, those institutions could pool your money with other people's savings and put your money to work by making a variety of investments.

diversification *spreading out investments to reduce risk*

Figure 11.1 Financial Intermediaries

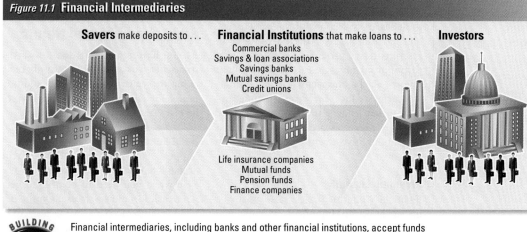

Savers make deposits to . . .

Financial Institutions that make loans to . . .

Commercial banks
Savings & loan associations
Savings banks
Mutual savings banks
Credit unions

Life insurance companies
Mutual funds
Pension funds
Finance companies

Investors

Financial intermediaries, including banks and other financial institutions, accept funds from savers and make loans to investors. Investors include entrepreneurs, businesses, and other borrowers. **Economic Institutions What advantages do financial intermediaries provide for savers?**

Block Scheduling Strategies

Consider these suggestions to take advantage of extended class time:

- Provide each student with a note card that lists information about a different fictitious individual: name, job status, income, and so on. At points around the room, post the names of various financial intermediaries as headings on sheets of posterboard. Have students visit the financial intermediaries in their assigned roles and record a transaction they might carry out there. After the activity, discuss with students their transactions at each location.
- Show the Economics Video Library segment "Getting Started," which explains how to save for retirement. Go over with students the statistics explained in the video, and explain the importance of starting to save early. Have students research investment opportunities and report on their findings.

Differentiated Instruction 

(Linguistic/Logical) Have students study the graphic on this page. Then ask them to write a paragraph in which they use this graphic to explain how the elements of the financial system—especially financial intermediaries—link savers to borrowers.

Differentiated Instruction 

Place English language learners in groups of three with two students who are proficient in English. Ask each group to name a local or regional example of each of the types of financial intermediaries explained in this section. Suggest that they find as much information as possible on each firm. ELL

Transparency Resource Package Economics Concepts, 11A: Financial Intermediaries

Differentiated Instruction 

Choose four active students to be representatives of financial companies: (1) a bank, (2) a mutual fund, (3) a life insurance company, and (4) a savings and loan. Have students research and determine the appropriate rates of interest or earnings versus risk each institution offers. Give each member of the rest of the class $1000 to invest. Allow the financial representatives to solicit investments one-on-one, writing down the names of the investors and amounts on a ledger. Compare results. Which company attracted the most money? How well did the investors diversify their money? SN

Answer to . . .

Building Key Concepts Financial intermediaries match savers with borrowers so that savers can gain interest on their money. Intermediaries also provide risk sharing, liquidity, and information to savers.

Learning Styles Activity
Learning Styles Lesson Plans folder, p. 27 asks student groups to create posters tracking the course of consumer savings as they move through the free enterprise system.

Differentiated Instruction L3

(Reteaching) Organize the class into four groups, and ask each group to work together as investment counselors for two investors, Tom and Rachel. They should evaluate each investor's personal and financial situation, assess trade-offs between risk and return, and then make recommendations about how much risk that investor should assume and the types of investments he or she should make. Share the following information with the class.

Tom is 26 years old and single, lives in a small studio apartment, works as a Web site designer, and has $50,000 to invest. His immediate plans include saving to buy a house, replacing his used car, and going to graduate school.

Rachel is 55 years old and a newly retired teacher. She and her husband own a home in the city and have a small summer cottage by a lake. Rachel has $50,000 in retirement funds to invest. Her immediate plans include vacationing in Italy and taking photography classes at the city's art museum. She and her husband plan to sell their home and purchase a condominium.

Transparency Resource Package
Economics Concepts, 11B: Risk and Return

Investors must weigh the risks explained in this chart against the potential rate of return on their investment.
Income What additional examples can you think of to illustrate each of the types of risk explained in the chart?

Figure 11.2 Types of Risk

Name	Description	Example
Credit risk	Borrowers may not pay back the money they have borrowed, or they may be late in making payments.	You lend $20 to your cousin, who promises to pay you back in two weeks. When your cousin fails to pay you on time, you don't have money for the basketball tickets you had planned to buy.
Liquidity risk	You may not be able to convert the investment back into cash quickly enough for your needs.	Your CD player is worth $100. You need cash to buy concert tickets, so you decide to sell your CD player. To convert your CD player into cash on short notice, you have to discount the price to $75.
Inflation rate risk	Inflation rates erode the value of your assets.	Ricardo lends Jeff $1,000 for one year at 10 percent interest. If the inflation rate is 12 percent, Ricardo loses money.
Time risk	You may have to pass up better opportunities for investment.	Lili invests $100 in May's cleaning business, to be repaid at 5 percent interest one year later. Six months later, Lili is unable to invest in Sonia's pet-sitting business, which pays 10 percent interest, because she has already invested her savings.

portfolio *a collection of financial assets*

prospectus *an investment report to potential investors*

return *the money an investor receives above and beyond the sum of money initially invested*

In other words, financial intermediaries diversify your investments and thus reduce the risk that you will lose all of your funds if a single investment fails.

Providing Information

Financial intermediaries are also good sources of information. Your local bank collects information about borrowers by monitoring their income and spending. So do finance companies when borrowers fill out credit applications. Mutual fund managers know how the stocks in their **portfolios,** or collections of financial assets, are performing. As required by law, all intermediaries provide this information to potential investors in an investment report called a **prospectus.** Financial intermediaries reduce the costs in time and money that lenders and borrowers would pay if they had to search out such information about investment opportunities on their own.

Providing Liquidity

Financial intermediaries also provide investors with liquidity. (Recall that liquidity is the ease with which people can convert an asset into cash.) It is intermediaries that provide this liquidity in the financial system.

Suppose, for example, that you decide to invest in a mutual fund. You keep the investment for two years, but then must sell it to pay your college tuition. If you had purchased an investment-quality painting instead, you would need to find another investor who would buy the art from you. As you can see, financial intermediaries and the liquidity they provide are crucial to meeting borrowers' and lenders' needs in our increasingly complex financial system.

Risk, Liquidity, and Return

As you have read, most decisions involve trade-offs. For example, the trade-off for going to a movie may be two additional hours of sleep. Saving and investing involves trade-offs as well.

Return and Liquidity

Suppose you save money in a savings account. Savings accounts are good ways to save when you need to be able to get to your cash for immediate use. On the other hand, savings accounts pay relatively low interest rates, about 2 to 3 percentage points below a certificate of deposit (CD). In other words, savings accounts are liquid, but they have a low return. **Return** is the

Answer to . . .

Building Key Concepts Students should think of at least one additional example for each type of risk. For example, for *credit risk* they may mention a transaction between a credit card company and a customer who fails to pay the company's bill.

Interdisciplinary Connections: Language Arts

Examining Words The word *prospectus* is derived from the Latin-based *prospect,* meaning "view" or "lookout." *Prospectus* entered the English language in 1765. In 1841 the British began to use *prospect* to mean "to explore an area, especially for mineral deposits." Gold miners in the United States were known as *prospectors.* In a sense a person who reads a prospectus is looking for "gold," since she or he hopes to gain wealth.

Making the Connection Ask students to volunteer other words that include the root *spect.* Ask what these words have in common. (Students may suggest *inspect, spectacles,* and *aspect,* and should note that all have to do with seeing or viewing something.)

money an investor receives above and beyond the sum of money initially invested.

What if, however, you suddenly inherit $5,000? You do not need ready access to those funds, since your part-time job pays your day-to-day expenses. If you are willing to give up some degree of ready access to your money, you can earn higher interest rates than offered by a savings account. For example, you can invest your money in a certificate of deposit that pays 4 percent interest. You would not be allowed to withdraw your money for, say, two years without paying a penalty. Therefore, before buying the CD, you would want to weigh the greater return on your investment against the loss of liquidity.

Return and Risk

Certificates of deposit (up to $100,000) are considered very safe investments because they are insured by the federal government. When you buy a CD, you are giving up liquidity for a certain period of time, but you are not risking losing any money. What if, however, you decided to invest the money in a new company that your friends are starting? If the company succeeds, you could double your investment. If it fails, however, you could lose all or part of the money you invested.

To take another example, suppose your savings account is earning 2 percent interest. Would you be willing to lend money to your friend Emily for that same 2 percent interest rate, knowing that she rarely pays back loans on time? Probably not. For you to lend Emily the money, she would have to offer you a higher return than the bank could offer. This higher return would help offset the greater risk that Emily will not repay the loan on time. Likewise, investors and lenders must consider the degree of risk involved in an investment and decide what return they would require to make up for that risk.

The higher the potential return, the riskier the investment. Whenever individuals evaluate an investment, they must balance the risks involved with the rewards they expect to gain from the investment.

THE WALL STREET JOURNAL. CLASSROOM EDITION

In the News Read more about return and risk in "How Much Risk Can You Tolerate," an article in The Wall Street Journal Classroom Edition.

Go Online
The Wall Street Journal Classroom Edition
For: Current Events
Visit: PHSchool.com
Web Code: mnc-4111

Section 1 Assessment

Progress Monitoring *Online*
For: Self-quiz with vocabulary practice
Web Code: mna-4115

Key Terms and Main Ideas

1. How does investing promote financial growth?
2. Explain how savers, borrowers, and **financial intermediaries** contribute to the **financial system.**
3. Describe three roles of financial intermediaries.
4. Explain the following statement in your own words. "The higher the potential **return** on an **investment,** the higher the risk."

Applying Economic Concepts

5. ***Critical Thinking*** Explain why a student with $500 in a savings account is participating in the American financial system.
6. ***You Decide*** Suppose your cousin Bill asks to borrow $50 from you for concert tickets. Bill has offered to pay you interest on the loan. What factors should you consider before you decide how much interest to charge?
7. ***Try This*** What are three questions concerning risk, return, and liquidity that you would ask a financial advisor before investing your savings?
8. ***You Decide*** Explain the potential risks and returns of the following savings plans and investments. **(a)** a savings account **(b)** a certificate of deposit **(c)** your neighbor's successful pet care service

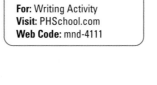

Go Online PHSchool.com
For: Writing Activity
Visit: PHSchool.com
Web Code: mnd-4111

Go Online PHSchool.com Typing in the Web Code when prompted will bring students directly to the article.

THE WALL STREET JOURNAL. CLASSROOM EDITION

For an additional article from *The Wall Street Journal Classroom Edition,* see the Source Articles folder in the **Teaching Resources,** pp. 33–35.

GTE Guide to the Essentials
Chapter 11, Section 1, p. 46 provides support for students who need additional review of the section content. Spanish support is available in the Spanish edition of the guide on p. 46.

Quiz Unit 4 folder, p. 14 includes questions to check students' understanding of Section 1 content.

Presentation Pro CD-ROM
Quiz provides multiple-choice questions to check students' understanding of Section 1 content.

Answers to . . .

Section 1 Assessment

1. Investing allows more money to be used by more people or firms, thus encouraging financial growth.
2. Savers provide funds for borrowers to use. Borrowers use that money to invest in financial and real assets. Financial intermediaries help channel funds from savers to borrowers.
3. Financial intermediaries share risk, allowing savers to diversify ways in which their money is saved; they provide information, gathering data on financial markets and assets for both savers and investors; and they provide liquidity, giving people the means to convert assets into cash.
4. Possible answer: Investments that offer the chance to earn a lot of money tend also to be risky investments.
5. The $500 is used by borrowers through financial intermediaries, providing assets for borrowers and businesses, thus contributing to the financial system.
6. Factors include how reliable you consider Bill to be, when you think he will pay you back, and what it will cost you to lend him the money.
7. Possible questions: How has this fund done in the last five years? What companies do you invest in? How easily can I convert my investment back into cash?
8. (a) low risk and low return (b) low risk and medium return (c) high risk and high potential return

Progress Monitoring *Online*
For additional assessment, have students access Progress Monitoring Online at **Web Code:** mna-4115

Go Online PHSchool.com Typing in the Web Code when prompted will bring students directly to detailed instructions for this activity.

ECONOMIC *Profile*
Warren Buffett

Background

In 2003 Warren Buffett was the second-richest person in the United States. Unlike some wealthy individuals, Buffett doesn't flash his bankroll. In fact, he is criticized by some people as being too cautious with his funds.

Buffett had always believed that private company jets were wasteful corporate expenditures. In 1986, however, he was persuaded to purchase a plane for Berkshire—it was a used one, of course. A few years later Buffett bought a more expensive model. In wry recognition of his previous stance against private jets, he named his new plane the *Indefensible.*

Over time Buffett grew to appreciate the plane, and in 1995 he bought a one-fourth share in a Hawker jet, this time for his personal use. Buffett's wife, who used the jet often, christened it the *Richly Deserved.* Finally acknowledging his new passion for private, pampered jet travel, Buffett himself renamed his jet the *Indispensible.*

Careers in Economics Activity Unit 4 folder, p. 22 gives students a closer look at the career path of a stockbroker.

Answers to . . .

1. Possible answer: Do your own research. Understand the business. Look for companies whose stock is selling for less than it is worth. Don't follow the crowd.
2. Advantages include minimizing the changes in value that accompany the daily buying and selling of shares. Disadvantages include potential difficulty for existing shareholders to sell their shares and lessened ability to attract new investors.
3. Answers should show evidence of research and an understanding of Berkshire Hathaway as well as the difference between a mutual fund and a holding company.

Entrepreneur

ECONOMIC

Profile

Warren Buffett (b. 1930)

When Warren Buffett was 5 years old, he set up a stand to sell lemonade—not in front of his own house, but at a friend's house on another street, where the traffic was heavier. The son of an Omaha, Nebraska, stockbroker, Buffett announced while still in grade school that he intended to be rich before he was 35. Today, Buffett is widely considered to be a financial genius and is one of the most successful investors in the world.

The Oracle of Omaha

At age 14, Warren Buffett bought 40 acres of land and rented it to a farmer. By the age of 21, Buffett had accumulated nearly $10,000. Nearly every dollar of the $20 billion he is worth today can be traced back to that original bankroll. Because of this phenomenal success, he is known as the financial "Oracle of Omaha."

Investing the Buffett Way

Buffett learned how to invest at Columbia University, where he earned a master's degree in business in 1951. A professor taught him to pick his investments by doing his own research. "You're not right or wrong because 1,000 people agree with you or disagree with you," the professor told him. "You're right because your facts and reasoning are right."

Buffett has continued to follow that advice to this day. He will not invest in a business he does not understand. For this reason, he has shied away from high-tech companies and focuses on communications, retail, and insurance companies. He avoided the rise and fall of the dot-coms.

Buffett chooses companies whose stock is selling for less than it is worth. If such a company is well managed, has few competitors, and is concentrating on what it does best, he will buy stock and wait for it to go up.

For example, many analysts predicted in 1963 that American Express would go out of business after it suffered a major financial setback. In Omaha, Buffett saw that people were still using their American Express charge cards. Ignoring the experts, he bought 5 percent of American Express. Five years later, the stock was worth nearly six times what he paid for it.

The Berkshire Hathaway Company

Buffett objects to those who label his Berkshire Hathaway investment company a mutual fund. Because it owns Dairy Queen, GEICO Insurance, and Executive Jet outright—and holds controlling interests in other corporations—Buffett prefers to think of it as a holding company.

The cost of Berkshire Hathaway stock, as much as $75,500 a share in 2003, puts it beyond the reach of most investors. That's fine with Buffett. Not only does the high price make Berkshire Hathaway the "Rolls Royce" of investing, it also limits trading in the company's shares on the stock market.

CHECK FOR UNDERSTANDING

1. **Source Reading** Summarize Warren Buffett's approach to investing by creating a list of his "dos" and "don'ts" when deciding whether to buy stock in a company.
2. **Critical Thinking** Why might it be a plus for a company to have such a high share price that trading in its stock is discouraged? What drawbacks might there be for a company in this situation?
3. **Problem Solving** Is Buffett's firm a mutual fund or a holding company? Use the Internet and other resources to learn more about Berkshire Hathaway in order to support your response.

Beyond the Classroom: Career Connections

Investment Banker Explain to students that if the high-stakes world of investing appeals to them, but they don't have a fortune to invest (or lose), they might enjoy working for an investment bank. When a corporation is ready to issue new securities, the investment bank purchases the entire issue from the corporation at a fixed price. Then the bank sells the securities in small units to investors at a price that covers the bank's costs and enables it to make a profit. Ask students to further investigate the world of investment banking and report on specific career opportunities in this area of the banking world.

Bonds and Other Financial Assets

Preview

Objectives

After studying this section you will be able to:

1. **Describe** the characteristics of bonds as financial assets.
2. **Identify** different types of bonds.
3. **Describe** the characteristics of other types of financial assets.
4. **Explain** four different types of financial asset markets.

Section Focus

Corporations and governments borrow money by selling bonds and other financial assets. The corporation or government pays the purchaser interest on the bonds and repays the principal, or money borrowed, at a specified time.

Key Terms

coupon rate
maturity
par value
yield
savings bond
municipal bond
corporate bond
Securities and Exchange Commission
junk bond
capital market
money market
primary market
secondary market

How do borrowers raise money for investment? One of the most important ways is by selling bonds. As you read in Chapter 8, bonds are certificates sold by a company or government to finance projects or expansion.

For example, starting in 1942, the United States Department of Treasury launched bond drives to encourage Americans to buy "war bonds"—government savings bonds that helped finance World War II. Movie stars and war heroes urged the public to buy bonds. Even school children brought their dimes and quarters to school each week, buying defense stamps that would eventually add up to the price of a war bond.

Bonds as Financial Assets

Bonds are basically loans, or IOUs, that represent debt that the government or a corporation must repay to an investor. Bonds typically pay the investor a fixed amount of interest at regular intervals for a fixed amount of time. Bonds are generally lower-risk investments. As you might expect from your reading about the relationship between risk and return, the rate of return on bonds is usually also lower than for other investments.

The Three Components of Bonds

Bonds have three basic components:

- *Coupon rate* The **coupon rate** is the interest rate that the bond issuer will pay to the bondholder.
- *Maturity* **Maturity** is the time at which payment to the bondholder is due.

coupon rate *the interest rate that a bond issuer will pay to a bondholder*

maturity *the time at which payment to a bondholder is due*

Don't Let That Shadow Touch Them
Buy WAR BONDS

◀ **This poster used powerful images to convince people to buy war bonds during World War II.**

Graphing the Main Idea

Interest Rates To build understanding of the concept of **interest rates** and investment opportunities, have students complete a tree map graphic organizer like the one shown at the right. Remind students that a tree map shows an outline of a main topic, main ideas, and supporting details. They should place the title "Financial Assets" at the top of the organizer. Each main heading in the section can go into one of the next tier of boxes, with supporting details listed below.

Section Reading Support Transparencies A template and the answers for this graphic organizer can be found in Chapter 11, Section 2 of the Section Reading Support Transparency System.

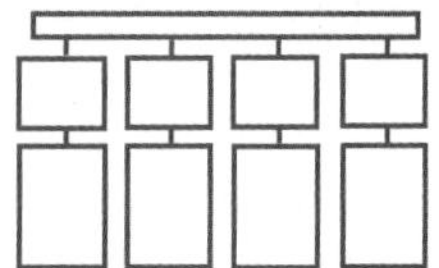

Section 2

Bonds and Other Financial Assets

Objectives You may wish to call students' attention to the objectives in the Section Preview. The objectives are reflected in the main headings of the section.

Bellringer Ask students whether they have ever heard the expression "His word is as good as his bond." Explain that it means that a person's word is as trustworthy as a financial arrangement for which a person has legal liability. Tell the class that in this section they will learn about bonds and promises.

Vocabulary Builder Have students read through the section to find the meaning of each key term. Then ask them to create a matching quiz with the key terms.

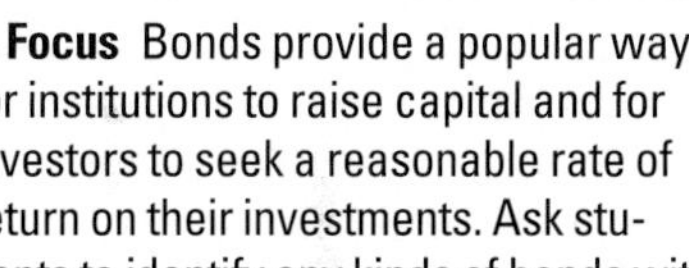

Lesson Plan

Teaching the Main Concepts (L3)

1. Focus Bonds provide a popular way for institutions to raise capital and for investors to seek a reasonable rate of return on their investments. Ask students to identify any kinds of bonds with which they are familiar.

2. Instruct Begin by explaining the characteristics and types of bonds. Explain how bonds are rated and what the ratings mean. Then introduce students to other types of financial assets along with the advantages and drawbacks of each. Finally, discuss financial asset markets.

3. Close/Reteach Remind students that borrowers and investors use bonds and other financial assets to achieve specific financial goals. Ask students to recall the different types of bonds and to rate their respective risks.

Guided Reading and Review Unit 4 folder, p. 15 asks students to identify the main ideas of the section and to define or identify key terms.

Differentiated Instruction 

Ask students to create a fact sheet that explains the characteristics of bonds as financial assets. Remind them that the fact sheet should be aimed at people who do not understand what bonds are or how they work. Encourage students to use a format (such as question and answer) that allows them to explain bonds concisely.

Background

Economics in History

The war bond drives of World War II featured famous entertainers and bolstered public support for the war. However, these bond drives added little to the nation's war chest. World War II cost the federal government about $321 billion, of which 41 percent came from taxes. Where did the rest of the money come from?

The answer lies in "defense economics," of which war finance is a branch. Generally wars are financed by taxes, compulsory loans, voluntary domestic loans, foreign loans, and printing of new money.

Compulsory loans are short-term, mandatory loans made to government by the public. Usually the public thinks of these "loans" as taxes. Voluntary domestic loans result from the sale of government bonds. Some are purchased by the public, in the form of war bonds, but the rest are financed by banks.

The least desirable form of war financing is the printing of new money. A government that is forced to print money has probably exhausted all other borrowing options. The more money it prints, the less that money is worth. If the government prints enough new money, the currency will become worthless.

par value *the amount that an investor pays to purchase a bond and that will be repaid to the investor at maturity*

yield *the annual rate of return on a bond if the bond were held to maturity*

Different bonds have different lengths of maturity. Bonds typically mature in 10, 20, or 30 years.

- *Par value* A bond's **par value** is the amount that an investor pays to purchase the bond and that will be repaid to the investor at maturity. Par value is also called *face value* or *principal.*

Suppose that you buy a $1,000 bond from the corporation Jeans, Etc. The investor who buys the bond is called the "holder." The seller of a bond is the "issuer." You are therefore the holder of the bond, and Jeans, Etc. is the issuer. The components of this bond are as follows:

- *Coupon rate:* 5 percent, paid to the bondholder annually
- *Maturity:* 10 years
- *Par Value:* $1,000

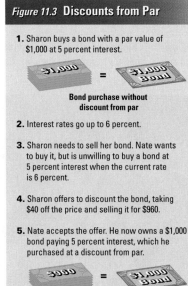

Figure 11.3 Discounts from Par

1. Sharon buys a bond with a par value of $1,000 at 5 percent interest.

Bond purchase without discount from par

2. Interest rates go up to 6 percent.
3. Sharon needs to sell her bond. Nate wants to buy it, but is unwilling to buy a bond at 5 percent interest when the current rate is 6 percent.
4. Sharon offers to discount the bond, taking $40 off the price and selling it for $960.
5. Nate accepts the offer. He now owns a $1,000 bond paying 5 percent interest, which he purchased at a discount from par.

$960 = $1,000 Bond

Bond purchase with discount from par

Investors can earn money by buying bonds at a discount, called a discount from par.
Interest Rates How do interest rates affect bond prices?

How much money will you earn from this bond, and over what period of time? The coupon rate is 5 percent of $1,000 per year. This means that you will receive a payment of $50 (.05 times $1,000) each year for ten years, or a total of $500 in interest. In ten years, the bond will have reached maturity, and Jeans, Etc. will retire the debt. This means that the company's debt to you will have ended, and that Jeans, Etc. will pay you the par value of the bond, or $1,000. Thus, for your $1,000 investment, you will have received $1,500 over a period of ten years.

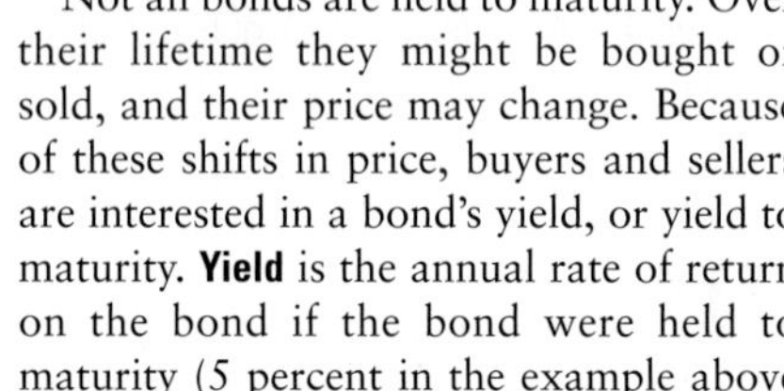

Not all bonds are held to maturity. Over their lifetime they might be bought or sold, and their price may change. Because of these shifts in price, buyers and sellers are interested in a bond's yield, or yield to maturity. **Yield** is the annual rate of return on the bond if the bond were held to maturity (5 percent in the example above involving Jeans, Etc.).

Buying Bonds at a Discount

Investors earn money from interest on the bonds they buy. They can also earn money by buying bonds at a discount, called a discount from par. In other words, if Nate were buying a bond with a par value of $1,000, he may be able to pay only $960 for it. When the bond matures, Nate will redeem the bond at par, or $1,000. He will thus have earned $40 on his investment, in addition to interest payments from the bond issuer.

Why would someone sell a bond for less than its par value? The answer lies in the fact that interest rates are always changing. For example, suppose that Sharon buys a $1,000 bond at 5 percent interest, which is the current market rate. A year later, she needs to sell the bond to help pay for a new car. By that time, however, interest rates have risen to 6 percent. No one will pay $1,000 for Sharon's bond at 5 percent interest when they could go elsewhere and buy a $1,000 bond at 6 percent interest. For Sharon to sell her bond at 5 percent, she will have to sell it at a discount. (See Figure 11.3.)

Econ 101: Key Concepts Made Easy

Interest Rates Explain to students that a bond's **maturity** is the time at which payment to the bondholder is due. At that point the bondholder receives the par value of the bond, and the company's debt is repaid. While the bond is maturing, the bondholder receives interest payments determined by the coupon rate. Ask students to work in pairs and present each other with various coupon rates, maturities, and par values. Each pair of students should calculate the return on the investment they describe.

Answer to . . .

Building Key Concepts Rising interests rates drive bond prices down.

Figure 11.4 Bond Ratings

Standard & Poor's		Moody's	
Highest investment grade	AAA	Best quality	Aaa
High grade	AA	High quality	Aa
Upper medium grade	A	Upper medium grade	A
Medium grade	BBB	Medium grade	Baa
Lower medium grade	BB	Possesses speculative elements	Ba
Speculative	B	Generally not desirable	B
Vulnerable to default	CCC	Poor, possibly in default	Caa
Subordinated to other debt rated CCC	CC	Highly speculative, often in default	Ca
Subordinated to CC debt	C	Income bonds not paying income	C
Bond in default	D	Interest and principal payments in default	D

Standard & Poor's and Moody's rate bonds according to their assessments of the issuer's ability to make interest payments and to repay the principal when the bond matures.
Income What bond rating carries the least risk?

Bond Ratings

How does an investor decide which bonds to buy? Investors can check bond quality through two firms that publish bond ratings. Standard & Poor's and Moody's rate bonds on a number of factors, including the issuer's ability to make future interest payments and to repay the principal when the bond matures. These companies' rating systems rank bonds from the highest investment grade (AAA in the Standard & Poor's system or Aaa in the Moody's rating system) to the lowest (D in both systems). A bond rating of D generally means that the bond is in default—that is, the issuer has not kept up with interest payments or has defaulted on paying principal.

The higher the bond rating, the lower the interest rate the company usually has to pay to get people to buy its bonds. For example, a AAA bond may be issued at a 5 percent interest rate. A BBB bond, however, may be issued at a 7.5 percent interest rate. The buyer of the AAA bond trades off a lower interest rate for lower risk. The buyer of the BBB bond trades greater risk for a higher interest rate.

Similarly, the higher the bond rating, the higher the price at which the bond will sell. For example, a $1,000 bond with an AAA (or "triple A") rating may sell at $1,100. A $1,000 bond with a BBB rating may sell for only $950 because of the increased risk that the seller could default.

In essence, holders of bonds with high ratings who keep their bonds until maturity face relatively little risk of losing their investment. Holders of bonds with lower ratings, however, take on more risk in return for potentially higher interest payments.

Advantages and Disadvantages to the Issuer

From the point of view of the investor, bonds are good investments because they are relatively safe. Bonds are desirable from the issuer's point of view as well, for two main reasons:

1. Once the bond is sold, the coupon rate for that bond will not go up or down. For example, when Jeans, Etc. sells bonds, it knows in advance that it will be making fixed payments for a specific length of time.
2. Unlike stockholders, bondholders do not own a part of the company. Therefore, the company does not have to share profits with its bondholders if the company does particularly well.

Block Scheduling Strategies

Consider these suggestions to take advantage of extended class time:

- Devote some class time to showing students how to read the business section of a newspaper. Provide small groups with copies of a national daily newspaper. Point out how the variety of information can help students invest wisely. Have students create their own how-to manual for reading these sections of the newspaper.
- Extend the first activity on this page by conducting an in-class tour of Web sites related to securities. Have students create a brochure pointing out what is offered at each site. Have students use the links provided in the *Economics: Principles in Action* segment in the Social Studies area at the following Web site: **www.phschool.com**

Differentiated Instruction 

Standard & Poor's and Moody's provide investment services other than bond ratings. Have a small group of students research both companies and create an illustrated presentation to explain their findings. Ask them to explore the types of investor services each company provides and how these services help investors to make informed choices. GT

Differentiated Instruction 

To help students understand bond ratings and the opportunity cost involved in choosing one bond over another, instruct pairs of students to complete the following exercise. First, ask each pair to read through the part of the section titled "Bonds as Financial Assets," starting on p. 277. Then, instruct one student to present a hypothetical bond to the other, including information about bond rating and interest rate. Ask the other student to respond verbally by describing the trade-off he or she would make by buying that bond. Then have students switch roles. *(Example: One student presents a bond with a AAA Standard & Poor's rating with an interest rate of 4.5 percent. The other student responds by saying that the buyer is giving up a higher interest rate to gain a secure investment.)*

Transparency Resource Package Economics Concepts, 11C: Bond Reports

Answer to . . .

Building Key Concepts AAA and Aaa

Background

Economics in History

The Securities and Exchange Commission (SEC) came into being as part of the Securities Exchange Act of 1934. The purpose of the act was to reform and regulate certain financial practices, which many people blamed for the Great Depression.

The SEC's mission is to prevent fraud and deception in the purchase and sale of stocks and bonds. Stockbrokers and companies that trade in securities must register with the SEC. Furthermore, any individual who owns more than 10 percent of a company's stock is required to submit reports at regular intervals to the SEC.

Another important aspect of the Securities and Exchange Act was to give the Federal Reserve authority to regulate margin requirements. *Margin* means the amount of money that an investor deposits with a broker. Stock bought on margin is financed largely with credit. Buying on margin was a popular way to invest before the Great Crash in 1929. In fact, one reason the market collapsed was that so much of the stock in circulation had been bought with credit. The Securities and Exchange Act gave the Federal Reserve the right to require that anyone who bought securities on margin had to deposit a minimum amount of cash with a broker before the rest of the purchase price could be financed.

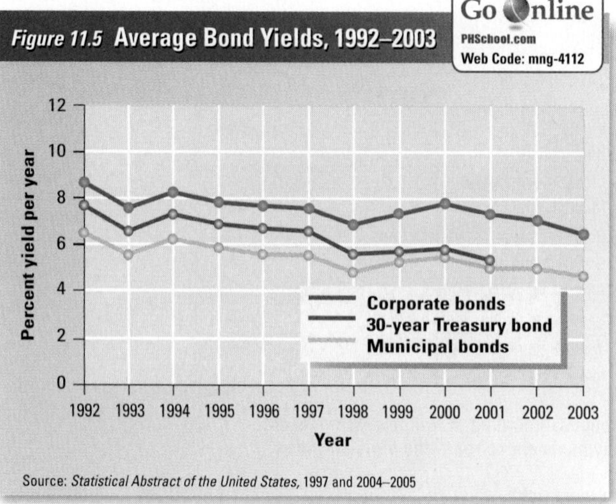

From the early 1990s to the start of the 2000s, bond yields dipped slightly for all three types of bonds shown. Corporate bonds, however, continued to have the highest yield. **Income Which of the three types of bonds would you expect to carry the least risk? Explain your answer.**

savings bond
low-denomination bond issued by the United States government

On the other hand, bonds also pose two main disadvantages to the issuer:

1. The company must make fixed interest payments, even in bad years when it does not make money. In addition, it cannot change its interest payments even when interest rates have gone down.
2. If the firm does not maintain financial health, its bonds may be downgraded to a lower bond rating and thus may be harder to sell unless they are offered at a discount.

Figure 11.6 Treasury Bonds, Notes, and Bills

	Treasury Bond	Treasury Note	Treasury Bill
Term	long-term	intermediate-term	short-term
Maturity	from 10 to 30 years	from 2 to 10 years	3, 6, or 12 months
Liquidity and safety	safe	safe	liquid and safe
Minimum purchase	$1,000	$1,000	$1,000
Denomination	$1,000	$1,000	$1,000

Treasury bonds, notes, and bills represent debt that the government must repay the investor.
Government How do these three types of government securities differ?

Types of Bonds

Despite these risks to the issuer, when corporations or governments need to borrow funds for long periods, they often issue bonds. There are several different types of bonds.

Savings Bonds

You may already be familiar with savings bonds, which are sometimes given to young people as gifts. **Savings bonds** are low-denomination ($50 to $10,000) bonds issued by the United States government. The government uses funds from the sale of savings bonds to help pay for public works projects like buildings, roads, and dams. Like other government bonds, savings bonds have virtually no risk of default, or failure to repay the loan.

The federal government pays interest on savings bonds. However, unlike most other bond issuers, it does not send interest payments to bondholders on a regular schedule. Instead, the purchaser buys a savings bond for less than par value. For example, you can purchase a $50 savings bond for only $25. When the bond matures, you receive the $25 you paid for the bond plus $25 in interest.

Treasury Bonds, Bills, and Notes

The United States Treasury Department issues Treasury bonds, as well as Treasury bills and notes (T-bills and T-notes). These investments offer different lengths of maturity, as shown in Figure 11.6. Backed by the "full faith and credit" of the United States government, these securities are among the safest investments in terms of default risk. The federal government temporarily stopped selling 30-year bonds in 2001, upsetting many investors who like safe, long-term investments.

Answer to . . .

Building Key Concepts Students may say Treasury bonds because they are backed by the federal government.

Building Key Concepts They differ mainly in their maturity and in the term.

Preparing for Standardized Tests

Have students read the section titled "Savings Bonds" and then answer the question below.

Which of the following is not a characteristic of savings bonds?

A They are issued by the government.
B They can be used to help pay for public works projects.
C They are sold in low denominations.
(D) They carry a high risk.

▲ Municipal bonds, or munis, help finance local projects such as libraries and schools.

Municipal Bonds

State and local governments and municipalities (government units with corporate status) issue bonds to finance such improvements as highways, state buildings, libraries, parks, and schools. These bonds are called **municipal bonds,** or "munis."

Because state and local governments have the power to tax, investors can assume that these governments will be able to keep up with interest payments and repay the principal at maturity. Standard & Poor's and Moody's therefore consider most municipal bonds to be safe investments, depending upon the financial health of a particular state or town. In addition, the interest paid on municipal bonds is not subject to income taxes at the federal level or in the issuing state. Because they are relatively safe and are tax-exempt, "munis" are very attractive to investors.

Corporate Bonds

As you read in Chapter 8, corporations issue bonds to help raise money to expand their businesses. These **corporate bonds** are issued in fairly large denominations, such as $1,000, $5,000, and $10,000. The interest on corporate bonds is taxed as ordinary income.

Unlike city and other governments, corporations have no tax base to help guarantee their ability to repay their loans, so these bonds have moderate levels of risk. Investors in corporate bonds must depend on the success of the corporation's sales of goods and services to generate enough income to pay interest and principal.

Corporations that issue bonds are watched closely not only by Standard & Poor's and Moody's, but also by the **Securities and Exchange Commission** (SEC). The SEC is an independent government agency that regulates financial markets and investment companies. It enforces laws prohibiting fraud and other dishonest investment practices.

Junk Bonds

Junk bonds, or high-yield securities, are lower-rated, and potentially higher-paying, bonds. They became especially popular investments during the 1980s and 1990s,

municipal bond *a bond issued by a state or local government or municipality to finance such improvements as highways, state buildings, libraries, parks, and schools*

corporate bond *a bond that a corporation issues to raise money to expand its business*

Securities and Exchange Commission *an independent agency of the government that regulates financial markets and investment companies*

junk bond *a lower-rated, potentially higher-paying bond*

Differentiated Instruction L2

Have students use the following method to take notes on this section. First have them draw a vertical line down their paper, about one third of the way in from the left side. Have them paraphrase important points from the section in the right column. Then, in the left column, ask them to write questions that can be answered by their notes. Explain to them that they can use these notes for review by covering up the right column with a sheet of paper and answering the questions in the left column. LPR

Differentiated Instruction 

(Reteaching) Have students identify the types of bonds described in this section (savings, Treasury, corporate, junk) in a poster, table, chart, or other graphic presentation. Display these projects on a bulletin board.

Interdisciplinary Connections: Math

Calculating Rate of Return Calculating interest rates and rates of return can be tedious work. Fortunately, some calculators have been designed specifically to handle interest rate calculations for both simple and compound interest over varying lengths of time. In addition, graphing calculators can be programmed to show data visually, enabling the user to enter data and track the progress of investments.

Making the Connection Ask students who own graphing calculators to bring them in. You may also be able to borrow some from your school's mathematics department. Have a knowledgeable student demonstrate their use, or lead a class demonstration with investment data.

Differentiated Instruction L4

You may wish to have students add the following to their portfolios. Ask them to write a brief essay comparing and contrasting certificates of deposit and money market mutual funds. Explain that their essays should describe the two types of financial assets and show how they are similar and different.

Economics Assessment Rubric
Economics Assessment Rubrics folder, pp. 6–7 provides sample evaluation materials for a writing assignment.

Differentiated Instruction L3

Ask groups of three to four students to design graphic organizers that use text and illustrations to show the differences and interrelationships among capital markets, money markets, primary markets, and secondary markets. Encourage students to go beyond the text to find additional information about these markets and incorporate that information into their graphic organizers.

Global Connections

International Bonds The United States government isn't the only government that issues bonds. Many other countries, including Saudi Arabia, Germany, and Japan, also issue bonds. International bonds are usually issued in large denominations, starting at $1 million. In addition, principal and coupon payments are often made in foreign currencies. The investors, therefore, cannot know what the value of payments will turn out to be. **What are two drawbacks to buying international bonds?**

when large numbers of aggressive investors made—but also sometimes lost—large sums of money buying and selling these securities.

Junk bonds have been known to pay over 12 percent interest at a time when government bonds are yielding only about 8 percent interest. On the other hand, junk bonds also carry bond ratings of "lower medium grade" or "speculative" (BB, Ba, or lower). Investors in junk bonds therefore face a strong possibility that some of the issuing firms will default on their debt. Nevertheless, in many cases junk bonds have enabled companies to undertake activities that would otherwise have been impossible to complete. (For more information on how to follow the progress of a stock by reading stock market reports, see page 284.)

"Gee, fellas - junk bonds."

▲ **From what you have read, how accurate is the cartoonist's view of junk bonds?**

Other Types of Financial Assets

In addition to bonds, investors may choose other financial assets. These include certificates of deposit and money market mutual funds, as well as stock. You will read more about stock in Section 3.

Certificates of Deposit

Certificates of deposit (CDs) are one of the most common forms of investment. As you read in Chapter 10, CDs are available through banks, which lend out the funds deposited in CDs for a fixed amount of time, such as 6 months or a year.

CDs are attractive to small investors because they cost as little as $100. Investors can also choose among many terms of maturity. This means that if an investor foresees a future expenditure, such as college tuition or a major home improvement, he or she can buy a CD that matures just before the expenditure is due.

Money Market Mutual Funds

Money market mutual funds are special types of mutual funds. As you read in Section 1, businesses collect money from individual investors and then buy stocks, bonds, or other financial assets to form a mutual fund.

In the case of money market mutual funds, intermediaries buy short-term financial assets. Investors receive higher interest on a money market mutual fund than they would receive from a savings account. On the other hand, money market mutual funds are not covered by FDIC insurance. (As you read in Chapter 10, FDIC insurance protects bank deposits up to $100,000 per account). This makes them slightly riskier than savings accounts.

Answer to . . .

Global Connections Students may point out that investments would not be regulated by the U.S. government or that certain political events, such as wars, could affect an investment negatively.

Cartoon Caption Students may say that junk bonds are not as worthless as the cartoonist suggests.

Preparing for Standardized Tests

Have students read the section titled "Certificates of Deposit" and then answer the question below.

Why are certificates of deposit attractive to small investors?

(A) They cost as little as $100.
B They are insured by the Securities and Exchange Commission.
C They pay higher interest than money market mutual funds.
D They are highly rated by Standard & Poor's.

Financial Asset Markets

Financial assets, including bonds, certificates of deposit, and money market mutual funds, are traded on financial asset markets. The various types of financial asset markets are classified in different ways.

Capital and Money Markets

One way to classify financial asset markets is according to the length of time for which funds are lent. This type of classification includes capital markets and money markets.

- *Capital markets* Markets in which money is lent for periods longer than a year are called **capital markets.** Financial assets that are traded in capital markets include long-term CDs and corporate and government bonds that require more than a year to mature.
- *Money markets* Markets in which money is lent for periods of less than a year are called **money markets.** Financial assets that are traded in money markets include short-term CDs, Treasury bills, and money market mutual funds.

Primary and Secondary Markets

Markets may also be classified according to whether assets can be resold to other buyers. This type of classification includes primary and secondary markets.

- *Primary markets* Financial assets that can be redeemed only by the original holder are sold on **primary markets.** Examples include savings bonds, which are non-transferable (that is, the original buyer cannot sell them to another buyer). Small certificates of deposit are also in the primary market because investors would most likely cash them in early rather than try to sell them to someone else.
- *Secondary markets* Financial assets that can be resold are sold on **secondary markets.** This option for resale provides liquidity to investors. If there is a strong secondary market for an asset, the investor knows that the asset can be resold fairly quickly without a penalty, thus providing the investor with ready cash. The secondary market also makes possible the lively trade in stock that is the subject of the next section.

capital market *market in which money is lent for periods longer than a year*

money market *market in which money is lent for periods of less than a year*

primary market *market for selling financial assets that can only be redeemed by the original holder*

secondary market *market for reselling financial assets*

Section 2 Assessment

Progress Monitoring *Online*
For: Self-quiz with vocabulary practice
Web Code: mna-4116

Key Terms and Main Ideas

1. Describe two ways in which investors can earn money from bonds.
2. Why are bond ratings useful to investors?
3. Describe five different types of bonds.
4. How do **capital markets** and **money markets** differ?

Applying Economic Concepts

5. ***Math Practice*** Suppose that you buy a bond for $100 that pays 4 percent interest per year. How much money will you have earned when the bond reaches maturity in five years?
6. ***Decision Making*** Suppose that you have saved $1,000. In which of the financial assets described in this section would you invest? Explain your choice.
7. ***Critical Thinking*** Which bond would you expect to be more expensive, a bond with a AAA rating or a bond with a BBB rating? (Assume that both bonds pay the same rate of interest.)
8. ***Try This*** Assume that you are an investment advisor with a client who is interested in buying bonds. Create a fact sheet that shows your client the different types of bonds and their characteristics.

For: Math Activity
Visit: PHSchool.com
Web Code: mnd-4112

GTE Guide to the Essentials
Chapter 11, Section 2, p. 47 provides support for students who need additional review of the section content. Spanish support is available in the Spanish edition of the guide on p. 47.

Quiz Unit 4 folder, p. 16 includes questions to check students' understanding of Section 2 content.

Presentation Pro CD-ROM
Quiz provides multiple-choice questions to check students' understanding of Section 2 content.

Answers to . . .

Section 2 Assessment

1. Investors earn money from interest on the bonds they buy. They can also earn money by buying bonds at a discount and cashing them in once they reach maturity.
2. Bond ratings give investors an indication of the quality or degree of default risk that various bonds carry.
3. Savings bonds are low-denomination ($50 to $10,000) bonds issued by the U.S. government. They involve little risk. Treasury bonds are bonds issued by the Treasury Department. They are safe investments, and their interest is exempt from state and local taxes. Municipal bonds are issued by state or local governments to help finance local improvements, are generally safe investments, and carry the added bonus that their interest is free from federal income tax. Corporate bonds are issued by corporations to raise large sums of money and involve moderate risk. Junk bonds are lower-rated, potentially higher-paying bonds issued by particular firms.
4. Capital markets include markets where money is lent for periods longer than one year (long-term CDs, corporate and government bonds). Money markets include markets where money is lent for periods of less than a year (short-term CDs, Treasury bills, money market mutual funds).
5. $20 in interest
6. Answers will vary with students' personal preference and familiarity with various investments. Students who prefer very safe investments may choose a certificate of deposit or a savings bond. Other students may choose money market funds for a higher return.
7. The AAA bond will generally be more expensive because of its lower risk.
8. Students should create a fact sheet showing accurate information about bonds and their characteristics.

Progress Monitoring *Online*
For additional assessment, have students access Progress Monitoring Online at **Web Code:** mna-4116

Go Online PHSchool.com Typing in the Web Code when prompted will bring students directly to detailed instructions for this activity.

Skills for LIFE

Predicting Consequences

1. Focus Although economic predictions are not infallible, careful analysis of past and current economic performance can yield important clues to future activity.

2. Instruct Explain to students that well-founded assumptions about future economic activity are often used to shape current economic decisions. Stress that economic variables are unpredictable, so economists do not always find that their predictions come true. Then work through the two stages of the activity with students evaluating economic activity patterns using the table provided.

3. Close/Reteach To provide additional practice, see the Economic Skills Activity below.

Economic Skills Activity
Unit 4 folder, p. 19, "Predicting Consequences," asks students to use past economic data to make predictions about future economic activity.

Social Studies Skills Tutor CD-ROM offers interactive practice in critical thinking and reading, visual analysis, and communication.

Answers

1. (a) GDP growth, discount rate on January 1 and December 31, rate change
2. (a) 1997 (b) Interest rates began the year at a high level but dropped to a very low level. (c) There may be a link between relatively high interest rates in 2000 and slow GDP growth in 2001.

Additional Practice

Students should locate recent articles about the economy and interest rates and list the indicators used to judge economic health. Students should then make logical predictions about the future movement of interest rates and give reasons for their predictions.

Skills for LIFE

Predicting Consequences

Economists, politicians, and entrepreneurs use economic data as a window into the future. On the basis of past events and the current situation, they sometimes try to predict how an economy or an individual market will behave. Thousands of variables and events have an impact on an economy, so predictions will not always come true. However, one can observe broad trends in an economy and try to imagine what will happen if these trends continue into the future. Follow the steps below to analyze the table and use the data to make predictions about the American economy.

1. **Identify the kinds of information in the table.** The table below lists the rate of growth of Gross Domestic Product (GDP) each year from 1996 to 2002. Also listed is the discount lending rate, one of the key factors that determines how expensive it is to borrow money to start a new business or invest in capital. The higher the discount rate, the more expensive it is to borrow money. A relatively high discount rate can cause slow GDP growth, while a low discount rate may encourage economic growth the following year. Because the discount rate can change several times during the year, rates are given for the end of December. Read the column headings and introductory notes for the table. (a) What information does this table give you for each year?

2. **Look for relationships within the data.** Lower interest rates encourage people to invest in new businesses because the cost of borrowing money is lower. Because too much borrowing can lead to inflation, the Federal Reserve Bank will raise the discount rate if there is a lot of new investment in the economy. (a) In which year did the U.S. economy grow most quickly? (b) How did the interest rates in 2001 compare with rates in other years? (c) What is a possible relationship between interest rates in 2000 and economic growth in 2001?

GDP Growth, 1996–2002

Year	GDP Growth (1996 dollars)	Discount rate on January 1	Discount Rate on December 31	Rate Change
1996	4.3%	5.25%	5%	–.25%
1997	4.4%	5%	5%	0%
1998	4.3%	5%	4.5%	–.5%
1999	4.1%	4.5%	5%	+.5%
2000	3.8%	5%	6%	+1%
2001	0.3%	6%	1.25%	–4.75%
2002	2.4%	1.25%	.75%	–.5%

Sources: Bureau of Economic Analysis; *The World Almanac 2003*

Additional Practice

Using the Internet or your local library, locate recent articles about the state of the economy and interest rates. What indicators do economists use to judge the health of the economy? Based on these indicators, do you think interest rates will go up, stay the same, or go down in the near future? Explain.

Interdisciplinary Connections: Literature

Predicting What Will Happen Next Today's students are taught to be active readers, and an essential element of active reading is predicting what will happen next in a literary work. Active readers think about what has gone on in a story and why; then they apply that knowledge by attempting to predict how a character will act, how a crisis may be sparked, or how a conflict will be resolved. Active readers, like economists, analyze the past to predict the future.

Have students work through the following activity: Ask students to think about what they learned in Section 1 of this chapter and use that knowledge to predict some of the content of Sections 2 and 3. After they read these sections, have students discuss the accuracy of their predictions.

Section 3 The Stock Market

Preview

Objectives

After studying this section you will be able to:

1. **Understand** the benefits and risks of buying stock.
2. **Describe** how stocks are traded.
3. **Identify** how stock performance is measured.
4. **Explain** the causes and effects of the Great Crash of 1929.

Section Focus

Corporations sell stock to raise money for starting, running, or expanding their businesses. Investors buy stocks to profit through regular payments, called dividends, or by selling the stock at a price higher than the purchase price. Stocks are traded on secondary markets called stock exchanges.

Key Terms

share
equities
capital gain
capital loss
stock split
stockbroker
brokerage firm
stock exchange
Nasdaq
OTC market
futures
options
call option
put option
bull market
bear market
The Dow
S & P 500
Great Crash
speculation

The New York Stock Exchange is a tangle of telephones, video monitors, computer screens, and frantic activity. The wrong decision may mean the difference between gaining or losing thousands of dollars. This is one of the places where stock is bought and sold—and fortunes are made and lost. Just what is stock, exactly how is it traded, and when is it a good investment?

Buying Stock

Besides bonds, corporations can raise funds by issuing stock, which represents ownership in the corporation. Stock is issued in portions known as **shares**. By selling shares of stock, corporations raise money to start, run, and expand their businesses. Stocks are also called **equities**, or claims of ownership in the corporation.

Benefits of Buying Stock

There are two ways for stockholders to make a profit:

- *Dividends* As you read in Chapter 8, many corporations pay out part of their profits as dividends to their stockholders. Dividends are usually paid four times a year (quarterly). The size of the dividend depends on the corporation's profit. The higher the profit, the larger the dividend per share of stock.

share *portion of stock*

equities *claims of ownership in a corporation*

▲ **Daytime at the Chicago Board of Trade (top photo) shows the frantic pace of trade. The frenzied pace of a day of trading is perhaps even better suggested by a view of the Chicago Stock Exchange at night (bottom photo).**

Graphing the Main Idea

Economic Institutions To build understanding of **economic institutions** and the causes and effects of the Great Crash, have students use a multi-flowchart graphic organizer like the one at the right. Remind students that a multi-flowchart shows causes and effects. They should place the heading "Great Crash of 1929" in the center box and show causes and effects in the other boxes.

Section Reading Support Transparencies A template and the answers for this graphic organizer can be found in Chapter 11, Section 3 of the Section Reading Support Transparency System.

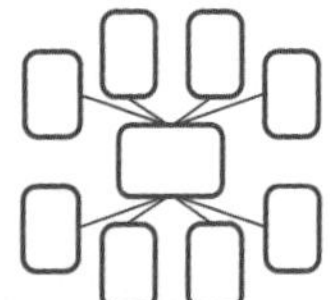

Section 3

The Stock Market

Objectives You may wish to call students' attention to the objectives in the Section Preview. The objectives are reflected in the main headings of the section.

Bellringer Ask students to think about the number of times they have heard or read about the stock market during the past year. Explain that in this section they will learn how the stock market works and why it plays such an important role in the world's economy.

Vocabulary Builder Have students read through the section to learn the meanings of the key terms. Ask them to use each key term in a sentence that reveals its meaning without repeating the definition.

Lesson Plan

Teaching the Main Concepts (L3)

1. Focus The stock market provides a forum for borrowers and investors to raise capital and to profit from wise investment strategies. Ask students to tell what they know about trading in the stock market.

2. Instruct Begin by discussing with students the benefits and risks of stock ownership. Then explain to students how stocks are traded. Help students to understand the intricacies of the options market and the recent Internet phenomenon of daytrading. Then explain how stock performance is measured. Finally, discuss the meaning of bull and bear markets, and explain how an unrestrained bull market resulted in the Great Crash of 1929.

3. Close/Reteach Fortunes have been made and lost in the stock market, but for most Americans the market remains a sound investment and an option for raising capital. Ask students to explain how bull and bear markets reflect the health of the nation's economy.

Guided Reading and Review
Unit 4 folder, p. 17 asks students to identify the main ideas of the section and to define or identify key terms.

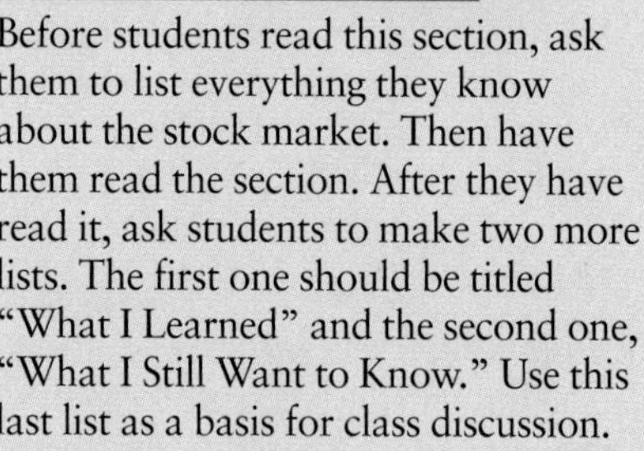

Differentiated Instruction L2

Before students read this section, ask them to list everything they know about the stock market. Then have them read the section. After they have read it, ask students to make two more lists. The first one should be titled "What I Learned" and the second one, "What I Still Want to Know." Use this last list as a basis for class discussion. LPR

Differentiated Instruction L3

Time: 90 minutes

Activity: Hold a panel discussion.

Grouping: Organize the class into two groups—panel members and audience.

Purpose: Students will discuss the benefits and risks of buying stock. The teacher should act as moderator, recording the main points and keeping the discussion moving. The panelists will represent groups of stockbrokers, successful and unsuccessful investors, and business owners. Allow panelists representing each group 20 minutes to prepare their points of view while audience members review section material and compose questions for the panel. Then have the audience begin asking the panel members questions about the benefits and risks of investing.

Roles: Stockbroker(s), successful investor(s), unsuccessful investor(s), business owner(s), audience members.

Outcome: Students will increase their understanding of the benefits and risks of buying stock.

Transparency Resource Package
Economics Concepts, 11D: Stock Splits

THE WALL STREET JOURNAL. CLASSROOM EDITION

In the News Read more about stock trading in "How to Get Started in Online Trading," an article in The Wall Street Journal Classroom Edition.

Go Online
The Wall Street Journal Classroom Edition
For: Current Events
Visit: PHSchool.com
Web Code: mnc-4113

capital gain *the difference between a higher selling price and a lower purchase price, resulting in a financial gain for the seller*

capital loss *the difference between a lower selling price and a higher purchase price resulting in a financial loss to the seller*

stock split *the division of a single share of stock into more than one share*

stockbroker *a person who links buyers and sellers of stock*

- *Capital gains* A second way an investor can earn a profit is to sell the stock for more than he or she paid for it. The difference between the higher selling price and the lower purchase price is called a **capital gain.** An investor who sells a stock at a price lower than the purchase price, however, suffers a **capital loss.**

Types of Stock

Stock may be classified in several ways, such as whether or not it pays dividends.

- *Income stock* This stock pays dividends at regular times during the year.
- *Growth stock* This stock pays few or no dividends. Instead, the issuing company reinvests its earnings in its business. The business (and its stock) thus increases in value over time.

Stock may also be classified as to whether stockholders have a vote in company policy.

- *Common stock* Investors who buy common stock are voting owners of the company. They usually receive one vote for each share of stock owned. They may use this vote, for example, to elect the company's board of directors. In some cases, a relatively small group of people may own enough shares to give them control over the company.
- *Preferred stock* Investors who buy preferred stock are nonvoting owners of the company. Owners of preferred stock, however, receive dividends before the owners of common stock. If the company goes out of business, preferred stockholders get their investments back before common stockholders.

Stock Splits

Owners of common stock may sometimes vote on whether to initiate a stock split. A **stock split** means that each single share of stock splits into more than one share. A company may seek to split a stock when the price of stock becomes so high that it discourages potential investors from buying it.

For example, suppose you own 200 shares in a sporting goods company called Ultimate Sports. Each share is worth $100. After the split, you own two shares of Ultimate Sports stock for every single share you owned, so that you now own 400 shares. Because the price is divided along with the stock, however, each share is now worth only $50. Although the split has not immediately resulted in any financial gain, shareholders like stock splits because prices tend to rise afterward.

Risks of Buying Stock

Purchasing stock is risky because the firm selling the stock may earn lower profits than expected, or it may lose money. If so, the dividends will be smaller than expected or nothing at all, and the market price of the stock will probably decrease. If the price of the stock decreases, investors who choose to sell their stock will get less than they paid for it, experiencing a capital loss.

How do the risk and rate of return on stocks compare to the risk and rate of return on bonds? As you have read, investors expect higher rates of return when they take on greater risk. Because of the laws governing bankruptcy, stocks are more risky than bonds. When a firm goes bankrupt, it sells its assets (such as land and equipment) and then pays its creditors, including bondholders, first. Stockholders receive dividends only if there is money left over after bondholders are paid. As you might expect, because stocks are riskier than bonds, the returns on stocks are generally higher.

How Stocks Are Traded

Suppose you decide that you want to buy stock. Do you call up the company and place an order? Probably not, because very few companies sell stock directly. Instead, you would contact a **stockbroker,** a person who links buyers and sellers of stock.

Econ 101: Key Concepts Made Easy

Economic Institutions To help students understand the background of the **stock market,** explain that an old-fashioned meaning of the term *stock* is "a supply of capital" or "money or capital invested or available for investment or trading." Stock exchanges grew out of medieval trading activities. Traders in European fairs found it convenient to use credit, which required documentation such as bank drafts and bills of exchange. Ask students to find out more about medieval trade fairs and the development of stock exchanges in France and elsewhere in Europe.

Stockbrokers usually work with individual investors, advising them to buy or sell particular stocks.

Stockbrokers work for **brokerage firms,** or businesses that specialize in trading stocks. Stockbrokers and brokerage firms cover their costs and earn a profit by charging a commission, or fee, on each stock transaction. Sometimes they also act as dealers of stock, meaning that they buy shares at a lower price and sell them to investors at a slightly higher price, profiting from the difference, or "spread."

Stock Exchanges

Stock is bought and sold on **stock exchanges,** or markets for buying and selling stock. These markets act as secondary markets for stocks and bonds. Most newspapers publish data on transactions in major stock exchanges. (See Figure 11.7 to learn how to read a newspaper stock market report.)

Major United States stock exchanges include the New York Stock Exchange (NYSE) and Nasdaq. In addition, a large number of people trade stocks on the Internet. (See Skills for Life on page 284 to learn more about reading a stock market report on the Internet.)

The New York Stock Exchange

The New York Stock Exchange (NYSE) is the country's largest and most powerful exchange. The NYSE began in 1792 as an informal, outdoor exchange under a now-famous buttonwood tree in New York's financial district. Over time, as the financial market developed and the demand to buy and sell financial assets grew, the exchange moved indoors and became restricted to a limited number of members, who buy "seats" allowing them to trade on the exchange. Today, new technologies make trading so fast that a transaction takes only an instant.

The NYSE handles stock and bond transactions for only the largest and most established companies in the country. The largest and best-known companies listed

brokerage firm *a business that specializes in trading stocks*

stock exchange *a market for buying and selling stock*

Figure 11.7 **Reading a Newspaper Stock Report**

Div: Most companies send dividends, or payments, to shareholders. **Div** shows the amount of the dividend in dollars per share.

Yld %: Yield is equal to the dividend as a percentage of the stock price.

Vol 100s: This column lists the number of shares sold (in hundreds). Multiply this number by 100 to find out how many shares were traded for that day.

Sym: the stock's symbol

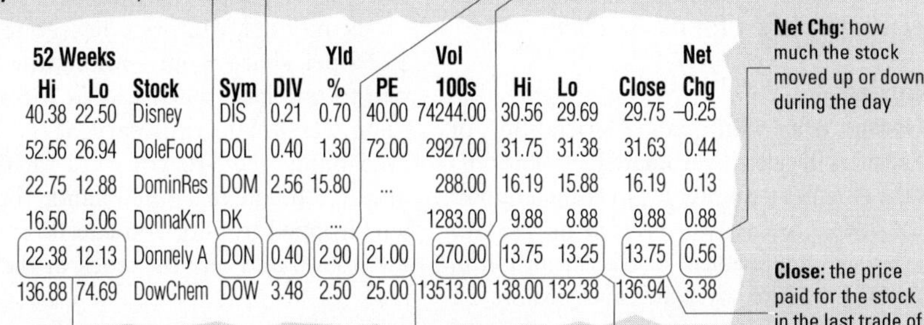

52 Weeks Hi	52 Weeks Lo	Stock	Sym	DIV	Yld %	PE	Vol 100s	Hi	Lo	Close	Net Chg
40.38	22.50	Disney	DIS	0.21	0.70	40.00	74244.00	30.56	29.69	29.75	–0.25
52.56	26.94	DoleFood	DOL	0.40	1.30	72.00	2927.00	31.75	31.38	31.63	0.44
22.75	12.88	DominRes	DOM	2.56	15.80	...	288.00	16.19	15.88	16.19	0.13
16.50	5.06	DonnaKrn	DK		...		1283.00	9.88	8.88	9.88	0.88
22.38	12.13	Donnely A	DON	0.40	2.90	21.00	270.00	13.75	13.25	13.75	0.56
136.88	74.69	DowChem	DOW	3.48	2.50	25.00	13513.00	138.00	132.38	136.94	3.38

Net Chg: how much the stock moved up or down during the day

Close: the price paid for the stock in the last trade of the day

52 Weeks Hi and **Lo:** the highest and lowest prices paid for the stock over the past year

PE: The price-to-earnings (PE) ratio is equal to the stock's current price divided by the company's earnings per share the previous year.

Hi and **Lo:** the highest and lowest prices paid for the stock on that day

BUILDING KEY CONCEPTS

Many newspapers publish daily reports of stock market transactions. The explanations of the abbreviations in this sample report will help you read stock market reports in your own daily paper.

Income Which of the companies listed pays the highest dividend?

Meeting NCEE Standards

Use the following benchmark activity from the **Voluntary National Content Standards in Economics** to evaluate student understanding of **Standard 10.**

Play the role of a business consultant hired to advise a partnership on the advantages it could enjoy by incorporating; write a letter outlining these benefits for their client.

Differentiated Instruction 

To help students assimilate material on how stocks are traded, organize the class into groups of five students. Have each group create a five-minute demonstration that will show various ways in which stocks are traded. They may use dialogue, narrative, signs/labels, or any other methods to illustrate the process. Give each group time to present its work.

Economic Skills Activity

Unit 4 folder, p. 19, "Reading a Stock Market Report," reinforces skills by asking students to read and interpret a stock market report.

Block Scheduling Strategies

Consider these suggestions to take advantage of extended class time:

- Create a list of terms that are not key terms but that are crucial to understanding this section (such as *NYSE* or *Nasdaq*). Then organize students into teams of two players each. Allow time for each student to create, for each key term and extra term, an extended definition that does not include the term itself. Then have individuals take turns reading a definition and having the other person offer a question that the definition would answer. *(Definition: A condition in which the stock market rises steadily over a period of time. Question: What is a bull market?)*
- Extend the Meeting NCEE Standards activity on this page by having groups of three to four students create and perform short dramatic presentations that show how a partnership that chose to incorporate could sell its stock on the stock market and gain capital.

Answer to . . .

Building Key Concepts DowChem

Differentiated Instruction L4

Ask students to research who buys stocks and create a profile of a typical stock owner. (One place where such information can be found is in a study by Peter D. Hart Research Associates for Nasdaq. Excerpts from this report may be found in almanacs such as *The Wall Street Journal Almanac.*) Have students write an essay discussing typical stock owners. GT

Background

Running Risks

In the 1980s merger and acquisition mania gave rise to a very risky—and potentially very lucrative—practice called *risk arbitrage.*

The process involves companies that are about to merge or to be acquired by another company. When Company A buys Company B, Company A usually offers Company B from 30 to 40 percent more than the market price of its stock as an incentive for Company B to accept the deal. As news of the proposed buyout leaks to the public, Company B's shares increase in value, almost to the price offered by Company A. Anyone who owns stock in Company B stands to make a handsome profit by selling at that time.

Risk arbitrageurs study the market closely and try to predict which companies are most likely to be taken over. The arbitrageurs then buy large blocks of stock in those companies. If one of the companies is indeed a takeover target, its stock will rise, and the arbitrageurs will profit by selling their holdings. If, however, the arbitrageurs are wrong, potential profits evaporate. Worse still, if a proposed buyout suddenly goes sour, the takeover target's stock price may tumble, and the arbitrageurs will have to sell their stock at a loss.

▲ Stockbrokers link buyers and sellers of stock.

OTC market *an electronic marketplace for stocks and bonds*

Nasdaq *American market for OTC securities*

futures *contracts to buy or sell at a specific date in the future at a price specified today*

options *contracts that give investors the choice to buy or sell stock and other financial assets*

call option *the option to buy shares of stock at a specified time in the future*

put option *the option to sell shares of stock at a specified time in the future*

on the NYSE are referred to as blue chip companies. Blue chip stocks are often in high demand because investors expect the companies to continue to do business profitably for a long time.

The OTC Market

Despite the importance of organized stock exchanges like the New York Stock Exchange, many stocks, as well as bonds, are not traded on the floor of stock exchanges. Instead, they are traded on the **OTC market,** that is, over-the-counter, or electronically. Investors may buy directly from a dealer or from a broker who will search the market for the best price.

Nasdaq

Nasdaq (the National Association of Securities Dealers Automated Quotations) is the American market for over-the-counter securities. Nasdaq was created in 1971 to help solve the problem of fragmentation in the OTC market by using automation. By the 1990s, it had grown into the second largest securities market in the United States and the third largest in the world, linking markets in the United States, Asia, and Europe. Because it does not have a trading floor, Nasdaq's trading information is simultaneously broadcast to some 360,000 computer terminals throughout the world.

Futures and Options

Futures are contracts to buy or sell commodities at a specific date in the future at a price specified today. For example, a buyer and seller might agree today on a price of $4.50 for a bushel of soybeans six or nine months in the future. The buyer would pay some portion of the money today, and the seller would deliver the goods in the future. Many of the markets in which futures are bought and sold are associated with grain and livestock exchanges. These markets include the New York Mercantile Exchange and the Chicago Board of Trade.

Similarly, **options** are contracts that give investors the choice to buy or sell stock and other financial assets. Investors may buy or sell a particular stock at a particular price up until a certain time in the future—usually three to six months. The option to buy shares of stock at a specified time in the future is known as a **call option.**

For example, you may pay $10 per share today for a call option. The call option gives you the right, but not the obligation, to purchase a certain stock at a price of, say, $100 per share. If at the end of six months, the price has gone up to $115 per share, your option still allows you to purchase the stock for the agreed-upon $100. You thus earn $5 per share ($15 minus the $10 you paid for the call option). If, on the other hand, the price has dropped to $80, you can throw away the option and buy the stock at the going rate.

The option to sell shares of stock at a specified time in the future is called a **put option.** Suppose that you, as the seller, pay $5 for the right to sell a particular stock that you do not yet own at $50 per share. If the price per share falls to $40, you can

Preparing for Standardized Tests

Have students read the section titled "Futures and Options" and then answer the question below.

A contract allowing a person to sell shares of stock at a specified time in the future is called:

A a call option.

B an over-the-counter trade.

C a put option.

D a daytrade.

buy the share at that price and require the contracted buyer to pay the agreed-upon $50. You would then make $5 on the sale ($10 minus the $5 you paid for the put option). If the price rises to $60, however, you can throw away the option and sell the stock for $60.

Daytrading

Most people who buy stock hold their investment for a period of time—sometimes many years—with the expectation that it will grow in value. Recently, however, a different type of stock trading, called daytrading, has become popular. Daytraders try to predict minute-by-minute price changes based on computer programs that tell the trader when to buy and sell. These traders might make dozens of trades a day in hopes of making a profit. Unfortunately, daytrading is a risky business in which traders can lose a great deal of money.

Measuring Stock Performance

You may have heard newscasters speak of a "bull" or "bear" market or of the market rising or falling. What do these terms mean and how are increases and decreases in the sale of stocks measured?

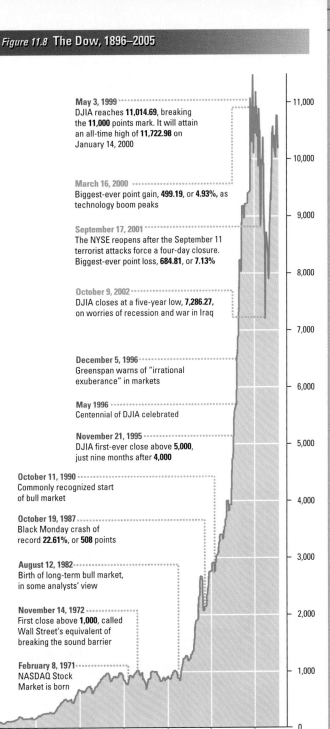

Figure 11.8 **The Dow, 1896–2005**

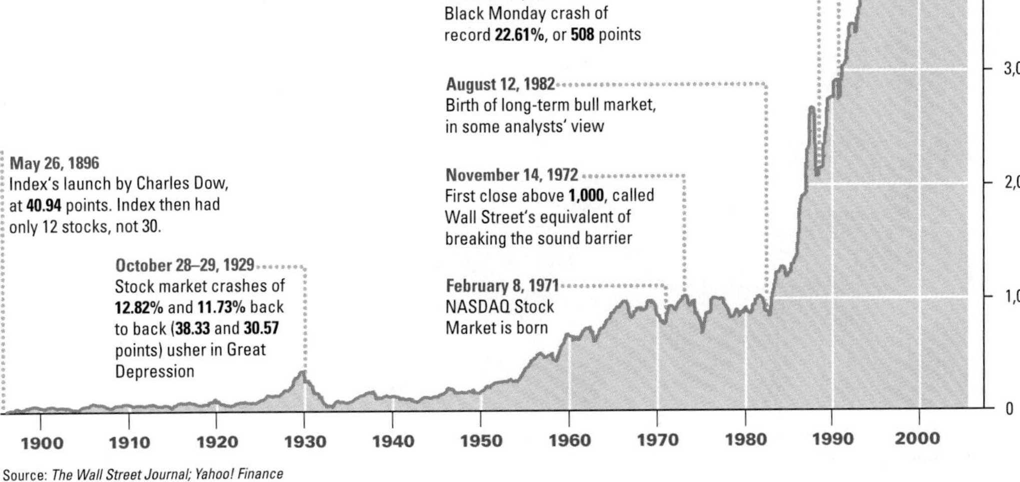
May 3, 1999
DJIA reaches 11,014.69, breaking the 11,000 points mark. It will attain an all-time high of 11,722.98 on January 14, 2000
March 16, 2000
Biggest-ever point gain, 499.19, or 4.93%, as technology boom peaks
September 17, 2001
The NYSE reopens after the September 11 terrorist attacks force a four-day closure. Biggest-ever point loss, 684.81, or 7.13%
October 9, 2002
DJIA closes at a five-year low, 7,286.27, on worries of recession and war in Iraq
December 5, 1996
Greenspan warns of "irrational exuberance" in markets
May 1996
Centennial of DJIA celebrated
November 21, 1995
DJIA first-ever close above 5,000, just nine months after 4,000
October 11, 1990
Commonly recognized start of bull market
October 19, 1987
Black Monday crash of record 22.61%, or 508 points
August 12, 1982
Birth of long-term bull market, in some analysts' view
November 14, 1972
First close above 1,000, called Wall Street's equivalent of breaking the sound barrier
February 8, 1971
NASDAQ Stock Market is born
May 26, 1896
Index's launch by Charles Dow, at 40.94 points. Index then had only 12 stocks, not 30.
October 28–29, 1929
Stock market crashes of 12.82% and 11.73% back to back (38.33 and 30.57 points) usher in Great Depression
11,000
10,000
9,000
8,000
7,000
6,000
5,000
4,000
3,000
2,000
1,000
0
1900
1910
1920
1930
1940
1950
1960
1970
1980
1990
2000

Source: *The Wall Street Journal; Yahoo! Finance*

Learning Styles Activity
Learning Styles Lesson Plans folder, p. 28 asks student groups to locate global stock exchanges and examine stock activity on these exchanges.

Economic Cartoon
Unit 4 folder, p. 23 gives students practice in interpreting cartoons about section content.

Transparency Resource Package
Economics Concepts, 11E: The Dow Jones Industrial Average

Differentiated Instruction 

Have students create a simple graphic titled "How Stock Performance Is Measured." Explain to them that their graphic should compare and contrast the Dow Jones Industrial Average with Standard & Poor's 500 and should define a bull market and a bear market. Have pairs of students exchange graphics and evaluate the clarity and accuracy of each other's efforts.

Background Note

Gold and Silver Futures

During the clean up efforts of the World Trade Center following the September 11 attacks, it was announced that in the smoldering basement under the rubble was approximately $243 million worth of precious metals belonging to futures traders of the New York Mercantile Exchange (NYME). The NYME is the world's largest physical commodity futures exchange, and, although the gold was only 0.3 percent of the 2000 world supply, there was genuine concern over the safety and recovery of these precious metals. It was not until mid-November 2001 that the metals were located and deposited into a Brink-licensed depository in Brooklyn. At that time, the recovered gold and silver were once again available for use on the Exchange.

Interdisciplinary Connections: Science & Technology

News at Your Fingertips The year 1867 marked an important milestone for the New York Stock Exchange (NYSE). That was the year the first stock ticker began operation. Before 1867 all stock exchange reports were either mailed or delivered by messenger—unthinkably slow methods by today's standards. Thomas Edison improved on the original ticker, but the advancements didn't stop there. The ticker got faster and faster until, in 1965, it was computerized. Today's Internet technology makes it possible for anyone to have stock information running across the top of his or her computer screen, providing instant information on the market's performance.

Making the Connection Have students use newspapers to find stock exchange information. Hold a class discussion about other possible ways to obtain this information.

Differentiated Instruction L2

Have students skim the section, noting unfamiliar words. Then ask them to define the words, using context clues or a dictionary. ELL

Differentiated Instruction L3

(Enrichment) Remind students that although the crash of 1929 might seem like ancient history, another crash occurred relatively recently—in 1987. Have students work in groups of three or four to research the 1987 crash, focusing their efforts on primary sources (such as newspaper and magazine articles or interviews with people who experienced the crash firsthand). Ask groups to prepare three- to five-page reports on the crash.

bull market *a steady rise in the stock market over a period of time*

bear market *a steady drop in the stock market over a period of time*

The Dow *index that shows how certain stocks have traded*

S & P 500 *index that shows the price changes of 500 different stocks*

Great Crash *the collapse of the stock market in 1929*

speculation *the practice of making high-risk investments with borrowed money in hopes of getting a big return*

Bull and Bear Markets

When the stock market rises steadily over a period of time, a **bull market** exists. On the other hand, when the stock market falls for a period of time, people call it a **bear market.** In a bull market, investors expect an increase in profits and thus buy stock. During a bear market, investors sell stock in expectation of lower profits. The 1980s and 1990s brought the longest sustained bull market in the nation's history. A multiyear bear market began in 2000.

The Dow Jones Industrial Average

The Dow (The Dow Jones Industrial Average) has shown how certain stocks have traded daily since 1896. To make sure that the stocks remain representative of the stock market as a whole, over the years the companies on the Dow have changed. Today, the stocks on the Dow represent 30 large companies in various industries, such as food, entertainment, and technology.

S & P 500

The **S & P 500** (Standard & Poor's 500) gives a broader picture of stock performance. It tracks the price changes of 500 different stocks as a measure of overall stock market performance. The S&P 500 reports mainly on stocks listed on the NYSE, but some of its stocks are traded on the Nasdaq and OTC markets.

▲ **As stock market prices fell in 1929, nervous investors crowded onto Wall Street hoping to hear the latest news.**

The Great Crash of 1929

Like the 1980s and 1990s, the 1920s saw a long-term bull market. Unfortunately, this period ended in a horrifying collapse of the stock market known as the **Great Crash.** The causes of this collapse contain important lessons for investors today.

Investing During the 1920s

When President Herbert Hoover took office in 1929, the United States economy seemed to be in excellent shape. The stock market is widely viewed as the nation's main economic indicator, and the stock market was soaring. In 1925, the market value of all stocks had been $27 billion. By early October 1929, combined stock values had hit $87 billion, rising by almost $11.4 billion in 1928 alone.

Signs of Trouble

Despite widespread optimism about continuing prosperity, there were signs of trouble. A relatively small number of companies and families held much of the nation's wealth. Many farmers and workers, on the other hand, were suffering financially. In addition, many ordinary people went into debt buying consumer goods such as refrigerators and radios—new and exciting inventions at the time—on credit. Finally, industries were producing more goods than consumers could buy. As a result, some industries, including the important automobile industry, developed large surpluses of goods, and prices began to slump.

Another economic danger sign was the debt that investors were piling up by playing the stock market. The dizzying climb of stock prices encouraged widespread **speculation,** the practice of making high-risk investments with borrowed money in hopes of getting a big return. To make matters worse, before World War I, only the wealthy had bought and sold

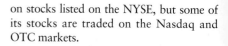

Preparing for Standardized Tests

Have students read the section titled "Signs of Trouble" and then answer the question below.

Purchasing a stock by paying only a fraction of its price and borrowing the remainder of the purchase price is called:

(A) buying on margin.
B buying in a bear market.
C buying on debt.
D buying in a bull market.

shares in the stock market. Now, however, the press was reporting stories of ordinary people making fortunes in the stock market. Small investors thus began speculating in stocks, often with their life savings.

To attract less-wealthy investors, stockbrokers encouraged a practice called buying on margin. Buying on margin allowed investors to purchase a stock for only a fraction of its price and borrow the rest from the brokerage firm. Brokers' loans to these investors went from about $5 million in mid-1928 to $850 million in September 1929. The Hoover administration did little to discourage such borrowing.

The Crash

By September 3, 1929, the Dow had reached an all-time high of 381. The rising stock prices dominated the news. Eager investors filled brokerage firms to catch the latest news coming in on ticker tape. Prices for many stocks soared far above their real values in terms of the company's earnings and assets.

After their peak in September, stock prices began to fall. Some brokers demanded repayment of loans. When the stock market closed on Wednesday, October 23, 1929, the Dow had dropped 21 points in an hour. The next day, worried investors began to sell, and stock prices fell further. Business and political leaders told the public not to worry about their losses, but widespread panic began.

By Monday, October 28, 1929, the value of shares of stock were dropping to a fraction of what people had paid for them. Investors all over the country were therefore racing to get what was left of their money out of the stock market. On October 29, 1929, known as Black Tuesday, a record 16.4 million shares were sold, compared with the average 4 to 8 million shares per day earlier in the year. The Great Crash had begun.

The Aftermath of the Crash

During the bull market that led up to the Crash, about 4 million people had invested in the stock market. Although they were the first to feel the effects of the Crash, eventually the whole country was affected. The Crash contributed to the Great Depression, in which millions of Americans lost their jobs, homes, and farms.

Mistakes in monetary policy slowed the nation's recovery. In 1929, the Fed had begun limiting the money supply in order to discourage excessive lending. With too little money in circulation, individuals and businesses could not spend enough to help the economy improve.

After the Depression, many people saw stocks as risky investments to be avoided. In 1980, only about 2.5 percent of American households held stock. Gradually, however, attitudes began to change. The development of mutual funds also made it easy to own a wide range of stocks. Americans became more comfortable with stock ownership.

After a period of very strong growth, stocks crashed again on "Black Monday," October 18, 1987. The Dow Jones

▲ **What does the cartoonist suggest about investors in the 1990s who assumed that the stock market would only keep climbing?**

FAST FACT

The story of the rise, fall, and recovery of General Motors offers a lesson for investors who saw technology stocks soar, then rapidly lose value in the late 1990s and early 2000s. When William C. Durant founded General Motors in the early 1900s, investment capital poured in. GM stock rose more than 5,500% from 1914 to 1920. When the overcrowded auto industry began to disappoint investors in the early 1920s, however, auto stocks plummeted, and GM stock lost two-thirds of its value in six months. Eventually, of course, GM recovered and prospered.

Differentiated Instruction 

Have students create a captioned time line about the events leading up to and following the Great Crash of 1929. Remind them that the time line should both orient the reader in time and show how one event affected or led to another, culminating in the Great Crash. When students have completed this assignment, display their time lines on a bulletin board.

Economic Detective Activity

Unit 4 folder, p. 21, "Sylvestor and Frugala Investor," provides an integrated application of chapter concepts.

Answer to . . .

Cartoon Caption The cartoonist suggests that these investors only consider other options when stock prices drop.

GTE Guide to the Essentials
Chapter 11, Section 3, p. 48 provides support for students who need additional review of the section content. Spanish support is available in the Spanish edition of the guide on p. 48.

Quiz Unit 4 folder, p. 18 includes questions to check students' understanding of Section 3 content.

Presentation Pro CD-ROM
Quiz provides multiple-choice questions to check students' understanding of Section 3 content.

Answers to . . .

Section 3 Assessment

1. Two benefits are dividends (amounts paid regularly) and capital gains (profits made from selling stock for a higher price than was paid for it). Risks include small dividends or stock that loses value.
2. Possible answer: The New York Stock Exchange (NYSE) is the largest exchange and handles trading of only the largest and most established companies. Nasdaq (National Association of Securities Dealers' Automated Quotation system) deals with slightly riskier stocks from smaller and less well-established companies.
3. The Dow Jones Industrial Average measures the performance of 30 representative companies. Standard & Poor's 500 measures 500 stocks as an indicator of overall stock market performance.
4. Possible answer: A relatively small number of companies and families held most of the nation's wealth; many people went into debt buying consumer goods on credit; certain industries had large surpluses of goods. Students may mention other factors.
5. Advantages would include the ease and lower cost of electronic trading. Disadvantages include possible fraud and greater potential losses for individuals because of their inexperience.
6. Advantages would include great returns on investments, and disadvantages would include losses due to wrong guesses about how prices would behave in the future. Students should provide specific examples.
7. Possible questions: What has been the average dividend in the last three years? Has this company's stock been on an upward or downward trend? What goods or services does this company sell?
8. Students' answers should demonstrate an understanding of daytrading. Students may advise against daytrading because of its risks.
9. Students may say that they would choose safe stocks or stocks that will rise in value quickly.

▶ Following the September 11, 2001, terrorist attacks, the American flag draped over the New York Stock Exchange symbolized American unity and patriotism.

lost 22.6% of its value that day—nearly twice the one-day loss that began the Crash of 1929. This time the market rebounded on each of the next two days, and impact on the economy was much less severe. The Fed moved quickly to add liquidity and reduce interest rates to stimulate economic growth. Within two years, the Dow returned to pre-crash levels.

The Market Today

During the second half of the 1990s, stock prices rose dramatically. Many people bought stock for the first time or invested in new technology companies. At the end of the 1990s, almost half of American households owned mutual funds.

By 2000, however, investors had become worried that most companies could not make enough money to justify their high stock prices. Stocks fell, and many investors lost most or all of their prior gains. The following year, an economic recession and terrorist attacks further battered the stock market.

In 2002, several large corporations, including Enron and WorldCom, declared bankruptcy and revealed that they had issued false financial reports for several years. Stock prices fell even more as investors questioned how much they really knew about the companies they had invested in. The federal government introduced new rules for corporations to restore confidence in the market. The stock market recovered, but it remained below the peak values reached during the bull market of the 1990s.

Section 3 Assessment

Progress Monitoring *Online*
For: Self-quiz with vocabulary practice
Web Code: mna-4117

Key Terms and Main Ideas

1. What are two benefits and two risks of buying stock?
2. Identify two **stock exchanges** and describe the differences between them.
3. Describe two popular indexes of stock performance.
4. What were three causes of the **Great Crash?**

Applying Economic Concepts

5. ***Critical Thinking*** Many people believe that electronic trading services will replace stockbrokers in the future. What might be the advantages and disadvantages of this development?
6. ***Critical Thinking*** What might be the advantages and disadvantages of trading in futures and options? Choose a specific example to support your conclusions.
7. ***Try This*** What three questions would you ask a stockbroker before buying a company's stock?
8. ***You Decide*** Would you advise a friend to become a daytrader? Explain your answer.
9. ***You Decide*** Suppose you were given $1,000 to invest in the stock market. How would your choice of stock be influenced by the fact that you will soon need to pay college tuition?

For: Research Activity
Visit: PHSchool.com
Web Code: mnd-4113

Progress Monitoring *Online*
For additional assessment, have students access Progress Monitoring Online at **Web Code:** mna-4117

Go Online PHSchool.com Typing in the Web Code when prompted will bring students directly to detailed instructions for this activity.

Real-life Case Study

Supply and Demand

The Fate of the Dot-Coms

The "dot-coms" are companies that sprang up to take advantage of the potential business opportunities offered by the Internet. The first of these companies to take off provided services directly relating to the Internet—companies like America Online and Netscape. Right behind them came a big group of "B2C" companies, businesses marketing products to consumers. Amazon.com is the best known of these, but there were hundreds—even thousands—more looking for a share of consumers' spending.

Unlimited Potential? Many dot-coms were started by young entrepreneurs with more vision than experience. Companies like Amazon declared that making a profit in the short term was less important than developing a large market share for the long run. Even though the companies were losing money, and often did not expect to be profitable for years, excited investors flocked to the stocks. Stock prices soared, which in turn generated more excitement, attracted more investors, and pushed stock prices even higher. Venture capitalists funded fledgling companies and pushed them quickly to market in order to take advantage of the hot stock market.

The Fall of the Dot-Coms In the middle of 2000, Internet stocks fell sharply as investors became concerned about the lack of profits. The companies could stay in business if investors were willing to put up more money or if they had profits to reinvest. Otherwise, they could quickly run out of money. Many dot-coms filed for bankruptcy protection or closed their doors entirely. Investors saw the value of their holdings plummet.

Dry Bones

IF I HAD SAVED UP ANY MONEY AT ALL...

I'D HAVE INVESTED IT IN HIGH TECH STOCKS...

AND I'D HAVE BEEN RUINED IN THE STOCK MARKET CRASH!

YOU MEAN?

YUP... POVERTY HAS KEPT ME FROM FINANCIAL RUIN!

YOU LUCKY DOG!

KIRSCHEN
JERUSALEM POST
Jerusalem
ISRAEL

▲ What does the cartoon suggest about investing in dot-coms?

The Future of the Dot-Coms After the fall of technology stocks, many formerly enthusiastic entrepreneurs and investors began to think that dot-coms would never be a good investment. In reality, they were probably never as good as people thought at the height of the market, or as bad as people thought after the fall. Certainly the Internet will continue to expand, and its use in business will grow. Companies that are able to develop useful Web-based services may find that they grow more steadily, but more reliably, than during the boom years.

▼ One technology stock, Cisco Systems, reflected the decline of the value of dot-coms in 2001.

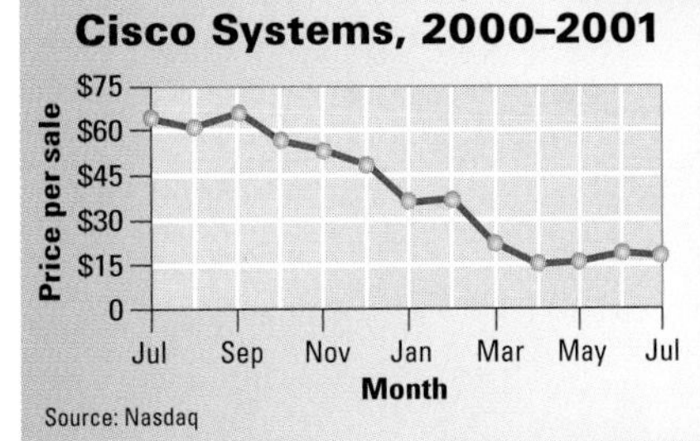

Applying Economic Ideas

1. Why did the initial success of dot-coms make it easier for other dot-com companies to get started?
2. What might a dot-com entrepreneur have done to avoid the "boom and bust" cycle that many technology stocks experienced?

Real-life Case Study: Supply and Demand

1. Focus Have students name some of the Internet businesses they are familiar with. How do these businesses make a profit? What goods or services do they offer? Recount how optimistic investors and venture capitalists embraced dot-coms with little regard to whether or when these companies would make a profit. When the Nasdaq began its fall in early 2001, many dot-coms proved risky investments.

2. Instruct Discuss with students how dot-coms met a demand in the developing Internet economy. It is not yet clear how the Internet companies will function or even how advertising will support them. In other words, there is a supply of dot-coms, but the demand is not yet well understood.

3. Close/Reteach The demand for technology stocks fell over the period from July 2000 to July 2001 and prices fell. As a result many dot-coms have gone out of business. Entrepreneurs, investors, and venture capitalists are likely to be wary for some time.

Case Studies Activity
Case Studies in Free Enterprise folder, pp. 22–23, "Edward L. Bernays," helps students apply economic principles in an additional case study.

Economic Detective Activity
Unit 4 folder, p. 21, "Sylvestor and Frugala Investor," provides an additional application of chapter concepts.

Interdisciplinary Connections: Language Arts

Coining New Terms *Jargon* is vocabulary that has special meaning within a particular industry. When junk bonds began to fuel a corporate takeover frenzy in the 1980s, the situation spawned its own jargon. For example, a *corporate raider* is an individual or company that targets a company for acquisition. If the management of the company in question does not want to sell it, the raider may initiate a *hostile takeover,* an attempt to acquire a publicly traded company by bypassing its management and offering its shareholders handsome profits if they vote to sell the company. To prevent such takeovers, some companies developed and "swallowed" a *poison pill,* a deliberate attempt to make the company unattractive to raiders through some action such as taking on excessive debt.

Making the Connection Ask students to offer lists of jargon in businesses or occupations with which they are familiar.

Answers to . . .

1. The stock prices of dot-coms soared, which generated excitement among investors who were eager to fund other technology companies. Venture capital companies responded with more money to finance similar businesses.
2. The entrepreneur might have built the company more slowly, aiming to make a profit in the short-term rather than to gather a giant market share.

Chapter 11 Assessment

Key Terms

1. diversification
2. capital gain
3. coupon rate
4. bull market
5. investment
6. financial intermediary
7. junk bonds
8. speculation
9. portfolio

Using Graphic Organizers

10. Students should fill circles with investment options and their descriptions, such as savings bonds (low-denomination, safe investments) and junk bonds (lower-rated, potentially higher-paying bonds).

Reviewing Main Ideas

11. Financial intermediaries help channel funds from savers to borrowers.
12. Bond ratings allow investors to check bond quality to determine if the return on the investment is worth the risk. They are established and published by Standard & Poor's and Moody's and based on factors such as the issuer's ability to make future interest payments and to repay the principal when the bond matures.
13. Stocks can be traded on a stock exchange through a stockbroker, in the over-the-counter market, or by daytrading.
14. Diversification distributes an investor's financial assets into several areas; if one portion of the portfolio does poorly, others may still be doing well.

Critical Thinking

15. Students' answers should demonstrate an understanding of the importance of savings and investments in the free enterprise system. For example, students may say that in order to be able to start and grow, private businesses must have access to capital, which is provided by investment. Investors will invest if they believe that they can make a profit; the profit motive is an important part of the free enterprise system.
16. Answers may include: savings bonds (low risk), treasury bonds (low to medium risk), corporate bonds (low to high risk), junk bonds (high risk), CDs (low risk), mutual funds (low to medium risk).
17. Students' answers should demonstrate an understanding of the causes of the Great Crash. They may suggest lessons such as not allowing wealth to become concentrated in the hands of a few, keeping consumer indebtedness under control, and watching the stock market carefully for signs that investors are engaging in dangerous practices.
18. Students' analyses should show an understanding of the importance of investment for the overall health of the economy. Answers may also analyze the impact on the individual investor in terms of the risks and returns on various investments.

Chapter 11 Assessment

Chapter Summary

A summary of major ideas in Chapter 11 appears below. See also the **Guide to the Essentials of Economics,** which provides additional review and test practice of key concepts in Chapter 11.

Section 1 Saving and Investing (pp. 271–275)

Saving and **investment** are essential parts of the American free enterprise system. In our financial system, institutions called **financial intermediaries** bring together savers and borrowers to channel funds for investment. Investors must weigh potential risks and **returns** when choosing among the many types of investments available.

Section 2 Bonds and Other Financial Assets (pp. 277–283)

Businesses and governments issue bonds and other financial assets in order to finance expansion. Bonds are relatively low-risk investments for purchasers, who generally receive the purchase price of the bond plus interest when the bond matures. Other financial assets, such as money market mutual funds and certificates of deposit, offer additional investment opportunities.

Section 3 The Stock Market (pp. 285–292)

The stock market is another way for people to invest their earnings. Stocks offer possibilities for high return, but also present certain risks. Major **stock exchanges** in the United States include the New York Stock Exchange and the **Nasdaq,** an electronic stock exchange. Stock performance is measured by **The Dow** and the **S & P 500.** The **Great Crash** of 1929 dealt the stock market one of its worst economic blows in our history. Following a period of distrust of the stock market in the decades after the Crash, however, investors returned to the stock market in great numbers.

Key Terms

Match the following terms with the definitions listed below. You will not use all of the terms.

brokerage firm	**portfolio**
junk bonds	**financial intermediary**
bull market	**maturity**
coupon rate	**diversification**
investment	**capital gain**
speculation	

1. Spreading out your investments to reduce risk
2. Difference between a higher selling price and a lower purchase price
3. The interest rate to be paid to the bondholder
4. A period of time during which the stock market steadily rises
5. An action taken today that will create benefits in the future
6. Institution that helps channel funds from savers to investors
7. Lower-rated, higher-paying bonds
8. The practice of making high-risk investments in hopes of getting a big return
9. Collection of financial assets

Using Graphic Organizers

10. On a separate sheet of paper, copy the web map below. Complete the web map by writing and describing examples of investment options in the circles. More circles may be added.

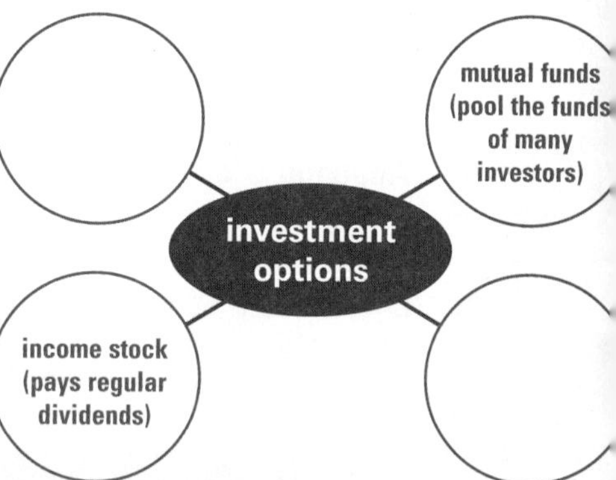

Reviewing Main Ideas

11. What do financial intermediaries do?

12. How do bond ratings influence which bonds investors buy? How are bond ratings established?

13. Describe three ways that stocks are traded.

14. How does diversification strengthen an investor's portfolio?

Critical Thinking

15. Drawing Conclusions Using evidence from the chapter, support the following statement: Savings and investments play an essential role in the free enterprise system.

16. Making Comparisons Compare different means by which savings can be invested and the risks each strategy poses to the consumer.

17. Drawing Conclusions Review the causes of the Great Crash of 1929. What lessons can investors learn from the Crash?

18. Demonstrating Reasoned Judgment Analyze the economic impact of investing in the stock and bond market.

Problem-Solving Activity

19. Suppose that you have been handed $10,000. Now, create your own hypothetical investment portfolio that best suits your needs and goals. What types of financial intermediaries will you use? Will you invest more money in stocks, bonds, or other financial assets?

Skills for Life

Predicting Consequences Review the steps shown on page 284; then answer the following questions using the table below.

20. What is the topic of the table?

21. What economic indicators does the table show?

22. What time period do the data cover?

23. Identify two trends that you can find in these data.

24. How might you explain these trends in the data?

Stock Market Data

	Number of Shares Traded (millions)	Dow Jones Industrial Average (average daily close)
January 2007	35,410	11,359.25
February 2007	42,491	12,014.98
March 2007	47,345	11,895.42
April 2007	41,109	11,012.01
May 2007	39,882	10,891.11

Data are fictional.

Economics Journal

Synthesizing Information Review the list of questions you created at the beginning of the chapter. Use what you have learned in the chapter to answer your questions. Research any remaining questions in the library or on the Internet.

Progress Monitoring *Online*

For: Chapter 11 Self-Test **Visit:** PHSchool.com
Web Code: mna-4111

As a final review, take the Economics Chapter 11 Self-Test and receive immediate feedback on your answers. The test consists of 20 multiple-choice questions designed to test your understanding of the chapter content.

Problem-Solving Activity

19. Students should create a portfolio that demonstrates understanding of chapter concepts and the trade-offs between risk, return, and liquidity in investments.

Skills for Life

20. Data from the stock market

21. The number of shares traded in a given month and the average daily close of the Dow Jones Industrial Average

22. January 2007 through May 2007

23. The number of shares traded rises until March 2007 and then drops significantly. The average daily close of the Dow Jones Industrial Average rises until February 2007, falls slowly the following month, and then drops much further in April and May.

24. Possible explanation: investors traded stocks heavily in a rising market, but began to trade less as the market began to fall.

Additional support materials and activities for Chapter 11 of *Economics: Principles in Action* can be found in the Social Studies area of **PHSchool.com**.

Economics Journal

Students should demonstrate an understanding of chapter material that will allow them to answer their initial questions or do successful research to find answers.

Review and Assessment

Vocabulary Practice Unit 4 folder, p. 20 uses a crossword puzzle to reinforce understanding of key terms.

GTE **Guide to the Essentials** Chapter 11 Test, p. 49

Test Bank CD-ROM Chapter 11 Test

Go Online PHSchool.com Students may use the Chapter 11 Self-Test on **PHSchool.com** to prepare for the Chapter Test.

Economics Simulation

Objectives Upon completion of this simulation, students should be able to:

- apply money management and investment knowledge in a simulated economic situation;
- demonstrate an understanding of the risks and choices involved when choosing investment or savings strategies;
- understand that risk is an important factor in any investment strategy.

Bellringer Inform students that they have just received a gift of $100,000. Ask them to volunteer their first thoughts about how they would invest a portion of it. Explain that this simulation will help them understand investment options and risks.

1. Focus Remind students that an investment strategy must focus on a goal. Ask them how the goals of the following persons might differ: A young couple plans to have children; a 25-year-old single man has inherited a large sum of cash; a single 63-year-old woman approaches retirement.

2. Instruct Have students prepare for and conduct the simulation, using the procedures noted in the text.

3. Close/Reteach Have students calculate their profits and losses. After they have presented their conclusions, discuss answers to the first four analysis questions as a class. Assign the Identifying Alternatives question as a follow-up.

Economic Simulation
Economic Simulations folder, pp. 21–27, "The Stock Market: Becoming a Wizard of Wall Street," provides an additional simulation on a unit topic.

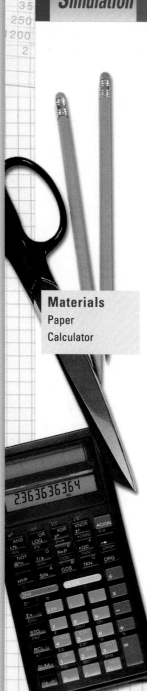

Economics Simulation Making Investment Decisions

Long ago, many people saved their money by tucking it away in a sugar bowl or underneath a mattress. These are relatively safe, but not very profitable, options for savings. Today, there are a wide number of investment options available to help your savings multiply. Banks offer various types of savings accounts and certificates of deposit (CDs). These are safe and accrue small amounts of interest. More agressive investments, such as mutual funds, government bonds, and stocks and bonds, potentially offer greater returns, but are relatively risky.

In this simulation, you and your group are trying to raise enough money to pay for all 100 students in your senior class to visit a nearby amusement park. You plan to take the trip in one year, and you have already saved some money. You want to earn as much interest or dividends as you can, but you only have one year. How will you make your money grow?

▲ How will you raise enough money to pay for a senior class trip to an amusement park?

Materials
Paper
Calculator

Preparing the Simulation

The best way to make sound investments is to understand your choices thoroughly. Your task in this simulation is to determine the best way to raise enough money for your senior trip in only one year.

Step 1: First, form fundraising groups of five to eight students. Each fundraising group will begin with $5,000 to invest for one year.

Step 2: Your goal is to raise enough money for everyone in your senior class to spend a Senior Weekend at a nearby amusement park. There are 100 students in your senior class, and you have figured out that it will cost $8,000 to buy two-day passes for everyone.

Conducting the Simulation

The simulation will consist of two parts. First, you will discuss your investment options and make your choices. Then you will calculate the results and discover how much you would have made—or lost.

Step 1: First, examine your investment options. Of all the options available, you have narrowed down your choices to the five shown in the investment choices chart. Some of your choices have guaranteed returns on your investment, but others do not. Be sure you understand the risks as well as the potential returns of each kind of investment.

Step 2: As a group, discuss your philosophy of investing. Do you want to take risks in hopes of a higher return? Would you rather avoid risk in your investments, but earn a smaller return?

As you discuss each fundraising choice, keep these questions in mind:
- Does this alternative guarantee a certain rate of return, or might the rate of return vary?
- Is this choice aggressive enough to earn the necessary amount of money in one year?
- What is the risk associated with this investment choice?

Step 3: Decide how to invest your group's $5,000. Make an investments and returns chart like the one on this page, and record your investment choices.

Step 4: Now, suppose it is one year later, and it is time to analyze the results of your investment decisions. Your teacher will provide you with the performance figures for each investment option. Using that information, calculate your profits and losses on stock and mutual funds. Figure out the interest you would have accumulated from bank deposits or CDs.

Investments and Returns Chart

Choices	Amount Invested	Amount of Return
Gibraltar Bank Savings Account	$	$
One-Year Certificate of Deposit (CD)	$	$
Rock Solid Mutual Fund	$	$
Hurrah! Stock	$	$
Wycombe and Marlow Health Care	$	$
Totals	$	$

Fundraising Options

Options	Potential Return
Deposit the money in a bank	
Gibraltar Bank Savings Acount A traditional savings account at your local bank is fully guaranteed by the FDIC, and deposits can be withdrawn at any time.	2% guaranteed
One-Year Certificate of Deposit This CD is fully guaranteed by the FDIC, but deposits may only be withdrawn after the end of one full year.	4% guaranteed
Invest in the stock market	
Rock Solid Mutual Fund This mutual fund invests in blue chip stocks, which are stocks for large, well-established companies that expect slow and steady growth.	8% return last year; return not guaranteed
Hurrah! (individual company stock) This brand-new technology company has been all over the news in the last few weeks. The new technology it developed has revolutionized how companies conduct business across the Internet.	brand new, no data to determine how this stock will perform
Wycombe and Marlow Health Care This company is in financial trouble but could turn itself around. The bonds it has issued are considered junk bonds; if the company is able to pay interest on the bonds, investors will make a healthy profit.	15%, if the company can pay the interest when it is due

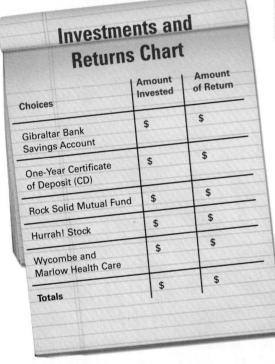

Simulation Analysis

As a final step, meet with the other fundraising groups and compare your investment choices and their results.

1. How many of the groups met their goal of turning their $5,000 into $8,000 in one year?
2. Which group's investments earned the most? Did this group take risks or make "safe" choices?
3. Did any groups lose money? Was it because they took risks? Or were there changes in the economy over the year?
4. **Identifying Alternatives** If you could do this simulation again, would you have made different investment choices? Why or why not?

Meeting NCEE Standards

Use the following benchmark activity from the **Voluntary National Content Standards in Economics** to evaluate student understanding of Standard 19.

Identify assets people can buy to protect themselves financially against inflation and discuss how much time people spend with this problem in times of high inflation (e.g., 1981) compared to times of low inflation (e.g. 1955).

Background

Economics in History

The Dow Jones Industrial Average is currently an index of 30 "blue chip" U.S. stocks. When the Dow Jones Average was begun more than 100 years ago, the following 12 stocks were averaged:
- American Cotton Oil
- American Sugar
- American Tobacco
- Chicago Gas
- Distilling & Cattle Feeding
- General Electric
- Laclede Gas
- National Lead
- North American
- Tennessee Coal & Iron
- U.S. Leather Preferred
- U.S. Rubber

Answers to . . .

1. Answers will depend on the investments chosen.
2. Answers will depend on the investments chosen.
3. Answers will depend on the investments chosen. Some students may point out that risky investments have the opportunity for greater gains but also for greater losses. Others may note that safer investments don't make as much money but also carry less risk.
4. Students should give answers that demonstrate understanding of this simulation and of the investment strategies they used.

Interdisciplinary Connections: Language Arts

Knowing About Investments Although more people than ever before are investing their money, they may not be especially well informed about the risks and benefits of investing. Everyone benefits from understanding investment strategy.

Making the Connection Organize students into groups of four or five. Tell them that they are to do research and then present a five-minute infomercial on investments. Have each group produce a script designed to educate the public about the differing financial instruments profiled in this simulation. Have students present their infomercials and then ask them to vote on the best script, judging it for accuracy, creativity, and quality of information.

Measuring Economic Performance

Introducing the Unit

Unit Summary

Unit 5 describes how economic performance is measured. Chapter 12 discusses the calculation and use of gross domestic product (GDP) and the significance of business cycles. This chapter also discusses economic growth and the factors that contribute to it. Chapter 13 examines the economic challenges of unemployment, inflation, and poverty. It also discusses the effects of these challenges on the economy.

Focus Activity

Introduce Unit 5 to students by asking them to complete the Focus Activity. Ask each pair that shared articles to present a brief oral summary of what they learned. Have students save the articles for review after completing the unit.

Measuring Economic Performance

National Council on Economic Education

The following Voluntary National Content Standards in Economics are addressed in this unit:

★ Standard 15 ★ Standard 19
★ Standard 18 ★ Standard 20

See the Chapter Openers on pp. 300 and 330 for a complete description of the standards addressed in each chapter.

Chapters in This Unit

12. *Gross Domestic Product and Growth*

13. *Economic Challenges*

New housing starts are up . . .

Every day, news reporters tell us how well or poorly the economy is performing. Analyzing an entire economy is a challenging task. However, there are key indicators such as the number of new housing starts, unemployment rates, and inflation rates that provide clues. After listening to the financial news, you may wonder:

- How do economists measure the health of the economy?
- What impact would a recession have on workers and businesses?
- What is inflation?
- What makes the economy grow?

In this unit, you'll read about the answers to these questions as you are introduced to macroeconomics—the branch of economics that looks at an economy as a whole.

Focus Activity

Summarize one recent news article that refers in some way to the health of the economy of the United States. Then share your article with a classmate.

Bibliography

Print

Alsop, Ronald J., ed., and staff of *The Wall Street Journal. The Wall Street Journal Almanac.* New York: Ballantine Books, 1998.

The Story of Inflation. New York: Federal Reserve Bank of New York, 1998.

Multimedia

Economics U$A Series. "U.S. Economic Growth." Color video, 30 minutes. The first segment on this videocassette documents the greatest achievements and failures in developing and using the GNP since its introduction in the 1930s. "Booms and Busts." Color video, 30 minutes. The second segment examines America's roller-coaster economy in light of several economic theories. Educational Film Center (Annandale, VA): Annenberg/CPB Collection.

Technology Center

Economics Video Library
Includes high-interest, chapter-specific segments produced by CNBC for

THE WALL STREET JOURNAL.
CLASSROOM EDITION

Simulations and Data Graphing CD-ROM
Provides interactive federal budget and stock market simulations and a data graphing tool designed to support instruction in economics.

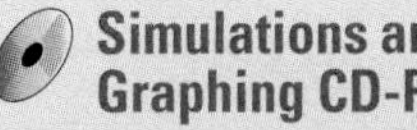

PRENTICE HALL
TeacherEXPRESS™
Plan • Teach • Assess

Teacher Express CD-ROM offers powerful lesson planning, resource management, testing, and an interactive Teacher's Edition.

Prentice Hall Presentation Pro CD-ROM
Allows you to create custom lectures for every chapter.

Social Studies Skills Tutor CD-ROM
Provides interactive practice in geographic literacy, critical thinking and reading, visual analysis, and communications.

Exam*View*® Test Bank CD-ROM
Allows you to create, edit, and print out chapter level tests.

Transparency Resource Package
Illustrates key economic concepts and provides useful forms and templates for enhancing classroom discussions.

Section Reading Support Transparency System
Delivers the main idea of each section in the student text through graphic organizers.

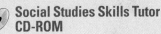

Go Online
PHSchool.com
Offers student-appropriate online activities and links as well as resources for the teacher. Be sure to check out this month's **eTeach** online discussion with a Master Economics Teacher.

Chapter Resource Manager

Chapter 12 Gross Domestic Product and Growth

For more pacing suggestions, see the Economics Pacing Guide in the Program Overview of the Teaching Resources.

Section Objectives	Print and Technology Resources
1 Gross Domestic Product *(pp. 301–308)* **Objectives** 1. Identify National Income and Product Accounts (NIPA). 2. Explain how gross domestic product (GDP) is calculated. 3. Explain the difference between nominal and real GDP. 4. List the main limitations of GDP. 5. Describe other income and output measures. 6. Identify factors that influence GDP.	• **Lesson Planner** Section 1 Lesson Plan, p. 51 • **Learning Styles Lesson Plans folder** Section 1 Lesson Plan, p. 29 • **Lesson Plans folder** Section 1 Lesson Plan, p. 44 • **Economics Assessment Rubrics folder** Writing Assignment, pp. 6–7 • **Unit 5 folder** Guided Reading and Review, p. 2 Economic Skills, p. 8 Section 1 Quiz, p. 3 • **Math Practice folder** Determining Economic Growth, p. 3 • **Presentation Pro CD-ROM** Section 1 • **Transparency Resource Package** Economics Organizers, G7: Tree Map Graphic Organizer Economics Concepts, 12A: Defining GDP Economics Concepts, 12B: Aggregate Supply Economics Concepts, 12C: Aggregate Demand Overlay • **Section Reading Support Transparency System** • **Social Studies Skills Tutor CD-ROM**
2 Business Cycles *(pp. 310–316)* **Objectives** 1. Identify the phases of the business cycle. 2. Describe four key factors that keep the business cycle going. 3. Explain how economists forecast fluctuations in the business cycle. 4. Analyze the impact of business cycles on U.S. history. 5. Analyze why U.S. business cycles may change in the future.	• **Lesson Planner** Section 2 Lesson Plan, p. 52 • **Lesson Plans folder** Section 2 Lesson Plan, p. 45 • **Unit 5 folder** Guided Reading and Review, p. 4 Careers in Economics, Technology Consultant, p. 11 Economic Cartoon, p. 12 Section 2 Quiz, p. 5 • **Presentation Pro CD-ROM** Section 2 • **Transparency Resource Package** Economics Organizers, G8: Flow Chart Graphic Organizer Economics Concepts, 12D: The Business Cycle Economics Concepts, 12E: Leading Economic Indicators • **Section Reading Support Transparency System**
3 Economic Growth *(pp. 318–324)* **Objectives** 1. Analyze how economic growth is measured. 2. Understand capital deepening and how it contributes to economic growth. 3. Analyze how saving and investment are related to economic growth. 4. Summarize the impact of population growth, government, and foreign trade on economic growth. 5. Identify the causes and impact of technological progress.	• **Lesson Planner** Section 3 Lesson Plan, p. 53 • **Learning Styles Lesson Plans folder** Section 3 Lesson Plan, p. 30 • **Lesson Plans folder** Section 3 Lesson Plan, p. 46 • **Economics Assessment Rubrics folder** Writing Assignment, pp. 6–7 • **Unit 5 folder** Guided Reading and Review, p. 6 Vocabulary Practice, p. 9 Economic Detective, p. 10 Section 3 Quiz, p. 7 • **Case Studies in Free Enterprise folder** Andrew Carnegie, pp. 24–25 • **Source Articles folder** The Psychology of Spending, pp. 36–38 • **Presentation Pro CD-ROM** Section 3 • **Transparency Resource Package** Economics Organizers, G9: Multi-Flow Chart Graphic Organizer Economics Concepts, 12F: Growth Rate of U.S. GDP Economics Concepts, 12G: Investment Spending as a Percentage of GDP • **Section Reading Support Transparency System**

Differentiated Instruction

Evaluating Online Sources (L2)

Remind students that when conducting research, they should use credible, accurate sources. To improve accuracy of the information gathered, provide students with these guidelines:

1. Identify the sponsor of the Web site. Think about whether the sponsor's credentials and expertise. Determine if the sponsor has any bias.

2. Check the time of the last update of the Web site. Ensure the information is current.

3. Use several sources to confirm information.

To model this skill, write the following possible sources on the board. For each one, have students decide whether or not it would be a good source to use for a research paper.

- Personal home page updated daily *(No, because the individual has no incentive to make sure the information is accurate.)*
- Web site sponsored by a publisher of reference materials *(Yes, because the group has an incentive to make sure the information is accurate.)*
- Government Web site last updated three years ago *(No, because the site will not have up-to-date information.)*
- Web site sponsored by a political group or business *(Possibly. Students should look at the information carefully, because the site might present information favorable to the sponsors' interests.)*

Go Online PHSchool.com

Visit the Social Studies area of the Prentice Hall Web site. There you can find additional links to enrich chapter content for *Economics: Principles in Action* as well as a self-test for students. Be sure to check out this month's **eTeach** online discussion with a Master Economics Teacher.

Web Code: mnf-5121

Running Out of Time?

- Use the **Presentation Pro CD-ROM** to create an outline for this chapter.
- Use the Chapter Summary in the **Chapter 12 Assessment,** p. 326.
- Use the Section Summaries for Chapter 12, from **Guide to the Essentials of Economics (English and Spanish).**

THE WALL STREET JOURNAL. CLASSROOM EDITION

Prentice Hall brings into the classroom the authoritative content of *The Wall Street Journal Classroom Edition.* See the Source Articles, Debating Current Issues, and You and Your Money folders in the **Teaching Resources**. Also, see Economics Video Library, "A New Era."

Assessment Resources

Chapter Assessment

Teaching Resources Unit 5, Chapter 12

- Section Quizzes, pp. 3, 5, 7

Exam *View*® Test Bank CD-ROM Chapter 12

Economics Assessment Rubrics

Chapter 12 Self-Test, **Web Code:** mna-5121

Reading and Skills Evaluation

Progress Monitoring Assessments

- Screening Test
- Diagnostic Test of Social Studies Skills

Cumulative Testing and Remediation

Progress Monitoring Assessments

- Benchmark Test #2

Standardized Test Preparation

Test Prep Workbook

Test-Taking Strategies With Transparencies

Differentiated Instruction Key

L1	Special Needs	LPR	Less Proficient Readers
L2	Basic to Average	AR	Advanced Readers
L3	All Students	SN	Special Needs Students
L4	Average to Advanced	GT	Gifted and Talented
		ELL	English Language Learner

Chapter 12

Gross Domestic Product and Growth

Introducing the Chapter

In this chapter students are introduced to the measurements economists use to analyze current economic performance and predict future performance. Additionally, the chapter discusses the fluctuations of business cycles and the factors that influence economic growth.

For additional links for *Economics: Principles in Action* provided by Prentice Hall and *The Wall Street Journal Classroom Edition,* visit the Social Studies area. Be sure to check out this month's **eTeach** online discussion with a Master Teacher.

Beyond the Lecture

You may cover the concepts in Chapter 12 in an activity-based style by using the following materials:

- **Technology Resources** appropriate for use with this chapter are noted on pp. 302, 306, 307, 308, 311, 314, 316, 319, 321, 324, and 327.
- **Presentation Pro CD-ROM** with animated graphs gives you an alternative method for organizing and delivering chapter content.
- **Activities** designed to meet the needs of students of mixed abilities and learning styles are noted throughout the chapter in the side columns.
- **Learning Styles Lesson Plans** provide alternate lessons for diverse learning styles. See pp. 29–30 of the Learning Styles Lesson Plans folder located in the Teaching Resources.

Economics Journal

Instruct students to summarize the evidence in their Economics Journals. Students may include completed journal entries in an Economics Portfolio.

Chapter 12

Gross Domestic Product and Growth

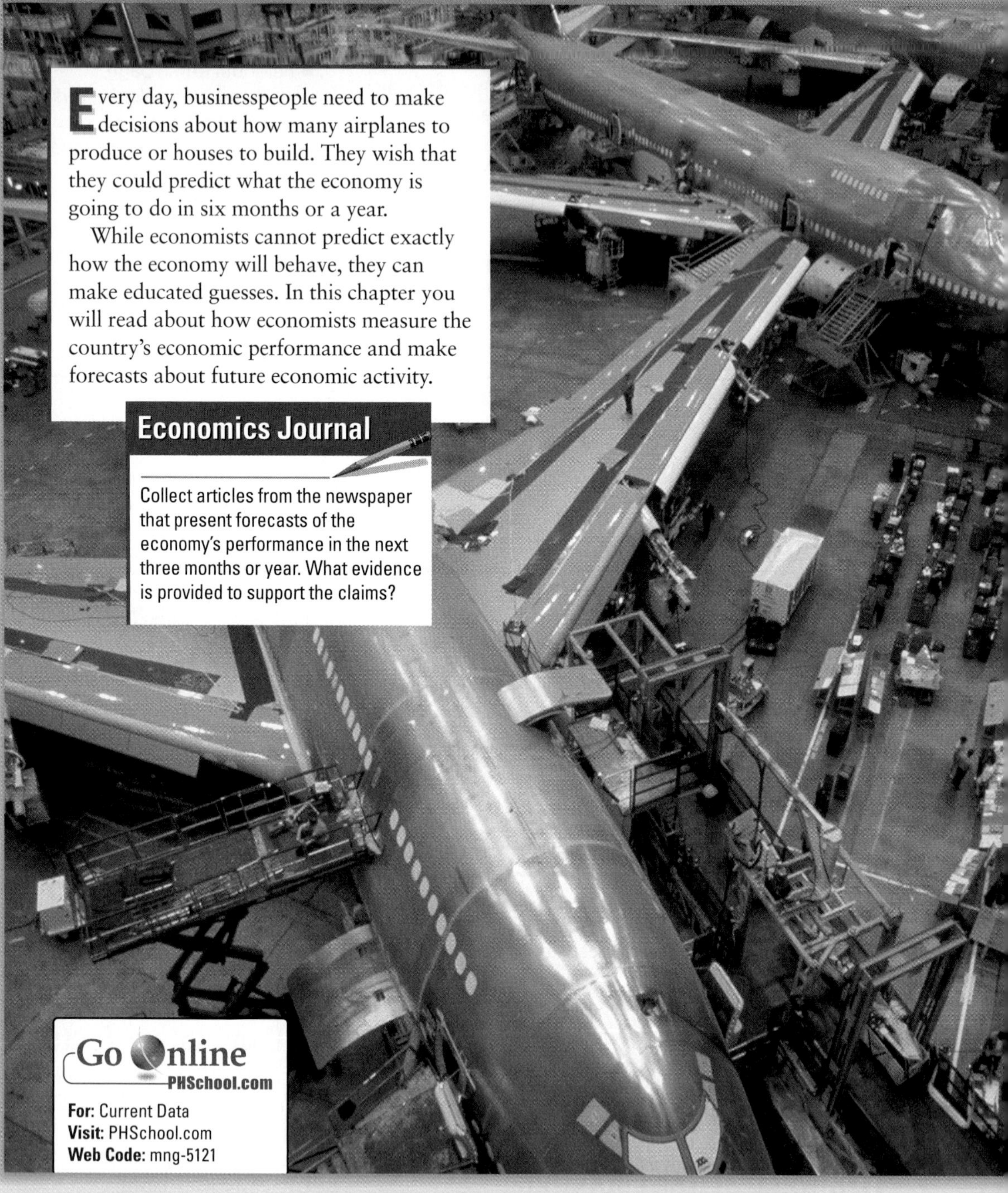

Every day, businesspeople need to make decisions about how many airplanes to produce or houses to build. They wish that they could predict what the economy is going to do in six months or a year.

While economists cannot predict exactly how the economy will behave, they can make educated guesses. In this chapter you will read about how economists measure the country's economic performance and make forecasts about future economic activity.

Economics Journal

Collect articles from the newspaper that present forecasts of the economy's performance in the next three months or year. What evidence is provided to support the claims?

Go Online
PHSchool.com

For: Current Data
Visit: PHSchool.com
Web Code: mng-5121

National Council on Economic Education

The following Voluntary National Content Standards in Economics are addressed in this chapter:

★ **Standard 15** Students will understand that: Investment in factories, machinery, new technology, and the health, education, and training of people can raise future standards of living.

★ **Standard 18** Students will understand that: A nation's overall levels of income, employment, and prices are determined by the interaction of spending and production decisions made by all households, firms, government agencies, and others in the economy.

For more information about the standards, contact the National Council on Economic Education

1140 Avenue of the Americas
New York, NY 10036
1-800-338-1192

Section 1 Gross Domestic Product

Preview

Objectives

After studying this section you will be able to:

1. **Identify** National Income and Product Accounts (NIPA).
2. **Explain** how gross domestic product (GDP) is calculated.
3. **Explain** the difference between nominal and real GDP.
4. **List** the main limitations of GDP.
5. **Describe** other income and output measures.
6. **Identify** factors that influence GDP.

Section Focus

There are several ways to evaluate a nation's economic performance. Gross domestic product (GDP) is the most important, despite its limitations. GDP changes in response to shifts in aggregate supply or aggregate demand.

Key Terms

national income accounting
gross domestic product
intermediate goods
durable goods
nondurable goods
nominal GDP
real GDP
gross national product
depreciation
price level
aggregate supply
aggregate demand

Early economists believed that a national economy would regulate itself. Periods of high unemployment and low income and output would be temporary and short-lived and would be corrected automatically.

These ideas about the economy lasted until the Great Depression, a severe economic decline that started in 1929 and lasted for over a decade. This economic avalanche, touched off by the Great Crash of the stock market in October 1929, devastated the U.S. economy. The length and depth of the Great Depression convinced many economists that they must find a way to monitor the macroeconomy's performance so that they could predict economic downturns and try to prevent them.

National Income and Product Accounts

Keeping track of the U.S. economy is an enormous task. Today, economists monitor important macroeconomic data using **national income accounting,** a system that collects statistics on production, income, investment, and savings. The data are compiled and presented in the form of National Income and Product Accounts (NIPA), which are maintained by the U.S. Department of Commerce. NIPA data are used to determine economic policies that you will read about in Chapters 15 and 16.

Gross Domestic Product

The most important of the measures in NIPA is **gross domestic product (GDP),** the dollar value of all final goods and services produced within a country's borders in a given year. This carefully worded definition conveys a lot of information that we should consider piece by piece.

Dollar value is the total of the selling prices of all goods and services produced in a country in one calendar year, which are added up to calculate GDP. *Final goods and services* are products in the form sold to consumers, as opposed to **intermediate goods,** which are used in the production of final goods. *Produced within a country's borders* is especially important to remember. For example, U.S. GDP includes cars made in Ohio by a Japanese car company.

national income accounting *a system that collects macroeconomic statistics on production, income, investment, and savings*

gross domestic product (GDP) *the dollar value of all final goods and services produced within a country's borders in a given year*

intermediate goods *goods used in the production of final goods*

Section 1

Gross Domestic Product

Objectives You may wish to call students' attention to the objectives in the Section Preview. The objectives are reflected in the main headings of the section.

Bellringer Ask students to recall what they have learned about the causes and effects of the Great Depression. Explain that the depression motivated economists to devise ways of measuring and predicting economic performance. These methods are the subject of this section.

Vocabulary Builder After students have read through the section, ask them to make flashcards for all of the key terms. On one side of each card, they should write the key term and on the other side, a definition in the student's own words.

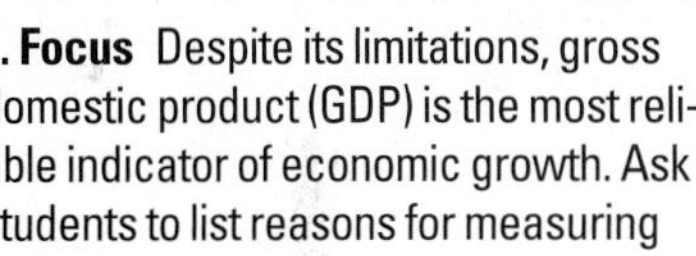

Teaching the Main Concepts (L3)

1. Focus Despite its limitations, gross domestic product (GDP) is the most reliable indicator of economic growth. Ask students to list reasons for measuring economic growth.

2. Instruct Begin by defining gross domestic product and then discussing how GDP is calculated. Be sure to emphasize the differences between the expenditure approach and the income approach. Then explain how nominal GDP differs from real GDP, and discuss the limitations of GDP as a measure of economic performance. Explain the other income and output measures that are derived from GDP. Finally, define aggregate supply (AS), aggregate demand (AD), and AS/AD equilibrium, explaining how they influence GDP.

3. Close/Reteach Remind students that the careful calculation of GDP can reveal much about economic trends and performance. Ask students to restate the definition of GDP and explain the difference between nominal and real GDP.

Graphing the Main Idea

Gross Domestic Product To build understanding of the concept of **gross domestic product,** have students complete a tree map graphic organizer like the one shown at the right. Remind students that a tree map shows an outline for a main topic, main ideas, and supporting details. They should place the title of the section in the top box, the main headings in the next row of boxes, and main ideas and supporting details in the row of boxes below that.

Section Reading Support Transparencies A template and the answers for this graphic organizer can be found in Chapter 12, Section 1 of the Section Reading Support Transparency System.

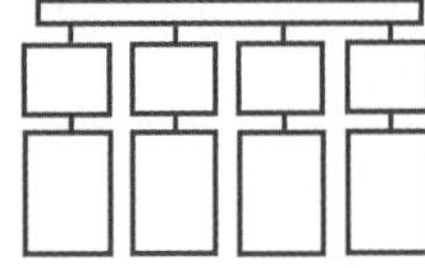

 **Guided Reading and Review**
Unit 5 folder, p. 2 asks students to identify the main ideas of the section and to define or identify key terms.

 **Transparency Resource Package**
Economics Concepts, 12A: Defining GDP

Differentiated Instruction L3
Have students identify National Income and Product Accounts (NIPA), describing where GDP fits in. Encourage students to find or create interesting illustrations depicting production, income, investment, and savings.

Differentiated Instruction L3
(Reteaching) Ask students to choose two of the following goods or services and explain how they would be added to the GDP, using first the expenditure approach and then the income approach: a refrigerator, a wide-screen television, an automobile assembly robot, a bag of potato chips, a cable television service, and a haircut.

durable goods *goods that last for a relatively long time, such as refrigerators, cars, and DVD players*

nondurable goods *goods that last a short period of time, such as food, light bulbs, and sneakers*

U.S. GDP does not include cars made in Brazil by an American automaker. You'll be able to see shortly why this distinction is important.

Let's look at the housing market for more examples of how GDP is compiled. Suppose that your neighbor sold his house this year. When the house was built, say in 1982, it was counted in that year's GDP. Thus, it would be inaccurate to count it again this year just because it changed hands. However, the fee paid to the real estate agent who handled the resale of the house would come from services performed this year, so that fee would be included in GDP.

Meanwhile, your neighbor has bought a newly built house. Would the lumber, nails, shingles, windows, and other items used to produce that house be included in GDP? No. Those are intermediate goods, and their value would be included in the price of the completed house. Thus, only the price of the completed house would be added to GDP.

Expenditure Approach

One way government economists calculate GDP is by using the expenditure approach, sometimes called the output-expenditure approach. It works this way: First, economists estimate the annual expenditures, or amounts spent, on four categories of final goods and services:

1. consumer goods and services
2. business goods and services
3. government goods and services
4. net exports or imports of goods and services

Consumer goods include **durable goods,** those goods that last for a relatively long time, such as refrigerators, cars, and DVD players. Consumer goods also include **nondurable goods,** those goods that last a short period of time, such as food, light bulbs, and sneakers.

Then, economists add together the amounts spent on all four categories to arrive at the total expenditures on goods

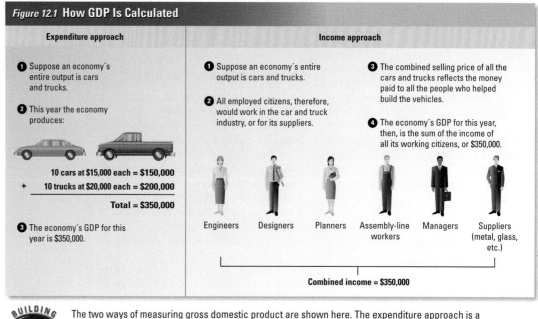

Figure 12.1 **How GDP Is Calculated**

Expenditure approach

1. Suppose an economy's entire output is cars and trucks.
2. This year the economy produces:

10 cars at $15,000 each = $150,000
+ 10 trucks at $20,000 each = $200,000
Total = $350,000

3. The economy's GDP for this year is $350,000.

Income approach

1. Suppose an economy's entire output is cars and trucks.
2. All employed citizens, therefore, would work in the car and truck industry, or for its suppliers.
3. The combined selling price of all the cars and trucks reflects the money paid to all the people who helped build the vehicles.
4. The economy's GDP for this year, then, is the sum of the income of all its working citizens, or $350,000.

Engineers | Designers | Planners | Assembly-line workers | Managers | Suppliers (metal, glass, etc.)

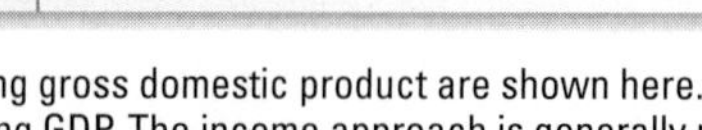

Combined income = $350,000

The two ways of measuring gross domestic product are shown here. The expenditure approach is a practical way of calculating GDP. The income approach is generally more accurate.
Gross Domestic Product Apply this example by using the expenditure approach and the income approach to explain how a new housing complex would add to GDP.

Econ 101: Key Concepts Made Easy

Gross Domestic Product Students will have an easier time remembering the definition of **gross domestic product** if they think about the meaning of each word in the phrase:

gross	=	entire; whole
domestic	=	within a country's borders
product	=	good or service

Thus GDP can be expressed as the whole amount of goods and services produced within a country's borders. As students cover this section, suggest this technique to help them remember other key terms.

Answer to . . .

Building Key Concepts A housing complex would add a specified number of dwellings at a particular price, totaling a specified amount (expenditure approach). It would also be reflected in the income paid to architects, construction workers, salespeople, and so on (income approach).

and services produced during the year. This total equals GDP. Figure 12.1 provides a simplified example of calculating GDP with the expenditure approach.

Income Approach

The expenditure approach gives economists a practical way to measure GDP. If they want better accuracy, however, they use the income approach. The income approach calculates GDP by adding up all the incomes in the economy.

Here's how it works: When a firm sells its product, the selling price represents income for the firm's owners and employees. For instance, suppose that your neighbor's newly built house sold for $115,000. This amount is added to GDP under the expenditure approach.

However, that $115,000 is also income that was shared by all of the people who helped build the house. The contractor, the bricklayer, the roofers, the window installers, and everyone else who worked on the house received some income directly from the house's selling price. Also, let's not forget the people who supplied the lumber, the nails, and all of the other materials that went into the house. The money that they received for these goods all comes from the selling price of the house, even though they may have been paid before the house was sold.

Each of these people may get only a small share of the house's selling price. However, if we added up all the shares, we would see that $115,000 of income was generated by the sale. In other words, the house's selling price is equal to the amount of income earned by all of the people who helped, however indirectly, to build the house. This same logic holds for all goods and services produced in the economy. Thus, we may calculate GDP by adding up all income earned in the economy. This process is the income approach, shown in Figure 12.1.

In theory, we can calculate GDP with either the income approach or the expenditure approach. Both calculations should give us the same total. In fact, federal economists often determine GDP using both approaches. Then they compare the two totals and make adjustments to offset any mistakes. This gives them a better result.

Figure 12.2 Circular Flow of Output and Income

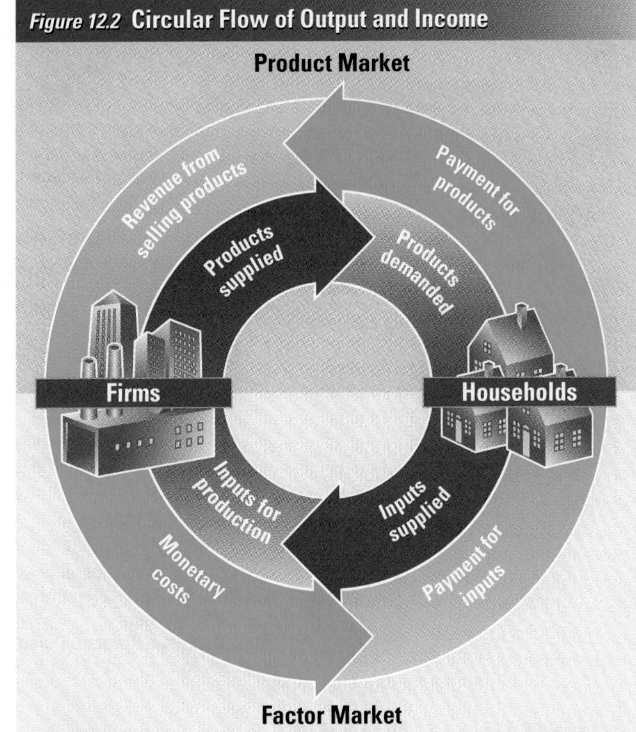

This circular flow diagram shows how the production of goods and services generates income for households and how households purchase goods and services produced by firms. **Gross Domestic Product (a) Which part of this diagram would you use to calculate GDP using the expenditure approach? (b) Which part would you use for the income approach?**

Nominal Versus Real GDP

Government policymakers measure gross domestic product to find out how well the economy is performing. The measurement must be as accurate as possible. Comparing the results of the expenditure and income approaches is one way to judge accuracy. To develop additional information about the economy, economists distinguish between two measures of GDP, nominal and real.

Differentiated Instruction  L2

Ask English language learners to customize the flashcards they created for the Vocabulary Builder activity by including a second definition on each flashcard—one that explains the term in that student's native language. ELL

Differentiated Instruction  L3

Organize students into groups of three or four. Ask each group to create a short oral presentation that explains the difference between nominal and real GDP. Encourage them to use any format (such as lecture or skit) that accomplishes their goal. Allow time for each group to make its presentation.

Differentiated Instruction L1

When comparing GDP data for several years, the figures may not give a very accurate picture. For example, in the 1950s, more people did their own house painting, cleaning, and gardening instead of hiring workers and none of their work was counted in the GDP. Similarly, people today are more likely to pump their own gasoline and withdraw money from a bank without help from a worker. Ask students to suggest other reasons that GDP data in the 1950s might not compare well with GDP today. Write the list on the chalkboard. Then have each student draw a cartoon that illustrates this concept. SN

Block Scheduling Strategies

Consider these suggestions to take advantage of extended class time:

- Have groups of two or three students search the Internet for National Income and Product Accounts data. Have groups report their findings, displaying at least one type of data. Use the links provided in the *Economics: Principles in Action* segment in the Social Studies area at the following Web site: **www.phschool.com**
- Extend the second activity on p. 302 by having small groups of students create an imaginary small country, providing data for a limited number of goods and services for a particular year. Ask them to calculate GDP for the country, using both expenditure and income approaches. Have groups present their GDP data in poster form.

Answer to . . .

Building Key Concepts (a) the outer circle (b) the outer circle

Learning Styles Activity
Learning Styles Lesson Plans folder, p. 29 asks students to create a chart showing how nominal GDP and real GDP are calculated over a period of three years.

Meeting NCEE Standards

Use the following benchmark activity from the **Voluntary National Content Standards in Economics** to evaluate student understanding of **Standard 18.**

Gather current and historical data on real GDP per capita for the United States, Japan, Somalia, and South Korea and state a relationship between real GDP and standard of living.

Math Practice Activity
Math Practice folder, p. 3, "Determining Economic Growth," allows students to calculate per capita GDP and examine how it can be used to measure economic growth.

Differentiated Instruction L2

The concepts in this section are fairly complex. Have less proficient readers copy the main headings from this section on a sheet of paper, leaving plenty of space beneath each heading. Then ask them to write five facts from each segment under each heading. LPR

Answer to . . .
Building Key Concepts $505,000 ($225,000 + 280,000)

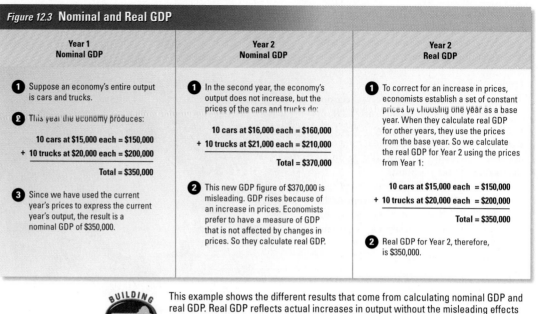

Figure 12.3 **Nominal and Real GDP**

Year 1 Nominal GDP	Year 2 Nominal GDP	Year 2 Real GDP
1 Suppose an economy's entire output is cars and trucks. **2** This year the economy produces: 10 cars at $15,000 each = $150,000 + 10 trucks at $20,000 each = $200,000 Total = $350,000 **3** Since we have used the current year's prices to express the current year's output, the result is a nominal GDP of $350,000.	**1** In the second year, the economy's output does not increase, but the prices of the cars and trucks do: 10 cars at $16,000 each = $160,000 + 10 trucks at $21,000 each = $210,000 Total = $370,000 **2** This new GDP figure of $370,000 is misleading. GDP rises because of an increase in prices. Economists prefer to have a measure of GDP that is not affected by changes in prices. So they calculate real GDP.	**1** To correct for an increase in prices, economists establish a set of constant prices by choosing one year as a base year. When they calculate real GDP for other years, they use the prices from the base year. So we calculate the real GDP for Year 2 using the prices from Year 1: 10 cars at $15,000 each = $150,000 + 10 trucks at $20,000 each = $200,000 Total = $350,000 **2** Real GDP for Year 2, therefore, is $350,000.

This example shows the different results that come from calculating nominal GDP and real GDP. Real GDP reflects actual increases in output without the misleading effects of price increases.
Gross Domestic Product Using Year 1 as the base year, calculate real GDP for Year 3, in which 15 cars and 14 trucks were sold.

nominal GDP *GDP measured in current prices*

real GDP *GDP expressed in constant, or unchanging, prices*

Nominal GDP

In Figure 12.1, we calculated **nominal GDP**—that is, GDP measured in current prices. (Sometimes it is called "current GDP.") To calculate nominal GDP, we simply use the current year's prices to calculate the value of the current year's output. Figure 12.3 shows how the definition of nominal GDP applies to the small economy that produces only cars and trucks.

Real GDP

Study how nominal GDP is calculated in Year 1 and Year 2. The diagram points out a problem with nominal GDP: A general increase in prices *appears* to make GDP rise, when in fact output has not risen. To correct for this distortion, economists determine **real GDP.** This is defined as GDP expressed in constant, or unchanging, prices.

Look again at Figure 12.3 and see how real GDP is calculated in Year 2. When real GDP rises, we can be certain whether an economy is producing more goods and services, regardless of changes in the prices of those items. In this example, we learn from calculating real GDP that output did not increase in Year 2.

Limitations of GDP

Even though economists can calculate it accurately, GDP is still not a perfect yardstick. For instance, GDP does not take into account certain economic activities, such as:

- *Nonmarket activities* GDP does not measure goods and services that people make or do themselves, such as caring for children, mowing the lawn, cooking dinner, washing the car. GDP *does* rise, however, when people pay someone else to do these things for them. When nonmarket activities are shifted to the market, GDP is pushed up somewhat, even though production has not really increased.
- *The underground economy* A large amount of production and income is never recorded or reported to the govern-

Transparency Resource Package
Economics Concepts, 12D: The Business Cycle

Figure 12.7 **Tracking a Business Cycle**

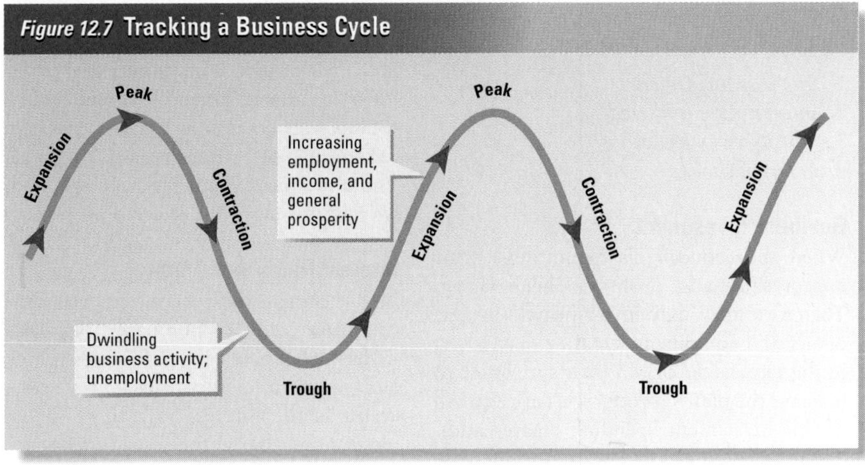

In a business cycle, a period of rising real GDP reaches a peak, then falls into a contraction. When the contraction reaches the low point, or trough, a new expansion begins. From 1854 to 1991, the United States had 31 business cycles. Excluding wartimes, the cycles averaged 48 months. **Gross Domestic Product** **In which part of a business cycle do you think the United States is right now—expansion or contraction? Give evidence to support your conclusion.**

4. *Trough* When the economy has "bottomed out," it has reached the **trough** (TRAWF), the lowest point in an economic contraction, when real GDP stops falling.

During the contraction phase, GDP is always falling. But other conditions, such as price levels and unemployment, may vary. Economists created terms to describe contractions with different characteristics and levels of severity. They include:

- *Recession* If real GDP falls for two consecutive quarters (at least six straight months), the economy is said to be in a recession. A **recession** is a prolonged economic contraction. Generally lasting from 6 to 18 months, recessions are typically marked by unemployment rising into the range of 6 percent to 10 percent.
- *Depression* If a recession is especially long and severe, it may be called a **depression.** The term has no precise definition but usually refers to a deep recession with features such as high unemployment and low factory output.
- *Stagflation* This term combines *stagnant*—a word meaning unmoving or decayed—and *inflation.* **Stagflation** is a decline in real GDP (output) combined with a rise in the price level (inflation).

Although economists know much about business cycles, they cannot predict any one cycle's behavior, nor can they tell exactly how long its phases will last. The only certainty is that a growing economy will eventually experience a downturn and will later bounce back.

What Keeps a Business Cycle Going?

The shifts that occur during a business cycle have many causes, some more predictable than others. Often, two or more factors will combine to push the economy into the next phase of a business cycle. Typically, a sharp rise or drop in some important economic variable will set off a series of events that bring about the

trough *the lowest point in an economic contraction, when real GDP stops falling*

recession *a prolonged economic contraction*

depression *a recession that is especially long and severe*

stagflation *a decline in real GDP combined with a rise in the price level*

Background

Economics in History

Inflation can hurt an economy. Hyperinflation can destroy it. Hyperinflation occurs when prices rise rapidly and uncontrollably. To counter rising prices a government may borrow heavily or print more money, which then quickly loses its value.

An example of hyperinflation can be found in the German economy just after World War I. German currency had so little value that workers had to be paid twice a day. Eventually many Germans abandoned the monetary system altogether and reverted to barter. People spent so much time trading for the things they needed that production almost stopped entirely. This hyperinflation may have been a contributing factor in the rise of Adolf Hitler.

Differentiated Instruction 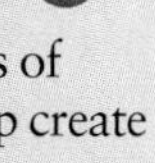

Organize the class into groups of three or four. Have each group create a poster illustrating the business cycle. Encourage students to be both informative and creative in their depictions of the business cycle.

Econ 101: Key Concepts Made Easy

Gross Domestic Product To help students understand the nuances of the **business cycle,** explain that not every expansion is a boom and not every contraction is a depression. In reality many phases of the business cycle represent subtle changes in economic direction, although the terms *peak* and *trough* may suggest otherwise.

Answer to . . .

Building Key Concepts Answers will vary based on the current state of the economy, but students should logically explain their reasoning and their choice of evidence.

Differentiated Instruction L2

Ask students to consult a thesaurus to find synonyms for the four major phases of the business cycle: expansion, peak, contraction, and trough. After each synonym, students should define that phase, using the synonyms to write the definition. Explain to students that using more than one synonym may make their definitions clearer.

Differentiated Instruction L3

Ask students to create cause-and-effect charts that illustrate the effects of business investment, interest rates and credit, consumer expectations, and external shocks on the business cycle. Remind students that these are the factors that keep the business cycle going.

next phase. Business cycles are affected by four main economic variables:

1. *business investment*
2. *interest rates and credit*
3. *consumer expectations*
4. *external shocks*

Business Investment

When the economy is expanding, firms expect sales and profits to keep rising. Therefore, they may invest heavily in new plants and equipment. Or they may invest in the expansion of old plants in order to increase the plants' productive capacity. All of this investment spending creates additional output and jobs, helping to increase GDP and maintain the expansion.

At some point, however, firms may decide that they have expanded enough or that demand for their products is dropping. They cut back on investment spending; as a result, aggregate demand falls. As Figure 12.8 shows, the result is a decline in the price level and in GDP. The drop in business spending reduces output and income in other sectors of the economy.

Figure 12.8 **Declining Business Investment**

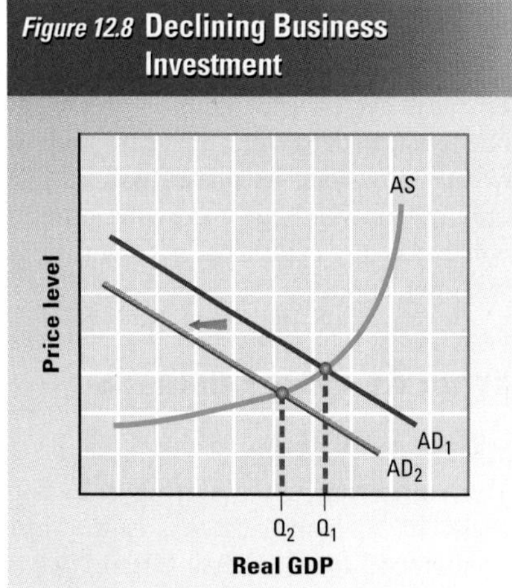

This graph shows how a drop in business investment can affect the business cycle.

Supply and Demand On this graph, when business investment declines, what happens to (a) aggregate demand? (b) real GDP? (c) the price level?

Then industries that produce capital goods slow production down and begin to lay off workers. Other industries might follow, causing unemployment to rise. Jobless workers cannot buy new cars, eat at restaurants, or perhaps even pay their rent. The downward spiral picks up speed, and we find ourselves in a recession.

Interest Rates and Credit

In the United States economy, consumers often use credit to purchase "big ticket" items—from new cars and houses to home electronics and vacations. The cost of credit is the interest rate that financial institutions charge their customers. If the interest rate rises, consumers are less likely to buy those new cars and appliances.

Businesses, too, look to interest rates in deciding whether or not to purchase new equipment, expand their facilities, or make any other large investments that must be financed. For businesses, interest rates are a part of the opportunity cost of investments.

When interest rates are low, companies borrow money to make new investments, often adding jobs to the economy. When interest rates climb, investment dries up, as does job growth. One result of rising interest rates, then, is less output and employment in the industries producing consumer and business goods. Such actions may lead the entire economy to shrink.

Consider one example of the impact of interest rates on the business cycle. In the early 1980s, high consumer interest rates helped bring on the worst economic slump in the United States since the Great Depression. Some credit-card interest rates reached 21 percent. As a result, the cost of expensive items usually bought on credit was too high for many Americans.

As consumers reduced their spending, the economy entered a recession. The recession eventually drove up unemployment rates to over 9 percent—the highest since the Depression.

You can see, therefore, why economists watch interest rates closely. The rise and fall of borrowing rates has a great impact on the level of spending and real GDP.

Block Scheduling Strategies

Consider these suggestions to take advantage of extended class time:

- Present the Background note on p. 311. Then have students use the library to research this period in Germany as well as similar periods in other places that experienced hyperinflation. Gather as a class after the research period to discuss their findings, including the effects of hyperinflation on individuals and the historical consequences of hyperinflation in the other countries they researched.
- Have students use a current almanac or another source to find historical statistics on business investment, interest rates, or other business cycle indicators. Have them use the Simulations and Data Graphing CD-ROM to create graphs of the data and to write paragraphs that explain its significance.
- Extend the Interdisciplinary Connection on p. 314 by asking students to create a "Readers' Theater" presentation of passages from *The Grapes of Wrath* or other Depression-era literature.

Answer to . . .

Building Key Concepts (a) It decreases. (b) It decreases. (c) It decreases.

Consumer Expectations

Consumer spending is determined partly by consumers' expectations. Fears of a weakening economy can cause consumer confidence to fall, meaning that a majority of people expect the economy to begin contracting. If that happens, consumers may start "saving for a rainy day," reducing their spending because they expect layoffs and lower incomes.

This reduced spending can actually help bring on a contraction, as firms respond to reduced demand for their products. Thus consumer expectations often become self-fulfilling prophecies, creating the very outcome that consumers fear. In spring 2003, expectations of war with Iraq influenced the economy as consumers and entrepreneurs postponed some purchases until the end of the conflict.

Of course, the opposite can occur. If people expect a rapidly growing economy, they will also expect abundant job opportunities and rising incomes. Thus, they will buy more goods and services, pushing up GDP. Consumers can help create the very prosperity they anticipate!

External Shocks

Of all of the factors that affect the business cycle, perhaps most difficult to predict are external shocks, which you read about in Chapter 6. External shocks can dramatically affect an economy's aggregate supply.

Examples of negative external shocks include disruptions of the oil supply, wars that interrupt normal trade relations, and droughts that severely reduce crop harvests.

Let's consider what might happen if a shock occurred. Suppose that the nation's oil supply were suddenly cut off. Immediately, the price of any remaining oil skyrockets.

This shock has a powerful effect on the economy. Oil is used to produce many goods, and petroleum products fuel the trucks, trains, and airplanes that transport goods from factories to stores. The oil shortage forces firms to reduce production and raise prices for their goods. In other words, GDP declines and the price level rises.

Figure 12.9 Negative External Shock

Hurricanes, drought, war, and trade disputes can cause negative external shocks to the economy. **Supply and Demand Compare the results of the negative shock shown on this graph with the results of declining business investment shown in Figure 12.8.**

Figure 12.9 illustrates this scenario. The negative shock raises costs of production and prices of final goods throughout the economy. The aggregate supply (AS) curve shifts to the left, reflecting higher prices and lower real GDP. This is the stagflation that you read about on page 311. It is particularly harmful to businesses and households and difficult for policymakers to fix.

Of course, an economy may also enjoy *positive* external shocks to its aggregate supply. The discovery of a large deposit of oil or minerals will contribute to a nation's wealth. A growing season with a perfect mix of sun and rain may create bountiful harvests that drive food prices down. Positive shocks tend to shift the AS curve to the right, lowering the price level and increasing real GDP.

External shocks usually come without much warning. The other key factors capable of pushing an economy from one phase of the business cycle to another are more predictable. So economists track

Economic Cartoon

Unit 5 folder, p. 12 gives students practice in interpreting cartoons about section content.

Differentiated Instruction 

(Enrichment) Have students search newspapers and magazines for examples of external shocks to world economies that have occurred in the last year. Ask students to find two articles on this subject, to write a short summary of each article, and to analyze the effects that these shocks had on the economies of the nations in which they occurred.

Differentiated Instruction 

Have students research various theories concerning business cycles, or economic fluctuations. Possible places to start are with agricultural theories (William Stanley Jevons); psychological theories (Arthur C. Pigou); political, demographic, or monetary theories; or underconsumption or investment theories. Ask students to present their findings in an essay, either supporting or disputing the theories. GT

Preparing for Standardized Tests

Have students read the section titled "External Shocks" and then answer the question below.

Which of the following best represents a positive external shock to an economy?

A outbreak of war
B drought
(C) discovery of extensive copper deposits
D trade embargo

Answer to . . .

Building Key Concepts Instead of decreasing, all factors increase.

Transparency Resource Package
Economics Concepts, 12E: Leading Economic Indicators

Differentiated Instruction L3

(Enrichment) Have students research the ten leading economic indicators. Ask them first to restate in summary form how economists forecast fluctuations in the business cycle. Then have students list each indicator, define it briefly, and explain how that indicator might help economists forecast future economic trends.

Go Online PHSchool.com Typing in the Web Code when prompted will bring students directly to detailed instructions for this activity.

Background

The Conference Board

The Conference Board is a not-for-profit business research and membership organization that has been in existence for more than 80 years. In December 1995 the Conference Board became the official source for the indexes of economic indicators. Until then these economic data were compiled and published by the U.S. Department of Commerce.

Global Connections

Global Economic Decline Like a deadly virus, the Great Depression quickly spread throughout much of the world. Latin America took a hard hit when U.S. markets for its goods dried up. Europeans depended on the United States for investments and loans, which became scarce. Industrial production fell by 40 percent in Germany, 14 percent in Britain, and 29 percent in France. "Hoovervilles," the makeshift shelters of the homeless named after President Hoover, sprang up in cities around the world. A photo from the era shows a British man wearing a sign that described the plight of many: "I know 3 trades / I speak 3 languages / Fought for 3 years / Have 3 children / And no work for 3 months / But I only want one job."

business investment, interest rates, and consumer expectations in order to more accurately forecast changes in the business cycle.

Business Cycle Forecasting

Predicting changes in a business cycle is difficult. To predict the next phase of a business cycle, forecasters must anticipate movements in real GDP before they occur. This is no easy task, given the large number of factors that influence the level of output in a modern economy.

Government and business decision makers need accurate economic predictions to respond to changes in a business cycle. For instance, if businesses expect a contraction, they may reduce inventories and postpone building new factories. If government policymakers expect a contraction, they may launch spending and taxation measures to try to prevent a recession.

leading indicators *key economic variables that economists use to predict a new phase of a business cycle*

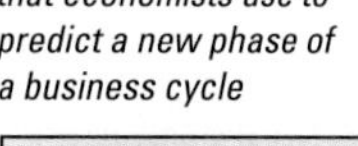

In the News Read more about the effects of terrorism on the business cycle in "The Last Straw?," an article in The Wall Street Journal Classroom Edition.

The Wall Street Journal Classroom Edition

For: Current Events
Visit: PHSchool.com
Web Code: mnc-5122

Economists have many tools available for making these predictions. The **leading indicators** are a set of key economic variables that economists use to predict a new phase of a business cycle.

The stock market is one leading indicator. Typically, the stock market turns sharply downward before a recession begins. For example, the Nasdaq crash of 2000 preceded the recession of 2001. Recessions do not *always* follow downturns in the stock market, but the pattern is fairly regular.

Interest rates are another indicator. Short-term interest rates show the cost of borrowing money for a few days or months. These rates change often and reflect current events. Long-term interest rates, such as those paid on 10-year and 30-year bonds, affect housing and large business investments. Long-term rates provide clues to the future health of the economy. Low rates may mean that businesses and consumers don't want to borrow money to invest, and so the economy may contract in coming years.

The Conference Board, a private business research organization, maintains an index of ten leading economic indicators, including stock prices, interest rates, and manufacturers' new orders of capital goods. Economists and policymakers closely watch this index, which is updated monthly. However, like the other important tools used to forecast changes in the business cycle, it is not altogether reliable, since it sometimes predicts events that don't occur. (See the Economic Atlas and Databank, pages 538–539, for data relating to the Index of Leading Economic Indicators and other economic measures.)

Business Cycles in American History

Economic activity in the United States has indeed followed a cyclical pattern. Periods of GDP growth alternate with periods of GDP decline.

The Great Depression

As you read earlier, before the 1930s many economists believed that when an economy declined, it would quickly recover on its own. This explains why, when the U.S. stock market crashed in 1929, and the economy took a nosedive, President Herbert Hoover felt little need to

Interdisciplinary Connections: Literature

The Dust Bowl When overcultivation and drought turned farmland into scrubland in the early 1930s, one of the most severe environmental catastrophes ever to hit the United States occurred: the Dust Bowl. Combined with the Great Depression, the Dust Bowl drove thousands of American families from their homes. John Steinbeck chronicled the plight of farmers who left Oklahoma to travel to California during this time in his classic novel *The Grapes of Wrath*.

Making the Connection Ask students to look for other novels, stories, plays, poems, and song lyrics that depict the harsh economic reality of the Dust Bowl or the Great Depression. Have them share their findings with the class.

change his economic policies. The crisis, however, did not just go away.

One look at Figure 12.10 shows that the Great Depression did not rapidly cure itself. Rather, it was the most severe economic downturn in the history of industrial capitalism. Between 1929 and 1933, GDP fell by almost one third, and unemployment rose to about 25 percent. One out of every four workers was jobless, and those who could find work often earned very low wages.

As the effects of the Great Depression spread throughout the world, it affected economists' beliefs about the macroeconomy. The Depression, along with the publication of John Maynard Keynes's *The General Theory of Employment, Interest, and Money,* pushed economists to consider the idea that modern market economies could fall into long-lasting contractions.

In addition, many economists accepted Keynes's idea that government intervention might be needed to pull an economy out of a depression. You'll read more about Keynes and his ideas in Chapter 15.

The depression also affected American politics. Rejecting Hoover, voters in 1932 elected the Democratic governor of New York, Franklin Delano Roosevelt, to the presidency. Roosevelt soon began a series of government programs designed to get people back to work.

Programs such as the Works Progress Administration and the Civilian Conservation Corps got able-bodied workers back on the job and earning income, which they would then spend supporting their families. In this way, spending increased throughout the economy.

Not until the United States entered into World War II did the country completely recover from the Great Depression. The sudden surge in government defense spending boosted real GDP well above pre-depression levels.

Figure 12.10 U.S. Real GDP, 1929–1945

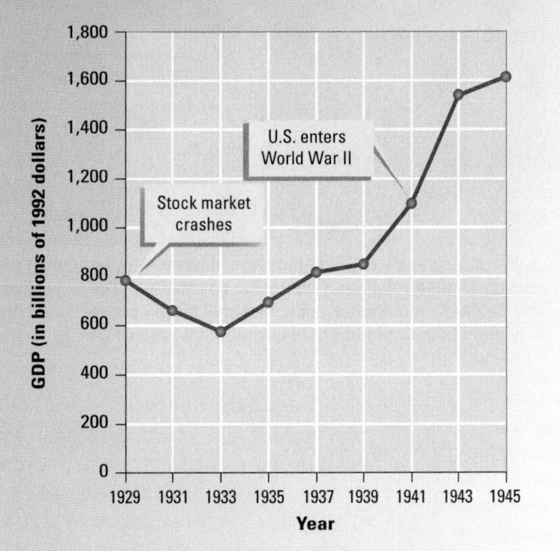

As this graph shows, output (real GDP) dropped dramatically during the Great Depression. With factories idle, thousands of Americans lost their jobs and their homes. **Unemployment What accounts for the rise in real GDP in the early 1940s?**

Some Later Recessions

Thankfully, no economic downturns since the 1930s have been nearly as severe as the Great Depression. We have had recessions, though.

In the 1970s, an international cartel, the Organization of Petroleum Exporting Countries (OPEC), launched an embargo on oil shipped to the United States and quadrupled the price of its oil. These actions caused external shocks in the American oil market. As oil prices skyrocketed, raw material costs rose, and the economy quickly contracted into a period of stagflation.

Reeling from higher-than-ever prices for gasoline and heating fuel prices, Americans began looking for ways to conserve energy. They turned down their heat, bought smaller, more fuel-efficient cars, and began researching energy alternatives to petroleum. When the United States and other nations developed more of their own energy resources, OPEC finally lowered its oil prices.

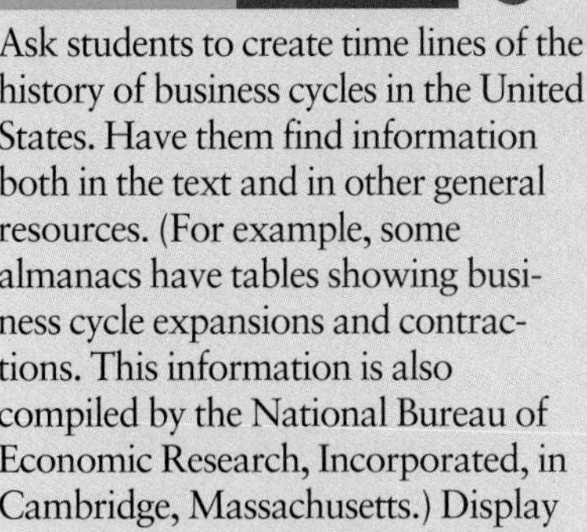

Differentiated Instruction L3

Ask students to create time lines of the history of business cycles in the United States. Have them find information both in the text and in other general resources. (For example, some almanacs have tables showing business cycle expansions and contractions. This information is also compiled by the National Bureau of Economic Research, Incorporated, in Cambridge, Massachusetts.) Display the time lines, or combine their data in a bulletin board display.

Differentiated Instruction 

(Reteaching) Have students write brief newspaper articles that explain common views of how U.S. business cycles may change in the future. Inform them that their articles should discuss why some people are optimistic about the future of business cycles while others counsel caution.

Preparing for Standardized Tests

Have students read the section titled "Some Later Recessions" and then answer the question below.

Which of the following describes how Americans responded to high prices for gasoline and fuel oil in the 1970s?

A They launched a campaign to bar the import of oil from OPEC countries.

B They began looking for ways to increase defense spending.

C They asked the government to subsidize the search for oil.

(D) They began looking for ways to conserve gasoline and fuel oil.

Answer to . . .

Building Key Concepts entry of the United States into World War II

GTE Guide to the Essentials
Chapter 12, Section 2, p. 51 provides support for students who need additional review of the section content. Spanish support is available in the Spanish edition of the guide on p. 51.

Quiz Unit 5 folder, p. 5 includes questions to check students' understanding of Section 2 content.

Presentation Pro CD-ROM
Quiz provides multiple-choice questions to check students' understanding of Section 2 content.

Answers to . . .

Section 2 Assessment

1. contraction
2. If interest rates rise too high, consumers will stop purchasing "big ticket" items, and businesses will not be able to afford to borrow the money they need in order to invest in their plants and equipment. Output will fall, a situation that marks the start of a contraction.
3. The stock market has historically given advance notice of a new phase of the business cycle. Typically it turns sharply downward a short time before a recession begins.
4. Instead of assuming that the macroeconomy would automatically recover from a recession, economists began to consider the possibility that modern market economies could fall into prolonged contractions and that government assistance would be necessary to pull them out.
5. Students who choose the peak may point out that it is the most prosperous point of an expansion, when output is highest. Students who choose the trough may say that although it is the worst point of a recession, when output is lowest and many people are unemployed, it also marks the beginning of an expansion, which can return an economy to prosperity.
6. Students should draw a graph that reflects the data, based on the model of Figure 12.10.

▲ **When the supply of OPEC petroleum decreased, gasoline prices shot up. Limited supplies closed some gas stations. The green flag at this California gas station meant that only those customers with even-numbered license plates could buy rationed gas that day.**

Once again the United States had suffered an economic downturn, although not as severe as the Great Depression. There were additional problems in the late 1970s and early 1980s. High interest rates and other factors caused real GDP to fall and the unemployment rate to rise to over 9 percent in the early 1980s.

The Business Cycle Today

Following a brief recession in 1991, the U.S. economy grew steadily, with real GDP rising each year during the 1990s. The country enjoyed record growth, low unemployment, and low inflation. Some economists began to suggest that the nature of the business cycle had changed. Perhaps we had learned how to control recessions and promote long-term growth.

As the dot-com boom of the 1990s ended, however, the U.S. growth slowed. Businesses and individuals invested billions of dollars in new technology that proved to be unprofitable and, in some cases, worthless. The negative effects of the technology crash spread throughout the economy to other industries. In March 2001, the country slipped into a recession.

Economists hoped the decline would prove short-lived, but then the terrorist attacks of September 11, 2001, resulted in a sharp drop in consumer spending. The hotel, airline, and tourism industries were especially affected. Many companies blamed their performance problems on September 11.

The recession ended in November 2001 when the economy began to grow slowly. The Fed cut interest rates to historic low levels to prevent the economy from slipping back into a recession. However, unemployment continued to rise steadily over the following years as companies laid off more workers and kept spending low. The economy's growth was not strong enough to dispel the feeling of bad times even though the recession had ended. Investors looked to the future for a true turn-around and confident economic growth.

Section 2 Assessment

Progress Monitoring *Online*
For: Self-quiz with vocabulary practice
Web Code: mna-5126

Key Terms and Main Ideas

1. Which phase of a **business cycle** can lead an economy into recession?
2. How can interest rates push a business cycle into a **contraction?**
3. Why is the stock market considered to be a **leading indicator** of economic change?
4. How did the Great Depression affect economists' beliefs about the macroeconomy?

Applying Economic Concepts

5. ***Critical Thinking*** At which point in a business cycle would you prefer to be, the peak or the trough? Why?
6. ***Try This*** Draw a line graph of a business cycle in which the peak occurs when the real GDP reaches $4.9 trillion ($4,900 billion) and the trough occurs at $4.3 trillion. Label the expansion, peak, contraction, and trough. Use Figure 12.10 as a model.

For: Primary Source Activity
Visit: PHSchool.com
Web Code: mnd-5122

Progress Monitoring *Online*
For additional assessment, have students access Progress Monitoring Online at **Web Code:** mna-5126

Go Online PHSchool.com Typing in the Web Code when prompted will bring students directly to detailed instructions for this activity.

Economist

Entrepreneur

ECONOMIC

Profile

ANDREW CARNEGIE (1835–1919)

Andrew Carnegie's hard work and determination helped him rise from poverty to wealth and power. He inherited a strong commitment to workers from his father, but he also was ruthless when dealing with his own employees. He was deeply committed to charity, and is remembered today for the his huge charitable endowments.

Escape from Poverty

If you had known the Carnegie family when Andrew was born, you would never have predicted his financial success. The Carnegies lived in Dunfermline, Scotland. The town formerly produced the finest damask linens in England, but the industry had declined and Andrew's father, a weaver, did not have enough work to support his family. Hearing that conditions were better in America, the family left Scotland and arrived in Pittsburgh, Pennsylvania, in 1848.

Pittsburgh was a booming industrial city, growing rapidly but suffering the effects of pollution. Carnegie later wrote that "if you washed your face and hands they were as dirty as ever in an hour. The soot gathered in the hair and irritated the skin . . . ." Carnegie was determined to improve his life.

At first, Carnegie worked as a telegraph messenger, then as the personal telegrapher to the superintendent of the western division of the Pennsylvania Railroad. Eventually, he became superintendent himself. By 1856, he had saved enough money to begin investing in other companies, and by 1863 he was earning $40,000 a year from his investments. In 1899, he founded the company that grew into Carnegie Steel Co., Ltd.

Mixed Treatment of Workers

Carnegie often spoke out in support of working people, no doubt remembering his own humble beginnings. But he ran his own business ruthlessly. In a brutal confrontation between striking workers and management guards, three workers and seven guards were killed. Carnegie expressed horror at the bloodshed. Once the union was crushed, however, Carnegie cut wages and imposed longer workdays. He gave his steel workers only one day off during the entire year: the Fourth of July.

Charitable Commitments

In 1901, Carnegie sold Carnegie Steel to J.P. Morgan. Carnegie personally earned $250 million from the sale—or about $4.5 billion in today's dollars. He then retired from business as one of the wealthiest people in the world.

In retirement, Carnegie gave more than $350 million to a wide range of philanthropic causes—over $3 billion in current dollars. He supported education, world peace, libraries, and research. Today, he is also remembered for creating music halls (the most famous one, in New York City, bears his name) and over 3,000 public libraries.

CHECK FOR UNDERSTANDING

1. Source Reading How did Andrew Carnegie use the technological developments of the Industrial Revolution to become one of the richest people in the world?

2. Critical Thinking Are today's entrepreneurs able to make the same degree of charitable contributions as Carnegie? Why or why not?

3. Learn More Use the Internet to learn more about major Carnegie endowments such as the Carnegie Endowment for International Peace.

Beyond the Classroom: Occupations and Institutions Change with the Economy

Both Andrew Carnegie and Bill Gates have contributed large amounts of their very large fortunes to libraries. Carnegie for the most part contributed to the construction of the physical buildings. Gates' funds provide for many aspects of computerization and technology. Have students research and compare the library interests and contributions of both Andrew Carnegie and Bill Gates. Point out that both the library and the work of librarians has changed over time as the technology around it has changed–just as the weavers' trade changed with the introduction of the power loom. Have students discuss how the library and the role of the librarian have changed. Invite a professional librarian to speak about the changes.

ECONOMIC Profile Andrew Carnegie

Background

Andrew Carnegie–a captain of 19th century American industry–was one of the richest entrepreneurs of his age. Born in Scotland in 1835, he watched as the industrial revolution replaced his father–a hand weaver–with a steam powered loom. When an aunt wrote from Pittsburgh, the iron manufacturing center of the United States, urging the family to join her, the family obliged.

Pittsburgh–its roaring furnaces, American ingenuity, and technology–symbolized the opportunity inherent in the industrial revolution, and Andrew Carnegie was determined to take advantage of it. He would not be hurt by change as his father was. Alert to opportunities, he soon headed up a company that was replacing wooden bridges with iron. He used a refining process developed by the Englishman Henry Bessemer to convert iron into steel, and soon he was producing more steel than Great Britain.

In 1901 Carnegie sold his company to J.P. Morgan for $250 million. "Congratulations," said Morgan. "You are now the richest man in the world." By the time he died in 1919, Carnegie had given away $350 million to charity.

Careers in Economics Activity
Unit 5 folder, p. 11 gives students a closer look at the career path of a technology consultant.

Answers to . . .

1. Answers will vary but should point out that Carnegie's wealth was based on using technology to convert iron into steel.
2. Student responses will vary but may include comparisons with Bill Gates' and other entrepreneurs' contributions to libraries and health and learning initiatives.

Section 3

Economic Growth

Objectives You may wish to call students' attention to the objectives in the Section Preview. The objectives are reflected in the main headings of the section.

Bellringer Ask students to define *standard of living* and then to list those qualities of life that characterize a high standard of living. Inform them that this section will explain the relationship between economic growth and standard of living.

Vocabulary Builder Have students read through the section to discover the meaning of each key term. Then ask them to write a paragraph that includes all of the key terms.

Lesson Plan

Teaching the Main Concepts L3

1. Focus The long-term growth of real GDP is powered by many economic variables, including capital deepening, savings and investment, trade, and technological progress.

2. Instruct Begin by defining economic growth. Then discuss with students those economic variables that influence growth in real GDP. Be sure that students understand that capital deepening includes both physical and human capital. Also, stress the importance of the relationship between saving and investing and GDP. Finally, discuss the contribution to economic growth that results from technological progress, emphasizing that such progress can take many forms.

3. Close/Reteach Remind students that economic growth can be sustained by a variety of economic variables that can lead to a higher standard of living. Ask students to list and define those economic variables.

Answer to . . .

Building Key Concepts by about $17,000

Section 3 Economic Growth

Preview

Objectives

After studying this section you will be able to:

1. **Analyze** how economic growth is measured.
2. **Understand** capital deepening and how it contributes to economic growth.
3. **Analyze** how saving and investment are related to economic growth.
4. **Summarize** the impact of population growth, government, and foreign trade on economic growth.
5. **Identify** the causes and impact of technological progress.

Section Focus

Economic growth is a steady, long-term increase in a nation's real GDP that tends to raise living standards. Primary contributors to long-term growth include capital deepening, saving and investing, and advances in technology. The other factors that affect economic growth are population, government, and foreign trade.

Key Terms

real GDP per capita
capital deepening
saving
savings rate
technological progress

Most of us would agree that as far as material possessions go, Americans are much better off today than they were 100 years ago. Why is this so?

Economic growth has allowed successive generations to have more and better goods and services than their parents. Long-term increases in real GDP allow an entire society to improve its quality of life, especially its standard of living. (See Chapter 3.)

A hundred years ago, most American families would have been able to own an icebox, a wood-burning stove, and a horse or bicycle. For most of us today, those necessities of life have turned into a refrigerator-freezer, a microwave oven, and a car or two. Think about the differences between these two sets of products!

BUILDING KEY CONCEPTS

Americans have been enjoying a fairly steady rise in their standard of living.

Standard of Living

By about how much did real GDP per capita increase between 1970 and 2004?

Go Online
PHSchool.com
Web Code: mng-5122

Figure 12.11 **Real GDP per Capita, 1970–2004**

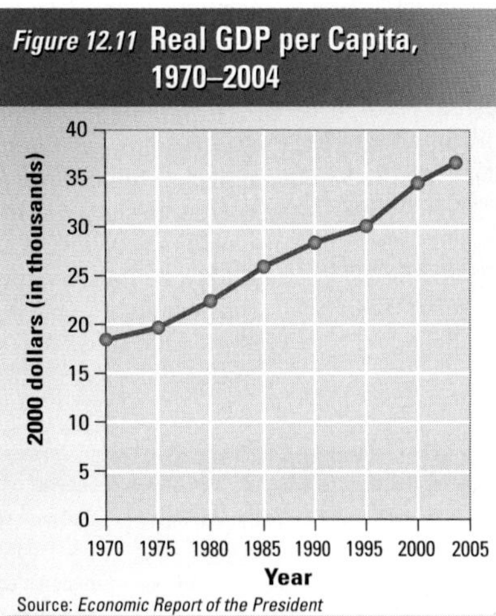

Source: *Economic Report of the President*

Measuring Economic Growth

The basic measure of a nation's economic growth rate is the percentage change of real GDP over a given period of time. For example, the real GDP in 1994 was $7.8 billion, and in 2004, it was $10.8 billion. The economic growth rate for this decade was about 38 percent (($10.8 billion – $7.8 billion) ÷ $7.8 billion × 100).

GDP and Population Growth

Over time, a nation's population tends to grow. Real gross domestic product, if it is to satisfy the needs of a nation's growing population, must keep up with the growth

Graphing the Main Idea

Gross Domestic Product To build understanding of how economic growth, which affects **gross domestic product,** is stimulated, have students complete a multi-flowchart graphic organizer like the one shown at the right. Remind students that a multi-flowchart shows causes and effects. Tell them to use the chart to show ways in which capital deepening, saving and investing, and other factors are related to economic growth.

Section Reading Support Transparencies A template and the answers for this graphic organizer can be found in Chapter 12, Section 3 of the Section Reading Support Transparency System.

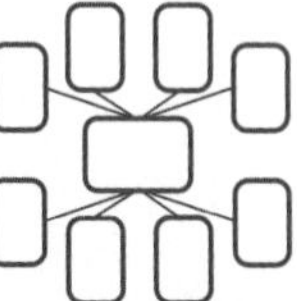

Figure 12.12 Economic Health of Selected Countries

Country	GDP per capita (2002 dollars, in thousands)	GDP growth (average annual % change in growth, 1991–2001)	School expenditure per student, 2001 (in dollars)	Life expectancy at birth, 2002 (men /women)	Unemployment rate (% of labor force, 2003, men /women)	% change in consumer prices, 2003
U.S.	36.1	+3.4	8,144	74.4/79.8	6.3/5.7	2.2
Czech Rep.	15.1	+1.6	2,819	72.1/78.7	6.2/9.8	0.2
France	27.2	+1.9	6,783	75.8/83.0	8.5/10.5	2.1
Germany	25.9	+1.5	6,055	75.6/81.3	10.0/9.2	1.1
Japan	27.0	+1.1	6,179	78.3/85.2	5.5/4.9	–0.3
Korea	17.0	+5.5	4,406	72.8/80.0	3.8/3.3	3.6
Mexico	9.2	+3.1	1,575	72.1/77.1	2.0/2.4*	4.6
Turkey	6.4	+2.7	not available	66.2/70.9	6.6/6.5*	25.0
U.K.	27.9	+2.7	5,324	75.7/80.4	5.5/4.3	2.9

* 2000
Sources: Organization for Economic Cooperation and Development, 2005

The statistics shown here are typically used as indicators of a country's living standards. **Standard of Living (a) How does the economic health of the United States compare to that of the other countries shown here? (b) What countries seem to have the most-healthy and the least-healthy economies?**

rate of the population. This is one reason that economists prefer a measure that takes population growth into account. For this, they rely on **real GDP per capita,** which is real GDP divided by the total population (*per capita* means "for each person").

real GDP per capita *real GDP divided by the total population*

This measure is considered the best measure of a nation's standard of living. As long as real GDP is rising faster than the population, real GDP per capita will rise, and so will the standard of living. Economists can see how the standard of living has changed over time by comparing real GDP per capita from two different time periods. They can also use per capita growth rates to compare the economies of two different nations.

GDP and Quality of Life

We can use GDP to measure standard of living, which relates to material goods. We cannot use it, however, as a complete measure of people's quality of life. As you read in Section 1, GDP excludes many factors that affect the quality of life, such as the state of the environment or the level of stress that individuals feel in their daily lives. In addition, while real GDP per capita represents the average output per person in an economy, it tells us nothing about how the output is distributed. A nation may have relatively high real GDP per capita, but if most of the income goes to relatively few people while the majority earn next to nothing, the typical person will not enjoy a very high standard of living.

Despite these facts, real GDP per capita is a good starting point for measuring a nation's quality of life. Nations with greater availability of goods and services usually enjoy better nutrition, safer and more comfortable housing, longer life spans, better education, and other indicators of a favorable quality of life.

Since economic growth has an enormous impact on quality of life, economists devote significant resources to figuring out what causes the nation's real GDP to rise. They

Guided Reading and Review
Unit 5 folder, p. 6 asks students to identify the main ideas of the section and to define or identify key terms.

Differentiated Instruction L3

(Enrichment) Ask students to consult an almanac to find the following information:

- The five nations with the highest real GDP per capita and the five nations with the lowest real GDP per capita
- The average life expectancy at birth in these ten nations

Then have students construct a chart or graph that shows the relationship between real GDP per capita and life expectancy. Finally, ask students to analyze this relationship and draw some conclusions about real GDP per capita and life expectancy.

Transparency Resource Package
Economics Concepts, 12 F: Growth Rate of U.S. GDP

Econ 101: Key Concepts Made Easy

Standard of Living To help students better understand **capital deepening,** ask them to think about how this economic concept works in their own lives. Tell them to consider any physical capital (such as a new calculator) they have invested in recently and what effect it has had. Ask students how they are deepening their human capital (in school or in training programs) and why it is worth the investment.

Answer to...
Building Key Concepts (a) Overall the economic health of the United States compares favorably.
(b) Most healthy: the United States, Japan, and Germany; Least healthy: Turkey, Czech Republic, and Mexico

Differentiated Instruction L3

Organize the class into four groups. Explain that each group must develop a capital-deepening plan to encourage growth at the company described below. Their plans should include five examples of capital deepening using physical capital and five examples of capital deepening using human capital. When the groups have completed their plans, have the class analyze each and decide which plan will best foster growth.

The *Princeville Post* is a newspaper in a midwestern city. The paper employs nearly 150 people—reporters, editors, electronic page layout specialists, press operators, and delivery truck drivers, among others. The paper has been located in the same building for 50 years.

Differentiated Instruction L2

Have English language learners use the flowchart on this page to explain the concept of capital deepening. Suggest that they first read the text and then examine the flowchart. Encourage them to use specific examples in their explanations. ELL

capital deepening *process of increasing the amount of capital per worker*

saving *income not used for consumption*

savings rate *the proportion of disposable income that is saved*

focus on the roles of capital goods, technology, and a few related factors.

Capital Deepening

Physical capital, the equipment used to produce goods and services, makes an important contribution to the output of an economy. With more physical capital, each worker can be more efficient and productive, producing more output per hour of work. Economists use the term *labor productivity* to describe the amount of output produced per worker.

With a labor force of a given size, more physical capital will lead to more output—in other words, to economic growth. This process of increasing the amount of capital per worker, called **capital deepening**, is one of the most important sources of growth in modern economies. (See Figure 12.13.)

Human capital, the productive knowledge and skills acquired by a worker through education and experience, also contributes to output. Firms, and employees themselves, can deepen human capital through training programs and on-the-job experience. Better-trained and more-experienced workers can produce more output per hour of work. As the United States moves toward a service-oriented economy, human capital becomes another vital source of growth.

Capital deepening—whether it be physical capital or human capital—increases output per worker. It also tends to increase workers' earnings. To understand why this happens, consider the effect of greater worker productivity on the demand for workers. As you read in Chapter 9, if workers can produce more output per hour, they become more valuable to their employers. As a result, employers will demand more workers. This increase in demand will increase the equilibrium wage rate in the labor market.

So, with a labor force of a given size, capital deepening will increase output and workers' wages. But how does an economy increase its stock of capital per worker? It does so through saving and investment.

Figure 12.13 Effects of Capital Deepening

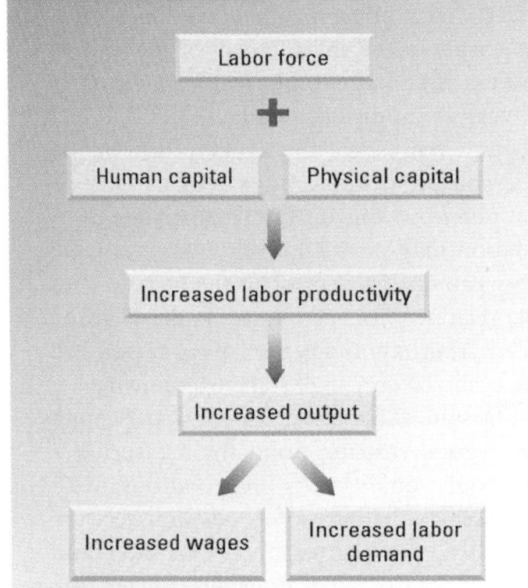

This diagram shows the beneficial effects of capital deepening.

Money **Suppose you own a small clothing shop. Why should buying a new line of clothes for an upcoming season and providing special training for sales staff result in capital deepening?**

Saving and Investment

To help us understand how saving and investment are related, let's consider an economy with no government sector and no foreign trade. In this simplified economy, consumers and business firms purchase all output. In other words, output can be used for consumption (by consumers) or investment (by firms). Income that is not used for consumption is called **saving.**

Since output can only be consumed or invested, whatever is not consumed must be invested. Therefore, in this simplified economy, saving is equal to investment. The proportion of disposable income that is saved is called the **savings rate.**

To see this another way, look at an individual's decision, as shown in Figure 12.14.

Answer to . . .

Building Key Concepts Both the new line of clothes and the special training for sales staff contribute to increased output and increased workers' earnings, which result in capital deepening.

Block Scheduling Strategies

Consider these suggestions to take advantage of extended class time:

- Show the Economics Video Library segment "A New Era," about the expected boom economy created by the effects of education, technology, and globalization. After showing the segment, assign each student one of the following topics: education, technology, or globalization. Then ask students to list developments within their categories that could lead to a boom economy. Discuss these developments as a class.
- Economic growth is often portrayed as being incompatible with environmental health. Discuss reasons for this view. Then have small groups of students develop lists of ways in which respect for the environment can spur economic growth and ways in which economic growth can contribute to a healthier environment.

Shawna had an after-tax income of $30,000 last year, but she spent only $25,000. That left her with $5,000 available for saving. She used some of her leftover income to purchase shares in a mutual fund (stocks and bonds). She put the rest of the money into her bank account.

Through her mutual-fund firm, her bank, and other intermediaries, Shawna's $5,000 was made available to businesses. The firms used the money to invest in new plants and equipment. So, when Shawna chose not to spend her entire income but to save a share, the amount that she saved became available for business investment.

If we consider the economy as a whole, the process works the same way. If total saving rises, more investment funds become available to businesses. Those firms will use most of these funds for capital investment—for expanding the stock of capital in the business sector.

Higher saving, then, leads to higher investment, and thus to higher amounts of capital per worker. In other words, higher saving leads to capital deepening. Now we can understand why most nations promote saving. In the long run, more saving will lead to higher output and income for the population, raising GDP and the standard of living. The United States has a low saving rate, but businesses and government successfully borrow from other countries with high saving rates.

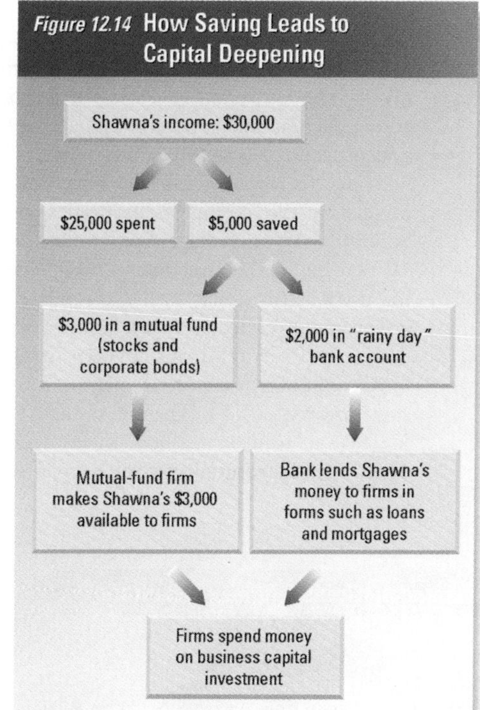

This diagram shows how saving adds to GDP by creating capital.
Money If people saved a high proportion of their incomes, how might the economy be affected?

Population, Government, and Trade

Now we will consider a slightly more realistic economy that has population growth, a government sector, and foreign trade. First, think about the effect of the population growth on capital accumulation.

Population Growth

Population growth does not necessarily preclude economic growth. However, if the population grows while the supply of capital remains constant, the amount of capital per worker will shrink. This process, the opposite of capital deepening, will lead to lower living standards. In fact, some relatively poor countries, such as India, have large labor forces but small capital stocks.

The result is that output per worker—and earnings per worker—are relatively low. Conversely, a nation with low population growth and expanding capital stock will enjoy significant capital deepening.

Government

Government can affect the process of capital deepening in several ways. If government raises tax rates to pay for additional services or to finance a war, households will have less money. People will reduce their saving, thus reducing investment. In these cases, the government is taxing households in order to pay for

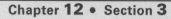

Differentiated Instruction L3

(Reteaching) Explain to students that personal savings in the United States declined from a high of $285.6 billion in 1992 to just $121.0 billion in 1997. This decline took place during a time of sustained economic growth. Ask students to think about the implications of these facts and then to write a brief essay that addresses the questions: Why did savings drop off during an economic expansion? What impact could this drop eventually have on economic growth?

Transparency Resource Package
Economics Concepts, 12G: Investment Spending as a Percentage of GDP

Preparing for Standardized Tests

Have students read the section titled "Saving and Investment" and then answer the question below.

The proportion of disposable income spent to income saved is called:

A per capita income.
(B) savings rate.
C investment output.
D savings.

Answer to . . .

Building Key Concepts More money saved would lead to higher investment and therefore higher amounts of capital per worker (capital deepening).

Differentiated Instruction 

Ask students to create a table that illustrates the positive and negative impacts on economic growth of population growth, government intervention, and foreign trade. Encourage students to think of or to research examples in addition to those given in the text.

Meeting NCEE Standards

Use the following benchmark activity from the **Voluntary National Content Standards in Economics** to evaluate student understanding of **Standard 15.**

Compare the material standard of living of individuals living in the United States in 1790, 1890, and 1990; explain the relationship between higher productivity levels, new technologies, and the standard of living.

Answer to . . .

Building Key Concepts Money from European lenders was used for capital expenditures such as new track and cars, thus fueling growth.

technological progress *an increase in efficiency gained by producing more output without using more inputs*

consumption spending, and the net effect is reduced investment.

On the other hand, if government invests the extra tax revenues in public goods, such as roads, telecommunications, and other infrastructure, investment will increase. To see why, consider what share of income the average household saves. Suppose that, on average, households save 10 percent of their income. In this case, for every extra dollar in tax revenue the government collects, household saving (and investment) drops by 10 cents. However, government investment in infrastructure rises by $1. The net result is an increase in total investment of 90 cents. This would promote capital deepening, since the government is taxing its citizens to provide investment goods.

Foreign Trade

Foreign trade can result in a trade deficit, a situation in which the value of goods a country *imports* is higher than the value of goods it *exports*. (You will read more about trade deficits in Chapter 17.) Running a trade deficit may not seem like a wise practice, but if the imports consist of investment goods, the practice can foster capital deepening. *Investment goods* are the structures and equipment purchased by businesses.

Capital deepening can help a country pay back its creditors because it is a source of economic growth. In the mid-1800s, for example, the United States financed the building of the transcontinental railroad in part by borrowing funds from investors in other countries. (See Figure 12.15.) The borrowing created a trade deficit, but it also helped create a much higher rate of economic growth than would have occurred without the borrowing. The railroad opened up vast areas to farming, which over time helped increase the nation's agricultural output by a huge amount.

Of course, not all trade deficits promote capital deepening. In this regard, trade deficits are similar to government taxation. Whether they encourage capital deepening and economic growth depends on how the funds are used. If they are used for short-term consumption, the economy will not grow any faster, and it will not have any additional GDP to pay back the debts. If the funds are used for long-term investment, however, they will foster capital deepening. The resulting economic growth will bring the country prosperity in the future.

Technological Progress

Another key source of economic growth is technological progress. This term usually brings to mind new inventions or new ways of performing a task, but in economics, it has a more precise definition. **Technological progress** is an increase in efficiency gained

Figure 12.15 Financing the Transcontinental Railroad

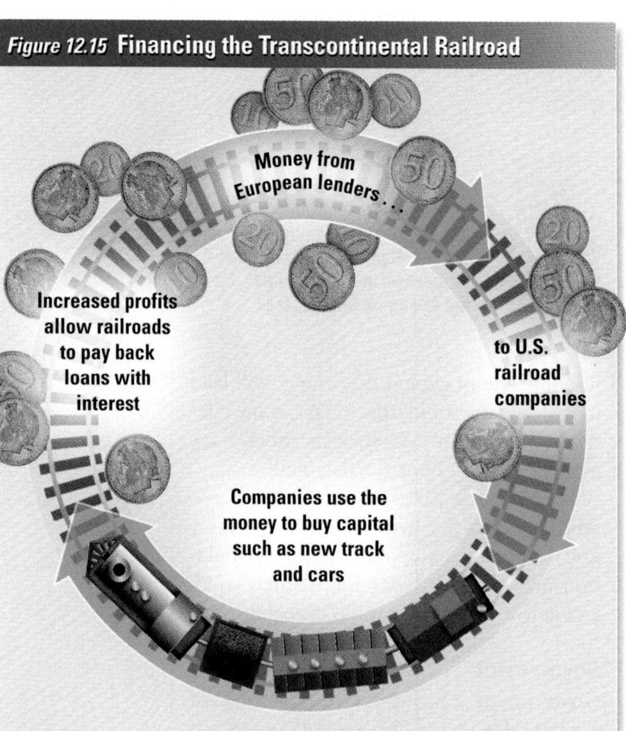
Money from European lenders . . .
to U.S. railroad companies
Companies use the money to buy capital such as new track and cars
Increased profits allow railroads to pay back loans with interest

BUILDING KEY CONCEPTS

In the mid-1800s, railroad companies, eager to build a transcontinental line, borrowed money from foreign investors. The railroad, which was completed in 1869, made enough money to pay off the loans and return a profit.
Money How is the scenario shown here an example of capital deepening?

Interdisciplinary Connections: History

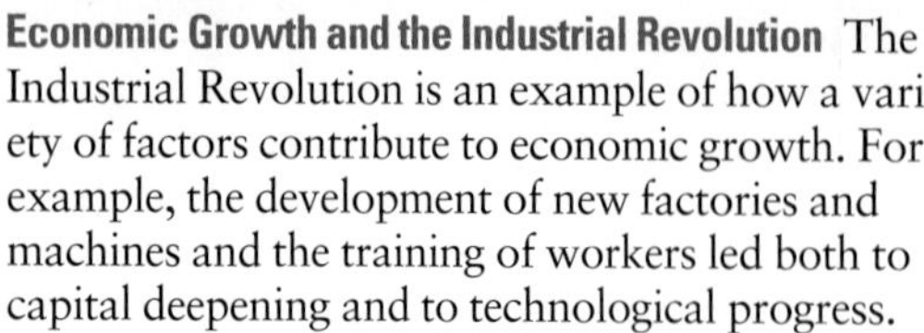

Economic Growth and the Industrial Revolution The Industrial Revolution is an example of how a variety of factors contribute to economic growth. For example, the development of new factories and machines and the training of workers led both to capital deepening and to technological progress.

Making the Connection Ask students to examine the factors associated with economic growth discussed in this section. Then have them review the history of the Industrial Revolution and relate these factors to economic growth during that period in history.

▲ **Inventions such as desktop computers (right) contribute to America's technological progress. Just as important are new manufacturing processes, such as the use of robots in assembly lines (left), and new knowledge, such as medical breakthroughs.**

by producing more output without using more inputs.

Technological progress occurs in many ways, as illustrated in the photographs above. It can come as new scientific knowledge that has practical uses. It can be a new machine that allows goods to be produced more efficiently. It may be a new method for organizing production. All of these advances raise a nation's productivity. Increased productivity means that we can produce more output with the same amounts of land, labor, and capital. With technological progress, a society can enjoy higher real GDP per capita, which leads to a higher standard of living.

Measuring Technological Progress

In most modern economies, the amount of physical and human capital changes all the time. So does the quantity and quality of labor and the technology used to produce goods and services. These interconnected variables work together to produce economic growth. How then can we isolate and measure the effects of technological progress?

Robert Solow, a 1987 Nobel Prize-winning economist from the Massachusetts Institute of Technology, developed a method for measuring the impact of technological progress on economic growth. Solow's method was to determine how much growth in output comes from increases in capital and how much comes from increases in labor. He concluded that any remaining growth in output must then come from technological progress.

Between 1929 and 1982, the average annual growth rate of real GDP was 2.92 percent. Using Solow's method, economist Edward Denison has estimated that technological progress boosted the real GDP 1.02 percent per year, on average. Increases in capital and labor were responsible for 0.56 percent and 1.34 percent of the average annual growth, respectively (2.92 – 0.56 – 1.34 = 1.02).

Causes of Technological Progress

Since technological progress is such an important source of economic growth, economists have looked for its causes. They have found a variety of factors that influence technological progress.

FAST FACT

Innovations in communication and transportation have revolutionized business efficiency in recent decades. Suppose a Michigan manufacturer needs a part from Japan to repair an essential tool on his automobile assembly line. He can contact the parts factory in Japan instantly through phone, fax, or email. Then, instead of waiting a week or more for the new part to arrive, he can receive the part in the morning through an overnight airline express service and have his assembly line up and running by afternoon.

Differentiated Instruction 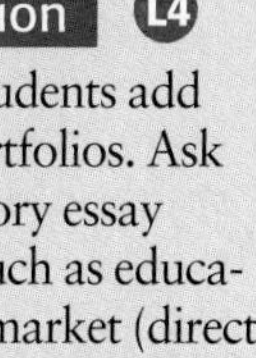 L4

You may wish to have students add the following to their portfolios. Ask them to write an expository essay describing how factors such as education and the scale of the market (direct students to the section titled "Causes of Technological Progress") have influenced one significant technological advance in the past 10 years. GT

Learning Styles Activity
Learning Styles Lesson Plans folder, p. 30 asks students to write one or two paragraphs on capital deepening, savings and investment, or technological progress, as described in a recent news story, and then to write a second paragraph explaining how the subject is related to economic growth.

Economics Assessment Rubric
Economics Assessment Rubrics folder, pp. 6–7 provides sample evaluation materials for a writing assignment.

Economic Detective Activity
Unit 5 folder, p. 10, "Colobano," provides an integrated application of chapter concepts.

Preparing for Standardized Tests

Have students read the section titled "Technological Progress" and then answer the question below.

Which of the following is not an example of technological progress?

A New scientific knowledge shows practical uses.

B A new piece of machinery allows goods to be produced more efficiently.

C An innovative method for organizing production raises productivity.

(D) The government invests in new roads and other infrastructure improvements.

Go Online PHSchool.com Typing in the Web Code when prompted will bring students directly to the article.

THE WALL STREET JOURNAL. CLASSROOM EDITION

For an additional article from *The Wall Street Journal Classroom Edition,* see the Source Articles folder in the **Teaching Resources,** pp. 36–38.

GTE Guide to the Essentials
Chapter 12, Section 3, p. 52 provides support for students who need additional review of the section content. Spanish support is available in the Spanish edition of the guide on p. 52.

Quiz Unit 5 folder, p. 7 includes questions to check students' understanding of Section 3 content.

Presentation Pro CD-ROM
Quiz provides multiple-choice questions to check students' understanding of Section 3 content.

THE WALL STREET JOURNAL. CLASSROOM EDITION

In the News Read more about productivity in "And a Silver Lining," an article in The Wall Street Journal Classroom Edition.

Go Online
The Wall Street Journal Classroom Edition
For: Current Events
Visit: PHSchool.com
Web Code: mnc-5123

1. *Scientific research* Scientific research can generate new or improved production techniques, improve physical capital, and result in better goods and services.
2. *Innovation* When new products and ideas are successfully brought to the market, output goes up, boosting GDP and business profits. Yet innovation often requires costly research. For companies to carry out research, they need some assurance that they will make a profit on the sale of a product.

That's why the government issues patents. A patent is an exclusive right to produce and sell a product for a given period, currently 20 years. A patent helps companies recover the cost of research by earning profits before its competitors are allowed to copy new products.

Government can aid innovation in several other ways as well. Through organizations such as the National Science Foundation and the National Institutes of Health, the United States government sponsors so-called basic research. Basic research is a term that describes theoretical research that is often expensive and might not bring a new product to market in a timely way.

3. *Scale of the market* Larger markets provide more incentives for innovation, since the potential profits are greater. For this reason, larger economies will come up with more technological advances.
4. *Education and experience* As you read earlier, firms can develop their human capital by providing education and on-the-job experience for workers. Human capital makes workers more productive and thus accelerates economic growth. It can also stimulate growth in another way. A more educated and experienced work force can more easily handle technological advances and may well create some new advances, too.
5. *Natural resource use* Increased natural resource use can create a need for new technology. For example, new technology can turn previously useless raw materials into usable resources. It can also allow us to obtain and use resources more efficiently, develop substitute new resources, and discover new resource reserves. Because price is based on the cost of obtaining a resource (and not necessarily on its scarcity), new technology can also lead to lower prices.

Section 3 Assessment

Key Terms and Main Ideas

1. **(a)** Why do economists measure **real GDP per capita?** **(b)** Why does real GDP per capita provide a better way to compare the economies of two different nations than does real GDP alone?
2. What is **capital deepening,** and how does it contribute to economic growth?
3. What role does **saving** play in the process of economic growth?
4. How do patents encourage **technological progress?**

Applying Economic Concepts

5. ***Critical Thinking*** You have read about the economic effects of the transcontinental railroad. What other communication and transportation systems might have similar effects? Write a paragraph analyzing these effects.
6. ***Using the Databank*** Turn to the graph "Personal Savings as a Percentage of Disposable Income" on page 540. What was the trend in savings between 1990 and 2004? How might this trend have affected capital deepening? Explain.

Go Online PHSchool.com
For: Presentation Activity
Visit: PHSchool.com
Web Code: mnd-5123

Answers to . . .

Section 3 Assessment

1. (a) Real GDP per capita provides a measure of how much each individual in an economy is producing. If real GDP per capita rises over time, the standard of living usually rises as well. (b) Even if two economies have the same real GDP, the standard of living will differ if there is a dramatic difference in population.
2. Capital deepening involves increasing the amount of capital per worker. Workers who have more capital to work with are likely to be more productive and will therefore contribute to economic growth.
3. Saving may be used by firms for business investment (loaned by banks), contributing to economic growth.
4. Patents give inventors sole rights to produce and sell their newly invented goods, providing economic incentive to be creative and thus contributing to technological progress.
5. Students' answers will vary and should illustrate an understanding of how technological advances affect the economy. They may include: digital fiber optics (Internet, telephone, and medical advances); aeronautical and mechanical engineering (faster planes and safer automobiles).
6. The trend was toward a sharp decrease in personal savings. This might have affected capital deepening in a negative way, because lower amounts of money in savings means less money available for capital investment.

Progress Monitoring *Online*
For additional assessment, have students access Progress Monitoring Online at **Web Code:** mna-5127

Go Online PHSchool.com Typing in the Web Code when prompted will bring students directly to detailed instructions for this activity.

Gross Domestic Product

How Has Technology Affected Productivity?

▲ High-tech underwater cameras help researchers study the ocean floor.

Technology, according to Peter Zentz, "is the cornerstone of all the products we make." Zentz is an executive with Benthos, Inc., a manufacturer of underwater equipment such as cameras that operate on the ocean floor. Benthos cameras took the first underwater pictures of the RMS *Titanic* after its discovery.

"The technology that continues to be developed in our industry," says Zentz, "is truly remarkable. But what strikes me every day is the way in which other types of technology have enabled us . . . to efficiently serve our customers, communicate effectively with them and our workers . . . and keep precise records."

Teleconferencing Rick Gifford, a Benthos sales executive, believes that one of the greatest advancements for business is the technology that makes teleconferencing possible. "We used to spend hours, even days, bringing our sales representatives, customers, and field workers into our office for important meetings," he explains. "Through teleconferencing we get it done just as effectively, eliminate enormous expense, and no one has to be uprooted."

Photocopiers Zentz and Gifford, however, both agree that the computer is not their most indispensable technological device. "Believe it or not," says Zentz, "we've found that the copy machine is our most important piece of equipment. The thought of hand-copying the thousands of designs, research reports, written correspondence, and other documents that we generate every year boggles my mind."

Zentz is not alone in his opinion. In a recent survey, most office workers indicated that the photocopier is important to their productivity. But whatever the ranking, one thing is certain. Technology has changed the business world forever.

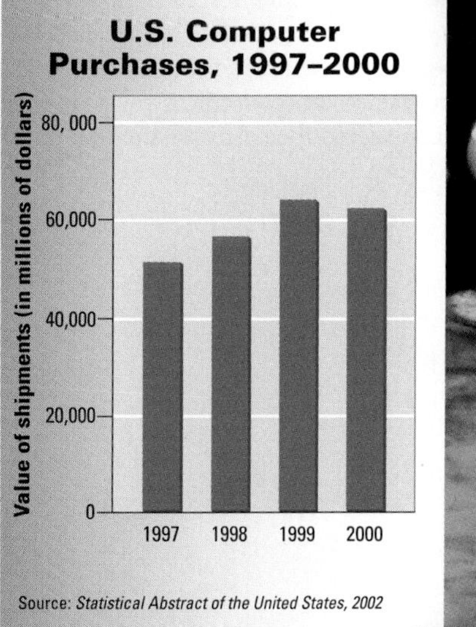

Source: *Statistical Abstract of the United States, 2002*

Applying Economic Ideas

1. How has technology affected office productivity?
2. The graph on the right shows the value of computers sold in the United States. What might this graph indicate about the growth of GDP in the late 1990s and early 2000s?

Real-life Case Study: Gross Domestic Product

1. Focus Technology that has made the workplace more efficient has had a significant impact on worker productivity.

2. Instruct Begin by asking students to think about technologies that have made them more productive as students and workers. Then discuss the difference between workplace technology (such as videoconferencing capabilities) and other types of technological development (such as the Hubble telescope). Finally, help students understand how workplace technology leads to increased efficiency and how this efficiency leads to increased productivity.

3. Close/Reteach Ask students to speculate about technology that will come about in the next five years that will make workers even more productive.

Case Studies Activity
Case Studies in Free Enterprise folder, pp. 24–25, "Andrew Carnegie," helps students apply economic principles in an additional case study.

Economic Detective Activity
Unit 5 folder, p. 10, "Colobano," provides an additional application of chapter concepts.

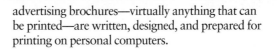

Interdisciplinary Connections: History

Advancing Printing Technology Ever since Johann Gutenberg revolutionized printing in the mid-1400s with his method of printing from movable type, technological advances have continually changed the way printed materials are manufactured. During the last two decades of the twentieth century, powerful computers and sophisticated software came together to spark a new printing revolution—desktop publishing. Today books, newspapers, magazines, advertising brochures—virtually anything that can be printed—are written, designed, and prepared for printing on personal computers.

Making the Connection Ask students who have worked with desktop publishing programs to present brief oral reports on how these programs work. Encourage them to bring materials they have printed to show to the class.

Answers to . . .

1. Office productivity has increased because of technological advances such as copy machines, fax machines, and computers. People can do jobs more quickly and more efficiently.
2. Greater spending on computers may have been one element of higher GDP growth.

Chapter 12 Assessment

Key Terms

1. Intermediate goods
2. business cycle
3. gross domestic product
4. Capital deepening
5. price level
6. recession

Using Graphic Organizers

7. Students should add to the web organizer components of the GDP such as business goods and services.

Reviewing Main Ideas

8. GDP does not include nonmarket activities; does not include the underground economy; does not include many negative externalities; and does not necessarily indicate quality of life.
9. business investment, interest rates and credit, consumer expectations, external shocks
10. Economists rely on real GDP per capita as well as examining the roles of capital deepening and technological progress.
11. Nominal GDP is GDP measured in current prices. Real GDP is GDP measured in constant prices.

Critical Thinking

12. In peak periods the business cycle is propelled by increased business investment, low interest rates, high consumer expectations, and positive external shocks. Answers about the factor with the strongest effect will vary, although many students may name interest rates. External shocks are the most uncontrollable factor.
13. Real GDP per capita is used because it provides a measure of how individuals function in an economy and whether the standard of living is becoming higher or lower (increased or decreased GDP per capita). It is effective because, in general, nations with higher real GDP per capita have a better quality of life.

Chapter 12 Assessment

Chapter Summary

A summary of major ideas in Chapter 12 appears below. See also the **Guide to the Essentials of Economics**, which provides additional review and test practice of key concepts in Chapter 12.

Section 1 Gross Domestic Product (pp. 301–308)

Gross domestic product (GDP) is the most important measure of a nation's economic performance. GDP changes in response to shifts in **aggregate supply** and **aggregate demand.** GDP does have its limitations, however. Other measures are often used in addition to GDP when evaluating a nation's economy. **National income accounting** is a system that collects macroeconomic statistics.

Section 2 Business Cycles (pp. 310–316)

A business cycle includes four phases: **expansion, peak, contraction,** and **trough.** Policymakers study business cycles to try to predict downturns in the economy and take steps to lessen their effects and speed economic recovery. **Leading indicators** help economists take the pulse of the macroeconomy.

Section 3 Economic Growth (pp. 318–324)

Economic growth is a steady, long-term increase in real GDP and often results in higher living standards. **Capital deepening, saving** and investment, population growth, government, foreign trade, and **technological progress** affect economic growth. **Real GDP per capita** is considered the best measure of a nation's standard of living.

Key Terms

Complete each sentence by choosing the correct answer from the list of terms below. You will not use all of the terms.

gross domestic product	**recession**
price level	**leading indicators**
capital deepening	**business cycle**
aggregate supply	**gross national product**
intermediate goods	

1. ____ are goods used in the production of final goods.
2. A ____ can be described as a period of macroeconomic expansion followed by a period of contraction.
3. Economists use the term ____ to describe the dollar value of all final goods and services produced within a country's borders in a given year.
4. ____ occurs when the amount of capital per worker increases.
5. The ____ is the average of all prices in the economy.
6. A prolonged economic contraction is known as a ____.

Using Graphic Organizers

7. On a separate sheet of paper, copy the web map below. Complete the web map by filling in the circles with components of GDP. You may add more circles.

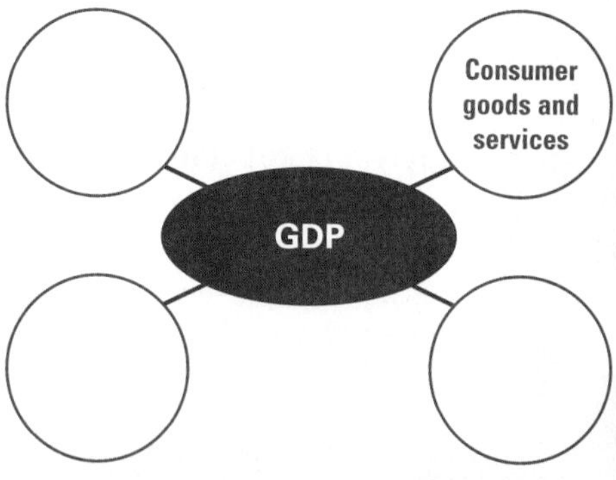

14. Although GDP has its drawbacks, it is still the most comprehensive measure economists have to evaluate an economy's performance.

Problem-Solving Activity

15. A possible drawback would be less money invested in research and development because of the reduced economic incentive to produce new products. Less investment in this area could mean fewer new drugs.

Reviewing Main Ideas

8. List three limitations of using GDP as a measure of the nation's economy.
9. Identify four factors that keep the business cycle going.
10. Summarize the ways in which economists measure economic growth.
11. What is the difference between nominal GDP and real GDP?

Critical Thinking

12. **Making Comparisons** Compare the factors that propel the business cycle in peak periods. Which factor affects you most? Which is the most uncontrollable factor?
13. **Drawing Inferences** Why is real per capita GDP used to measure economic growth? In which ways is this measure more effective than other measures?
14. **Synthesizing Information** Explain why GDP is an accepted way of measuring the economy, despite its known drawbacks.

Problem-Solving Activity

15. A group of consumers claims that drug companies earn excessive profits because of the patents they have on drugs. They recommend cutting the length of time that a drug company can hold a patent to five years. They argue that this will lead to lower prices for drugs because competitors will enter the market after the five-year period. Are there any drawbacks to this proposal?

Skills for Life

Cost-Benefit Analysis Review the steps shown on page 309. Then answer the following questions using the table below describing two transportation plans for a town that would like to reduce car traffic and pollution.

16. (a) What are the two possible solutions the town is considering? (b) Does each of these solutions address the town's problems?
17. (a) What are the financial costs of each system? (b) What other non-financial costs does each system include?
18. (a) What quantitative data can you find about the benefits of each system? (b) What other, non-financial benefits does each system provide?
19. What is the cost for each system as measured by the additional dollar cost per new rider?
20. Consider the answer to the question above. Should the town choose the system which costs less, in dollars, per new rider? Why or why not?

Transportation Choices

Catagory	New Bus Routes	Light Rail Line
Cost	$10,000,000	$85,000,000
New riders served	2,000	6,000
Advantages	Reduces traffic, routes can change easily for market needs	Less pollution, reduces traffic, regular schedule
Disadvantages	More local air pollution, buses get caught in traffic	Route cannot change, expensive to run

Economics Journal

Making Comparisons Compare the forecasts you collected. How are they similar? How do they differ? On what indicator does each article base its forecast? Which forecast is considered most reliable?

Progress Monitoring *Online*

For: Chapter 12 Self-Test **Visit:** PHSchool.com
Web Code: mna-5121

As a final review, take the Economics Chapter 12 Self-Test and receive immediate feedback on your answers. The test consists of 20 multiple-choice questions designed to test your understanding of the chapter content.

Skills for Life

16. (a) new bus routes or a light rail line (b) yes
17. (a) $10,000,000 for the bus routes; $85,000,000 for the light rail line (b) buses increase pollution; trains are committed to certain routes
18. (a) number of new riders served (b) reduces traffic or lowers pollution
19. $5,000 per bus rider; $14,167 per light rail rider
20. Answers will vary. Students should consider both the various costs and benefits associated with each choice when making a decision.

Go Online
PHSchool.com

Additional support materials and activities for Chapter 12 of *Economics: Principles in Action* can be found in the Social Studies area of **PHSchool.com.**

Economics Journal

Students should analyze the forecasts they collected, determining similarities and differences and evaluating reliability.

Review and Assessment

Vocabulary Practice Unit 5 folder, p. 9 uses a word puzzle to reinforce understanding of key terms.

GTE **Guide to the Essentials** Chapter 12 Test, p. 53

Test Bank CD-ROM Chapter 12 Test

Go Online PHSchool.com Students may use the Chapter 12 Self-Test on **PHSchool.com** to prepare for the Chapter Test.

Economics Simulation

Objectives Upon completion of this simulation, students should be able to:

- explain the effect of division of labor on productivity;
- explain how investments in capital can increase productivity, noting that such investments involve opportunity costs and economic risks.

Bellringer Review how businesses and individuals measure productivity levels. Ask students whether they have ever taken measures to increase their productivity in completing school assignments or working at a part-time job.

1. Focus Ask students to brainstorm a list of ways to increase productivity. *(Possible answers: Workers can learn and perfect new skills; use tools or machinery to do a task; apply advances in technology; or invest in physical and human capital.)*

2. Instruct Have students prepare for and conduct the simulation, using the procedures noted in the text.

3. Close/Reteach Have students complete the productivity chart and then, as a class, discuss their answer to the first three analysis questions. Assign the Identifying Alternatives question as a follow-up.

Economic Simulation
Economic Simulations folder, pp. 28–34, "Inflation: Creating a Teenage Consumer Price Index," provides an additional simulation on a unit topic.

Databank pp. 538–539 contains a variety of charts and graphs that may be useful in this and other simulations.

Economics Simulation Increasing Productivity

Resources are limited, and people's wants and needs often exceed what is available. As a result of scarcity, people "economize" by trying to get the greatest benefits from their limited resources. In other words, they try to get as much as possible from those resources by increasing productivity. Productivity is usually measured by the amount of output per worker. In this lab you will explore how businesses try to obtain the greatest possible benefits from the fewest possible resources.

Materials
50 sheets of plain $8\frac{1}{2}$" x 11" paper
6 student desks
3 scissors
10 pencils

▲ **Specialization at this assembly line can lead to increased productivity.**

Preparing the Simulation

One way that producers attempt to increase productivity is by dividing production into steps and assigning a step to each worker. Your task in this lab is to determine the impact this specialization, or division of labor, has on productivity.

Step 1: With a group of six of your classmates, form a "company" that builds paper airplanes. As a group, experiment and agree on a simple design for your company's airplane using only one half of an $8\frac{1}{2}$" x 11" piece of paper ($8\frac{1}{2}$" x $5\frac{1}{2}$"). Next, choose a company name, and print the name on both sides of the plane's fuselage. Each member of the company should practice making an airplane before beginning the lab activity.

Step 2: Gather your company's production resources as shown in the Materials box above. You already have one factor of production—your group's labor. Select one member to be quality control manager. The other members will be production workers. The quality control manager should inspect each worker's "practice" airplane using the following criteria: The plane must be made from the correct size paper, it must be properly folded, and the company name should be printed correctly on both sides.

Step 3: As the "workers" assemble the factors of production, the quality control manager should prepare a chart by copying, on a separate sheet of paper, the Productivity Chart shown at right.

Conducting the Simulation

This simulation will consist of three four-minute "shifts," each of which is described on the next page. During each shift the group's six workers will "manufacture" airplanes. All workers must cease work immediately at the end of each shift.

Shift 1

Materials:
1 pair of scissors
1 pencil
2 desks
Procedure: Each worker must work alone to make his or her airplanes. The materials must be shared. After the four minutes is up, the quality control manager should inspect the airplanes and record the number of acceptable airplanes completed in the Shift 1 column on the Productivity Chart.

Shift 2

Materials:
1 pair of scissors
1 pencil
2 desks
Procedure: Before this shift begins, work as a group to break the production process into a series of steps. Include cutting the paper, folding, and writing the company name. Before the shift begins, assign group members to one of the steps and organize the new assembly line. When the shift ends, the quality control manager should record the number of acceptable airplanes completed in the Shift 2 column on the Productivity Chart.

Shift 3

Materials:
Using the costs listed on the Productivity Chart, decide as a group whether to purchase additional desks, scissors, or pencils for the purposes of increasing productivity or of adding a second assembly line. You may acquire a maximum of 6 desks, 3 scissors, and 10 pencils.
Procedure: Before the shift begins, record the costs of any new capital in the Shift 3 column on the chart and reorganize the new assembly line or lines. At the end of the shift, record the number of airplanes completed in the Shift 3 column on the chart.

Productivity Chart

	Shift 1	Shift 2	Shift 3
a number of acceptable airplanes completed			
b number of workers			
c cost of materials (25¢ per plane)			
d wages ($1.00 per worker)			
e factory rent ($1.00 per desk)	2.00	2.00	
f investment in equipment (50¢ per scissors) (25¢ per pencil)	.75	.75	
g total cost (c + d + e + f)			
h cost per airplane (g ÷ a)			
i total time worked (b x 4 minutes)			
j output per minute (a ÷ i)			
k productivity per worker (a ÷ b)			

Simulation Analysis

Complete the productivity chart as a group; then discuss the following questions.

1. What effect did the division of labor in Shift 2 have on productivity?
2. What effect did investing in additional capital goods for Shift 3 have on productivity?
3. For which shift was the cost per airplane the lowest? The highest?
4. **Identifying Alternatives** If instead of making an additional capital investment in Shift 3, the company had laid off one or two workers, how might total production, costs, and productivity per worker (rows a, g, h, j, and k on the productivity chart) have been affected?

Meeting NCEE Standards

Use the following benchmark activity from the **Voluntary National Content Standards in Economics** to evaluate student understanding of Standard 15.

Discuss the advantages and disadvantages of investing in a riding mower, given the following information: A teenager mows lawns to earn income. If she purchases a riding mower, she can mow more lawns in less time and possibly earn more income.

Background

Decline in Productivity

From 1950 to 1973, real GDP in the United States grew at a rate of 3.58 percent annually. From 1974 to 1995, however, real GDP grew at a slower annual rate of 2.66 percent. This slowed growth was matched by a decline in labor productivity, the amount produced by each worker.

Labor productivity depends on many factors, including the amount of machinery, buildings, and equipment in an economy as well as the economy's level of technology. A slowdown in productivity is significant because standards of living can continue to rise only if labor productivity continues to rise.

Interdisciplinary Connections: Math

Graphing Productivity Real GDP is one measure of productivity. Another way to measure productivity is to measure output per hour of work. The U.S Bureau of Labor Statistics maintains statistics on this and many other topics.

Making the Connection Have students visit the Bureau of Labor Statistics Web site to find statistics on productivity. Ask them to locate the statistics for private nonfarm businesses. After they print this material in table format, have them use the Simulations and Data Graphing CD-ROM to create a line graph that displays this data from 1970 to the most current year for which statistics are provided. Ask students to study their graphs, and then hold a class discussion about the implications of these statistics for the economy. Have students use the links provided in the *Economics: Principles in Action* segment of the Social Studies area at the following Web site: **www.phschool.com**

Answers to . . .

1. Productivity should have increased with the division of labor.
2. Productivity should have increased even more than it did in Shift 2.
3. Answers will vary, depending on the number of planes produced and investments in equipment. In most groups Shift 3 will have the lowest cost per plane and Shift 1 the highest.
4. Total production would be most likely to stay the same as in Shift 2 or to drop. Cost would decline because wages would be lower, and there would be no additional investment in equipment. Productivity would probably not rise because there would still be an insufficient amount of supplies to complete the task.

Chapter 13 Economic Challenges

For more pacing suggestions, see the Economics Pacing Guide in the Program Overview of the Teaching Resources.

Section Objectives	Print and Technology Resources	
1 Unemployment *(pp. 331–336)* **Objectives** 1. Describe frictional, seasonal, structural, and cyclical unemployment. 2. Describe how full employment is measured. 3. Explain why full employment does not mean that every worker is employed.	• **Lesson Planner** Section 1 Lesson Plan, p. 54 • **Learning Styles Lesson Plans folder** Section 1 Lesson Plan, p. 31 • **Lesson Plans folder** Section 1 Lesson Plan, p. 47 • **Economics Assessment Rubrics folder** Graphing Data, pp. 8–9 • **Unit 5 folder** Guided Reading and Review, p. 13 Economic Skills, p. 19 Section 1 Quiz, p. 14 • **Source Articles folder** My Job Just Vanished, pp. 39–41 • **Presentation Pro CD-ROM** Section 1	• **Transparency Resource Package** Economics Organizers, G7: Tree Map Graphic Organizer Economics Concepts, 13A: Types of Unemployment Economics Concepts, 13B: Underemployment Economics Concepts, 13C: Unemployment Rates • **Section Reading Support Transparency System** • **Social Studies Skills Tutor CD-ROM**
2 Inflation *(pp. 338–343)* **Objectives** 1. Explain the effects of rising prices. 2. Understand the use of price indexes to compare changes in prices over time. 3. Identify the causes and effects of inflation. 4. Describe recent trends in the inflation rate.	• **Lesson Planner** Section 1 Lesson Plan, p. 55 • **Learning Styles Lesson Plans folder** Section 2 Lesson Plan, p. 32 • **Lesson Plans folder** Section 2 Lesson Plan, p. 48 • **Unit 5 folder** Guided Reading and Review, p. 15 Careers in Economics, Fund-Raiser, p. 22 Economic Cartoon, p. 23 Section 2 Quiz, p. 16 • **Math Practice folder** Choosing Between Job Offers, p. 11	• **Presentation Pro CD-ROM** Section 2 • **Transparency Resource Package** Economics Organizers, G9: Multi-Flow Chart Graphic Organizer Economics Concepts, 13D: Inflation Economics Concepts, 13E: Components of the Consumer Price Index Economics Concepts, 13F: CPI Annual Average • **Section Reading Support Transparency System**
3 Poverty *(pp. 345–350)* **Objectives** 1. Define who is poor, according to government standards. 2. Describe the causes of poverty. 3. Analyze the distribution of income in the United States. 4. Summarize government policies intended to combat poverty.	• **Lesson Planner** Section 1 Lesson Plan, p. 56 • **Lesson Plans Folder** Section 3 Lesson Plan, p. 49 • **Economics Assessment Rubrics folder** Writing Assignment, pp. 6–7 • **Unit 5 folder** Guided Reading and Review, p. 17 Vocabulary Practice, p. 20 Economic Detective, p. 21 Section 3 Quiz, p. 18 • **Case Studies in Free Enterprise folder** Fred Smith, pp. 26–27	• **Presentation Pro CD-ROM** Section 3 • **Transparency Resource Package** Economics Organizers, G9: Multi-Flow Chart Graphic Organizer Economics Concepts, 13G: Poverty Rates Economics Concepts, 13H: Income Distribution • **Section Reading Support Transparency System**

Differentiated Instruction

Oral History L1 L2

To help students become engaged in more recent historical events, have them conduct an oral history. First, have students select a focus for the oral history. It could be either a topic, such as unemployment during a recession, or a question, such as, what was it like to live with high inflation in the late 1970s and early 1980s? As a class, brainstorm types of questions and specific questions for an interview. The class can use these questions with a guest speaker or with their own interviewee. Offer students a choice as to how they will report their findings: essay, poster, or skit.

To conclude the activity, have students compare and contrast their findings with a partner and with the information presented in this textbook. Remind students to analyze their sources when they compare findings. For example, a participant who experienced inflation as a young student may have different experiences than a parent trying to buy food for a family on a fixed income.

Vocabulary: Use Context Clues L3

Explain that students can help determine the meaning of vocabulary words by looking for clues in the surrounding text. The sentences' context can provide clues to the words meaning.

Model this skill by pointing out the word *cyclical* in the first paragraph under the heading *Cyclical Unemployment* in Section 1. The surrounding words explain that this type of unemployment rises and falls with the business cycle and is not permanent. From this context, we can conclude that *cyclical* refers to a trend that goes up and down, through cycles, without permanence.

Visit the Social Studies area of the Prentice Hall Web site. There you can find additional links to enrich chapter content for *Economics: Principles in Action* as well as a self-test for students. Be sure to check out this month's **eTeach** online discussion with a Master Economics Teacher.

Web Code: mnf-5131

Running Out of Time?

- Use the **Presentation Pro CD-ROM** to create an outline for this chapter.
- Use the Chapter Summary in the **Chapter 13 Assessment,** p. 352.
- Use the Section Summaries for Chapter 13, from **Guide to the Essentials of Economics (English and Spanish).**

THE WALL STREET JOURNAL. CLASSROOM EDITION

Prentice Hall brings into the classroom the authoritative content of *The Wall Street Journal Classroom Edition.* See the Source Articles, Debating Current Issues, and You and Your Money folders in the **Teaching Resources**. Also, see Economics Video Library, "Pink Slips."

Assessment Resources

Chapter Assessment

Teaching Resources Unit 5, Chapter 13

- Section Quizzes, pp. 14, 16, 18

Exam *View*® Test Bank CD-ROM Chapter 13

Economics Assessment Rubrics

Chapter 13 Self-Test, **Web Code:** mna-5131

Reading and Skills Evaluation

Progress Monitoring Assessments

- Screening Test
- Diagnostic Test of Social Studies Skills

Standardized Test Preparation

Test Prep Workbook

Test-Taking Strategies With Transparencies

Differentiated Instruction Key

L1	Special Needs	LPR	Less Proficient Readers
L2	Basic to Average	AR	Advanced Readers
L3	All Students	SN	Special Needs Students
L4	Average to Advanced	GT	Gifted and Talented
		ELL	English Language Learner

Chapter 13

Economic Challenges

Introducing the Chapter

In this chapter students will learn about some of the major challenges to our economy: unemployment, inflation, and poverty. Students will examine the causes and effects of each of these challenges as well as actions the government takes to decrease their negative effects.

Go Online
PHSchool.com

For additional links for *Economics: Principles in Action* provided by Prentice Hall and *The Wall Street Journal Classroom Edition,* visit the Social Studies area. Be sure to check out this month's **eTeach** online discussion with a Master Teacher.

Beyond the Lecture

You may cover the concepts in Chapter 13 in an activity-based style by using the following materials:

- **Technology Resources** appropriate for use with this chapter are noted on pp. 333, 335, 336, 337, 339, 343, 346, 348, 350, and 353.
- **Presentation Pro CD-ROM** with animated graphs gives you an alternative method for organizing and delivering chapter content.
- **Activities** designed to meet the needs of students of mixed abilities and learning styles are noted throughout the chapter in the side columns.
- **Learning Styles Lesson Plans** provide alternate lessons for diverse learning styles. See pp. 31–32 of the Learning Styles Lesson Plans folder located in the Teaching Resources.

Economics Journal

Instruct students to write their responses to the question in their Economics Journals. Students may include completed journal entries in an Economics Portfolio.

Chapter 13 Economic Challenges

Even in times of prosperity, unemployment, inflation, and poverty can affect large numbers of Americans. This chapter addresses the causes and effects of these economic challenges.

Economics Journal

The United States Census Bureau indicates that about 13 percent of Americans live in poverty. What images come to mind when you think of poverty? Think about these images. Then answer the following question in your journal: What is poverty?

Go Online
PHSchool.com

For: Current Data
Visit: PHSchool.com
Web Code: mng-5131

National Council on Economic Education

The following Voluntary National Content Standards in Economics are addressed in this chapter:

★ **Standard 19** Unemployment imposes costs on individuals and nations. Unexpected inflation imposes costs on many people and benefits some others because it arbitrarily redistributes purchasing power. Inflation can reduce the rate of growth of national living standards, because individuals and organizations use resources to protect themselves against the uncertainty of future prices.

★ **Standard 20** Federal government budgetary policy and the Federal Reserve System's monetary policy influence the overall levels of employment, output, and prices.

For more information about the standards, contact the National Council on Economic Education

1140 Avenue of the Americas
New York, NY 10036
1-800-338-1192

Section 1 Unemployment

Preview

Objectives

After studying this section you will be able to:

1. **Describe** frictional, seasonal, structural, and cyclical unemployment.
2. **Describe** how full employment is measured.
3. **Explain** why full employment does not mean that every worker is employed.

Section Focus

Even in good economic times, unemployment affects millions of Americans. The unemployment rate provides an important clue to the health of the entire economy.

Key Terms

frictional unemployment
seasonal unemployment
structural unemployment
cyclical unemployment
census
unemployment rate
full employment
underemployed
discouraged worker

Unemployment is not just a personal issue. It is an issue for the national economy as well. Economists can measure how healthy the economy is at any given time by counting the number of people who are unemployed. Congress, the President, and other policymakers pay close attention to these statistics so they can take the necessary action to get people back to work.

Economists look at four basic kinds of unemployment: frictional, seasonal, structural, and cyclical. The various kinds of unemployment have different effects on the economy as well as on the people who are unemployed.

Frictional Unemployment

Unemployment always exists, even in a booming economy. **Frictional unemployment** occurs when people take time to find a job. For example, people might change jobs, be laid off from their current jobs, need some time to find the right job after they finish their schooling, or take time off from working for a variety of other reasons. In the following examples Hannah, Jorge, and Liz are all considered frictionally unemployed.

- Hannah was not satisfied working as a nurse in a large hospital. Last month she left her job to begin looking for a position at a small health clinic.
- Since Jorge graduated from law school three months ago, he has been interviewing with various law firms to find the one that best suits his needs and interests.
- Liz left her sales job two years ago to care for an aging parent. Now she is trying to return to the work force.

None of these three people found work immediately after beginning his or her search. While they are looking for work, they are considered frictionally unemployed. In an economy as large and diverse as that of the United States, economists expect to find many people in this category.

Unemployment insurance, which provides an income to laid-off workers seeking jobs, may contribute slightly to frictional unemployment. A worker receiving unemployment insurance faces less financial pressure to find a new job immediately.

frictional unemployment *unemployment that occurs when people take time to find a job*

Seasonal Unemployment

Gregory is a brick mason for a small construction company in the northeastern United States. Every winter Gregory's

Graphing the Main Idea

Unemployment and Inflation To build understanding of the types of unemployment and their roles in the economic challenges of **unemployment** and **inflation,** have students use a tree map graphic organizer like the one at the right to record information. Have them write the label "Types of Unemployment" in the top box and the four types in the next row of boxes. Beneath each heading they should record main ideas and supporting details.

Section Reading Support Transparencies A template and the answers for this graphic organizer can be found in Chapter 13, Section 1 of the Section Reading Support Transparency System.

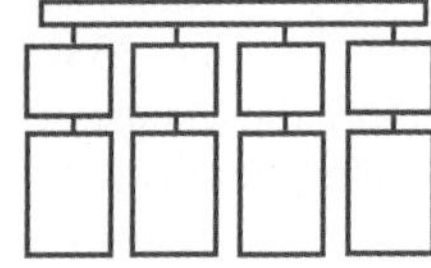

Section 1

Unemployment

Objectives You may wish to call students' attention to the objectives in the Section Preview. The objectives are reflected in the main headings of the section.

Bellringer Display the word *unemployment,* and ask students to think of all the words that they associate with this concept. Explain that in this section they will learn that unemployment is of concern not just to individuals but also to governments, economists, and politicians. Point out that the unemployment rate is one way of judging an economy's health.

Vocabulary Builder Ask students to examine the meanings of the key terms. Have them create, for each term, a collage that shows other meanings of the descriptive part of the term (friction, season, structure, cycle). On the back of each collage, ask them to explain how these meanings are related to the term.

Lesson Plan

Teaching the Main Concepts 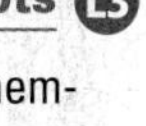

1. Focus Inform students that unemployment has many different causes and varied effects. Ask volunteers to suggest two possible causes and two possible effects of unemployment.

2. Instruct Discuss the four kinds of unemployment, explaining their causes and effects. Make sure that students understand how the unemployment rate is determined and what *full employment* means: the level of employment that is reached when there is no cyclical unemployment.

3. Close/Reteach In recent years the average number of years a worker spends at one job has decreased. Ask students what kind of unemployment results from this fact *(frictional)* and what effects it might have on the economy.

 **Guided Reading and Review**
Unit 5 folder, p. 13 asks students to identify the main ideas of the section and to define or identify key terms.

Differentiated Instruction L3
To help students comprehend seasonal unemployment and the workers whom it affects, have students find as many images as they can of migrant workers, construction workers, and other seasonal workers. Tell them to attach a short description to each picture, explaining why that form of employment is seasonal.

Differentiated Instruction L3
(Reteaching) Organize students into groups of three or four. Ask each group to come up with one additional example of each of the causes of structural unemployment covered in this section. Have a representative from each group present its examples to the class.

 **Learning Styles Activity**
Learning Styles Lesson Plans folder, p. 31 asks students to create diary entries of fictional unemployed persons, describing how they became unemployed, how they feel about it, and what they have done to find a job.

Databank, pp. 532–547 contains a variety of graphs that can be used to extend and reinforce section concepts.

▲ **Seasonal unemployment affects migrant farm workers, who can be without work once the harvest season is over.**

seasonal unemployment *unemployment that occurs as a result of harvest schedules or vacations, or when industries slow or shut down for a season*

structural unemployment *unemployment that occurs when workers' skills do not match the jobs that are available*

employer lays off all seven of his employees when cold weather forces an end to outdoor work. In the spring, he hires the workers back again to begin a new construction season. Gregory's yearly pattern of steady work followed by a predictable period of unemployment marks him as a seasonal worker.

In general, **seasonal unemployment** occurs when industries slow or shut down for a season or make seasonal shifts in their production schedules. It can also occur as a result of harvest schedules or vacations. When this school year ends, you or your friends may need some time to find the perfect summer job. If so, economists will count you as seasonally unemployed.

As with frictional unemployment, economists expect to see seasonal unemployment throughout the year. Government policymakers do not take steps to prevent this kind of unemployment, because it is a normal part of a healthy economy.

Still, the lives of seasonally unemployed workers can be extremely difficult. Migrant agricultural workers, for example, travel throughout the country to pick fruits and vegetables as various crops come into season. They know that their work will likely end when winter arrives. Migrant workers can also have periods of unemployment even during harvest season, depending on weather patterns that year. Heat, cold, rain, and drought can all ruin harvest schedules by causing fruits and vegetables to ripen sooner or later than expected. Instead of moving smoothly from crop to crop, migrant workers might lose work time waiting for a crop to be ready for picking.

Structural Unemployment

As you read in Chapter 9, the structure of the American economy has changed over time. Two centuries ago, people needed basic farming skills to survive. As the country developed an industrial economy, farm workers moved to urban areas to work in factories. Today, service industries are rapidly replacing manufacturing industries, and information services are expanding at breakneck speed.

All these shifts lead to upheavals in the labor market. When the structure of the economy changes, the skills that workers must have in order to succeed in the economy also change. Workers who lack the necessary skills lose their jobs. **Structural unemployment** occurs when workers' skills do not match the jobs that are available.

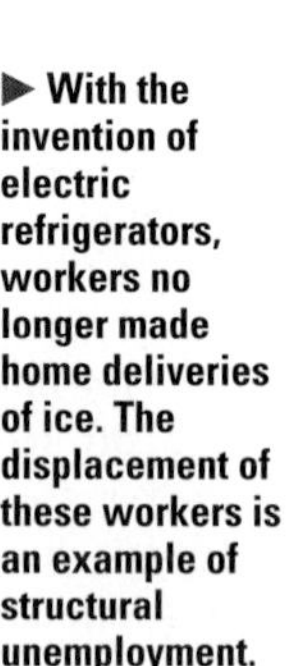

▶ **With the invention of electric refrigerators, workers no longer made home deliveries of ice. The displacement of these workers is an example of structural unemployment.**

Econ 101: Key Concepts Made Easy

Unemployment and Inflation One of the key concepts in this section is **structural unemployment.** This type of unemployment occurs whenever there is a shift in the economy on the macroeconomic level: the development of new technology, the discovery of new resources, or any of the other factors mentioned on p. 333. Students should recognize that the changes that lead to structural unemployment are permanent changes in the economy.

Tell students to consider this example: Music reproduction technology is currently approaching a point at which music can be purchased over the Internet and downloaded to a hard drive. The new technology could greatly reduce the demand for a physical product such as a compact disc. Ask students to explain who would be affected if compact discs were no longer produced and how this could cause structural unemployment.

There are five major causes of structural unemployment.

- *The development of new technology* New inventions and ideas often push out older ways of doing things. For example, after the compact disc was introduced in 1982, fewer people bought phonograph records. Many workers who produced records and record players had to look for work in another field.
- *The discovery of new resources* New resources replace old resources and the industries that provide them. The discovery of petroleum in Pennsylvania in 1859 severely hurt the whale-oil industry and put many whaling ship crews out of work.
- *Changes in consumer demand* Consumers often stop buying one product in favor of another. Many people today favor sneakers over more traditional kinds of shoes. As a result, traditional shoemaking jobs have declined.
- *Globalization* The international mobility of capital and labor has fueled a shift from local to global markets. As a result, companies often relocate jobs or entire facilities to other countries. Celia, for example, had spent many years working on an automobile assembly line in Michigan. Then, the removal of trade barriers led her company to move much of its auto assembly work to Mexico, where labor is less expensive. Celia lost her job. More recently, this trend has affected call center operators and computer programmers.
- *Lack of education* People who drop out of school or fail to acquire the minimum skills needed for today's job market may find themselves unemployed, employed part-time, or stuck in a low-wage job. For example, Martin only barely managed to graduate from high school. When he was hired as a clerk by a local clothing store, he had trouble using the computerized checkout register. The store manager fired Martin after just two months because Martin lacked the skills needed for the job.

Policymakers in the 1990s and 2000s recognized that computer technology, globalization, and other structural changes threatened the futures of many workers. As a result, they developed job-training programs to help workers gain new skills, especially computer skills.

Retraining takes a long time, however, and the new skills do not assure the trainees a high-wage job. Some companies have begun offering their own training programs. In this way, they can tailor the training to fit their exact labor needs. This approach gives more trainees the specific skills that can make them valued employees.

Cyclical Unemployment

Unemployment that rises during economic downturns and falls when the economy improves is called **cyclical unemployment.** During recessions, or downturns in the business cycle, the demand for goods and services drops. The resulting slowdown in production causes the demand for labor to drop as well, and companies begin to lay off employees. Many of these laid-off employees will be rehired when the recession ends and the business cycle resumes an upward trend. Although economists expect cyclical unemployment, it can severely

cyclical unemployment *unemployment that rises during economic downturns and falls when the economy improves*

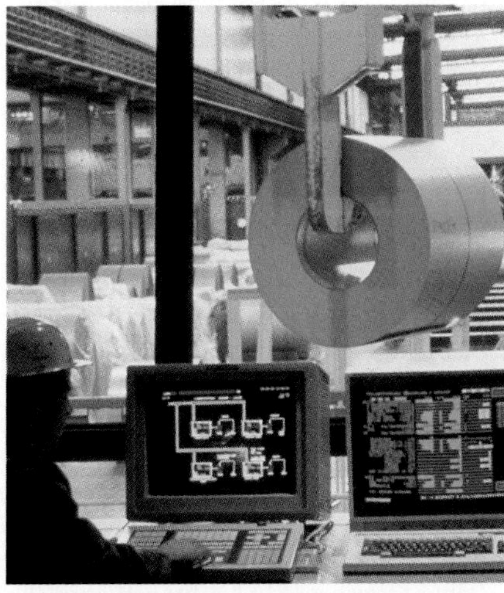

◀ Cyclical unemployment can affect workers in industries sensitive to changes in the business cycle, such as workers in the steel industry.

Differentiated Instruction L4

The 1993 North American Free Trade Agreement (NAFTA) between the United States, Canada, and Mexico has transformed much of the Western Hemisphere into a free-trade bloc. Many types of industries can operate free of tariffs and other barriers to trade.

Have students research the following question: How does NAFTA contribute to globalization? How might this result in more structural unemployment? Have students present their findings in written form. GT

Transparency Resource Package Economics Concepts, 13A: Types of Unemployment

Meeting NCEE Standards

Use the following benchmark activity from the **Voluntary National Content Standards in Economics** to evaluate student understanding of **Standard 19.**

Give examples of each type of unemployment, analyze the differences among them, and identify which types cause more serious problems in the economy.

Block Scheduling Strategies

Consider these suggestions to take advantage of extended class time:

- Organize the class into small groups, and have each group write and perform a skit that demonstrates the causes and effects of one of the types of unemployment discussed in this section. Then hold a class discussion about the issues raised.
- Organize the class into groups of three or four, and let each group choose from a list of several jobs that interest them. Then have each group research employment projections for those jobs or fields. Ask a member of each group to report orally on the group's findings.
- Show the Economics Video Library segment "Pink Slips," about the effects of downsizing, including the retraining of individuals for new jobs. Ask students to analyze the pros and cons of the new labor market, and have them list personal qualities and skills that would help a person adjust to a job change.

Differentiated Instruction L3

Ask students to describe in a step-by-step fashion how the Bureau of Labor Statistics determines the unemployment rate. Have students create a flowchart or time line illustrating the process.

Differentiated Instruction L3

Unemployment statistics are an important factor in determining monetary policy. Organize the class into groups of three or four, and ask groups to suppose that unemployment is low and that statistics show that wages are rising. Then ask them to predict how these factors might affect a proposed increase in the minimum wage. Have groups present their analyses orally.

"Our days of living from pay check to pay check are over... I was laid-off."

▲ **What might be the effects of the mother's job loss on her family?**

strain the economy and greatly distress the unemployed.

The most damaging example of cyclical unemployment in the twentieth century was the Great Depression. During the Great Depression, one out of every four workers was unemployed. Many remained jobless for years. To help these unemployed workers, President Franklin D. Roosevelt proposed, and Congress passed, the Social Security Act of 1935. In addition to providing payments for people who cannot support themselves, this act established a program of unemployment insurance. Today, this insurance provides weekly payments to workers who have lost their jobs. The payments usually provide about half of a worker's lost wages each week for a limited amount of time.

Measuring Employment

The amount of unemployment in the nation is an important clue to the health of the economy. For this reason, the government keeps careful track of how many people are unemployed, and why.

census *an official count of the population*

unemployment rate *the percentage of the nation's labor force that is unemployed*

The United States Bureau of the Census conducts a monthly census relating to the size and other characteristics of the population. (A **census** is an official count of the population.) Each month, the Bureau of Labor Statistics (BLS), a branch of the U.S. Department of Labor, polls a sample of the population. This sample, consisting of about 50,000 families, is designed to represent the entire population of the United States. The interviewers poll families about employment during that month. From this poll, called the Current Population Survey, the BLS identifies how many people are employed and how many are unemployed. Using these numbers, the BLS computes the **unemployment rate,** or the percentage of the nation's labor force that is unemployed.

Determining the Unemployment Rate

As you read in Chapter 9, the labor force is composed of civilians age 16 and older who have a job or are actively looking for a job. To determine the unemployment rate, BLS officials add up the number of employed and unemployed people. That figure equals the total labor force. Then they divide the number of unemployed people by the total labor force and multiply by 100. As Figure 13.1 shows, the result is the percentage of people who are unemployed.

For example, in March 2005, the Current Population Survey showed that 140.5 million people were employed, and

Figure 13.1 **Calculating the Unemployment Rate**

To calculate the unemployment rate, use the following formula:

Number of people unemployed **divided by** number of people in the civilian labor force **multiplied by** 100

For example,
if the number of people unemployed = 7.7 million and the number of people in the civilian labor force = 148.2 million

then,
7.7 ÷ 148.2 = .052
.052 x 100 = 5.2

Therefore,
the unemployment rate is 5.2%.

To calculate the unemployment rate, follow the steps above. **Unemployment In 1982, the civilian labor force was 110.2 million, and 10.68 million were unemployed. What was the unemployment rate?**

Answer to...

Cartoon Caption They won't have enough money to live.
Building Key Concepts The rate of unemployment is 9.7 percent.

7.7 million were unemployed. The total labor force, therefore, was 148.2 million. Dividing 7.7 million by 148.2 million, and then multiplying the result by 100, yields an unemployment rate of 5.2 percent for that month.

When you see the unemployment rate for a particular month, it has usually been "seasonally adjusted." This means that the rate has been increased or decreased to take into account the level of seasonal unemployment. Seasonally adjusting unemployment levels allows economists to compare unemployment rates from month to month in order to detect changing economic conditions.

The unemployment rate is only an average for the nation. It does not reflect differences from region to region, state to state, or even city to city. Some areas, such as the coal-mining region of Appalachia in the southeastern United States, have long had a higher-than-average unemployment rate. The BLS and individual state agencies therefore establish unemployment rates for states and other geographic areas. These rates help pinpoint trouble areas on which policymakers can focus attention.

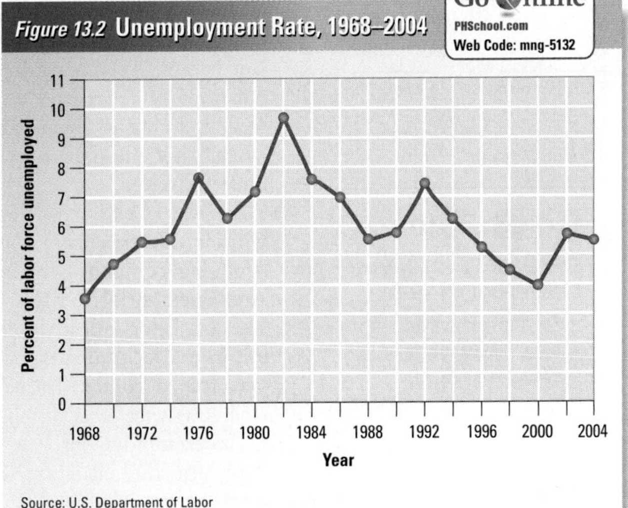

The unemployment rate reached a 40-year peak in 1982. **Unemployment In what years was the unemployment rate between 4 and 6 percent, the rate considered normal for a healthy economy?**

Full Employment

Look at Figure 13.2. Notice the low levels of unemployment in the late 1960s and late 1990s. Do you think it is possible for the economy to reach an unemployment rate of 0 percent? As you read earlier, zero unemployment is not an achievable goal in a market economy, even under the best of circumstances. Economists generally agree that in an economy that is working properly, an unemployment rate of around 4 to 6 percent is normal. Such an economy would still experience frictional, seasonal, and structural unemployment. In other words, **full employment** is the level of employment reached when no cyclical unemployment exists.

Underemployment

Full employment means that nearly everyone who wants a job has a job, but are all those people satisfied with their jobs? Not necessarily. Some people working at low-skill, low-wage jobs may be highly skilled or educated in a field with few opportunities. They are **underemployed,** that is, working at a job for which they are over-qualified, or working part-time when they desire full-time work.

For example, Jim was a philosophy major in college. He went on to earn a graduate degree in philosophy. When he left school, Jim found that although the economy was booming, he could not find

full employment *the level of employment reached when there is no cyclical unemployment*

underemployed *working at a job for which one is over-qualified, or working part-time when full-time work is desired*

Global Connections

A Shorter Workweek During the early months of 1998, protests erupted throughout France. The reason—the nation's high 12.5 percent unemployment rate. In response, the French government signed into law a shorter, 35-hour workweek that went into effect in January 2000. This new workweek, down from the standard 39 hours a week, was intended to create more than 200,000 new jobs. Many entrepreneurs and economists were skeptical of this solution. Although unemployment did decline in the early 2000s, many businesses and some workers disliked the law and the government repealed it in September 2002. **How would a mandatory shorter workweek affect employment?**

Transparency Resource Package
Economics Concepts, 13B: Underemployment
Economics Concepts, 13C: Unemployment Rates

Differentiated Instruction L4

You may wish to have students add the following to their portfolios. Have students conduct an unemployment survey of 25 of their schoolmates. Caution them to differentiate between those who are actively looking for jobs and those who are not. Ask them to record the numbers and develop graphs to display their data. GT

Economics Assessment Rubric
Economics Assessment Rubrics folder, pp. 8–9 provides sample evaluation materials for a data graphing assignment.

Interdisciplinary Connections: Geography

Geography and Employment As one might expect of such a large and diverse nation as the United States, unemployment can vary dramatically by region. The Northeast, once the industrial heart of the United States, lost ground in the last half of the twentieth century to the so-called Sun Belt states, where newer, higher-technology industries had developed. Meanwhile, some areas, such as Appalachia and parts of the South, maintain high levels of unemployment.

Making the Connection Organize students into groups of three or four to have them find out more about economic changes within an area of the United States and how these changes affected unemployment. Students might examine states such as California, Texas, or Michigan or entire regions such as the Northeast or the Midwest. Have them present their data orally or in a written report, or work with students to construct a bulletin board display of the data.

Answer to . . .

Building Key Concepts In the following years: 1968–1974; 1988–1990; 1996–2004

Global Connections More workers would be needed to accomplish the same amount of work so unemployment would probably decrease, but each worker would earn less.

Go Online PHSchool.com Typing in the Web Code when prompted will bring students directly to the article.

THE WALL STREET JOURNAL. CLASSROOM EDITION

For an additional article from *The Wall Street Journal Classroom Edition*, see the Source Articles folder in the **Teaching Resources**, pp. 39–41.

GTE Guide to the Essentials Chapter 13, Section 1, p. 54 provides support for students who need additional review of the section content. Spanish support is available in the Spanish edition of the guide on p. 54.

Quiz Unit 5 folder, p. 14 includes questions to check students' understanding of Section 1 content.

Presentation Pro CD-ROM Quiz provides multiple-choice questions to check students' understanding of Section 1 content.

Answers to . . .

Section 1 Assessment

1. Frictional unemployment occurs when people take time to find a job—for example, the time spent looking for a job after schooling is finished; structural unemployment occurs when workers' skills do not match the available jobs, as when compact disc technology reduced the need for workers who made vinyl phonograph records.
2. Cyclical unemployment occurs during economic downturns.
3. The unemployment rate is calculated by dividing the number of unemployed people by the total labor force and multiplying the result by 100.
4. Even when an economy is working properly, it will experience frictional, seasonal, and structural unemployment.
5. 5.5 percent (125.4 + 7.3 = 132.7; 7.3 ÷ 132.7 x 100 = 5.5)
6. Santo's situation is an example of frictional unemployment; he had to take time off because of an injury, not for seasonal or structural reasons.
7. Students should demonstrate an understanding of the nature of underemployment and the discouraged worker as described in the section. Students may also mention that people in these categories are not included in the unemployment rate calculation, although they would like to find suitable jobs.

Progress Monitoring *Online*

For additional assessment, have students access Progress Monitoring Online at **Web Code:** mna-5135

Go Online PHSchool.com Typing in the Web Code when prompted will bring students directly to detailed instructions for this activity.

THE WALL STREET JOURNAL. CLASSROOM EDITION

In the News Read more about unemployment in "Rethinking Layoffs," an article in The Wall Street Journal Classroom Edition.

The Wall Street Journal Classroom Edition

For: Current Events
Visit: PHSchool.com
Web Code: mnc-5131

jobs in which he could apply his knowledge of philosophy. Jim had many job choices, but none of them paid very well, and none of them challenged his mind. He was underemployed.

So was Celia, the auto worker described earlier. After her company sent her auto-assembly job to Mexico, she could not find a similar job in the local area, so she was forced to take a low-skill, low-wage job.

Underemployment also describes the situation of people who want a permanent, full-time job but have not been able to find one. Many part-time workers and seasonal workers fit this category.

discouraged worker *a person who wants a job but has given up looking*

Discouraged Workers

Some people, especially during a long recession, give up hope of finding work. These **discouraged workers** have stopped searching for employment and may need to rely on other family members or savings to support them. Discouraged workers, although they are without jobs, do not appear in the unemployment rate determined by the Bureau of Labor Statistics because they are not actively looking for work.

Effects of Terrorism

By late 2001, the employment picture had changed from the low levels of unemployment of the late 1990s and 2000. Even before the September 11 attacks on the World Trade Center and the Pentagon, the economic slowdown had brought U.S. unemployment to a four-year high. Studies estimate that the terrorist attacks cost the country an additional 1.5 to 2 million jobs.

Many of the lost jobs were in travel and tourism. The largest drop-off was in air transportation, accounting for about 20 percent of jobs lost.

The area of New York City around the World Trade Center site was especially hard-hit, with New York City losing some 150,000 jobs. Employment in New York City and in the nation as a whole was expected to improve as the economy returned to normal and New York began rebuilding.

Section 1 Assessment

Progress Monitoring *Online*
For: Self-quiz with vocabulary practice
Web Code: mna-5135

Key Terms and Main Ideas

1. How do **frictional** and **structural unemployment** differ? Give an example of each.
2. When does **cyclical unemployment** take place?
3. How is the **unemployment rate** calculated?
4. Why isn't **full employment** the same as zero unemployment?

Applying Economic Concepts

5. ***Math Practice*** Determine the unemployment rate for a month in which 125.4 million people were employed and 7.3 million people were unemployed.
6. ***Critical Thinking*** After a car accident, Santo needed six months to recover. Since his recovery, he has spent the last year trying to find work in his former occupation, medical technology. So far, he has failed, even though the economy is booming. Which of the four kinds of unemployment best describes Santo's situation? Explain.
7. ***Try This*** Create two fictional workers, one a discouraged worker and one an underemployed worker. Write a paragraph explaining each person's employment situation. Include why these workers are discouraged or underemployed, their current financial situation, and their view of the future.

For: Current Events Activity
Visit: PHSchool.com
Web Code: mnd-5131

Skills for
LIFE

Analyzing Bar Graphs

A bar graph is a useful way to present information visually and to condense large amounts of data. Bar graphs allow us to see the relationships between two or more sets of data, and to discern trends. Use the following steps to study and analyze the bar graph below.

1. **Identify the subject.** Bar graphs show one or more sets of data for a small group of items, such as cities, countries, or people. The title, axis labels, and key tell the reader what the graph depicts. (a) What is the title of the graph below? (b) What do the bars represent?

2. **Read the data.** While some graphs measure all data on the same scale, this bar graph uses two different scales for the *y*-, or vertical, axis. Two different scales are needed to show home prices and average income. Per capita income is shown on the left scale, while home prices are shown on the right scale. (a) What is the per capita income in Houston? (b) Which city has the lowest housing costs? (c) How much does the average house cost in this city?

3. **Interpret the graph.** Look at the data and consider what you can learn from the bar graph. (a) Judging from the three cities with the least expensive houses, what conclusion can you draw about the relationship between geographic location and housing costs? (b) What does it mean if the housing bar is much taller than the income bar? (c) Compare the average income and housing cost in Phoenix with those in Houston. Which city is relatively cheaper to live in (housing costs divided by average per capita income)?

Income and Housing Costs in U.S. Cities

Source: *The Wall Street Journal Almanac*

Additional Practice

Construct a bar graph using two sets of recent data on the economies of the United States, Canada, Germany, and Japan, such as inflation rate, income per capita, or unemployment rate. What can you infer from your bar graph about these economies? What other statistics might you have used instead?

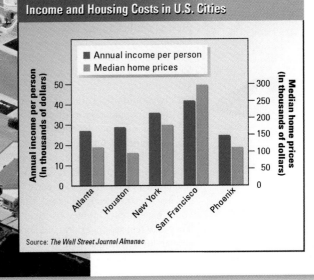

Interdisciplinary Connections: Math

Choosing Scales for Graphs It is important to select the right scale for a bar graph. For example, if the annual income scale for the graph on this page increased in increments of $25,000 rather than $10,000, the differences between incomes in these five cities would be hard to see. Sometimes, as in the graph on this page, two scales are needed for two types of data. Because incomes are calculated on a yearly basis and housing prices are calculated on a one-time basis, both cannot be shown on the same scale.

Have students work through the following activity: Tell students to choose one of the bar graphs in the Databank on pp. 532–547. Then ask them to think of another type of data that could be added to the graph for comparison. Have them explain whether a different scale would be needed, and why.

Skills for LIFE

Analyzing Bar Graphs

1. Focus Students will use bar graphs to compare and contrast income and housing costs in five U.S. cities.

2. Instruct Have volunteers look at the graph before reading the text. Ask them to explain what they think the graph is intended to show. (If necessary, explain the term *median home price.*) Then have students work through the three steps outlined in the feature evaluating economic patterns using the graph provided.

3. Close/Reteach To provide additional practice, see the Economic Skills Activity below.

Economic Skills Activity
Unit 5 folder, p. 19, "Analyzing Bar Graphs," asks students to interpret a bar graph on unemployment.

Simulations and Data Graphing CD-ROM offers data graphing tools so that students can practice creating and interpreting graphs.

Social Studies Skills Tutor CD-ROM offers interactive practice in critical thinking and reading, visual analysis, and communication.

Databank, pp. 532–547 contains a variety of graphs that can be used to extend and reinforce the skills lesson.

Answers

1. (a) Income and Housing Costs in U.S. Cities (b) The bars represent per capita annual income and median housing costs.
2. (a) about $30,000 (b) Houston (c) about $100,000
3. (a) Housing costs are lower in the South and Southwest. (b) It is relatively more expensive to own a house in that city. (c) Houston

Additional Practice

Students should construct an accurate bar graph as directed. Inferences should be supportable from the data graphed; such as, if a country has higher inflation and unemployment rates than another, infer that its economy is weaker than the others'.

Section 2

Inflation

Objectives You may wish to call students' attention to the objectives in the Section Preview. The objectives are reflected in the main headings of the section.

Bellringer Hold up any familiar object that was manufactured in a similar form in 1960 (for example, a pencil or notebook). Ask students about how much it costs today and how much they think it cost in 1960. Then have them compute their guesses as a percentage increase in price. Inform students that in this section they will learn why inflation occurs and how it is computed in this section.

Vocabulary Builder Have students work in pairs to find the definition for each key term. One member of each pair should then explain the term's meaning to the other. Students should switch roles for each term.

Lesson Plan

Teaching the Main Concepts (L3)

1. Focus Inform students that inflation can have terrible effects on the economy; at its worst it can make currency practically worthless. Ask students whether they can name a time and place in history when this occurred.

2. Instruct Explain the effects of rising prices and the use of price indexes to compare inflation rates. Move into a discussion of the causes and effects of inflation, explaining the theories described in the text. Finally, describe recent trends in the inflation rate.

3. Close/Reteach Ask students to recall any statements they have heard about inflation. Ask them how this section helps them understand these statements.

Answer to . . .

Building Key Concepts Workers' incomes have increased at a greater rate than automobile prices.

Section 2 Inflation

Preview

Objectives

After studying this section you will be able to:

1. **Explain** the effects of rising prices.
2. **Understand** the use of price indexes to compare changes in prices over time.
3. **Identify** the causes and effects of inflation.
4. **Describe** recent trends in the inflation rate.

Section Focus

Economists use indexes to keep track of rising prices and to calculate the inflation rate. The level of inflation in the economy can affect wages, purchasing power, and other aspects of everyday life.

Key Terms

inflation
purchasing power
price index
Consumer Price Index (CPI)
market basket
inflation rate
core inflation rate
hyperinflation
quantity theory
demand-pull theory
cost-push theory
wage-price spiral
fixed income
deflation

inflation *a general increase in prices*

You may have heard your grandparents or other relatives talk about the "good old days," when you could get an ice cream for a nickel or a movie ticket for a quarter. They aren't kidding. Prices really were much lower years ago. On the other hand, although prices have generally risen, wages have risen, too. If you asked your older relatives how much they earned when they were young, you might find that it was difficult to scrape up that quarter for the movie ticket. In this section, you will learn why prices have risen, how economists measure their rise, and the effects of rising prices across the economy.

Figure 13.3 Effect of Inflation on Auto Prices

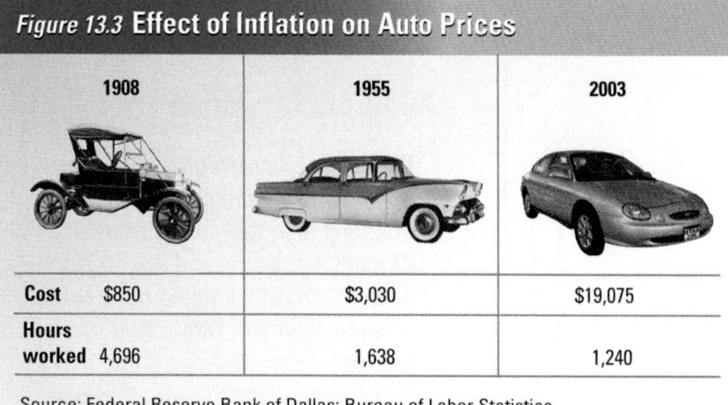

	1908	1955	2003
Cost	$850	$3,030	$19,075
Hours worked	4,696	1,638	1,240

Source: Federal Reserve Bank of Dallas; Bureau of Labor Statistics

Inflation has driven up the price of an automobile even though the number of hours a worker must work to earn the money to pay for an automobile has decreased. **Income Why can more people afford automobiles today than they could in 1908, despite much higher auto prices?**

The Effects of Rising Prices

Josephine and Jack Barrow have owned the same house for 50 years. Recently, they had a real estate agent estimate the house's present market value. The Barrows were astounded. They had bought the house for $12,000, and now it was worth nearly $150,000—a rise in value of more than 1,100 percent.

How could the value of a house, or anything else, increase so much? The main reason is inflation. **Inflation** is a general increase in prices. Over the years prices rise and fall, but in the American economy, they have mostly risen. Since World War II, real estate prices have risen greatly.

The Barrows were pleased that they could get so much money for their house. They also realized that they could not buy a similar house in their area for $12,000 or even $120,000. Inflation had raised the

Graphing the Main Idea

Unemployment and Inflation To build understanding of the major theories of the causes of inflation and its role in the economic challenges of **unemployment** and **inflation,** have students use multi-flowchart graphic organizers like the one at the right. Inform students that a multi-flowchart graphic organizer shows causes and effects and can be used to show the factors that lead to inflation.

Section Reading Support Transparencies A template and the answers for this graphic organizer can be found in Chapter 13, Section 2 of the Section Reading Support Transparency System.

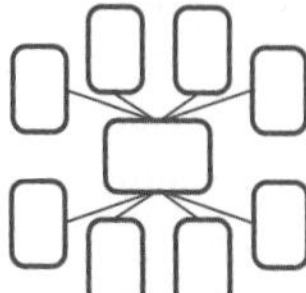

prices of all houses, just as it had also raised wages and the price of most other goods and services.

Another way to look at the Barrows' situation is that inflation had shrunk the value, or purchasing power, of the Barrows' money. **Purchasing power** is the ability to purchase goods and services. As prices rise, the purchasing power of money declines. That is why $12,000 can buy much less now than it could 50 years ago.

Price Indexes

Housing costs are just one element that economists consider when they study inflation. The economy has thousands of goods and services, with millions of individual prices. How do economists compare the changes in all these prices in order to measure inflation? The answer is that they do not compare individual prices; instead, they compare price levels. As you read in Chapter 12, price level is the cost of goods and services in the entire economy at a given point in time.

To help them calculate price level, economists usually turn to a price index. A **price index** is a measurement that shows how the average price of a standard group of goods changes over time. A price index produces an average that economists can compare to earlier averages to see how much prices have changed over time.

Using Price Indexes

Price indexes help consumers and businesspeople make economic decisions. For example, after Marina read in the newspaper that consumer prices had been rising, she decided to increase the amount of money she had been saving to buy a new car. She wanted to be sure that when the time came to buy the car, she would have saved enough money for her purchase.

The government also uses indexes in making policy decisions. A member of Congress, for example, might push for an increase in the minimum wage if she thinks inflation has shrunk purchasing power.

Figure 13.4 **CPI Market Basket Items**

Category	Examples
Food and drinks	cereals, coffee, chicken, milk, restaurant meals
Housing	rent, homeowners' costs, fuel oil
Apparel and upkeep	men's shirts, women's dresses, jewelry
Transportation	airfares, new and used cars, gasoline, auto insurance
Medical care	prescription medicines, eye care, physicians' services
Entertainment	newspapers, toys, musical instruments
Education and communication	tuition, postage, telephone services, computers
Other goods and services	haircuts, cosmetics, bank fees

Source: Bureau of Labor Statistics

The CPI market basket helps economists calculate the average inflation rate for the country. **Inflation Why might an individual family experience an inflation rate that is higher or lower than the national average?**

The Consumer Price Index

Although there are several price indexes, the best-known index focuses on consumers. **The Consumer Price Index (CPI)** is computed each month by the Bureau of Labor Statistics (BLS). The CPI is determined by measuring the price of a standard group of goods meant to represent the "market basket" of a typical urban consumer. This **market basket** is a representative collection of goods and services. By looking at the CPI, consumers, businesses, and the government can compare the cost of a group of goods this month with what the same or a similar group cost months or even years ago.

As you can see from Figure 13.4, the CPI market basket is divided into eight categories of goods and services. Figure 13.4 shows these categories and a few examples of the many items in each group.

About every 10 years, the items in the market basket are updated to account for shifting consumer buying habits. The BLS determines how the market basket should change by conducting a Consumer Expenditure Survey. The BLS conducted one such survey from 1993 to 1995. For

purchasing power *the ability to purchase goods and services*

price index *a measurement that shows how the average price of a standard group of goods changes over time*

Consumer Price Index (CPI) *a price index determined by measuring the price of a standard group of goods meant to represent the "market basket" of a typical urban consumer*

market basket *a representative collection of goods and services*

Econ 101: Key Concepts Made Easy

Unemployment and Inflation Students may be confused by the use of the term *index* in the terms *price index* and *Consumer Price Index*. Students probably know that an index is also the list of topics covered in a book, referenced by page number. Both uses of the term come from the same Latin root, *indicare*, a word meaning "to point out" or "to indicate." (The same root is found in the term *index finger*, the "pointer" finger.) A price index is used to "point to" change from a standard.

Guided Reading and Review
Unit 5 folder, p. 15 asks students to identify the main ideas of the section and to define or identify key terms.

Differentiated Instruction L3

Organize students into groups of three or four. Ask each group to restate the information on the effects of rising prices by writing several paragraphs about an original example like the one given in the text. Challenge students to create a meaningful example that is different from the one in the text to demonstrate their understanding of the effects of inflation.

Transparency Resource Package
Economics Concepts, 13D: Inflation
Economics Concepts, 13E: Components of the Consumer Price Index
Economics Concepts, 13F: CPI Annual Average

Background

Global Connections

As the countries of the European Union (EU) integrate their economic activities, they are finding it useful to integrate their statistical information as well. Eurostat is the statistical office of the European Community. It collects European statistics on various economic indicators from member countries, standardizes the information, and then makes it accessible to people all over the world. Although Eurostat was founded in 1953, the coming of the single European market in the 1990s and the increased integration of EU member nations extended Eurostat's activities and increased its public role.

Answer to . . .

Building Key Concepts Each family buys a somewhat different combination of goods; price changes may vary significantly for different goods.

Differentiated Instruction L3

(Reteaching) Organize the class into pairs, and give each pair a copy of Consumer Price Index data from an almanac. To help students to use appropriate mathematical skills to interpret social studies information, ask them to create a poster that shows how these numbers can be used to calculate, compare, and contrast inflation rates. Students must show, step by step, how to calculate inflation rates for two different periods of time. Then have them compare the rates. For example, they may calculate the rate between 1994 and 1995 and between 2002 and 2003 and compare the two. (The earlier rate is significantly greater than the later one.)

Learning Styles Activity
Learning Styles Lesson Plans folder, p. 32 asks groups of students to create a market basket of goods, whose prices they increase to calculate a Consumer Price Index and the rate of inflation.

Math Practice Activity
Math Practice folder, p. 11, "Choosing Between Job Offers," allows students to evaluate the cost of living index for several cities to make a decision in a hypothetical job-hunting situation.

Answer to . . .
Building Key Concepts The inflation rate is 13.5 percent.

inflation rate *the percentage rate of change in price level over time*

core inflation rate *the rate of inflation excluding the effects of food and energy prices*

each of these years, 4,800 families provided information on their spending habits. Another 4,800 families kept diaries in which they noted everything they purchased during a two-week period for each of the years. This process resulted in the list of market basket items used today.

Price Indexes and the Inflation Rate

Economists also find it useful to calculate the **inflation rate,** or the percentage rate of change in price level over time. Although there are other price indexes, the CPI is the index you will most often hear about, so we will focus on it. How does the BLS determine the CPI and use it to calculate the inflation rate?

Determining the CPI

To determine the CPI, the BLS establishes a base period to which it can compare current prices. Currently, the base period is 1982–1984. The cost of the market basket for that period is assigned the index number 100. Every month, BLS representatives update the cost of the same market basket of goods and services by rechecking all the prices. Each updated cost is compared with the base-period cost to determine the index for that month. As costs rise, the index rises.

The BLS determines the CPI for a given year using the following formula.

$$\text{CPI} = \frac{\text{updated cost}}{\text{base period cost}} \times 100$$

For example, suppose the market basket cost $200 during the base period and costs $360 today. The CPI for today would be:

$$\frac{\$360}{\$200} \times 100 = 180$$

In this example, the CPI rose from 100 in the base period to 180 today.

Calculating the Inflation Rate

To figure the inflation rate from one year to the next, you would use the steps shown in Figure 13.5. You can also determine the rate of inflation from month to month using the same basic formula that you see in this chart. Just substitute "Month A" and "Month B" for "Year A" and "Year B."

To calculate the inflation rate, follow the steps shown in the chart.
Inflation **CPI for 1979 was 72.6. For 1980, CPI was 82.4. Calculate the inflation rate for 1980.**

Figure 13.5 Calculating the Inflation Rate

To calculate the inflation rate, use the following formula:

CPI for Year A **minus** CPI for Year B
divided by CPI for Year B
multiplied by 100

For example,
if the CPI for 2004 (Year A) = 188.9
and the CPI for 2003 (Year B) = 184.0

then,
188.9 – 184.0 = 4.9
4.9 ÷ 184.0 = .027
.027 x 100 = 2.7

Therefore,
the inflation rate for 2004 was 2.7%.

Types of Inflation

Inflation rates in the United States have changed greatly over time. From Figure 13.6, you can see that the inflation rate stayed fairly low in the 1960s. When the inflation rate stays low and averages between 1 and 3 percent, it does not typically cause problems for the economy. Businesses and governments can plan in this environment. However, economists have noted that when the inflation rate exceeds 5 percent, the inflation rate itself becomes unstable and unpredictable. This makes planning very difficult.

As you can also see in figure 13.6, the inflation rate sometimes spikes up sharply, as in 1974 and 1980. These sharp increases in the inflation rate were due in part to increases in prices in world food and oil markets. In order to study long-term trends in the inflation rate, analysts need to set aside temporary spikes in food and fuel prices. To do this, economists have developed the concept of core inflation rate. The **core inflation rate** is the rate of inflation excluding the effects of food and energy prices.

Block Scheduling Strategies

Consider these suggestions to take advantage of extended class time:

- Extend the Background note on p. 339 by having small groups research Eurostat on the Internet. Ask students to access some of the statistics available from Eurostat. Each group should prepare a written report on its findings. Students may use the links offered in the *Economics: Principles in Action* segment of the Social Studies area of the Prentice Hall Web site. **PHSchool.com**
- Have students use the Simulations and Data Graphing CD-ROM to create line graphs, similar to the one on p. 341, that track the inflation rate over particular periods of time. Some students could graph inflation rates during the 1990s and others over a longer span of time. Tables showing rates from 1914 onward are available in several sources, including almanacs.

By far the worst kind of inflation is **hyperinflation**, or inflation that is out of control. During periods of hyperinflation, inflation rates can go as high as 100 or even 500 percent per month, and money loses much of its value. This level of inflation is rare, but when it occurs it often leads to a total economic collapse.

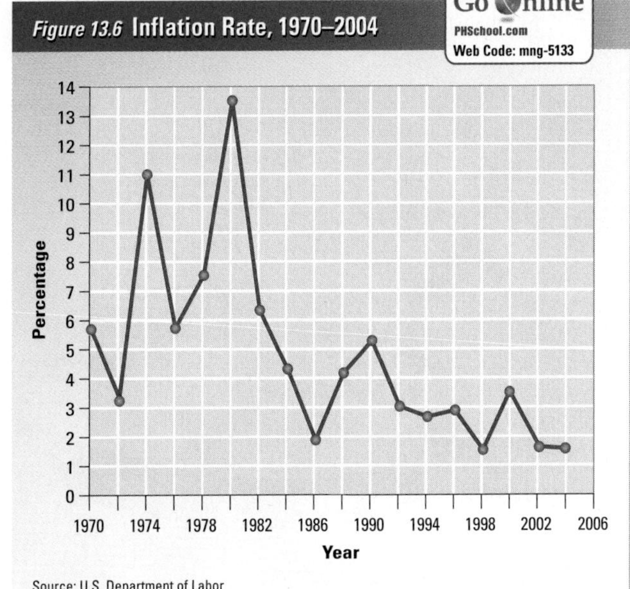

Figure 13.6 **Inflation Rate, 1970–2004**

Source: U.S. Department of Labor

Sharp inflation rate increases in 1974 and 1980 were due in part to increases in food and oil prices. An inflation rate of 1 to 3 percent does not typically cause economic problems. **Inflation In what years was the inflation rate at a level where it would not cause problems for the economy?**

Causes of Inflation

Where does inflation come from? Price levels can rise steeply when demand for goods and services exceeds the supply available at current prices, such as during wartime. They can also rise steeply when productivity is restricted, such as when a long drought leads to poor harvests.

Nobody can explain every instance of rising price levels. Economists, however, offer several theories about the causes of inflation. These include the quantity theory, the demand-pull theory, and the cost-push theory.

A full explanation of the reasons for inflation incorporates all three theories. Economists therefore look at all elements of this picture when they try to understand the inflation process.

The Quantity Theory

The **quantity theory** of inflation states that too much money in the economy causes inflation. Therefore, the money supply should be carefully monitored to keep it in line with the nation's productivity as measured by real GDP.

Economists at the University of Chicago developed a popular version of this theory in the 1950s and 1960s. They maintained that the money supply could be used to control price levels in the long term. The key to stable prices, they said, was to increase the supply of money at the same rate as the economy was growing.

Demand-Pull Theory

The **demand-pull theory** states that inflation occurs when demand for goods and services exceeds existing supplies. During wartime, for example, the needs of the government put pressure on producers. The heavy demand for new equipment, supplies, and services makes those items more valuable, forcing their prices up. Wages also rise as the demand for labor increases along with the demand for goods.

Cost-Push Theory

According to the **cost-push theory**, inflation occurs when producers raise prices in order to meet increased costs. Higher prices for raw materials can cause costs to increase. Wage increases, however, are most often the biggest reason, since wages are the largest single production cost for most companies.

Wage increases can come when low unemployment leads employers to offer higher wages in an effort to attract workers. Wage increases can also occur as a result of collective bargaining.

Assume, for example, that Jen is a union laborer at Am-Gro Fertilizer. Her

hyperinflation *inflation that is out of control*

quantity theory *theory that too much money in the economy causes inflation*

demand-pull theory *theory that inflation occurs when demand for goods and services exceeds existing supplies*

cost-push theory *theory that inflation occurs when producers raise prices in order to meet increased costs*

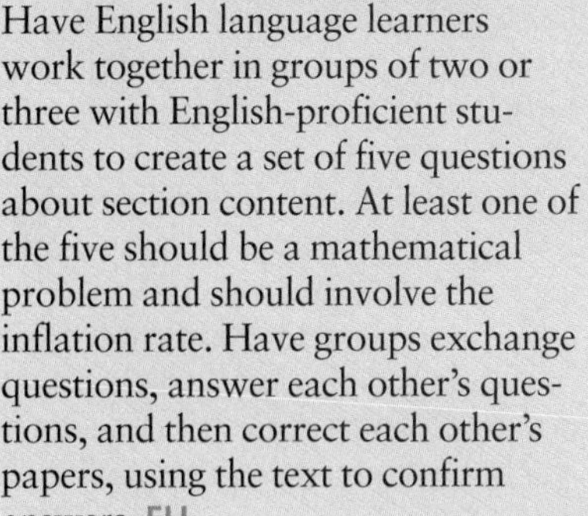

Differentiated Instruction L2

Have English language learners work together in groups of two or three with English-proficient students to create a set of five questions about section content. At least one of the five should be a mathematical problem and should involve the inflation rate. Have groups exchange questions, answer each other's questions, and then correct each other's papers, using the text to confirm answers. ELL

Meeting NCEE Standards

Use the following benchmark activity from the **Voluntary National Content Standards in Economics** to evaluate student understanding of **Standard 20.**

Explain why inflation occurs after participating in two rounds of an auction where the number of goods available remains constant, but the money in circulation increases in round two.

Differentiated Instruction 

Simulate the effects of inflation. Year One: Give each student $5,000 worth of fake money. Offer several used cars for sale for $5,000 each. Tell students that they may buy one car now or save their money and buy a better car later, when they will have more money. In Year Two give each student another $5,000. Announce that a used car now costs $8,000. Students may buy one or save their money until Year Three. In Year Three, give each student another $5,000. Announce that a used car now costs. $12,000. After sales are completed ask students why it was better to have spent their money in Year One. SN

Interdisciplinary Connections: History

OPEC and Inflation In the 1970s the cost-push theory of inflation was proven true when the members of OPEC (Organization of Petroleum Exporting Countries) raised prices on oil in retaliation for the West's support of Israel during the 1973 Arab-Israeli war. For a while OPEC even ordered a ban on sales to the United States by member countries. The higher price of oil caused a wave of inflation to sweep across the economy as manufacturers passed their higher transportation and manufacturing costs on to the consumer.

Making the Connection Have students research the wide-ranging effects of higher oil prices in the 1970s on the American economy. Ask students to find out what solutions were proposed to make sure that such a situation did not develop again.

Answer to . . .

Building Key Concepts In the following years: 1966; 1986; 1992–1998; 2002–2004

Differentiated Instruction L3

Have students use role-playing to demonstrate understanding of the causes and effects of inflation. Organize the class into groups of four or five students. Inform students that after preparation each group will conduct a five-minute press conference in front of the class. One student will act as a leading economist, holding the press conference; the other students will be television interviewers.

Differentiated Instruction L3

(Reteaching) Ask students to write a short newspaper article describing recent trends in the inflation rate as described in the text. Encourage them to convey the text information in a reportorial style, not in the style of a textbook.

Economic Cartoon
Unit 5 folder, p. 23 gives students practice in interpreting cartoons about section content.

Background

Menu Costs

One type of cost of inflation that students may not be familiar with is what economists refer to as the *menu costs.* Menu costs are the costs that arise from actually making a change in prices. Any business that posts prices must expend labor and capital to change the posted prices when they rise. These are called menu costs because one of the most obvious categories of business affected is a restaurant, which must print new prices on every menu.

Answer to . . .

Building Key Concepts Higher food prices tend to cause workers to seek wage increases; increased wages lead to higher prices as producers try to regain their profits.

Figure 13.7 **The Wage-Price Spiral**

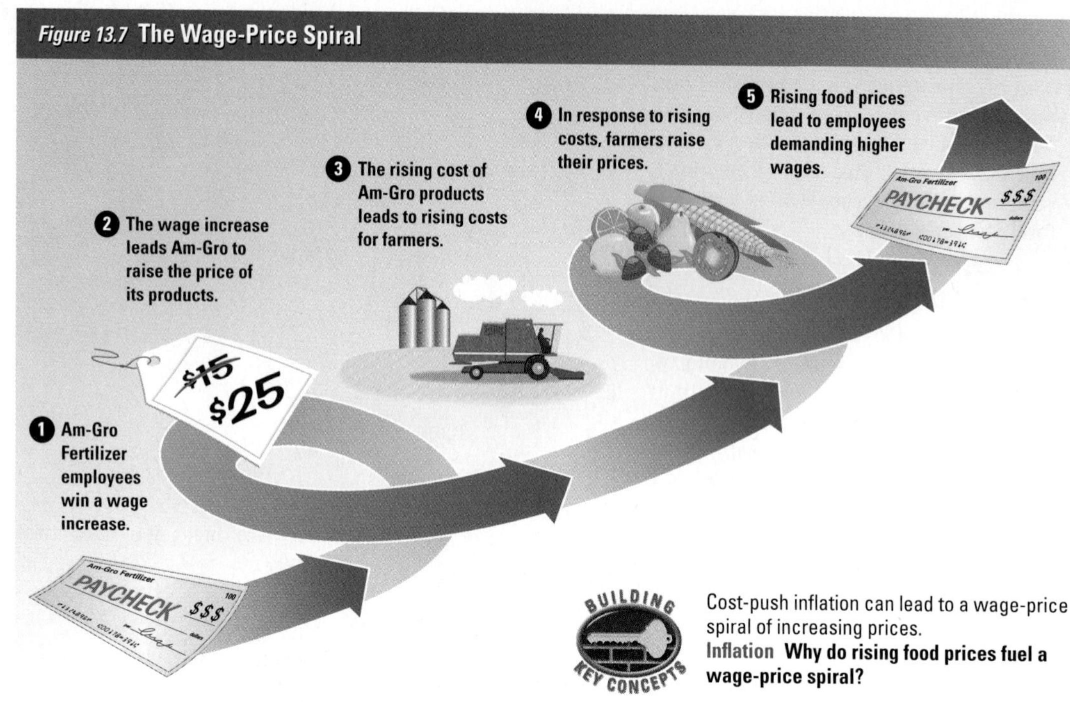
1 Am-Gro Fertilizer employees win a wage increase.
2 The wage increase leads Am-Gro to raise the price of its products.
3 The rising cost of Am-Gro products leads to rising costs for farmers.
4 In response to rising costs, farmers raise their prices.
5 Rising food prices lead to employees demanding higher wages.
$15
$25
Am-Gro Fertilizer
PAYCHECK $$$
Am-Gro Fertilizer
PAYCHECK $$$

BUILDING KEY CONCEPTS
Cost-push inflation can lead to a wage-price spiral of increasing prices.
Inflation Why do rising food prices fuel a wage-price spiral?

wage-price spiral *the process by which rising wages cause higher prices, and higher prices cause higher wages*

union recently won a large wage increase. This new cost has led Am-Gro to raise its prices to meet the higher payroll and maintain its profits.

Cost-push inflation can lead to a spiral of ever-higher prices. That is, one increase in costs leads to an increase in prices, which leads to another increase in costs, and on and on. The process by which rising wages cause higher prices, and higher prices cause higher wages, is known as the **wage-price spiral.** Figure 13.7 above shows how a wage-price spiral would affect Am-Gro Fertilizer.

Effects of Inflation

High inflation is a major economic problem, especially when inflation rates change greatly from year to year. Buyers and sellers find planning for the future difficult, if not impossible. The effects of inflation can be seen mainly in purchasing power, income, and interest rates.

Purchasing Power

You have seen, in the example of Jack and Josephine Barrow's house, how inflation can erode purchasing power. In an inflationary economy, a dollar will not buy the same number of goods that it did in years past. To take a simple example, suppose $1.00 would buy $1.00 worth of goods last year. If the inflation rate is 10 percent this year, however, $1.00 will buy the equivalent of only $.90 worth of goods today.

Income

Inflation sometimes, but not always, erodes income. If wage increases match the inflation rate, a worker's real income stays the same. People who don't receive their income as wages, such as doctors, lawyers, and businesspeople, can often increase their incomes to keep up with inflation by raising the prices they charge.

Not all people are so fortunate. The Barrows, for example, could be hit hard by inflation because they are retired and

Preparing for Standardized Tests

Have students read the section titled "Effects of Inflation" and then answer the question below.

Which one of the following is not a typical effect of inflation?

A Prices for goods and services rise over time.
B Purchasing power is eroded.
C Savers lose money if the interest rate is lower than the inflation rate.
(D) Income from wages drops.

living on a **fixed income**, or income that does not increase even when prices go up. The portion of their income from Social Security rises with the price level, because the government raises Social Security benefits to keep up with inflation. Much of their income, however, comes from a pension fund that pays them a fixed amount of money each month. Inflation steadily eats away at the real value of that pension check.

Interest Rates

People receive a given amount of interest on money in their savings accounts, but their true return depends on the rate of inflation. For example, Sonia had her savings in an account that paid 7 percent interest. At the same time, the annual inflation rate was 5 percent. The purchasing power of Sonia's savings increased that year by 2 percent, not by 7 percent, because 5 percent of her savings was needed to keep up with inflation.

When a bank's interest rate matches the inflation rate, savers break even. The amount they gain in interest is taken away by inflation. Savers may even lose money if the inflation rate is higher than their bank's interest rate.

Recent Trends

Americans over age 30 have experienced positive inflation rates for most of their lifetimes. In the late 1990s, unemployment levels reached record low levels. Typically, low unemployment leads to higher inflation because companies compete for scarce workers by offering higher wages. Rising wages can push the inflation rate up, as you know from the discussion of the wage-price spiral. However, inflation crept along at less than 3 percent. Some economists suggested that the economy was going through a lucky streak. Others maintained that the economy was returning to the normal levels of unemployment that had existed in the 1950s and 1960s.

As the economy entered a period of recession and slow growth in the 2000s, inflation decreased further to less than 2 percent. Rising unemployment and falling capital investment removed two factors that might have led to cost-push inflation. Prices at times seemed to be falling. Some experts even predicted a period of **deflation**, or a sustained drop in the price level. However, the economy recovered and inflation remained at a comfortably low level for consumers.

fixed income *income that does not increase even when prices go up*

deflation *a sustained drop in the price level*

Section 2 Assessment

Progress Monitoring *Online*
For: Self-quiz with vocabulary practice
Web Code: mna-5136

Key Terms and Main Ideas

1. How does **inflation** affect **purchasing power**? Give an example.
2. What is the purpose of the **Consumer Price Index (CPI)**?
3. What causes a **wage-price spiral**, and what can it lead to?
4. Why did the existence of low inflation and low unemployment in the 1990s puzzle some economists?

Applying Economic Concepts

5. ***Math Practice*** Suppose that the CPI for last year was 164 and that for this year it is 168. Calculate the inflation rate from last year to this year.
6. ***Critical Thinking*** If you had never experienced inflation, how might that affect your expectations about annual wage increases?
7. ***Using the Databank*** Turn to the chart on page 538 that shows the CPI Market Basket. **(a)** Which category of the CPI receives the highest percentage weighting? **(b)** Does this answer surprise you? Why or why not?

For: Presentation Activity
Visit: PHSchool.com
Web Code: mnd-5132

GTE Guide to the Essentials
Chapter 13, Section 2, p. 55 provides support for students who need additional review of the section content. Spanish support is available in the Spanish edition of the guide on p. 55.

Quiz Unit 5 folder, p. 16 includes questions to check students' understanding of Section 2 content.

Presentation Pro CD-ROM
Quiz provides multiple-choice questions to check students' understanding of Section 2 content.

Answers to . . .

Section 2 Assessment

1. It reduces the purchasing power of money. For example, a movie ticket that cost a quarter 50 years ago might cost $7 today. That quarter no longer has the same purchasing power that it did 50 years ago.
2. The CPI is a tool for measuring inflation. Consumers and business people use it in making economic decisions.
3. One increase in costs—such as a wage hike—leads to an increase in prices, which leads to another increase in costs, and so on. The result is a cycle of increasing wages and increasing prices, called the wage-price spiral.
4. Low unemployment is usually accompanied by a rise in inflation.
5. 2.43 percent; $(168–164) \div 164 = 0.0243 \times 100 = 2.43$
6. Students may say that they would not automatically expect a wage increase each year.
7. (a) housing (b) Some students will not be surprised, especially if they know what their families spend on rent or mortgage payments. Other students may expect food or clothing to be the largest expense.

Progress Monitoring *Online*
For additional assessment, have students access Progress Monitoring Online at **Web Code:** mna-5136

Go Online PHSchool.com Typing in the Web Code when prompted will bring students directly to detailed instructions for this activity.

ECONOMIC *Profile*
Oprah Winfrey

Background

Oprah Winfrey's entertainment credentials are impressive: an Academy Award nomination for her role in Steven Spielberg's *The Color Purple,* seven Emmy Awards for Outstanding Talk Show Host, and the National Academy of Television Arts & Sciences' Lifetime Achievement Award. On top of these achievements, in the late 1990s she decided to make an attempt at reenergizing America's flagging interest in reading. Winfrey often features a notable new book on her show, catapulting more than one novel onto the bestseller lists. In 2003, Forbes magazine revealed that Winfrey had become the first African-American woman billionaire. She has also established scholarships and donated millions of dollars to colleges and universities. It's no surprise that *Time* magazine named her one of the 100 Most Influential People of the Twentieth Century.

Careers in Economics Activity Unit 5 folder, p. 22 gives students a closer look at the career path of a fund-raiser.

Answers to . . .

1. She has used her popular talk show as a forum to increase public awareness, has herself contributed millions of dollars to programs to help needy Americans, and has encouraged her viewers and celebrity guests to do the same.
2. Answers will vary but should recognize that poverty limits individual opportunity and that widespread poverty impacts almost every aspect of economic life, including production and consumption; distribution of wealth; and taxing, spending, and fiscal policy.
3. Students should prepare brief reports that describe specific public or private programs to improve the lives of poor people.

ECONOMIC

Profile

Economist

Entrepreneur

Oprah Winfrey (b. 1954)

Determination and an uncanny ability to connect with her audience enabled Oprah Winfrey to become one of the richest and most powerful women in America. Remembering her roots, Oprah has used her substantial power in the media to raise awareness of important social and economic issues.

Raised in Poverty

Born in rural Mississippi, Oprah Winfrey spent her early childhood in extreme poverty on a farm, where she was raised by her grandmother after her mother moved north in search of work. At age 6, Winfrey was sent to Milwaukee, Wisconsin, to live with her mother and half brothers. The family struggled to survive on her mother's monthly $50 income as a servant.

Winfrey spent her early teens in and out of trouble until she went to live with her father in Nashville, Tennessee. Winfrey credits his strict discipline with saving her life. He required her to learn five new vocabulary words each day and read one book per week. "Getting my library card was like citizenship," Winfrey recalls. She soon excelled in school, and in her senior year, she got a part-time job reading the news for a local radio station.

The Oprah Winfrey Show

While studying speech and drama at Tennessee State University, Winfrey was offered a job anchoring the evening news at a local TV station. "Sure I was a token," she says, "But, honey, I was one happy token." After graduating in 1976, Winfrey took a job with a station in Baltimore, Maryland. When the station demoted her from news anchor to talk show host, she discovered what she "was born to do."

In 1984, Winfrey moved to Chicago to take over a similar show. In 1985, it became *The Oprah Winfrey Show,* and the next year it began to air nationwide. By 1987, in a business dominated by white men, this African American woman had the most-watched talk show in America.

Oprah Gives Back

In exploring topics related to family abuse, poverty, and opportunity, Winfrey has confronted her own past in front of a national television audience. By offering a forum for such subjects, she has increased public awareness of important social and economic issues. Winfrey has also shared her success by contributing millions of dollars to schools and to her own Family for Better Lives foundation.

Through her show, Winfrey continues to influence America's culture and economy. Oprah's Book Club, launched in 1996 and revived in 2003, encourages millions of viewers to read new novels and classic fiction. Winfrey's desire to share her favorite books has also helped the book publishing industry to prosper.

CHECK FOR UNDERSTANDING

1. **Source Reading** Describe three ways in which Oprah Winfrey has used her position to address the issue of poverty in America.
2. **Critical Thinking** How are poverty and opportunity related? What effects does widespread poverty have on the nation's economy?
3. **Learn More** Use the Internet and other resources to learn more about efforts to improve the lives of poor people in the United States. Prepare a brief report on one specific public or private program.

Beyond the Classroom: Career Connections

Television Producer Television producers are the people who are ultimately responsible for what viewers see on their television screens. Producers work in all areas of television, from local news to made-for-TV movies. While directors exert creative control, producers exercise financial control. They are usually responsible for coordinating the activities of writers, directors, and actors and may also be responsible for a host of details such as selecting scripts and hiring personnel. Ask students to describe qualities that they think would be important in a television producer. (Possible answers include *creativity, organizational skills, a competitive spirit,* and *tenacity.*)

Section 3 Poverty

Preview

Objectives

After studying this section you will be able to:

1. **Define** who is poor, according to government standards.
2. **Describe** the causes of poverty.
3. **Analyze** the distribution of income in the United States.
4. **Summarize** government policies intended to combat poverty.

Section Focus

Despite the tremendous success of our nation's economy, millions of Americans remain poor. The government develops public policies and programs to try to combat poverty.

Key Terms

poverty threshold
poverty rate
income distribution
food stamps
Lorenz Curve
enterprise zone
block grant
workfare

What image comes to mind when you think of poverty? You might associate poverty with a homeless person on a city street or a poorly clothed child in a small rural house. Despite the success of the American economy, many Americans lack sufficient food, clothing, and shelter. In this section you'll read about the nature and causes of poverty, the distribution of income in the United States, and government programs designed to combat poverty.

The Poor

As you have read, the United States Bureau of the Census conducts extensive surveys to gather data about the American people. Then its economists analyze the data and organize it to reveal important characteristics, such as how many families and households live in poverty. The Census Bureau defines a family as a group of two or more people related by birth, marriage, or adoption who live in the same housing unit. A household is all people who live in the same housing unit, regardless of how they are related.

The Poverty Threshold

According to the government, a poor family is one whose total income is less than the amount required to satisfy the family's minimum needs. The Census Bureau determines the income level, known as the poverty threshold, needed to meet those minimum needs. The **poverty threshold** is the income level below which income is insufficient to support a family or household.

The poverty threshold, or poverty line, varies with the size of the family. For example, in 2004, the poverty threshold for a single parent under age 65 with one child

poverty threshold *the income level below which income is insufficient to support a family or household*

Go Online
PHSchool.com
Web Code: mng-5134

Figure 13.8 **Poverty Rate, 1964–2002**

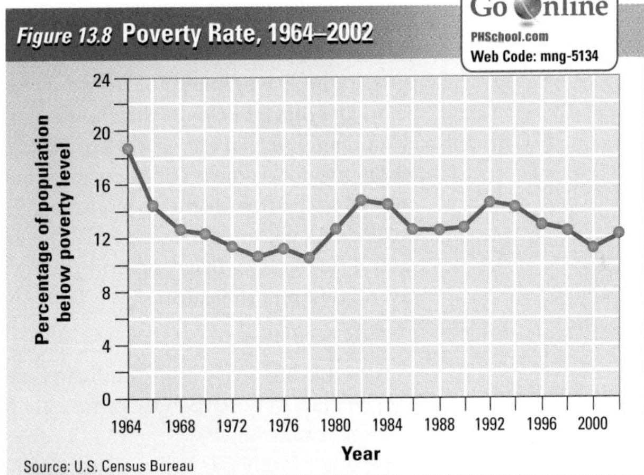

The poverty rate began to decline during the 1960s, partly as a result of anti-poverty programs.
Income **How did poverty rates during the 2000s compare with poverty rates during the 1960s?**

Building Key Concepts: Graphing the Main Idea

Public Policy To build understanding of the causes of poverty and how they shape **public policy** attempts to deal with poverty, have students use a multi-flowchart graphic organizer like the one at the right. Inform students that a multi-flowchart shows causes and effects. They should place the label "Poverty" in the center and record causes in the outer boxes.

Section Reading Support Transparencies A template and the answers for this graphic organizer can be found in Chapter 13, Section 3 of the Section Reading Support Transparency System.

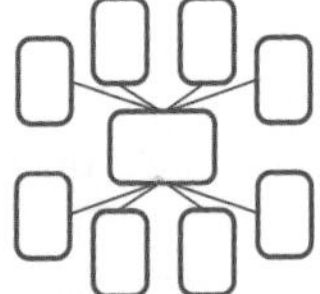

Section 3 Poverty

Objectives You may wish to call students' attention to the objectives in the Section Preview. The objectives are reflected in the main headings of the section.

Bellringer Organize students into small groups, and have them brainstorm a list of words that they associate with the subject of poverty. Inform them that in this section they will learn about poverty in the United States.

Vocabulary Builder Organize students into pairs. Have them take turns explaining the key terms to their partners, using graphics from the section where necessary.

Lesson Plan

Teaching the Main Concepts 

1. Focus To introduce this section, inform students that economics is not simply an abstract science. Economics can be used to battle poverty. Ask students how successful they think our nation is at fighting poverty.

2. Instruct Using the lists from the Bellringer activity, ask students what they think poverty is. Then discuss the methods the government uses to measure poverty and the factors that contribute to poverty. Explain the distribution of income in the United States, and describe government policies intended to combat poverty. Remind students that in a democracy like ours, these policies are the subject of political debate.

3. Close/Reteach Inform students that most societies feel a responsibility to help those in need but that people disagree on how best to do that. Ask students to describe and analyze recent articles in newspapers or news magazines that address this issue.

Answer to . . .

Building Key Concepts Poverty rates were lower in the 2000s.

Guided Reading and Review
Unit 5 folder, p. 17 asks students to identify the main ideas of the section and to define or identify key terms.

Differentiated Instruction L3

Have students create a question-and-answer sheet explaining who is poor, as defined by government standards. Explain that their sheets should include these questions: Who collects the data? What is the definition of a family? What is the poverty threshold for a family of four with two children? They should also include concise answers based on the textbook material.

Transparency Resource Package
Economics Concepts, 13G: Poverty Rates

Background

Careers in Economics

For those who are interested in fighting poverty and helping others, social work may be an excellent career choice. Social workers often aid people with psychological, medical, or family problems; many also help their clients find work and develop their job skills. Social workers with master's degrees or doctorates often become involved in public policy debates on poverty, focusing on action that can be taken to alleviate it. To become a social worker, a bachelor's degree is necessary. Advancement often requires a master's degree in social work.

Answer to . . .
Building Key Concepts 24.3 percent

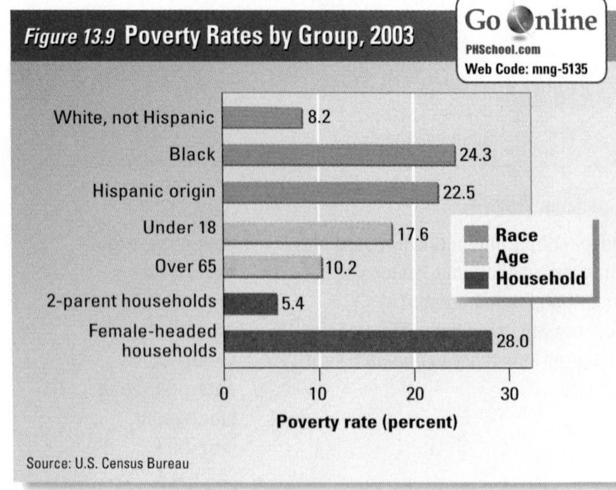

Households headed by women, African Americans, and Hispanics are more likely than other groups to have incomes below the poverty threshold, as this recent data shows.
Income What percentage of African American families have incomes below the poverty threshold?

poverty rate *the percentage of people who live in households with income below the official poverty line*

was $12,490. For a family of four with two children, it was $18,850. If a family's total income is below the poverty threshold, everyone in the family is counted as poor.

The Poverty Rate

Figure 13.9 shows poverty rates for various groups. The **poverty rate** is the percentage of people who live in households with income below the official poverty threshold.

We can use poverty rates to discover whom the government considers to be poor and what factors seem to contribute to poverty. As you read in Chapter 3, poverty rates differ sharply by groups, according to several different indicators:

- *Race and ethnic origin* The poverty rate among African Americans and Hispanics is more than twice the rate for white Americans.
- *Type of family* Families with a single mother have a poverty rate almost six times greater than that of two-parent families.
- *Age* The percentage of children living in poverty is significantly larger than that for any other age group. Young adults make up the next largest group in this category.
- *Residence* People who live in the inner city have double the poverty rate of those who live outside the inner city. People who live in rural areas also have a higher poverty rate, especially in regions where job prospects are limited.

Causes of Poverty

Put simply, a family is poor when the adults in the family fail to earn enough income to provide for its members' basic needs. This failure to earn adequate income is often the result of unemployment.

As you read in Section 1, millions of Americans are unemployed, for a variety of reasons. While they are out of a job, their families might well fall below the poverty threshold. Many other poor adults are not even considered a part of the labor force. Some suffer from chronic health problems or disabilities that prevent them from working.

Many poor adults do have jobs, however. In fact, more than half of poor households have someone who works at least part-time, and one in five have a full-time, year-round worker. For these "working poor," the problem is usually low wages or a limited work schedule, rather than the lack of a job. For example, Ray makes $7.90 an hour as a full-time clerk in a clothing store. While he is at work, his wife stays at home with their two young children. Although Ray works 40 hours per week, and his salary is well above minimum wage, his annual earnings amount to just over $16,400, which is below the poverty threshold for a family of four.

Economists agree that poverty and lack of income go hand in hand, but have different ideas about the causes of poverty. Here are some of the most important explanations for why some people are poor.

Lack of Education

The median income of high school dropouts in 2003 was $18,344, which was just above the poverty threshold for a family of

Econ 101: Key Concepts Made Easy

Public Policy One of the key concepts in this section is that of a **poverty threshold.** The poverty threshold, at its most basic, represents a government estimate of the amount of money necessary to satisfy the minimum needs of a particular number of people. Poverty definitions were originally developed in 1964 and were based on an estimate of food costs. Because the government had determined that families generally spend about one third of their income on food, the thresholds were set at three times the estimated cost of food.

Ask students whether they think that a poverty threshold based primarily on food costs makes sense. Ask them to suggest a variety of factors that affect how much a person or a family needs in order to live.

four in that year. High-school graduates earned about one third more than dropouts, and college graduates earned about three times as much.

Location

In most cities of the United States, racial minorities are concentrated in the inner cities, far from the higher-wage jobs in suburban areas. Many inner-city residents do not own cars, and mass-transit systems are often not an efficient means of commuting from the inner city to the suburbs. As a result, people who live in the inner city earn less than people living outside the inner city. Similar obstacles exist for many people living in rural areas.

Racial and Gender Discrimination

White workers generally earn more than minority workers, and men generally earn more than women. Much of this income inequality can be explained by differences in hours worked, education, and work experience. Part of the inequality, however, results from racial and gender discrimination. Even when all the workers in a group are equally productive, whites are often paid more than African Americans, and men are often paid more than women. Economists agree, however, that this kind of discrimination has been diminishing.

Economic Shifts

People who lack education and skills are not very productive workers. For this reason they are often the "last hired and first fired." They are hired when the economy is expanding, and workers are hard to find, but they are the first to lose their jobs when the economy slows down. Also, workers without college-level skills have suffered in recent decades from the ongoing decline of manufacturing and the rise of service and high-technology jobs.

Shifts in Family Structure

The divorce rate has risen significantly since the 1960s, as has the number of children born to unmarried parents. These demographic shifts tend to result in more single-parent families and more children living in poverty.

Income Distribution

In 2003, the median household income in the United States was $43,318, which means that half the households earned more than this amount and half earned

THE WALL STREET JOURNAL.
CLASSROOM EDITION

In the News Read more about poverty in "A Grim Undertaking," an article in The Wall Street Journal Classroom Edition.

The Wall Street Journal Classroom Edition

For: Current Events
Visit: PHSchool.com
Web Code: mnc-5133

▼ People with college and advanced degrees generally earn much higher incomes than people with only high-school diplomas.

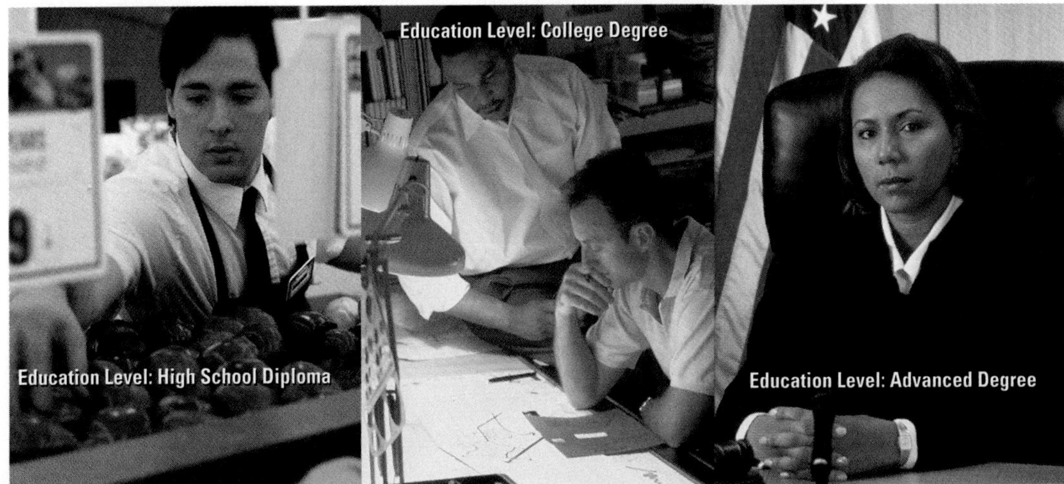

Go Online PHSchool.com Typing in the Web Code when prompted will bring students directly to the article.

Differentiated Instruction 

Organize students into groups of three or four. Ask the groups to read through the section titled "Causes of Poverty" and then to work together to create a graphic organizer that summarizes this material. The organizer may be in the form of a web, a cause-and-effect chart, a flow chart, or any other format that illustrates these concepts. When groups have finished, display their work on a bulletin board.

Differentiated Instruction 

You may wish to have students add the following to their portfolios. As this section indicates, people with few skills and little education are more likely to be unemployed or poor. The contrary, of course, is also true. Have students do research to find out what skills and college degrees will be the most marketable in the next ten years. Then ask them to write a newspaper article discussing their findings. GT

Economics Assessment Rubric
Economics Assessment Rubrics folder, pp. 6–7 provides sample evaluation materials for a writing assignment.

Block Scheduling Strategies

Consider these suggestions to take advantage of extended class time:

- Extend the Econ 101 activity at the bottom of p. 346 by having students examine the history of poverty thresholds. Students can obtain Bureau of the Census information on the development of poverty thresholds from library resources. Ask them to report on their findings.
- Extend the first activity on this page by conducting a panel discussion about the causes of poverty. Assign five students as panel members, each supported by a group of three. Have each group research one of the causes of poverty highlighted in the text. Then hold the discussion, allowing the class to ask questions.
- Ask students to locate articles concerning poverty and government poverty programs. Have them bring in the articles and present short oral summaries. Then hold a class discussion about regional and national poverty issues.

Differentiated Instruction 

(Reteaching) Ask students to demonstrate understanding of the Lorenz Curve and the distribution of income in the United States by creating a captioned version of Figure 13.10 on this page. Call on students to show how their numbers were derived and present any conclusions that can be drawn from the figure.

Transparency Resource Package
Economics Concepts, 13H: Income Distribution

Background

Global Connections

On a global scale as well as on a national scale, the distribution of income is unequal. The 1999 United Nations Human Development Report included this statistic: The combined wealth of the world's top three billionaires is worth more than the combined gross national product of the 48 least-developed countries where 600 million people live.

income distribution *how the nation's total income is distributed among its population*

food stamps *government-issued coupons that recipients exchange for food*

less. This figure, however, tells only part of the income story. In order to fully understand poverty in the United States, you also need to understand **income distribution,** or how the nation's total income is distributed among its population.

Income Inequality

The United States has millions of poor people, but it also has the one of the highest per capita GDPs in the world. How can that be? The answer lies in how the market distributes income. Figure 13.10 shows how income is distributed in the United States. These figures do not take into account the effects of taxes or noncash government aid such as housing subsidies, health care, or food stamps. **Food stamps** are government-issued coupons that recipients exchange for food.

Look at the table on the left side of Figure 13.10. To compute the numbers in the table, economists take four steps.

1. First, they rank the nation's households according to income.
2. Second, they divide the list into fifths, or quintiles, with equal numbers of households in each fifth. The lowest fifth, which appears at the top of the list, includes the poorest 20 percent of households. The highest fifth, which appears at the bottom of the list, includes the richest 20 percent of households. The first column in Figure 13.10 shows this division into quintiles.
3. Next, they compute each group's average income by adding up the incomes of all the households in the group, and then dividing by the number of households.
4. Finally, they compute each group's share, or percentage, of total income by dividing the group's total income by the total income of all the groups. The second column shows each group's share. The third column shows the cumulative total. (For example, the lowest two fifths of households earned 12.1 percent of total income.)

Compare the share of the poorest fifth with that of the richest fifth. If you divide richest by poorest, you will see that the typical household in the richest fifth receives more than 13 times the income of the typical household in the poorest fifth.

Now look at the graph on the right side of Figure 13.10. It shows that the numbers for shares of total income, when they are plotted on a graph, form a curve. This

The table (left side) shows family income ranked by category. When plotted on a Lorenz Curve (right side), these data show the distribution of income in the United States.
Income What percent of total income did the lowest three fifths of households make in 2003?

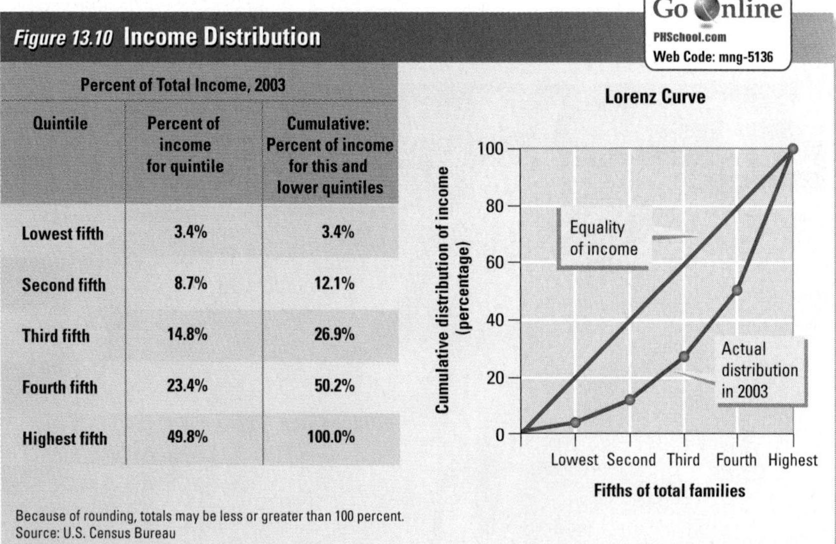

Figure 13.10 **Income Distribution**

Go Online PHSchool.com Web Code: mng-5136

Percent of Total Income, 2003

Quintile	Percent of income for quintile	Cumulative: Percent of income for this and lower quintiles
Lowest fifth	3.4%	3.4%
Second fifth	8.7%	12.1%
Third fifth	14.8%	26.9%
Fourth fifth	23.4%	50.2%
Highest fifth	49.8%	100.0%

Because of rounding, totals may be less or greater than 100 percent.
Source: U.S. Census Bureau

Interdisciplinary Connections: Math

Figuring Income Distribution The procedure economists use to find out how income is distributed across households of varying economic status involves fairly simple arithmetic. Students can create a simplified Lorenz Curve from hypothetical statistics.

Making the Connection Imagine that the government of a country of 12 people has divided the population into three income groups. Compute income distribution, using these figures and the procedure on this page.

Group A Incomes: $34,500, $38,000, $32,000, $33,000

Group B Incomes: $60,400, $65,000, $58,000, $59,300

Group C Incomes: $80,400, $95,000, $100,000, $102,000

(Answers: Group A Total/Average Income: $137,500/$34,375; Group B: $242,700/$60,675; Group C: $377,400/$94,350; Percentages: 18 percent; 32 percent; 50 percent.)

Answer to . . .

Building Key Concepts 26.8 percent

graph, called the **Lorenz Curve,** illustrates the distribution of income in the economy.

Let's see what this Lorenz Curve tells you. First, read the label on each axis. Then look at the straight line running diagonally across the graph. This reference line represents complete equality. Under conditions of complete equality, each quintile would receive one fifth of total income. That means the lowest 20 percent of households would receive 20 percent of total income, as shown by the point (lowest, 20). Similarly, the lowest 40 percent (the first two quintiles) would receive 40 percent of total income, as shown by the point (second, 40), and so on.

In 2003, the distribution of income was not equal, as the Lorenz Curve indicates. For example, the point (lowest, 3.4) shows that the lowest 20 percent, or one fifth, of households received just 3.4 percent of the nation's total income. The point (second, 12.1) shows that the lowest 40 percent, or two fifths, of households received only 12.1 percent of the income. The area on the graph between the line of equality and the Lorenz Curve represents the amount of inequality in income distribution. The larger the area between the curves, the greater the income inequality.

Income Gap

As you can see from Figure 13.10, the wealthiest fifth of American households earned nearly as much income (49.8 percent) as the bottom four-fifths combined. A study published in 1999 showed that the richest 2.7 million Americans receive as much income after taxes are deducted as the poorest 100 million Americans. Why are there such differences in income among Americans? Here are some factors.

- *Differences in skills and education* Some people are more highly skilled than others, so they earn higher wages. Labor skills are determined in part by education and training and in part by a worker's natural ability.
- *Inheritances* Some people inherit large sums of money and earn income by investing it. Others inherit businesses that produce income from profits.
- *Field of work* Wages are determined by the demand for labor. As you read in Chapter 9, labor demand is a "derived demand" because it is set by demand for what people produce. People who produce goods with a low market value usually earn lower wages.

In the last two decades, the distribution of income has become less equal. Since 1977, the share of income earned by the lowest three fifths has decreased by 12 percent, while the share earned by the top 1 percent has more than doubled.

▲ **Young adults who volunteer for the AmeriCorps program help combat poverty.**

Antipoverty Policies

As you read in Chapter 3, the government spends billions of dollars on programs designed to reduce poverty. This money is spent mainly on cash assistance, education, medical benefits, and noncash benefits such as food stamps and subsidized housing.

Many antipoverty programs have drawn criticism from those who say that much of the money is wasted. Many people also argue that the programs themselves harm the very people they are intended to help. In recent years, these criticisms have led to new policies and proposals for reform. These include the establishment of enterprise zones, job training and other forms of employment assistance, and welfare reform.

Lorenz Curve *the curve that illustrates income distribution*

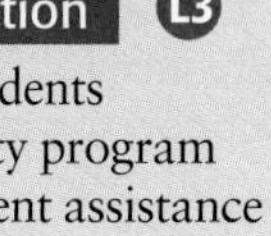

Differentiated Instruction L3

(Reteaching) Have students research one antipoverty program that involves employment assistance and another that involves welfare reform. Then ask them to summarize the programs they researched and the effects these programs have had.

Differentiated Instruction L4

Inheritance and estate taxes have traditionally been some of the heftiest of all tax burdens, up to 55 percent for extremely wealthy individuals. Ask students to write several paragraphs explaining why they think the government taxes inheritances heavily and how this might affect income distribution. GT

Background

Market Solutions

During times of economic instability or recession, many more families and individuals face personal economic hardship. Many people argue that market-based efforts, charitable organizations, religious institutions, and individuals can actually be more effective than the government at lessening the impact of economic instability.

Preparing for Standardized Tests

Have students read the section titled "Income Gap" and then answer the question below.

Which of the following statements is supported by the text?

(A) In recent years the richest segment of the population has become richer.
B Skill and effort have little to do with income differences in the population.
C In recent years income distribution has become more equal.
D Inheritances are rarely invested.

GTE Guide to the Essentials
Chapter 13, Section 3, p. 56 provides support for students who need additional review of the section content. Spanish support is available in the Spanish edition of the guide on p. 56.

Quiz Unit 5 folder, p. 18 includes questions to check students' understanding of Section 3 content.

Presentation Pro CD-ROM
Quiz provides multiple-choice questions to check students' understanding of Section 3 content.

Answers to . . .

Section 3 Assessment

1. The poverty threshold determines how many people are included in the poverty rate (people below the poverty threshold).
2. lack of education, location, racial and gender discrimination, economic shifts, shifts in family structure
3. The Lorenz Curve illustrates the distribution of income in the economy. It suggests that there is an unequal distribution of income in the United States.
4. Programs focus on cash assistance, education, medical benefits, and subsidized housing. Enterprise zones attempt to revitalize inner city areas. Other programs focus on job training.
5. The working adult(s) may be paid low wages or have a limited work schedule.
6. Students' responses should reflect an understanding of employment assistance and welfare/welfare reform programs.
7. Answers for family of four: Two parents at \$5.15/hr working 40 hr/week = \$10.30 ×40 hr×52 weeks = \$21,424. This income is above the poverty threshold of \$16,530 for a family of four. Some students will accept this as adequate; others will say that a family of four would need more than this to support decent living conditions.
8. Block grants are lump sums of money rather than open-ended commitments of money to operate programs that require many administrators and expand or contract as the number of people who qualify for aid changes.

enterprise zone *area where companies can locate free of certain local, state, and federal taxes and restrictions*

block grant *federal funds given to the states in lump sums*

workfare *a program requiring work in exchange for temporary assistance*

Enterprise Zones

Enterprise zones, which became popular in the 1980s, are areas where companies can locate free of certain state, local, and federal taxes and restrictions. Zones benefit businesses and residents because people can find work near their homes. Rundown areas, such as inner cities, can begin to be revitalized.

Employment Assistance

The lack of an adequate income may result from inadequate skills or simply a lack of opportunity. In recent decades, federal and state governments have designed job-training programs to deal with the problem of workers who lack skills. In addition, the federal government has made a minimum wage mandatory since 1938. The minimum wage ensures that workers' hourly pay will not fall below a certain point.

Welfare Reform

Poor people often cannot afford basic needs, such as food and medical care. The United States has long had a welfare system that provides for those basic needs, especially for children and the elderly. That system underwent major reform when President Clinton signed the Personal Responsibility and Work Opportunity Reconciliation Act of 1996.

This welfare-reform plan responded to criticisms that welfare encouraged poor people to remain unemployed in order to keep receiving aid. It replaced the traditional antipoverty program for poor families (Aid to Families with Dependent Children, or AFDC) with a new program called Temporary Assistance for Needy Families (TANF). TANF eliminated cash assistance for poor families. Instead, the federal government provides **block grants,** or lump sums of money, to the states. As a result of this welfare-reform act, the states are now responsible for designing and implementing programs to move most poor adults from welfare dependence to employment. TANF also set a 5-year limit on receipt of benefits.

The plan calls for a shift from welfare to **workfare**—a program requiring work in exchange for temporary assistance. The resulting surge of new employees has increased the number of low-skilled people in the labor market. In theory, this could lower the wages of the least-skilled workers. On the other hand, welfare reform has the potential to reduce poverty by providing poor Americans with labor skills and access to a steady, adequate income.

Tough economic times in the early 2000s tested the new plan's limits. States cut spending for workfare jobs while private firms were hiring fewer new workers. The future of the plan will depend on its success in a difficult economy.

Section 3 Assessment

Progress Monitoring *Online*
For: Self-quiz with vocabulary practice
Web Code: mna-5137

Key Terms and Main Ideas

1. How is the **poverty threshold** related to the **poverty rate?**
2. Identify five reasons that help account for poverty.
3. What is the **Lorenz Curve,** and what does it suggest about the distribution of income in the United States?
4. How do existing government policies deal with poverty?
5. Explain how a family can include working adults but still have an income below the poverty threshold.

Applying Economic Concepts

6. ***Try This*** Suppose that you are in charge of creating an antipoverty program for your state. Create a list of at least five proposals for your program.
7. ***Math Practice*** Do you think the minimum wage in 2005 (\$5.15 per hour) was adequate to lift most families out of poverty? Explain your answer.
8. ***Critical Thinking*** How might the distribution of block grants help the federal government control its budget?

For: Current Events Activity
Visit: PHSchool.com
Web Code: mnd-5133

Progress Monitoring *Online*
For additional assessment, have students access Progress Monitoring Online at **Web Code:** mna-5137

Go Online PHSchool.com Typing in the Web Code when prompted will bring students directly to detailed instructions for this activity.

Unemployment in a Changing Economy

In the late 1990s, the United States found itself in the midst of an economic boom that would have been unimaginable only a decade earlier. Demand for workers continued to grow to such an extent that by 2000, the final year of the boom, there were more than 143 million jobs in the nation. Unemployment dipped below 4 percent.

▲ Job seekers can use the Internet to help them find the right job.

Looking for Work During such a period of frenzied demand for workers, some people thought that anyone who wanted a job could get one. They were wrong. Even in periods of so-called full employment, there are always qualified people without jobs. Some companies move, while others fail. Some workers live in areas where there are few jobs available that match their skills.

Take Rick Taber, for example, a highly educated, skilled accountant who lives about 100 miles from Boston. When the company he worked for was purchased by another firm, he lost his job. There were jobs available in Boston, but Rick didn't want to move there. He spent almost a year searching for a job near his home that would match his skills and experience, but eventually had to take a job for which he was overqualified.

Older Workers Sometimes older workers have trouble finding jobs because of the emphasis on youth in the job marketplace. Many energetic men and women in their 50s and 60s, with years of experience in their fields, have difficulty finding work because some companies prefer to hire younger employees, who tend to work for smaller salaries.

Effects of Technology In addition, the technology that helped create millions of new jobs in high tech industries has also eliminated jobs in other areas. Many bank tellers, for example, have lost their jobs because computers and machines do many of their tasks more cheaply and efficiently. Telephone operators are being replaced by automated phone systems. As technology continues to perform routine tasks more efficiently, more and more Americans will find themselves switching jobs, and perhaps occupations.

Applying Economic Ideas

1. Why are some people jobless during periods of high employment?
2. How might technological changes in the workplace affect the unemployment rate?

Career Planning

✓ Preparing for Standardized Tests

Have students read the case study and then answer the question below.

In the case study the author's main point is that:

A Unemployment is primarily a result of technological changes.

B Becoming an accountant does not always mean that one will be able to find a satisfactory job.

(C) Some unemployment will always exist, no matter how strong the economy is.

D High demand for workers means that workers often have to take jobs for which they are overqualified.

Real-life Case Study: Unemployment

1. Focus Remind students that in a free enterprise economy some unemployment is inevitable. Before they read the case study, ask students whether they can think of any reasons unemployment may exist even in periods of sustained economic expansion.

2. Instruct As students read the case study, have them jot down the author's main points and identify the main argument. Tell them to pay close attention to the topic sentences to find the main points. Ask students to answer this question: How do the points the author makes contribute to his main argument?

3. Close/Reteach Have students write a paragraph explaining why the author uses the example of Rick Taber and what unemployment issues this example illustrates.

Case Studies Activity
Case Studies in Free Enterprise folder, pp. 26–27, "Fred Smith," helps students apply economic principles in an additional case study.

Economic Detective Activity
Unit 5 folder, p. 21, "Troubles in Hitechum," provides an additional application of chapter concepts.

Databank, pp. 532–547 contains a variety of graphs that can be used to extend and reinforce case study concepts.

Answers to . . .

1. Company failures and moves, technological advances, and seasonal trends all contribute to unemployment during good economic times.
2. Technological changes may increase the need for certain workers while decreasing the need for others.

Chapter 13 Assessment

Key Terms

1. structural unemployment
2. poverty rate
3. inflation
4. wage-price spiral
5. price level
6. full employment
7. Lorenz Curve

Using Graphic Organizers

8. frictional—caused by people changing jobs, getting laid off, and taking time off for a variety of reasons; seasonal—caused by industries slowing or shutting down for a season or a holiday; structural—caused by shifts that cause workers not to have the skills to match the jobs available; cyclical—caused by economic downturns

Reviewing Main Ideas

9. erodes purchasing power, as when this year's dollar purchases only $.90 worth of goods in last year's terms; sometimes erodes income, as when a person has a fixed income and inflation decreases its value; reduces the value gained from interest, as when the interest rate on savings is 5 percent, but the inflation rate is 3 percent, so the saver really gains only 2 percent
10. The rate of inflation is calculated by using data from the Consumer Price Index, which shows how the average prices of certain goods change over time.
11. Students should describe three antipoverty policies such as subsidized housing (paying part of the cost of housing for poor families), enterprise zones (areas where companies can locate free of certain tax restrictions), and job-training programs.
12. The quantity theory states that inflation occurs when there is too much money. The demand-pull theory states that inflation occurs when demand exceeds supply. The cost-push theory states that when costs rise, producers raise prices and inflation occurs.
13. The unemployment rate is determined by calculating the labor force and then dividing the number of unemployed people by the total labor force and multiplying by 100.
14. Poverty rates are highest for female-headed households (27.8 percent) and for people of Hispanic origin (22.8 percent) as well as African Americans (23.6 percent).

Critical Thinking

15. Students who agree with it will probably say that it encourages those who can work to do so and helps them in the long run, as well as helping the economy. Those who disagree will say that it may help some people but cuts off others from needed help.
16. Full employment can be a problem when employers find it difficult to recruit workers; competition for workers leads to wage increases and thus to inflation

Chapter 13 Assessment

Chapter Summary

A summary of major ideas in Chapter 13 appears below. See also the **Guide to the Essentials of Economics,** which provides additional review and test practice of key concepts in Chapter 13.

Section 1 Unemployment (pp. 331–336)

Unemployment affects millions of Americans each year. Causes of unemployment vary, so unemployment is categorized into **seasonal, frictional, structural,** and **cyclical unemployment.** The Bureau of Labor Statistics tracks unemployment and determines the **unemployment rate.** Economists use the unemployment rate as an indicator of the health of the overall economy.

Section 2 Inflation (pp. 338–343)

A general increase in prices is known as **inflation.** Economists use indexes to measure inflation and its effects on consumers and producers. The best-known index is the **Consumer Price Index (CPI),** which uses prices of a group of consumer goods called the **market basket.** Inflation affects many aspects of our everyday lives, from how much we earn to how much our earnings can purchase.

Section 3 Poverty (pp. 345–350)

Despite the tremendous success of our nation's economy, millions of Americans remain poor. Causes of poverty range from lack of education to racial and gender discrimination. Federal, state, and local governments administer programs to help people whose incomes place them below the **poverty threshold,** the income level needed to meet a family's minimum needs.

Key Terms

Match the following definitions with the terms listed below. You may not use all of the terms.

inflation	**discouraged workers**
full employment	**deflation**
poverty rate	**price level**
wage-price spiral	**Lorenz Curve**
structural unemployment	**poverty threshold**

1. occurs when the skills that workers have do not match the jobs that are available
2. the percentage of people in a particular group who live in households below the official poverty threshold
3. an increase in the general level of prices
4. process by which rising wages cause higher prices and higher prices cause higher wages
5. an average of the prices of goods and services in the economy
6. the level of employment reached when there is no cyclical unemployment
7. illustrates the distribution of income in the economy

Using Graphic Organizers

8. On a separate sheet of paper, copy the tree map below. Chart the four types of unemployment, and list the causes of each.

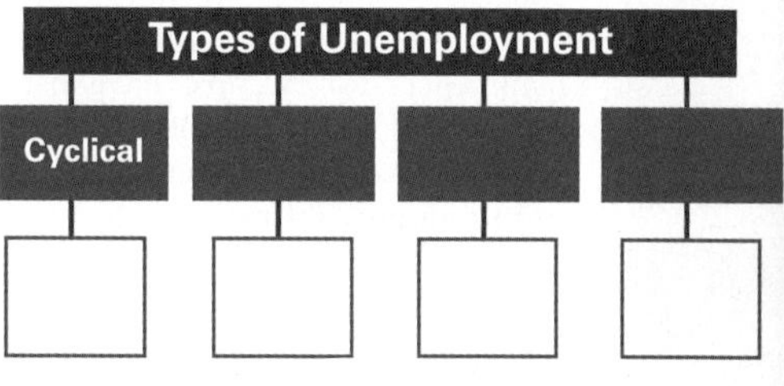

Reviewing Main Ideas

9. What are three effects of inflation? Give an example of each.
10. What role does the Consumer Price Index play in calculating inflation?
11. List and describe at least three ways in which the government combats poverty.
12. What are three causes of inflation, and how do they differ?
13. How is the unemployment rate determined?
14. Which groups are most affected by poverty? Use data from the chapter to support your answer.

Critical Thinking

15. **Analyzing Information** Review the characteristics of the Personal Responsibility and Work Opportunity Reconciliation Act of 1996 decribed on page 350. Do you agree with the basic aim of the program? Explain your answer.
16. **Expressing Problems Clearly** How can full employment be a problem? What issues arise when the economy reaches full employment?
17. **Recognizing Cause and Effect** What cause-and-effect relationship exists in the cost-push theory of inflation?

Problem-Solving Activity

18. Assume you are about to run for local political office. Your area is currently affected by high poverty rates and unemployment. Write a proposal for alleviating poverty and unemployment in your area.

Skills for Life

Analyzing Bar Graphs Review the steps shown on page 337; then answer the following questions using the bar graphs below.

19. What is the subject of these bar graphs?
20. Did the total number of people in poverty in the United States increase or decrease between 1998 and 2001?
21. Which regions of the country had poverty rates lower than the national rate?
22. Did any regions have a poverty rate greater than the national rate? If so, which ones?
23. What additional data might you want to consult to help you interpret these graphs?

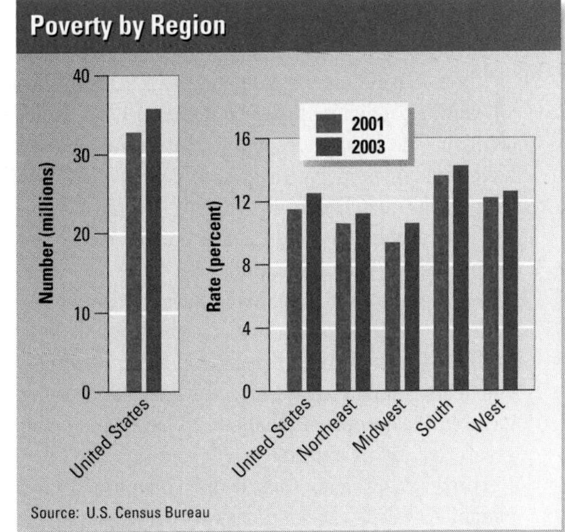

Economics Journal

Making Comparisons How do your perceptions of poverty in the United States compare with the data presented in this chapter? How does your definition of poverty compare with that of the Bureau of the Census? What do you think are the primary causes of poverty?

Progress Monitoring *Online*

For: Chapter 13 Self-Test **Visit:** PHSchool.com
Web Code: mna-5131

As a final review, take the Economics Chapter 13 Self-Test and receive immediate feedback on your answers. The test consists of 20 multiple-choice questions designed to test your understanding of the chapter content.

17. When costs rise (the cause), this leads producers to raise prices (the effect). Then, when prices rise (the cause), inflation occurs (the effect).

Problem-Solving Activity

18. Students should write proposals that are clear and that demonstrate an understanding of the economic concepts in this chapter. For example, they could suggest building a downtown aquarium that would provide jobs, bring revenue and tourists into the city, and boost the local economy.

Skills for Life

19. poverty rates in various regions of the United States
20. increased
21. the Northeast and Midwest
22. the South and the West
23. Students might suggest employment or other economic data for the region or population figures.

Additional support materials and activities for Chapter 13 of *Economics: Principles in Action* can be found in the Social Studies area of **PHSchool.com**.

Economics Journal

Students' responses will vary depending on their initial impressions. They should effectively compare their original answers with chapter data and speculate on the causes of poverty.

Review and Assessment

Vocabulary Practice Unit 5 folder, p. 20 uses a word puzzle to reinforce understanding of key terms.

GTE **Guide to the Essentials** Chapter 13 Test, p. 57

Test Bank CD-ROM Chapter 13 Test

Go Online PHSchool.com Students may use the Chapter 13 Self-Test on **PHSchool.com** to prepare for the Chapter Test.

THE WALL STREET JOURNAL.
CLASSROOM EDITION

DEBATE: EASY CREDIT

1. Focus Have students find the meaning of each of these words before they begin to read: *credit, debit, democratization, disposable income, gleam, mortgage,* and *prudently.*

Explain to students that they will be conducting a debate on easy credit and its impact on the economy. Inform them that they will be responsible for arguing one side of the issue. Remind students that a well-prepared debater supports a position with valid evidence, logical arguments, and responsible appeals to emotion.

2. Instruct The authors have both researched the impact of easy credit on businesses, consumers and the economy. Have students conduct further research on the advantages and disadvantages of access to credit from credible sources before conducting the debate.

Remind students that they should use the following debate format:
The affirmative side will:

- State the problem. Why is this problem significant?
- Explain who or what is harmed if the problem is not resolved. Use factual evidence to quantify the harm.
- Propose a plan of action. Explain why it is better than the current system.
- Provide factual evidence to show how this plan will solve the problem.

The opposing side will:

- Refute the arguments of the affirmative side, using factual evidence to quantify and support its position.
- If necessary, support the status quo's ability to solve the problem.

3. Close/Reteach When the debate is concluded, encourage students to discuss their opinions on the issue. Ask them whether they were persuaded by the other side's arguments. Conclude by having students write their own statements on the impact of easy credit on the economy.

THE WALL STREET JOURNAL.
CLASSROOM EDITION

DEBATING CURRENT ISSUES: *Easy Credit*

For many Americans, borrowing money is easier than ever. But some economists worry that all that borrowing is setting the economy up for a fall.

In this debate from *The Wall Street Journal Classroom Edition,* Allen Grommet, a senior economist at the Cambridge Consumer Credit Index, and Ruth Ann Marshall, President of MasterCard North America, discuss the benefits and drawbacks of expanding consumer credit.

YES *Is Easy Credit Good for the Economy?*

BY RUTH ANN MARSHALL

If you like old movies, you know this scene: A hard-working individual goes to the local bank to get a loan. The banker responds, "Sorry, but you don't have enough property to guarantee the loan." Well, that wasn't just Hollywood fiction. Not too long ago, the only people who could easily borrow money were people who already had money.

Today, millions of Americans have access to credit, with the major determining factor being their ability to repay. How did credit become more democratic? For one, federal laws enacted over the past 30 years have ensured that people of all ages and backgrounds have greater access to credit.

Thirty years ago, Americans traveling overseas bought traveler's checks or risked carrying cash. Now a debit or credit card gets you local currency almost anywhere in the world. College students have learned the value of having a card in an emergency when their cars break down far from home. And payment cards give small businesses financial flexibility that was unknown in the 1960s.

Then there's e-commerce—a category of spending that would be just a gleam in a futurist's eye if it weren't for debit and credit cards and the protections behind them.

Some critics believe the price for democratization of credit is too high, yet the truth is the vast majority of consumers use credit responsibly. That said, we believe one consumer in trouble with credit is one too many. But the answer doesn't lie in making credit harder to get. The answer lies in improved financial education in schools and more widespread teaching of basic money-management skills.

Because of the efforts of the financial-services industry, Americans now have more choices and more technologically advanced ways of managing their money than ever before. If the past three decades are any guide, those choices and advances will only continue to grow in the coming years.

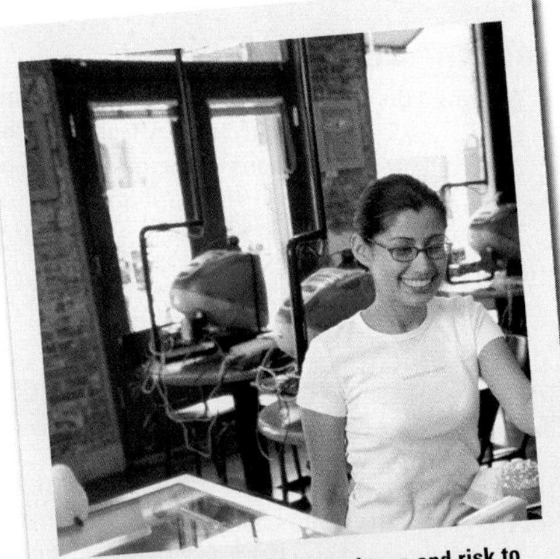

Credit cards offer both convenience and risk to consumers who may be tempted to borrow more money than they can afford to pay back.

Debate Activity Debating Current Issues folder, p. 17 asks students to determine the advantages and disadvantages of easy credit. Have students consider how access to easy credit can help and hurt businesses, consumers and the economy.

Economic Assessment Rubric Economics Assessment Rubrics folder, pp. 14–15 provides sample evaluation materials for participation in debates.

Background

About the Authors

Allen Grommet, senior economist at the Cambridge Consumer Credit Index, thinks inflation is a danger arising from too much credit. Ruth Ann Marshall, president of MasterCard North America, argues that easier credit represents a democratization of lending that has helped not only individuals but the economy as well—particularly the burgeoning e-commerce market.

NO Is Easy Credit Good for the Economy?

By Allen Grommet

Easy credit has many consequences. It allows individuals to spend more than they are capable of paying. It adds more purchasing power to the economy than the amount of efficient production of goods and services, leading to inflation. Given that easy credit is rarely extended evenly throughout the economy, it inevitably leads to distortions in the proportion of goods and services offered to various groups of consumers.

Research shows a growing number of consumers are unable to prudently handle the number of credit offers thrust upon them. The combination of all service payments from mortgages and other consumer debts has been staying around the historically high 14% of disposable personal income. This is up from the previous low point of about 12% in 1992 and 1993.

People are borrowing money against their credit cards more than ever. Credit-card debt, most home-equity loans, and other variable-rate forms of consumer debt will add to this already high level of debt service as interest rates rise and people will have to pay more each month on existing debts.

Higher interest rates could also hurt the housing market, causing many consumers to lose value in their homes. This is because an increase in interest rates requires new homebuyers to spend more to borrow the same amount of money. People will offer lower bids on houses to keep mortgage payments low and the whole market suffers. For example, a family that bought a $250,000 house by borrowing $220,000 for a mortgage could suddenly find the value of their home fall to $210,000 if interest rates rise. Their $30,000 in home equity would be wiped out because they borrowed too heavily when credit was easy.

With bankruptcies, foreclosures, and charge-offs already at high levels, the dangers of easy credit are more critical than normal. Many financial institutions offering credit will find themselves unprofitable if the situation turns only slightly worse.

Despite the warning signs, lenders are not tightening up. Instead, credit card issuers are continuing to aggressively recruit new accounts with millions of letters offering new credit cards.

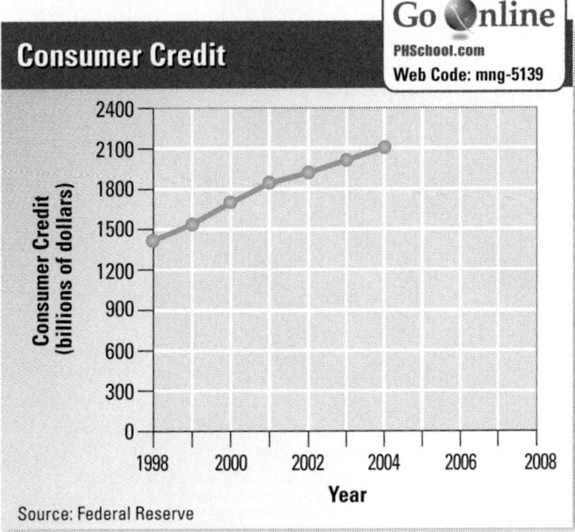

Rising consumer credit—the amount of money that consumers have borrowed from financial institutions—has aided the growth of the economy.

DEBATING THE ISSUE

1. According to Ruth Ann Marshall, what has enabled millions of Americans to have access to credit on competitive terms?
2. What data does Allen Grommet use to show that consumers aren't handling credit offers well?
3. **Drawing Conclusions** The authors disagree on whether consumers can accurately judge the risks of borrowing money for online purchases or home improvements. Which author do you find more convincing? Why?
4. **Reading Graphs** How much money did Americans owe in the form of consumer credit in 1999? By how much had this debt increased five years later?

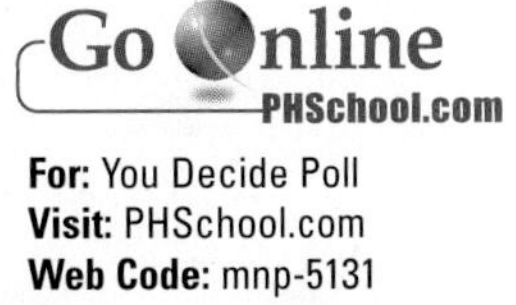

For: You Decide Poll
Visit: PHSchool.com
Web Code: mnp-5131

Differentiated Instruction 

Americans' taste for consumer products is crucial to economic growth. For each dollar a consumer spends, the financial impact on the economy will be many times that single dollar. The spending *multiplier* is an important economic concept.

Have students use their own community and the concept of the multiplier to discuss and analyze the economic impact of consumer spending choices.

In groups, have students select a retail business in the area such as a clothing store, a gas station, a car dealer, or a supermarket.

Have students draw a diagram or write a description of how $100 spent at this business will flow back through consumers and businesses at least three times in the community. Then see if the students can expand the flow to include businesses and consumers outside of the community or the United States.

Ask students to report to the class. What conclusions or observations can be made about the impact of consumer spending on the economy? Would consumers charging these purchases to credit cards have a positive or negative effect? Why?

Go Online PHSchool.com Students can find additional links related to the debate by visiting the *Economics: Principles in Action* at **PHSchool.com.**

Interdisciplinary Connections: History

Credit in History In past generations, it was more difficult for the average American to get a loan. Credit cards were non-existent. Today, millions of consumers use credit to finance an education, buy a car or home, or start a business. The Federal Equal Credit Opportunity Act, established in 1974, ensures that all consumers are given an equal chance to obtain credit. It prohibits discrimination on the basis of age, sex, race, color, religion, national origin, marital status, or reliance on income from public assistance.

Making the Connection Have students research this law to find out their rights and how to report violations if discrimination is suspected. Then ask students to use newspapers and other media sources to find examples of credit discrimination. Would students agree that easy credit is equally extended to every American? Why?

Answers to . . .

1. Federal laws ensure that people of all ages and backgrounds have greater access to credit based on their ability to repay.
2. The sum of all debt service payments from mortgages and other consumer debts has been staying around the historically high rate of 14% of disposable income since early 2001; this is up from 12% in 1992 and 1993.
3. Answers will vary.
4. About $1,500 billion; about $600 billion.

Government and the Economy

Introducing the Unit

Unit Summary

Unit 6 discusses ways that the government obtains and spends resources as well as how it intervenes in the economy. In Chapter 14 students learn about taxes and federal spending. Chapter 15 discusses fiscal policy and the varied ways in which economists have viewed the role of government in the economy. Chapter 16 explains monetary policy, including the money creation process, bank regulation, and the role of the Federal Reserve.

Focus Activity

Introduce Unit 6 to students by asking them to complete the Focus Activity. Remind them that the tax they are tracking is primarily sales tax, a small percentage of the overall taxes the government collects. Have students work in groups of three or four to list other taxes paid by Americans.

Government and the Economy

National Council on Economic Education

The following Voluntary National Content Standards in Economics are addressed in this unit:

★ Standard 12 ★ Standard 17
★ Standard 16 ★ Standard 20

See the Chapter Openers on pp. 358, 386, and 414 for a complete description of the standards addressed in each chapter.

Chapters in This Unit

14. *Taxes and Government Spending*

15. *Fiscal Policy*

16. *The Federal Reserve and Monetary Policy*

It's April 15. Where's your tax return?

Every year Americans rush to file their Federal Income Tax return by midnight on or around April 15. Whether you'll be receiving a refund or have to pay, you're probably asking yourself a few questions as you slip the envelope addressed to the IRS into the mail slot:

- What does the government do with all the money it collects?
- Why does the government sometimes spend more than it takes in?
- Is the national debt too large?

Governments, whether federal, state, or local, all need money to operate. This unit focuses on how governments gather financial resources, how they spend these resources, and the actions that the government sometimes takes to help ensure the health of the nation's economy.

Focus Activity

Keep track of all the transactions you make in one day—whether you're buying a bottle of juice or putting money in a parking meter. Calculate what portion of all of your spending goes to the local, state, or federal government.

Bibliography

Print

Alsop, Ronald J., ed., and staff of *The Wall Street Journal*. *The Wall Street Journal Almanac*. New York: Ballantine Books, 1998.

Understanding the Federal Debt and Deficit. New York: The Federal Reserve Bank of New York, 1994.

Multimedia

"Tax Whys—Understanding Taxes." Video. Introduces major issues of taxation and stresses the impact taxes have on individual consumers and producers. Joint Council on Economic Education and the Agency for Instructional Technology, distributed by the Federal Reserve Bank of St. Louis.

"The Federal Reserve." A comprehensive package of video and ancillary materials for teaching, produced by the Federal Reserve. Available at no cost to teachers from the Federal Reserve Bank of San Francisco.

Technology Center

Economics Video Library

Includes high-interest, chapter-specific segments produced by CNBC for

THE WALL STREET JOURNAL.
CLASSROOM EDITION

Simulations and Data Graphing CD-ROM

Provides interactive federal budget and stock market simulations and a data graphing tool designed to support instruction in economics.

PRENTICE HALL
TeacherEXPRESS™
Plan • Teach • Assess

Teacher Express CD-ROM offers powerful lesson planning, resource management, testing, and an interactive Teacher's Edition.

Prentice Hall Presentation Pro CD-ROM

Allows you to create custom lectures for every chapter.

Social Studies Skills Tutor CD-ROM

Provides interactive practice in geographic literacy, critical thinking and reading, visual analysis, and communications.

Exam*View*® Test Bank CD-ROM

Allows you to create, edit, and print out chapter level tests.

Transparency Resource Package

Illustrates key economic concepts and provides useful forms and templates for enhancing classroom discussions.

Section Reading Support Transparency System

Delivers the main idea of each section in the student text through graphic organizers.

Offers student-appropriate online activities and links as well as resources for the teacher. Be sure to check out this month's **eTeach** online discussion with a Master Economics Teacher.

Chapter 14 Taxes and Government Spending

For more pacing suggestions, see the Economics Pacing Guide in the Program Overview of the Teaching Resources.

Section Objectives	Print and Technology Resources	
1 What Are Taxes? *(pp. 359–363)* **Objectives** 1. Understand how the government uses taxes to fund programs. 2. Identify the roots of the concept of taxation in the United States Constitution. 3. Describe types of tax bases and tax structures. 4. List the characteristics of a good tax. 5. Identify who bears the burden of a tax.	• **Lesson Planner** Section 1 Lesson Plan, p. 57 • **Learning Styles Lesson Plans folder** Section 1 Lesson Plan, p. 33 • **Lesson Plans folder** Section 1 Lesson Plan, p. 50 • **Unit 6 folder** Guided Reading and Review, p. 2 Economic Skills, p. 10 Economic Cartoon, p. 14 Section 1 Quiz, p. 3 • **Source Articles folder** More Income Taxes, Please, pp. 42–44	• **Presentation Pro CD-ROM** Section 1 • **Transparency Resource Package** Economics Organizers, G7: Tree Map Graphic Organizer Economics Concepts, 14A: Tax Structures Economics Concepts, 14B: Economic Impact of Taxes • **Section Reading Support Transparency System** • **Social Studies Skills Tutor CD-ROM**
2 Federal Taxes *(pp. 365–369)* **Objectives** 1. Describe the process of paying individual income taxes. 2. Explain the basic characteristics of corporate income taxes. 3. Understand the purpose of Social Security, Medicare, and unemployment taxes. 4. Identify other types of taxes.	• **Lesson Planner** Section 2 Lesson Plan, p. 58 • **Lesson Plans folder** Section 2 Lesson Plan, p. 51 • **Unit 6 folder** Guided Reading and Review, p. 4 Careers in Economics, Tax Preparer, p. 13 Section 2 Quiz, p. 5 • **Presentation Pro CD-ROM** Section 2	• **Transparency Resource Package** Economics Organizers, G5: Web Graphic Organizer Economics Concepts, 14C: Major Sources of Federal Government Income Economics Concepts, 14D: Federal Taxes Economics Concepts, 14E: Value-Added Tax • **Section Reading Support Transparency System**
3 Federal Spending *(pp. 371–374)* **Objectives** 1. Distinguish between mandatory and discretionary spending. 2. Describe major entitlement programs. 3. Identify categories of discretionary spending. 4. Explain the impact of federal aid to state and local governments.	• **Lesson Planner** Section 3 Lesson Plan, p. 59 • **Lesson Plans folder** Section 3 Lesson Plan, p. 52 • **Economics Assessment Rubrics folder** Writing Assignment, pp. 6–7 • **Unit 6 folder** Guided Reading and Review, p. 6 Section 3 Quiz, p. 7 • **Presentation Pro CD-ROM** Section 3	• **Transparency Resource Package** Economics Organizers, G5: Web Graphic Organizer Economics Concepts, 14F: Federal Spending • **Section Reading Support Transparency System**
4 State and Local Taxes and Spending *(pp. 375–380)* **Objectives** 1. Explain how states use a budget to plan their spending. 2. Identify where state taxes are spent. 3. List the major sources of state tax revenue. 4. Describe local government spending and sources of revenue.	• **Lesson Planner** Section 4 Lesson Plan, p. 60 • **Learning Styles Lesson Plans folder** Section 4 Lesson Plan, p. 34 • **Lesson Plans folder** Section 4 Lesson Plan, p. 53 • **Economics Assessment Rubrics folder** Position Paper, pp. 22–23 • **Unit 6 folder** Guided Reading and Review, p. 8 Vocabulary Practice, p. 11 Economic Detective, p. 12 Section 4 Quiz, p. 9	• **Case Studies in Free Enterprise folder** John F. Kennedy, pp. 28–29 • **Presentation Pro CD-ROM** Section 4 • **Transparency Resource Package** Economics Organizers, G7: Tree Map Graphic Organizer Economics Concepts, 14G: State and Local Spending • **Section Reading Support Transparency System**

Differentiated Instruction

Considering Alternate Perspectives L2

Learning the perspectives of all sides of a conflict can help students understand the complex web of factors that influence a historical event. Asking students to consider alternate perspectives can aid them in understanding the event's outcome. Similar practices can help students understand complex debates in economics, including contemporary debates about taxes and government spending.

To begin, break students into groups and assign each group a particular nation involved in a conflict. Using outside research, have each group prepare a written statement expressing their nation's views and perspectives on a certain world event. Ask each group to answer the following questions in the context of their prepared statement:

- Why did your nation become involved in this conflict?
- Who is at fault for creating this conflict?
- What options did your nation have? Why did it ultimately choose one option?
- How could this conflict or issue have been presented?
- What were the circumstances occurring at the time in your nation that influenced decisions?

Then have the groups share their conclusions with the class. Point out that occasionally, all sides of an issue feel that their actions were inevitable. Ask students to brainstorm ways that the involved parties could have avoided the conflict at hand.

Visit the Social Studies area of the Prentice Hall Web site. There you can find additional links to enrich chapter content for *Economics: Principles in Action* as well as a self-test for students. Be sure to check out this month's **eTeach** online discussion with a Master Economics Teacher.

Web Code: mnf-6141

Running Out of Time?

- Use the **Presentation Pro CD-ROM** to create an outline for this chapter.
- Use the Chapter Summary in the **Chapter 14 Assessment,** p. 382.
- Use the Section Summaries for Chapter 14, from **Guide to the Essentials of Economics (English and Spanish).**

THE WALL STREET JOURNAL. CLASSROOM EDITION

Prentice Hall brings into the classroom the authoritative content of *The Wall Street Journal Classroom Edition.* See the Source Articles, Debating Current Issues, and You and Your Money folders in the **Teaching Resources**. Also, see Economics Video Library, "Private Prisons."

Assessment Resources

Chapter Assessment

Teaching Resources Unit 6, Chapter 14
- Section Quizzes, pp. 3, 5, 7, 9

Exam *View*® Test Bank CD-ROM Chapter 14

Economics Assessment Rubrics

Chapter 14 Self-Test, **Web Code:** mna-6141

Reading and Skills Evaluation

Progress Monitoring Assessments
- Screening Test
- Diagnostic Test of Social Studies Skills

Standardized Test Preparation

Test Prep Workbook

Test-Taking Strategies With Transparencies

Differentiated Instruction Key

L1	Special Needs	LPR	Less Proficient Readers
L2	Basic to Average	AR	Advanced Readers
L3	All Students	SN	Special Needs Students
L4	Average to Advanced	GT	Gifted and Talented
		ELL	English Language Learner

Chapter 14

Taxes and Government Spending

Introducing the Chapter

In this chapter, students will learn about the taxes levied by federal, state, and local governments. This chapter discusses the types of taxes, how they are collected, and how they are used by governments to provide services for people.

For additional links for *Economics: Principles in Action* provided by Prentice Hall and *The Wall Street Journal Classroom Edition,* visit the Social Studies area. Be sure to check out this month's **eTeach** online discussion with a Master Teacher.

Beyond the Lecture

You may cover the concepts in Chapter 14 in an activity-based style by using the following materials:

- **Technology Resources** appropriate for use with this chapter are noted on pp. 361, 363, 366, 367, 368, 369, 373, 374, 379, 380, and 383.
- **Presentation Pro CD-ROM** with animated graphs gives you an alternative method for organizing and delivering chapter content.
- **Activities** designed to meet the needs of students of mixed abilities and learning styles are noted throughout the chapter in the side columns.
- **Learning Styles Lesson Plans** provide alternate lessons for diverse learning styles. See pp. 33–34 of the Learning Styles Lesson Plans folder located in the Teaching Resources.

Economics Journal

Instruct students to record the taxes they pay in their Economics Journals. Students may include completed journal entries in an Economics Portfolio.

Chapter 14 Taxes and Government Spending

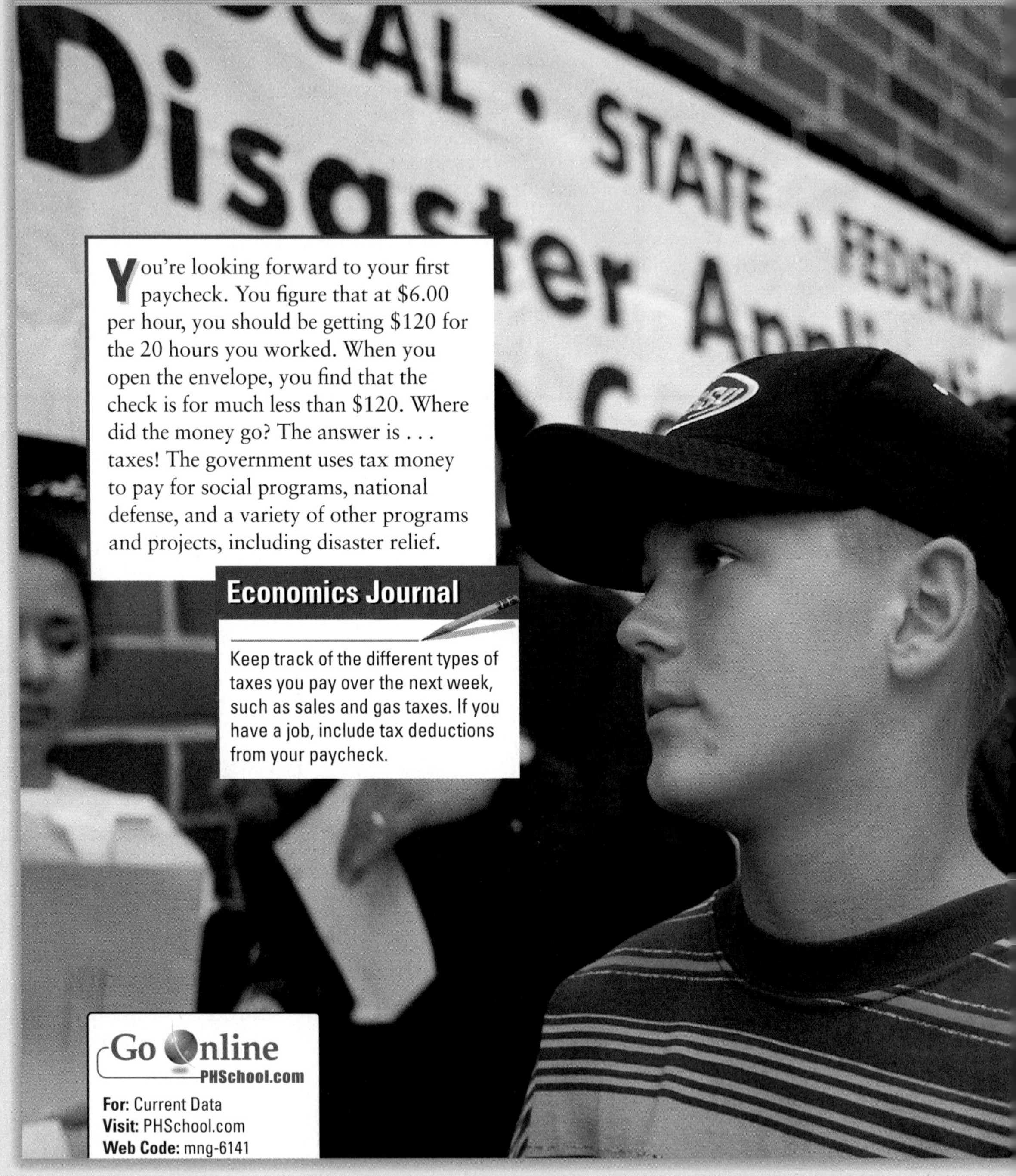

You're looking forward to your first paycheck. You figure that at $6.00 per hour, you should be getting $120 for the 20 hours you worked. When you open the envelope, you find that the check is for much less than $120. Where did the money go? The answer is . . . taxes! The government uses tax money to pay for social programs, national defense, and a variety of other programs and projects, including disaster relief.

Economics Journal

Keep track of the different types of taxes you pay over the next week, such as sales and gas taxes. If you have a job, include tax deductions from your paycheck.

Go Online PHSchool.com
For: Current Data
Visit: PHSchool.com
Web Code: mng-6141

National Council on Economic Education

The following Voluntary National Content Standard in Economics is addressed in this chapter:

★ **Standard 16** Students will understand that: There is an economic role for government to play in a market economy whenever the benefits of a government policy outweigh its costs. Governments often provide for national defense, address environmental concerns, define and protect property rights, and attempt to make markets more competitive. Most government policies also redistribute income.

For more information about the standards, contact the National Council on Economic Education

1140 Avenue of the Americas
New York, NY 10036
1-800-338-1192

Section 1 What Are Taxes?

Preview

Objectives

After studying this section you will be able to:

1. **Understand** how the government uses taxes to fund programs.
2. **Identify** the roots of the concept of taxation in the United States Constitution.
3. **Describe** types of tax bases and tax structures.
4. **List** the characteristics of a good tax.
5. **Identify** who bears the burden of a tax.

Section Focus

Local, state, and national governments generate revenue by charging taxes. The Constitution spells out specific limits on governments' powers to tax. Taxation can take several different forms, and people disagree over which method of taxation is most fair.

Key Terms

tax
revenue
tax base
individual income tax
sales tax
property tax
corporate income tax
proportional tax
progressive tax
regressive tax
incidence of a tax

Looking at all of the taxes taken from your paycheck can be discouraging. It can feel like all of that money is being taken from you for someone else's use. Frustration over taxes is, after all, what led American colonists to go to war against Britain and declare independence. How, then, is anything different today?

Although money is taken from your paycheck, it is not done without your consent. As citizens of the United States, we authorize the government, through the Constitution and our elected representatives in Congress, to raise money in the form of taxes. Why?

Funding Government Programs

A **tax** is a required payment to a local, state, or national government. Taxation is the primary way that the government collects money. Taxes give the government the money it needs to operate.

The income received by a government from taxes and other nontax sources is called **revenue.** Without revenue from taxes, the government would not be able to provide the goods and services that we not only benefit from, but that we expect the government to provide. For example, we authorize the government to provide national defense, highways, education, and law enforcement. We also ask the government to provide help to people in need.

All of these goods and services cost money—in workers' salaries, in materials, in land and labor. All members of our society share these costs through the payment of taxes.

tax *a required payment to a local, state, or national government*

revenue *income received by a government from taxes and nontax sources*

Taxes and the Constitution

Taxation is a powerful tool. The founders of the United States did not, without careful consideration, give their new government the power to tax. The Constitution they created spells out specific limits on the government's power to tax.

The Power to Tax

The Framers of the Constitution gave each branch of government certain powers and duties. The first power granted to Congress is the power to tax. This is Article 1, Section 8, Clause 1:

To lay and collect taxes, duties, imposts and excises, to pay the debts, and provide

Section 1 What Are Taxes?

Objectives You may wish to call students' attention to the objectives in the Section Preview. The objectives are reflected in the main headings of the section.

Bellringer Ask students to recall the colonists' cry of "No taxation without representation!" Have students explain what the colonists were angry about and why it is important that people who are taxed be represented in government. Then explain that this section will introduce them to types of taxes.

Vocabulary Builder Most of the key terms in this section have other meanings in other contexts. Ask students to choose three key terms and link their economic meaning to another meaning. For example, if they choose *progressive tax,* they may say that someone who is progressive is always moving ahead. A progressive tax rate "moves ahead" with income level.

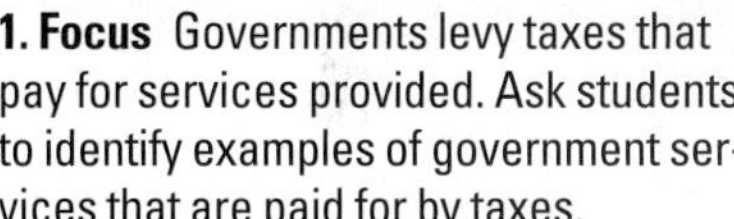

Lesson Plan

Teaching the Main Concepts L3

1. Focus Governments levy taxes that pay for services provided. Ask students to identify examples of government services that are paid for by taxes.

2. Instruct Begin by explaining the purpose of taxation and the historical background that led to constitutional limits on this practice. Then introduce students to the three tax structures: proportional, progressive, and regressive. Discuss the four characteristics of a good tax. Finally, help students to understand how principles of supply and demand can affect the amount of tax they pay.

3. Close/Reteach Remind students that different tax structures distribute the tax burden among taxpayers in different ways. Ask them to distinguish among proportional, progressive, and regressive taxes, and have them create an organizer highlighting these differences.

Building Key Concepts: Graphing the Main Idea

Government To build understanding of how and why the **government** collects taxes, have students complete a tree map graphic organizer like the one at the right. Remind students that a tree map shows an outline for a main topic, main ideas, and supporting details. Encourage students to use the main heads and subheads in the section to organize their tree maps.

Section Reading Support Transparencies A template and the answers for this graphic organizer can be found in Chapter 14, Section 1 of the Section Reading Support Transparency System.

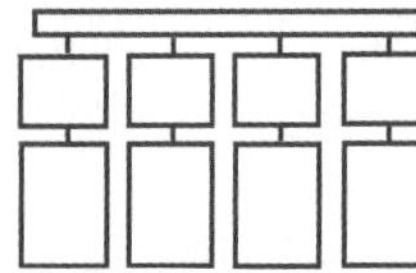

 **Guided Reading and Review**
Unit 6 folder, p. 2 asks students to identify the main ideas of the section and to define or identify key terms.

Differentiated Instruction L3
(Reteaching) Ask students to create two lists. The first list should include the limits that the Constitution places on the federal government's authority to create and collect taxes. The second list should include examples of how taxes are used to fund federal programs.

Background

Economics in History

Tax Freedom Day (TFD) has occurred later and later each year since the early years of the twentieth century. What is it?

Economists track the number of days average Americans must work to satisfy their federal, state, and local tax obligations. The day after the last day of working for the government is called Tax Freedom Day: the day when people begin working for themselves. In 1913 TFD came on January 30. By 1930 TFD had slipped all the way to February 13. Near the start of World War II, in 1940, Americans were working for the government until March 8.

TFD continued to fall later and later in the year until tax cuts and a recession reduced tax revenues. In 2000, TFD fell on April 30. By 2003, it had moved back to April 19. Because federal income taxes are progressive, most Americans enjoyed a personal Tax Freedom Day before this date.

tax base *income, property, good, or service that is subject to a tax*

individual income tax *a tax on a person's earnings*

sales tax *a tax on the dollar value of a good or service being sold*

property tax *a tax on the value of a property*

corporate income tax *a tax on the value of a company's profits*

for the common defense and general welfare of the United States; but all duties, imposts, and excises shall be uniform throughout the United States.

This clause is the basis for federal tax laws.

Limits on the Power to Tax

The Constitution specifically limits certain kinds of taxes. Two of those limits are in the taxation clause. First, the purpose of a tax must be for the "common defense and general welfare." A tax cannot bring in money that goes to individual interests. Second, federal taxes must be the same in every state. The federal gas tax, for example, cannot be $.04 a gallon in Maryland and $.10 a gallon in South Dakota.

Other provisions of the Constitution also limit the kinds of taxes Congress can impose. For example, Congress cannot tax church services because that would violate the freedom of religion promised by the First Amendment. Another clause of the Constitution prohibits taxing exports. The government can collect taxes only on imports—goods brought into the United States. (Congress can limit or prohibit the export of certain goods, however, such as technology or weaponry.)

Yet another clause of the Constitution (Article 1, Section 9, Clause 4) prohibits Congress from levying, or imposing, taxes unless they are divided among the states according to population. Because of this provision, it took the Sixteenth Amendment to legalize the income tax. This amendment was ratified in 1913.

Tax Bases and Tax Structures

Despite these limits, the government actually collects a wide variety of taxes. Economists describe these taxes in different ways. First, they describe a tax according to the value of the object taxed. Second, they describe how the tax is structured.

Tax Bases

A **tax base** is the income, property, good, or service that is subject to a tax. The tax base might be a person's earnings (**individual income tax**), the dollar value of a good or service being sold (**sales tax**), the value of a property (**property tax**), or the value of a company's profits (**corporate income tax**). When government policymakers create a

Figure 14.1 **Three Types of Tax Structures**

Type of Tax	Description	Example	Ron's taxes on $50,000 income	Mary's taxes on $150,000 income
Proportional	A constant percentage of income is taken in taxes as income increases	"Flat" tax	$7,500, or 15 percent of income	$22,500, or 15 percent of income
Progressive	A larger percentage of income is taken in taxes as income increases	Income tax	$5,000, or 10 percent of income	$45,000, or 30 percent of income
Regressive	A smaller percentage of income is taken in taxes as income increases	Sales tax	$2,000, or 5 percent of total purchases of $40,000; tax bill is 4 percent of income	$3,000, or 5 percent of total purchases of $60,000; tax bill is 2 percent of income

This chart shows how three different tax structures would affect a taxpayer named Ron with an income of $50,000 and a taxpayer named Mary with an income of $150,000.
Income How does Mary's higher income affect the taxes she pays in each type of tax structure?

Econ 101: Key Concepts Made Easy

Markets and Prices To help students understand the **incidence of a tax**, briefly review the principles of supply and demand, especially elasticity of demand, found in Chapter 5. Help them to see that if people will buy the same amount of a good even when the price rises—that is, if the demand is inelastic—the tax burden is likely to fall mainly on consumers. If, however, demand is elastic, so that people buy less of a good when the price rises, producers will bear the greater burden.

Ask students to make a list of goods that are (or might be) taxed. Then have students characterize the elasticity of demand for each good and the incidence of a tax on that item.

Answer to . . .

Building Key Concepts Mary pays much higher taxes with a proportional or a progressive tax structure; her taxes are highest under a progressive tax structure. With a regressive structure she pays little more than Ron.

new tax, they first decide what the base will be for the tax: income, sales, property, profits, or some other category.

Next, the government decides how to structure the tax on that particular base. As shown in Figure 14.1, economists describe three different tax structures: proportional, progressive, and regressive.

Proportional Taxes

A **proportional tax** is a tax for which the percentage of income paid in taxes remains the same for all income levels. Leslie Wilson, a corporate executive, earns $350,000 a year. Tony Owens, a nurse, earns $50,000 a year. If a 6 percent proportional tax were levied on their incomes, Leslie would pay 6 percent of $350,000, or $21,000, in taxes. Tony would pay 6 percent of $50,000, or $3,000. With a proportional income tax, whether income goes up or down, the percentage of income paid in taxes stays the same.

Progressive Taxes

A **progressive tax** is a tax for which the percentage of income paid in taxes increases as income increases. As income rises, the percentage of income paid in taxes also rises. People with very small incomes might pay no tax at all.

The federal income tax is the clearest example of a progressive tax in the United States. A sample progressive income tax system is shown in Figure 14.2. Notice that the tax rate in this example rises from 15, to 25, and then to 30 percent as income rises. This is a progressive tax rate structure because as income rises, the percentage of income paid in taxes also rises.

Regressive Taxes

A **regressive tax** is a tax for which the percentage of income paid in taxes decreases as income increases. For example, although the sales tax rate remains constant, a sales tax is regressive. This is because higher-income households spend a lower proportion of their incomes on taxable goods and services. As a result, although they may pay more actual dollars in sales taxes, the proportion of their income spent on sales taxes is lower than that of lower-income households.

Figure 14.2 **Progressive Income Tax**

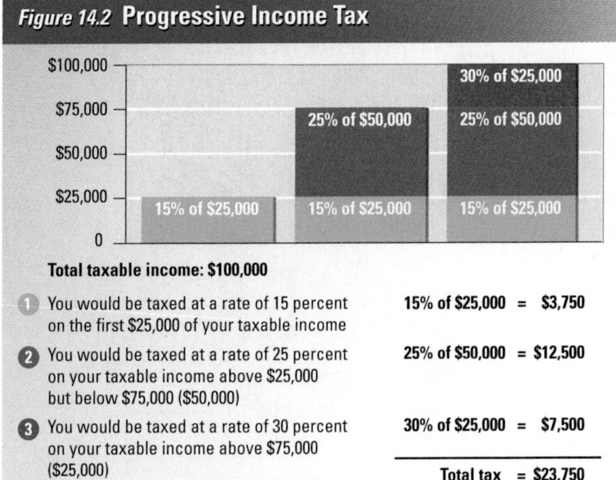

$100,000
$75,000
$50,000
$25,000
0
15% of $25,000
25% of $50,000
30% of $25,000
Total taxable income: $100,000
1 You would be taxed at a rate of 15 percent on the first $25,000 of your taxable income
15% of $25,000 = $3,750
2 You would be taxed at a rate of 25 percent on your taxable income above $25,000 but below $75,000 ($50,000)
25% of $50,000 = $12,500
3 You would be taxed at a rate of 30 percent on your taxable income above $75,000 ($25,000)
30% of $25,000 = $7,500
Total tax = $23,750

In a progressive tax structure, the higher a taxpayer's income, the greater percentage he or she must pay in taxes. This chart shows a sample progressive income tax for a taxpayer with total taxable income of $100,000.
Income According to the chart, what would be the total tax on taxable income of $65,000?

Characteristics of a Good Tax

Though it is sometimes difficult to decide whether a specific tax is proportional, progressive, or regressive, economists do generally agree on what makes a good tax. A good tax should have four characteristics: simplicity, efficiency, certainty, and equity, or fairness.

- *Simplicity* Tax laws should be simple and easily understood. Taxpayers and businesses should be able to keep the necessary records, prepare their own tax forms, and pay the taxes on a predictable schedule.
- *Efficiency* Government administrators should be able to collect taxes without spending too much time or money. Similarly, taxpayers should be able to pay taxes without giving up too much time. They should also not have to pay too much money in fees.

proportional tax *a tax for which the percentage of income paid in taxes remains the same for all income levels*

progressive tax *a tax for which the percentage of income paid in taxes increases as income increases*

regressive tax *a tax for which the percentage of income paid in taxes decreases as income increases*

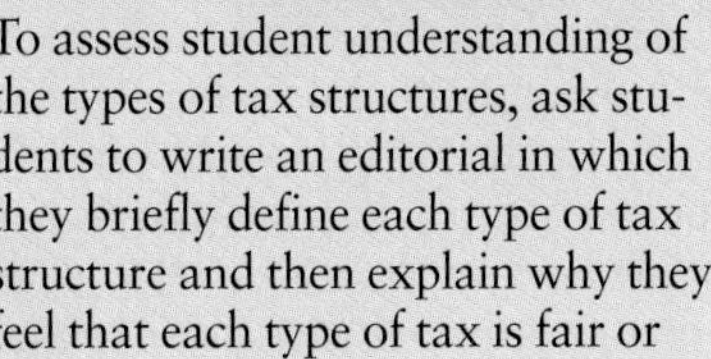

Differentiated Instruction L3

To assess student understanding of the types of tax structures, ask students to write an editorial in which they briefly define each type of tax structure and then explain why they feel that each type of tax is fair or unfair.

Learning Styles Activity
Learning Styles Lesson Plans folder, p. 33 asks pairs of students to create brochures supporting or criticizing the idea of a proportional tax structure for individual income tax.

Differentiated Instruction 

Have students use the following method to take notes on the section. Tell them first to draw a line down the length of their paper, about one third of the way from the left side. Have them paraphrase important points from the section in the right column. Then, in the left column, tell them to write questions that can be answered by their notes. Tell them that they can use these notes for review by covering up the right column with a sheet of paper and answering the questions from the left column. LPR

Transparency Resource Package
Economics Concepts, 14A: Tax Structures

Economic Cartoon
Unit 6 folder, p. 14 gives students practice in interpreting cartoons about section content.

Block Scheduling Strategies

Consider these suggestions to take advantage of extended class time:

- Organize students into pairs. Have one student in each pair investigate the taxes that the British imposed on the American colonists and find out how those taxes were collected. Have the other student in the pair investigate why the colonists were opposed to the taxes and how they made their displeasure known. Then have each pair create a summary of its findings.
- Have groups of three to four students search through newspapers and magazines for letters to the editor, editorials, or cartoons about taxes. Then have each group make a presentation about what they have found, drawing conclusions about how people view taxes and are affected by them.

Answer to . . .
Building Key Concepts $13,750

Differentiated Instruction L3

(Enrichment) After students have read about the characteristics of good taxes, organize the class into several "taxing bodies." Explain that each taxing body must create a tax that satisfies the four characteristics of a good tax. Each group must also show how its tax satisfies the two principles of fairness. Finally, ask the class to determine which of the proposed taxes is the best tax and to explain why.

Differentiated Instruction L2

Ask students to look up the dictionary definitions of *simplicity, efficiency, certainty,* and *equity.* For each word they are likely to find several shades of meaning. Ask them to choose the meaning that they think is most appropriate in the context of taxes and then to explain their choices. ELL

Differentiated Instruction L3

Organize students into small groups. Assign each group a different type of manufactured product. (Choose goods that are common but that vary in their elasticity of demand.) Then explain to students that the government has just imposed a 10 percent tax on all manufactured goods. Ask each group to prepare a brief oral presentation explaining who bears the burden of this tax as it applies to their assigned product. Remind them to consider the elasticity of demand for their particular good.

Go Online PHSchool.com Typing in the Web Code when prompted will bring students directly to the article.

▲ **This political cartoon makes fun of the saying, "The only sure things in life are death and taxes." Why are taxes necessary?**

- *Certainty* Certainty is also a characteristic of a good tax. It should be clear to the taxpayer when a tax is due, how much money is due, and how the tax should be paid.
- *Equity* The tax system should be fair, so that no one bears too much or too little of the tax burden.

Determining Fairness

Although everyone agrees that a tax system should be fair, people often disagree on what "fair" means. Over time, economists have proposed two different ideas about how to measure the fairness of a tax.

The first idea is called the benefits-received principle. According to this principle, a person should pay taxes based on the level of benefits he or she expects to receive. People who drive, for example, pay gasoline taxes that are used to build and maintain highways. In this way, the people who receive the most benefit from the roads also contribute the most to their upkeep.

THE WALL STREET JOURNAL. CLASSROOM EDITION

In the News Read more about taxes in "Hard Habit to Break," an article in The Wall Street Journal Classroom Edition.

Go Online
The Wall Street Journal Classroom Edition
For: Current Events
Visit: PHSchool.com
Web Code: mnc-6141

The second idea about fairness is called the ability-to-pay principle. According to this principle, people should pay taxes according to their ability to pay. The ability-to-pay principle is the idea behind a progressive income tax: people who earn more income pay more taxes.

Balancing Tax Revenues and Tax Rates

How much revenue does a good tax generate? The answer is "enough, but not too much." That is, enough so that citizens' needs are met, but not so much that the tax discourages production. For example, if a company has to pay $100,000 in taxes, it will not be able to use that $100,000 to expand production. If tax rates are lower, however, the company can use more of its income to stimulate production rather than to pay taxes. Ultimately, many people argue, the economy benefits from lower, rather than higher, tax rates.

Who Bears the Tax Burden?

To fully evaluate the fairness of a tax, it is important to think about who actually bears the burden of the tax. Taxes affect more than just the people who send in the checks to pay them. Why? The answer lies in supply and demand analysis.

Suppose that the government imposes a gasoline tax of $.50 per gallon and collects the tax from service stations. You may think that the burden of the tax falls only on the service stations, because they mail the checks to the government. Graphs A and B in Figure 14.3, however, provide a different set of answers.

Both Graphs A and B show two supply curves: an original supply line and a line showing the supply after the $.50 tax is imposed. When a tax is imposed on a good, the cost of supplying the good increases. The supply of the good then decreases at each and every price level. This shifts the supply curve to the left.

Before the tax, the market was in equilibrium, and consumers bought gas at $1.00

Preparing for Standardized Tests

Have students read the section titled "Characteristics of a Good Tax" and then answer the question below.

When taxpayers know when a tax is due, how much is due, and how it is to be paid, which requirement of a good tax is being fulfilled?

A equity
B simplicity
(C) certainty
D efficiency

Answer to . . .

Cartoon Caption Taxes are necessary to fund public goods and services and to fund the functions of government.

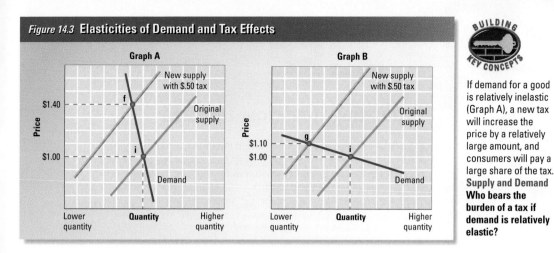

Figure 14.3 Elasticities of Demand and Tax Effects

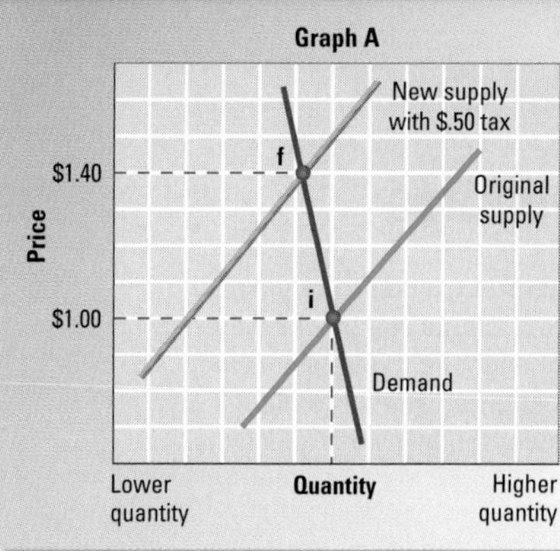

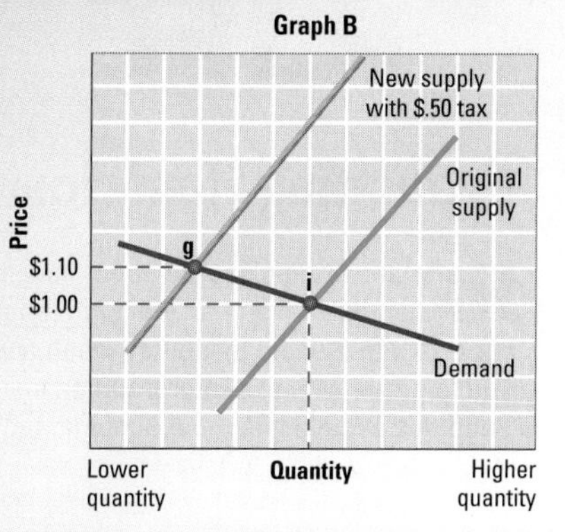

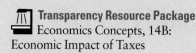

If demand for a good is relatively inelastic (Graph A), a new tax will increase the price by a relatively large amount, and consumers will pay a large share of the tax. **Supply and Demand Who bears the burden of a tax if demand is relatively elastic?**

per gallon. This is shown as point i on Graph A above. If demand for gas is relatively inelastic (that is, if consumers buy about the same amount no matter what the price), the tax will increase the price of each gallon by a relatively large amount. Consumers will bear a large share of the tax. This is shown in Graph A. Demand is inelastic, so the demand curve is relatively steep, and a $.50 tax increases the equilibrium price by $.40 (from $1.00 to $1.40 from point i to point f). In other words, consumers pay about four fifths of the tax.

In contrast, if demand is relatively elastic, the demand curve will be relatively flat, as in Graph B. Consumers will pay a relatively small part of the tax. As Graph B shows, a $.50 tax increases the equilibrium price by only $.10 (from $1.00 to $1.10 from point i to point g). In this case, consumers pay only one fifth of the tax. The service stations pay the other four fifths.

This example shows the **incidence of a tax**—that is, the final burden of a tax. When policymakers consider a new tax, they examine who will actually bear the burden. As in the example above, producers can "pass on" the burden to consumers. Generally, the more inelastic the demand, the more easily the seller can shift the tax to consumers. The more elastic the demand, the more the seller bears the burden.

incidence of a tax *the final burden of a tax*

Section 1 Assessment

Progress Monitoring *Online*
For: Self-quiz with vocabulary practice
Web Code: mna-6145

Key Terms and Main Ideas

1. Why do governments impose taxes?
2. What is the difference between a **progressive tax** and a **regressive tax?**
3. What are the four characteristics of a good tax?
4. Describe the benefits-received principle. How does it differ from the ability-to-pay principle?

Applying Economic Concepts

5. ***Try This*** Suppose that your town decides to levy a tax to raise funds for construction, maintenance, and other expenses for local schools. Should the tax be proportional, progressive, or regressive? Explain your answer.
6. ***Critical Thinking*** Analyze the impact of the power to tax as expressed in the Constitution on tax policies today.

For: Discussion Activity
Visit: PHSchool.com
Web Code: mnd-6141

Progress Monitoring *Online*
For additional assessment, have students access Progress Monitoring Online at **Web Code:** mna-6145

Go Online PHSchool.com Typing in the Web Code when prompted will bring students directly to detailed instructions for this activity.

Transparency Resource Package Economics Concepts, 14B: Economic Impact of Taxes

GTE Guide to the Essentials Chapter 14, Section 1, p. 58 provides support for students who need additional review of the section content. Spanish support is available in the Spanish edition of the guide on p. 58.

Quiz Unit 6 folder, p. 3 includes questions to check students' understanding of Section 1 content.

Presentation Pro CD-ROM Quiz provides multiple-choice questions to check students' understanding of Section 1 content.

Answers to . . .

Section 1 Assessment

1. To provide public goods and services and to fund the functions of government.
2. A progressive tax is a tax that causes the percentage of income paid in taxes to increase as income increases. A regressive tax is a tax in which the percentage of income paid in taxes goes down as income increases.
3. simplicity, efficiency, certainty, and equity
4. The benefits-received principle states that people should pay taxes based on the level of benefits they receive from the government. In contrast, the ability-to-pay principle states that people should pay taxes according to their ability to pay.
5. Possible answers: The tax should be proportional because the school is a public resource, so everyone should pay an equal portion of their income to fund it. The tax should be progressive because the ability to pay varies. The tax should be regressive because people who make the most money are already paying the most in taxes.
6. Although the Constitution grants Congress the power to tax, it also limits certain kinds of taxes; for example, a federal tax such as the gas tax must be the same rate in every state.

Answer to . . .

Building Key Concepts Producers or intermediaries bear the burden.

Skills for LIFE

Evaluating Historical Debates

1. Focus Ask student to define "point of view."

2. Instruct Explain to students that it is the task of historians to interpret events, putting them into perspective and making generalizations. When they do this, their interpretations are often based on a particular point of view. Two historians, using the same facts, may make differing generalizations and draw dissimilar conclusions. The reader must be able to discern the author's point of view.

3. Close/Reteach To provide additional practice, see the Economic Skills Activity below.

Economic Skills Activity
Unit 6 folder, p. 10

Social Studies Skills Tutor CD-ROM offers interactive practice in critical thinking and reading, visual analysis, and communication.

Skills for LIFE

Evaluating Historical Debates

Historians often disagree about how to interpret events in the past. Sometimes a historian will write about past events in a biased way. It's important to be able to identify when a writer might be trying to convince you to agree with one interpretation instead of giving you a broader view. Read this sample historical account and answer the following questions.

1. **Identify statements that might be misleading.** Authors will sometimes oversimplify their statements or use broad generalizations in order to make their arguments look stronger than they really are. (a) List three sentences from the passage that seem to be using misleading oversimplications. (b) Why do you think those sentences are oversimplifications?

The Social Security program was developed during the Great Depression. At first, Social Security was proposed as a public pension system that would save some amount of a worker's earnings and then give that amount back to him when he was elderly. The people who needed money most were already elderly when the plan was announced, though, and they wouldn't get anything from it because they hadn't already been paying in. Congress and the general public had no interest in the plan.

The only enthusiastic supporters of Social Security were a team of economists who came up with a plan for old-age insurance. In this plan, the pension would be supported by a general revenue tax, like the income tax. President Roosevelt changed the plan so that the pension payments came out of a special payroll tax instead. This change was supposed to help the system be more self-sufficient.

Although no one really wanted to pass Social Security legislation, President Roosevelt had been convinced by the economists that it was the right answer for the country's problems. In order to convince Congress, Roosevelt had to make some deals. He offered to fund other social service programs in return for support for Social Security. After all the deals were made, Congress passed Roosevelt's flawed version of the economists' plan for Social Security.

2. **Determine the author's point of view or interpretation.** If you think that an author is misleading to persuade you, think about what the author's point of view is. (a) Based on this passage, what do you think the author's opinion of the Social Security system is? (b) What specific sentences or phrases led you to that conclusion?

3. **Look at how facts are used to support the author's interpretation.** Historical accounts should always be based on facts, but individual facts can be used to support different interpretations. (a) Identify three facts in the passage that could be verified by other sources. (b) Show how the author uses those facts to support her interpretation of the historical event. (c) Think of another interpretation that could be supported by the same facts.

Additional Practice

Think of an event in your own past that could have more than one interpretation. Write a short historical account that supports one possible interpretation, and then write a second account that uses the same facts but supports a different interpretation.

Answers

1. (a) "Congress and the general public had no interest in the plan." "The only enthusiastic supporters of Social Security were a team of economists . . . ." "Although no one really wanted to pass Social Security legislation, President Roosevelt had been convinced. . . ." (b) They are generalizations that are too broad to be entirely true.
2. (a) The author believes that Social Security was flawed from the beginning. (b) ". . .Roosevelt had to make some deals." ". . . Congress passed Roosevelt's flawed version of the economists' plan. . . ."
3. (a) "At first, Social Security was proposed as a public pension system that would save some of the worker's earnings. . . . Congress and the general public had no interest in the plan. President Roosevelt changed the plan so that the pension payments came out of a special payroll tax instead." (b) The author uses the fact that Social Security was changed by President Roosevelt and deals were made with Congress to support the idea that the President's version was flawed. (c) Another author may believe that Roosevelt's changes improved the original plan.

Additional Practice

Student essays should illustrate the ability to think critically about an issue and present competing viewpoints.

Section 2 Federal Taxes

Preview

Objectives

After studying this section you will be able to:

1. **Describe** the process of paying individual income taxes.
2. **Explain** the basic characteristics of corporate income taxes.
3. **Understand** the purpose of Social Security, Medicare, and unemployment taxes.
4. **Identify** other types of taxes.

Section Focus

The federal income taxes that households and families pay help to fund government programs. Other types of taxes are levied on specific items for specific purposes.

Key Terms

withholding
tax return
taxable income
personal exemption
deductions
FICA
Social Security
Medicare
estate tax
gift tax
tariff
tax incentive

During fiscal year 2004, the federal government took in about $1.88 trillion in taxes. If you divide up this federal tax revenue among all the people in the United States, it comes to about $6,300 per person. How does the government get all this money?

The federal government has six major sources of tax revenue. They are individual and corporate income taxes, social insurance taxes, excise taxes, estate and gift taxes, and taxes on imports.

Individual Income Taxes

The federal government levies a tax on individuals' taxable income. As Figure 14.4 shows, individual income taxes make up the federal government's main source of revenue. About 45 percent of the federal government's revenues come from the payment of individual income taxes.

"Pay-As-You-Earn" Taxation

The amount of federal income tax a person owes is determined on an annual basis. In theory, the federal government could wait until the end of the tax year to collect individual income taxes. In reality, that would be a problem for both taxpayers and the government. Like other employers, the government has to pay regularly for rent, supplies, services, and employees' salaries. A single annual payment from all the nation's taxpayers at once would make meeting these expenses difficult.

Similarly, many people might have trouble paying their taxes in one large sum. For these reasons, federal income tax is collected in a "pay-as-you-earn" system. This means that individuals usually pay

Figure 14.4 **Federal Revenue, 2004**

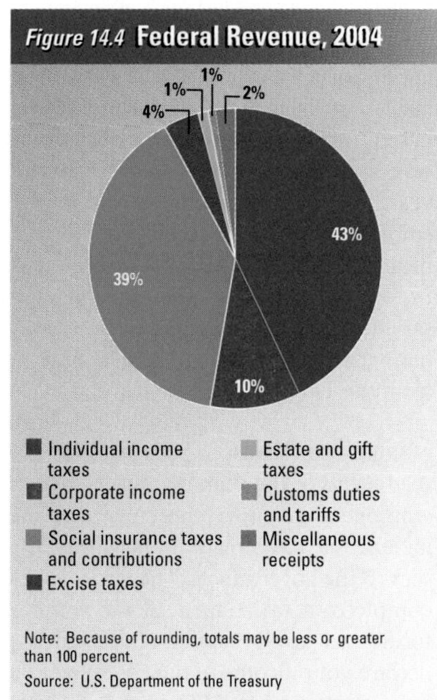

Note: Because of rounding, totals may be less or greater than 100 percent.
Source: U.S. Department of the Treasury

Sources of government revenue include the taxes shown on this graph. **Government Analyze the categories of revenue in the federal budget. What are the largest sources of federal revenue?**

Go Online
PHSchool.com
Web Code: mng-6142

Graphing the Main Idea

Government To build understanding of the information on taxes collected by the **government,** ask students to complete two web graphic organizers. Tell them to make an organizer like the one at the right for income taxes and another for Social Security, Medicare, and unemployment taxes. Remind students that a web shows a main idea and its supporting details.

Section Reading Support Transparencies A template and the answers for this graphic organizer can be found in Chapter 14, Section 2 of the Section Reading Support Transparency System.

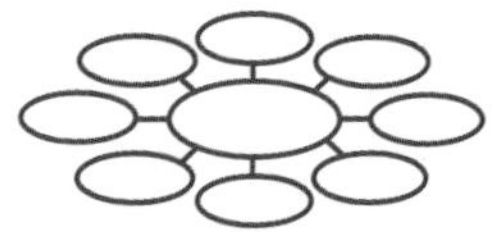

Section 2

Federal Taxes

Objectives You may wish to call students' attention to the objectives in the Section Preview. The objectives are reflected in the main headings of the section.

Bellringer Ask students to consider why employees are required to fill out and submit tax returns on April 15 if employers send taxes to the federal government during the year. Explain that this section will answer that question and others about taxes and the federal government.

Vocabulary Builder Ask students to create a quiz of 11 fill-in-the-blank questions about the terms. Have students exchange quizzes, complete them, and return them to the authors for correction.

Lesson Plan

Teaching the Main Concepts 

1. Focus The federal government collects six major types of taxes to keep the government running and to provide services for people who live in the United States. Ask students to list as many types of federal taxes as they can.

2. Instruct Begin by discussing individual income taxes—what they are and how they are collected. Then compare them with corporate income taxes. Go on to explain the other types of federal taxes that are withheld from an employee's paycheck and the tax paid by employers. Finally, compare and contrast excise, estate, gift, and import taxes.

3. Close/Reteach Remind students that the federal government collects taxes from individuals, corporations, and employers. Ask students to explain how each tax is collected.

Answer to . . .

Building Key Concepts The largest sources of federal revenue are individual income taxes and social insurance taxes and contributions.

Guided Reading and Review
Unit 6 folder, p. 4 asks students to identify the main ideas of the section and to define or identify key terms.

Transparency Resource Package
Economics Concepts, 14C: Major Sources of Federal Government Income

Differentiated Instruction L2

Before students read this section, ask them to list everything they know about federal taxes and also what they would like to know. Then instruct them to look for answers as they read the section. Have them create a study guide to show what they learn. Discuss with students anything they wanted to know that was not covered in the section. LPR

Differentiated Instruction 

Ask students to create a flow chart that illustrates the process of paying income taxes. The flow chart should begin with a new employee filling out a W-4 form, declaring deductions, and so on, and end with the employee submitting a tax return.

Answer to . . .

Photo Caption roughly 13 percent (FICA and federal); 16 percent (total)

HOURS AND EARNINGS		TAXES AND DEDUCTIONS	
Hours	Earnings	Description	Amount
20	200.00	FICA	15.20
		Federal	10.25
		State	5.10
		City	1.00
		Total Taxes	**31.55**
TOTAL			
Taxable Wages		**Less Taxes**	**Net Pay**
200.00		31.55	168.45

SAFE CHECK

▲ **This young worker's pay stub shows that her employer, as required by law, has withheld part of her earnings for taxes. What percentage of this worker's pay was withheld for federal taxes? For total taxes?**

withholding *taking tax payments out of an employee's pay before he or she receives it*

tax return *form used to file income taxes*

taxable income *income on which tax must be paid; total income minus exemptions and deductions*

personal exemption *set amount that you subtract from your gross income for yourself, your spouse, and any dependents*

deductions *variable amounts that you can subtract, or deduct, from your gross income*

most of their income tax throughout the year as they earn income. In mid-April, they pay any additional income taxes they owe.

Tax Withholding

Employers are responsible in part for carrying out the system for collecting federal income taxes. They do so by **withholding,** or taking payments out of your pay before you receive it. The amount they withhold is based on an estimate of how much you will owe in federal income taxes for the entire year. After withholding the money, the employer forwards it to the federal government as an "installment payment" on your upcoming annual income tax bill. On the sample pay stub shown above, the employer has withheld $10.25 in federal income taxes from this employee's paycheck.

Filing a Tax Return

At the end of the year, employers give their employees a report showing how much income tax has already been withheld and sent to the government. The employee then completes a tax return. A **tax return** is a form used to file income taxes. On it you declare your income to the government and figure out your taxable income.

Taxable income is a person's gross (or total) income minus exemptions and deductions. Gross income includes earned income—salaries, wages, tips, and commissions. It also includes income from investments such as interest on savings accounts and dividends from stock.

Personal exemptions are set amounts that you subtract from your gross income for yourself, your spouse, and any dependents. **Deductions** are variable amounts that you can subtract, or deduct, from your gross income. Deductions include such items as interest on a mortgage, donations to charity, some medical expenses, and state and local tax payments.

Completing a tax return allows you to determine whether the amount of income taxes you have already paid was higher or lower than the actual amount of tax you owe. If you have paid more than you owe, the government sends you a refund. If you have paid less than you owe, you must pay the balance to the government. All federal income tax returns must be sent to the Internal Revenue Service, or IRS, by midnight on April 15 (or the next business day if April 15 falls on a weekend).

Econ 101: Key Concepts Made Easy

Trade To help students understand **tariffs,** explain that a tariff is a kind of economic ticket of admission to the United States for foreign goods. Paying the tariff gets products in the market door, so to speak, so that they can be sold. Be sure that students understand that American citizens also pay tariffs—called customs duties—when they return from a foreign country with goods they purchased in that country that exceed a certain value set by the U.S. government. Ask students who have traveled in foreign countries to describe the customs process. If no students have traveled abroad, invite faculty members who have done so to talk about their experiences.

Tax Brackets

The federal income tax is a progressive tax. In other words, the tax rate rises with the amount of taxable income. The tax rate schedule in Figure 14.5 shows that in 2005, there were six rates. Each applied to a different range of income, or tax bracket. For example, married couples who filed a return together (a joint return) and had a taxable income of $14,600 or less paid 10 percent income tax. The highest rate—35 percent—was paid by high-income single people or married couples on the portion of their taxable incomes that exceeded $326,450. Each year, the IRS publishes new tax rate schedules that reflect any changes in the federal tax code.

Corporate Income Taxes

Like individuals, corporations must pay federal income tax on their taxable income. Corporate taxes made up less than 10 percent of federal revenues in recent years.

Determining a corporation's taxable income can be a challenge because businesses can take many deductions. That is, they can subtract many expenses from their income before they reach the amount of income that is subject to taxation. For example, companies deduct the cost of employees' health insurance. Many other costs of doing business can also be deducted.

Like individual income tax rates, corporate income tax rates are progressive. In 2005, rates began at 15 percent on the first $50,000 of taxable income. The highest corporate income tax rate was 35 percent on all taxable corporate income above $10,000,000.

Social Security, Medicare, and Unemployment Taxes

In addition to withholding money for income taxes, employers withhold money for taxes authorized under the Federal Insurance Contributions Act, or FICA. **FICA** taxes fund two large government programs, Social Security and Medicare. Employees and employers share FICA payments.

Social Security Taxes

Most of the FICA taxes you pay go to the Social Security Administration to fund Old-Age, Survivors, and Disability Insurance (OASDI), or **Social Security.** Social Security was established in 1935 to ease the hardships of the Great Depression.

FICA *taxes that fund Social Security and Medicare*

Social Security *Old-Age, Survivors, and Disability Insurance (OASDI)*

Go Online
PHSchool.com
Web Code: mng-6143

Figure 14.5 **Federal Income Tax Rates, 2005**

Schedule	If your taxable income is over–	but not over–	the tax is	of the amount over–
Schedule X– use if your filing status is **single**	$0	$7,300	.... 10%	$0
	$7,300	$29,700	$730.00 plus 15%	$7,300
	$29,700	$71,950	$4,090.00 plus 25%	$29,700
	$71,950	$150,150	$14,652.40 plus 28%	$71,950
	$150,150	$326,450	$36,548.50 plus 33%	$150,150
	$326,450	....	$94,727.50 plus 35%	$326,450
Schedule Y– use if your filing status is **married filing jointly**	$0	$14,600	.... 10%	$0
	$14,600	$59,400	$1,460.00 plus 15%	$14,600
	$59,400	$119,950	$8,180.00 plus 25%	$59,400
	$119,950	$182,800	$23,317.50 plus 28%	$119,950
	$182,800	$326,450	$40,915.50 plus 33%	$182,800
	$326,450	....	$88,320.00 plus 35%	$326,450

According to these sample individual income tax tables, a single individual with $5,000 of taxable income would pay $5,000 X .10, or $500 in taxes.
Income What would be the tax for a married couple filing jointly with $75,000 in taxable income?

Transparency Resource Package Economics Concepts, 14D: Federal Taxes

Differentiated Instruction 

(Reteaching) Ask students to create a Venn diagram to review how individual income taxes and corporate income taxes are alike and how they are different. Have them conclude the activity by discussing what they included in each circle (for example, withholding by employers in the "personal income taxes" area, deductions for the costs of doing business in the "corporate income taxes" area, and progressive taxes in the common area).

Differentiated Instruction 

Organize the class into three groups—a Social Security group, a Medicare group, and an unemployment compensation group. Tell each group that it is responsible for researching the purpose of its assigned program and preparing and delivering an illustrated five-minute oral presentation on it. The presentation should include at least one chart or graph.

Block Scheduling Strategies

Consider these suggestions to take advantage of extended class time:

- Bring in multiple blank copies of federal tax return forms. Distribute the forms to groups of students. Then go through the form line by line with the students, having them explain the information requested on each line and clarifying such information for them where necessary.
- Extend the Learning Styles Activity on this page by having students do additional research, using the Simulations and Data Graphing CD-ROM to create several graphs for their group's presentation. Provide extra time for each presentation, and work with the class to display the graphs on a class bulletin board.
- Have students use the Internet to find examples of cartoons about taxes. Links can be found within *Economics: Principles in Action* in the Social Studies area of the Prentice Hall Web site: **www.phschool.com**

Answer to . . .
Building Key Concepts $12,080

Differentiated Instruction L3

(Reteaching) Organize students into groups of three or four. Have them look in recent almanacs for information on U.S. budget receipts by source. They should collect data on the most recent year for which figures are available. First have students figure out what percentage of the total revenue came from individual income taxes, corporate income taxes, social insurance taxes (such as Social Security), excise taxes, and other types of taxes each year. Then have each group use the Simulations and Data Graphing CD-ROM to create a circle graph similar to the one in Figure 14.4 on page 365 that displays this information. (Their graphs will be for a more recent year, however.) Have them accompany their graphs with a brief glossary that defines each of the types of taxes mentioned in the section.

Simulations and Data Graphing CD-ROM offers data graphing tools so that students can practice creating and interpreting graphs.

Transparency Resource Package Economics Concepts, 14E: Value-Added Tax

Global Connections

Value-Added Tax Individual income taxes and sales taxes play a smaller role in generating government revenue in many European nations than they do in the United States. Instead, in much of Europe, a value-added tax, or VAT, has been implemented. A VAT taxes the increase in value that a good gains in each step of its production. For example, in the United States, consumers usually pay taxes when they buy a car. Under a VAT system, the price of a car already includes the tax paid by the mine that extracts the iron ore used to make the car. It also includes the tax the steel mill paid based on the value added to the iron ore when it was turned into steel. Similarly, the car's price includes the tax the car manufacturer paid on the value the steel gained when it was made into a car. In this way, the consumer doesn't directly pay the tax. Rather, the total price of the car already includes the tax. **Would you recommend a VAT for the United States? Why or why not?**

Medicare *a national health insurance program that helps pay for health care for people over age 65 or with certain disabilities*

estate tax *a tax on the estate, or total value of the money and property, of a person who has died*

gift tax *a tax on money or property that one living person gives to another*

Originally, Social Security was simply a retirement fund to provide old-age pensions to workers. Today, it also provides benefits to surviving family members of wage earners and to people whose disabilities keep them from working.

Each year the government establishes an income cap for Social Security taxes. In 2005, the cap was $90,000. No Social Security taxes could be withheld from a taxpayer's wages and salaries above that amount.

Medicare Taxes

FICA taxes also fund Medicare. The **Medicare** program is a national health insurance program that helps pay for health care for people over age 65. It also covers people with certain disabilities.

Both employees and self-employed people pay the Medicare tax on all their earnings. There is no ceiling as for Social Security payments.

Unemployment Taxes

The federal government also collects an unemployment tax, which is paid by employers. In effect, the tax pays for an insurance policy for workers. If workers are laid off from their jobs through no fault of their own, they can file an "unemployment compensation" claim and collect benefits for a fixed number of weeks. In order to collect unemployment benefits, an unemployed person usually must show that he or she is actively looking for another job. The unemployment program is financed by both state and federal unemployment taxes.

Other Types of Taxes

What are the taxes on gasoline and cable television service called? If you inherit money from your great aunt, will you have to pay a tax? Why are some imported products so expensive? To answer these questions, you need to look at excise, estate, gift, and import taxes.

Excise Taxes

As you read in Chapter 5, an excise tax is a general revenue tax on the sale or manufacture of a good. Federal excise taxes apply to gasoline, cigarettes, alcoholic beverages, telephone services, cable television, and other items.

Estate Taxes

An **estate tax** is a tax on the estate, or total value of the money and property, of a person who has died. It is paid out of the person's estate before the heirs receive their share. A person's estate includes not only money, but also real estate, cars, furniture, investments, jewelry, paintings, and insurance.

In 2005, if the total value of the estate is $1.5 million or less, there is no federal estate tax. Because an estate tax is a progressive tax, the rate rises with increasing value. That is, a $5 million estate will be taxed by the federal government at a higher rate than a $2 million estate.

Gift Taxes

The **gift tax** is a tax on money or property that one living person gives to another. The goal of the gift tax, established in 1924, was to keep people from avoiding estate taxes by giving away their money before they died. The tax law sets limits on gifts, but still allows the tax-free transfer of fairly

Preparing for Standardized Tests

Have students read the section titled "Other Types of Taxes" and then answer the question below.

Which of the following taxes is likely to show up on a telephone bill?

(A) excise tax
B FICA tax
C estate tax
D gift tax

Answer to . . .

Global Connections Answers will vary. Some students may favor a VAT as a way to collect revenue. Others will recommend against it so as to limit taxes.

large amounts each year. Under current law, a person can give up to $11,000 a year tax-free to each of several different people.

Import Taxes

Taxes on imported goods (foreign goods brought into the country) are called **tariffs.** Today, most tariffs are intended to protect American farmers and industries from foreign competitors rather than to raise revenue. Tariffs raise the price of foreign items and help keep the price of American products competitive. You will read more about tariffs in Chapter 17.

Taxes That Affect Behavior

The basic goal of taxation is to create revenue. However, governments sometimes use tax policies to discourage the public from buying harmful products. Taxes are also used to encourage certain types of behavior. The use of taxation to encourage or discourage behavior is called a **tax incentive.**

Federal taxes on tobacco products and alcoholic beverages are examples of so-called sin taxes. While they do bring in revenue, their main purpose is to discourage people from buying and using tobacco and alcohol.

▲ **The owner of this house is installing solar panels. He or she may be able to take advantage of tax incentives designed to encourage energy conservation.**

Taxes have also been imposed on the purchase of vehicles that get low gas mileage. The goal of these taxes is to encourage people to purchase more fuel-efficient cars. Similarly, certain tax deductions encourage energy conservation. Homeowners and businesses may deduct some of the cost of certain improvements, such as adding solar heating, from their taxable income.

tariff *a tax on imported goods*

tax incentive *the use of taxation to encourage or discourage certain behavior*

Section 2 Assessment

Progress Monitoring *Online*
For: Self-quiz with vocabulary practice
Web Code: mna-6146

Key Terms and Main Ideas

1. Explain "pay-as-you-earn" taxation.
2. Describe **withholding** and explain how it would affect a student with a part-time job.
3. What is the purpose of **FICA?**

Applying Economic Concepts

4. ***Critical Thinking*** The founders of the United States wanted to avoid establishing a permanent aristocracy, or group of wealthy families who could control a great deal of the nation's wealth. How is this idea related to estate and gift taxes?
5. ***Try This*** Contributions to organizations such as the American Cancer Society are tax deductible (that is, they can be deducted from taxable income). Explain the reason for this tax policy.
6. ***Using the Databank*** Study the bar graph showing Government Receipts by Source on page 543 of the Databank. Approximately how much money (in billions of dollars) do the top three sources of government income generate?

Go Online PHSchool.com
For: Research Activity
Visit: PHSchool.com
Web Code: mnd-6142

GTE Guide to the Essentials
Chapter 14, Section 2, p. 59 provides support for students who need additional review of the section content. Spanish support is available in the Spanish edition of the guide on p. 59.

Quiz Unit 6 folder, p. 5 includes questions to check students' understanding of Section 2 content.

Presentation Pro CD-ROM
Quiz provides multiple-choice questions to check students' understanding of Section 2 content.

Answers to . . .

Section 2 Assessment

1. Pay-as-you-earn taxation means that individuals usually pay most of what they owe over the year as they earn income.
2. Withholding is a portion of income taken out of an employee's paycheck. It is forwarded to the federal government as an installment payment on the person's annual tax. A student with a part-time job would have a portion of salary withheld.
3. FICA taxes fund two large government programs—Social Security and Medicare.
4. Estate and gift taxes tax money that transferred from one individual to another. If large sums are given or inherited, some of that amount is taxed and paid to the government. Therefore, no inheritance can be passed along among a few individuals or families without losing some of its value.
5. Donations are deductible in order to encourage people to give to worthy organizations. The money is donated to a nonprofit organization, which furthers the public good.
6. approximately $1,700 billion

Progress Monitoring *Online*
For additional assessment, have students access Progress Monitoring Online at **Web Code:** mna-6146

Go Online PHSchool.com Typing in the Web Code when prompted will bring students directly to detailed instructions for this activity.

ECONOMIC *Profile* Henry J. Aaron

Background

In the late 1990s the U.S. government was faced with budget surpluses that were expected to last for 15 years and total perhaps $5 trillion. Some groups proposed sizable tax cuts; others favored new spending.

In February 1999 Henry J. Aaron wrote in a *Newsday* article that the prudent course was to find a way to increase saving and that a plan unveiled by President Clinton in his State of the Union message that year would do that. Aaron noted that surpluses allow the government to buy back publicly held bonds. The government debt is reduced; investors get new funds for economic growth.

The President's plan also called for creating new savings accounts to include matching government funds, prompting increased saving. According to Aaron, the President's plan supports saving on all levels—including within the government. Although Aaron's plan was not implemented, many economists still believe the federal government should encourage private saving.

Careers in Economics Activity Unit 6 folder, p. 13 gives students a closer look at the career path of a tax preparer.

Answers to . . .

1. The growing ratio of retirees to workers will be offset by a decline in the number of people dependent on workers' wages. Current proposals would require a lengthy transition and huge tax increases, and they might trigger changes in consumer habits that could hurt the economy.
2. Factors include lowered birth rates, the "baby boom" generation reaching retirement age, and lengthened life spans. Some studies predict that the Social Security system will go bankrupt.
3. Reports may include recent increases in the age at which a retiree can draw Social Security and increases in the amount of money retirees can earn without affecting their benefits.

Economist

Entrepreneur

ECONOMIC *Profile*

Henry J. Aaron (b. 1936)

During the 1990s, a movement to "save Social Security" became a major crusade among Washington politicians. The debate worried many Americans, who wondered if the nation's retirement system was about to collapse. A prominent economist says, however, that the Social Security system works, so don't try to fix it.

The Sky Is Not Falling

Many studies predict that the Social Security system will go bankrupt once the Baby Boom generation begins to retire, despite hikes in the Social Security tax and huge surpluses in the program today. Not everyone agrees. Among the harshest critics of this alarming prediction is economist Henry Aaron.

An Expert on Entitlements Issues

Henry Aaron is senior fellow in economic studies at the Brookings Institution, a Washington "think tank" that analyzes economic and social issues. Before joining Brookings, he served on the staff of the Council of Economic Advisors, and in the 1970s, served as Assistant Secretary for Planning in the Department of Health, Education, and Welfare.

In 1978, Aaron was selected to chair the Social Security Advisory Council, which reviews the status of the Social Security system every four years. He has become recognized as an expert on government entitlements and tax policy.

The Dangers of Unwise Reforms

Much of the concern over Social Security has arisen because increasing numbers of retirees are being supported by the taxes of working Americans. Aaron agrees that the ratio of retirees to workers will continue to rise. However, he argues that this increase is offset by a lower ratio of children to workers and by growing numbers of women entering the work force. Both trends reduce the ratio of nonworking dependents per worker, Aaron argues, so the overall tax burden on workers' wages will remain about the same.

One popular proposal is to replace Social Security with a private retirement savings program. Aaron warns that this would require a 50-year transition, during which people would have to make their private contributions while also supporting current retirees through a 10 percent sales tax.

For those who would reform the existing system by raising the retirement age or reducing benefits, Aaron has dire warnings. He notes that no one really knows how expectations about old age affect the saving, working, and spending decisions that people make. Aaron cautions that major changes in the current system could have unforeseen consequences for the entire economy.

CHECK FOR UNDERSTANDING

1. **Source Reading** Summarize in your own words the argument that Aaron makes to oppose any major changes in the Social Security system.
2. **Critical Thinking** What trends and conditions are responsible for the increase in the ratio of retirees to workers? Why might this development be a potential threat to the future of Social Security?
3. **Learn More** Research and report on changes that Congress has made in Social Security in recent years.

Beyond the Classroom: Workplace Skills

Preparing and Monitoring Budgets In any type of business, the finance department is a major nerve center. It is here that revenues are calculated and budgets—plans for the amounts of money that will be spent by various areas of the company—are developed. In addition to preparing budgets, this department forecasts revenue and spending, keeps the company's financial records, and adjusts budgets throughout the year in light of revenue shortfalls or surpluses. Ask students to search business school sites on the Internet and list the types of instruction available for budgeting and financial forecasting.

Section 3 Federal Spending

Preview

Objectives

After studying this section you will be able to:

1. **Distinguish** between mandatory and discretionary spending.
2. **Describe** major entitlement programs.
3. **Identify** categories of discretionary spending.
4. **Explain** the impact of federal aid to state and local governments.

Section Focus

Although the federal budget is extremely large, about three quarters of the government's spending is required by current laws. Major categories of government spending include Social Security, defense, interest on the national debt, Medicare, and health care.

Key Terms

mandatory spending
discretionary spending
entitlement
Medicaid

Suppose that each year you were given almost $1.9 trillion to spend. So much money! So many choices! In reality, when the federal government receives this amount of revenue in the form of taxes, most of it is already accounted for. That is, after the government fulfills all its legal obligations, only about 26 percent of the money remains. In this section you will look at the many items on which the federal government spends its tax revenues. In Chapter 15, you will read about how the federal government, as part of the budget process, plans for that spending.

Mandatory and Discretionary Spending

The graph in Figure 14.6 shows the major categories of federal spending. Some of these categories, such as Social Security and Medicare, are "mandatory." **Mandatory spending** refers to money that lawmakers are required by existing laws to spend on certain programs or to use for interest payments on the national debt. Others, such as defense and education, are "discretionary." **Discretionary spending** is spending about which government planners can make choices.

In general, the percentage of federal spending that is mandatory has grown in recent years. The percentage of discretionary spending has decreased. These trends worry many budget planners and politicians.

mandatory spending *spending on certain programs that is mandated, or required, by existing law*

discretionary spending *spending category about which government planners can make choices*

Figure 14.6 **Federal Spending, 2004**

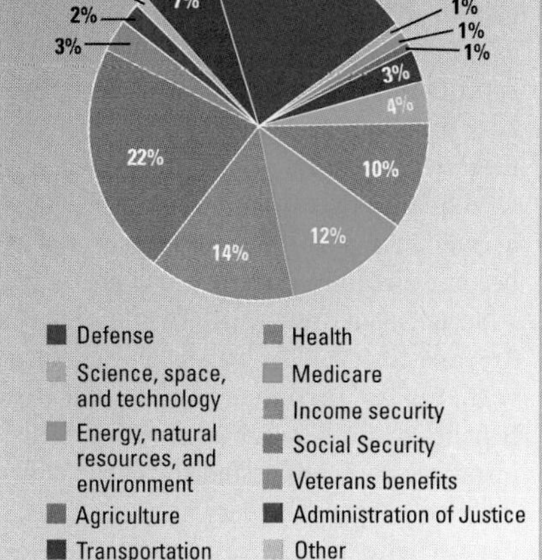

Note: Because of rounding, totals may be less or greater than 100 percent.
Source: Office of Management and Budget

The federal government spends the funds it collects from taxes and other sources on a variety of programs. **Government Analyze the categories of expenditures in the federal budget. Which categories receive the most federal funds?**

Go Online
PHSchool.com
Web Code: mng-4164

Graphing the Main Idea

Government To help students understand mandatory spending and discretionary spending by the **government,** have them complete a web graphic organizer like the one at the right for each of the types of spending. Remind students that a web shows a main idea and its supporting details.

Section Reading Support Transparencies A template and the answers for this graphic organizer can be found in Chapter 14, Section 3 of the Section Reading Support Transparency System.

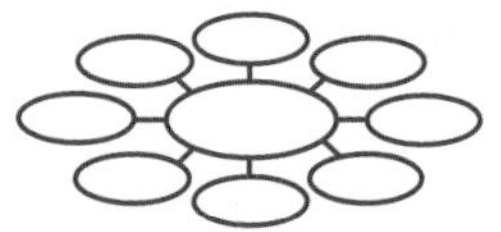

Section 3 Federal Spending

Objectives You may wish to call students' attention to the objectives in the Section Preview. The objectives are reflected in the main headings of the section.

Bellringer Ask students to describe how they think most workers spent their most recent paychecks. Do they think that workers were able to choose freely how their money was spent, or did some of the money have to go toward required expenses? Explain that this section will detail how the government allocates its financial resources.

Vocabulary Builder Have students read through the section to discover the meaning of the key terms. Ask them to write each term and its definition in their Economics Journals.

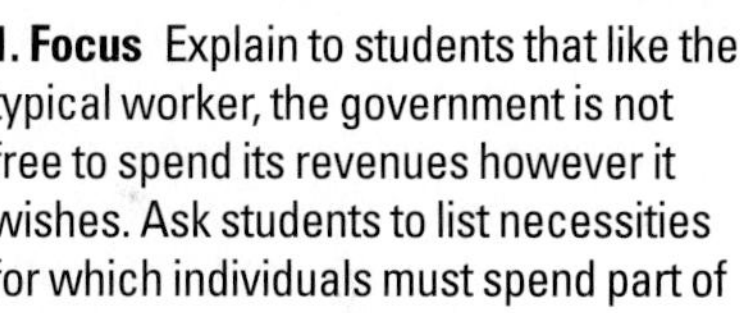

Lesson Plan

Teaching the Main Concepts L3

1. Focus Explain to students that like the typical worker, the government is not free to spend its revenues however it wishes. Ask students to list necessities for which individuals must spend part of their earnings.

2. Instruct Begin by stating the differences between mandatory and discretionary spending. Then discuss each type of spending in depth, introducing students to the concept of entitlement programs. Finally, explain how federal tax dollars find their way back to the states and to local governments.

3. Close/Reteach After the federal government has funded its mandatory entitlement programs, it allocates its remaining financial resources as Congress and the executive branch see fit. Ask students to explain the purpose of entitlement programs.

Answer to . . .

Building Key Concepts Social Security, defense, income security, Medicare, health

 **Guided Reading and Review**
Unit 6 folder, p. 6 asks students to identify the section's main ideas and to define or identify key terms.

Differentiated Instruction L2

Ask students to consult a dictionary to learn the pronunciation and meaning of the words *mandate* and *discretion.* Have them state each definition in their own words, and ask them to explain how those definitions help them to understand mandatory and discretionary spending. ELL

Differentiated Instruction L3

(Reteaching) Have students list everything they can remember spending money for over the past several weeks. Then ask them to divide their lists into two categories: mandatory spending and discretionary spending. Ask how they decided which category best described each expense. Finally, ask them to relate these categories to spending by the government and to list examples of government expenses that fall into each category.

Differentiated Instruction L3

Organize the class into six groups, and assign one of the following topics to each group: Social Security, Medicare, Medicaid, food stamps, Supplemental Security Income (SSI), and child nutrition. Ask each group to create a fact sheet about its topic that answers the following questions:

- Who benefits from the program?
- What benefits does the program offer?
- When was the program started?
- Why was the program initiated?
- How does the program work?

Photocopy and distribute the fact sheets so that everyone has information on all of these programs.

▲ **People who receive entitlement benefits such as Social Security, Medicare, and Medicaid include veterans, people with disabilities, and the elderly.**

entitlement *social welfare program that people are "entitled to" if they meet certain eligibility requirements*

Entitlement Programs

Except for interest on the national debt, most of the mandatory spending items in the federal budget are for entitlement programs. **Entitlements** are social welfare programs that people are "entitled to" if they meet certain eligibility requirements, such as being at a certain income level or age. The federal government guarantees assistance for all those who qualify. As the number of people who qualify rises, mandatory spending rises as well. As a result, managing costs has become a major concern.

Some, but not all, entitlements are "means-tested." In other words, people with higher incomes may receive lower benefits or no benefits at all. Medicaid, for instance, is means-tested, or dependent on income. Social Security is not. A retired person who has worked and paid Social Security taxes is entitled to certain benefits. Similarly, military veterans and retired federal employees are entitled to receive pensions from the government.

Entitlements are a largely unchanging part of government spending. Once Congress has set the requirements, it cannot control how many people become eligible for each kind of benefit. Congress can change the eligibility requirements or reduce the amount of the benefit in order to try to keep costs down. Such actions, however, require a change in the law.

Social Security

Social Security is the largest category of federal spending. More than 50 million retired or disabled people and their families and survivors receive monthly benefits. The Social Security Administration became an independent agency in 1995. Before that, its spending was part of the budget for the Health and Human Services Department.

Medicare

Medicare serves about 42 million people, most of them over 65 years old. The program pays for hospital care and for the costs of physicians and medical services. It also pays health care bills for people who suffer from certain disabilities and diseases.

Econ 101: Key Concepts Made Easy

Government Explain to students that the concept of **entitlement** entered the English language as recently as 1944. The word is derived from *entitle,* which itself comes from the Latin *intitulare,* meaning "give a title to." Someone bestowed with a title had certain rights and privileges. Thus, to be *entitled* means to have a right to something.

Ask students to examine the debate that has gone on for some time about whether individuals are actually "entitled" to programs that are called entitlements. Encourage students to see how the words that are used to talk about something can reveal a person's attitude toward it.

Medicare is funded by taxes withheld from people's paychecks. Monthly payments paid by people who make certain levels of taxable income and receive Medicare benefits also pay for the program.

Medicaid

Medicaid benefits low-income families, some people with disabilities, and elderly people in nursing homes. It is the largest source of funds for medical and health-related services for America's poorest people. The federal government shares the costs of Medicaid with state governments. The state share of the costs varies from 50 percent to 83 percent. In 2004, 54.6 million people were covered by Medicaid—about 18 percent of Americans.

Other Mandatory Spending Programs

Other means-tested entitlements benefit people and families whose incomes fall below a certain level. Requirements vary from program to program. Federal programs include food stamps, Supplemental Security Income (SSI), and child nutrition. The federal government also pays retirement benefits and insurance for federal workers, as well as veterans' pensions and unemployment insurance.

The Future of Entitlement Spending

Spending for both Social Security and Medicare has increased enormously in recent years and is expected to increase further in the next few decades. Social Security payments will rise as people in the large "baby boomer" generation, born between 1945 and 1964, start to retire. When the "baby boomers" reach 65, they will become eligible for Medicare as well.

Medicare costs have been growing rapidly, partly as a result of expensive technology, but also because people are living longer. Who will pay these costs? The following fact indicates the basic problem facing Medicare. In 1995, there were four people paying Medicare taxes for every Medicare recipient. By 2050, there will only be two people paying taxes for every recipient.

Discretionary Spending

Spending on defense accounts for about half of the federal government's discretionary spending. The remaining funds available for discretionary spending are divided among a wide variety of categories.

Defense Spending

Defense spending has dropped somewhat since the end of the cold war as a percentage of the total federal budget. As you can see from the graph in Figure 14.6, defense spending consumes about 20 percent of the federal budget.

The Department of Defense spends most of the defense budget. It pays the salaries of all the men and women in the army, navy, air force, and marines, as well as the department's civilian employees. There are about 1.4 million men and women in uniform, along with about 654,000 civilian workers, working for the armed forces.

Defense spending, of course, also buys weapons, missiles, battleships, tanks, airplanes, ammunition, and all the other equipment the military needs. The defense budget also includes funds for maintaining equipment and military bases.

Other Discretionary Spending

You may be surprised at how small a portion of federal spending goes into the category that could be labeled "everything else." Here are some of the many programs that this category of federal spending pays for.

- education
- training
- scientific research
- student loans
- technology
- national parks and monuments
- law enforcement
- environmental cleanup
- housing

THE WALL STREET JOURNAL.
CLASSROOM EDITION

In the News Read more about federal spending in "Rethinking the Digital Divide," an article in The Wall Street Journal Classroom Edition.

The Wall Street Journal Classroom Edition

For: Current Events
Visit: PHSchool.com
Web Code: mnc-6143

Medicaid *entitlement program that benefits low-income families, some people with disabilities, and elderly people in nursing homes*

Go Online PHSchool.com Typing in the Web Code when prompted will bring students directly to the article.

Differentiated Instruction 

(Enrichment) Assign each student one of the categories of discretionary spending discussed in this section. Instruct students to locate recent real-life examples of spending for their assigned categories. Then have each student compose a brief description of the example. You may want to have students also create "Dubious Discretionary Doings" lists to document strange or seemingly wasteful discretionary spending that they uncover in their research. Depending on the time available, have the information presented orally or in a class report and combined list.

Differentiated Instruction 

You may wish to have students add the following to their portfolios. Ask them to read the part of this section titled "Federal Aid to State and Local Governments." Then have students research one type of federal aid to your state or local government to find out what kinds of restrictions come along with the funds. Have them write several paragraphs, first briefly describing the general impact of federal aid on state and local governments and then focusing on their research. GT

Economics Assessment Rubric
Economics Assessment Rubrics folder, pp. 6–7 provides sample evaluation materials for a writing assignment.

Transparency Resource Package
Economics Concepts, 14F: Federal Spending

Block Scheduling Strategies

Consider these suggestions to take advantage of extended class time:

- Distribute a table that details government spending. (Almanacs usually include this information, but it is also available from the Office of Management and Budget.) Then work with students to analyze the chart. First identify which spending is mandatory and which is discretionary. Then identify categories that get the most and the least spending. Finally, have students do research to analyze how spending in various categories has changed over time.
- Extend the second activity on this page by having students debate the following question: *Should the federal government fund state and local programs and projects without imposing any requirements or regulations?* After each side has presented its case, have the class decide which team made the most convincing arguments.

GTE Guide to the Essentials
Chapter 14, Section 3, p. 60 provides support for students who need additional review of the section content. Spanish support is available in the Spanish edition of the guide on p. 60.

Quiz Unit 6 folder, p. 7 includes questions to check students' understanding of Section 3 content.

Presentation Pro CD-ROM
Quiz provides multiple-choice questions to check students' understanding of Section 3 content.

Answers to . . .

Section 3 Assessment

1. Discretionary spending is spending about which government planners can make choices. Mandatory spending is spending that is required by existing law.
2. An entitlement program is a social welfare program that people are "entitled to" if they meet certain eligibility requirements.
3. Social Security costs are expected to increase as the "baby boomer" generation, a large segment of today's society, reaches retirement age.
4. Defense is the largest category of discretionary spending. Other examples may include education, training, scientific research, student loans, technology, national parks and monuments, law enforcement, environmental cleanup, housing, land management, transportation, disaster aid, foreign aid, farm subsidies, and salaries of civilian employees of the federal government.
5. (a–b) Answers will vary, but students should demonstrate an understanding of entitlement programs and be able to support their answers by suggesting needs that are not met (requiring added programs) or examples of waste or inefficiency (requiring modifying or cutting of programs).
6. Answers should demonstrate an understanding of federal spending and be well supported. For example, students may want to lower defense spending because the United States is the strongest world power, or they may want to spend more on environmental clean-up because many areas are damaged.

Answer to . . .

Cartoon Caption State governments are portrayed as being low on funds and therefore unprepared.

▲ As the federal government reduces its size, the burden of providing public assistance programs falls more heavily on the states. How does the cartoonist portray the ability of state governments to handle this responsibility?

- land management
- transportation
- disaster aid
- foreign aid
- farm subsidies

This part of the federal budget also pays the salaries of the millions of people who work for the civilian branches of the federal government. They include members of Congress, Cabinet secretaries, park rangers, FBI agents, file clerks, geologists, CIA agents, meat inspectors, and many others.

Federal Aid to State and Local Governments

Some federal tax dollars find their way to state and local governments. In total, about $406 billion a year in federal monies is divided among the states. This is an average of about $1,400 per person.

As you have read, state and federal governments share the costs of some social programs, including Medicaid, unemployment compensation, and some of the programs that help children, families, refugees, and others. State and federal governments also share the costs of some highway construction. Additional federal money goes to the states for education, lower-income housing, mass-transit, health care, highway construction, employment training, and dozens of other programs.

Federal grants-in-aid are grants of federal money for certain closely defined purposes. States must use the federal funds only for the purpose specified and obey the federal guidelines for which aid is given. Beginning with the Reagan administration in the early 1980s, many grant-in-aid programs were converted to a block grant format. As you read in Chapter 13, block grants are lump sums of money intended to be used in a broadly defined area of public need, such as education or highways.

Section 3 Assessment

Progress Monitoring *Online*
For: Self-quiz with vocabulary practice
Web Code: mna-6147

Key Terms and Main Ideas

1. How does **discretionary spending** differ from **mandatory spending?**
2. What is an **entitlement** program?
3. Why is the cost of the Social Security program expected to increase in the next decades?
4. What is the largest category of **discretionary spending?** Identify three additional examples of discretionary spending.

Applying Economic Concepts

5. ***Try This*** Suppose that you are running for political office. **(a)** Would you propose any new entitlement programs? If so, what would they be? **(b)** Would you propose eliminating or modifying any existing entitlement programs? Explain your answers.
6. ***You Decide*** Which categories of federal spending would you lower? Which would you raise? Give specific reasons for the changes you suggest.

For: Debate Activity
Visit: PHSchool.com
Web Code: mnd-6143

Progress Monitoring *Online*
For additional assessment, have students access Progress Monitoring Online at **Web Code:** mna-6147

Go Online PHSchool.com Typing in the Web Code when prompted will bring students directly to detailed instructions for this activity.

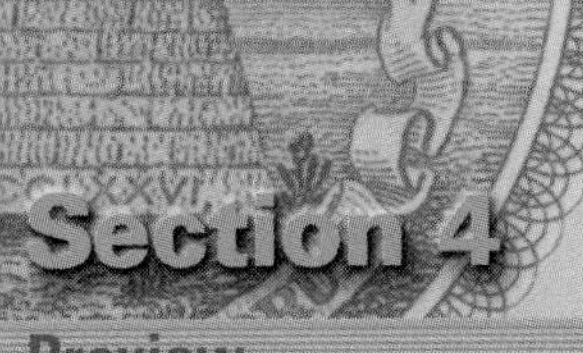

State and Local Taxes and Spending

Preview

Objectives

After studying this section you will be able to:

1. **Explain** how states use a budget to plan their spending.
2. **Identify** where state taxes are spent.
3. **List** the major sources of state tax revenue.
4. **Describe** local government spending and sources of revenue.

Section Focus

Like the federal government, state and local governments use the revenue from taxes to pay for a variety of programs and services. In general, states spend the largest amounts on grants to local governments, education, and public welfare.

Key Terms

operating budget
capital budget
balanced budget
tax exempt
real property
personal property
tax assessor

You and your family are thinking about colleges. Which one offers the courses you want? How much does it cost? During your research, you find that colleges within your state's university system are far less expensive than private schools. The reason is that your state government is paying part of the cost of running the state colleges. In fact, higher education is one of the largest areas of state government spending.

What else do states spend money on? In this section you will look at patterns of taxing and spending by state and local governments.

State Budgets

Like families and individuals, governments must plan their spending ahead of time. The federal government has just one budget for all kinds of spending. States have two budgets: operating budgets and capital budgets.

Operating Budgets

A state's **operating budget** pays for day-to-day expenses. Those include salaries of state employees, supplies such as computers or paper, and maintenance of state facilities, from the state capitol to recreation areas and roadside parks.

Capital Budgets

A state's **capital budget** pays for major capital, or investment, spending. If the state builds a new bridge or building, the money comes from this budget. Most of these expenses are met by long-term borrowing or the sale of bonds.

operating budget *budget for day-to-day expenses*

capital budget *budget for major capital, or investment, expenditures*

▲ **State colleges and universities, such as the University of Texas at Austin, receive state funding.**

Graphing the Main Idea

Government To build understanding of the ways in which state and local **governments** collect and spend taxes, ask students to complete a tree map graphic organizer like the one at the right. Remind students that a tree map shows the main topic, main ideas or divisions, and supporting details. They should place the title of the section in the top box and the main headings in the next row of boxes, followed by supporting details.

Section Reading Support Transparencies A template and the answers for this graphic organizer can be found in Chapter 14, Section 4 of the Section Reading Support Transparency System.

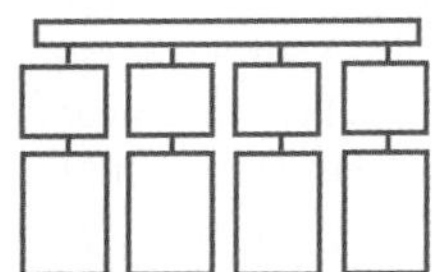

Section 4

State and Local Taxes and Spending

Objectives You may wish to call students' attention to the objectives in the Section Preview. The objectives are reflected in the main headings of the section.

Bellringer Ask students who purchased their economics textbooks or who provides the buses and trains that transport people around your community. (Adjust questions as needed to reflect state or local expenditures.) Explain that this section will discuss how state and local taxes are used.

Vocabulary Builder Ask students to review the meaning of each key term and to give a real-life example of the term or of a situation in which they would encounter an example of the term.

Teaching the Main Concepts L3

1. Focus Like the federal government, state and local governments collect taxes to finance the operations of the government and to provide services for their populations. Have students list services that their local taxes provide.

2. Instruct Begin by explaining the difference between an operating budget and a capital budget. Then discuss the various ways in which states spend their tax dollars. Next, talk about the kinds of taxes that states collect and how they are similar to and different from federal taxes. Finally, explain what is meant by local government, and discuss the taxation and spending policies of such governments.

3. Close/Reteach In addition to funds distributed by the federal government, state budgets are supported by taxes levied at the state and local levels. Ask students to list the types of services that state and local governments offer.

Guided Reading and Review
Unit 6 folder, p. 8 asks students to identify the main ideas of the section and to define or identify key terms.

Differentiated Instruction 

(Reteaching) Have students work in pairs to complete this activity. Ask them to create two lists: one titled "Operating Budget" and the other titled "Capital Budget." Have students include at least five expenses in each list. Expenses in the capital budget list should be based on actual capital improvements in your state. Ask pairs to review their lists, discuss why they placed each item in each list, and correct misplaced expenses.

Learning Styles Activity
Learning Styles Lesson Plans folder, p. 34 asks pairs of students to create circle graphs showing how a state allocates its revenue to its operating budget.

Answer to...
Building Key Concepts
Intergovernmental revenue, insurance trust expenditure, education, and public welfare

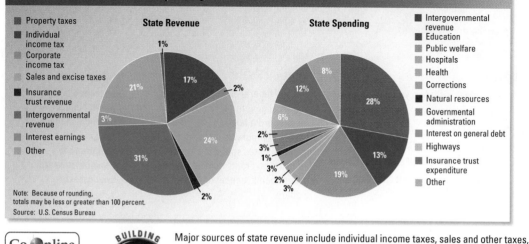

Figure 14.7 **State Revenue and Spending, 2002**

State Revenue

- Property taxes 1%
- Individual income tax 17%
- Corporate income tax 2%
- Sales and excise taxes 24%
- Insurance trust revenue 2%
- Intergovernmental revenue 31%
- Interest earnings 3%
- Other 21%

State Spending

- Intergovernmental revenue 28%
- Education 13%
- Public welfare 19%
- Hospitals 3%
- Health 2%
- Corrections 3%
- Natural resources 1%
- Governmental administration 3%
- Interest on general debt 2%
- Highways 6%
- Insurance trust expenditure 12%
- Other 8%

Note: Because of rounding, totals may be less or greater than 100 percent.
Source: U.S. Census Bureau

Major sources of state revenue include individual income taxes, sales and other taxes, insurance premiums, and local and federal funds ("intergovernmental revenue").
Government What are the major categories of state government spending?

balanced budget *budget in which revenues are equal to spending*

Balancing State Budgets

In most states, the governor prepares the budget with the help of a budget agency. The legislature then discusses and eventually approves the budget.

Unlike the federal government, 49 states require **balanced budgets**—budgets in which revenues are equal to spending. These laws, however, apply only to the operating budget, not the capital budget. That makes it easier to balance state budgets than to balance the federal budget.

Some states can borrow money for several years. In other states, lawmakers must cut programs or raise taxes to balance the budget. In the early 2000s, deficits forced cuts and tax hikes in many states.

Where Are State Taxes Spent?

Spending policies differ among the fifty states. You are probably most familiar with state spending on education, highways, police protection, and state recreation areas. You can see other significant spending categories in Figure 14.7.

Education

Every state has at least one public state university. Some, such as California, have large systems with many campuses throughout the state. In many states, tax dollars also support agricultural and technical colleges, teacher's colleges, and two-year community colleges.

State governments also provide financial help to their local governments, which run elementary, middle, and high schools. Some states pay a larger share of local schools' costs than other states do. The amount of money that each state spends per student also varies. The national average is $7,920 per student per year.

Public Safety

State police are a familiar sight along the nation's highways. This police force enforces traffic laws and helps motorists in emergencies. State police also maintain crime labs that can assist local law-enforcement agencies.

State governments build and run corrections systems. These institutions house people convicted of state crimes.

Econ 101: Key Concepts Made Easy

Monetary and Fiscal Policy Help students understand **balanced budgets** by drawing an analogy to two common types of credit cards—one with revolving credit and one without. In the latter case, card holders are obligated to pay their monthly balances in full, so they can only spend as much as they are willing and able to pay at the end of each billing cycle. In other words their credit card budgets are in balance at the end of each month. A card that carries revolving credit, however, requires cardholders to pay only a portion of the monthly balance. In this case, the holders' credit card budgets may not be balanced—they may maintain a deficit.

Ask students why they think states are required to balance their operating budgets. Then ask how the existence of a deficit affects a governmental organization.

Highways and Transportation

Building and maintaining highway systems is another major state expense. State crews resurface roads and repair bridges. Some money for roads comes from the federal government. In turn, states contribute money to federal and interstate highway systems.

States pay at least some of the costs of other kinds of transportation facilities, such as waterways and airports. Money for such projects may also come from federal and local government budgets.

Public Welfare

States look after the health and welfare of the public in various ways. State funds support some public hospitals and clinics. State regulators inspect water supplies and test for pollution.

As you read in Section 2, states also help pay for many of the federal programs that assist individuals, such as unemployment compensation benefits. Because states determine their own benefits, they can meet local needs better than the federal government can. For example, during a local recession, they may decide to extend the number of weeks that people can claim benefits.

Arts and Recreation

If you've hiked in a state forest or picnicked in a state park, you've enjoyed another benefit of state tax dollars. Parks and nature reserves preserve scenic and historic places for people to visit and enjoy. States also run museums and help fund music and art programs.

Administration

Besides providing services, state governments need to spend money just to keep running. Like the federal government, state governments have an executive branch (the governor's office), a legislature, and a court system. State tax revenues pay the salaries of all these and other state workers, including maintenance crews in state parks, the governor, and state court judges.

State Tax Revenue

For every dollar a state spends, it must take in a dollar in revenue. Otherwise, it cannot maintain a balanced budget. The 50 states now take in more than $500 billion a year from taxes. Where does this money come from? Sales and individual income taxes provide the largest part of state revenues. The pie chart on the left in Figure 14.7 shows you other sources of state revenue.

Limits on State Taxation

Just as the United States Constitution limits the federal government's power to tax, it also puts limits on the states. Because trade and commerce are considered national enterprises, states cannot tax imports or exports. They also cannot tax goods sent between states.

State governments cannot tax federal property, such as military bases. Nonprofit organizations, religious groups, and charities are usually **tax exempt**; that is, they are not subject to taxes.

tax exempt *not subject to taxes*

◀ Funds for plowing state highways are included in state budgets. Would you expect these funds to be included in a state's operating budget or capital budget?

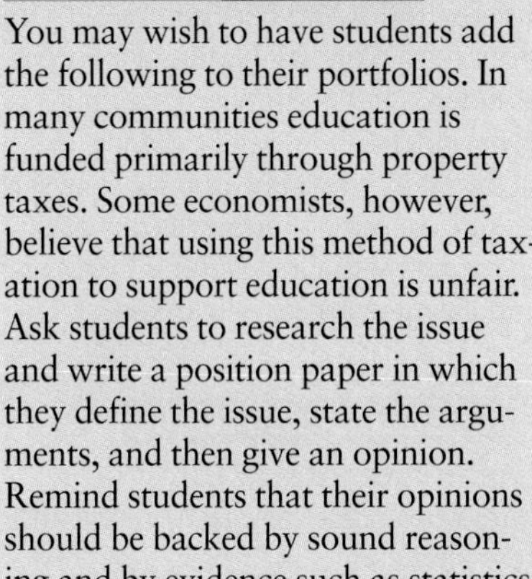

Differentiated Instruction L4

You may wish to have students add the following to their portfolios. In many communities education is funded primarily through property taxes. Some economists, however, believe that using this method of taxation to support education is unfair. Ask students to research the issue and write a position paper in which they define the issue, state the arguments, and then give an opinion. Remind students that their opinions should be backed by sound reasoning and by evidence such as statistics and judicial decisions. GT

Economics Assessment Rubric

Economics Assessment Rubrics folder, pp. 22–23 provides sample evaluation materials for a position paper.

Differentiated Instruction L3

Ask students to create a web graphic organizer that shows where state taxes are spent. They should use the categories listed in the section but also add at least two categories that reflect spending in their own state.

Block Scheduling Strategies

Consider these suggestions to take advantage of extended class time:

- Extend the second activity on this page by obtaining a summary of your state's most recent budget and analyzing it with students. (These are often available on-line at your state's Web site.) Ask questions such as: How much revenue did the state collect? How did the state allocate these resources? What changes might students like to see in the budget? Have students write a paragraph that summarizes their answers to these questions.
- Show the Economics Video Library segment "Private Prisons," about the trend toward privatizing prisons and its effect on state budgets. Have students investigate whether your state has privatized the prison system. If it has, have students research how well the system is working. If it has not, have them find articles on any relevant debate that may be occurring in your state.

Answer to . . .

Photo Caption These funds would be included in the operating budget because plowing keeps state-owned roads operating properly.

Meeting NCEE Standards

Use the following benchmark activity from the **Voluntary National Content Standards in Economics** to evaluate student understanding of **Standard 16.**

Explain why state and local governments use public money to pay for elementary education and why tobacco and gasoline are heavily taxed.

Differentiated Instruction 

Have students research their own state's taxes. Use a search engine and key words such as "taxes," or "revenue" and your state name. Make a list of all the types of taxes that your state uses. What are the main sources of revenue? SN

real property *physical property such as land and buildings*

personal property *possessions such as jewelry, furniture, and boats*

Sales Tax

As Figure 14.7 shows, sales taxes are a main source of revenue for state governments. As you read in Section 1, a sales tax is a tax on goods and services. The tax—a percentage of the purchase price—is added on at the cash register and paid by the purchaser.

All but a few of the 50 states collect sales taxes. Sales tax rates range from 3 to 8 percent. Some local governments have their own, additional, sales tax.

In every state, some categories of products are exempt from sales tax. Many states do not charge sales tax on basic needs such as food and clothing. Some do not tax prescription medicines.

Even states without a sales tax impose excise taxes that apply to specific products and activities. Some are sin taxes—taxes that are intended to discourage harmful behavior—on products like alcoholic beverages and tobacco. Other taxes apply to hotel and motel rooms, automobiles, rental cars, and insurance policies. Many states also tax gasoline. This state gasoline tax is in addition to the federal tax.

State Income Taxes

Individual income taxes are another large contributor to many states' budgets. People pay this state income tax in addition to the federal income tax. Figure 14.7 shows that state individual income taxes contribute about 17 percent of state revenue.

Some states tax incomes at a flat percentage rate (that is, as a proportional tax). Some charge a percentage of a person's federal income tax. Others have progressive rates, with a tax structure like the federal income tax. A few states tax only interest and dividends from investments, not wages and salaries.

Corporate Income Tax

Most states collect corporate income taxes from companies that do business in the state. Some states levy taxes at a fixed, flat rate on business profits. A few charge progressive rates—that is, higher tax rates for businesses with higher profits.

As you can see from Figure 14.7, corporate income taxes contribute only a small percentage of state tax revenues—about 2 percent. Nevertheless, corporate income taxes can influence a state's economy.

Low corporate taxes, along with a well-educated work force and good public services, can make it easier to attract new businesses to a state. Politicians deciding on state corporate tax rates keep this fact in mind when they determine their state's policies.

Other State Taxes

Besides the corporate income tax, businesses pay a variety of other state taxes and fees. Do you want to be a hairdresser, a carpenter, or a building contractor? If so, you will have to pay a licensing fee. A licensing fee is a kind of tax that people pay to carry on different kinds of business within a state.

Some states charge a transfer tax when documents such as stock certificates are transferred and recorded. Other states tax the value of the stock shares that corporations issue.

Many states have rich natural resources, such as gold, oil, natural gas, fish, or lumber. Some states place a tax, called a severance tax, on companies that take (or "sever") these resources from the state's land and waters.

As you read in Section 2, the federal government taxes the estate of a person who has died. States, in turn, usually charge an inheritance tax on the value of the property that goes to each heir.

Some states also tax property. That includes **real property,** such as land and buildings, or "real estate." It also includes **personal property,** such as jewelry, furniture, and boats. Some states even tax intangible property, such as bank accounts, stocks, and bonds. Today, however, most property taxes, especially on real estate, are levied by local governments.

FAST FACT

New Hampshire legislators were faced with a dilemma: how to fund the state's education system, without placing undue hardship on low- and middle-income taxpayers. Their solution: establish an education trust fund. This fund created a uniform statewide education property tax with provisions for tax relief for certain qualified taxpayers. It also dedicated to education revenue from increases in the tobacco tax and from tobacco settlement funds, as well as from various tax increases on businesses.

Preparing for Standardized Tests

Have students read the section titled "Limits on State Taxation," and then answer the question below.

Which of the following cannot be taxed by state governments?

A prescription medicines

B corporate income

C individual income

(D) federal property

public education, and if so, how much it wants to give. Each group can choose to contribute between $0 and $10 in each session. Record your contribution on your Contributions and Refunds Record, and give the money in cash to the state treasurer.

The state budget director adds up all the first session's contributions to education. Then he or she figures the state's budget savings using the Budget Worksheet, keeping in mind that every dollar collected for education results in three dollars saved from welfare and criminal justice. The state budget director gives this information to the state treasurer, who then gives each citizen-group its refund in dollars. If no cash is available, the treasurer will issue IOUs.

Session 2: Each citizen-group again decides whether to make a contribution to public education. Even if you have received a refund, you can still contribute only $10 each day. Record your contribution on your Contributions and Refunds Record, and give the money to the treasurer.

The state budget director again adds up the total contributions, using the Budget Worksheet. He or she figures the savings, and the treasurer gives each citizen-group its refund.

Session 3: Each citizen-group decides again whether to make a contribution to education, using the same process as in earlier sessions. When refunds for this session have been calculated and given, each group adds up all the money it has in cash and IOUs. The total amount of money is the citizen-group's score.

Budget Table for a 10-Citizen State

Total Contributions	State Budget Savings	Tax Refund per Citizen
$20.00	$60.00	$6.00
$50.00	$150.00	$15.00
$80.00	$240.00	$24.00
$100.00	$300.00	$30.00

Contributions and Refunds Record

	Session 1	Session 2	Session 3
Balance at beginning of session	$	$	$
– Contribution	– $	– $	– $
+ Refund	+ $	+ $	+ $
= New balance	= $	= $	= $

Budget Worksheet

	Session 1	Session 2	Session 3
Total contributions x $3.00 = Total budget savings	$ X $3.00 $	$ X $3.00 $	$ X $3.00 $
Total budget savings ÷ Number of citizen-groups = Tax refund per citizen-group	$ ÷ $	$ ÷ $	$ ÷ $

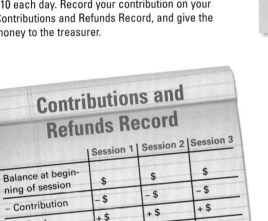

Simulation Analysis

Discuss these questions as a group.

1. From the state treasurer's Budget Worksheet, analyze whether all the citizen-groups were equally generous in their contributions. Did any citizens try to get a free or almost-free ride? Did this tactic pay off for them? How did that affect other groups that did make contributions?
2. Each citizen-group began with $30. How does this compare with the amount that each one has now?
3. Which session brought in the largest total amount of contributions to education?
4. **Determining Relevance** What does this experiment demonstrate about the need for governments to use taxes to pay for public services?

Differentiated Instruction L3

Public radio and television stations receive only a small portion of their funding from the government. As a result they must rely on voluntary contributions. Ask students to consider how free riders take advantage of public radio and television. Have students write several paragraphs expressing their opinions.

Background

Economics in History

A movement to change one of the most fundamental of all public services—public education—has developed. Proponents of school "vouchers" believe that allowing parents to send their children to any school they wish—public or private, religious or nonreligious—would improve education through free market mechanisms. Controversies have surrounded the movement. For example, some people worry about the constitutionality of funding religious schools, even indirectly. Others are concerned about moving away from one goal of public schooling: to bring Americans from all creeds, ethnic groups, races, and income levels into the classroom to learn together.

Answers to . . .

1. Answers will depend on the Budget Worksheet, but it is likely that some citizens would get a free ride. The tactic would pay off for them in the short term. In any case groups that contributed might feel the free riders benefited unfairly.
2. Answers will depend on the results of the simulation.
3. Answers will depend on the results of the simulation.
4. Students should realize that, because of the free rider problem, governments need to require payment for public services through taxes. Otherwise the services would not be funded adequately.

Interdisciplinary Connections: Math

Graphing the Results Students can illustrate graphically the results of this simulation. Different types of graphs will be appropriate for differing types of data.

Making the Connection Have students choose data from the simulation to graph, such as contributions of particular groups over time or total contributions compared to total refunds. Ask students also to create a graph that shows each group's contributions in comparison to those of other groups. Display the finished graphs on a bulletin board.

Chapter Resource Manager

Chapter 15 Fiscal Policy

For more pacing suggestions, see the Economics Pacing Guide in the Program Overview of the Teaching Resources.

Section Objectives	Print and Technology Resources	
1 Understanding Fiscal Policy *(pp. 387–393)* **Objectives** 1. Describe how the government uses fiscal policy as a tool for achieving its economic goals. 2. Explain how the government creates the federal budget. 3. Analyze the impact of fiscal policy decisions on the economy. 4. Identify the limits of fiscal policy.	• **Lesson Planner** Section 1 Lesson Plan, p. 61 • **Learning Styles Lesson Plans folder** Section 1 Lesson Plan, p. 35 • **Lesson Plans folder** Section 1 Lesson Plan, p. 54 • **Economics Assessment Rubrics folder** Writing Assignment, pp. 6–7 • **Unit 6 folder** Guided Reading and Review, p. 15 Economic Skills, p. 21 Section 1 Quiz, p. 16 • **Presentation Pro CD-ROM** Section 1	• **Simulations and Data Graphing CD-ROM** Data Graphing Tools • **Transparency Resource Package** Economics Organizers, G9: Multi-Flow Chart Graphic Organizer Economics Concepts, 15A: Fiscal Policy Economics Concepts, 15B: Wrestling with the Budget • **Section Reading Support Transparency System** • **Social Studies Skills Tutor CD-ROM**
2 Fiscal Policy Options *(pp. 395–401)* **Objectives** 1. Compare and contrast classical economics and Keynesian economics. 2. Explain the basic principles of supply-side economics. 3. Understand the role that fiscal policy has played in American history.	• **Lesson Planner** Section 2 Lesson Plan, p. 62 • **Learning Styles Lesson Plans folder** Section 2 Lesson Plan, p. 36 • **Lesson Plans folder** Section 2 Lesson Plan, p. 55 • **Unit 6 folder** Guided Reading and Review, p. 17 Careers in Economics, Accountant, p. 24 Section 2 Quiz, p. 18 • **Source Articles folder** Four Trillion Gone, pp. 45–47 • **Presentation Pro CD-ROM** Section 2	• **Transparency Resource Package** Economics Organizers, G7: Tree Map Graphic Organizer Economics Concepts, 15C: Effects of Keynesian Economics Economics Concepts, 15D: The Multiplier Effect Economics Concepts, 15E: The Great Depression • **Section Reading Support Transparency System**
3 Budget Deficits and the National Debt *(pp. 403–408)* **Objectives** 1. Explain the importance of balancing the budget. 2. Analyze how budget deficits add to the national debt. 3. Summarize the problems caused by the national debt. 4. Identify how a government can reduce budget deficits and the national debt.	• **Lesson Planner** Section 3 Lesson Plan, p. 63 • **Lesson Plans folder** Section 3 Lesson Plan, p. 56 • **Economics Assessment Rubrics folder** Position Paper, pp. 22–23 • **Unit 6 folder** Guided Reading and Review, p. 19 Economic Cartoon, p. 25 Vocabulary Practice, p. 22 Economic Detective, p. 23 Section 3 Quiz, p. 20 • **Case Studies in Free Enterprise folder** Paul Ehrlich, pp. 30–31	• **Math Practice folder** Per Capita Share of the National Debt, p. 12 • **Presentation Pro CD-ROM** Section 3 • **Transparency Resource Package** Economics Organizers, G10: Venn Diagram Economics Concepts, 15F: Federal Budget Deficits and Surpluses Economics Concepts, 15G: The National Debt • **Section Reading Support Transparency System**

Differentiated Instruction

Finding Patterns in History (L4)

Learning to find patterns in economics and history helps students make connections among events and time periods and to see relevance to their own times. Comparing the economy during the Great Depression and today requires higher level thinking and presents an excellent opportunity for this exercise.

Suggest that students keep a "Patterns Diary" in which they make comparisons between the two eras as they read Chapter 10. One column should be labeled Great Depression and the other Today. Categories may include

- Prices
- Unemployment
- Role of Government
- Popular Economic Theories

Students may also work together to brainstorm their own list of categories. When they have completed their reading, have students draw three to five conclusions from their Patterns Diaries.

Analyze Text Structure (L3)

Remind students that authors organize their text to suit a specific purpose. For example, an advertisement and a newspaper article will probably be set up differently, since the advertisement's goal is to persuade while the article's goal is to inform. Write these guidelines for evaluating text format on the board:

1. Head structure: What is the largest head on the page? What information do these heads provide?

2. Images: What images are included? Where? How do the images support information in the text? What is their purpose?

3. Organization: What information appears on the first page? Why? What information appears inside? Why?

To model this skill, bring in a copy of a newspaper article, advertisement, and brochure and use these guidelines to evaluate each text. Show students how each text structure supports the authors' purpose, whether it is to inform, entertain, or persuade.

Visit the Social Studies area of the Prentice Hall Web site. There you can find additional links to enrich chapter content for *Economics: Principles in Action* as well as a self-test for students. Be sure to check out this month's **eTeach** online discussion with a Master Economics Teacher.

Web Code: mnf-6151

Running Out of Time?

- Use the **Presentation Pro CD-ROM** to create an outline for this chapter.
- Use the Chapter Summary in the **Chapter 15 Assessment,** p. 410.
- Use the Section Summaries for Chapter 15, from **Guide to the Essentials of Economics (English and Spanish).**

THE WALL STREET JOURNAL. CLASSROOM EDITION

Prentice Hall brings into the classroom the authoritative content of *The Wall Street Journal Classroom Edition.* See the Source Articles, Debating Current Issues, and You and Your Money folders in the **Teaching Resources.** Also, see Economics Video Library, "New Economic Era?"

Assessment Resources

Chapter Assessment

Teaching Resources Unit 6, Chapter 15

- Section Quizzes, pp. 16, 18, 20

Exam*View*® Test Bank CD-ROM Chapter 15

Economics Assessment Rubrics

Chapter 15 Self-Test, **Web Code:** mna-611

Reading and Skills Evaluation

Progress Monitoring Assessments

- Screening Test
- Diagnostic Test of Social Studies Skills

Standardized Test Preparation

Test Prep Workbook

Test-Taking Strategies With Transparencies

Differentiated Instruction Key

L1 Special Needs	LPR Less Proficient Readers
L2 Basic to Average	AR Advanced Readers
L3 All Students	SN Special Needs Students
L4 Average to Advanced	GT Gifted and Talented
	ELL English Language Learner

Chapter 15

Fiscal Policy

Introducing the Chapter

In this chapter, students will learn how the government makes fiscal policy, how fiscal policy has changed over time, and how Keynesian and supply-side economics differ. Students will also learn about the national debt and deficit: what they are, what causes them, and how they are affected by fiscal policy.

For additional links for *Economics: Principles in Action* provided by Prentice Hall and *The Wall Street Journal Classroom Edition,* visit the Social Studies area. Be sure to check out this month's **eTeach** online discussion with a Master Teacher.

Beyond the Lecture

You may cover the concepts in Chapter 15 in an activity-based style by using the following materials:

- **Technology Resources** appropriate for use with this chapter are noted on pp. 388, 389, 393, 394, 397, 398, 400, 401, 404, 406, 408, and 411.
- **Presentation Pro CD-ROM** with animated graphs gives you an alternative method for organizing and delivering chapter content.
- **Activities** designed to meet the needs of students of mixed abilities and learning styles are noted throughout the chapter in the side columns.
- **Learning Styles Lesson Plans** provide alternate lessons for diverse learning styles. See pp. 35–36 of the Learning Styles Lesson Plans folder located in the Teaching Resources.

Economics Journal

Instruct students to record their lists in their Economics Journals. Students may include completed journal entries in an Economics Portfolio.

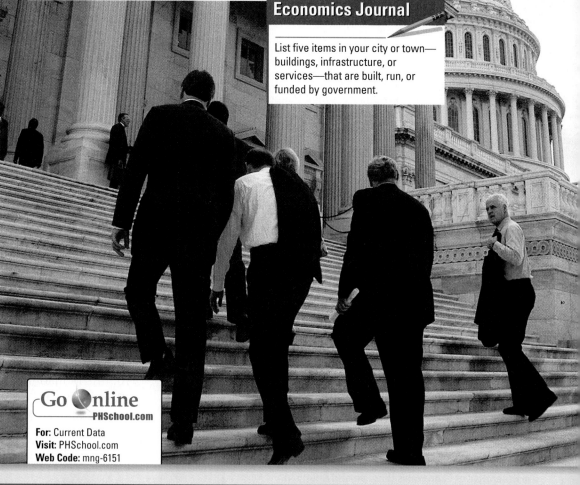

Chapter 15 Fiscal Policy

Spending more money than you earn is usually a bad idea. But what if you face an unexpected need for more cash than you have? How do you decide whether you should borrow money or not spend the money at all?

The federal government deals with this dilemma every year when it prepares its budget. Sometimes borrowing money is the best choice for the economy. Other times, borrowing money causes more problems than it solves.

Economics Journal

List five items in your city or town—buildings, infrastructure, or services—that are built, run, or funded by government.

Go Online
PHSchool.com

For: Current Data
Visit: PHSchool.com
Web Code: mng-6151

National Council on Economic Education

★ **Standard 17** Students will understand that: Costs of government policies sometimes exceed benefits. This may occur because of incentives facing voters, government officials, and government employees, because of actions by special interest groups that can impose costs on the general public, or because social goals other than economic efficiency are being pursued.

★ **Standard 20** Students will understand that: Federal government budgetary policy and the Federal Reserve System's monetary policy influence the overall levels of employment, output, and prices.

For more information about the standards, contact the National Council on Economic Education

1140 Avenue of the Americas
New York, NY 10036
1-800-338-1192

Section 1 Understanding Fiscal Policy

Preview

Objectives

After studying this section you will be able to:

1. **Describe** how the government uses fiscal policy as a tool for achieving its economic goals.
2. **Explain** how the government creates the federal budget.
3. **Analyze** the impact of fiscal policy decisions on the economy.
4. **Identify** the limits of fiscal policy.

Section Focus

The federal government takes in money for the budget through taxation and borrowing. The decisions the government makes about taxing and spending can have a powerful impact on the overall economy.

Key Terms

fiscal policy
federal budget
fiscal year
Office of Management and Budget (OMB)
Congressional Budget Office (CBO)
appropriations bill
expansionary policies
contractionary policies

The word *fiscal* comes from the Latin word *fisc*, which means "basket" or "bag." Over time, the word came to be linked with a bag of money. Specifically, it meant the "bag," or pool, of money held by the government. In Chapter 14, you read about how the government collects money, primarily through taxes, and how the government spends its money on a wide variety of programs. In this section you will read about fiscal policy. **Fiscal policy** is the use of government spending and revenue collection to influence the economy.

Fiscal Policy as a Tool

As you learned in Chapter 14, the federal government takes in and spends huge amounts of money. The federal government spends about $250 million every hour, $6 billion every day, and about $2.3 *trillion* a year. The tremendous flow of cash into and out of the economy has a large impact on aggregate demand and supply in the economy.

Fiscal policies are used to achieve economic growth, full employment, and price stability. Fiscal policy decisions—how much to spend and how much to tax—are among the most important decisions the federal government makes. These decisions are made each year during the creation of the federal budget.

The Federal Budget

The **federal budget** is a written document indicating the amount of money the government expects to receive for a certain year and authorizing the amount the

fiscal policy *the use of government spending and revenue collection to influence the economy*

federal budget *a plan for the federal government's revenues and spending for the coming year*

▲ **Federal budget costs include Transportation Security Administration workers who screen airline passengers and luggage for security threats.**

Section 1

Understanding Fiscal Policy

Objectives You may wish to call students' attention to the objectives in the Section Preview. The objectives are reflected in the main headings of the section.

Bellringer Ask students whether they or their families have ever made a budget. Ask how they make decisions about how much to spend on various items. Explain that in this section they will learn that the government must answer similar questions when setting fiscal policy for the entire country.

Vocabulary Builder As they read, have students create graphic organizers to show relationships between the key terms. Ask them to write a short definition of each term in their organizers and to supply labels that show interrelationships. (For example, between the boxes for *Office of Management and Budget* and *federal budget*, students might write the label *prepares.*)

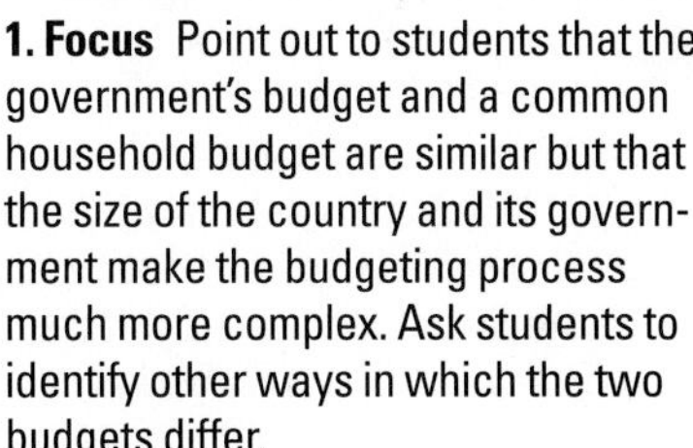

Lesson Plan

Teaching the Main Concepts L3

1. Focus Point out to students that the government's budget and a common household budget are similar but that the size of the country and its government make the budgeting process much more complex. Ask students to identify other ways in which the two budgets differ.

2. Instruct Define fiscal policy and explain its relationship to the federal budget. Explain how the federal budget is created. Distinguish between policies designed to expand and to contract the economy, and explain the purpose of each. Finally, identify the limitations of fiscal policy.

3. Close/Reteach To check students' understanding of the effects of fiscal policy on the economy, have them provide oral summaries of the graphics on pp. 389–390.

Building Key Concepts: Graphing the Main Idea

Monetary and Fiscal Policy To build understanding of how **public policy** is expressed fiscally, have students complete two multi-flowchart graphic organizers like the one at the right. One covering expansionary policies; the other covering contractionary policies. Students should place the expansionary (or contractionary) policies in the outside boxes and the effect (encouraging or slowing growth) in the center.

Section Reading Support Transparencies A template and the answers for this graphic organizer can be found in Chapter 15, Section 1 of the Section Reading Support Transparency System.

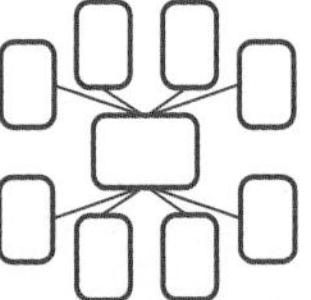

 **Guided Reading and Review**
Unit 6 folder, p. 15 asks students to identify the main ideas of the section and to define or identify key terms.

Differentiated Instruction L3
Have students write a letter to a foreign friend who has asked what fiscal policy is, how it affects the economy, and how the federal budget is related to fiscal policy. Students should summarize the budget process itself as well as the role of each branch of government in creating a budget. Encourage students to use language and sentence structure that would be easily understood by someone who is not a native speaker of English.

 **Transparency Resource Package**
Economics Concepts, 15A: Fiscal Policy

Differentiated Instruction L4
Have students locate a copy of the publication "A Citizen's Guide to the Federal Budget," published by the Government Printing Office. Ask students to examine the guide, especially the charts and graphs. Have them choose a graphic that they think is particularly clear or informative and share it with the class. Explain to students that this will help all students understand important aspects of the budget.
GT

 ***Take It to the NET***
This publication is available on-line. Have students use the links provided in the *Economics: Principles in Action* segment in the Social Studies area at the following Web site: **www.phschool.com**

Figure 15.1 **Creating the Federal Budget**

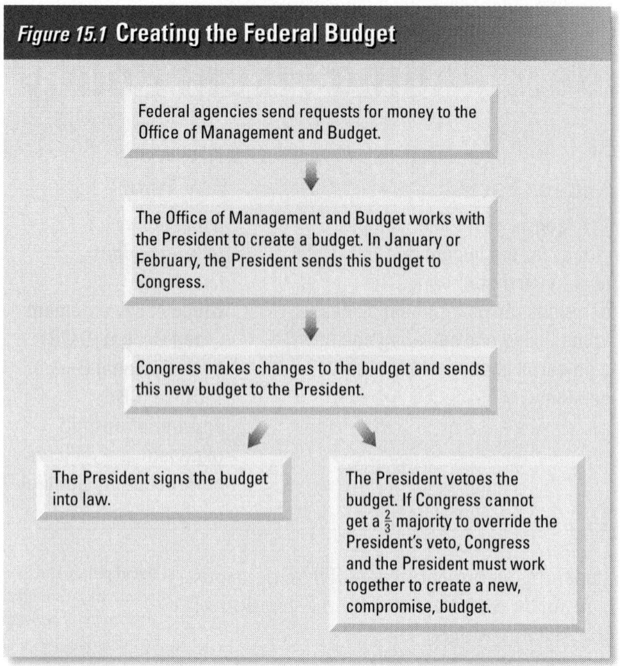

Federal agencies send requests for money to the Office of Management and Budget.
The Office of Management and Budget works with the President to create a budget. In January or February, the President sends this budget to Congress.
Congress makes changes to the budget and sends this new budget to the President.
The President signs the budget into law.
The President vetoes the budget. If Congress cannot get a $\frac{2}{3}$ majority to override the President's veto, Congress and the President must work together to create a new, compromise, budget.

Congress and the White House work together over the course of the year to put together a federal budget.
Government Who takes the first step in the budget process?

government can spend that year. The federal budget is just a plan to pay for the federal government's expenditures. Much like a family's budget, it lists expected income and shows exactly how the money will be spent.

The federal government prepares a new budget for each fiscal year. A **fiscal year** is a twelve-month period that is not necessarily the same as the January-to-December calendar year. The federal government uses a fiscal year that runs from October 1 through September 30.

The federal budget takes about 18 months to prepare. During this time, citizens, Congress, and the President debate the government's spending priorities. There are four basic steps in the federal budget process.

fiscal year *a twelve-month period that can begin on any date*

Office of Management and Budget (OMB) *government office that manages the federal budget*

Congressional Budget Office (CBO) *government agency that provides economic data to Congress*

Spending Proposals

The federal budget must fund many offices and agencies in the federal government, and Congress cannot decide all of their needs. Before the budget can be put together, each federal agency writes a detailed estimate of how much it expects to spend in the coming fiscal year.

These spending proposals are sent to a special unit of the executive branch, the **Office of Management and Budget (OMB).** The OMB is part of the Executive Office of the President. As its name suggests, the OMB is responsible for managing the federal government's budget. Its most important job is to prepare the federal budget.

In the Executive Branch

The OMB holds several meetings to review the Federal agencies' spending proposals. Representatives from the agencies must explain their spending proposals to the OMB and convince the OMB to give them as much money as they have asked for. Usually, OMB gives each agency less than they say they need.

The OMB then works with the President's staff to combine all of the individual agency budgets into a single budget document. This document gives the President's overall spending plan for the coming fiscal year. The President presents the budget to Congress in January or February.

In Congress

The President's budget is only a starting point, and the number of changes Congress makes depends on the relationship between the President and Congress. Congress carefully considers, debates, and modifies the President's proposed budget. For help, members of Congress rely on the assistance of the **Congressional Budget Office (CBO).** Created in 1974, the CBO gives Congress independent economic data to help with its decisions.

Much of the work done by Congress—the House of Representatives and the Senate—is done by small committees. Working at the same time in different houses of Congress, committees in the House and Senate analyze the budget and hold hearings at which agency officials and others can speak out about the budget. The

Monetary and Fiscal Policy One of the key concepts in this section is the use of a **budget.** The text compares family budgets to the federal budget. These comparisons are helpful, but students need to comprehend the much greater complexity of the federal budgeting process.

Briefly summarize a typical family budgeting process. Then ask students to create a Venn diagram that shows the similarities and differences between a family budget and the federal budget.

Answer to . . .
Building Key Concepts Federal agencies send requests for money to the Office of Management and Budget.

House Budget Committee and Senate Budget Committee combine their work to propose one initial budget resolution, which must be adopted by May 15 of the year. This resolution is not intended to be final, but gives initial estimates for revenue and spending to guide the legislators as they continue working on the budget.

Then, in early September, the Budget Committees for each house of Congress propose a second budget resolution that sets binding spending limits. Congress must pass this resolution by September 15, after which Congress cannot pass any new bills that would spend more money than the budget resolution allows.

Finally, the Appropriations Committees for each house submit bills to authorize specific spending. By this time, the new fiscal year is about to start and Congress faces pressure to get these **appropriations bills** adopted and submitted to the President quickly before the previous year's funding ends on September 30. If Congress cannot finish in time, it must pass short-term emergency spending legislation known as "stop-gap funding" to keep the government running. If Congress and the President cannot even agree on temporary funding, the government "shuts down" and all but the most essential federal offices will close.

In the White House

Congress sends the appropriations bills to the President, who can sign them into law. If he vetoes any of these bills, Congress must either come up with enough votes to override the veto—usually, this is impossible—or work with the President to write an appropriations bill on which both sides can agree. Once that is completed, the President signs the new budget into law.

Fiscal Policy and the Economy

Government officials who take part in the budget process debate how much should be spent on specific programs such as defense, education, and scientific research. They also consider how much should be spent in total. The total level of government spending can be changed to help increase or decrease the output of the economy. Similarly, taxes can be raised or lowered to help increase or decrease the output of the economy.

Fiscal policies that try to increase output are known as **expansionary policies.** Fiscal policies intended to decrease output are called **contractionary policies.** By carefully choosing to follow expansionary or contractionary fiscal policies, the federal government tries to make the economy run as smoothly as possible.

Expansionary Fiscal Policies

Governments use expansionary fiscal policies to raise the level of output in the economy. That is, they use expansionary policies to encourage growth, either when the economy is in a recession or to try to prevent a recession. Recall from Chapter 12 that a recession is the part of the business

appropriations bill *a bill that sets money aside for specific spending*

expansionary policies *fiscal policies, like higher spending and tax cuts, that encourage economic growth*

contractionary policies *fiscal policies, like lower spending and higher taxes, that reduce economic growth*

Figure 15.2 Effects of Expansionary Fiscal Policy

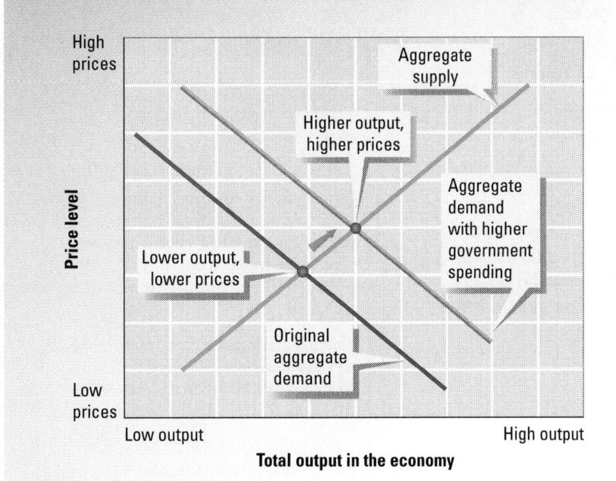

Expansionary fiscal policy helps the economy by increasing aggregate demand and output.
Supply and Demand **How do increases in government spending affect aggregate supply?**

Differentiated Instruction L3

Ask students to examine the section and the flowchart on p. 388. Then ask the question: "Who are the main players in the budgetary process?" *(federal agencies, the Office of Management and Budget, the President, Congress)* Have students locate more specific information about the role of each arm of government in the budgetary process. Finally, ask them to write out a list of responsibilities for each of these groups.

Transparency Resource Package Economics Concepts, 15B: Wrestling with the Budget

Differentiated Instruction 

Have students print out several years of federal government budgets in major categories from the *Statistical Abstract of the United States* or from another Internet site. Compare the increases in spending by category, and discuss reasons for the difference in rates of increase or decrease. SN

Block Scheduling Strategies

Consider these suggestions to take advantage of extended class time:

- Extend the first activity on p. 388 by having each student exchange letters with a partner. Each partner should read the other's letter and then write a letter back asking for more clarification where it is needed. The writer of each original letter should then make these clarifications and resubmit the letter.
- Show the Economics Video Library segment "New Economic Era?" about America's strong economic growth, unaccompanied by inflation. The phenomenon has caused economists to reexamine whether old patterns still hold true. After students view the segment, provide copies of several articles that reflect this debate, and hold a discussion on economic growth and fiscal policy.

Answer to . . .

Building Key Concepts Government spending increases aggregate supply, encouraging the economy to expand.

Differentiated Instruction L3

(Enrichment) To help students understand a real-life issue in fiscal policy, have them research the capital-gains tax. Capital gains are made when selling assets, especially shares of stock. Have students investigate arguments for and against cutting the tax. Then have them write an essay explaining which side they support and whether that policy is expansionary or contractionary.

Differentiated Instruction L3

Organize students into groups of three. Ask each group to create three economic scenarios that involve such factors as recession, unemployment, or inflation. (Encourage students to examine the headings titled "Expansionary Fiscal Policies" and "Contractionary Fiscal Policies" to find ideas for their scenarios.) Then have groups exchange scenarios and suggest specific expansionary or contractionary fiscal policies to deal with each situation. Groups should be able to explain why they suggested the remedies they did.

Learning Styles Activity

Learning Styles Lesson Plans folder, p. 35 asks students to compose letters to representatives in Congress asking that a budget allocation be created or retained for a specific need or project.

cycle that occurs when output declines for two quarters, or three-month periods, in a row. Expansionary fiscal policies fall into either or both of two categories: increasing government spending and cutting taxes.

Increasing Government Spending

If the federal government increases its spending or buys more goods and services, it triggers a chain of events that raises output and creates jobs. Government spending increases aggregate demand, which causes prices to rise. (See Figure 15.2.) According to the law of supply, higher prices encourage suppliers of goods and services to produce more. To do this, firms will hire more workers. In short, an increase in demand will lead to lower unemployment and to an increase in output, as shown in Figure 15.3. The economy will be encouraged to expand.

Cutting Taxes

Tax cuts work much like higher government spending to encourage the economy to expand. If the federal government cuts taxes, individuals have more money to spend, and businesses keep more of their profits. Consumers will have more money to spend on goods and services, and firms will have more money to spend on land, labor, and capital. These actions will increase demand, prices, and output.

The goal of expansionary fiscal policy is to add money to the economy. **Government How might cutting taxes have similar effects to those shown in the chart?**

Figure 15.3 Flowchart of Effects of Expansionary Fiscal Policy

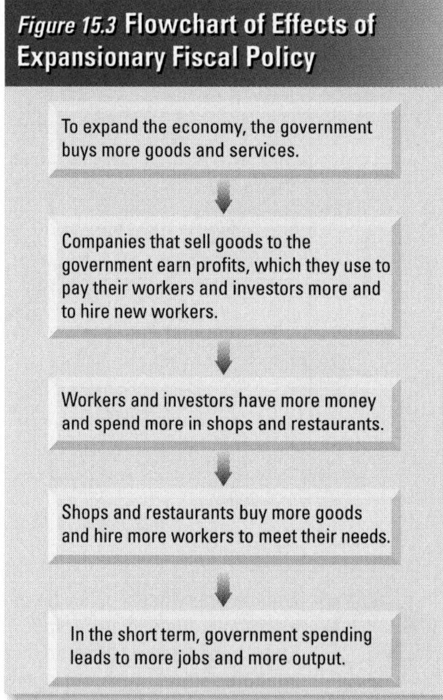

To expand the economy, the government buys more goods and services.
Companies that sell goods to the government earn profits, which they use to pay their workers and investors more and to hire new workers.
Workers and investors have more money and spend more in shops and restaurants.
Shops and restaurants buy more goods and hire more workers to meet their needs.
In the short term, government spending leads to more jobs and more output.

Contractionary Fiscal Policies

At some stages in the business cycle, the government may choose contractionary fiscal policies. Contractionary fiscal policies try to decrease aggregate demand, and by decreasing demand, reduce the growth of economic output. If contractionary fiscal policies are strong enough, they may slow the growth of output to zero, or even lead to a fall in GDP.

The government sometimes tries to slow down the economy because fast-growing demand can exceed supply. When demand exceeds supply, producers must choose between raising output and raising prices. If producers cannot expand production enough, they will raise their prices, which leads to high inflation. As you read in Chapter 12, inflation is an increase in prices over time. Inflation cuts into consumers' purchasing power and discourages economic growth and stability. Fiscal policies aimed at slowing the growth of total output generally fall into either or both of two categories: decreasing government spending and raising taxes.

Decreasing Government Spending

If the federal government spends less, or buys fewer goods and services, it triggers a chain of events that may lead to slower GDP growth. A decrease in government spending leads to a decrease in aggregate demand because the government is buying less than before. Decreased demand tends to cause lower prices. According to the law of supply, lower prices encourage suppliers to cut their production and possibly fire workers. Lower production lowers the growth rate of the economy and may even reduce GDP.

Answer to . . .

Building Key Concepts Like government spending, tax cuts provide consumers with more money to spend and businesses with more profits, all of which increase demand, prices, and output.

Preparing for Standardized Tests

Have students read the section titled "Contractionary Fiscal Policies" and then answer the question below.

According to the text, what occurs—or may occur—when the government pursues a contractionary economic policy?

A Economic growth may be reduced.

B Taxes may be raised.

C Government spending may be reduced.

(D) all of the above

This chain of events is the exact opposite of what happens when the government increases spending. The government uses the same tools to try to influence the economy in both cases, but in different ways, and with very different goals.

Increasing Taxes

When the federal government raises taxes, individuals have less money to spend on goods and services or to save for the future. Firms keep less of their profits and decrease their spending on land, labor, and capital. As a result of these decreases in demand, prices tend to fall. Producers of goods and suppliers of services tend to cut production. This slows the growth of GDP.

Figure 15.4 Effects of Contractionary Fiscal Policy

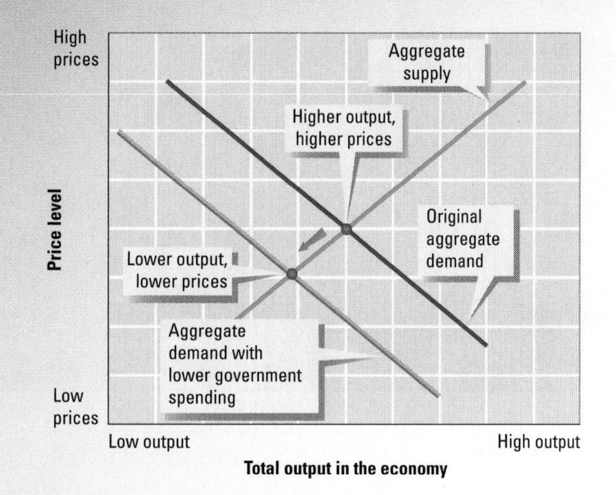

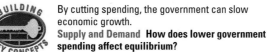

By cutting spending, the government can slow economic growth.
Supply and Demand How does lower government spending affect equilibrium?

Limits of Fiscal Policy

On paper, fiscal policies look like powerful tools that can keep the economy in perfect balance. In reality, fiscal policies can be clumsy and difficult to put into practice.

Difficulty of Changing Spending Levels

Increasing or decreasing the amount of federal spending is not an easy task. As you read in Chapter 14, many of the spending categories in the federal budget are entitlements that are fixed by law. Nearly 60 percent of the federal budget is set aside for programs such as Medicaid, Social Security, and veterans' benefits before Congress even begins the budget process. The government cannot change spending for entitlements under current law. As a result, significant changes in federal spending generally must come from the small part of the federal budget that includes discretionary spending. This gives the government less leeway for increasing or lowering spending.

Predicting the Future

Governments use fiscal policies to prevent big changes in the level of GDP. Despite the statistics, however, it is difficult to know the current state of the economy. As you read in Chapter 12, no one can predict how quickly the business cycle will move from one stage to the next, nor can anyone identify exactly where the economy is at any specific point in the cycle. Economists often disagree about the meaning of statistics, whether they show the economy is in good condition or ready for a recession.

Predicting future economic performance is even more difficult. As a result, lawmakers may put off making changes in fiscal policy until they know more about how the economy is performing. By then, it may be too late to act.

In addition, when lawmakers put fiscal policies in place, they base their decisions partly on the past behaviors of individuals. It is risky to assume that people will, for example, respond the same way to a tax cut in the future as they have in the past.

Delayed Results

Although changes in fiscal policy affect the economy, changes take time. Once government officials decide when and how to change fiscal policy, they have to put these changes into effect within the federal budget, which itself takes over a year to

Differentiated Instruction L4

You may wish to have students add the following to their portfolios. The battle over the federal budget is a year-round process, and therefore the flow of news on the budget is usually continuous. For a period of several weeks, ask students to read daily newspapers for articles on the budgetary process. Have students clip the articles or photocopy them and add them to their portfolios. At the end of this period, ask students to write a short summary of the articles they found. GT

Economics Assessment Rubric
Economics Assessment Rubrics folder, pp. 6–7 provides sample evaluation materials for a writing assignment.

Background

Global Connections

An often surprising part of the political budgeting process is called "pork barrel legislation." This refers to spending packages members of Congress attach to bills; packages that aid only their own constituents. The extra funding generally has nothing to do with the main purpose of the bill. For example, in the spring of 1999, President Clinton made a $6 billion emergency spending request to aid war refugees in Kosovo and tornado victims in the midwestern United States. By the time Congress was ready to vote on it, the bill had expanded to $14.7 billion, including $3 million to aid commercial reindeer herders in Alaska and a permit to open a controversial gold mine on a mountain in Washington State.

Econ 101: Key Concepts Made Easy

Monetary and Fiscal Policy The notion of **contractionary fiscal policies** may be difficult for some students to comprehend. Tell students to think of the economy as a person who has gained a few pounds and is unable to fit into his or her old clothing. If the economy's demand is too high (the economic equivalent of an increased appetite), inflation (like unwanted weight) may result. By reducing spending, the government puts the economy on a diet. By raising taxes, the government makes the economy exercise a bit more, with the burned calories flowing into government coffers. Ask students to apply this example to **expansionary fiscal policies** either orally or in writing.

Answer to . . .

Building Key Concepts Lower government spending *leads to a decrease* in aggregate demand, causing lower output, possibly lower prices, and the potential for recession. If the economy has been expanding too quickly, the market will move toward equilibrium.

Differentiated Instruction 

(Reteaching) To help students understand the limits of fiscal policy, ask them to contribute to a list of the reasons why fiscal policies are difficult to put into practice. As each reason is suggested, challenge students to name a real-life example of this reason. For example, for difficulty of changing spending levels, they may recall mandatory spending information from Chapter 14.

Background

Careers in Economics

For those interested in combining an interest in economics and a talent for writing, journalism may be an excellent career choice. Journalists who have a thorough understanding of economics will always be in demand because of their ability to translate the intricacies of fiscal policy and the economic ideas behind them into language that can be understood by the typical newspaper reader.

▲ **Cutting government spending is difficult because some voters will object to cuts that impact their interests.**

develop. Finally, they have to wait for the change in spending or taxing to affect the economy.

By the time the policy takes effect, the economy might be moving in the opposite direction. The government could propose massive public spending on highways in the middle of a recession, only to have the economy recover before construction begins. In these cases, fiscal policy would only add to the new trend, instead of correcting the original problem. If the government continued to spend lots of money on highways in the middle of a recovery, it could lead to high inflation and a labor shortage.

Global Connections

Experimenting in Japan Japan used expansionary fiscal policies in the 1990s to try to end an economic slump. When real estate prices and stock prices decreased sharply in Japan in the early 1990s, investors, businesses, and banks lost much of their wealth. Consumers and businesses spent less, and banks could not afford to lend money for new investment, so the economy suffered. The Japanese government tried to increase demand by spending money on new roads, government-sponsored loans, and tax cuts. Between 1992 and 1999, the government passed nine major bills spending a total of $1.1 trillion, or nearly $90,000 for every man, woman, and child in Japan. The plan failed to revive the economy and burdened the government with enormous debts. By 2004, government debt had reached 173% of GDP but the economy was still struggling.

Political Pressures

The President and members of Congress, who develop the federal budget and the federal government's fiscal policies, are elected officials. If they wish to be reelected, they must make decisions that benefit the people who elect them, not necessarily decisions that are good for the overall economy.

For example, government officials have an incentive to practice expansionary fiscal policies by increasing government spending and lowering taxes. These actions are usually popular with voters, although in Section 3 you will read about why some people disapprove of government spending. Government spending benefits the firms that receive government contracts and the individuals who receive direct payments from the government. Lower taxes leave more disposable income in people's pockets.

On the other hand, contractionary fiscal policies that decrease government spending or raise taxes are often unpopular. Firms and individuals that expect income from the government are not happy when the income is reduced or cut off. No one likes to pay higher taxes, unless the tax revenue is spent on a specific, highly valued good or service.

Coordinating Fiscal Policy

For fiscal policies to be effective, various branches and levels of government must plan and work together. This is very difficult to do. For example, if the federal government is pursuing contractionary policies, ideally state and local governments should pursue consistent fiscal policies. Yet, state and local governments may be pursuing different goals for fiscal policy than the federal government.

For example, after the federal government cut income taxes in 2001 and 2003, many state and local governments raised income and property taxes to close budget deficits and avoid deep spending cuts. The federal goverment was willing to cut taxes and run a deficit in poor economic times, but most state and local goverments were legally forbidden to do so.

Businesspeople, politicians, and economists often disagree about how well the economy is performing, and what the goals of the fiscal policy should be. Also, different regions of the economy can experience very different conditions. California and Hawaii may have high unemployment while Nebraska and Massachusetts face rising prices and a labor shortage.

In addition, in order for the federal government's fiscal policy to be effective, it must also be coordinated with the monetary policies of the Federal Reserve. You'll read more about monetary policy in the next chapter.

Even when all of these obstacles are overcome, fiscal policy faces still another limitation. The short-term effects of fiscal policy can be different from the long-term effects. A tax cut or increased government spending will give a temporary boost to economic production and to employment. However, as the economy returns to full employment, high levels of government spending combined with market spending will lead to increased inflation as the economy overheats.

Similarly, an increase in taxes or a decrease in government spending may "cool" the economy and lead to a recession. However, in the long run, reduced government spending will allow other types of spending to increase without risking higher inflation. If there is more private investment spending, this could lead to higher economic growth in the long run. In this way, slow growth or even recession in the short term can lead to prosperity and more jobs in the future.

◀ **New community-built pools, like this one in California, have an economic impact on the local level by providing jobs.**

Section 1 Assessment

Progress Monitoring *Online*
For: Self-quiz with vocabulary practice
Web Code: mna-6155

Key Terms and Main Ideas

1. Explain **fiscal policy** and how it relates to the **federal budget.**
2. When does the federal government's **fiscal year** begin?
3. What role does the **Office of Management and Budget (OMB)** play in creating the federal budget?
4. What are two types of **expansionary policies?**

Applying Economic Concepts

5. ***Critical Thinking*** Explain how a tax cut can lead to a higher GDP in the short run.
6. ***Try This*** Which fiscal policy strategy do you think policymakers would use in each of these scenarios? Explain your answers. **(a)** Inflation is rising, and real GDP is up by 4 percent. **(b)** GDP is down, and the unemployment rate has increased to 10 percent.
7. ***Using the Databank*** The Consumer Confidence Index measures how optimistic American consumers are that the economy will do well. The graph on page 539 of the Databank measures consumer confidence in recent years. If you had been a policymaker in 2004, would you have recommended expansionary or contractionary fiscal policies? Explain your answer.

For: Simulation Activity
Visit: PHSchool.com
Web Code: mnd-6151

Progress Monitoring *Online*
For additional assessment, have students access Progress Monitoring Online at **Web Code:** mna-6155

Go Online PHSchool.com Typing in the Web Code when prompted will bring students directly to detailed instructions for this activity.

GTE Guide to the Essentials
Chapter 15, Section 1, p. 63 provides support for students who need additional review of the section content. Spanish support is available in the Spanish edition of the guide on p. 63.

Quiz Unit 6 folder, p. 16 includes questions to check students' understanding of Section 1 content.

Presentation Pro CD-ROM
Quiz provides multiple-choice questions to check students' understanding of Section 1 content.

Answers to . . .

Section 1 Assessment

1. Fiscal policy is government use of taxing and spending to stabilize the economy. The federal budget is the revenue and spending plan based on fiscal policy decisions. The two are related because the federal budget expresses the government's current fiscal policy.
2. The federal fiscal year begins October 1.
3. The Office of Management and Budget (OMB) is the part of the Executive Office of the President that prepares the federal budget based on spending proposals received from federal agencies.
4. Two expansionary policies are increasing government spending and cutting taxes.
5. A tax cut makes more money available to consumers to spend on goods and services. Firms keep more profits that they can reinvest in labor, land, and capital. All of these factors increase GDP in the short run.
6. (a) Students may suggest raising taxes to slow consumer and producer spending, curbing both inflation and economic growth. (b) Students may suggest cutting taxes, allowing firms to reinvest in more labor and allowing consumers to purchase more goods and services. Both will raise GDP.
7. Some students may suggest neither type of policy because consumer confidence was moderate. Some may suggest contractionary policies because confidence was rising.

Skills for LIFE

Comparing Circle Graphs

1. Focus Circle graphs show visually the relationships of parts to a whole and allow comparisons of different categories over time.

2. Instruct Explain to students that all circle graphs should have a main heading, representing a whole, and subcategories, representing the parts of that whole. Then have students work through the three steps outlined in the skills feature. Have students analyze the information to find the main idea and draw inferences and conclusions from the graphs.

3. Close/Reteach To provide additional practice, see the Economic Skills Activity below.

Economic Skills Activity
Unit 6 folder, p. 21, "Comparing Circle Graphs," asks students to compare two circle graphs on Medicaid.

Simulations and Data Graphing CD-ROM offers data graphing tools so that students can practice creating and interpreting graphs.

Social Studies Skills Tutor CD-ROM offers interactive practice in critical thinking and reading, visual analysis, and communication.

Answers

1. (a) 18 percent (b) 18 percent (c) Social Security
2. (a) Social Security, Veterans Benefits, Health (Medicaid), Other (b) Defense, Social Security, and Interest (c) Defense, Social Security, and Income Security
3. Students may suggest that the increased spending on Social Security is due to the growing number of retired individuals receiving benefits.

Additional Practice

Students should draw an accurate circle graph showing budget data for any year between 1941 and 1945 and then describe how that budget differs from the 2004 budget. Noticeable differences will be the percentage of the budget devoted to defense spending and social security.

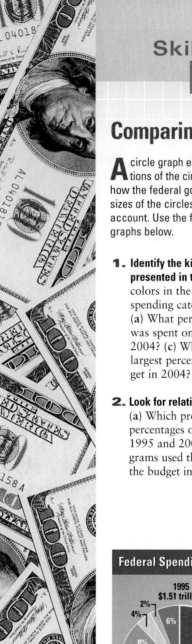

Skills for LIFE

Comparing Circle Graphs

A circle graph enables you to compare parts with a whole. Together, the sections of the circle add up to 100 percent. The circle graphs below show how the federal government spent its money in 1995 and 2004. The different sizes of the circles reflect the increase in spending before taking inflation into account. Use the following steps to analyze the circle graphs below.

1. **Identify the kind of information presented in the graph.** Match the colors in the circle graph to the spending categories listed in the key. (a) What percentage of the budget was spent on defense in 1995? (b) In 2004? (c) What program used the largest percentage of the federal budget in 2004?

2. **Look for relationships among the data.** (a) Which programs increased their percentages of the budget between 1995 and 2004? (b) Which three programs used the largest percentages of the budget in 1995? (c) In 2004?

3. **Use the graphs to draw conclusions.** Social Security benefits grew by 23 percent between 1995 and 2004. Based on this figure, some people might argue that government is providing more benefits to each recipient. What is another way to interpret this statistic?

Additional Practice

Locate federal budget data for any year between 1941 and 1945. Draw a circle graph showing all the programs that accounted for at least 3 percent of the budget. How does this budget differ from the 2004 budget?

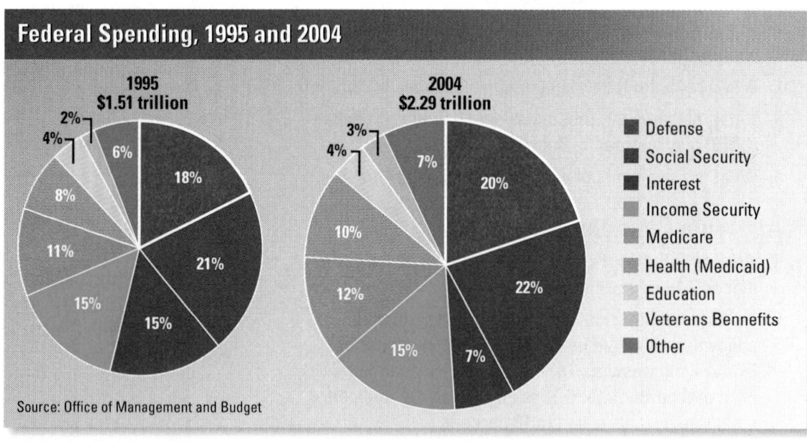

Interdisciplinary Connections: Geography

Using Circle Graphs Remind students that circle graphs can be used to represent the relationship of any part to a whole and can therefore be used in many fields other than economics. Discuss with students types of data for which a circle graph might be preferable to a bar graph.

Have students work through the following problem: Land use in an area could be graphed in this way. Have interested students conduct research in a local library or go to municipal government offices for information on land use in your school district. Students should be able to find out total square mileage for your district as well as square mileage devoted to various purposes. Have them design circle graphs with separate categories for each type of land use. Typical categories might include heavy industrial, light industrial, commercial, residential, and recreational.

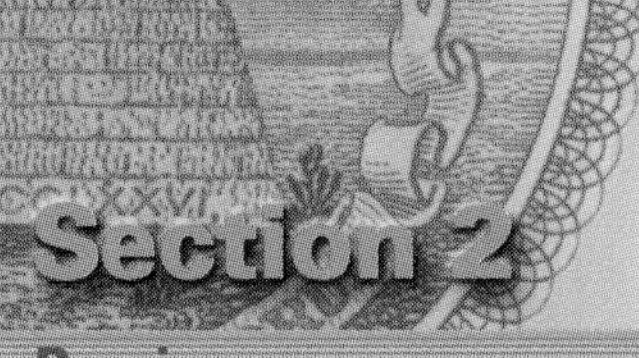

Section 2 Fiscal Policy Options

Preview

Objectives

After studying this section you will be able to:

1. **Compare and contrast** classical economics and Keynesian economics.
2. **Explain** the basic principles of supply-side economics.
3. **Understand** the role that fiscal policy has played in American history.

Section Focus

Fiscal policy is the use of government spending and taxes to work toward low unemployment, low inflation, and steady economic growth. Keynesian economic theories and supply-side economic theories suggest two very different ways for government to encourage growth.

Key Terms

classical economics
productive capacity
demand-side economics
Keynesian economics
multiplier effect
automatic stabilizer
supply-side economics
Council of Economic Advisers (CEA)

For thousands of years, governments have collected taxes and spent money. Until the 1930s, however, most economists believed that a government should keep its role in the economy small. These economists belonged to a school of thought called classical economics.

Classical Economics

Throughout this book, you have read about the workings of a free market economy. In a free market, people act in their own self-interest, causing prices to rise or fall so that supply and demand will always return to equilibrium. This idea that free markets regulate themselves is at the heart of a school of thought known as **classical economics.** Adam Smith, David Ricardo, and Thomas Malthus are all considered classical economists. For more than a century, classical economics dominated economic theory and government policies.

The Great Depression that began in 1929 challenged this thinking. Prices fell over several years, so demand should have increased enough to stimulate production as consumers took advantage of low prices. Instead, demand also fell as people lost their jobs and bank failures wiped out their savings. According to classical economics, the market should have reached equilibrium, with full employment. But it didn't, and millions suffered from unemployment and other hardships. Many people were too poor to buy enough food for their families, while farmers lost their farms because corn was selling for seven cents a bushel, beef for two and a half cents a pound, and apples were five for a penny.

classical economics *the idea that free markets can regulate themselves*

▼ **The economic hardships brought about by the Great Depression challenged the ideas of classical economics.**

Graphing the Main Idea

Monetary and Fiscal Policy To build understanding of **public policy** and economic theory, have students use a tree map graphic organizer like the one at the right to illustrate the ideas behind classical, Keynesian, and supply-side economics. Remind students that a tree map includes a main topic, main ideas or subtopics, and supporting details.

Section Reading Support Transparencies A template and the answers for this graphic organizer can be found in Chapter 15, Section 2 of the Section Reading Support Transparency System.

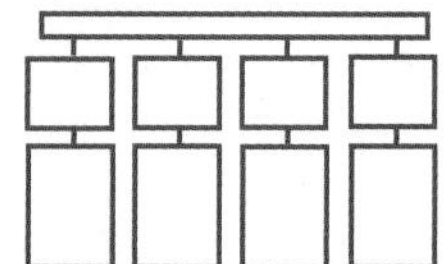

Section 2 Fiscal Policy Options

Objectives You may wish to call students' attention to the objectives in the Section Preview. The objectives are reflected in the main headings of the section.

Bellringer Ask students whether they have ever been so frustrated by the way a job was being done that they felt they had to develop a new way of doing it. Point out that new theories in economics, as well as in other social sciences, often develop because of similar frustrations.

Vocabulary Builder Have students create flashcards with definitions of the key terms. Then organize the class into pairs, and have students quiz each other, using their flashcards.

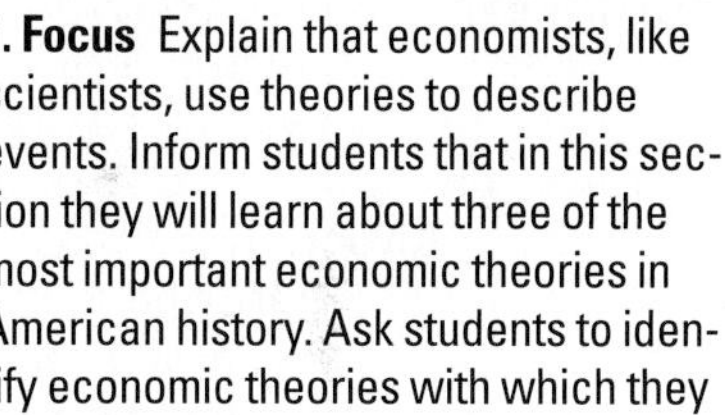

Lesson Plan

Teaching the Main Concepts L3

1. Focus Explain that economists, like scientists, use theories to describe events. Inform students that in this section they will learn about three of the most important economic theories in American history. Ask students to identify economic theories with which they are familiar.

2. Instruct Explain the differences among the economic theories described in this section. Continue by explaining how governments use fiscal policy. Make sure that students understand the role that fiscal policy has played in American history.

3. Close/Reteach The battles continue among economists over which, if any, of the theories covered in this section should drive fiscal policy. Ask students to read business magazines and news magazines to find out what kind of fiscal policy debates are going on now and which economists strongly influence the U.S. economy.

Guided Reading and Review
Unit 6 folder, p. 17 asks students to identify the main ideas of the section and to define or identify key terms.

Differentiated Instruction 

Have students use the graph on this page and section material about the theories of John Maynard Keynes to answer the following questions:

- In what way does the left column of the graph represent what occurred during the Depression? *(During the Depression neither producers nor consumers had an incentive to spend enough to cause an increase in production. Therefore, actual production fell short of productive capacity.)*
- What was Keynes's recommendation for helping the economy to reach its productive capacity? *(Keynes proposed that the government, with its resources, begin spending to boost the economy.)*
- What are the three sectors of the economy, according to Keynes? *(producers, consumers, and government)*

Differentiated Instruction 

(Verbal) To review concepts learned in this section, have students imagine themselves to be Keynes in the 1930s. Have them prepare 5-minute speeches in which they advocate his methods for alleviating the Great Depression. Before they begin work, review persuasive techniques that students might use in their speeches.

productive capacity *the maximum output that an economy can produce without big increases in inflation*

demand-side economics *the idea that government spending and tax cuts help an economy by raising demand*

Keynesian economics *a form of demand-side economics that encourages government action to increase or decrease demand and output*

The Great Depression highlighted a problem with classical economics: it did not address *how long* it would take for the market to return to equilibrium. Classical economists recognized it could take some time, and looked to the "long run" for equilibrium to reestablish itself. One economist, who was not satisfied with the idea of simply waiting for the economy to recover on its own, commented: "In the long run we are all dead." That man was John Maynard Keynes (pronounced CANES).

Keynesian Economics

British economist John Maynard Keynes developed a new theory of economics to explain the Depression. Keynes presented his ideas in 1936 in a book called *The General Theory of Employment, Interest, and Money.* He wanted to develop a comprehensive explanation of economic forces. Such an explanation should, he argued, tell economists and politicians how to get out of economic crises like the Great Depression. It should also tell them how to avoid crises in the first place. In sharp contrast to classical economics, Keynes wanted to give government a tool it could use now, in the short run.

A Broader View

A key to Keynes's ideas was a broader view of a country's economy. Classical economists had always looked at the equilibrium of supply and demand for *individual products.* In contrast, Keynes focused instead on the economy *as a whole.*

Keynes looked at the productive capacity of the entire economy. **Productive capacity,** often called full-employment output, is the maximum output that an economy can sustain over a period of time without increasing inflation. Keynes attempted to answer the difficult question posed by the Great Depression: why does the actual production in an economy sometimes fall far short of its productive capacity?

Keynes argued that the Great Depression was continuing because neither consumers nor businesses had an incentive to spend enough to cause an increase in production. After all, why would a company spend money to increase production when no one had enough money to buy its products? How could unemployed consumers spend money they didn't have? The only way to end the Depression would be if someone, somewhere, started spending.

A New Role for Government

Keynes thought that the spender should be the government. In the early 1930s, only the government still had the resources to spend enough to affect the whole economy. In effect, the government could make up for the drop in private spending by buying goods and services on its own. This, Keynes argued, would encourage production and increase employment. Then, as people went back to work, they would spend their wages on more goods and services, leading to even higher levels of production. This ever-expanding cycle would carry the economy out of the depression, and the government could then step back and reduce its spending. This is known as **demand-side economics** because it involves changing demand to help the economy.

These ideas form the basis of Keynesian economics. **Keynesian economics** is basically the idea that the economy is composed of

Figure 15.5 Keynesian Economics

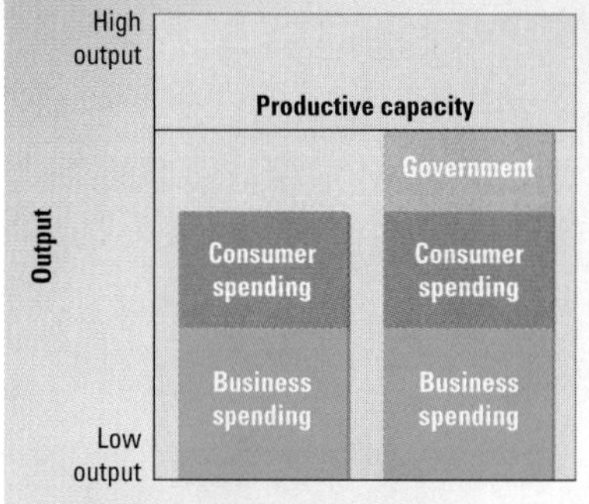

In a recession or depression, businesses and consumers do not demand as much as the economy can produce. Keynes argued that government spending can bring the economy up to its productive capacity.

Keynes added government spending to the classical model of demand.
Government What role did Keynes envision for government in the economy?

Econ 101: Key Concepts Made Easy

Monetary and Fiscal Policy Classical economists believed that there were strong forces that would push the economy back into equilibrium after shocks that had caused high levels of unemployment. **John Maynard Keynes,** however, suggested that this did not occur because there was a failure of coordination in the economy. Because there was insufficient demand for goods, factories produced less and employed fewer people. With fewer people employed, there were fewer consumers, and demand fell still further. Keynes believed that the government had to step in and create the needed demand.

Ask students to draw cartoons to show the difference between the classical approach and Keynes's approach. Display students' cartoons in class.

Answer to...

Building Key Concepts Keynes believed that the government could help restore equilibrium, making up for changes in the consumer and business sectors of the economy.

three sectors—individuals, business, and government—and that government actions can make up for changes in the other two. Keynesian economics proposes that by using fiscal policy the government can, and should, help the economy.

Avoiding Recessions and Depressions

Keynes argued that fiscal policy can be used to fight the two fundamental macroeconomic problems. These two opposing problems are periods of recession/depression and periods of inflation.

The federal government, Keynes argued, should keep track of the total level of spending by consumers, businesses, and government in the economy. If total spending begins to fall far below the level required to keep the economy running at full capacity, the government should watch out for the possibility of an upcoming recession or depression.

The government can respond by increasing its own spending until spending by the private sector returns to a higher level. Or, it can cut taxes, so that spending and investment by consumers and businesses increases. As you read in the previous section, raising government spending and cutting taxes are expansionary fiscal policies.

President Franklin D. Roosevelt carried out expansionary fiscal policies after his election in 1932. His New Deal put people to work building dams, planting forests, and constructing schools across the country, all paid for by the government.

Many people argue that instead of creating new jobs, such public works projects only shift employment from the private to the public sector. The taxes required to pay for them reduce demand in the private sector as much as they increase it in the public sector. In addition, work relief jobs are less productive than private sector jobs because their goal is employment, not efficient production.

Controlling Inflation

Keynes also argued that the government could use a contractionary fiscal policy to prevent inflation or reduce its severity. The government can reduce inflation either by increasing taxes or by reducing its own spending. Both of these actions decrease overall demand.

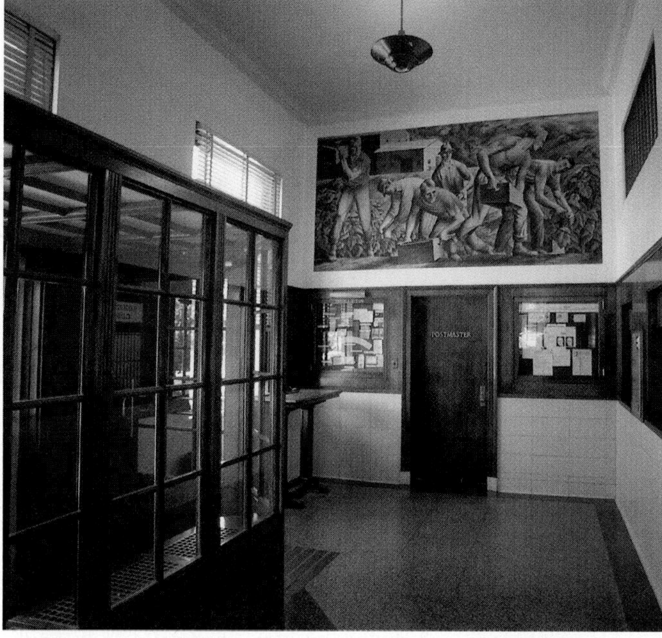

▲ **During the Depression, the government's Works Progress Administration (WPA) hired artists to paint murals in public places like this California post office.**

The Multiplier Effect

Fiscal policy, although difficult to control, is an extremely powerful tool. The key to its power is the **multiplier effect.** The multiplier effect in fiscal policy is the idea that every one dollar change in fiscal policy—whether it be an increase in spending or a decrease in taxes—creates a *greater than* one dollar change in the national income. In other words, the effects of changes in fiscal policy are multiplied.

Suppose the federal government finds that business investment is dropping. It fears a recession. To prevent a recession, in the next budget, the government decides to spend an extra $10 billion to stimulate the economy. How will this affect the economy?

With this government spending, demand, income, and GDP will increase by $10 billion. After all, if the government buys an extra $10 billion of goods and services, then

multiplier effect *the idea that every one dollar of government spending creates more than one dollar in economic activity*

THE WALL STREET JOURNAL. CLASSROOM EDITION

For an article from *The Wall Street Journal Classroom Edition,* see the Source Articles folder in the **Teaching Resources,** pp. 45–47.

Transparency Resource Package
Economics Concepts, 15C: Effects of Keynesian Economics

Differentiated Instruction L2

Have English language learners work in groups with at least two students who are proficient in English. Have the groups come up with one question and answer about each heading in this section. If time allows, have groups answer each other's questions. ELL

Block Scheduling Strategies

Consider these suggestions to take advantage of extended class time:

- Explain to students that *stagflation* is the name for what is described on this page: a slowing of economic growth accompanying a rise in inflation. Have students research this phenomenon and then use their data to write several paragraphs explaining why the economic developments of the late 1960s and early 1970s gave people reason to doubt the effectiveness of Keynesian economics.
- Organize students into pairs to complete the "Thinking About the Case Study" questions in the activity on Paul Ehrlich, Case Studies in Free Enterprise folder, pp. 30–31. When they have completed these questions, ask them to research Thomas Malthus (1766–1834). Have them work together to create a graphic that shows similarities and differences between the theories of these two men.

Transparency Resource Package Economics Concepts, 15D: The Multiplier Effect

Differentiated Instruction 

(Reteaching) Have groups of three to four students demonstrate their understanding of the multiplier effect by creating a scenario similar to the one supplied in the text. Ask them to present their scenario in poster form, showing how the effects of government spending are multiplied.

Differentiated Instruction 

Ask students to write several paragraphs to accompany the graph on this page. The paragraphs should explain the role of automatic stabilizers in the U.S. economy, using information from the graph to illustrate the concepts.

an extra $10 billion of goods and services have been produced. However, the GDP will increase by more than $10 billion. Here's why:

The businesses that sold the $10 billion in goods and services to the government have earned an additional $10 billion. These businesses will spend their additional earnings on wages, raw materials, and investment, sending money to workers, other suppliers, and stockholders. What will the recipients do with this money? They will spend part of it, perhaps 80 percent, or $8 billion. The businesses that benefit from this second round of spending will then pass it back to households, who will again spend 80 percent of it, or $6.4 billion. The next round will add an additional $5.1 billion to the economy, and so on. When all of these rounds of spending are added up, the initial government spending of $10 billion leads to an increase of $50 billion in GDP. The multiplier effect gives fiscal policy initiatives a much bigger kick than the initial amount spent.

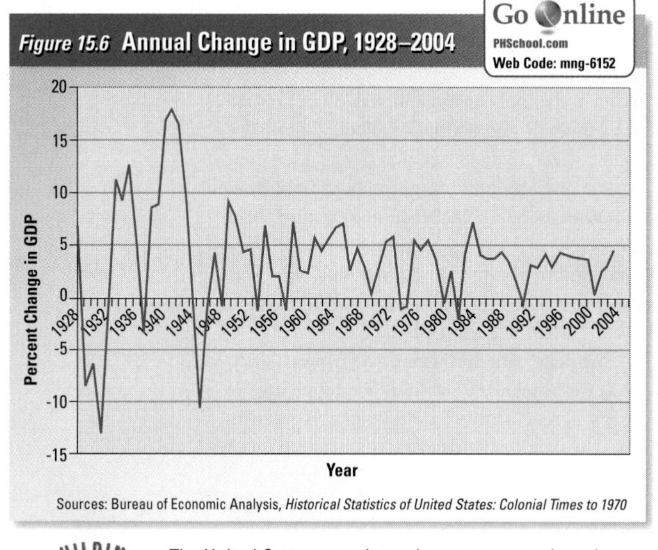

Figure 15.6 **Annual Change in GDP, 1928–2004**

Sources: Bureau of Economic Analysis, *Historical Statistics of United States: Colonial Times to 1970*

The United States experienced strong economic swings before World War II.

Government How do the years after the war show the effect of automatic stabilizers on the economy?

Automatic Stabilizers

Fiscal policy is used to achieve many economic goals. One of the most important things that fiscal policy can achieve is a more stable economy. A stable economy is one in which there are no rapid changes in the economic indicators you read about in Chapter 12. What's more, set up properly, fiscal policy can come close to stabilizing the economy *automatically*.

Figure 15.6 shows how real GDP in the United States changed each year from 1928 to 2004. Prior to World War II, there were much larger changes in GDP from year to year than after World War II. Although GDP still fluctuates, these fluctuations have not been as large as they were before World War II. Economic growth has been much more stable in the United States in the last 50 years.

Why did this happen? After the war, federal taxes and spending on transfer payments—two key tools of fiscal policy—increased sharply. Taxes and transfer payments, or transfers of cash from the government to consumers, stabilize economic growth. When national income is high, the government collects more in taxes and pays out less in transfer payments. Both of these actions take money away from consumers, and therefore reduce spending. This decrease in spending balances out the increase in spending that results from rising income in a healthy economy.

The opposite is also true. When income in the country is low, the government collects less in taxes and pays out more in transfer payments. Both actions increase the amount of money held by consumers, and thus increase spending. This increase in spending balances against the decrease in spending that results from falling income.

As the graph shows, taxes and transfer payments do not eliminate changes in the rate of growth of GDP, but they do make these changes smaller. They are known as stabilizers because they work to stabilize economic growth. It is important to note that policymakers do not have to make changes in taxes and transfer payments for them to have their stabilizing effect. Taxes

Preparing for Standardized Tests

Have students read the section titled "The Multiplier Effect" and then answer the question below.

Which of the following best summarizes the multiplier effect?

A Prices rise as demand rises.

(B) Every one-dollar change in fiscal policy creates a greater-than-one-dollar change in the national income.

C Fiscal policy automatically stabilizes the economy over the long run.

D A productive economy will sustain its maximum output over a long period of time.

Answer to . . .

Building Key Concepts Automatic stabilizers kept the economy from experiencing the drastic swings that occurred before the war.

and most transfer payments are tied to the GDP and to personal income, so they change automatically. Thus, taxes and transfer payments are known as **automatic stabilizers.**

Some stabilizers are no longer automatic. The former Aid to Families with Dependent Children, often called "welfare," lost its entitlement status in 1996 and was renamed Temporary Assistance for Needy Families (TANF). Now, the federal government gives the states a set amount of money each year to spend as they wish. However, the stabilizer effect was not completely lost. When the economy boomed in the late 1990s, state spending on TANF fell.

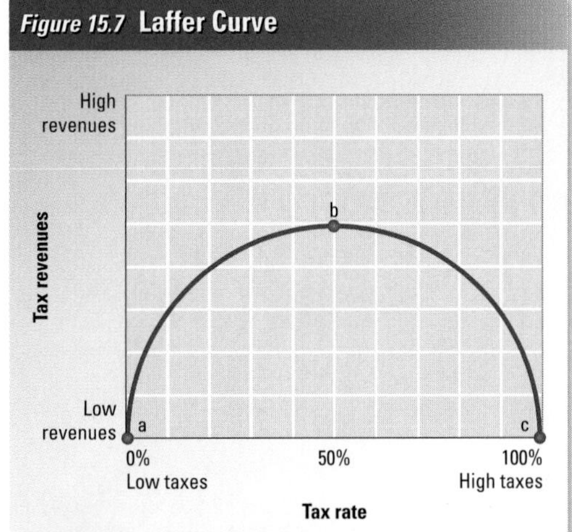

According to the Laffer curve, both a high and a low tax rate can produce the same revenues. **Incentives** **Why do higher tax rates sometimes cause revenues to fall?**

Supply-Side Economics

Another school of economic thought, supply-side economics, promotes a different direction for fiscal policy. **Supply-side economics** stresses the influence of taxation on the economy. Supply-siders believe that taxes have strong negative influences on economic output. While Keynesian economics uses government to change aggregate demand, supply-side economics tries to increase economic growth by increasing aggregate supply.

The Laffer Curve

Supply-side economists often use the Laffer curve, named after the economist Arthur Laffer, to illustrate the effects of taxes. The Laffer curve shows the relationship between the tax rate set by the government and the total tax revenue that the government collects. The total revenue depends on both the tax rate and the health of the economy. The Laffer curve illustrates that high tax rates may not bring in much revenue if these high tax rates cause economic activity to decrease.

Figure 15.7 depicts the Laffer curve. Suppose the government imposes a tax on the wages of workers. If the tax rate is zero, as at point a on the graph, the government will collect no revenue, although the economy will prosper from the lack of taxes. As the government raises the tax rate, it starts to collect some revenue. Follow this change in Figure 15.7 by tracing the curve from no taxes at point a to x percent taxation at point b.

To the left of point b on the curve, higher tax rates will discourage some people from working as many hours and prevent companies from investing and increasing production. The net effect of a higher tax rate and a slightly lower tax base is an increase in revenue.

To the right of point b, the decrease in workers' effort is so large that the higher tax rate *decreases* total tax revenue. In other words, high rates of taxation will eventually discourage so many people from working that tax revenues will fall sharply. In the extreme case of a 100 percent tax rate, no one would want to work! In this case, shown at point c on the curve, the government would collect no revenue.

Taxes and Output

The heart of the supply-side argument is that a tax cut increases total employment so much that the government actually collects more in taxes at the new, lower tax rate. Suppose the initial tax on labor is $3 an hour, and the typical worker works 30

automatic stabilizer *a government program that changes automatically depending on GDP and a person's income*

supply-side economics *a school of economics that believes tax cuts can help an economy by raising supply*

Background

Biography

Arthur Laffer is a conservative economist, best known for his supply-side theories. His theories were in favor among Republicans in the 1970s and 1980s.

Laffer studied economics at Yale and Stanford, earning a Ph.D. in 1972. He was chief economist at the Office of Management and Budget, and he advised President Ronald Reagan on economic issues. He made an unsuccessful run for the U.S. Senate in 1986. Several years later he founded an economics consulting firm with a longtime partner, Victor A. Canto.

Differentiated Instruction 

Time: 90 minutes

Activity: Hold a panel discussion.

Grouping: Organize the class into three groups: classical, Keynesian, and supply-side economists.

Purpose: Students will engage in a discussion of economic theories and solutions. Choose a moderator, who will ask the questions and summarize the main arguments. The panel will consist of nine students—three members from each group. Each group of economists should research that school's point of view on major issues. The moderator should create a list of historic economic problems (the Depression, the stagflation of the 1960s and 1970s) and ask panel members how they would deal with them.

Roles: Moderator, classical economists, Keynesian economists, and supply-side economists

Outcome: Students will be able to compare and contrast classical economics, Keynesian economics, and supply-side economics.

Interdisciplinary Connections: Math

The Laffer Curve The Laffer curve shows the relationship between tax rates and the total tax revenue that the government collects. The assumption is that fewer people will work, or that people will work fewer hours, when they are taxed more heavily.

Have students work through the following activity: To explore this assumption, have students develop a survey that asks 10 classmates how many hours they would work for $8 an hour at the following tax rates: 10 percent, 25 percent, 50 percent, 75 percent, 90 percent, and 100 percent. Have students average the 10 responses and then figure tax revenue at each percentage. Finally, have them plot these numbers on a graph, placing tax rates on the x-axis and tax revenues on the y-axis. Discuss the graphs, their similarity to or divergence from the Laffer curve, and the implications of the findings.

Answer to . . .

Building Key Concepts Higher tax rates may discourage people from working and prevent companies from investing and increasing production, causing tax revenues to fall.

Differentiated Instruction 

Ask students to make up five questions about section content. Each question should begin with one of the following words: *Who, What, When, Where,* or *Why.* Then have students answer their own questions. Remind them that this strategy can be used for just about any topic. ELL

Transparency Resource Package
Economics Concepts, 15E: The Great Depression

Differentiated Instruction 

Have students use section content and outside research as needed to create a captioned time line that shows the role that fiscal policy has played in American history since 1929. Although the text covers history through the 1980s, ask students to try to add at least one entry for the 2000s.

Learning Styles Activity
Learning Styles Lesson Plans folder, p. 36 asks student groups to create cartoons depicting weaknesses in the three economic theories discussed in this section.

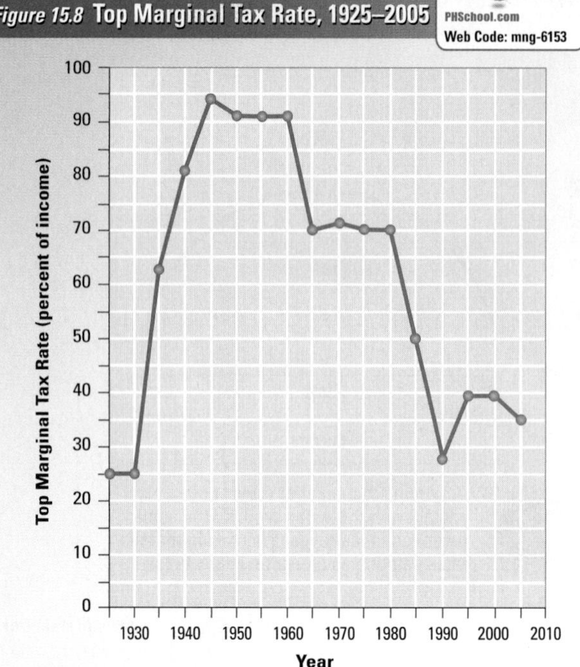

Note: The top marginal tax rate is applied to individual income above a certain level, which varied from about $30,000 in the late 1980s to $5,000,000 from 1936 to 1941. The top tax rate of 35% in 2005 applied to income above approximately $326,450, close to the historic average.
Source: National Taxpayers Union

Tax rates varied widely throughout the last century. Government **When were top marginal income tax rates at their highest?**

Council of Economic Advisers (CEA) *a group of three respected economists that advise the President on economic policy*

hours per week, paying a total of $90 in taxes each week. If the government cuts the tax on labor to $2 an hour, and the worker responds by working 50 hours per week, the worker will pay $100 in taxes a week, an increase of $10. If all workers respond to the tax cut by working this much harder, the tax cut will increase total revenue.

Actual experience has proven that while a tax cut encourages some workers to work more hours, the end result is a relatively small increase in the number of hours worked. In the example above, if the tax cut increased the hours worked from 30 hours to 35 hours, the worker would pay only $70 in taxes ($2 per hour times 35 hours), down from $90 ($3 per hour times 30 hours). In general, taxpayers do not react strongly enough to tax cuts to increase tax revenue.

◀ **Increasing production during World War II finally ended the high unemployment of the 1930s.**

Fiscal Policy in American History

As you recall, Keynes presented his ideas at the same time that the world economy was still engulfed in the Great Depression. President Herbert Hoover, influenced by classical economics, thought that the economy was basically sound and would return to equilibrium on its own. His popular successor, President Franklin D. Roosevelt, was much more willing to increase government spending to help lift the economy out of depression. After the Democratic party won landslide victories in the 1932 and 1934 federal elections, Roosevelt started several programs to pump money into the economy.

World War II

Keynes's theory was fully tested in the United States during World War II. As the country geared up for war, government spending increased dramatically. The government spent large sums of money to feed soldiers and equip them with everything from warplanes to rifles to medical supplies. This money was given to the private sector in exchange for goods. Just as Keynesian economics predicted, the additional demand for goods and services moved the country sharply out of the Great Depression and toward full productive capacity. After the war, Congress created the **Council of Economic Advisers (CEA)**, a group of three respected economists that could advise the President on economic policy.

Preparing for Standardized Tests

Have students read the section titled "World War II" and then answer the question below.

How did World War II help move the United States out of the Depression?

A The Council of Economic Advisers was formed.
B Demand for goods and services fell.
C Tax cuts stimulated demand.
(D) The government spent large sums of money on goods in the private sector.

Answer to . . .
Building Key Concepts
They were highest in the mid-1940s.

The Kennedy Administration

Between 1945 and 1960, the U.S. economy was healthy and growing, despite a few minor recessions. The last recession continued into the term of President John F. Kennedy, with unemployment at 6.7 percent.

Kennedy's chief financial policy advisor was Walter Heller, a Keynesian who thought that the economy was below its productive capacity. Heller believed that unemployment would fall to 4 percent if the economy were at full capacity. He convinced Kennedy that tax cuts would stimulate demand and bring the economy closer to full productive capacity.

As Figure 15.8 shows, tax rates were extremely high in the early 1960s. The highest individual income tax rate was about 90 percent, compared to about 40 percent today. The top business rate was 52 percent, compared with 35 percent in recent years. So Kennedy proposed tax cuts, both because he agreed with Heller, and because tax cuts are popular.

A modified version of Kennedy's tax cuts was enacted in 1964, after Kennedy's assassination. At the same time, the Vietnam War raised government spending. Over the next two years, the economy grew rapidly. Consumption and the GDP increased by more than 4 percent a year. While there is no way to prove that the tax cut caused this increase, the result is what Keynesian economics had predicted.

Supply-Side Policies in the 1980s

Keynesian economics was used on many other occasions in the 1960s and 1970s to try to adjust the national economy. During the late 1970s, however, unemployment and inflation rates soared. Ronald Reagan became President in 1981 and instituted new policies based on supply-side economics. In 1981, Reagan proposed a tax cut that was put in place and reduced taxes by 25 percent over three years. Unlike Keynes, Reagan did not believe that government spending should be used to bring the economy out of a recession. After a brief but harsh recession in 1982, caused partly by the Fed's tightening of the money supply to reduce inflation, the economy recovered and flourished.

For many reasons, however, government spending continued to rise each year while Reagan was in office. During the Reagan and George H.W. Bush presidencies and the first years of Bill Clinton's first term, the federal government spent much more money than it took in. This gap caused increasing concern among economists and policymakers. In the next section, you'll read about these concerns in detail.

THE WALL STREET JOURNAL. CLASSROOM EDITION

In the News Read more about tax policy in "Deficit Dilemma," an article in The Wall Street Journal Classroom Edition.

The Wall Street Journal Classroom Edition
For: Current Events
Visit: PHSchool.com
Web Code: mnc-6152

Section 2 Assessment

Progress Monitoring *Online*
For: Self-quiz with vocabulary practice
Web Code: mna-6156

Key Terms and Main Ideas

1. What is the central idea of **classical economics?**
2. Why is full-employment output another way to describe **productive capacity?**
3. Compare and contrast **Keynesian economics** and **supply-side economics.**
4. Explain the **multiplier effect.**

Applying Economic Concepts

5. *Critical Thinking* Why can low tax rates encourage investment and increase employment and wages?
6. *Try This* Keynes suggested that building pyramids was good for the Egyptian economy. Why would Keynes have suggested this, and can you think of an analogy in our society for the building of the pyramids? Explain your answer.

Go Online PHSchool.com
For: Research Activity
Visit: PHSchool.com
Web Code: mnd-6152

Progress Monitoring *Online*
For additional assessment, have students access Progress Monitoring Online at **Web Code:** mna-6156

Go Online PHSchool.com Typing in the Web Code when prompted will bring students directly to detailed instructions for this activity.

Go Online PHSchool.com Typing in the Web Code when prompted will bring students directly to the article.

GTE Guide to the Essentials
Chapter 15, Section 2, p. 64 provides support for students who need additional review of the section content. Spanish support is available in the Spanish edition of the guide on p. 64.

Quiz Unit 6 folder, p. 18 includes questions to check students' understanding of Section 2 content.

Presentation Pro CD-ROM
Quiz provides multiple-choice questions to check students' understanding of Section 2 content.

Answers to . . .

Section 2 Assessment

1. The central idea of classical economics is that free markets regulate themselves.
2. Productive capacity is the maximum output that an economy can sustain over time. Therefore it is the output at full employment.
3. Keynesian economics uses government to increase aggregate demand through both spending and tax cuts. Supply-side economics tries to increase aggregate supply through tax cuts.
4. The multiplier effect is the idea that every one-dollar change in fiscal policy creates a greater-than-one-dollar change in national income.
5. Cutting taxes provides consumers with more money to spend on goods and services and allows businesses to keep more of their profits, which allows them to invest in land, labor, and capital.
6. By building the pyramids, the Egyptian economy was stimulated through an increased labor demand and increased producer spending. Possible comparisons in today's society include the space program in the 1960s or the building of highways.

ECONOMIC *Profile*
John Maynard Keynes

Background

As a young man John Maynard Keynes was educated at Eton, the famous private school of Britain's elite. He then went on to Cambridge, where he studied mathematics. There he fell under the influence of the economist Alfred Marshall, who turned Keynes's intellectual focus to politics and economics.

Keynes had interests outside these areas, however. He was part of the famous Bloomsbury group, a gathering of freethinking intellectuals whose members included writers Virginia Woolf and Lytton Strachey. Keynes's later career was characterized by government service and heavy involvement in Great Britain's economic planning during World War II and afterward. Today Keynes stands as one of the dominant economic theorists of the twentieth century.

Careers in Economics Activity Unit 6 folder, p. 24 gives students a closer look at the career path of an accountant.

Answers to . . .

1. Keynes is saying that in the past only war brought countries out of depressions because military spending in times of emergency provided the only reason why governments would engage in deficit spending.
2. Students should note that government spending pumps more money into the economy. Public works projects create jobs as well as profits for the firms that hire the workers and provide the materials. The wages workers receive allow them to buy more, which increases demand.
3. Students' research should lead them to discover that Keynes played an important role in the establishment of the World Bank and the International Monetary Fund. Students should discuss the influence of Keynes's ideas on these institutions.

Economist

Entrepreneur

ECONOMIC

Profile

John Maynard Keynes

(1883–1946)

A government official, teacher, and writer, John Maynard Keynes is one of a handful of economists who have substantially affected the course of history. His revolutionary theories on supply, demand, and unemployment led to the first use of government programs to help manage the nation's economy.

Early Career and Accomplishments

Keynes graduated from the University of Cambridge with a degree in mathematics in 1905. Rising through government service, he served as Britain's economic advisor at the Versailles Conference, where the peace treaty to end World War I was drafted.

Upset over the harsh treaty, Keynes resigned from government and returned to Cambridge to teach. In 1919, he wrote *The Economic Consequences of the Peace,* which correctly predicted that the treaty's economic penalties on Germany would lead to future problems in Europe.

Keynes and the Great Depression

At the height of the Great Depression in 1936, Keynes completed his most famous book, *The General Theory of Employment, Interest and Money*. In analyzing the causes and effects of the Depression, he revolutionized thinking about government's role in a nation's economy.

Before Keynes, most economists believed that government should leave the economy alone as it passed through the low points of the business cycle. In this view, the laws of supply and demand—as they applied to employment and wages, consumption and production, and prices—would lead to economic recovery.

Keynesian Economics

Keynes claimed that in a depression, a natural recovery is impossible because the private sector cannot consume all it can produce. He argued that government should lower interest rates and taxes to encourage investment and increase spending on public projects to stimulate demand for goods and create jobs. Keynes recognized that raising spending while cutting taxes would lead to budget deficits, but he accepted that liability if it boosted employment and led to economic recovery.

Keynes's theories were controversial at the time, and remain so today, even though other economists have greatly revised and expanded upon his ideas. In the United States, politicians have followed his program of government intervention in good economic times as well as bad. This has led some critics to blame Keynesian economics for the huge federal budget deficits that the United States built up from the 1960s to the mid-1990s.

CHECK FOR UNDERSTANDING

1. Source Reading Explain the following Keynes statement: "Formerly there was no expenditure out of the proceeds of borrowing that it was thought proper for the State to incur except for war. . . . Therefore, we have not infrequently had to wait for a war to terminate a major depression."

2. Critical Thinking How would government spending programs stimulate employment, consumption, and production in the private sector of the economy?

3. Learn More Find out what involvement Keynes had with international economic institutions after World War II, and explain how these institutions now reflect Keynes's economic theories.

Beyond the Classroom: Workplace Skills

Reasoning Explain to students that reasoning skills, which involve forming judgments and drawing conclusions, are sought after by employers. Reasoning skills are important for problem solving. Individuals with good reasoning skills will recognize problems and then develop plans of action to overcome them. Ask students to list ways in which they use reasoning skills in their schoolwork. Then ask them to imagine how they might use these same skills in the workplace.

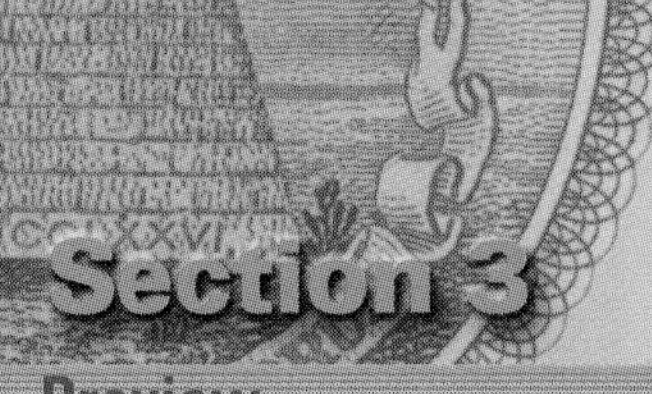

Section 3 Budget Deficits and the National Debt

Preview

Objectives

After studying this section you will be able to:

1. **Explain** the importance of balancing the budget.
2. **Analyze** how budget deficits add to the national debt.
3. **Summarize** the problems caused by the national debt.
4. **Identify** how a government can reduce budget deficits and the national debt.

Section Focus

Fiscal policy decisions can lead the federal government to spend more money than it brings in, causing budget deficits and a national debt. Economists, lawmakers, and citizens debate whether the benefits of government spending outweigh the costs of debt.

Key Terms

balanced budget
budget surplus
budget deficit
hyperinflation
Treasury bill
Treasury note
Treasury bond
national debt
crowding-out effect

As you have learned, the federal government uses fiscal policy—taxing and spending—to make changes in the economy. Fiscal policy is a powerful tool. It can be used to help stimulate demand, increase production, create jobs, increase GDP, avoid recessions, control inflation, and stabilize economic growth. As you'll read in this section, raising government spending can lead to yearly budget deficits that add up to an enormous debt. The costs of this debt must be measured against the benefits of higher government spending.

Balancing the Budget

The basic tool of fiscal policy is the federal budget. It is made up of two fundamental parts: revenue (taxes) and expenditures (spending programs). When the federal government's revenues equal its expenditures in any particular year, the federal government has a **balanced budget.** There is the same amount of money going into and coming out of the Treasury.

In reality, the federal budget is almost never balanced. Usually, it is either running a *surplus* or a *deficit*. A **budget surplus** occurs in any year when revenues exceed expenditures. In other words, there is more money going into the Treasury than coming out of it. A **budget deficit** occurs in any year when expenditures exceed revenues. In other words, there is more money coming out of the Treasury than going into it.

balanced budget *a budget in which revenues are equal to spending*

budget surplus *a situation in which the government takes in more than it spends*

budget deficit *a situation in which the government spends more than it takes in*

◀ **In the early 2000s, the national debt, the sum of all the money owed by the federal government, seemed to be spiraling out of control.**

Graphing the Main Idea

Monetary and Fiscal Policy To build understanding of **government** and fiscal policy, have students use a Venn diagram like the one at the right to differentiate between debt and deficit. Remind students that a Venn diagram shows two concepts (debt and deficit in this case) and their supporting details in their individual circles, and any details shared by both concepts in the middle section.

Section Reading Support Transparencies A template and the answers for this graphic organizer can be found in Chapter 15, Section 3 of the Section Reading Support Transparency System.

Section 3

Budget Deficits and the National Debt

Objectives You may wish to call students' attention to the objectives in the Section Preview. The objectives are reflected in the main headings of the section.

Bellringer Ask students whether they have ever borrowed money from anyone. Explain that until they paid back the loan, they were in debt. Tell students that in this section they will learn that the government itself is often in debt and that this situation sometimes leads to problems.

Vocabulary Builder Ask students to read the text to find the meanings of the key terms. Then ask them to personify the terms verbally. Other students should try to guess which term they are personifying. (For example, for *budget surplus* a student might say: *"I occur in any year when revenues exceed expenditures."*)

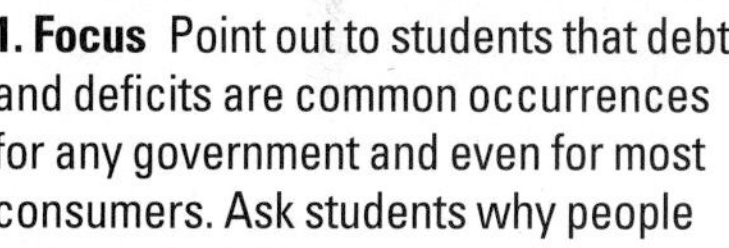

Lesson Plan

Teaching the Main Concepts (L3)

1. Focus Point out to students that debt and deficits are common occurrences for any government and even for most consumers. Ask students why people try to avoid debt.

2. Instruct Discuss the difference between a budget surplus and a budget deficit, and distinguish between *deficit* and *debt.* Describe the effects of the national debt on the government and on businesses. Finally, discuss how governments can reduce budget deficits and the national debt.

3. Close/Reteach Hold a class discussion on the various methods suggested to reduce the deficit. Ask which one students think provides the best solution.

Guided Reading and Review
Unit 6 folder, p. 19 asks students to identify the main ideas of the section and to define or identify key terms.

Differentiated Instruction L3

To reinforce the concepts of surplus and deficit as discussed in this section, try this activity. Bring to class a bag of candy and two blank IOUs. Count out enough candy before class so that you have two pieces for each student. (Put the rest aside; it will not be used in this activity.) Pass two pieces of candy to each student. Then tell students that you are the government. Demand a tax of one piece of candy, and have students deposit their candy on your desk. Next, redistribute some, but not all, of the candy randomly among the students. Ask students whether you have a surplus or deficit, and have them explain why.

Collect the same tax again, and redistribute all of it plus the surplus you had left over last time. Ask two students if you may borrow some of their candy; then write each of them an IOU and distribute the candy you have borrowed. Now ask students whether you have a surplus or deficit, and have them explain why.

Transparency Resource Package
Economics Concepts, 15F: Federal Budget Deficits and Surpluses

Figure 15.9 Budget Surpluses and Deficits, 1940–2004

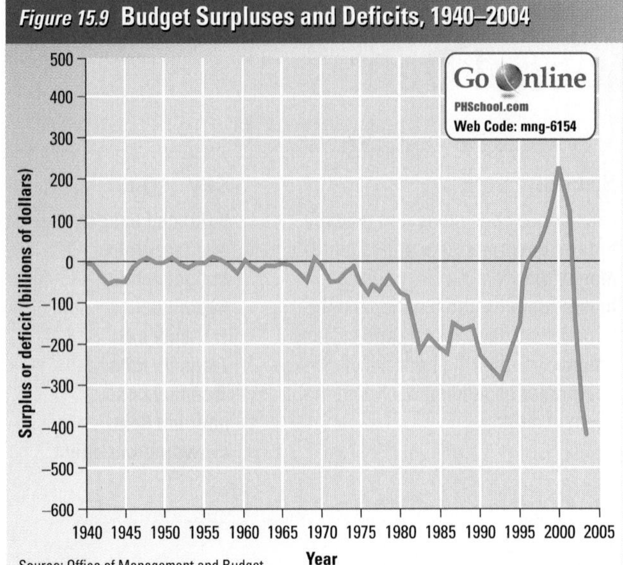

Source: Office of Management and Budget

Budget deficits swelled in the early 2000s due to recession, tax cuts, and defense spending. **Government What was the dominant trend in deficits in the late 1990s?**

hyperinflation *very high inflation*

Assume the federal government starts with a balanced budget. If the government decreases expenditures without changing anything else, it will run a budget surplus. Similarly, if it increases taxes—revenues—without changing anything else, it will run a surplus.

The same sort of analysis describes budget deficits. If the government increases expenditures without changing anything else, it will run a deficit. Similarly, if it decreases taxes without changing anything else, it will run a deficit. The deficit can grow or shrink because of forces beyond the government's control. During a recession, fewer people are working, and tax revenues fall as spending on antipoverty programs rises. Surpluses and deficits can be very large figures. The largest deficit was about $400 billion, in 2004.

Responding to Budget Deficits

When the government runs a deficit, that means it did not take in enough revenue to cover its expenses for the year. When this happens, the government must find a way to pay for the extra expenditures. There are two basic actions the government can take to do so.

Creating Money

The government could create new money to pay salaries for its workers and benefits for citizens. Traditionally, governments simply printed the bills they needed. Today, the government can create money electronically by depositing money in people's bank accounts. The effect is the same. This approach works for relatively small deficits, but can cause severe problems when there are large deficits. Why?

When the government creates more money, it increases the amount of money in circulation. This increases the demand for goods and services and can increase output. But once the economy reaches full employment, output cannot increase. The increase in money will mean that there are more dollars, but the same amount of goods and services. Prices in the economy rise so that a greater amount of money will be needed to purchase the same amount of goods and services. In other words, prices go up, and the result is inflation. As you read in Chapter 13, high levels of inflation are a serious economic problem.

Covering very large deficits by printing more money can cause very high inflation, called **hyperinflation**. This happened in Germany and Russia after World War I, Brazil and Argentina in the 1980s, and Ukraine in the 1990s. If the United States experienced hyperinflation, a shirt that cost $30 in June might cost $50 in July, $80 in August, and $400 in December!

Borrowing Money

As an alternative to creating money to cover a budget deficit, the federal government can borrow money. The government commonly borrows money by selling bonds. As you read in Chapter 11, a bond is a type of loan: a promise to repay money in the future, with interest. Consumers and businesses buy bonds from the government. The government thus has the money

Econ 101: Key Concepts Made Easy

Monetary and Fiscal Policy One of the key concepts in this section is the difference between the **national debt** and the **deficit.** To further student understanding, explain that the same concepts can be applied to an individual's finances. The deficit is simply the name for spending that exceeds income, or revenue. Each year that someone spends more than he or she earns, that person creates a deficit for that year. The person's debt is the cumulative sum of each year's deficit. Demonstrate with the following chart.

Year	Income	Spending	Deficit	Debt
2006	$20,000	$21,000	$1,000	$1,000
2007	$23,000	$25,000	$2,000	$3,000
2008	$24,000	$24,000	0	$3,000

The person's total debt is $3,000. In three years this person has achieved a balanced budget only once and has not repaid the loans that allowed him or her to spend more than he or she earned. This means that the debt is $3,000.

Answer to . . .

Building Key Concepts Deficits decreased in the late 1990s; there were budget surpluses.

to cover its budget deficit. In return, the purchasers of the bonds earn interest on their investment over time.

United States Savings Bonds allow millions of Americans to lend small amounts of money to the federal government for a period as brief as three months or as long as 30 years. In return, they earn interest on the bonds. Other common forms of government borrowing are **Treasury bills, Treasury notes,** and **Treasury bonds.** Treasury bills are short-term bonds that must be repaid within a year or less. Treasury notes cover periods from two to ten years. Treasury bonds may be issued for as long as 30 years.

Federal borrowing lets the government undertake more projects than it could otherwise afford. These include projects such as building airports, highways, and national parks. Wise borrowing allows the government to create more public goods and services. Federal borrowing, however, also has serious disadvantages.

◀ **By purchasing a U.S. Savings Bond, you are lending money to the federal government. A savings bond represents a small piece of the national debt.**

The National Debt

One problem with the government borrowing money is that it creates a national debt. The **national debt** is the total amount of money the federal government owes to bondholders. Every year that there is a budget deficit, and the federal government borrows money to cover it, the national debt will grow.

The national debt is owed to investors who hold Treasury bonds, bills, and notes. If you have a federal savings bond, that bond represents money you have loaned the government.

Bonds issued by the United States federal government are considered to be one of the safest investments in the world. The national debt is owned by investors in the United States and around the world who have put their money and their trust in the federal government. In this way, a modest national debt is good because it offers a safe investment for individuals and businesses.

Because the United States federal government is widely viewed as stable and trustworthy, the federal government can borrow money at a lower rate of interest than private citizens or corporations can. Lower interest rates benefit taxpayers by reducing the cost of government borrowing.

The Difference Between Deficit and Debt

Many people are confused about the difference between the deficit and the debt. The deficit is the amount of money the government borrows for one budget, representing one fiscal year. The debt, on the other hand, is a sum of all the government borrowing up to that time, minus the borrowings that have been repaid. The debt is the total of all deficits and surpluses.

Measuring the National Debt

In dollar terms, the size of the national debt is extremely large. In 2004, it exceeded $7 trillion! Such large numbers can be confusing. A more useful way to evaluate the size of the debt is to look at it as a percentage of GDP.

Historically, debt as a percentage of GDP rises during wartime, when government spending increases faster than taxation, and falls during peacetime. This can be seen in the graph in Figure 15.10.

Treasury bill *a government bond that is repaid within three months to a year*

Treasury note *a government bond that is repaid within two to ten years*

Treasury bond *a government bond that can be issued for as long as 30 years*

national debt *all the money the federal government owes to bondholders*

Background

Economics in History

After World War I the large debt Germany had built up financing the war and the punishing reparations it was forced to pay wreaked havoc on its economy, spurring hyperinflation. A loaf of bread that cost 20,000 marks in the morning might cost 5,000,000 marks in the afternoon. By November of 1923, one dollar was worth 4.2 trillion marks.

How did this happen? By 1923 Germany had fallen behind in its reparation payments. In response France and Belgium occupied the heavily industrialized Ruhr Valley, hoping to extract payment in the form of goods from German industry. Germany refused to cooperate and, in fact, ordered its workers not to report to work in the occupied zone. The German government, however, continued to pay workers' salaries simply by printing more money. Soon inflation was completely out of control.

Economic Cartoon

Unit 6 folder, p. 25 gives students practice in interpreting cartoons about section content.

Meeting NCEE Standards

Use the following benchmark activity from the **Voluntary National Content Standards in Economics** to evaluate student understanding of **Standard 20.**

Explain the difference between the budget deficit and the national debt. Then determine how long it would take to pay off all of the national debt at the current rate of GDP if all GDP were devoted to that purpose.

Differentiated Instruction 

Have students create flow-charts titled "Responding to Budget Deficits." They should show the ways in which governments respond to budget deficits and the effects that occur because of these responses.

Block Scheduling Strategies

Consider these suggestions to take advantage of extended class time:

■ Extend the Background Note on this page by asking groups of three to four students to research reasons for and effects of other examples of hyperinflation. (See the examples on the opposite page of the text under "Creating Money.") Allow class time for students to present their findings orally.

■ Have student pairs complete the Economic Cartoon activity in the Unit 6 folder, p. 25. Then have pairs create their own economic cartoons based on key concepts from this section. Display the cartoons on a bulletin board.

■ Hold a debate between two imaginary presidential candidates, one in favor of a balanced-budget amendment and one opposed to it. Organize the class into two groups, one to support each candidate. Give groups time to gather research and craft their arguments; then hold the debate.

Differentiated Instruction 

(Enrichment) Have students demonstrate their understanding of the effects of the national debt by writing a brief editorial titled "The Two Sides of the National Debt." One part of the editorial should warn of the dangers of a high national debt; the other should caution readers not to become alarmists about this issue. Students may use material from the text as well as outside research to write their editorials.

Transparency Resource Package
Economics Concepts, 15G: The National Debt

Meeting NCEE Standards

Use the following benchmark activity from the **Voluntary National Content Standards in Economics** to evaluate student understanding of **Standard 17.**

Explain why, although most Americans say they are in favor of reducing the deficit, Congress does not vote to increase taxes.

Databank, p. 542 contains graphs that can be used to illustrate section content.

Math Practice Activity
Math Practice folder, p. 12, "Per Capita Share of the National Debt," allows students to examine figures on the national debt and population, analyzing changes over time.

Notice how the pattern changed in the 1980s, when the United States began to run a large debt, even though the country wasn't at war. The debt was in part a result of increases in spending during President Ronald Reagan's terms. As you read in the previous section, the Reagan administration also lowered tax rates to pull the economy out of a recession. The combined effect of higher spending and lower tax rates was several years of increased budget deficits. The government borrowed billions of dollars to cover these deficits, adding to the national debt. Meanwhile, an economic downturn in 1981–1982 reduced GDP. As a result, the ratio of debt to GDP grew very large for peacetime.

Is the Debt a Problem?

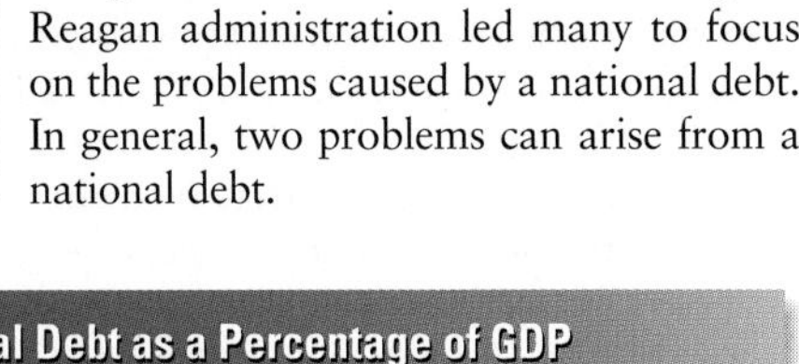

crowding-out effect *the loss of funds for private investment due to government borrowing*

The growth of the national debt during the Reagan administration led many to focus on the problems caused by a national debt. In general, two problems can arise from a national debt.

***Figure 15.10* National Debt as a Percentage of GDP**

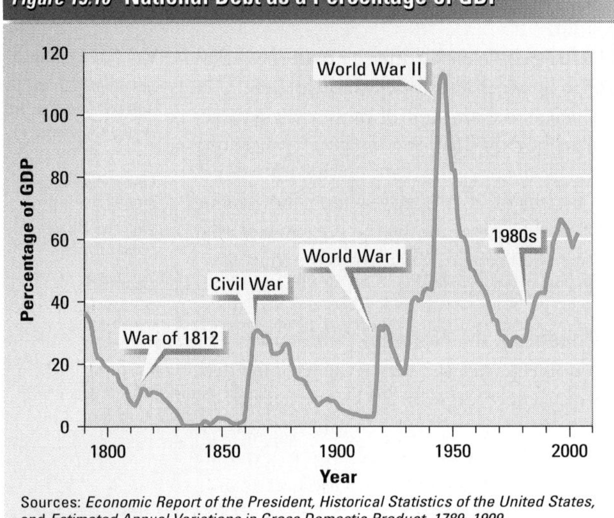

Sources: *Economic Report of the President, Historical Statistics of the United States,* and *Estimated Annual Variations in Gross Domestic Product, 1789–1909* by Thomas Senior Berry

War puts special strains on government spending, and governments borrow money to pay the high costs. **Government What must governments do when the war ends?**

Problems of a National Debt

The first problem with a national debt is that it reduces the funds available for businesses to invest. This is because in order to sell its bonds, the government must offer a high interest rate to attract buyers. Individuals and businesses, attracted by the high interest rates and the security of investing in the government, use their savings or profits to buy government bonds.

However, every dollar spent on a government bond is one fewer dollar that can be invested in private business. Less money is available for companies to expand their factories, conduct research, and develop new products, and interest rates rise. Economists call this the **crowding-out effect,** because federal borrowing "crowds out" private borrowing by making it harder for private businesses to borrow. A national debt, then, can hurt investment and slow economic growth over the long run. On the other hand, more investment in the private sector can lead to lower prices, more jobs, and overall higher standards of living.

The second problem with a high national debt is that the government must pay interest to bondholders. The more the government borrows, the more interest it has to pay. Paying the interest on the debt is sometimes called *servicing the debt.* Over time, the interest payments have become very large. At the beginning of the twenty-first century, the federal government spent about $250 billion a year servicing the debt. Moreover, there is an opportunity cost—dollars spent servicing the debt cannot be spent on something else, like defense, health care, or infrastructure.

Other Views of a National Debt

Not everyone agrees that the national debt is such a large problem. Traditional Keynesian economists believe that fiscal policy is an important tool that can be used to help achieve full productive capacity. To these analysts, the benefits of a productive economy outweigh the costs of interest on national debt.

However, a budget deficit can only be an effective tool if it is temporary. If the

Interdisciplinary Connections: History

War and Peace and the National Debt Through much of American history, the national debt as a percentage of GDP rose sharply during wartime because of the cost of financing war. After the end of each war, debt fell. This occurred in other nations as well, with debt relative to GDP rising during periods of conflict and falling in peacetime. Starting in the 1980s, however, the United States began to have large peacetime deficits.

Making the Connection The text gives some explanation for the rising deficits of the 1980s (increased defense spending). Ask students to research other reasons for rising deficits and to write a short report on their findings.

Answer to . . .

Building Key Concepts
Governments must help the economy return to equilibrium.

Figure 15.11 **Effects of the Budget Deficit**

The federal government spends more than it takes in, and has to borrow money to cover the deficit.

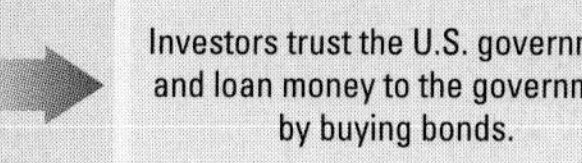

Investors trust the U.S. government and loan money to the government by buying bonds.

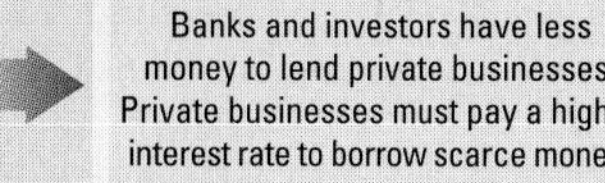

Banks and investors have less money to lend private businesses. Private businesses must pay a higher interest rate to borrow scarce money.

Government borrowing "crowds out " private investment by taking away some funds that could have been invested in private business.
Incentives **Why do lenders put their money in government bonds?**

government runs large budget deficits each year, the costs of the growing debt will eventually outweigh the benefits.

Deficits, Surpluses, and the National Debt

During the 1980s and into the 1990s, annual budget deficits added substantially to the national debt. Several factors frustrated lawmakers in their attempts to control the deficits. As we have seen, much of the budget consists of entitlement spending that is politically difficult to change. Another large part of the budget consists of interest that must be paid to bondholders. Finally, specific budget cuts are often opposed by groups affected.

Efforts to Reduce Deficits

Concerns about the budget deficits of the mid-1980s caused Congress to pass the Gramm-Rudman-Hollings Act, which created automatic across-the-board cuts in federal expenditures if the deficit exceeded a certain amount. This saved lawmakers from having to make difficult decisions about individual funding cuts. The Act exempted significant portions of the budget (such as interest payments and many entitlement programs) from the cuts.

When the Supreme Court found that significant portions of the Act were unconstitutional, Congress attempted to correct the flaws. In 1990, however, lawmakers realized that the deficit was going to be much larger than expected. Because Congress had exempted so many programs from automatic cuts, funding for nonexempt programs would be dramatically reduced.

To resolve the crisis, President George H.W. Bush and congressional leaders negotiated a new budget system that replaced Gramm-Rudman-Hollings. The 1990 Budget Enforcement Act created a "pay-as-you-go" system that requires Congress to raise enough revenue to cover increases in direct spending, so that the budget deficit cannot grow larger.

In addition, at various times citizens and politicians have suggested amending the Constitution to require a balanced budget. In 1995, a balanced budget amendment passed in the House and failed by only a single vote in the Senate. Supporters argued that the amendment would force the federal government to be more disciplined about its spending. Opponents objected that a constitutional amendment would not be flexible enough to deal with rapid changes in the economy.

End-of-Century Surpluses

The late 1990s brought a welcome reversal of fortune. For the first time in thirty years, the President and the Office of Management and Budget (OMB) were able to announce that the government was running a surplus. How did this happen? First, the new budget procedures begun

FAST FACT

Unlike the federal government, most states already require a balanced budget. However, what works well at the state level may not work for the federal government. State requirements range from strict to very weak. At least ten states can carry over budget deficits into the next year or borrow money to cover the deficit. Also, many states have a "rainy day" fund, where surplus money is stored to pay for future deficits. Neither would be allowed under a federal balanced budget amendment.

Differentiated Instruction L4

You may wish to have students add the following to their portfolios. Ask them to read the text material on government responses to deficit and debt. Then have them research to find out more about these solutions and the controversies that surround them. Ask students to write a position paper in which they support a particular method of reducing deficit and debt and give reasons for choosing this method above others. GT

Economics Assessment Rubric

Economics Assessment Rubrics folder, pp. 22–23 provides sample evaluation materials for a position paper.

Differentiated Instruction L2

Ask students to rewrite the following incorrect statements as correct statements.

- A budget surplus occurs in any year when *expenditures exceed revenues. (revenues exceed expenditures)*
- United States Savings Bonds, Treasury bonds, and Treasury bills are methods of dealing with budget deficits by *printing money. (government borrowing)*
- The *debt* is the amount of money the government borrows for one fiscal year, while the *deficit* is the sum of all the government borrowing up to that time. (*deficit* [one fiscal year]; *debt* [sum]) LPR

Economic Detective Activity

Unit 6 folder, p. 23, "Troubles in Westfed," provides an integrated application of chapter concepts.

Preparing for Standardized Tests

Have students read the section titled "Deficit and Debt Reduction" and then answer the question below.

Which of the following could be categorized as a legislative solution to reducing the deficit?

A selling additional bonds
(B) the Gramm-Rudman laws
C a balanced-budget amendment
D increasing spending

Answer to . . .

Building Key Concepts Government bonds are a safe investment. Some lenders may also feel that they are helping the nation.

GTE Guide to the Essentials
Chapter 15, Section 3, p. 65 provides support for students who need additional review of the section content. Spanish support is available in the Spanish edition of the guide on p. 65.

Quiz Unit 6 folder, p. 20 includes questions to check students' understanding of Section 3 content.

Presentation Pro CD-ROM
Quiz provides multiple-choice questions to check students' understanding of Section 3 content.

Answers to . . .

Section 3 Assessment

1. A balanced budget is a budget in which revenues are equal to expenditures.
2. A budget deficit occurs when spending is greater than revenue. Continued budget deficits, without sufficient counteracting budget surpluses, can lead to national debt.
3. A Treasury note is a government bond that is repaid within 2 to 10 years. A Treasury bill is a government bond that is repaid within a year or less.
4. Students' proposals should demonstrate understanding of fiscal policy. For example, a student might suggest that the surplus be balanced between investment (to boost the economy) and purchasing back of bonds (to lower interest payments).
5. (a) $55 billion (b) $20 billion (c) $290 billion (d) about $400 billion (2004)
6. During the 1980s the deficit grew and the federal debt began a sharp rise. During the 1990s the debt continued to rise, but the deficit grew smaller and by the late 1990s there was a budget surplus. Deficits returned in 2002 and the debt was projected to grow substantially.
7. Students' charts will vary, but should show how government creation of money can lead to increased output, and when full employment is reached, inflation results.

under President Bush and extended under President Clinton did help Congress control the growth of government spending. Second, tax increases by President Clinton in 1993 resulted in more federal revenue. Finally, the strong economy and low unemployment during the 1990s meant that more individuals and corporations were earning more money—and thus paying more in taxes.

Return to Deficits

The changeover from deficits to surplus brought with it a different set of political concerns. Investors who had come to rely heavily upon Treasury bonds as the basic "safe" investment worried that the federal government would remove all bonds from the market as it repaid its debt. As a 2000 presidential candidate, George W. Bush pledged to use the surplus to guarantee Social Security into the new century, provide additional medical benefits to seniors, and reduce income taxes.

However, the surplus was short-lived. The end of the stock market boom, an economic slowdown, and a new federal income tax cut reduced federal revenues. The terrorist attacks of September 11, 2001 dealt a double blow to the federal budget by disrupting the economy and imposing new defense and rebuilding costs. In response, the federal government returned to deficit spending. President Bush announced that national security and economic growth, not a balanced budget, were his administration's primary goals.

In 2003, President Bush signed a second tax bill that further lowered taxes on regular income, dividends, and capital gains. The president promised the bill would energize the American economy and create jobs for unemployed workers. However, the 2004 federal budget included an approximately $400 billion deficit with even more borrowing projected for future years.

In the short term, deficit spending may help create jobs and encourage economic growth. The long-term outlook for the federal budget is uncertain. Federal spending on Social Security and Medicare is projected to rise sharply in the next thirty years as large numbers of Baby Boomers leave the job market and retire. With new retirees outnumbering new workers, balancing the budget is expected to become ever more difficult.

Section 3 Assessment

Progress Monitoring *Online*
For: Self-quiz with vocabulary practice
Web Code: mna-6157

Key Terms and Main Ideas

1. What is a **balanced budget?**
2. How might a **budget deficit** be related to the **national debt?**
3. How does a **Treasury note** differ from a **Treasury bill?**

Applying Economic Concepts

4. ***Try This*** You're a lawmaker, and you get to decide what to do with this year's budget surplus. Write a brief proposal explaining whether the surplus should be used for new spending, tax cuts, or to buy back bonds and cut interest payments. Include explanations for your proposals.
5. ***Math Practice*** Use the data in Figure 15.9 to determine the approximate size of the largest budget deficits in each of the following decades: **(a)** 1940s **(b)** 1970s **(c)** 1990s **(d)** 2000s.
6. ***Using the Databank*** Study the Federal Debt and Federal Deficit graphs on page 542 of the Databank. Summarize the trends shown in the data for the period from 1980 to 1990 and the period from 1990 to 2004.
7. ***Critical Thinking*** Create a flowchart showing how the creation of money by the government to pay for a budget deficit can lead to inflation.

For: Current Events Activity
Visit: PHSchool.com
Web Code: mnd-6153

Progress Monitoring *Online*
For additional assessment, have students access Progress Monitoring Online at **Web Code:** mna-6157

Go Online PHSchool.com Typing in the Web Code when prompted will bring students directly to detailed instructions for this activity.

Real-life Case Study

Public Policy

Will Social Security Survive?

Until the 1930s, paying for retirement was almost entirely up to the individual. During the 1930s, however, the Great Depression left nearly half of all senior citizens unable to support themselves. To help them, the federal government created the Social Security program in 1935.

Social Security System Here's how the program works. Workers pay a Social Security tax, which is matched by their employers. After they retire, workers receive Social Security payments for the rest of their lives.

Social Security is a "pay as you go" system. Most of the Social Security taxes paid by today's workers are used to pay benefits to today's retirees. Any surplus is put into trust funds to earn interest. In 2001, there were 3.4 workers paying taxes for every retiree receiving benefits.

▲ President Franklin D. Roosevelt signed the Social Security Act into law in 1935.

Trouble Ahead Many economists are concerned about what will happen to Social Security in the future. If the system continues unchanged, experts warn that Social Security payments will exceed revenues in the year 2018. By 2042, the Social Security trust fund will be exhausted.

Why will this system be broke by the 2040s? The reason is the "baby boom," the period between 1945 and 1964 when there was a large increase in the number of babies born. As baby boomers retire, there will only be two workers for every retiree receiving benefits. Also, life expectancies are rising, which means that Americans will collect benefits longer.

Possible Solutions In the early 2000s, the President and Congress began to focus their attention on saving Social Security. But how should it be done? Some people believe that the age of retirement should be further increased. Others believe that the government should invest Social Security reserves in the stock market. However, all agree that depriving Americans of Social Security would be disastrous.

Projected Population, 2000–2050 (in thousands)

Year	Americans aged 25-64	Americans aged 65 and over
2000	142,883	34,709
2010	155,660	39,408
2020	161,999	53,220
2030	162,252	69,379
2040	171,360	75,233
2050	182,621	78,859

Source: U.S. Census Bureau

Applying Economic Ideas

1. Do you think that paying Social Security taxes should be mandatory? Explain.
2. How do baby boomers present a challenge to the future of Social Security?

Real-life Case Study: Public Policy

1. Focus Point out to students that problems with Social Security may affect them directly. Ask them whether they think that the Social Security system is a good idea.

2. Instruct Make sure that students understand how Social Security works and why changing demographics are affecting the system. Help students to see that the Social Security debate is part of the larger debate about fiscal policy.

3. Close/Reteach Ask students to examine the possible solutions to the Social Security problem identified in the text. Have them evaluate these solutions as well as others that they may have seen mentioned in news reports.

Case Studies Activity
Case Studies in Free Enterprise folder, pp. 30–31, "Paul Ehrlich," helps students apply economic principles in an additional case study.

Economic Detective Activity
Unit 6 folder, p. 23, "Troubles in Westfed," provides an additional application of chapter concepts.

Interdisciplinary Connections: Science

The Economics of Aging In the 1930s the life span of the average American was much shorter than it is today. Part of the problem with the Social Security system is that its developers never expected that people would be able to live for so many years beyond the age of retirement.

Making the Connection Recent advances in medical science have significantly extended human life expectancy. Have students find out about scientific developments that are lengthening life expectancy today (for example, advances in nutritional science, better treatments for cancer, organ transplants, and gene therapy). Ask students to find out what the average life expectancy is for people born in the year of their birth. Then have them compare this number with the expectancy for a person born in 1935.

Answers to . . .

1. Students may say yes, that it is a program that provides for the needs of everyone. Others may say no, that people should be allowed to invest their money for retirement as they see fit.
2. As baby boomers reach retirement age, there will be only two workers paying into Social Security for every three retirees receiving benefits. Since people are living longer, payments will be needed for a longer time.

Chapter 15 Assessment

Key Terms

1. Expansionary policies
2. classical economics
3. Treasury bond
4. Budget surpluses
5. productive capacity
6. fiscal policy
7. national debt

Using Graphic Organizers

8. Students should complete the web map by filling in appropriate characteristics of classical, Keynesian, and supply-side economics.

Reviewing Main Ideas

9. Limits include difficulty of changing spending levels, political pressures, and problems in predicting future economic activity.
10. The multiplier effect states that the effects of government fiscal policy are multiplied in the marketplace; every dollar of change in fiscal policy translates into more than a dollar of change in national income.
11. The economy was healthy from 1945 to 1960. During the Kennedy administration fiscal policy took a Keynesian approach, so taxes were lowered to boost the economy. Keynesian policies remained in force through the 1960s and 1970s. During the Reagan administration supply-side economics came into fashion, and taxes were lowered once again, although government spending continued to rise, increasing the national debt. In the 1990s fiscal policy focused on reducing deficits and the national debt. In the early 2000s, taxes were reduced to encourage economic growth, but continued higher spending led to large deficits.
12. The national debt is the sum of government borrowing to date. Usually it is measured by comparing it to GDP; the debt is calculated as a percentage of GDP.
13. The national debt is all of the money that the federal government owes. The deficit is the amount of money the government borrows for one fiscal year.
14. Options include legislative acts that require a balanced budget or a constitutional amendment. Governments could also cut spending or increase taxes to balance the budget.

Chapter 15 Assessment

Chapter Summary

A summary of major ideas in Chapter 15 appears below. See also the **Guide to the Essentials of Economics,** which provides additional review and test practice of key concepts in Chapter 15.

Section 1 Understanding Fiscal Policy (pp. 387–393)

The government can try to stabilize the economy through **fiscal policy,** or changing how much it taxes and spends. The tool it uses is the **federal budget,** which lists how much money the government expects to take in and how it will spend that money. **Expansionary policies** include lowering taxes and spending more to increase output. **Contractionary policies** include raising taxes and cutting spending to lower economic growth.

Section 2 Fiscal Policy Options (pp. 395–401)

The Great Depression of the 1930s seemed to disprove the idea that free markets always return to equilibrium. John Maynard Keynes argued that government spending can raise demand and help an economy recover. **Keynesian economics** drove American policy from the 1930s to the 1970s. In the 1980s, Ronald Reagan tried to increase output by putting **supply-side economics** into practice. He cut taxes to encourage people and businesses to work harder.

Section 3 Budget Deficits and the National Debt (pp. 403–408)

When the government spends more than it takes in, it runs a **budget deficit** and must create new money or borrow money to cover the difference. The government borrows money by issuing bonds. The **national debt** is all of the money the government owes to bondholders. The United States debt grew tremendously during the 1980s and early 1990s, causing problems for private businesses and leading to a public backlash against deficit spending. After a brief period of budget surpluses in the late 1990s, recession, tax cuts, and war caused massive new deficits in the early 2000s.

Key Terms

Choose the italicized word in parentheses that best completes each sentence.

1. *(Contractionary policies/Expansionary policies)* are used to increase overall demand and GDP.
2. The theory that states that the economy regulates itself best is known as *(classical economics/Keynesian economics)*.
3. A *(Treasury note/Treasury bond)* is a long-term bond, issued sometimes for as long as 30 years.
4. *(Budget surpluses/Budget deficits)* occur when the government has money left over after paying all of its expenses for the year.
5. The maximum sustainable economic output of a society is known as its *(productive capacity/automatic stabilizer)*.
6. A government's *(fiscal year/fiscal policy)* is the use of taxing and spending to affect the overall economy.
7. The *(national debt/balanced budget)* is the total amount of money the federal government owes.

Using Graphic Organizers

8. Copy the web map below on a separate sheet of paper. Complete the diagram by filling in the primary characteristics of classical, Keynesian, and supply-side economics.

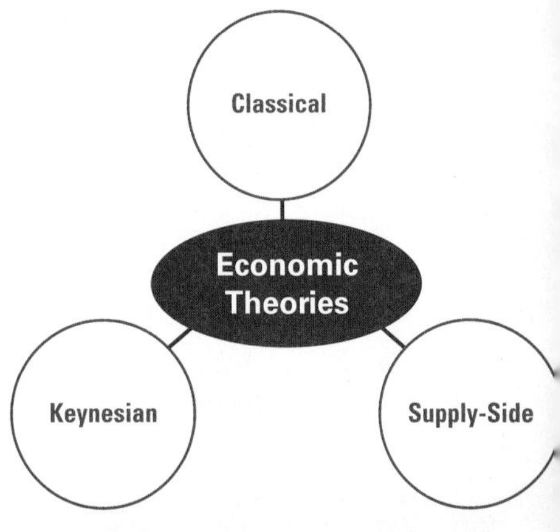

Critical Thinking

15. Classical economics states that the free market can regulate itself, whereas Keynesian economics supports government interaction in the market system. The Great Depression led to the development of Keynesian economics.
16. Students' lists will vary but may include taxes, especially sales taxes, or certain entitlement programs such as Social Security.
17. Automatic stabilizers attempt to keep large economic upswings and downturns to a minimum and keep the economy growing at a steady pace. Without them the economy could experience hyperinflation or depression.

Reviewing Main Ideas

9. Describe three problems that limit fiscal policy.
10. Describe the multiplier effect in your own words.
11. Summarize the ways in which fiscal policy has affected our country since World War II.
12. How is the national debt measured?
13. What is the difference between the national debt and the budget deficit?
14. What options does the government have to respond to an annual budget deficit?

Critical Thinking

15. **Making Comparisons** What fundamental differences exist between classical economics and Keynesian economics? What events led to the popularization of Keynesian economics?
16. **Drawing Inferences** Make a list of ways in which fiscal policy affects your daily life. Which aspects of fiscal policy have the greatest effect on you?
17. **Recognizing Cause and Effect** How do automatic stabilizers affect our economy? What would our economy be like without them?
18. **Analyzing Information** Use your own words to describe the crowding-out effect. Explain why it can influence economic growth over the long run.
19. **Drawing Conclusions** What would be the benefits and drawbacks of a balanced budget amendment? Would you support such an amendment?

Problem-Solving Activity

20. Recommend your own proposal for debt reduction. Consider the examples in Section 3 when creating your proposal.

Skills for Life

Comparing Circle Graphs Review the steps shown on page 394; then answer the following questions using the circle graphs below.

21. How did the percentage of federal spending on interest payments change between 1980 and 2004?
22. Which category of federal spending has seen the largest percentage decrease since 1980?
23. How have human resource outlays changed as a percentage of the federal budget?

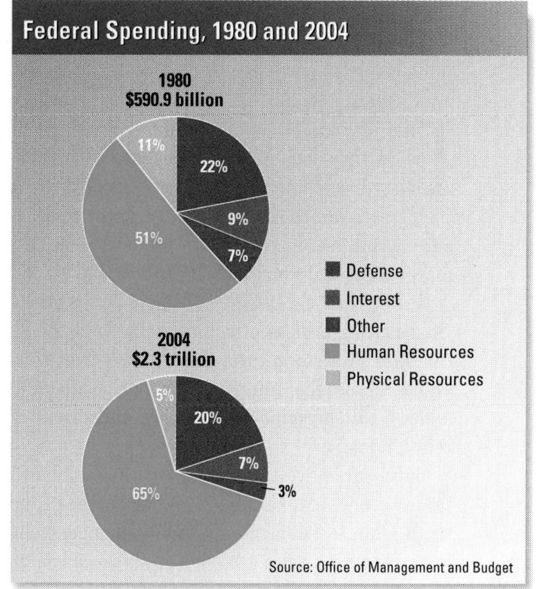

Economics Journal

Essay Writing Look at your list of items paid for by the government. Which ones do you think are essential services of government, and which do you think represent unnecessary spending, if any? In what ways has government funding helped your local economy?

Progress Monitoring *Online*

For: Chapter 15 Self-Test **Visit:** PHSchool.com
Web Code: mna-6151

As a final review, take the Economics Chapter 15 Self-Test and receive immediate feedback on your answers. The test consists of 20 multiple-choice questions designed to test your understanding of the chapter content.

18. When the government needs to borrow money, there is less money available to invest in businesses. If people do not invest in businesses, economic growth will slow down.
19. Students should list advantages and disadvantages of a balanced budget amendment and use these examples to explain why they would or wouldn't support one.

Problem-Solving Activity

20. Student proposals should demonstrate an appreciation for the complexities of fiscal policy and the effects of various methods of reducing debt.

Skills for Life

21. Interest decreased from 9 percent to 8 percent.
22. Physical resources has seen the largest decrease.
23. Human resource outlays have increased from 51 percent to 66 percent.

Additional support materials and activities for Chapter 15 of *Economics: Principles in Action* can be found in the Social Studies area of **PHSchool.com.**

Economics Journal

Students should describe which of the items on their list are essential and which are nonessential. They should also list specific ways in which government spending has helped the local economy.

Review and Assessment

Vocabulary Practice Unit 6 folder, p. 22 uses a fill-in-the-blanks word puzzle to reinforce understanding of key terms.

GTE **Guide to the Essentials** Chapter 15 Test, p. 66

Test Bank CD-ROM Chapter 15 Test

Go Online PHSchool.com Students may use the Chapter 15 Self-Test on **PHSchool.com** to prepare for the Chapter Test.

THE WALL STREET JOURNAL.
CLASSROOM EDITION

DEBATE: INTERNET TAXATION

1. Focus Have students find the meaning of each of these words before they begin to read: *complexities, forfeit, impede, moratorium, opt, sovereignty,* and *transaction.*

Explain to students that they will be conducting a debate on taxing sales made online. Inform them that they will be responsible for arguing one side of the issue. Remind students that a well-prepared debater supports a position with valid evidence, logical arguments, and responsible appeals to emotion.

2. Instruct The authors have both researched the impact of taxing online sales. Have students conduct further research on Internet commerce from credible sources before conducting the debate.

Remind students that they should use the following debate format:

The affirmative side will:

- State the problem to be solved. Why is this problem significant?
- Explain who or what is harmed if the problem is not resolved. Use factual evidence to quantify the harm.
- Propose a plan of action. Explain why it is better than the current system.
- Provide factual evidence to show how this plan will solve the problem.

The opposing side will:

- Refute the arguments of the affirmative side, using factual evidence to quantify and support its position.
- If necessary, support the status quo's ability to solve the problem.

3. Close/Reteach When the debate is concluded, encourage students to discuss their opinions on the issue. Ask them whether they were persuaded by the other side's arguments. Conclude by having students write their own statements supporting or opposing taxing Internet commerce.

THE WALL STREET JOURNAL.
CLASSROOM EDITION

DEBATING CURRENT ISSUES: *Internet Taxation*

In 1998, Congress adopted the Internet Tax Freedom Act, which placed a three-year moratorium on taxing many online activities, including retail sales. The moratorium has been renewed and extended.

In this debate from *The Wall Street Journal Classroom Edition,* Maureen Riehl, vice president and industry-relations counsel for the National Retail Federation, and Grover Norquist, president of Americans for Tax Reform, argue the benefits and drawbacks of taxing e-commerce.

YES *Should Internet Commerce Be Taxed?*

BY MAUREEN RIEHL

Internet retailers enjoy an unfair price advantage when they don't have to collect sales tax from out-of-state customers. Not collecting sales tax means their prices can be as much as 10% lower than bricks-and-mortar merchants. In an industry where profit margins can be as small as 1% to 2%, that's a killer.

Retailers should be able to compete under the same tax rules, regardless of whether they sell their merchandise in a store, through the mail, over the telephone, or on the Internet. Tax policy shouldn't be allowed to determine the winners and losers in the retail industry.

Opponents have tried to portray an Internet sales tax as a new tax. Nothing could be further from the truth. Online customers and catalog shoppers who live in states with a sales tax have always owed sales tax. They are legally obligated to report purchases where sales tax wasn't collected and pay "use" tax on their state income-tax forms. Unfortunately, few people pay and enforcement has been lax.

Opponents also claim taxation would discourage new technology investment and employment growth. Not true. This is not a tax on an Internet company, it is a tax on the consumer/customer making the purchase.

When sales tax isn't collected, everyone suffers. Bricks-and-mortar retailers experience unfair competition. But the police departments, fire departments, and local schools that depend on sales-tax revenue for their funding suffer far more.

This isn't an "us vs. them" issue—the National Retail Federation includes both bricks-and-mortar and Internet members. And modern retailers are increasingly multichannel retailers who sell their merchandise through whatever medium the customer demands.

Collecting sales tax won't kill the Internet—a Jupiter Research study found that the convenience of online shopping is far more important to consumers than pricing. Instead, it will put Internet retailing on the same footing with bricks-and-mortar retailing, where everyone can compete fairly and freely.

A worker at an Internet retailer gathers books in a warehouse to meet a customer's order. Should sales over the Internet be taxed like local purchases?

Debate Activity Debating Current Issues folder, p. 20 asks students to complete a graphic organizer to evaluate the issue of taxing Internet commerce and the problems created by this policy.

Economic Assessment Rubric Economics Assessment Rubrics folder, pp. 14–15 provides sample evaluation materials for participation in debates.

Background

About the Authors

Maureen Riehl, vice president and industry-relations counsel for the National Retail Federation, argues that the tax will even the playing field for retailers. Grover Norquist, president of Americans for Tax Reform and a member of the federal advisory commission on electronic commerce, believes that taxing e-commerce introduces many new problems.

NO Should Internet Commerce Be Taxed?

BY GROVER NORQUIST

The Internet has become increasingly more important to the U.S. economy as the number of companies and jobs created by its existence continue to increase. Yet, some politicians want to tax Internet purchases across state lines.

Such taxation would discourage new technology investment and employment growth. A study by the National Bureau of Economic Research found that Internet taxation will reduce the number of people purchasing goods on the Internet by 25%. And fewer purchases means fewer jobs and more corporate bankruptcies.

Additionally, online taxes impede new technological growth by limiting people's access to and use of the Internet. Small businesses that sell goods over the Internet will be subject to more than 7,500 different tax rates on transactions with consumers. As such, Internet taxation will not simplify the tax code. It will add new complexities and will limit the goods available to consumers online because fewer retailers will opt to sell their goods on the Internet.

Proponents of the tax also argue that Internet retailers enjoy a price advantage over regular retailers. That is not the case as the shipping costs for an online transaction can cancel out any price advantage.

Today's economy demands a new business model, one that employs both an Internet and physical presence. This has allowed Main Street businesses to enter a worldwide market, while giving consumers a greater choice of products. Successful companies have readjusted to the changing times, and the retailers pushing for Internet taxation are the companies who fail to realize the new realities of the marketplace.

Finally, allowing states to tax out-of-state residents will force states to forfeit sovereignty over their individual tax laws and reverse 300 years of American history by leading to "taxation without representation." Politicians will have an unchecked ability to raise taxes on consumers in other states who are not permitted to vote for or against them, thus damaging the American political system.

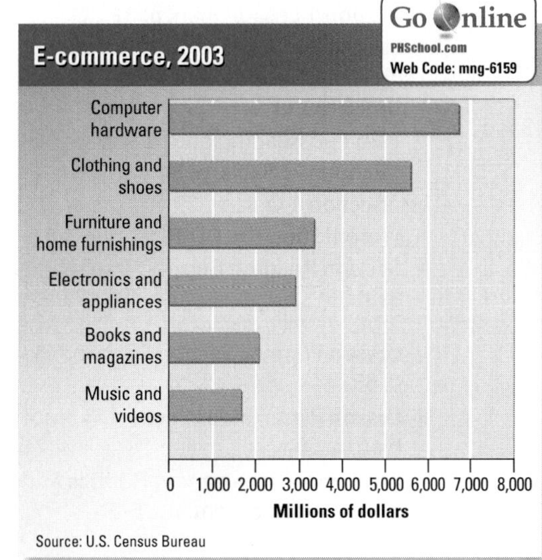

Billions of dollars worth of goods are sold over the Internet each year.

DEBATING THE ISSUE

1. Why does Maureen Riehl state that Internet retailers have an "unfair price advantage" when they don't collect sales tax from out-of-state customers?
2. Why does Grover Norquist disagree with Riehl's statement?
3. **Distinguishing Fact from Opinion** Agree or disagree with the following statement: Taxing the Internet would discourage new technology investment and employment growth.
4. **Synthesizing Information** Why do you think the value of computer hardware purchased online was so much greater than the value of books or clothing purchased online?

For: You Decide Poll
Visit: PHSchool.com
Web Code: mnp-6151

Differentiated Instruction 

Have students research and discuss reasons for imposing new laws on the Internet and the impact of new regulations on consumers, businesses and the economy. Then have them use media resources to research the status of the Internet Tax Freedom Law. What is the current government view of taxing such services as Internet access? If new rules are imposed, how will this change the way consumers and businesses use the Internet? How would requiring all Internet retailers to collect state taxes affect competition in the marketplace?

Go Online PHSchool.com Students can find additional links related to the debate by visiting the *Economics: Principles in Action* site at **PHSchool.com.**

Interdisciplinary Connections: History

Government and Cyberspace In 1996, John Perry Barlow's "Declaration of the Independence of Cyberspace" warned government to leave the Internet alone. The world of cyberspace is a world "where anyone, anywhere may express his or her beliefs, no matter how singular, without fear of being coerced into silence or conformity." Mr. Barlow thinks the only rule governing cyberspace is the Golden Rule.

Making the Connection Ask students to read and discuss the "Declaration of the Independence of Cyberspace." Then have them use their knowledge of the Internet and other factual evidence to agree or disagree with Mr. Barlow's views. The declaration can be found in its entirety at **PHSchool.com** **Web Code:** mne-6151.

Answers to . . .

1. By not collecting sales tax, Internet retailers can lower prices by as much as 10% over bricks-and-mortar merchants.
2. He argues that shipping costs for online transactions cancel out any price advantage.
3. Answers will vary.
4. Individual computers are much more expensive than books or music.

Chapter 16 The Federal Reserve and Monetary Policy

For more pacing suggestions, see the Economics Pacing Guide in the Program Overview of the Teaching Resources.

Section Objectives	Print and Technology Resources	
1 The Federal Reserve System *(pp. 415–418)* **Objectives** 1. Understand banking history in the United States. 2. Explain why the Federal Reserve Act of 1913 led to further reform. 3. Describe the structure of today's Federal Reserve System.	• **Lesson Planner** Section 1 Lesson Plan, p. 64 • **Learning Styles Lesson Plans folder** Section 1 Lesson Plan, p. 37 • **Lesson Plans folder** Section 1 Lesson Plan, p. 57 • **Unit 6 folder** Guided Reading and Review, p. 26 Economic Skills, p. 34 Section 1 Quiz, p. 27 • **Presentation Pro CD-ROM** Section 1 • **Section Reading Support Transparency System**	• **Transparency Resource Package** Economics Concepts, 16A: Structure of the Federal Reserve Economics Concepts, 16B: The Board of Governors Economics Concepts, 16C: Federal Reserve Districts Economics Concepts, 16D: Federal Open Market Committees • **Social Studies Skills Tutor CD-ROM**
2 Federal Reserve Functions *(pp. 420–423)* **Objectives** 1. Describe how the Federal Reserve serves the federal government. 2. Describe how the Federal Reserve serves banks. 3. Describe how the Federal Reserve regulates the banking system. 4. Understand the Federal Reserve's role in regulating the nation's money supply.	• **Lesson Planner** Section 2 Lesson Plan, p. 65 • **Lesson Plans folder** Section 2 Lesson Plan, p. 58 • **Economics Assessment Rubrics folder** Writing Assignment, pp. 6–7 • **Unit 6 folder** Guided Reading and Review, p. 28 Careers in Economics, Wire Transfer Analyst, p. 37 Section 2 Quiz, p. 29	• **Presentation Pro CD-ROM** Section 2 • **Transparency Resource Package** Economics Organizers, G5: Web Graphic Organizer Economics Concepts, 16E: How the Fed Clears a Check Economics Concepts, 16F: The Money Supply • **Section Reading Support Transparency System**
3 Monetary Policy Tools *(pp. 425–429)* **Objectives** 1. Describe the process of money creation. 2. Explain how the Federal Reserve uses three basic tools—reserve requirements, the discount rate, and open market operations—to implement U.S. monetary policy. 3. Understand why some monetary policy tools are favored over others.	• **Lesson Planner** Section 3 Lesson Plan, p. 66 • **Learning Styles Lesson Plans folder** Section 3 Lesson Plan, p. 38 • **Lesson Plans folder** Section 3 Lesson Plan, p. 59 • **Unit 6 folder** Guided Reading and Review, p. 30 Section 3 Quiz, p. 31 • **Source Articles folder** Greenspan Confronts Criticism of Fed Decision-Making Methods, pp. 48–50	• **Presentation Pro CD-ROM** Section 3 • **Transparency Resource Package** Economics Organizers, G8: Flow Chart Graphic Organizer Economics Concepts, 16G: Monetary Policy Tools and Their Effects • **Section Reading Support Transparency System**
4 Monetary Policy and Macroeconomic Stabilization *(pp. 430–434)* **Objectives** 1. Understand how monetary policy works. 2. Explain the problems of timing and policy lags in implementing monetary policy. 3. Explain how predictions about the length of a business cycle affect monetary policy. 4. Describe two distinct approaches to monetary policy.	• **Lesson Planner** Section 4 Lesson Plan, p. 67 • **Lesson Plans folder** Section 4 Lesson Plan, p. 60 • **Unit 6 folder** Guided Reading and Review, p. 32 Economic Cartoon, p. 38 Vocabulary Practice, p. 35 Economic Detective, p. 36 Section 4 Quiz, p. 33	• **Case Studies in Free Enterprise folder** Amartya Sen, pp. 32–33 • **Presentation Pro CD-ROM** Section 4 • **Transparency Resource Package** Economics Organizers, G6: Double Web Graphic Organizer Economics Concepts, 16H: Fiscal and Monetary Policy Tools • **Section Reading Support Transparency System**

Differentiated Instruction

Making Predictions L1 L2

One way to help struggling readers with effective reading skills is to have students practice making predictions. To begin, offer these guidelines and model the process.

1. Preview the pictures in the section prior to reading the text

2. Ask questions prompted by the graph, photograph, or painting.

3. Make predictions that will answer these questions.

4. Read the text and answer the questions they think were addressed.

Finding Viewpoints in the Media L4

Many students are aware of issues of credibility and bias in the media. As you present events in the text, ask students to consider how the accompanying visuals are constructed. To begin, have students look at the visuals in the text and answer the following questions

1. Who produced or sponsored the image?

2. Who is the target audience? How is the message tailored specifically to them?

3. What is implied in this image?

4. What tools are used to create the message?

5. What perspective is absent from the image? What is left out of the image that might be important to know?

Visit the Social Studies area of the Prentice Hall Web site. There you can find additional links to enrich chapter content for *Economics: Principles in Action* as well as a self-test for students. Be sure to check out this month's **eTeach** online discussion with a Master Economics Teacher.

Web Code: mnf-6161

Running Out of Time?

- Use the **Presentation Pro CD-ROM** to create an outline for this chapter.
- Use the Chapter Summary in the **Chapter 16 Assessment,** p. 436.
- Use the Section Summaries for Chapter 16, from **Guide to the Essentials of Economics (English and Spanish).**

THE WALL STREET JOURNAL. CLASSROOM EDITION

Prentice Hall brings into the classroom the authoritative content of *The Wall Street Journal Classroom Edition.* See the Source Articles, Debating Current Issues, and You and Your Money folders in the **Teaching Resources**. Also, see Economics Video Library, "Market Manias."

Assessment Resources

Chapter Assessment

Teaching Resources Unit 6, Chapter 16
- Section Quizzes, pp. 27, 29, 31

Exam *View*® Test Bank CD-ROM Chapter 16
Economics Assessment Rubrics
Chapter 16 Self-Test, **Web Code:** mna-6161

Reading and Skills Evaluation

Progress Monitoring Assessments
- Screening Test
- Diagnostic Test of Social Studies Skills

Standardized Test Preparation

Test Prep Workbook
Test-Taking Strategies With Transparencies

Differentiated Instruction Key

- L1 Special Needs
- L2 Basic to Average
- L3 All Students
- L4 Average to Advanced
- LPR Less Proficient Readers
- AR Advanced Readers
- SN Special Needs Students
- GT Gifted and Talented
- ELL English Language Learner

Chapter 16

The Federal Reserve and Monetary Policy

Introducing the Chapter

In this chapter, students will learn about the Federal Reserve System. They will find out about the history of this institution, its function in the American economy, and how it regulates the economy through the banking system.

For additional links for *Economics: Principles in Action* provided by Prentice Hall and *The Wall Street Journal Classroom Edition,* visit the Social Studies area. Be sure to check out this month's **eTeach** online discussion with a Master Teacher.

Beyond the Lecture

You may cover the concepts in Chapter 16 in an activity-based style by using the following materials:

- **Technology Resources** appropriate for use with this chapter are noted on pp. 416, 417, 418, 421, 423, 428, 429, 431, 433, 434, and 437.
- **Presentation Pro CD-ROM** with animated graphs gives you an alternative method for organizing and delivering chapter content.
- **Activities** designed to meet the needs of students of mixed abilities and learning styles are noted throughout the chapter in the side columns.
- **Learning Styles Lesson Plans** provide alternate lessons for diverse learning styles. See pp. 37–38 of the Learning Styles Lesson Plans folder located in the Teaching Resources.

Economics Journal

Instruct students to write their terms and definitions in their Economics Journals. Students may include completed journal entries in an Economics Portfolio.

Chapter 16 The Federal Reserve and Monetary Policy

Suppose you have a checkbook that allows you to write as many checks as you wish for any amount you desire. There is no need to worry about the balance in your account, and the checks will always be cashed, no matter how much you spend. Of course, no person has an account like this, but the Federal Reserve, our nation's central bank, very nearly does.

Economics Journal

Skim recent newspapers for references to policies of the Federal Reserve. List terms you don't understand. Jot down their definitions as you read this chapter.

For: Current Data
Visit: PHSchool.com
Web Code: mng-6161

National Council on Economic Education

The following Voluntary National Content Standards in Economics are addressed in this chapter:

★ **Standard 12** Students will understand that: Interest rates, adjusted for inflation, rise and fall to balance the amount saved with the amount borrowed, thus affecting the allocation of scarce resources between present and future uses.

★ **Standard 20** Students will understand that: Federal government budgetary policy and the Federal Reserve System's monetary policy influence the overall levels of employment, output, and prices.

For more information about the standards, contact the National Council on Economic Education

1140 Avenue of the Americas
New York, NY 10036
1-800-338-1192

Section 1 The Federal Reserve System

Preview

Objectives

After studying this section you will be able to:

1. **Understand** banking history in the United States.
2. **Explain** why the Federal Reserve Act of 1913 led to further reform.
3. **Explain** the structure of the Federal Reserve System.

Section Focus

To stabilize the nation's banking system, Congress created the Federal Reserve System in 1913. The Federal Reserve is owned by individual member banks. It is overseen by a small but powerful Board of Governors. As a private institution serving a public function, the Federal Reserve is a central bank relatively free from government control.

Key Terms

Board of Governors
monetary policy
Federal Reserve Districts
Federal Advisory Council (FAC)
Federal Open Market Committee (FOMC)

The American banking system is a compromise between supporters and opponents of a central bank. As a symbol of this compromise, the Federal Reserve System is the privately owned, publicly controlled central bank of the United States.

Banking History

As you read in Chapter 10, the issue of a central bank has been debated hotly since 1790, when Federalists lined up in favor of a central bank. The first bank of the United States issued a single currency. It also reviewed banking practices and helped the federal government carry out its duties and powers. Partly because of the continued debate over state versus federal powers, however, the first bank lasted only until 1811. At that time, Congress refused to extend its charter.

Congress established the Second Bank of the United States in 1816 to restore order in the monetary system. However, many people feared that a central bank placed too much power in the hands of the federal government. Political opposition toppled the Second Bank in 1836 when its charter expired.

A period of confusion followed. States chartered some banks, while the federal government chartered and regulated others. Reserve requirements—the amount of reserves that banks are required to keep on hand—were difficult to enforce, and the nation experienced a series of serious bank runs. The Panic of 1907 finally convinced Congress to act.

The nation's banking system needed to address two issues. First, consumers and businesses needed access to increased sources of funds to encourage business expansion. Second, banks needed a source of emergency cash to prevent depositor panics that resulted in bank runs.

▲ The Federal Reserve System is headed by the Federal Reserve Board of Governors. The first Federal Reserve Board of Governors, here, was seated in 1914.

Federal Reserve Act of 1913

Congress created the National Monetary Commission (NMC) in 1908 to propose solutions to the nation's banking problems. Based on the NMC's recommendations, Congress passed the Federal Reserve Act in 1913. The resulting Federal Reserve System, now often referred to simply as "the Fed," was composed of a group of twelve independent regional banks. This central group of banks could lend to other banks in times of need.

Graphing the Main Idea

Economic Institutions To build understanding of the concept of **public policy** as it is related to the history of banking in the United States, you may wish to have students complete a flowchart graphic organizer like the one at the right. Remind students that a flowchart shows a sequence of events. Ask students to use it to record the most important events in the history of banking.

Section Reading Support Transparencies A template and the answers for this graphic organizer can be found in Chapter 16, Section 1 of the Section Reading Support Transparency System.

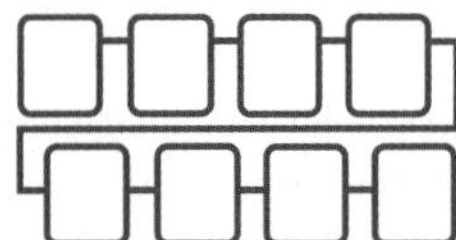

Section 1 The Federal Reserve System

Objectives You may wish to call students' attention to the objectives in the Section Preview. The objectives are reflected in the main headings of the section.

Bellringer Ask students whether they have ever heard of "The Fed." Explain that this is a common nickname for the Federal Reserve System, which regulates the nation's banks and administers monetary policy. Tell students that in this section they will learn what the Fed is, how it came into existence, and what it does.

Vocabulary Builder Ask students to give a brief definition for each key term. Then tell them to use information from the section to describe a type of news story that might include the term. (For example, for *Board of Governors* students may write *article about new presidential appointment to the board.*)

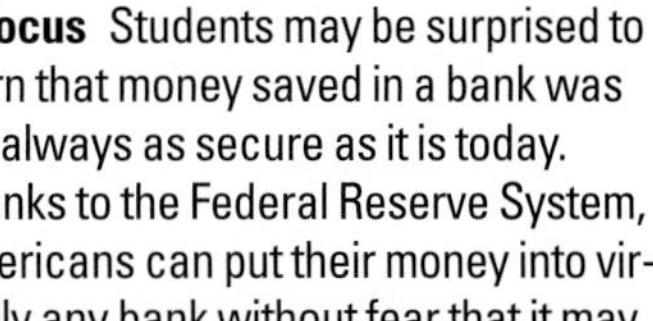

Lesson Plan

Teaching the Main Concepts L3

1. Focus Students may be surprised to learn that money saved in a bank was not always as secure as it is today. Thanks to the Federal Reserve System, Americans can put their money into virtually any bank without fear that it may not be available when they need it. Ask students why this is so.

2. Instruct Explain to students that before 1913 the banking system was not centralized. Discuss the reasons for this, and explain why the Federal Reserve was established. Help students to understand that the Fed as we know it today was developed only after many banking failures. Then describe the structure of the Fed.

3. Close/Reteach Ask students to suggest ways in which the Fed affects their lives.

 **Guided Reading and Review**
Unit 6 folder, p. 26 asks students to identify the main ideas of the section and to define or identify key terms.

 **Differentiated Instruction** L3
Organize the class into groups of three, and have each group create a captioned time line showing the history of banking in the United States, including the development of the Federal Reserve. Encourage students to check other resources to add events and explanations not included in the text. Have groups display time lines in order to determine what might need to be added or changed.

Differentiated Instruction L4
To expand understanding of why the terms of the members of the Fed's Board of Governors are staggered, have students make some predictions about what might happen if one U.S. President were able to appoint the entire Board of Governors. Ask them to consider how it would affect the stability of the financial system. Have them write their answers in a short paragraph. GT

Transparency Resource Package
Economics Concepts, 16A: Structure of the Federal Reserve
Economics Concepts, 16B: The Board of Governors

Learning Styles Activity
Learning Styles Lesson Plans folder, p. 37 asks students to plan and present a series of interviews depicting important stages in the development of the U.S. banking system.

Continued Need for Reform

Although the Federal Reserve System helped to restore confidence in the banking system beginning in 1914, it has also learned through trial and error the best ways to fulfill its responsibilities. During the Great Depression, the financial crises of 1930–1933 were exactly the kinds of problems that the NMC had hoped to avoid by creating the Federal Reserve System. The system did not work well, however, because the twelve regional banks each acted independently. Their separate actions often canceled one another out. The Governor of the Federal Reserve Bank of New York (a bank with a close relationship to Wall Street and the investment community) believed that to counteract the growing recession, the government needed to pump money into investment and help Americans get back to work. Many of the other regional governors disagreed about what kinds of action to take. They were more concerned about maintaining gold reserves and with administrative issues than with helping the economy to recover from the widespread recession. By the time Congress forced the Fed to take strong action in 1932, it was too little, too late. The financial crisis had deepened to the point that recovery became long and difficult.

Board of Governors *the seven-member board that oversees the Federal Reserve System*

A Stronger Fed

In 1935, Congress adjusted the Federal Reserve's structure so that the system could respond more effectively to future crises. These reforms created the Federal Reserve System as we know it today. The new Fed enjoys more centralized power so that the regional banks can act consistently with one another while still representing their own districts' banking concerns.

Figure 16.1 **Structure of the Federal Reserve System**

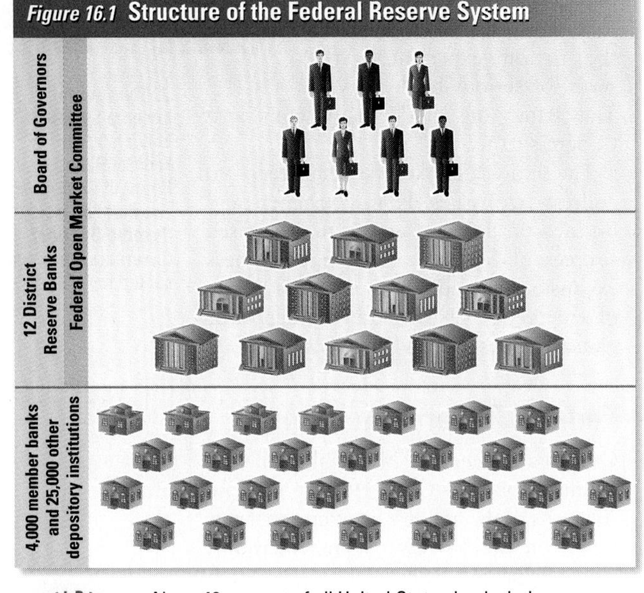

About 40 percent of all United States banks belong to the Federal Reserve. These members hold about 75 percent of all bank deposits in the United States.
Government How does the structure of the Fed reflect a compromise between centralized power and regional powers?

Structure of the Federal Reserve

Member banks themselves own the Federal Reserve System. Like so many American institutions, the structure of the Federal Reserve System represents compromises between centralized power and regional powers. (See Figure 16.1.)

The Board of Governors

The Federal Reserve System is overseen by the **Board of Governors** of the Federal Reserve. The Board of Governors is headquartered in Washington, D.C. Its seven members are appointed for staggered fourteen-year terms by the President of the United States with the advice and consent of the Senate. The terms are staggered to prevent any one President from appointing a full Board of Governors and to protect board members from day-to-day political pressures. Members cannot be reappointed after serving a full term. Geographical restrictions on these appointments ensure that no one district is over-represented.

The President also appoints, from among these seven members, the chair of the Board of Governors. The Senate confirms the

Answer to . . .
Building Key Concepts The Board of Governors is appointed by the President with the approval of the Senate. However, member banks within each district own shares in their own Federal Reserve District Bank.

Econ 101: Key Concepts Made Easy

Monetary and Fiscal Policy One of the key concepts in this section is **monetary policy.** Monetary policy consists simply of the actions taken by the Federal Reserve to ensure that the economy is working at its best, neither overheating and risking inflation or moving too slowly and risking a recession.
Ask students to consider similarities between the seven members of the Board of Governors and a sports team. *(Like members of a team, everyone on the Board has the same goal, and they will do their best to accomplish it. However, individuals may disagree about what the best course of action is. Therefore, most teams have a leader—like a quarterback—who provides guidance. The Chair of the Federal Reserve does much the same thing.)*

Figure 16.2 **Federal Reserve Districts**

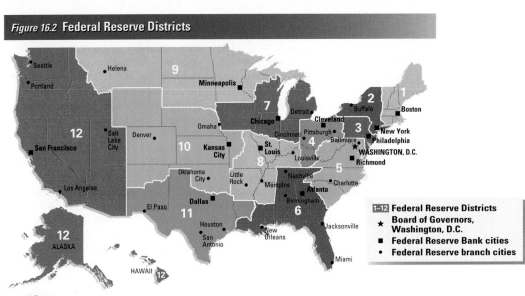

1–12 Federal Reserve Districts
★ Board of Governors, Washington, D.C.
■ Federal Reserve Bank cities
• Federal Reserve branch cities

Most Federal Reserve Districts contain a variety of agricultural, manufacturing, and service industries as well as rural and urban areas.
Government How does the makeup of the Federal Reserve Districts help ensure that no single region is dominant?

appointment. Chairs serve four-year terms, which can be renewed. The chair acts as the main spokesperson for monetary policy for the country. **Monetary policy** refers to the actions the Fed takes to influence the level of real GDP and the rate of inflation in the economy.

Recent chairs of the Fed have been economists from business, academia, or government. Alan Greenspan, whose previous career was in building economic forecasting models, has been the most notable chair of the Fed in recent years. He took office in 1987, serving both Republican and Democratic administrations. (See page 424 for a profile of Greenspan.)

Twelve District Reserve Banks

The Federal Reserve Act divided the United States into twelve **Federal Reserve Districts,** as shown on Figure 16.2. One Federal Reserve Bank is located in each of the twelve districts.

Each Federal Reserve Bank monitors and reports on economic and banking conditions in its district. Each Federal Reserve District is made up of more than one state. The Federal Reserve Act aimed to establish a system in which no one region could exploit the central bank's power at another's expense.

Congress also regulated the makeup of each Bank's board of nine directors to make sure that many groups' interests would be represented. Member banks elect three bankers and three leaders in industry, commerce, or other businesses to their district boards. The remaining three directorships, appointed by the Board of Governors of the Federal Reserve, represent broad public interests. The district president is then elected from among these nine directors.

Member Banks

All nationally chartered banks are required to join the Federal Reserve System. The remaining members are state-chartered banks that join voluntarily. Since 1980, all banks have equal access to Fed services like

monetary policy *the actions the Federal Reserve takes to influence the level of real GDP and the rate of inflation in the economy*

Federal Reserve Districts *the twelve banking districts created by the Federal Reserve Act*

FAST FACT

In 1913, when the Fed was established, economic and financial power was concentrated in the East and Midwest. Notice that no Federal Reserve Bank exists in Los Angeles, now one of the largest cities in the country.

Differentiated Instruction 

Ask students to create their own graphic representations of the structure of the Federal Reserve. They may use the illustration on p. 416 as a guide, but encourage them to portray the structure in a unique way.

Transparency Resource Package
Economics Concepts, 16C: Federal Reserve Districts
Economic Concepts, 16D: Federal Open Market Committee

Block Scheduling Strategies

Consider these suggestions to take advantage of extended class time:

- Extend the Vocabulary Builder activity by having students bring articles to class that mention key terms or other important terms from the section. Photocopy the articles and have students read one for each term. Have students summarize the articles, telling how they increased their understanding of the terms.
- Have small groups of students examine the Web sites of the Board of Governors and the 12 Federal Reserve Banks. Ask each group to present an oral report that gives an overview of the site they examined as well as any interesting features it contains. Use the links provided in the *Economics : Principles in Action* segment in the Social Studies area at the following Web site: **www.phschool.com**

Answer to . . .

Building Key Concepts The districts are comprised of several states and a variety of agricultural, manufacturing, and service industries in rural and urban areas. Their design will thus not allow for one single region to be dominant.

Transparency Resource Package Economics Concepts, 16D: Federal Open Market Committee

Guide to the Essentials Chapter 16, Section 1, p. 67 provides support for students who need additional review of the section content. Spanish support is available in the Spanish edition of the guide on p. 67.

Quiz Unit 6 folder, p. 27 includes questions to check students' understanding of Section 1 content.

Presentation Pro CD-ROM Quiz provides multiple-choice questions to check students' understanding of Section 1 content.

Answers to . . .

Section 1 Assessment

1. The seven members are usually economists from business, academia, or government who are appointed by the President of the United States with the approval of a majority of the Senate.
2. Monetary policy consists of the actions the Fed takes to influence the level of real GDP and the rate of inflation in the nation's economy.
3. Each district is made up of more than one state. Federal Reserve Districts include a mixture of agricultural, manufacturing, and service industries as well as rural and urban areas.
4. The Federal Advisory Council (FAC) collects information about each district and reports to the Board of Governors about economic conditions within each district. The FAC is a research arm of the Fed.
5. The Federal Open Market Committee makes key decisions about interest rates and the growth of the U.S. money supply.
6. The Federal Reserve System is owned by its member banks themselves, not by any part of the federal government.
7. Answers will vary based on the location of your school. Students should be able to locate their district, list the states that it comprises, and note economic variety within the district.

Federal Advisory Council (FAC) *the research arm of the Federal Reserve*

Federal Open Market Committee (FOMC) *Federal Reserve committee that makes key decisions about interest rates and the growth of the United States money supply*

check clearing and reserve loans, whether or not they are Fed members.

Each of the approximately 4,000 Fed member banks contributes a small amount of money to join the system. In return, they receive stock in the system. This stock earns them dividends from the Fed at a rate of up to 6 percent.

A research arm of the Fed, the **Federal Advisory Council (FAC),** collects information about each district and reports to the Board of Governors about economic conditions within their districts. It consists of one member from each Federal Reserve District—twelve members in all. The FAC's main function is to provide feedback and advice to the Board of Governors concerning the overall financial health of each district. The FAC meets with the Board of Governors four times a year.

The fact that the banks themselves, rather than a government agency, own the Federal Reserve gives the system a high degree of political independence. This independence helps the Fed to make decisions that best suit the interests of the country as a whole.

The Federal Open Market Committee

The **Federal Open Market Committee (FOMC)** makes key decisions about interest rates and the growth of the United States money supply. The committee meets about eight times a year in private to discuss the cost and availability of credit, for business and consumers, across the country. Announcements of the FOMC's decisions can affect the financial markets, the rates for home mortgages, and many other economic institutions around the world. You will read more about the effects of monetary policy later in this chapter.

Members of the Federal Open Market Committee are drawn from the Board of Governors and the twelve district banks. All seven members of the Board of Governors sit on the FOMC. Five of the twelve district bank presidents also sit on the committee. The president of the New York Federal Reserve Bank is a permanent member. The four other district presidents serve one-year terms on a rotating basis. The Board of Governors holds a majority of the seats on the FOMC, giving them effective control over the committee's actions.

After meeting with the FOMC, the chair of the Board of Governors announces the committee's decisions to the public. The Federal Reserve Banks and financial markets spring into action as they react to Fed decisions. In the next section, you will read about how the Fed's decisions are carried out and what functions the Federal Reserve serves.

Section 1 Assessment

Progress Monitoring *Online*
For: Self-quiz with vocabulary practice
Web Code: mna-6165

Key Terms and Main Ideas

1. Who serves on the **Board of Governors** of the Federal Reserve?
2. What is **monetary policy?**
3. Describe the makeup of the **Federal Reserve Districts.**
4. What does the **Federal Advisory Council (FAC)** do?
5. What is the role of the **Federal Open Market Committee (FOMC)?**

Applying Economic Concepts

6. ***Critical Thinking*** How does the banking system of the United States reflect a free enterprise economy?
7. ***Try This*** Locate your Federal Reserve District on the map on page 417. What states make up your district? What mixture of agricultural, manufacturing, and service industries does your district contain? Is it made up of both rural and urban areas?

For: Current Events Activity
Visit: PHSchool.com
Web Code: mnd-6161

Progress Monitoring *Online*

For additional assessment, have students access Progress Monitoring Online at **Web Code:** mna-6165

Go Online PHSchool.com Typing in the Web Code when prompted will bring students directly to detailed instructions for this activity.

Skills for LIFE

Recognizing Bias in Writing

Bias is the particular opinion or point of view held by a writer on a specific topic. An author's bias is not always obvious at first glance. As a critical reader, you must take steps to identify whether or not a piece of writing contains bias. Any piece of writing relating to economic topics may reflect the author's point of view on a particular public policy or institution. Read the selection on the Federal Reserve Board below, and then answer the questions that follow to help you identify any bias that is reflected in the writing.

1. **Identify the source.** Begin your critical reading of a piece by identifying who the author is, who the audience is, and any obvious signs of bias. (**a**) Who is the author of the excerpt below? (**b**) Is this a personal letter, diary entry, or public document? (**c**) Do you detect any obvious bias?

2. **Look for evidence of bias.** Next, search the excerpt for words or phrases that may reflect the author's bias. (**a**) What words does the author use to describe Mr. Greenspan and his actions? (**b**) Which phrases describe the author's attitude toward the Federal Reserve Board? (**c**) How does the author describe Humphrey-Hawkins?

3. **Draw conclusions.** Take any signs of bias into account when drawing conclusions about the topic. What point is the author trying to make in this article?

> This morning lawmakers will summon Fed Chairman Alan Greenspan over to the Hill for his mandatory semi-annual gabfest. Accountability is a useful requirement for all political figures, even mighty central bankers who stand watch over multitrillion dollar markets, so we have no trouble with the notion that Congress has the power to require Mr. Greenspan's presence and his report. We do have trouble with Humphrey-Hawkins, the law that prescribes the Chairman's testimony. Its terms assume that the Fed's job is essentially to choose between two dark scenarios. The first is growth, accompanied by inflation. The second is no growth, accompanied by no inflation. . . . We'd like to suggest that the parties involved take a deep breath here while we repeat ourselves: There are plenty of signs out there that the economy is growing without inflation.
>
> *"Phillips Think" [Editorial-Review & Outlook],* The Wall Street Journal, *February 26, 1997*

Additional Practice

Locate an editorial from a newspaper on a topic relating to economics, and identify any bias in the writing.

Interdisciplinary Connections: Language Arts

Identifying Bias Most news organizations attempt to be fair and accurate in reporting news. Even so, the people who write and edit the articles have opinions and views. These views and opinions can surface as bias. One way to detect bias is to try to understand the underlying assumptions that the writer of a piece makes.

Have students work through the following activity: Below are two statements from a news story. Display both, asking students to point out bias and try to detect the writer's assumptions.

(1) For many of the underprivileged in south central Los Angeles, the recent cutbacks in welfare spending mean that crime is their only recourse, and for many selling drugs is the only way they can get by in an area with little industry and few jobs.

(2) The poor in south central Los Angeles are victims of a culture that does not know how to say no. Southern California is booming, yet many choose the path of least resistance, turning to selling drugs instead of finding work.

Skills for LIFE

Recognizing Bias in Writing

1. Focus Students will read a short opinion piece on an economic issue to learn to recognize bias and analyze a writer's point of view.

2. Instruct Discuss with students why recognizing bias is an important skill. Explain that they can get the most out of what they read if they read it carefully and critically. Then have students work through the steps outlined in the skills feature and explain the point of view of the economic issue described.

3. Close/Reteach To provide additional practice, see the Economic Skills Activity below.

Economic Skills Activity
Unit 6 folder, p. 34, "Recognizing Bias in Writing," asks students to examine an excerpt from an article for evidence of bias.

Social Studies Skills Tutor CD-ROM offers interactive practice in critical thinking and reading, visual analysis, and communication.

Answers

1. (a) an editor of *The Wall Street Journal* (b) public document (c) Students should detect some bias in the tone of the article.
2. (a) He says that Greenspan is "summon(ed)" for his "gabfest." (b) He calls the Fed "mighty central bankers who stand watch over multitrillion dollar markets." (c) By saying that he has "trouble" with it and that the bill "assume(s) that the Fed's job is essentially to choose between two dark scenarios."
3. Answers should recognize that the author is saying that the law limits the context of Greenspan's remarks, and that he says that the law prevents Greenspan from acknowledging the real economic situation: growth without inflation.

Additional Practice

Answers will vary depending on the chosen article, but students should choose an appropriate editorial and demonstrate understanding of any bias it expresses.

Section 2

Federal Reserve Functions

Objectives You may wish to call students' attention to the objectives in the Section Preview. The objectives are reflected in the main headings of the section.

Bellringer Ask students whether they have ever written a check or received one from someone else. Have they ever wondered about the process by which a check clears? Explain that in this section they will learn about the role the Federal Reserve plays in processing checks.

Vocabulary Builder Have students read through the section to determine the meanings of the key terms. Then have them create a fill-in-the-blanks quiz, writing one sentence for each of the five terms. Have students exchange quizzes, fill in the answers, and return them for correction.

Lesson Plan

Teaching the Main Concepts (L3)

1. Focus Explain that in this section students will learn about the functions of the Federal Reserve. Ask them to describe any of its roles about which they have heard in the news.

2. Instruct Begin by pointing out that the Federal Reserve has many functions. Describe first how it serves the federal government and then how it serves banks. Explain to students that the Fed regulates the banking system in the United States and that it has an important role to play in monitoring the nation's money supply.

3. Close/Reteach Have students picture themselves as consultants for a country that has recently embraced capitalism and wants to reform its banking system to make it function better in a market economy. Ask students to write several paragraphs showing how a system like the Federal Reserve can help the country accomplish that goal.

Section 2 Federal Reserve Functions

Preview

Objectives

After studying this section you will be able to:

1. **Describe** how the Federal Reserve serves the federal government.
2. **Describe** how the Federal Reserve serves banks.
3. **Describe** how the Federal Reserve regulates the banking system.
4. **Understand** the Federal Reserve's role in regulating the nation's money supply.

Section Focus

The Federal Reserve functions as the government's banker and as a banker's bank. It regulates the nation's banking system. It also monitors and regulates the nation's money supply.

Key Terms

check clearing
bank holding company
federal funds rate
discount rate
net worth

As the central bank of the United States, the twelve district banks that make up the core of the Federal Reserve System carry out several important functions. The Federal Reserve System does the following:

- provides banking and fiscal services to the federal government
- provides banking services to member and nonmember banks
- regulates the banking industry
- tracks and manages the national money supply to meet current demand and to stabilize the economy

▼ **The Department of the Treasury does its banking at the Federal Reserve.**

Serving Government

The United States government has an operating budget of about $2.3 trillion. It raises about $1.1 trillion annually in taxes. It makes about $1 trillion in transfer payments through programs such as Medicare and Social Security. For its banking needs, the federal government turns to the Federal Reserve.

Federal Government's Banker

The Federal Reserve serves as banker for the United States government. It maintains a checking account for the Treasury Department. It processes payments such as social security checks, IRS refunds, and other government payments. For example, if you receive a check from the federal government and cash it at your local bank, the Federal Reserve deducts the amount from the Treasury's account.

Government Securities Auctions

The Federal Reserve also serves as a financial agent for the Treasury Department and other government agencies. The Fed sells, transfers, and redeems government bonds, bills, and notes, or securities. It also makes interest payments on these securities.

Graphing the Main Idea

Monetary and Fiscal Policy To build understanding of the concept of **monetary and fiscal policy** and the functions of the Federal Reserve, have students use a web graphic organizer like the one at the right. Remind students that a web shows a main idea and its supporting details. In this case the details will be about the functions of the Fed.

Section Reading Support Transparencies A template and the answers for this graphic organizer can be found in Chapter 16, Section 2 of the Section Reading Support Transparency System.

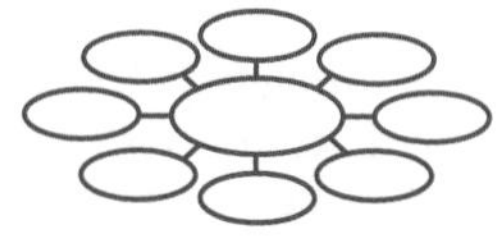

The Treasury Department periodically auctions off government bills, bonds, and notes to finance the government's activities. The funds raised from these auctions are automatically deposited into the Federal Reserve Bank of New York.

Issuing Currency

Under the Federal Reserve System, only the federal government can issue currency. The Department of the Treasury issues coins minted at the United States Mint. The district Federal Reserve Banks issue paper currency (Federal Reserve Notes), which is printed at the Bureau of Engraving and Printing. As bills become worn or torn, the Federal Reserve takes them out of circulation and replaces them with fresh ones.

Serving Banks

The Federal Reserve also provides services to banks throughout the nation. Its most visible function is in its check-clearing services. In addition, it safeguards bank reserves and lends reserves to banks that need to borrow to maintain legally required reserves.

Check Clearing

Figure 16.3 shows how checks "clear" within the Fed system. **Check clearing** is the process by which banks record whose account gives up money and whose account receives money when a customer writes a check. The Fed can clear millions of checks at any one time using high-speed equipment. Most checks clear within two days—a remarkable achievement when you consider that the Fed deals with about 20 billion checks per year.

Supervising Lending Practices

To ensure stability in the banking system, the Federal Reserve monitors bank reserves throughout the system. Each of the twelve Federal Reserve Banks sends out bank examiners to check up on lending and other financial activities of member banks.

They also study proposed bank mergers and bank holding company charters to ensure competition in the banking and financial industries. A **bank holding company** is a company that owns more than one bank. The Board of Governors approves or disapproves mergers and charters based on the findings and recommendations of the Reserve Banks.

The Federal Reserve also protects consumers by enforcing truth-in-lending laws, which require sellers to provide full and accurate information about loan terms. Under a provision called Regulation Z, millions of consumers receive information about retail credit terms, auto loans, and home mortgages every year.

Lender of Last Resort

Under normal circumstances, banks lend each other money on a day-to-day basis, using money from their reserve balances.

check clearing *the process by which banks record whose account gives up money and whose account receives money when a customer writes a check*

bank holding company *a company that owns more than one bank*

Figure 16.3 The Path of a Check

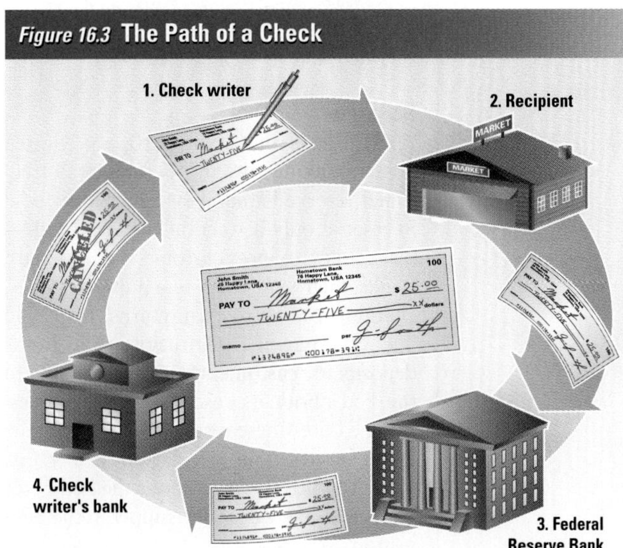

After you write a check, the recipient presents it at his or her bank. The check is then sent to a Federal Reserve Bank. The reserve bank collects the necessary funds from your bank and transfers them to the recipient's bank. Your processed check is returned to you by your bank or is available for you to view on the Internet. **Economic Institutions** **In what other ways does the Fed serve banks?**

Guided Reading and Review
Unit 6 folder, p. 28 asks students to identify the main ideas of the section and to define or identify key terms.

Differentiated Instruction L3

Organize the class into small groups. Ask each group to create a five-minute skit that shows the three basic ways in which the Federal Reserve serves the federal government. Allow time for students to practice and perform their skits for the rest of the class.

Differentiated Instruction L3

(Reteaching) To reinforce understanding of how the Federal Reserve serves banks, have students write advertising copy for the Federal Reserve System. Ask them to create a brief pamphlet aimed at a bank that is considering joining the system. The pamphlet should describe the services the Federal Reserve can provide and explain how these services can help a bank.

Transparency Resource Package
Economics Concepts, 16E: How the Fed Clears a Check
Economics Concepts, 16F: The Money Supply

Differentiated Instruction L2

As students read, ask them to change each of the headings and subheadings in this section into a question. Then have them answer each of their questions after a careful reading of the section. LPR

Econ 101: Key Concepts Made Easy

Economic Institutions An important concept in this section is that of **bank holding companies.** The Federal Reserve examines bank holding company charters in order to ensure competition. Typically a large holding company, such as Citicorp, owns a controlling interest in a number of banks around the nation. Citicorp traces its roots back to the City Bank of New York, incorporated in 1812. In the late 1970s Citicorp was the first to install a network of Automated Teller Machines (ATMs) throughout its branch offices. Today Citicorp is one of the most powerful financial institutions in the world, with about 3,000 branches.

Answer to . . .

Building Key Concepts It supervises lending practices and acts as a lender of last resort.

Differentiated Instruction L4

You may wish to have students add the following to their portfolios. Ask them to write a short illustrated report that shows how the Federal Reserve regulates the banking system. Tell them to describe regulation in relation to reserves as well as how bank examinations are conducted. Encourage students to include charts and graphs and to search general resources (such as encyclopedias and almanacs) for additional information. GT

Economics Assessment Rubric
Economics Assessment Rubrics folder, pp. 6–7 provides sample evaluation materials for a writing assignment.

Meeting NCEE Standards

Use the following benchmark activity from the **Voluntary National Content Standards in Economics** to evaluate student understanding of **Standard 20.**

Write an article for the business section of the local newspaper explaining what monetary policy is and how changes in monetary policy affect the money supply and interest rates. Using this information, advise a teenager about taking out a car loan and his/her opportunities for obtaining summer employment in the construction trade when the Federal Reserve is contracting the money supply.

federal funds rate *interest rate banks charge each other for loans*

discount rate *rate the Federal Reserve charges for loans to commercial banks*

net worth *total assets minus total liabilities*

These funds are called federal funds. The interest rate that banks charge each other for these loans is the **federal funds rate.**

Banks can also borrow from the Federal Reserve. They do so routinely and especially in financial emergencies such as severe recessions. The Federal Reserve acts as a lender of last resort, making emergency loans to commercial banks so that they can maintain required reserves. The rate the Federal Reserve charges for these loans is called the **discount rate.** You will read more about the role of the discount rate in the economy of the United States in Section 3.

Regulating the Banking System

Banks, savings and loan companies, credit unions, and bank holding companies are supervised by various state and federal authorities. The Fed coordinates all regulatory activities.

Reserves

As you read in Chapter 10, the United States banking system operates as a fractional reserve banking system. Banks hold in reserve only a fraction of their funds—just enough to meet customers' daily needs. Banks then lend their remaining reserves, charging interest to earn returns.

Each financial institution that holds deposits for customers must report daily to the Fed about its reserves and activities. The Fed uses these reserves to control how much money is in circulation at any one time. You'll read more about the Fed's role in controlling the money supply in the next section.

Bank Examinations

The Federal Reserve and other regulatory agencies also examine banks periodically to make sure that each institution is obeying laws and regulations. Examiners may make unexpected bank visits to make sure that banks are following sound lending practices.

Bank examiners can force banks to sell risky investments or to declare loans that will not be repaid as losses. If examiners find that a bank has taken excessive risks, they may classify that institution as a problem bank and force it to undergo more frequent examinations. Examiners would take the same action for banks that have low net worth. **Net worth** equals total assets minus total liabilities. In addition, any bank that goes to the Fed for emergency loans too often will be subject to financial review and close government supervision.

Regulating the Money Supply

The Federal Reserve is best known for its role in regulating the nation's money supply. You will recall from Chapter 10 that economists and the Fed watch several indicators of the money supply. M1 is simply a measure of the funds that are easily accessible or in circulation. M2 includes the funds counted in M1 as well as money market accounts and savings instruments. Economists also measure M3. M3 goes even further to include large time deposits and some government securities. The Fed's job is to consider these various measures of the money supply and compare those figures with the likely demand for money.

Factors That Affect Demand for Money

People hold money for a variety of reasons. The amount of money that firms or individuals hold depends generally on four factors:

1. cash needed on hand
2. interest rates
3. price levels in the economy
4. general level of income

People and firms need to have a certain amount of cash on hand to make economic transactions—to buy groceries, supplies, clothing, and so forth. The more of your wealth you hold as money, the easier it will be to make economic transactions.

Of course, we can't earn interest on money that we hold as cash. As interest rates rise, it becomes more expensive for

Block Scheduling Strategies

Consider these suggestions to take advantage of extended class time:

- Extend the Bellringer activity by having students create bulletin board displays titled "The Life of a Check." They should display visually and with captions what occurs from the time when the check is written until it returns to the writer with a checking account statement. Have volunteers explain to the class the steps they depicted.
- Extend the Econ 101: Key Concepts Made Easy feature by having small groups research one of the following holding companies: Chemical New York Corporation, Manufacturers Hanover Corporation, or Transamerica Corporation. Ask students to prepare an oral report that describes the activities of the corporation and its importance in banking.

individuals to hold money as cash rather than placing it in assets that pay returns, such as bonds, stocks, or savings accounts. So as interest rates rise, people and firms will generally keep their wealth in assets that pay returns. In other words, they demand less money in the form of cash. (See Figure 16.4.)

The general price level in the economy affects the demand for money, too. As price levels rise, so does the demand for cash. If your usual cost for an outing with your friends is $25 and prices rise 10 percent, you will now need $27.50 for a night out.

The final factor that influences money demand is the general level of income. On a personal level, if you take an after-school job that pays you $75 per week, you will likely carry around more cash than you did before. On a national level, as GDP or real income rises, families and firms keep more of their wealth or income in cash.

Figure 16.4 **Demand for Money**

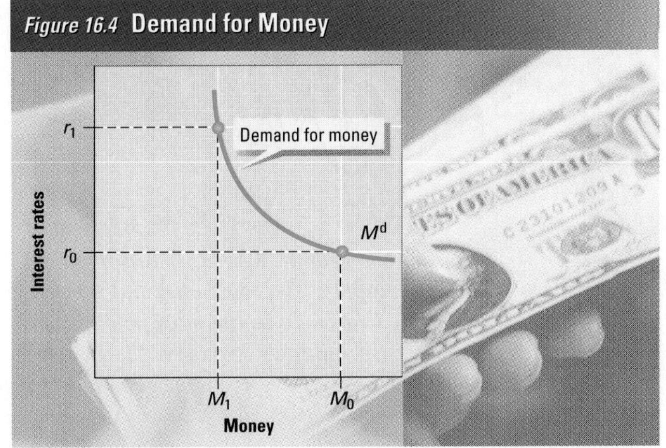

As interest rates increase from r_0 to r_1, the quantity of money demanded falls from M_0 to M_1. **Incentives Explain demand for money in terms of incentives.**

Stabilizing the Economy

The laws of supply and demand affect money, just as they affect everything else in the economy. Too much money in the economy leads to a general rise in prices, or inflation. A glut of dollars lessens their value. In inflationary times, it will take more money to purchase the same goods and services. It is the Fed's job to keep the money supply stable.

In an ideal world, in which real GDP grew smoothly and the economy stayed at full employment, the Fed would increase the money supply just to match the growth in the demand for money. If the Fed could accomplish this, the country would experience very low inflation rates and, ideally, the economy would remain at full employment. As you read in Chapter 15, however, it is hard to predict economic effects.

The Fed uses its tools to stabilize the economy as best it can. In the next section, you will read about the tools that the Fed can use to help the economy function at full employment without contributing to inflation.

Section 2 Assessment

Progress Monitoring *Online*
For: Self-quiz with vocabulary practice
Web Code: mna-6166

Key Terms and Main Ideas

1. What is **check clearing?**
2. What is a **bank holding company?**
3. What is the difference between the **federal funds rate** and the **discount rate?**
4. How is **net worth** calculated?

Applying Economic Concepts

5. ***Try This*** Create a graphic organizer showing how the Federal Reserve serves the federal government and banks.
6. ***Critical Thinking*** What are the advantages of having the Federal Reserve oversee the regulation of the banking system?

For: Current Events Activity
Visit: PHSchool.com
Web Code: mnd-6162

GTE Guide to the Essentials
Chapter 16, Section 2, p. 68 provides support for students who need additional review of the section content. Spanish support is available in the Spanish edition of the guide on p. 68.

Quiz Unit 6 folder, p. 29 includes questions to check students' understanding of Section 2 content.

Presentation Pro CD-ROM
Quiz provides multiple-choice questions to check students' understanding of Section 2 content.

Answers to . . .

Section 2 Assessment

1. Check clearing is the process by which banks record whose account gives up money and whose account receives money when a customer writes a check.
2. A bank holding company is a company that owns more than one bank.
3. The federal funds rate is the interest rate banks charge each other for loans. The discount rate is the rate the Federal Reserve charges for emergency loans to commercial banks.
4. Net worth is calculated by computing total assets minus total liabilities.
5. Students should create graphic organizers illustrating how the Federal Reserve serves the federal government and how it serves banks.
6. The Fed provides banking and fiscal services to the federal government; regulates the banking industry; regulates the money supply; provides check clearing services; ensures stability in the banking system; stabilizes the economy.

Progress Monitoring *Online*
For additional assessment, have students access Progress Monitoring Online at **Web Code:** mna-6166

Go Online PHSchool.com Typing in the Web Code when prompted will bring students directly to detailed instructions for this activity.

Answer to . . .

Building Key Concepts As interest rates rise, it becomes more expensive to hold money as cash, creating an incentive to demand less money in cash.

ECONOMIC *Profile*
Alan Greenspan

Background

As the voice of the Fed, Alan Greenspan wields great power to affect markets, both in the United States and in the rest of the world. Greenspan's speeches are closely watched by brokers, economists, and politicians for clues as to what actions the Fed might take next. Although his statements are often cryptic, in December of 1996 Greenspan dropped a bombshell that had repercussions around the world. Commenting on the amazing increase in stock prices over the past few years, Greenspan warned against "irrational exuberance and unduly escalating stock prices." Greenspan's statement came after the close of the New York Stock Exchange, but halfway around the world, in Japan, markets were just opening. There traders interpreted his comments to mean that U.S. stocks were overvalued and that interest rates might go up. Markets around the world responded quickly by going into a downward spiral.

Careers in Economics Activity
Unit 6 folder, p. 37 gives students a closer look at the career path of a wire transfer analyst.

Economist

Entrepreneur

ECONOMIC
Profile

Alan Greenspan (b. 1926)

The Federal Reserve Board (the Fed) helps to control the nation's money supply. The economist and former professional pop musician at its head may be the most powerful person in America when it comes to the nation's economy. Alan Greenspan's careful handling of the Federal Reserve won him credit for the remarkable economic boom of the 1990s and a place in the administrations of four presidents.

The Chairman of the Fed

Alan Greenspan's first term as chairman of the Federal Reserve Board began in a dramatic fashion. Soon after he took office in August 1987, the stock market crashed. Investors feared that lenders would adopt a tight-money policy, as banks had done after the last great market crash in 1929. Instead, Greenspan responded with actions that boosted the nation's money supply. The stock market quickly recovered, and the nation avoided the economic meltdown that could have followed.

Hard Times

Having grown up during the Great Depression, Greenspan knows hard economic times. As a young child he showed a gift for numbers and amazed his parents' friends with his ability to do math problems in his head. After high school, however, he decided to develop his musical talents, and enrolled at New York's Juilliard School of Music. During the 1940s, he toured with a swing band.

Soon tiring of life on the road, Alan Greenspan returned to New York City and earned bachelor's and master's degrees in economics at New York University. Moving to Columbia University to pursue a Ph.D., he had to quit school when he ran short of money. In 1954, he and a friend started an economic consulting firm.

The Transition to Public Life

Alan Greenspan first went to Washington, D.C., in 1974 to chair the President's Council of Economic Advisors. In 1977, he returned to New York to complete his Ph.D., but 10 years later, President Ronald Reagan recalled him to Washington to head the Federal Reserve. At the time, many people were critical of the Fed's heavy-handed role in shaping monetary policy. The previous chairman had thrown the economy into recession in the early 1980s when he raised interest rates in an effort to halt high inflation.

Although Greenspan strongly opposes inflation, he is sensitive to the loss of jobs that accompanies any major attempt to slow the growth of the money supply. Under Greenspan, interest rate adjustments were frequent but generally small in scale. He preferred to use monetary policy to make minor adjustments in the economy's course rather than to drive it in a new direction. As a result, Greenspan's terms as Fed chairman witnessed the longest period of economic growth in the nation's history.

CHECK FOR UNDERSTANDING

1. **Source Reading** Describe Greenspan's approach to using the powers of the Federal Reserve to influence the nation's economy.
2. **Critical Thinking** Explain how a sharp increase in interest rates by the Fed could slow inflation but also lead to higher unemployment and a recession.
3. **Learn More** Visit the Federal Reserve's Web site and summarize the most recent Fed activities that are reported there.

Answers to . . .

1. He prefers to use monetary policy to make minor adjustments in the economy's course rather than attempt to force it in a predetermined direction.
2. A sharp increase in interest rates would slow inflation by discouraging borrowing. At the same time, however, it would slow economic growth. Less spending would result in job loss and an eventual decline in economic activity.
3. Responses should accurately reflect the activities currently reported on the Web site of the Federal Reserve.

Beyond the Classroom: Workplace Skills

Decision Making Remind students that the ability to make decisions, which involves analyzing possible courses of action for their outcomes, is important in the workplace as well as in other areas of life. A responsible person sets goals, considers alternative ways to reach them, and then chooses the best course of action. Ask students to consider the types of decisions that Alan Greenspan and other members of the Board of Governors must make. Have students list ways in which these decisions are similar to and different from decisions made by individual business owners.

Section 3 Monetary Policy Tools

Preview

Objectives

After studying this section you will be able to:

1. **Describe** the process of money creation.
2. **Explain** how the Federal Reserve uses reserve requirements, interest rates, and open market operations to implement U.S. monetary policy.
3. **Understand** why some monetary policy tools are favored over others.

Section Focus

Banks create money in their day-to-day operations. The Federal Reserve uses the tools of monetary policy to control the amount of money in circulation.

Key Terms

money creation
required reserve ratio (RRR)
money multiplier formula
excess reserves
prime rate
open market operations

In early 2001, when it appeared that economic growth was slowing, the Fed began reducing interest rates. The September 11 terrorist attacks further increased the need for such changes in economic policy. By early 2003, the Fed had cut interest rates 13 times, to 45-year lows. By reducing the cost of borrowing, the Fed hoped to encourage consumers to spend more money and stimulate economic growth. In this section you will see why the Fed uses these tactics to influence economic growth.

Money Creation

The Department of the Treasury is responsible for manufacturing money. The Federal Reserve is responsible for putting dollars into circulation. How does this money get into the economy? The process is called **money creation,** and it is carried out by the Fed and by banks all around the country. Recall from Chapter 15 the multiplier effect of government spending. The multiplier effect in fiscal policy holds that every one dollar change in fiscal policy creates a change greater than one dollar in the economy. The process of money creation works in much the same way.

How Banks Create Money

Money creation does not mean the printing of money. Banks create money not by printing it, but by simply going about their business.

For example, suppose you take out a loan of $1,000. You decide to deposit the money in a checking account. Once you have deposited the money, you now have a balance of $1,000. Since demand deposit account balances, such as your checking account, are included in M1, the money supply has now increased by $1,000. The process of money creation begins here.

▲ The daily activities of banks and their customers create money through the multiplier effect.

Banks make money by charging interest on loans. Your bank will lend part of the $1,000 that you deposited. The amount that the bank is allowed to lend is determined by the **required reserve ratio (RRR)**—the fraction of the deposit that must be kept on reserve. This is calculated as the ratio of reserves to deposits. The RRR is the fraction of deposits that banks are required to keep in reserve. The required reserve ratio, which is established by the Federal Reserve, ensures that banks will have enough funds to supply customers' withdrawal needs.

Suppose in our example that the RRR is 0.1, or 10 percent. This means that of your $1,000 demand deposit balance, the bank is allowed to lend $900.

money creation *the process by which money enters into circulation*

required reserve ratio (RRR) *ratio of reserves to deposits required of banks by the Federal Reserve*

Building Key Concepts: Graphing the Main Idea

Monetary and Fiscal Policy To build understanding of the concept of **monetary and fiscal policy** and the process of money creation, have students use a flowchart graphic organizer like the one at the right. Remind them that a flowchart organizer shows a sequence of events. They may illustrate the example found in the section or use an example of their own.

Section Reading Support Transparencies A template and the answers for this graphic organizer can be found in Chapter 16, Section 3 of the Section Reading Support Transparency System.

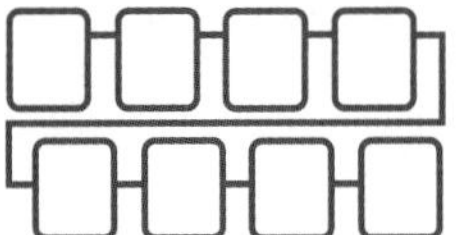

Section 3

Monetary Policy Tools

Objectives You may wish to call students' attention to the objectives in the Section Preview. The objectives are reflected in the main headings of the section.

Bellringer Hold up a single dollar bill and explain to students that in this section they will learn about money creation—not printing currency, but increasing the money supply. Ask students how they think the money supply could increase without more money being printed.

Vocabulary Builder Ask students to write a sentence using each key term in a way that shows how it is involved in monetary policy. *(The Fed could increase the money supply by reducing the required reserve ratio.)*

Lesson Plan

Teaching the Main Concepts (L3)

1. Focus Explain to students that monetary policy affects everyone's life. Interest rate hikes by the Fed can mean that a car loan or a mortgage may be more costly. Ask students what they think people would do if interest rates were high—would they save more or spend more? *(They would save more.)*

2. Instruct Make sure that students understand that money is not simply cash; if necessary, review the material on M1 and M2 in Chapter 10. Describe money creation and explain how the Federal Reserve uses reserve requirements, the discount rate, and especially open market operations to bring about changes in the money supply.

3. Close/Reteach Have students design a review chart on the tools of monetary policy. Tell them to base their charts on the graphics in this section.

Guided Reading and Review
Unit 6 folder, p. 30 asks students to identify the main ideas of the section and to define or identify key terms.

Go Online PHSchool.com Typing in the Web Code when prompted will bring students directly to the article.

THE WALL STREET JOURNAL. CLASSROOM EDITION

For an additional article from *The Wall Street Journal Classroom Edition,* see the Source Articles folder in the **Teaching Resources**, pp. 48–50.

Differentiated Instruction L3

Have students create a comic strip that shows the process of monetary creation after a student receives a gift of $1,000 and deposits the money in the bank. The strip should include all the steps in the process, from the initial deposit to the lending of the bank's new reserves to someone who is seeking a loan. Encourage volunteers to share their comic strips with the class.

Differentiated Instruction L4

Organize students into groups of three, and ask them to create a scenario that would show how the money multiplier formula works in the real world. To start students off, explain that many people do not spend all of the money that they receive as a gift or loan but often keep some as cash. Ask students to write a fictional scenario with several characters to show how this might take place. For example, Angela receives $1,000 in pay at the end of November, but she deposits only $800 of it. The bank lends only $500 of this money—it wants to keep its reserves high because people generally make more withdrawals during the December holiday season. Ask students to calculate, using a reserve ratio of 3 percent, the amount of new money that would be created in their scenarios. GT

THE WALL STREET JOURNAL. CLASSROOM EDITION

In the News Read more about monetary policy in "Alan Who?," an article in The Wall Street Journal Classroom Edition.

Go Online
The Wall Street Journal Classroom Edition
For: Current Events
Visit: PHSchool.com
Web Code: mnc-6163

Let's say the bank lends that $900 to Elaine, and she deposits it in her checking account. Elaine now has $900 she didn't have before. Elaine's $900 is now included in M1. You still have your $1,000 demand deposit account balance, on which you can write a check at any time. Thus, your initial deposit to the bank, and the subsequent loan, have caused the money supply to increase by $1,000 + $900 for a total of $1,900.

money multiplier formula *amount of new money that will be created with each demand deposit, calculated as 1 ÷ RRR*

Now suppose that Elaine uses the $900 to buy Joshua's old car. Joshua deposits the $900 from Elaine into his checking account. His bank keeps 10 percent of the deposit, or $90, as required reserves. It will lend the other $810 to its customers. So, Joshua has a demand deposit balance of $900, which is included in the money supply, and the new borrower gets $810, which is also added to the money supply. This means that the money supply has now increased by $1,000 + $900 + $810 = $2,710—all because of your initial $1,000 deposit. (See Figure 16.5.)

The Money Multiplier

This process will continue until the loan amount, and hence the amount of new money that can be created, becomes very small. The amount of new money that will be created, in the end, is given by the **money multiplier formula,** which is calculated as 1 ÷ RRR. The money multiplier tells us how much the money supply will increase after an initial cash deposit to the banking system. To apply the formula, we multiply the initial deposit by the money multiplier:

$$\text{Increase in money supply} = \text{initial cash deposit} \times \frac{1}{\text{RRR}}$$

In our example the RRR is 0.1, so the money multiplier is 1 ÷ 0.1 = 10. This means that the deposit of $1,000 leads to a $10,000 increase in the money supply.

As of 2003 in the United States, banks were required to hold 3 percent reserves against demand deposit assets up to $41.3 million and 10 percent on all demand deposit assets exceeding $41.3 million.

In the real world, however, people hold some cash outside of the banking system, meaning that some funds leak out of the money multiplier process. Also, banks

BUILDING KEY CONCEPTS

In this example of money creation, the money supply increases by $2,710 after four rounds.

Money Suppose Joshua deposited only $500 of Elaine's payment into his account. How much would the money supply increase then?

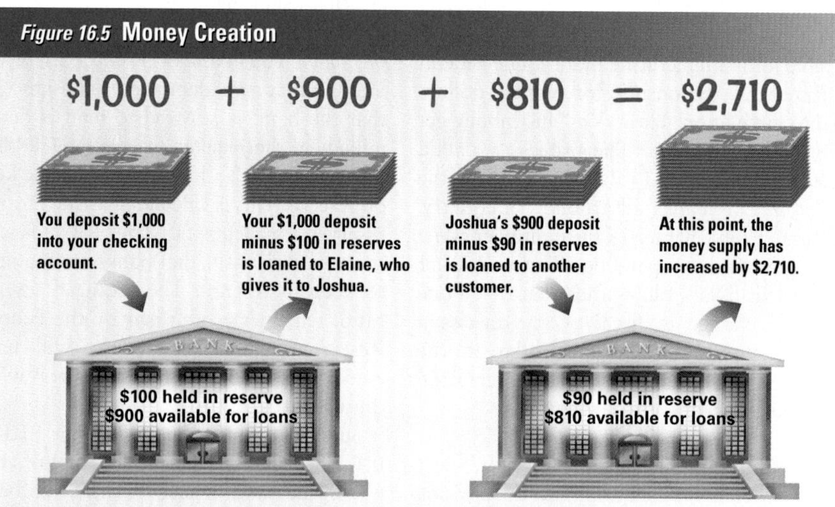
$1,000 + $900 + $810 = $2,710
You deposit $1,000 into your checking account.
Your $1,000 deposit minus $100 in reserves is loaned to Elaine, who gives it to Joshua.
Joshua's $900 deposit minus $90 in reserves is loaned to another customer.
At this point, the money supply has increased by $2,710.
BANK
$100 held in reserve
$900 available for loans
BANK
$90 held in reserve
$810 available for loans

Figure 16.5 **Money Creation**

Econ 101: Key Concepts Made Easy

Monetary and Fiscal Policy Two of the key concepts in this section are the roles of the **money multiplier formula** and the **required reserve ratio** in the creation of money. The relationship between the two is fairly simple: When reserve requirements are raised, the money multiplier effect is lower because less money is available for banks to loan. The reverse is also true.

Have students continue to carry out the math for the example on this page to see how this works. The new borrower takes $810 and deposits it, and then the bank lends $729 of it, keeping $81 in reserve. Ask students to use the money multiplier formula to determine how much money would be created at various reserve requirement ratios.

Answer to . . .

Building Key Concepts $2,350 ($1,000+ $900 + [$500-$50])

sometimes hold **excess reserves,** which are reserves greater than the required amounts. These excess reserves ensure that banks will always be able to meet their customers' demands and the Fed's reserve requirements. The actual money multiplier effect in the United States is estimated to be between 2 and 3.

The Federal Reserve has three tools for adjusting the amount of money in the economy. These tools are reserve requirements, the discount rate, and open market operations.

Reserve Requirements

The simplest way for the Fed to adjust the amount of reserves in the banking system is to change the required reserve ratio. It is not, however, the tool most used by the Fed.

Reducing Reserve Requirements

A reduction of the RRR would free up reserves for banks, allowing them to make more loans. It would also increase the money multiplier. Both effects would lead to a substantial increase in the money supply.

Increasing Reserve Requirements

The process also works in reverse. Even a slight increase in the RRR would force banks to hold more money in reserves. This would cause the money supply to contract, or shrink.

Although changing reserve requirements can be an effective means of changing the money supply, the Fed does not use this tool often because it is disruptive to the banking system. Even a small increase in the RRR would force banks to call in significant numbers of loans, that is, to require the borrower to pay the entire outstanding balance of the loan. This may be difficult for the borrower. For this reason, the Fed rarely changes reserve requirements.

Setting Rates

As you read in Section 2, the discount rate is the interest rate that the Federal Reserve charges on loans to financial institutions. In the past, the discount rate was changed to increase or decrease the money supply. Today, the discount rate is primarily used as a mechanism to insure that sufficient funds are available in the economy. For example, during a financial crisis, there may not be enough funds available in the banking system to provide the necessary loans to businesses and individuals. In that case, the ability of banks to borrow at the discount rate from the Federal Reserve provides an important safety valve.

Today, when the Federal Reserve makes its decisions on monetary policy, it does so by setting a target for the federal funds rate, which is the rate that banks lend reserves to one another. The Federal Reserve keeps the discount rate above the funds rate. Banks will initially borrow from one another at the federal funds rate. But if they need additional funds, they will turn to the Federal Reserve and borrow at the discount rate.

excess reserves *reserves greater than the required amounts*

Figure 16.6 **Reserve Requirements**

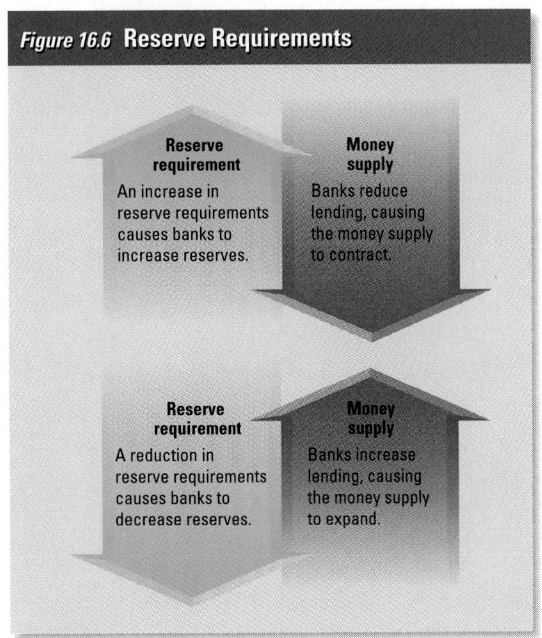

Reserve requirement
An increase in reserve requirements causes banks to increase reserves.
Money supply
Banks reduce lending, causing the money supply to contract.
Reserve requirement
A reduction in reserve requirements causes banks to decrease reserves.
Money supply
Banks increase lending, causing the money supply to expand.

When the Fed increases reserve requirements, the money supply decreases. **Monetary and Fiscal Policy What is the effect of reducing reserve requirements? Why?**

Background

Interdisciplinary

Ratios are a useful way of showing the relationship between numbers. The required reserve ratio (RRR) is the relationship between the amount of money banks must keep in reserve and the total amount of deposits. Ratios are also used in many other fields. Most educational specialists, for example, believe that schools where classes are smaller allow students to perform better. As one measure of a school's effectiveness, they use a student-teacher ratio. To determine the student-teacher ratio at your school, simply divide the number of students by the number of teachers. For instance, if there are 800 students and 40 teachers at your school, then there are 20 students for every teacher, or a ratio of 20:1. Explain to students that a student-teacher ratio can be made to seem lower by counting part-time faculty and coaches. Then ask students to consider whether the RRR might be manipulated in a similar way by banks.

Differentiated Instruction 

(Reteaching) Organize students into groups of three. Within the groups, have students take turns explaining how the Federal Reserve might use open market operations, reserve requirements, and the discount rate to bring about changes in the money supply. Each student should explain one tool to the others, and each listener should ask one clarifying question.

Block Scheduling Strategies

Consider these suggestions to take advantage of extended class time:

- Stage a money creation simulation. Distribute board game money and then award a gift amount to one student, explaining that at least part of it must be deposited. Simulate deposits, loans, and reserves. Then have students write summaries of their observations.
- Organize the class into small groups, and have them search the Internet for the Federal Reserve Bank of New York publication *Understanding Open Market Operations.* Assign different groups different sections of the publication to read and summarize in oral reports for the class. Use the links provided in the *Economics: Principles in Action* segment of the Social Studies area at the following Web site: **www.phschool.com**

Answer to . . .

Building Key Concepts Reducing reserve requirements causes the money supply to expand because banks have more money to lend.

Transparency Resource Package
Economics Concepts, 16G: Monetary Policy Tools and Their Effects

Differentiated Instruction 

The concepts and terminology in this section may be difficult for English language learners. Pair these students with students who are proficient in English, and have each pair work together to write explanations of each of the graphics on pp. 427 and 428. ELL

Learning Styles Activity
Learning Styles Lesson Plans folder, p. 38 asks students to construct graphs to depict changes in the discount rate over past periods and relate the changes to the Fed's assessment of the macroeconomy.

prime rate *rate of interest banks charge on short-term loans to their best customers*

open market operations *the buying and selling of government securities to alter the supply of money*

When the Federal Reserve increases or decreases the federal funds rate, the discount rate will rise or fall with it. Changes in the federal funds rate and the discount rate affect the cost of borrowing to banks or financial institutions. In turn, these changes in interest rates affect the prime rate. The **prime rate** is the rate of interest that banks charge on short-term loans to their best customers—usually large companies with good credit ratings. Changes in the federal funds rate and discount rate are reflected in the prime rate.

The discount rate, federal funds rate, and prime rate are short-term rates. They determine the cost of borrowing money for a few hours, days, or months. As you read in Chapter 12, short-term rates have a limited impact on the long-term growth of the economy. To influence long-term interest rates, the Federal Reserve must use other tools.

Open Market Operations

The most important monetary policy tool is **open market operations.** Open market operations are the buying and selling of government securities to alter the supply of money. Open market operations are by far the most-used monetary policy tool.

Bond Purchases

When the Federal Open Market Committee (FOMC) chooses to increase the money supply, it orders the trading desk at the Federal Reserve Bank of New York to purchase a certain quantity of government securities on the open market.

Figure 16.7 **Federal Funds Rate**

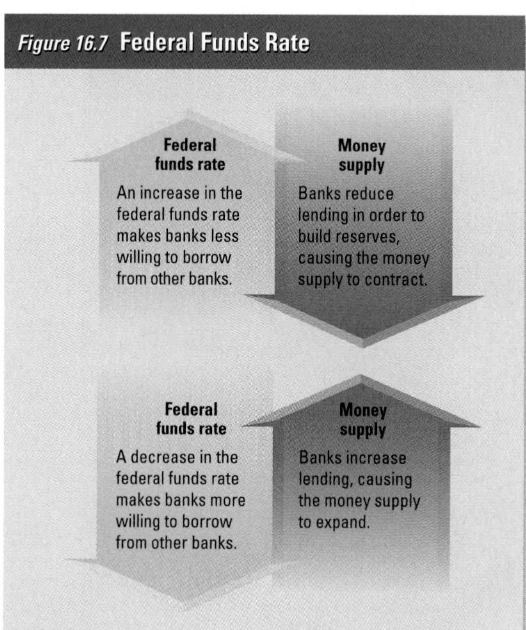

Federal funds rate
An increase in the federal funds rate makes banks less willing to borrow from other banks.
Money supply
Banks reduce lending in order to build reserves, causing the money supply to contract.
Federal funds rate
A decrease in the federal funds rate makes banks more willing to borrow from other banks.
Money supply
Banks increase lending, causing the money supply to expand.

Figure 16.8 **Open Market Operations**

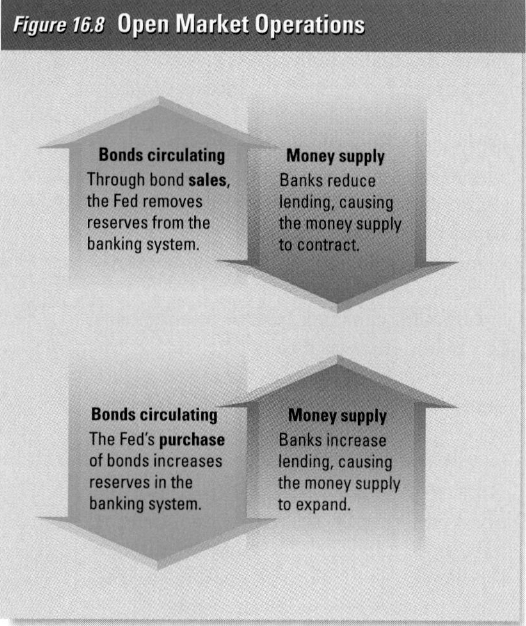

Bonds circulating
Through bond sales, the Fed removes reserves from the banking system.
Money supply
Banks reduce lending, causing the money supply to contract.
Bonds circulating
The Fed's purchase of bonds increases reserves in the banking system.
Money supply
Banks increase lending, causing the money supply to expand.

Because an increase in the federal funds rate makes borrowing more costly, the money supply contracts. Banks are more willing to borrow and lend money when the federal funds rate is low (left). Open market operations (right), however, are the most-used monetary policy tool.
Fiscal and Monetary Policy **How do open market operations differ from the monetary policy tools shown in Figures 16.6 and 16.7?**

Preparing for Standardized Tests

Have students read the section titled "Open Market Operations" and then answer the question below.

Which of the following is the most accurate description of open market operations?

A changing of reserve requirements
B reduction of the rate the Federal Reserve charges on loans to financial institutions
(C) buying and selling of government securities to change the supply of money
D calling in loans

Answer to . . .

Building Key Concepts Open market operations use purchase and sale of bonds, while monetary policy tools address how banks operate.

The Federal Reserve Bank buys these securities with a check drawn on Federal Reserve funds. The bond seller then deposits the money from the bond sales in its bank. In this way, funds enter the banking system, setting in motion the money creation process described earlier.

Bond Sales

If the FOMC chooses to decrease the money supply, it must make an open market bond sale. In this case, the Fed sells government securities back to bond dealers, receiving from them checks drawn on their own banks. After the Fed processes these checks, the money is out of circulation. This operation reduces reserves in the banking system. Banks reduce their outstanding loans in order to keep reserves at the required levels. The money multiplier process then works in reverse, resulting in a decline in the money supply that is greater than the value of the initial securities purchase.

Global Connections

Global Monetary Policy Before 12 European countries adopted a single common currency in 2002, the European System of Central Banks (ESCB) was created to handle the European Union monetary policy. The ESCB includes the new European Central Bank as well as the central banks of all European Union member nations. Its job is similar to that of the Federal Reserve. The ESCB conducts monetary policy for the European Union nations, conducts foreign exchange operations, and provides banks with services such as check cashing. The ESCB's monetary policy tools include open market operations as well as reserve requirements. **How do the monetary policy tools of the ESCB resemble those of the Federal Reserve?**

Using Monetary Policy Tools

Open market operations are the most used of the Federal Reserve's monetary policy tools. They can be conducted smoothly and on an ongoing basis to meet the Fed's goals. The Fed changes the discount rate less frequently. It usually follows a policy of keeping the discount rate in line with other interest rates in the economy in order to prevent excess borrowing by member banks from the Fed. (See the graph "Key Interest Rates" on page 542 in the Economic Atlas and Databank.)

Today, the Fed does not change reserve requirements to conduct monetary policy. Changing reserve requirements would force banks to make drastic changes in their plans. Open market operations or changes in the discount rate do not disrupt financial institutions.

The Federal Reserve uses these monetary policy tools to adjust the money supply. Why the Fed would want to change the money supply, and the effects of monetary policy, are the subjects of the next section.

Section 3 Assessment

Progress Monitoring *Online*
For: Self-quiz with vocabulary practice
Web Code: mna-6167

Key Terms and Main Ideas

1. What is **money creation?**
2. What is the **required reserve ratio (RRR)?**
3. State the **money multiplier formula.**
4. Why do banks sometimes hold **excess reserves?**
5. If the discount rate rose, would you expect the **prime rate** to rise or fall?
6. What are **open market operations?**

Applying Economic Concepts

7. ***Math Practice*** Suppose the RRR is 0.15. Use the money multiplier formula to determine by how much a $2,000 checking account deposit will increase the money supply.
8. ***Critical Thinking*** Will the money supply actually increase by the amount you calculated in Question 7? Why or why not?

For: Current Events Activity
Visit: PHSchool.com
Web Code: mnd-6163

GTE Guide to the Essentials
Chapter 16, Section 3, p. 69 provides support for students who need additional review of the section content. Spanish support is available in the Spanish edition of the guide on p. 69.

Quiz Unit 6 folder, p. 31 includes questions to check students' understanding of Section 3 content.

Presentation Pro CD-ROM
Quiz provides multiple-choice questions to check students' understanding of Section 3 content.

Answers to . . .

Section 3 Assessment

1. Money creation is the process by which money enters into circulation.
2. The required reserve ratio (RRR) is the required ratio of reserves to deposits—the fraction of deposits that banks are required to keep on reserve.
3. The money multiplier formula is the amount of new money that will be created with each demand deposit, calculated as 1/RRR.
4. Banks hold excess reserves in order to be sure that they can meet customers' demands and Federal Reserve requirements.
5. rise
6. Open market operations are purchases and sales of government securities to alter the supply of money.
7. 2000 ÷ 0.15 = $13,333.33
8. Students should realize that the money supply is unlikely to increase by that amount because, in reality, people hold on to some money instead of placing all of it back into the system.

Progress Monitoring *Online*
For additional assessment, have students access Progress Monitoring Online at **Web Code:** mna-6167

Go Online PHSchool.com Typing in the Web Code when prompted will bring students directly to detailed instructions for this activity.

Answer to . . .

Global Connections Open market operations and reserve requirements are also two tools of the Federal Reserve.

Section 4

Monetary Policy and Macroeconomic Stabilization

Objectives You may wish to call students' attention to the objectives in the Section Preview. The objectives are reflected in the main headings of the section.

Bellringer Based on what students have read in the previous sections, have them review briefly the tools of fiscal policy. Ask students to think of reasons why the Fed uses these tools.

Vocabulary Builder Four of the key terms in this section are easily divided into two pairs of near opposites. Ask students to write several sentences for each pair that compare and contrast the terms.

Lesson Plan

Teaching the Main Concepts (L3)

1. Focus Explain to students that the tools they learned about in the last section are methods that the Fed uses to regulate the overall operation of the economy. Ask students what they think the overall goal of the Fed is in regulating the economy.

2. Instruct Begin with an overview of how monetary policy works. Describe how problems with timing and policy lags affect the implementation of monetary policy. Then explain to students how the Federal Reserve must anticipate the business cycle in order to make decisions about monetary policy. Finally, distinguish between interventionist and laissez-faire money policies.

3. Close/Reteach Discuss with students their opinions on monetary policy. Ask them what kind of policy they favor, and have them explain why they favor that policy.

Guided Reading and Review Unit 6 folder, p. 32 asks students to identify the main ideas of the section and to define or identify key terms.

Section 4 Monetary Policy and Macroeconomic Stabilization

Preview

Objectives

After studying this section you will be able to:

1. **Understand** how monetary policy works.
2. **Explain** the problems of timing and policy lags in implementing monetary policy.
3. **Explain** how predictions about the length of a business cycle affect monetary policy.
4. **Describe** two distinct approaches to monetary policy.

Section Focus

The Federal Reserve uses monetary policy to try to tame business cycles. The unpredictable length of business cycles, however, makes it difficult to determine when it is wise to intervene in the economy.

Key Terms

monetarism
easy money policy
tight money policy
inside lag
outside lag

monetarism *the belief that the money supply is the most important factor in macroeconomic performance*

Adherents of **monetarism** believe that the money supply is the most important factor in macroeconomic performance. How, then, does monetary policy influence macroeconomic performance?

How Monetary Policy Works

Monetary policy alters the supply of money. The supply of money, in turn, affects interest rates. As you read earlier, interest rates affect the level of investment and spending in the economy.

▶ **Keeping the economy stable requires a delicate balancing act.**

The Money Supply and Interest Rates

It is easy to see the cost of money if you are borrowing it. The cost—the price that you as borrower pay—is the interest rate. Even if you have your own money, however, the interest rate still affects you. The interest rate is also the cost of having money, because you are giving up interest by not saving or investing. Thus, the interest rate is always the cost of money.

The market for money is like any other market. If the supply is higher, the price—the interest rate—is lower. If the supply is lower, the price—the interest rate—is higher. In other words, when the money supply is low, interest rates are high. When the money supply is high, interest rates are low.

Interest Rates and Spending

Recall from Chapter 12 that interest rates are important factors of spending in the economy. Lower interest rates encourage greater investment spending by business firms. This is because a firm's cost of borrowing—or of using its own funds—decreases as the interest rate decreases.

Firms find that lower interest rates give them more opportunities for profitable

Graphing the Main Idea

Monetary and Fiscal Policy To build understanding of the concept of **monetary and fiscal policy,** have students use a double web graphic organizer like the one at the right. Remind students that a double web graphic organizer can be used to compare and contrast information about two topics. Ask them to use the double web to examine the differences between an easy money policy and a tight money policy.

Section Reading Support Transparencies A template and the answers for this graphic organizer can be found in Chapter 16, Section 4 of the Section Reading Support Transparency System.

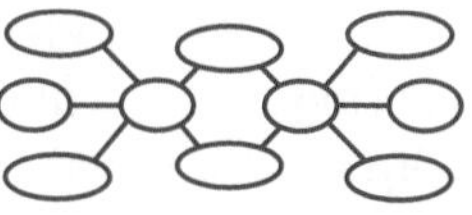

monetary and fiscal policy. For fiscal policy, the outside lag lasts as long as is required for new government spending or tax policies to take effect and begin to affect real GDP and the inflation rate. This time period can be relatively short, as with a tax rebate that returns government revenues to households eager for spending money. One statistical model concluded that an increase in government spending would increase GDP after just six months.

Outside lags can be much longer for monetary policy, since they primarily affect business investment plans. Firms may require months or even years to make large investment plans, especially those involving new physical capital, such as a new factory. Thus, a change in interest rates may not have its full effect on investment spending for several years. This conclusion is supported by several studies that suggest that the outside lag for monetary policy is probably rather long. More than two years may pass before the maximum impact of monetary policy is felt.

Given the longer inside lag for fiscal policy and the longer outside lag for monetary policy, it is not obvious which policy has the shorter total lag. In practice, partisan politics and budgetary pressures often prevent the President and Congress from agreeing on fiscal policy. Because of the political difficulties of implementing fiscal policy, we rely to a greater extent on the Fed to use monetary policy to soften the business cycle.

▲ Unprecedented economic growth in the 1990s led some economists to predict an end to the peaks and troughs of past business cycles. Recession in the early 2000s, however, showed the cycle beginning again.

Predicting Business Cycles

The Federal Reserve must not only react to current trends. It must also anticipate changes in the economy. How should policymakers decide when to intervene in the economy?

Monetary Policy and Inflation

You have already read that expansionary policy, if enacted at the wrong time, may push an economy into high inflation, thus reducing any beneficial impact. This is the chief danger of using an easy money policy to get the economy out of a recession.

An inflationary economy can be tamed by a tight money policy, but the timing is again crucial. If the policy takes effect as the economy is already cooling off on its own, the tight money could turn a mild contraction into a full-blown recession.

The decision of whether to use monetary policy, then, must be based partly on our expectations of the business cycle. Some recessions are short-run phenomena that will, in the long run, disappear. Some inflationary peaks may also be expected to last for the short run and end in the long run. Given the timing problems of monetary policy, in some cases it may be wiser to allow the business cycle to correct itself rather than run the risk of an ill-timed policy change.

If a recession is expected to turn into an expansion in a short time, the best course of action may be to take a laissez-faire approach to the economy and let the economy correct itself. On the other hand, if we expect a recession to last several years, then all but the most conservative onlookers

THE WALL STREET JOURNAL. CLASSROOM EDITION

In the News Read more about monetary policy in "Retirees Forced to Pinch Pennies," an article in The Wall Street Journal Classroom Edition.

Go Online
The Wall Street Journal Classroom Edition
For: Current Events
Visit: PHSchool.com
Web Code: mnc-6164

Differentiated Instruction 

To assess students' understanding of how predictions about the length of a business cycle affect monetary policy, have students write a script for a five-minute news presentation. Explain to them that their job is to write a script that explains the topic concisely and clearly. Instruct them to describe any visuals that they think would clarify their presentations.

Economic Detective Activity
Unit 6 folder, p. 36, "Fulla Favors the Fed," provides an integrated application of chapter concepts.

Differentiated Instruction 

(Enrichment) Have students create a double web graphic organizer that compares and contrasts the two approaches to monetary policy: interventionist and laissez faire. Have them add to the information located in this section by including economists discussed in other chapters of the textbook, showing which of the policies each would probably follow and why.

Transparency Resource Package
Economics Organizers, G6: Double Web Graphic Organizer

Go Online PHSchool.com Typing in the Web Code when prompted will bring students directly to the article.

Preparing for Standardized Tests

Have students read the section titled "Predicting the Business Cycle" and then answer the question below.

A laissez-faire economic policy would:

A increase the money supply quickly.
B alter the business cycle.
(C) allow the economy to fix itself.
D decrease the money supply quickly.

GTE Guide to the Essentials
Chapter 16, Section 4, p. 70 provides support for students who need additional review of the section content. Spanish support is available in the Spanish edition of the guide on p. 70.

Quiz Unit 6 folder, p. 33 includes questions to check students' understanding of Section 4 content.

Presentation Pro CD-ROM
Quiz provides multiple-choice questions to check students' understanding of Section 4 content.

Answers to . . .

Section 4 Assessment

1. An easy money policy is enacted to increase the money supply and expand the economy.
2. A tight money policy is enacted to decrease the money supply and contract the economy.
3. An inside lag is a delay in implementing monetary policy. Inside lags occur because it is not always immediately obvious, even to economists, exactly how the economy is performing, and because economic data usually take time to be gathered, analyzed, and reacted to in the form of economic policy.
4. Outside lags may be long because they mainly affect business investment plans. Firms may take months or years to make and carry out these plans.
5. Monetarism is the belief that the money supply is the most important factor in macroeconomic performance.
6. It is not always easy to know where in the business cycle an economy is at a given time or how long a particular part of the cycle will last.
7. Students should prepare well-crafted and logical arguments for each side of the debate, based on textbook material.
8. Economic performance was good.

Answer to . . .

Building Key Concepts Both fiscal and monetary policy affect the nation's economy. However, fiscal policy is created by Congress while monetary policy is created by the Fed.

Figure 16.11 Fiscal and Monetary Policy Tools

	Fiscal policy tools	Monetary policy tools
Expansionary tools	1. increasing government spending 2. cutting taxes	1. open market operations: bond purchases 2. decreasing the federal funds rate 3. decreasing reserve requirements
Contractionary tools	1. decreasing government spending 2. raising taxes	1. open market operations: bond sales 2. increasing the federal funds rate 3. increasing reserve requirements

Both the federal government and the Federal Reserve can influence the nation's economy.
Fiscal and Monetary Policy **How are fiscal and monetary policy similar? How do they differ?**

would recommend an active policy. So the question is this: How long will a recessionary or inflationary period last?

How Quickly Does the Economy Self-Correct?

Economists disagree on the answer to this question. Their estimates for the U.S. economy range from two to six years. Since the economy may take quite a long time to recover on its own from an inflationary peak or a recessionary trough, there is time for policymakers to guide the economy back to stable levels of output and prices.

Approaches to Monetary Policy

In practice, the lags discussed here make monetary and fiscal policy difficult to apply. Interventionist policy, a policy encouraging action, is likely to make the business cycle worse if the economy self-adjusts quickly. Laissez-faire economists who believe that the economy will self-adjust quickly will recommend against enacting new policies. Economists who believe that economies emerge slowly from recessions, however, will usually recommend enacting fiscal and monetary policies to move the process along.

The rate of adjustment may also vary over time, making policy decisions even more difficult. This debate over which approach to take with monetary policy will probably never be settled to the satisfaction of all economists.

Section 4 Assessment

Progress Monitoring *Online*
For: Self-quiz with vocabulary practice
Web Code: mna-6168

Key Terms and Main Ideas

1. Why would the Federal Reserve enact an **easy money policy?**
2. Why would the Federal Reserve enact a **tight money policy?**
3. What are **inside lags,** and why do they occur?
4. Why does monetary policy have such long **outside lags?**
5. What is **monetarism?**

Applying Economic Concepts

6. ***Critical Thinking*** Why do business cycles make monetary policy difficult to time?
7. ***Try This*** With a partner, stage a debate on monetary policy. One of you will take an interventionist approach, encouraging action, the other a laissez-faire approach, discouraging action. Use information from your textbook to help craft your argument.
8. ***Using the Databank*** Examine the graphs on Economic Indicators in the Economic Atlas and Databank on pages 538–539. How would you describe the economic performance of the United States at the end of the twentieth century?

For: Presentation Activity
Visit: PHSchool.com
Web Code: mnd-6164

Progress Monitoring *Online*
For additional assessment, have students access Progress Monitoring Online at **Web Code:** mna-6168

Go Online PHSchool.com Typing in the Web Code when prompted will bring students directly to detailed instructions for this activity.

Monetary and Fiscal Policy

Banking, Monetary Policy, and the Great Depression

In 1929, the collapse of the stock market touched off a period of economic devastation known as the Great Depression. Millions of Americans found themselves unemployed and lost their homes, farms, and life savings.

Bank Failures In late October 1929, dropping stock prices caused many panicked investors to sell their stocks, which resulted in the collapse of the stock market on October 29, 1929. Banks had invested heavily in the stock market and lost huge sums. Fearful that banks would run out of money, people rushed to their banks demanding their money. To pay back these deposits, banks had to recall loans from borrowers, but they could not do so fast enough to pay all the depositors demanding their money. Thousands of banks failed.

▲ Countless investors lost everything in the Crash of 1929.

Emergency Action In 1933, President Franklin D. Roosevelt took emergency action and declared a bank "holiday." All banks closed temporarily to stop the banking panic. Congress then passed the Banking Act of 1933, which created the Federal Deposit Insurance Corporation (FDIC) to insure deposits. This meant that even if a bank failed, deposits would be guaranteed by the federal government.

Meanwhile, banks became extremely cautious. They made fewer loans and kept enough cash on hand in case depositors all came at once to withdraw their funds. Banks began to hold substantial reserves, far in excess of those required by the Federal Reserve.

Federal Reserve Response These excess reserves concerned the Federal Reserve, which feared that banks might distribute that money, possibly causing inflation. In 1937, the Fed raised reserve requirements for the banks, thus lowering the money supply to prevent inflation. Banks responded by cutting back their loans even further to have enough cash for depositors.

This Federal Reserve policy had an unintended negative result. Banks reduced lending, which led to a recession. Since that time the Fed has learned not to make sharp increases in reserve requirements.

Applying Economic Ideas

1. Why did the Federal Reserve raise reserve requirements in 1937?
2. Were banks justified in holding excess reserves in the 1930s? Why or why not?

Real-life Case Study: Monetary and Fiscal Policy

1. Focus The Great Depression had many causes. Unfortunately, policies enacted by the Federal Reserve prolonged slow economic activity. Explain to students that in this case study they will learn why the Fed rarely changes reserve requirements today.

2. Instruct Ask students to read the case study, looking for examples of fiscal and monetary policy in action. Ask them to create a cause-and-effect chain to show how the stock market crash eventually led to the collapse of banks. Then ask students why they think the government feared that inflation might rise.

3. Close/Reteach Discuss with students why raising the reserve requirements was a mistake. Ask them to point to information in this chapter that shows what the government learned from its experience during the Great Depression.

Case Studies Activity
Case Studies in Free Enterprise folder, pp. 32–33, "Amartya Sen," helps students apply economic principles in an additional case study.

Economic Detective Activity
Unit 6 folder, p. 36, "Fulla Favors the Fed," provides an additional application of chapter concepts.

Preparing for Standardized Tests

Have students read the case study on this page and then answer the question below.

How did the raising of reserve requirements by the Federal Reserve affect the economy in the long run?

A People rushed to banks, demanding their money.
(B) Banks reduced lending, triggering a recession.
C The Great Crash of 1929 occurred.
D Banks increased lending, triggering inflation.

Answers to . . .

1. The Fed feared that banks might distribute their excess reserves to their depositors, causing inflation.
2. The banks held the reserves because of the recent banking panics. Many students will think that the banks were justified in their caution. Others will say that the banks should have anticipated the long-term effects of holding these reserves.

Chapter 16 Assessment

Key Terms

1. discount rate
2. money creation
3. Board of Governors
4. tight money policy
5. excess reserves
6. check clearing
7. outside lag

Using Graphic Organizers

8. Students may fill in the top boxes with "Increasing reserve requirements" and "Reducing the discount rate." In the box below "Open market operations," they may write "Increasing or decreasing money supply through bond purchases or sales." Below "Increasing reserve requirements" they may put "Decreasing money supply." Under "Reducing the discount rate" they can put "Increasing money supply."

Reviewing Main Ideas

9. The Fed was established to regulate and supervise the banking system and to act as lender of last resort to avert banking panics.
10. check clearing (recording transactions involving checks), supervising lending practices (monitoring reserves and examining banks and holding companies), and acting as lender of last resort (source for funds in emergencies)
11. The money multiplier formula is the amount of new money that will be created with each demand deposit, calculated as 1/RRR. Students should summarize this idea in their own words.
12. The Federal Reserve can set the federal funds rate or use open market operations, including bond purchases and sales, to change short-term rates. The Fed has no direct influence over long-term rates.
13. Inside and outside lags create delays in implementing monetary policy.
14. Easy money policies aim to expand the money supply; tight money policies aim to contract the money supply.

Chapter 16 Assessment

Chapter Summary

A summary of major ideas in Chapter 16 appears below. See also the **Guide to the Essentials of Economics**, which provides additional review and test practice of key concepts in Chapter 16.

Section 1 The Federal Reserve System (pp. 415–418)

To stabilize the nation's banking system, Congress created the Federal Reserve System. The Federal Reserve is made up of twelve **Federal Reserve Districts** and is overseen by a small but powerful **Board of Governors.** As a private institution serving a public function, the Federal Reserve is a central bank relatively free from government control.

Section 2 Federal Reserve Functions (pp. 420–423)

The Federal Reserve serves the banking needs of the government and of individual banks. It regulates the nation's banking system. It also monitors and regulates the nation's money supply.

Section 3 Monetary Policy Tools (pp. 425–429)

Money creation occurs through the day-to-day operations of banks. The Federal Reserve uses three tools of monetary policy to control the amount of money in circulation. The three tools are changing the required reserve ratio, changing the discount rate, and buying or selling bonds on the open market.

Section 4 Monetary Policy and Macroeconomic Stabilization (pp. 430–434)

The Federal Reserve enacts monetary policy to lessen the effects of business cycles. The unpredictable length of business cycles, however, makes it difficult to determine when it is wise to intervene in the economy. **Inside lags** and **outside lags** make it difficult to conduct monetary and fiscal policy.

Key Terms

Match the following definitions with the terms listed below. You will not use all of the terms.

inside lag	**tight money policy**
discount rate	**money creation**
Board of Governors	**outside lag**
federal funds rate	**easy money policy**
excess reserves	**prime rate**
Federal Reserve District	**check clearing**

1. Rate the Federal Reserve charges for loans to commercial banks
2. Process by which money enters into circulation
3. The seven-member board that oversees the Federal Reserve System
4. Monetary policy that reduces the money supply
5. Reserves greater than the required amounts
6. The process by which banks record whose account gives up money and whose account receives money when a customer writes a check
7. The time it takes for monetary policy to have an effect

Using Graphic Organizers

8. On a separate sheet of paper, copy the tree map below. Complete the tree map with the tools of monetary policy and their expected effects on the economy.

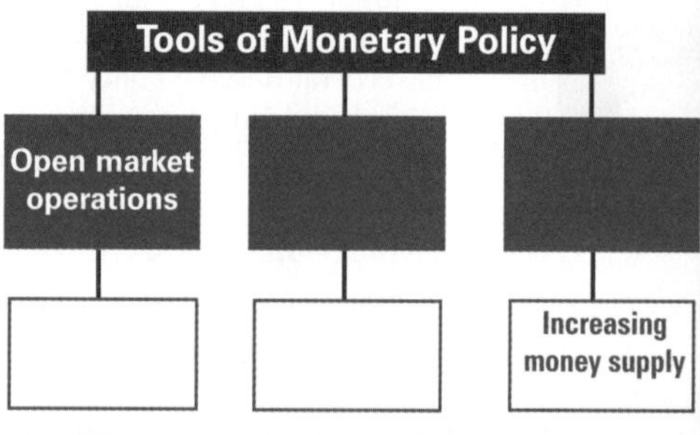

Critical Thinking

15. Student responses will vary. Some students will see everyday check clearing as the most crucial service, whereas others may see the supervisory role of the Fed over lending practices as important in preventing bank failures. Students who find the regulatory aspects most important may also note the Fed's bank examinations and control of reserves.
16. Open market operations have an almost immediate effect on the money supply (increasing with bond purchases, decreasing with bond sales), a fact that gives them an advantage over other monetary policy tools that may take a longer time to implement. Also, open market operations do not disrupt financial institutions.
17. Fed actions to implement an easy money policy would aim to expand the money supply through open market operations (bond sales) and lowering of interest rates. An increased money supply encourages investment spending and economic growth. Such actions might be taken if the economy is experiencing a contraction.

Reviewing Main Ideas

9. What was the reasoning behind the creation of the Federal Reserve?
10. List and describe three services the Federal Reserve offers banks.
11. Describe the money multiplier formula in your own words.
12. Explain the different methods the Federal Reserve uses to change short-term interest rates and long-term interest rates.
13. How do inside lags and outside lags affect monetary policy?
14. What is the difference between easy money policies and tight money polices?

Critical Thinking

15. **Analyzing Information** Review the services the Federal Reserve offers banks and the regulations it places on banks. Which service or regulation do you think is most important to the American banking system?
16. **Analyzing Information** Why are open market operations the most commonly used actions taken by the Fed? What advantages do open market operations have over other monetary policy tools?
17. **Recognizing Cause and Effect** If the Federal Reserve Board were to implement an easy money policy, what actions would it take? What would be the expected results of this policy? What conditions could lead the Fed to take such actions?

Problem-Solving Activity

18. Suppose the economy is experiencing a high rate of inflation. As chair of the Federal Reserve Board, what actions would you take to put the economy back on track?

Economics Journal

Organizing Information Review your list of terms and definitions. Use your list and other information from the chapter to create a graphic organizer summarizing the role of the Fed in the United States economy.

Skills for Life

Recognizing Bias in Writing Review the steps shown on page 419; then complete the following activity based on the passage on inflation below.

19. Who is the author of the excerpt below?
20. Is this a personal letter, diary entry, or public document?
21. What words does the author use to describe the actions of Alan Greenspan?
22. Do you detect any obvious bias?
23. What economic attitudes may have influenced the author's opinion?

"In the late 1960s, after 20 years in which the gross domestic product had grown 4% a year, inflation had remained below 2%, and the Dow Jones Industrial Average had increased fivefold, the U.S. economy began a long slide into an economic abyss. Inflation and interest rates shot up, stock prices stagnated, and by the late 1970s, few thought the U.S. economy could ever recover.

Today, many believe this same fate is once again awaiting the U.S. economy. According to the pessimists, the U.S. stock market is in a bubble that is about to burst, and inflation is about to explode. The recent dip in the stock market—prompted by more gloomy warnings from Alan Greenspan—appeared to give credence to these worrywarts. But they are wrong."

Brian S. Wesbury, chief economist at Griffin, Kubik, Stephens & Thompson, "Have No Fear, Inflation Isn't Here" [Commentary], *The Wall Street Journal Interactive Edition,* October 21, 1999

Progress Monitoring *Online*

For: Chapter 16 Self-Test **Visit:** PHSchool.com
Web Code: mna-6161

As a final review, take the Economics Chapter 16 Self-Test and receive immediate feedback on your answers. The test consists of 20 multiple-choice questions designed to test your understanding of the chapter content.

Problem-Solving Activity

18. This activity's results will be based on students' interpretation of Federal Reserve monetary policy and on their individual ingenuity. A possible solution would be to expand the money supply through open market operations or by lowering the discount rate.

Skills for Life

19. Brian S. Wesbury, chief economist at Griffin, Kubik, Stephens & Thompson
20. public document
21. "gloomy warnings"
22. Students should recognize bias. The author clearly means to convince the reader that Greenspan is wrong.
23. Answers will vary. Students may point out that Wesbury is a chief economist for a firm whose revenues may be affected by actions taken by Greenspan and the Fed.

Additional support materials and activities for Chapter 16 of *Economics: Principles in Action* can be found in the Social Studies area of **PHSchool.com**

Economics Journal

Students should review their terms and definitions and use them to create a graphic organizer summarizing the role of the Fed.

Review and Assessment

Vocabulary Practice Unit 6 folder, p. 35 uses a crossword puzzle to reinforce understanding of key terms.

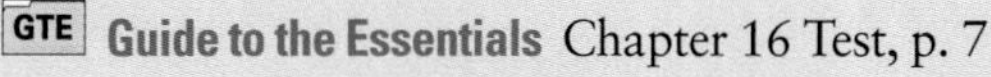

GTE **Guide to the Essentials** Chapter 16 Test, p. 71

Test Bank CD-ROM Chapter 16 Test

Go Online PHSchool.com Students may use the Chapter 16 Self-Test on **PHSchool.com** to prepare for the Chapter Test.

UNIT 7

The Global Economy

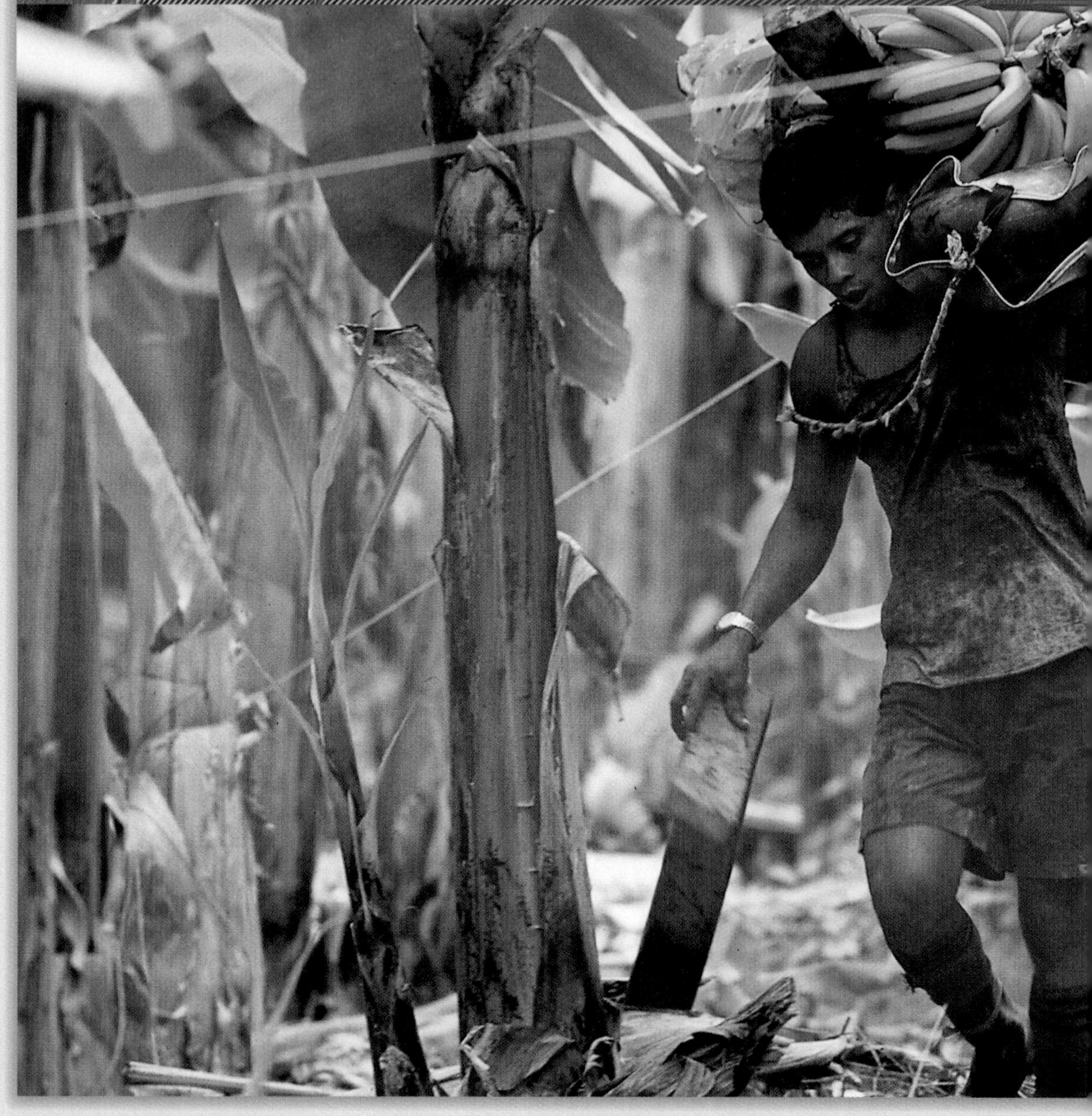

Introducing the Unit

Unit Summary

Unit 7 teaches students about international trade and economic development. Chapter 17 discusses reasons why nations trade and barriers to trade as well as international cooperation and ways in which trade is measured. In Chapter 18 students examine levels of economic development and the changes that are sweeping much of the world today.

Focus Activity

Introduce Unit 7 to students by asking them to complete the Focus Activity. Have students make their lists, and let them compare their lists with a classmate's. Then collect the lists, and compile results on a poster or in a bulletin board display. Keep the results in view as you work through the two chapters in this unit.

National Council on Economic Education

The following Voluntary National Content Standards in Economics are addressed in this unit:

★ Standard 5 ★ Standard 7
★ Standard 6 ★ Standard 15

See the Chapter Openers on pp. 440 and 470 for a complete description of the standards addressed in each chapter.

Chapters in This Unit

17. *International Trade*
18. *Economic Development and Transition*

These bananas were grown in Costa Rica.

Your shoes were made in Indonesia and your backpack in China. While many people take the global economy for granted, when you step back to consider the entire flow of goods, services, and money around the world, the result is mind-boggling.

- Who made your shirt, and how much were they paid for their labor?
- Which goods does the United States export, and which goods are imported?
- How does international trade affect the economy of the United States?

In this unit you'll read about why nations trade and actions nations take to restrict or increase trade. Finally, you'll look at why standards of living vary greatly from country to country and the impact of the global economy on everyone's future.

Focus Activity

Choose five items you own, and identify where they were made. Compare your list of items and countries with that of a classmate.

Bibliography

Print

Virtual Economics: An Interactive Center for Economics Education. CD-ROM. Gonnelli, Adam. *The Basics of Foreign Trade and Exchange.* EconomicsAmerica, National Council on Economic Education, 1997.

National Council on Economic Education. *Focus: International Economics.* New York: National Council on Economic Education.

Multimedia

Economics U$A Series. "International Trade." Color video, 30 minutes. The first segment on this videocassette focuses on the effects of international trade, tariffs, and quotas. "Exchange Rates." Color video, 30 minutes. The second segment discusses how governments seek to control exchange rates. Educational Film Center (Annandale, VA): Annenberg/CPB Collection.

Technology Center

Economics Video Library

Includes high-interest, chapter-specific segments produced by CNBC for

THE WALL STREET JOURNAL.
CLASSROOM EDITION

Simulations and Data Graphing CD-ROM

Provides interactive federal budget and stock market simulations and a data graphing tool designed to support instruction in economics.

PRENTICE HALL
TeacherEXPRESS™
Plan • Teach • Assess

Teacher Express CD-ROM offers powerful lesson planning, resource management, testing, and an interactive Teacher's Edition.

Prentice Hall Presentation Pro CD-ROM

Allows you to create custom lectures for every chapter.

Social Studies Skills Tutor CD-ROM

Provides interactive practice in geographic literacy, critical thinking and reading, visual analysis, and communications.

Exam*View*® Test Bank CD-ROM

Allows you to create, edit, and print out chapter level tests.

Transparency Resource Package

Illustrates key economic concepts and provides useful forms and templates for enhancing classroom discussions.

Section Reading Support Transparency System

Delivers the main idea of each section in the student text through graphic organizers.

Offers student-appropriate online activities and links as well as resources for the teacher. Be sure to check out this month's **eTeach** online discussion with a Master Economics Teacher.

Chapter 17 International Trade

For more pacing suggestions, see the Economics Pacing Guide in the Program Overview of the Teaching Resources.

Section Objectives	Print and Technology Resources	
1 Why Nations Trade *(pp. 441–447)* **Objectives** 1. Analyze the locations of resources and evaluate the significance of these locations. 2. Explain the concepts of absolute and comparative advantage and apply the concept of comparative advantage to explain why and how countries trade. 3. Analyze the impact of U.S. imports and exports on the United States and its trading partners.	• **Lesson Planner** Section 1 Lesson Plan, p. 68 • **Lesson Plans folder** Section 1 Lesson Plan, p. 61 • **Economics Assessment Rubrics folder** Writing Assignment, pp. 6–7 • **Unit 7 folder** Guided Reading and Review, p. 2 Economic Skills, p. 8 Section 1 Quiz, p. 3 • **Presentation Pro CD-ROM** Section 1	• **Transparency Resource Package** Economics Organizers, G7: Tree Map Graphic Organizer Economics Concepts, 17A: Absolute and Comparative Advantage Economics Concepts, 17B: U.S. Trade Partners Economics Concepts, 17C: Major U.S. Exports and Imports • **Section Reading Support Transparency System** • **Social Studies Skills Tutor CD-ROM**
2 Trade Barriers and Agreements *(pp. 449–456)* **Objectives** 1. Define various types of trade barriers. 2. Compare the effects of free trade and trade barriers on economic activities. 3. Understand arguments in favor of protectionism. 4. Evaluate the benefits and costs of participation in international trade agreements. 5. Explain the role of multinationals in the global market.	• **Lesson Planner** Section 2 Lesson Plan, p. 68 • **Learning Styles Lesson Plans folder** Section 2 Lesson Plan, p. 39 • **Lesson Plans folder** Section 2 Lesson Plan, p. 62 • **Economics Assessment Rubrics folder** Writing Assignment, pp. 6–7 • **Unit 7 folder** Guided Reading and Review, p. 4 Careers in Economics, Exporter, p. 11 Section 2 Quiz, p. 5 • **Source Articles folder** Two-Way Street, pp. 51–53	• **Presentation Pro CD-ROM** Section 2 • **Transparency Resource Package** Economics Organizers, G5: Web Graphic Organizer Economics Concepts, 17D: Trade Barriers Economics Concepts, 17E: Protectionism Economics Concepts, 17F: Major Trade Organization Members • **Section Reading Support Transparency System**
3 Measuring Trade *(pp. 458–464)* **Objectives** 1. Analyze how changes in exchange rates of world currencies affect international trade. 2. Describe the effect of various exchange rate systems. 3. Analyze the effects of changes in exchange rates on the balance of trade.	• **Lesson Planner** Section 3 Lesson Plan, p. 68 • **Learning Styles Lesson Plans folder** Section 3 Lesson Plan, p. 40 • **Lesson Plans folder** Section 3 Lesson Plan, p. 63 • **Unit 7 folder** Guided Reading and Review, p. 6 Economic Cartoon, p. 12 Vocabulary Practice, p. 9 Economic Detective, p. 10 Section 3 Quiz, p. 7 • **Case Studies in Free Enterprise folder** Soichiro Honda, pp. 34–35	• **Math Practice folder** Applying Foreign Exchange Rates, p. 13 • **Presentation Pro CD-ROM** Section 3 • **Simulations and Data Graphing CD-ROM** Data Graphing Tools • **Transparency Resource Package** Economics Organizers, G7: Tree Map Graphic Organizer Economics Concepts, 17G: The U.S. Balance of Trade • **Section Reading Support Transparency System**

Differentiated Instruction

Shared Reading L1 L2

Depending on their skill level, some readers may be unable to successfully complete a reading assignment at home or independently. They may only be able to understand the content sufficiently if the selection of text is read aloud in class and the meaning is clarified by the teacher. You may choose to do this in several ways:

- **As a Class** Call on each student to read a paragraph out loud to the class, using stronger readers for longer selections and weaker readers for shorter selection. After each paragraph, ask the class a question to check for understanding of key concepts, and wait for volunteers.
- **In Small Groups** Break the class into small groups, assigning each group a small selection of text. Each group is responsible for bullet pointing key information from that selection to present to the class. All members of the class should take notes as selections of text are presented.

Revising the Text L4

Advanced readers typically understand that when one conflict has two sides, the groups' perspectives on an event can differ tremendously. To reinforce this, ask students to rewrite a section of text explaining a conflict from one side's perspective. Provide students with the following steps:

1. Assign members of the class a selection of reading from their text. Be sure that this selection discusses an event or conflict that involves more than one nation or group.

2. Ask students to choose one of the nations involved to represent. They should research the role of this particular nation and develop a thorough understanding of its involvement in this event.

3. Students should re-write or revise the assigned selection of text to reflect the perspective of the assigned country.

Revisions should include changes in use of vocabulary that may make the reader more sympathetic to the assigned nation, mention of events concerning the assigned nation that were omitted from this text, and the inclusion of rationales for why the assigned nation or group acted in a certain way.

Go Online PHSchool.com

Visit the Social Studies area of the Prentice Hall Web site. There you can find additional links to enrich chapter content for *Economics: Principles in Action* as well as a self-test for students. Be sure to check out this month's **eTeach** online discussion with a Master Economics Teacher.

Web Code: mnf-7171

Running Out of Time?

- Use the **Presentation Pro CD-ROM** to create an outline for this chapter.
- Use the Chapter Summary in the **Chapter 17 Assessment,** p. 466.
- Use the Section Summaries for Chapter 17, from **Guide to the Essentials of Economics (English and Spanish).**

THE WALL STREET JOURNAL. CLASSROOM EDITION

Prentice Hall brings into the classroom the authoritative content of *The Wall Street Journal Classroom Edition.* See the Source Articles, Debating Current Issues, and You and Your Money folders in the **Teaching Resources**. Also, see Economics Video Library, "The Euro, Part 2."

Assessment Resources

Chapter Assessment

Teaching Resources Unit 7, Chapter 17

- Section Quizzes, pp. 3, 5, 7

Exam *View*® Test Bank CD-ROM Chapter 17

Economics Assessment Rubrics

Chapter 17 Self-Test, **Web Code:** mna-7171

Reading and Skills Evaluation

Progress Monitoring Assessments

- Screening Test
- Diagnostic Test of Social Studies Skills

Standardized Test Preparation

Test Prep Workbook

Test-Taking Strategies With Transparencies

Differentiated Instruction Key

L1 Special Needs	LPR Less Proficient Readers
L2 Basic to Average	AR Advanced Readers
L3 All Students	SN Special Needs Students
L4 Average to Advanced	GT Gifted and Talented
	ELL English Language Learner

Chapter 17

International Trade

Introducing the Chapter

In this chapter, students are introduced to international trade. They will learn about the economic forces that make trade desirable, the controls and barriers that nations impose to maximize their gains from trade, and the effects of international monetary policies and currency fluctuations on the conduct of trade.

For additional links for *Economics: Principles in Action* provided by Prentice Hall and *The Wall Street Journal Classroom Edition,* visit the Social Studies area. Be sure to check out this month's **eTeach** online discussion with a Master Teacher.

Beyond the Lecture

You may cover the concepts in Chapter 17 in an activity-based style by using the following materials:

- **Technology Resources** appropriate for use with this chapter are noted on pp. 443, 446, 447, 450, 451, 454, 456, 459, 463, 464, and 467.
- **Presentation Pro CD-ROM** with animated graphs gives you an alternative method for organizing and delivering chapter content.
- **Activities** designed to meet the needs of students of mixed abilities and learning styles are noted throughout the chapter in the side columns.
- **Learning Styles Lesson Plans** provide alternate lessons for diverse learning styles. See pp. 39–40 of the Learning Styles Lesson Plans folder located in the Teaching Resources.

Economics Journal

Instruct students to write their responses to the question in their Economics Journals. Students may include completed journal entries in an Economics Portfolio.

Chapter 17 International Trade

In today's global economy, many products that Americans use every day were produced in other countries. We drive Japanese cars, wear clothes from China, and sit on furniture from Canada. These products come by trucks and trains or arrive at United States ports aboard huge freighters like the one you see here.

Check the labels on clothing, appliances, electronics, and other items that you use every day. Then make a list of the items and the countries in which they were made. What does your list suggest about the importance of international trade?

For: Current Data
Visit: PHSchool.com
Web Code: mng-7171

National Council on Economic Education

★ **Standard 5** Voluntary exchange occurs only when all participating parties expect to gain. This is true for trade among individuals or organizations within a nation, and among individuals or organizations in different nations.

★ **Standard 6** When individuals, regions, and nations specialize in what they can produce at the lowest cost and then trade with others, both production and consumption increase.

★ **Standard 7** Markets exist when buyers and sellers interact. This interaction determines market prices and thereby allocates scarce goods and services.

For more information about the standards, contact the National Council on Economic Education

1140 Avenue of the Americas
New York, NY 10036
1-800-338-1192

Section 1 Why Nations Trade

Preview

Objectives

After studying this section you will be able to:

1. **Analyze** the locations of resources and evaluate the significance of these locations.
2. **Explain** the concepts of absolute and comparative advantage and apply the concept of comparative advantage to explain why and how countries trade.
3. **Analyze** the impact of U.S. imports and exports on the United States and its trading partners.
4. **Describe** the effects of trade on employment.

Section Focus

International trade is based on resources that one country needs and another can provide. Each country in the world possesses different resources. By specializing in the production of certain goods and services, nations can use their resources more efficiently. Specialization and trade can benefit all nations.

Key Terms

absolute advantage
comparative advantage
law of comparative advantage
export
import

Have you logged on to a computer today? Ridden in a car or bus? Bought a new sweatshirt or jacket? Chances are these items all have one thing in common. They—or some of their components—were likely made outside the United States.

We know that the United States produces many products, such as jeans, machinery, and some types of computers. We don't, however, produce most of the world's video game systems or VCRs. Why? The answer lies with resources and their distribution. The unequal distribution of resources prevents countries from producing everything their citizens need and want. This is also why we trade.

Resource Distribution

As you read in Chapter 1, the resources that are used to make goods and services are called the factors of production. They include natural resources (land), human resources (labor), and capital resources.

Natural Resources

As you have read, natural resources include those materials found in nature that people use to make goods and provide services. Natural resources include arable land (land that can be farmed), mineral deposits, oil and gas deposits, water, and raw materials like timber.

It is easy to see why a region with fertile soil, such as the central United States, is likely to have an economy based on agriculture. Similarly, you can predict that a region with large oil and natural gas reserves—such as Southwest Asia—is likely to have an economy based on income from the sale of these resources.

Natural resources, as well as climate and location, help determine what goods and services an economy produces. They are not, however, the only influences.

Human Capital

You learned in Chapter 1 that human capital is the knowledge and skills gained by a worker through education and experience. Every job requires some human capital. To be a surgeon you must learn about anatomy and acquire surgical skills. To be a taxi driver, you must know the layout of the city streets.

How do you measure the amount of human capital available in a country? One measure is the literacy rate, or percentage

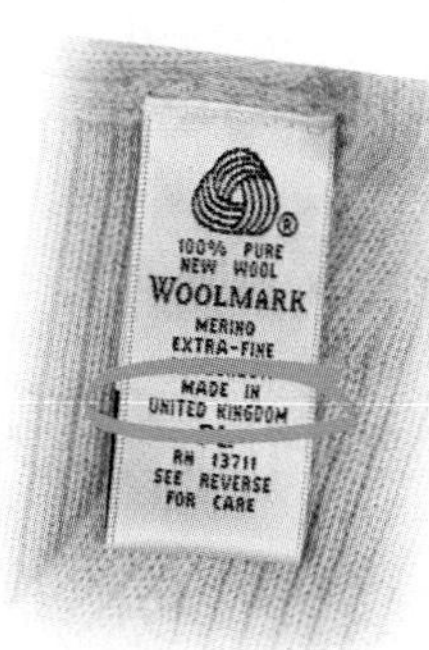

▲ **Many items of clothing are traded internationally.**

Section 1

Why Nations Trade

Objectives You may wish to call students' attention to the objectives in the Section Preview. The objectives are reflected in the main headings of the section.

Bellringer Ask students to recall times when they have traded parts of their lunches with other students. Have volunteers explain their motivation for trading. Lead students to see that trade occurs whenever each of two parties has something that the other party wants or needs.

Vocabulary Builder Ask students to read Section 1 to discover the meanings of the key terms. Have students use each term in a sentence that demonstrates understanding of the concept.

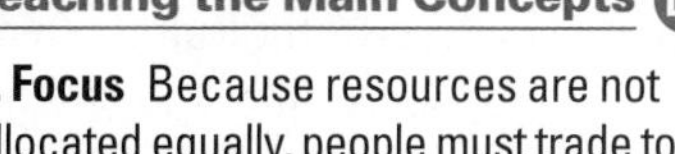

Teaching the Main Concepts (L3)

1. Focus Because resources are not allocated equally, people must trade to satisfy wants and needs. Ask students to identify trades in their everyday lives.

2. Instruct Discuss the types of resources used to produce goods and services and how their unequal distribution leads to trade. Help students understand how the law of comparative advantage enables trading partners to determine which goods and services to produce. Finally, discuss the conduct of trade between the United States and its trading partners and how such trade affects employment.

3. Close/Reteach Remind students that without trade, nations would lack many of the goods and services necessary for economic growth and the well-being of their citizens. Have students make a list of the items they use every day that are produced in other countries.

Building Key Concepts: Graphing the Main Idea

Trade and **Specialization** To build understanding of the concepts of **trade** and **specialization,** have students complete a tree map graphic organizer like the one at right. Remind students that a tree map shows an outline for a main topic, main ideas, and supporting details. Have students place the title "Why Nations Trade" in the top box and the main headings of the section in the boxes below. Boxes below the heading should include supporting details.

Section Reading Support Transparencies A template and the answers for this graphic organizer can be found in Chapter 17, Section 1 of the Section Reading Support Transparency System.

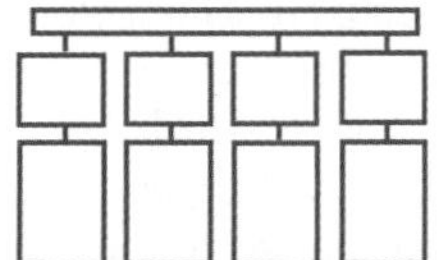

 **Guided Reading and Review**
Unit 7 folder, p. 2 asks students to identify the main ideas of the section and to define or identify key terms.

Differentiated Instruction 
Organize the class into groups of four to six students. Tell each group to skim the section material on resource distribution. Then tell groups to plan and perform a five-minute skit that illustrates how unequal resource distribution affects trade.

Differentiated Instruction (L4)
You may wish to have students add the following to their portfolios. David Ricardo was an influential political economist of the early 1800s. Assign students to investigate his theories about comparative advantage and other economic issues. Ask them to write an essay that explains Ricardo's contribution to economic theory. Have students share their work with the class. GT

Economics Assessment Rubric
Economics Assessment Rubrics folder, pp. 6–7 provides sample evaluation materials for a writing assignment.

Answer to . . .
Building Key Concepts Resources determine the capital that is available to a nation and what goods a nation can produce most efficiently.

Go Online
PHSchool.com
Web Code: mng-7172

Figure 17.1 **Resource Distribution**

	India	Peru	United Kingdom	United States
Total area (sq km)	3,287,590	1,285,220	244,820	9,629,091
Arable land (sq km)	1,664,986	38,400	60,398	1,740,202
Natural resources	Coal, iron ore, manganese, mica, bauxite, titanium ore, chromite, natural gas, diamonds, petroleum, limestone, arable land	Copper, silver, gold, petroleum, timber, fish, iron ore, coal, phosphate, potash, hydropower	Coal, petroleum, natural gas, tin, limestone, iron ore, salt, clay, chalk, gypsum, lead, silica, arable land	Coal, copper, lead, phosphates, molybdenum, uranium, bauxite, gold, iron, mercury, nickel, potash, silver, tungsten, zinc petroleum, natural gas, timber
Population	1.1 billion	27,949,639	59,778,002	291,765,169
Labor force	406 million	7.5 million	29.7 million	147 million
Literacy rate	52%	88.3%	99%	97%
Telephones*	27 per 1,000 people	64 per 1,000 people	585 per 1,000 people	697 per 1,000 people
Airports	335	239	470	14,695

*non-cellular
Sources: *CIA World Factbook*; U.S. Census Bureau

These countries each possess different natural, human, and physical resources.
Specialization How do a nation's resources determine what that nation produces?

of people over 15 who can read and write. A country with a high literacy rate is likely to have an educated, skilled work force.

Physical Capital

Physical capital includes objects made by men and women that are used to produce goods and services. Examples include factories, machinery, and computers. Physical capital also includes the public infrastructure, such as roads and bridges, that allows raw materials and finished goods to be manufactured and transported.

Economic Activity Patterns

Five major economic activities are producing, exchanging, consuming, saving, and investing. Patterns of production, distribution, and use develop as the economic activities become concentrated in urban, industrial, or agricultural areas. Geographic and human factors also influence patterns of economic activity. Ski resorts develop in the mountains, farming in the valleys, and mining where there are ore deposits. Saving and investment also follow patterns, becoming concentrated in areas of potential growth.

Unequal Resource Distribution

Each country in the world possesses different types and quantities of land, labor, and capital resources. Some of these resources are determined by nature. Others are not. A nation's culture and history affect its human and physical resources. For example, if a nation has experienced prolonged civil wars, it may not have been able to develop its resources fully.

The table in Figure 17.1 provides data on different types of resources in selected countries. You can see that the availability of resources differs greatly from country to country. For example, the United Kingdom has over twice as many airports as Peru despite its smaller land area, suggesting that the United Kingdom has more physical capital than Peru. Economists can confirm this fact with additional data. As you might expect, because countries differ in resources, they also differ in their capacities to produce different goods and services.

The Need for Trade

Specialization occurs when producers—either individuals or nations—decide to produce only certain goods and services,

Econ 101: Key Concepts Made Easy

Specialization To help students understand **comparative advantage,** ask them to think about the qualities that make a sports team successful. Explain that success is assured when talented people with differing abilities combine their strengths efficiently and effectively. Trade works the same way. When each trading partner produces only those goods and services which that partner can produce most efficiently, it is bringing its strengths, or comparative advantage, to the marketplace.

Ask students to think about where many consumer electronics, such as VCRs, are made. Ask them to write a brief explanation of why the United States imports many of these items. Have them share their responses with the class. *(Students may suggest that Japan produces many of these items because it has the technology to do so at a lower cost than the United States.)*

rather than producing all the goods and services they need. Specialization is determined by a nation's natural resources and by its human and physical capital. For example, the world's wheat is grown in regions with a cool climate. In the United States, we grow wheat, soybeans, and other crops for which we have appropriate soil and climate conditions. We cannot, however, produce diamonds or coffee.

When nations specialize in producing only certain goods, they obtain the goods they don't or can't produce through trade. For example, Costa Rica specializes in producing coffee and exports a large quantity of coffee beans. The country then uses the money it earns from coffee exports to buy products that it does not produce.

What about a nation that enjoys an abundance of resources, including a rich natural environment, a well-educated work force, and the latest technologies? It can, in theory, produce almost all that it needs by itself, without trade. If you were in charge of such a country, would you engage in large-scale trading? Or, would you decide to rely mostly on your country's own resources and be largely self-sufficient? Although self-sufficiency may sound appealing, it actually is better for countries to specialize in some products and trade for others.

Figure 17.2 Productivity per Hour

	T-shirts per hour	Birdhouses per hour
Kate	6	2
Carl	1	1

Kate has an absolute advantage in producing both T-shirts and birdhouses.
Specialization In which good should each person specialize?

As shown in Figure 17.2, Kate can either print six T-shirts or make two birdhouses per hour. Carl can print one T-shirt or make one birdhouse per hour. In other words, Kate is more productive than Carl in making both T-shirts and birdhouses. In economic terms, Kate has an absolute advantage over Carl in producing both goods.

Suppose that each person is initially self-sufficient. Both Kate and Carl produce their own T-shirts and their own birdhouses. Because Kate enjoys an absolute advantage in both goods, should she remain self-sufficient? Or would Kate be better off if she specialized in either T-shirts or birdhouses? What should Carl produce—T-shirts, birdhouses, or both?

Countries have to face the same sorts of questions as individuals. Should a wealthy country with many resources be self-sufficient, or should it specialize in a few products and trade for the goods it doesn't produce? How does a poorer nation decide what to produce? The answer to these questions lies with the concept of comparative advantage.

Absolute and Comparative Advantage

Trading relationships benefit countries with abundant resources as well as countries with few resources. To see why, you need to look at two related concepts—absolute advantage and comparative advantage.

Absolute Advantage

A person or nation has an **absolute advantage** when it can produce more of a given product using a given amount of resources. A simple example can illustrate this idea.

Suppose that two of your friends, Carl and Kate, want to make some extra money. They decide to print designs on T-shirts and make birdhouses.

Comparative Advantage

Early in the nineteenth century, British political economist David Ricardo argued that the key to determining which country should produce which goods is opportunity cost. Remember that the opportunity cost is what you give up in order to produce a certain product. The nation that has the lower opportunity cost in producing a

absolute advantage *the ability to produce more of a given product using a given amount of resources*

Background

Economics in History

One of the world's best-known trade routes illustrates the far-reaching effects of international trade. The Silk Road was a caravan route that stretched 4,000 miles, from eastern Asia to the Mediterranean, linking the two great civilizations of China and Rome. The route began at Xi'an in eastern China, followed the Great Wall to the northwest, bypassed the Takla Makan, traversed mountains and rivers, and ended at the Mediterranean Sea.

The caravans that traveled the Silk Road were laden with exotic goods. From Europe came gold, silver, wools, and wine. From Asia came Chinese spices, silk, and other luxury goods.

The Silk Road caravans carried more than just goods from one trading outpost to another. Works of art, customs, and religious ideas were also passengers on this fabled route. Buddhist missionaries, for example, traveled the Silk Road from India to China, bringing the principles of Buddhism. Likewise, Muslim religious leaders from the Middle East brought Islamic beliefs and practices eastward.

Transparency Resource Package Economics Concepts, 17A: Absolute and Comparative Advantage

Block Scheduling Strategies

Consider these suggestions to take advantage of extended class time:

- Have students search the Foreign Trade Statistics Web site. Ask them to choose a set of statistics from the site and to use the Simulations and Data Graphing CD-ROM to create a graph of the data. Have students use the links provided in the *Economics: Principles in Action* segment in the Social Studies area at the following Web site: **www.phschool.com**
- Have students work alone or in pairs to find export and import statistics for four countries. Then have them create bar graphs that give comparative data for their four countries.
- Arrange a conversation about trade between the class and a trade representative. This conversation can take place in person, over a speakerphone, or as a live Internet chat.

Answer to . . .

Building Key Concepts Kate should specialize in T-shirts; Carl should specialize in birdhouses.

Meeting NCEE Standards

Use the following benchmark activity from the **Voluntary National Content Standards in Economics** to evaluate student understanding of **Standard 6.**

Apply the concepts of opportunity cost and comparative advantage to the following problem: The Netherlands can produce in one day either four drill presses or eight embroidered tablecloths. Using the same amount of resources, Portugal can produce either two drill presses or seven embroidered tablecloths. Which country should specialize in drill presses and import tablecloths, and why? Which country should specialize in tablecloths and import drill presses, and why?

Kate gives up three T-shirts for each birdhouse she produces. Carl gives up only one T-shirt for each birdhouse he produces.
Opportunity Costs
What are Kate and Carl's opportunity costs for T-shirts and birdhouses?

Figure 17.3 **Opportunity Costs for Kate and Carl**

	Opportunity cost of a T-shirt	Opportunity cost of a birdhouse
Kate	$\frac{1}{3}$ birdhouse	3 T-shirts
Carl	1 birdhouse	1 T-shirt

certain good has a comparative advantage in producing that good. A country has a **comparative advantage** in the product that it can produce most efficiently given all the products it could choose to produce. It is the nation with the comparative advantage—not necessarily the absolute advantage—that should specialize in producing that good.

According to the **law of comparative advantage,** a nation is better off when it produces goods and services for which it has a comparative advantage. Each nation can then use the money it earns selling those goods to buy other goods that it cannot produce as efficiently. We can use the example of Kate and Carl to illustrate the benefits from trade that is based on comparative advantage.

comparative advantage *the ability to produce a product most efficiently given all the other products that could be produced*

law of comparative advantage *the idea that a nation is better off when it produces goods and services for which it has a comparative advantage*

The Importance of Opportunity Cost

To determine comparative advantage in the example involving Kate and Carl, you need to look at the opportunity costs of producing T-shirts and birdhouses.

- *Kate's opportunity costs* In an hour, Kate can make either six T-shirts or two birdhouses. She therefore sacrifices three T-shirts for every birdhouse she produces. In other words, the opportunity cost of a birdhouse is the three T-shirts she could have produced instead. Conversely, the opportunity cost of a T-shirt is one third of a birdhouse.
- *Carl's opportunity costs* Carl sacrifices only one T-shirt for every birdhouse. His opportunity cost for a birdhouse is the one T-shirt that he could have produced instead.

As you have read, each person should produce the good for which he or she has a comparative advantage—that is, a lower opportunity cost than another person. Carl's opportunity cost for producing a birdhouse (one T-shirt) is lower than Kate's (three T-shirts), so it is sensible for Carl to produce birdhouses. Kate's opportunity cost for producing a T-shirt (one third of a birdhouse) is lower than Carl's (one birdhouse), so Kate should produce T-shirts.

Why is it sensible for Carl to specialize in birdhouses? Although Kate has an absolute advantage in making birdhouses, Carl has a comparative advantage in birdhouses because he has a lower opportunity cost. Remember that in order to make a birdhouse, Kate has to give up three T-shirts. In order to make a birdhouse, Carl has to give up only one T-shirt.

Benefits for Trading Partners

As you might remember from trading baseball cards or small toys when you were younger, trade usually involves bargaining. Each side tries to make the best deal it can. In a modern economy, we don't exchange goods directly—we use money. The main principle, however, remains the same: both sides agree on a price that benefits both.

When Kate wants a birdhouse, she can either produce it herself or produce some shirts and trade some of them for a birdhouse made by Carl. Suppose Kate and Carl agree to trade two T-shirts for one birdhouse. In this case, Kate will be better off producing T-shirts and trading for a birdhouse. That's because in the time she could have taken to produce her own birdhouse, Kate can produce three T-shirts. Once she pays Carl two T-shirts to get a birdhouse, she will still have one T-shirt left over. In other words, trade makes her better off by one T-shirt. (See Figure 17.4.)

When Carl wants two more T-shirts, he can either make them himself, or make some birdhouses and trade some of them for shirts made by Kate. If Kate and Carl agree to trade one birdhouse for two T-shirts, Carl will be better off producing birdhouses and trading for shirts. In the time he could have taken to produce two T-shirts for himself, he can produce two

Answer to . . .

Building Key Concepts Kate's opportunity cost for producing a birdhouse is production of three T-shirts. Her opportunity cost for producing a T-shirt is production of one-third of a birdhouse. Carl's opportunity cost for producing a birdhouse is production of one T-shirt. His opportunity cost for producing a T-shirt is production of one birdhouse.

Preparing for Standardized Tests

Have students read the section titled "Comparative Advantage" and then answer the question below.

Which of the following is a restatement of the law of comparative advantage?

A Nations should produce those goods that they have experience in producing.
B Nations should produce those goods for which they have the largest amounts of resources.
C Nations should produce those goods that they can produce with little labor.
(D) Nations should produce those goods and services that they can produce most efficiently.

birdhouses. Once he pays one birdhouse to Kate to get two T-shirts, he will still have one birdhouse left over. Trade makes him better off by one birdhouse.

Kate and Carl both benefit from trade. Each person specializes in the production of the good for which he or she has a comparative advantage, and then trades for the other good. The same is true with nations—both sides benefit from trade.

Comparative Advantage and Trade

The lessons from this example apply to trade between nations. According to Ricardo, the nation that has the lower opportunity cost in producing a good has a comparative advantage in producing that good. Remember that comparative advantage is the ability of one nation to produce a good at a lower opportunity cost than that of another nation. It is the nation with the comparative advantage—not necessarily the absolute advantage—that should specialize in producing that good.

Suppose two countries, A and B, produce bananas and sugar. If A must sacrifice 2 tons of sugar to produce a ton of bananas, the opportunity cost of a ton of bananas is 2 tons of sugar. If the opportunity cost of a ton of bananas in B is 3 tons of sugar, A has a comparative advantage in producing bananas. That's because A's opportunity cost (2 tons of sugar) is lower than B's (3 tons of sugar). If A specializes in producing bananas, it could use the money earned from selling bananas to buy other goods and services.

International trade leads to greater interdependence. When countries are interdependent, events in one country's economy influence the other economies as well. Mexico and the United States have become more interdependent since 1994.

The United States and Trade

The United States enjoys a comparative advantage in producing many goods and services. What, then, is its position as an

Differentiated Instruction L4

Ask students to research and write about the roles played by President Millard Fillmore and Commodore Matthew Perry in opening Japanese ports to trade with the United States. Have students answer the following questions in their reports: Why did the United States believe that this trade was vital to its interests? How did Perry convince the reluctant Japanese to honor his request? Was this trade based on mutual need? GT

Differentiated Instruction 

Have students find out which five countries are the top exporters of goods and services to the United States and which five countries are the top importers of goods and services from the United States. Have students create two circle graphs that illustrate the relative percentage of exports and imports for each country. Students may examine circle graphs in the text to get ideas on how to compose their own graphs.

Figure 17.4 **Benefits From Specialization and Trade for Carl and Kate**

Carl			Kate		
Specialization	Trade	Net Effect	Specialization	Trade	Net Effect
Carl specializes, switching 2 hours from T-shirt production to birdhouse production.	Carl trades 1 birdhouse for 2 T-shirts.	Net effect is same number of T-shirts and 1 more birdhouse.	Kate specializes, switching one half-hour from birdhouse production to T-shirt production.	Kate trades 2 T-shirts for 1 birdhouse.	Net effect is the same number of birdhouses and 1 more T-shirt.

Kate and Carl both benefit from specialization and trade.
Trade What is the net effect of trade for Kate and Carl? Why are they both better off trading?

Interdisciplinary Connections: History

Trading With the Pilgrims Not long after the Pilgrims landed at Plymouth Rock, they realized that the Native Americans in that part of North America had commodities and skills that they themselves lacked. Soon the two groups were trading to their mutual benefit.

Making the Connection Have students use American history textbooks and other sources to research the nature of this trade. Ask students to find out how trade was conducted, what goods and services were exchanged, and how each group benefited.

Answer to . . .

Building Key Concepts The net effect for Carl is one birdhouse. The net effect for Kate is one T-shirt. By trading, each partner can produce the largest possible amount of goods at the lowest opportunity cost and has access to more kinds of goods.

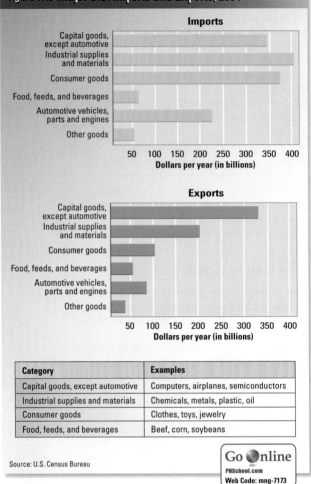

Figure 17.5 Major U.S. Imports and Exports, 2004

Imports

Capital goods, except automotive
Industrial supplies and materials
Consumer goods
Food, feeds, and beverages
Automotive vehicles, parts and engines
Other goods

50 100 150 200 250 300 350 400
Dollars per year (in billions)

Exports

Capital goods, except automotive
Industrial supplies and materials
Consumer goods
Food, feeds, and beverages
Automotive vehicles, parts and engines
Other goods

50 100 150 200 250 300 350 400
Dollars per year (in billions)

Category	Examples
Capital goods, except automotive	Computers, airplanes, semiconductors
Industrial supplies and materials	Chemicals, metals, plastic, oil
Consumer goods	Clothes, toys, jewelry
Food, feeds, and beverages	Beef, corn, soybeans

Source: U.S. Census Bureau

Go Online
PHSchool.com
Web Code: mng-7173

The United States is both the world's largest importer and its largest exporter. **Trade Judging from these graphs, does the United States export more than it imports or import more than it exports? Explain.**

export *a good that is sent to another country for sale*

import *a good that is brought in from another country for sale*

importer and exporter on the world market? In the language of international trade, an **export** is a good sent to another country for sale. An **import** is a good brought in from another country for sale.

As you can see from the map on page 545 of the Databank, the main U.S. trading partners are Canada, Mexico, Japan, and China. Trade with China has grown tremendously in recent years.

The United States as an Exporter

The United States is the world's leading exporter, followed by Germany and Japan. One reason for the success of the United States as an exporter is the wide range of its exports, from telecommunications equipment to soybeans. Another reason is that the United States has a commanding lead in manufacturing such products as computer software, medical equipment, and other advanced technology.

The United States is also in a good position to benefit from increased trade in services. Goods make up the bulk of international trade, but services are also traded on the world market. These include education, information services, computer and data processing, financial services, and medical care. Exports of services have grown rapidly over the last decade. The United States is the world's top exporter of services, so it stands to gain significantly from this trend.

The United States as an Importer

Besides being the world's largest exporter, the United States is also the world's top importer, and by a significant amount. The United States imports nearly $1.4 trillion in goods and services, or 17.3 percent of the world's total. That amount exceeds total imports for Germany and Japan combined, the world's largest importers after the United States.

The Effects of Trade on Employment

Trade allows nations to specialize in producing a limited number of goods while consuming a greater variety of goods. However, specialization can also dramatically change a nation's employment patterns.

Specialization and Employment

To help you better understand the effects of international trade on employment, think back to the example of Kate and Carl. As you have read, Kate can make six T-shirts or two birdhouses by herself in an hour.

Differentiated Instruction 

Have students use the bar graphs on this page as well as information in the text to create a poster titled "U.S. Trade." The poster should identify the major exports and imports of the United States as well as the major trading partners of the United States. Tell students to include a world map with a key that also displays trade information.

Differentiated Instruction 

(Reteaching) Have students create cause-and-effect charts that demonstrate understanding of the effects of trade on employment. Encourage students to use specific real-life examples whenever possible. Display these charts in the classroom.

Databank, pp. 532–547 contains a variety of charts and graphs that can be used to extend and reinforce graphing skills.

Transparency Resource Package
Economics Concepts, 17B: U.S. Trade Partners
Economics Concepts, 17C: Major U.S. Exports and Imports

Answer to . . .

Building Key Concepts The United States imports more than it exports. Added together, the bars on the import graph represent a larger number of dollars than do those on the export graph.

Interdisciplinary Connections: Science

Trading Ideas When people think of trade, they usually focus on the exchange of goods and services. The exchange of ideas, however, is also a part of international trade. Scientists from many parts of the world, for example, regularly exchange information that often leads to exciting breakthroughs in technology development and medical research.

Making the Connection Ask students to find out how scientists trade information. Have them write a brief report describing each method of information trading. *(Students should report that the scientists' "marketplace" includes scientific journals, professional conferences, and specialized Internet forums.)*

Suppose she hires Ari to help her build birdhouses. She later realizes that she should specialize only in T-shirts since that is where her comparative advantage lies. She no longer needs Ari to help her. Unfortunately, Ari's only skill is making birdhouses.

Ari now faces three possibilities: unemployment, retraining, or relocating to a part of the country where his skills are in demand. Ari may be able to find a training program and learn to make T-shirts or another product. He might even find himself better off than he was making birdhouses.

If Ari relocates, he may or may not be better off. How well he does depends on housing prices, the quality of his new neighborhood, the impact on his family, and a variety of other factors.

Government assistance is often available to help retrain laid-off workers for new jobs or to help them relocate to fit shifts in employment patterns. However, especially in the case of older workers or workers with families, retraining or relocation is not an easy (or sometimes not a possible) option. Some workers may become unemployed or be forced to take lower-paying jobs.

Specialization and Employment in the United States

In the United States, significant changes in employment patterns have occurred in the past two decades as a result of specialization and international trade. For example, during the 1970s, specialization, new technologies like robotics, and high productivity gave Japan a comparative advantage in producing automobiles. As a result, Japanese cars became less expensive than many comparable American-made cars. As more consumers bought Japanese cars, many American workers lost jobs in automobile-producing centers such as Detroit.

Many other shifts in employment have also taken place in the United States in recent decades as a result of world trade and other factors. The overall result has been a shift in population from the manufacturing states of the Midwest to the Sunbelt states of the South and Southwest.

▲ Workers who lose their jobs can often learn new skills.

Section 1 Assessment

Progress Monitoring *Online*
For: Self-quiz with vocabulary practice
Web Code: mna-7175

Key Terms and Main Ideas

1. How do nations obtain goods and services for which they lack adequate resources?
2. Susan grows coffee in a North Dakota greenhouse under sunlamps. Growing coffee this way takes a lot of effort and money. She also grows sunflowers, which are easy to grow in the dry climate in which she lives. In which crop does she probably have a **comparative advantage?**
3. Why is a nation with abundant resources better off trading than being self-sufficient?
4. Specialization and trade can result in shifting employment patterns. **(a)** What possibilities are available to people who lose their jobs due to changes in employment patterns? **(b)** What are the advantages and disadvantages of each possibility?

Applying Economic Concepts

5. ***Critical Thinking*** Suppose a nation has a great deal of human capital but few natural resources. In what kinds of products might it specialize?
6. ***Try This*** Make a Productivity Table for yourself and a friend using the table on page 443 as a model. Choose your own goods and estimate production times. Then decide where you and your friend have a comparative advantage.
7. ***Using the Databank*** Turn to the map showing United States trading partners on page 545. Considering geographical location and resources, give reasons to explain why the countries shown are major U.S. trading partners.

For: Research Activity
Visit: PHSchool.com
Web Code: mnd-7171

GTE Guide to the Essentials
Chapter 17, Section 1, p. 72 provides support for students who need additional review of the section content. Spanish support is available in the Spanish edition of the guide on p. 72.

Quiz Unit 7 folder, p. 3 includes questions to check students' understanding of Section 1 content.

Presentation Pro CD-ROM
Quiz provides multiple-choice questions to check students' understanding of Section 1 content.

Answers to . . .

Section 1 Assessment

1. Nations acquire necessary goods and services through trade.
2. Susan has a comparative advantage with sunflowers, since she can produce them in greater amounts more easily.
3. Trade allows that nation to specialize and produce the most goods at the lowest opportunity cost.
4. (a) People may relocate or retrain. (b) Relocation could lead to better opportunities, but will be disruptive. Retraining may also lead to better opportunities, but could result in a less desirable job.
5. This nation may specialize in providing services rather than goods.
6. Answers will vary but should show clear understanding of comparative advantage.
7. Reasons for U.S. trading partner nations include: Canada and Mexico are neighboring countries and signatories in NAFTA; Germany and Japan are highly industrialized countries with many products to trade; China is a newly-industrialized country very interested in building its worldwide trade; the U.K. and France are traditional trading partners.

Progress Monitoring *Online*
For additional assessment, have students access Progress Monitoring Online at **Web Code:** mna-7175

Go Online PHSchool.com Typing in the Web Code when prompted will bring students directly to detailed instructions for this activity.

Skills for LIFE

Creating a Multimedia Presentation

1. Focus Students will create a written, oral, and visual presentation of social studies information. They will plan a multimedia presentation by choosing a topic, investigating sources of information, planning a script, and selecting visuals, text, and music.

2. Instruct Discuss with students the importance of media in today's world. Stress that messages can often be delivered more effectively by combining media. Then have students work through the three steps outlined in the skills feature.

3. Close/Reteach To provide additional practice, see the Economic Skills Activity below.

Economic Skills Activity
Unit 7 folder, p. 8, "Creating a Multimedia Presentation," asks students to prepare a multimedia presentation.

Social Studies Skills Tutor CD-ROM offers interactive practice in critical thinking and reading, visual analysis, and communication.

Answers

1. (a) Possible topics related to the global economy and its effects on people living in their region. (b) They should present an outline with logical divisions.
(c) Their outlines should show how these are related.
2. (a) Advantages include ease of coordinating resources and less time spent recording interviewees. Disadvantages include possible monotony of single monologue and requiring too much of one person.
(b) Students should be able to support their opinions adequately.
3. (a) They should create a list showing good planning skills and an understanding of the material. (b) Perhaps interviewing local politicians, business owners, and residents. (c) They should explain their reasoning logically.

Additional Practice

Students should prepare a complete preproduction chart like the one shown.

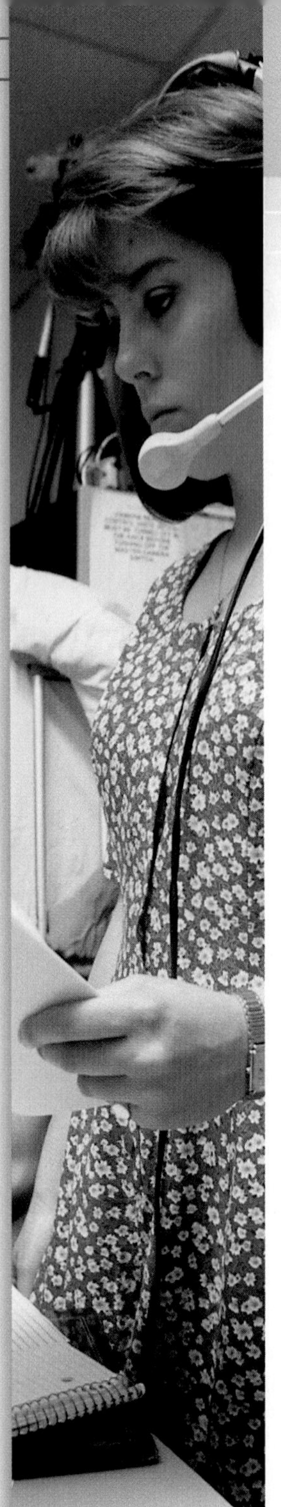

Skills for LIFE

Creating a Multimedia Presentation

Multimedia presentations communicate information in a variety of forms, both audio and visual. The preproduction, or planning, stage of a presentation requires a considerable amount of work if the production stage and final product are to go well. During the preproduction stage, the producer drafts an outline and script, decides what media to use and where, arranges interviews or photography sessions, selects images, and chooses music.

Suppose that you have been assigned to produce a multimedia presentation on how the global economy affects the lives of people in your region. Use the following steps and a copy of the preproduction topic analysis sheet below to prepare your presentation.

1. **Plan your content.** Select a topic for your presentation. (**a**) What possible topics might you focus on? (**b**) How could you break up your presentation into different segments? (**c**) How do these segments connect with one another?

PREPRODUCTION TOPIC ANALYSIS SHEET

Assignment: The impact of the global economy on the local community

Possible topics:
1. __________
2. __________
3. __________
My choice: __________
Sources for topic information:__________
Intended audience: __________
Information to be presented: __________

Segment description and sequence:
1. __________
2. __________
3. __________
Mood:__________
Type of narration: __________
Graphics/illustrations, interviews, music
Segment #1 __________
Segment #2 __________
Segment #3 __________

2. **Plan a script.** You must decide whether to use a running commentary by a single narrator, comments by several interviewees, or a combination. (**a**) What are the advantages and disadvantages of using a single narrator? (**b**) Which script style do you feel would be most appropriate for a presentation on the local impact of the global economy, and why?

3. **Make a list of images, interviews, and music.** The images you choose will help viewers visualize your message. (**a**) What images would fit the content and mood of each segment? (**b**) Which people could you interview? (**c**) What pieces or types of music would best enhance the mood of your presentation?

Additional Practice

Suppose that you are planning a multimedia presentation on some aspect of life at your school. Prepare a preproduction chart like the one shown here for your presentation.

Interdisciplinary Connections: Literature

Bringing Literature to Film Literary works are often brought to life on film. Filmmakers present personal interpretations of literature by selecting settings, costumes, and music that mirror their feelings about the work. In addition, they employ the techniques of filmmaking—camera movement, order of scenes, camera angles—to define their visions further.

Have students work through the following activity: Have each student select a poem that has special meaning, perhaps because of its rich imagery, its hypnotic rhythms, or its playful rhymes. Ask students to think about how they would present their interpretations of the poems on videotape, and then to plan such a presentation. Have students consider the following questions: What visual effects would they use to represent the poem's imagery? What music would best set the tone? How would they want the narrator to read the poem? How would the presentation flow, from the opening scene to the final shot?

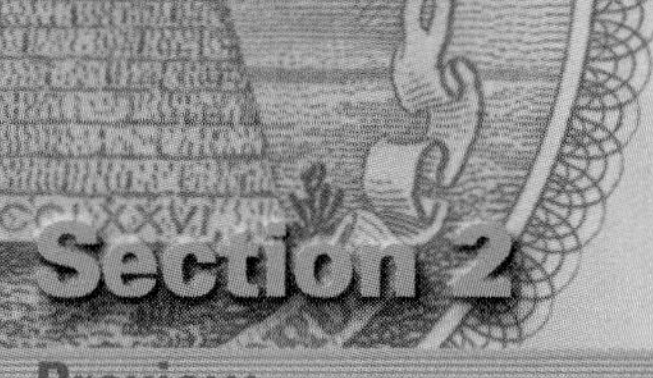

Section 2 Trade Barriers and Agreements

Preview

Objectives

After studying this section you will be able to:

1. **Define** various types of trade barriers.
2. **Compare** the effects of free trade and trade barriers on economic activities.
3. **Understand** arguments in favor of protectionism.
4. **Evaluate** the benefits and costs of participation in international trade agreements.
5. **Explain** the role of multinationals in the global market.

Section Focus

The free exchange of goods can be restricted by barriers to trade, such as tariffs, quotas, and voluntary export restraints. International trade agreements and organizations work to reduce trade barriers.

Key Terms

- trade barrier
- import quota
- voluntary export restraint (VER)
- customs duty
- tariff
- trade war
- protectionism
- infant industry
- international free trade agreement
- World Trade Organization (WTO)
- European Union (EU)
- euro
- free-trade zone
- NAFTA

So far, our discussion of trade has assumed that international trade is not subject to government regulations. Many people, however, argue that governments should regulate trade in order to protect certain industries and jobs from foreign competition.

Trade Barriers

Most countries have some form of trade barriers that hinder free trade. A **trade barrier,** or trade restriction, is a means of preventing a foreign product or service from freely entering a nation's territory. Trade barriers take three common forms: import quotas, voluntary export restraints, and tariffs.

Import Quotas

An **import quota** is a limit on the amount of a good that can be imported. For example, the United States limits the annual amount of raw (unprocessed) cotton coming into the country from other nations. Quotas limit India and Pakistan to 908,764 kilograms of cotton, China to 621,780 kilograms, and Egypt and Sudan to 355,532 kilograms. The United States will accept no more than these amounts of cotton from these countries. Other nations that produce cotton must also observe quotas of various amounts.

Voluntary Export Restraints

An import quota is a law. A **voluntary export restraint (VER)** is a self-imposed limitation on the number of products that are shipped to a particular country. Under a voluntary export restraint, a country voluntarily decreases its exports in an attempt to

trade barrier *a means of preventing a foreign product or service from freely entering a nation's territory*

import quota *a limit on the amount of a good that can be imported*

voluntary export restraint (VER) *a self-imposed limitation on the number of products shipped to a particular country*

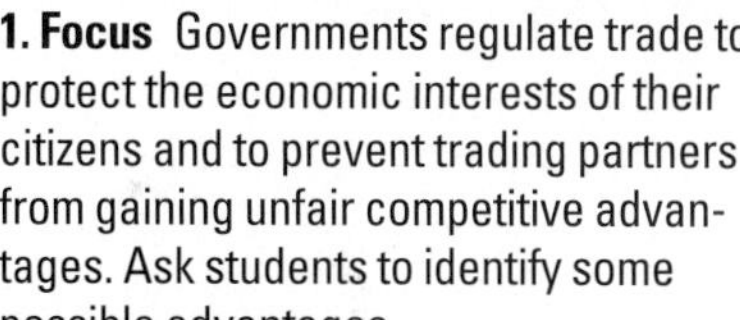

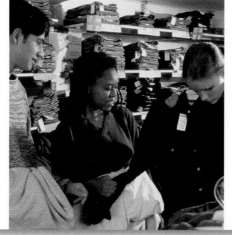

◀ **The cotton used to make much of the clothing Americans wear is subject to import quotas.**

Graphing the Main Idea

Trade To build understanding of the concepts of **trade,** have students create two web graphic organizers like the one shown at the right. One should show the types and effects of trade barriers. The other should list arguments in favor of protectionism. Remind students that a web illustrates a main idea and its supporting details.

Section Reading Support Transparencies A template and the answers for this graphic organizer can be found in Chapter 17, Section 2 of the Section Reading Support Transparency System.

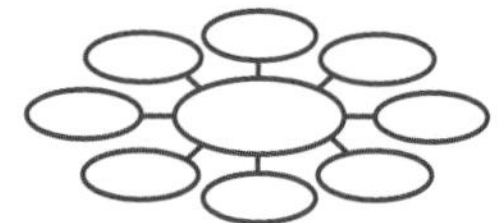

Section 2

Trade Barriers and Agreements

Objectives You may wish to call students' attention to the objectives in the Section Preview. The objectives are reflected in the main headings of the section.

Bellringer Discuss with students how the flow of automobile traffic would be affected if there were no traffic laws or signs. Would drivers regulate their own behavior? Explain that in this section they will learn how the flow of trade is regulated by national and international policies.

Vocabulary Builder Have students create a matching quiz with the key terms from the Section Preview. Ask them to exchange quizzes and try to match each term with its definition.

Lesson Plan

Teaching the Main Concepts (L3)

1. Focus Governments regulate trade to protect the economic interests of their citizens and to prevent trading partners from gaining unfair competitive advantages. Ask students to identify some possible advantages.

2. Instruct Begin by discussing with students the various types of trade barriers governments impose to regulate trade. Lead students to understand that trade barriers have both positive and negative consequences. Go over the arguments for and against protectionism. Finally, discuss the various agreements and organizations that have been created to control international trade.

3. Close/Reteach Remind students that nations employ a variety of trade barriers and become partners in trade organizations and agreements to regulate the conduct of international trade. Ask them to speculate on what might happen if there were no global trade barriers.

Guided Reading and Review
Unit 7 folder, p. 4 asks students to identify the main ideas of the section and to define or identify key terms.

Transparency Resource Package
Economics Concepts, 17D: Trade Barriers

Differentiated Instruction 

Have students work in groups of three or four to create two examples of each of the types of trade barriers discussed on pp. 449–451. (The examples need not be real, but they should be realistic.) Have students write each example on a separate slip of paper. Then have volunteers from each group take turns reading their examples. The rest of the class should attempt to identify from the description what kind of trade barrier is described.

Meeting NCEE Standards

Use the following benchmark activity from the **Voluntary National Content Standards in Economics** to evaluate student understanding of **Standard 5.**

Analyze the political and economic implications of a proposed ban on imported television sets.

Answer to...

Building Key Concepts Tariffs were heavily used through the mid-1930s, then they began to decline. In recent decades, tariff rates have reached their lowest levels.

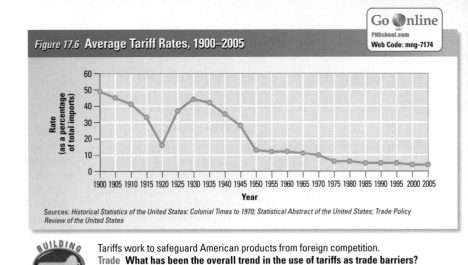

Go Online
PHSchool.com
Web Code: mng-7174

Figure 17.6 **Average Tariff Rates, 1900–2005**

Sources: *Historical Statistics of the United States: Colonial Times to 1970; Statistical Abstract of the United States; Trade Policy Review of the United States*

Tariffs work to safeguard American products from foreign competition.
Trade **What has been the overall trend in the use of tariffs as trade barriers?**

customs duty *a tax on certain items purchased abroad*

tariff *a tax on imported goods*

reduce the chances that the importing country will set up trade barriers.

Tariffs

If you have traveled to a foreign country, you might have had to pay a tax called a **customs duty** on certain items you purchased abroad. You might also have seen "duty free" stores at international borders and airports selling luxury items like perfume and chocolate. Countries have agreed that items purchased in these shops will be free of customs duty.

Customs duty is one kind of **tariff,** or tax on imported goods. As you read in Chapter 14, both individuals and businesses have to pay tariffs. For example, the United States collects tariffs on steel, foreign-made cars, and many other products that are brought into the country. As you can see from Figure 17.6, however, tariffs have become far less important sources of government revenue than they were in the late 1800s and early 1900s.

Other Barriers to Trade

Governments sometimes use less formal methods to limit imports. For example, sometimes a government will require foreign companies to obtain a license to sell goods in that country. High licensing fees or slow licensing processes act as informal trade barriers.

Health and safety regulations and requirements are often used by governments as subtle trade barriers. For example, suppose a nation treats the fruit it grows with an insecticide that is widely accepted in its own country. Another nation that wants to discourage imports of this product might ban any fruit treated with that insecticide. The importing nation hopes that it will be too troublesome for potential sellers to meet this condition. In this way, imports will be sharply reduced or eliminated.

Effects of Trade Barriers

Trade barriers have a number of effects, some negative and some positive. Simply put, trade barriers limit supply. You will recall that the United States limits cotton imports through import quotas. These quotas ensure that the United States manufacturers of jeans and other cotton clothing will probably not be able to meet their needs for cotton with imported cotton alone. Instead, clothing manufacturers will have to buy some cotton grown in the

Econ 101: Key Concepts Made Easy

Trade Some students may have difficulty remembering the differences between **import quotas** and **voluntary export restraints.** Explain that both are trade barriers, but they differ in intensity and also in their point of origination. An import quota is more strict and is imposed on one country by another. A voluntary export restraint is self-imposed. Ask students to identify why a country would voluntarily impose export restraints on itself.

United States to make up their shortfall. In this way, American cotton growers benefit from quotas on cotton.

Increased Prices for Foreign Goods

Although producers of many products may benefit from trade barriers, consumers can lose out. That's because trade barriers result in higher prices. For example, suppose the market price of an imported car is $20,000. The United States wants to use a tariff to restrict the number of imported cars coming into the country. The United States government thus places a 10 percent tariff on all foreign-auto imports. With this tariff, the price of the $20,000 imported car now rises to $22,000.

As a result of this price increase, American car makers can compete more easily in the market. American manufacturers and workers therefore benefit through increased sales. On the other hand, consumers must now pay higher prices for foreign-made cars. In addition, American manufacturers lose the economic incentive to become more efficient and produce their cars less expensively.

Trade Wars

Escalating economic conflict is another possible outcome of trade barriers. When one country restricts imports, its trading partner may impose its own restrictions against that country. Such a cycle of increasing trade barriers is known as a **trade war.**

Trade wars often lead to a substantial decrease in trade for both countries. As you read in Section 1, trade benefits both trading partners. Conversely, a decrease in trade hurts both trading partners.

Perhaps the largest and most dangerous trade war in United States history was launched by the Smoot-Hawley tariff in 1930. This tariff raised the average tariff on all products to 50 percent. When the federal government passed this law, the economy had begun to slide into a depression. Consumers were spending less, and many workers had lost their jobs. Congress hoped the tariff would protect American workers from foreign competition.

Other countries responded by raising tariffs against American-made goods. The trade war that resulted decreased international trade and deepened the worldwide depression of the 1930s. Most economists blame the Smoot-Hawley tariff for increasing American unemployment. The trade war had closed foreign markets to American goods and reduced world-wide demand for all goods.

Trade wars still break out between the United States and other countries, but most disputes center on a few products instead of all imports. Recent conflicts include the Beef War of 1999 and the Steel Tariff of 2002.

European countries launched the Beef War by banning the import of American beef from cows raised with hormones. The United States responded by imposing tariffs on European clothing and specific foods, including certain cheeses, meats, and mustards.

The Steel Tariff dispute began when the United States introduced temporary tariffs on imported steel to help American steel producers recover from bankruptcy. Angry European nations sued and threatened to retaliate. An international panel (see page 454) ruled these tariffs illegal in 2003.

trade war *a cycle of increasing trade restrictions*

◀ Trade wars have at times resulted in increased prices for some imported foods such as this mustard from France.

Transparency Resource Package
Economics Concepts, 17E: Protectionism

Differentiated Instruction L1

Trade with China has become the fastest growing trade relationship for the United States. But trade relations with China have become controversial because many Americans worry about business failures and job losses. Have students conduct a panel discussion of U.S. and China trade policy. Students should research the current state of the controversy on the Internet. Use phrases such as "U.S. China trade," "China trade deficit," "imports from China." SN

Block Scheduling Strategies

Consider these suggestions to take advantage of extended class time:

- Extend the Global Connections feature found on p. 452 by holding a class debate. Have two teams of students gather information either in support of further development of genetically altered crops or against such development. Remind students to consider the validity and reliability of the information they find, both pro and con. Direct a third group of students to observe the debate and choose a winner.
- Extend the first activity on p. 453 by asking volunteers to deliver their speeches in class. Stress that students should employ effective persuasive strategies. Ask listeners to critique the delivery and content of the speeches.
- Have groups of three to four students work on the Case Studies in Free Enterprise activity on Soichiro Honda. Tell them to prepare the report called for as part of the activity as an oral presentation. Allow time for students to present their reports.

Background

Global Connections

After World War II the Japanese economy was in disarray. Nevertheless, from 1955 to 1973, Japanese leaders nearly quadrupled their nation's per capita gross domestic product (GDP), from $3,500 to $13,500. How did the Japanese accomplish this economic miracle? They encouraged exports and fiercely protected Japanese industries, continuing to do so long after their infant industries had matured.

While some of Japan's protected companies, such as Sony and Toyota, became world leaders, many others grew lazy. With no real competition and an abundance of government subsidies, these firms had no incentive to become efficient or to price their products fairly. The Japanese construction industry is a good example. In 1998 the Japanese government accepted bids on 767 construction orders. However, because of various protectionist policies, including bureaucratic red tape that foreign companies have a difficult time negotiating, only five of these orders were won by non-Japanese companies. With no genuine foreign competition, Japanese construction costs in 1999 were 30 percent higher than those in the United States, costs that had to be paid by the Japanese government with its citizens' tax dollars.

protectionism *the use of trade barriers to protect a nation's industries from foreign competition*

infant industry *a new industry*

Arguments for Protectionism

Why does a country impose trade barriers? There are three main arguments that support **protectionism,** the use of trade barriers to protect industries from foreign competition. These include protecting workers' jobs, protecting infant industries, and safeguarding national security.

Protecting Jobs

One argument for protectionism is that it shelters workers in industries that would be hurt by foreign competition. This reasoning led to the Smoot-Hawley tariff in 1930. For example, suppose that nations in East Asia have a comparative advantage in producing textiles. If the United States reduced existing tariffs on textile imports, domestic manufacturers may not be able to compete with East Asian imports. They would have to close their factories and lay off workers.

In an ideal world, the laid-off workers would take new jobs in other industries. In practice, however, as you read in Section 1, retraining and relocation can be difficult. Many workers do not have the skills to work in other industries, and obtaining such skills takes time and money.

In addition, industry and political leaders often do not want to shut down existing industries and lose jobs in their home regions. For example, the textile industry is heavily concentrated in the southeastern United States. Politicians and industry leaders from the Southeast might try to keep textile tariffs in place to prevent loss of jobs and business.

Protecting Infant Industries

Suppose you are learning a new skill, such as playing ping-pong. At first you find it difficult to hit the ball, but as you play more your skills improve. This process is called "learning by doing."

Similarly, new industries need time and practice to become efficient producers. Tariffs and other protectionist policies are often defended on the grounds that they protect new industries in the early stages of their development. A new industry is often called an **infant industry.**

A tariff shields a young industry from the competition of its more mature rivals. After the infant industry grows up—that is, acquires the ability to produce goods efficiently and at a competitive price—the tariff can be eliminated because the industry is able to compete.

Two main difficulties arise, however. First, a protected infant industry lacks the incentive to become more efficient and competitive. Second, once an industry is given tariff protection, it is difficult to take the protection away. In other words, the infant may never "grow up."

Safeguarding National Security

Certain industries may require protection from competition because their products are essential to defending the country. In the event of a war, the United States would need steel and other products from heavy industries. It would also need industries that provide energy and advanced technologies. For this reason, the government wants to ensure that these industries remain active in the United States.

Even supporters of free trade agree that some industries need to be protected—or at least receive government financial help—so

Global Connections

Frankenstein Food? When free trade and the worries of the everyday consumer conflict, trade wars may result. Companies in the United States have developed genetically modified (GM) crops to be hardier, more nutritious, and more resistant to pests than unmodified crops. Today, much of the grain used to feed American livestock and bake bread comes from GM plants.

Many European consumers and governments strongly oppose genetically modified crops, known in Britain as "Frankenstein Food." European regulators banned GM crops for five years on the grounds that they were unsafe to eat, although they lacked scientific evidence for this claim. The ban prevents American farmers from selling grain to Europe. In addition, American businesses can not sell GM seeds to farmers in other countries that export crops to Europe. Many people argue that the ban is an illegal tactic to protect European farmers from competition. In 2003, the United States sued the European Union to end the ban. **Who are the winners and losers in a trade war?**

Preparing for Standardized Tests

Have students read the section titled "Arguments for Protectionism" and then answer the question below.

Which of the following is a harmful effect of protectionism?

A protection of workers' jobs

B protection of infant industries

(C) protection of inefficient industries

D protection of national security

Answer to . . .

Global Connections Students should point out that individual growers or industries in a country may be winners, but other producers lose. Consumers also lose in trade wars.

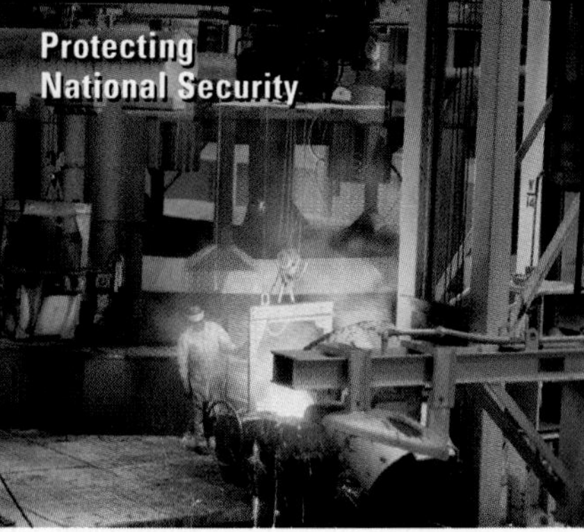

Protectionists argue in favor of trade barriers based on protecting infant industries, jobs, and national security.
Competition How does protectionism reduce foreign competition?

that the United States will not have to depend on other nations during a crisis. Free trade supporters argue, however, that certain industries claim trade protection when in fact their products are not essential to national security at all.

International Agreements

Recent trends favor lowering trade barriers and increasing trade. Many people argue that free trade is the best way to pursue comparative advantage, raise living standards, and further international peace.

To increase free trade, a number of international free trade agreements have developed. An **international free trade agreement** results from cooperation between at least two countries to reduce trade barriers and tariffs and to trade with each other.

The Reciprocal Trade Agreement Act

Today's free trade movement began in the 1930s when the United States began to promote international trade, which had declined due to tariffs and depression. The Reciprocal Trade Agreements Act of 1934 gave the president the power to reduce tariffs by as much as 50 percent.

The Act also allowed Congress to grant most-favored-nation (MFN) status to U.S. trading partners. Today, MFN status is called normal trade relations status, or NTR. A country with NTR status pays the same tariffs as those paid by all NTR partners. Therefore, if the United States lowers the tariff on imported rice from 25 percent to 15 percent for one NTR nation, all other NTR nations automatically receive the reduction. (Non-NTR nations may still be taxed at the higher rate, however.)

The World Trade Organization

In 1948, GATT, the General Agreement on Tariffs and Trade, was established to reduce tariffs and expand world trade. The **World Trade Organization (WTO)** was founded in 1995 to ensure compliance with GATT, to negotiate new trade agreements, and to resolve trade disputes. Various conferences, or rounds, of tariff negotiations have advanced the goals of GATT and the WTO. For example, the Uruguay round of negotiations, completed in 1994, decreased average global tariffs by about a third. From 1930 to 1995, the average tariff in the United States dropped from about 59 percent to about 5 percent.

The World Trade Organization also acts as a referee, enforcing the rules agreed upon by the member countries. For example, when the Beef war erupted

international free trade agreement *agreement that results from cooperation between at least two countries to reduce trade barriers and tariffs and to trade with each other*

World Trade Organization (WTO) *a worldwide organization whose goal is freer global trade and lower tariffs*

Differentiated Instruction L3

Ask students to reflect on and write about what they have learned concerning protectionism. Ask them first to explain in their own words the most powerful arguments for and against protectionism. Then read them the following scenario:

As President, you are faced with a dilemma. Imports of steel are threatening the domestic steel industry. The imported steel is less expensive because the technology used to produce it is more advanced, enabling foreign workers to be more efficient and productive. In addition, foreign workers are paid much lower wages than domestic workers. If domestic steel plants close, thousands of Americans will be out of work, and an important industry may collapse. The U.S. steel industry wants you to erect trade barriers. United States companies that use steel, however, want to be able to buy the less expensive imported steel. What decision do you make, and why? Write a brief speech explaining your decision.

Differentiated Instruction L4

Ask students to create scenarios in which protecting or failing to protect a particular industry might affect national security. Some students may want to write their scenarios in short-story or dramatic script form. GT

Econ 101: Key Concepts Made Easy

Public Policy Students may have a difficult time grasping the connection between **protectionist policies** and **national security.** Certain industries are essential to national security, so that their disappearance from the market in the United States would compromise safety. In other words, the United States must not become dependent on other countries for certain critical supplies. The text gives the example of the steel industry as an industry that must be protected. Ask students to suggest additional industries that might be protected in the name of national security, and have them explain why. *(Students might suggest wheat or other important food products, automobiles, electronics, airplanes, or weaponry.)*

Answer to . . .

Building Key Concepts
Protectionism subjects foreign exports to trade barriers such as import quotas, custom duties, tariffs, and special licensing.

Differentiated Instruction L2

Ask students to read carefully the presentation of trade agreements and international trade organizations. Then ask them to explain the purpose of each agreement or organization in their own words.

Differentiated Instruction L3

(Reteaching) Assign groups of three students each a particular trade organization or agreement. Ask students to write a summary statement for their organization or agreement that describes its basic purpose. Then ask groups to come up with examples—these should be either realistic inventions or references to actual news stories—that show how their organization or agreement affects the world economy and efforts toward international cooperation. Have a volunteer from each group present the information to the class.

Transparency Resource Package Economics Concepts, 17F: Major Trade Organization Members

European Union (EU) *a regional trade organization made up of European nations*

euro *a single currency that replaces individual currencies among members of the European Union*

free-trade zone *a region where a group of countries agrees to reduce or eliminate trade barriers*

NAFTA *agreement that will eliminate all tariffs and other trade barriers between Canada, Mexico, and the United States*

between the United States and the European Union, the case was brought before the WTO. The WTO allowed the United States tariffs to remain in effect. In 2003, the WTO ruled against the United States in the case of the steel tariffs.

The European Union

In recent years, many countries have formed customs unions—agreements that abolish tariffs and trade restrictions among union members, and that adopt uniform tariffs for nonmembers. The most successful example is the **European Union (EU)**.

The European Union as we know it today developed slowly over time. In 1957, six western European nations set up the Common Market to coordinate economic and trade policies. In the years that followed, additional European nations joined the Common Market. In 1986, member nations agreed to eliminate tariffs on one another's exports. They thereby created a single market, called the European Economic Community (EEC).

The development of the EU illustrates how the global economy and free trade can change the role of international political borders and territorial sovereignty. In 1993, the European Economic Community nations formed the European Union. The EU has a parliament and a council in which all member nations are represented. It also has its own flag, its own anthem, and celebrates Europe Day on May 9. Most EU citizens can cross borders freely and work in other EU countries. In early 2002, twelve member nations replaced their individual currencies with a single currency called the **euro.**

FAST FACT

Europe and the United States account for 55 percent of world trade, 60 percent of trade in services, and 80 percent of world wealth.

NAFTA

In other parts of the world, countries have developed **free-trade zones,** or regions where a group of countries agrees to reduce or eliminate trade barriers. **NAFTA** (the North American Free Trade Agreement) will eliminate all tariffs and other trade barriers between Canada, Mexico, and the United States by 2009. The resulting free-trade zone is the largest in the world.

Key NAFTA provisions include the following:

1. Tariffs on all farm products and on some 10,000 other goods are to be eliminated over 15 years.
2. Automobile tariffs are to be phased out over 10 years.
3. Special judges have authority to resolve trade disputes.
4. The agreement cannot be used to override national and state environmental, health, or safety laws.
5. Trucks are to have free access across borders and throughout the three member countries.

Before the agreement was signed, the NAFTA measure aroused a great deal of controversy in the United States. NAFTA opponents worried that American factories would relocate to Mexico, where wages were lower and government regulations, such as environmental controls, were less strict. The result would be a loss of jobs in the United States. Supporters of NAFTA claimed that the measure would instead create more jobs in the United States as a result of increased exports to Mexico and Canada.

▼ **NAFTA has resulted in increased trade across the Rio Grande.**

Preparing for Standardized Tests

Have students read the section titled "The European Union" and then answer the question below.

Which of the following statements is not supported by the text?

(A) The EU no longer trades with the United States.
B The EU developed slowly over time.
C The EU's goal is to create a single regional economy.
D The EU has chosen to move toward a common currency, the euro.

Figure 17.7 Major Trade Organization Members

Many countries are members of major regional trade organizations.
Trade What is the purpose of these organizations?

The United States Senate ratified NAFTA on January 1, 1994, after a bruising Congressional battle. In 1997, the government's first study of NAFTA revealed that while some jobs had been created, an almost equal number had been eliminated. At the same time, trade between the United States, Canada, and Mexico increased significantly. From 1993 to 2002, United States exports to Mexico increased from $41 billion to $98 billion. Imports from Mexico to the United States more than tripled, from $40 billion to $135 billion. To the north, United States exports to Canada during that time increased by one half, from $100 billion to $161 billion. Imports nearly doubled from $111 billion in 1994 to $211 billion in 2002.

Today, the United States government is working to negotiate trade agreements with other countries, including Chile and Singapore. In 2002, Congress granted the president "fast track" authority to draft trade agreements with minimal interference from Congress.

Other Regional Trade Agreements

Throughout the world, many countries have entered into other regional trade agreements. In fact, about 100 regional trading organizations operate in the world today. The largest of these organizations include the following.

- *APEC* The Asia-Pacific Economic Cooperation includes countries that lie along the Pacific Rim, including the United States, Mexico, and Canada. These nations have signed a nonbinding agreement to reduce trade barriers among their nations.
- *MERCOSUR* The Southern Common Market is similar to the European Union

Interdisciplinary Connections: Science

Trade Laws and Environmental Protection An emerging concern in the last decades of the twentieth century was the effect of increased trade on the environment. One issue that sparked controversy was the killing of dolphins by people who fished commercially for tuna. When tuna are caught with a large net, dolphins—which swim with the tuna—are also caught and usually die. Environmental protection groups hoped that a U.S. boycott of tuna from nations that allowed such fishing methods would be effective, but the World Trade Organization (WTO) forced the United States to stop the boycott.

Making the Connection Ask students to research this boycott and the WTO ruling. Have them discuss the controversy and what responsibility, if any, trade organizations have to preserve the environment.

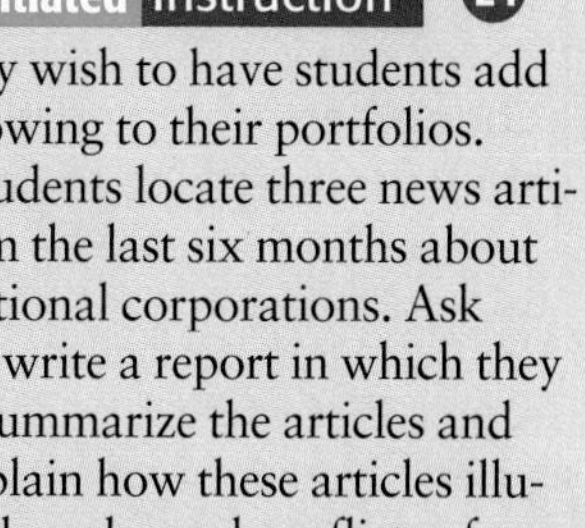

Differentiated Instruction L4

You may wish to have students add the following to their portfolios. Have students locate three news articles from the last six months about multinational corporations. Ask them to write a report in which they briefly summarize the articles and then explain how these articles illuminate the roles and conflicts of multinationals in the global market. GT

Economics Assessment Rubric
Economics Assessment Rubrics folder, pp. 6–7 provides sample evaluation materials for a writing assignment.

Learning Styles Activity
Learning Styles Lesson Plans folder, p. 39 asks student groups to create charts showing selected economic facts about world trade zones.

Answer to . . .

Building Key Concepts Their purposes vary, but most support cooperation and the lowering of trade barriers between member nations.

Go Online PHSchool.com Typing in the Web Code when prompted will bring students directly to the article.

GTE Guide to the Essentials
Chapter 17, Section 2, p. 73 provides support for students who need additional review of the section content. Spanish support is available in the Spanish edition of the guide on p. 73.

Quiz Unit 7 folder, p. 5 includes questions to check students' understanding of Section 2 content.

Presentation Pro CD-ROM
Quiz provides multiple-choice questions to check students' understanding of Section 2 content.

Answers to . . .

Section 2 Assessment

1. All are means of preventing a foreign product or service from freely entering a country. An import quota is a limit on the amount of a good that can be imported. A voluntary export restraint (VER) is a self-imposed limitation on the quantity of products a country ships to another country. A tariff is a tax on an imported good.
2. Trade barriers often make imported goods more expensive for consumers, so they aid domestic manufacturers and workers but harm foreign manufacturers and workers. If retaliatory trade barriers are established, domestic industries can be harmed.
3. Advantages: new industries can be protected in their early stages of development, and a nation's output can be diversified. Disadvantages: a protected industry may not have the incentive to become more efficient, and protections are difficult to take away.
4. Students may argue that protectionism shelters domestic jobs, encourages the growth of new industries, and helps protect national security.
5. Answers will vary depending on which trade organization or agreement is chosen. The WTO, for example, ensures compliance with GATT, negotiates new trade agreements, and resolves trade disputes.
6. Some students may favor increasing trade barriers to give video game companies in the United States more of a share of the market. Other students may want to decrease them, hoping that the price of games would decrease.
7. Placing a tariff on foreign movies will make them more expensive for the consumer, placing the products of NewMovies, Inc., in a better competitive position.
8. Advantages include more trade, booming economies, and friendship between nations that are linked by agreements. Disadvantages might include resentment and possible conflict with nations who are not part of a particular agreement.

Progress Monitoring *Online*
For additional assessment, have students access Progress Monitoring Online at **Web Code:** mna-7176

Go Online PHSchool.com Typing in the Web Code when prompted will bring students directly to detailed instructions for this activity.

THE WALL STREET JOURNAL. CLASSROOM EDITION

In the News *Read more about the impact of internation trade in "The Shrinking of the 'Big Three'," an article in* The Wall Street Journal Classroom Edition.

Go Online
The Wall Street Journal Classroom Edition
For: Current Events
Visit: PHSchool.com
Web Code: mnc-7172

in its goals. Its members are Brazil, Argentina, Paraguay, and Uruguay.

• *CARICOM* The Caribbean Community and Common Market includes countries from South America and the Caribbean.

The Role of Multinationals

Multinational corporations (MNCs) also contribute to international trade. As you read in Chapter 8, a multinational is a large corporation that sells goods and services throughout the world. For example, an automobile company might design its cars in the United States. The same company might import parts from Asia and assemble its cars in Canada and Mexico. As a result, although you might purchase the automobile from a company based in the United States, it is not a purely domestic product.

Many goods besides cars are produced globally. Some brands of athletic shoes are designed in the United States but are produced in East Asia. Some personal computers are designed in the United States and assembled abroad with parts and components from the United States.

The decision to build production facilities in a foreign country benefits both the multinational corporation and the host nation. By locating abroad, the corporation avoids some shipping fees and tariffs. It may also benefit from cheaper labor in much of Asia and Latin America. The host nation benefits by gaining jobs and tax revenue on the corporation's income, profits, and property.

On the other hand, host nations worry about the effect of multinationals on their countries. Multinationals in a small country with a less developed economy could gain excessive political power. In addition, host nations are concerned that multinationals could replace the host country's domestic industries and exploit their workers. In order to address these concerns, nations have instituted rules that require multinationals to export a certain percentage of their products. Host nations hope that such requirements will help protect their domestic industries.

Section 2 Assessment

Progress Monitoring *Online*
For: Self-quiz with vocabulary practice
Web Code: mna-7176

Key Terms and Main Ideas

1. Describe the similarities and differences among the following barriers to free trade: **import quotas, voluntary export restraints (VERs),** and **tariffs.**
2. Explain the effects of **trade barriers** on manufacturers, workers, and consumers.
3. What are the advantages and disadvantages of protecting an **infant industry?**
4. Describe the three arguments in favor of **protectionism.**
5. Choose one of the trade organizations or agreements described in the section and explain its purpose.

Applying Economic Concepts

6. ***You Decide*** Suppose that you were in charge of trade policy in the United States. Would you recommend that the United States increase or decrease trade barriers on video game systems? Explain your answer.
7. ***Problem Solving*** Suppose that a company called NewMovies, Inc., located in Country X, has decided to produce and distribute movies. NewMovies, Inc., would like the government of Country X to impose a tariff on foreign-made movies. Why?
8. ***Critical Thinking*** What are the advantages of international trade agreements? What might be some disadvantages?

For: Current Events Activity
Visit: PHSchool.com
Web Code: mnd-7172

ECONOMIC

Profile

Economist

Entrepreneur

Carla Anderson Hills (b. 1934)

Although a strong believer in free trade, U.S. Trade Representative Carla Anderson Hills was not afraid to use tariffs and quotas as tools to pry open foreign markets. Her approach to eliminating overseas barriers to American trade earned her the nickname "the Velvet Crowbar."

An Advocate for Free Trade

"The case for free trade does not easily fit on a bumper sticker," Carla Anderson Hills observes. Free trade, she says, results in a stronger economy with more innovation and technological development.

As U.S. Trade Representative from 1989 to 1993, Hills was charged with carrying out U.S. trade policy. She earned a reputation as a tough advocate for U.S. rights in world trade. "With less than 5 percent of the world's population, we produce more than 20 percent of the world's output," Hills asserts. "We need access to foreign markets to sell the goods we produce."

From Law to International Trade

After graduating from Stanford University, Hills earned a law degree from Yale in 1958. She joined her husband and three other attorneys to found their own law firm in 1962. In 1974, she left California to work in the Justice Department.

In 1975, President Gerald Ford named Hills Secretary of Housing and Urban Development. After Jimmy Carter became president, Hills returned to the private practice of law, where she remained until President George Bush appointed her U.S. Trade Representative in 1989. Today her firm, Hills & Company, provides advice on trade to U.S. businesses.

The Velvet Crowbar

Hills described her negotiating approach as "a handshake wherever possible [and] a crowbar where necessary." To open the Japanese market to U.S. electronic and wood products, Hills threatened U.S. retaliation against Japanese goods. She said, "I'll never say I'm satisfied until their market is as open to our entrepreneurs as ours is to theirs."

In 1992, Hills threatened to pull the United States out of global trade talks unless the European Union agreed to cut government subsidies to its farmers. When France resisted, she slapped a 200 percent tariff on French wine and farm products.

In general, however, Hills opposes this kind of trade protection. She labels it "the worst possible policy option to deal with jobs thought to be lost to foreign competition, because in the long run it will cost more jobs by making our companies less competitive."

CHECK FOR UNDERSTANDING

1. **Source Reading** Explain the reasoning in the following Hills statement: "It is in our interest to persuade our trading partners to lower their barriers. That is particularly true with respect to nations of Asia and Latin America, the two fastest-growing regions in the world."
2. **Critical Thinking** As U.S. trade representative, why would Hills have opposed European governments who provided subsidies to European farmers?
3. **Decision Making** Some opponents of free trade contend that it costs American workers jobs. If you were the U.S. Trade Representative, would you try to protect American companies from foreign competition?

Beyond the Classroom: Workplace Skills

Using Computers to Process Information Explain to students that computer literacy has become an essential skill in today's workplace. Accessing information, designing documents, and using spreadsheets are just some of the computer-related tasks a worker must master to achieve success. Ask students to go to the *Economics: Principles in Action* segment in the Social Studies area of the Prentice Hall Web site (**www.phschool.com**) to find trade statistics from the World Trade Organization (WTO). Then ask them to use the Simulations and Data Graphing CD-ROM to turn at least one set of their statistics into a graph.

ECONOMIC Profile
Carla Anderson Hills

Background

Carla Hills's term as U.S. Trade Representative ended in 1993, but her interest in the issues surrounding global trade has remained strong. She started her own business, Hills & Company, to advise U.S. firms about investment, trade, and risk issues. In an on-line interview with readers of the *Washington Post* in April 1999, Hills reaffirmed her belief in the importance of free trade.

When asked whether the United States should force countries with which it has a trade deficit to reduce their exports to America, Hills offered four reasons for welcoming imports. First, certain imports provide Americans with goods and services that can be obtained only from outside the United States. Second, imports offer Americans greater choice and often lower prices. Third, the development of technologies in other nations can end up benefiting American business. Finally, Hills noted that imports provide competition that forces American business to innovate.

Careers in Economics Activity Unit 7 folder, p. 11 gives students a closer look at the career path of an exporter.

Answers to . . .

1. It is important to increase U.S. trade opportunities in these two regions because their fast-growing populations make them good markets.
2. Answers should reflect the understanding that such subsidies would give European farmers a competitive advantage over American farmers on world markets and thus are (indirectly) barriers to U.S. trade.
3. Some students may feel that foreign competition costs jobs and should be restricted. Others may point to America's productive capacity, arguing that the United States cannot block a country's exports and expect it to encourage U.S. imports.

Section 3

Measuring Trade

Objectives You may wish to call students' attention to the objectives in the Section Preview. The objectives are reflected in the main headings of the section.

Bellringer Ask students if they have ever traveled in a foreign country that uses an unfamiliar currency. Ask them to describe their experiences with the foreign currency. Explain that in this section they will learn how fluctuating currency exchange rates can affect the value of goods and services worldwide.

Vocabulary Builder After students have read the section to learn the meaning of each key term, have them add the terms and their definitions to their Economics Journals. Ask students to provide examples that apply to each term and situations that do not apply to show their understanding.

Lesson Plan

Teaching the Main Concepts L3

1. Focus Explain to students that because different nations have their own currencies that fluctuate in value, the costs of imported and exported goods and services also vary.
2. Instruct Begin by discussing how exchange rates are calculated and why they change. Explain that a currency can either appreciate or depreciate in value relative to other currencies. After discussing types of exchange rate systems, explain how the fluctuating value of currencies affects the balance of trade between nations.
3. Close/Reteach Remind students that because currencies fluctuate, the value of goods and services that nations trade also fluctuates. Ask students to list some reasons currencies change in value.

Guided Reading and Review Unit 7 folder, p. 6 asks students to identify the main ideas of the section and to define or identify key terms.

Section 3

Measuring Trade

Preview

Objectives

After studying this section you will be able to:

1. **Analyze** how changes in exchange rates of world currencies affect international trade.
2. **Describe** the effect of various exchange rate systems.
3. **Analyze** the effects of changes in exchange rates on the balance of trade.

Section Focus

International trade is complicated by the fact that different nations have different currencies. Countries pay for imports in their own currencies and receive foreign currency for exports. If a nation imports more than it exports, or vice versa, a trade imbalance is created.

Key Terms

exchange rate
appreciation
depreciation
foreign exchange market
fixed exchange-rate system
flexible exchange-rate system
trade surplus
trade deficit
balance of trade

exchange rate *the value of a foreign nation's currency in terms of the home nation's currency*

Have you ever traveled to a foreign country? If so, you may have been unable to purchase goods in that country using U.S. dollars. Similarly, tourists buying goods in the United States need to exchange their home country's money for U.S. dollars. In order for foreign visitors to buy something in another country, they usually must obtain that country's currency before making any purchases.

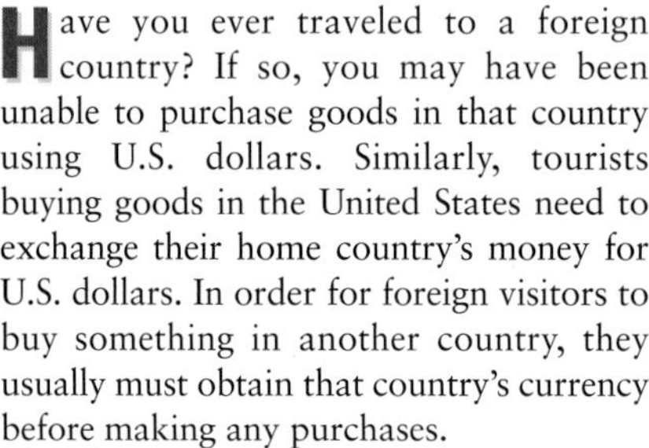

▼ **Tourists can exchange their currency for that of the country they are visiting at currency exchange outlets or centers.**

Exchange Rates

International trade takes place whenever a good or service is produced in one country and sold in another. Trade between countries is more complex than buying and selling within the same country because of the world's many currencies and their changing values.

Foreign Exchange

If you want to buy a newspaper in Beijing, you will need to change your American dollars for Chinese renminbi. If a Mexican visitor to New York wants to buy lunch, she must change her pesos to dollars.

Changing money from one currency to another is not a simple matter of exchanging, say, one peso for one American dollar. A dollar might be worth 11 pesos—or 104 Japanese yen, or 8 Chinese renminbi.

The value of a foreign nation's currency in relation to your own currency is called the foreign exchange rate, or simply the **exchange rate.** The exchange rate enables you to convert prices in one currency to prices in another currency.

Reading an Exchange Rate Table

Exchange rates are listed on the Internet and in many major newspapers. Figure 17.8 shows a table of sample exchange rates. If you read down the first column, for example, you will see that one U.S. dollar can be exchanged for about one-and-a-quarter (1.28) Australian dollars, for a bit less than one euro (0.772), and so forth.

It is important to realize that these rates are what one U.S. dollar is worth on one particular day. Exchange rates go up and down daily.

Determing the Rate of Exchange

The following example will help you calculate exchange rates. Suppose your family is planning a trip to Mexico this summer and wants to determine the cost of staying in a

Graphing the Main Idea

Trade To build understanding of the concept of **trade**, have students complete a tree map graphic organizer like the one shown at the right. Remind them that a tree map shows an outline for a main topic, main ideas, and supporting details. The label "Measuring Trade" can go in the top box and main headings in the boxes below, followed by supporting details.

Section Reading Support Transparencies A template and the answers for this graphic organizer can be found in Chapter 17, Section 3 of the Section Reading Support Transparency System.

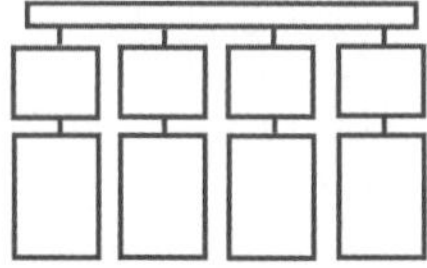

Figure 17.8 **Foreign Exchange Rates**

	U.S. $	Aust $	U.K. £	Canadian $	¥en	€uro	Mexican peso	Chinese renminbi
U.S. $	1	0.781	1.906	0.804	0.0096	1.296	0.0914	0.121
Australian $	1.281	1	2.442	1.03	0.0122	1.66	0.117	0.155
U.K. £	0.525	0.41	1	0.422	0.00502	0.68	0.04799	0.0635
Canadian $	1.244	0.972	2.372	1	0.0112	1.612	0.114	0.151
¥en	104.4	81.5	199	83.9	1	135.3	9.5	12.6
€uro	0.772	0.603	1.471	0.62	0.00734	1	0.071	0.0934
Mexican peso	10.935	8.54	20.84	8.77	0.105	14.1	1	1.323
Chinese renminbi	8.277	6.464	15.748	6.623	0.0794	10.71	0.757	1

Read down the first column of the chart to find what one U.S. dollar was worth in foreign currencies on this particular day. (Example: One U.S. dollar was worth 0.5245 British pounds.) Read across the top row to find out how much a selected foreign currency was worth in U.S. dollars. (Example: One British pound cost 1.9064 U.S. dollars or about $1.91.) **Money How much were 8.28 Chinese renminbi worth in U.S. dollars?**

hotel. If a hotel room in Mexico costs 500 pesos per night and the exchange rate is 10.0 pesos per dollar, a hotel room will cost $50:

$$\frac{500 \text{ pesos}}{10.0 \text{ pesos per dollar}} = \$50.00$$

If your family decides to go to Mexico the following fall, however, the exchange rate will probably have changed. If by fall, the exchange rate is 11.0 pesos per dollar, the hotel room will cost only about $45 a night (assuming that the hotel still charges 500 pesos per night):

$$\frac{500 \text{ pesos}}{11.0 \text{ pesos per dollar}} = \$45.45$$

By fall, the exchange rate might, however, be only 9.0 pesos per dollar. In that case, your family would need to spend more money on your visit. The hotel room would now cost about $56 per night:

$$\frac{500 \text{ pesos}}{9.0 \text{ pesos per dollar}} = \$55.55$$

Strong and Weak Currencies

You have probably heard newscasters talk about a "strong" or "weak" dollar or a currency like the Japanese yen "rising" or "falling." What do these terms mean, and are they good news or bad news for the United States economy?

An increase in the value of a currency is called **appreciation**. When a currency appreciates, it becomes "stronger." If the exchange rate between the dollar and the yen increases from 100 yen per dollar to 120 yen per dollar, one dollar will purchase more yen. Since the dollar has increased in value, we say that the dollar has appreciated against the yen. This appreciation means that people in Japan will have to spend more yen to purchase a dollar's worth of goods from the United States.

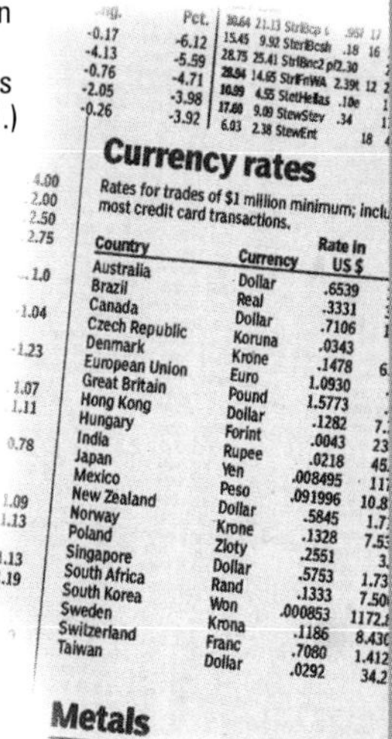

Currency rates

Rates for trades of $1 million minimum; inclu... most credit card transactions.

Country	Currency	Rate in US $
Australia	Dollar	.6539
Brazil	Real	.3331
Canada	Dollar	.7106
Czech Republic	Koruna	.0343
Denmark	Krone	.1478
European Union	Euro	1.0930
Great Britain	Pound	1.5773
Hong Kong	Dollar	.1282
Hungary	Forint	.0043
India	Rupee	.0218
Japan	Yen	.008495
Mexico	Peso	.091996
New Zealand	Dollar	.5845
Norway	Krone	.1328
Poland	Zloty	.2551
Singapore	Dollar	.5753
South Africa	Rand	.1333
South Korea	Won	.000853
Sweden	Krona	.1186
Switzerland	Franc	.7080
Taiwan	Dollar	.0292

Metals

When a nation's currency appreciates, that nation's products become more expensive in other countries. For example, a strong dollar makes American goods and services more expensive for Japanese consumers. Japan will therefore probably import fewer products from the United States. That means that total United States exports to Japan will likely decline.

On the other hand, a strong dollar means that foreign products will be less expensive for consumers in the United States. A strong dollar is therefore likely to lead consumers in the United States to purchase imported goods.

A decrease in the value of a currency is called **depreciation**. You might also hear depreciation referred to as "weakening." If the dollar exchange rate fell to 80 yen per

appreciation *an increase in the value of a currency*

depreciation *a decrease in the value of a currency*

Econ 101: Key Concepts Made Easy

Money Students may have an easier time understanding **appreciation** and **depreciation** through this sports analogy. Maria Santana and Lorna Howe are two professional soccer players whose careers went in opposite directions. Maria's career took off like a rocket. She was voted Rookie of the Year and was named to the all-star team each of her first three seasons. Lorna, on the other hand, was beset by injuries from the start, and she was forced to retire after three injury-plagued seasons. Maria's rookie trading card appreciated, or grew more valuable, every time she took the field. Lorna's rookie card depreciated every time she twisted an ankle or tore a ligament.

Invite students to speculate about the value of a Roger Maris trading card after both Mark McGuire and Sammy Sosa broke his home run record two years in a row. Then ask them to explain how these situations are similar to and different from the way currencies change in value.

Differentiated Instruction L3

(Enrichment) Organize the class into groups of two or three. Assign each group a major international currency. Have each group research the value of its currency as compared to the United States dollar on the last day of each month for the preceding year. Then ask groups, with those values in hand, to create line graphs that show the fluctuations of their currencies in relation to the U.S. dollar for the past year. Ask students to speculate about how these changes affected international trade.

Simulations and Data Graphing CD-ROM offers data graphing tools so that students can practice creating and interpreting line graphs.

Meeting NCEE Standards

Use the following benchmark activity from the **Voluntary National Content Standards in Economics** to evaluate student understanding of **Standard 7.**

Use the following scenario to analyze the effects on trade of a change in exchange rates: In one year, the American dollar equaled 250 Japanese yen; in the following year, the American dollar equaled 150 yen; and in the third year, it equaled 200 yen. If a Nikon camera costs 75,000 yen and a Sony Walkman radio costs 25,000 yen: (1) What will be the price in dollars of these two products in each year for an American? (2) Will an American want to buy more or fewer Japanese products in year one, year two, or year three? Explain.

Answer to . . .

Building Key Concepts They equal about 1 U.S. dollar.

Background

Global Connections

Students may be surprised to discover that the United States is not the only country where *dollar* is the name of the monetary unit. Many countries around the world also issue dollars as their currency of choice.

For example, both Hong Kong and Canada have been issuing dollars since the last half of the 1800s. During the mid-1960s, Australia and New Zealand also began issuing dollars, followed shortly thereafter by many former British possessions in the Caribbean.

George Washington is not, however, to be found staring out from the front of a Canadian dollar. Each country that issues dollars prints its own money, using its own designs. Canada's dollar coin, for example, shows an image of Queen Elizabeth II.

All of these dollars not only look different but also have different values. For example, on July 15, 2005, the U.S. dollar was averaging $1.22 in Canadian dollars, $1.33 in Australian dollars, and $7.78 in Hong Kong dollars.

Economic Cartoon
Unit 7 folder, p. 12 gives students practice in interpreting cartoons about section content.

Learning Styles Activity
Learning Styles Lesson Plans folder, p. 40 asks students to construct bar graphs showing foreign currency exchange rates for a ten-year period.

Answer to . . .
Building Key Concepts A strong dollar leads to an increase in imports. A weak dollar leads to a decrease in imports.

Figure 17.9 **Effects of a Strong or Weak Dollar on Exports**

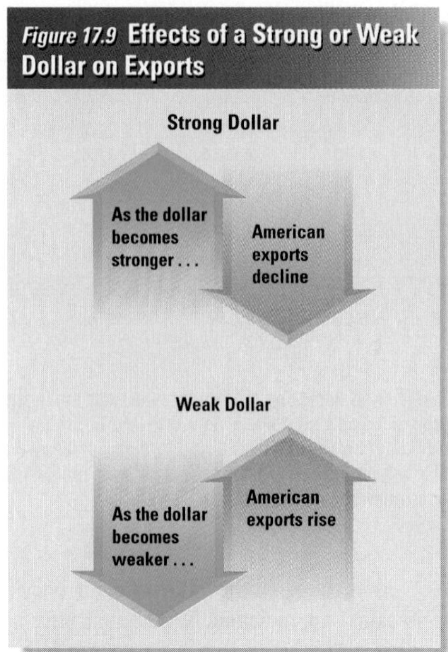
Strong Dollar
As the dollar becomes stronger . . .
American exports decline
Weak Dollar
As the dollar becomes weaker . . .
American exports rise

BUILDING KEY CONCEPTS

A strong dollar leads to a decrease in exports. A weak dollar leads to an increase in exports. **Trade** **What is the effect of a strong or weak dollar on imports?**

foreign exchange market *the banks and other financial institutions that facilitate the buying and selling of foreign currencies*

dollar, you would get fewer yen for each dollar. In other words, the dollar has depreciated against the yen.

When a nation's currency depreciates, its products become cheaper to other nations. A depreciated, or weak, dollar means that foreign consumers will be able to better afford products made in the United States. As you can see from Figure 17.9, exports are likely to increase as a result of a weakened dollar. At the same time, other nations' products become more expensive for consumers in the United States, so imports are likely to decrease.

The Foreign Exchange Market

When a company in the United States sells computers in Japan, that company is paid in yen. It must, however, pay its United States workers in dollars. The company must therefore exchange its yen for dollars in order to pay its workers. This exchange takes place on the foreign exchange market. Because each nation uses a different currency, international trade would not be possible without this market.

The **foreign exchange market** consists of about 2,000 banks and other financial institutions that facilitate the buying and selling of foreign currencies. These banks are located in various financial centers around the world, including New York, London, Paris, Singapore, Tokyo, and many other cities. Wherever they are located, the banks that make up the foreign exchange market maintain close links to one another through telephones and computers. This technology allows for the instantaneous transmission of market information and rapid financial transactions.

Exchange Rate Systems

As you read in Chapter 10, currencies varied in value from state to state in early America. In the United States today, of course, it doesn't matter whether you are in California, New York, or Texas—all prices are in dollars, and all dollars have the same value. No one asks whether your dollars came from San Francisco or Miami. Within the United States, a dollar is just a dollar.

Think how much more complicated it would be to do business if each state still had different currencies. To buy goods from a mail-order company in Indiana, for instance, you would have to find out the exchange rate between your local dollar and the Indiana dollar. Any large business in the United States would be overwhelmed by its efforts to keep track of all the exchange rates among the states. The economy would become less efficient as individuals and businesses spent time dealing with exchange rates.

You can understand from the above example how complex transactions would become if states had different exchange rates. The same ideas also apply to exchange rates among nations.

Block Scheduling Strategies

Consider these suggestions to take advantage of extended class time:

- Extend the first activity on p. 459 by holding an in-class international bazaar. Offer 10 to 15 imaginary products, such as a Moroccan rug, a Chinese jade figure, and a Swiss watch. Price each item in the currency of the country where it is produced, and have students figure out how much each product would cost in U.S. dollars.
- Show the Economics Video Library segment "The Euro, Part 2," about the transition to a single currency in Europe. Present the Background note on p. 462, and then encourage students to check newspapers and news magazines from the past six months to find recent news about the European Union.

Fixed Exchange-Rate Systems

Wouldn't it be easier if all countries either used the same currency or fixed their exchange rates against one another? Then no one would have to worry about shifts in exchange rates. A currency system in which governments try to keep the values of their currencies constant against one another is called a **fixed exchange-rate system.**

In a typical fixed exchange-rate system, one country with a stable currency is at the center. Other countries fix, or "peg," their exchange rates to the currency of this central country.

Normally, the fixed exchange-rate is not just a single value, but is kept within a certain prespecified range (for example, plus or minus 2 percent). If the exchange rate moves outside of this range, governments usually step in—or intervene—to help maintain the rate.

How do governments intervene to maintain an exchange rate? Like the price of any product or service, the exchange rate relies on supply and demand. To preserve its exchange rate, a government may buy or sell foreign currency in order to affect a currency's supply and demand. It will follow this course of action until the exchange rate is back within the prespecified limits.

The Bretton Woods Conference

In 1944, as World War II was drawing to a close, representatives from 44 countries met in Bretton Woods, New Hampshire. Their purpose was to make financial arrangements for the postwar world after the expected defeat of Germany and Japan.

The Bretton Woods conference resulted in the creation of a fixed exchange-rate system for the Untied States and much of western Europe. Because the United States was the strongest economic power with the most stable currency, the U.S. dollar was at the center of the new system. Beginning in 1945, the conference participants agreed to fix their currencies to the U.S. dollar.

The Bretton Woods conference also established the International Monetary Fund (IMF) to make the new system work. Today this organization promotes international monetary cooperation, currency stabilization, and international trade. You will read more about the International Monetary Fund in Chapter 18.

Flexible Exchange-Rate Systems

Although fixed exchange-rate systems make it easier to trade, they require countries to maintain similar economic policies, including similar inflation and interest rates. By the late 1960s, changes were continually occurring in the international trading system, and worldwide trade was growing rapidly. At the same time, the war in Vietnam was causing inflation in the United States. These factors made it increasingly difficult for many countries to rely on a fixed exchange-rate system.

fixed exchange-rate system *a currency system in which governments try to keep the values of their currencies constant against one another*

Figure 17.10 **Exchange Rates of the Dollar and Pound**

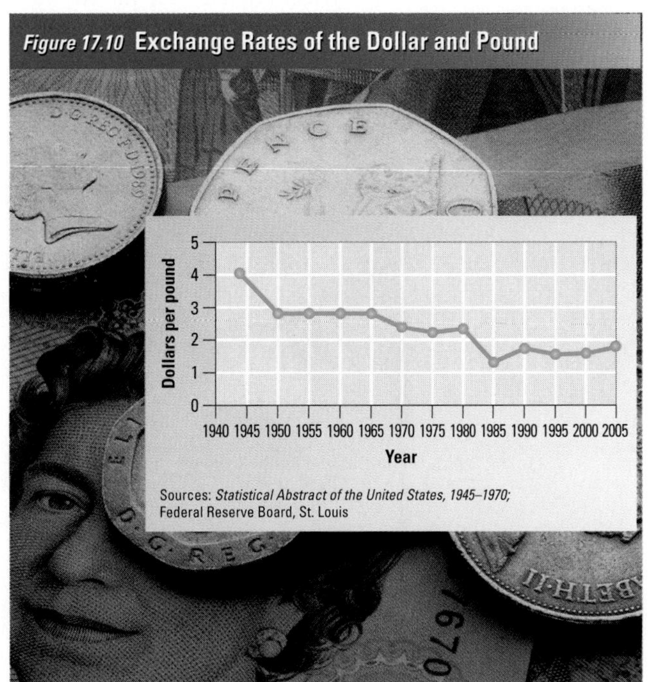

Sources: *Statistical Abstract of the United States, 1945–1970;* Federal Reserve Board, St. Louis

The United States and Britain shifted from a fixed rate to a flexible exchange-rate system in the early 1970s.
Money How did this shift affect exchange rates between the dollar and the pound?

Differentiated Instruction 

Organize the class into groups of three or four. Have each group create a table or other graphic presentation (chart, Venn diagram) that has as its subject the fixed exchange-rate system and the flexible exchange-rate system. Each group should use its chosen graphic method to compare and contrast the two systems and the effects of each system.

Differentiated Instruction 

Have individual students prepare reports on specific examples of foreign exchange market intervention in the last several years (situations in which the Federal Reserve or other central banks in the United States and elsewhere have purchased or sold currencies, hoping to influence the market exchange rate). Have students prepare short oral or written reports on the circumstances surrounding these interventions, and ask them to assess the impact of these interventions. GT

Math Practice Activity
Math Practice folder, p. 13, "Applying Foreign Exchange Rates," gives students additional practice in working with exchange rates.

Interdisciplinary Connections: Math

Travel and Exchange Rates Keeping track of your expenses on vacation in another country can be a challenge. However, with a calculator and some division and multiplication skills, it can be a snap.

Making the Connection Ask students to solve this problem: You're traveling through Europe, and your friends are expecting some souvenirs when you return. You've decided to spend $12 on each of four friends, purchasing one souvenir in each of the four countries you will visit. How much of the following currencies will you need for your souvenirs: British pounds, French euros, Swiss francs, and Russian roubles? Use current exchange rates for your calculations. *(Answers will depend on current exchange rates. Answers based on July 2005 exchange rates are 6.85 pounds, 9.96 euros, 15.53 francs, and 344.34 roubles.)*

Answer to . . .

Building Key Concepts Relative currency values between the two countries change daily, determined by supply and demand.

Background

Economics in History

The European Union, or EU, was established by a treaty approved in December 1991. The official name of the treaty is the Treaty on European Union, but it is often called the Maastricht Treaty after the city in the Netherlands where it was finalized. The treaty established the EU, an organization of Western European states working together toward economic and political integration.

The European Union is not the first group of its kind, however. Since the late 1950s organizations in Europe, such as the European Economic Community (EEC or EC) and the European Free Trade Association (EFTA), had been working toward goals such as the creation of a single market with a common currency and a common central bank. A common currency, the euro, began circulating in 2002. At that point francs, marks, lire, and other currencies of participating countries disappeared.

FAST FACT

In general, the United States has a negative trade balance. While the United States may experience an overall trade deficit, however, trade with any one country may run a surplus. For example, the United States has recently had trade surpluses with The Netherlands, Hong Kong, Belgium, and Australia, as well as with Brazil, Argentina, and Egypt.

flexible exchange-rate system *a currency system that allows the exchange rate to be determined by supply and demand*

trade surplus *the result of a nation exporting more than it imports*

trade deficit *the result of a nation importing more than it exports*

balance of trade *the relationship between a nation's imports and its exports*

In 1971, the West German and Dutch governments abandoned the fixed exchange-rate system. By 1973, many countries, including the United States, had adopted a system based on flexible, or floating, exchange rates.

In contrast to the fixed rate system, the **flexible exchange-rate system** allows the exchange rate to be determined by supply and demand. With a flexible exchange-rate system, exchange rates need not fall into any prespecified range.

Today, the countries of the world use a mixture of fixed and flexible exchange rates. Most major currencies, however—including the U.S. dollar and the Japanese yen—use the flexible exchange-rate system. This system accounts for the day-to-day changes in currency values that you read about earlier in this section.

When the flexible exchange-rate system was first adopted, some economists worried that changes in the exchange rate might interrupt the flow of international trade. In fact, the flexible exchange-rate system has worked reasonably well since the breakdown of the Bretton Woods fixed-rate system. World trade has grown at a rapid rate, and more nations trade today than ever before.

The Euro

Although the flexible exchange-rate system works well, some countries whose economies are closely tied together want the advantages of fixed exchange rates. One way to enjoy the advantages but avoid some of the difficulties of fixed exchange rates is to abolish individual currencies and establish a single currency.

This is just what most of the European Union countries have done. The EU has established a new currency, which twelve EU member nations have adopted. As you read in Section 2, this single currency is called the euro. Use of this common currency requires participating countries to coordinate their economic policies, but it also simplifies trade.

▲ **Most members of the European Union have phased out their individual currencies in favor of a single currency, the euro.**

The Balance of Trade

When a nation exports more than it imports, it has a **trade surplus.** When a nation imports more than it exports, it creates a **trade deficit.** The relationship between a nation's imports and its exports is called its **balance of trade.**

When a large difference between a nation's imports and exports arises, it is said to have a trade imbalance. A nation that exports more goods than it imports has a positive trade balance. A nation that imports more than it exports has a negative trade balance.

Understanding the Balance of Trade

Nations seek to maintain a balance of trade with values of imports equal to values of exports. By balancing trade, a nation can protect the value of its currency on the international market. If a trade imbalance continues, with one country importing more

Preparing for Standardized Tests

Have students read the section titled "Flexible Exchange-Rate Systems" and then answer the question below.

The flexible exchange-rate system allows the exchange rate to be determined by

A a single central bank.

B the European Union.

(C) supply and demand.

D the Federal Reserve.

than it is exporting, the value of its currency falls. For example, in the 1980s the United States imported considerably more than it exported, and the foreign exchange market was glutted with dollars. As the value of the dollar fell, the prices of imports increased and consumers paid more for the goods.

A trade imbalance can be corrected by limiting imports or increasing the number and/or quality of exports. Both of these actions affect trading partners, of course, who may retaliate by raising tariffs. Maintaining a balance of trade thus requires international cooperation and fair trade.

The United States Trade Deficit

Although the United States sells many goods abroad (supercomputers, movies, and CDs, for example), in general it buys more goods from abroad than it sells (cars, clothing, and VCRs, for example). The result is that the United States is running a large trade deficit, and has been for several decades.

The United States trade deficit has existed since the early 1970s. At that time, the Organization of Petroleum Exporting Countries (OPEC) dramatically raised the price of oil. The United States had to increase the money spent on foreign oil, thus increasing the money spent on imports. The total cost of imports to the United States then exceeded the income from exports, and a trade deficit developed. (See the United States Trading Partners map on page 545 of the Databank for the names of the countries that belong to OPEC.)

As you can see from Figure 17.11, the United States suffered record trade deficits in 1986 and 1987. In the early 1990s, the trade deficit began to fall. By the late 1990s, however, the deficit had skyrocketed to record levels, largely as a result of increasing oil prices and an economic boom that fueled consumer buying.

The United States trade deficit totaled over $617 billion in 2004, with the largest amounts owed to China, Japan, Canada, Mexico, Germany, and oil exporting countries, such as Venezuela. Imported petroleum accounted for about 20 percent of the deficit.

Reducing the Trade Deficit

You have read that trade deficit occurs when United States businesses and consumers purchase more goods and services from foreign producers than foreigners buy from the United States during the same time period. This means that Americans are spending more than they produce.

For the United States to run a trade deficit, other countries must be willing to finance the deficits by lending to the United States or buying American assets. When Americans are buying more goods abroad than they sell, extra dollars end up in the hands of foreigners. The foreigners can then use these dollars to purchase American assets. As a result of America's persistent trade deficits, people

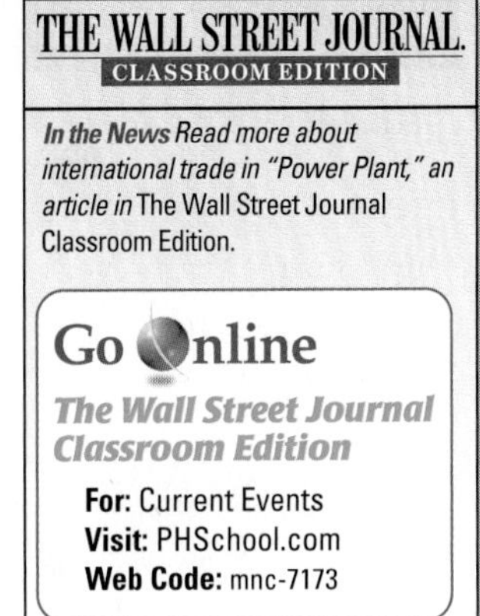

THE WALL STREET JOURNAL.
CLASSROOM EDITION
In the News Read more about international trade in "Power Plant," an article in The Wall Street Journal Classroom Edition.
Go Online
The Wall Street Journal Classroom Edition
For: Current Events
Visit: PHSchool.com
Web Code: mnc-7173

Go Online PHSchool.com Web Code: mng-7175

Figure 17.11 U.S. Balance of Trade, 1976–2004

Balance of trade (billions of dollars): 40 to −800; Year: 1976–2004

Source: U.S. Department of Commerce

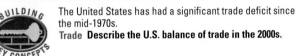

The United States has had a significant trade deficit since the mid-1970s.
Trade Describe the U.S. balance of trade in the 2000s.

Go Online PHSchool.com Typing in the Web Code when prompted will bring students directly to the article.

Transparency Resource Package
Economics Concepts, 17G: The U.S. Balance of Trade

Differentiated Instruction 

Have students check a current almanac for data on which countries of the world have the largest trade deficits and which have the largest trade surpluses. Ask students to examine the reasons given in their textbook for the size of the trade deficit of the United States. Then have students write several paragraphs proposing why the other listed countries have large deficits or surpluses.

Databank, pp. 532–547 contains maps and graphs that can be used to gain information about world trade and to extend and reinforce skills.

Differentiated Instruction 

Before students read the section, have them skim it, identifying the main idea of each subsection. When students have finished reading the section, ask them to write one or more paragraphs in which they summarize the section content. Tell students to include all of the key terms in their paragraphs. LPR

Economic Detective Activity
Unit 7 folder, p. 10, "Learning to Trade," provides an integrated application of chapter concepts.

Preparing for Standardized Tests

Have students read the section titled "The Balance of Trade" and then answer the question below.

Last year the Utopian Democratic Republic (U.D.R.) exported $3.5 trillion in goods and services. That same year, the U.D.R. imported $2.7 trillion in goods and services. Which of the following best describes the state of trade in the U.D.R. last year?

(A) trade surplus
B trade balance
C trade barrier
D trade deficit

Answer to . . .

Building Key Concepts The U.S. trade deficit declined slightly from 2000 to 2001 and then increased sharply through 2004.

GTE Guide to the Essentials
Chapter 17, Section 3, p. 74 provides support for students who need additional review of the section content. Spanish support is available in the Spanish edition of the guide on p. 74.

Quiz Unit 7 folder, p. 7 includes questions to check students' understanding of Section 3 content.

Presentation Pro CD-ROM
Quiz provides multiple-choice questions to check students' understanding of Section 3 content.

Answers to . . .

Section 3 Assessment

1. Knowing the exchange rate is important because other countries do not use the U.S. dollar as their currency. The exchange rate tells you how much your dollars are worth and what your spending power will be.
2. A strong U.S. dollar is a situation in which the dollar has increased in value in relation to other currencies. A weak dollar is a situation in which the U.S. dollar has decreased in value in relation to other currencies. A strong dollar makes imports less expensive. A weak dollar makes them more expensive.
3. A fixed exchange-rate system attempts to keep currency values between two or more countries constant. A flexible exchange-rate system allows the value of a currency to be determined by supply and demand. Changes in the international trading system along with inflation in the United States led to the adoption of a flexible exchange-rate system.
4. A trade deficit occurs when a nation imports more than it exports. The United States has been experiencing a trade deficit for several decades.
5. This is good news for American tourists because American dollars will now have an increased value in Canada, so their purchasing power will be greater.
6. It will cost about $58.
7. Students should prepare notes that accurately represent text information on one topic.

Answer to . . .

Building Key Concepts Every country listed grew as importers and exporters

Figure 17.12 Leading Exporters and Importers, 2003

Exporters	$ Billions	% Change 2002–2003	Importers	$ Billions	% Change 2002–2003
Germany	748.3	22	United States	1303.1	9
United States	723.8	4	Germany	607.1	23
Japan	471.8	13	China	413.1	40
China	437.9	34	United Kingdom	390.8	13
France	386.7	17	France	390.5	19
United Kingdom	304.6	9	Japan	382.9	14
Netherlands	294.1	20	Italy	290.8	18
Italy	292.1	15	Netherlands	262.8	20
Canada	272.7	8	Canada	245.0	8
Belgium	255.3	18	Belgium	235.4	18

Note: Billions are in U.S. dollars
Source: World Trade Organization

Go Online
PHSchool.com
Web Code: mng-7176

Many of the countries listed on this chart are becoming world trade powerhouses. **Trade Which countries grew as exporters and importers in 2003?**

from other countries now own a bigger piece of the American economy. They have used the surplus dollars they received from sales to Americans to purchase American land, stocks, bonds, and other assets.

Some worry that foreign investment might not always support the trade deficit. Federal Reserve Chairman Alan Greenspan has commented that "we do not know how long net imports and U.S. external debt can rise before foreign investors become reluctant to continue to add to their portfolios of claims against the United States." The U.S. Trade Deficit Review Commission reported in 2000 that "Maintaining large and growing trade deficits is neither desirable nor likely to be sustainable for the extended future."

To reduce the trade deficit, individuals and companies could purchase fewer foreign goods or they could sell more domestic products abroad. Nationally, the country could cut back spending by adjusting its monetary or fiscal policy. Or it could appreciate the exchange rate in order to make its own goods more expensive on the world market and make other countries' goods correspondingly less expensive. All of these approaches would result in fewer surplus dollars ending up in the hands of foreigners.

Section 3 Assessment

Progress Monitoring *Online*
For: Self-quiz with vocabulary practice
Web Code: mna-7177

Key Terms and Main Ideas

1. Explain why you need to know the **exchange rate** when you travel to a foreign country.
2. Explain what is meant by a strong or a weak dollar. How do a strong or a weak dollar affect prices of imports and exports?
3. What is the difference between a **fixed exchange-rate system** and a **flexible exchange-rate system?** Why did the United States shift to a flexible exchange-rate system in the early 1970s?
4. What is a **trade deficit?** How would you describe the current **balance of trade** in the United States?

Applying Economic Concepts

5. ***Critical Thinking*** Assume you have just heard that the Canadian dollar has weakened. Is this good news or bad news for travelers from the United States visiting Canada? Explain your answer.
6. ***Math Practice*** Suppose you are planning to take a train between the Chinese cities of Beijing and Xian. A ticket costs 480 renminbi. Use the exchange rate table in Figure 17.8 to calculate how much money in U.S. dollars the ticket will cost.
7. ***Try This*** You have been invited to a local high school to explain one of the following topics: **(a)** Understanding exchange rates or **(b)** The United States balance of trade. Choose one of the above topics and prepare notes for a brief presentation.

For: Comparison Activity
Visit: PHSchool.com
Web Code: mnd-7173

Progress Monitoring *Online*
For additional assessment, have students access Progress Monitoring Online at **Web Code:** mna-7177

Go Online PHSchool.com Typing in the Web Code when prompted will bring students directly to detailed instructions for this activity.

Trade

NAFTA: Is Free Trade a Good Idea?

In the 1980s and early 1990s, debate raged over the North American Free Trade Agreement (NAFTA). The goal of this agreement was to eliminate all trade restrictions among Mexico, Canada, and the United States. It included provisions for more than 9,000 products and services.

▲ NAFTA has given Mexico's electronics assembly industry a boost.

Pro-NAFTA Arguments Supporters of NAFTA argued it would benefit the economies of all three nations. They believed NAFTA would increase trade and promote healthy competition. They also argued that employment in some U.S. industries would increase, as the elimination of tariffs made American goods less expensive in Mexico and Canada.

Anti-NAFTA Arguments NAFTA critics argued that without tariffs, items produced in Mexico would be cheaper than American-made goods, resulting in widespread unemployment among American industrial workers. The authors of NAFTA anticipated this possibility and reduced its effects by slowly phasing out tariffs and by providing compensation to many workers who lost jobs because of NAFTA.

Consequences NAFTA went into effect January 1, 1994. By 2005, it was clear that NAFTA had a generally positive impact on the economies of all three trading partners. American exports of farm products, technology, and textiles to Mexico increased over pre-NAFTA levels. Canada's trade with the United States increased by 80 percent, while its trade with Mexico doubled. And although the United States did lose thousands of jobs because of increased imports, the growth in exports to Canada and Mexico resulted in thousands of newly created jobs.

Major Provisions of NAFTA

Automobile manufacturing
- **20% Mexican tariff on U.S. cars eliminated**

Agriculture
- **57% of all Canadian, U.S., and Mexican tariffs on farm products eliminated immediately**
- **Remaining tariffs phased out over 15 years**

Clothing and Textiles
- **Canadian and U.S. tariffs phased out over 10 years**
- **Mexican tariffs eliminated immediately**

Trucking
- **Mexican, Canadian, and U.S. truck drivers allowed to drive and deliver goods anywhere in North America**

Banking
- **U.S. banks and brokerage firms to have unlimited access to doing business in Mexico**

Applying Economic Ideas

1. How has NAFTA benefited the economies of all three nations that signed it?
2. The table shows some of the major provisions of NAFTA. Which of these provisions benefit the United States? Which have a negative impact? Explain.

Real-life Case Study: Trade

1. Focus Despite opposition from some critics, the North American Free Trade Agreement (NAFTA) has had a generally positive effect on trade among Mexico, the United States, and Canada.

2. Instruct Remind students why nations establish free trade agreements. Then discuss how NAFTA has benefited Canada, the United States, and Mexico.

3. Close/Reteach Ask students why two U.S. Presidents and members of Congress would support a treaty that they knew would probably result in some job losses in the United States.

Case Studies Activity
Case Studies in Free Enterprise folder, p. 34–35, "Soichiro Honda," helps students apply economic principles in an additional case study.

Economic Detective Activity
Unit 7 folder, p. 10, "Learning to Trade," provides an additional application of chapter concepts.

Interdisciplinary Connections: History

Trade and War Surprisingly, it was the *lack* of free trade that fostered the unrest that led to the American colonies' Revolutionary War against Great Britain. The British had passed a number of "Navigation Acts" in the 1600s and 1700s. Simply stated, these acts detailed how imports to and exports from Britain were to be transported. To protect British shipping, the acts decreed that certain goods coming into and going out of England had to be transported on British ships. The British tightened the acts in 1764, angering the American colonists and fueling their desire for independence from England.

Making the Connection Ask students to look up *mercantilism* in a reference work. Have them explain how this restrictive policy affected trade.

Answers to . . .

1. Overall trade levels between Canada, Mexico, and the United States have increased.
2. Students may suggest that the elimination of the tariff on American cars and the access to business in Mexico are beneficial. They might suggest that eliminating U.S. tariffs could have a negative impact in that a demand for cheaper Mexican goods might cause U.S. unemployment.

Chapter 17 Assessment

Key Terms

1. exchange rate
2. tariff
3. trade surplus
4. appreciation
5. exports
6. comparative advantage
7. infant industry

Using Graphic Organizers

8. Students should provide examples and brief descriptions of trade organizations, such as "APEC Pacific Rim countries" who have signed a nonbinding agreement to reduce trade barriers.

Reviewing Main Ideas

9. Trade and specialization benefit both trading partners by allowing nations to pursue a comparative advantage, raising living standards overall, and furthering friendly exchanges between nations.
10. A flexible exchange-rate system allows currency values to be based on supply and demand.
11. Students should list and describe three arguments such as the protection of jobs, the protection of infant industries, and the safeguarding of national security.
12. The United States stands to benefit because the U.S. economy is becoming more service-oriented.

Critical Thinking

13. Many jobs would probably be lost because American companies would stop making computers, and this is an important industry in the United States.
14. (a) A strong dollar will cause imports to increase and exports to decline. (b) A strong dollar will allow American tourists to buy more with their dollars.
15. The United States might have an emerging clock industry that it wants to protect. Effects could include retaliatory tariffs from other clock-making countries or the boycotting of American clocks by other nations.

Chapter 17 Assessment

Chapter Summary

A summary of major ideas in Chapter 17 appears below. See also the **Guide to the Essentials of Economics**, which provides additional review and test practice of key concepts in Chapter 17.

Section 1 Why Nations Trade (pp. 441–447)

Because resources are distributed unevenly throughout the world, nations specialize in producing certain goods and services, then trade to acquire the goods and services that they cannot produce. Nations, like individuals, specialize in producing goods and services based on the **law of comparative advantage:** that is, nations should specialize in producing the goods for which they have the lowest opportunity cost. As a result of specialization, both sides in the trading relationship benefit from trade.

Section 2 Trade Barriers and Agreements (pp. 449–456)

Import quotas, voluntary export restraints (VERs), and **tariffs** are three types of **trade barriers.** Their overall effect is to raise prices and protect domestic industries from foreign competition. People who favor **protectionism** argue that these measures are necessary to protect the jobs of domestic workers, shelter **infant industries,** and safeguard national security. Current trends, however, generally favor international cooperation, regional trade agreements, and an overall reduction in trade barriers.

Section 3 Measuring Trade (pp. 458–464)

After World War II, the United States and many of its trading partners used a **fixed exchange-rate system** in which exchange rates were fixed relative to the U.S. dollar. Today, most countries use a **flexible exchange-rate system** in which exchange rates shift according to market forces. As exchange rates change, currencies weaken and strengthen relative to other currencies. The difference between a nation's imports and exports is called the **balance of trade.** When a country imports more than it exports, it has a **trade deficit.** The United States has generally had a large trade deficit since the 1970s.

Key Terms

Complete each sentence by choosing the correct answer from the list of terms below. You will not use all of the terms.

comparative advantage	**imports**
appreciation	**infant industry**
exchange rate	**protectionism**
exports	**tariff**
free-trade zone	**trade surplus**
	depreciation

1. The ____ determines how much a foreign currency is worth in a certain nation.
2. Nations may choose to impose a ____, or tax, on imports from other countries.
3. A ____ occurs when one nation exports more goods than it imports.
4. Economists use the term ____ to refer to one nation's currency rising in value in comparison to another country's currency.
5. Goods shipped abroad for sale are ____.
6. A country has a ____ when it has the lowest opportunity cost of producing a good.
7. A young business that is shielded from foreign competition is called a(n) ____.

Using Graphic Organizers

8. On a separate sheet of paper, copy the web map below to help you organize information about trade organizations. Complete the web map by writing examples of trade organizations. Include a brief description of each organization in the blank circles.

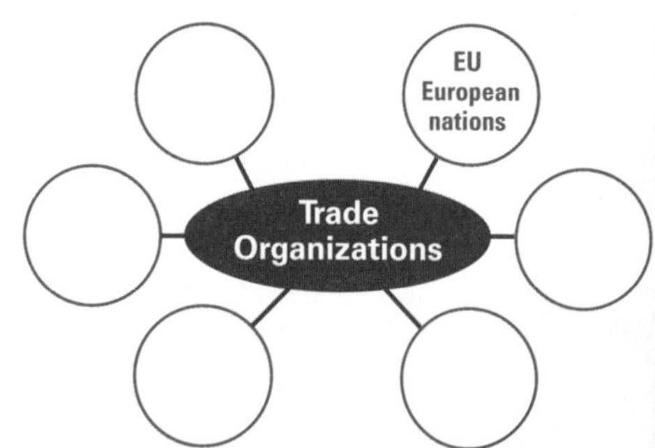

Reviewing Main Ideas

9. How do specialization and trade benefit both trading partners?
10. Explain the concept of a flexible exchange-rate system.
11. List and describe three arguments in favor of trade barriers.
12. Why does the United States stand to benefit from increased trade in services?

Critical Thinking

13. **Analyzing Information** Suppose the United States loses its comparative advantage in producing computers. How would this loss affect employment in the United States?
14. **Drawing Conclusions** Suppose you have heard that the U.S. dollar is strong on world markets. (a) What does this news mean for imports and exports? (b) How will it affect American tourists in other countries?
15. **Recognizing Cause and Effect** Assume the United States has established a tariff on clocks. Why would the United States establish this tariff, and what are two possible effects of its enactment?

Problem-Solving Activity

16. Divide your class into small groups, each group representing a country. Have each country answer the following questions: What goods and services will you produce? With which other countries will you trade? Will tariffs and import quotas exist? Discuss the implications of your choices for the other countries in your class.

Economics Journal

Organizing Ideas Review your Economics Journal entry for Chapter 17. Then answer the following questions: Which countries do the items represent? Do the countries you have listed have any similarities, such as where they are located? What generalizations about the comparative advantages of these countries or regions can you make?

Skills for Life

Creating a Multimedia Presentation Review the steps shown on page 448; then use the chart below to help you plan your presentation. You have been asked to create a multimedia presentation on NAFTA.

17. Review the discussion of NAFTA on pages 454–455 and in the Chapter 17 Case Study on page 465. What aspects of NAFTA should you learn more about?
18. Into what segments will you divide your presentation?
19. What types of sources might you use for your presentation?
20. What sort of audio-visual aids could you use?

PREPRODUCTION TOPIC ANALYSIS SHEET

Assignment: North American Free Trade Agreement

Aspects of NAFTA to consider: ____________
1. ____________
2. ____________

My choice: ____________

Segment description and sequence:
1. ____________
2. ____________
3. ____________

Sources of information: ____________

____

Audio-Visual Aids: ____________

____

____

Progress Monitoring *Online*

For: Chapter 17 Self-Test **Visit:** PHSchool.com
Web Code: mna-7171

As a final review, take the Economics Chapter 17 Self-Test and receive immediate feedback on your answers. The test consists of 20 multiple-choice questions designed to test your understanding of the chapter content.

Problem-Solving Activity

16. Answers will vary among groups, but students should demonstrate an understanding of international trade, comparative advantage, and other chapter concepts.

Skills for Life

17. Students should use the chart to organize their own information. Students may suggest learning about the provisions of the agreement, reactions to them, and their effects.
18. Students may suggest segments based on the provisions with spoken reactions to each by political leaders and individual citizens.
19. Students may suggest almanacs, newspaper and magazine reports, and government documents.
20. Students may suggest videotaped interviews, conference calls, or the Internet.

Additional support materials and activities for Chapter 17 of *Economics: Principles in Action* can be found in the Social Studies area of **PHSchool.com**

Economics Journal

Students should provide accurate information about the items they listed and make reasonable generalizations about countries and regions of the world, based on the items.

Review and Assessment

Vocabulary Practice Unit 7 folder, p. 9 uses a crossword puzzle to reinforce understanding of key terms.

GTE **Guide to the Essentials** Chapter 17 Test, p. 75

Test Bank CD-ROM Chapter 17 Test

Go Online PHSchool.com Students may use the Chapter 17 Self-Test on **PHSchool.com** to prepare for the Chapter Test.

Economics Simulation

Objectives Upon completion of this simulation, students should be able to:
- explain the effects of protectionist policies on the prices of goods;
- explain why protectionist policies are bad for consumers but beneficial to domestic industries.

Bellringer Ask students why countries might want to protect their industries. (*The industry needs time to mature; politicians want to save jobs in the industry; the industry is suffering from a temporary downturn that could damage it badly if inexpensive, foreign substitutes flood the market.*) Explain that in this simulation they will see some of the effects of protectionist policies.

1. Focus Explain that protectionist policies have a long history as a tool of government policy. Tell students that in the long run, protectionism tends to harm consumers by raising prices and that in this simulation they will see how tariffs and bans on foreign goods can cause prices to rise but protect domestic producers.

2. Instruct Have students prepare for and conduct the simulation, using the procedures noted in the text.

3. Close/Reteach Have students complete the transaction chart. As a class, discuss their answers to the first three analysis questions. Assign the Drawing Conclusions question as a follow-up.

Economic Simulation
Economic Simulations folder, pp. 40–45, "Foreign Exchange and International Trade," provides an additional simulation on a unit topic.

Economics Simulation Protectionist Policies

The laws of supply and demand apply in international trade as well as in the domestic market. Consumers and producers negotiate to find a price they can agree on. In international trade, though, there is often another player—government. Governments may put certain kinds of restrictions on particular goods in order to protect industries and workers at home. In this simulation, you will explore some effects that protectionist policies have on trade.

▲ How might protectionist policies affect the cost of these foreign-produced coats?

Materials
20 slips of paper (one color)
10 slips of paper (contrasting color)
10 slips of paper (third color)
2 small boxes
notebook paper

Preparing the Simulation

In this simulation, you will role-play foreign and domestic producers who are competing to sell wool coats. Labor costs and other factors make domestic coat manufacturing more expensive. Certain government policies try to make up for this to protect domestic manufacturing. You will discover how different kinds of protectionist policies affect the workings of supply and demand.

Step 1: Your class will be divided into two equal groups: Consumers and Producers.

Step 2: The Consumers group will prepare 20 slips of colored paper that represent the prices a Consumer is willing to pay for a coat. Number these slips from $15 to $110 by fives ($15, $20, $25, and so on). Put these slips into a box.

Step 3: Meanwhile, the Producers group will prepare two sets of ten slips each (each set in a different color). These slips will represent the costs to produce a coat. One color will designate Foreign Producers. Number the Foreign Producers' slips from $10 to $50 by tens ($10, $20, etc.). The other color will designate Domestic Producers. Number the Domestic Producers' slips from $60 to $100 by tens ($60, $70, etc.). Each amount will be used twice—two $60 slips, two $70 slips, and so on. Put all the Producer slips into a second box.

Step 4: Each member of the Consumer group will draw a slip from the Consumer box. This is the maximum price you are willing to pay for a coat. Each member of the Producer group should draw a slip from the Producer box. The color indicates whether you are a Foreign or a Domestic Producer, and the amount represents your cost to make a coat.

Conducting the Simulation

There will be three trading periods. Your goal in each trading period is to make the best deal you can—to buy below your maximum price if you are a Consumer, and to sell for more than your cost if you are a Producer.

If you are a Consumer, your score is your savings—the difference between the maximum price you were willing to pay and the price you actually paid for a coat. For example, if the price on your slip is $50, and you succeed in buying a coat for only $30, your score is $20. If you are a Producer, your score is your profit—the difference between your cost to produce the coat and the price at which you can sell it.

You do not have to buy or sell a coat in any trading period, but if you do not, your score for that round will be $0. Your teacher will keep a record of all the transactions. You should also keep a record of your own scores. The final score is the sum of all savings (Consumers) or profits (Producers).

Trading Period 1

Producers and Consumers will meet in a trading area and try to make deals. Each person can buy or sell one coat in each trading period. When you reach an agreement, report the price and your own score to the teacher. The trading period will end when no more pairs of Producers and Consumers can make a deal. Your teacher will list the prices at which coats were sold and their origins (domestic or foreign) in this trading period.

Trading Period 2

Now you will see the results of one kind of protectionist policy. The government has imposed a tariff—an import tax—of $30 on each imported coat. If you are a Foreign Producer, add $30 to your cost amount. Then trade as before. Record your transaction with your teacher.

Trading Period 3

Another government policy changes the market. Politicians from textile-manufacturing states have succeeded in banning imports of wool coats. As a result, the Foreign Producers cannot take part in this trading period. Consumers must try to buy coats from the remaining Domestic Producers. Record your transaction with your teacher.

Transactions Chart

	Trading Period 1	Trading Period 2	Trading Period 3
Number of deals made			
Number of Consumers unable to buy			
Number of Producers unable to sell			
Average price for a wool coat			
Lowest price			
Highest price			

Simulation Analysis

Use a sheet of notebook paper to create a transaction chart like the one on this page. As a class, complete the transaction chart using information that you reported to your teacher. Discuss the following questions as a group.

1. In which trading period were the largest number of coats sold?
2. In Trading Period 2, what were the effects of the tariff on the Foreign Producers? On Consumers? How did the tariff affect Domestic Producers?
3. What happened to coat prices when imports from Foreign Producers were banned in Trading Period 3? Why?
4. **Drawing Conclusions** In the real world, what would domestic coat producers probably do if imported coats were banned? Why?

Interdisciplinary Connections: Current Events

Protectionism in the News Countries continue to put protectionist policies in place and to accuse other nations of protecting their own products in an unfair manner. By searching the international news students can see how protectionism works out in real situations.

Making the Connection Have individual students search news sources from the last year for stories about protectionism. Ask them to clip or photocopy at least two articles and write a summary that compares and contrasts the effects of the policies.

Differentiated Instruction L3

Organize students into groups of four. Have each group research an industry in the United States that is suffering or has suffered from foreign competition. Have two students in each group plan an argument for protectionism based on this situation. Have the other two students argue against protectionism and in favor of a free market without trade barriers. Allow groups to present their opposing arguments to the class.

Background

Economics in History

Voices have been raised against protectionism for more than 100 years. As protectionist sympathies were spreading in France in the mid-1800s, French economist Claude-Frédéric Bastiat (1801-1851) wrote a fictitious letter from French candlemakers against their "unfair" competition. The letter pleaded with the French government to take measures against this competitor by ordering that windows, skylights, curtains, and blinds be kept shut. Bastiat's wry protest, of course, was against the natural light of the sun!

Answers to . . .

1. Students will probably note that the most coats were sold in Trading Period 1.
2. The effects of the tariff on Foreign Producers would be to reduce their profits because fewer foreign coats would be sold. Consumers would save less money because the coats they bought would generally cost more. Domestic Producers would benefit because more Consumers would buy their coats.
3. Average coat prices would generally be higher because the cheaper foreign coats could no longer be offered for sale.
4. Domestic producers would probably raise their prices because they would not have to worry about consumers purchasing cheaper foreign coats.

Chapter Resource Manager

Chapter 18 Economic Development and Transitions

For more pacing suggestions, see the Economics Pacing Guide in the Program Overview of the Teaching Resources.

Section Objectives	Print and Technology Resources	
1 Levels of Development *(pp. 471–476)* **Objectives** 1. Understand what is meant by developed nations and less developed countries. 2. Identify the tools used to measure levels of development. 3. Describe the characteristics of developed nations and less developed countries. 4. Understand how levels of development are ranked.	• **Lesson Planner** Section 1 Lesson Plan, p. 71 • **Lesson Plans folder** Section 1 Lesson Plan, p. 24 • **Unit 7 folder** Guided Reading and Review, p. 13 Careers in Economics, Regional Planner, p. 24 Economic Cartoon, p. 25 Section 1 Quiz, p. 14 • **Math Practice folder** Determining Economic Growth, p. 4	• **Presentation Pro CD-ROM** Section 1 • **Transparency Resource Package** Economics Organizers, G7: Tree Map Graphic Organizer Economics Concepts, 18A: World Political Map Economics Concepts, 18B: Levels of Development (Overlay) Economics Concepts, 18C: Per Capita Energy Consumption (Overlay) • **Section Reading Support Transparency System**
2 Issues in Development *(pp. 478–483)* **Objectives** 1. Identify the causes and effects of rapid population growth. 2. Describe the effects of the unequal distribution of the factors of production. 3. Understand the importance of human capital to development. 4. Analyze how political factors and debt are obstacles to development.	• **Lesson Planner** Section 2 Lesson Plan, p. 72 • **Learning Styles Lesson Plans folder** Section 2 Lesson Plan, p. 41 • **Lesson Plans folder** Section 2 Lesson Plan, p. 65 • **Unit 7 folder** Guided Reading and Review, p. 15 Economic Skills, p. 21 Section 2 Quiz, p. 16	• **Source Articles folder** Moscow Diary, pp. 54–56 • **Presentation Pro CD-ROM** Section 2 • **Transparency Resource Package** Economics Organizers, G9: Multi-Flow Chart Graphic Organizer Economics Concepts, 18D: Per Capita Calorie Supply (Overlay) • **Section Reading Support Transparency System** • **Social Studies Skills Tutor CD-ROM**
3 Financing Development *(pp. 485–488)* **Objectives** 1. Understand the role investment plays in development. 2. Identify the purposes of foreign aid. 3. Describe the functions of various international economic institutions.	• **Lesson Planner** Section 3 Lesson Plan, p. 73 • **Lesson Plans folder** Section 3 Lesson Plan, p. 66 • **Economics Assessment Rubrics folder** Writing Assignment, pp. 6–7 • **Unit 7 folder** Guided Reading and Review, p. 17 Section 3 Quiz, p. 18	• **Presentation Pro CD-ROM** Section 3 • **Transparency Resource Package** Economics Organizers, G5: Web Graphic Organizer Economics Concepts, 18E: International Economic Institutions • **Section Reading Support Transparency System**
4 Transitions to Free Enterprise *(pp. 489–494)* **Objectives** 1. Identify some important steps in moving from a centrally planned economy toward a free market economy. 2. Describe the political and economic changes that have taken place in Russia in recent decades. 3. Describe the actions that China's communist government has taken to introduce free market reforms into China.	• **Lesson Planner** Section 4 Lesson Plan, p. 74 • **Learning Styles Lesson Plans folder** Section 4 Lesson Plan, p. 42 • **Lesson Plans folder** Section 4 Lesson Plan, p. 67 • **Unit 7 folder** Guided Reading and Review, p. 19 Vocabulary Practice, p. 22 Economic Detective, p. 23 Section 4 Quiz, p. 20 • **Case Studies in Free Enterprise folder** George Soros, pp. 36–37	• **Presentation Pro CD-ROM** Section 4 • **Transparency Resource Package** Economics Organizers, G6: Double Web Graphic Organizer Economics Concepts, 18F: Transition to Free Enterprise in Russia Economics Concepts, 18G: Economies in Transition • **Section Reading Support Transparency System**

Differentiated Instruction

Descriptive Phrases L2

To further English language learners' acquisition of vocabulary, ask them to create descriptive phrases for key economic concepts, key inventions, and key events. Assign students to work either individually or with a partner and find examples of the concept, figure, or event. Instruct students to create a bulleted list of descriptive phrases and adjectives that describe their given topic. Provide students with a thesaurus to assist them with the assignment. Then ask students to read their list of descriptive phrases to the class. Allow members of the class guess what is being described. Write the list of possible items on the board to assist students in guessing the right name.

Independent Research L4

Challenge advanced readers by asking them to independently research material that goes beyond what is presented in the textbook. By honing their research skills, these advanced readers are learning to be independent thinkers and are developing skills that will aid them in future studies. The text provides an excellent base knowledge that can be used to springboard individual student research. You may assign students to research the personal backgrounds and biographies of individuals mentioned in a particular chapter. Students can be asked to conduct in-depth research on events that are only given passing mention by the text. Students should present their research to the class via a multimedia presentation or oral report.

Go Online
PHSchool.com

Visit the Social Studies area of the Prentice Hall Web site. There you can find additional links to enrich chapter content for *Economics: Principles in Action* as well as a self-test for students. Be sure to check out this month's **eTeach** online discussion with a Master Economics Teacher.

Web Code: mnf-7181

Running Out of Time?

- Use the **Presentation Pro CD-ROM** to create an outline for this chapter.
- Use the Chapter Summary in the **Chapter 18 Assessment,** p. 496.
- Use the Section Summaries for Chapter 18, from **Guide to the Essentials of Economics (English and Spanish).**

THE WALL STREET JOURNAL. CLASSROOM EDITION

Prentice Hall brings into the classroom the authoritative content of *The Wall Street Journal Classroom Edition.* See the Source Articles, Debating Current Issues, and You and Your Money folders in the **Teaching Resources**. Also, see Economics Video Library, "ABCs of the IMF."

Assessment Resources

Chapter Assessment

Teaching Resources Unit 7, Chapter 18

- Section Quizzes, pp. 14, 16, 18, 20

Exam *View*® Test Bank CD-ROM Chapter 18

Economics Assessment Rubrics

Chapter 18 Self-Test, **Web Code:** mna-1011

Reading and Skills Evaluation

Progress Monitoring Assessments

- Screening Test
- Diagnostic Test of Social Studies Skills

Cumulative Testing and Remediation

Progress Monitoring Assessments

- Benchmark Test #3

Standardized Test Preparation

Test Prep Workbook

Test-Taking Strategies With Transparencies

Differentiated Instruction Key

L1 Special Needs	LPR Less Proficient Readers
L2 Basic to Average	AR Advanced Readers
L3 All Students	SN Special Needs Students
L4 Average to Advanced	GT Gifted and Talented
	ELL English Language Learner

Chapter 18

Economic Development and Transition

Introducing the Chapter

This chapter describes issues that confront less developed countries and discusses opportunities for financing development. Students will also learn about the steps Russia and China are taking as they move from centrally planned to market-based economies.

For additional links for *Economics: Principles in Action* provided by Prentice Hall and *The Wall Street Journal Classroom Edition,* visit the Social Studies area. Be sure to check out this month's **eTeach** online discussion with a Master Teacher.

Beyond the Lecture

You may cover the concepts in Chapter 18 in an activity-based style by using the following materials:

- **Technology Resources** appropriate for use with this chapter are noted on pp. 472, 475, 476, 481, 483, 487, 488, 492, 493, 494, and 497.
- **Presentation Pro CD-ROM** with animated graphs gives you an alternative method for organizing and delivering chapter content.
- **Activities** designed to meet the needs of students of mixed abilities and learning styles are noted throughout the chapter in the side columns.
- **Learning Styles Lesson Plans** provide alternate lessons for diverse learning styles. See pp. 41–42 of the Learning Styles Lesson Plans folder located in the Teaching Resources.

Economics Journal

Instruct students to write their responses to the question in their Economics Journals. Students may include completed journal entries in an Economics Portfolio.

Chapter 18 Economic Development and Transition

The path to development is long and difficult. As nations struggle to improve their economies and their standards of living they are met with a variety of complex issues.

Economics Journal

Examine the photo on this page. What can you infer about the standard of living in this woman's country? List your ideas on a separate piece of paper.

Go Online
PHSchool.com
For: Current Data
Visit: PHSchool.com
Web Code: mng-7181

National Council on Economic Education

The following Voluntary National Content Standard in Economics is addressed in this chapter:

★ **Standard 15** Students will understand that: Investment in factories, machinery, new technology, and the health, education, and the training of people can raise future standards of living.

For more information about the standards, contact the National Council on Economic Education

1140 Avenue of the Americas
New York, NY 10036
1-800-338-1192

Section 1 Levels of Development

Preview

Objectives

After studying this section you will be able to:

1. **Understand** what is meant by developed nations and less developed countries.
2. **Identify** the tools used to measure levels of development.
3. **Describe** the characteristics of developed nations and less developed countries.
4. **Understand** how levels of development are ranked.

Section Focus

Nations throughout the world exhibit varying levels of economic well-being. Many tools are used to measure a nation's level of development.

Key Terms

development
developed nation
less developed country
per capita gross domestic product (per capita GDP)
industrialization
subsistence agriculture
literacy rate
life expectancy
infant mortality rate
infrastructure
newly industrialized country (NIC)

Three billion people—half the world's population—live in extreme poverty. The United Nations estimates that 1 billion people live on less than $1 a day. Concern over these startling statistics has led to close examination of the world's economies.

Social scientists measure the economic well-being of a nation in terms of its level of development. **Development** is the process by which a nation improves the economic, political, and social well-being of its people.

development *the process by which a nation improves the economic, political, and social well-being of its people*

developed nation *nation with a higher average level of material well-being*

less developed country *nation with a low level of material well-being*

Developed Nations and Less Developed Countries

Some nations enjoy a high standard of living. Wealthy nations, such as the United States, Canada, the nations of Western Europe, Australia, New Zealand, and Japan, are called developed nations. **Developed nations** are those nations with a higher average level of material well-being. Most nations, however, have low levels of material well-being. These are the **less developed countries** (LDCs). LDCs include the world's poorest countries, such as Bangladesh, Nepal, Albania, and the nations of Central and Southern Africa. They also include nations such as Mexico, Poland, Saudi Arabia, and the former republics of the Soviet Union. The countries in this second group of nations are not the world's poorest, but they have yet to achieve the high standard of living of the world's developed nations.

It is important to remember that development refers to a nation's material well-being. It is not a judgment of the worth of a nation or its people. The level of development does not indicate cultural superiority or inferiority. Rather, the level of development indicates how well a nation is able to feed, clothe, and shelter its people. It indicates how healthy people are, how well they are educated, and how productive they are.

Measuring Development

Life expectancy, diet, access to health care, literacy, energy consumption, and many other factors are used to measure development. As you will read below, the primary measure of a country's development, however, is per capita gross domestic product (GDP).

Graphing the Main Idea

BUILDING KEY CONCEPTS

Standard of Living To build understanding of the tools used to measure **standard of living,** have students complete a tree map graphic organizer like the one at the right. Remind students that a tree map graphic organizer shows an outline for a main topic, main ideas, and supporting details. Suggest that students place the section title in the top box, the main headings in the next boxes, and main points and supporting details in the next row of boxes.

Section Reading Support Transparencies A template and the answers for this graphic organizer can be found in Chapter 18, Section 1 of the Section Reading Support Transparency System.

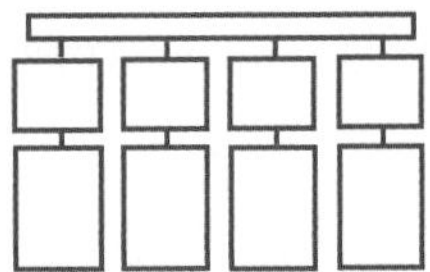

Section 1

Levels of Development

Objectives You may wish to call students' attention to the objectives in the Section Preview. The objectives are reflected in the main headings of the section.

Bellringer Ask students whether they have ever traveled in other countries. Ask those who have traveled abroad to describe their first impressions of the places they visited. Would they describe these places as prosperous or impoverished? What factors support this judgment? Tell students that in this section they will look at the tools used to measure levels of development.

Vocabulary Builder Have students skim this section to find out the meanings of the key terms. Then ask pairs of students to examine recent almanacs and to report on what they discovered about these terms in the almanacs.

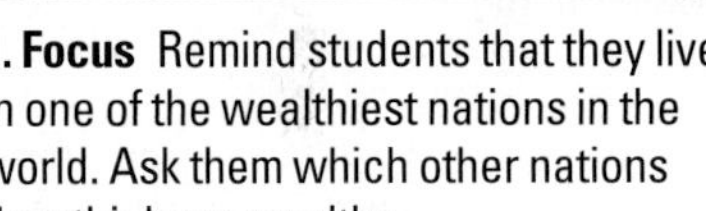

Lesson Plan

Teaching the Main Concepts L3

1. Focus Remind students that they live in one of the wealthiest nations in the world. Ask them which other nations they think are wealthy.
2. Instruct Explain the differences between developed nations and less developed countries. Discuss the tools that are used to measure development, showing how these are related to the material well-being of citizens. Use these measurement tools to contrast the characteristics of developed nations and less developed countries.
3. Close/Reteach Remind students that these rankings are economic and have to do with material well-being. Ask them how the United States benefits from cultural exchange with less developed countries.

Guided Reading and Review
Unit 7 folder, p. 13 asks students to identify the main ideas of the section and to define or identify key terms.

Transparency Resource Package
Economics Concepts, 18A: World Political Map

Differentiated Instruction L3

(Reteaching) To confirm students' understanding of what is meant by developed and less developed countries, have students create a Venn diagram. Tell them to label the circles *Developed Nations* and *Less Developed Countries.* Then, in the separated areas, have them list names of countries and characteristics that are unique to each grouping. In the area of overlap, students should list shared characteristics such as governmental structure and traditions.

Meeting NCEE Standards

Use the following benchmark activity from the **Voluntary National Content Standards in Economics** to evaluate student understanding of **Standard 15.**

Analyze per capita real GDP data for several periods in history, identifying periods during which the United States experienced rapid economic growth; identify the factors that contributed to this growth.

Economic Cartoon
Unit 7 folder, p. 25 gives students practice in interpreting cartoons about section content.

Math Practice Activity
Math Practice folder, p. 3, "Determining Economic Growth," allows students to calculate per capita GDP and examine how it can be used to measure economic growth.

Answer to . . .

Building Key Concepts United States, highest; Mali, lowest

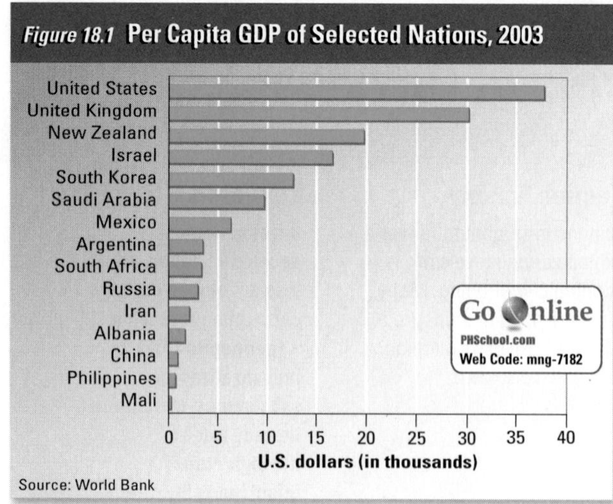

BUILDING KEY CONCEPTS Per capita GDP varies greatly among nations.
Standard of Living Which nation on this graph do you think has the highest standard of living. The lowest?

Per Capita GDP

As you read in Chapter 12, gross domestic product, or GDP, is the total market value of all the final goods and services produced within an economy in a given year. It is used to measure the economic activity of a nation. GDP measures the value of production and also provides a measure of income for an economy. **Per capita gross domestic product (per capita GDP)** is a nation's GDP divided by its total population.

Development experts use per capita GDP figures because GDP alone is not adequate to compare the living standards within nations. For example, Australia and India have similar GDPs, around $465 billion for Australia and around $540 billion for India. Yet, Australia enjoys a high standard of living, while India is very poor. What accounts for this difference? The answer is population size.

Australia's $465 billion is shared by fewer than 20 million people. India's $540 billion is shared by about 1.1 billion people. This is why economists use per capita GDP to compare levels of development. Australia's per capita GDP is around $23,570. India's per capita GDP is around $500. (See Figure 18.2.)

per capita gross domestic product (per capita GDP) *a nation's gross domestic product (GDP) divided by its total population*

industrialization *the extensive organization of an economy for the purpose of manufacture*

subsistence agriculture *level of farming in which a person raises only enough food to feed his or her family*

These per capita figures indicate that the average Australian can more easily meet basic needs than the average Indian. The average Australian also has income left over to spend on nonessentials or to save.

Using per capita GDP to measure a nation's economic health has its limitations, however. Per capita GDP does not take into account a country's distribution of income. Within every nation, some people are wealthier than most, while others are poorer than most. In many less developed countries, the gap between rich and poor is especially wide. In some LDCs, a small, wealthy elite controls much of the wealth while most of the nation's population remains poor.

Energy Consumption

Energy consumption is another way to measure development. The amounts of fossil fuel, hydroelectricity, and nuclear energy a nation uses depends on its level of industrialization. **Industrialization** is the extensive organization of an economy for the purpose of manufacture. Industrial processes generally require large amounts of energy. For this reason, low levels of energy use tend to indicate low levels of industrial activity. High levels of energy use tend to indicate high levels of industrial activity. Because most of the developed nations of the world are highly industrialized, they are sometimes referred to as "industrialized nations."

Nations that have low levels of per capita energy consumption tend to have little industry. Most of the people in such nations are farmers working with simple tools and few machines. This is true of many LDCs, where large portions of the population engage in **subsistence agriculture.** That is, they are able to raise only enough food to feed their families.

Labor Force

What does it mean for the economy if a nation has low industrialization? It means that most of the labor force is devoted to agriculture. If most of the people are working simply to raise food for them-

Econ 101: Key Concepts Made Easy

Standard of Living Students may have difficulty understanding how the methods of measuring **development** can really reflect the quality of life in a nation. Point out that the methods discussed here have the advantage of being backed by hard data: production numbers, energy consumption rates, numbers of people in various occupations, and so on. Although these do not give a full picture of the quality of life within a nation, they provide standards for comparing conditions among nations. Ask students what other statistics might be compared to give a more complete picture of economic similarities and differences among nations.

selves, few are available to work in industry. As a result, there is little opportunity for workers to specialize. (Recall from Chapter 2 that specialization makes economies more efficient.) If individuals—or nations—are unable to produce specialized goods to sell, they are unable to generate cash income.

Consumer Goods

The quantity of consumer goods a nation produces per capita can also indicate its level of development. A large number of consumer goods in an economy means that people have enough money to meet their basic needs and still have some money left over for nonessential goods. Social scientists look to the number of large consumer goods per person to measure development. They count, for example, how many people have televisions, automobiles, refrigerators, washing machines, or telephones.

Literacy

Usually, the more a country's people attend school, the higher its level of development. This makes sense because the greater the number of people that can read and write, the more productive a population can be at both industrial and agricultural jobs.

A country's **literacy rate** is the proportion of the population over age 15 that can read and write. A well-educated nation has a high literacy rate. A low literacy rate indicates a poorly educated nation.

Life Expectancy

Life expectancy is the average expected life span of an individual. It indicates how well an economic system supports life and fends off death. A population that is well nourished and housed, as well as protected from disease, will have a long life expectancy. A population that has a poor diet and shelter and that is exposed to poor sanitation and disease will have a shorter life expectancy.

literacy rate *the proportion of the population over age 15 that can read and write*

life expectancy *the average expected life span of an individual*

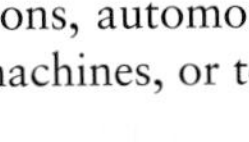

Australia (left) and India (right) have very different standards of living.
Gross Domestic Product **What do the photos below tell you about the population levels of Australia and India? How do their population levels affect the measurement of per capita GDP?**

Figure 18.2 Comparing Australia and India

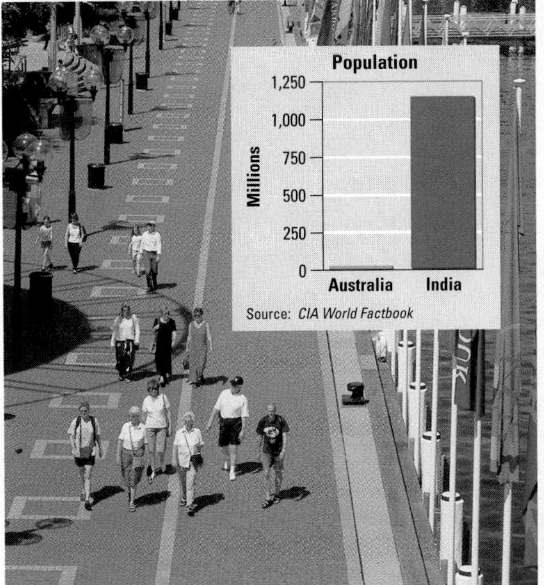

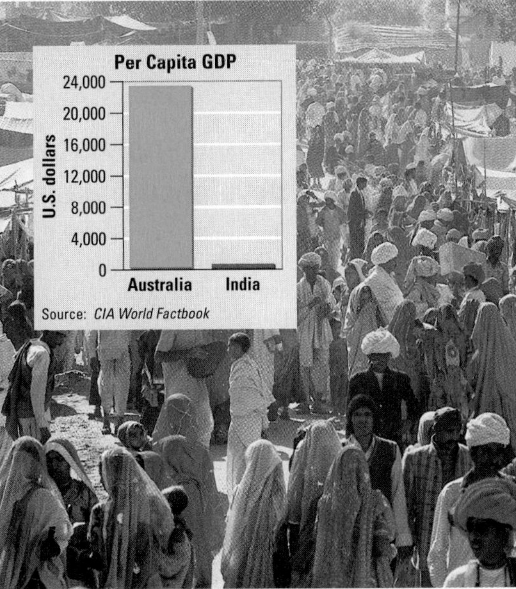

Differentiated Instruction L4

You may wish to have students add the following to their portfolios. Ask them to make a list of the tools used to measure development. Then instruct them to create captioned posters that briefly describe each of these measurement tools and give sample statistics from two nations of the world. Have copies of recent almanacs available as resources for students. GT

Databank, pp. 546–547 contains a variety of graphs that can be used as resources for study of global development issues.

Background

Careers in Economics

Social science is a broad occupational category that includes people who study all aspects of human society. Social scientists examine everything from how societies distribute goods and services to the ways in which groups within a society relate to each other. Economists are social scientists, and they often work closely with others in this larger field. Here are some of the main groups of social scientists:

- *Anthropologists* study the origins of human beings and their physical, social, and cultural development.
- *Geographers* analyze how the distribution of physical and cultural elements affects regions and groups.
- *Political scientists* study the origins, development, and functioning of political systems and public policy.
- *Urban and regional planners* develop comprehensive plans and programs for the use of land.

Block Scheduling Strategies

Consider these suggestions to take advantage of extended class time:

- Extend the Vocabulary Builder and combine it with the first activity on this page. Have groups of three to four students select three countries that they believe are at differing levels of development. Ask the groups to create the posters as instructed in the portfolio activity, adding visuals (graphs or charts) for their selected nations within each development category.
- Extend the Background note on this page by having students find out more about one of the categories of social science. Encourage students to interview professionals from the fields they choose and give oral reports.
- Have students choose two nations and examine economic data that is available on each from at least two different sources. Ask them to prepare a report on their findings, including an analysis of discrepancies between the sources.

Answer to . . .

Building Key Concepts India's population is much larger, so the per capita GDP is much smaller.

Differentiated Instruction L3

Organize students into groups of four or five. Tell them to create short news presentations that will illuminate the differences between developed nations and less developed countries. Have them use the information in the section as they prepare their reports, but suggest that they check other sources as well. Encourage them to use visuals and simulated interviews in their presentations.

Differentiated Instruction L2

Ask students to copy the main headings from this section (Developed Nations and Less Developed Countries, Measuring Development, and so on) onto a piece of paper. Have them write five facts from the appropriate section under each heading. LPR

▶ **In the developed world, the infant mortality rate is 8; in the less developed world, it is 62.**

infant mortality rate *the number of deaths that occur in the first year of life per 1,000 live births*

infrastructure *the services and facilities necessary for an economy to function*

Infant Mortality Rate

Another measure of development related to nutrition and health care is a country's infant mortality rate. A country's **infant mortality rate** indicates the number of deaths that occur in the first year of life per 1,000 live births. For example, the United States has an infant mortality rate of 6.4. This means that out of every 1,000 infants born alive in a given year, 6.4 of them die before they reach their first birthdays. Like most measures of development, infant mortality rate is an average. Not all regions of a country or sectors of a population have the same infant mortality rates.

Characteristics of Developed Nations

Developed nations have high per capita GDPs, and a majority of their populations are neither very rich nor very poor. Developed nations enjoy a higher degree of economic and political freedom than do less developed countries. They also have a high degree of consumer spending. For example, in the United States, the average household has at least two television sets.

In most developed nations, agricultural output is high, but relatively few people work on farms. Use of advanced irrigation techniques, fertilizers, pesticides, seed varieties, and heavy machinery makes farmers very productive. In the United States a single farmer can feed 80 people. Compare this to many LDCs, where a single farmer can support only his or her own family.

Since only a small portion of the labor force is needed in agriculture in a developed nation, most of the labor force is available to work in industry and services. High per capita energy use in developed nations reflects a high level of industrialization. Widespread use of technology increases the productivity of the work force.

The populations of developed nations are generally very healthy. Infant mortality rates are low, while life expectancy is high. People in developed nations tend to be well educated, and literacy rates are high.

Developed nations have been urbanized for many generations. That is, most of their populations live in cities and towns and have done so for many years. A solid infrastructure has grown along with these cities and towns. **Infrastructure** is the services and facilities necessary for an economy to function. Transportation and communication systems, roads, power plants, schools, and banks are all part of a nation's infrastructure, which determines that nation's capacity to produce.

▶ **Technology plays a huge role in agricultural productivity.**

Interdisciplinary Connections: Geography

Risky Business Dun & Bradstreet, an English firm specializing in business information, publishes a report called the *International Risk and Payment Review.* It assesses the relative risk of doing business with 120 countries throughout the world. Information about such factors as currency fluctuations, speed of payment, and political activity support comparative ratings of the countries with which it is most risky to do business and those with which it is least risky.

Making the Connection In 1998–1999 the four highest-risk countries with which to do business were the Democratic Republic of the Congo, Albania, Myanmar, and Yugoslavia. The four least risky were the United States, Denmark, Luxembourg, and France. Ask students to suggest factors that would affect placement of each of these countries on the lists.

Characteristics of Less Developed Countries

Less developed countries have low per capita GDPs. Low per capita energy consumption signals their low level of industrialization. Many in the labor force work on their own farms and grow only enough food to feed themselves and their families. Unemployment rates are high, often around 20 percent. In addition, much of the labor force is underemployed. That is, some people have work, but not enough. They cannot support themselves or their families because they work less than eight hours a day.

Even if an LDC could produce consumer goods, most of the population would be unable to buy them. Subsistence-level agriculture does not provide a family with an income. It is so labor-intensive that farmers have no time for other work, even if they could find it.

The impoverished economy of an LDC has trouble educating the populace. Resources for schools are limited. In addition, children in subsistence-level economies are often needed to work on the family farm, limiting the amount of time they can spend in school.

Literacy rates in LDCs are very low. In Cambodia, for example, only 35 percent of the people over 15 years old can read and write. Compare this figure with the United States, where the literacy rate is nearly 100 percent.

Global Connections

Global Development and the Environment In 1997, the Kyoto Protocol was signed by 159 nations in an effort to reduce greenhouse gas emissions. Less developed countries, such as Brazil, China, India, and Mexico, voiced concern over who would pay for these measures, and whether they would hamper economic growth. In further discussions, participants recognized that less developed countries may not be able to raise environmental standards while trying to develop their economies. The United States has not signed the Kyoto Protocol. **Do you think less developed countries should be held to the same standards as developed nations?**

In the world's poorest countries, housing is of poor quality. Diet is, too. Along with limited access to health care, these factors lead to high infant mortality rates and short life expectancy.

There are additional characteristics common to most LDCs. In the next section, you will read about some of the difficult issues challenging less developed countries.

Levels of Development

Economic development commonly occurs in the following stages.

- *Primitive equilibrium* Economy has no formal economic organization or monetary system. It exists in equilibrium based on tradition.
- *Transition* Cultural traditions begin to crumble and people adopt new living patterns.
- *Takeoff* New industries grow and profits are reinvested.
- *Semidevelopment* Economy expands significantly and enters the international market.
- *Highly developed* Basic human needs are met easily. Economy is focused on consumer goods and public services.

Some of the more successful of the developing countries are referred to as **newly industrialized countries (NICs).** NICs are less

newly industrialized country (NIC) *less developed country that has shown significant improvement in the measures of development*

Differentiated Instruction L3

To help students understand how levels of development are ranked, ask them to use the map on p. 476 to explain the differences between high-income, middle-income, and low-income economies. Have them integrate material from the entire section to describe these categories as they are shown on this map. Students who prefer to present materials linguistically or visually may use an outline map to reproduce the visual, adding explanatory captions. Students who prefer to present material verbally should give a short oral report, using the map as a visual aid.

Differentiated Instruction L2

Place English language learners in groups with at least two native English-speaking students. Tell each group to study the illustrations in this section. Have groups use the photos to write sentences or short paragraphs that explain the section's main ideas. ELL

Transparency Resource Package
Economics Concepts, 18B: Levels of Development (Overlay)
Economics Concepts, 18C: Per Capita Energy Consumption (Overlay)

Preparing for Standardized Tests

Have students read the section titled "Characteristics of Less Developed Countries" and then answer the question below.

Which of the following are characteristics of less developed countries?

(A) limited access to health care and low per capita GDP
B high literacy rate and large percentage of the population engaged in subsistence agriculture
C high per capita GDP and limited resources for schools
D poor diet and high literacy rate

Answer to . . .

Global Connections Students may say yes, that protection of the environment is crucial or that developed nations could finance some of the costs. Other students may say no, that these nations should be allowed to reach a higher economic level before they are required to meet these standards.

GTE Guide to the Essentials
Chapter 18, Section 1, p. 76 provides support for students who need additional review of the section content. Spanish support is available in the Spanish edition of the guide on p. 76.

Quiz Unit 7 folder, p. 14 includes questions to check students' understanding of Section 1 content.

Presentation Pro CD-ROM
Quiz provides multiple-choice questions to check students' understanding of Section 1 content.

Answers to . . .

Section 1 Assessment

1. Development is the process by which a nation improves the economic, political, and social well-being of its people.
2. Developed nations usually have adequate industrial facilities for producing consumer and capital goods, and they are therefore sometimes referred to as industrialized nations.
3. Per capita GDP shows how much of the nation's product is being created per person, rather than the total production of the country. It can also indicate people's living standard, depending on income distribution within the country.
4. The quality of infrastructure determines that nation's capacity to produce.
5. Developed nations: increased consumer spending, fully industrialized, high agricultural output, healthy population, educated population, developed infrastructure; Less developed countries: low per capita GDP and energy consumption, low level of industrialization, subsistence agriculture, low literacy rate.
6. List items will vary, but students may include literacy rate, per capita GDP, public health statistics, or industrial status. Student proposals will also vary depending on interpretation of problems facing LDCs.

Although income is only one measure of development, it gives a good indication of a nation's standard of living.

Income Can you see a pattern in the locations of developed nations and less developed countries?

Figure 18.3 **Levels of Development**

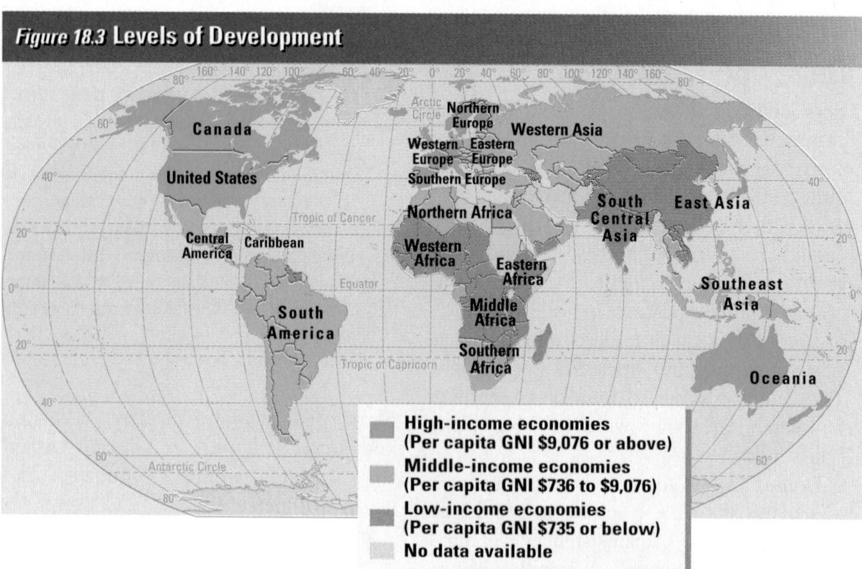

developed countries that have shown significant improvement in development. Newly industrialized countries include Mexico, Brazil, Malaysia, Thailand, Singapore, Hong Kong, South Korea, and Taiwan. The most successful of these—Singapore, Hong Kong, South Korea, and Taiwan—are known collectively as "the four Asian tigers." These countries now have incomes comparable to those of some developed nations.

The World Bank is an international organization devoted to assisting development. It uses per capita gross national income (GNI) to categorize nations as *high income, middle income,* and *low income.* High-income economies are the developed nations. Middle- and low-income economies are the less developed countries. See the map in Figure 18.3 for the distribution of these nations.

Section 1 Assessment

Progress Monitoring *Online*
For: Self-quiz with vocabulary practice
Web Code: mna-7185

Key Terms and Main Ideas

1. What is **development?**
2. Why are **developed nations** sometimes referred to as industrialized nations?
3. Why is **per capita GDP** a better measure of development than GDP?
4. What role does **infrastructure** play in a nation's development?
5. List and describe three characteristics of **developed nations** and three characteristics of **less developed countries.**

Applying Economic Concepts

6. ***Decision Making*** Create a list of three factors used to measure a nation's development. If you were in charge of an LDC, how would you attempt to obtain higher levels of development in those three areas?
7. ***Using the Databank*** Turn to the charts showing the health expenditures as a percent of GDP on page 547. **(a)** Which countries spend the least percentage of GDP on health care? **(b)** How do those countries' figures compare to the amount spent in the United States?

Go Online PHSchool.com
For: Comparison Activity
Visit: PHSchool.com
Web Code: mnd-7181

7. (a) Mexico, South Korea, and Turkey (b) These countries spend half or less than half of what the United States spends in total health-related expenditures.

Progress Monitoring *Online*
For additional assessment, have students access Progress Monitoring Online at **Web Code:** mna-7185

Typing in the Web Code when prompted will bring students directly to detailed instructions for this activity.

Answer to . . .

Building Key Concepts Most of the nations with the highest incomes are in the Northern Hemisphere, especially in North America and Europe, and most with the lowest incomes are in the Southern Hemisphere.

ECONOMIC

Profile

Economist

Entrepreneur

W. Arthur Lewis (1915–1991)

W. Arthur Lewis rose from working as a file clerk to become a world authority on economic development. Through his economic models, Lewis hoped to bring nations in Africa, Asia, and Latin America into the global marketplace and to help poor farm workers escape from poverty.

A Man of Ideas

William Arthur Lewis grew up on the island of St. Lucia, a poor British colony in the Caribbean. Leaving school at age 14, he went to work as a clerk in a government office. A few years later, he applied for a scholarship to go to college in Great Britain. He enrolled as a business student at the London School of Economics, and received a Ph.D. in 1940.

Lewis taught economics in Britain until 1958. In 1963, he accepted a position at Princeton University, where he became well respected for stressing ideas over numbers.

A Theory of Economic Development

Lewis focused his research and teaching on developing nations. In 1954, Lewis identified a "dual economy" in poor nations—a small, profitable "capitalist" sector dominated by a large, inefficient "traditional" agricultural sector. In 1955, he expanded his ideas into a book, *The Theory of Economic Growth*.

Lewis drew the path of economic development as an upside-down U. Countries grow rich by moving excess farm workers to factory jobs. On the left of the U were poor countries like Bangladesh, where growth was slow because too many people worked in the countryside. On the right were rich countries like the United States, with large manufacturing sectors and efficient farms. Growth in these wealthier countries was also slow, Lewis argued, because "the gains from diverting labour out of agriculture are almost all exploited." At the top, with the fastest-growing economies, were countries like South Korea, where the labor shifted from agriculture helped fuel manufacturing.

Lewis concluded that poor countries should move workers from farm to factory. This idea provided a model for many developing nations.

International Economic Advisor

Lewis put his ideas into practice as advisor to Ghana and as president of the Caribbean Development Bank. Britain's Queen Elizabeth II knighted him in 1963, and in 1979, Lewis was awarded a Nobel Prize in economics.

Because Lewis supported foreign investment in developing countries, critics once attacked his work as justifying capitalist exploitation. The collapse of socialism in most developing nations in the 1980s and early 1990s helped redeem his work.

CHECK FOR UNDERSTANDING

1. **Source Reading** Explain what Lewis meant when he said that economic growth in developed nations is slow because "the gains from diverting labour out of agriculture are almost all exploited."
2. **Critical Thinking** Why might Lewis's ideas have encouraged developing countries' governments to limit economic freedoms?
3. **Learn More** Research economic growth in an African or Asian nation and describe how closely it has followed Lewis's model for development.

Beyond the Classroom: Workplace Skills

Problem Solving Explain to students that the ability to recognize and solve problems is an important skill in every workplace. An effective problem solver sees the problem, correctly identifies the factors that led to it, and creates and carries out a plan of action that will resolve the problem. An important aspect of problem solving is monitoring the progress of a plan and making changes in it as needed. Ask students how they act as problem solvers in their school lives. Allow them to provide examples to show how they use the steps in problem solving. Then point out that these skills can be transferred to the workplace.

ECONOMIC Profile
W. Arthur Lewis

Background

William Arthur Lewis credited his parents with much of his own success. In speeches and lectures he painted a picture of hard-working parents who made sacrifices to give the best they could to their children.

Lewis's parents were both teachers. His intelligence allowed him to move at an accelerated rate through the school system. In fourth grade, at the age of 7, an illness forced him to stay home for an extended period. His father chose to teach him at home for the next three months. Upon returning to school, Lewis turned out to have learned so much that he was promoted to sixth grade.

Unfortunately, Lewis's father died later that year. In the years that followed, according to Lewis, it was his mother's self-discipline and hard work, along with her love and gentleness, that allowed each of her children to succeed. By the time Lewis left school at the age of 14, he had completed the curriculum.

Careers in Economics Activity
Unit 7 folder, p. 24 gives students a closer look at the career path of a regional planner.

Answers to . . .

1. He meant that in industrialized countries most former farm workers have already made the shift to more productive industrial work, so opportunities for further economic growth are limited.
2. Students may point out that forcing a nation's economy into a predetermined direction would probably involve loss of the freedom to make decisions, a feature of a democratic, market-based society.
3. Students should do the necessary research, and their responses should demonstrate effective analysis of the data as well as an understanding of Lewis's theories.

Section 2

Issues in Development

Objectives You may wish to call students' attention to the objectives in the Section Preview. The objectives are reflected in the main headings of the section.

Bellringer Ask students to suggest what would be different in your classroom if five new students joined the class each day. Tell them to assume that the size of the room cannot increase and that the number of desks, books, and other resources would not increase as quickly as the number of students. Explain that in this section they will learn how rapid population growth, among other issues, affects less developed countries.

Vocabulary Builder Have students read this section to find the meaning of each key term. Then ask groups of three students each to find a graphic (photo, table, graph, or other) that illustrates an aspect of each key term and discuss how it is related to the term.

Lesson Plan

Teaching the Main Concepts L3

1. Focus Tell students that in this section they will examine the obstacles that developing countries face. Before students begin the section, ask what some of these obstacles might be.
2. Instruct Explain the causes and effects of rapid population growth. You may want to review the definitions of *resources, physical capital,* and *human capital* before discussing how each of these influences development. Use as many current examples as possible to help students understand how political factors and debt can block development.
3. Close/Reteach Point out that despite many obstacles, many developing countries have made great progress in recent years. Ask students to suggest examples of such success stories. Tell students that in this section they will examine the obstacles that developing countries face. Before students begin the section, ask what some of these obstacles might be.

Section 2

Issues in Development

Preview

Objectives

After studying this section you will be able to:

1. **Identify** the causes and effects of rapid population growth.
2. **Describe** the effects of the unequal distribution of the factors of production.
3. **Understand** the importance of human capital to development.
4. **Analyze** how political factors and debt are obstacles to development.

Section Focus

Less developed countries face a variety of complex issues. These include rapid population growth, a lack of natural resources, inadequate quantities of physical and human capital, political instability and government corruption, and debt.

Key Terms

population growth rate
natural rate of population increase
arable
malnutrition

population growth rate *the increase in a country's population in a given year, expressed as a percentage of the population figure at the start of the year*

natural rate of population increase *the difference between the birth rate and the death rate*

If you were an official in the government of a less developed country, you'd quickly discover that there are no easy solutions for ending decades of underdevelopment. The fortunate discovery of oil, diamonds, or some other valuable natural resource could certainly help. Natural resources, however, are but one factor in development.

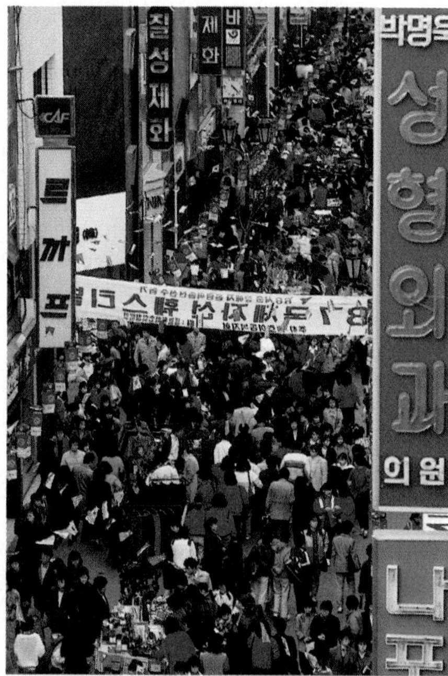

▶**Rapid population growth has created new challenges for South Korea, particularly in its capital, Seoul.**

Rapid Population Growth

One of the most pressing issues in development is the rapid population growth experienced by many less developed countries. Some economists point out that a population's quality of life depends on economic productivity, not on population density. Very dense populations can have rising living standards where free markets foster growth. Nevertheless, the already poor economies of many LDCs have trouble meeting the needs of rapidly growing populations.

Causes of Rapid Population Growth

The **population growth rate** is the increase in a country's population in a given year. It is expressed as a percentage of the population figure at the start of the year. The population growth rate takes into account the number of births, deaths, and the number of people migrating to or from a country.

When analyzing population growth in less developed countries, development experts often focus on the **natural rate of population increase.** This is the difference between the birth rate and the death rate.

Many LDCs are experiencing an increase in life expectancy. This is good news for individuals and families. However, while life expectancy has increased, birth rates have not decreased, at least not significantly.

Graphing the Main Idea

Scarcity To build understanding of the concepts of **scarcity** and economic development, have students use a multi-flowchart graphic organizer like the one at right to show the effects of various factors on economic development. Have them place the label "Economic Development" in the center of the organizer. In the boxes around it, suggest that they indicate factors that influence development and details about their influence.

Section Reading Support Transparencies A template and the answers for this graphic organizer can be found in Chapter 18, Section 2 of the Section Reading Support Transparency System.

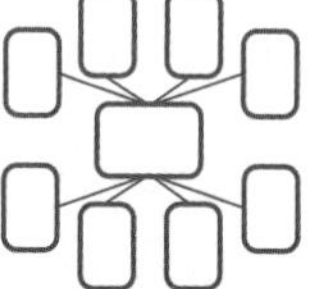

What this means is that births are far outpacing deaths, leading to rapid population growth.

The age structure of LDCs also contributes to rapid population growth. In many LDCs, a high proportion of the population is of childbearing age. In developed nations, the largest segment of the population is older. Populations in developed nations therefore increase at a much slower rate. Figure 18.5 compares the age structure of low-income economies and high-income economies.

Consequences of Rapid Population Growth

The average population growth rate of the less developed countries of the world is estimated to be around 1.7 percent. This may sound low to you, but at this rate the population of LDCs will double from their 1990 figure of 4.1 billion to over 8 billion by the year 2031. Compare this to the growth rate of developed nations, which is 0.5 percent. Their population is not expected to double until 2129.

To stay at its current level of development, a country that doubles its population must also double employment opportunities, health facilities, teachers and schoolrooms, agricultural production, and industrial output. To increase its level of development, an economy must do even more. With all the obstacles less developed countries face, achieving this level of growth is a daunting task.

Population growth is only one factor in development. Many people in LDCs are concerned with sustainable development. Sustainable development describes economic growth that takes into account the health and future of the environment and natural resources. With sustainable development, present economic development lays the groundwork for long-term economic growth in that community or nation.

There are many factors that affect development, as described below. All these factors interact with each other, making both the causes of and solutions to underdevelopment difficult to identify.

Go Online
PHSchool.com
Web Code: mng-7183

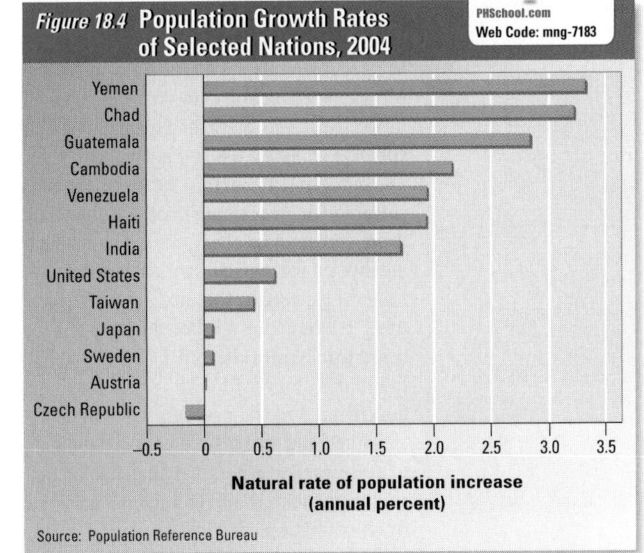

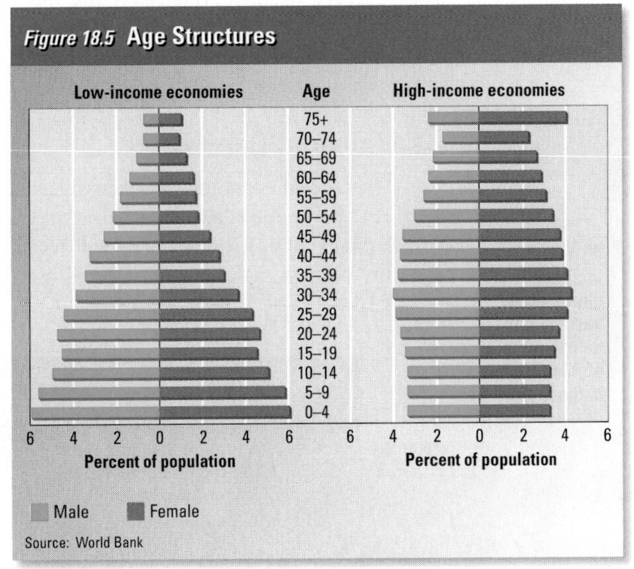

Rapid population growth results in a large proportion of the population being young and dependent. If the largest segment of the population is too young to work, then production does not increase along with the population.

Standard of Living What is Yemen's natural rate of population increase? Describe the shapes of the age structure graphs for low-income and high-income economies. Which shape would you expect Yemen's age structure to have? Why?

Guided Reading and Review
Unit 7 folder, p. 15 asks students to identify the main ideas of the section and to define or identify key terms.

Differentiated Instruction L3

Organize the class into an even number of groups of three to four students each. Ask each group to create a list of six statements. Each statement should represent either a cause or an effect of rapid population growth but should not be identified as one or the other. Tell students to list the statements in random order. Then have groups exchange lists and identify each statement on the list they have received as a cause or an effect of rapid population growth. Groups should prepare a one- or two-sentence explanation of why they identified each statement as they did. Finally, combine groups that exchanged statements and instruct them to work through each other's responses to identify corresponding causes and effects.

Differentiated Instruction L1

While population growth may be a problem in LDCs, experts predict that population decline may become a problem in industrialized Europe. Low birth rates and shrinking populations in some European nations have led some to consider immigration to sustain a stable population. Italy's population could shrink 28 percent to 41 million by 2050. This has sparked a debate in Italy between those who believe the economy needs immigrants and those who believe that admitting millions of new residents who speak different languages could change Italy dramatically. Choose a panel of six "Italian leaders" to debate this issue. SN

Econ 101: Key Concepts Made Easy

Scarcity To help students understand the roles of **resource distribution, physical capital,** and **human capital** in development, ask them to speculate about the production capability of a farm in an area with fertile land and good rainfall, where the means of transportation are good and where there are skilled workers. Then have them speculate about the production capability of a farm in a desert or mountainous area with uneven rainfall, poor transportation, and few workers. Ask students to suggest ways in which various countries have made up for deficiencies in resources or capital.

Answer to . . .

Building Key Concepts Yemen's natural rate of population increase is about 3.3 percent. Low-income economies have a pyramid shape, with a larger percentage of the population among the young. High-income economies have a more even distribution. Chad's graph would likely be pyramid-shaped because Chad has a very low per capita income.

THE WALL STREET JOURNAL. CLASSROOM EDITION

For an additional article from *The Wall Street Journal Classroom Edition,* see the Source Articles folder in the **Teaching Resources,** pp. 54–56.

Differentiated Instruction L3

(Reteaching) To enable students to understand how the supplies of resources and physical capital influence development, form heterogeneous groups of four to six students each. Ask each group to use an almanac, encyclopedia, or another reference source to create a brief profile of a less developed country. (Assign each group a different country.) In the profiles students should evaluate the resources and physical capital that the assigned countries possess and show how these have been used for development. Obstacles to development should be noted along with successes. Have students post the profiles in the classroom and analyze similarities and differences.

Differentiated Instruction L4

Have pairs of students each choose a less developed country and prepare an analysis of that nation in light of at least two of the factors described in this section: population growth, resources, physical capital, human capital, political factors, and debt. Ask them to present their results in graphic form or in an oral report. GT

arable *suitable for producing crops*

Factors of Production

In parts of Africa, Asia, and Latin America, physical geography makes development more difficult. Natural resources are not spread evenly across the globe. Only about 10 percent of Earth's land is **arable,** or suitable for producing crops. Some land is more fertile than other land. Some climates are better for agriculture than others. Key mineral resources, too, are unevenly distributed across the globe. Harsh climates, uncertain rainfall, and lack of good farmland or mineral resources have contributed to the problems of some LDCs.

Sometimes the problem isn't the absence of resources. Rather, it is that the means to utilize resources are lacking in less developed countries.

Technology may help LDCs develop the resources they do have. Technology, however, is costly to develop and requires much capital. As you will read below, the formation of capital is another important issue in development.

Physical Capital

The lack of economic productivity typical of LDCs is due in part to a lack of physical capital. Physical capital, you will recall, is any human-made resource that is used to create goods and services. Without capital, industry cannot grow. Agricultural output remains low.

What's more, the resulting subsistence-level agriculture does not give individuals or households the opportunity to save. Neither does the presence of a large dependent segment of a population. A large proportion of dependents means a large number of people who don't produce and who must be supported by others. No savings means no money for purchasing capital.

Some countries turn to foreign investment to boost capital. However, as you will read below, that won't happen unless LDCs invest in human capital.

Human Capital

Human capital is the skills and knowledge gained by a worker through education and experience. Health and nutrition, as well as education and training, are important to the development of human potential. Human capital is crucial to the functioning of an economy. It is the people who develop and utilize technology, who work in agriculture, industry, and services. It is the people who manage businesses and government. When a country doesn't invest in human capital, the supply of skilled workers, industry leaders, entrepreneurs,

▼ How might increased physical and human capital help to remedy the problems shown in these photos?

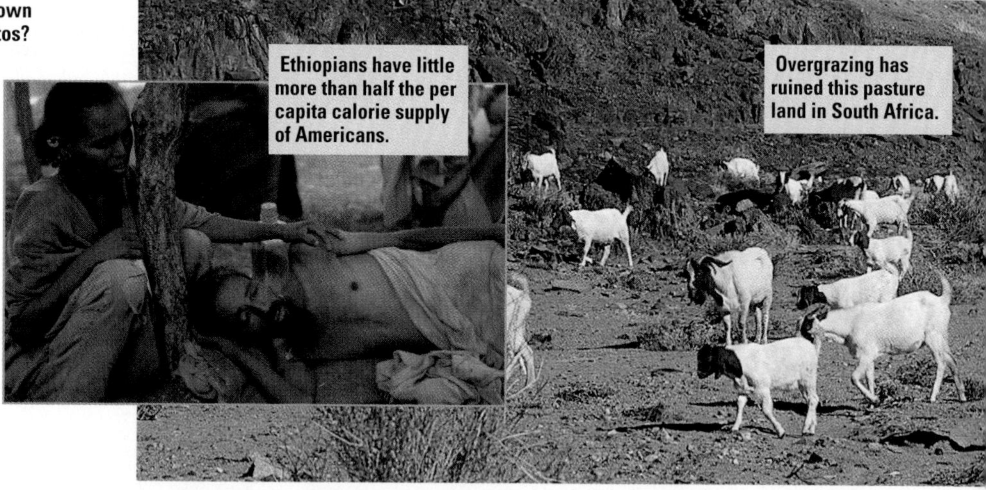

Ethiopians have little more than half the per capita calorie supply of Americans.

Overgrazing has ruined this pasture land in South Africa.

Block Scheduling Strategies

Consider these suggestions to take advantage of extended class time:

- Provide students with newspapers and magazines, and ask them to find articles and political cartoons on section-related issues. Tell students to choose three items and to write summaries of the issues and solutions they present. Then have the class work together to post their items as part of an "Issues in Development" bulletin board.
- Ask groups of three to four students to create a country profile (showing natural resources as well as human and physical capital) for an imaginary less developed country. Ask groups to create a brief economic plan that would show how the country could improve its development. Allow class time for students to present their plans.

Answer to . . .

Photo Caption Increased physical and human capital could allow for growth and industrialization, with more wealth for citizens and fewer people dependent on subsistence agriculture.

government leaders, doctors, and other professionals is limited. As a result, foreign investors become discouraged because investment is profitable only if there is a skilled work force to use it.

Health and Nutrition

Proper food and nutrition are necessary not only for survival, but also for physical and mental growth and development. An individual's performance and productivity depend on the benefits of good nutrition.

Inadequate nutrition is called **malnutrition.** The populations of many less developed countries suffer chronic malnutrition. Malnourished mothers may give birth to infants with low birth weight, brain damage, and birth defects. Malnutrition in children slows or delays their physical and mental development. In adults, it can cause lethargy, heart disease, diabetes, and other health problems.

Education and Training

To be able to use technology and move beyond mere subsistence, a nation must have an educated work force. Education and training let people develop new skills and adapt to new technologies and processes. It also helps them develop new and better ways of doing things.

Many less developed countries have low literacy rates. Access to education and participation in education are limited. Adult literacy in many countries is below 40 percent. Only three out of four children in LDCs who begin primary school are still in school four years later. Throughout the world, many children are needed at home to work on the farm, and have no time to go to school.

Improvements in literacy rates in many countries are held back by the gender gap in education. In highly developed nations, the literacy rates for men and women are nearly identical. In many LDCs, however, women's literacy lags behind that of men. The greatest difference in literacy rates between men and women exists in regions that have poor social and economic conditions for women. Some of the factors that discourage families from investing in the education of girls are the following:

- early child-bearing age
- limited job opportunities for women
- lower wages for women
- cultural factors that devalue women

malnutrition *inadequate nutrition*

THE WALL STREET JOURNAL. CLASSROOM EDITION

In the News Read more about investing in human capital in "Spreading the Wealth," an article in The Wall Street Journal Classroom Edition.

The Wall Street Journal Classroom Edition

For: Current Events
Visit: PHSchool.com
Web Code: mnc-7182

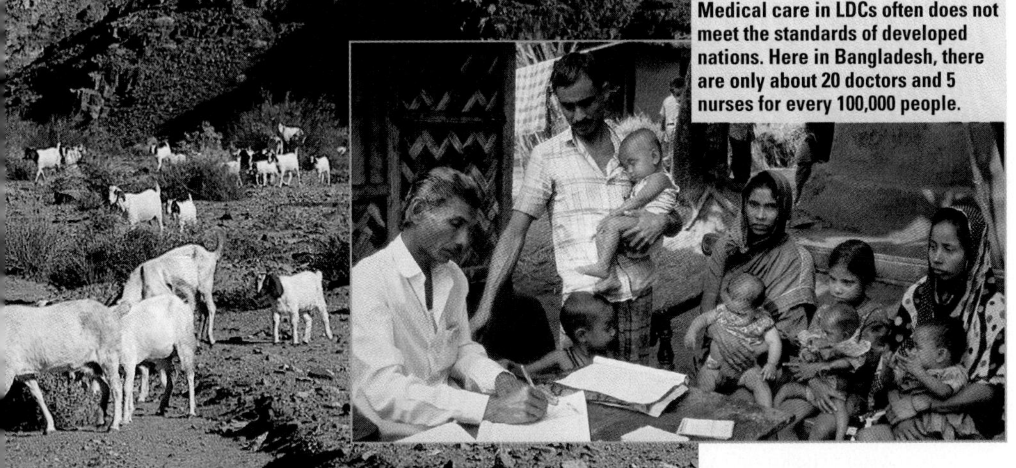

Medical care in LDCs often does not meet the standards of developed nations. Here in Bangladesh, there are only about 20 doctors and 5 nurses for every 100,000 people.

Go Online PHSchool.com Typing in the Web Code when prompted will bring students directly to the article.

Differentiated Instruction 

Ask students to create charts of causes and effects, based on the material in the section titled "Human Capital." Remind them that their charts should show clearly the importance of human capital to development.

Background

Global Connections

President John F. Kennedy established the Peace Corps in 1961 to assist developing countries. The Peace Corps has endured as an example of investment in human capital. Peace Corps volunteers use their own skills, knowledge, and training to assist people in other countries in their development efforts. President Kennedy declared in a 1960 election campaign speech: "There is not enough money in all America to relieve the misery of the underdeveloped world in a giant and endless soup kitchen. But there is enough know-how and knowledgeable people to help those nations help themselves."

Agriculture, health care, and education are just a few of the areas in which Peace Corps volunteers use their own skills and knowledge to increase human capital. Volunteer services similar to the Peace Corps were later initiated in countries as diverse as France, Canada, Finland, Japan, and New Zealand.

Interdisciplinary Connections: Health

Doctors Without Borders The world's largest independent international medical relief agency is called Doctors Without Borders. The objective of this group is to provide medical relief to populations that are in crisis. Experienced medical personnel—including surgeons, nurses, and nutritionists—offer their expertise freely for at least six months. Each year, more than 2,000 volunteers, representing 45 nationalities, support this organization in more than 80 nations.

Making the Connection Ask students to consider whether Doctors Without Borders is an investment in human capital. Have them locate the Web page for this organization and find out where it has been active in the last six months.

Learning Styles Activity
Learning Styles Lesson Plans folder, p. 41 asks student groups to create posters that depict problems faced by less developed countries.

Transparency Resource Package
Economics Concepts, 18D: Per Capita Calorie Supply (Overlay)

Differentiated Instruction L3

To help students understand how political factors and debt are obstacles to development, hold a panel discussion. Organize the class into four groups. Assign each group one of the factors described in the text: colonial dependency/central planning, government corruption, political instability, and debt. Have each group work cooperatively to prepare a set of notes on the topic and to appoint a panel representative. Then hold a discussion, with you as moderator, in which the representatives from all of the groups discuss ways in which these factors have hindered development as well as possible solutions.

Differentiated Instruction L2

Ask students to rewrite the following incorrect statements so that they become true statements:

- Arable land is *unsuitable* for producing crops. *(suitable)*
- *Physical* capital consists of skills and knowledge gained through education and experience. *(Human)*
- A low literacy rate indicates that a country's population *has* adequate access to education. *(does not have)*
- Central planning *helped* long-term economic growth in countries that were emerging from colonial dependence. *(hindered)*
- Foreign debt *is not a problem in most* LDCs. *(is a problem in many)*

LPR

Answer to . . .

Building Key Concepts School enrollment and literacy rates correlate highly. Less developed countries have lower school enrollment for females and lower overall literacy as well as female literacy.

Go Online PHSchool.com Web Code: mng-7184

Figure 18.6 **Education and Literacy**

	School enrollment rate (percentage enrolled)		Literacy rate (percentage literate)	
Country	**Female**	**Male**	**Female**	**Male**
United States	99	91	97	97
Peru	79	81	83	94.5
Indonesia	61	68	84.1	92.9
Nigeria	41	49	60.6	75.7
Yemen	29	72	30	70.5
Chad	20	42	39.3	56
Niger	12	20	9.7	25.8

Sources: United Nations Development Program, *CIA World Factbook*

These Saudi Arabian women (right) are participating in a university course. Since 1960, public education has been opened to Saudi women—if they have permission from their families. **Standard of Living** **Examine the table. What patterns do you see in the school enrollment and literacy rates of males and females?**

"Brain Drain"

Wealthy people in LDCs have the most access to education. Yet, many of the best-educated citizens leave to live and work in developed nations. The scientists, engineers, teachers, and entrepreneurs of LDCs are often attracted to the enormous opportunities developed nations can offer. This loss of educated citizens to the developed world is called "brain drain."

Political Factors

Political factors have limited and even reduced the development of many poor nations. These factors include dependence on former colonial powers, experiments with central planning, and corrupt and unstable governments.

From Colonial Dependency to Central Planning

Many LDCs are former colonies of European powers. As colonies, they had to supply their rulers with agricultural products and raw materials. In turn, they were forced to rely on their colonizers for manufactured goods. This relationship prevented the development of industry within the colonies.

After achieving independence following World War II, many of these new nations turned to central planning, rather than free enterprise, in an effort to modernize their economies quickly. They made some gains in the 1950s and 1960s. In the long run, however, central planning hindered economic growth. As you will read in Section 4, many LDCs are now making the transition to free enterprise.

Government Corruption

Corruption in the governments of many LDCs also holds back development. Leaders often make political decisions and laws to benefit themselves and their friends, not the country at large. Economic policies often benefit only the urban minority, which has greater political influence.

For example, Mobutu Sese Seko, the president of Zaire (now the Democratic Republic of Congo) from 1965 to 1997, ran a government noted for its corruption and mismanagement. Mobutu Sese Seko used his position to accumulate one of the largest personal fortunes in the world. As he plundered the nation's treasury and natural resources, Zaire's infrastructure crumbled for lack of funding. Today, the country is one of the poorest in the world, with a per capita GDP of only $98.

Preparing for Standardized Tests

Have students read the section titled "Political Factors" and then answer the question below.

Which of the following is *not* a political factor that has hindered growth in poor nations?

A Some nations adopted central planning.
B Some governments are corrupt.
(C) Some nations are making the transition to free enterprise.
D Civil wars and social unrest plague some nations.

Political Instability

Civil wars and social unrest plague many less developed countries. El Salvador, Lebanon, Cambodia, and Rwanda, for example, suffered years of civil unrest.

In these countries, war has killed millions of people and created millions of refugees. Military leaders spend huge sums of money on weapons and warfare instead of on education, housing, health care, or other investments in development.

◀ **Closed shops and uncollected trash in Al Kut, Iraq, following the overthrow of Saddam Hussein illustrate the economic costs of political instability.**

Debt

In the 1970s and 1980s, many less developed countries acquired loans from foreign governments and private banks to finance development. Events in the world economy, however, have hindered repayment of these loans.

In 1973, a political crisis in the Middle East prompted the oil-producing nations of the Organization of Petroleum Exporting Countries (OPEC) to reduce oil exports, and then to raise prices. The price of crude oil rose from $8 a barrel to $35 a barrel. Many LDCs, like most of the world, depend heavily on oil from OPEC. Many had to borrow yet more money to import oil. Increased debt made repayment of loans difficult, if not impossible, for many LDCs.

Between 1980 and 1985, the value of the U.S. dollar appreciated, or increased in value against other currencies, on the world market. Since most of their loans were based on U.S. dollars, LDCs, as a result, had further difficulty in repayment.

Between 1970 and 1984, the combined debt of LDCs increased by 1,000 percent to $700 billion. Today it exceeds $1.5 trillion. In some countries, the foreign debt is greater than the annual gross domestic product. In the next section, you will read about the ways debt repayment is being handled.

Section 2 Assessment

Progress Monitoring *Online*
For: Self-quiz with vocabulary practice
Web Code: mna-7186

Key Terms and Main Ideas

1. What is **population growth rate?**
2. How does **arable** land play an important role in a nation's development?
3. How does a lack of physical capital hinder development?
4. What is the connection between human capital and foreign investment?
5. How does **malnutrition** affect human capital?
6. Why are many less developed countries carrying a large burden of debt?

Applying Economic Concepts

7. ***Math Practice*** The United States has a population of about 291 million and a population growth rate of about 0.97 percent. By how many people do you expect the nation's population to increase over the next year?
8. ***Critical Thinking*** How does the formation of physical capital relate to resource development?
9. ***Decision Making*** As leader of a less developed country, what measures could you undertake to limit "brain drain"?

For: Writing Activity
Visit: PHSchool.com
Web Code: mnd-7182

GTE Guide to the Essentials
Chapter 18, Section 2, p. 77 provides support for students who need additional review of the section content. Spanish support is available in the Spanish edition of the guide on p. 77.

Quiz Unit 7 folder, p. 16 includes questions to check students' understanding of Section 2 content.

Presentation Pro CD-ROM
Quiz provides multiple-choice questions to check students' understanding of Section 2 content.

Answers to . . .

Section 2 Assessment

1. Population growth rate is the increase in a country's population in a given year, expressed as a percentage of the population figure at the start of the year.
2. The amount of arable land—land that can be used for farming—affects the agricultural output of a nation.
3. With little physical capital a country cannot industrialize and thus produce the necessary goods and services needed for economic growth.
4. A lack of human capital discourages foreign investment because there are not enough skilled workers to produce a good return on the investment.
5. Malnutrition causes low birth weight, brain damage, and birth defects in infants; slows the physical and mental development of a nation's youth; and causes lethargy, heart disease, diabetes, and other health problems in adults. Such problems greatly hinder the development of human capital.
6. In the 1970s and 1980s many LDCs borrowed to finance development. Rising oil prices, which necessitated more borrowing, and the appreciation of the U.S. dollar hindered repayment.
7. It will grow by about 2.8 million people.
8. Without adequate physical capital the basic elements of an industrial economy cannot be produced, and resources cannot be adequately developed.
9. Student responses will vary but should include creating incentives for educated people to remain in the LDC.

Progress Monitoring *Online*
For additional assessment, have students access Progress Monitoring Online at **Web Code:** mna-7186

Go Online PHSchool.com Typing in the Web Code when prompted will bring students directly to detailed instructions for this activity.

Skills for LIFE

Using the Writing Process

1. Focus Students will examine and practice the steps in the writing process.

2. Instruct Present the steps in the writing process. Remind students to use the social studies terminology correctly as well as following standard grammar, spelling, sentence structure, and punctuation rules. Then have students work through the three steps presented in the skills feature.

3. Close/Reteach To provide additional practice in using the writing process, see the Economic Skills Activity below.

Economic Skills Activity
Unit 7 folder, p. 21, "Using the Writing Process," asks students to examine the writing process as it might be used to plan a biographical essay on Mohandas Gandhi.

Social Studies Skills Tutor CD-ROM offers interactive practice in critical thinking and reading, visual analysis, and communication.

Answers

1. (a) a comparison of the economies of the United States, Sweden, and China (b) They represent three major types of economic systems. (c) Possible title: Three Economic Systems at Work
2. (a) a teacher and possibly other students (b) The essay should have a formal tone. (c) an analytical approach—the chart shows comparisons and contrasts between the systems (d) Possible topic sentence: The three major economic systems in the world today show both similarities and differences.
3. (a/b) Students should report comments from a classmate and make appropriate revisions.

Additional Practice

Students may say that some facts will not fit easily into a chart or that there could be too much information for a chart. Possible alternative ways to organize are lists, note cards, and web graphic organizers.

Skills for LIFE

Using the Writing Process

Good writers generally follow three steps in the writing process: prewriting, writing, and revising. During the prewriting stage, the writer decides what to write about and gathers information. In the writing stage, the writer decides the purpose of the writing, the audience, and the best form for the work. The writer then prepares a first draft. During the revising stage, the writer reviews the draft for sense, style, and errors, and shapes the work into its final form. Use the following steps to learn more about the writing process.

1. **Prewriting: Develop ideas for writing and organize your information.** Decide upon a general topic, and then brainstorm several possible areas to explore within the topic. Research these subtopics in the library or on the Internet, and list what you have found under each topic. Organize your research findings into a chart like the one below. Use the chart to answer the following questions. (a) What has this student chosen to research for his essay? (b) Why do you think he chose these three countries? (c) What is a likely title for his essay?

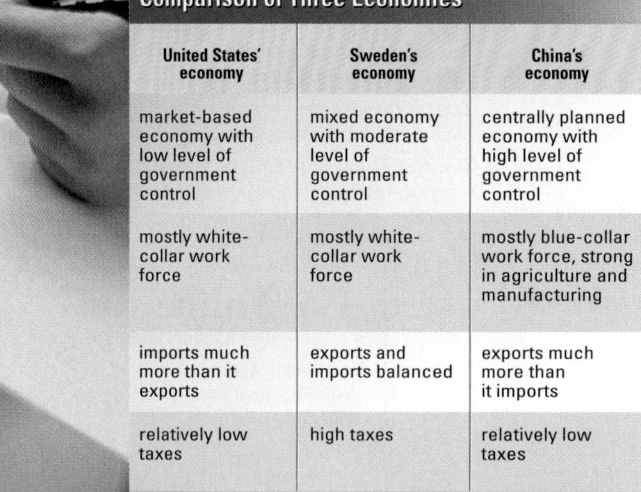

Comparison of Three Economies

United States' economy	Sweden's economy	China's economy
market-based economy with low level of government control	mixed economy with moderate level of government control	centrally planned economy with high level of government control
mostly white-collar work force	mostly white-collar work force	mostly blue-collar work force, strong in agriculture and manufacturing
imports much more than it exports	exports and imports balanced	exports much more than it imports
relatively low taxes	high taxes	relatively low taxes

2. **Writing: Identify who will read the work and what the purpose is, and write a first draft.** (a) Who are the likely readers of this essay? (b) How should this affect the tone and style of the writing? (c) Would the writer be likely to use an eyewitness approach, an analytical approach, or a biographical approach? Why? (d) Write a topic sentence for the first draft of this essay.

3. **Revising: Review your writing to see whether it makes sense.** Ask one of your classmates to read your topic sentence and make suggestions for improving it. (a) What changes were suggested? (b) Rewrite your sentence based on any useful suggestions your classmate gave you.

Additional Practice

What problems do you foresee with using a chart to organize ideas? Can you think of an alternative way to organize your research findings?

Interdisciplinary Connections: Literature

Writing and Reading One of the best ways to become an effective writer is to spend time reading well-written literature. Reading can be an enjoyable way to absorb the principles of good writing. Effectively written literature, whether fiction or nonfiction, displays good organization, effective word choice, and logical sequencing skills.

Have students work through the following activity: Tell students to read an article or a short story by a writer whose work they enjoy. If students have difficulty thinking of a writer, check with a language arts instructor for several appropriate suggestions related in some way to economics. Have students examine the article or story for organization, approach, and overall effectiveness.

Foreign Aid

In Section 2, you read about development loans given to LDCs by foreign governments. Sometimes, foreign governments give, rather than loan, money and other forms of aid for development. Many developed nations provide aid to less developed countries for building schools, sanitation systems, roads, and other infrastructure. Such assistance can be motivated by humanitarian concern for the welfare of fellow human beings.

However, there are also military, political, economic, and cultural reasons for one country to extend aid to another. For example, in the early 1940s, the United States gave nearly $50 billion in food, weapons, ammunition, and other supplies to its allies in World War II. Government officials believed that this aid would help win the war. More recently, the United States has supplied large amounts of military aid to nations such as Israel, Egypt, and Taiwan.

In the years following World War II, political and economic concerns motivated American foreign aid policies. American officials noted that the Soviet Union had extended its power by establishing more Communist governments with centrally planned economies around the world. Such actions threatened both democracy and free market economic systems. Containment, or prevention of such expansion, became the cornerstone of American foreign policy.

In 1947, Secretary of State George C. Marshall unveiled a plan to help restore the war-torn countries of Europe so that they might create stable democracies and achieve economic recovery. Congress approved the plan in 1948. Over the next four years, the United States sent $13 billion in grants and loans to Western Europe. The region's economies soon recovered, and the United States gained new markets for American goods.

During the 1990s, the same logic that motivated foreign aid under the Marshall Plan prompted many countries to fund the redevelopment of the war-torn Balkan nations. In the early 2000s, the United States promised funds to help Afghanistan and Iraq recover from years of dictatorship and fighting. Figure 18.7 shows the top five recipients of aid from the United States.

International Institutions

Several international economic institutions promote development. Among the most prominent are the World Bank, the United Nations Development Program, and the International Monetary Fund.

World Bank

The largest provider of development assistance is the **World Bank,** founded in 1940. The World Bank raises money on the financial markets and accepts contributions from the wealthier member nations.

The World Bank offers loans, advice, and other resources to more than 100 LDCs. The World Bank also coordinates with other organizations to promote development throughout the world.

United Nations Development Program

The **United Nations Development Program (UNDP)** is dedicated to the elimination of poverty through development. The UNDP

World Bank *the largest provider of development assistance*

United Nations Development Program (UNDP) *United Nations program dedicated to elimination of poverty through development*

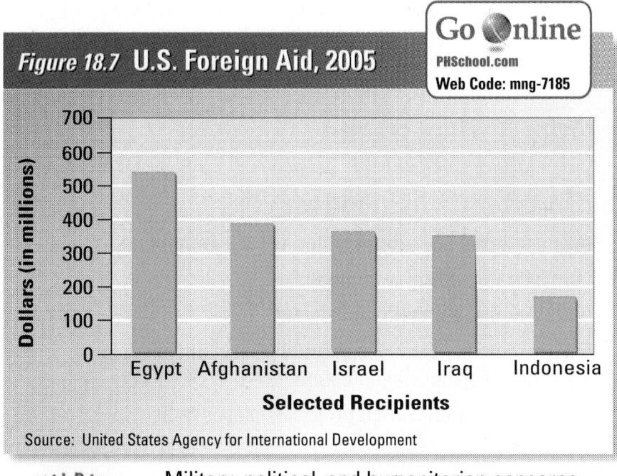

Military, political, and humanitarian concerns motivate the United States to extend aid.
Government Why might it benefit the United States to provide aid to Afghanistan?

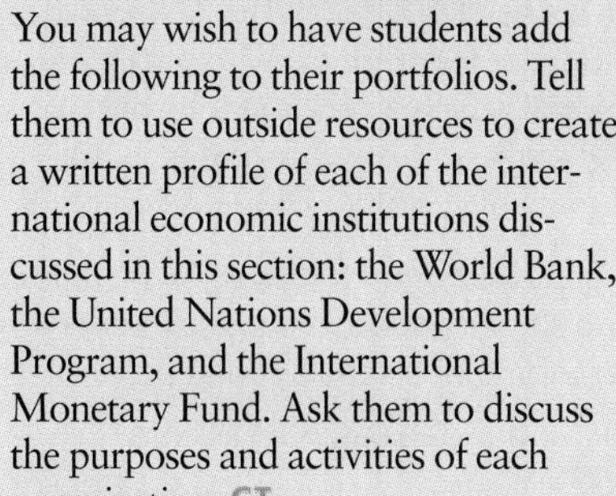

Differentiated Instruction L4

You may wish to have students add the following to their portfolios. Tell them to use outside resources to create a written profile of each of the international economic institutions discussed in this section: the World Bank, the United Nations Development Program, and the International Monetary Fund. Ask them to discuss the purposes and activities of each organization. GT

Economics Assessment Rubric
Economics Assessment Rubrics folder, pp. 6–7 provides sample evaluation materials for a writing assignment.

Differentiated Instruction 

(Enrichment) Have students find newspaper articles about the work of the World Bank and the International Monetary Fund in the world today. Encourage them to analyze the varied work of these organizations and the impact that they have on the world economy. Have them present their findings in oral or written reports.

Transparency Resource Package
Economics Concepts, 18E: International Economic Institutions

Block Scheduling Strategies

Consider these suggestions to take advantage of extended class time:

- Extend the first activity on p. 486 by having students find information about foreign direct investment by the United States in a recent year. First have them compare this data to the overall U.S. budget. Then ask students to use the Simulations and Data Graphing CD-ROM to create graphs displaying the data.
- Show the Economics Video Library segment "ABCs of the IMF," which presents a history of the IMF. After students view the segment, ask them to research and prepare short oral reports about the outcomes of the loans to Russia and Asian countries. After the reports have been presented, discuss conflicting views among developed nations about the IMF.

Answer to . . .

Building Key Concepts Reasons include the importance of building a stable, prosperous society to discourage terrorism.

GTE Guide to the Essentials
Chapter 18, Section 3, p. 78 provides support for students who need additional review of the section content. Spanish support is available in the Spanish edition of the guide on p. 78.

Quiz Unit 7 folder, p. 18 includes questions to check students' understanding of Section 3 content.

Presentation Pro CD-ROM
Quiz provides multiple-choice questions to check students' understanding of Section 3 content.

Answers to . . .

Section 3 Assessment

1. Internal financing is derived from the savings of a country's own citizens, whereas foreign investment consists of assets from foreign countries.
2. Foreign direct investment is the establishment of an enterprise by a foreigner.
3. Foreign portfolio investment is the entry of funds into a country when foreigners make purchases in the country's stock and bond markets.
4. The World Bank offers loans, advice, and other resources to LDCs. The UNDP provides grants for economic and social development. The IMF offers policy advice and technical assistance to LDCs.
5. A stabilization program is an agreement between a debtor nation and the IMF in which the debtor nation agrees to revise its economic policy to provide incentives for higher export earnings and to reduce imports. In order for a LDC to have its debt rescheduled, it must agree to accept a stabilization program.
6. Possible economic factors: state of country's infrastructure, availability of labor force. Possible ethical factors: fair wages, safety issues. Possible political factors: stability of government, level of corruption in government.
7. Students should compose a speech that encourages internal financing. Speeches may appeal to national pride or present statistics to show that domestic investment will be profitable.

▲ **Some international institutions, like the Red Cross and the World Food Program, support development by providing disaster relief. Here, workers delivered food aid to victims of Rwanda's ethnic turmoil.**

International Monetary Fund (IMF) *organization formed to stabilize international exchange rates and facilitate development*

debt rescheduling *lengthening the time of debt repayment and forgiving, or dismissing, part of the loan*

stabilization program *an agreement between a debtor nation and the IMF in which the nation agrees to revise its economic policy*

is one of the world's largest sources of grant funding for economic and social development. It devotes 90 percent of its resources to 66 low-income nations, where 90 percent of the world's poorest people live. The UNDP is funded by the voluntary contributions of United Nations member states and agencies.

International Monetary Fund

The **International Monetary Fund (IMF)** was originally developed in 1946 to stabilize international exchange rates. The IMF has expanded its role to facilitate development through policy advice and technical assistance to LDCs. It also intervenes when LDCs need help in financing their international transactions.

The International Monetary Fund is often viewed as a last resort for struggling LDCs. If a country has trouble repaying a debt, it may ask its lenders to reschedule it. **Debt rescheduling** involves lengthening the time of debt repayment and forgiving, or dismissing, part of the loan. In return, the debtor nation is expected to accept an IMF stabilization program.

A **stabilization program** is an agreement between a debtor nation and the IMF. The nation agrees to change its economic policies to provide incentives for higher export earnings and to lower imports. By increasing exports, an LDC can earn more foreign money to pay off its debt.

Stabilization programs are sometimes controversial because they can have a negative impact on the poor in the short term. They often require the lifting of wage and price controls, causing wages to go down while prices go up. They may also include cuts in government spending on food, health, and education services. Stabilization programs may also decrease domestic consumption of goods in order to increase exports. After negative experiences in East Asia and Argentina in the 1990s and 2000s, many critics have questioned whether IMF policies are the most effective way to repair a troubled economy.

Section 3 Assessment

Progress Monitoring *Online*
For: Self-quiz with vocabulary practice
Web Code: mna-7187

Key Terms and Main Ideas

1. How do **internal financing** and **foreign investment** differ?
2. What is **foreign direct investment?**
3. What is **foreign portfolio investment?**
4. What are some of the ways international economic institutions help less developed countries?
5. What roles do **stabilization programs** play in **debt rescheduling?**

Applying Economic Concepts

6. ***Decision Making*** Your corporation is thinking about opening a factory in a less developed country. What economic factors will you consider? What ethical factors will you consider? What political factors might be important to consider?
7. ***Try This*** Suppose that you are the president of a less developed country. Write a speech to persuade the wealthy elite of your country to invest at home.

For: Simulation Activity
Visit: PHSchool.com
Web Code: mnd-7183

Progress Monitoring *Online*
For additional assessment, have students access Progress Monitoring Online at **Web Code:** mna-7187

Go Online PHSchool.com Typing in the Web Code when prompted will bring students directly to detailed instructions for this activity.

Section 4 Transitions to Free Enterprise

Preview

Objectives

After studying this section you will be able to:

1. **Identify** some important steps in moving from a centrally planned economy toward a free market economy.
2. **Describe** the political and economic changes that have taken place in Russia in recent decades.
3. **Describe** the actions that China's communist government has taken to introduce free market reforms into China.

Section Focus

Making the transition from a command economy to a market economy is a difficult process. The shift requires tremendous changes on the part of the government and workers.

Key Terms

privatization
work ethic
glasnost
perestroika
light industry
special economic zones

As you read in Section 2, many less developed countries have discovered that a centrally planned economy limits development. For this reason, many communist nations are reshaping their economies. Some, like the former Soviet Union, are dismantling their centrally planned economic systems entirely and replacing them with market-based systems. Others, like China, are modifying their centrally planned economies to incorporate some free market practices.

The transition to free markets and capitalism is a huge adjustment for an economy and a nation. As you will read below, Russia has had to adjust to rapid changes in the economy and political system. China, on the other hand, is slowly introducing market reforms within its existing communist system. Both have given up some sovereign control of their economies to join in the global marketplace.

Toward a Market Economy

One of the key elements of a centrally planned economy is that the government, not individuals, owns and controls the factors of production. The government answers the three key economic questions of what to produce, how to produce it, and how to distribute goods and services. In contrast, in a market-based economy, the factors of production are owned by individuals. Individual buyers and sellers answer the three economic questions. One of the first steps, then, in moving from a centrally planned economy to a market economy is privatization.

Privatization

Privatization is the sale or transfer of government-owned businesses to individuals. Private ownership gives individuals, rather than the government, the right to

privatization *the sale or transfer of state-owned businesses to individuals*

▼ **Hungary slowly began privatizing its economy in the 1960s. Instead of raising his flock on a collective, today this goose farmer raises geese at his own expense. He then sells the meat and feathers to a cooperative, keeping all the profits.**

Graphing the Main Idea

Government To help students understand the concept of **government** and the transitions in Russia and China, have students complete a double web graphic organizer like the one at the right. Remind students that a double web can be used to compare and contrast information about two groups. In this case they are comparing the transitions made in Russia and in China.

Section Reading Support Transparencies A template and the answers for this graphic organizer can be found in Chapter 18, Section 4 of the Section Reading Support Transparency System.

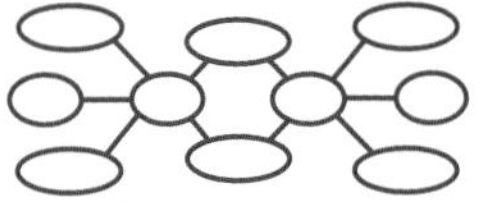

Section 4

Transitions to Free Enterprise

Objectives You may wish to call students' attention to the objectives in the Section Preview. The objectives are reflected in the main headings of the section.

Bellringer Ask students what they know about the term *Cold War.* Explain that it describes a period of conflict between two major political and economic systems during the latter half of the twentieth century. Tell students that in this section they will learn how some Cold War issues have been resolved in the economic sphere.

Vocabulary Builder Have students skim the section to find the meaning of each key term. Then ask them to create a five-item, fill-in-the-blanks quiz. Ask students to exchange papers, complete the quizzes, and then re-exchange for correction.

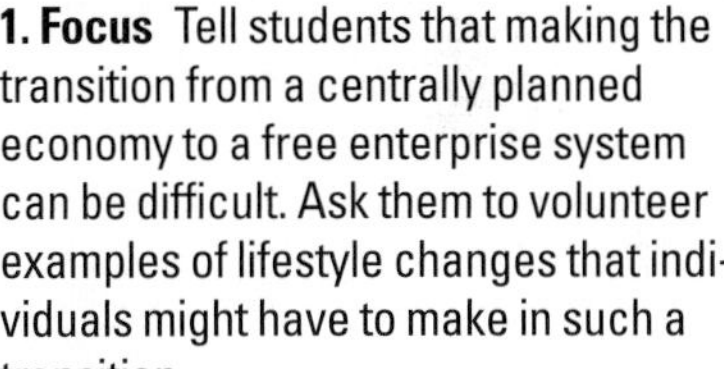

Lesson Plan

Teaching the Main Concepts L3

1. Focus Tell students that making the transition from a centrally planned economy to a free enterprise system can be difficult. Ask them to volunteer examples of lifestyle changes that individuals might have to make in such a transition.

2. Instruct Examine the steps in changing from a centrally planned economy to a free enterprise system and the problems that occur during such transitions. Move on to a discussion of how these issues have been handled in Russia. Compare this transition with that of China, the other major nation that is moving away from a centrally planned economy.

3. Close/Reteach Emphasize the enormous changes involved in shifts like the ones discussed in this section. Ask students to imagine themselves in the place of a Russian or Chinese citizen during these years of change and to describe how they might have felt.

 **Guided Reading and Review**
Unit 7 folder, p. 19 asks students to identify the main ideas of the section and to define or identify key terms.

 **Differentiated Instruction** L3

To help students understand the steps in a transition from a centrally planned economy to a market economy, have them display this information in a flowchart graphic organizer format. Their charts should show sequences of events and their consequences, based on section information.

Differentiated Instruction L3

(Enrichment) Have students examine the map on this page. Ask them to use the map key to locate the former Soviet satellite nations and the former Soviet Union. Have them choose one former Soviet satellite and report on the events leading up to its break with the Soviet Union.

make decisions about what to produce and how much to produce.

There are several ways in which a government can privatize a state-owned business. First, it can simply sell the business to one owner. Another option is to sell shares in the business to interested individuals. A third method is to give every citizen a voucher or certificate that can be used to purchase shares in the businesses when they are privatized.

Simple as this may sound, privatization is a complicated process. One difficulty in privatizing is that only the profitable production facilities will continue to operate. No one will want to buy unprofitable facilities, so many people will lose their jobs. Other job opportunities will eventually appear as successful operations are expanded. However, there may be a period when total employment drops. Some people oppose privatization because it means the end of secure, lifelong government jobs with little or no competition. In a free market, jobs are not guaranteed.

Another difficulty is that there may be only one or two firms in a certain market. Even after firms are privatized, there will be little competition with so few privatized firms.

Protecting Property Rights

Even when it gives up its role as the owner and decision maker, the government still plays a vital role in ensuring the success of a new market-based economy. Legal systems under central planning do not include laws guaranteeing private property rights. A free market cannot function without such rights. As a result, the government must create new sets of laws that ensure a person's right to own and transfer property.

If property rights are uncertain, entrepreneurs will not be willing to make large

Figure 18.8 Communist and Noncommunist Nations

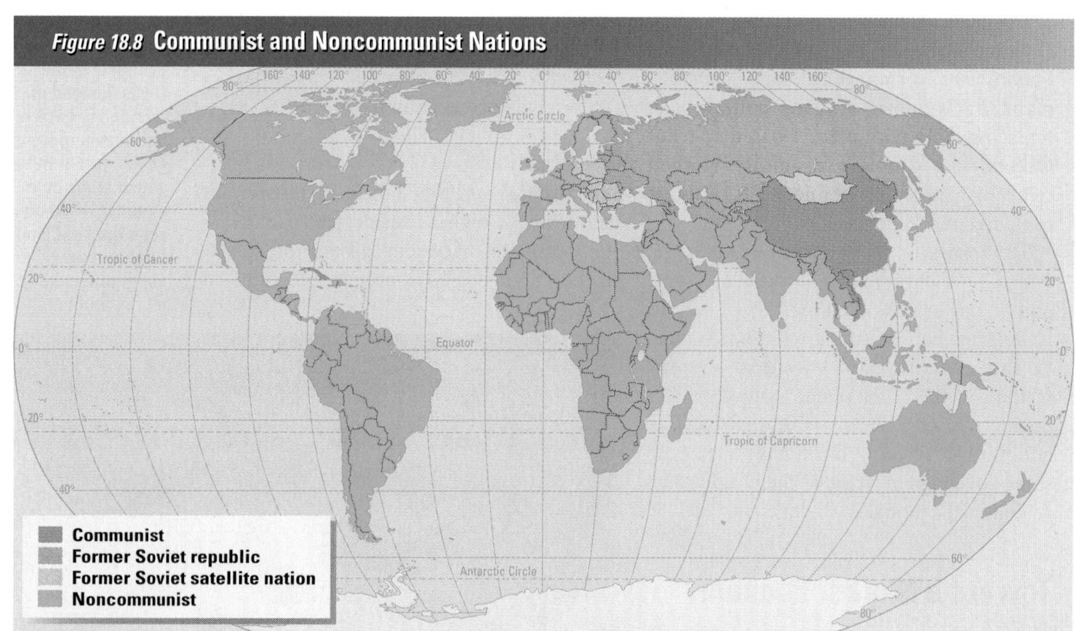

Beginning in the late 1980s, communism in Eastern Europe began to collapse. Countries such as East Germany, Poland, Hungary, and Czechoslovakia made profound changes in their governments and their economies.

Economic Systems **Roughly what percentage of the world remains communist?**

Econ 101: Key Concepts Made Easy

Economic Systems Because most students have lived all their lives under a **free enterprise system,** they may have difficulty understanding what life would be like in a **centrally planned economy.** Use the information in this section to help them comprehend some of the major differences.

If time allows, invite a speaker who has lived under such a system, or locate first-person accounts that will allow students to see themselves in the place of a Russian or Chinese citizen. Then have students summarize what they have learned in a short report.

Answer to . . .

Photo Caption Less than 10 percent

investments and take risks because there will be no guarantee they will benefit from successful projects. Entrepreneurs need law and order to prevent criminals from stealing the profits from legitimate enterprises. They also need a legal system that prevents the government from unduly interfering with their everyday business activities.

It will take time to develop the legal culture necessary to support a market-based economy. To have a successful market-based economy, the government must establish property rights, enforce laws, and provide a framework of regulation. Western market economies have developed the roles of government gradually over many decades. Economies making the transition to free markets need to develop these roles more rapidly.

More New Roles for Government

During privatization, government must be prepared to deal with the unrest that might develop from rising unemployment. A government could, for example, institute unemployment insurance.

The government can also play a role in helping workers make the transition from a centrally planned economy to a market economy. Workers in transition often need to learn a new **work ethic,** or system of values that gives central importance to work. In a free market, incentives, not quotas, influence people's labor.

Transition in Russia

Russia was once the dominant republic of the Soviet Union and the world's most powerful communist nation. In the latter part of the twentieth century, the lagging Soviet economy prompted economic and social reform. Change came quickly to Russia, as economic freedom led to the desire for political freedom.

Communism in Russia

As you read in Chapter 2, the Soviet Union arose out of a pair of revolutions in Russia in 1917, followed by three years of civil war in which the Communists, led by Vladimir Lenin, won control of the government. Under the repressive control of the Communist party, central planning was introduced during the 1920s.

The Soviet government reorganized farmland into state farms and collective farms. State farm workers received wages, similar to factory workers. On the collectives, workers shared any surpluses that remained after the required quantity of products was sold and expenses were paid. Few incentives existed to encourage farmers to work hard. As a result, agricultural output remained low.

Soviet policy also emphasized the development of heavy industry. By 1940, the Soviet Union was the second-largest producer of iron and steel in Europe. The growth of heavy industry, however, came at a great opportunity cost. With so much land, labor, and capital being devoted to heavy industry, little was left over to produce consumer goods. Everyday items such as soap and shoes were in short supply.

Glasnost and Perestroika

In the late 1980s, a new leader, Mikhail Gorbachev, began a series of radical political and economic reforms. Because Gorbachev believed that economic prosperity could not happen without political freedom, he introduced ***glasnost.*** A policy of "openness," *glasnost* encouraged Soviet citizens to say what they wished without fear of government persecution.

▲ **Entrepreneurs in the former Soviet Union had a lot to learn about free market systems.**

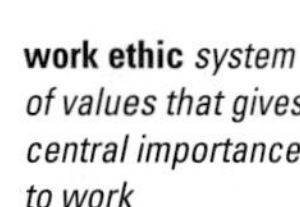

work ethic *system of values that gives central importance to work*

glasnost *a policy of political "openness" introduced into the Soviet Union in the late 1980s*

Background

Interdisciplinary

The leaders of the Soviet Union had hoped to seal the dominance of the Communist Party with Article 6 of the Soviet constitution, which guaranteed a Communist Party monopoly. In early 1990, however, this article was removed. Hundreds, even thousands, of new parties sprang up. In areas that had long resented Russian rule, including the Baltic states, these new parties crystallized opposition to Russian rule. Lithuania declared its independence in the spring of 1990, followed quickly by Estonia and Latvia.

Differentiated Instruction 

Ask students to contrast the amounts and quality of information about the marketplace available to central economic planners and to individuals in a free enterprise system. This information is provided in a free enterprise system through demand, supply, and prices. Ask students to write an analysis several paragraphs long that ties availability of information to economic efficiency. GT

Block Scheduling Strategies

Consider these suggestions to take advantage of extended class time:

- Extend the Vocabulary Builder activity on p. 489 by asking small groups of students to create dramatizations of the key terms. For example, they may dramatize problems with privatization or the effects of *glasnost.* Allow time for these skits to be presented to the class.
- Extend the second activity on p. 490 by having groups search news sources to prepare a brief report on the struggles and successes of this nation since it broke with the Soviet Union. Make these reports available to other students in the class, or allow students to present them orally.
- Extend the activity on p. 493 by having students search news sources for articles that discuss these reforms. Ask students to give brief oral reports on their findings.

Differentiated Instruction L3

To help students understand political and economic changes that have taken place in Russia in recent decades, ask them to create a time line showing these events and changes. Have them write captions that explain the significance of at least three of these events.

Differentiated Instruction L2

Have students use information from the section to answer each of the following questions:

- What is the name for the sale or transfer of government-owned businesses to individuals? *(privatization)*
- What kind of industry did the Soviet Union concentrate on? *(heavy industry)*
- What are *glasnost* and *perestroika?* (glasnost *was a policy of openness in which Soviet citizens could speak their minds;* perestroika *was economic restructuring; both were policies of Gorbachev*)
- Which Chinese leader began market-based reforms after Mao's death? *(Deng Xiaoping)* LPR

Learning Styles Activity

Learning Styles Lesson Plans folder, p. 42 asks students to compare and contrast the methods used by China and Russia in their transitions to market-based economies.

Transparency Resource Package

Economics Concepts, 18F: Transition to Free Enterprise in Russia

FAST FACT

Corruption and unfair market conditions have hampered Russia's development. ***Foreign direct investment*** *in Russia equals only about 1 percent of its GDP.*

Gorbachev's economic reform was a plan for economic restructuring, called ***perestroika.*** *Perestroika* called for a gradual change from a centrally planned system to free enterprise. Gorbachev's main desire was to incorporate the use of markets and incentives into the existing structure of communism.

perestroika *Soviet leader Gorbachev's plan for economic restructuring*

Under *perestroika,* the government began to allow factory managers, rather than central planners, to decide what goods to produce and how much to charge for them. It converted several factories from the production of military goods to the production of consumer goods. Many factories set goals to improve the quality of goods produced. For the first time in decades, people were allowed to start their own businesses.

Farmers were granted long-term leases on land. By making farmers their own bosses, Gorbachev hoped to increase food production.

With little experience in democracy and free enterprise, however, the transition to a market economy proved difficult. Economic reform produced some initial hardships. People lost secure government jobs, benefits, and pensions. Many people, especially the elderly, were hurt financially. Other Russians, however, quickly began to make the new system work for them, starting their own businesses. Many prospered.

▼ In 1991, Communist hard-liners failed in their efforts to overthrow the democratically elected government of Boris Yeltsin. Yeltsin supporters blocked the Soviet army from the parliament building during the coup.

Collapse of Communism

Enjoying the newfound freedoms of *glasnost* and *perestroika,* many people called for a complete end to communism and the domination of the central government. In 1991, Russians voted in their first democratic election. They chose Boris Yeltsin as president of the Russian Republic. A few months later, some officials and army officers tried unsuccessfully to restore old-style communism. The attempt backfired. One by one, the Soviet republics declared themselves independent nations. At the end of the year, Gorbachev resigned as leader, announcing the end of the Soviet Union.

Transition to the Free Market

Yeltsin came to power by promising rapid progress towards a market-based economy. Under Yeltsin's administration, there were improvements. But many hardships continued. Prices of goods in the Soviet Union were kept artificially low by the government. In 1992, Yeltsin lifted price controls. Now that prices were controlled not by the government, but by the workings of supply and demand, prices tripled.

The distribution of wealth tended to be concentrated in the urban centers such as Moscow. The uneven distribution of income led many to call for additional change. It also led to extensive corruption and widespread organized crime.

Billions of dollars in financial aid flooded into the country from the World Bank, the International Monetary Fund, and through independent donations. However, due to mismanagement and corruption, the funds were not used efficiently.

Today, Russia's economy is smaller than that of the Netherlands, although its population is nine times larger. Russia and the former Soviet republics have great potential as producers and markets, however. Russia has only begun to tap large reserves of oil, natural gas, and other natural resources for sale on the world market.

Preparing for Standardized Tests

Have students read the sections titled "Collapse of Communism" and "Transition to the Free Market" and then answer the question below.

Hardships that the people of the former Soviet Union experienced after the collapse of communism included:

A an absence of free elections.

B the institution of price controls.

C lack of foreign aid.

(D) rapidly rising prices.

Transition in China

In the first half of the twentieth century, China struggled with civil war. In 1949, the supporters of communism, led by Mao Zedong, defeated the anticommunist nationalists. The Nationalist party retreated to what is now Taiwan. The communists took power in China's capital city, Beijing. Since then, China developed its own version of communism.

The Great Leap Forward

In 1958, Mao introduced an ambitious development plan called the Great Leap Forward. The Great Leap Forward was intended to turn China into a world economic power in the shortest time possible. All of the country's land was taken over by the central government. The people were organized into self-sufficient settlements called People's Communes.

These communes, sometimes with as many as 25,000 people, contained both farms and industries. Life in a People's Commune resembled life in the military. Communist party officials made all the decisions about what goods were made and who received them. The people's task was simply to work in the fields or factories. They received the same rewards no matter how much or how little they produced.

The Great Leap Forward was a huge disaster. Without incentives for workers, production fell. In the ensuing famine, about 20 million people starved to death under this development plan.

The Cultural Revolution

In the 1960s, Mao instituted a Cultural Revolution. His intention was for China to further embrace communism by destroying all traces of the past. Mao organized an army of radical young men and women, called the Red Guards, to carry out his policy. The Red Guards persecuted people in their attempt to eradicate what Mao called "the Four Olds": old ideology, old thought, old habits, and old customs. Mao succeeded only in further damaging the Chinese economy.

▲ **During China's Cultural Revolution, Mao's sayings were collected and distributed in what became known as Mao's "little red book."**

Transition to the Free Market

Mao died in 1976. He was succeeded by Deng Xiaoping. Deng introduced a new approach that not only shifted more power to local government, but also used the tools of the free market to improve productivity.

Deng began a program of economic reform called the Four Modernizations. The goals of the program were to improve agriculture, industry, science and technology, and defense as quickly as possible. Deng was not afraid to use free enterprise as a means of accomplishing these goals.

Deng replaced the People's Communes with the contract responsibility system. Under this arrangement, the government rented land to individual farm families. Each family then decided for themselves what to produce. The families contracted with the government to provide a certain amount of crops at a set price. Once the contract was fulfilled, they were free to sell any extra crops at markets for whatever prices they could get.

Under this system, farmers had the incentive to grow more crops. Farmers increased their production by about 8 percent. In the first eight years of the program, their incomes tripled.

Industry

As in the Soviet Union, when the communists came to power in China they had used most of the nation's resources to increase

Background

Entrepreneurship's Changing Face

In Russia and China in the 1990s, central planning systems weakened, and the two nations became more open to market-based influences. Both nations began to provide a welcome environment for direct selling. Two companies shrewd enough to benefit from this greater openness were Avon Products and Mary Kay Corporation.

Both firms are leading sellers of cosmetics in the United States. Russian and Chinese women were attracted to the sales forces of the two companies.

The relationship proved to be a win-win situation. Avon and Mary Kay experienced great increases in revenue. Women in Russia and China gained financial opportunities and job satisfaction. In Russia female doctors and engineers gladly left their old jobs for a more reliable source of income: selling Mary Kay cosmetics. In China there were reports of women who left their state jobs to sell full time for Avon and began to earn several times their former salaries.

Differentiated Instruction  L3

(Reteaching) Have students create a list of actions that China's communist government has taken to introduce market-based reforms in China. Ask them to comment on the success of each of these reforms in moving China toward a market-based system.

Economic Detective Activity
Unit 7 folder, p. 23, "South Gamara," provides an integrated application of chapter concepts.

Transparency Resource Package
Economics Concepts, 18G: Economies in Transition

Interdisciplinary Connections: History

Returning Hong Kong to China China lost Hong Kong to Great Britain after the first Opium War in the mid-1800s. In 1898 Britain was given a 99-year lease on the island. During the term of this lease, Hong Kong became a haven for refugees from Chinese communism as well as a thriving free enterprise zone. At 12:00 midnight on June 30/July 1, 1997, Hong Kong was officially returned to China.

Making the Connection Have students research the transition (including agreements concerning the autonomy of Hong Kong) and find out about economic conditions in Hong Kong today. Ask them to write a news article describing what they have found.

Go Online PHSchool.com Typing in the Web Code when prompted will bring students directly to the article.

GTE Guide to the Essentials
Chapter 18, Section 4, p. 79 provides support for students who need additional review of the section content. Spanish support is available in the Spanish edition of the guide on p. 79.

Quiz Unit 7 folder, p. 20 includes questions to check students' understanding of Section 4 content.

Presentation Pro CD-ROM
Quiz provides multiple-choice questions to check students' understanding of Section 4 content.

Answers to . . .

Section 4 Assessment

1. privatization, protecting property rights, accepting new roles for government
2. Privatization gives individuals, rather than government, the right to decide what to produce and how much to produce, which is a basis of free market economies.
3. *Glasnost* was a policy of political "openness" introduced in the Soviet Union in the late 1980s.
4. *Perestroika* was Soviet leader Gorbachev's plan for economic restructuring, which called for a gradual change from a centrally planned system to free enterprise.
5. The Great Leap Forward failed because it provided little incentive for workers, so it caused a decrease in production and eventual famine.
6. Heavy industry is industry that requires a large capital investment and that produces items used in other industries. Light industry involves the production of small consumer goods.
7. China's special economic zones incorporate many aspects of a market-based system, allowing businesses to make most of their own investment and production decisions. Most of China's rapid economic growth has occurred in these zones.
8. Russia's transition to a market-based system happened very rapidly; China's has been more gradual.

THE WALL STREET JOURNAL. CLASSROOM EDITION

In the News Read more about population growth in China in "Baby Bust," an article in The Wall Street Journal Classroom Edition.

Go Online
The Wall Street Journal Classroom Edition
For: Current Events
Visit: PHSchool.com
Web Code: mnc-7184

heavy industry. By the time Deng came to power, however, Chinese technology was outdated.

Deng had two goals for industry. First, he wanted people to spend more money on consumer goods. Therefore he changed the focus on production to **light industry,** or the production of small consumer goods such as clothing, appliances, and bicycles. He also wanted factories to increase production. To accomplish this, Deng gave more decision-making power to factory managers. He started a system of rewards for managers and workers who found ways to make factories more productive.

light industry *the production of small consumer goods*

special economic zones *designated regions in China where foreign investment is encouraged, businesses can make most of their own investment and production decisions, and foreign companies are allowed to operate*

Economic Zones

In addition, Deng set up four **special economic zones** along China's east coast. In these zones, local governments are allowed to offer tax incentives to foreign investors. Businesses are allowed to make most of their own investment and production decisions. Foreign companies are allowed to operate in these zones. Deng located these first four zones near Hong Kong and Taiwan. He hoped to attract foreign investment, companies, and technology from these economic giants. The zones have proved so successful that China now has hundreds of these zones.

Most of China's rapid economic growth has taken place in the special economic zones of the coastal cities. The interior regions lag far behind. Massive projects like the controversial Three Gorges Dam are designed to bring economic growth to the interior. Nevertheless, the population has shifted dramatically. About 120 million people have left inland villages to seek their fortunes in the booming cities. Rapid urban growth has resulted in an increase in crime and life-threatening air and water pollution.

Despite these negative effects, the economy has benefited. Since the start of Deng's reforms, China's economy has quadrupled in size. The question now at hand is whether or not China's political leaders will be able to maintain their Communist regime in the face of pressures for cultural freedom brought about by economic freedom. China's leadership continues to come under criticism for its violations of human rights and political repression.

Section 4 Assessment

Progress Monitoring *Online*
For: Self-quiz with vocabulary practice
Web Code: mna-7178

Key Terms and Main Ideas

1. Identify three factors necessary for the transition to free enterprise.
2. Why is **privatization** necessary to create a free market economy?
3. What is ***glasnost?***
4. What is ***perestroika?***
5. Why was the Great Leap Forward such a disaster for China?
6. How does **light industry** differ from heavy industry?
7. What role do **special economic zones** play in China's transition to free enterprise?

Applying Economic Concepts

8. ***Critical Thinking*** What is the main difference between transition in Russia and transition in China?
9. ***Problem Solving*** How could China expand its economic success to the interior?

Go Online PHSchool.com
For: Map Activity
Visit: PHSchool.com
Web Code: mnd-7184

9. Answers will vary, but students may suggest the creation of additional special economic zones.

Progress Monitoring *Online*
For additional assessment, have students access Progress Monitoring Online at **Web Code:** mna-7178

Go Online PHSchool.com Typing in the Web Code when prompted will bring students directly to detailed instructions for this activity.

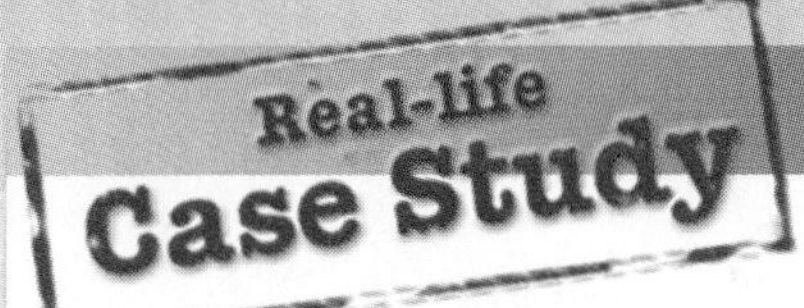

Economic Institutions

The World Bank and Economic Assistance

As World War II drew to a close, much of Europe lay in ruins, and the World Bank was created to help finance the reconstruction. Within a few years, the World Bank changed its mission from helping rebuild war-torn areas to helping developing nations achieve stable economic growth.

Function The primary function of the World Bank is to make loans to countries unable to borrow from other sources. Its loans are used for many purposes: to improve health care, to build transportation networks, and to promote economic reforms. The Bank makes about $20 billion in new loans each year.

The World Bank raises most of its money in financial markets by issuing bonds. In addition, it receives contributions from its member nations, including industrialized nations such as the United States and Japan. Even some developing nations, once borrowers from the World Bank themselves, make contributions.

▲ The World Bank helps finance highway construction in developing nations such as Colombia.

Controversy Despite its worthwhile goals, the World Bank has sometimes been a source of controversy. Some critics have argued that the United States would be better off using its money to help less fortunate American citizens. Others have criticized the Bank for not holding developing nations fully accountable for effectively carrying out projects it has funded.

Accomplishments Still, the World Bank can boast of many significant accomplishments. It has helped many developing countries improve roads, hospitals, schools, and water supplies. In addition, by strengthening the economies of less developed countries, the World Bank has helped build new markets for American goods, which in turn benefits the economy of the United States.

Per Capita Earnings in Selected Countries

GNI per Capita Earnings	Countries	
High income (more than $9,076)	Germany Japan	South Korea United States
Upper middle income ($2,936–$9,075)	Malaysia Mexico	Poland Saudi Arabia
Lower middle income ($736–$2,935)	China Iran	Jamaica Philippines
Low income ($735 or less)	Indai Keyna	North Korea Vietnam

Source: The World Bank

Applying Economic Ideas

1. How does the World Bank work to improve conditions in developing nations?
2. The table shows how the World Bank classifies selected countries according to per capita GNI. What factors might have led to some countries being poor for so long?

Real-life Case Study: Economic Institutions

1. Focus The World Bank provides loans to less developed countries that might not otherwise be able to secure loans. However, its activities have both supporters and critics.

2. Instruct Explain the reasons why the World Bank was created, its functions, and its accomplishments. Then discuss controversies that have arisen about the activities of the World Bank.

3. Close/Reteach Ask students to find and summarize orally news reports about World Bank activities from the last six months.

Case Studies Activity
Case Studies in Free Enterprise folder, p. 36–37, "George Soros," helps students apply economic principles in an additional case study.

Economic Detective Activity
Unit 7 folder, p. 23, "South Gamara," provides an additional application of chapter concepts.

✓ Preparing for Standardized Tests

Have students examine the table on this page and then answer the question below.

Which countries have GNI per capita earnings of more than $2,936?

A Vietnam and the Philippines
(B) Germany and Mexico
C China and Iran
D Jamaica and North Korea

Answers to . . .

1. The World Bank provides loans and financial assistance to countries in need. Many nations have used these loans to improve standards of living and to put themselves on the road to economic success.
2. Students may mention factors such as lack of resources, colonial dependency, interference from stronger nations, poor economic policies, or continued conflict.

Chapter 18 Assessment

Key Terms

1. literacy rate
2. Malnutrition
3. light industry
4. Foreign direct investment
5. infrastructure
6. debt rescheduling
7. Industrialization
8. internal financing

Using Graphic Organizers

9. Students should complete the tree map by filling in the appropriate financing options. Examples include internal financing (derived from the savings of the country's citizens), foreign direct investment (the establishment of an enterprise by a foreigner), foreign portfolio investment (purchases by foreigners in the country's stock and bond markets), and foreign aid (money granted for development by other countries).

Reviewing Main Ideas

10. LDCs have the following characteristics: low per capita GDP; presence of malnutrition, illiteracy, and subsistence agriculture; low level of industrialization; unavailability of consumer goods; high infant mortality rate; and low life expectancy.
11. (a) less developed (b) developed (c) newly industrialized (d) less developed (e) developed
12. Issues involve short-term effects on the poor. Wages may go down, prices may rise, and there may be cuts in government spending.
13. Both *glasnost* and *perestroika* were used by Gorbachev as an initial step toward integrating some market-based reforms into the Soviet system.
14. Special economic zones have allowed some aspects of a market-based system to develop in China, encouraging foreign investment and overall economic growth.

Chapter 18 Assessment

Chapter Summary

A summary of major ideas in Chapter 18 appears below. See also the **Guide to the Essentials of Economics**, which provides additional review and test practice of key concepts in Chapter 18.

Section 1 Levels of Development (pp. 471–476)
Nations throughout the world exhibit varying levels of economic success. The most prosperous are called **developed nations.** Nations with relatively low standards of living are called **less developed countries. Per capita gross domestic product** is the primary measure of development.

Section 2 Issues in Development (pp. 478–483)
Less developed countries face a wide range of issues. A high **population growth rate,** lack of natural resources, inadequate human and physical capital, political instability and corruption, and foreign debt often inhibit development.

Section 3 Financing Development (pp. 485–488)
Less developed countries turn to many sources to finance their development, including **internal financing, foreign investment,** and foreign aid and loans. Help also comes in the form of policy advice and technical assistance.

Section 4 Transitions to Free Enterprise (pp. 489–494)
Some communist and former communist nations, such as China and Russia, are making transitions to free enterprise in order to boost their lagging economies. The move to free enterprise requires **privatization** of industry and changes in the legal system.

Key Terms

Complete each sentence by choosing the correct answer from the list of terms below. You will not use all of the terms.

malnutrition	**light industry**
infrastructure	**work ethic**
industrialization	**foreign direct investment**
literacy rate	**life expectancy**
internal financing	
debt rescheduling	

1. Measuring a nation's ____ provides data on how many people in that country can read or write.
2. ____ may cause disease in adults, and may cause infants to be born with brain damage or birth defects.
3. The production of small consumer goods is referred to as ____.
4. ____ is the establishment of an enterprise in a country by a foreigner.
5. The services and facilities necessary for an economy to function are called ____.
6. A country undergoing ____ is allowed more time to pay off its loans and have a portion of its loans forgiven.
7. ____ is the extensive organization of an economy for the purpose of manufacture.
8. Economists use the term ____ to describe investment derived from the savings of a country's citizens.

Using Graphic Organizers

9. On a separate sheet of paper, copy the tree map below. Chart financing options for less developed countries by filling in each box with an example and description of a financing option.

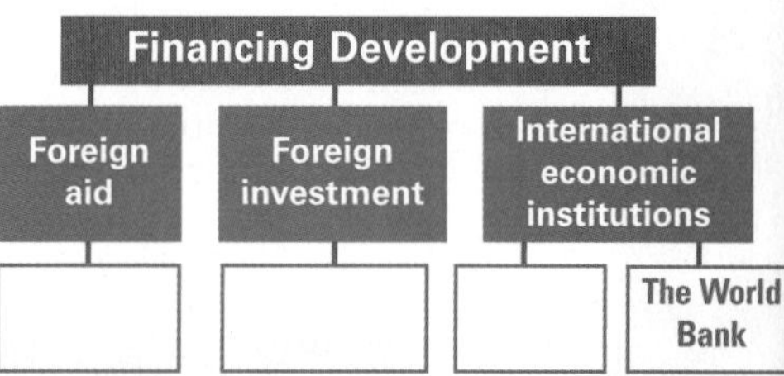

Critical Thinking

15. High energy consumption by a labor force reflects a high level of industrialization. Low energy consumption indicates a lower level of development.
16. Some students may point to physical capital, saying that without it industry cannot grow, so that people cannot move beyond subsistence agriculture. Students who favor human capital may point out that high levels of physical capital are not productive without the knowledge and skills to use them effectively.
17. Students should note that if a country's economic development does not keep pace with its population growth, problems will occur in areas such as employment, health, and education. They may also mention problems related to a large segment of the population being dependent.

Reviewing Main Ideas

10. List and describe three characteristics of less developed countries.
11. Which development status (developed, less developed, or newly industrialized) does each of the following characteristics describe? **(a)** low per capita GDP **(b)** many consumer goods available **(c)** shows significant improvement in the measures of economic performance **(d)** high infant mortality rate **(e)** high life expectancy
12. What issues arise when less developed countries adopt a stabilization program?
13. How did *glasnost* and *perestroika* factor in Russia's transition to a free market economy?
14. What role do special economic zones play in China's transition to a free market economy?

Critical Thinking

15. **Drawing Conclusions** In measuring development, what relationship exists between the activities of the labor force and energy consumption?
16. **Making Comparisons** Which do you believe is more important for a nation's development—physical capital or human capital? Why?
17. **Recognizing Cause and Effect** Describe four consequences faced by nations experiencing rapid population growth.

Problem-Solving Activity

18. Compare and contrast the transitions to free market economies in China and Russia. Describe three unique aspects of each country's transition. Which country do you believe will be most successful in the long run?

Economics Journal

Essay Writing Review your comments on the chapter opener photo. What comments can you add, based on your reading of the chapter? Write a brief essay to accompany the photo. Then, check an encyclopedia or other resource for information on Ghana, the country shown. Revise your essay as needed.

Skills for Life

Using the Writing Process Review the steps shown on page 484; then complete the following activity based on the information below.

19. Study the chart below. **(a)** Who is involved in each of these organizations? **(b)** How could these organizations be compared?
20. You have been assigned the task of writing an essay comparing these three organizations. **(a)** What is a possible title for your essay? **(b)** Compose a topic sentence for your essay.
21. Exchange your topic sentence with a classmate. Analyze each other's topic sentences; then revise your sentence based on your classmate's input.
22. Use the information in the chart below to write a rough draft of an essay. Ask your classmate to read your draft and comment on it.

Global Economic Organizations

	World Trade Organization	G-8 Countries	International Monetary Fund
Membership characteristics	Entrance granted by vote of existing member countries	Top eight industrialized nations	Finances supported by members
Function	Establishes agreements on lowering or abolishing tariffs on a global level	Summit meetings allow members to discuss international issues	Provides monetary services and loans in attempts to stabilize global trade
Countries involved	145 as of 2005	United States, Japan, France, Germany, Italy, Great Britain, Russia, Canada	184 as of 2005

Progress Monitoring *Online*

For: Chapter 18 Self-Test **Visit:** PHSchool.com
Web Code: mna-7181

As a final review, take the Economics Chapter 18 Self-Test and receive immediate feedback on your answers. The test consists of 20 multiple-choice questions designed to test your understanding of the chapter content.

Problem-Solving Activity

18. Students should present various aspects of China's and Russia's economic transitions, including *glasnost, perestroika,* and special economic zones. Predictions will vary depending on individual interpretations of both countries' transitions to date.

Skills for Life

19. (a) WTO: 142 nations in 2003; G-8: top eight industrialized nations; IMF: 184 nations in 2003 (b) membership characteristics, function, countries involved
20. (a) Possible answer: "Comparison of Global Economic Organizations" (b) Students should construct an appropriate topic sentence for comparing these organizations.
21. Answers will vary but should be based on individual student analysis.
22. Students should prepare rough drafts of their essays and allow peer review.

Additional support materials and activities for Chapter 18 of *Economics: Principles in Action* can be found in the Social Studies area of **PHSchool.com.**

Economics Journal

Students' essays should reflect an understanding of chapter concepts as they relate to this photograph.

Review and Assessment

Vocabulary Practice Unit 7 folder, p. 22 uses a crossword puzzle to reinforce understanding of key terms.

GTE **Guide to the Essentials** Chapter 18 Test, p. 80

Test Bank CD-ROM Chapter 18 Test

Go Online PHSchool.com Students may use the Chapter 18 Self-Test on **PHSchool.com** to prepare for the Chapter Test.

THE WALL STREET JOURNAL.
CLASSROOM EDITION

DEBATE: TARIFFS AND TRADE

1. Focus Have students find the meaning of each of these words before they begin to read: *attributable, chronic, consumption, deficit, economies of scale, retaliating,* and *specialize.*

Explain to students that they will be conducting a debate on whether the U.S. government should impose tariffs on imported goods. Inform them that they will be responsible for arguing one side of the issue. Remind students that a well-prepared debater supports a position with valid evidence, logical arguments, and responsible appeals to emotion.

2. Instruct The authors have both researched the impact of import tariffs on domestic goods. Have students conduct further research on taxing international trade from credible sources before conducting the debate.

Remind students that they should use the following debate format:
The affirmative side will:

- State the problem to be solved. Why is this problem significant?
- Explain who or what is harmed if the problem is not resolved. Use factual evidence to quantify the harm.
- Propose a plan of action. Explain why it is better than the current system.
- Provide factual evidence to show how this plan will solve the problem.

The opposing side will:

- Refute the arguments of the affirmative side, using factual evidence to quantify and support its position.
- If necessary, support the status quo's ability to solve the problem.

3. Close/Reteach When the debate is concluded, encourage students to discuss their opinions on the issue. Ask them whether they were persuaded by the other side's arguments. Conclude by having students write their own statements supporting or opposing tariffs placed on international goods.

THE WALL STREET JOURNAL.
CLASSROOM EDITION

DEBATING CURRENT ISSUES: *Tariffs and Trade*

Tariffs are taxes on imported goods. Supporters say tariffs protect American jobs, while critics reply that they hurt consumers by making imported products more expensive.

In this debate from *The Wall Street Journal Classroom Edition,* Jock Nash, a lawyer who represents textiles producer Milliken & Co., and Daniel T. Griswold, an associate director of the Center for Trade Policy Studies at the Cato Institute, discuss whether the United States sould set tariffs on imports to protect American industry.

YES *Should industries be protected by tariffs?*

BY JOCK NASH

There is little made in America that cannot be made cheaper and just as well elsewhere. This is made clear by our nation's chronic and growing manufacturing trade deficit—which is running at the rate of $1.4 billion dollars a day. Currently, we are consuming more than we are producing in goods and services, by a margin of a million dollars a minute.

A growing part of this deficit is attributable to U.S.-based companies moving overseas part or all of their production of goods and services destined for consumption in the U.S. market—not in foreign markets, as the companies claim. Obviously, these companies would not be manufacturing offshore if a tariff prevented their products from entering the U.S. market at a profit.

In 2003, U.S. manufacturing employed 16 million people. This was after losing two million manufacturing jobs in 24 months. Most reports indicate that the majority of these newly unemployed workers drop out of the middle class only to join the countless working poor in the service economy. They are not finding new employment at their previous salaries.

The move to put production of goods destined for sale in the U.S. in other countries effectively destroys the ability of many American workers to earn a good living, as they traditionally have, by adding value to a product whose costs and pricing reflect the realities of the U.S. market. Without protection of some kind—like a tariff—U.S. manufacturing workers are forced to compete head-to-head with foreign workers in the same industry who may be earning pennies an hour. This situation applies to every U.S. industrial sector, from advanced technology products to basic industries.

Nations become great by producing, not consuming. Manufacturing, not trade, is the main source of prosperity. Manufacturing is the engine that increases national productivity and creates wealth. It is worth protecting—by a tariff if necessary.

Many factories have closed down as manufacturing jobs have left the United States for countries with cheaper labor. Would higher tariffs help or hurt workers and consumers?

Debate Activity Debating Current Issues folder, p. 23 asks students to determine who is helped and who is hurt by the use of tariffs to protect domestic industries.

Economic Assessment Rubric Economics Assessment Rubrics folder, pp. 14–15 provides sample evaluation materials for participation in debates.

Background

About the Authors

Presenting an argument in favor of tariffs is Jock Nash, a lawyer in Washington, D.C., who represents Milliken & Co., a large producer of textiles based in Spartanburg, S.C. The case against tariffs comes from Daniel T. Griswold, associate director of the Center for Trade Policy Studies at the Cato Institute, a think tank in Washington, D.C.

NO *Should industries be protected by tariffs?*

By Daniel T. Griswold

An import tariff is a tax, plain and simple. By taxing international trade, tariffs impose higher prices on millions of workers, families, and import-using industries for the benefit of a small number of "protected" domestic producers.

Consider steel and sugar. In 2002, the U.S. government imposed tariffs of as much as 30% on imported steel. But domestic steel producers, to improve their earnings, then raised their prices in line with the now higher-priced imports. As a result, the tariffs kept a few extra U.S. steel mills open by allowing them to raise their prices. However, those higher prices hurt American workers in steel-using industries, such as automobiles, home appliances, and construction. In the same way, restrictions on imported sugar benefit a small number of domestic producers at the expense of candy makers and soft-drink producers. And millions of families suffer because they must pay more for all those products at the store.

Imagine how much poorer your family would be if you had to grow your own food and make all your own clothes, furniture, and appliances. The same truth applies to nations. Trade allows people and countries to specialize in what they do best, exchanging their surplus production for what others can produce most efficiently. Through economies of scale—meaning the more you produce of any given product, the less each item costs to produce—trade reduces the cost of such goods as automobiles, jet airliners, and medicines by spreading the high, up-front costs of research and capital among millions of consumers worldwide. Trade brings new technology to poor countries and protects consumers from domestic monopolies.

It's a myth that manufacturing has declined in the U.S. because of trade. American workers can and do compete successfully with lower-paid foreign workers because better-educated Americans produce so much more per hour of work. Indeed, U.S. factories today produce a greater volume of goods and more sophisticated products than in decades past. Those jobs that have migrated overseas tend to be the lower-paying manufacturing jobs in industries that have been in decline for decades. Protecting such industries with tariffs just keeps wages down by slowing our transition to higher-skilled and better paying jobs.

Go Online
PHSchool.com
Web Code: mng-7189

U.S. Trade Deficit, 1994–2004

Period	Balance (millions of dollars)	Exports (millions of dollars)	Imports (millions of dollars)
1994	-97,188	702,622	799,811
1995	-95,069	793,725	888,794
1996	-102,869	850,877	953,746
1997	-107,048	933,873	1,040,920
1998	-163,153	932,558	1,095,711
1999	-261,202	957,146	1,219,383
2000	-375,384	1,070,054	1,445,438
2001	-357,819	1,007,580	1,365,399
2002	-418,038	974,107	1,392,145
2003	-495,508	1,020,503	1,517,011
2004	-617,075	1,147,181	1,764,256

Source: U.S. Census Bureau

The trade deficit has widened as more and more manufactured goods sold in the United States are imported from other countries.

DEBATING THE ISSUE

1. What is a manufacturing trade deficit?
2. Both authors focus on the loss of U.S. manufacturing jobs. What impact do you think competition from foreign workers has had on these jobs?
3. **Distinguishing Fact from Opinion** Agree or disagree with Jock Nash's statement: "There is little made in America that cannot be made cheaper and just as well elsewhere." Be sure to support your answer with facts.
4. **Recognizing Consequences** According to Daniel T. Griswold, what happens to consumption when tariffs are placed on imported goods?
5. **Reading Graphs** By how much did U.S. imports increase, in dollars, from 1994 to 2004?

For: You Decide Poll
Visit: PHSchool.com
Web Code: mnp-7181

Differentiated Instruction L3

In 1994, the North American Free Trade Agreement (NAFTA) was ratified. NAFTA established a free trade zone among Mexico, Canada, and the United States for the purpose of eliminating or reducing trade barriers by 2009.

Many other countries have entered into regional trade agreements. In groups, have students select one of the following trade zones and research the pros and cons of eliminating or reducing trade barriers within that zone. Some trade zones to include are NAFTA; APEC, the Asia-Pacific Economic Cooperation; MERCOSUR, the Southern Common Market; and CARICOM, the Caribbean Community and Common Market.

Ask students to prepare a report to the class on the member nations of the chosen trade zone and the impact of trade on their economies. How have trade agreements affected political stability, economic growth, unemployment, business investment, exports, and imports?

Go Online PHSchool.com Students can find additional links related to the debate by visiting the *Economics: Principles in Action* site at **PHSchool.com**.

Interdisciplinary Connections: History

Trade Barriers The Smoot-Hawley Act of 1930 imposed stiff tariffs on a wide variety of goods imported into the United States But when foreign countries sold fewer goods in the United States as a result, their own purchasing power and willingness to buy United States goods were also reduced, which helped fuel a global economic depression. Trade barriers returned most recently in 2002 when the United States government imposed tariffs of as much as 30% on imported steel.

Making the Connection Trade barriers protect industries from foreign competition. Ask students to research the history of other trade barriers and the outcome of imposing these tariffs. Why were these barriers imposed? What happened to prices and jobs as a result of these tariffs? Then have students apply the concepts of voluntary exchange and specialization to determine if trade barriers support economic growth and productivity.

Answers to . . .

1. A deficit indicates that the United States is consuming more than it is producing in goods and service.
2. Many manufacturing jobs have moved overseas because foreign workers will often work for low wages.
3. Answers will vary.
4. Tariffs impose higher prices on millions of workers, families, and import-using industries. Higher prices cause families to consume less of a given product whether it is made in the U.S. or in foreign countries.
5. $964,445

박명욱
성형외과
의원

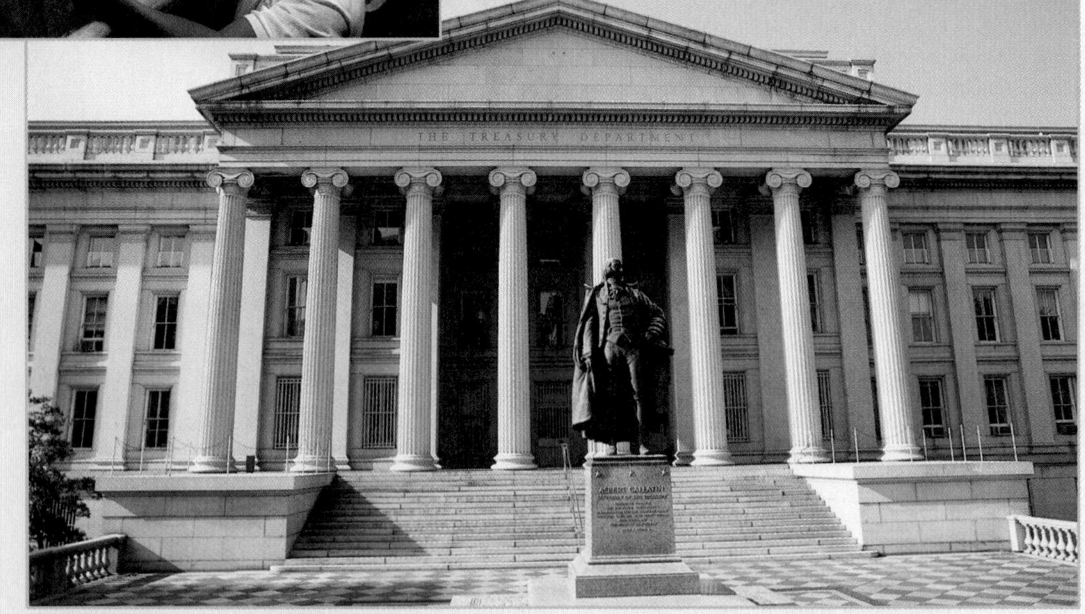

THE TREASURY DEPARTMENT

Reference Section

Personal Finance Handbook 502
- Creating a Budget 502
- Opening and Managing a Checking Account 504
- Saving and Investing 506
- Financial Institutions and Services 510
- Credit and Debt 512
- Paying for Education 516
- Buying a Car 520
- Renting an Apartment 522
- Buying Insurance 524
- Getting a Job 526
- Paying Taxes 528

Economic Atlas and Databank 532
- Natural Resources 532
- Americans at Work 536
- Economic Indicators 538
- The American Consumer 540
- The United States Government 542
- Trade 544
- The United States and the World 546

Glossary 548

Spanish Glossary 559

Index 573

Acknowledgments 591

Personal Finance Activities
"Creating a Budget," p. 2 provides activities to help students practice personal finance skills.

Creating a Budget

A tiny drip from your bathtub faucet can send thousands of gallons of water down the drain each year. Your money can dribble away, too.

An $8 pizza, a $12 pair of sunglasses, $20 at the movies—they don't seem like much at the time. But a lifetime pattern of careless spending can be painful, even ruinous. Money problems can cause stress, wreck personal relationships, and trap people in jobs they don't like just so they can pay their bills. What a way to live your life!

Start a better way. Budget your money.

Calculate Income Versus Spending

Budgeting begins simply with writing how much money you receive and how much you spend. Try these steps:

Four Steps to Successful Budgeting

1. Make a list of your earnings like the one below right. Then calculate your total monthly income.
2. For one month, keep a record of everything you spend money on, from car payments to candy bars. You can jot down each purchase on a scrap of paper, and toss all the scraps in a shoebox. Or carry a small notebook to list items and amounts.
3. At the end of the month, organize the records of your purchases into categories such as food, clothing, entertainment, car payments, and so on. Find the total for each category.
4. On a sheet of paper or on a computer spreadsheet, make a list similar to the one on the next page. Fill in the expenditures and the amounts. Then calculate your total monthly spending.

This record of your income and spending can be very revealing. Do you have a little money left over at the end of the month? Or do you spend more than you earn? Experts recommend that you put about 10 percent of your income into savings. If you have very little left over—or worse, if you spend more than you earn—it's time to create a budget.

Living Within Your Budget

Look at your expenditures and find areas in which you can cut spending. For instance, buy a frozen pizza from the grocery store instead of ordering take-out. Get together at friends' houses instead of at the mall. Shop end-of-season clothing sales. And be careful with automatic teller machines! ATMs make it too easy to drain your bank account.

Fill in the first two columns of a chart like the one on the next page. Then in the third column, enter the reduced amounts you think you can spend. Keep cutting until you can reserve 10 percent of your earnings as savings. This is your new **budget,** a plan for saving and spending.

If you have a difficult time staying within your budget, enlist a friend or family member to review your expenditures each week to help keep you on track. Distinguish between "needs" and "wants." Try not to rationalize impulse buying. After all, you'll only be kidding yourself.

My Earnings

SOURCE	MONTHLY INCOME
Restaurant job	$392
Computer tutoring	$68
Baby-sitting	$20
TOTAL	**$480**

My Spending and Saving Plan

MONTHLY EXPENDITURE	CURRENT EXPENSES	BUDGET
Car		
Payment	$120	$120
Insurance	$42	$42
Gasoline	$27	$14
Maintenance (estimated)	$30	$30
Food		
Lunches at school	$58	$35
Snacks	$34	$20
Movies		
Theater	$28	$7
Rentals	$4	$8
Clothes		
Shoes	$16	$7
Other clothes	$39	$25
Savings for school trip	$50	$50
Magazine subscription	$5	$0
CDs	$24	$12
Gifts	$0	$35
Savings	$0	$48
Emergencies	$0	$27
TOTALS	**$477**	**$480**

Costs such as car payments are fixed.

Bike or carpool instead of driving. Savings: one tank of gas a month.

Cut out chips at lunch. Savings: $23 a month! (It's healthier, too.) Even better: Pack a lunch.

Items such as new clothes are optional expenses. Wear last year's shirt for one more season.

Borrow magazines from friends or the library. Savings: $5 a month

By cutting expenses, you can set aside money for savings, holiday gifts, and emergency needs.

Check Your Understanding

1. **Key Terms** Why is it important to create a **budget?**
2. **Review** Reread the suggested ways for saving money, and brainstorm others to add to the list.

Answers to . . .

Check Your Understanding

1. Having a budget allows you to track where your money comes from and how you spend it. By sticking to a budget, you can keep yourself out of debt, know exactly how much money you should have, and have more organized personal finance records.
2. Ways to save: buy food at the supermarket rather than eating out, spend more time at home rather than at the mall, shop at "sale" times rather than in-season, and be wary of ATM use. Other options: buy generic goods at the store instead of brand name varieties and ride your bicycle or take public transportation instead of driving somewhere.

Personal Finance Activities
"Opening and Managing a Checking Account," p. 4 provides activities to help students practice personal finance skills.

Opening and Managing a Checking Account

If your piggy bank is bursting, consider opening a checking account.

Before banks dotted every streetcorner in America, some people stuffed their money under the mattress for safekeeping. It wasn't very safe.

Today virtually everyone has access to a bank. It's a safe place to store your money, and it offers conveniences such as check writing, electronic banking, and interest on your money.

Choosing a Bank

The most common types of bank accounts are checking and savings. If you plan to take money out of your account frequently, you probably need a checking account. Savings accounts and other savings options are discussed on page 506.

Opening a checking account is fairly easy. First you'll need some kind of identification, such as a driver's license or a pay stub. You'll also need a Social Security number. (If you don't yet have a Social Security number, you can apply on-line at the Web site of the Social Security Administration.) Finally, you'll need at least a small sum of money to deposit when you open your account.

How to Choose a Checking Account

- ❑ Do I have to keep a **minimum balance,** or amount of money, in the account to avoid fees?
- ❑ Is there a monthly fee? How much is it?
- ❑ Will I be charged check writing fees?
- ❑ How many checks can I write per month?
- ❑ Will the bank return my canceled checks each month or keep them on file?
- ❑ Will I be charged ATM fees?
- ❑ What other fees are associated with this account?

It pays to shop around for the best checking account. Although the interest that most banks pay on checking accounts ranges from little to none, other features, such as fees, vary widely. The chart above lists some of the criteria to consider when selecting a checking account.

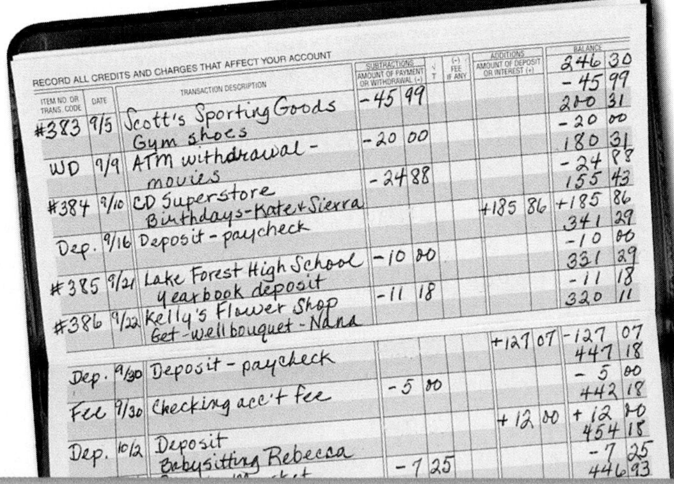

RECORD ALL CREDITS AND CHARGES THAT AFFECT YOUR ACCOUNT
#383 9/5 Scott's Sporting Goods Gym shoes -45 99
WD 9/9 ATM withdrawal - movies -20 00
#384 9/10 CD Superstore Birthdays-Kate+Sierra -24 88
Dep. 9/16 Deposit - paycheck +185 86
#385 9/21 Lake Forest High School yearbook deposit -10 00
#386 9/22 Kelly's Flower Shop Get-well bouquet - Nana -11 18
Dep. 9/30 Deposit - paycheck +127 07
Fee 9/30 Checking acc't fee -5 00
Dep. 10/2 Deposit Babysitting Rebecca +12 00

Keeping Records

When you open an account, you'll receive a checkbook that includes sequentially numbered checks and a **check register,** a booklet in which you'll record your account transactions. You'll make your life a lot easier if you decide from the start to be a good recordkeeper. Every time you write a check, make a deposit, or use an ATM, take a few seconds to jot it down in your check register.

You won't believe how glad you'll be that you have your own records of your financial business. For example, if you earn money, the Internal Revenue Service could ask at any time to see

Journey of a Personal Check

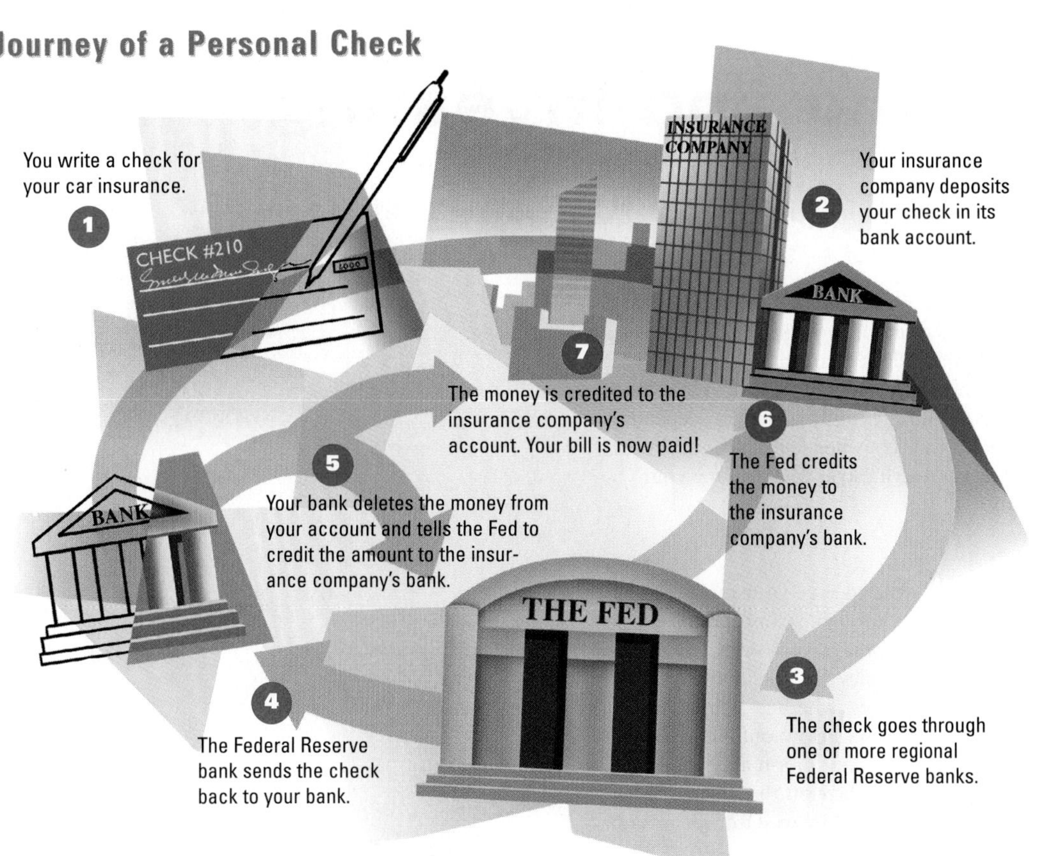

your financial records for the past three years. Also, your bank could make a mistake. Bank records are rarely wrong, but it does happen. The ATM receipt you shoved in your wallet is your proof that you withdrew $50, not $500!

You write a check for your car insurance.
1
CHECK #210
INSURANCE COMPANY
2
Your insurance company deposits your check in its bank account.
BANK
7
The money is credited to the insurance company's account. Your bill is now paid!
6
The Fed credits the money to the insurance company's bank.
5
Your bank deletes the money from your account and tells the Fed to credit the amount to the insurance company's bank.
BANK
THE FED
3
The check goes through one or more regional Federal Reserve banks.
4
The Federal Reserve bank sends the check back to your bank.

Balancing Your Checkbook

Each month you'll receive a statement, a record of your checking account activity during the last month. It lists deposits, withdrawals, ATM transactions, interest paid, and fees charged. Any checks you wrote that were cashed during the month may be returned to you in the statement, although some banks keep the originals in storage. The diagram above shows where your check goes before it is returned to you.

It's extremely important to balance your checkbook every month. That means comparing the transactions in the bank statement to your own records to make sure they agree. Most statements have a worksheet on the back to help you balance your account in a few easy steps. If you have any trouble balancing your checkbook, someone at your bank's local branch office can assist you.

Check Your Understanding

1. **Key Terms** **(a)** How is your account balance different from your **minimum balance?** **(b)** Why is it a good idea to use a **check register?**
2. **Evaluate** If you were going to open a checking account today, which criteria listed above would be most important and least important to you? Why?

Answers to . . .

Check Your Understanding

1. **(a)** The account balance is the actual amount of funds available, whereas your minimum balance is the lowest amount of funds that can be in your account before incurring a service charge. **(b)** Carrying a check register with you allows for quick notation of all the transactions you make. It is also a handy place to keep ATM and store receipts.
2. Students should compare the amount of money available to open an account with possible minimum balance fees. They should also estimate the usage of their checking account to determine which service to use to avoid excessive fees.

Personal Finance Activities "Saving and Investing," p. 7 provides activities to help students practice personal finance skills.

Saving and Investing

It's never too early to prepare for your financial future, whether that means holiday shopping, next year's vacation, college, or retirement.

Paving the way to a sound financial future involves more than getting a job and living within a budget. Managing your money also involves saving and investing. How much you save and how much you invest depends on the lifestyle you choose for yourself in the present and the lifestyle you plan for your future.

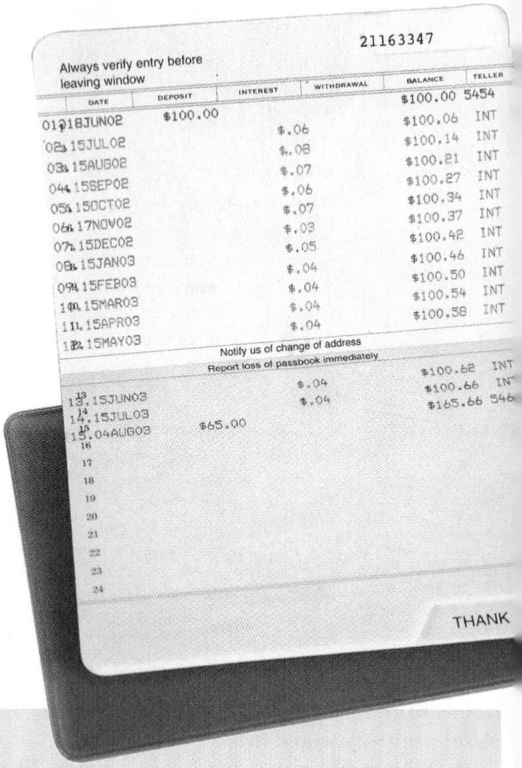

Saving

Why do you need to save your money? While you might have enough earnings to meet your daily expenses, saving is a way to make sure you have money for special purchases and future expenses, whether planned or unplanned. The box below outlines the main types of bank or credit union accounts for saving money. The box on the next page provides questions to help you select an account.

Types of Accounts

Banks offer several ways for you to save your money. Each account has different features and restrictions.

Savings Accounts It's a good idea to use a **savings account** for savings that you may need to use within a short period of time. When you deposit money in a savings account, your bank or credit union will record deposits, withdrawals, fees, and any **interest** earned by your account. The interest rate is the rate of interest an account will earn on funds deposited for a full year.

Money Market Accounts A money market deposit account (MMDA) will let you save and write a limited number of checks. It usually earns higher interest than a savings account, but also usually requires a higher minimum balance and has more fees. MMDAs have a variable interest rate, which can be a benefit or a drawback depending on whether rates move up or down.

Time Deposits A **time deposit,** such as a certificate of deposit (CD), offers a guaranteed interest rate for a fixed period of time. In general, the longer the term, the higher the interest rate. Most banks will charge you a high penalty fee if you withdraw from the CD account before the term expires, or "matures." Open a CD account only if you think you won't need access to that money during the term of the CD.

How to Choose a Savings Account

Deposits and withdrawals
- ❑ What is the minimum balance?
- ❑ When can I make my first withdrawal?
- ❑ How many deposits and withdrawals am I allowed to make each month?
- ❑ Am I limited in the dollar amount of my withdrawals?
- ❑ What are the penalties for early withdrawal?
- ❑ Can I use an automated teller machine (ATM) to make deposits and withdrawals?

Interest
- ❑ What is the interest rate?
- ❑ Is it compounded? How frequently?
- ❑ What is the minimum balance required to earn interest?
- ❑ When is the interest paid?

Fees
- ❑ What fees apply?
- ❑ What is the minimum balance needed to avoid fees?
- ❑ Do certain transactions carry penalty fees?
- ❑ What ATM fees apply?

Truth in Savings The **Truth in Savings Act** is a federal law that requires banks to provide you with certain information about the accounts they offer, including
- annual percentage yield—the amount of interest you will earn on a deposit
- interest rates
- fees and other charges that apply
- features, such as the minimum balance needed to avoid fees

Use this information to help you choose the bank and the type of account that is best for you.

Investing

Saving is a great way to plan for your future. Many experts advise saving 10 percent of your earnings annually. While keeping your money in a savings account is safe, investing your money can give your dollars the opportunity to grow. Bonds, stocks, and mutual funds are among the many investment options available to you.

Bonds A **bond** is an IOU issued by a corporation or by the government as a way for them to borrow money. When you buy a bond, you buy the right to receive a fixed amount of money at some future date as well as an annual interest payment. The face value of the bond is the fixed amount agreed upon. Corporate bonds can be risky, depending on the financial health of the firm. If the firm goes bankrupt, it won't be able to pay what it owes you. Government bonds are more secure because the government is unlikely to declare bankruptcy.

Government bonds can be purchased through your bank and are available in small denominations. Interest earned is subject to federal tax, but not state or local taxes. They are a secure investment, although the return is low compared to other types of investment.

A word about interest rates Interest rates are expressed as percentages and indicate the rate of interest an account will earn on funds deposited for a full year. Interest is compounded when it is added to your principal. In effect, compound interest is interest on interest.

Stocks A popular form of investment, **stock** represents ownership in an organization. If a firm issues and sells 10,000 shares of stock, and you purchase 1,000 of them, you own 10 percent of the firm. By purchasing a corporation's stock, you are buying the right to receive a fraction of its profit.

The two potential benefits from owning stock are dividends and capital gains. **Dividends** are portions of a corporation's profit paid to stockholders. **Capital gain** is the profit you make if you can sell your stock for more than you paid for it. Not all stocks pay dividends. Some companies reinvest their profits, rather than pay out dividends. Such "growth" stocks are attractive to investors because they expect the stock price to increase as the company grows.

Stock is available in two forms: **common stock** and **preferred stock**. Preferred stock earns dividends fixed at an annual rate, whereas any dividends earned by common stock are dependent on market fluctuations. Preferred shareholders are paid dividends before common shareholders.

Corporate stocks are bought and sold on stock markets. Most investors rely on the services of a stockbroker to purchase stock. You'll want to compare reputations, transaction fees, insurance, and services of various brokerage firms before you choose one. Many people rely on the advice of a professional financial advisor or investment advisor when choosing stock. Make sure you check an advisor's credentials.

Stocks are riskier than bonds, because stock price is based on the expectation of profit. If the firm turns out to be less profitable than expected, dividends will be smaller than expected and the market price of shares may decrease. You may find yourself selling your shares for less money than you paid for them.

Experts warn that if you get into the stock market, you should be prepared to ride the ups and downs. Sometimes you will win, and sometimes you will lose. And don't go into the stock market

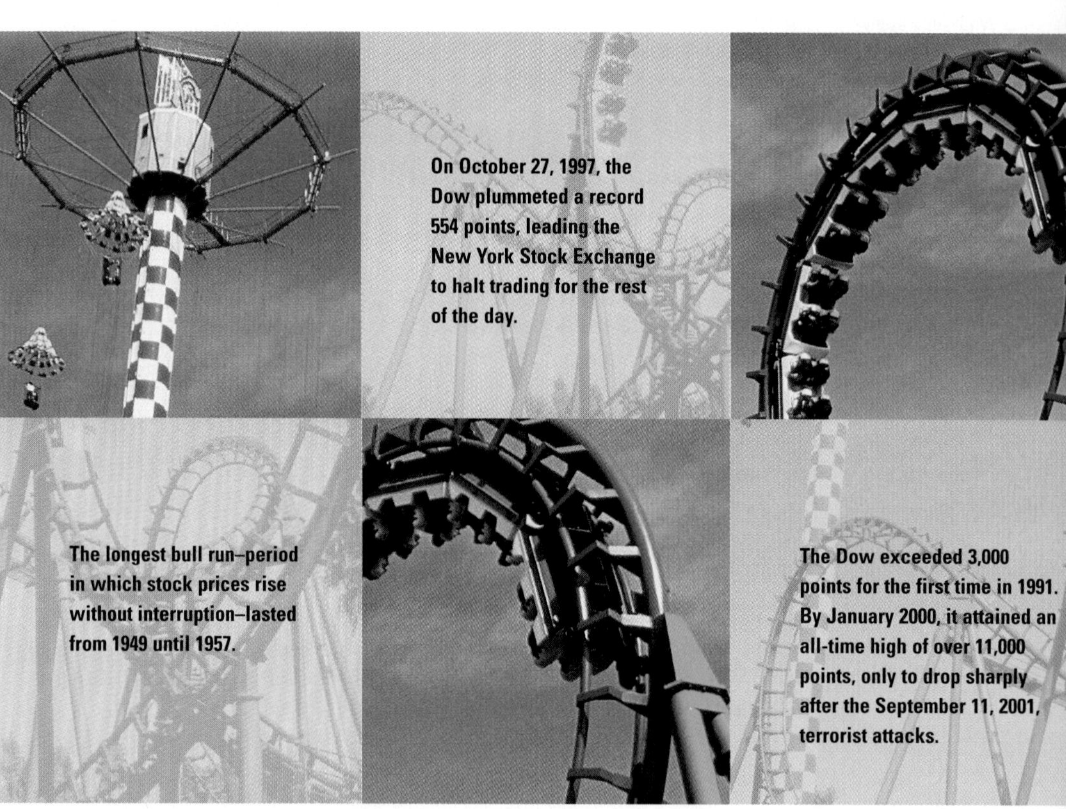
On October 27, 1997, the Dow plummeted a record 554 points, leading the New York Stock Exchange to halt trading for the rest of the day.
The longest bull run–period in which stock prices rise without interruption–lasted from 1949 until 1957.
The Dow exceeded 3,000 points for the first time in 1991. By January 2000, it attained an all-time high of over 11,000 points, only to drop sharply after the September 11, 2001, terrorist attacks.

Comparing Investment Options

Type of investment	Income generated	Growth potential	Risk level
Bonds	very steady	little or none	low risk
Common stock	variable	good	high risk
Preferred stock	less variable than common stock	good	moderate risks

to make a quick profit for something crucial, like school tuition. If you do, the stock could take a tumble right at the time you need to sell it, and you could lose all of your investment.

Mutual Funds You might choose to invest your money in a **mutual fund,** which is an investment in an investment company. Investment companies sell stock in their mutual funds. Instead of producing a product or service, however, they take the money they receive for their stock and invest it in the stocks and bonds of other corporations. The mutual fund will combine the money you invest with that of other investors in order to make substantial investments in other companies.

A major benefit of investing in a mutual fund is that it provides instant diversification to your portfolio. This means that the money you invest in a mutual fund is spread out among all the different companies in which the mutual fund invests its money.

Mutual funds include stocks of varying risk levels. There are three categories of mutual funds:

- *Money market funds* are short-term, low risk investments. The money you invest will be used to make short-term loans to businesses or the government. (Do not confuse money market funds with money market deposit accounts, which are described on page 506.)
- *Bond funds* are, as the name implies, investments in bonds. They usually have higher potential yields than money market funds, but they are also riskier.
- *Stock funds,* though riskiest, offer the highest potential returns. As long-term investments, they perform better than money market funds and bond funds.

As with any investment, you must do your homework before you commit to a mutual fund. Even though a professional money manager will control your investment, mutual funds are not without risk.

Risk Versus Payout You have many options when it comes to investing your money. What you choose depends on what rate of return you'd like on your money and how much risk you are willing to accept. You also need to consider the length of your investment, the ease of making the transaction, and any tax burdens the investment may carry. In general, the safer the investment, the lower the return. High-risk investments have the potential for high returns because investors demand higher rates of return to compensate for the risk they face.

Despite stock tips, hype about hot stocks or "sure things," you should not approach investing as if you were a gambler in a casino. Informed decisions and careful planning are your best strategies for successful investment.

Check Your Understanding

1. **Key Terms (a)** What is the difference between a **bond** and a **stock? (b)** How does a **dividend** differ from a **capital gain? (c)** Explain the difference between **common stock** and **preferred stock. (d)** What makes a **mutual fund** an attractive investing option?
2. **Identifying Alternatives** Think about your future financial needs. Are you planning to buy a car? Do you need money for an apartment deposit or college tuition? Use the information on these pages to design a savings and investment plan that will help you reach your goals.

Answers to . . .

Check Your Understanding

1. (a) A bond is a note stating that you have lent money to a company or the government and will be paid interest on that loan. In comparison, stocks represent partial ownership in a company and may offer dividends as a form of payment, although that is not guaranteed. (b) A dividend is a portion of a corporation's profit paid to stockholders. Capital gain is the profit made by selling a stock for more than its purchase price. (c) Preferred stock earns dividends fixed at an annual rate, whereas any dividends earned by common stock are dependent on market fluctuations. (d) Mutual funds allow your money to be combined with other people's money and managed by one group, therefore giving all the people involved more purchasing power and hopefully more profits, although that is never guaranteed.
2. Students should list specific goals and identify savings and investment plans appropriate to these goals.

Personal Finance Activities
"Financial Institutions and Services," p. 9 provides activities to help students practice personal finance skills.

Financial Institutions and Services

If you have money, you're going to need the services of a bank or credit union—to save money, to manage it, and transfer it to others. If you need more money, a bank can lend it to you.

The city or town you live in probably has many banks, both large and small. Behind all that brick and chrome and glass, what are their differences? How do you choose? Begin by familiarizing yourself with the different types of banks and the various services they offer, then determine which one best suits your needs.

Types of Financial Institutions

A bank is an institution for receiving, keeping, and lending money. There are four basic types of banks:

- *commercial banks*
- *savings and loan associations*
- *savings banks*
- *credit unions*

Each offers a different range of services, although recent deregulation of the American banking industry has made them more similar than different. Whatever type of bank you choose, make sure that it is federally insured. That way, if the bank fails, you won't lose your money. Federal deposit insurance protects your deposit up to a limit of $100,000.

Banking Services

Automated teller machines (ATMs) and bank cards
A bank card and an ATM allow you 24-hour access to your accounts, although services and withdrawal amounts are limited.

Debit cards
Debit cards are used much like checks. When you make a purchase with a debit card, money is electronically deducted from your account and credited to the seller's account. Many stores let you use your ATM card as a debit card.

Credit cards
You can obtain a credit card that is directly linked to your bank account. Payments are automatically withdrawn from your bank account, making payment of your credit card bill more convenient.

Overdraft privileges
Your bank may give your checking account a small line of credit to protect you from bouncing checks.

Electronic banking
Using a computer and a modem, you can do much of your banking without entering a bank.

Direct deposit
You can move money directly from one account to another by authorizing a wire transfer.

Automatic withdrawal
You can arrange to have your regular bills, such as your car payment, deducted directly from your account.

Commercial Banks The bank that provides the most services and plays the biggest role in our economy is the **commercial bank.** Commercial banks provide checking accounts, savings accounts, and money market accounts, and they accept time deposits (CDs). Individuals as well as businesses maintain accounts at commercial banks. Commercial banks also make loans to both individuals and businesses. Many have begun to offer stock brokerage services as well.

Savings and Loans **Savings and loans associations,** as the name implies, traditionally accepted deposits from customers and specialized in offering long-term financing for homes. They were originally intended to promote savings and home ownership. Recent deregulation, however, has expanded scope of their services.

Savings Banks **Savings banks** accept deposits and specialize in low-risk investments, such as government bonds. Some of the larger ones offer some of the same services as commercial banks, such as checking accounts.

Credit Unions **Credit unions** are nonprofit banks owned by their members, usually employees of a single organization such as a company or trade union. Their ties to industry and their tax-exempt nonprofit status enable credit unions to pay slightly higher interest rates than commercial banks. They also finance consumer loans at competitive rates.

Other Financial Institutions You may also turn to mutual fund companies, brokerage firms, and insurance subsidiaries for some financial services. Mutual fund companies and brokerage firms are useful for investing. Insurance companies can provide you with tax-deferred savings and may let you take out loans against your insurance policy. These institutions, however, do not offer a full range of banking services.

How to Choose A Bank

It can be challenging to find the right bank or credit union to suit your needs. When choosing a financial institution, be sure to get answers to the following questions:

- ❑ Is it conveniently located?
- ❑ Does it have convenient hours?
- ❑ Are ATMs available?
- ❑ What services does it offer?
- ❑ How high are the fees?
- ❑ Is it federally insured?

Wire transfers
Your employer can credit your pay directly to your account, giving you speedy access to your earnings.

Business and consumer loans
Banks can help you finance your education, automobile purchase, or other large purchase.

Investment services
You can purchase stocks through the brokerage services now offered by many of the larger commercial banks.

Safe deposit boxes
You can secure important documents and valuables by renting a safe deposit box, which is kept in the bank's vault.

Check Your Understanding

1. **Key Terms** How does a **commercial bank** differ from a **savings and loan association?** How does a commercial bank differ from a credit union?
2. **Organizing Information** Review the chart on banking services. Rank them in order of importance to you.

Answers to . . .

Check Your Understanding

1. Commercial banks offer a wide range of services usually including checking and savings accounts as well as certificates of deposit. Savings and loan associations offer limited services (savings and loans), usually for homeowners. A credit union is a publicly owned bank, sometimes owned by a certain labor or service union, which provides services to its owners.
2. Student's lists should contain all services mentioned in the chart. They should also include unique factors relevant to each student.

Personal Finance Activities "Credit and Debt," p. 11 provides activities to help students practice personal finance skills.

Credit and Debt

Credit gives extra punch to your purchasing power; but reckless handling of credit can bury you in debt.

Seems like everyone wants to lend you money. Each year, credit-card companies bombard American consumers with alluring offers of easy money. "Congratulations—you are qualified to receive $10,000!" "You will not be turned down!" "Why postpone your dreams? Apply today."

Why do they want to lend you money? Because that's how they make money. Banks and other financial institutions lend money to both businesses and consumers. Borrowers, in return, pay fees, and those fees can be hefty. If you must borrow—for a car, for college, or for other expenses that you lack the cash to cover—learn how to borrow wisely.

Don't let the credit card monster consume you!
10%
18%

Are You Credit Worthy?

Loans, credit cards, and other methods of deferred payment are known as **credit.** For a bank or other institution to extend you credit, it must be confident that you will repay all the money you borrow, plus any additional interest and fees. You, on the other hand, must understand what you're getting into before you sign on the dotted line.

Creditors, the folks who lend you money, aren't going to give you money just on your word. They are going to ask many questions about your financial past and demand evidence of your financial health to determine if you are able and willing to pay them back.

The Four Cs Creditors look for *capacity, capital, character,* and *collateral* when judging your credit worthiness. *Capacity* is your ability to repay the debt. Creditors will want to know where you work, how long you've worked there, and how much money you make. They will also want to know how much you spend.

Capital is your regular income plus the money in your savings and checking accounts.

Character is your willingness to repay your debts. Creditors will obtain a record of your past borrowing, your bill-paying habits, and your ability to live within your means. Much of this information they will obtain from an organization called a **credit bureau.** If you fail to maintain a good **credit rating,** you will find it very difficult to obtain credit. Creditors will also look for signs of stability in your life. How long have you lived at your current address? How often have you moved in the past few years? Do you own or rent your home?

Some loans require **collateral,** which is property used to secure a loan. If you default on the loan or fail to repay it, the creditor takes ownership of the collateral. Often the item that the loan is used to purchase serves as collateral. This is usually the case with car loans and home mortgages. If you fail to keep up with your car payments, you may find yourself walking to work.

Four Steps to Establishing Credit

1. **Maintain savings and checking accounts.** While these are not credit, they can be used to show that you know how to manage your money. You can use your canceled checks to prove that you pay bills promptly.
2. **Get a department-store charge card.** Store cards, which can be used only to make purchases from that particular retailer, are usually easier to obtain than bank credit cards or other forms of credit. Responsible use of a store charge card can help you establish good credit.
3. **Use your bank deposits as collateral for a credit card.** Your limit, or the maximum amount you're allowed to borrow, would not exceed the amount of your deposits.
4. **Have someone with good credit cosign your credit application.** A cosigner agrees to pay your debt if you fail to do so. With a cosigner, you can use someone else's good credit to establish your own.

Information Creditors Can't Use The federal government has passed laws protecting consumers from being discriminated against when applying for credit. The Equal Credit Opportunity Act forbids creditors from using age, gender, marital status, race, color, religion, national origin, or public assistance income when establishing your credit worthiness. Nor can creditors discriminate against you for exercising certain rights, such as filing a billing error notice with a creditor.

Maintaining Good Credit As you begin to make purchases with loans and credit cards, credit might seem to you like free money, but it's not. When you borrow money from a financial institution, you are, in effect, renting money. Eventually you have to pay it all back, along with interest and fees, called **finance charges.** Finance charges can be quite expensive and add up rapidly. If you're not paying attention, you can quickly lose control of your debt.

Making late payments, missing payments, or borrowing more than you can pay back will damage your credit history. A poor credit history can haunt you for seven years or more. If you are irresponsible with your credit card, you're going to have a hard time financing that new car you plan to buy.

To maintain good credit, you need to develop good credit behavior. Don't overborrow or overspend, make sure you pay your bills promptly, and protect your credit cards from loss or theft. It is also crucial for you to understand the different forms of credit available to you and how their finance charges are calculated. That way, you can make sound decisions that will keep you out of financial hot water.

Types of Credit

Different forms of credit are suited to different purposes. You know that you shouldn't use your credit card to pay for a new car. And you wouldn't take out a loan to pay for dinner and a movie on Friday night. There is much more you need to know, however, about credit.

Loans Loans come in two forms: single-payment loans and installment loans. Single-payment loans are short-term loans paid off in one lump sum. Installment loans, on the other hand, are repaid at regularly scheduled intervals, or installments, usually monthly. Each installment payment is for the same amount. Each payment is applied to both the principal (the amount borrowed) and the interest (the fee for borrowing the money). Although you pay the same number of dollars each month, at first, more of the payment goes toward interest than principal. An automobile loan is an example of an installment loan. (See "Buying a Car" on pages 520–521.)

Loans that require collateral are called secured loans. Loans that don't require collateral are called unsecured loans. Credit for these loans, also known as signature loans, is based on the borrower's references and credit rating. A Guaranteed Student Loan is an example of an unsecured loan.

Credit Cards One of the most popular forms of credit in the United States today is the credit card. It is a form of open-ended, or revolving, credit. A credit card lets you borrow money on an ongoing basis, up to a prearranged limit, to buy goods and services. Any amount you pay back you are able to reborrow.

Many people find credit cards more convenient than cash. You can order movie tickets, buy clothes, pay for a meal, or just about anything else using a credit card. Bank cards such as Visa and MasterCard are the most widely accepted.

As a cardholder you receive a monthly bill and are required to pay at least some portion of the balance (the amount you owe) each month. Annual fees, interest rates, and other charges vary greatly among credit card issuers, so you should carefully compare the terms of several card offers before making any commitments. Some nonprofit organizations on the Internet offer listings of good credit card deals and guidance in applying for them.

Another form of credit is a travel and entertainment (T&E) card. It is similar to a credit card, but the borrower is required to pay the total amount owed each month. Because you pay your debt in full each month, you aren't charged interest. Usually you are required to pay an annual membership fee. American Express and Diners Club are popular travel and entertainment cards.

Finance Charges and Terms

As a borrower, you pay for the privilege of borrowing money. Interest is the primary fee for borrowing money. Just as a bank will pay you interest to use your money, you must pay your creditors to use theirs. A creditor, however, may charge you additional fees. The total dollar amount you pay to use credit is called the finance charge. It includes interest and other fees that may apply.

Annual Percentage Rate An important number for you to understand when applying for credit is the **annual percentage rate (APR)**. The APR tells you what your credit will cost. It is the finance charge expressed as an annual rate. Comparing the annual percentage rates, rather than the interest rates, offered by lenders is a good way to compare loans. Be sure you understand how your lender calculates the APR for the credit cards you are considering.

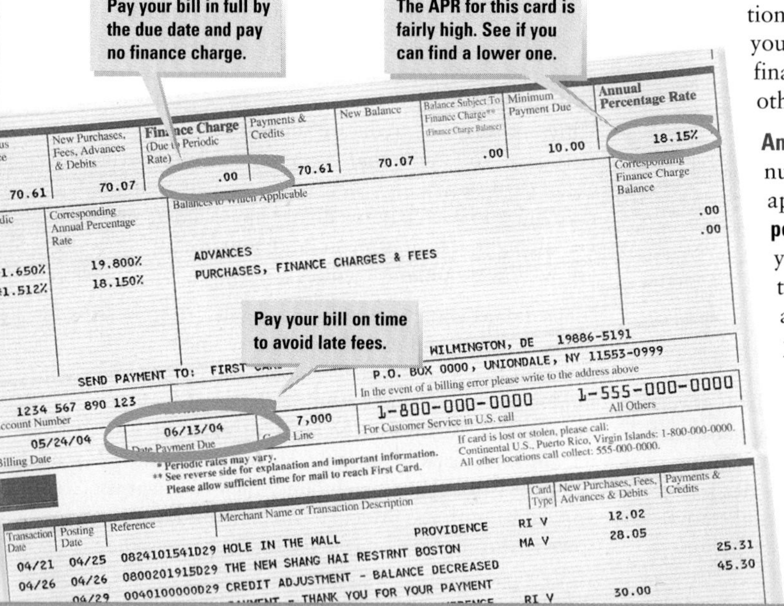
Pay your bill in full by the due date and pay no finance charge.
The APR for this card is fairly high. See if you can find a lower one.
Pay your bill on time to avoid late fees.

New Purchases, Fees, Advances & Debits	Finance Charge (Due to Periodic Rate)	Payments & Credits	New Balance	Balance Subject To Finance Charge**	Minimum Payment Due	Annual Percentage Rate
70.07	.00	70.61	70.07	.00	10.00	18.15%

Periodic	Corresponding Annual Percentage Rate	Balances to Which Applicable	Corresponding Finance Charge Balance
1.650%	19.800%	ADVANCES	.00
1.512%	18.150%	PURCHASES, FINANCE CHARGES & FEES	.00

SEND PAYMENT TO: FIRST CARD WILMINGTON, DE 19886-5191
P.O. BOX 0000, UNIONDALE, NY 11553-0999
In the event of a billing error please write to the address above
1234 567 890 123 Account Number
05/24/04 Billing Date
06/13/04 Date Payment Due
7,000 Credit Line
1-800-000-0000 For Customer Service in U.S. call
1-555-000-0000 All Others
* Periodic rates may vary.
** See reverse side for explanation and important information.
Please allow sufficient time for mail to reach First Card.
If card is lost or stolen, please call: Continental U.S., Puerto Rico, Virgin Islands: 1-800-000-0000. All other locations call collect: 555-000-0000.

Transaction Date	Posting Date	Reference	Merchant Name or Transaction Description		Card Type	New Purchases, Fees, Advances & Debits	Payments & Credits
04/21	04/25	0824101541D29	HOLE IN THE WALL	PROVIDENCE	RI V	12.02	
04/26	04/26	0800201915D29	THE NEW SHANG HAI RESTRNT BOSTON		MA V	28.05	
			CREDIT ADJUSTMENT - BALANCE DECREASED				25.31
	04/29	0040100000D29	PAYMENT - THANK YOU FOR YOUR PAYMENT				45.30

Comparing APR

EXAMPLE a $150,000, 30-year home mortgage

	Plan A	Plan B
Interest rate	6.0%	6.0%
Points	0	2.0
Other closing costs	$1,500	$1,000
APR	6.094	6.278

Comparing Terms on an Installment Loan

EXAMPLE a $13,500 loan with 12.5% interest

	3-year loan	5-year loan
Number of monthly payments	36	60
Amount of each payment	$451.62	$303.72
Total interest paid	$2,758.32	$4,723.20

Terms Another important factor to consider is the term, or length, of your loan. For example, if you arrange to pay for your new car in three years rather than five, your monthly payments will be higher, but in the end, you will pay less interest.

How to Choose a Credit Card

When selecting a credit card, be sure you understand all the terms of the credit-card offer before you make a commitment.

What is the APR? You may want to choose the card with lowest APR, especially if you carry a balance on your account.

Is the APR fixed or variable? A fixed APR will stay the same. A variable APR will rise and fall as the prime rate or other economic indicator changes.

What is the periodic rate? The periodic rate is the interest rate that is applied to your account balance each billing period.

How are finance charges computed? Most creditors use your average daily balance to determine the finance charge. The average daily balance is calculated by adding up all daily balances and dividing them by the number of days in a billing period.

Is there a grace period? Many creditors will charge you no interest if you pay your bill in full before the due date.

What fees does the creditor charge? Many credit cards charge an annual membership fee, as well as fees for late payments, cash advances, or exceeding the credit limit.

Know Your Rights Credit card issuers and other lenders are required by **Truth in Lending laws** to disclose certain information. Institutions extending loans must tell you the exact finance charge on your loan. Credit card issuers must disclose monthly interest rates, the APR, and the method of finance charge calculation.

The Fair Credit Reporting Act protects you from errors on credit reports issued by credit bureaus. You are entitled to know the reason for any negative activity on your report and to have any errors corrected. Similarly, the Fair Credit Billing Act lets you dispute and correct billing information.

If you find yourself in debt and subject to debt collection, be aware that debt collectors must ensure the accuracy of the bill in question and allow you to dispute the bill if you believe it to be in error. Debt collectors may not threaten, harass, or otherwise abuse you in pursuit of the debt.

Check Your Understanding

1. **Key Terms** **(a)** Name two types of **credit** and explain how they are different. **(b)** How does **collateral** discourage borrowers from defaulting on a loan? **(c)** How do the Equal Credit Opportunity Act and **Truth in Lending laws** protect consumers?
2. **Analyzing Information** Analyze the credit card offers your household receives in the mail or that you see advertised. Make a chart comparing their features and finance charges. Identify and explain which credit card is the best deal.

Answers to . . .

Check Your Understanding

1. (a) Two types of credit are loans and credit cards. They differ in that a loan is taken out for a certain amount of money, with set limits for repayment, and a credit card is an open-ended, or revolving, form of borrowing money and repaying it. (b) Collateral is collected when a loan defaults. It discourages defaulting because the collateral on the loan is often the item that the loan paid for itself or something else of equal or greater value. (c) The Equal Opportunity in Lending Act prevents discrimination based on age, gender, marital status, race, color, religion, national origin, or public assistance income when assessing credit worthiness. The Truth in Lending Act ensures that consumers are given all information on interest rates and fees before getting a loan or credit card.
2. Students should show an understanding of the significance of APR, finance charge calculation, grace periods, and fees.

Personal Finance Activities
"Paying for Education," p. 13 provides activities to help students practice personal finance skills.

Paying for Education

Learning how to finance your tuition is an education in itself.

By the time you finish paying for college, you may have shelled out enough money to buy a luxury car, a small yacht, or perhaps even a house. And that doesn't count the cost of graduate or professional school.

The car won't last, however, while education affects your earning power for the rest of your life. So the short-term sacrifice is generally worth the potential long-term gain. But how on Earth are you going to pay for it?

Decisions, Decisions

The hard facts about paying for college are these: even after adjusting for inflation, the average cost of tuition at public and private universities nearly doubled between 1990 and 2005, while average salaries rose only slightly. **Tuition** is the cost of enrolling in courses. In recent years, schools have added on many other costly fees. Second, financial aid rose to meet the increased need, but mostly in terms of loans, not scholarships. How can you achieve your educational goals without jeopardizing your financial future? Start by thinking about the type of school you want to attend. For example:

- *What school do you want to attend, and why?* Examine your goals. Can you find the educational resources you need at a less-expensive public school? The answer, often, is yes. However, if only private schools have what you're looking for, don't rule them out because of cost. Although private schools are generally more costly than public schools, private schools often can be more generous in providing financial aid.
- *How much does location matter to you?* According to the College Board, tuition costs vary considerably from region to region. Schools in the Southwest are generally less expensive than those in the East.
- *How much debt do you want to incur?* If you expect to be a freelance artist after you graduate, you might want to take on less debt than if you're planning a career as a doctor.

The costs of attending college have been rising faster than the rate of inflation. This chart, adjusted for inflation to 2004 dollars, shows how the average annual costs of attending four-year private and public colleges and universities have risen since 1985.

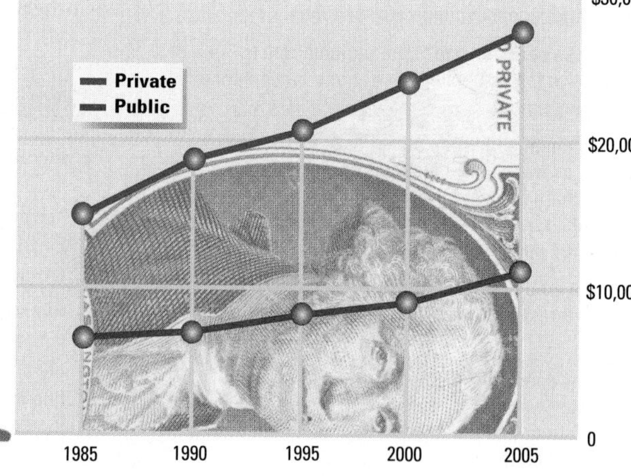

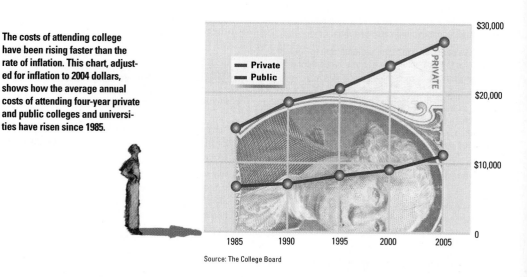

Source: The College Board

The ABCs of Financial Aid

Each year, millions of dollars are made available to help students pay for college. The three major types of financial aid are (a) grants and scholarships; (b) work-study programs; and (c) loans. These categories are described in the box below.

One simple equation cuts through the confusing information about financing:

Total Cost – Total Aid = What you owe

So the idea is to reduce the amount you're going to owe by applying for as many sources of aid as possible. Most students qualify for some kind of financial aid. How much you receive depends on the following criteria:

- income—yours and your parents'
- the number of college students in your family
- family assets and expenses
- the available pool of aid at the school you plan to attend
- the number of students applying for aid in a given year and their financial need compared with yours.

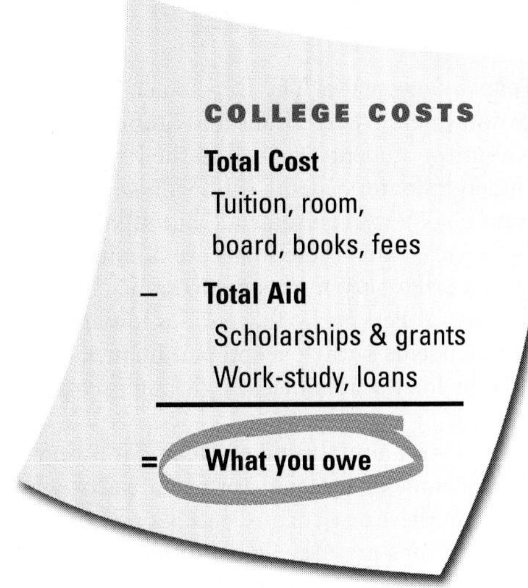

COLLEGE COSTS
Total Cost
Tuition, room,
board, books, fees
– Total Aid
Scholarships & grants
Work-study, loans
= What you owe

Types of Lenders

Regardless of your income, you can qualify for some type of government loan. You might need to supplement it with a loan from your school or with a commercial loan.

Three Types of Financial Aid

Grants and Scholarships

Scholarships are often based on academic or athletic performance. But don't count yourself out if you're not valedictorian or captain of the basketball team.

All kinds of people can qualify for "free money." Federal Pell Grants and Federal Supplemental Educational Opportunity Grants are given to students with "exceptional financial need." Other grants are available to students of a certain gender or ethnic group or members of a certain club or civic organization. Companies often offer scholarships to children of their employees. If you already know what you want to major in, there are scholarships for just about every field. You can find scholarship directories in the reference section of your library, on the Web, through your guidance counselor, and through college financial aid offices.

The Reserve Officer's Training Corps (ROTC) program, offered by all branches of the armed forces, gives merit-based scholarships. These pay for tuition, fees, and books and give you a monthly living allowance in return for service in the military after you graduate.

Work-study

Many American college students work their way through school. Many colleges offer work-study programs that provide on-campus jobs for students receiving financial aid. Most work-study programs are federally funded.

Loans

Both students and parents can apply for college loans. Most college loans have a low interest rate and a generous repayment schedule.

Loans can be subsidized or unsubsidized. On a federally subsidized loan, the government pays the interest during the years you're in school, and you don't begin paying back the loan until you leave school.

The Federal Government The Department of Education offers Direct Loans and Stafford Loans for parents or students, as well as the Parent Loan for Undergraduate Students (PLUS). Each loan has different eligibility requirements, but all have a cap on the interest rate. These loans are administered by agencies that vary from state to state.

The Federal Perkins Loan provides low-interest funds to students with "exceptional financial need." The loan is administered through schools themselves.

Students who go on to take teaching jobs in certain low-income or teacher-shortage areas or who volunteer in the Americorps, Peace Corps, or VISTA programs may be eligible to have their federal loans partially repaid or even canceled.

INFORMATION SOURCES

The Internet is the best thing that ever happened to students seeking financial aid. If you have or can get Internet access, you'll save yourself many hours of searching for financial aid information. In addition, you can file on-line for most scholarships and loans. Several sites have calculators that allow you to estimate your Expected Family Contribution, the amount of your aid awards, and the amount of your loan payments.

Some good starting places include:

- The Access Group
- Scholarship Search and CSS/Financial Aid PROFILE, programs of the College Board
- Federal Student Aid Information Center
- SallieMae (the commonly used nickname for the acronym SLMA, or Student Loan Marketing Association; site includes a listing of major private lenders)

Private Sources If money from government loans does not cover your college expenses, many other sources are available. Banks and other financial institutions offer regular commercial loans for education. These loans generally carry higher interest rates than federal loans. Trade organizations and educational institutions also provide loans, as do a variety of for-profit companies on the Web.

Pay Up! A word to the wise: Repay your student loans. Computerization and more vigorous collection efforts are resulting in more cheaters getting caught and penalized. If you run into trouble repaying your loan, call your lender, who can help you work out a manageable repayment plan.

Some loans allow you to pay just the interest for a certain period of time. Or you might get a graduated payment schedule, in which the monthly amount starts out low—when your income is relatively low—and rises later on, when presumably you can better afford to pay.

Pay off unsubsidized loans, which accrue interest while you're in school, before government **subsidized** loans, which do not.

Applying for Financial Aid

Filling out financial aid applications has gotten easier, but it still requires some time and organization.

Required Forms To qualify for any type of government financial aid, you must complete the Free Application for Federal Student Aid (FAFSA). You can obtain the form from your high school, the local library, or the U.S. Department of Education's Web site. The information you provide on the FAFSA form is used to calculate your Expected Family Contribution (EFC). The EFC is determined according to a formula established by Congress.

To receive nonfederal aid, many schools require you to fill out the PROFILE form. The College Board's financial aid program, the College Scholarship Service (CSS), runs the PROFILE program. You can request the form on paper from CSS or complete it on-line at the CSS Web site.

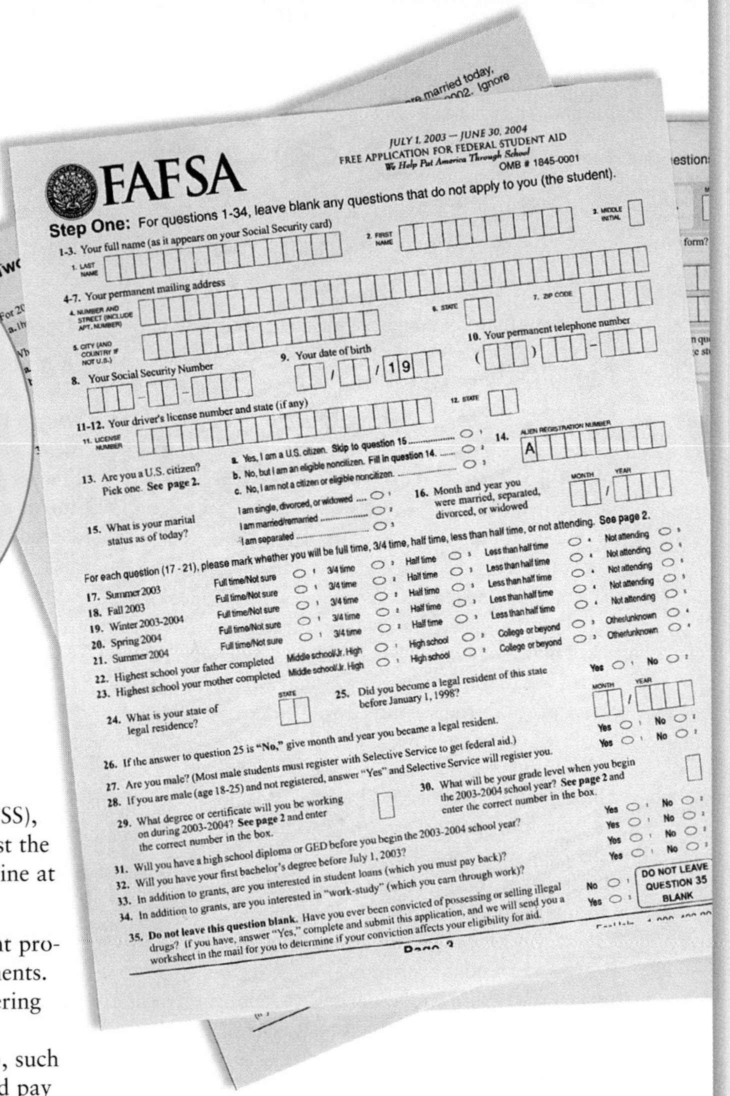

Required Documents As with any government program, you'll need documents—many documents. Don't wait until deadline time to start gathering them. They include:

- Proof of income (yours and your parents'), such as most recent tax returns, W-2 forms, and pay stubs
- Mortgage statements
- Proof of any unusual financial hardships, such as high medical expenses

Tip If you have savings, use it to pay off any debts you may have before applying for aid. You don't get a break for having high credit card debt, but you will be expected to contribute about one third of all savings. So use your savings to pay down your debt first.

RULES TO LIVE BY

1. Never miss a filing deadline; the federal government doesn't accept "my dog ate my application" as an excuse.
2. Photocopy everything you submit; you may need to refer to it later.
3. Use consistent information from form to form, including the spelling of your name.

Check Your Understanding

1. **Key Terms (a)** What are some of the ways that students deal with skyrocketing **tuition** costs? **(b)** Why is it smart to pay off an unsubsidized loan before paying off a **subsidized** loan?
2. **Analyze** What factors might influence your own decision making about college? Explain your reasoning.

Answers to . . .

Check Your Understanding

1. **(a)** Prospective college students can apply for scholarships, grants, and loans to help subsidize increasing tuition costs. **(b)** Subsidized loans have the interest paid by the government while you are in school, while unsubsidized loans do not and therefore accrue interest at a faster pace (you pay more).
2. Students should provide information on the basics of their college decision-making process, including location, costs, field of study, and post-undergraduate plans.

Personal Finance Activities
"Buying a Car," p. 15 provides activities to help students practice personal finance skills.

Buying a Car

Don't think of a car as a status symbol or a personal statement. The best car is the one that suits your needs—and that you can afford.

A car is one of the biggest purchases you will make. With a small investment in time and effort, you can learn what you need to make a sensible decision—and get a good deal.

Getting the Best Deal on a New Car

Most car-buying guides recommend that you identify the invoice price of the base model of the new car you want. Then request bids—in writing—from five dealers in your area, asking them how much above or below that price they will sell the car for. Save time and avoid hassling with dealers by communicating by fax if you can. Once you have received all the bids, approach the second-lowest bidder to see if he or she will beat the lowest bid.

When purchasing your car, know in advance which options you want. Don't let a dealer talk you into spending more for options than you can afford. Be especially wary of important-sounding but unnecessary add-ons such as fabric protection, paint sealant, rustproofing, and an extended warranty. An extended warranty is a service contract purchased from the dealer by the buyer. Do not confuse it with the manufacturer's warranty that comes with the car. Extended warranties are expensive and often cover repairs already covered by the manufacturer's warranty.

Financing

Before you buy your car, research the costs of auto loans at banks and other lending institutions. Compare the annual percentage rates they offer with that of the financing offered by your car dealer. Consider how much of a down payment you can afford to make. The more money you can put down, the less you have to borrow. (For more information on loans, see Credit and Debt on pages 512–515.)

Used Cars

Automobiles quickly **depreciate,** or lose their value. The new car you drive off the lot today will be worth half what you paid for it in three years. After three years, the rate of depreciation slows down. By the sixth year, it is down to 3 percent per year. You might consider buying a car that has already depreciated substantially. That way, not only will you pay a lot less for it, but it will retain its value a lot longer than a new car.

You can buy used cars from many sources: dealers, rental and leasing companies, or individuals.

To make sure the car you're buying is reliable, try to obtain all service records on the car. This way

you can determine how well the car has been cared for. Calculate the average annual mileage. Anything over 15,000 miles per year indicates a car that has experienced an excessive amount of wear and tear.

You should also arrange to have an independent mechanic inspect the car for you before you buy it. Look in the Yellow Pages under "Automotive Diagnostic Service" for a certified mechanic.

Dealers are required by federal law to post a Buyer's Guide on the used cars they offer for sale. The Buyer's Guide must specify whether the vehicle is being sold "as is" or with a warranty, and what percentage of the repair costs the dealer will pay.

Avoiding High-Pressure Tactics

Let's face it, a professional car dealer has much more experience in selling cars than you do in buying them. How can you avoid being pressured into spending more money than you want to?

- Be prepared. Know what you want, what you don't want, and obtain bids based on the invoice price.

PRACTICALITY

- Don't be talked into options you don't want. If the dealer doesn't have the exact car you want, have him or her try to get it from another dealer, or go to another dealer yourself.
- Don't discuss trade-ins until after you've settled on a sale price. Do not let the dealer consider the trade-in of your old car as a reduction in dealer sticker price. To "trade in" your old car is simply to sell it to the dealer. It has nothing to do with the price of the new car.
- Don't be pushed into a decision. If you're at a dealership just to look, don't let a dealer talk you into buying that day, no matter what one-day specials he or she dangles before you. If you're negotiating a price and the dealer says, "Take it or leave it," don't be afraid to leave it. If you can't find a better deal elsewhere, you can always come back.
- Get it in writing. If a dealer is not willing to put all agreements in writing, walk away.

If you are feeling bullied, confused, or pressured by a dealer, just walk away. Your ability to get up and leave is the best leverage you have.

How to Choose a Car

There are so many makes and models of cars, both new and used. How can you pick the one that's right for you? Identify your needs to help you narrow your search. Here are some questions to ask yourself:

- ❑ How many people does my car need to seat?
- ❑ How much cargo space do I need?
- ❑ What weather and road conditions will my car be subject to?
- ❑ How often will I use my car? Daily? Weekly?
- ❑ How many miles do I expect to put on my car each year?
- ❑ What do I consider acceptable gas mileage (number of miles per gallon of gasoline)?

And the most important question:

- ❑ How much can I afford to pay?

Your local library has many car-buying guides to help you choose a make and model. Check the Internet and nonprofit consumer publications for prices and evaluations of the performance, comfort, and safety of new and used cars.

Check Your Understanding

1. **Key Terms** Why is it a wise idea to buy a car that has already **depreciated** a great deal?
2. **Analyze** **(a)** What four features would matter most to you in buying a car? List them in order, for example, a certain price range, two-door vs. four-door, or a sun roof. **(b)** What do you have to sacrifice in order to get your most-wanted feature? In other words, what is the opportunity cost of that choice?

Answers to . . .

Check Your Understanding

1. Purchasing a car that has already depreciated in value provides a lower purchasing cost and less depreciation in value in the future.
2. (a) Students should list the four options most important to them and explain why they selected those options. (b) The opportunity cost should be in terms of wanted options lost due to other options gained. For instance, a person might have to give up automatic locks so that they can afford a CD player.

Personal Finance Activities
"Renting an Apartment," p. 17 provides activities to help students practice personal finance skills.

Renting an Apartment

Home is more than a place to hang your hat. Choosing the right place to live can go a long way toward making you happy.

Renting your first apartment is an exciting prospect, but don't rush into a decision you might regret. Research your options carefully, and know your rights and responsibilities before making a commitment.

Choosing the Right Place

To locate apartments to rent, look through the real estate section of a newspaper, search the Internet, read community bulletin boards, or use the services of a realtor. Keep in mind that realtors will charge you a fee for finding you an apartment, often half a month's rent or more. Find several listings that seem attractive to you. Make appointments with the landlords or their representatives to view the apartments.

Rent and Other Costs

A good rule of thumb is to have one month's rent and utility payments equal no more than one week's take-home pay. Estimate your utility bills by asking the landlord or a previous tenant what the average monthly heating and electricity costs were for the apartment during the previous year.

Keep in mind that you will probably need a large supply of cash up front. Many landlords require in advance the first and last month's rent. Some also ask for a **security deposit**, a sum of money that you pay the landlord to ensure that you will leave the apartment in the same condition you found it in. The security deposit is usually equal to a full month's rent. After you give up the apartment, the landlord will inspect it. If you have damaged the property, the landlord will use money from your security deposit to make repairs and will return any unused portion to you. If the apartment is undamaged, you will get back your entire deposit, sometimes with interest.

Signing the Lease

Finding an apartment you like is half the battle. The other half is convincing the landlord that you'll

reno.	renovated
sngl fam.	single family
ranch	ranch-style home
br	bedrooms
eik	eat-in kitchen
d&d	dishwasher and disposal
w/d	washer and dryer
ac	air conditioned
hwf	hardwood floors
pkg	parking
wlk to T	walk to public transportation

How to Choose an Apartment

Finding the right apartment can be difficult. Be sure to get answers to the following questions during your search.

- ❑ How many rooms does it have?
- ❑ What condition is it in?
- ❑ Are the door and window locks sturdy?
- ❑ Are there working smoke detectors?
- ❑ Are the walls soundproof?
- ❑ Does it have adequate closet space?
- ❑ Are there laundry facilities?
- ❑ What is the condition of the bathroom fixtures?
- ❑ Is parking available?
- ❑ Are pets allowed?
- ❑ Does the neighborhood appear safe?
- ❑ Is it convenient to where you work or attend school?
- ❑ Will you have access to public transportation?
- ❑ How close is the nearest grocery store?
- ❑ What are the terms of the lease?

be a responsible tenant. Remember, you may be competing with other prospective tenants for the apartment.

You will be asked to fill out a rental application. Most applications ask you for details such as:

- The names and phone numbers of your present and previous landlords
- Your social security number
- Your employer, job position, and income
- Your bank name, address, and account numbers
- Personal references

The landlord may also perform a credit check on you—another good reason to maintain a good credit history.

If this is your first apartment rental, you'll have to rely on your personal references, rather than previous landlords, to vouch for your character. Ask responsible adults who know you well, such as a teacher, coach, employer, or clergy member, to provide you with written references.

Once you've been approved to take the apartment, you will be required to sign a **lease,** a rental agreement between landlord and tenant. Most leases require a one-year commitment and monthly rent payments. The lease also spells out rules such as whether pets are allowed, or whether a fee will be charged if your rent is late. Some landlords will let you rent month to month without a set end date other than the amount of notice previously agreed upon.

Read any lease or rental agreement carefully, and make sure you understand it before you sign. Discuss the terms with your landlord, along with any changes you'd like to make. Bear in mind that what you are signing is a **contract,** a binding legal agreement. Both you and your landlord are required to live up to its obligations.

Rights and Responsibilities Know your tenant rights. While a landlord has the right to ask for references and perform a credit check, it is against the law to discriminate against a potential tenant on the basis of race, color, national origin, religion, sex, familial status, or handicap. Contact your state's office of Housing and Urban Development for more information.

Landlords are required to provide a dwelling that is structurally safe and sanitary and that has heat, water, and electricity. Your landlord has the right to enter your apartment only to make repairs or to show it to a prospective tenant, and sometimes he must give you notice before doing so.

Rental laws vary in different locations. For example, in rent-controlled neighborhoods, landlords are limited in the amount of rent they can charge. Check with your local housing or consumer affairs office for information.

At the same time, tenants have responsibilities. As a tenant, you must pay your rent on time, keep your apartment clean and undamaged, follow the terms of your lease or rental agreement, and be considerate of your neighbors.

Check Your Understanding

1. **Key Terms** **(a)** What is the purpose of a **security deposit?** **(b)** How does a **lease** benefit both landlord and tenant?
2. **Analyze** What three factors would be most important to you when searching for an apartment? Explain your reasoning.

Answers to . . .

Check Your Understanding

1. **(a)** A security deposit is collateral for the landlord in case a tenant damages his or her apartment. **(b)** Leases set terms that need to be met by both the landlord (structurally sound apartment, basic utilities, sanitary facilities, repairs, etc.) and tenant (no damage to the apartment, clean environment, courtesy to neighbors) while the tenant is renting the apartment.
2. Students should include examples from both the "How to Choose an Apartment" checklist as well as the text of the article.

Personal Finance Activities
"Buying Insurance," p. 19 provides activities to help students practice personal finance skills.

Buying Insurance

We hate to pay for it, but we're sometimes glad we did.

When we're young, we tend to think that nothing bad will ever happen to us. But sooner or later we usually find ourselves wanting the benefits that insurance offers.

How Insurance Works

Insurance is essentially a bet between you and your insurance company. You are betting that some type of accident will happen to you: illness or damage to your car or home. The company, on the other hand, is betting that you will not have such a problem. It bases its judgment on complicated formulas of probable risk.

Insurance Costs

In the event of an accident, you could suffer devastating financial losses. So you pay the insurance company a sum of money called a **premium.** The company then promises to pay compensation in the event of an accident. The amount the insurance company pays out could be many times what you paid in premiums.

If you remain accident-free, the company makes money. It uses part of that money to pay policyholders who do sustain some type of loss.

Most insurance policies include a **deductible,** an amount of expenses that you must pay before the insurer will cover any expenses. For example, if your car insurance policy has a $1,000 deductible, and you have an accident, you'll have to pay the first $1,000 in damages yourself, then the insurance company will pay the rest, up to a certain limit.

Coverage

Before you buy auto or home insurance, find out if the policy covers replacement cost, the amount of money needed to buy a new item to replace the lost or damaged one. Some companies only cover actual cash value (ACV), the amount that the lost or damaged item would have been worth on the market before the accident. If, for instance, your two-year-old computer is stolen, its ACV is not nearly as much as it would cost you to buy a new computer to replace the stolen one, because computers lose their value quickly.

Shop for a policy that requires the lowest possible premium while giving you the amount of coverage you need, no more and no less. But beware: Insurance policies contain complicated language and lots of fine print. Make sure you read carefully. Get estimates from several companies before you sign. Or go to a fee-only insurance advisor, an impartial expert who can help you evaluate policies and recommend the one that's right for you.

Auto Insurance

If you drive, most states require you to have your own auto insurance or to be listed as a driver on someone else's policy. If you drive a car with the owner's permission, you're usually covered.

Most insurance companies offer several types of auto insurance. Collision insurance covers damage to your vehicle regardless of who is at fault in an accident. Comprehensive insurance pays for other types of damage to your car, such as theft, broken glass, vandalism, and natural disasters. If you are at fault in an accident, liability insurance covers property damage and bodily injuries to people who are not on your policy, as well as your court costs. Other provisions pay medical costs for you and others riding in your car.

Health Insurance

Even if you're healthy, having health insurance is a good idea. Insurance plans cover a variety of health-care needs, such as hospitalization, surgeries, routine medical care, preventive care, visits to specialists, medicines, mental health care, and dental care.

The problem, however, is finding affordable care. Health insurance premiums are costly. The best rates are available through group insurance plans offered by employers and other large organizations. Purchasing an individual plan can cost hundreds of dollars a month. Health insurance companies offer a variety of plans, so you can buy the level of coverage you need to feel protected.

Dental insurance policies cover procedures and products such as fillings, crowns, extractions, bridgework, and dentures. These plans usually require deductibles and copayments.

Health insurance plans vary according to several factors:

1. The degree to which you can choose your doctors
2. The types of procedures covered
3. The amount of deductible required
4. The amount of **copayment**, which is the percentage of each visit or procedure that the patient must pay
5. Annual limits on the total amount of care covered

Property Insurance

Think for a moment about the value of your belongings: stereo, computer, television, VCR, bicycle, books, clothes, coin collection, etc. What if your apartment caught fire? What if your building were destroyed by a tornado or other natural disaster? Would you need a lot of money to replace what you own? If so, then you should insure it.

Renter's insurance is generally a type of homeowner's policy. It protects your belongings against destruction from fire, wind, lightning, explosions, and theft. It can cover your liability if someone is injured in your home. Most policies do not protect you against flood damage; you need to purchase a separate flood insurance policy for that kind of coverage. You might need to keep receipts and other records of major household items to have them covered.

Check Your Understanding

1. **Key Terms** **(a)** Explain the difference between a **premium,** a **deductible,** and a **copayment.** **(b)** Why is a policy that covers replacement cost better than one that covers actual cash value? **(c)** Why do you think some states require drivers to carry liability insurance but not collision insurance or comprehensive insurance?
2. **Using Graphic Organizers** Create a chart that shows the opportunity costs of buying auto insurance, health insurance, and property insurance.

PERSONAL FINANCE HANDBOOK

Answers to . . .

Check Your Understanding

1. (a) A premium is the amount you pay each year to the insurance company. A deductible is the amount of money that you have to pay before the insurance company will start covering your losses. A copayment is the amount of each doctor's visit or prescription you pay out of pocket. (b) A policy that covers replacement cost will pay you in order to purchase a new unit, whereas a policy that covers actual cash value will only reimburse you for the value of the unit in today's market. The actual cash value can be, and often is, much lower than the cost to purchase a new unit. (c) Liability insurance covers the damage that happens to others involved in an accident, making sure that society's losses are accounted for. States might not require collision or comprehensive insurance because they only cover individuals and not society as a whole.
2. Students should prepare a chart showing what benefits they receive or forgo with each type of insurance and the costs involved in purchasing each type of insurance.

Personal Finance Activities "Getting a Job," p. 21 provides activities to help students practice personal finance skills.

Getting a Job

Finding work can seem like a full-time job in itself.

But the harder you search, the better the job you'll get. Nobody likes looking for a job. It's tedious and time consuming. You have to steel yourself for rejections and forge ahead. But remember: All you need is for one employer to say, "You're hired."

The Résumé

One of the most important tools in your job hunt is your **résumé,** a document that summarizes your employment experience, education, and other information a potential employer wants to know. Many job postings will instruct you to send in your résumé.

Reviewing résumés is the employer's first step in eliminating candidates for a job, so you'll want to make sure yours is as well-prepared as it can be.

The Cover Letter

When you send out a résumé, accompany it with a cover letter addressed to a particular individual—ideally, the hiring manager. You should mention your interest in the company and where you learned about the job opening. Your cover letter is an opportunity to highlight or add detail to points in your résumé. Keep your letter brief, however.

Heading Include your name, address, phone number, and any other contact information, such as fax number or e-mail address.

Objective Identify the type of position you seek.

Education Outline your educational achievements (degrees, diplomas, or certificates earned) .

Experience Describe your work experience and the job skills you have demonstrated.

Activities and **Other Skills** Provide any other information pertinent to the job you seek.

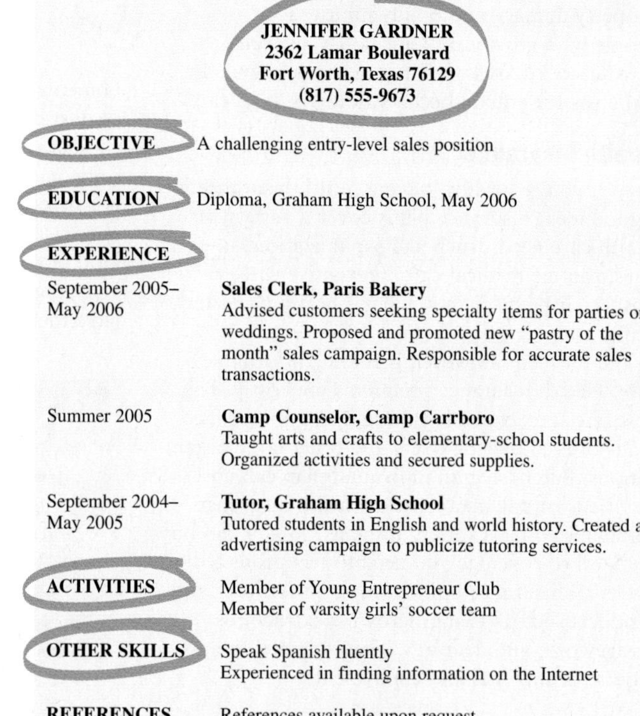

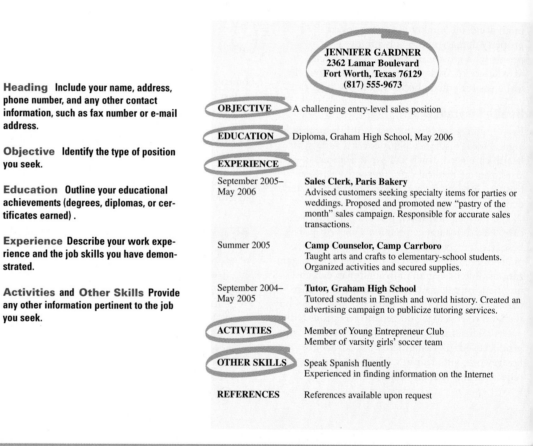

JENNIFER GARDNER
2362 Lamar Boulevard
Fort Worth, Texas 76129
(817) 555-9673

OBJECTIVE A challenging entry-level sales position

EDUCATION Diploma, Graham High School, May 2006

EXPERIENCE

September 2005–May 2006 — **Sales Clerk, Paris Bakery**
Advised customers seeking specialty items for parties or weddings. Proposed and promoted new "pastry of the month" sales campaign. Responsible for accurate sales transactions.

Summer 2005 — **Camp Counselor, Camp Carrboro**
Taught arts and crafts to elementary-school students. Organized activities and secured supplies.

September 2004–May 2005 — **Tutor, Graham High School**
Tutored students in English and world history. Created an advertising campaign to publicize tutoring services.

ACTIVITIES
Member of Young Entrepreneur Club
Member of varsity girls' soccer team

OTHER SKILLS
Speak Spanish fluently
Experienced in finding information on the Internet

REFERENCES References available upon request

It's not enough to send your résumé out into the world and then sit back and wait for phone calls. Your résumé may wind up sitting in a stack of hundreds on somebody's desk. In your cover letter, mention when and how you will follow up the letter—and make sure you do.

Identifying Job Openings

The more information you have, the better your job hunt. You need to learn not only about the field you're interested in, but about the companies you're seeking a position with. Use as many information sources as you can to get the complete picture.

Networking There's a grain of truth to the adage "It's not what you know, it's who you know." Friends and family can put you in contact with people in the fields you're interested in. Talking with friends, family, and acquaintances about job leads is called networking.

Help Wanted Ads Newspapers' help wanted sections carry many advertisements for jobs. But the ads are often brief, offering few details about the job or the company. Competition for these jobs is keen, since many people turn to the help wanted ads when they are looking for a job. Respond promptly to help wanted ads, and keep a record of employers you contact.

The Internet Some Web sites let you post your résumé on-line. For example, the U.S. Department of Labor, in conjunction with state-run employment services, maintains a Web site called America's Job Bank. It offers career resources, occupational projections, job listings, and a place to post your résumé.

Employment Services Public employment services can match your qualifications with available jobs. State-run job services are free. Check the state government listing in your phone directory for the office nearest you.

Many community job centers provide job placement services, too. They may offer résumé writing tips, interview practice, testing, and job counseling. And don't forget your school guidance counselor's office for job placement and counseling.

Private employment services are also available. These businesses will charge you or your employer a high fee for placing you in a job. Find out who will be paying the fee and what guarantees the agency offers before you sign up with them.

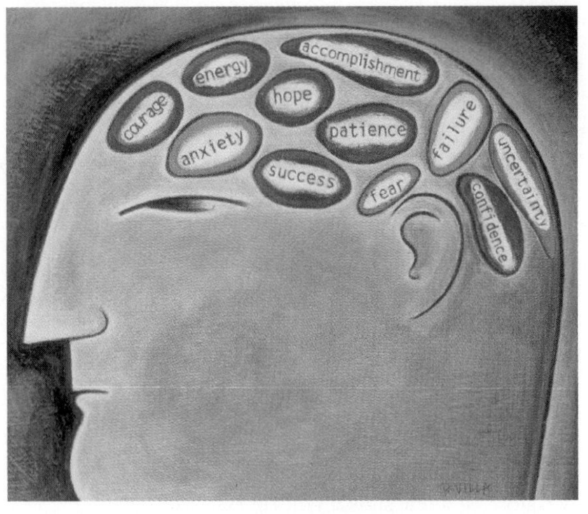

Interviewing

At the interview, the interviewer will talk with you to determine whether you are able and willing to do the job and whether you share the company's goals. Prepare for the interview by finding out as much about the company as you can. You'll also want to go into the interview with information about the standard salary ranges for similar positions. The employer may want to discuss salary during the interview.

Be ready to answer questions about your qualifications and goals. Also be prepared to ask questions about the position and the company. An interview can determine not only whether you're right for the job, but also whether the job is right for you.

Check Your Understanding

1. **Key Terms** To an employer, what qualities might distinguish a good **résumé** from a poor one?
2. **Formulating Questions** Plan a mock interview. Write down five questions an employer might ask you and five questions you might ask an employer.

Answers to . . .

Check Your Understanding

1. A good résumé should be neat, clear, spell-checked, grammatically correct, and well-organized and should summarize your schooling and work experience.
2. Students should provide five questions related to a possible job or field of employment that is relevant to them. They should also prepare five questions to ask the employer, incorporating such ideas as wages, benefits, working conditions, company goals and expectations, and company policies.

Paying Taxes

Uncle Sam wants his share of your paycheck; but don't give him too much.

When the Sixteenth Amendment to the Constitution took effect in 1913, the federal income tax became a fact of life. Every year of your working life you will go through the ritual of filing a federal tax return, the form(s) on which you calculate how much tax you owe. So why not decide to get organized from the start? By following a few simple guidelines, you can save time, effort, and maybe some money.

The American Tax System

Perhaps the three most dreaded letters in American English are "IRS." They stand for the **"Internal Revenue Service."**

The IRS The IRS, an agency within the Treasury Department, interprets and applies federal income tax laws passed by Congress. The agency generates tax forms and collects taxes.

The IRS will also come after you if you don't pay what you owe. In the past, the agency's aggressive pursuit of delinquent taxpayers and the surly attitude of some of its agents earned it a bad reputation. But public pressure for reform finally brought about changes in the late 1990s intended to make the IRS more helpful to citizens—most of whom are honest taxpayers.

Understanding the Tax System The current federal tax system includes a progressive tax, one in which people with the highest incomes have the highest tax rates. The system includes hundreds of tax breaks for people with special financial burdens, such as people paying for college or starting a business, or who have high medical bills. By finding out which tax deductions you qualify for and taking advantage of them, you can save hundreds of dollars a year in taxes.

People in many places have three bites taken out of their income: federal, state, and local taxes. Therefore, it is especially important to understand how to prepare for tax time.

Withholding

The federal government used to collect taxes at the end of every year. The problems were that (a) the government needed money throughout the year, not just at the end, and (b) many people weren't very good about setting aside some tax money out of every paycheck, so by tax time, they had no money to give to the tax collector.

In 1943, in need of money to finance World War II, the government introduced on a permanent basis the idea of withholding, that is, taking a certain percentage of your earnings before you get your paycheck. The amount that is withheld is shown on the **payroll withholding statement** attached to your paycheck. The money withheld goes into the federal Treasury. At the end of the year, you figure out

Employee's Withholding Allowance Certificate

▶ For Privacy Act and Paperwork Reduction Act Notice, see page 2.

OMB No. 1545-0

2005

irst name and middle initial: A | Last name: PINKHAM | Your social security number: 012 34 5678

nber and street or rural route): HESTNUT ST.

3 ☒ Single ☐ Married ☐ Married, but withhold at higher Single

Note: If married, but legally separated, or spouse is a nonresident alien, check the "Singl

and ZIP code: VA 00000

4 If your last name differs from that shown on your social securi card, check here. You must call 1-800-772-1213 for a new card

allowances you are claiming (from line H above or from the applicable worksheet on page 2) 5 2

nt, if any, you want withheld from each paycheck . . . . 6 $

on from withholding for 2003, and I certify that I meet both of the following conditions for exemption:

d a right to a refund of all Federal income tax withheld because I had no tax liability and

pect a refund of all Federal income tax withheld because I expect to have no tax liability.

n conditions, write "Exempt" here . . . . ▶ 7

I certify that I am entitled to the number of withholding allowances claimed on this certificate, or I am entitled to claim exempt status

Sam A. Pinkham Date ▶ 3/20/05

and 10 only if sending to the IRS.) 9 Office code (optional) 10 Employer identification numb

Be sure to enter your Social Security number correctly.

The worksheet on page 2 of this form will help you figure out how many deductions you can take.

Don't forget to sign and date the form!

the amount of tax you owe. If you had too much money withheld from your paychecks, the surplus is returned to you as a tax refund. If you did not have enough money withheld during the year, you have to pay the balance.

Too Much, Too Little Tax laws require most people to have a certain minimum percentage withheld from their paychecks. Beyond that, you choose how much to have set aside. Do you want to make sure that you won't have to pay more taxes at the end of the year? Do you want to get a big tax refund? If so, have a generous amount withheld.

The disadvantage of having a large amount withheld is that the government is holding on to your money all year and giving it back to you at the end. That's like giving the government a no-interest loan. Instead, you could put that money into savings and earn interest on it all year, then use it to pay whatever you owe at tax time. Make sure, however, that you at least have the legal minimum amount withheld, or you will be subjected to stiff penalties.

The W-4 Form To figure out how much money to have withheld from your paychecks, you must complete a Form W-4, which is shown above. When you start a new job, the employer will give you the form to complete and return. It includes worksheets to help you do the calculations required.

The W-4 form gives you the option of taking certain personal allowances that will lower the amount of tax withheld from your income. For example, you may take an exemption for yourself, your spouse, and any dependents you have. An exemption lowers the amount of your income that is taxed. The more exemptions you have, the lower your taxable income.

Estimated Taxes Under certain circumstances—if you are self-employed, for instance—you can choose not to have taxes withheld. However, you still must pay an estimated tax. Those who estimate can pay a lump sum at the beginning of the year or make quarterly estimated payments. The IRS will provide you with the forms for estimating and filing your payments.

Tax Preparation

The tax "season" runs from January to April 15. During that time, you need to fill out and file the appropriate tax forms.

The W-2 Form Some time in January or early February you should receive a Form W-2. You will get a W-2 from any employer you worked for who withheld taxes from your pay. If you don't receive this form by mid-February, contact your employer and ask about it. Employers must send out W-2s by January 31.

Save these important tax documents! The W-2s must be attached to your tax return when you file.

Personal Finance Activities
"Paying Taxes," p. 24 provides activities to help students practice personal finance skills.

What you'll need to fill out your tax return

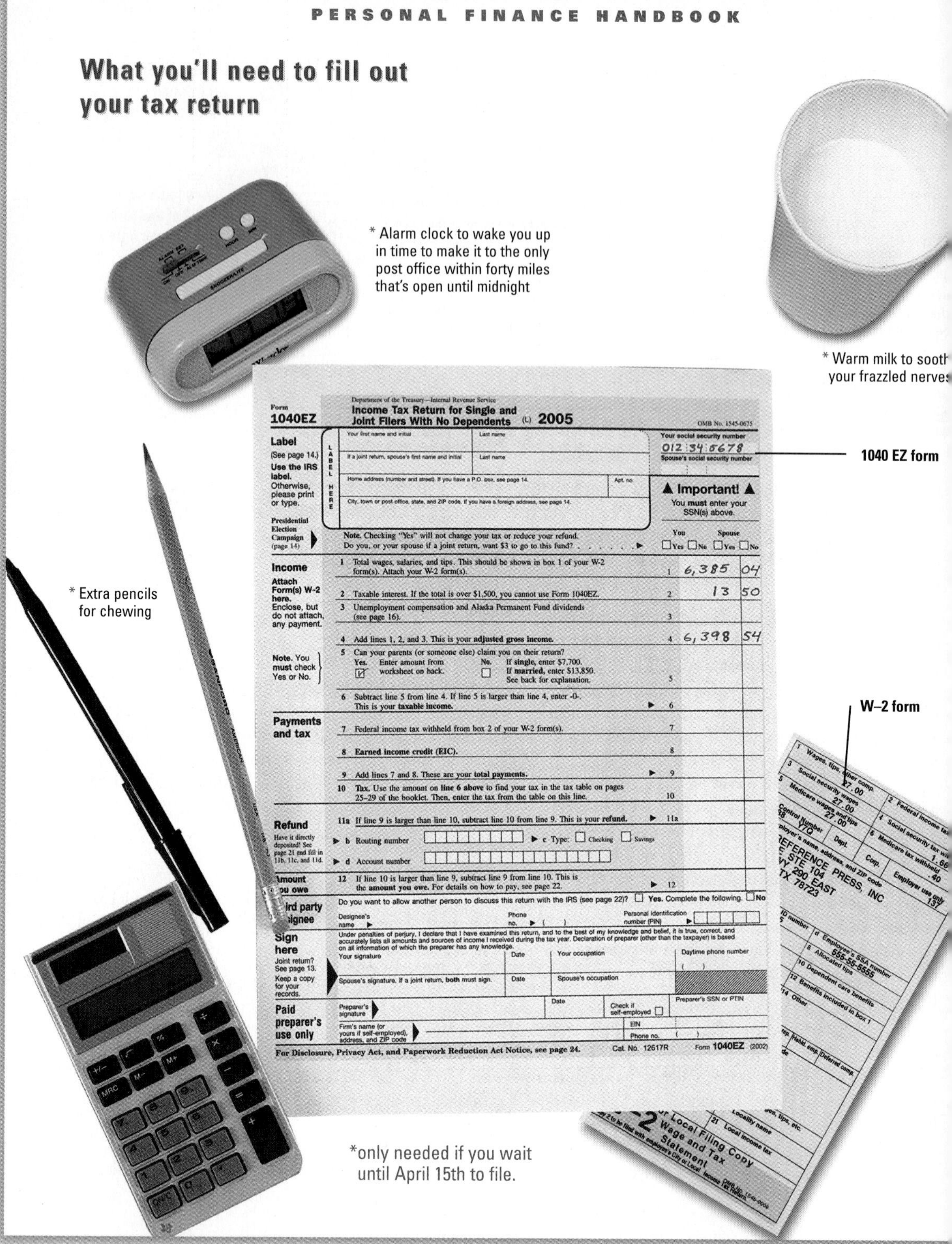

Preparing Your Return

The Internal Revenue Service publishes dozens of tax forms that require you to provide information about your income and certain financial activities from the previous year. Then, following the directions on the forms, you calculate how much tax you owe, or how much should be refunded to you.

Federal tax forms and instruction booklets are usually available free from January through April at many post offices, public libraries, and banks. You can also quickly download dozens of forms at the IRS Web site, or receive certain forms via fax through the IRS's TaxFax Service.

Many unmarried people with no children qualify to use Form 1040EZ, which is the simplest tax form. As you can see from the sample on page 530, the 1040EZ asks you questions that you should be able to answer by looking at your W-2 and interest statements.

If you have more complicated financial circumstances, you may need to file a Form 1040A or standard Form 1040, which are more complex. Use one of these forms if you're able to claim deductions. A deduction is a provision that allows you to deduct, or subtract, money from your taxable income. The lower your taxable income, the less tax you owe. If you paid for any of the following items, they may be tax-deductible:

- *college tuition*
- *child or parental care*
- *high medical expenses*
- *a home mortgage*
- *business expenses you paid yourself*
- *business losses (if you're self-employed)*

Never put any false information on a tax form. If the IRS suspects that you've cheated on your taxes, you'll be called in for an audit, a detailed examination of your financial transactions. (Occasionally, perfectly innocent people get audited, too.) Penalties for tax fraud are severe.

What if you make an honest mistake on your tax return? If it's a simple math error, the IRS will generally catch it, inform you of it, and recalculate your tax. If you make a significant error, you may need to file an amended form as soon as possible. These mistakes generally are not considered fraudulent.

Help!

If preparing your tax return seems too daunting, don't merely guess—get help. Each form has step-by-step instructions, but they might not answer all your questions. Here are some other places to turn to:

- The Internal Revenue Service Web site is a friendly, helpful site with lots of information. Try out TaxInteractive, an on-line information service sponsored by the IRS and the American Bar Association.
- Call the IRS anytime at 1-800-829-1040. You can get help over the telephone, schedule an appointment, or take advantage of a walk-in service at certain locations and times.
- Tax-preparation services and tax accountants will fill out your tax return for you for a fee. They provide the forms, make suggestions, and answer questions. Some will file your return for you.

Ways to File Your federal tax return usually must be postmarked by midnight on April 15. If you file late, you could be hit with substantial penalties and interest charges.

If you prepare your return on paper, you must send it to the IRS Service Center listed in the instruction booklets and at the IRS Web site. There are several ways to prepare and file your return electronically. Filing electronically will get you a faster tax refund but you usually have to pay a fee. If you owe money, you can pay by check or credit card. Call the IRS or visit its Web site for details.

Check Your Understanding

1. **Key Terms** **(a)** Why must people who earn an income file a tax return? **(b)** Who might benefit most from a progressive tax, people with a low income or people with a high income? **(c)** How do you qualify for a tax refund? **(d)** How do exemptions and deductions benefit taxpayers?
2. **Drawing Comparisons** What are the advantages of having a large amount of money withheld for taxes? What are the advantages of having the minimum amount withheld? Which would you choose, and why?

Answers to . . .

Check Your Understanding

1. (a) Income tax is part of the Constitution (16th Amendment) and a requirement of every U.S. citizen that gains income. A tax return is the government's way of tracking your tax payments. (b) Lower income people benefit most from progressive taxes, in theory. (c) Tax refunds occur from having more taxes withheld than necessary or as a result of qualifying for the numerous deductions and exemptions that lower your taxable income. (d) Deductions and exemptions allow people with special circumstances to have a more affordable tax burden.
2. Having a lot of money withheld for taxes means that you would pay less additional money when filing your taxes in April, possibly even getting a refund. Having the minimum amount of money withheld puts more money in your possession right away but will result in a higher tax bill in April. Students should evaluate their own personal finances and decide which option is best for them, and explain their reasoning.

Natural Resources

Economists use the term *land* to refer to all the natural resources used to produce goods and services. The United States enjoys an abundance of natural resources.

United States Economic Activity and Resources

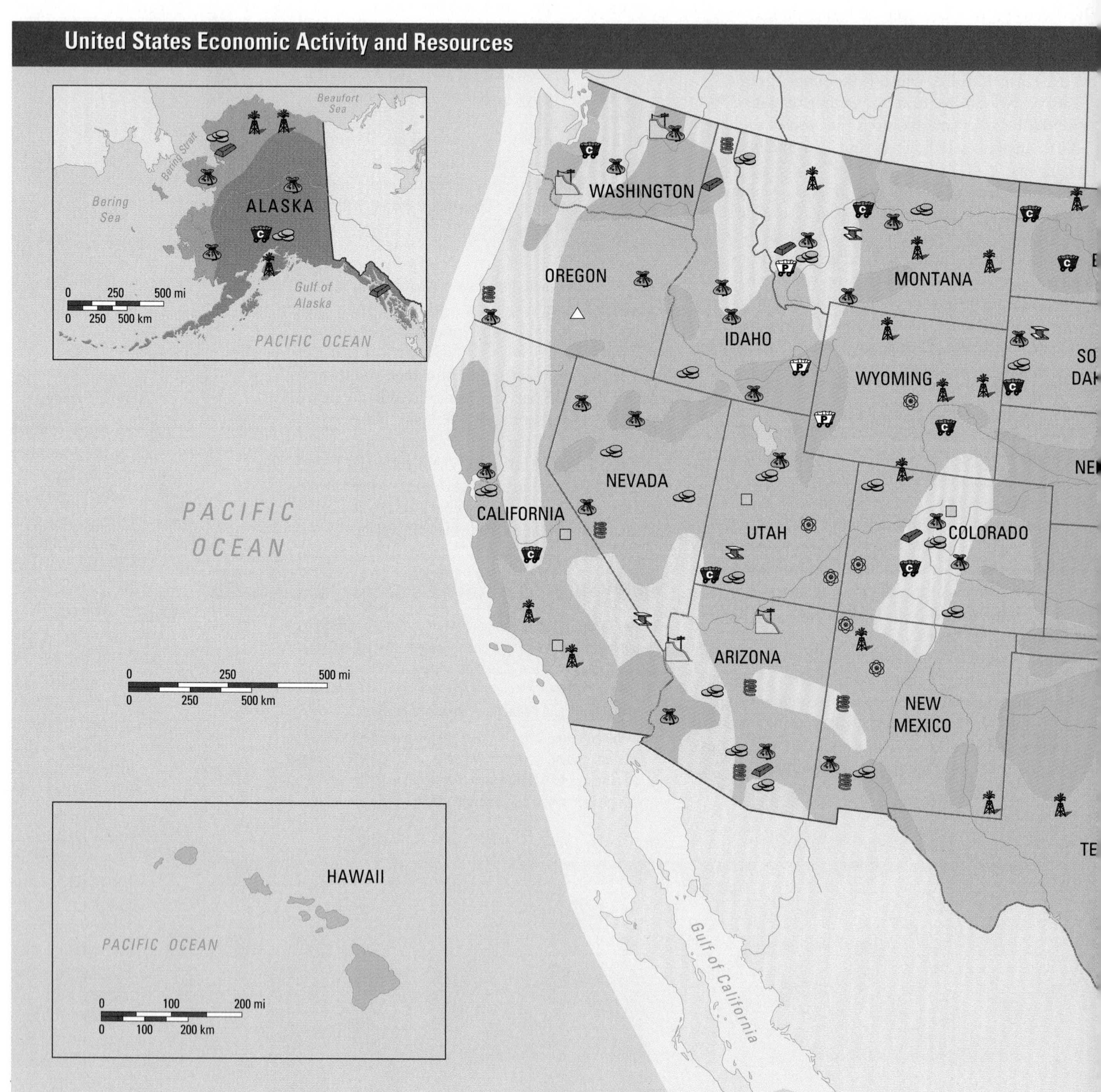

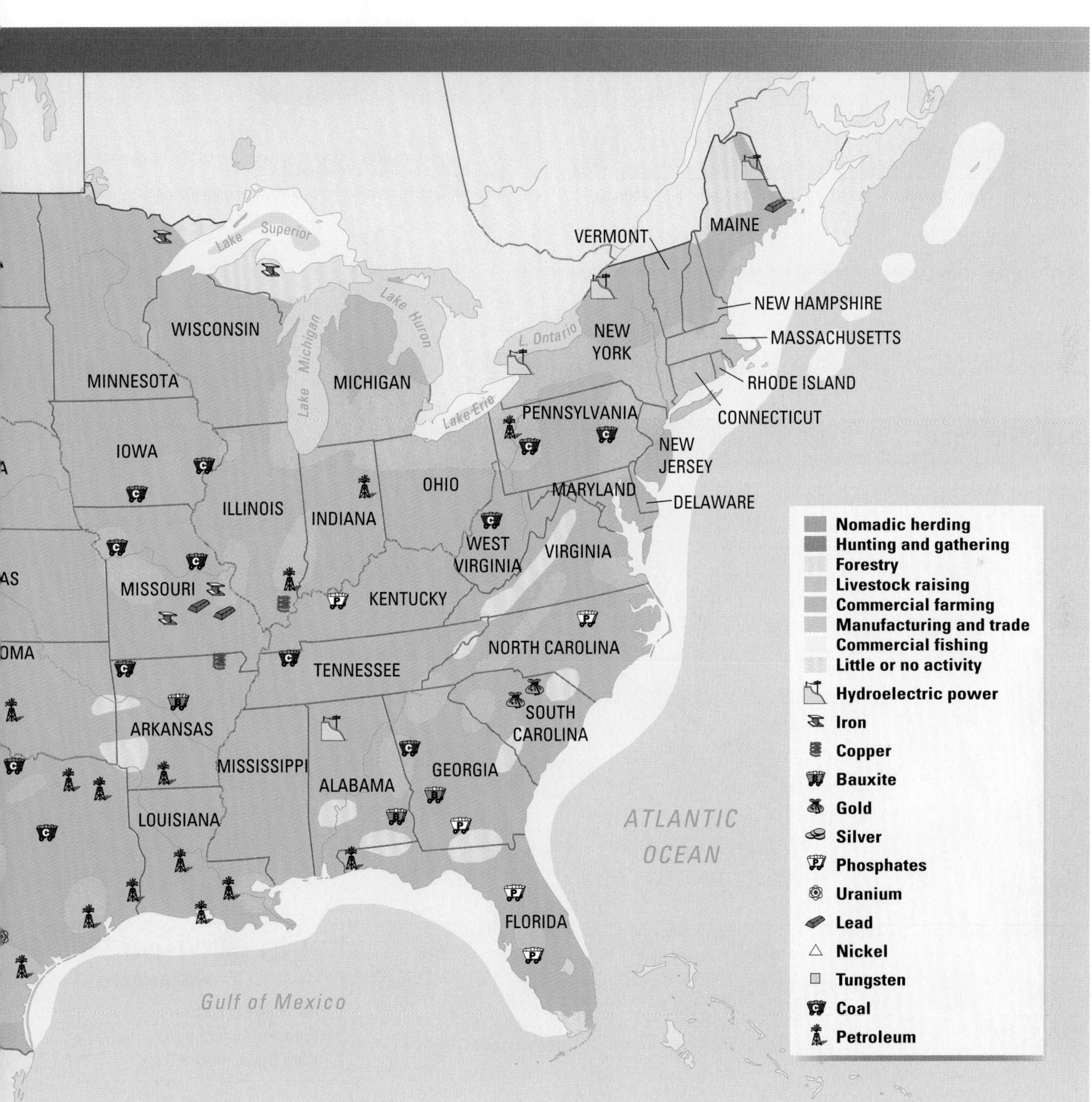
Lake Superior
Lake Michigan
Lake Huron
L. Ontario
Lake Erie
WISCONSIN
MINNESOTA
MICHIGAN
IOWA
ILLINOIS
INDIANA
OHIO
PENNSYLVANIA
NEW YORK
VERMONT
MAINE
NEW HAMPSHIRE
MASSACHUSETTS
RHODE ISLAND
CONNECTICUT
NEW JERSEY
MARYLAND
DELAWARE
WEST VIRGINIA
VIRGINIA
KENTUCKY
MISSOURI
TENNESSEE
NORTH CAROLINA
SOUTH CAROLINA
ARKANSAS
MISSISSIPPI
ALABAMA
GEORGIA
LOUISIANA
FLORIDA
ATLANTIC OCEAN
Gulf of Mexico
Nomadic herding
Hunting and gathering
Forestry
Livestock raising
Commercial farming
Manufacturing and trade
Commercial fishing
Little or no activity
Hydroelectric power
Iron
Copper
Bauxite
Gold
Silver
Phosphates
Uranium
Lead
Nickel
Tungsten
Coal
Petroleum

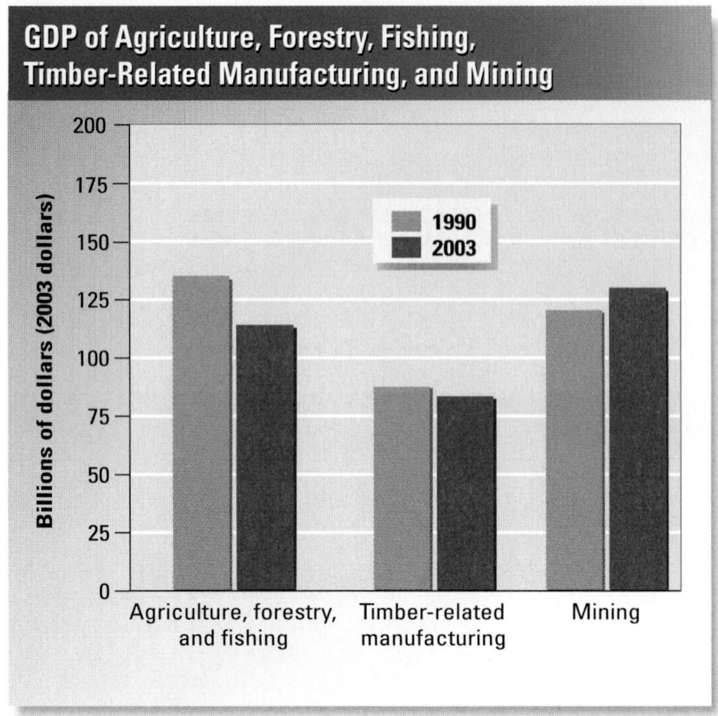
GDP of Agriculture, Forestry, Fishing, Timber-Related Manufacturing, and Mining
Billions of dollars (2003 dollars)
200
175
150
125
100
75
50
25
0
1990
2003
Agriculture, forestry, and fishing
Timber-related manufacturing
Mining

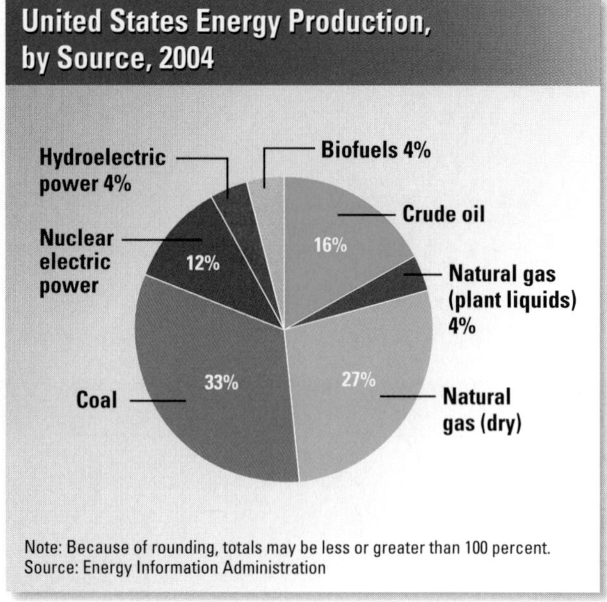
United States Energy Production, by Source, 2004
Hydroelectric power 4%
Biofuels 4%
Crude oil
16%
Nuclear electric power
12%
Natural gas (plant liquids) 4%
Coal
33%
27%
Natural gas (dry)
Note: Because of rounding, totals may be less or greater than 100 percent.
Source: Energy Information Administration

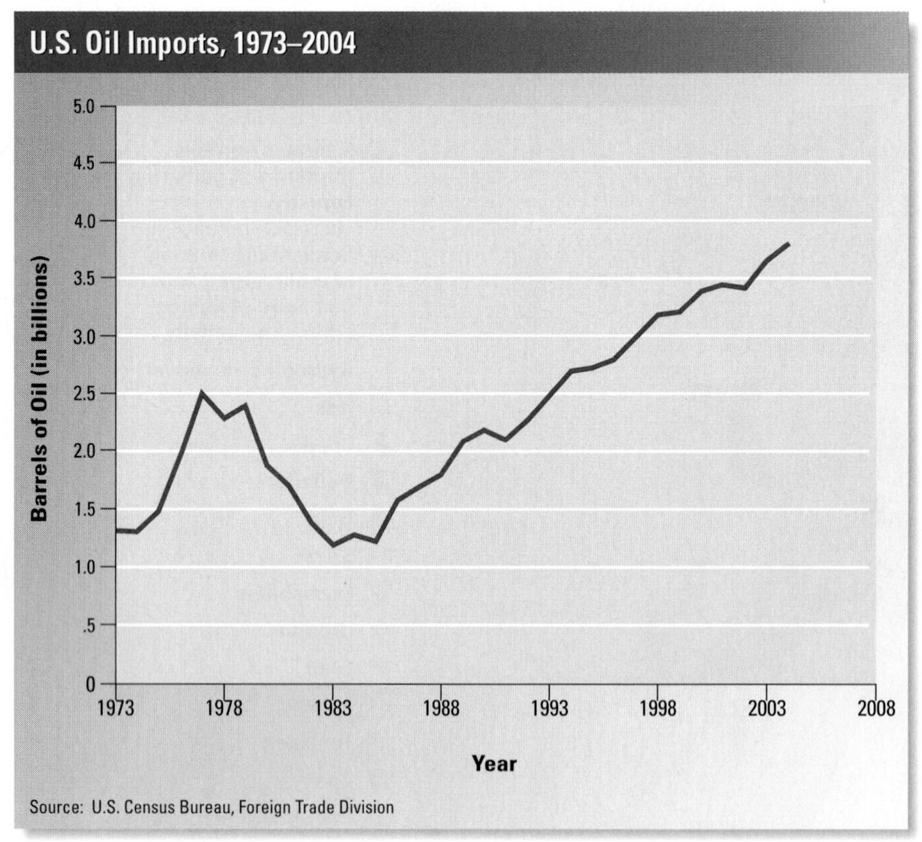
U.S. Oil Imports, 1973–2004
Barrels of Oil (in billions)
5.0
4.5
4.0
3.5
3.0
2.5
2.0
1.5
1.0
.5
0
1973
1978
1983
1988
1993
1998
2003
2008
Year
Source: U.S. Census Bureau, Foreign Trade Division

Go Online
PHSchool.com

For: Current Data
Visit: PHSchool.com
Web Code: mng-8012

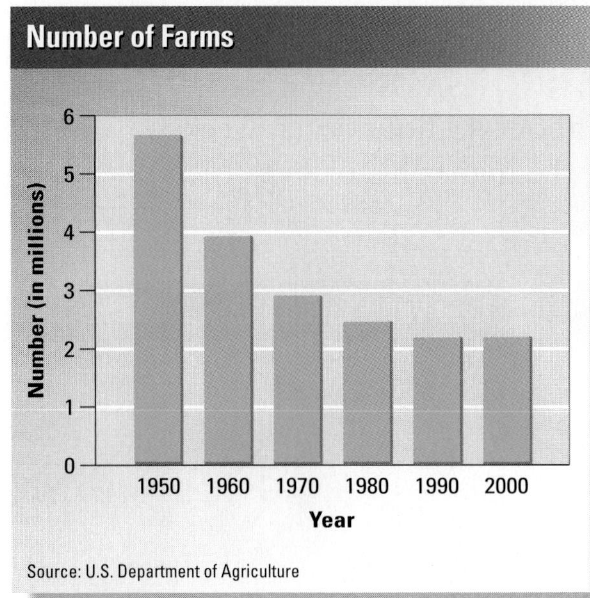

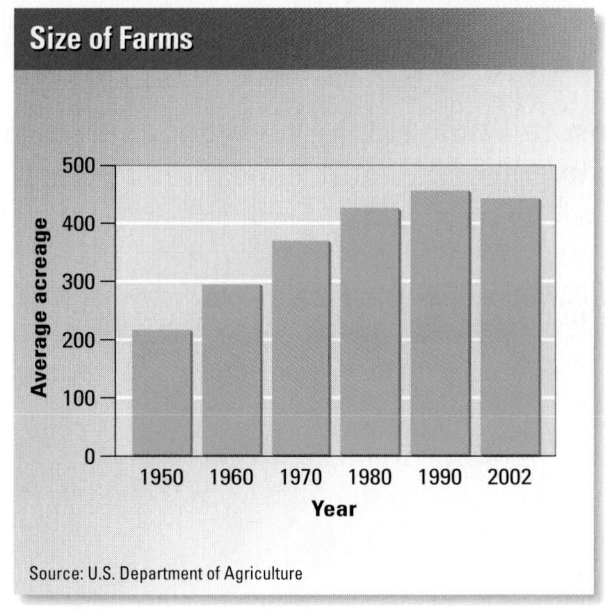

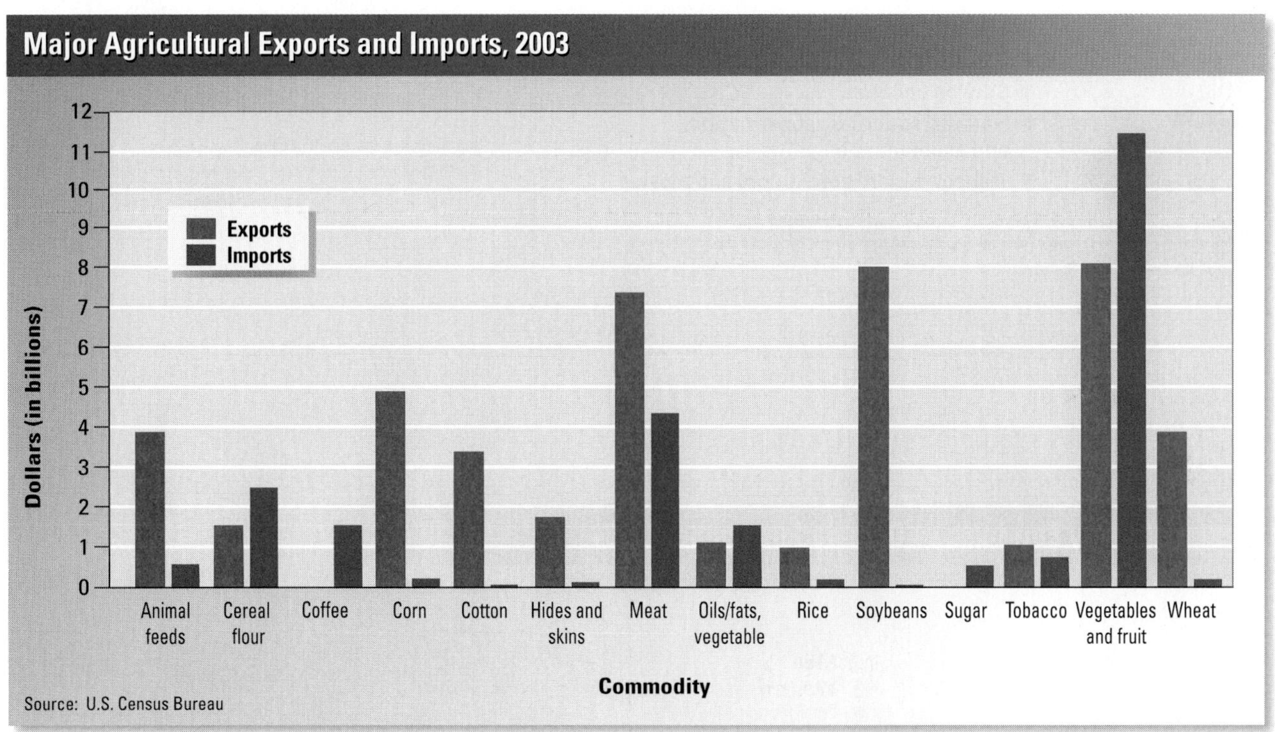

For: Current Data
Visit: PHSchool.com
Web Code: mng-8013

Americans at Work

Most full-time employees work an average of about 43 hours each week. On average, the more education a person has, the higher his or her hourly wage.

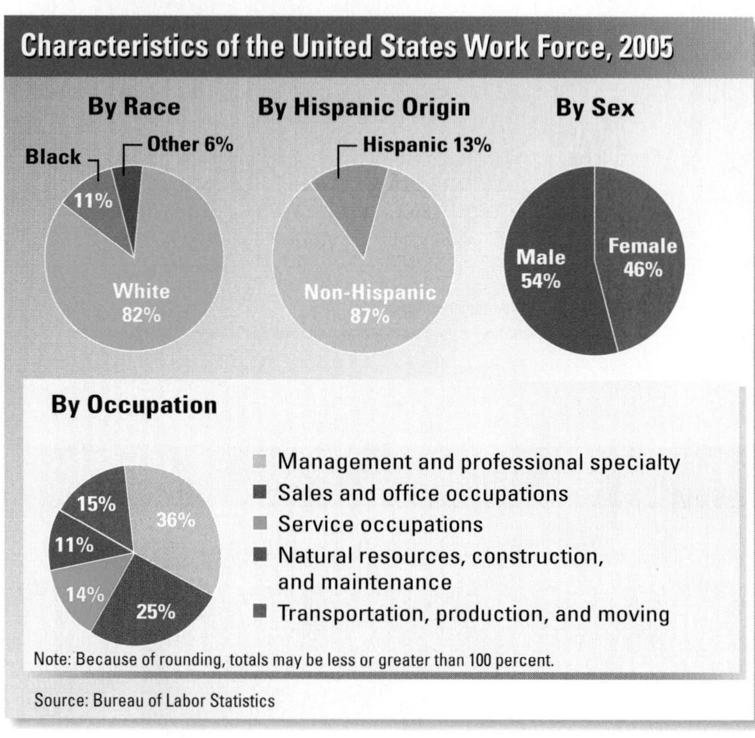

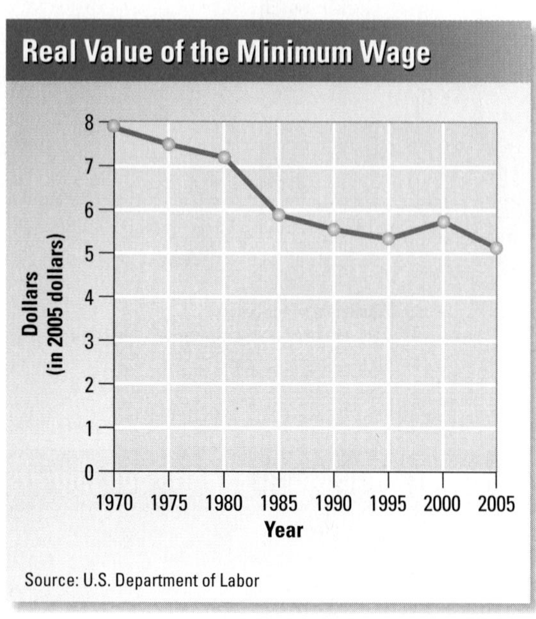

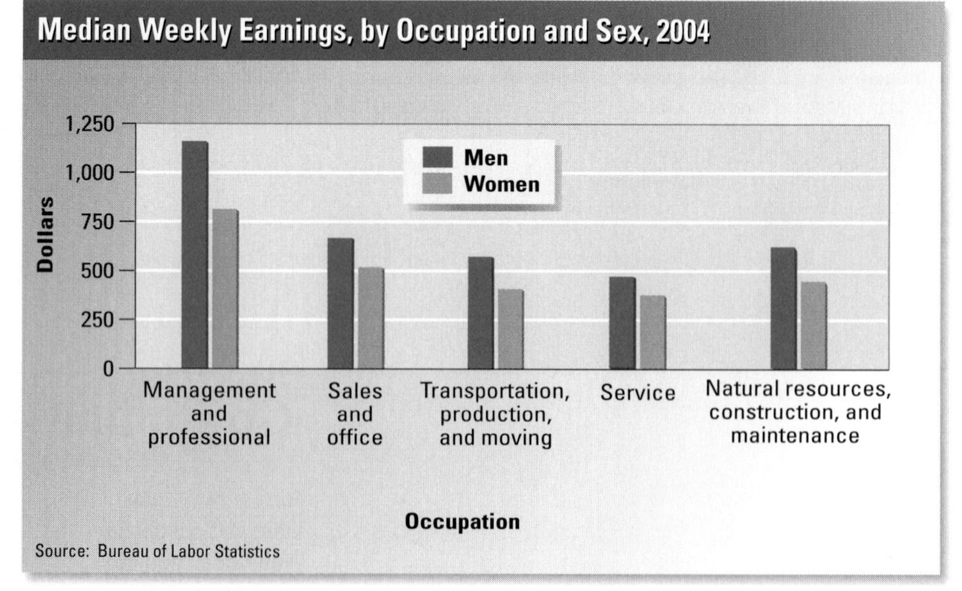

For: Current Data
Visit: PHSchool.com
Web Code: mng-8014

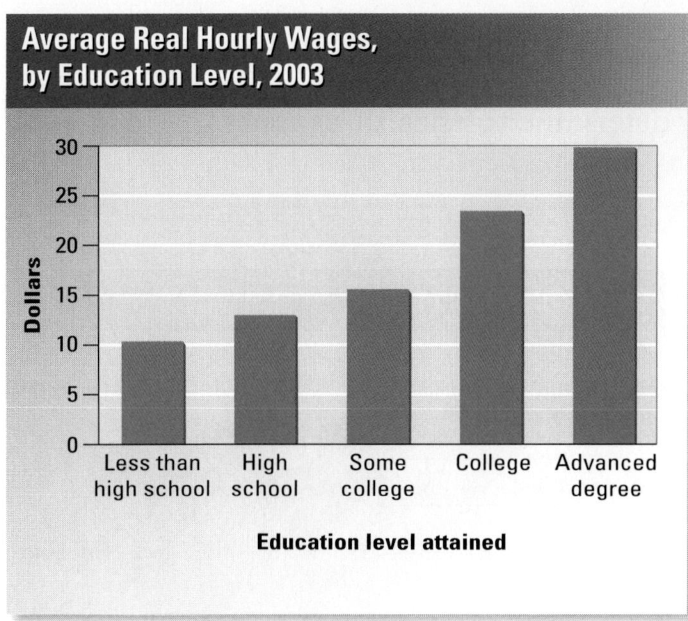
Average Real Hourly Wages, by Education Level, 2003
Dollars
30
25
20
15
10
5
0
Less than high school
High school
Some college
College
Advanced degree
Education level attained

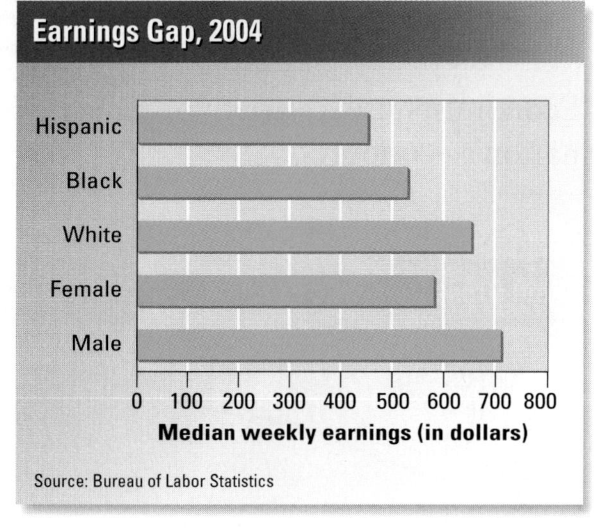
Earnings Gap, 2004
Hispanic
Black
White
Female
Male
0 100 200 300 400 500 600 700 800
Median weekly earnings (in dollars)
Source: Bureau of Labor Statistics

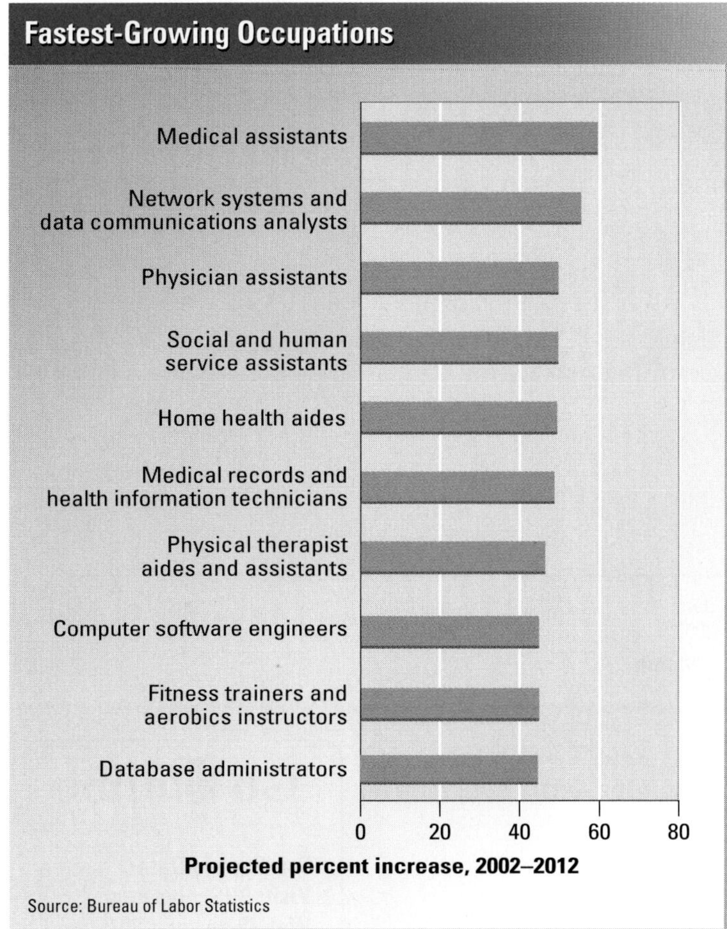
Fastest-Growing Occupations
Medical assistants
Network systems and data communications analysts
Physician assistants
Social and human service assistants
Home health aides
Medical records and health information technicians
Physical therapist aides and assistants
Computer software engineers
Fitness trainers and aerobics instructors
Database administrators
0 20 40 60 80
Projected percent increase, 2002–2012
Source: Bureau of Labor Statistics

Go Online
PHSchool.com

For: Current Data
Visit: PHSchool.com
Web Code: mng-8015

Economic Indicators

Economists use a variety of indicators to determine the health of the nation's economy.

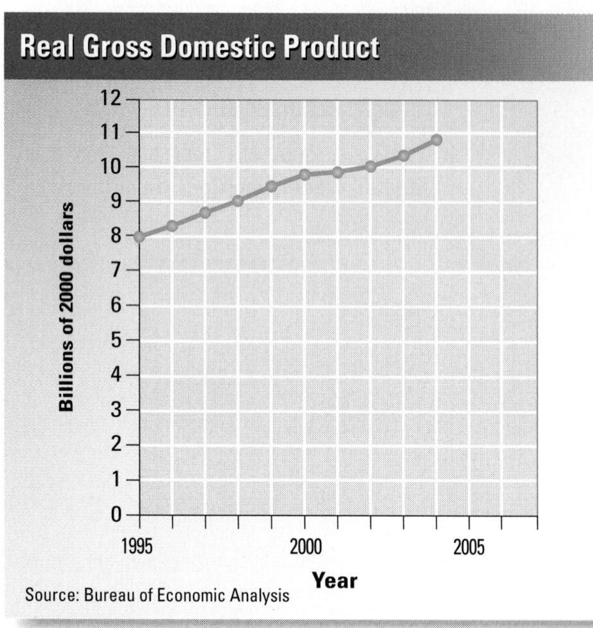

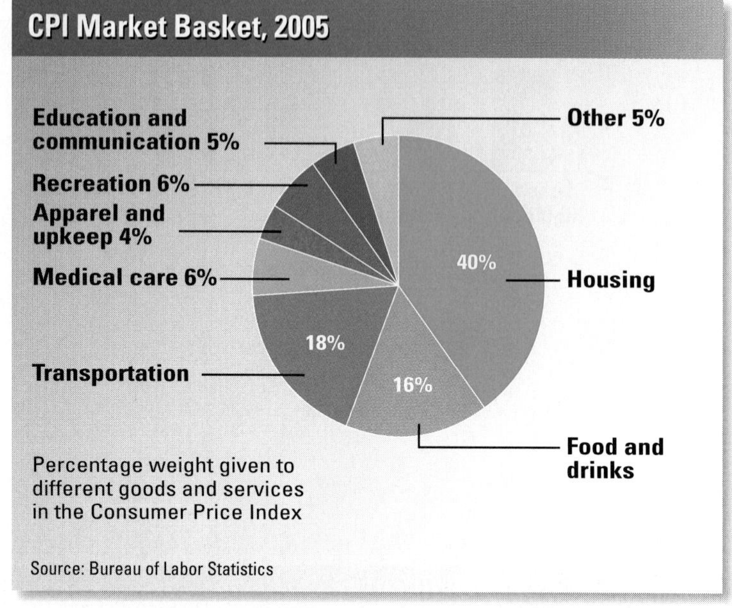

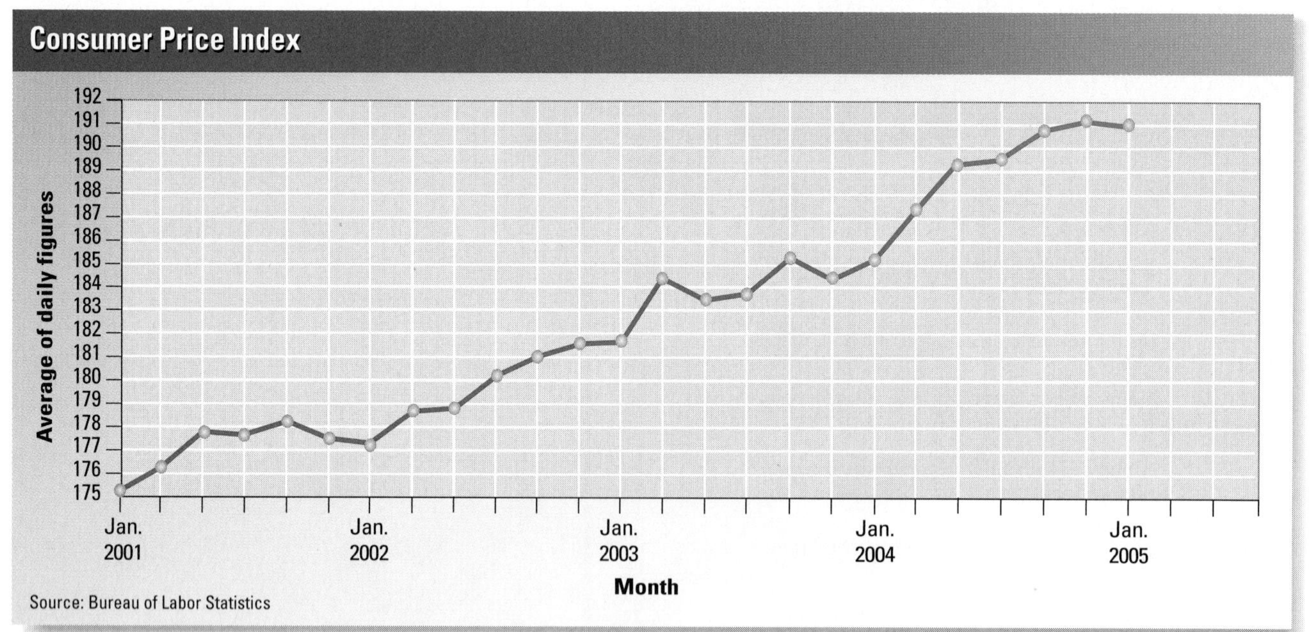

For: Current Data
Visit: PHSchool.com
Web Code: mng-8016

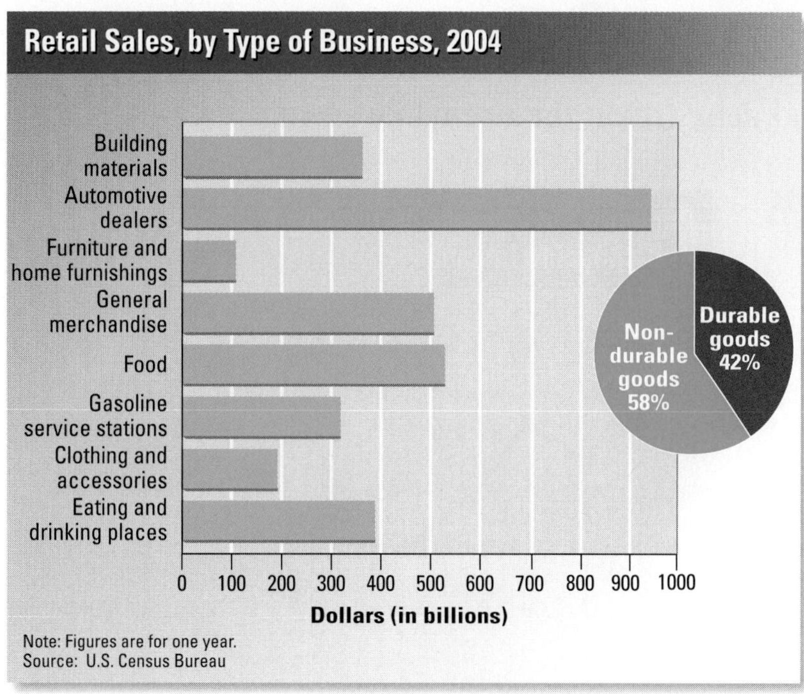
Retail Sales, by Type of Business, 2004
Building materials
Automotive dealers
Furniture and home furnishings
General merchandise
Food
Gasoline service stations
Clothing and accessories
Eating and drinking places
0 100 200 300 400 500 600 700 800 900 1000
Dollars (in billions)
Non-durable goods 58%
Durable goods 42%
Note: Figures are for one year.
Source: U.S. Census Bureau

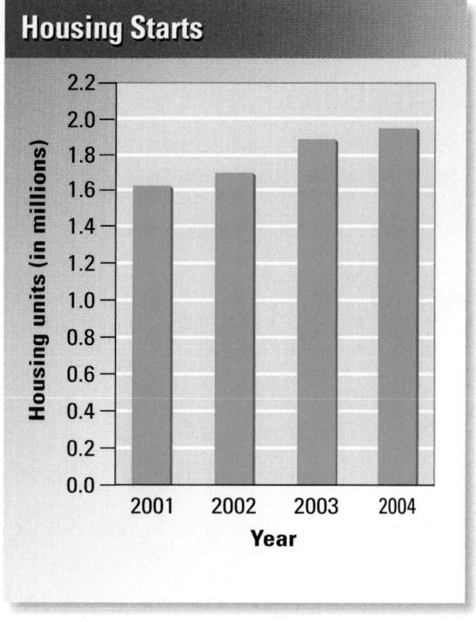
Housing Starts
Housing units (in millions)
0.0 0.2 0.4 0.6 0.8 1.0 1.2 1.4 1.6 1.8 2.0 2.2
2001 2002 2003 2004
Year

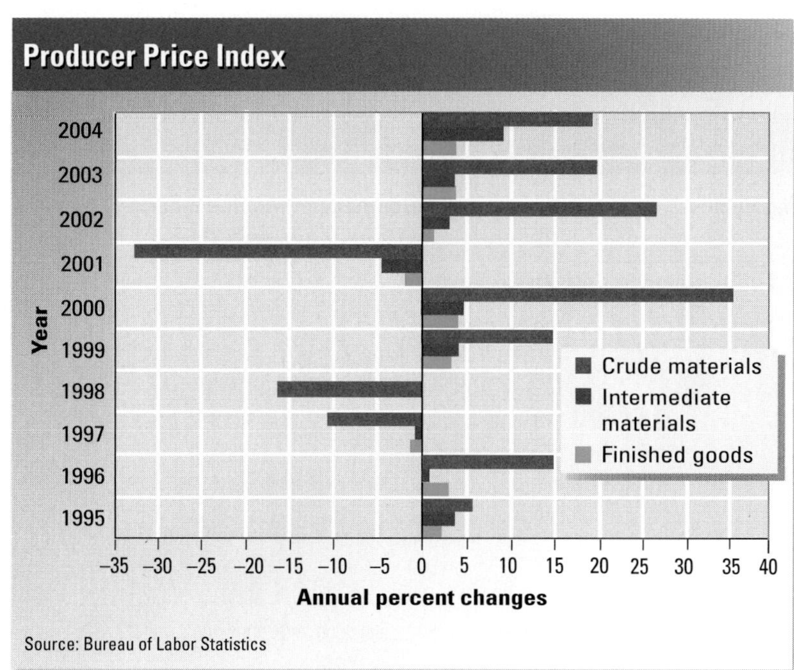
Producer Price Index
Year
2004 2003 2002 2001 2000 1999 1998 1997 1996 1995
Crude materials
Intermediate materials
Finished goods
–35 –30 –25 –20 –15 –10 –5 0 5 10 15 20 25 30 35 40
Annual percent changes
Source: Bureau of Labor Statistics

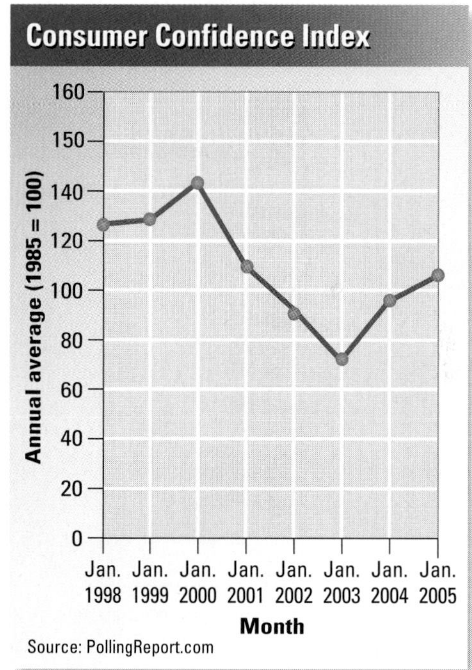
Consumer Confidence Index
Annual average (1985 = 100)
0 20 40 60 80 100 120 140 160
Jan. 1998 Jan. 1999 Jan. 2000 Jan. 2001 Jan. 2002 Jan. 2003 Jan. 2004 Jan. 2005
Month
Source: PollingReport.com

Go Online
PHSchool.com

For: Current Data
Visit: PHSchool.com
Web Code: mng-8017

The American Consumer

In the United States, spending and debt are on the rise while savings dwindle.

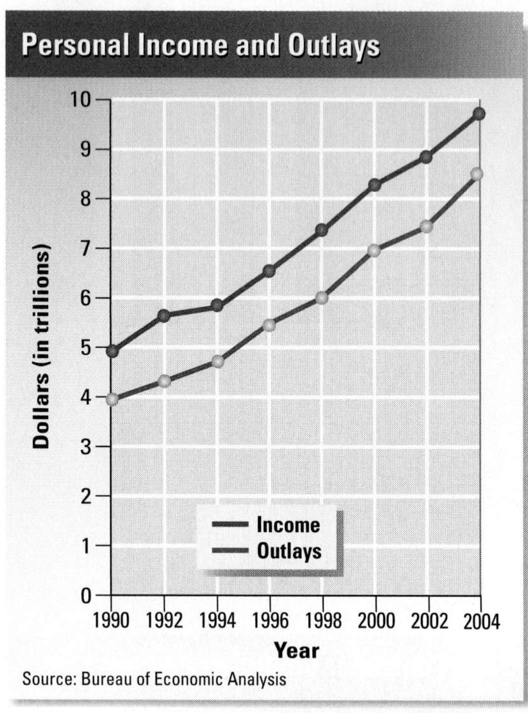

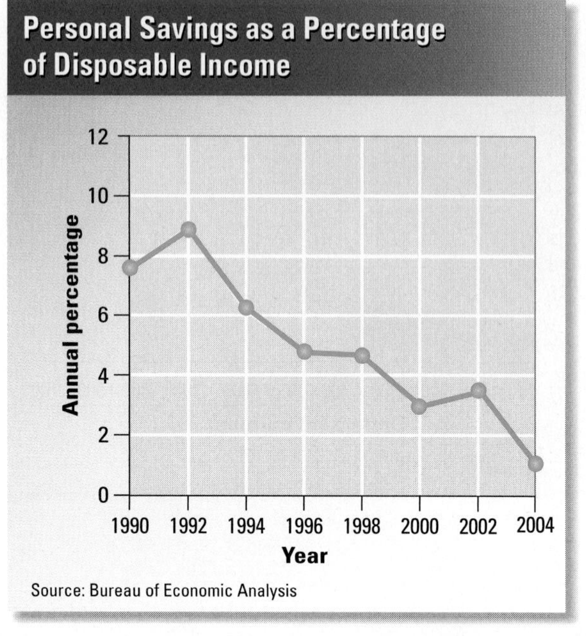

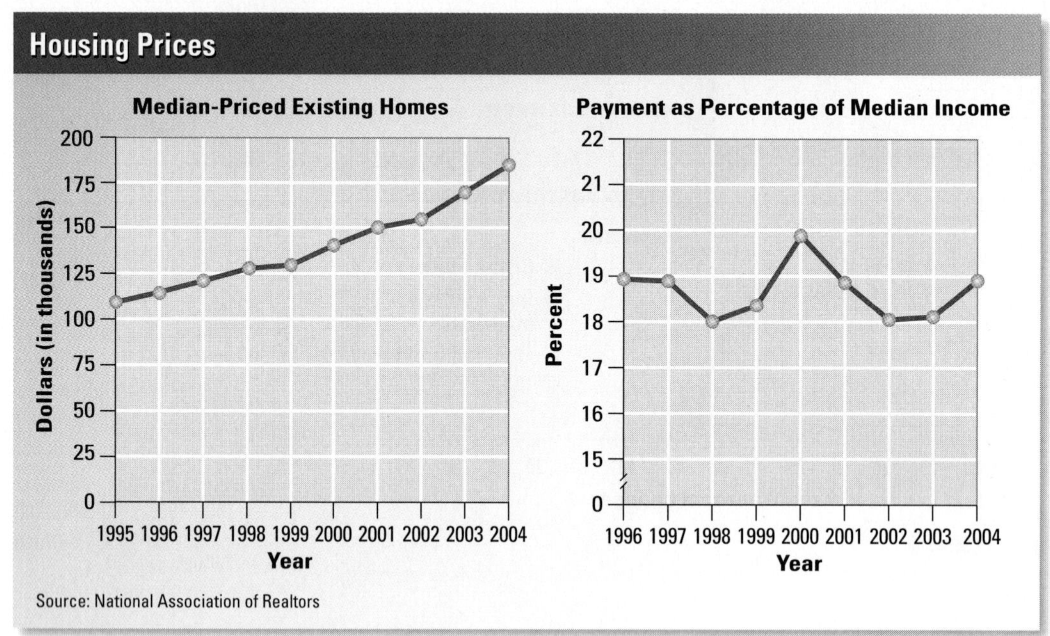

For: Current Data
Visit: PHSchool.com
Web Code: mng-8018

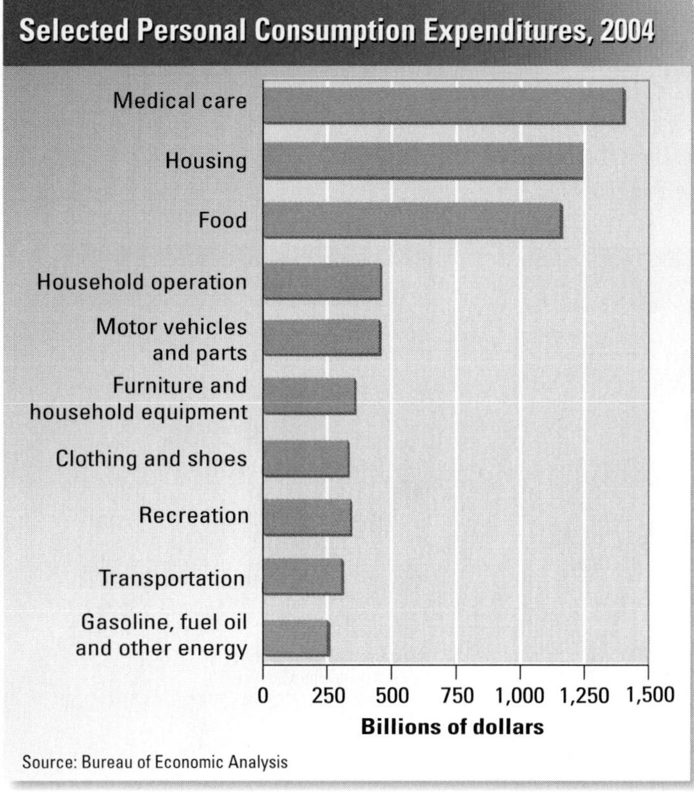

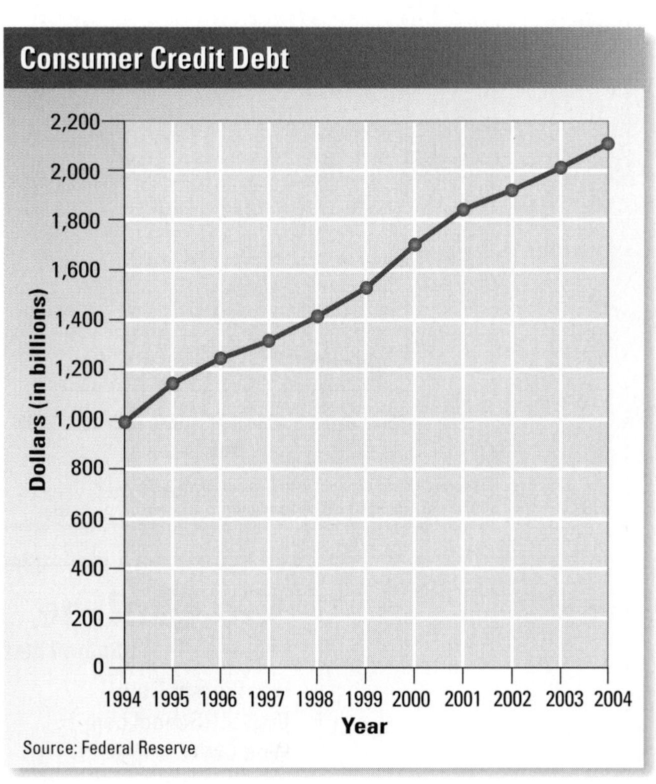

Per Capita Energy Consumption

Rank	State	Btu (in millions)
1	Alaska	999.5
2	Louisiana	887.1
3	Wyoming	844.3
4	Montana	658.2
5	North Dakota	570.1
6	Texas	553.2
7	Kentucky	461.6
8	Indiana	456.1
9	Alabama	444.2
10	Maine	439.5
11	West Virginia	411.7
12	Oklahoma	405.6
13	Arkansas	404.7
14	Mississippi	401.5
15	Idaho	393.4
16	Pennsylvania	389.2
17	Delaware	384.9
18	Kansas	384.8
19	Iowa	375.5
20	Washington	367.9
21	South Carolina	367.1
22	Tennessee	355.3
23	Illinois	355.3
24	Ohio	352.3
25	Minnesota	342.3
26	New Mexico	340.8
27	Nebraska	340.7
28	Georgia	336.6
29	Wisconsin	335.0
30	South Dakota	325.6
31	Virginia	324.3
32	New Jersey	321.1
33	Utah	320.4
34	Oregon	314.8
35	Michigan	313.7
36	Nevada	313.5
37	North Carolina	309.7
38	Missouri	296.1
39	Maryland	286.2
40	Colorado	277.5
41	Massachusetts	271.0
42	Vermont	270.0
43	New Hampshire	265.4
44	Connecticut	253.1
45	California	250.5
46	Florida	245.7
47	New York	243.3
48	Rhode Island	238.4
49	Arizona	235.4
50	Hawaii	218.4

Source: Corporation for Enterprise Development

For: Current Data
Visit: PHSchool.com
Web Code: mng-8019

The United States Government

The government raises and spends trillions of dollars each year.

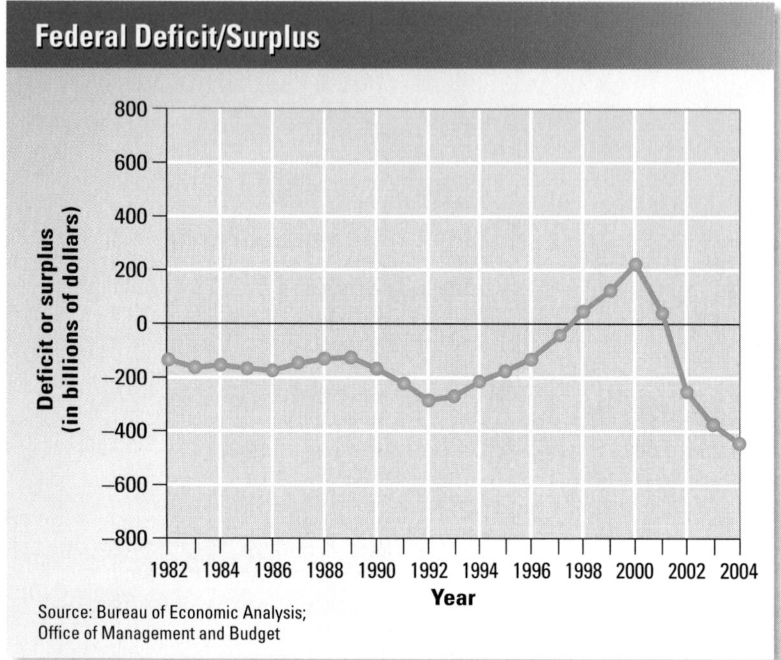

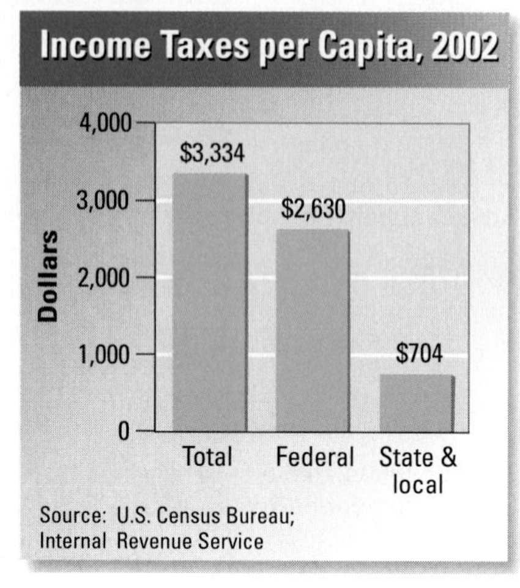

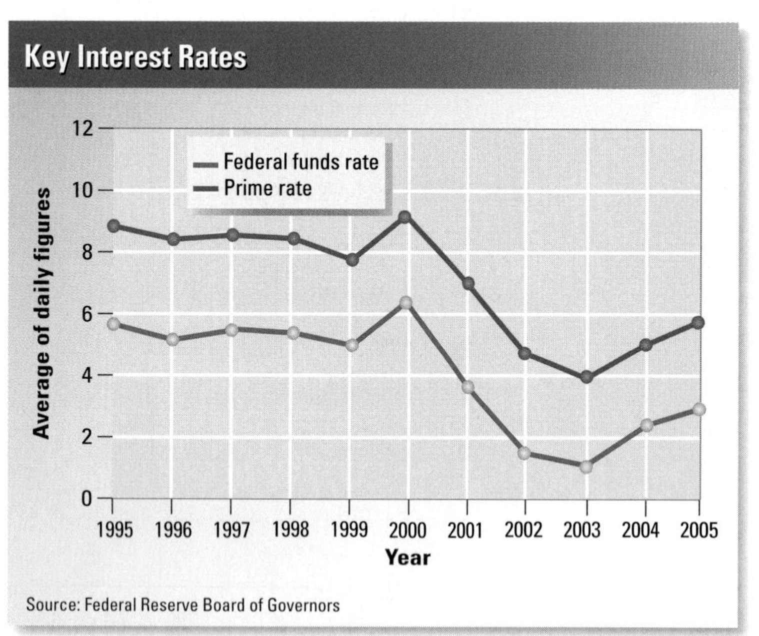

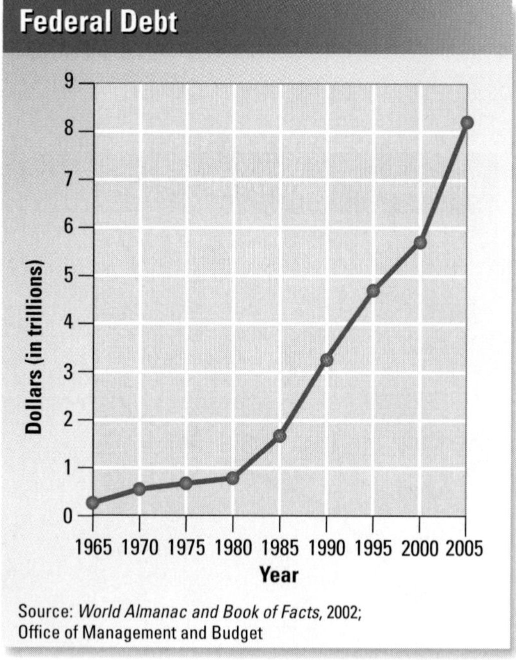

For: Current Data
Visit: PHSchool.com
Web Code: mng-8021

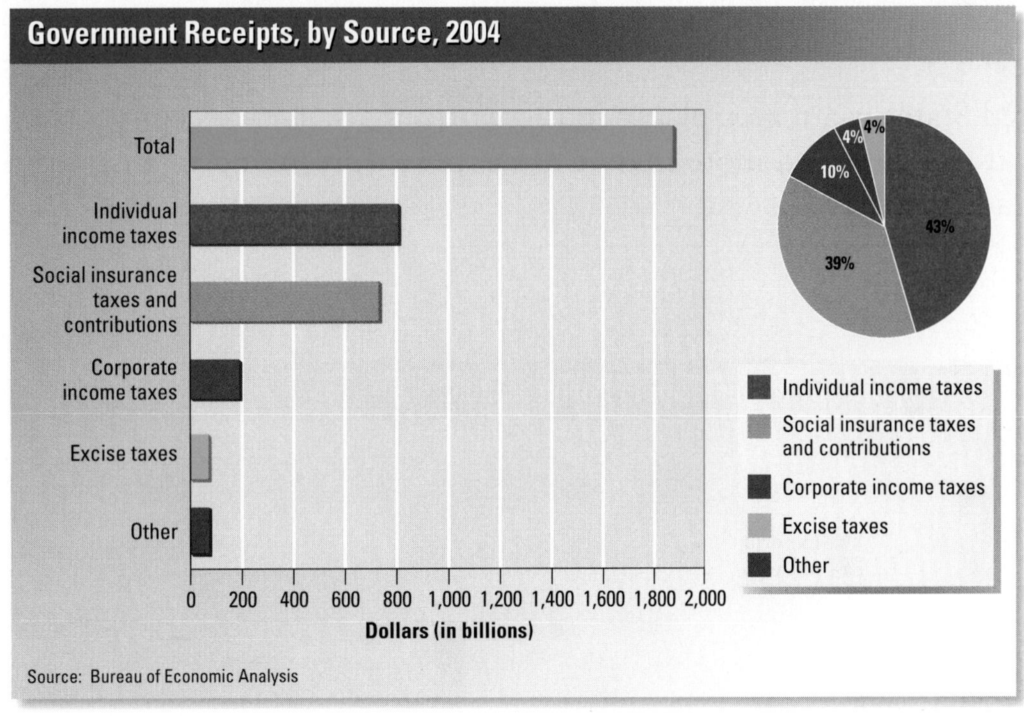
Government Receipts, by Source, 2004
Total
Individual income taxes
Social insurance taxes and contributions
Corporate income taxes
Excise taxes
Other
0
200
400
600
800
1,000
1,200
1,400
1,600
1,800
2,000
Dollars (in billions)
43%
39%
10%
4%
4%
Individual income taxes
Social insurance taxes and contributions
Corporate income taxes
Excise taxes
Other
Source: Bureau of Economic Analysis

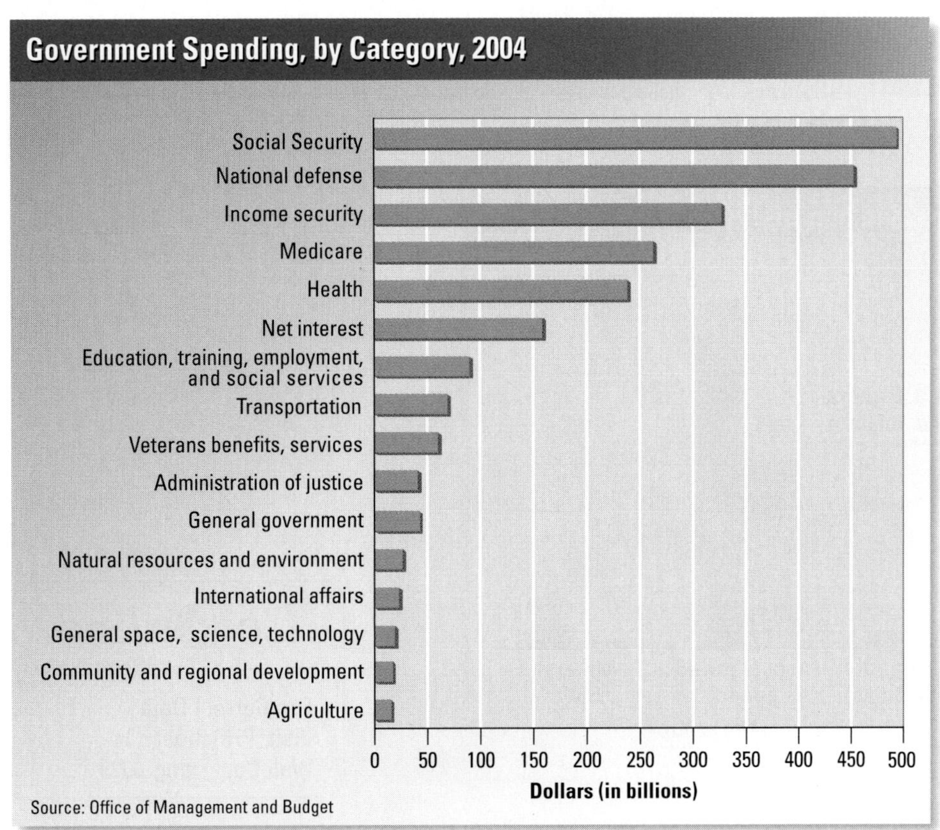
Government Spending, by Category, 2004
Social Security
National defense
Income security
Medicare
Health
Net interest
Education, training, employment, and social services
Transportation
Veterans benefits, services
Administration of justice
General government
Natural resources and environment
International affairs
General space, science, technology
Community and regional development
Agriculture
0
50
100
150
200
250
300
350
400
450
500
Dollars (in billions)
Source: Office of Management and Budget

Go Online
PHSchool.com

For: Current Data
Visit: PHSchool.com
Web Code: mng-8022

Trade

The United States is a major player in the world market. In recent years, however, it has imported more than it has exported, resulting in an annual trade deficit.

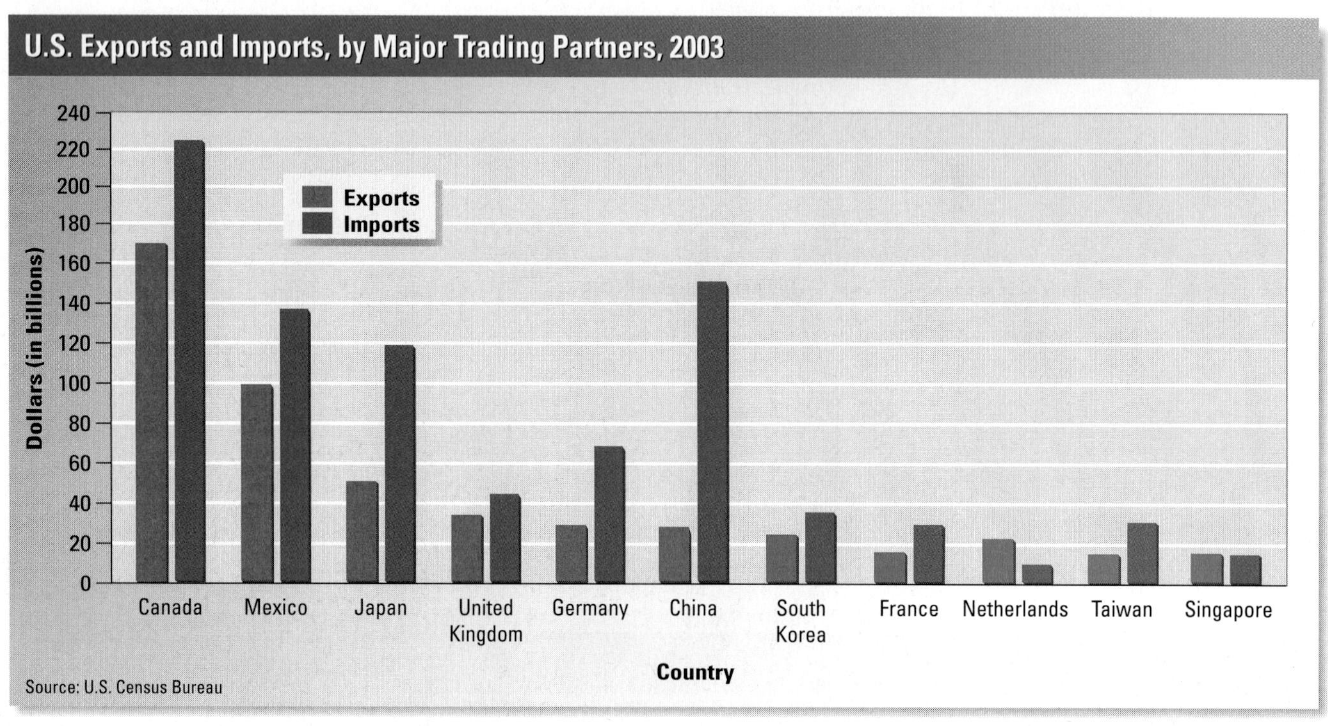

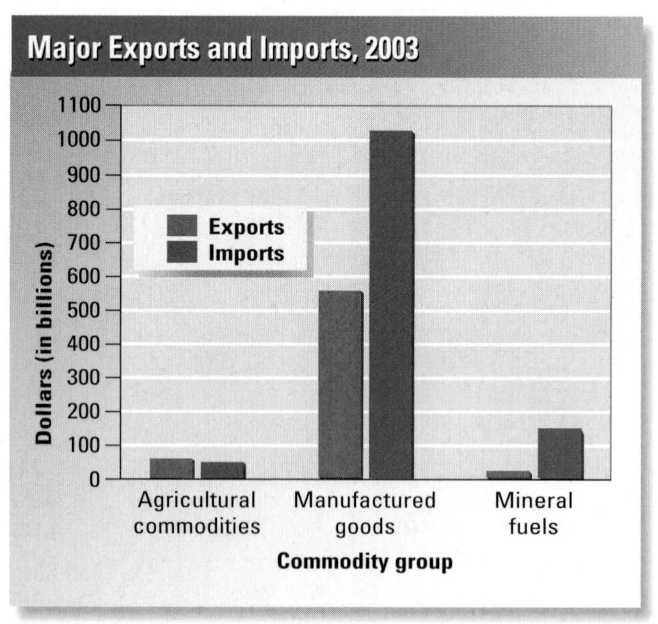

For: Current Data
Visit: PHSchool.com
Web Code: mng-8023

United States Trading Partners

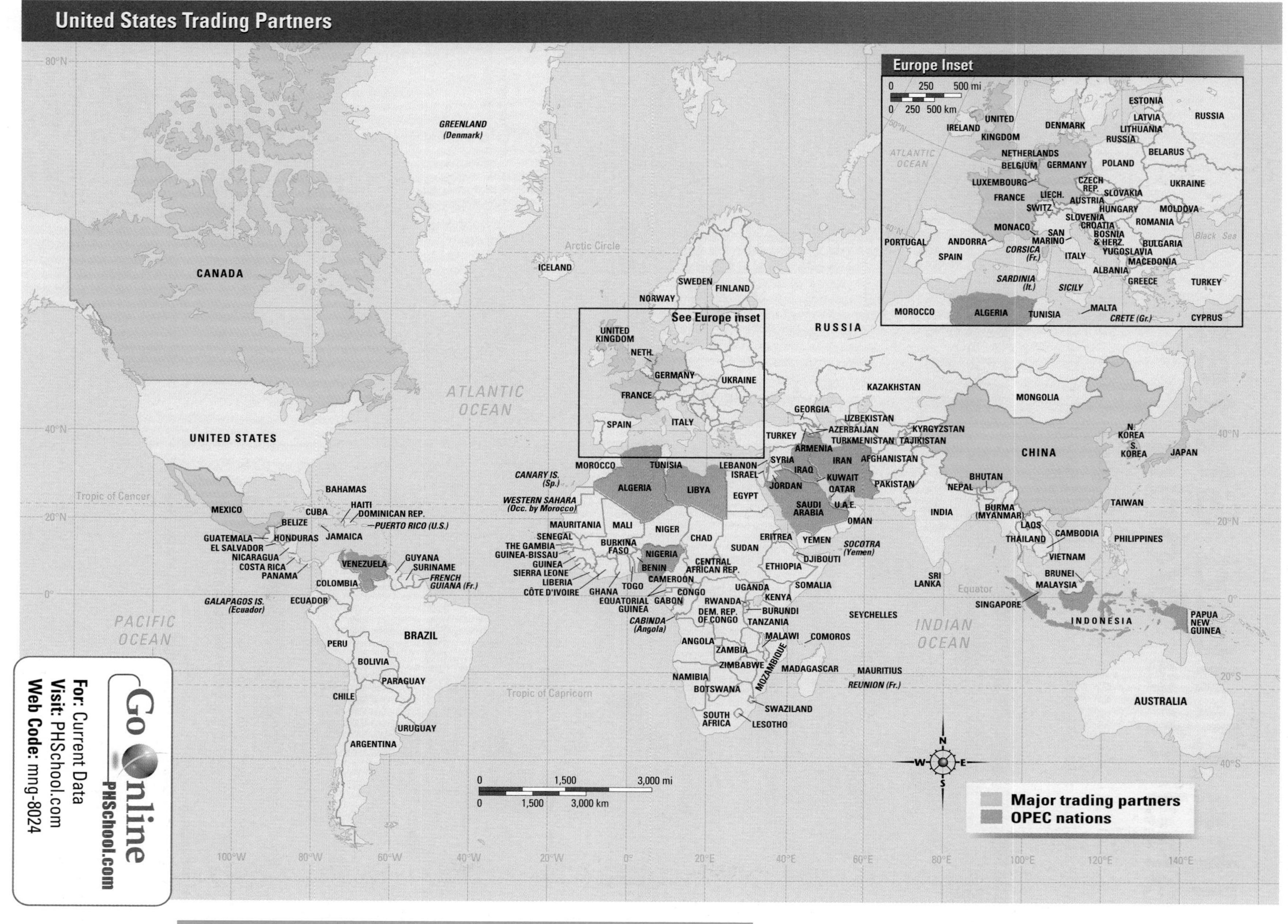

Go Online
PHSchool.com
For: Current Data
Visit: PHSchool.com
Web Code: mng-8024

The United States and the World

The United States enjoys one of the highest standards of living in the world and one of the lowest tax burdens of the industrialized nations.

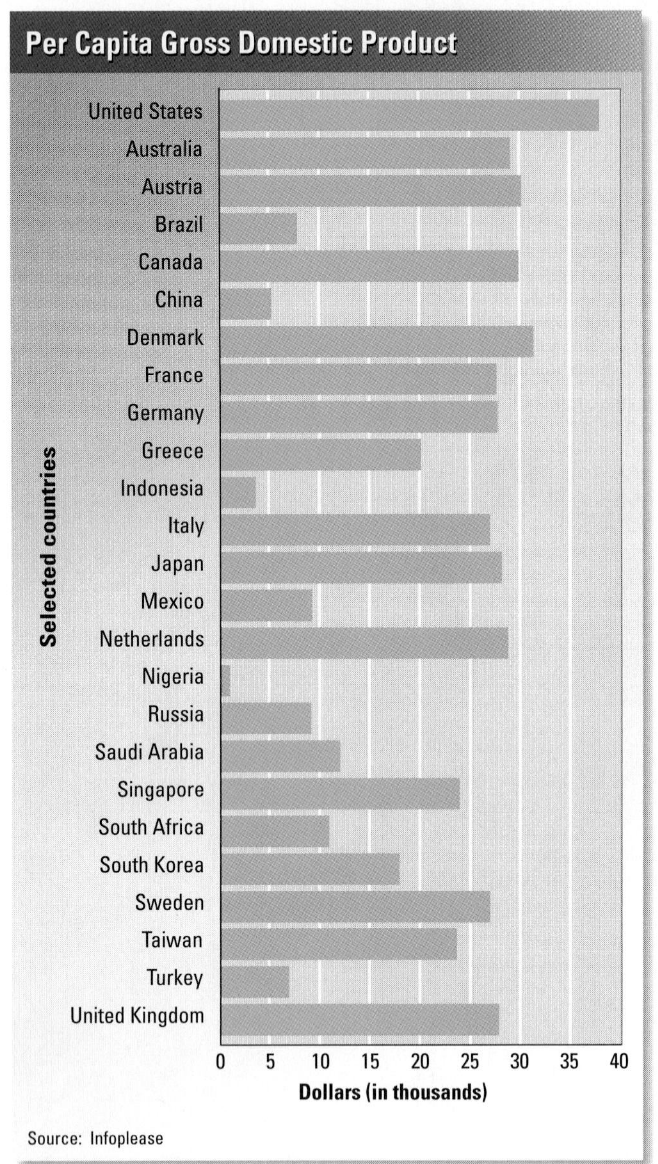

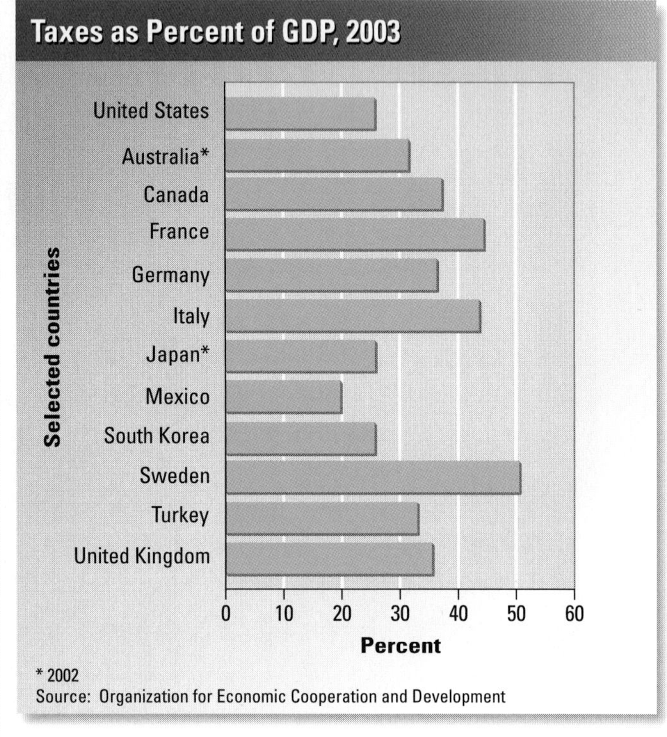

For: Current Data
Visit: PHSchool.com
Web Code: mng-8025

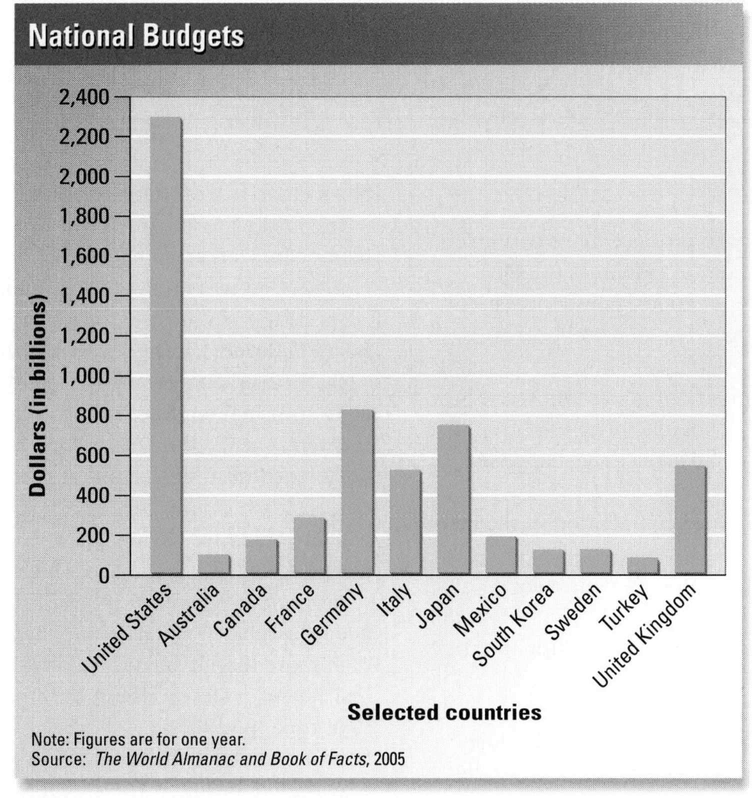
National Budgets
2,400
2,200
2,000
1,800
1,600
1,400
1,200
1,000
800
600
400
200
0
Dollars (in billions)
United States
Australia
Canada
France
Germany
Italy
Japan
Mexico
South Korea
Sweden
Turkey
United Kingdom
Selected countries
Note: Figures are for one year.
Source: The World Almanac and Book of Facts, 2005

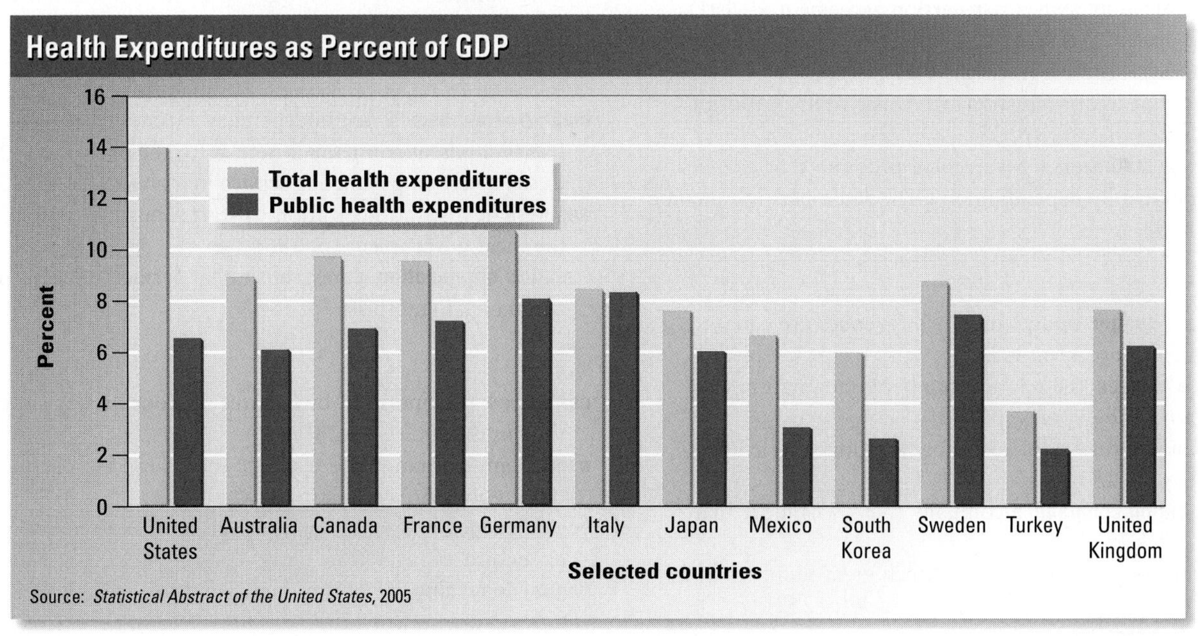
Health Expenditures as Percent of GDP
16
14
12
10
8
6
4
2
0
Percent
Total health expenditures
Public health expenditures
United States
Australia
Canada
France
Germany
Italy
Japan
Mexico
South Korea
Sweden
Turkey
United Kingdom
Selected countries
Source: Statistical Abstract of the United States, 2005

Go Online
PHSchool.com

For: Current Data
Visit: PHSchool.com
Web Code: mng-8026

Glossary

A

absolute advantage the ability to produce more of a given product using a given amount of resources (p. 443)

aggregate demand the amount of goods and services in the economy that will be purchased at all possible price levels (p. 307)

aggregate supply the total amount of goods and services in the economy available at all possible price levels (p. 307)

annual percentage rate (APR) a finance charge expressed as an annual rate (p. 514)

antitrust laws laws that encourage competition in the marketplace (p. 173)

appreciation an increase in the value of a currency (p. 459)

appropriations bill a bill that sets money aside for specific spending (p. 389)

arable suitable for producing crops (p. 480)

arbitration a settlement technique in which a third party reviews the case and imposes a decision that is legally binding for both sides (p. 234)

articles of partnership a partnership agreement (p. 191)

assets money and other valuables belonging to an individual or business (p. 192)

authoritarian requiring strict obedience to an authority, such as a dictator (p. 35)

automatic stabilizer a government program that changes automatically depending on GDP and a person's income (p. 399)

B

balanced budget budget in which revenues are equal to spending (pp. 376, 403)

balance of trade the relationship between a nation's imports and exports (p. 462)

bank an institution for receiving, keeping, and lending money (p. 250)

bank holding company a company that owns more than one bank (p. 421)

bank run widespread panic in which great numbers of people try to redeem their paper money (p. 252)

barrier to entry any factor that makes it difficult for a new firm to enter a market (p. 153)

barter the direct exchange of one set of goods or services for another (p. 243)

bear market a steady drop in the stock market over a period of time (p. 290)

black market a market in which goods are sold illegally (p. 142)

block grant federal funds given to states in lump sums (p. 350)

blue-collar worker someone who works in an industrial job, often in manufacturing, and who receives wages (p. 231)

Board of Governors the seven-member board that oversees the Federal Reserve System (p. 416)

bond a formal contract to repay borrowed money with interest at fixed intervals (pp. 197, 507)

brokerage firm a business that specializes in trading stocks (p. 287)

budget a plan for saving and spending (p. 502)

budget deficit a situation in which the government spends more than it takes in (p. 403)

budget surplus a situation in which the government takes in more than it spends (p. 403)

bull market a steady rise in the stock market over a period of time (p. 290)

business association nonprofit organization that promotes collective business interests for a city, state, or other geographical area, or for a group of similar businesses (p. 204)

business cycle a period of macroeconomic expansion followed by a period of contraction (pp. 57, 310)

business franchise a semi-independent business that pays fees to a parent company in return for the exclusive right to sell a certain product or service in a given area (p. 201)

business license authorization to start a business issued by the local government (p. 186)

business organization an establishment formed to carry on commercial enterprise (p. 185)

C

call option the option to buy shares of stock at a specified time in the future (p. 288)

capital any human-made resource that is used to create other goods or services (p. 4)

capital budget budget for major capital, or investment, expenditures (p. 375)

capital deepening process of increasing the amount of capital per worker (p. 320)

capital gain the difference between a higher selling price and a lower purchase price, resulting in a financial gain for the seller (pp. 286, 508)

capital loss the difference between a lower selling price and a higher purchase price, resulting in a financial loss for the seller (p. 286)

capital market market in which money is lent for periods longer than a year (p. 283)
cartel a formal organization of producers that agree to coordinate prices and production (p. 171)
cash transfers direct payments of money to eligible poor people (p. 69)
census an official count of the population (p. 334)
central bank bank that can lend to other banks in times of need (p. 254)
centrally planned economy economic system in which the central government makes all decisions on the production and consumption of goods and services (p. 27)
certificate of incorporation license to form a corporation issued by state government (p. 197)
ceteris paribus a Latin phrase that means "all other things held constant" (p. 85)
check clearing the process by which banks record whose account gives up money and whose account receives money when a customer writes a check (p. 421)
check register a booklet used to record checking account transactions (p. 504)
classical economics the idea that free markets can regulate themselves (p. 395)
closely held corporation corporation that issues stock to only a few people, often family members (p. 196)
collateral property used to secure a loan (p. 513)
collective large farm leased from the state to groups of peasant farmers (p. 36)
collective bargaining the process in which union and company representatives meet to negotiate a new labor contract (p. 233)
collusion an agreement among firms to divide the market, set prices, or limit production (p. 171)
command economy economic system in which the central government makes all decisions on the production and consumption of goods and services (p. 27)
commercial bank a bank that provides checking accounts, savings accounts, and money market accounts and that accepts time deposits (p. 511)
commodity a product that is the same no matter who produces it, such as petroleum, notebook paper, or milk (p. 152)
commodity money objects that have value in themselves as well as for use as money (p. 246)
common stock stock whose dividends are based on market fluctuations (p. 508)
communism a political system characterized by a centrally planned economy with all economic and political power resting in the hands of the central government (p. 35)
comparative advantage the ability to produce a product most efficiently given all the other products that could be produced (p. 444)
competition the struggle among producers for the dollars of consumers; the rivalry among sellers to attract customers while lowering costs (pp. 31, 53)
complements two goods that are bought and used together (p. 88)
conglomerate business combination merging more than three businesses that make unrelated products (p. 199)
Congressional Budget Office (CBO) government agency that provides economic data to Congress (p. 388)
consumer cooperative retail outlet owned and operated by consumers (p. 203)
Consumer Price Index (CPI) a price index determined by measuring the price of a standard group of goods meant to represent the typical "market basket" of a typical urban consumer (p. 339)
consumer sovereignty the power of consumers to decide what gets produced (p. 32)
contingent employment temporary jobs or part-time jobs (p. 215)
continuum a range with no clear divisions (p. 43)
contract a binding legal agreement (p. 523)
contraction period of economic decline marked by falling real GDP (p. 310)
contractionary policies fiscal policies, like lower spending and higher taxes, that reduce economic growth (p. 389)
cooperative a business organization owned and operated by a group of individuals for their mutual benefit (p. 202)
copayment part of the cost of a medical visit or procedure that the patient must pay out of pocket (p. 525)
core inflation rate the rate of inflation excluding the effects of food and energy prices (p. 340)
corporate bond a bond that a corporation issues to raise money in order to expand its business (p. 281)
corporate income tax a tax on the value of a corporation's profits (p. 360)
corporation a legal entity owned by individual stockholders (p. 195)
cost to an economist, cost is an alternative that is given up as the result of a decision (p. 16)
cost-push theory theory that inflation occurs when producers raise prices to meet increased costs (p. 341)
Council of Economic Advisers (CEA) a group of three respected economists that could advise the President on economic policy (p. 400)
coupon rate the interest rate that a bond issuer will pay to a bondholder (p. 277)
credit any form of deferred payment (p. 512)
credit bureau organization providing information on individuals' borrowing and bill-paying habits (p. 512)
credit card a card entitling its holder to buy goods and services based on the holder's promise to pay for these goods and services (p. 261)
creditor person or institution to whom money is owed (p. 264)
credit rating an evaluation made by credit bureaus of a borrower's overall credit history (p. 512)

credit union nonprofit bank owned by its members, often members of a single organization or trade union (p. 511)

crowding-out effect the loss of funds for private investment due to government borrowing (p. 406)

currency coins and paper bills used as money (p. 245)

customs duty a tax on certain items purchased abroad (p. 450)

cyclical unemployment unemployment that rises during economic downturns and falls when the economy improves (p. 333)

D

debit card a card used to withdraw money (p. 263)

debt rescheduling lengthening the time of debt repayment and forgiving, or dismissing, part of the loan (p. 488)

deductible amount of expenses that must be paid out of pocket before an insurer will cover any expenses (p. 524)

deductions variable amounts that you can subtract, or deduct, from your gross income (p. 366)

default failure to pay back a loan (p. 261)

deflation a sustained drop in the price level (p. 343)

demand the desire to own something and the ability to pay for it (p. 79)

demand curve a graphic representation of a demand schedule (p. 82)

demand deposit the money in checking accounts (p. 258)

demand-pull theory theory that inflation occurs when demand for goods and services exceeds existing supplies (p. 341)

demand schedule a table that lists the quantity of a good a person will buy at each different price (p. 81)

demand-side economics a school of economics that believes government spending and tax cuts help an economy by raising demand (p. 396)

depreciation the loss of the value of capital equipment that results from normal wear and tear (pp. 305, 520), or, a decrease in the value of a currency (p. 459)

depression a recession that is especially long and severe (p. 311)

deregulation the removal of some government controls over a market (p. 175)

derived demand demand that is derived from demand for another service or good (p. 219)

developed nation country with a higher average level of material well-being (p. 471)

development the process by which a nation improves the economic, political, and social well-being of its people (p. 471)

differentiation making a product different from other similar products (p. 167)

diminishing marginal returns a level of production in which the marginal product of labor decreases as the number of workers increases (p. 109)

discount rate rate the Federal Reserve charges for loans to commercial banks (p. 422)

discouraged worker a person who wants a job but has given up looking (p. 336)

discretionary spending spending category about which government planners can make choices (p. 371)

disequilibrium describes any price or quantity not at equilibrium; when quantity supplied is not equal to quantity demanded in a market (p. 126)

diversification spreading out investments to reduce risk (p. 273)

dividend the portion of corporate profits paid out to stockholders (pp. 198, 508)

The Dow index that shows how certain stocks have traded (p. 290)

durable goods goods that last for a relatively long time, such as refrigerators, cars, and DVD players (p. 302)

E

easy money policy monetary policy that increases the money supply (p. 431)

economic growth steady, long-term increase in real GDP (p. 310)

economics the study of how people seek to satisfy their needs and wants by making choices (p. 3)

economic system the method used by a society to produce and distribute goods and services (p. 23)

economies of scale factors that cause a producer's average cost per unit to fall as output rises (p. 157)

efficiency using resources in such a way as to maximize the production of goods and services (p. 15)

elastic describes demand that is very sensitive to a change in price (p. 90)

elasticity of demand a measure of how consumers react to a change in price (p. 90)

elasticity of supply a measure of the way quantity supplied reacts to a change in price (p. 104)

enterprise zone area where companies can locate free of certain local, state, and federal taxes and restrictions (p. 350)

entitlement social welfare program that people are "entitled" to if they meet certain eligibility requirements (p. 372)

entrepreneur ambitious leader who combines land, labor, and capital to create and market new goods or services (p. 6)

equilibrium the point at which quantity demanded and quantity supplied are equal (p. 125)

equilibrium wage the wage rate that produces neither an excess supply of workers nor an excess demand for workers in the labor market (p. 220)

equities claims of ownership in a corporation (p. 285)

estate tax a tax on the estate, or total value of the money and property, of a person who has died (p. 368)

euro a single new currency that replaces individual currencies among members of the European Union (p. 454)

European Union (EU) a regional trade organization made up of European nations (p. 454)

excess demand when quantity demanded is more than quantity supplied (p. 126)

excess reserves in banking, reserves of cash more than the required amounts (p. 427)

excess supply when quantity supplied is more than quantity demanded (p. 128)

exchange rate the value of a foreign nation's currency in terms of the home nation's currency (p. 458)

excise tax a tax on the production or sale of a good (p. 118)

expansion a period of economic growth as measured by a rise in real GDP (p. 310)

expansionary policies fiscal policies, like higher spending and tax cuts, that encourage economic growth (p. 389)

export a good that is sent to another country for sale (p. 446)

externality an economic side effect of a good or service that generates benefits or costs to someone other than the person deciding how much to produce or consume (p. 65)

F

factor market market in which firms purchase the factors of production from households (p. 29)

factor payments the income people receive for supplying factors of production: land, labor, or capital (p. 24)

factors of production land, labor, and capital; the three groups of resources that are used to make all goods and services (p. 4)

featherbedding the practice of negotiating labor contracts that keep unnecessary workers on a company's payroll (p. 225)

Federal Advisory Council (FAC) the research arm of the Federal Reserve (p. 418)

federal budget a plan for the federal government's revenues and spending for the coming year (p. 387)

Federal Deposit Insurance Corporation (FDIC) the government agency that insures customer deposits if a bank fails (p. 255)

federal funds rate interest rate banks charge each other for loans (p. 422)

Federal Open Market Committee (FOMC) Federal Reserve committee that makes key decisions about interest rates and the growth of the United States money supply (p. 418)

Federal Reserve Districts the twelve banking districts created by the Federal Reserve Act (p. 417)

Federal Reserve note the national currency we use today in the United States (p. 255)

Federal Reserve System the nation's central banking system (p. 254)

fiat money money that has value because the government has ordered that it is an acceptable means to pay debts (p. 248)

FICA taxes that fund Social Security and Medicare (p. 367)

finance charge interest accrued on, and fees charged for, some forms of credit (p. 513)

financial asset claim on the property or income of a borrower (p. 272)

financial intermediary institution that helps channel funds from savers to borrowers (p. 272)

financial system the system that allows the transfer of money between savers and borrowers (p. 272)

firm an organization that uses resources to produce a product, which it then sells (p. 29)

fiscal policy the use of government spending and revenue collection to influence the economy (p. 387)

fiscal year a twelve-month period that can begin on any date (p. 388)

fixed cost a cost that does not change, no matter how much of a good is produced (p. 111)

fixed exchange-rate system a currency system in which governments try to keep the values of their currencies constant against one another (p. 461)

fixed income income that does not increase even when prices go up (p. 343)

flexible exchange-rate system a currency system that allows the exchange rate to be determined by supply and demand (p. 462)

food stamps government-issued coupons that recipients exchange for food (p. 348)

foreign direct investment the establishment of an enterprise by a foreigner (p. 486)

foreign exchange market the banks and other financial institutions that facilitate the buying and selling of foreign currencies (p. 460)

foreign investment investment originating from other countries (p. 485)

foreign portfolio investment the entry of funds into a country when foreigners make purchases in the country's stock and bond markets (p. 486)

fractional reserve banking a banking system that keeps only a fraction of funds on hand and lends out the remainder (p. 260)

franchise the right to sell a good or service within an exclusive market (p. 159)

free contract the concept that people may decide what agreements they want to enter into (p. 53)

free enterprise an economic system characterized by private or corporate ownership of capital goods; investments that are determined by private decision rather than by state control; and determined in a free market (p. 43)

free rider someone who would not choose to pay for a certain good or service, but who would get the benefits of it anyway if it were provided as a public good (p. 63)

free-trade zone a region where a group of countries has agreed to reduce or eliminate trade barriers (p. 454)

frictional unemployment unemployment that occurs when people take time to find a job (p. 331)

fringe benefit payment other than wages or salaries (p. 188)

full employment the level of employment reached when there is no cyclical unemployment (p. 335)

futures contracts to buy or sell at a specific date in the future at a price specified today (p. 288)

G

general partnership partnership in which partners share equally in both responsibility and liability (p. 190)

gift tax a tax on money or property that one living person gives to another (p. 368)

glasnost a policy of "openness" introduced into the Soviet Union in the late 1980s (p. 491)

glass ceiling an unofficial, invisible barrier that prevents women and minorities from advancing in businesses dominated by white men (p. 224)

gold standard a monetary system in which paper money and coins are equal in value to a certain amount of gold (p. 253)

goods physical objects such as clothes or shoes (p. 3)

government monopoly a monopoly created by the government (p. 159)

Great Crash the collapse of the stock market in 1929 (p. 290)

Great Depression the severe economic decline that began in 1929 and lasted for more than a decade (p. 255)

greenback paper currency issued by the North during the Civil War (p. 253)

gross domestic product (GDP) the total value of all final goods and services produced in a particular economy; the dollar value of all final goods and services produced within a country's borders in a given year (pp. 57, 301)

gross national product (GNP) the annual income earned by U.S.-owned firms and U.S. residents (p. 305)

guns or butter a phrase that refers to the trade-off that nations face when choosing whether to produce more or less military or consumer goods (p. 8)

H

heavy industry industry that requires a large capital investment and that produces items used in other industries (p. 37)

household a person or a group of people living in the same residence (p. 29)

horizontal merger the combination of two or more firms competing in the same market with the same good or service (p. 199)

human capital the skills and knowledge gained by a worker through education and experience (p. 5)

hyperinflation inflation that is out of control; very high inflation (pp. 341, 404)

I

imperfect competition a market structure that does not meet the conditions of perfect competition (p. 153)

import a good that is brought in from another country for sale (p. 446)

import quota a limit on the amount of a good that can be imported (p. 449)

incentive an expectation that encourages people to behave in a certain way (p. 31)

incidence of a tax the final burden of a tax (p. 363)

income distribution how the nation's total income is distributed among its population (p. 348)

income effect the change in consumption resulting from a change in real income (p. 80)

increasing marginal returns a level of production in which the marginal product of labor increases as the number of workers increases (p. 109)

individual income tax a tax on a person's earnings (p. 360)

industrialization the extensive organization of an economy for the purpose of manufacturing (p. 472)

inelastic describes demand that is not very sensitive to a change in price (p. 90)

infant industry a new industry (p. 452)

infant mortality rate the number of deaths that occur in the first year of life per 1,000 live births (p. 474)

inferior good a good that consumers demand less of when their incomes increase (p. 87)

inflation a general increase in prices (p. 338)

inflation rate the percentage rate of change in price level over time (p. 340)

infrastructure the services and facilities necessary for an economy to function (p. 474)

in-kind benefits goods and services provided for free or at greatly reduced prices (p. 70)

inside lag delay in implementing monetary policy (p. 432)

interest the price paid for the use of borrowed money (p. 261), or, money earned by deposited funds (p. 506)

interest group a private organization that tries to persuade public officials to act or vote according to group members' interests (p. 54)

intermediate goods goods used in the production of final goods (p. 301)

internal financing financing derived from the savings of a country's citizens (p. 485)

Internal Revenue Service agency within the U.S. Department of the Treasury responsible for interpretation and application of federal tax law (p. 528)

international free trade agreement agreement that results from cooperation between at least two countries to reduce trade barriers and tarriffs and to trade with each other (p. 453)

International Monetary Fund (IMF) organization formed to stabilize international exchange rates and facilitate development (p. 488)

investment the act of redirecting resources from being consumed today so that they may create benefits in the future; the use of assets to earn income or profit (p. 271)

invisible hand term economists use to describe the self-regulating nature of the marketplace (p. 32)

J

junk bond a lower-rated, potentially higher-paying bond (p. 281)

K

Keynesian economics form of demand-side economics that encourages government action to increase or decrease demand and output (p. 396)

L

labor the effort that people devote to a task for which they are paid (p. 4)

labor force all nonmilitary people who are employed or unemployed (p. 211)

labor union an organization of workers that tries to improve working conditions, wages, and benefits for its members (p. 225)

laissez faire the doctrine that states that government generally should not intervene in the marketplace (p. 41)

land natural resources that are used to make goods and services (p. 4)

law of comparative advantage the idea that a nation is better off when it produces goods and services for which it has a comparative advantage (p. 444)

law of demand economic law that states that consumers buy more of a good when its price decreases and less when its price increases (p. 79)

law of increasing costs as we shift factors of production from making one good or service to another, the cost of producing the second item increases (p. 17)

law of supply tendency of suppliers to offer more of a good at a higher price (p. 101)

leading indicators key economic variables that economists use to predict a new phase of the business cycle (p. 314)

learning effect the theory that education increases productivity and results in higher wages (p. 214)

lease a rental agreement between landlord and tenant (p. 523)

legal equality the concept of giving everyone the same legal rights (p. 53)

less developed country nation with a low level of material well-being (p. 471)

liability the legally bound obligation to pay debts (p. 187)

license a government-issued right to operate a business (p. 159)

life expectancy the average expected life span of an individual (p. 473)

light industry the production of small consumer goods (p. 494)

limited liability partnership (LLP) partnership in which all partners are limited partners (p. 190)

limited partnership partnership in which only one partner is required to be a general partner (p. 190)

liquidity the ability to be used as, or directly converted to, cash (p. 258)

literacy rate the proportion of the population over age 15 that can read and write (p. 473)

Lorenz Curve the curve that illustrates income distribution (p. 349)

M

macroeconomics the study of the behavior and decision making of entire economies (p. 57)

malnutrition inadequate nutrition (p. 481)

mandatory spending spending on certain programs that is mandated, or required, by existing law (p. 371)

marginal cost the cost of producing one more unit of a good (p. 111)

marginal product of labor the change in output from hiring one additional unit of labor (p. 108)

marginal revenue the additional income from selling one more unit of a good; sometimes equal to price (p. 112)

market an arrangement that allows buyers and sellers to exchange things (p. 28)

market basket a representative collection of goods and services (p. 339)

market demand schedule a table that lists the quantity of a good all consumers in a market will buy at every different price (p. 82)

market economy economic system in which decisions on production and consumption of goods and services are based on voluntary exchange in markets (p. 27)

market failure a situation in which the market does not distribute resources efficiently (p. 64)

market power the ability of a company to change prices and output like a monopolist (p. 163)

market supply curve a graph of the quantity supplied of a good by all suppliers at different prices (p. 104)

market supply schedule a chart that lists how much of a good all suppliers will offer at different prices (p. 103)

maturity the time at which payment to a bondholder is due (p. 277)

mediation a settlement technique in which a neutral mediator meets with each side to try to find a solution that both sides will accept (p. 234)

Medicaid entitlement program that benefits low-income families, some people with disabilities, and elderly people in nursing homes (p. 373)

Medicare a national health insurance program that helps pay for health care for people over age 65 or who have certain disabilities (p. 368)

medium of exchange anything that is used to determine value during the exchange of goods and services (p. 243)

member bank bank that belongs to the Federal Reserve System (p. 254)

merger combination of two or more companies into a single firm (p. 174)

microeconomics the study of the economic behavior and decision making of small units, such as individuals, families, and businesses (p. 57)

minimum balance an amount of money required in a bank account to avoid fees (p. 504)

minimum wage a minimum price that an employer can pay a worker for an hour of labor (p. 130)

mixed economy economic system that combines the free market with limited government involvement (p. 27)

monetarism the belief that the money supply is the most important factor in macroeconomic performance (p. 430)

monetary policy the actions the Federal Reserve takes to influence the level of real GDP and the rate of inflation in the economy (p. 417)

money anything that serves as a medium of exchange, a unit of account, and a store of value (p. 243)

money creation the process by which money enters into circulation (p. 425)

money market market in which money is lent for periods less than a year (p. 283)

money market mutual fund a fund that pools money from small savers to purchase short-term government and corporate securities (p. 259)

money multiplier formula amount of new money that will be created with each demand deposit; 1 ÷ RRR (p. 426)

money supply all the money available in the United States economy (p. 258)

monopolistic competition a market structure in which many companies sell products that are similar but not identical (p. 166)

monopoly a market dominated by a single seller (p. 156)

mortgage a specific type of loan that is used to buy real estate (p. 261)

multinational corporation (MNC) large corporation that produces and sells its goods and services throughout the world (p. 199)

multiplier effect the idea that every dollar of spending creates more than one dollar in economic activity (p. 397)

municipal bond a bond issued by a state or local government or municipality to finance such improvements as highways, state buildings, libraries, parks, and schools (p. 281)

mutual fund fund that pools the savings of many individuals and invests this money in a variety of stocks, bonds and other financial assets (pp. 272, 509)

N

NAFTA agreement that will eliminate all tariffs and other trade barriers between Canada, Mexico, and the United States (p. 454)

Nasdaq American market for OTC securities (p. 288)

national bank a bank chartered, or licensed, by the national government (p. 251)

national debt all the money the federal government owes to bondholders (p. 405)

national income accounting a system that collects macroeconomic statistics on production, income, investment, and savings (p. 301)

natural monopoly a market that runs most efficiently when one large firm supplies all of the output (p. 158)

natural rate of population increase the difference between the birth rate and the death rate (p. 478)

need something like air, food, or shelter that is necessary for survival (p. 3)

net worth total assets minus total liabilities (p. 422)

newly industrialized country (NIC) less developed country that has shown significant improvement in the measures of development (p. 475)

nominal GDP gross domestic product measured in current prices (p. 304)

nondurable goods goods that last a short period of time, such as food, light bulbs, and sneakers (p. 302)

nonprice competition a way to attract customers through style, service, or location, but not a lower price (p. 167)

nonprofit organization institution that functions much like a business, but does not operate for the purpose of generating profits (p. 203)

normal good a good that consumers demand more of when their incomes increase (p. 86)

O

Office of Management and Budget (OMB) government office that manages the federal budget (p. 388)

oligopoly a market structure in which a few large firms dominate a market (p. 169)

open market operations the buying and selling of government securities to alter the supply of money (p. 428)

open opportunity the concept that everyone can compete in the marketplace (p. 53)

operating budget budget for day-to-day expenses (p. 375)

operating cost the cost of operating a facility such as a store or factory (p. 113)

opportunity cost the most desirable alternative given up as the result of a decision (p. 9)

options contracts that give investors the choice to buy or sell stock and other financial assets (p. 288)

OTC market the over-the-counter market; an electronic marketplace for stock that is not listed or traded on an organized exchange (p. 288)

outside lag the time it takes for monetary policy to have an effect (p. 432)

P

partnership a business organization owned by two or more persons who agree on a specific division of responsibilities and profits (p. 190)

par value the amount that an investor pays to purchase a bond and that will be repaid to investor at maturity (p. 278)

patent a license that gives the inventor of a new product the exclusive right to sell it for a certain period of time (p. 159)

patriotism the love of one's country; the passion that inspires a person to serve his or her country (p. 25)

payroll withholding statement document attached to a paycheck detailing the amount of money withheld (p. 528)

peak the height of an economic expansion, when real GDP stops rising (p. 310)

per capita gross domestic product (per capita GDP) a nation's gross domestic product (GDP) divided by its total population (p. 472)

perestroika Soviet leader Mikhail Gorbachev's plan for economic restructuring (p. 492)

perfect competition a market structure in which a large number of firms all produce the same product (p. 151)

personal exemption set amount that you subtract from your gross income for yourself, your spouse, and any dependents (p. 366)

personal property possessions such as jewelry, furniture, and boats (p. 378)

physical capital all human-made goods that are used to produce other goods and services; tools and buildings (p. 4)

population growth rate the increase in a country's population in a given year, expressed as a percentage of the population figure at the start of the year (p. 478)

portfolio a collection of financial assets (p. 274)

poverty rate the percentage of people who live in households with income below the official poverty line (p. 346)

poverty threshold an income level below which income is insufficient to support families or households (pp. 67, 345)

predatory pricing selling a product below cost to drive competitors out of the market (p. 173)

preferred stock stock whose dividends are based on a fixed annual rate (p. 508)

premium money paid to an insurance company for a policy (p. 524)

price ceiling a maximum price that can be legally charged for a good or service (p. 128)

price discrimination division of customers into groups based on how much they will pay for a good (p. 163)

price fixing an agreement among firms to charge one price for the same good (p. 171)

price floor a minimum price for a good or service (p. 128)

price index a measurement that shows how the average price of a standard group of goods changes over time (p. 339)

price level the average of all prices in the economy (p. 307)

price war a series of competitive price cuts that lowers the market price below the cost of production (p. 171)

primary market market for selling financial assets that can only be redeemed by the original holder (p. 283)

prime rate rate of interest banks charge on short-term loans to their best customers (p. 427)

principal the amount of money borrowed (p. 261)

private property property owned by individuals or companies, not by the government or the people as a whole (p. 41)

private property rights the concept that people have the right and priviledge to control their own possessions as they wish (p. 53)

private sector the part of the economy that involves the transactions of individuals and businesses (p. 63)

privatization the sale or transfer of state-owned businesses to individuals (p. 489)

privatize to sell to individuals state-run firms, which are then allowed to compete with one another in the marketplace (p. 43)

producer cooperative agricultural marketing cooperatives that help members sell their products (p. 203)

product market the market in which households purchase the goods and services that firms produce (p. 30)

production possibilities curve a curve that shows alternative ways to use an economy's resources (p. 13)

production possibilities frontier the line on a production possibilities graph that shows the maximum possible output for a specific economy (p. 14)

productive capacity the maximum output that an economy can produce without big increases in inflation (p. 396)

productivity value of output produced (p. 219)

professional labor labor that requires advanced skills and education (p. 221)

professional organization nonprofit organization that works to improve the image, working conditions, and skill levels of people in particular occupations (p. 203)

profit the financial gain made in a transaction (p. 29)

profit motive the force that encourages people and organizations to improve their material well-being (p. 53)

progressive tax a tax for which the percentage of income paid in taxes increases as income increases (p. 361)

property tax a tax on the value of a property (p. 360)

proportional tax a tax for which the percentage of income paid in taxes remains the same for all income levels (p. 361)

prospectus an investment report to potential investors (p. 274)

protectionism the use of trade barriers to protect a nation's industries from foreign competition (p. 452)

public disclosure laws laws requiring companies to provide full information about their products (p. 54)
public good a shared good or service for which it would be impractical to make consumers pay individually and to exclude nonpayers (p. 62)
public interest the concerns of the public as a whole (p. 54)
publicly held corporation corporation that sells stock on the open market (p. 196)
public sector the part of the economy that involves the transactions of the government (p. 63)
purchasing power the ability to purchase goods and services (p. 339)
put option the option to sell shares of stock at a specified time in the future (p. 288)

Q

quantity supplied the amount a supplier is willing and able to supply at a certain price (p. 101)
quantity theory theory that too much money in the economy causes inflation (p. 341)

R

rationing a system of allocating scarce goods and services using criteria other than price (p. 141)
real GDP gross domestic product expressed in constant, or unchanging, prices (p. 304)
real GDP per capita real gross domestic product divided by the total population (p. 319)
real property physical property such as land and buildings (p. 378)
recession a prolonged economic contraction (p. 311)
regressive tax a tax for which the percentage of income paid in taxes decreases as income increases (p. 361)
regulation government intervention in a market that affects the production of a good (p. 118)
rent control a price ceiling placed on rent (p. 129)
representative money objects that have value because the holder can exchange them for something else of value (p. 247)
required reserve ratio (RRR) ratio of reserves to deposits required of banks by the Federal Reserve (p. 425)
résumé a document summarizing an individual's employment experience, education, and other information a potential employer needs to know (p. 526)
return the money an investor receives above and beyond the sum of money initially invested (p. 274)
revenue income received by a government from taxes and nontax sources (p. 359)
right-to-work law a measure that bans mandatory union membership (p. 231)
royalty share of earnings given as payment (p. 202)

S

S & P 500 index that shows the price changes of 500 different stocks (p. 290)
safety net government programs that protect people experiencing unfavorable economic conditions (p. 26)
sales tax a tax on the dollar value of a good or service being sold (p. 360)
saving income not used for consumption (p. 320)
savings account a bank account used for depositing money that may be needed within a short period of time (p. 506)
savings and loans associations banks that accept deposits and specialize in offering long-term financing for homes (p. 511)
savings bank a bank that accepts deposits and specializes in low-risk investments (p. 511)
savings bond low-denomination bond issued by the United States government (p. 280)
savings rate the proportion of disposable income that is saved (p. 320)
scarcity limited quantities of resources to meet unlimited wants (p. 4)
screening effect the theory that the completion of college indicates to employers that a job applicant is intelligent and hard-working (p. 214)
search costs the financial and opportunity costs consumers pay when searching for a good or service (p. 136)
seasonal unemployment unemployment that occurs as a result of harvest schedules or vacations, or when industries slow or shut down for a season (p. 332)
secondary market market for reselling financial assets (p. 283)
Securities and Exchange Commission an independent agency of the government that regulates financial markets and investment companies (p. 281)
security deposit a sum of money paid to a landlord or other lessor to ensure goods are returned in the same condition as originally rented (p. 522)
self-interest one's own personal gain (p. 31)
semi-skilled labor labor that requires minimal specialized skills and education (p. 221)
service cooperative cooperative that provides a service, rather than a good (p. 203)
services actions or activities one person performs for another (p. 3)
share portion of stock (p. 285)
shortage a situation in which a good or service is unavailable (p. 4), or a situation in which the quantity demanded is greater than the quantity supplied, also known as excess demand (p. 136)
skilled labor labor that requires specialized skills and training (p. 221)
socialism a social and political philosophy based on the belief that democratic means should be used to evenly distribute wealth throughout a society (p. 35)
Social Security Old-Age, Survivors, and Disability Insurance (OASDI) (p. 367)

sole proprietorship a business owned and managed by a single individual (p. 185)

special economic zones designated regions in China where foreign investment is encouraged, businesses can make most of their own investment and production decisions, and foreign companies are allowed to operate (p. 494)

specialization the concentration of the productive efforts of individuals and firms on a limited number of activities (p. 29)

speculation the practice of making high-risk investments with borrowed money in hopes of getting a big return (p. 290)

spillover costs costs of production that affect people who have no control over how much of a good is produced (p. 144)

stabilization program an agreement between a debtor nation and the IMF in which the nation agrees to revise its economic policy (p. 488)

standard of living level of economic prosperity (p. 26)

stagflation a decline in real GDP combined with a rise in the price level (p. 311)

start-up costs the expenses a firm must pay before it can begin to produce and sell goods (p. 153)

stock a certificate of ownership in a corporation (pp. 195, 507)

stock exchange a market for buying and selling stock (p. 287)

stock split the division of a single share of stock into more than one share (p. 286)

stockbroker a person who links buyers and sellers of stock (p. 286)

store of value something that keeps its value if it is stored rather than used (p. 244)

strike an organized work stoppage intended to force an employer to address union demands (p. 229)

structural unemployment unemployment that occurs when workers' skills do not match the jobs that are available (p. 332)

subsidized loans loans for which the government pays the interest while the student is attending school (p. 518)

subsidy a government payment that supports a business or market (p. 117)

subsistence agriculture level of farming in which a person raises only enough food to feed his or her family (p. 472)

substitutes goods used in place of each other (p. 88)

substitution effect when consumers react to an increase in a good's price by consuming less of that good and more of other goods (p. 80)

supply the amount of goods available (p. 101)

supply curve a graph of the quantity supplied of a good at different prices (p. 104)

supply schedule a chart that lists how much of a good a supplier will offer at different prices (p. 103)

supply shock a sudden shortage of a good (p. 141)

supply-side economics a school of economics that believes tax cuts can help an economy by raising supply (p. 399)

surplus situation in which quantity supplied is greater than quantity demanded; also known as excess supply (p. 134)

T

tariff a tax on imported goods (pp. 369, 450)

tax a required payment to a local, state, or national government (p. 359)

taxable income income on which tax must be paid; total income minus exemptions and deductions (p. 366)

tax assessor an official who determines the value of a property (p. 380)

tax base income, property, good, or service that is subject to a tax (p. 360)

tax exempt not subject to taxes (p. 377)

tax incentive the use of taxation to encourage or discourage certain behavior (p. 369)

tax return form used to file one's income taxes (p. 366)

technological progress an increase in efficiency gained by producing more output without using more inputs (p. 322)

technology the process used to produce a good or service (p. 59)

thinking at the margin deciding whether to do or use one additional unit of some resource (p. 10)

tight money policy monetary policy that reduces the money supply (p. 431)

time deposit a deposit offering guaranteed interest for a fixed period of time (p. 506)

total cost fixed costs plus variable costs (p. 111)

total revenue the total amount of money a firm receives by selling goods or services (p. 95)

trade association nonprofit organization that promotes the interests of a particular industry (p. 204)

trade barrier a means of preventing a foreign product or service from freely entering a nation's territory (p. 449)

trade deficit the result of a country importing more than it exports (p. 462)

trade-off an alternative we sacrifice when we make a decision (p. 8)

trade surplus the result of a nation exporting more than it imports (p. 462)

trade war a cycle of increasing trade restrictions (p. 451)

traditional economy economic system that relies on habit, custom, or ritual to decide questions of production and consumption of goods and services (p. 26)

transition period of change in which an economy moves away from a centrally planned economy toward a market-based system (p. 43)

Treasury bill a government bond that is repaid within three months to a year (p. 405)

Treasury bond a government bond that can be issued for as long as 30 years (p. 405)

Treasury note a government bond that is repaid within two to ten years (p. 405)

trough the lowest point in an economic contraction, when real gross domestic product stops falling (p. 311)

trust like a cartel, an illegal grouping of companies that discourages competition (p. 173)

Truth in Savings Act federal law requiring banks to provide customers with information on accounts they offer (p. 507)

Truth in Lending laws regulations requiring institutions extending loans to disclose exact finance charges, monthly interest rates, annual percentage rates, and finance charge calculation methods (p. 515)

tuition the cost of enrolling in educational courses (p. 516)

U

underemployed working at a job for which one is overqualified, or working part-time when full-time work is desired (p. 335)

underutilization using fewer resources than an economy is capable of using (p. 15)

unemployment rate the percentage of the nation's labor force that is unemployed (p. 334)

Uniform Partnership Act (UPA) act ordering common ownership interests, profit and loss sharing, and shared management responsibilities in a partnership (p. 191)

unitary elastic describes demand whose elasticity is exactly equal to 1 (p. 91)

United Nations Development Program (UNDP) United Nations program dedicated to elimination of poverty through development (p. 487)

unit of account a means for comparing the values of goods and services (p. 244)

unskilled labor labor that requires no specialized skills, education, or training (p. 221)

V

variable a factor that can change (p. 103)

variable cost a cost that rises or falls depending on how much is produced (p. 111)

vertical merger the combination of two or more firms involved in different stages of producing the same good or service (p. 199)

voluntary exchange the concept that people may decide what and when they want to buy and sell (p. 53)

voluntary export restraint (VER) a self-imposed limitation on the number of products shipped to a particular country (p. 449)

W

wage-price spiral the process by which rising wages cause higher prices and higher prices cause higher wages (p. 342)

want an item that we desire but that is not essential to survival (p. 3)

welfare government aid to the poor (p. 68)

white-collar worker someone in a professional or clerical job who usually earns a salary (p. 232)

withholding taking tax payments out of an employee's pay before he or she receives it (p. 366)

work ethic a commitment to the value of work and purposeful activity; system of values that gives central importance to work (pp. 59, 491)

workfare a program requiring work in exchange for temporary assistance (p. 350)

World Bank the largest provider of development assistance (p. 487)

World Trade Organization (WTO) a worldwide organization whose goal is freer global trade and lower tariffs (p. 453)

Y

yield the annual rate of return on a bond if the bond were held to maturity (p. 278)

Z

zoning law law in a city or town that designates separate areas for residency and for business (p. 187)

Spanish Glossary

A

absolute advantage/ventaja absoluta capacidad que tiene una persona o nación de producir un producto a un costo más bajo que otra persona o nación (pág. 443)

aggregate demand/demanda global cantidad de productos y servicios que se pueden adquirir en todos los niveles de precios (pág. 307)

aggregate supply/suministros totales cantidad total de productos y servicios que están disponibles en todos los niveles de precios (pág. 307)

annual percentage rate (APR)/tasa porcentual anual carga financiera que se expresa como tasa anual (pág. 514)

antitrust laws/legislación antimonopolios leyes que estimulan la competencia en el mercado (pág. 173)

appreciation/revalorización aumento en el valor de una moneda (pág. 459)

appropriations bill/proyecto de ley de asignación de fondos proyecto de ley que asigna dinero para gastos específicos (pág. 389)

arable/cultivable tierras adecuadas para cosechas (pág. 480)

arbitration/arbitraje técnica de acuerdo en la cual una tercera parte estudia un caso e impone una decisión final legalmente obligatoria para las dos partes en litigio (pág. 234)

articles of partnership/contrato de asociación acuerdo de asociación (pág. 191)

assets/activos dinero y otros haberes que pertenecen a un individuo o a una empresa (pág. 192)

authoritarian/autoritario que exige obediencia estricta a una autoridad, como por ejemplo, un dictador (pág. 35)

automatic stabilizers/estabilizadores automáticos beneficio estatal que cambia automáticamente según el PIB y los ingresos de un individuo (pág. 399)

B

balanced budget/presupuesto equilibrado presupuesto en el cual las entradas son iguales a los gastos (págs. 376, 403)

balance of trade/balanza comercial relación entre los productos que una nación importa y exporta (pág. 462)

bank/banco institución que recibe, guarda y presta dinero (pág. 250)

bank holding company/compañía tenedora de bancos compañía dueña de más de un banco (pág. 421)

bank run/pánico bancario pánico muy difundido durante el cual un gran número de personas intentan recuperar su dinero (pág. 252)

barrier to entry/barreras a la entrada cualquier factor que dificulta la entrada de una nueva empresa a un mercado (pág. 153)

barter/trueque o permuta intercambio directo de un grupo de productos o servicios por otro (pág. 243)

bear market/mercado de bajistas caída sostenida en la bolsa de valores durante cierto período de tiempo (pág. 290)

black market/mercado negro venta clandestina e ilegal de productos (pág. 142)

block grant/transferencia global fondos federales asignados a un estado en una suma global (pág. 350)

blue-collar worker/obrero persona que trabaja en una industria, a menudo la manufacturera, a cambio de un salario (pág. 231)

Board of Governors/Junta de Gobernadores consejo formado por siete miembros que supervisa el Sistema de la Reserva Federal (pág. 416)

bond/bono certificado emitido por el estado u otra corporación pública, la cual se compromete a reembolsar con interés la cantidad que pidió prestada al comprador (págs. 197, 507)

brokerage firm/oficina de corredores de bolsa empresa que se especializa en el comercio de valores (pág. 287)

budget/presupuesto registro de ingresos y gastos (pág. 502)

budget deficit/déficit presupuestario situación en la cual el estado gasta más de lo que recibe (pág. 403)

budget surplus/superávit presupuestario situación en la cual el estado recibe más de lo que gasta (pág. 403)

bull market/mercado de alcistas alza sostenida en la bolsa de valores durante cierto período de tiempo (pág. 290)

business association/sociedad no pecunaria organización sin fines de lucro que fomenta intereses comerciales colectivos para una ciudad, un estado u otra región geográfica, o para un grupo de empresas afines (pág. 204)

business cycle/ciclo económico período de expansión macroeconómica seguido por un período de contracción (págs. 57, 310)

business franchise/franquicia comercial empresa semi-independiente que paga derechos a una compañía matriz a cambio de los derechos exclusivos para vender cierto producto o servicio en una área determinada (pág. 201)

business license/licencia comercial permiso emitido por las autoridades locales para poder iniciar un negocio o empresa (pág. 186)

business organization/organización comercial establecimiento que se forma con el fin de llevar a cabo empresas comerciales (pág. 185)

C

call option/opción de compra opción para comprar acciones en un futuro determinado (pág. 288)

capital/capital cualquier recurso humano que se usa para producir otros bienes o servicios (pág. 4)

capital budget/presupuesto de capital presupuesto asignado para gastos o inversión de capital importantes (pág. 375)

capital deepening/aumento de capital aumento en la cantidad de capital por trabajador (pág. 320)

capital gain/ganancia de capital diferencia entre un precio de venta mayor y un precio de compra menor, que resulta en ganancias financieras para el vendedor (págs. 286, 508)

capital loss/pérdida de capital diferencia entre un precio de venta menor y un precio de compra mayor, que resulta en una pérdida financiera para el vendedor (pág. 286)

capital market/mercado de capitales mercado en el cual los préstamos financieros se otorgan por más de un año (pág. 283)

cartel/cartel agrupación formal de productores que convienen en coordinar la producción y los precios (pág. 171)

cash transfers/transferencias de efectivo pagos directos de dinero a personas de escasos recursos que reúnen los requisitos (pág. 69)

census/censo cuenta oficial de la población (pág. 334)

central bank/banco central banco que puede hacer préstamos a otros bancos en tiempos de adversidad (pág. 254)

centrally planned economy/economía de planificación centralizada sistema económico en el cual el gobierno central toma todas las decisiones sobre la producción y consumo de bienes y servicios (pág. 27)

certificate of incorporation/certificado de incorporación permiso para formar una sociedad anónima emitido por el estado (pág. 197)

ceteris paribus/ceteris paribus expresión en latín que significa "todo lo demás permanece inalterable" (pág. 85)

check clearing/liquidación de cheques operación bancaria en la cual se lleva un control tanto de la cuenta donde se retira dinero como de la cuenta donde se recibe dinero cuando se cobra un cheque (pág. 421)

check register/registro de cheques librito que se usa para llevar un control de las transacciones en las cuentas corrientes (pág. 504)

classical economics/economía clásica sistema económico o corriente de pensamiento que cree en la autorregulación de los mercados libres (pág. 395)

closely held corporation/corporación cerrada empresa que emite acciones sólo a unos cuantos individuos quienes son, a menudo, miembros de la familia (pág. 196)

collateral/garantía propiedad que se utiliza para garantizar u obtener un préstamo (pág. 513)

collective/granja colectiva granja que el estado arrienda a grupos de labradores (pág. 36)

collective bargaining/negociación colectiva proceso en el que tanto representantes de un sindicato como del patrón se reúnen para negociar un nuevo contrato laboral (pág. 233)

collusion/colusión acuerdo secreto entre empresas con el fin de dividir el mercado, fijar precios o limitar la producción (pág. 171)

command economy/economía dirigida sistema económico en el que el gobierno central toma todas las decisiones referentes a la producción y el consumo de bienes y servicios (pág. 27)

commercial bank/banco comercial banco que ofrece cuentas corrientes, de ahorro y del mercado de valores y que acepta depósitos a plazo (pág. 511)

commodity/producto básico producto que no cambia no importa quien lo produzca. Por ejemplo, el petróleo crudo, el papel para cuadernos o la leche (pág. 152)

commodity money/valor de materia prima productos que poseen valor propio y monetario (pág. 246)

common stock/acciones ordinarias acciones cuyos dividendos se basan en las fluctuaciones del mercado (pág. 508)

communism/comunismo sistema político que se caracteriza por una economía de planificación centralizada. Todo el poder económico y político descansa en las manos del gobierno central (pág. 35)

comparative advantage/ventaja comparativa capacidad que posee una persona o una nación para producir un artículo a un costo de oportunidad que es menor al de otra persona o nación (pág. 444)

competition/competencia el esfuerzo entre productores por obtener los dólares de los consumidores (págs. 31, 53)

complements/complementos dos bienes que se compran y venden juntos (pág. 88)

conglomerate/conglomerado fusión de más de tres empresas que fabrican productos muy diferentes (pág. 199)

Congressional Budget Office (CBO)/Agencia presupuestaria del Congreso organismo fiscal que proporciona información económica al Congreso (pág. 388)

consumer cooperative/cooperativa de consumidores mercado de ventas al detalle cuyos dueños y administradores son los consumidores mismos (pág. 203)

Consumer Price Index (CPI)/Índice de precios al consumidor (IPC) índice de precios que se determina al medir el precio de un grupo estándar de bienes los cuales representan la "canasta familiar" típica de un consumidor urbano (pág. 339)

consumer sovereignty/soberanía del consumidor facultad que tienen los consumidores de determinar lo que se debe producir (pág. 32)

contingent employment/empleo contingente trabajos temporales y trabajos parciales (pág. 215)

continuum/continuo extensión sin divisiones claras (pág. 43)

contract/contrato convenio legal obligatorio (pág. 523)

contraction/contracción período de depresión económica marcado por una baja real del producto interno bruto (pág. 310)

contractionary policies/políticas de austeridad políticas fiscales que disminuyen el crecimiento económico, como por ejemplo, la reducción de gastos y el aumento de impuestos (pág. 389)

cooperative/cooperativa sociedad comercial que se constituye entre productores, vendedores o consumidores, para el beneficio común de los socios (pág. 202)

copayment/copago porcentaje de cada visita o procedimiento médico que el paciente debe pagar de su propio bolsillo (pág. 525)

core inflation rate/índice de inflación básica el índice de inflación, excluidos los precios de los alimentos y la energía (pág. 340)

corporate bond/bono corporativo bono emitido por una sociedad o empresa anónima para recaudar fondos con el fin de expandir su actividad comercial (pág. 281)

corporate income tax/impuesto sobre ingresos corporativos impuesto sobre el valor de las ganancias de una corporación (pág. 360)

corporation/corporación o sociedad anónima entidad legal cuyos dueños son accionistas individuales (pág. 195)

cost/costo en términos económicos, el costo es una alternativa a la cual se renuncia como resultado de una decisión (pág. 16)

cost-push theory/teoría de costos teoría que afirma que el aumento de costos en los salarios y las materias primas provoca inflación (pág. 341)

Council of Economic Advisers (CEA)/Consejo de Asesores Económicos grupo de tres economistas distinguidos cuyo papel es asesorar al presidente en políticas económicas (pág. 400)

coupon rate/tipo de interés tasa de interés que el emisor de bonos debe pagar al tenedor de bonos (pág. 277)

credit/crédito cualquier forma de pagos diferidos (pág. 512)

credit bureau/agencia informativa sobre solvencia organismo que proporciona información sobre los hábitos de endeudamiento y pago de las personas (pág. 512)

credit card/tarjeta de crédito tarjeta con la que el portador puede comprar bienes y servicios a cambio de su promesa de pagar por ellos (pág. 261)

creditor/acreedor individuo o asociación a quien se le debe dinero (pág. 264)

credit rating/clasificación crediticia evaluación realizada por las agencias informativas sobre solvencia acerca de la historia crediticia total de un prestatario (pág. 512)

credit union/cooperativa de crédito organismos bancarios sin fines de lucro cuyos miembros son los dueños, los cuales suelen ser miembros de una organización o gremio individual (pág. 511)

crowding-out effect/efecto de desplazamiento pérdida de fondos para inversiones privadas debido a los fondos pedidos prestados por el gobierno (pág. 406)

currency/moneda monedas y billetes que se usan como dinero (pág. 245)

customs duty/derechos aduaneros impuesto que se aplica a ciertos artículos adquiridos en el extranjero (pág. 450)

cyclical unemployment/desempleo cíclico desempleo que aumenta durante períodos de contracción económica pero que disminuye cuando la economía mejora (pág. 333)

D

debit card/tarjeta de débito tarjeta que se utiliza para retirar dinero de una cuenta (pág. 263)

debt rescheduling/reajuste de los vencimientos de la deuda alargar el período de reembolso de la deuda y/o condonar o anular parte del préstamo (pág. 488)

deductible/deducible cantidad de gastos que se deben pagar en efectivo antes de que una aseguradora cubra cualquier gasto (pág. 524)

deductions/deducciones cantidad variable que una persona puede sustraer o deducir de sus ingresos brutos (pág. 366)

default/incumplimiento fallo en pagar una deuda (pág. 261)

deflation/deflación baja sostenida en el nivel general de precios (pág. 343)

demand/demanda el deseo de poseer algo y la capacidad de pagar por ello (pág. 79)

demand curve/curva de demanda representación gráfica de una tabla de demanda (pág. 82)

demand deposit/depósito a la vista dinero en una cuenta corriente (pág. 258)

demand-pull theory/teoría de la atracción de la demanda teoría que afirma que la inflación se produce por una gran demanda de productos y servicios (pág. 341)

demand schedule/tabla de demanda tabla que enumera la cantidad de un producto que una persona comprará a cada precio diferente (pág. 81)

demand-side economics/economía de demanda doctrina económica que afirma que el gasto fiscal y la reducción de impuestos ayudan a una economía mediante el aumento de la demanda (pág. 396)

depreciation/depreciación pérdida del valor de los bienes de capital debido a un desgaste normal o una devaluación de la moneda (págs. 305, 520)

depression/depresión recesión económica larga y severa (pág. 311)

deregulation/desregulación eliminación de algunas restricciones del gobierno para ciertos mercados (pág. 175)

derived demand/demanda derivada demanda que deriva de la demanda por otro servicio o bien (pág. 219)

developed nation/país desarrollado país que posee un promedio elevado de bienestar material (pág. 471)

development/desarrollo proceso por el cual una nación mejora el bienestar económico, político y social de su población (pág. 471)

differentiation/diferenciación hacer diferente un producto de otros productos semejantes (pág. 167)

diminishing marginal returns/rendimientos marginales decrecientes nivel de producción en el cual el producto de mano de obra marginal disminuye cuando el número de trabajadores se aumenta (pág. 109)

discount rate/tasa de descuento tasa que la Reserva Federal les cobra a los bancos comerciales por crédito de urgencia (pág. 422)

discouraged worker/trabajador desalentado persona que quiere un trabajo pero deja de buscarlo (pág. 336)

discretionary spending/gastos discrecionales categoría de gastos sobre los cuales pueden tomar decisiones los organismos de planificación del gobierno (pág. 371)

disequilibrium/desequilibrio describe cualquier precio o cantidad que no está equilibrada; cuando en el mercado la oferta no es igual a la demanda (pág. 126)

diversification/diversificación expansión de las inversiones con el fin de disminuir los riesgos (pág. 273)

dividend/dividendo parte de las ganancias de una empresa que les corresponde a los accionistas (págs. 198, 508)

The Dow/índice Dow Jones índice que muestra la compra y venta de ciertas acciones selectas (pág. 290)

durable goods/bienes duraderos productos que tienen un período de duración relativamente largo, como por ejemplo, los refrigeradores, los carros y los reproductores de DVD (pág. 302)

E

easy money policy/política de dinero abundante política monetaria que aumenta el medio circulante (pág. 431)

economic growth/crecimiento económico aumento sostenido y a largo plazo en el producto interno bruto (pág. 310)

economics/economía estudio de cómo los seres humanos buscan satisfacer sus necesidades y deseos mediante la toma de decisiones (pág. 3)

economic system/sistema económico método que utiliza una colectividad humana para producir y distribuir bienes y servicios (pág. 23)

economies of scale/economía de escala factores que provocan la caída de los costos medios de un productor conforme aumenta la producción (pág. 157)

efficiency/rendimiento uso eficaz de los recursos con el fin de maximizar la producción de bienes y servicios (pág. 15)

elastic/elástica describe la demanda que es muy sensible a la variación de precios (pág. 90)

elasticity of demand/elasticidad de la demanda medida de cómo reaccionan los consumidores a una variación de precio (pág. 90)

elasticity of supply/elasticidad de la oferta medida de cómo reacciona el volumen de la oferta a una variación de precio (pág. 104)

enterprise zone/zona empresarial área donde las compañías pueden operar libres de ciertos impuestos y restricciones locales, estatales y federales (pág. 350)

entitlement/derecho reglamentario programa que proporciona pagos a personas que cumplen ciertos requisitos, como por ejemplo, edad o ingresos (pág. 372)

entrepreneur/empresario líder con ambiciones que reúne factores como bienes, mano de obra y capital para crear y lanzar al mercado nuevos productos o servicios (pág. 6)

equilibrium/equilibrio económico el punto en el cual se nivelan la oferta y la demanda (pág. 125)

equilibrium wage/salario de equilibrio escala de salarios que no produce ni un número excesivo de trabajadores ni una demanda excesiva de trabajadores en el mercado laboral (pág. 220)

equities/acciones ordinarias título de propiedad en una sociedad anónima (pág. 285)

estate tax/impuesto sucesorio impuesto sobre la herencia, o valor total del dinero y la propiedad, de una persona que ha fallecido (pág. 368)

euro/euro nueva moneda que reemplaza las monedas individuales de las naciones de la Unión Europea (pág. 454)

European Union (EU)/Unión Europea (U.E.) organización mercantil regional formada por países europeos (pág. 454)

excess demand/exceso de demanda cuando el volumen de la demanda es mayor que el de la oferta (pág. 126)

excess reserves/reservas excedentes en las operaciones bancarias, reservas en efectivo mayores que las cantidades necesarias (pág. 427)

excess supply/exceso de oferta cuando el volumen de la oferta es mayor que el volumen de la demanda (pág. 128)

exchange rate/tipo de cambio valor de la moneda de un país en relación a la moneda de otros países (pág. 458)

excise tax/impuesto sobre el consumo impuesto sobre la producción o venta de un bien (pág. 118)

expansion/expansión período de desarrollo económico medido por un aumento en el producto interno bruto verdadero (pág. 310)

expansionary policies/políticas expansionistas políticas fiscales (tal como mayores gastos y reducción de impuestos) que estimulan el crecimiento económico (pág. 389)

export/artículo exportado producto que se vende a otro país (pág. 446)

externality/factor externo efecto secundario económico de un bien o servicio que genera beneficios o costos a alguien que no sea la persona que decide la cantidad de producción o de consumo (pág. 65)

F

factor market/mercado de factores mercado en el cual las compañías adquieren los factores de producción de las unidades familiares (pág. 29)

factor payments/pagos por factores los ingresos que un individuo recibe por suministrar factores de producción: bienes, mano de obra o capital (pág. 24)

factors of production/factores de producción bienes, mano de obra y capital; los tres grupos de recursos que concurren en la producción de todos los bienes y servicios (pág. 4)

featherbedding/prebendaje práctica de negociación de contratos laborales que mantienen en la planilla un número innecesario de trabajadores (pág. 227)

Federal Advisory Council (FAC)/Consejo Asesor Federal la autoridad de estudios de investigación de la Reserva Federal (pág. 418)

federal budget/presupuesto federal plan de entradas y gastos del gobierno federal para el año siguiente (pág. 387)

Federal Deposit Insurance Corporation (FDIC)/Agencia Aseguradora Federal de Depósitos agencia gubernamental que asegura los depósitos de los clientes en caso de una quiebra bancaria (pág. 255)

federal funds rate/tasa de fondos federales tasa de interés que los bancos se cobran entre sí por préstamos (pág. 422)

Federal Open Market Committee (FOMC)/Comité del Mercado Libre Federal comité de la Reserva Federal que toma decisiones clave sobre tasas de interés y el crecimiento del medio circulante de Estados Unidos (pág. 418)

Federal Reserve Districts/Distritos de la Reserva Federal los doce distritos bancarios creados por la Ley de la Reserva Federal (pág. 417)

Federal Reserve note/billetes de reserva federal dinero que actualmente circula en Estados Unidos (pág. 255)

Federal Reserve System/sistema bancario de la Reserva Federal el sistema bancario central de Estados Unidos (pág. 254)

fiat money/moneda fiduciaria dinero que posee valor porque el gobierno ha dispuesto que es un medio aceptable de pagar deudas (pág. 248)

FICA/FICA, Acta federal de contribuciones de seguros impuestos que financian el Seguro Social y *Medicare* (pág. 367)

finance charges/cargo por financiamiento interés que se acumula y derechos que se cobran por algunas formas de crédito (pág. 513)

financial asset/inmovilización financiera derecho sobre la propiedad o sobre los ingresos de un prestatario (pág. 272)

financial intermediary/intermediario financiero institución que ayuda a canalizar fondos de los ahorradores a los prestatarios (pág. 272)

financial system/sistema financiero sistema que permite el traspaso de dinero entre ahorradores y prestatarios (pág. 272)

firm/firma organización que utiliza recursos para fabricar un producto y luego venderlo (pág. 29)

fiscal policy/política fiscal normas tributarias y de gasto que aplica un gobierno con el fin de estabilizar la economía (pág. 387)

fiscal year/año fiscal período de doce meses que puede iniciarse en cualquier fecha (pág. 388)

fixed cost/costo fijo costo que no cambia sea cual sea la cantidad de producción (pág. 111)

fixed exchange-rate system/sistema de cambio fijo sistema monetario en el que un gobierno intenta mantener constante el valor de su moneda contra el de otros gobiernos (pág. 461)

fixed income/renta fija ingreso que no está sujeto a un aumento a un cuando los precios suben (pág. 343)

flexible exchange-rate system/sistema de cambio flexible sistema monetario que permite que la oferta y la demanda determinen el tipo de cambio (pág. 462)

food stamps/cupones de alimentos cupones que emite el gobierno y que se canjean por alimentos (pág. 348)

foreign direct investment/inversión extranjera directa compañía creada por extranjeros (pág. 486)

foreign exchange market/mercado de divisas bancos y otras instituciones financieras que facilitan la compra y venta de monedas extranjeras (pág. 460)

foreign investment/inversiones extranjeras inversiones provenientes de otros países (pág. 485)

foreign portfolio investment/inversión de cartera extranjera fondos que entran en un país cuando inversionistas extranjeros realizan adquisiciones en sus mercados de valores y bonos (pág. 486)

fractional reserve banking/operaciones bancarias de reserva fraccionada sistema bancario que mantiene sólo una fracción de los fondos y da prestado el resto (pág. 260)

franchise/franquicia derecho para vender un bien o un servicio dentro de un mercado exclusivo (pág. 159)

free contract/contrato libre concepto que define los acuerdos en los que quieren participar las personas (pág. 53)

free enterprise/libre empresa sistema económico que se caracteriza por la propiedad privada or corporativa sobre los bienes de capital; las inversiónes son determinadas por vías privadas y no por el gobierno; y determinada en un mercado libre (pág. 43)

free rider/aprovechador individuo que se niega a pagar por un bien o un servicio pero que toma los beneficios que éste ofrece si se le proporciona como un bien o servicio público (pág. 63)

free-trade zone/zona de libre comercio zona donde un grupo de países ha acordado disminuir las barreras comerciales entre sí (pág. 454)

frictional unemployment/desempleo friccional desempleo que surge cuando una persona busca otro trabajo (pág. 331)

fringe benefit /beneficios complementarios o extrasalariales pagos que se reciben además del sueldo o salario (pág. 188)

full employment/empleo pleno nivel de empleo que se alcanza cuando no existe el desempleo cíclico (pág. 335)

futures/futuros contratos de compra y venta en una fecha específica en el futuro a un precio específico actual (pág. 288)

G

general partnership/sociedad colectiva sociedad en la cual los socios comparten el mismo grado de responsabilidad (pág. 190)

gift tax/impuesto sobre donaciones y legados impuesto que una persona viva debe pagar sobre una donación monetaria valorada por sobre una cierta cantidad (pág. 368)

glasnost/glásnost política de apertura emprendida en la Unión Soviética a fines de la década de 1980 (pág. 491)

glass ceiling/techo de vidrio barrera invisible y oficiosa que impide que las mujeres y las minorías logren promociones o puedan superarse en organizaciones dominadas por hombres blancos (pág. 224)

gold standard/patrón oro sistema monetario en el cual billetes y monedas tienen igual valor a una cierta cantidad de oro (pág. 253)

goods/bienes objetos físicos como la ropa o los zapatos (pág. 3)

government monopoly/monopolio fiscal monopolio credo por el gobierno (pág. 159)

Great Crash/Quiebre de la Bolsa caída de la bolsa de valores en 1929 (pág. 290)

Great Depression/Gran Depresión grave crisis económica que empezó en 1929 y que duró más de una decada (pág. 255)

greenback/*greenback* papel moneda que emitió el Norte durante la Guerra Civil (pág. 253)

gross domestic product (GDP)/producto interno bruto (PIB) valor de todos los bienes y servicios finales producidos por un país dentro de su territorio en un año dado (págs. 57, 301)

gross national product (GNP)/producto nacional bruto (PNB) ingresos anuales de compañías y residentes norteamericanos (pág. 305)

guns or butter/armas o alimentos término que se refiere al dilema que enfrentan las naciones cuando deben decidir si producir una mayor o una menor cantidad de bienes militares o para el consumidor (pág. 8)

H

heavy industry/industria pesada industria que requiere grandes inversiones de capital y que produce artículos que se usan en otras industrias (pág. 37)

household/casa o unidad familiar persona o grupo de personas que viven juntos (pág. 29)

horizontal merger/fusión horizontal combinación de dos o más empresas de productos o servicios similares que compiten en el mismo mercado (pág. 199)

human capital/capital humano destrezas y conocimientos que adquiere un trabajador gracias a su educación y experiencia (pág. 5)

hyperinflation/hiperinflación inflación fuera de control (págs. 341, 404)

I

imperfect competition/competencia imperfecta estructura del mercado que no reúne las condiciones de una competencia perfecta (pág. 153)

import/artículo importado producto que se trae de otro país (pág. 446)

import quota/cuota de importación límite sobre la cantidad que se puede importar de un producto (pág. 449)

incentive/incentivo estímulo que mueve a una persona a comportarse de cierta manera (pág. 31)

incidence of a tax/incidencia de los impuestos peso final de un impuesto (pág. 363)

income distribution/distribución de ingresos la manera en que los ingresos totales de un país se distribuyen entre la población (pág. 348)

income effect/efecto de ingreso cambio en el consumo debido a un cambio en los ingresos reales (pág. 80)

increasing marginal returns/rendimiento marginal creciente nivel de producción en el que el producto de mano de obra marginal crece cuando el número de trabajadores se aumenta (pág. 109)

individual income tax/contribución individual sobre ingresos impuesto sobre los ingresos de una persona (pág. 360)

industrialization/industrialización organización extensiva de una economía para la elaboración de bienes (pág. 472)

inelastic/inelástica o fija describe la demanda que no es muy sensible a una variación de precios (pág. 90)

infant industry/industria naciente industria nueva (pág. 452)

infant mortality rate/tasa de mortalidad infantil número de muertes que ocurren en el primer año de vida por cada mil bebés nacidos vivos (pág. 474)

inferior good/bien o producto subordinado bien o producto que sufre una menor demanda cuando aumentan los ingresos de los consumidores (pág. 87)

inflation/inflación alza general de precios (pág. 338)

inflation rate/índice de inflación cambio porcentual en el nivel de precios en un período de tiempo (pág. 340)

infrastructure/infraestructura servicios e instalaciones que son necesarios para el funcionamiento de una economía (pág. 474)

in-kind benefits/beneficios en especie bienes y servicios gratis o a precios muy reducidos (pág. 70)

inside lag/demora interna retraso en la implementación de políticas monetarias (pág. 432)

interest/interés precio que se paga por el uso de dinero prestado (pág. 261), o, dinero que ganan los fondos depositados (pág. 506)

interest group/grupo de intereses agrupación privada que intenta persuadir a funcionarios públicos de que tomen medidas o voten a favor de los intereses de los miembros del grupo (pág. 54)

intermediate goods/bienes intermedios bienes utilizados en la producción de bienes finales (pág. 301)

internal financing/autofinanciación financiación que proviene de los ahorros de los ciudadanos de un país (pág. 485)

Internal Revenue Service/Servicio de Impuestos Internos organismo del Ministerio de Hacienda de Estados Unidos responsable de la interpretación y aplicación del derecho tributario federal (pág. 528)

international free trade agreement/tratado internacional de libre comercio acuerdo que resulta de la cooperación de un mínimo de dos países para eliminar barreras e impuestos comerciales en el comercio mutuo (pág. 453)

International Monetary Fund (IMF)/Fondo Monetario Internacional (F.M.I.) organismo cuyo fin es garantizar la estabilidad de los tipos de cambio internacionales y facilitar el desarrollo (pág. 488)

investment/inversión la acción de cambiar el uso de los recursos para evitar consumirlos hoy de modo que puedan crear beneficios en el futuro; el uso de activos para obtener ingresos o utilidades (pág. 271)

invisible hand/mano invisible término usado por economistas para describir la naturaleza autorreguladora del mercado (pág. 32)

J

junk bond/bono de calidad inferior bono de precio menor pero que potencialmente puede rendir un pago mayor (pág. 281)

K

Keynesian economics/economía keynesiana tipo de economía de demanda que fomenta la acción del gobierno con el fin de aumentar o disminuir la demanda y la producción (pág. 396)

L

labor/trabajo esfuerzo que se dedica a una tarea por la cual una persona es remunerada (pág. 4)

labor force/mano de obra o fuerza de trabajo todos los individuos civiles (excluyendo las fuerzas militares) que están empleados o desempleados (pág. 211)

labor union/sindicato obrero agrupación de trabajadores cuyo objetivo es mejorar las condiciones laborales, los salarios y los beneficios de sus miembros; también conocido como gremio (pág. 225)

laissez faire/política de mínima interferencia o laissez faire doctrina que afirma que, por lo general, el gobierno no debe interferir en el mercado (pág. 41)

land/tierras recursos naturales que se usan en la producción de bienes y servicios (pág. 4)

law of comparative advantage/ley de la ventaja comparativa ley que afirma que las naciones están en mejores condiciones cuando producen bienes y servicios que les signifícan una ventaja comparativa al ofrecerlos en el mercado (pág. 444)

law of demand/ley de la demanda ley que afirma que los consumidores compran una mayor cantidad de un producto cuando su precio disminuye y una menor cantidad cuando su precio aumenta (pág. 79)

law of increasing costs/ley de costos crecientes cuando ocurre un cambio en los factores de producción en la elaboración de un bien o un servicio a otro, esto significa el aumento del costo de producción del segundo bien o servicio (pág. 17)

law of supply/ley de la oferta tendencia de los proveedores a ofrecer una cantidad mayor de un producto a un precio más alto (pág. 101)

leading indicators/indicadores anticipados variables económicas clave que utilizan los economistas para pronosticar una fase nueva del ciclo comercial (pág. 314)

learning effect/efecto del aprendizaje teoría que afirma que la educación aumenta la productividad, lo que resulta en salarios más altos (pág. 214)

lease/arrendamiento acuerdo de renta entre un propietario y un arrendatario (pág. 523)

legal equality/igualdad legal dar a cada persona los mismos derechos legales (pág. 53)

less developed country/país menos desarrollado nación con un nivel bajo de bienestar material (pág. 471)

liability/responsabilidad (legal) obligación con fuerza legal para pagar una deuda (pág. 187)

license/permiso autorización emitida por el gobierno para conducir un negocio (pág. 159)

life expectancy/expectativa de vida promedio de vida que se espera de un individuo (pág. 473)

light industry/industria ligera producción de bienes de consumo pequeños (pág. 494)

limited liability partnership (LLP)/sociedad de responsabilidad limitada sociedad comercial en la que todos los socios son socios colectivos (pág. 190)

limited partnership/sociedad en comandita simple sociedad comercial en la que se requiere que solamente uno de los socios sea un socio colectivo (pág. 190)

liquidity/liquidez capacidad de usar o de convertir directamente en efectivo (pág. 258)

literacy rate/índice de analfabetismo porcentaje de la población que no sabe ni leer ni escribir (pág. 473)

Lorenz Curve/curva Lorenz curva gráfica que muestra ingresos totales y que ilustra la distribución del ingreso (pág. 349)

M

macroeconomics/macroeconomía estudio del comportamiento y de la toma de decisiones de economías completas (pág. 57)

malnutrition/desnutrición alimentación deficiente (pág. 481)

mandatory spending/gastos obligatorios gastos requeridos por ley para efectuarse sobre ciertos programas (pág. 371)

marginal cost/costo límite o marginal costo de producir una unidad más de un bien (pág. 111)

marginal product of labor/producto de mano de obra marginal cambio en producción que resulta al contratar una unidad adicional de mano de obra (pág. 108)

marginal revenue/ingresos marginales ingreso adicional que resulta al producir una unidad más de un bien; por lo general, es igual al precio (pág. 112)

market/mercado convenio que permite que compradores y vendedores intercambien cosas (pág. 28)

market basket/cesta de compras colección representativa de bienes y servicios (pág. 339)

market demand schedule/cuadro de la demanda del mercado tabla que enumera la cantidad de un bien que comprarán todos los consumidores de un mercado a precios diferentes (pág. 82)

market economy/economía de mercado sistema económico en el que las decisiones sobre producción y consumo de bienes y servicios se basan en intercambios voluntarios en los mercados (pág. 27)

market failure/fracaso del mercado situación en la cual el mercado no distribuye los recursos de manera eficaz (pág. 64)

market power/poder de mercado capacidad de una empresa de cambiar precios y producción como si fuera un monopolio (pág. 163)

market supply curve/curva de oferta del mercado gráfica que muestra el volumen de la oferta de todos los proveedores en todos los niveles de precios (pág. 104)

market supply schedule/cuadro de oferta del mercado tabla que enumera la cantidad de un bien que ofrecen todos los proveedores a precios diferentes (pág. 103)

maturity/vencimiento fecha en que se vence el pago a un tenedor de bonos (pág. 277)

mediation/mediación técnica de arreglo en la que un mediador neutral se reúne con cada parte en litigio para hallar una solución, sin imponérsela (pág. 234)

Medicaid/*Medicaid* programa de derecho reglamentario que beneficia a familias de bajos ingresos, a personas discapacitadas y a personas de edad avanzada que viven en hogares de ancianos (pág. 373)

Medicare/*Medicare* programa nacional de seguro médico que ayuda a pagar el cuidado de salud para personas mayores de 65 años o que sufren de alguna invalidez (pág. 368)

medium of exchange/medio de cambio cualquier cosa que se usa como medida de valor durante el intercambio de bienes y servicios (pág. 243)

member bank/banco afiliado banco que pertenece al Sistema de Reserva Federal (pág. 254)

merger/fusión unión de dos o más compañías en una sola empresa (pág. 174)

microeconomics/microeconomía estudio del comportamiento económico y de la toma de decisiones de unidades pequeñas, como por ejemplo, individuos, familias y negocios (pág. 57)

minimum balance/balance mínimo cantidad de dinero que se requiere en una cuenta bancaria para evitar comisión y gastos por servicio (pág. 504)

minimum wage/salario mínimo precio mínimo que puede pagar un patrón a un empleado por hora de trabajo (pág. 130)

mixed economy/economía mixta sistema económico que mezcla el sistema tradicional y el mercado libre con una participación mínima del gobierno (pág. 27)

monetarism/monetarismo creencia de que el volumen de la masa monetaria es el factor más importante en el rendimiento macroeconómico (pág. 430)

monetary policy/política monetaria medida que lleva a cabo la Reserva Federal para influir sobre el nivel del producto interno bruto real y la tasa de inflación en la economía (pág. 417)

money/dinero cualquier cosa que sirve como medio de cambio, unidad de cuenta y reserva de valor (pág. 243)

money creation/poner el dinero en circulación proceso por el cual el dinero entra en circulación (pág. 425)

money market/mercado monetario mercado en el cual se presta dinero por períodos menores de un año (pág. 283)

money market mutual fund/fondo común de inversiones fondo que atrae dinero de ahorradores pequeños para adquirir bonos del gobierno o de sociedades anónimas a corto plazo (pág. 259)

money multiplier formula/fórmula multiplicadora de dinero cantidad de dinero nuevo que se crea con cada depósito a la vista, calculada como 1 ÷ CRR (coeficiente de reservas requerido) (pág. 426)

money supply/masa monetaria todo el dinero disponible en la economía de Estados Unidos (pág. 258)

monopolistic competition/competencia monopolista estructura del mercado en la cual muchas empresas venden productos semejantes pero no idénticos (pág. 166)

monopoly/monopolio mercado controlado por un solo vendedor (pág. 156)

mortgage/hipoteca tipo específico de préstamo que se usa para comprar bienes raíces (pág. 261)

multinational corporation/corporación multinacional empresa o grupo industrial o financiero que vende sus bienes y servicios en distintas partes del mundo (pág. 199)

multiplier effect/efecto multiplicador la idea de que cada dólar invertido crea más de un dólar de actividad económica (pág. 397)

municipal bond/bono municipal bono emitido por un gobierno o una municipalidad estatal o local para financiar mejoras a carreteras, edificios, bibliotecas, parques y escuelas (pág. 281)

mutual fund/fondo mutuo fondo constituído por los ahorros de muchos inversionistas y que invierteeste dinero en una diversidad de valores y bonos (págs. 272, 509)

N

NAFTA/Tratado de Libre Comercio (T.L.C.) convenio que elimina todos los aranceles y otras barreras comerciales entre Canadá, México y Estados Unidos (pág. 454)

Nasdaq/Nasdaq (por sus siglas en inglés para National Association of Securities Dealers Automated Quotation System y American Stock Exchange Inc.) mercado que se especializa en valores de alta tecnología y energía americanos (pág. 288)

national bank/banco nacional banco registrado por el gobierno nacional (pág. 251)

national debt/deuda nacional todo el dinero que el gobierno federal les debe a los tenedores de bonos (pág. 405)

national income accounting/contabilidad del ingreso nacional sistema que reúne estadísticas macroeconómicas sobre producción, ingresos, inversiones y ahorros (pág. 301)

natural monopoly/monopolio natural mercado que opera con mucha eficacia cuando una empresa mayor suministra toda la producción (pág. 158)

natural rate of population increase/índice demográfico diferencia entre la tasa de nacimientos y la tasa de mortalidad (pág. 478)

need/necesidad algo como, por ejemplo, el aire, los alimentos o un refugio que es necesario para la supervivencia (pág. 3)

net worth/valor o activo neto activos totales menos pasivos totales (pág. 422)

newly industrialized country (NIC)/país recientemente industrializado país menos desarrollado que ha demostrado mejoras significativas en las medidas de desarrollo (pág. 475)

nominal GDP/PIB nominal producto interno bruto que se mide en precios actuales (pág. 304)

nondurable goods/bienes perecederos bienes de duración relativamente corta. Ejemplos: alimentos, bombillos de luz y zapatos tenis (pág. 302)

nonprice competition/competencia no basada en precio manera de atraer a clientes mediante estilo, servicio o ubicación, pero no a un precio menor (pág. 167)

nonprofit organization/organización sin fines de lucro empresa que funciona en forma muy parecida a una empresa comercial pero que no opera con el fin de generar ganancias (pág. 203)

normal good/producto o bien normal bien que disfruta de una mayor demanda de los consumidores cuando los ingresos de éstos aumentan (pág. 86)

O

Office of Management and Budget (OMB)/Dirección de Administración y Presupuesto agencia gubernamental que administra el presupuesto federal (pág. 388)

oligopoly/oligopolio estructura del mercado en la que unas cuantas empresas mayores controlan un mercado (pág. 169)

open market operations/operaciones de mercado abierto compra y venta de títulos del Estado con el fin de alterar el medio circulante (pág. 428)

open opportunity/oportunidad abierta concepto que define la posibilidad de que todos puedan competir en el mercado (pág. 53)

operating budget/presupuesto operativo presupuesto para los gastos diarios (pág. 375)

operating cost/gastos de operación costo de operación de una instalación como, por ejemplo, una tienda o una fábrica (pág. 113)

opportunity cost/costo de oportunidad alternativa más deseada a la que se ha renunciado como resultado de una decisión (pág. 9)

options/opciones contratos que les proporcionan a los inversionistas la opción de comprar o vender valores y otros activos financieros (pág. 288)

OTC market/mercado extrabursátil mercado electrónico para valores que no aparecen o que no se comercializan en una bolsa organizada (pág. 288)

outside lag/demora externa tiempo que tarda una política monetaria en entrar un efecto (pág. 432)

P

partnership/sociedad personal organización comercial de dos o más personas que convienen en una repartición específica de responsabilidades y ganancias (pág. 190)

par value/valor a la par cantidad que se debe pagar a un inversionista de bonos cuando el bono se vence, sin tener en cuenta el interés (pág. 278)

patent/patente derecho que concede al inventor de un producto nuevo su venta exclusiva, durante un determinado período de tiempo (pág. 159)

patriotism/patriotismo el amor por el propio país; la pasión que inspira a una persona a servir a su país (pág. 25)

payroll witholding statement/estado de cuenta de retención de nómina documento adherido al cheque de pago que indiqua la suma retenida (pág. 310)

peak/apogeo el punto más alto de una expansión económica, cuando el producto interno bruto real deja de aumentar (pág. 310)

per capita gross domestic product (per capita GDP)/producto interno bruto per cápita (PIB per cápita) el producto interno bruto de una nación dividido por su población total (pág. 472)

perestroika/perestroika plan económico puesto en marcha por el líder soviético Mikhail Gorbachev para llevar a cabo una reforma económica (pág. 492)

perfect competition/competencia perfecta estructura del mercado en la que un vasto número de empresas elaboran el mismo producto (pág. 151)

personal exemption/exención personal una suma que resta una persona de sus ingresos brutos para si mismo, su esposo, y unos dependientes (pág. 366)

personal property/bienes personales pertenencias como joyas, muebles y embarcaciones (pág. 378)

physical capital/bienes materiales todos los bienes producidos por el ser humano que se utilizan en la producción de otros bienes y servicios; herramientas y edificios (pág. 4)

population growth rate/tasa de crecimiento demográfico aumento en la población de un país en un año determinado, expresado como porcentaje de la cifra de habitantes al comienzo del año (pág. 478)

portfolio/cartera conjunto de activos financieros (pág. 274)

poverty rate/índice de pobreza porcentaje de un grupo de la población que vive en casas con ingresos por debajo del nivel de pobreza oficial (pág. 346)

poverty threshold/umbral de pobreza nivel de ingresos bajo el cual los ingresos son insuficientes para poder mantener a una familia (págs. 67, 345)

predatory pricing/precio para eliminar competidores vender un producto bajo costo para alejar a los competidores del mercado (pág. 173)

preferred stock/acciones preferentes acciones cuyos dividendos se basan en una tasa anual fija (pág. 508)

premium/prima dinero que se paga a una compañía aseguradora por una póliza (pág. 524)

price ceiling/tope de precios precio máximo que se puede pagar por un bien o un servicio (pág. 128)

price discrimination/discriminación de precios división de clientes en grupos según la cantidad de dinero que pagarán por un producto (pág. 163)

price fixing/fijación de precios convenio entre empresas para cobrar un precio por el mismo producto (pág. 171)

price floor/precio mínimo precio más bajo que se debe pagar por un bien o un servicio (pág. 128)

price index/índice de precios medida que muestra cómo cambia con el tiempo el precio promedio de un grupo estándar de bienes (pág. 339)

price level/nivel de precios promedio de todos los precios en una economía (pág. 307)

price war/guerra de precios serie de rebaja de precios que reduce el precio del mercado por debajo del costo de producción (pág. 171)

primary market/mercado primario mercado de venta de activos financieros que sólo el tenedor original puede redimir (pág. 283)

prime rate/tasa de interés preferencial tasa de interés que cobran los bancos a sus mejores clientes cuando éstos solicitan préstamos a corto plazo (pág. 427)

principal/capital o principal cantidad de dinero que se presta (pág. 261)

private property/propiedad privada la propiedad que poseen los individuos o las compañías, no el gobierno o el conjunto del pueblo (pág. 41)

private property rights/derecho a la propiedad privada concepto que define el derecho y privilegio de las personas a controlar sus posesiones como deseen (pág. 53)

private sector/sector privado parte de la economía que envuelve las transacciones de individuos y de empresas (pág. 63)

privatization/privatización venta o traspaso de empresas estatales al sector privado (pág. 489)

privatize/privatizar vender al sector privado empresas estatales, las cuales pueden competir entre sí en el mercado (pág. 43)

producer cooperative/cooperativa de producción cooperativas de comercialización agrícola que ayudan a sus miembros a vender sus productos (pág. 203)

product market/mercado de productos mercado en el cual las personas compran los bienes y servicios que producen las empresas (pág. 30)

production possibilities curve/curva de posibilidades de producción gráfica que muestra maneras alternativas para usar los recursos de una economía (pág. 13)

production possibilities frontier/límite de posibilidades de producción en una gráfica de posibilidades de producción, la línea que muestra la producción máxima posible para una economía específica (pág. 14)

productive capacity/capacidad de producción producción máxima que puede realizar una economía sin grandes alzas inflacionarias (pág. 396)

productivity/productividad valor de producción efectuada (pág. 219)

professional labor/trabajo profesional trabajo que requiere destrezas y educación avanzadas (pág. 221)

professional organization /organización profesional agrupación sin fines de lucro cuyo objetivo es mejorar la imagen, las condiciones laborales y los niveles de destrezas de individuos de un determinado oficio (pág. 203)

profit/ganancias utilidades financieras que se producen en una transacción (pág. 29)

profit motive/ánimo de lucro la fuerza que anima a las personas y organizaciones a mejorar sus condiciones materiales (pág. 53)

progressive tax/impuesto progresivo impuesto para el cual el porcentaje de ingresos que se paga en impuestos aumenta conforme lo hacen los ingresos (pág. 361)

property tax/impuesto de la propiedad impuesto sobre el valor de una propiedad (pág. 361)

proportional tax/impuesto proporcional impuesto en el que el porcentaje de ingresos que se paga es inalterable para todos los niveles de ingresos (pág. 361)

prospectus/prospecto informe de inversiones para inversionistas potenciales (pág. 274)

protectionism/proteccionismo uso de restricciones comerciales con el fin de proteger las industrias de un país de la competencia extranjera (pág. 452)

public disclosure laws/leyes de divulgación pública reglas que obligan a las empresas a proporcionar información sobre sus productos (pág. 54)

public good/bien público bien o servicio compartido que no sería práctico que los consumidores pagaran individualmente ni excluir a los que no pagan (pág. 62)

public interest/interés público inquietudes del público en general (pág. 54)

publicly held corporation/empresa pública compañía que vende valores en el mercado libre (pág. 196)

public sector/sector público parte de la economía que implica las transacciones del gobierno (pág. 63)

purchasing power/poder adquisitivo capacidad de comprar bienes y servicios (pág. 339)

put option/opción de venta opción para vender acciones en un tiempo determinado en el futuro (pág. 288)

Q

quantity supplied/volumen de oferta cantidad que un proveedor está dispuesto a, y es capaz de, producir a un precio determinado (pág. 101)

quantity theory/teoría cuantitativa del dinero teoría que afirma que demasiado dinero en la economía produce inflación (pág. 341)

R

rationing/racionamiento sistema para asignar o distribuir bienes y servicios escasos pero sin considerar los precios (pág. 141)

real GDP/PIB real producto interno bruto expresado en precios constantes o invariables (pág. 304)

real GDP per capita /PIB real per cápita producto interno bruto real dividido por la población total (pág. 319)

real property/bienes inmuebles propiedades físicas como tierras y edificios (pág. 378)

recession/recesión contracción prolongada de la economía (pág. 311)

regressive tax/impuesto regresivo impuesto para el cual el porcentaje de ingresos que se paga en impuestos disminuye conforme aumentan los ingresos (pág. 361)

regulation/regulación intervención del gobierno en un mercado que afecta la producción de un bien (pág. 118)

rent control/congelación de rentas precio máximo que se asigna a los alquileres (pág. 129)

representative money/dinero representativo artículos que poseen valor porque el tenedor puede intercambiarlos por otro objeto de valor (pág. 247)

required reserve ratio (RRR)/coeficiente de reserva requerido (CRR) coeficiente de reservas para los depósitos en los bancos requerido por la Reserva Federal (pág. 425)

résumé/resumé documento que resume la experiencia laboral, los estudios realizados y otros datos que califican a una persona, y que necesita saber un patrón potencial (pág. 526)

return/ganancia dinero que recibe un inversionista mucho más allá de la suma de dinero que invirtió inicialmente (pág. 274)

revenue/ingresos rentas públicas que recibe el gobierno por concepto de impuestos y otras fuentes exentas de impuestos (pág. 359)

right-to-work law/ley sobre libertad laboral medida que prohibe el ingreso obligatorio a un sindicato (pág. 231)

royalty/regalía participación de ganancias dada como pago (pág. 202)

S

S & P 500/*S & P 500* (por sus siglas en inglés para Standard and Poor's Corporation) índice que representa los precios de 500 valores diferentes (pág. 290)

safety net/red de asistencia: programas del gobierno que protegen a las personas que pasan por condiciones económicas adversas (pág. 26)

sales tax/impuesto sobre las ventas impuesto sobre el valor del dólar de un bien o producto en venta (pág. 360)

saving/ahorros ingresos que no se usan para el consumo (pág. 320)

savings account/cuenta de ahorros cuenta bancaria que se usa para depositar dinero que se pudiera necesitar en un tiempo relativamente corto (pág. 506)

savings and loans associations/sociedades de ahorro y préstamo bancos que aceptan depósitos y que se especializan en financiamientos a largo plazo (pág. 511)

savings bank/caja de ahorros banco que acepta depósitos y que se especializa en inversiones de bajo riesgo (pág. 511)

savings bond/bono de ahorro bono de bajo valor emitido por el gobierno de Estados Unidos (pág. 280)

savings rate/tasa de ahorros proporción de los ingresos disponibles gastados a los ingresos ahorrados (pág. 320)

scarcity/escasez cantidades limitadas de recursos para poder satisfacer necesidades ilimitadas (pág. 4)

screening effect/efecto pantalla teoría que afirma que completar los estudios universitarios les indica a los patrones que un candidato a un puesto es una persona inteligente y trabajadora (pág. 214)

search costs/costos de indagación costos financieros y de oportunidad que pagan los consumidores cuando buscan un bien o un servicio (pág. 136)

seasonal unemployment/desempleo estacional desempleo que ocurre como resultado de cosechas programadas, días festivos y vacaciones o cuando las industrias reducen sus actividades o cierran por una temporada (pág. 332)

secondary market/mercado secundario mercado para la reventa de activos financieros (pág. 283)

Securities and Exchange Commission/Comisión del Mercado de Valores organismo independiente del gobierno que regula los mercados financieros y las compañías inversionistas (pág. 281)

security deposit/depósito de garantía suma de dinero que se paga a un arrendador con el fin de asegurar que los bienes se devuelvan en las mismas condiciones que tenían al momento de arrendarse (pág. 522)

self-interest/interés propio ganancia personal propia (pág. 31)

semi-skilled labor/mano de obra semicalificada mano de obra que requiere educación y destrezas de especialización mínimas (pág. 221)

service cooperative/cooperativa de servicios cooperativa que proporciona un servicio en lugar de un bien o producto (pág. 203)

services/servicios medidas o actividades que una persona realiza para otra (pág. 3)

share/acción parte de valores o títulos (pág. 285)

shortage/insuficiencia situación en la cual un bien o un servicio no se encuentra disponible (pág. 4), o una situación en la cual el volumen de demanda es mayor que el volumen de oferta (pág. 136)

skilled labor/mano de obra calificada mano de obra que requiere educación y destrezas especializadas (pág. 221)

socialism/socialismo filosofía social y política que se basa en la creencia de que se deben utilizar medios democráticos para distribuir la riqueza uniformemente en una sociedad (pág. 35)

Social Security (OASDI)/Seguro Social Seguro de edad avanzada, sobrevivientes y invalidez (pág. 367)

sole proprietorship/negocio propio negocio que pertenece a una sola persona, la cual lo administra (pág. 185)

special economic zones/zonas económicas especiales regiones designadas en China donde se fomenta la inversión extranjera, las empresas pueden tomar la mayoría de sus propias decisiones sobre inversiones y producción y donde se permite que operen las compañías extranjeras (pág. 494)

specialization/especialización concentración de los esfuerzos productivos de individuos y de empresas en un número limitado de actividades (pág. 29)

speculation/especulación práctica de realizar inversiones de alto riesgo con dinero prestado con la esperanza de lograr grandes ganancias (pág. 290)

spillover costs/costos indirectos costos de producción que influyen sobre las personas que no tienen ningún control sobre la manera en que se produce un bien (pág. 144)

stabilization program/programa de estabilización convenio entre una nación deudora y el FMI (Fondo Monetario Internacional) por el cual la nación acuerda revisar su política económica (pág. 488)

standard of living/nivel de vida nivel de prosperidad económica (pág. 26)

stagflation/estanflación disminución del PIB real conjuntamente con un aumento del nivel de precios (pág. 311)

start-up costs/costos iniciales gastos que debe pagar una empresa antes de poder producir y vender bienes (pág. 153)

stock/valores o títulos acción que representa una parte de la participación accionaria en una sociedad anónima (págs. 195, 507)

stock exchange/bolsa de valores mercado para la compra y venta de valores (pág. 287)

stock split/división de acciones división de una acción en más de una (pág. 286)

stockbroker/corredor o agente de bolsa persona que es el vínculo entre compradores y vendedores de valores (pág. 286)

store of value/reserva de valor algo que mantiene su valor si se guarda en lugar de usarlo (pág. 244)

strike/huelga paro organizado de trabajadores cuyo objetivo es obligar a un patrón a considerar peticiones sindicales (pág. 229)

structural unemployment/desempleo estructural o endémico desempleo que ocurre cuando las destrezas que poseen los trabajadores no coinciden con los trabajos disponibles (pág. 332)

subsidized loans/préstamos subvencionados préstamos en los cuales gobierno paga el interés mientras el estudiante asiste a la escuela o la universidad (pág. 518)

subsidy/subvención ayuda económica que otorga el gobierno para auxiliar una empresa o un mercado (pág. 117)

subsistence agriculture/agricultura de subsistencia nivel de agricultura en el cual una persona produce sólo los alimentos suficientes para alimentar a su familia (pág. 472)

substitutes/substitutos productos que se usan en lugar de otros (pág. 88)

substitution effect/efecto de substitución cuando los consumidores reaccionan a un alza en el precio de un producto consumiendo una menor cantidad de ese producto y una mayor cantidad de otros productos (pág. 80)

supply/oferta la cantidad de bienes disponible (pág. 101)

supply curve/curva de la oferta gráfica del volumen de oferta de un producto en cada precio posible (pág. 104)

supply schedule/cuadro de oferta tabla que muestra una lista de la cantidad de un producto que un proveedor ofrecerá a precios diferentes (pág. 103)

supply shock/contracción de la oferta escasez repentina de un producto (pág. 141)

supply-side economics/economía de oferta doctrina económica que establece que una reducción de los impuestos puede ayudar a la economía al aumentar la oferta (pág. 399)

surplus/superávit situación en la cual el volumen de oferta es mayor que el volumen de demanda; oferta excedente (pág. 134)

T

tariff/arancel aduanero impuesto sobre los bienes importados (págs. 369, 450)

tax/impuesto pago obligatorio a un gobierno local, estatal o nacional (pág. 359)

taxable income/ingreso imponible ingresos sobre los cuales se debe pagar impuestos; ingresos totales menos las exenciones y deducciones (pág. 366)
tax assessor/tasador de impuestos oficial que evalúa propiedades (pág. 380)
tax base/base imponible ingresos, propiedad, bien o servicio sujetos a impuestos (pág. 360)
tax exempt/exento de impuestos no sujeto a pagar impuestos (pág. 377)
tax incentive/incentivo de impuesto el uso de los impuestos para alentar o desalentar ciertas acciónes específicas (pág. 369)
tax return/declaración de impuestos formulario que utiliza una persona para presentar los impuestos sobre sus ingresos (pág. 366)
technological progress/progreso tecnológico aumento que se logra en el rendimiento al producir más sin usar más recursos (pág. 322)
technology/tecnología proceso que se usa para producir un bien o un servicio (pág. 59)
thinking at the margin/pensar en el margen decidir si se debe hacer o usar una unidad adicional de algún recurso (pág. 10)
tight money policy/política de dinero escaso política monetaria que reduce el medio circulante (pág. 431)
time deposit/depósito a plazo depósito que ofrece interés garantizado durante un período de tiempo fijo (pág. 506)
total cost/costo total costos fijos más costos variables (pág. 111)
total revenue/total de ingresos cantidad total de dinero que recibe una empresa al vender bienes o servicios (pág. 95)
trade association/asociación mercantil organismo sin fines de lucro que fomenta los intereses de una industria en particular (pág. 204)
trade barrier/barrera comercial medios para evitar que un producto o servicio extranjero entre libremente al territorio de una nación (pág. 449)
trade deficit/déficit de la balanza comercial resultado de un país importar más de lo que exporta (pág. 462)
trade-off/concesión mutua alternativa que sacrificamos cuando tomamos una decisión (pág. 8)
trade surplus/superávit de la balanza comercial resultado de un país exportar más de lo que importa (pág. 462)
trade war/guerra comercial ciclo que ocurre cuando un país restringe las importaciones y su socio comercial impone sus propias restricciones (pág. 451)
traditional economy/economía tradicional sistema económico que descansa en hábitos, costumbres y normas para tomar decisiones sobre la producción y consumo de bienes y servicios (pág. 26)
transition/transición período de cambios en el cual una economía se aleja de una economía dirigida o planificada para acercarse a un sistema de mercado (pág. 43)
Treasury bill/obligación del Tesoro a corto plazo bono del gobierno pagadero entre tres meses a un año (pág. 405)
Treasury bond/bono del Tesoro a largo plazo bono del gobierno que se puede emitir hasta 30 años (pág. 405)
Treasury note/pagaré del Tesoro bono del gobierno pagadero entre dos a diez años (pág. 405)
trough/depresión punto más bajo en una contracción económica cuando el producto bruto nacional real deja de caer (pág. 311)
trust/consorcio monopolista agrupación ilegal de compañías que desalientan la competencia (pág. 173)
Truth in Savings Act/Ley de divulgación de información sobre intereses ley federal que dispone que los bancos deben divulgar a sus clientes información pertinente a las cuentas que ofrece el banco que producen intereses (pág. 507)
Truth in Lending laws/leyes de divulgación de información sobre préstamos reglamentos que disponen que las instituciones que otorgan préstamos deben divulgar cargos por financiamiento exactos, tasas de interés mensual, tasas de porcentaje annual y métodos que se utilizan en el cálculo de los cargos por financiamiento (pág. 515)
tuition/matrícula costo de la enseñanza (pág. 516)

U

underemployed/subempleado trabajar en un puesto para el cual la persona está sobrecalificada, o trabajar medio tiempo cuando se desea trabajar tiempo completo (pág. 335)
underutilization/subutilización usar menos recursos de lo que una economía puede usar (pág. 15)
unemployment rate/tasa de desempleo porcentaje de la mano de obra del país que se encuentra desempleada (pág. 334)
Uniform Partnership Act (UPA)/Ley de Uniformidad de las Sociedades Personales ley que dispone intereses comunes de participación accionaria, participación en pérdidas y ganancias y responsabilidades administrativas compartidas en una sociedad personal (pág. 191)
unitary elastic/elástica unitaria describe la demanda cuya elasticidad es exactamente igual a 1 (pág. 91)
United Nations Development Program (UNDP)/Programa de las Naciones Unidas para el Desarrollo programa de las Naciones Unidas dedicado a la eliminación de la pobreza por medio del desarrollo (pág. 487)
unit of account/unidad de cuenta medida que se usa para comparar los valores de bienes y servicios relativos entre sí (pág. 244)
unskilled labor/mano de obra no calificada trabajo que no requiere destrezas, educación o capacitación especializada (pág. 221)

V

variable/variable factor que puede cambiar (pág. 103)
variable cost/costo variable costo que sube o baja según la cantidad que se produzca (pág. 111)

vertical merger/fusión vertical unión de dos o más empresas implicadas en etapas diferentes de producción del mismo bien o servicio (pág. 199)

voluntary exchange/intercambio voluntario concepto que define la libertad de la gente para decidir qué y cuándo quieren comprar o vender (pág. 53)

voluntary export restraint (VER)/limitación voluntaria de las exportaciones limitación autoimpuesta sobre el número de productos que se envían a un determinado país (pág. 449)

W

wage-price spiral/espiral de salarios y precios proceso mediante el cual los salarios que aumentan pueden provocar precios más altos y, a su vez, los precios más altos fomentan salarios más altos (pág. 342)

want/deseo artículo que deseamos pero que no es indispensable para sobrevivir (pág. 3)

welfare/asistencia social auxilio económico para los necesitados que ofrece el gobierno (pág. 68)

white-collar worker/oficinista persona que tiene un trabajo de oficina y que, por lo general, recibe un sueldo (pág. 232)

withholding/retención retirar pagos del salario de un empleado antes de éste que lo reciba (pág. 366)

work ethic/ética profesional sistema de valores que da importancia principal al trabajo (págs. 59, 491)

workfare/asistencia social a cambio de trabajo programa de asistencia social temporal en el que se requiere que los recipientes realicen un trabajo de servicio público, por lo general (pág. 350)

World Bank/Banco Mundial el proveedor más grande de asistencia técnica y financiera para el desarrollo (pág. 487)

World Trade Organization (WTO)/Organización Mundial del Comercio (O.M.C.) organismo mundial cuya meta es lograr una mayor liberalización del comercio internacional y aranceles aduaneros más bajos (pág. 453)

yield/rendimiento tasa anual de ganancias de un bono si éste no se pagara hasta su vencimiento (pág. 278)

Z

zoning law/ley de zonificación ley municipal que designa áreas separadas para viviendas y para empresas (pág. 187)

Index

Note: An italicized entry with a page number preceded by a *c* indicates a chart; a *g* indicates a graph; an *m* indicates a map; and a *p* indicates a photo.

A

Aaron, Henry J., 370, *p370*
ability-to-pay principle, 362
absolute advantage, 443, *p443*
ACH. *See* Automated Clearing House.
acid rain, 66
actual cash value, 524
ACV. *See* actual cash value.
ADC. *See* Aid to Dependent Children (ADC).
advertising
  in franchises, 202
  nonprice competition and, 168
  professional organizations and, 204
  shifts in demand and, 87–88
AFDC. *See* Aid to Families with Dependent Children (AFDC).
AFL. *See* American Federation of Labor.
Africa, less developed countries in, 471
African Americans, *c224*, 344, *p344*, *c536*, *g537*
  entrepreneurs, 115
  poverty rate and, 346, *c346*, 347
  wage discrimination and, 224–226, *g225*, *g226*
aggregate demand, 307–308, *g307*, *g308*, 399
aggregate supply, 306–307, *g307*, *g308*, 313, 399
agricultural marketing cooperatives, 203
agriculture, *g534*
  arable, 480
  imports and exports, *g535*
  location of production, 119–120
  price supports and, 131
  in Soviet Union, 36–37, *p36*, 491
  subsistence, 472, 480
  technology and, *p474*
Aid to Dependent Children (ADC), *c68*
Aid to Families with Dependent Children (AFDC), *c68*, 69, *c69*, 399
Afghanistan, 487, *487c*
airline industry
  deregulation of, 175, 176
  oligopolies and, 170
  targeted discounts and, 163, 164
Alabama
  energy consumption, *g541*
  natural resources, *m532–533*
Alaska
  energy consumption, *g541*
  natural resources, *m532–533*
Albania, 471, *p483*
allocation of resources, 62–66
  externalities, 65–66, *p65*
  public goods, 62–64
Amazon.com, 293
America Online, 293
American Bar Association, 204
American Federation of Labor (AFL), 229
American Management Association, 204
American Marketing Association, 204
American Medical Association, 204
American Revolution, 248
American Telephone & Telegraph (AT&T), 174, *c175*
American Tobacco Company, 174
annual percentage rate (APR), 514–515
Antifederalists, 250–251
antitrust laws, 173, *p173*
APEC. *See* Asian Pacific Economic Cooperation.
appreciation, 459
appropriations bills, 389
APR. *See* annual percentage rate.
arable land, 441, 480
arbitration, 234
Argentina, 404, *m455*, 456, 488
Arizona
  energy consumption, *g541*
  housing costs, *g337*
  natural resources, *m532–533*
Arkansas
  energy consumption, *g541*
  Federal Reserve district, *m417*
  natural resources, *m532–533*
Articles of Confederation, 248
articles of partnership, 191
Ash, Mary Kay, 97
Asian Americans, 189, *p189*
Asian Pacific Economic Cooperation (APEC), 455, *m455*
Assessment, 20–21, 46–47, 72–73, 98–99, 122–123, 146–147, 178–179, 206–207, 236–237, 266–267, 294–295, 326–327, 352–353, 382–383, 410–411, 436–437, 466–467, 496–497
  See also Self-assessment.
Assessment
  6, 11, 18, 20–21, 27, 32, 38, 44, 46–47, 55, 60, 66, 70, 72–73, 83, 88, 96, 98–99, 106, 114, 120, 122–123, 131, 137, 144, 146–147, 154, 164, 171, 176, 178–179, 188, 193, 200, 204, 206–207, 217, 226, 234, 236–237, 248, 256, 264, 266–267, 275, 283, 292, 294–295, 308, 316, 324, 326–327, 336, 343, 350, 352–353, 363, 369, 374, 380, 382–383, 393, 401, 408, 410–411, 418, 423, 429, 434, 436–437, 447, 456, 464, 466–467, 476, 483, 488, 494, 496–497
assets, 192
ATF. *See* Bureau of Alcohol, Tobacco, and Firearms (ATF).
Atlanta, Georgia, *g337*, *m417*
Atlantic City, New Jersey, 97, *p97*
ATM. *See* Automated Teller Machine.
AT&T. *See* American Telephone & Telegraph (AT&T).
Australia
  balanced trade and, 462
  as developed nation, 471
  national budget of, *g547*
  per capita gross domestic product, 472, *g473*
  population, 472
Austria, *g547*
authoritarian, 35
Automated Clearing House (ACH), 264
Automated Teller Machine (ATM), 225, 263, *p263*
automatic stabilizers, 398–399
automobiles
  buying, 520–521
  inflation and, *c338*
  in Japan, 447
  labor unions in manufacturing of, *p228*
  pollution from, 118
  price changes and, 94–95, *p94*
  safety, 19, *p19*
  supply curve and, 135–136
  trade barriers and, 451
automobile insurance, 525

B

baby boomers, 87, 373, 408
Background 7, 33, 56, 68, 89, 115, 138, 165, 189, 227, 238, 257, 276, 317, 344, 370, 402, 424, 457, 477; Airline Policy 174; Article Authors 354; The Beef Battle 87; Biography 37, 203, 253, 399, 432; Careers in Economics 346, 392, 473; Common Misconceptions 81, 233, 247, 261; Comparing Economic Performance 36; Consumer Preferences 25; Corporate Downsizing 110; Currency Transactions 269; The Dangers of Lead 75; Decline in Productivity 329; Double Taxation 368; Economics in History 5, 26, 29, 41, 49, 52, 93, 159, 170, 173, 255, 278, 280, 297, 311, 360, 385, 405, 443, 462, 469; Effects of Welfare Reform 355; Entrepreneurship's Changing Face 493; Excise Taxes 118; Global Connections 149, 163, 339, 348, 391, 452, 460, 481; Gold and Silver Futures 289; Good Business? 413; Government Intervention 498; Interdisciplinary 14, 158, 245, 427, 491; Investment Clubs 272; Keeping the Playing Field Level 198; Luring Workers 216; Market District to Market Phenomenon 102; Market Solutions 349; Menu Costs 342; The Minimum Wage 130;

Monopoly and Patents 161; The Pokemon Craze 209; Profits and More Profits 113; Public-Choice Economics 64; Reforming Welfare 69; Risky Business 192; Running Risks 288; Stress Sometimes Pays 223; A Striking Decline 232; Subminimum Wage 181; Supply and Demand 136; Taking the Economy's Temperature 59; The Conference Board 314; Thinking at the Margin and Blackberry Picking 10; The Two Faces of Money 259; The Workers Minstrel 230
balanced budget, 376, 403, 404, 407, 408
balanced budget amendment, 407
balance of trade, 462–464, *g463*, *c464*
Balkan nations, 487
Baltimore, Maryland, *m160*, 172
Bangladesh, 471
bank holding company, 421
bank holiday, 255
banking, 257
checking accounts, 504–505
before Civil War, 250–252, *p250*, *p251*
during Civil War, 253, *p253*
deregulation of, 175, 176, 256
developments in American, 250–256, *c254*
electronic, 263–264, *p263*
Free Banking era, 252, *p252*
Great Depression and, 255, *p255*, 435
history, 415–416, *p415*
reforms, 255
regulating, 422
role of money in, 241
savings accounts, 259, 275, 506–510
services, 259–262
See also Federal Reserve System.
Banking Act (1933), 435
Bank of America, 257
Bank of the United States, first and Second, 251–252, 415
bank run, 252, *p255*
banks, 250
economic stability of, 58
examinations of, 422
Federal Reserve System and, 421–422
as financial intermediaries, 272
foreign exchange market, 460
loans and, 260–261
member banks of the Federal Reserve System, 254
mergers of, 265
money creation and, 425–426, *c426*
profit and, 262, *c262*
regulations, 58
services of, 259–262, 510–511
types of, 510–511
unifying American, 253
See also commercial banks; savings banks.
bargaining, 444
bar graphs, 337, 351, 353
barriers to entry
defined, 153
monopolies and, 156, 167
in oligopoly, 170
start-up costs, 153
technology, 153
barter, 243
baseball, 121
bear market, 290
Becker, Gary, 7, *p7*
Beef War (1999), 451
Beige Book, 418
Bellringer
3, 8, 13, 23, 28, 34, 40, 48, 51, 57, 62, 67, 79, 85, 90, 101, 108, 116, 125, 133, 139, 148, 151, 156, 166, 172, 190, 195, 201, 208, 211, 219, 228, 243, 250, 258, 271, 277, 285, 301, 310, 318, 331, 338, 345, 359, 365, 371, 375, 387, 395, 403, 415, 420, 425, 430, 441, 449, 458, 471, 478, 485, 489
benefits
collective bargaining, 233
of public goods, 62–63
thinking at the margin and, 11
trends in, 216–217, *p216*
benefits-received principle, 362
Berkshire Hathaway Company, 276
BET. *See* Black Entertainment Television (BET).
Better Business Bureau, 204
Beyond The Classroom
Career Connections 89, 138, 165, 189, 257, 276, 344; Occupations and Institutions Change with the Economy 317; Workplace Skills 7, 33, 56, 227, 370, 402, 424, 457, 477
bias, recognizing, 419, 437
Biddle, Nicholas, 252
Biography
Aaron, Henry J., 370, *p370*
Becker, Gary, 7, *p7*
Buffett, Warren, 276, *p276*
Carnegie, Andrew, 317, *p317*
Dell, Michael, 138, *p138*
Gates, Bill, 165, *p165*
Giannini, Amadeo P., 257, *p257*
Greenspan, Alan, 424, *p424*
Haubegger, Christy, 89, *p89*
Hills, Carla Anderson, 457, *p457*
Johnson, Robert L., 115, *p115*
Keynes, John Maynard, 402, *p402*
Lewis, W. Arthur, 477, *p477*
Marx, Karl, 227, *p227*
Rivlin, Alice, 56, *p56*
Smith, Adam, 33, *p33*
Winfrey, Oprah, 344, *p344*
Yang, Jerry, 189, *p189*
Birdseye, Clarence, 6
Black Americans. *See* African Americans.
Black Entertainment Television (BET), 115
black market, 142, 304–305
Black Tuesday, 291
block grants, 350, 374
Block Scheduling
5, 10, 15, 25, 30, 36, 42, 53, 59, 64, 69, 81, 87, 92, 103, 110, 118, 127, 135, 141, 153, 158, 168, 174, 187, 192, 197, 203, 213, 222, 232, 245, 252, 260, 273, 279, 287, 303, 312, 320, 333, 340, 347, 361, 367, 373, 377, 389, 397, 405, 417, 422, 427, 432, 443, 451, 460, 473, 480, 487, 491
blue-collar workers, 231–232
board of directors, 196
Board of Governors, 416–417
Bolsheviks, 36
bond funds, 509
bond ratings, 279, *c279*
bonds, 197, 405, 507
advantages and disadvantages of, 279–280
buying at a discount, 278
components of, 277–278
in corporations, 197
as financial assets, 277–280, *p277*, *c278*, *g280*
purchases of, 428–429
sales of, 429
types of, 280–282, *c280*, *p281*
See also loans.
borrowers, 272
Boston, Massachusetts, *m417*
brain drain, 482
Brazil, *p28*, 404, *p485*
as newly industrialized country, 476
Southern Common Market, *m455*, 456
Bretton Woods Conference, 461
brokerage firms, 287
budget, creating a, 502–503
budget deficit, 403, 404, *g404*, 406–408, *c407*
budget surplus, 381, 403, 404, *g404*, 407, 408
Buffett, Warren, 276, *p276*
bull market, 290
Bureau of Labor Statistics (BLS), 211, 212, 217, 334, 340
Burr, Aaron, 251
Bush, George H.W., 401, 407, 408
Bush, George W.
airlines and, 176
concerns of business, 55
faith-based initiatives, *c69*, 70
tax cuts, 381, 408
business associations, 203, 204
business cycles
business investment and, 312, *g312*
consumer expectations and, 313
defined, 57
external shocks, 313–314, *g313*
forecasting, 314
future of, 316
history of, 314–316
interest rates and credit, 312–313
phases of, 310–314, *c311*
recession and, 312–313, 433
stabilization policy and, 433–434, *g432*
business investment, 312, *g312*
business license, 186
business loans, 261
business name, 186
business organizations
categories of, 183
cooperative organizations, 202–203, *p202*
corporations, 195–198
defined, 185
entrepreneurs and, 185–186
franchises, 201–202, *p201*
mergers, 198–199, *c198*
multinational corporations, 199–200, *p200*
nonprofit organizations, 203–204, *p203*, *p204*
partnerships, 190–193

retail sales of, *g539*
shutting down, 113–114, *p114*
sole proprietorships, 185–188, *p185*, *c186*, *p187*
business tax, 378
buyers, 29
decisions of consumers, 53
in perfect competition, 151, 152
buying on margin, 291
buying power, 202

C

Cable Television Consumer Protection Act (1992), 177
California, 67–68, 107, 119–120, *m160*, 172, 257, *p316*, 393, *p393*, *p397*, 417, *m417*
currency in, 460
deregulation in, 176
education in, 376
energy consumption, *c541*
Federal Reserve district, *m417*
franchises in, 202
housing costs, *g337*
natural resources, *m532–533*
toxic-waste cleanup in, 74–75, *p74*, *g75*
call option, 288
Cambodia, 475, 483
Canada
Asian Pacific Economic Cooperation, 455, *m455*
national budget of, *g547*
North American Free Trade Agreement, 454–455, *m455*, 465
taxes in, 368
as trading partner, 446, *g544*, *m545*
United States trade deficit and, 463
capital
in corporations, 197
defined, 4, *c5*
human capital, 5, 188, 225
increased mobility, 213, 333
marginal returns and, 110
in partnerships, 192
physical capital, 4–5, 188
capital budget, 375
capital deepening, 320, *c320*, 322, *c322*
capital gains, 285–296, 508
capital gains tax, 198
capital goods, 4. *See also* physical capital.
capital loss, 286
capital markets, 283
careers, *g537*
Caribbean Community and Common Market, *m455*, 456
CARICOM. *See* Caribbean Community and Common Market.
Carnegie, Andrew, 51, 97, 317, *p317*
Carnegie Steel Company, *c198*, 317
cartels, 171, 173
Carter, Jimmy, 176
cash assistance, 349
cash transfers, 69
catalytic converter, 66
cause and effect, recognizing, 123, 132, 147, 467, 497
CBO. *See* Congressional Budget Office.
CDs. *See* certificates of deposit.
CEA. *See* Council of Economic Advisers.
Celler-Kefauver Act (1950), 175
cellular technology, 159
census, 334, 345
Census Bureau, 68, 345
central bank, 254
centrally planned economy
defined, 27
as economic system, 27
incentives in, 36, 37
Internet Activities and, 38
organization of, 34–36
problems of, 38
in Soviet Union, 36–37, *p36*, *p37*
transitions to free enterprise, 489–494, *p489*, *m490*, *p491*, *p492*, *p493*
central planning, 482
certificate of incorporation, 197
certificates of deposit, 259
as financial assets, 282
return and risk of, 275
ceteris paribus, 85, 86, 101
change in demand, 86
checking accounts, 259
check clearing, 421
demand deposits and, 258
opening and managing, 504–505
Chicago, Illinois, *p285*
Chicago Board of Trade, 288
child labor, 229
Chile, 455
China, *p143*
economy of, 484
fast-food industry in, 43
Hong Kong and, 44
import quotas, 449
poverty in, 494
as trading partner, *g544*, *m545*
transition to market-based economy, 489, 493–494, *p493*
as U.S. trading partner, 446, 463
Chrysler Corporation, 199
CIO. *See* Congress of Industrial Organizations.
circle graphs, 394
circular flow diagram
free market economy and, 29, *c30*
of mixed economy, 42–43, *c42*
output and income, *c303*
Civil Rights Act (1964), 223
Civil War, 120
classical economics, 395–396, *p395*
Clayton Antitrust Act (1914), 174
Cleveland, Ohio, *m160*
Clinton, Bill, 56, 408
fiscal policy, 401
welfare reform and, 350
closely held corporations, 196
coffee industry, 203, 443
collateral, 513
collective bargaining, 233
collectives, 36–37, 491
college, financing, 516–519, *g516*
College Scholarship Service, 518–519
collusion, 171
colonies, 482
Colorado
energy consumption, *g541*
Federal Reserve District, *m417*
natural resources, *m532–533*
command economy, 141–142
See also centrally planned economy.
Commerce, Department of, 301
commercial banks, 262, 510–511
commodity, 152
commodity money, 246–247, *c247*
Common Agricultural Policy (CAP), 118
Common Market, 454
common stock, 286, 508
communication systems
in developed nations, 474
as physical capital, 442
communism, 35–36, 39
collapse of, *p38*, *m490*, 492
Karl Marx and, 227
in Russia, 491
The Communist Manifesto **(Marx),** *p36*, 227
comparative advantage, 443–444, 445
competition, 31
deregulation and, 175
free market system and, 31, *p31*, *p52*, 53
mergers and, 199
and monopolistic competition, 169
complements, 88
compound interest, 261
computers, 229, *g325*
input costs and, 117
opportunity cost and, *g18*
personal, 137
software, 165
See also e-commerce.
Conference Board, 314
conflict, 193, *p193*
conglomerates, 199, *a199*
Congress, U.S.
antitrust laws and, 173, *p173*
balanced budget, 407
Bank of the United States and, 251
entitlements and, 372
federal budget and, 388–389, *c388*
Federal Reserve and, 416
government shutdown and, 381
labor unions and, 231
taxes and, 359–360
wage discrimination and, 223
Congressional Budget Office (CBO), 388
Congress of Industrial Organizations (CIO), *c229*
Connecticut
energy consumption, *g541*
natural resources, *m532–533*
consequences, predicting, 309
Conservation International Foundation, 203
Constitution, U.S., 359–360, 363
constitutional protections, 52–53
consumer confidence index, *g539*
consumer cooperatives, 203
consumer credit debt, *g355*, *g541*

consumer demand, 333
consumer economics, 512–515, 516–519, 520–521, 522–523, 524–525, 526–527, 528–531
consumer expectations, 313
consumer goods, *p13*, 473
Consumer Price Index(CPI), 339–340, *c339*, *g538*
consumer products
safety of, 54–55, *c55*
Consumer Product Safety Commission (CPSC), *c55*
consumer protection
government and, 54–55, *c55*
consumers, *g540*, *g541*
buying decisions of, 53
expectations of, 87, *p87*
free enterprise system and, 31, *p31*, 53
income effect, 80–81, *c80*, *p81*
law of demand and, 79–80, *c79*, *p79*, *c80*
protection of, 204
public disclosure laws and, 54
public policy and, 54
in the Soviet Union, 37, *p37*
substitution effect, 80, *c80*
tastes and advertising, 87–88
teenage, 87
consumer skills, 504–505, 506–510, 510–511, 512–515, 516–519, 520–521, 522–523, 524–525, 526–527, 528–531
consumer sovereignty, 32
Consumer's Savings Bank, 263
consumption expenditures, *g541*
containment, 487
Continental Congress, Second, 248
contingent employment, 215, 217
continuum, 43
contraction, 310, *c311*
contractionary policy, 389, 390–391, *c391*, 392, 397, *c434*
contracts, 523
free enterprise system and, *p52*
control, in corporations, 198
cooperative organizations, 202–203, *p202*, *p203*
copyright, 60
core inflation, 340
corporate bonds, 281
corporate charters, 197
corporate combinations, 198–199, *c198*, *c199*
corporate income tax, 360, 367, 378
corporations, 195–198
advantages of, 196–197
characteristics of, *c196*
corporate bonds and, 281
defined, 195
disadvantages of, 197–198
officers, 196
structure, 196
types of, 196
cost/benefit analysis, 10–11, 309, 327
Costa Rica, 439
cost-push theory, 341–342
costs, 16
input, 116–117
opportunity cost and, 16
production, 108–114, *p108*, *g109*, *p110*, *c111*, *c112*, *g113*, *p114*
of public goods, 64, *c64*
setting output, 112–113, *g112*, *g113*
thinking at the margin and, 11, *c11*
Council of Economic Advisers (CEA), 400
coupon rate, 277
cover letters, 526
CPI. *See* consumer price index.
CPSC. *See* Consumer Product Safety Commission (CPSC).
credit
business cycles and, 312–313
establishing, 512–513
finance charges and, 514–515
types of, 513–514
credit bureau, 512
credit cards, 261, 354–355, *p354*, *g355*, 514
creditor, 264
credit rating, 512
credit unions, 203, 263, 272, 510–511
Critical Thinking Activity
analyzing information, 467
automatic stabilizers, 401
block grants, 350
business cycles, 316
business organizations, 207
cause and effect, 123, 467, 497
chapter assessment, 21, 47, 73, 99, 123, 147, 179, 207, 237, 267, 295, 327, 353, 383, 411, 437, 467, 497
corporations, 200
demand, 99
differences in wages, 226
drawing conclusions, 467, 497
economic transitions, 494
elastic demand, 96
fact and opinion, 364
foreign exchange rates, 464
franchises, 204
gross domestic product measurement, 308
human capital, 447
inflation, 343
international trade, 456, 467
labor force, 217
law of demand, 83
law of supply, 106, 120
making comparisons, 123, 497
partnerships, 193
production costs, 114
real GDP, 324
tax cuts, 393
unemployment, 336
crowding-out effect, 406, *c407*
Cuba, 143
Cultural Revolution, 493, *p493*
currency, 245, 252, *p252*
euro, 454, 462, *p462*
in European Union, 429
exchange rates, 458–462, *c460*
Federal Reserve System and, 421
fixed exchange-rate systems, 461, *g461*
flexible exchange-rate systems, 461–462, *g461*
history of, 256
strong and weak, 459–460, *c460*
customers, 163–164
customs duty, 450, *c450*
cyclical unemployment, 333–334, *p333*
Czech Republic, *c319*

D

Daimler-Benz, 199
DaimlerChrysler, 199
Dallas, Texas, *m417*
Darrow, Charles, 97
Das Kapital **(Marx),** 227
Databank Activity, 18, 27, 88, 120, 131, 171, 188, 226, 264, 324, 343, 369, 380, 393, 408, 434, 447, 476
daytrading, 289, 292
Debating Current Issues, 74–75, 180–181, 238–239, 268–269, 354–355, 412–413, 498–499
debit cards, 263–264
debt, 405
consumer credit, *g541*
development and, 483
rescheduling, 488
in sole proprietorships, 187
decentralized decision making, 29
decision making, 1
Decision Making Activity, 83, 106, 114, 120, 217, 234, 248, 476, 483, 488
decision-making grid, 9–11, *c10*, *c11*
deductible, 524
deductions, 366
default, 261
Defense, Department of, 373
defense spending, 373, *p387*
deficit, 403
deflation, 343
Delaware
energy consumption, *g541*
natural resources, *m532–533*
Dell, Michael, 138, *p138*
Dell Computer Corporation, 138
demand
elasticity of, 90–96, *p90*, *g92*, *p93*, *p94*, *c95*, *c96*
fiscal policy and, 390–391
income effect, 80–81, *p81*, *c80*
law of, 79–80, *c79*, *p79*, *c80*
monopolies and, 157, 161
prices of related goods, 88
shifts in, 85–88, *g86*
substitution effect, 80, *c80*
demand curve, 82–83, *g82*, *g83*
shifts in the, 85–88, *g86*, 136–137, *g136*
demand deposits, 258
demand notes, 253
demand-pull theory, 341
demand schedule, 81–82, *c81*, 125, *c161*
demand-side economics, 396
excess demand, 126–128, *g127*
Democratic Republic of Congo, 482
demographics, 347
Deng Xiaoping, 493–494
Denison, Edward, 323
Denmark, *g547*
Denver, Colorado, *m417*

depreciate, 305, 459, 520
depressions, 311, 397.
See also Great Depression.
deregulation
of banking, 175, 176, *c176*, 256
of electricity, 176, *p179*
government and, 175–176, *c176*
of television, 177
derived demand, 219, 349
developed nations, 471
characteristics of, 474, *p474*
consumer goods, 473
debt and, 483
education in, 481, *g482*, *p482*
energy consumption, 472
health and nutrition in, 481, *p481*
human capital, 480–481, *p480*
infant mortality rate, 474, *p474*
labor force, 472–473
life expectancy, 473
literacy rate, 473
per capita gross domestic product, 472
physical capital, 480, *p480*
political factors, 482–483, *p483*
population in, 474
resource distribution and, 479–480
development
defined, 471
financing, 485–488, *p485*, *p486*, *g487*, *p488*
foreign aid and, 487
foreign direct investment, 486
foreign portfolio investment, 486
human capital, 480–481, *p480*
internal financing, 485–486
levels of, 476, *m476*
measuring, 471–474, *g472*, *g473*
physical capital, 480, *p480*
political factors, 482–483, *p483*
population growth, 478–479, *p478*, *g479*
ranking, 475–476
resource distribution and, 480
sustainable, 479
diamonds, *p156*
Differentiated Instruction Activity
4, 9, 10, 14, 15, 16, 17, 24, 25, 26, 29, 30, 31, 35, 36, 37, 42, 43, 49, 52, 53, 54, 58, 59, 63, 64, 65, 68, 69, 80, 81, 82, 86, 87, 91, 92, 93, 94, 95, 103, 104, 105, 109, 111, 112, 113, 117, 118, 119, 126, 127, 128, 129, 134, 135, 140, 141, 142, 143, 152, 153, 157, 158, 159, 160, 161, 162, 163, 167, 168, 169, 173, 174, 175, 181, 186, 187, 191, 192, 196, 197, 198, 199, 202, 212, 213, 214, 216, 220, 223, 224, 225, 229, 231, 232, 233, 239, 244, 246, 251, 252, 253, 254, 259, 260, 262, 263, 269, 272, 273, 274, 278, 279, 281, 282, 286, 287, 288, 289, 290, 291, 302, 303, 304, 305, 306, 307, 311, 312, 313, 314, 315, 319, 320, 321, 322, 323, 332, 333, 334, 335, 339, 340, 341, 342, 346, 347, 348, 349, 355, 360, 361, 362, 366, 367, 368, 372, 373, 376, 377, 379, 385, 388, 389, 390, 391, 392, 396, 397, 398, 399, 400, 404, 405, 406, 407, 413, 416, 417, 421, 422, 426, 427, 428, 431, 432, 433, 442, 445, 446, 450, 453, 454, 455, 459, 461, 463, 469, 472, 473, 474, 475, 479, 480, 481, 482, 486, 487, 490, 491 492, 493, 499
differentiation, 167
diminishing marginal returns, 109–110, *g109*
disabled persons, 68, 70, *p372*
disaster relief, 25, *p25*, 358
discount rate, 422, 427–428
discounts, targeted, 163–164
discouraged workers, 336
discretionary spending, 371, *c371*, 373–374, 391
disequilibrium, 126–128, *g127*, 134–135
supply curve and, 134–135
disposable personal income, 306
District of Columbia, *c541*
diversification, 273, 274
dividends, 198, 285, 507–508
divorce rate, 347
dollar
appreciation of, 483
effect of, on exports, *c460*
value of, 301, 460
See also money.
dot-coms, 293
double taxation, 197–198
Dow Jones Industrial Average, *g289*, 290, 291
drug industry, 88, *p93*
dual economies, *p486*
durable goods, 302
duty free goods, 450

E

earnings, *g537*
easy money policy, 431, 433
e-commerce, 293, *p305*, 412–413, *p412*, *g413*
Econ 101
4, 9, 14, 24, 29, 35, 41, 52, 58, 63, 68, 80, 86, 91, 102, 105, 109, 117, 126, 128, 134, 140, 143, 152, 157, 167, 173, 186, 191, 196, 202, 212, 220, 229, 244, 251, 259, 272, 278, 286, 302, 307, 311, 319, 332, 339, 346, 360, 366, 372, 376, 388, 391, 396, 404, 416, 421, 426, 431, 442, 450, 453, 459, 472, 479, 486, 490
economic activity patterns, 442
economic assistance, 495
***The Economic Consequences of the Peace* (Keynes),** 402
economic citizenship, 58–59
economic development, theory of, 477
economic efficiency, 25, *c25*, 32
economic equity, 26, *c25*
economic freedom, 25, *c25*, 32
free enterprise system and, *p52*
public interest and, 54–55
economic goals, 25–26, *c25*, 57–59
economic growth, *c25*, 26, 32, 310, *c311*
capital deepening, 320, *c320*, 322, *c322*
foreign trade and, 322
measuring, 318–320, *g318*, *c319*
population growth and, 321
saving and investment, 320–321, *c321*
technological progress, 322–324, *p323*
Economic Growth and Tax Relief Reconciliation Act of 2001, 381
economic indicators, *g538*, *g539*
economic institutions, 510–511
economic organizations, *c497*
economic questions, 23–25
economic rights, 53
economics
decision making, 3
defined, 2, 3
personal decisions and, 8
economic systems, 22–47
analyzing, 299
defined, 23
four types of, 26–27
simulation of, 48–49
traditional economy, 26–27
economic zones, 494
economies of scale
defined, 157
effect of, *c157*
mergers and, 199
in monopoly, 157–158
in oligopoly, 170
economists
Aaron, Henry J., 370, *p370*
Becker, Gary, 7, *p7*
Greenspan, Alan, 417, 424, *p424*, 432, 498
Hills, Carla Anderson, 457, *p457*
Jevons, William Stanley, 310
Keynes, John Maynard, 402, *p402*
Lewis, W. Arthur, 477, *p477*
Marx, Karl, 227, *p227*
Rivlin, Alice, 56, *p56*
Smith, Adam, 30–31, 32, 33, *p33*, 41, 143–144
women, 56, 457
Edison, Thomas, 59, *p59*
education
development and, 481, *g482*, *p482*
financing an, 516–519, *g516*
government funding for, 70
human capital and, 324
income and, 213–214, *g214*
literacy rate, 473
as a positive externality, 66
poverty and, 346–347, *p347*
relationship between income and, *g21*
state government and, 376
taxes and, 378
unemployment and, 333
of women, *p482*
EEC. *See* European Economic Community.
EEOC. *See* Equal Employment Opportunity Commission.
EFC. *See* Expected Family Contribution.
efficiency, 15
Egypt, 449
Eisenhower, Dwight D., *p71*
elastic demand, 90, *g92*, *p93*, 93, 94
revenue and, 95, *c96*
values of, 91
elasticity, 104–106, *c105*, *p106*
elasticity of demand, 90–96, *p90*, *g92*, *p93*, *p94*, *c95*, *c96*

INDEX

calculating, 90–91
factors affecting, 91–95
prices and, 90–91, 96
revenue and, 95–96
tax effects, *c363*
values of, 91
elderly persons, 26, *58*
health care for, 70
Social Security and, 69
electricity deregulation, 176, *p179*
electronic banking, 263–264, *p263*
electronic paper, 16
El Salvador, 483
e-mail, 117
employees
of corporations, 196
of partnerships, 192
in sole proprietorships, 188
employment, 26, 183, 211, *c212*, *g536*, *g537*
changes in, by industry, 212–213, *g213*
child labor, 229, 238–239, *p238*, *c239*
as economic goal, 58
effects of trade on, 446–447
getting a job, 526–527
minimum wage and, 130–131, *p130*, *g131*, 238–239
specialization and, 447
unemployment and, 335–336
employment assistance, 350
employment services, 527
energy consumption, 180–181, *g181*, 472, *g541*
energy production, *p119, p180, g534*
Engels, Friedrich, *p36*
Enron, 176, *p176*
enterprise zones, 349, 350
entitlements, 370, 372–373, *p372*, 391
entrepreneurs, 5, *c5*, 6, 97, 188
Ash, Mary Kay, , 89, *p89*
Buffett, Warren, 276, *p276*
business organizations and, 185–205
Dell, Michael, 138, *p138*
economic growth and, 32
Gates, Bill, 165, *p165*
Giannini, Amadeo P., 257, *p257*
Haubegger, Christy, 89, *p89*
Johnson, Robert L., 115, *p115*
Morison, George Abbot, 205
property rights and, 490–491, *p491*
qualities of, 186
simulation of, 208–209
start-up costs and, 153
Winfrey, Oprah, 344, *p344*
women, 89, 344
Yang, Jerry, 189, *p189*
environmental policy report, 107
environmental protection, 26
government and, 54–55
Environmental Protection Agency (EPA), *c55*, 66
EPA. *See* Environmental Protection Agency.
Equal Employment Opportunity Commission (EEOC), *c55*, 223
Equal Pay Act (1963), 223
equilibrium, 125–126, *g126*, 133–137, *g134*, *g135*, *g136*
taxes and, 363
equilibrium aggregate, 308, *g308*
equilibrium wage, 220, *c221*
equities, 285
estate taxes, 368
ethics statements, 194, 205
EU. *See* European Union.
euro, 454, 462, *p462*
Europe
currency in, 429
value-added tax, 368
European Economic Community (EEC), 451, 454
European System of Central Banks, 429
European Union (EU), *m455*
currency in, 252
farm subsidies in the, 118
international cooperation and agreements of, 454, *m455*
trade wars and the, 452
as U.S. trading partner, 446
excess demand, 126–128, *g127*
excess reserves, 427
excess supply, 128
exchange rates, 458–462
calculating, 458–459
fixed systems, 461, *g461*
flexible systems, 461–462, *g461*
foreign exchange market, 460
reading tables, 458, *c459*
systems, 460–462, *g461*
excise tax, 118, 368, 378, 380, *g543*
expansion, 310, *c311*
expansionary policy, 389–390, *c389*, *c390*, 392, 433–434, *c434*
Expected Family Contribution (EFC), 518
exports, 322, 445
agricultural, *g535*
balance of trade and, 463
coffee, 443
defined, 446
effect of dollar on, *c460*
mineral fuels, *g534*
taxes and, 360
trading partners, *g544*, *m545*
of United States, 446, *g446*
voluntary restraints, 449–450
external investment. *See* foreign investment.
externalities, 65–66, *c65*
external shocks, 313–314, *g313*

F

FAA. *See* Federal Aviation Administration.
FAC. *See* Federal Advisory Council.
fact and opinion, distinguishing, 364, 383
factor market, 29, *c303*
free market economy and, 29, *c30*
government in, 42
factor payments, 24
factor resources
in centrally planned economy, 34–35
opportunity costs and, *c24*
factors of production, 480
capital and, 4
defined, 4, *c5*
factor payments and, 24
labor and, 4
land and, 4
natural resources and, 4
FAFSA. *See* Free Application for Federal Student Aid.
Fair Credit Billing Act, *515*
Fair Credit Reporting Act, *515*
Fair Deal, *c58*
Fair Labor Standards Act (1938), 224, *c229*
faith-based initiatives, *c69*, 70
family structure, 347
farms, *g535*
farm subsidies, 117
Fast Fact
balanced budget, 407
balanced trade, 462
Birdseye, Clarence, 6
Chinese economy, 43
education in New Hampshire, 378
electronic banking, 264
Federal Reserve System, 417
foreign direct investment, 492
franchises, 202
free market and, 32
General Motors, 291
law of demand, 80
schooling, 475
marginal returns, 110
natural monopoly, 159
pennies, 248
pollution permits, 66
tax rates, 368
technological progress, 212, 323
technology and resources, 60
top employers, 219
tourism industry, 127
underground economy, 305
fast-food industry, 43
FCC. *See* Federal Communications Commission.
FDA. *See* Food and Drug Administration.
FDIC. *See* Federal Deposit Insurance Corporation.
featherbedding, 225–226, 230
Fed. *See* Federal Reserve System.
Federal Advisory Council (FAC), 418
federal aid, 374, *p374*
Federal-Aid Highway Act (1956), 71
Federal Aviation Administration (FAA), *c55*
Federal Communications Commission (FCC), *c55*, 160, 177
federal budget
balanced budget, 403, 404, 407
budget deficit, 403, 404, *g404*, 406–408, *c407*
budget surplus, 403, 404, *g404*, 407, 408
creating a, *c388*
fiscal policy and, 387–389, *c389*
federal debt, *g542*
federal deficit, *g542*
Federal Deposit Insurance Corporation (FDIC), 255, 262, 435
Federal Emergency Relief Administration (FERA), *c68*

federal funds rate, 422, 427–428, *428c*
Federal Highway Act (1921), 71
Federal Insurance Contributions Act (FICA), 367
See also Social Security.
Federalists, 250–251, 415
Federal Open Market Committee (FOMC), 418, 428–429, 432, 434
Federal Perkins Loan, 518
federal regulatory agencies, *c55*
Federal Reserve Act (1913), 254, 415–416
Federal Reserve Bank of New York, 416, 428–429
Federal Reserve Board, 254, 424
Federal Reserve Districts, 417, *m417*
Federal Reserve notes, 255
Federal Reserve System
banks and, 421–422
commercial banks and, 262
development of, 254–255
districts of, 417, *m417*
during Great Depression, 291
fiscal policy, 393
functions of, 420–423, *p420*, *c421*, *g423*
government and, 420–421, 426
history, 415–416, *p415*
monetary policy and, 417, 425–429, *p425*, *c426*, *c427*, *c428*, 430–435, *c431*, *g432*, *p433*, *c434*
money circulation and the, 246
structure of, 416–418, *c416*
See also banking.
federal spending, *g394*
Federal Trade Commission (FTC), *c55*, 80, 173, 175
FEMA. *See* Federal Emergency Management Agency.
fiat money, *c247*, 248
FICA. *See* Federal Insurance Contributions Act.
Filo, David, 189
finance charges, 513, 514–515
finance companies, 263, 272
financial aid, 517–519
financial assets, 272
bonds as, 277–280, *p277*, *c278*, *g280*
types of, 282–283
financial assistance
for education, 516–519, *g516*
in franchises, 202
financial cooperatives, 203
financial institutions, 510–511
economic stability of, 58
foreign exchange market, 460
types of, 262–263
Financial Institutions Reform, Recovery, and Enforcement Act (FIRREA), 256
financial intermediaries, 272–274, *c273*
financial system, 271–272
firms, 29
free market economy and, 29
in monopolistic competition, 167
nonprice competition and, 167–168
FIRREA. *See* Financial Institutions Reform, Recovery, and Enforcement Act.
fiscal policy
automatic stabilizers, 398–399
contractionary policies and, 389, 390–391, *c391*, 392
economy and, 389
expansionary policies and, 389–390, *c389*, *c390*
federal budget and, 387–389, *c388*
Federal Reserve and, 393
limits on, 391–393, *p392*, *p393*
multiplier effect, 397–398
options, 395–401
supply-side economics, 399–400, *g399*, 401
fiscal year, 388
fishing, *g534*
fixed costs, *p110*, 111, *c111*
fixed exchange-rate systems, 461, *g461*
fixed income, 342–343
flat tax, *c360*
flexible exchange-rate systems, 461–462,*g461*
Florida, *p50*
energy consumption, *c541*
Federal Reserve District, *m417*
natural resources, *m532–533*
Focus Activity, 1, 77, 183, 241, 299, 357, 439
FOMC. *See* Federal Open Market Committee (FOMC).
Food and Drug Administration (FDA), *c55*, 66, 159
food stamps, 69, 348, 349, 373
Ford, Henry, 212
foreign aid, 487, *g487*
foreign competition, 232
foreign direct investment, 486, 492
foreign exchange market, 460
foreign investment, 464, 485, 486
foreign policy, 487
foreign portfolio investment, 486
foreign trade, 322, 439, *g544*, *m545*
North American Free Trade Agreement (NAFTA), 465, *p465*
See also international trade.
forestry, *g534*
Form 1040, 531
Four Modernizations, 493
Four Olds, 493
Four tigers, 476
fractional reserve banking, 260–261, *c260*
France
informed buyers in, 152
national budget of, *g547*
subsidies in, 117, *p118*
as trading partner, *g544*, *m545*
unemployment in, 335
franchises, 159–160, 201–202, *p201*
advantages of, 202
defined, 159
disadvantages of, 202
fraud, 252
Free Application for Federal Student Aid (FAFSA), 518
Free Banking era, 252, *p252*
free contract, 53
free enterprise system, 43, 53
business cycles and, 57
constitutional protections of, 52–53
consumers and, 53–54
features of the, *p52*
government and, 54–55
inventions in a, 59–60
investing and, 271
principles of, 53
producers and, 53
protection versus, 54
public interest and, 54–55
tradition of, 51
transitions to, 489–494, *p489*, *m490*, *p491*, *p492*, *p493*
in United States, 44, 51–52
free market economy, 29
circular flow diagram and, 29, *c30*
classical economics, 395–396, *p395*
factor market and, 29, *c30*
and Graphic Organizer Activity, 46
households and firms and, 29
prices in, 139–140
product market and, 29–30, *c30*
property rights and, 490–491, *p491*
public interest and, 54
See also market economy.
free market entry, 152–153
free market system, 31, *p31*, 32
free rider, 63–64
free-trade zones, 454, 457
frictional unemployment, 331
fringe benefits, 188
frozen foods industry, 6
FTC. *See* Federal Trade Commission.
futures, 288

G

gas deposits, 441
gasoline crisis, 144
Gates, Bill, 5, 165, *p165*
GATT. *See* General Agreement on Tariffs and Trade.
G-8 countries, 497
GDP. *See* gross domestic product.
gender discrimination, 347
General Agreement on Tariffs and Trade (GATT), 453
General Motors, 291
general partnerships, 190
The General Theory of Employment, Interest and Money **(Keynes),** 315, 396, 402
genetically modified food, 452
Georgia
energy consumption, *g541*
Federal Reserve District, *m417*
housing costs, *g337*
natural resources, *m532–533*
Germany
bonds in, 282
economic health of, *c319*
hyperinflation in, 404
national budget of, *g547*
as trading partner, *g544*, *m545*
United States trade deficit and, 463
Giannini, Amadeo P., 257, *p257*
gift taxes, 368–369
glasnost, 491
glass ceiling, 224
Glass-Steagall Act (1933), 256

INDEX

Global Connections
distribution of goods in Cuba, 143
elasticity of demand, 91
environment, 475
European System of Central Banks, 429
Great Depression, 314
India, 91
informed buyers, 152
international bonds, 282
Japan's fiscal policy, 392
new business in Russia, 54
nonprofit organizations, 203
production workers salaries, 225
rubles, 246
subsidies in the European Union, 118
Sweden, 41
trade wars, 452
trade-offs, 9
unemployment in France, 335
value-added tax, 368
global economy, 439
Global Connections, 9, 41, 54, 91, 118, 143, 152, 203, 225, 246, 282, 314, 335, 368, 392, 429, 452, 475
protectionist policies, 468–469
supply and demand in the, 119
Sweden, 41
trade-offs, 9
World Bank and, 495
globalization, 333
GNP. *See* gross national product.
gold, 248
loans and, 260–261
gold standard, 253
Gompers, Samuel, 229
goods
choice of, 141–142
complements, 88
consumers of, 24–25
defined, 3
demand for, *c84*
determining what to produce, 23
how to produce, 23–24
substitutes, 88
Gorbachev, Mikhail, 491–492
GOSPLAN, 141
government, *g542, g543*
blocking mergers, 174–175
bonds, 405
breaking up monopolies by, 174
centrally planned economy and, 27, 34–38, *p34*
communist, 35–36
consumer protection and, 54
corruption in, 482
deregulation and, 175–176
economic goals of, 57–59
educational funding by, 70, 518
encouragement of innovation by, 59–60
entitlements, 372–373, *p372*
environmental protection and, 54–55
in the factor market, 42
federal budget, 403–408
federal regulating agencies, *c55*
Federal Reserve System and, 420–421, 426
financial resources of, 357
fiscal policy, 387–408
free enterprise system and, 54
influence on supply, 117–119
Keynesian economics and, 396–399, *c396*
laissez faire, 33
medical benefits funding by, 70
minimum wage and the, 25, 130–131, *p130, g131*, 238–239, *p238, g239, g536*
in mixed economies, 40–44, *c42, c43*
national debt, *p403*, 405–407, *g406*
natural monopolies and, 158
partnerships and, 191
prices and intervention by, 128–131, *g129*
privatization, 489–490, *p489*
in the product market, 42–43
programs, 359
public goods and, 66
public interest and, 54
public policy and, 54
redistribution programs of, 68–70
regulation by the, 54–55, 173–174
rent control and, 129–130, *g129*, 131
role of, in the economy, 54
socialist, 35
sole proprietorships and, 186–187
spending, 357, 371–374, *c371, p372*, 390
transferring money and, 43
See also taxes.
government bonds, 280–282, *c280, p281*
government monopolies, 159–160
government securities auctions, 420–421
Gramm-Rudman-Hollings Act, 407
grants, 517
grants-in-aid, 374
Graphic Organizer Activity
banking services, 266
business organizations, 206
demand curve, 98
economic theories, 410
factors of production, 20
government deregulation, 178
government effect on prices, 146
gross domestic product, 326
investment options, 294
mixed economy, 46
monetary policy tools, 436
multiflow maps, 122
public policy goals, 72
revenue sources, 382
trade organizations, 466
unemployment, 352
wage rates, 236
Graphing the Main Idea
3, 8, 13, 23, 28, 34, 40, 51, 57, 62, 67, 79, 85, 90, 101, 108, 116, 125, 133, 139, 151, 156, 166, 172, 185, 190, 195, 201, 211, 219, 228, 243, 250, 258, 271, 277, 285, 301, 310, 318, 331, 338, 345, 359, 365, 371, 375, 387, 395, 403, 415, 420, 425, 430, 441, 449, 458, 471, 478, 485, 489
graphs, interpreting line, 21
Great Britain, 200, 231
Great Crash, 290–292, 301, 314–315
Great Depression, 68, 291, 301, 314, 402, 435
banking and, 255, *p255*
business cycles, 314–315
classical economics and, 395–396, *p395*
Federal Reserve System and, 416
fiscal policy and, 400
unemployment in, 334
unions and the, 230
Great Society, *c69*
Greece, *g547*
greenbacks, 253
greenhouse effect, 475
Greenspan, Alan, 417, 424, *p424*, 432, 464, 498
gross domestic product (GDP), 57, 58, *g58*, 59, 417, 431, 471, *g472, g534, g538*
business cycles and, 310, *c311, g312*, 312–314
calculation of, 302–303, *c302, c303*
contractionary policies and, 390–391
depressions and, 311
durable goods, 302
Great Depression and, 315, *g315*
gross national product and, 305–306, *c306*
income approach, *c302*, 303, *c303*
influences on, 306–308, *g307, g308*
intermediate goods, 301–302
limitations of, 304–305
multiplier effect and, 397–399, *g398*
national debt and, 405–407, *g406*
nominal and real, 303–304, *c304*
nondurable goods, 302
outside lags and, 433
population growth and, 318–319
quality of life and, 319–320, *c319*
quantity theory, 341
recessions and, 311
stagflation and, 311
taxes as percent of, *g546*
gross national product, 305–306, *c306*
growth, 16
as economic goal, 58
growth stock, 286
Guatemala, *p26*
guns or butter, 8

H

Hamilton, Alexander, 250–251, *p250*
Harding, Warren G., 51
Haubegger, Christy, 89
Hawaii, 393, 499
energy consumption, *g541*
natural resources, *m532–533*
Head Start, *c69*
health care
costs, 74–75
development and, 481, *p481*
for elderly persons, 70
expenditures in United States, *g547*
government agencies and, 54
poll, 249
health codes, 187
health insurance, *g75*, 216, 525
heavy industry, 37, 491
Heller, Walter, 401
high-income economies, 476, *m476*
highway systems, 71, 377, *p377*
Hills, Carla Anderson, 457, *p457*

Hispanics. *See* Latinos; specific nationalities.
home banking, 264
home-based businesses, *p187*
Hong Kong, 44, 475, 494
Hoover, Herbert, 290, 315
horizontal merger, *c198*, 199
household, 29
housing
costs, *g337*
inflation and, 338–339
prices, *g540*
renting an apartment, 522–523
starts, 299, *g539*
subsidized, 70, 349
Houston, Texas, *m160, g337*
human capital, 5, 18, 188, 225, 320, 480–481, *p480*
education and, 324
international trade and, 441
Hungary, *p489*
hydroelectric plants, 157–158
hyperinflation, 340–341, 404

I

IBM, 212
Idaho
energy consumption, *g541*
natural resources, *m532–533*
Illinois, 252
energy consumption, *g541*
natural resources, *m532–533*
IMF. *See* International Monetary Fund.
imports, 322
agricultural, *g535*
balance of trade and, 463
defined, 446
fastest-growing, *c463*
mineral fuels, *g534*
quotas on, 449, *p449*
restrictions on, 119
trading partners, *g544, m545*
of United States, 446, *g446*
import taxes, 369
incentives, 31
in centrally planned economies, 37
for innovation, 59–60
monetary and non-monetary, 31, 80
preserving, 175
incidence of a tax, 363
income, *g337*
education and, 213–214, *g214*
inflation and, 342–343
personal, *g540*
relationship between education and, *g21*
shifts in demand and, 86–87
income approach, *c302*, 303, *c303*
income distribution, 348–349, *g348*
income effect, 80–81, *c80*, *p81*
income gap, 349
income inequality, 348–349, *g348*
income stock, 286
income tax, 357, 361, *c361*, 380, 528–531, *g542*, *g543*
individual, 360, *c360*, 365–367, *c365*, *c366*, *c367*
state government and, 378
incorporation
advantages of, 196–197
disadvantages of, 197–198
India, *p29*, 91
import quotas, 119, 449
per capita gross domestic product, 472, *g473*
population, 472
resource distribution in, *c442*
Indiana
energy consumption, *g541*
natural resources, *m532–533*
individual income tax, 360, *c360*, 365–367, *c365*, *c366*, *c367*
Individual Retirement Account, 381
Indonesia
subsidies in, 117
industrialization, 472
industrialized nations. *See* developed nations.
industrial organizations, 160
Industrial Revolution, 229
industry
in China, 493–494
regulation of, 54–55
in Soviet Union, 37, 491
inelastic demand, *g92*, 93, 94
defined, 90
revenue and, 95–96, *c96*
values of, 91
inelasticity, 105
infant industry, 452, *p453*
infant mortality rate, 474, *p474*
inferior goods, 87
inflation, 417
causes of, 341–342, *c342*
core, 340
effects of, 342–343
hyperinflation, 340–341, 404
interest rates and, 343
Keynesian economics and, 397
monetary policy and, 433–434, *c434*
price indexes, 339–341, *c339*, *c340*
prices and, 119–120, *p120*, 338–339
rate of, 340–341, *c340*, *g341*, 343
unemployment and, 343
Information Age, 212
infrastructure, 474
inheritances, 349
tax on, 378
in-kind benefits, 70
innovations, 324
incentives for, 59–60
in technology, 26
input costs, 116–117
inside lags, 432
installment loans, 263, 513–514
insurance, 273, 524–525
interdependence, 445
Interdisciplinary
Dramatic Arts 112; Current Events 469; Geography 17, 170, 194, 335, 394, 474; Government 107, 145; Health 481; History 49, 61, 75, 155, 160, 175, 181, 235, 239, 247, 254, 269, 322, 325, 341, 355, 406, 413, 445, 465, 493, 499; Language Arts 215, 249, 274, 293, 297, 419; Literature 94, 224, 233, 265, 284, 309, 314, 379, 448, 484; Math 12, 130, 218, 281, 329, 337, 348, 385, 399, 461; Music 121; Philosophy 132; Science 45, 84, 97, 149, 198, 209, 225, 364, 409, 446, 455; Science & Technology 289
interest, 261
interest groups, 54
interest rates, 68, 314, *g542*
business cycles and, 312–313
inflation and, 343
money supply and, 430
short-term and long-term, 280–281, 314
spending and, 430–431
intermediate goods, 301–302
internal financing, 485–486
Internal Revenue Service (IRS), 357, 528–531
international free trade agreement, 453
International Monetary Fund, 461, 488, 492, 497
international trade, 440–467, 457
absolute and comparative advantage, 443–445, *p443*, *c444*
comparative advantage, 443–444, 445
cooperation and agreements, 452–456, *p454*, *m455*
human capital and, 441
measuring, 458–464
money, 458–462
natural resources and, 441
opportunity costs and, 443, 444, *c444*
physical capital and, 442
protectionism and, 452–453, *p453*, 498–499, *p498*, *g499*
reasons for, 441–447, *p441*
resource distribution, 441–443, *p441*, *c442*
trade barriers, 449–457
unequal resource distribution, 442
See also foreign trade.
Internet
employment opportunities and the, 527
exchange rates on the, 458
law of supply, 106
markets on the, 153
Microsoft and the, 173
research on the, 194
using, for research, 207
Yahoo!, 189
Internet Activity, 7, 12, 18, 27, 33, 38, 45, 56, 61, 66, 70, 84, 89, 96, 107, 115, 120, 132, 138, 144, 155, 165, 171, 176, 189, 194, 200, 204, 218, 227, 234, 249, 257, 264, 276, 284, 292, 309, 317, 324, 337, 344, 350, 364, 370, 374, 380, 394, 402, 408, 419, 424, 429, 434, 448, 457, 464, 477, 484, 488, 494
Self-Test, 21, 47, 73, 99, 123, 147, 179, 207, 237, 267, 295, 327, 353, 383, 411, 437, 467, 497
interstate highway system, 71
interventionist policy, 434
interviews, job, 527
investing, 268–269, *p268, g269,* 286
investment goods, 322
investments, 16, 271, 286, 320–321, *c321*
private enterprise and, 271

simulation of, 296–297, *c297*
invisible hand
defined, 32
free market economy and, 31–32
Iowa
energy consumption, *g541*
natural resources, *m532–533*
Iraq, 313, *p483,* 487, *487c*
IRS. *See* Internal Revenue Service.
Italy
multinational corporations in, 200
national budget of, *g547*

J

Jackson, Andrew, 251–252, *p251*
Japan
automobile industry, 447
bonds in, 282
as developed nation, 471
economic health of, *c319*
fiscal policy, 392
imports from, 119
multinational corporations in, 200
national budget of, *g547*
taxes in, 368
as trading partner, 446, *g544*, *m545*
United States trade deficit and, 463
Jefferson, Thomas, 250–251, *p250*
Jevons, William Stanley, 310
job discrimination, 222, 223
job security, 233
job training, 349, 350
jobs, protecting, 452, *p453*
Jobs and Growth Tax Relief Reconciliation Act of 2003, 381
Johnson, Lyndon B., 68, *g70*
Johnson, Robert L., 115, *p115*
Journal Activity, 2, 21, 22, 47, 50, 73, 78, 99, 100, 123, 124, 147, 150, 179, 184, 207, 210, 237, 242, 267, 270, 295, 300, 327, 330, 353, 358, 383, 386, 411, 414, 437, 440, 467, 470, 497
junk bonds, 281–282, *p282*
Justice, Department of, 173, 174

K

Kansas
energy consumption, *g541*
natural resources, *m532–533*
Kennedy, John F., 401
Kentucky
energy consumption, *g541*
Federal Reserve district, *m417*
natural resources, *m532–533*
Kern-McGillicuddy Act, *c68*
Keynes, John Maynard, 315, 396, 402, *p402,* 408
Keynesian economics, 396–399, *c396,* 402
inflation, 397
multiplier effect, 397–398
national debt and, 406–407, 408
productive capacity, 396
recessions and depressions, 397
World War II and, 400
Knights of Labor, 228
Kyoto Protocol (1997), 475

L

labor
defined, 4, *c5*
demand for, 219–220, *g221*
impact on supply and demand, 183
increased mobility, 213, 333
marginal product of, 108–109
output and, 108–110, *c109*
supply of, 220, *g221*
temporary workers, 215
unemployment and, 331–336
wages and, 219–226
See also labor unions; organized labor.
Labor Day, 228
labor force, 211–212, *p211, c212*
education and, 213–214, *g214*
temporary workers, 215
women in, 214–215, *g215*
labor market, 211–217
trends, 211–217
labor movement, 229–233, *c229, p230, p231, g232, m232, g233*
labor productivity, 320
labor statistics, 212
labor unions, 204, 225, 228, *g233*
blue-collar workers, 231–232
collective bargaining, 233
Congress and, 231
featherbedding, 225–226, 230
right-to-work laws, 231
strikes, *p228,* 234
wages and, 225–226, *p226*
white-collar workers, 232
yellow-dog contracts, 230
See also labor; organized labor.
Laffer, Arthur, 399
Laffer curve, 399–400, *g399, g400*
laissez faire, 33, 434
defined, 41
limits of, 41
land, 4, *c5*
arable, 441
natural resources, *m532–533*
land-grant colleges, 60
Latina, 89
Latinos, 89, *g536, g537*
poverty rate and, 346, *c346*
wage discrimination and, *g224*
law of comparative advantage, 444
law of increasing costs
defined, 17, *c17*
production possibilities frontier and, 17
LDC. *See* less developed countries.
leading indicators, 314, 538–539
learning effect, 214
lease, 522–523
Lebanon, 483
legal equality, 53
Lenin, Vladimir, 36, *p36, p38,* 491
less developed countries, 471
brain drain in, 482
characteristics of, 475, *p475*
consumer goods, 473
debt and, 483
education in, 481, *g482, p482*
energy consumption, 472
foreign aid and, 487
foreign investment, 486
health and nutrition in, 481, *p481*
human capital, 480–481, *p480*
infant mortality rate, 474, *p474*
internal financing, 485–486
International Monetary Fund, 488
labor force, 472–473
life expectancy, 473
literacy rate, 473, 481
multinational corporations and, 200, 486
per capita gross domestic product, 472, *g472, g473*
physical capital, 480, *p480*
political factors, 482–483, *p483*
population, *g473,* 478–479, *g479*
resource distribution and, 479–480
Lewis, W. Arthur, 477, *p477*
liability, 187
in corporations, 197
in partnerships, 190–193
in sole proprietorships, 187
licenses, 170
defined, 159
franchises and, 159–160
as trade barriers, 450
licensing fee, 378, 450
life expectancy, 473
life insurance companies, 273
light bulb, invention of, 59, *p59*
light industry, 494
limited liability partnerships, 190–191, 192–193
limited partnerships, 190
line graphs, 12
liquidity, 258, 274–275
literacy rate, 441, *c442,* 473, 475, 481, *c482*
LLP. *See* limited liability partnerships
loans, 513–514
banks and, 260–261
educational, 517–518
short-term, 254–255
See also bonds.
local government
federal aid to, 374, *p374*
forms of, 379
jobs of, 379
other taxes of, 380
property taxes and, 380
location, nonprice competition and, 168, *p168*
loose money policy. *See* easy money policy.
Lorenz curve, 348–349, *g348*
Los Angeles, California, 67–68, *m160,* 172, 417, *m417*
Louisiana, 6
energy consumption, *g541*
natural resources, *m532–533*
low-income economies, 476, *m476*
luxuries, versus necessities, 93–94, *p94*

M

M1, 258, *c259*, 422
M2, 258–259, *c259*, 422
M3, 422
macroeconomics, 299
  business cycles and, 310–316
  defined, 57
  Federal Reserve System and, 425–429
  measurement of, 301–306, *c306*
  monetary policy and, 430–434
Maine
  energy consumption, *g541*
  natural resources, *m532–533*
Major League Baseball, 160
Malaysia, 117, 476
malnutrition, 481
Malthus, Thomas, 395
management training, 202
mandatory spending, 371–373, *c371*
manufacturers, targeted discounts and, 163
manufacturing economy, 212–213, *g213*
Mao Zedong, 493
maps
  changing economies, *m490*
  communism, *m490*
  Federal Reserve Districts, *m417*
  job migration, *m*232
  levels of development, *m476*
  Missouri, *m67*
  monopoly decisions, *m160*
  National Football League, *m160*
  natural resources, *m532–533*
  Roman Empire, *m245*
  trade organizations, *m455*
  United States trading partners, *m545*
marginal cost, 111–112, *c111*, *g112*, 116
marginal product of labor, 108–109, *g109*
marginal returns, 109–110, *g109*
marginal revenue, 161–162, *c161*
  setting output, 112–113, *g113*
market
  buying and selling, 29
  defined, 28
  Internet, 153
  self-regulating nature of, 30–31
  specialization, 28–29
market basket, 339, *c339*, *g538*
market demand schedule, 81–82, *c81*
  shifts in the, 85–88, *g86*
market disequilibrium, 126–128, *g127*, 134–135, *g135*
market economy
  defined, 27
  as economic system, 27
  Internet Activity and, 38
  See also free market economy.
market entry, law of supply and, 102–103
market equilibrium, 125–126, *g126,* 133–137, *g134*, *g135*, *g136*, *g154*
  changes in, 133–137, *g134*, *g135*, *g136*
  price ceilings and, 129–130, *g129*
  price floors and, 130–131, *g131*
  simulation of, 148–149
market failure, 64
marketplace, invisible hand of the, 32, 33
market power, 172–173
  defined, 163
  predatory pricing and, 173
  price discrimination and, 163–164
market structures, 150–179
  comparison of, *c170*
  monopoly, 156–164, 166–169
  oligopoly, 169–171
  perfect competition, 151–154
market supply curve, 104
market supply schedule, 103–104, *c104*
market system
  demand in the, 78–99, *c79*, *c80*
  supply and demand in the, 125–131
Marshall, George C., 487
Marshall Plan, 487
Marx, Karl, *p36*, 227, *p227*
Maryland, *m160*, 172
  energy consumption, *g541*
  Federal Reserve District, *m417*
  natural resources, *m532–533*
  taxes in, 360
Massachusetts, 393
  banking in, 263
  energy consumption, *g541*
  Federal Reserve District, *m417*
  natural resources, *m532–533*
  representative money in colonial, 247–248
  unemployment in, 351
Massachusetts Institute of Technology (MIT), 60
mass transit systems, 172
Math Practice Activity, 70, 83, 88, 96, 114, 131, 137, 283, 308, 336, 343, 350, 408, 429, 464, 483
maturity, 277–278
McGuire, Peter J., 228
mediation, 218
Medicaid, *c69*, 70, *g70*, 372–373, *p372*, 391
medical care, 70
Medical Care Act, *c69*
Medicare, *c69*, 70, *g70*, 372–373, *p372*
  taxes and, 368, 408
medium of exchange, 243–245, *c244*
Meeting Standards
  4, 10, 24, 31, 54, 59, 80, 86, 111, 117, 136, 149, 153, 186, 197, 209, 220, 222, 244, 252, 272, 287, 297, 304, 322, 329, 333, 341, 378, 405, 406, 422, 431, 444, 450, 459, 472
member banks, 254
MERCOSUR. *See* Southern Common Market
mergers, 198–199
  blocked by government, 174–175
  preserving incentives, 175
  types of, 198–199, *c198*
Mexico, 471
  Asian Pacific Economic Cooperation, 455, *m455*
  economic health of, *c319*
  as newly industrialized country, 476
  North American Free Trade Agreement, 454–455, *m455*, 465, *p465*
  trade with the United States, 455
  as trading partner, 446, *g544*, *m545*
  United States trade deficit and, 463, *g463*
MFN. *See* most-favored nation status.
Miami, Florida, *p50*, *m417*
Michigan, *p217*, 333
  energy consumption, *g541*
  Federal Reserve District, *m417*
  natural resources, *m532–533*
microeconomics, 57
Microsoft Corporation, 165, 173, 175
middle-income economies, 476, *m476*
migrant workers, 332, *p332*
mineral deposits, 441
mineral fuels, *g534*
minimum wage, 41, 130–131, *p130*, *g131*, 224, 350, *g536*
mining, *g534*
Minnesota
  energy consumption, *g541*
  Federal Reserve District, *m417*
  natural resources, *m532–533*
Mint, United States, 421
Mississippi, 344
  energy consumption, *g541*
  natural resources, *m532–533*
Missouri, 67, *m67*, *p67*
  energy consumption, *g541*
  Federal Reserve District, *m417*
  natural resources, *m532–533*
mixed economy
  circular flow diagram of, 41–43, *c42*
  comparing, 43–44
  defined, 27
  as economic system, 27
  and Graphic Organizer Activity, 46
  rise of, 40–41
MNC. *See* multinational corporations.
monetarism, 430
monetary policy
  approaches to, 434
  effects of, *c431*
  Federal Reserve System and, 417, 425–429, *p425*, *c426*, *c427*, *c428*, 431–434, *c431*, *g432*, *p433*, *c434*
  inflation and, 433–434, *c434*
  macroeconomy and, 430–434
money
  borrowing, 404–405
  characteristics of, 245–246
  commodity money, 246–247, *c247*
  creation of, 404, 425–426, *c426*
  exchange rates, 458–462
  fiat money, *c247*, 248
  international trade and, 458–464
  measuring supply of, 258–259, *c259*
  representative money, 247–248, *c247*
  role of, 241
  saving, 259–260
  source of value of, 246–248, *c247*
  transferring of, 42–43
  uses of, 243–245, *c244*
money market accounts, 259, 506
money market funds, 509
money market mutual funds, 259, 282
money markets, 283
money multiplier formula, 426–427
money supply, 258–259, *c259*
  interest rates and, 430

INDEX

regulating the, 422–423, *g423*
monopolistic competition, 166–169, *p166*, *c167*, 170, *c170*
conditions of, 167
defined, 166
output in, 169
price in, 168–169
profits in, 169
monopoly, *p158*, *c170*
defined, 156–157
dilemmas of, 161
economies of scale and, 157–158
forming a, 157–159
franchises and licenses, 159–160
government and, 159–160, 174
industrial organizations, 160
marginal revenue in, 161–162
output decisions, 160–163
price discrimination in, 163–164, *p163*
profits in, 162–163
setting a price, 162, *g162*
technological, 159
See also natural monopoly.
Montana
energy consumption, *g541*
Federal Reserve District, *m417*
natural resources, *m532–533*
Moody's, 279, *c279*, 281
Morison, George Abbot, 205
Morrill Acts (1862, 1890), 60
mortgages, 261
most-favored nation status, 453
multimedia presentations, 448, 467
multinational corporations, 199–200, *p200*, 456
advantages of, 200
disadvantages of, 200
less developed countries and, 486
taxation of, 199–200
multiplier effect, 397–398
municipal bonds, 281, *p281*
munis. *See* municipal bonds.
music industry, 102–103, *p102*
mutual funds, 292, 509
as financial intermediaries, 272
money market, 282
mutual savings banks, 263

N

NAFTA. *See* North American Free Trade Agreement
NASA. *See* National Aeronautics and Space Administration
Nasdaq, 287, 288
National Aeronautics and Space Administration (NASA), 60
National Association of Securities Dealers' Automated Quotation (Nasdaq), 288
national bank, 251
National Banking Acts (1863 and 1864), *p253*
national debt, *p403*, 405–407, *g406*, 408
National Education Association, 203–204
National Football League, 77, *m160*
national income, 306
national income accounting, 301
National Income and Product Accounts (NIPA), 301, 305
National Monetary Commission (NMC), 415
National Park Service, 159
national security, 452, *p453*
natural gas industry, 441
deregulation of, 175
natural monopoly, 158
natural resources, 324, *m532–533*
factors of production and, 4
international trade and, 441
management of, 66
Nebraska, 6, 277
energy consumption, *g541*
Federal Reserve District, *m417*
natural resources, *m532–533*
necessities, versus luxuries, 93–94, *p94*
need, 3
negative externalities, 65–66, 305
Negotiable Order of Withdrawal (NOW), 263
Nepal, 471
Netherlands, 462, 492
balanced trade and, 462
multinational corporations in, 200
as trading partner, *g544*, *m545*
net national product, 305–306, *c306*
Netscape, 293
net worth, 422
Nevada
energy consumption, *g541*
natural resources, *m532–533*
New Deal, *c68*, 397
New Hampshire, 205
Bretton Woods Conference, 461
education in, 378
energy consumption, *g541*
natural resources, *m532–533*
New Jersey, 97, *p97*, 499
energy consumption, *g541*
natural resources, *m532–533*
newly industrialized countries, 475–476
New Mexico
energy consumption, *g541*
natural resources, *m532–533*
New York
currency in, 460
energy consumption, *g541*
Federal Reserve Bank of New York, 416, *m417*, 418, 428–429
housing costs, *g337*
Labor Day parade, 228
natural resources, *m532–533*
New York Stock Exchange, 196, 287–288, *p292*
Panic of 1907, 254, *c254*
subway system, *p87*
taxes in, 380
terrorist attacks, 176, 292, 316, 336, 408, 425
New York City, 129, 228, *g337*, *m417*
New York Mercantile Exchange, 288
New York Stock Exchange, 196, 287–288
New Zealand, 471
Nicholas II (czar of Russia), 36
NICs. *See* newly industrialized countries.
NIPA. *See* National Income and Product Accounts.
NMC. *See* National Monetary Commission.
NNP. *See* net national product.
nominal GDP, 303–304, *c304*
nondurable goods, 302
nonmarket activities, 304
nonprice competition, 167–168
nonprofit organizations, 192, 203–204, *p203*, *p204*
normal goods, 86–87
normal trade relations status, 453
Norris-LaGuardia Act (1932), *c229*
North American Free Trade Agreement (NAFTA), 454–455, *m455*, 465, *p465*, 467
North Carolina
energy consumption, *g541*
Federal Reserve District, *m417*
natural resources, *m532–533*
North Dakota
energy consumption, *g541*
natural resources, *m532–533*
North Korea, 43, *p142*
NOW. *See* Negotiable Order of Withdrawal.
NRC. *See* Nuclear Regulatory Commission.
NTR. *See* normal trade relations status.
Nuclear Regulatory Commission (NRC), *c55*
nutrition, development and, 481, *p481*
NYSE. *See* New York Stock Exchange.

O

Oakland, California, *m160*
OASDI. *See* Old-Age, Survivors, and Disability Insurance.
Occupational Safety and Health Administration (OSHA), *c55*
occupational trends, 212-213, *c213*
occupations, *g537*
Office of Faith-Based Initiatives, 70
Office of Management and Budget (OMB), 56, 388, *c388*
Office of Price Administration, 141
Ohio, *m160*
energy consumption, *g541*
Federal Reserve District, *m417*
natural resources, *m532–533*
oil industry, 180–181, *p180*, *g181*, *c198*, 313, 315–316, *p316*, 441
price changes and, 94–95, *p94*
United States trade deficit and, 463
Oklahoma
energy consumption, *g541*
Federal Reserve District, *m417*
natural resources, *m532–533*
Old-Age, Survivors, and Disability Insurance (OASDI), 367
See also Social Security.
older workers, 346, *c346*, 351, *p372*, 447
oligopoly, 169–171, *c169*, *c170*
barriers to entry, 170
cooperation and collusion in, 170–171
defined, 169

economies of scale in, 170
OMB. *See* Office of Management and Budget.
OPEC. *See* Organization of Petroleum Exporting Countries.
open market operations, 428–429, *c428*
open opportunity, 53
operating budget, 375
operating cost, 113
opportunity costs, *c444*
auto safety, 19
computers and, *g18*
cost and, 16
decision-making grid and, 9–10, *c10*
defined, 9
factor resources and, *c24*
importance of, 444
international trade and, 443, 444, *c444*
production possibilities graph and, *g14*, *g15*, *g16*
public goods and, *c64*
The Oprah Winfrey Show, 344
options, 288
Oregon
energy consumption, *g541*
natural resources, *m532–533*
Organization of Petroleum Exporting Countries (OPEC), 315–316, *p316*, 463, 483
organized labor
blue-collar workers, 231–232
labor movement, 229–233, *c229*, *p230*, *p231*, *g232*
right-to-work laws, 231
strikes, *p228*, 229
white-collar workers, 232
yellow-dog contracts, *c229,* 230
OSHA. *See* Occupational Safety and Health Administration.
OTC market, 288
output
labor and, 108–110, *c109*
in monopolistic competition, 169
in oligopoly, 170
in perfect competition market, 153–154
setting, 112–113, *g112*, *g113*
output decisions, 160–162
output-expenditure approach, 302
outside lags, 432–433

P

Pacific Rim, 455, *m455*
Pakistan, 449
Panic of 1907, 254, 415
Paraguay, *m455*, 456
parent companies, 201
Parent Loan for Undergraduate Students (PLUS), 518
partnership agreement, 191
partnerships, 190–193
advantages of, 191–192
characteristics of, *g191*
defined, 190
disadvantages of, 192–193
liability and, 192–193
types of, 190–191, *g191*
par value, 278, *c278*
PATCO. *See* Professional Air Traffic Controllers Organization.
patents, 6, 60, 159, 170, 324
patriotism, 25
pay-as-you-earn taxation, 365–366
payroll withholding statement, 528–529
peak, 310, *c311*
pennies, 248
Pennsylvania, 7, 317
energy consumption, *g541*
Federal Reserve District, *m417*
natural resources, *m532–533*
pension funds, 216, 273
People's Communes, 493
per capita gross domestic product, 472
perestroika, 492
perfect competition, *c170*
conditions for, 151–153
defined, 151
perfect competition market, *c153*
barriers to entry in, 153
market equilibrium in, *g154*
output in, 153–154
price in, 153–154
personal computer industry, *g18*, 230, *p323, g325*
personal finance, 502–503, 504–505, 506–510, 510–511, 512–515, 516–519, 528–531
Personal Finance Handbook, 502–531
personal income, 306
personal property, 378
Personal Responsibility and Work Opportunity Reconciliation Act (1996), 350
Peru, *c442*
philanthropy, 317, 488
Phoenix, Arizona, *g337*
physical capital, 4, 18, 188, 225, 320, 480, *p480*
benefits of, 5
defined, 4
international trade and, 442
See also capital goods.
Pittsburgh, Pennsylvania, 317
PLUS. *See* Parent Loan for Undergraduate Students.
Poland, 471
political cartoons, 90, 155, *p179*, 408
pollution, 118–119, *p119*
population
in developed nations, 474
gross domestic product and, 318–319
growth, 478–479, *p478*, *g479*
less developed countries, 478
natural rate of increase, 478
per capita gross domestic product, 472
projected, *c409*
shifts in, 447
shifts in demand and, 87
portfolios, 274
positive externalities, 65
poverty
antipoverty policies, 349–350, *p349*
causes of, 346–347
in China, 494
economic shifts and, 347
education and, 346–347, *p347*
income distribution and, 347–349, *g348*
income inequality and, 348–349, *g348*
location and, 347
minimum wage and, 350
problem of, 67–68, *p67*, *p68*
rate, *g345*, 346, *g348*
statistics, 471
poverty line, 345
poverty threshold, 67, 345
predatory pricing, 164, 173
preferred stock, 286, 508
premium, 524
Preparing for Standardized Tests
16, 19, 26, 31, 37, 39, 43, 54, 65, 71, 82, 93, 95, 104, 111, 113, 119, 129, 136, 142, 159, 162, 163, 169, 177, 199, 205, 214, 221, 223, 230, 231, 246, 253, 255, 261, 263, 280, 282, 288, 290, 305, 306, 313, 315, 321, 323, 342, 349, 351, 362, 368, 378, 381, 390, 398, 400, 407, 428, 433, 435, 444, 452, 454, 462, 463, 475, 482, 492, 495
President, U.S., 388, *c388*, 389
price ceilings, 128–130, *g129*
price controls, 142
price discrimination, *c174*
defined, 163
limits of, 164
in a monopoly, 163–164, *p163*
price fixing, 171
price floors, 128, 130–131, *g131*
price indexes, 339–341, *c339*, *c340*
price levels, 58, 307
prices
advantages of, 140–141
black market and, 142
changes in, 94, 113
disequilibrium and, 126–128, *g127*, 134–135
effects of rising, 338–339
elasticity of demand and, 90–91
equilibrium and, 125–126, *g126*, 133–137, *g134*, *g135*, *g136*
falling, 343
flexibility of, 140–141
in free market, 139–140
future expectations of, 119–120
government intervention and, 128–131, *g129*
as incentives, 140, 143–144
inflation and, 119–120
law of supply, 101–103, *c101*
minimum wage and, 130–131, *p130*, *g131*
in monopolistic competition, 167, 168–169
nonprice competition and, 167–168
in oligopoly, 170
in perfect competition, 152, 153
rationing and, 141, *p141*, 142, 143
of related goods, 88
rent control and, 129–130, *g129*, 131
resource allocation and, 142–143
responding to changes, 113, *g113*
role of, 139–144
setting in a monopoly, 162, *g162*

shortages and, 136–137, 142
as signals, 140
spillover costs and, 144
supply and demand and, 125–137, 140
surpluses and, 134–135
trade barriers and, 450–451, *p451*
price supports, 131
price war, 171
primary markets, 283
primary sources, 61, 73
prime rate, 427
primitive equilibrium, 475
privacy, 256
private enterprise, 271
privately held corporations, 196
private property, 41, 52, 53
private sector, 63, 65
privatization, 43, 489–490, *p489*
Problem Solving Activity
chapter assessment, 21, 47, 73, 99, 123, 147, 179, 207, 237, 267, 295, 327, 353, 383, 411, 437, 456, 467, 494, 497
cooperative organizations, 207
economic transitions, 494, 497
international trade, 467
law of supply, 106, 123
tariffs, 456
Uniform Partnership Act, 193
producer cooperatives, 203
producer price index, *g539*
producers, free enterprise system and, 53
production
in centrally planned economy, 34–35
elasticity of supply and, 104–106
law of supply, 101–103, *c101*
marginal product of labor, 108–109
production costs, 108–114, *p108*, *c109*, *g109*, *p110, c111*, *g112*, *g113*, *p114*
excise tax, 118
fixed costs, 111, *p110*, *c111*
marginal cost, 112–113, *g112*
total cost, 111, *c111*
variable costs, 111, *p110*, *c111*
production possibilities frontier, 59
defined, 14
efficiency and, 15
law of increasing costs and, 17
production possibilities graph
defined, 13–15, *g14*, *g15*, *g16*
opportunity cost and, *g14*, *g15*, *g16*
shifts in, 16
trade-offs and, *g15*
productive capacity, 396
productive resources, 13
productivity, 219, *g443*
simulation of, 328–329, *c329*
technology and, 325
product market, *c303*
defined, 30
free market economy and, 29–30, *c30*
government in, 42–43
products
in franchises, 202
in monopolistic competition, 166–167, *p166*, *c167*
in perfect competition, 152
product standards, 450
professional labor, 221
professional organizations, 203–204
PROFILE, 518–519
profit incentives, 139, 143–144
profit motive
free enterprise system and, *p52,* 53
investing and, 271
profits, 29
banks and, 262, *c262*
in corporations, 198
law of supply and, 102
in monopolistic competition, 169
in a monopoly, 162–163
in partnerships, 191
in sole proprietorships, 187
progressive tax, *c360*, 361, *g361*, 367
property insurance, 525
property rights, 52, 53, 490–491
property tax, 360, 378
proportional tax, *c360*, 361
proprietorships
characteristics of, *g186*
See also sole proprietorships.
prospectus, 274
protectionism, 498–499
free enterprise system versus, 54
international trade and, 451, 452–453, *p453*
public interest and, 54
protectionist policies, 468–469
public disclosure laws, 54
public goods, 62–65
characteristics of, 62–63, *p63*
costs and benefits of, 63–64, *c64*
defined, 62
externalities, 65–66, *p65*
free-rider problem, 63–64
government and, 66
opportunity costs and, *c64*
public interest
defined, 54
economic freedom and, 52
free enterprise system and, 51–53, *p52*
protection and, 54, 55, *c55*
publicly held corporation, 196, 198
public opinion polls, 249, 267
public policy
consumers and, 53, 54
defined, 54, 55
government and, 54, 55
Graphic Organizer Activity, 72
interest groups and, 54
public safety, 376
public sector, 63
public works projects, 397. *See also* work relief.
purchasing power, 339, 342
pushcarts, *p152*
Putin, Vladimir, 39
put option, 288–289

Q

quality of life, 305, 319–320, *c319*
quantity supplied, 101, 103
quantity theory, 341

R

racial discrimination, 347
radio, 160
railroad industry, 175, *c322*
ration coupons, *p13*
rationing, 141, *p141*, 142, 143
R&D. *See* research and development (R&D)
Reagan, Ronald
fiscal policy, 401
national debt and, 406
real GDP, 303–304, *c304*, 314, 315, *g315*, 318–320, *g318*
Real Life Case Studies, 19, 39, 71, 97, 121, 145, 177, 205, 235, 265, 293, 325, 351, 381, 409, 435, 465, 495
real property, 378
rebates, 163–164
recession, 315–316, 401, 432
business cycles and, 312–313, 433
gross domestic product and, 311
Keynesian economics and, 397
Reciprocal Trade Agreement Act (1934), 453
Red Cross, *p488*
Red Guards, 493
redistribution programs, 68–70
regressive tax, *c360*, 361
regulation
negative effects of, 55
of corporations, 198
regulatory agencies, *c55*
supply and, 118, *p119*
Regulation Z, 421
relocating, 447
rent control, 129–130, *g129*, 131
representative money, 247–248, *c247*
required reserve ratio (RRR), 425
reserves, 422
excess, 427
requirements, 427, *c427*
resource allocation, 142–143
resource distribution, 480
in international trade, 441–443, *p441*, *c442*
resumés, 526
retail facilities, spatial distribution of, 119–120
retail sales, *g539*
retirement benefits, 26, 373
retraining, 333, 447
return, risk and, 274–275
revenue, 359, 377
computing a firm's total, 95
elasticity of demand and, 95–96, *c96*
inelastic demand and, 95–96, *c96*
table, *c95*
Rhode Island
energy consumption, *g541*
natural resources, *m532–533*
Ricardo, David, 395, 443
right-to-work laws, 231
risk
return and, 274–275
sharing, 273
types of, *c274*
Rivlin, Alice, 56, *p56*
Robinson-Patman Act (1936), 174

robot technology, 117, *p323*
Rockefeller, John D., 51, 174, *c198*, 212
Roman Empire, 245, *m245*
Roosevelt, Franklin Delano, 68, 409, *p409*, 435
banking reforms and, 255
Great Depression and, 315, 400
minimum wage and, 180
New Deal, 397
Reciprocal Trade Agreement Act (1934) and, 453
Social Security and, 334
Roosevelt, Theodore, 174
royalty, 202
RRR. *See* required reserve ratio.
Rubin, Robert, 498
rubles, 246
Russia, 36
collapse of communist system in, 39
communism in, 491
currency of, 246
import of oil from, 119
inflation in, *p120*
hyperinflation in, 404
Rwanda, 483

S

safety, government agencies and, 54
safety net, 26, 68
St. Louis, Missouri, 67, *m67*, *p67*, *m417*
sales tax, 360, 361, 378, 380
San Diego, 488
San Francisco, California, *g337*, *m417*
Saudi Arabia, 471
bonds in, 282
savers, 272
savings, 320–321, *c321*, *g540*
savings accounts, 259
personal investing and, 506–510
return and risk of, 275
savings and loan associations, 176, 262, 510–511
as financial intermediaries, 272
crisis in, 256
savings banks, 263, 510–511
savings bonds, 280, 405
savings rate, 320–321, *c321*
scale of the market, 324
scanners, 174
scarce resources, 6
scarcity, 3–4, *p4*, 23
defined, 4
shortages and, 4
scholarships, 517
Scotland, 317
screening effect, 231
search costs, 136, 137
seasonal unemployment, 331–332, *p332*
Seattle, Washington, 6
SEC. *See* Securities and Exchange Commission.
secondary markets, 283
secured loan, 514
Securities and Exchange Commission (SEC), 198, 281
security deposit, 522
Seko, Mobutu Sese, 482
Self-assessment, 21, 47, 73, 99, 123, 147, 179, 207, 237, 267, 295, 327, 353, 383, 411, 437, 467, 497. *See also* Assessment.
self-interest, 30–31
defined, 31
free enterprise system and, *p52*
Selig, Bud, *p121*
sellers, in perfect competition, 151, 152
selling, market, 29
semi-skilled labor, 221
senior citizens, targeted discounts and, 164
September 11 attacks, 176, 292, 316, 336, 408, 425
service
cooperatives, 203
nonprice competition and, 168
service economy, 213, *c213*
services
consumers of, 24–25
defined, 3
determining what to produce, 23
how to produce, 23–24
severance tax, 378
shares, 285
See also stock.
Shen Qing, 43
Sherman Antitrust Act (1890), 173, 174, *c198*
shortages, 4, 136–137, 142
shutdown, company, 113–114, *p114*
silver certificates, 248
simple interest, 261
Simulations, 48–49, 148–149, 208–209, 296–297, 328–329, 384–385, 468–469
Singapore, 476
as newly industrialized country, 475
as trading partner, 455, *g544*, *m545*
sin taxes, 369, 378
site permits, 186
Sixteenth Amendment, 360, 528
skilled labor, 221
Skills Activity
analyzing tables, 84, 99
cause and effect, 132, 147
critical thinking, 132, 309, 364, 419
fact and opinion, 364, 383
flowcharts, 45, 47
graphs and charts, 12, 20, 21, 45, 84, 337, 353, 394, 411
Internet research skills, 194, 207
line graphs, 21
multimedia presentations, 448, 467
political cartoons, 155, 179
predicting consequences, 309, 327
primary sources, 61, 73
public opinion polls, 249, 267
reading stock market reports, 284, 295
recognizing bias, 419, 437
social studies, 61, 107, 155, 249, 484
statistics, 218, 237
technology, 194, 293, 448
test-taking, 107, 123
writing process, 484, 497
small business, 208–209
smart cards, 264
Smith, Adam, 30–31, 32, 33, *p33*, 41, 143–144, 395
Smoot-Hawley Tariff (1930), 451, 452, 453
socialism, 35
Social Security, 43, 234, 364, 370, 372, *p372*, 373, 391, 408, 409
taxes and, 367–368
Social Security Act (1935), 334, 409, *p409*
Social Security Administration, *c68*, 69, 70, 409, *p409*
social welfare programs, 372, *p372*
societal values, 26, 27, 41
sole proprietorships
advantages of, 185–187
defined, 185
disadvantages of, 187–188
role of, 185
Solow, Robert, 323
South Africa, *p156*
South Carolina
energy consumption, *g541*
natural resources, *m532–533*
South Dakota
energy consumption, *g541*
natural resources, *m532–533*
taxes in, 360
Southern Common Market, 455, *m455*
South Korea
economic health of, *c319*
health expenditures, *g547*
multinational corporations in, 200
national budget of, *g547*
as newly industrialized country, 476
population, *p478*
as trading partner, *g544*, *m545*
Southwest Asia, 441
sovereignty, 454, 489
Soviet Union
centrally planned economy of, 36–37, *p36*, *p37*
communism in, 491
five-year plans in, 38
goods in, 142
GOSPLAN in, 141
transition to market-based economy, 489, 491–492, *p491*, *p492*
S & P 500. *See* Standard & Poor's 500.
space technology, 60
specialization, 28–29, *p328*
defined, 29
employment and, 446–447
marginal production of labor and, 109
resources and, 443
unemployment and, 447
specie, 248, 251
speculation, 290–291
spending
consumer expectations and, 313
discretionary, 371, *c371*, 373–374
interest rates and, 430–431
mandatory, 371–373, *c371*
spillover costs, 144
spinoffs, 70
sports marketing, 160, *m160*
SSI. *See* Supplemental Security Income.

stability, economic, 58
stabilization policy, 430–434, *g432*, 488
Stafford Loans, 518
stagflation, 311, 313
Stalin, Joseph, 38
standard of living, 58, 235, 439, *g546*, *g547*
defined, 26
in free market economy, 41
growth of, 58
Standard Oil Company, *c198*
Standard Oil Trust, 174
Standard & Poor's 500, 279, *c279*, 281, 290
start-up costs, 153
state government
administration of, 377
arts and recreation, 377
balanced budget, 407
budgets, 375–376
business tax, 378
corporate income tax, 378
education and, 376
federal aid to, 374, *p374*
highways and transportation and, 377, *p377*
income tax, 378
public safety and, 376–377
sales tax, 378
tax revenues, 377
Statistical Abstract of the United States, 212
statistics, analyzing, 218, 237
steel industry, *p152*, *p198*, 232, 317, 451
stock, 197, 507
buying, 285–286, *p285*
defined, 195
measuring performance of, 289–290, *g289*
risks of, 286
trading of, 286–289
types of, 286
stockbroker, 286–287, *p288*, 292
stock exchanges, *p285*, 287–289
stock funds, 509
stock market
dot-coms, 293
Great Crash, 290–292
as leading indicator, 314
prices, 314
reading reports, *c287*, 295
regulation of, 198
stock splits, 286
stock trading, 58
stored value card, 264, 268–269, *p268*, *g269*
store of value, 244–245, *c244*
strikes, labor, *p228*, 234
structural unemployment, 332–333, *p332*
students, targeted discounts and, 164
subsidies, 117
subsistence agriculture, 472, 480
substitutes, 88
availability of, 91, 93
substitution effect, 80, *c80*
Sudan, 449
sunspot theory, 310
Super Bowl, 77
supermarkets, 174
Supplemental Security Income (SSI), 373
supply
changes in, 116–120, *p116*, *c117*, *p118*, *p119*, *p120*
government influence on, 117–119
import restrictions and, 119
in labor, 220
regulations and, 118–119
subsidies and, 117–118
taxes and, 118
supply, law of
elasticity and, 104–106, *c105*, *p106*
market entry, 102–103
prices, 101–103, *c101*
production, 101–103, *c101*
supply curve, 104, *c104*, *g105*
supply schedule, 103–104, *c103*, *c104*
supply and demand, *m160*
affecting wages, 121
combining, 125–131
disequilibrium, 126–128, *g127*, 134–135
equilibrium, 125–126, *g126*, 133–137, *g134*, *g135*, *g136*
fiscal policy and, 390–391
flexible exchange-rate system and, 462
government intervention in, 128–131, *g129*
government spending and, 390
gross domestic product and, 306–308, *g307*, *g308*
labor's impact on, 183
price ceilings, 128–130, *g129*
price floors, 130–131, *g131*
prices and, 125–137, 140
profit incentives and, 143–144
protectionist policies and, 468–469
rationing and, 141, *p141*, 142
resource allocation and, 142–143, 144
supply shock, 141
taxes and, 362–363, *c363*
supply curve, 104, *c104*, *g105*, 133–137, *g134*, *g135*, *g136*
shifts in the, 133–135, *g134*, *g135*
supply graph. *See* supply curve.
supply schedule, 103–104, *c103*, *c104*, 125
excess supply, 128
supply shock, 141
supply-side economics, 399–400, *g399*, 401
Supreme Court, U.S., 407
surplus, 134–135
surplus value, theory of, 227
sustainable development, 479
Sweden, 41
economy of, 484
national budget of, *g547*
taxes in, 368

T

tables, analyzing, 84, 99
Taft-Hartley Act (1947), 231
Taiwan, 494
as newly industrialized country, 476
as trading partner, *g544*, *m545*
United States trade deficit and, 463
TANF. *See* Temporary Aid for Needy Families (TANF).
targeted discounts, 163–164
tariffs, 369, 450, *g450*, 498–499, *p498*, *g499*
infant industry and, 452
trade wars and, 451
taxable income, 366
tax assessor, 380
taxation
of corporations, 196, 197–198
double, 197–198
of partnerships, 192
taxation clause, 360
tax base, 360–361, *c360*
tax credits, 381
tax cuts, 364, 381, 408
taxes
balancing revenues and rates, 362
brackets, 367, *c367*, 381
characteristics of good, 361–362
Constitution and, 52–53, 359–360
corporate income, 367
cutting, 390, 401
deductions and, 366
defined, 359
e-commerce, 412–413
education and, 378
excise, 118, 368, 378, 380, *g543*
exports and, 360
fairness and, 362
federal, 365–369, *c365*, *c366*, *c367*
filing returns, 366–367
increasing, 391
individual income tax, 365–367, *c365*, *c366*, *c367*
limits on, 360
Medicare and, 368
paying, 528–531
as percent of gross domestic product, *g546*
public goods and, 62
revenue, 359
Social Security and, 367–368
state and local government and, *p374*, 375–380, *g376*, *p377*, *g379*
supply and demand and, 362–363, *g363*
types of, 368–369
unemployment and, 368
withholding, 366
See also government.
tax exempt, 377
tax incentive, 369
tax rate, 399–400, *g399*, *g400*, 401
tax returns, 366–367
tax structures, 360, *c360*
T-bills. *See* Treasury bills.
technological monopoly, 159
technological progress, 322–324, *p323*
technology
agriculture and, *p474*
as barrier to entry, 153
defined, 59
education and, 481
effect on economy, 351
innovations in, 59
input costs and, 117
Internet Activity and, 18
natural monopolies and, 158
productivity and, 325
progress of, 59–60

resources and, 18
role of government, 60
unemployment and, 333
teleconferencing, 325
telephone companies, 158–159, *p158,* 174
telephone service, 175
television industry, 115, 160
deregulation of, 175, 177
Temporary Assistance for Needy Families (TANF), 59, *c59,* 350, 399
temporary workers, 215–216, 217
Tennessee
energy consumption, *g541*
natural resources, *m532–533*
terrorism, 176, 292, 316, 336, 408, 425
Texas
currency in, 460
energy consumption, *g541*
Federal Reserve District, *m417*
housing costs, *g337*
monopoly decision, *m160*
natural resources, *m532–533*
Texas A&M University, 60
Thailand, *p28,* 475
***The Theory of Economic Growth* (Lewis),** 477
thinking at the margin, 10
Three Gorges Dam, 494
thrifts, 262
tight money policy, 431, 433
time deposits, 506
T-notes. *See* Treasury notes
total cost, 111, *c111*
total revenue, 95–96, *c95, c96*
tourism industry, 127, *p498,* 499
toy industry, 145, *p145*
trade
benefits of, *c445*
effects of, on employment, 446–447
foreign, *g544, m545*
international, 440–467
NAFTA, 465, *p465*
See also balance of trade.
trade associations, 204
trade barriers, 449–457
effects of, 450–451
import quotas, 449, *p449*
international cooperation and agreements, 453–456, *p454, m455*
tariffs, 450, *g450,* 498–499, *p498, g499*
voluntary export restraints, 449
trade deficit, 322
reasons for, 463
reducing the, 463, 464
United States, 463
trade-offs, *p8, p9,* 11
defined, 8
global, 9
law of increasing costs and, 17, *c17*
production possibilities graph and, *g15*
trade surplus, 464
trade union, 213
trade wars, 451, 452
trading partners, 445–446, *g544, m545*
traditional economy, 26–27
training programs, 333
transfer tax, 378
transition, 43
transition economy, 475
transnational corporations, 199
transportation, 172, 377, *p377*
in developed nations, 474
as physical capital, 442
Transportation Security Administration, 387
travel and entertainment (T & E) card, 514
traveler's checks, 258
Treasury bills, 280, 405
Treasury bonds, 280, 405
Treasury Department, U.S., 280, 420
Bank of the United States and, 251
Treasury notes, 280, 405
Triangle Shirtwaist Factory, *p230*
trough, 311, *c311*
trucking industry, 175, 176
trusts, 160, 173
Truth in Lending laws, 421, 515
Truth in Savings Act, 507
tuition, 516
Turkey, *c319*
Ty, Inc., *p145*

U

Ukraine, 404
underemployment, 335–336
underground economy, 304–305
underutilization, 15
UNDP. *See* United Nations Development Program.
unemployment, *g61,* 211–212, *c212, c218,* 299, 351
business cycles and, 312–314
consumer demand and, 333
cyclical, 333–334, *p333*
education and, 333
frictional, 331
full employment and, 335–336
in Great Depression, 334
inflation and, 343
rate, 334, *c334, g335*
seasonal, 331–332, *p332*
specialization and, 446–447
structural, 332–333, *p332*
taxes and, 368
technology and, 333
unemployment insurance, 69
unemployment taxes, 368
Uniform Partnership Act, 191
Union Pacific Corp., 74
union shop, 216
unitary elastic demand, 91, *g92*
United Kingdom
economic health of, *c319*
national budget of, *g547*
resource distribution in, *c442*
as trading partner, *g544, m545*
United Mine Workers, *p230*
United Nations Development Program, 487–488
United States, *g542, g543*
Asian Pacific Economic Cooperation, 455, *m455*
balanced trade and, 462
as developed nation, 471
economic health of, *c319*
economy of, 484
energy production, *g534*
as exporter, 446, *g446*
foreign aid and, 487, *g487*
free enterprise system in, 51–52
free market economy of, 43, 44
government agencies, 44
government regulation in, 51–52
health expenditures in, *g547*
as importer, 446, *g446*
import quotas, 449
infant mortality rate, 474
multinational corporations in, 200
national budget of, *g547*
North American Free Trade Agreement, 454–455, *m455,* 465
resource distribution in, *c442*
statistics, 57
subsidies in, 117–118
trade deficit, 463
Trade Deficit Review Commission, 464
trade with Mexico, 455
trading partners, 445–446, *g544, m545*
unit of account, 244, *c244*
unsecured loan, 514
unskilled labor, 221
UPA. *See* Uniform Partnership Act
Uruguay, *m455,* 456
Utah
energy consumption, *g541*
natural resources, *m532–533*
utilities, deregulation of, 176

V

value-added tax, 368
variable costs, *p110,* 111, *c111*
variables, 103
VAT. *See* value-added tax.
VER. *See* voluntary export restraints.
Vermont
energy consumption, *g541*
natural resources, *m532–533*
vertical merger, *c198,* 199
veterans, 373
Vietnam War, 401, 461
Virginia
in Civil War, 120
energy consumption, *g541*
Federal Reserve District, *m417*
natural resources, *m532–533*
Vocabulary Activity, 20, 46, 72, 98, 122, 146, 178, 206, 236, 266, 294, 326, 352, 382, 410, 436, 466, 496
Vocabulary Builder
3, 8, 13, 23, 28, 34, 40, 51, 57, 62, 67, 79, 85, 90, 101, 108, 116, 125, 133, 139, 151, 156, 166, 172, 190, 195, 201, 211, 219, 228, 243, 250, 258, 271, 277, 285, 301, 310, 318, 331, 338, 345, 359, 365, 371, 375, 387, 395, 403, 415, 420, 425, 430, 441, 449, 458, 471, 478, 485, 489
voluntary contributions, 384–385

voluntary exchange, *p52,* 53
voluntary export restraints, 449
volunteerism, 488

W

wage determinants, 224–225
wage discrimination, 222–224, *g223, g224*
wage-price spiral, 342, *c342*
wages, *g217*
  collective bargaining and, 233
  comparison of, 220–222, *g222, g223*
  equilibrium wage, 220, *c221*
  labor and, 219–226
  labor supply and, 220, *c221*
  labor unions and, 225–226
  responses to, 225
  skill levels and, 220–222
  trends in, 216–217
  working conditions and, 224–225
Wagner Act (1935), *c229*
The Wall Street Journal Classroom Edition, 5, 16, 37, 53, 69, 87, 102, 135, 170, 175, 188, 192, 222, 252, 260, 275, 286, 314, 324, 336, 347, 362, 373, 401, 426, 433, 456, 463, 481, 494
  credit, 354–355
  e-commerce, 412–413
  health care, 74–75
  minimum wage, 238–239
  oil, 180–181
  regulating financial markets, 268–269
  tariffs, 498–499
want, 3
war, 313
war bonds, *p277*
Warner, Ty, *p145*
War on Poverty, 68, *g70*
Washington, 6
  energy consumption, *g541*
  natural resources, *m532–533*
Washington, D.C., 8, 67, 416, *m417*
water companies, 158
water resources, 441
***The Wealth of Nations* (Smith),** 30–31, 33, 143–144
welfare, 399
welfare reform, 349, 350
Western Europe, 471
West Germany, 462
West Virginia
  energy consumption, *g541*
  natural resources, *m532–533*
W-2 form, 529
W-4 form, 529, *p529*
wheat, 443
white-collar workers, 232
wildcat banks, 252
Wildcat Era, 252
Windows software, 165
Winfrey, Oprah, 344, *p344*
Wisconsin, 344, 355
  energy consumption, *g541*
  natural resources, *m532–533*
withholding, 366
women
  economists, 56, 457
  education of, *p482*
  employment, *g536*
  entrepreneurs, 89, 344
  glass ceiling and, 224
  in labor force, 214–215, *g215,* 223–224, *g224*
  in labor unions, 232, *c232*
  in management, 223–224
  poverty rate and, 346, *c346*
  in Saudi Arabia, *p482*
  unemployment rates of, *c218*
  wage discrimination and, 223–224, *g223, g224*
workers' compensation, 69
work ethic, 59, 491
workfare, 350
work force, characteristics of, *g536*
working conditions, 222, 235
working poor, 346
workplace safety, *c55*
work relief. *See* public works projects.
work-study, 517
World Bank, 476, 487, 492, 495
World Food Program, *p488*
World Trade Organization, 453, 497
World War II, 13, 400
  consumer goods during, *p13*
writing process, using the, 484, 497
WTO. *See* World Trade Organization.
Wyoming
  energy consumption, *g541*
  natural resources, *m532–533*

Y

Yahoo!, 189
Yang, Jerry, 189, *p189*
yellow-dog contracts, 230
Yellowstone National Park, 62, *p63*
Yeltsin, Boris, 492
yen, 488
yield, 278, *g280*

Z

Zaire, 482
Zentz, Peter, 325
zoning laws, 187

Acknowledgments

Team Credits The people who made up the ***Economics: Principles in Action*** team—representing editorial, editorial services, design services, market research, on-line services/multimedia development, product marketing, production services, and publishing processes—are listed below. Bold type denotes core team members.

Joyce Barisano, Barbara Bertell, **Peter Brooks,** Margaret Broucek, **Todd Christy,** Lisa J. Clark, Lori-Anne Cohen, Bob Craton, Kathy Dempsey, Gabriela Perez Fiato, Paul Gagnon, Sandy Graff, **Mary Ann Gundersen,** Katharine Ingram, Tim Jones, Lynne Kalkanajian, Russ Lappa, James Lonergan, Dotti Marshall, Grace Massey, **William McAllister,** Baljit Nijjar, Jill Ort, Elizabeth Pearson, Judi Pinkham, Mairead Reddin, Colleen Searson, Emily Soltanoff, **Mark Staloff,** Susan Swan, Merce Wilczek

Contributing Editors
Douglas Kinnear, Trish Taylor

Cover Design
Suzanne Schineller, Sweetlight Creative Partners, The Concept Bank
Front Cover Image, Ralph Mercer Photography

Illustration
Maps: Mapquest.com, Inc. **Charts, graphs and tables:** Precision Graphics, Inc.; J/B Woolsey and Associates; Accurate Art, Inc. **Creative art::** John Bleck **24**; Doug Bowles **528**; Adam Cohen **505;** Jon Conrad **512;** John Edwards and Associates **17;** Neil Stewart **30, 42, 153, 158, 167, 169, 244, 260, 262, 273, 302, 303, 322, 342, 416, 421, 426, 445, 510;** J/B Woolsey and Associates **198, 199, 278**

Picture Research
Kerri Hoar, PoYee Oster, Robin Samper, Siri Schwartzman

Photography
Table of Contents, Page i, Ralph Mercer; **iv t,** Corel Corp.; **iv tm,** Jan Halaska/Photo Researchers; **iv bm,** Dick Luria/FPG International; **iv b,** Ralph Pleasant/FPG International; **v t,** Todd Davidson/Image Bank/PNI; **v m,** Stone/Don Smetzer; **v b,** Tony Freeman/PhotoEdit; **vi t,** The Granger Collection, New York; **vi m,** Stone/Paul Chesley; **vi b,** James Marshall/The Stock Market; **vii t,** Richard Strauss/National Museum of American History, Smithsonian Institution; **vii m,** Russ Lappa; **vii b,** Stone/Brian Seed; **ix l,** A. Ramey/Stock Boston; **ix m,** AP/Wide World Photos; **ix r,** Jim Harrison/Stock Boston; **xviii,** Farmhouse Productions/Image Bank; **xix bl,** Phil McCarten/PhotoEdit; **xix br,** Index Stock Imagery; **xx l,** Eastcott/Momatiuk/Woodfin Camp & Associates; **xx r,** Stone/Paula Bronstein; **xxi,** Stock Boston, Inc./PictureQuest; **xxii,** Peter Gridley/ FPG International; **xxiv,** Bonnie Kamin/PhotoEdit; **xxv l,** Stone/Jon Riley; **xxv m,** Stone/Charles Gupton; **xxv r,** Arthur D'Arazien/Superstock; **xxvi l,** John S. Dykes/ Stock Illustration Source; **xxvi r,** Bob Rowan; Progressive Image/Corbis.

UNIT 1 Page xvi-xvii, Neal Preston/Corbis; **2 teens,** David Young-Wolff/PhotoEdit; **2 mall background,** PhotoDisc.; **4,** Jim Felt/Studio 3; **5 tl,** Garry McMichael/Photo Researchers; **5 ml,** William Taufic/The Stock Market; **5 bl,** Roger Ball/Picturesque Stock Photo; **5 m,** Stone/ Steven Peters; **5 r,** Richard Paslet/Stock Boston/PNI; **7 tl,** Ludovic/Rea/SABA Press Photos; **7 background,** Stone/Stuart McClymont; **8,** Ron Kimball/Ron Kimball Stock; **9,** Reprinted with permission of King Features Syndicate; **12,** Chris Trotman/Duomo; **13 l,** Jeff Tinsley/Smithsonian Institution; **13 r,** The Bancroft Library, Kaiser Pictorial Collections; **14,** ©Tribune Media Services, Inc. All Rights Reserved. Reprinted with permission.; **19 background,** Stone; **19 r,** David Young-Wolff/PhotoEdit; **22,** Stone/Tim Macpherson; **25,** Bob Daemmrich/Stock Boston; **26,** Jean-Gerard Sidaner/Photo Researchers; **28 l,** Stone/Paul Chesley; **28-29,** Jan Halaska/Photo Researchers; **29 inset,** Paul Stepan/Photo Researchers; **31 t,** From *The Wall Street Journal*-Permission, Cartoon Features Syndicate; **31 b,** Bryan F. Peterson /The Stock Market; **33 tl,** Corbis/Bettmann; **33 background,** Museum der Stadt, Vienna, Austria/ET Archive, London/Superstock; **34 l,** Judi Pinkham; **34 r,** A. Keler/Corbis Sygma; **35,** B. Bisson/Corbis Sygma; **36 l,** Corbis/Bettmann; **36 m, r,** Sovfoto; **36-37,** Jeff Greenberg/dMRp/Photo Researchers; **37 t,** Shepard Sherbell/SABA Press Photos; **38,** Ricki Rosen/SABA Press Photos; **39 background,** Charles Steiners/The Image Works; **39 tr,** Stone/Steven Weinberg; **40,** Stone/Bob Handelman; **41,** David M. Grossman/Photo Researchers; **44,** John Banagan/ Image Bank; **45,** Jeff Isaac Greenberg; **48-49 background,** Prentice Hall; **48 l,** Russ Lappa; **48 r,** Thomas R. Fletcher/Stock Boston; **49 bl,** Prentice Hall; **50,** Angelo Cavalli/Image Bank; **51,** Bob Rowan; Progressive Image/Corbis; **52 tl, bl,** Russ Lappa; **52 ml,** Tony Freeman/PhotoEdit; **52 tr, br,** Tony Freeman/PhotoEdit; **53,** National Highway Traffic Safety Administration; **54,** Stone/David Young-Wolff; **56 tl,** Brooks/Glogau Photographers/Federal Reserve Board; **56 background,** Vivian Ronay/Liaison Agency; **57,** Brian Orland/ East St. Louis Action Research Project/University of Illinois at Urbana-Champaign; **58 both,** Library of Congress; **59 tl,** Frank Siteman/The Picture Cube; **59 bl,** Tony Freeman/PhotoEdit; **59 tr,** Corbis Sygma; **59 br,** AP/Wide World Photos; **61,** Library of Congress; **63 background,** Stone/Baron Wolman; **63 tl,** MacDonald Photography/Index Stock Imagery; **63 bl,** Bud Freund/Index Stock Imagery; **63 tm,** Michael J. Howell/Index Stock Imagery; **63 tr,** Charles Schoffer/Index Stock Imagery; **63 br,** Stone/Frank Siteman; **64,** Nancy Simmerman/AllStock/PNI; **65 l,** PhotoDisc.; **65 r,** John Elk III/Stock Boston; **66,** Bill Horsman/Stock Boston; **68,** Russ Lappa; **69 l,** Silver Burdett Ginn; **69 r,** AP/Wide World Photos; **71 background,** Superstock; **71 tr,** AP/Wide World Photos; **74-75 background,** Russ Lappa; **74,** Jose Luis Pelaez/Corbis.

UNIT 2 Page 76-77, Chris Trotman/Duomo; **78,** Bill Aron/PhotoEdit; **79,** Stone/Robert Torrez; **81,** Sears Roebuck & Co.; **82,** Index Stock Imagery; **84,** Stone/Ron Sherman; **85,** Jõso Azel/Aurora/PNI; **86,** Stone/Joseph Sohm; **87 t,** Dick Luria/FPG International; **87 b,** Bruce Fier/Liaison Agency; **88,** Stone/Mark Junak; **89 background,** Russ Lappa; **89 inset,** AP/Wide World Photos; **90,** Glasbergen/Rothco Cartoons; **93 l,** Bonnie Kamin/PhotoEdit; **93 r,** Sonda Dawes/The Image Works; **94 t,** Ken Giese/Superstock; **94 bl,**Volkswagen America, Inc.; **94 br,** Stone/Donald Johnston; **97 background,** Craig Hammell/The Stock Market; **97 tr,** Superstock; **100,** Stone/Andy Sacks; **101,** Telegraph Colour Library 1998/FPG International; **102 tl,** Rick Gayle/The Stock Market; **102 bl,** Dennis Hallinan/FPG International; **102br,** Lynn Goldsmith/Corbis; **106 t,** Myrleen Ferguson/PhotoEdit; **106 b,** Ralph Pleasant/FPG International; **107,** Galen Rowell/Corbis; **108,** Richard Haynes; **110,** Stone/Jeff Zaruba; **114,** Todd Gipstein/Corbis; **115 background,** Superstock; **115 tl,** Black Entertainment Television; **116 tl,** PhotoDisc.; **116 bl,** Russ Lappa; **116 the rest,** PhotoDisc.; **119,** ML Sinibaldi/The Stock Market; **120,** Tim Page/Corbis; **121 background,** Jerry Arcieri/SABA Press Photos; **121 tr,** Darren Carroll/Duomo; **123,** Baloo/Rothco Cartoons; **124,** Stone/Charles Gupton; **125,** Phil McCarten/Photo Edit; **128,** Stone/Peter Pearson; **130,** David Young-Wolff/Photo Edit; **132 ,** Russ Lappa; **133,** Todd Davidson/Image Bank/PNI; **136,** Russ Lappa; **138 background,** B. Daemmrich/The Image Works; **138 tl,** B.Daemmrich/Corbis Sygma; **139, 140,** Russ Lappa; **141,** H. Armstrong Roberts; **142,** Greg Girard/Contact Press; **143,** David McIntyre/Black Star; **143 inset,** Stone/Keren Su; **144,** Stone/Craig Wells; **145 background,** Kerrick James Photo/Getty Images; **145 insert,** Randy Faris/Corbis; **148-149 background,** Prentice Hall; **148 l,** Russ Lappa; **148 r,** PhotoDisc.; **149 bl,** Prentice Hall; **150,** Stan Sholik/FPG International; **151,** Mark Tomalty/Masterfile; **152 l,** Miro Vintoniv/Index Stock Imagery; **152 r,** Mark Tomalty/Masterfile; **155 l,** Superstock; **155 br,** ©Tribune Media Services, Inc. All Rights Reserved. Reprinted with permission.; **156,** G. Biss/Masterfile; **158,** David J. Carol/Image Bank; **159,** A. Ramey/Stock Boston; **163 l,** Stone/David Young Wolff; **163 m,** Brent Jones/Stock Boston; **163 r,** Will McIntyre/Photo Researchers; **165 tl,** Courtesy of Microsoft; **165 background,** Stone/Peter Poulides; **166,** Stock Boston, Inc./PictureQuest; **168,** L. Mulvehill/The Image Works; **171,** David Young-Wolff/PhotoEdit; **172,** Stone/John Elk; **173, 174 l,** Culver Pictures; **174 r,** Brown Brothers; **175 tl,** Stone/Jon Ortner; **175 tr,** AP/Wide World Photos; **175 bm,** Corbis; **176,** James Nielson/Liaison/Getty Images, Inc.; **177 background,** Mark Peterson/SABA Press Photos; **177 tr,** John Coletti/Stock Boston; **177 br,** Corel Corp.; **179,** Russell Hodin/New Times; **180-181 background,** Russ Lappa; **180,** Mark A. Leman/Getty Images, Inc.

UNIT 3 Page 182-183, Peter Vandemark/Stock Boston; **184,** Walter Bibikow/FPG International; **185,** Stone/Don Smetzer; **187,** Jose Luis Pelaez Inc./The Stock Market; **189 background,** David Young-Wolfe/PhotoEdit; **189 tl,** Courtesy of Yahoo!; **190,** Tony Freeman/PhotoEdit; **192,** The New Yorker Collection 1995 Roz Chast from cartoonbank.com. All Rights Reserved.; **193,** Stone/Bruce Ayres; **194,** Jon Feingersh; **195,** Leonard Harris/Stock Boston; **200,** Les Stone/Corbis Sygma; **201,** Index Stock Imagery; **202,** Young-Wolff/PhotoEdit; **203,** Bob Daemmrich/Stock Boston; **204 l,** The American Veterinary Medical Association for Veterinarians; **204 tm,** Better Business Bureau; **204 tr,** Lake Norman Chamber of Commerce; **204 br,** American Dental Association; **205 background,** Brian Seed; **205 both,** Courtesy of the Hitchiner Corporation; **208-209 background,** Prentice Hall; **208 l,** Russ Lappa; **208 r,** Bill Bachmann/Stock Boston; **209 bl,** Prentice Hall; **210,** Superstock; **211,** Stone/Steve Smith; **213 l,** The Granger Collection, New York; **213 r,** Corbis/Bettmann; **214,** Corbis/Bettmann; **217,** Bill Pugliano/Liaison Agency; **219 background,** Richard Faverty/Liaison Agency; **219 tr,** Donald C. Johnson/The Stock Market; **219 br,** Corel Corp.; **220,** Stone/Gene Peach; **222,** Charlie Wasterman/Liaison Agency; **227,** Ed Quinn/SABA Press Photos; **228 tl,** Library of Congress; **228 background,** Culver Pictures; **232,** DILBERT reprinted by permission of United Feature Syndicate, Inc.; **234,** Russ Lappa; **235 background,** Ewing Galloway/Index Stock; **235 inset,** Farmhouse Productions/Image Bank; **238-239 background,** Russ Lappa ; **238,** J.L.Bulcao/Liaison Agency.

UNIT 4 Page 240-241, T. DelAmo/H. Armstrong Roberts; **242,** B. Kraft/Corbis Sygma; **245,** The Granger Collection, New York; **247 l,** John Colwell/Grant Heilman Photography; **247 m,** Courtesy of the Federal Reserve Bank of San Francisco; **247 r,** Russ Lappa; **249,** Rhoda Sidney/ PhotoEdit; **250 t,** Columbiana Collection, Columbia University; **250 b,** "Jefferson" by Rembrandt Peale © White House Historical Association/ Photo by National Geographic Society; **251,** The New York Historical Society; **252 all,** Courtesy of the Federal Reserve Bank of San Francisco; **253 t,** Archive Photos; **253 b,** Phil Schermeister/Corbis; **254 t,m,** Courtesy of the Federal Reserve Bank of San Francisco; **254 b,** Bob Daemmrich/Uniphoto Picture Agency; **255,** Brown Brothers; **256,** Rothco Cartoons; **257 background,** Richard Berenholtz/The Stock Market; **257 tl,** AP/ Wide World Photos; **258,** Russ Lappa; **263 t,** Hulton Getty/Liaison Agency; **263 b,** Myrleen Cate/Photo Network/PNI; **265 background,** Emanuel Fuare/Superstock; **265 tr,** David R. Frazier Photolibrary; **265 br,** Corel Corp.; **268-269 background,** Russ Lappa; **268,** Mario Tama/Getty Images, Inc.; **270,** Stone/Greg Pease; **271,** David C. Chen/Stock Illustration Source; **272 all,** Russ Lappa; **276 background,** AP Photo/Mark Lennihan; **276 tl,** Ira Wyman/Corbis Sygma; **277,** National Archive; **281 t,** Rhoda Sidney/The Image Works; **281 b,** Stone/Gary Holscher; **282,** Langdon/Rothco Cartoons; **284 background,** GALA/Superstock; **284 tl,** Wesley Bocxe/Photo Researchers; **285 t,** Stone/Michael Beasley; **285 b,** Stone/Paul Chesley; **288,** Stone/David Austen; **290,** Corbis; **291,** Tom Toles/Universal Press Syndicate; **292,** AFP/Henry Ray Abrams; **293 background,** Courtesy of the Ebay Corporation; **293 inset,** Kirschen; Dry Bones/Cartoonist and Writers Syndicate/cartoonweb.com; **296-297 background,** Prentice Hall; **296 l,** Russ Lappa; **296 r,** Stone/Bob Torrez; **297 bl,** Prentice Hall.

UNIT 5 Page 298-299, Martin Rogers/Prism/ FPG International; **300,** Louie Psihoyos/Matrix International, Inc.; **305,** Bonnie Kamin/PhotoEdit; **309,** Phil Schermeister/Corbis; **313,** Stone/Churchill & Klehr; **316,** Tom McHugh/Photo Researchers; **317 background,** Hulton-Deutsch Collection/Corbis; **317 inset,** Bettman/Corbis; **323 l,** Rene Burri/Magnum Photos;**323 r,** Richard Nowitz/PhotoTake; **325 background,** Bonnie Kamin/PhotoEdit; **325 tr,** Ralph White/Corbis; **325 br,** Corel Corp.; **328-329 background,** Prentice Hall; **328 l,** Russ Lappa; **328 r,** James A. Sugar/Black Star/PNI; **329 bl,** Prentice Hall; **330,** Stone/Chip Henderson; **332 t,** Jack Parsons/Omni-Photo Communications; **332 b,** Brown Brothers; **333,** Stone/Michael Rosenfeld; **334,** Carol Simpson/Rothco Cartoons; **337,** Stone/George Lepp; **338 l,** Brown Brothers; **338 m,** Brown Brothers; **338 r,** Michael Newman/PhotoEdit; **344 background,** Terry Thompson/Sipa Press; **344 tl,** Gregory Pace/Corbis Sygma; **347 l,** Tony Freeman/PhotoEdit; **347 m,** Stone/Steven Peters; **347 r,** Stone/David Young-Wolff; **349,** Piet van Lier/Impact Visuals; **351 background,** Richard Pasley/Stock Boston; **351 tr,** M. Greenlar/The Image Works; **354-355 background,** Russ Lappa **354,** Michael Newman/PhotoEdit.

UNIT 6 Page 356-357, Stone/John Lawrence; **358,** Steve Lehman/SABA Press Photos; **362,** Schwadron/Rothco Cartoons; **364,** Boden/Ledingham/Masterfile; **366,** Chuck Savage/The Stock Market; **369,** P.M. Chock/Stock Boston; **370 background,** Stone/Dale Durfee; **370 tl,** Richard A. Bloom/SABA Press Photos; **372 l,** Mike Valeri/FPG International; **372 r,** Stone/Steven Peters **372 m,** Bob Daemmrich/The Image Works; **374,** Leiderman/Rothco Cartoons; **375,** David R. Frazier Photolibrary; **377,** James Marshall/The Stock Market; **380,** Mark Burnett/Stock Boston; **381 background,** Prentice Hall School Division; **381 inset,** Ron Edmonds/AP Wide World Photos; **384-385 background,** Prentice Hall; **384 l,** Russ Lappa; **384 r,** Stone/Robert E. Daemmrich; **385 bl,** Prentice Hall; **386,** Dennis Brack/Black Star; **387,** Doug McFadd/Getty Images, Inc.; **392,** AP Photo/Angela Rowlings; **393,** Mark C. Burnett/Stock Boston/PNI; **394,** Christian Michaels/FPG International; **395,** FPG International; **397,** Spencer Grant/Liaison Agency; **400,** Richard Strauss/National Museum of American History, Smithsonian Institution; **402 background,** UPI/Corbis-Bettmann; **402 tl,** Brown Brothers; **403,** Rommel Pecson/The Image Works; **405,** Susan Van Etten/PhotoEdit; **408,** Tomm Gibb-The Tribune-Democrat, PA/Rothco Cartoons; **409 background,** Paul Barton/The Stock Market; **409 tr,** Corbis/Bettmann; **409 br,** Corel Corp.; **412-413 background,** Russ Lappa; **412,** AP/Wide World Photos; **414,** M. Dwyer/Stock Boston; **415,** Stock Montage; **419,** Charles Gupton/Stock Boston; **420,** Peter Gridley/FPG International; **423,** H. Armstrong Roberts; **424 background,** Doug Mills/AP Photo; **424 tl,** Jeffrey Markowitz/Corbis Sygma; **425,** Larry Edwards/The Stock Market; **430,** Janusz Kapusta/Stock Illustration Source; **433,** Mick Stevens/cartoonbank.com; **435 background,** Brown Brothers; **435 tr,** UPI/Corbis-Bettmann.

UNIT 7 Page 438-439, Martin Rogers/Stock Boston; **440,** Maersk Inc., HO/AP Photo; **441 all, 443 both,** Russ Lappa; **447,** Michael Newman/PhotoEdit; **448,** Terry Wild Studio; **449,** Stone/Penny Tweedie; **451 both,** Kelvin Thomas; **453 l,** Stone/Jon Riley;**453 m,** Stone/Charles Gupton; **453 r,** Arthur D'Arazien/Superstock; **454,** Kenneth Jarecke/Contact Press; **457 background,** Barry Sweet/AP Photo; **457 tl,** R. Maiman/Corbis Sygma; **458,** Bill Cardoni/Liaison Agency; **459,** Russ Lappa; **461,** Superstock; **462,** John S. Dykes/Stock Illustration Source; **465 background,** Tom Carroll/Phototake/PNI; **465 tr,** Stone/Mark Segal; **465 br,** Corel Corp.; **468-469 background,** Prentice Hall; **468 l,** Russ Lappa; **468 r,** Catherine Ursillo/Photo Researchers;**469 bl,** Prentice Hall; **470,** Stone/Brian Seed; **473 l,** James Marshall/The Stock Market; **473 r,** Superstock; **474 t,** Eastcott/Momatiuk/Woodfin Camp & Associates; **474 b,** Superstock; **475,** Stone/Paula Bronstein; **477 background,** Stone/Ian Murphy;**477 tl,** UPI/Corbis-Bettmann; **478,** Nathan Benn/Woodfin Camp & Associates; **480 l,** Thomas S. England/Photo Researchers; **480-481,** Nigel J. Dennis/Photo Researchers; **481 r,** S. Noorani/Woodfin Camp & Associates; **482,** Jodi Cobb/NGS Image Collection; **483,** Oleg Nikishin/Getty Images, Inc.; **484,** Superstock; **485 both,** Stephanie Maze/NGS Image Collection; **486,** Keith Dannemiller/SABA Press Photos; **488,** Steve Lehman/SABA Press Photos; **489,** Tomaz Tomaszewski/NGS Image Collection; **491,** ©Wiley Miller, San Francisco Examiner; **492,** Shepard Sherbell/SABA Press Photos; **493,** Paolo Koch/Photo Researchers; **495 background,** Stone/Paul Kenward; **495 tr,** Superstock; **495 br,** Corel Corp.; **498-499 background,** Russ Lappa; **498,** Rudi Von Briel/PhotoEdit.

Reference Table of Contents
Page 500 tl, Stone/Gene Peach; **500 bl,** Stone/Charles Gupton; **500 m,** Myrleen Cate/Photo Network/PNI; **500 tr,** Nathan Benn/Woodfin Camp & Associates; **500 br,** Peter Gridley/FPG International.

Personal Finance Handbook
Page 502, 503, 504, 506, Russ Lappa; **508,** Stone/Bob Torrez; **514,** Russ Lappa; **516,** Prentice Hall; **519,** Russ Lappa; **520 t,** Stone/Alan Levenson; **520 br,** Photo Disc.; **521,** George E. Jones/Photo Researchers; **522 both, 529, 530, 530,** Russ Lappa.

Debating Current Issues
The Debating Current Issues features are excerpts from articles originally published in *The Wall Street Journal Classroom Edition.* All excerpts are used by permission of Dow Jones & Company.